# STRATEGY AND ORGANIZATION
Text and cases in general management

# Strategy and organization
## TEXT AND CASES IN
## GENERAL MANAGEMENT

**HUGO E. R. UYTERHOEVEN,** Dr. Jur., Dr. en Droit, M.B.A., D.B.A.
Professor of Business Administration

**ROBERT W. ACKERMAN,** S.B., M.B.A., D.B.A.
Assistant Professor of Business Administration

**JOHN W. ROSENBLUM,** A.B., M.B.A., D.B.A.
Assistant Professor of Business Administration

*All of the*
*Graduate School of Business Administration*
*Harvard University*

 1973

**RICHARD D. IRWIN, INC.** Homewood, Illinois 60430
IRWIN-DORSEY INTERNATIONAL London, England WC2H 9NJ
IRWIN-DORSEY LIMITED Georgetown, Ontario L7G 4B3

*First Printing, May 1973*
*Second Printing, November 1973*
*Third Printing, January 1974*
*Fourth Printing, June 1974*
*Fifth Printing, September 1974*
*Sixth Printing, December 1974*
*Seventh Printing, May 1975*

Case material of the Harvard Graduate School of
Business Administration is made possible by the
cooperation of business firms who may wish to remain
anonymous by having names, quantities, and other
identifying details disguised while maintaining basic
relationships. Cases are prepared as the basis for
class discussion rather than to illustrate either effective
or ineffective handling of administrative situations.

ISBN 0-256-01448-5
Library of Congress Catalog Card No. 72–95395
*Printed in the United States of America*

# Preface

THIS IS A BOOK about business policy. It deals with the general management tasks of strategy formulation and organizational implementation. Its focus is not limited to those who are or want to be company presidents, because general management is not the exclusive province of the chief executive. The modern divisionalized corporation has several intermediate levels of general managers. In addition, executives at functional operating levels or in advisory staff positions need general management skills. The general management viewpoint is also important to professions dealing with a business firm from the outside, such as management consultants, financial analysts, commercial or investment bankers, and lawyers.

The text is oriented to the practitioner, describing a conceptual framework for strategic and organizational action. It is not intended to be a theory of the firm. Rather, as an operational guide, its purpose is to help in application: for the businessman in the real situation and for the student in the classroom through the study of the real-life case situations described in this book. The text, while benefiting from contributions of his coauthors, was written by Hugo Uyterhoeven, who for the past ten years has taught Business Policy at the Harvard Business School, has been head of the MBA Business Policy course, and is currently chairman of both the Advanced Management Program and the Business Policy Area.

The cases focus on the management of transition and change. They portray companies in dynamic situations involving opportunities for growth or competitive and other environmental threats. While both large and small companies are described, smaller firms predominate. This choice is deliberate: the total company is easier to comprehend when small, thus permitting a more thorough and meaningful analysis. The cases describe both domestic and international business situations, with the latter covering both the developing and industrial world.

A great variety of industries is covered. In manufacturing, they range from textiles, firearms, cigarettes, pickles, paints, detergents, and tableware to watches, video cassettes, electronics, and medical products. Other industries included are shipping, retailing, wholesaling, bottling, and construction. The growing service sector is represented by mutual fund management and investment banking, income tax services, movie theaters, and broadcasting. Some of these industries are aiming for the same consumer time and dollar: movie theaters, broadcasting, and video cassettes.

The cases are all current, reflecting environmental and other strategic as well as organizational issues that will confront managers in the 1970s. Published for the first time, these cases have been taught in a variety of programs at the Harvard Business School, including the Business Policy course in the MBA Program, the Advanced Management Program, the Program for Management Development, the International Teachers Program, and Executive Education Seminars. Several of the cases also have been used in other universities, in-house company programs, and industry association seminars. They have been tested in class with both graduate students and experienced executives.

All cases, with four exceptions, were either authored or coauthored by one of us. The remaining four cases were originally written by colleagues, but in these too we participated in preparing the revised versions which appear in this book. In developing several of the cases, we were assisted by: Allen R. Adler, Robert J. Berman, Robert J. Boehlke, Charles E. Fienning, W. Edward Massey, William J. Michaelcheck, Edwin A. Murray, Jr., Audrey T. Sproat, and Charles R. Weigle. We are particularly grateful for the major contributions made by Ralph Z. Sorenson in writing the Central American material, by Howard H. Stevenson in developing the Anglo-Norness cases, by Frederick T. Knickerbocker in the watch note, by Charles E. Summer in the BCI case, and by John Archer and Ralph M. Hower in the United Latex case.

This book would not have been possible without the support and stimulus of the Business Policy Area at the Harvard Business School. Its conceptual framework was developed over many years through joint efforts. It represents the collective product of the members of the Business Policy teaching group, which through the sixties was guided by its senior members: Robert W. Austin, Kenneth R. Andrews, and

C. Roland Christensen. We equally owe much to our other colleagues who have helped shape the Business Policy course through many years of teaching and research: Francis J. Aguilar, Norman A. Berg, Charles A. Bliss, Joseph L. Bower, Stephen H. Fuller, William D. Guth, Frederick T. Knickerbocker, John B. Matthews, Jr., Robert W. Merry, David C. D. Rogers, Malcolm S. Salter, Bruce R. Scott, Howard H. Stevenson, John M. Stopford, and Michael von Clemm.

We owe special notes of thanks to Helen Ford for her superb efforts in editing the cases and supervising the final assembly of the material and to Nancy Hayes for her help and dedication in typing and coordinating completion of the text.

We are grateful to the Director and the Trustees of IMEDE for letting us use a number of cases copyrighted by them. Also, several of the cases in this book were prepared with the support of the Young Presidents' Organization, for which we are most indebted. Our thanks also go to Dean Lawrence E. Fouraker and Senior Associate Dean George F. F. Lombard for their leadership at the Harvard Business School, which in the last analysis provided the impetus for this book.

*Harvard University*
*April 1973*

HUGO E. R. UYTERHOEVEN
ROBERT W. ACKERMAN
JOHN W. ROSENBLUM

# Contents

**Part II**
**THE GENERAL MANAGER AS ORGANIZATION BUILDER**

14.   **General management at the divisional level** . . . . . . **107**

Job of the middle-level general manager: *Managing multiple relationships. Acting as "playing coach." Translating goals into action. Translating action into measurement. Assuming full responsibility and limited authority. Managing in a "political" environment.* Implications of the middle-level general management job. Advantages of the middle-level general management job.

15.   **General management at the corporate level** . . . . . . **118**

The job of the corporate staff manager: *The illusionary power of the system. The illusion of neutrality. Managing relationships. Challenge of the corporate staff job. Possible roles of the corporate planner.* The job of the corporate general manager: *Managing the strategic process. Managing structure and systems. Managing relationships. Managing executive selection and development.*

16.   **The transition to general management** . . . . . . . **129**

*Major career transition. Resentment. Newcomer. Experimental leadership. Ratification. Accommodation and compromise. Job strategy.*

**Cases for part I**
**The general manager as strategist**

THE PROCESS OF CORPORATE STRATEGY

CORPORATE STRATEGY AND ENVIRONMENTAL CHANGE

STRATEGIC ALTERNATIVES AND CORPORATE CHOICE

**Cases for part II**
**The general manager as organization builder**

GENERAL MANAGEMENT IN THE
FUNCTIONAL ORGANIZATION

GENERAL MANAGEMENT IN THE
DIVISIONALIZED ORGANIZATION

# Part I

## The general manager as strategist

# 1

# General management is everybody's business

## THE GENERAL MANAGER AS STRATEGIST AND ORGANIZATION BUILDER

GENERAL MANAGEMENT, or business policy, focuses on a company in its totality: its external posture (corporate strategy) as well as its internal structure (corporate organization). The general manager, therefore, provides leadership both as strategist and as organization builder. The two major tasks are closely interwoven. A strategic response depends on the organizational ability to implement it. More importantly, the process of strategic decision making occurs within an organizational context. While in theory strategy determines organization, in practice strategy depends heavily on organizational inputs.

As strategist, the general manager defines the corporate purpose. The first part of this text portrays a dynamic framework for formulating strategy, relating the company's internal situation to its evolving external conditions. It involves several steps as well as a number of skills which are discussed in Chapters 2 through 9.

As organization builder, the general manager provides leadership by managing his people as a cohesive unit to accomplish the corporate strategic mission. Again, the challenge is a dynamic one: Today's action must be taken in view of tomorrow's needs. In many ways, the organizational aspects of the general manager's job are the most difficult, especially where they involve the management of transition. While strategy formulation, to a large extent, is an intellectual activity involving abstract

3

plans and physical or financial resources, organizational leadership, in contrast, is an administrative activity involving people, their tasks and their relationships. The general manager is concerned with both organizational diagnosis and action. Chapters 10 through 15 cover the organizational aspects of the general management task. Chapter 16 concludes this text by focusing on the most critical transition in a manager's career, that from specialist to general management.

## THE GENERAL MANAGEMENT POINT OF VIEW

To a manager of people, the respect for human dignity comes first and foremost. The general manager greatly influences the quality of the professional life of many people. Obviously, the quality of one's professional environment has a major impact on the quality of one's personal and family life and on the fabric of society. One key element in striving for respect for human dignity is the point of view, stressed in this text, of seeing oneself both as a superior and subordinate. By simultaneously viewing human relationships from both sides, it is possible to provide professional leadership. In a democratic society, one can govern only with the consent of those being governed.

The human element confronting the general manager makes his task a political one. He must deal with the personal and organizational realities: with ambitions, desires, and goals of individuals. These realities will influence motivation and cooperation, particularly when power is sought and contested and when rivalries and conflicts emerge. In fact, politics are a phenomenon of all human interaction, whether in the church, in government, in universities, or in business. The general manager must have a sense—and a stomach—for the political dimension of his organization.

A diagnostic ability is also required. General managers must be able to discover, select, and use the facts. This challenge is more demanding for the generalist because he is confronted by a multiplicity of dimensions. Furthermore, strategic and organizational facts do not manifest themselves as neatly and overtly as do technical or financial facts.

The ability and willingness to make decisions, however, is the most critical aspect of the general manager's job. He must integrate and balance the many elements of the total situation. His actions usually involve long time spans, necessitating a sense of timing. Frequently, he confronts major risks, making the decision process a dangerous and lonely task. Also, he must communicate his decisions to his organization and enlist support for their implementation.

General management is not an exact science. Those striving for clarity, purity, and certainty will never acquire a general management point of view. General management is fuzzy, complicated, and imprecise. Balancing the many elements of the total company equation requires trade-offs, compromises, and accommodations. Timing means predicting and anticipating future events, sequencing one's moves accordingly, and proceeding on a path which involves a continuous back and forth of action and response. General management skills, therefore, are not just analytical. They are judgmental and political as well. It is more important for a general manager to be wise than to be smart.

## GENERAL MANAGEMENT IS EVERYBODY'S BUSINESS

Traditionally, the job of the general manager has been equated with that of a company's chief executive. Yet, increasingly, corporate organizations are providing for general management positions at levels below the chief executive, and as a result the number of general management positions is rising.

General management positions at the intermediate level of the corporate hierarchy are a direct outgrowth of the movement toward the divisional organization. While the functional organization requires only one general manager, the divisional organization provides for a variety of business units, each requiring a general manager. Often the process of divisionalization extends several levels down into the organization (that is, group, division, department), further increasing the need for general managers at lower levels. As a result of divisionalization, the number of general managers has increased greatly during the last few decades. Today, in all likelihood, the majority of general managers are not chief executives.

General management, however, is of importance not just to the chief executive and the general managers of operating divisions. Every manager continuously makes operating decisions which have policy implications. In theory, a company's strategic and organizational posture results from definitive statements issued by top management. In practice, however, no statement can give categorical guidance when dealing with an uncertain future and highly complex situations. Policy statements, while superficially clear and often confining, typically require clarification and interpretation. Just as no legislature can write crystal-clear laws, so is it impossible for top management to issue unambiguous directives. The inevitable need for clarification and interpretation gives the manager a great deal of discretion which puts him, whether he wants it or not, in a general management position. In implementing guidance from above, the manager greatly influences it. Policies evolve and become clarified through a manager's daily activities. Every manager, therefore, is a policy maker, even though he may not have the formal authority. His role typically is broader than codified in his job description. If he wants to assume this broader role, however, he must be aware of it, because he cannot discharge a responsibility he does not recognize.

Strategic and organizational action involves all managers; it is part of their daily activities; and it is a continuous process. Because all managers make frequent operating decisions of a policy nature, it is important that everybody in the organization make general management his business. The general management approach in these situations serves as a frame of mind, an awareness, a point of view which guides the manager in recognizing and anticipating the policy implications of his daily activities.

The general management point of view is relevant to managers not only in the conduct of company affairs but also in approaching their own jobs and careers. Just as it is possible to formulate a corporate strategy, so is it feasible to develop a job strategy. The same framework can be used. In fact, the quality of corporate management depends heavily on how each individual manages his own professional life. The general management process and viewpoint help the manager in meeting this critical challenge.

# 2

# The general manager
# as strategist

## THE PURPOSE OF CORPORATE STRATEGY

CORPORATE STRATEGY can best be defined by looking at the purposes
it serves: to provide both direction and cohesion to the enterprise. Providing direction is the traditional objective assigned to corporate strategy: to give the company a sense of purpose and mission. Providing
cohesion, on the other hand, is an objective of corporate strategy which
is often ignored. Yet it is not only important but also more essential
than providing direction.

Rhetorically, advocates of corporate strategy often pose the alternatives for a company of either having or not having a corporate strategy.
In the latter case, they will cite the famous statement that "if you don't
know where you are going, any road will take you there." However,
lack of a corporate strategy does not necessarily entail a lack of direction.
Rather, in the absence of a corporate strategy, other goals and objectives
will fill the vacuum. Every company consists of various units—for example, marketing, manufacturing, research and development, and administration in a functional organization. Each unit will have its own functional strategy. Manufacturing may wish to mechanize its facilities to
the utmost in order to reduce the labor component in its cost structure;
research and development may wish to explore the frontiers of knowledge; and marketing may aim for a broad and constantly changing product line. The strategy of each unit, furthermore, will be influenced also
by the goals and ambitions of the executive in charge. Functional and

personal strategies of the various units will fill the vacuum which may exist in the absence of a corporate strategy.

Unit strategies may prevail even where a corporate strategy has been formulated because members of the organization identify more readily with their units, which are both smaller and closer, than with the corporation, which appears to many managers as remote and unfamiliar.

The choice usually is not between either having or not having a corporate strategy but between the primacy of corporate goals and objectives over those of the units, or vice versa. When the unit strategies take over (notwithstanding the lip service middle managers may continue to pay to company-wide objectives), corporate responses to external opportunities and threats become an arbitrary outgrowth of these multiple unit strategies. Because these unit strategies pull in their own and often different directions, they may create conflicts, thereby preventing the corporation from responding consistently as an entity. Such conflicting and haphazard responses are particularly dangerous when resources are limited or when the external threats are severe. Only by establishing the primacy of the corporate strategy over that of the units is it possible to achieve the internal cohesion which permits effective utilization of corporate resources and quick responses to external opportunities and threats.

In providing cohesion, corporate strategy influences the unit strategies rather than permitting the latter to shape the corporate response. This poses no problem where both corporation and unit pursue similar goals. Where the corporate strategy runs counter to that of the unit, however, strategic leadership requires convincing members of the unit to pursue policies which are not their "first" choice. Corporate strategy may require responses which run counter to the conventional functional wisdom. For example, a company with limited resources operating in a highly cyclical industry may emphasize the need for a low break-even point by minimizing fixed expenses. As a result, it will have to rely heavily on outside suppliers, minimizing its investment in manufacturing plant and equipment even at the penalty of foregoing cost-reducing automation. Such an approach clearly runs counter to conventional manufacturing wisdom.

In establishing cohesion, furthermore, corporate strategy must establish priorities among the units. Rarely can all their shopping lists be satisfied; choices must be made. As a result, some units will be treated as more equal than others. For instance, a company with a weak market share may give preference to bolstering its distribution setup before devoting funds to manufacturing or engineering. Likewise, where the industry is cyclical, debt may be repaid (avoiding future fixed interest and repayment charges) before money is invested in plant and equipment (which would increase fixed expenses).

Finally, cohesion requires that the activities of the various units be interrelated. For example, are product and distribution policy mutually supportive and do they reinforce each other? Do the total actions of marketing, manufacturing, engineering, and finance result in a coordinated response? This integration aspect not only provides a common sense of direction to the units but also permits the total organizational response to be more effective than that of the sum of its parts. This is the final test of a cohesive organization.

## THE PROCESS OF CORPORATE STRATEGY

The process of corporate strategy involves several steps. It is useful to begin with a thorough understanding of a company's *strategic profile.* A company may have made its strategy explicit or its strategy can be derived implicitly from the company's actual behavior. The two are not always identical, in which case the strategist judges a company by what it does, not by what it says. The strategic profile concerns itself with how a company has defined (1) its business, (2) its competitive posture, and (3) its concept of itself.

The next step is to arrive at a *strategic forecast.* A first phase sets the framework by identifying the various environmental dimensions, while a second phase involves predicting their future developments. Analysis focuses on the (1) political, social, and economic; (2) market; (3) product and technological; and (4) competitive dimensions. The strategic forecast thus encompasses the company's total external environment. Furthermore, it is a dynamic process: the existing environmental dimensions are not only identified but their future scope is predicted as well. The strategist explores both current as well as future opportunities and threats.

The third step of the strategic process involves the *resource audit.* Here the focus is on the internal dimensions: operational, financial, and managerial. Corporate resources are both identified and evaluated. The strategist defines a company's strengths as well as its weaknesses.

The subsequent step builds upon the preceding two: within the external and internal framework a variety of *strategic alternatives* are explored. What is the range of strategic responses, given the environmental opportunities and threats and the corporate strengths and weaknesses? The purpose of this step is to provide the strategist with a range of choice broader than the company's existing strategic profile and to prevent a myopic focus on either company traditions or on prevailing industry fashions. Given the earlier dynamic appraisal of environment and resources, the development of strategic alternatives aims particularly at the pursuit of future opportunities and the avoidance of emerging threats and risks.

The fifth step of the strategic process entails the *test of consistency*. The existing strategic profile and various strategic alternatives are evaluated by testing their consistency with the external and internal dimensions, both in their identified current and in their predicted future scope. The strategist relates what a company is *able* to do with respect to its resources to what is *possible* in its external environment.

Following the evaluation of a company's strategic options, the strategist moves to the final step: He makes his *strategic choice*. Either the existing corporate strategy is reaffirmed or a new strategic profile is developed. Commitment to a specific strategic plan usually will require not only definition of the elements of the strategic profile but also basic choices in terms of degree of risk and timing.

The steps of the strategic process thus move from the strategic profile to the strategic forecast and the resource audit, followed by the development of strategic alternatives. These, in turn, are put to the test of consistency which leads to the necessity for strategic choice. Three comments are in order. First, the framework of strategy formulation is simple in concept. It is easily described and understood. It is basic rather than esoteric. It represents common sense and will not strike anyone as a profound revelation. Yet this apparent simplicity should not fool its user. While simple in concept, the framework of corporate strategy is difficult to apply. The gap between understanding and application is extraordinarily wide. The test of a successful strategist is based on the latter, not the former.

Second, the framework of corporate strategy is a dynamic one. It deals with today's answers to tomorrow's issues. This requires not only an analytical approach to today's facts but also predictive judgments of tomorrow's conditions. By necessity, therefore, corporate strategy formulation is an inexact science. Those seeking certainty should not aspire to become strategists.

Third, the framework of corporate strategy operates in two ways. It can be used to appraise an existing strategy by relating it to the external environment and the internal resources. Alternatively, one can begin with an analysis of environment and resources to arrive at a number of strategic alternatives from which a desirable strategy is chosen.

## THE SKILLS OF THE STRATEGIST

In its application, the conceptually simple process of strategy formulation places high demands on the strategist. It requires a variety of skills. The first one, identification, is easily overlooked. Every manager will claim that he knows his own business. Yet it is surprising how many elements are discovered or seen in clearer perspective by embarking on a systematic and explicit process of identifying the company's strategic profile as well as its external and internal conditions.

While many executives carry the data on their strategy and their environment in their heads, it is extremely difficult to assess objectively the completeness and relevance of these data without making them explicit. It is a common experience that thoughts which appear perfect when they flash through one's head pale considerably once they are put down on paper and assessed with detachment. Likewise, being explicit about strategy, environment, and resources is an essential prerequisite if a complete and objective analysis is to take place.

Identification is primarily an analytic process. As such, it has to be thorough to ensure that all factors have been considered; it must be precise in order to give focus to the analysis; and it should be as concise as possible to avoid overburdening the decision process. More importantly, the process of identification establishes the parameters within which the strategic analysis must proceed. Given the multiplicity of dimensions involved as well as their changes over time, it is highly desirable to give structure and analytical discipline to the strategic process. Identification greatly influences the quality of the final outcome.

Analytical skills do not suffice. The predictive elements of the strategic process, especially strategic forecasting, require judgmental skills. The future cannot be identified; it must be predicted. Predictions cannot be based solely on an objective analysis but also require subjective judgments. Where no major environmental changes are anticipated, the role of the strategist is minimal. He earns his way by responding to changes or by bringing them about. Given the usually long lead times needed for strategic decisions, such responsiveness requires anticipation of these changes. This anticipation requires uncertain and difficult predictive judgments.

The skills of identification and prediction, of analysis and judgment, have to be complemented by a third skill: that of innovation. In developing strategic alternatives the strategist has to apply creative skills: he has to be an innovator. Within the context of environment and resources a broad range of strategic options has to be explored. As evidenced by several cases in this book, the rewards of a unique and imaginative strategy can be great.

After identification, prediction, and innovation comes evaluation as a fourth skill. While the test of consistency at first glance appears to be an instrument of logic, in reality it requires both analysis and judgment. In the dynamic framework of strategy formulation the test of consistency matches not only current environment and resources but also predictions of the future external and internal conditions. Because the latter are products of judgment, so also is the process of evaluation.

Furthermore, the test of consistency does not always result in neat and precise outcomes, again forcing the strategist to rely on his judgment.

The final step of the process confronts the strategist with the necessity of choice, requiring decisiveness. Because strategic decisions usually involve major commitments which have to be made in anticipation of future events and years may pass before the results are known, decisiveness is no easy task. Faced with an uncertain future, several options, and the need to embark on a specific course of action requiring the irrevocable commitment of major resources, decisiveness involves risk taking. It demands not only a clear head but also a strong stomach. The strategist must exhibit both nerve and courage.

The task of strategist, therefore, is not easy. It requires skills of identification, prediction, innovation, evaluation, and decisiveness. These skills require qualities which go beyond those of logical analysis. They demand sound judgments, imagination, and creativity, and a great deal of nerve and courage.

In summary, the strategic process consists of:

| Elements \ Skills | Identification | Prediction | Evaluation | Innovation | Decision |
|---|---|---|---|---|---|
| Strategic profile | Step 1 | | | | |
| Environmental dimensions | Step 2 | | | | |
| Strategic forecast | | Step 3 | | | |
| Company resources | Step 4 | | Step 4 | | |
| Strategic alternatives | | | | Step 5 | |
| Test of consistency | | | Step 6 | | |
| Strategic choice | | | | | Step 7 |

# 3

# The strategic profile

EVERY COMPANY, whether it has an explicit strategy or not, has a *strategic profile*. This profile is based on the actions of a company, not on the statements of its executives. Hence, strategic profiles are not secrets to the sensitive and perceptive analyst. They can be deduced from a company's actual behavior by insiders and outsiders alike. Thus, identification of the strategic profile is a feasible and useful exercise both for one's own company and for its competitors.

Every company in the conduct of its business faces some critical choices which shape its strategic profile. These choices are not entirely free; they are constrained both by the company's internal resources and by its external environment. Within these constraints, however, some basic choices are typically made. Such choices are not always the result of explicit decisions. They may have been inadvertent or may have gradually evolved over time.

The strategic profile consists of three major elements:

—how a company defines its business,
—how a company defines its competitive posture,
—how a company defines its concept of itself.

## HOW A COMPANY DEFINES ITS BUSINESS

Typically, a company faces some basic choices in terms of its scope of operations: horizontally, vertically, and geographically.

13

## Product scope: The horizontal choices

Every company defines, by one means or another, the business(es) it participates in. A first choice relates to the horizontal range of products: from specializing in a single product or a narrow segment of an industry, on one extreme, to broad diversification into a wide variety of unrelated products on the other. From a strategic and organizational point of view, the choice between participation in a single business versus that of engaging in multiple businesses is a critical one, the organizational implications of which will be discussed in later chapters. At this point, suffice it to say that in a diversified company the strategic process must be undertaken not only at headquarters for the corporation as a whole but also for each separate business unit before the total strategic plan can be formulated. Usually the former focuses on financial goals and the composition of the portfolio of businesses, while the latter deals with specific product-market relationships. Thus, the strategic process takes place on a corporate basis for the single product company and on a divisional (or even lower) as well as the corporate level for the diversified enterprise.

Within the single business entity, a number of options are typically available. Most businesses are characterized by a range of products that can be grouped along several dimensions, among them price (and quality), product features, and product utility. For instance, in the light aircraft industry planes are sold in various price categories having numerous configurations (single engine, twin engine, turboprop, etc.) for use in several markets (recreational, business, and commercial). The companies in the industry differ in the extent to which they attempt to blanket the market. Some opt for a relatively narrow segment; others seek a full product line.

Within the diversification choice, different approaches are possible depending on the degree of "relatedness" of the various activities. The business units, each catering to a different product and market, may share commonalities in technology, production processes, distribution, and customer base. For example, Litton Industries, in its early years, although represented in numerous fields including computer and control systems, radar systems, and navigational devices, maintained a relatively homogeneous technical and customer base. Or the relatedness between the units may be virtually nonexistent, as happened later when the company branched out into calculators, cash registers, geophysical research and exploration, shipbuilding, paper, restaurants, and other activities. The common thread became increasingly difficult to find.

## Degree of vertical integration

The flow of a product, from its basic raw materials until it reaches the ultimate user, usually involves several stages. For example, crude oil or natural gas are the feedstock for some chemical building blocks which are transformed into chemical intermediates which, in turn, are converted into chemical end products used to manufacture a great variety of products such as plastic toys, pipes, or packaging. In some instances, companies have integrated vertically along the product flow to protect or provide markets for intermediate products and to capture a greater share of the value added. In other cases, they have confined their activities to certain aspects of the product flow. The large oil companies, for example, are fully integrated from the well to the gasoline station but also sell by-products of their refineries on a merchant basis, providing feedstock for the chemical companies.

A company situated along the vertical product flow faces both an opportunity and a threat. It can decide to integrate either forward or backward. Concurrently, it is exposed to the threat of either its suppliers or its customers doing likewise. The strategic profile will indicate what choices a company as well as its competitors, customers, and suppliers have made in terms of their involvement along the vertical product flow. These strategic postures raise questions not only in terms of opportunities and threats but also in terms of the competitive conditions of an industry as reflected, for example, in costs, prices, or purchasing patterns.

The tire industry is a well-known example. Fearful of backward integration by the automobile companies, the tire companies have sold to the original equipment market at near cost, relying for their profitability largely on the replacement market. Within the framework of such a strategy, the introduction of longer lasting tires such as radials which delay the replacement cycle has significant strategic implications.

## Geographic coverage

The strategic profile also registers a company's geographic involvement. *The New York Times* has achieved leadership only in one section of the country; its western and European editions were failures, and in spite of its international reputation, its sales are geographically confined. *The Wall Street Journal,* in contrast, has successfully achieved national distribution. Geographic coverage, moreover, confronts a company with the choice of extending its operations to other countries. The degree, or absence, of its international commitment may have important strategic implications, for example, in terms of growth opportunities, manufacturing strength, competitive or economic vulnerability. Within the same industry, international coverage may vary significantly among the various companies.

The geographic choices complete the profile of how a company has defined its business. The strategic profiles resulting from these various choices can differ markedly, even for companies in the same industry.

The example below has been taken from the farm equipment industry and represents the percentage of total sales in 1965 that each of three major companies derived from North American, international, and non-farm equipment sales.

| | *Percentage of 1965 sales derived from—* | | |
|---|---|---|---|
| | *North American farm equipment sales* | *Overseas farm equipment sales* | *Nonfarm equipment sales* |
| Deere . . . . . . . . . . . . | 70 | 14 | 16 |
| Massey Ferguson . . . . . | 28 | 49 | 23 |
| White Motor . . . . . . . . | 30 | 1 | 69 |

## HOW A COMPANY DEFINES ITS COMPETITIVE POSTURE

### The choice of competitive weapons

An industrial company typically competes on the basis of its marketing, manufacturing, engineering, research and development, and financial capabilities. In other business sectors, such as shipping, publishing, construction, mutual fund management, or broadcasting, competition is based on different, though often analogous, activities. Because resources and capabilities are limited, companies often place different emphases on these various operational aspects. In effect, they choose the competitive weapons to be used in securing an advantage in the marketplace. For some it may be the posture of the low-cost producer. For others it may be rapid delivery and extensive customer service. For still others it may be product innovation or creative marketing. John Deere, in the example referred to above, achieved leadership in the farm equipment industry through emphasis first on distribution, then on the extension of credit, and finally on product development. Clearly, not every company places special emphasis on one or more aspects of its operations. However, most successful enterprises have a concept of how they wish to compete.

### A company's relative position

Beyond a concern for the company's choice of competitive weapons, the strategist identifies its rank relative to its competitors. What is the company's role in the industry? Does it exhibit leadership along some dimensions or does it follow industry convention? Is its leadership based on a unique strategic design or simply on overpowering muscle? Size, of course, does not necessarily connote leadership, nor is the company with the largest market share necessarily the most profitable or the most likely to secure growth in the future. Indeed, being the biggest in an industry often creates penalties and .constraints as well as rewards and opportunities.

## HOW A COMPANY DEFINES ITS CONCEPT OF ITSELF

### Mentality and culture

A company has a mentality and a mode of behavior of its own. In some instances, the company may be a reflection of the drive and leadership style of its chief executive. It was difficult in 1972 to separate Polaroid from Dr. Land, or ITT from Mr. Geneen, for example. In other instances, there is a pervasive atmosphere, which may range from aggressiveness, quick responses, and a hard-nosed orientation, as was the case for some of the newer conglomerates, to complacency, slow responses, and paternalism, a not uncommon characteristic of some of the older, long-established firms. These conditions influence not only a company's strategic posture but also its range of potential responses to competitive challenges and environmental changes.

### A company's performance goals

A final but important element of a company's strategic profile is the performance goals which management has decided to pursue and which, for the benefit of financial analysts or for internal guidance, have often been made explicit. These goals may be expressed in terms of earnings growth (often expressed as a rate of growth in earnings per share), sales growth, industry position, or in other ways (for example, in terms of sales breakdown, such as between government and civilian sales). Of increasing importance is the intended relationship between the company and various constituencies, such as employees, customers, and the community, which extends beyond the traditional financial and stewardship obligations to ownership interests. In some instances, performance in these areas is also included among the company's goals.

It is important to note that this identification deals with what a company hopes to achieve, not what it has achieved. In order to place these future goals in perspective it is useful to relate them to the actual performance to date. Where goals significantly exceed previous achievements, they provide an indication of the stress that will be placed on future strategy. Thus, performance goals serve as a point of departure for the subsequent steps in the strategic process.

# 4

# The environmental dimensions

## IDENTIFICATION OF THE
## ENVIRONMENTAL DIMENSIONS

In IDENTIFYING the conditions prevailing in the external environment, four major dimensions typically have to be considered:

—political, social, and economic dimension;
—market dimension;
—product and technological dimension;
—competitive dimension.

Identification of the external dimensions does not imply that they should be solely considered as "givens." Obviously, they influence a company's strategic flexibility. On the other hand, a company's strategic response may influence or change many of the environmental dimensions. Thus, the interaction between strategy and environment goes both ways: they influence each other. In this chapter, however, the focus will be exclusively on environmental analysis. The strategic response will be discussed later.

The process of identifying the external dimensions begins with the broad political, social, and economic environment within which business operates. From there, the more specific market dimension is considered. It describes the terrain on which the competitive battle will be waged. Then the product and technological dimensions must be identified, revealing the weapons with which the competitive battle will be fought.

Finally, the competitive dimension itself must be analyzed. Who are the opponents to be faced on the battlefield?

## POLITICAL, SOCIAL, AND ECONOMIC DIMENSION

Political factors have become vastly more important to businessmen in recent years. Rare nowadays are the general managers who can ignore the political consequences of their decisions or the impact of public policy on future decisions. Some of the elements which influence the strategic equation have been with us for years, such as tariffs and other trade restrictions or antitrust legislation. Others have surfaced lately, either through private actions in the courts and at stockholder meetings, or through congressional and other government activities. The public concern today over such issues as ecology, equal opportunity, and consumer protection may, in retrospect, appear to have been the inevitable consequences of clearly visible social change. However, few companies devoted time and resources a decade ago to diagnosing or preparing for this more complicated political and social environment.

The economic dimension is also an important input to the strategic equation. In part, the concerns are those traditionally having an influence on supply and demand: economic growth and cyclicality. How does a company's strategy relate to the business cycle? How is it affected by rising affluence and changing spending patterns? For instance, among the case studies in this book, the fortunes of the Wellington Management Company, one of the largest mutual fund management firms, are intimately related to the performance of the economy. However, given the expanding scope of governmental intervention in the private sector, the relationship between market opportunities and threats and public policy becomes even closer. Thus, Wellington must also assess the economic impact of government-sponsored regulations concerning negotiated brokerage fees and institutional membership on major stock exchanges.

The political, social, and economic dimension is one over which the strategist clearly has the least control. As a result, many general managers view those factors rather fatalistically as inevitable constraints. However, in many instances they may constitute opportunities. For example, antitrust actions may provide opportunities to the small newcomer. A major event permitting the growth of General Cinema was the breakup after World War II of the integrated companies which had dominated the production, distribution, and exhibition of movies. While the remnants of these giant companies, as they tried to diversify, floundered through an industry depression created in part by television, General Cinema capitalized on an array of social and economic trends to emerge by 1972 as the leading theater exhibition company.

Four elements of the political, social, and economic dimension will be discussed in more detail:

—international and national economic policies,
—traditional government regulation of business,
—recent political and social developments,
—economic developments.

## International and national economic policies

A relatively recent but highly important phenomenon is economic integration. Spearheaded by the European Common Market, attempts at economic integration have been undertaken by countries in a number of other trading areas as well. The reduction of tariff barriers and the harmonization of other economic policies broaden the market. Not only does economic integration stimulate economic growth but it also permits business strategies hitherto impossible because of the limitations of small fragmented national markets. However, opportunities for some constitute threats to others. The opening of national markets results in the entry of foreign competitors. Historic market positions may be attacked and competitive behavior may be upset by newcomers. More is at stake for participants in the enlarged competitive battle than market shares and prices. Changes in industry structure with the elimination of marginal firms may also result. Patterns of direct investment, manufacturing rationalization, and distribution may be altered as well.

Tariffs and other trade restrictions, such as import quotas or currency regulations, constitute other important elements influencing business strategy. The Swiss watch industry for decades and even centuries pursued an export strategy, supplying world markets from its local production sources. The post–World War II import restrictions, particularly in the developing world, upset this pattern.

Economic policies at the national level also influence corporate strategy. For instance, government attempts to tighten credit may affect the manufacturer of consumer durables which typically sells a large percentage of its products on an installment basis. Price controls may reduce marketing flexibility and, coupled with increasing costs, place pressure on margins. Tax policies, such as investment credits, may have a bearing on capital investment decisions.

## Traditional government regulation of business

While the above government actions influence businesses indirectly, other government activities have a direct impact on corporate strategy. Antitrust has already been mentioned. Regulatory agencies, such as the

Federal Communications Commission (FCC) or the Food and Drug Administration (FDA), shape the strategic options available to the industries they regulate. It can be argued that stricter testing by the FDA, while protecting the consumer, also benefits the established pharmaceutical companies and constitutes an additional entry barrier for newcomers. Policies established or interpreted by the FCC are critical inputs to the strategic process for radio and television firms such as the Arkana Broadcasting Company, which is described in a subsequent case.

### Recent political and social developments

In recent years, new developments having significant potential consequences have occurred. Consumerism or consumer protection is one of them. It manifests itself in a concern for reasonable prices, as happened in the pharmaceutical industry; for safety, which has become a major issue in the automotive and tire industries; and for truth in packaging, which has affected many consumer goods companies. It is impossible for the Marlin Firearms Company to avoid a concern for product safety and indeed the more pervasive issue of gun controls.

The issue posed by discrimination and equal employment has become another major environmental factor of strategic importance. For example, industries heretofore relying on low-cost minority or female labor, whether in agriculture, manufacturing, or services, are directly confronted by a different and rising cost structure. The more difficult task of integrating women and minorities into the ranks of top and middle management is only now being tackled. The physical and psychic energy consumed in racial disputes is enormous; the risks lie in the company's ability to attract competent managers as well as the diversion of attention from the competitive aspects of the business.

Another set of issues arises from the evolving public policy aimed at the protection of our physical environment. Emissions from manufacturing processes into the air and water are now being widely regulated. The businessman is confronted with rapidly changing laws at federal, state, and local levels which are sometimes at variance with one another. Moreover, the standards are often such that the best available technology is insufficient to ensure compliance. Under these uncertain conditions, the potential cost in the next decade to clean up certain industries including steel, paper, and copper is staggering. Decisions involving marginal facilities and businesses, product policy, and new plant locations will increasingly have to incorporate the direct and indirect (for example, higher fuel rates) costs of environmental protection.

These newer forces in many instances constrain existing strategies. Sometimes they call for revisions, and often they entail higher costs. While threatening or costly to some industries, they present opportunities to others and competitive advantages to more fortunate or farsighted companies in a single industry. As the quality of life increasingly takes precedence over the quantity of output, these environmental trends pose challenges that call for imaginative and novel strategies. However, by virtue of their new and evolving character, coupled with the great uncertainties clouding the formulation of public policy, the strategist often receives unclear and—worse—conflicting signals.

### Economic developments

The broad economic development of a country or market obviously is an important input into the strategic equation. The emerging economies of the Central American countries, on the verge of an era of industrialization, create different opportunities and problems than does the large and diverse industrial economy of the United States. In contrast to the relatively unsaturated markets of the developing world, the industrialized nations present the strategist with the problems of maturity and the opportunities associated with affluence. It is difficult to extend the capacity of a full stomach or to find products for the "person who has everything." In fact, deepening concern for ecology has given rise to proposals for a zero growth policy as the only way to halt mankind's predatory use of its limited global resources. Needless to say, a zero growth economy, or one in which energy or raw materials are rationed, has far-reaching implications for many corporate strategies.

Even if growth is to continue, its mix is certain to change. After food and shelter needs have been satisfied, economic activities are directed toward consumer durables, resulting in the vast mechanization of our daily activities, from transportation to household chores. But here, too, saturation becomes evident; with the second automobile and the electric carving knife, consumption tapers off. Expenditures for leisure activities, often of a service nature, then begin to grow. People travel more, increasingly eat in restaurants, and seek a wider variety of entertainment. Function alone ceases to suffice. Convenience and beauty are additional requirements. As such products or services gain acceptance, they move from a class to a mass market, permitting new strategies and industries.

While the structure of the economy changes, the strategist will also have to cope with the traditional and yet continually important phenomenon of the business cycle. The recession which occurred as we moved into the seventies has reminded many companies, often painfully, of the importance of this element. Admittedly, the business cycle affects various industries differently. Yet the phenomenon of declining margins coupled with rising working capital and fixed asset requirements has adversely affected many companies. The pattern is a common one. As the economy stagnates, companies fight more fiercely for a stagnant market, almost inevitably narrowing the spread between competitive prices and inflationary costs. In an attempt to keep costs under control, more mechanization is called for, resulting in higher fixed asset expenditures which—if debt financed—result in increased interest charges as well. At the same time, the use of customer service as a compensatory competitive weapon frequently results in larger inventories and receivables. Unable to finance these asset requirements internally with a shrinking cash flow, companies have to resort to more debt, thereby raising their fixed charges and vulnerability still further. The remedy, severe cost cutting, is then instituted, which may choke off those programs in product development and marketing which have been designed to fuel future growth.

Strategies have to be geared to a variety of economic conditions. A strategy which is viable only under good economic conditions is a highly risky proposition. Yet, obvious as this statement sounds, it is surprising how many strategies are in violation of it. Psychologically, it is difficult to plan for disaster under euphoric conditions. Indeed, it is usually during the periods of economic boom that the seeds of disaster are planted, through errors both of commission and omission. Regarding the former, shortages during boom periods pressure a company into plant expansion. Failure to respond to these pressures would result in a loss in market share and would leave the company behind in terms of modern and efficient manufacturing facilities. Thus, it is a matter of economic and competitive necessity for a company to ride with the economic boom. Such behavior, however, aggravates the condition as the business cycle turns downward. The larger manufacturing facilities create a severe excess capacity problem, compounded by a cost structure which, especially for modern, highly efficient plants, includes a high ratio of fixed costs. Where fixed costs are high and incremental variable costs low, the normal reaction is to attempt to maintain volume, even if it entails reducing price. Where everyone has the same idea in a period of declining demand, the obvious result is a vicious circle, with prices being pushed down severely as all manufacturers attempt to avoid a loss in volume. Thus, the logical behavior during economic boom creates conditions which are likely to lead to behavior which aggravates the damage of a subsequent economic downturn.

Errors of omission occur because boom conditions cover up weaknesses which may prove critical during a subsequent recession. Product characteristics and distribution strengths are not truly tested while shortages prevail. Yet they may prove critical in the subsequent fight for a share of a declining market. Because it is easy to gain a false impression of a company's competitive posture during good years, management fails to strengthen its products and distribution. When an economic downturn brutally uncovers competitive weaknesses, it is often too late and too costly.

Strategists in companies subject to changing economic conditions must be cognizant of these dangers. As a result, the strategic demands during an economic boom are twofold: to develop responses for benefiting from the prevailing favorable conditions, while simultaneously to prepare the company's competitive and financial posture for coping with a subsequent economic downturn.

## MARKET DIMENSION

The market dimension focuses on the terrain on which the competitive battle is being fought: the customers which are being served; the channels of distribution which are being used; and, importantly, the size and segmentation of market demand. This section will discuss the assessment of:

—market demand,
—market requirements,
—distribution requirements.

### Market demand

Determination of market size is an obvious step in identifying a company's environment. Every strategy has to be geared to available opportunities. In doing so, a shortsighted view of the limits of the market is a common error. The dangers are twofold. First, market opportunities may be artificially constrained by too narrow a product-market focus. And, second, competitive interdependencies among alternative means of satisfying demand may be overlooked or minimized. Thus, manufacturers of glass bottles, serving the packaging market, should at least be alert to trends affecting metal, paper, and plastic containers as well as glass.

Paradoxically, too general a view of market size may also mask opportunities and threats. Possible segmentations of market demand also have to be explored. HMH Publishing Company with its flagship, *Playboy*, is a famous (or infamous) example of a fantastic success story in a depressed publishing industry which counts the well-known *Saturday Evening Post, Life,* and *Look Magazine* among the victims of its declining competitive position among entertainment, news, and advertising media. Arthur Keller's company, the introductory case in this book, faces both major growth opportunities and severe market declines in the mature textile industry. General Cinema built its success in a depressed industry, first with drive-in theaters which were least affected by television and subsequently with shopping center movie houses. As a result, a corporate strategist has to focus not only on the size and growth of his company's total market but also on existing and potential segments within this market. The outlook for these segments is often markedly different from that for the industry as a whole. In fact, even in a stagnating or declining business it may be possible to discover segments providing a company with major growth opportunities.

At the same time, a prediction as to market growth is equally essential. Estimates of growth have to be based on predictions, not solely on projections. Determination of the future size of the market requires strategic judgments. Often other environmental dimensions will influence the outcome. For example, an estimate of Philip Morris' future market will have to include an assessment of the potential impact of government regulation and public response to the alleged dangers of cigarette smoking. Likewise, Marlin Firearms' market potential may be greatly influenced by gun legislation. Consequently, the past cannot always be taken as an accurate guide for the future. Yet the strategist must be cognizant of the impact of the political, social, and economic dimension on historic demand. He must be able to interpret the record of the past with a sensitivity that will enlighten his judgments of the future.

### Market requirements

A major input in the determination of market potential is the analysis of market requirements. Customer needs may not be satisfied by existing products and strategies. Needs may be changing, providing opportunities to those who are willing to adapt. Or new needs may emerge.

New needs provide the impetus for an entrepreneurial strategic design. Cartridge Television is a classic example; its strategy is based on the premise of a rapid and significant emergence of a consumer video cassette market. Success, of course, is by no means assured. For instance, General Cinema is betting that movie theaters in suburban locations will continue to draw large audiences. Since these two companies will compete for the same consumer time and dollar with very different products, their assessments of consumer needs are evidently different. The validity of their analysis, involving such factors as price, convenience, and product variety, will be critical for their relative success.

Changing needs are equally important. In some instances, they may result from changes in consumer desires. In other situations, consumers will shift their purchasing patterns because alternate products compete for their time or money. Sometimes these products are directly competitive; for example, cheaper ball-point pens and pin-lever watches damaged the market for more expensive fountain pens and jewel-lever watches, respectively. Or these alternate products may be only indirectly competitive. These instances are equally damaging yet harder to recognize. Frozen foods and other forms of food preservation have an indirect but important impact on the market for tin cans. Television, by competing for leisure-time activities, has been a major competitive threat to both the publishing and the movie exhibition industries.

An assessment of market requirements is one of the critical but difficult steps in identifying and predicting a company's environment. This question looms large for several of the companies portrayed in this book. Wellington faces an uncertain future in the mutual fund industry, Philip Morris in cigarettes, and Marlin Firearms for guns.

### Distribution requirements

Most businesses have to operate within a distributive infrastructure. The strategist asks: What impact does the distribution structure have on the formulation of a growth strategy? Are new or rapidly growing products able to find sufficient and qualified outlets? Sometimes a company faces a crucial dilemma: the use of existing channels may permit rapid product introduction but may entail longer run disadvantages, while a restructuring of distribution may be preferable for long-term growth but may create an initial start-up handicap.

Changes in the distribution infrastructure also have a strategic impact. Major changes, for example, may be occurring in mutual fund distribution, which raise important questions for Wellington. Will brokerage houses that have started their own funds continue to be aggressive salesmen for Wellington? What impact will the growth of "no load" funds which shortcut the salesman altogether have on distribution patterns and product line policy? Likewise, the decline of the jewelry trade greatly influences the strategies of the established watch companies.

Two major trends in distribution are frequently encountered. One is the shift from the use of independent channels to that of captive branches. As technological changes place greater emphasis on sophisticated sales effort and skilled service operations, many companies have integrated forward into these activities. Given the costs of operating one's captive and exclusive branches, this trend frequently favors the larger, wider line companies. Economies of scale sometimes are more critical in distribution than in manufacturing. If the tradeoff between benefits and costs for the company with the largest market share favors a direct sales force, the same conclusion may not be appropriate for competing firms. They may have to absorb a higher cost burden per unit sold if they create their own captive distribution network. Their alternative, however, may leave them with a competitively inferior distribution setup as they continue to rely on independent channels which may not have the required skills and resources and may divide their attention among a large number of unrelated products.

Another major trend is the so-called "retail revolution," characterized by the growth of large-scale department stores and supermarkets, on the one hand, and specialty chain stores on the other. In either case, the net effect is greater leverage for the retail outlet in terms of securing price and service concessions from manufacturers, more aggressive merchandising, and, on balance, lower retail prices. The shifting patterns of influence in the distribution system are manifested by the emergence of private brands and, in some instances, moves by the retail company to own or control its sources of supply. Thus, the emergence of the department store as a major outlet for ladies' dresses has an important impact on Arthur Keller's company. Marlin Firearms is faced with the increasing penetration by discount stores into the merchandising of guns.

These trends favor not only size but innovation. The continuous flux in retailing and particularly the large number of recent successes in discount retailing or convenience eating places, such as McDonald's, are vivid testimony to the opportunities open to innovators. In some industries, the many small outlets attempt to stem the tide, as, for example, the neighborhood drugstores and local stockbrokers. Yet even in these industries revolutionary changes in distribution are slowly breaking through. The degree and pace of change has far-reaching implications for the strategies of pharmaceutical and mutual fund companies. Finally, there is the inevitable problem of the middleman. A. G. Brown, a food broker, is affected by the establishment of captive sales forces by food manufacturers, on one end, and by the growing strength of supermarkets and their private brands on the other.

## PRODUCT AND TECHNOLOGICAL DIMENSION

The product and technological dimension deals with the weapons with which the competitive battle is being fought: the products or services which are being offered and the processes which are being used to get the goods out the door. In assessing this dimension it is useful to focus on three characteristics:

—the products and services themselves,
—the process required to produce the products,
—the ingredients or materials used in the manufacture of the products.

### Products

A critical element in the strategic profile is a company's product-market relationship. The identification of market size and competitive requirements deals with one aspect of this equation; the product and technological dimension focuses on the other. In the second instance, the product policies pursued by the various participants in the industry are highlighted. How broad are the product lines being offered? Do companies pursue "specialist" strategies or do they follow a full-line approach? Also, what choices have been made in terms of price and quality? In the light aircraft industry, for example, Piper has pursued a low-price, basic-quality strategy while Beech has been the leader in the high-price, high-quality segment, producing, as stated by company executives, the Cadillac of the industry. The largest company in the industry, Cessna, markets a line which, with only minor gaps, blankets the field. Tying price, quality, and product policy to the previously discussed market segmentation permits the identification of markedly different strategies even within the same industry.

Products are subject to continuous change as participants in the competitive arena attempt to secure marketing advantages. New products may be seen as competitive weapons to differentiate one's own strategy from that of competitors or as responses to new market needs or even as efforts to create markets. Often competitive and market elements will be intertwined. General Motors' product proliferation strategy that evolved under Alfred Sloan may have been primarily a competitive response, albeit haphazard at first, to differentiate the company from Henry Ford's then highly successful single-product strategy. Yet this strategy turned out to be in line with the changing market needs as the U.S. automobile market matured.

Product innovation may provide major competitive advantages and growth opportunities. For example, in the farm equipment industry the development of highly specialized, sophisticated, laborsaving machinery, geared to the large and increasingly specialized farms, has injected new life into an otherwise relatively stable and mature industry. More dramatically, product innovation has permitted the emergence of entirely new industries and companies. Snowmobiles are a recent example. Industry sales have grown from a few thousand dollars in the early sixties to around $600 million by the end of the decade, creating an estimated employment of around 100,000 people. Interestingly, this new industry is dominated by two newcomers, Bombardier and Arctic, while subsidiaries of large established companies are left with small market shares and often unprofitable operations. It is important to keep in mind, however, the limitations imposed by market size and competitive reaction. Products have life cycles which imply the existence of different strategies as the product passes from an untried innovation in a wary but untouched market to a standard item in a replacement market. During the early seventies, replacement sales began to exceed original purchases of snowmobiles, and the issue of market saturation became critical.

Product innovation may also change the rules of the game in an industry. The advent of supertankers, as described in the Anglo Norness cases, had a major impact on the competitive requirements of bulk shipping. While providing substantial operating economies to shipowners which could be shared with clients, the supertankers require a heavy initial investment, are expensive to have idle, and are relatively inflexible as to cargo. Predictably, the nature of the relationship between owners and shippers has begun to focus on longer term contracts which promise greater price stability. The strategic implications of new products can be far-reaching and have to be fully analyzed.

Product innovation is not without risks. The mortality rate of new products is high. But even where success has been achieved, it may prove to be ephemeral. The rate of technological change may be so rapid that it reduces the time span during which a company can reap the benefits of its product developments and hence requires a continuing commitment of development funds to stay in the vanguard of progress. Among marketing companies, brand proliferation may have an analogous effect. The cigarette industry, dominated in the 1920s by three brands, now boasts nearly a hundred, the most popular having less than 20% of the market. Launching a successful brand, defined as one having at least 1% of the market, is expensive and risky affair.

More critically, a company with an initial winner does not always find success possible to replicate. In many industries technological change has raised important strategic implications for the participants. Calculators are an example. For years, the industry worked peacefully on improvements and cost reductions for mechanical calculators. Then electromechanical calculators came along, and the technological pace quickened somewhat. It permitted Olivetti to emerge from its position as a small Italian company to that of a major worldwide factor in the office equipment industry. The shift toward electronics shifted the competitive constellation, providing Japanese companies with sizable growth opportunities. The pace of electronic innovation, however, has quickened even more, providing U.S. semiconductor manufacturers with technological and cost advantages that permit them to enter the end-use market for hand calculators. As wave upon wave of new products reached the market, prices eroded, threatening marginal producers who had hoped to ride along on the crest of a growing market.

Product and technological innovation does not always reward its supporters. Sometimes, those who are left behind may turn out to be the beneficiaries. The desire for product differentiation and the flow of ideas from the laboratories may overshoot market requirements. Not all innovation is either needed or accepted. A famous example is George Romney's American Motors which by staying with its old product in the late 1950s became unique, while the "Big Three" introduced larger and larger cars. The traditional American Motors car, later dubbed "the compact," better satisfied the needs of many consumers during those years than the so-called (by Romney) "dinosaurs" of the Big Three. In the packaging industry during the last decade there was a major push toward new and revolutionary packaging materials and techniques, leading some observers to write the obituary of the tin can. As it turned out, the performance of metal container companies was far better than that of many of the companies marketing new materials. Thus, product and technological innovation should not be endorsed automatically but should rather be submitted to a thorough strategic evaluation.

## Process innovation

Innovation takes place not only for products and services but for processes and ingredients as well. Innovation in these areas may also have far-reaching strategic implications, and many of the comments made above apply equally to them.

Process innovation has been particularly important in capital intensive commodity industries, such as steel or chemicals, where low manufacturing costs are critical. Innovation in such instances is often combined with increased facility size in an effort to attain greater economies of scale. The benefits, however, do not always accrue to the industry, though the implications of not innovating may be still less attractive because of foreign or interindustry competition. A cost or productivity breakthrough by one firm often triggers a competitive reaction. The result may be an expansion of industry capacity beyond current market needs which, of course, leads to price cutting and a lower-than-expected return on investment. This sequence of events has characterized the experience in recent years of many basic industries.

Process innovation is also important in those industries facing labor shortages and rising wage rates. The typical response in manufacturing areas under these circumstances is to seek ways of substituting capital equipment for manpower. Thus, Marlin Firearms, while continuing to manufacture and assemble in the United States, is attempting to remain competitive with European and Japanese imports through increased mechanization, requiring highly automated equipment. Process innovation in service industries has often been overlooked, though here, too, it may be significant. For instance, by locating multiple auditoriums in the same theater, General Cinema was able to reduce both construction and operating costs per dollar of revenue. In general, where costs are an essential input into the strategic equation, process innovation is a frequent companion.

Cost reduction is, of course, not the only goal of process innovation. It also may provide product-quality improvements and better customer service. New processes may also be linked to new ingredients. Thus, the strategist should bear in mind a number of questions: Have process technologies changed frequently or dramatically? Have plant sizes or machine speeds escalated? Has labor productivity increased and, if so, have capital expenditures followed suit?

### New ingredients or raw materials

Finally, new ingredients often permit both cost reductions and product innovations. Frequently, innovations in ingredients originate outside the user industry. Moreover, users do not always possess the technology required to apply these innovations and are sometimes inclined to ignore them. Their impact has to be broadly identified and carefully assessed, since potential opportunities and threats are easily overlooked. Classic examples of this phenomenon are the substitutions of aluminum for steel in beer cans, synthetic fibers for cotton and wool in textiles, and plastic for wood in furniture. In some instances, the innovator has sought or been forced to bypass the manufacturers who would normally be its customers and enter the market for end-use products.

## COMPETITIVE DIMENSION

The competitive dimension spotlights a company's opponents: the number and characteristics of one's competitors. The first question here is to ask: "Who are our competition?" The general manager is likely to greet the question with laughter. He knows who his competitors are. He already has the answer. However, a visit to a pathology lab of the corporate hospital reveals as a common cause of death: killed by a competitor one did not know or did not take seriously. IBM, which did not make manual typewriters, destroyed Underwood's leadership position in the typewriter business with its electric typewriter. Yet for many years Underwood paid more attention to its traditional rivals, Smith-Corona and Royal-McBee. IBM was seen as a remote outsider with a special luxury product, not as a serious and dangerous challenger. In some ways newcomers are more dangerous than established competitors. In identifying the competitive dimension, the strategist should not limit himself to familiar faces. He should also view the lesser known and, more importantly, potential competitors.

A second question in dealing with the competitive dimension is: "How do we compare?" Often this analysis focuses on a comparison of resources. Clearly, a count of the number of troops which can be sent into battle is important. It will provide clues as to relative strength and probable results. Of greater importance, however, is an assessment of the quality of the strategies. The larger company is not necessarily the one most likely to succeed. One must compare not only the size of available resources but also the characteristics of the respective strategies. John Deere is smaller than the Ford Motor Company yet more successful in farm equipment. Vlasic Foods has achieved leadership in the U.S. pickle market even though it is smaller than its major competitor, Heinz.

In some instances, the single-business company is able to outperform its competitors who accommodate a wide range of products. This is particularly true where new products damage the position of established ones. The electric typewriter, for example, was a threat to the market for manual machines. IBM, unburdened by a position in manuals, could focus all its efforts and attention on promoting and selling the electrics. Underwood, Smith-Corona, and Royal-McBee, on the other hand, were reluctant to endanger the position of their manuals, which accounted for the bulk of their output, and consequently sold the electric typewriter defensively at best. Unless properly trained and compensated, a salesman is not going to endanger his established bread-and-butter line by an uncertain, although potentially desirable, product.

A third question in identifying the competitive dimension is: "How do we compete?" Competitive behavior varies from industry to industry. It is in part a function of how participating companies have chosen to compete, a result of their strategic profiles. It is also influenced by the structure of the industry, its operational requirements, and the number and strength of the companies involved. The metal container industry is dominated by Continental and American Can. Their huge market shares and financial resources impose major restrictions on their smaller competitors, such as Crown Cork and Seal and National Can. At the same time, such a structure creates opportunities because can purchasers are often anxious to have one of the smaller companies as a second supplier. The combination of industry structure, operational requirements, and strategic profiles permits the strategist to identify the degree and type of competition which may be encountered.

Competitive weapons vary from industry to industry. In farm equipment, competition occurred on several fronts: price, product development, dealers, and credit. In the duplicating industry it involved product development, systems development, price, service, and advertising. An analysis of competitive behavior must precede the resource audit, which will be discussed in a later chapter. The adequacy of a company's resources can be judged only in light of the competitive requirements of its industry.

A fourth and final question in terms of this dimension is a determination of the impact of competition. Does competition permit the entry of new companies into the industry? Are the industry leaders increasing their market share at the expense of the smaller participants, as has happened in the beer industry? Of great importance is an identification of price levels and cost-price relationships. In certain industries, competition results in a deterioration of price levels, while in others prices remain at reasonable or even high levels in spite of competition. Cost-price relationships are equally important. It is not unusual for industries to have their margins squeezed between low prices and uncontrollable costs. As the IBM electric typewriter began to take an increasing share of the office typewriter market, the traditional Big Three in manuals competed so fiercely for the declining manual typewriter market that their margins almost completely disappeared. Rising costs resulting from inflationary pressures approached the highly competitive price levels. Trapped by such low margins, the Big Three were unable to generate the resources for either a competitive counterattack or for effective and durable diversification.

Several cases in this book permit an exploration of the competitive dimension, especially those dealing with the Central American paint and detergent industries, where both local and international companies are locking horns. The Philip Morris case permits the exploration of competitive behavior in an oligopolistic industry, while Anglo Norness in the shipping industry illustrates close to pure competition as the forces of supply and demand interact relatively freely.

# 5

# Strategic forecasting

## PREDICTIVE JUDGMENTS

THE DESCRIPTION of the environmental dimensions has made clear that they have to be looked at in terms of both the present and the future. The strategist is interested not only in today's market size but also in tomorrow's market growth. Competitive conditions have to be assessed both in current and future terms. In sum, the environmental framework, if it is to be useful to the strategist, must be a dynamic rather than a static description of prevailing conditions. As a result, the focus is not solely on the environment "as is" but also on the environmental trends. While the former requires the analytical skill of identification, the latter involves a predictive skill which is predominantly judgmental in character. Forecasting the environmental trends necessitates primarily strategic judgments and will be referred to here as strategic forecasting.

Strategic forecasting, therefore, is the judgmental process through which the strategist attempts to predict the future shape of the environmental dimensions. It involves the totality of the dimensions and therefore is more than just a market forecast. It includes a forecast of the economic, political, market, technological, and competitive dimensions. Once the forecasts of the various dimensions have been made, the total picture must be viewed.

Given the broad scope of the forecast and the difficulty in predicting many of the dimensions, strategic forecasting by necessity is a highly uncertain process. It is one where judgments by reasonable people may

34

vary significantly. As a result, critics contend that the general manager may as well throw a pair of dice. Yet uncertain and conflicting strategic judgments made explicitly are preferable to jumping haphazardly with one's eyes closed. The process of strategic forecasting makes the areas of judgment explicit. These areas can be fully analyzed, benefiting from a variety of inputs. And even though the forecast is a judgmental one, if made explicitly it can be monitored subsequently, so that changes can be made quickly if later events disprove the basis on which the judgment was made.

Anyone who is called on to forecast, in this day and age, almost feels a moral obligation to predict change. Change is glamorous, it gets the publicity, and it provides the justification for modifying one's strategic posture. Also, the grim stories of those companies which failed to respond to changing conditions make the headlines and are fresh in everybody's mind. Yet strategic forecasting should be done with an open mind. There are many situations which are not subject to appreciable change. In fact, many a strategic forecast will come to the conclusion that conditions will remain the same. No one should be ashamed of such a conclusion. However, it must be based on a thorough predictive analysis rather than on traditional thinking, which satisfies itself that tomorrow will be a carbon copy of yesterday because "that is the way it has been over the last several decades."

Strategic change is often characterized by its suddenness. Conditions which have been stable for years change abruptly, often without warning. It frequently happens in those industries where change is least expected: the older, mature ones. The challenge for the strategic forecaster is to call these sudden major changes in industries which have been stable for years. It is, in many respects, more difficult than predicting changes in industries which are in constant turmoil.

## PREDICTIONS, NOT PROJECTIONS

Strategic forecasting involves primarily predictions, not projections. Yet the strategic forecaster will constantly seek refuge in the latter. Projections have their roots in the past. They are essential in making operational forecasts. However, even if dressed up with the most elegant, esoteric, and modern analytical techniques, a projection still has its roots in the past. While the general manager can learn from history, history should not be the sole basis for his prediction of the future, especially when strategic change involves major structural change as well.

Major change cannot be predicted by relying on past experience. New products may either dislodge existing ones or they may satisfy hitherto unfulfilled needs. Projecting history into the future would not have predicted Heublein's phenomenal success with vodka during the fifties and sixties. During the early fifties the liquor industry was faced with a stagnating market; vodka accounted for only a minimal share of alcoholic beverages consumption. Yet vodka sales, and especially those of Heublein's Smirnoff brand, rose rapidly in the next decade, increasing vodka's share of the liquor market from about 2% to roughly 10%. This success was based on structural changes in liquor consumption; on the increased involvement of women and young people who preferred to dilute alcohol with the familiar taste of tomato juice, orange juice, or soft drinks rather than swallow straight rye or bourbon. The trend toward long drinks also helped, as did the trend toward lightness. Furthermore, the growth of the vodka market was greatly enhanced by Heublein's aggressive and imaginative marketing policies, coupled with the absence of immediate competitive retaliation. Heublein's larger competitors were busy diversifying outside the liquor industry and were also reluctant to endanger their other well-established products by aggressively marketing vodka.

This vodka example indicates some of the variables entering into the strategic forecast. As has already been stated, they cover all or several of the environmental dimensions. The anticipated competitive response was one variable. Would Heublein have been able to make Smirnoff the leading vodka brand if competition had retaliated immediately and vigorously? The strategic forecaster has to judge whether such a response is likely or whether a preoccupation with established lines and diversification will give the new entrant several years of grace. The market dimension as it relates to changing consumer needs was another key variable in the Smirnoff success. So was the product dimension, in that Smirnoff was not just another alcoholic beverage; Heublein's marketing approach made it much more than that. In fact, to achieve product differentiation and premium prices with a product that is tasteless, colorless, and odorless must rank among the major marketing achievements.

During the sixties, Heublein attempted to repeat its Smirnoff success with bottled cocktails. Here again, history was a most inadequate guide to the future. The strategic forecast required judgments in terms of competitive response, the uniqueness of the product, and the needs and desires of the market.

Another strategic forecast relates to the future of the metal container. Will users continue to rely on it as the staple package, or will the need for food processing techniques or beverage characteristics permit or even force a switch to other forms of packaging? Will new raw materials be developed with characteristics superior to those of the metal container? Will the established can companies have access to these new technologies or will they be developed by material companies who may supply the users directly? Will new technologies be developed by a single can company, giving it a major competitive advantage over its rivals? Or will new technologies encourage backward integration through increased self-manufacture by users? Alternatively, will rapid technological change discourage backward integration as users avoid freezing their commitment to a single technology, retaining their freedom of choice of where they want to obtain their packaging materials?

Uncomfortable as it may be, the strategist must predict the answers to such questions as these and, further, be prepared to allocate resources to strategic action programs based on his environmental assessments. In making these judgments, he should be guided by an analysis that encompasses the multiplicity of dimensions described earlier and the interdependencies among them.

## CYCLICAL OR STRUCTURAL CHANGE

A critical dilemma frequently faced by the strategic forecaster is whether the industry is suffering from a common cyclical decline or is confronted with major structural change. The farm equipment industry during the early fifties suffered a sales decline. Some executives in the industry interpreted it as a cyclical slump which they saw as inevitable after the postwar boom had satisfied the prevailing shortages. Others saw a concurrent structural change resulting from fewer but larger farms with different and more sophisticated product needs. The former group simply set out to weather the storm, whereas the latter concluded that changes in strategy were called for. The Strang Company discussed in this book is faced with a sales decline which may be caused by the recession and cutbacks in defense spending during the late sixties or by a declining competitive position in terms of product development and marketing.

The same dilemma may be posed during times of economic prosperity. IBM's electric typewriter counted its first successes during the immediate post–World War II period. Was this an indication of forthcoming structural change, a major shift from manual to electric typewriters? With the benefit of hindsight we now know that such a strategic forecast would have been correct. Yet at that time one could have argued persuasively that IBM's success with electrics was the result of the then prevailing shortages and that once the pent-up war demand was satisfied industry would return to purchasing low-cost and lower maintenance manual typewriters for all but a very specialized market segment. Who would have dared to predict in 1948 that electric typewriters would conquer virtually the entire office typewriter market rather than remaining the Cadillac of the industry with its use limited to the presidential secretary?

The strategic forecast dilemma, whether we are confronted with the impact of the business cycle or with basic structural change, does not solely confront the businessman. The London *Economist,* in its November 6, 1971, issue, posed the same dilemma for the United States:

. . . the chances of the United States recovering its confidence in the reasonably near future are either even worse than they seem at the moment, or rather better than most people think; and it cannot be ruled out that the trouble in America goes so deep that the Americans may be incapable of running a coherent foreign policy for years to come. The United States may be experiencing something that no other country has yet had to go through. It may be experiencing the first full flowering of the Protestant revolution. What happened in the sixteenth century was the rebirth of an idea that had long lain dormant: the idea that the responsibility of the individual is the ultimate criterion of both politics and religion. The rebirth of that idea changed the face of Europe; among other things, it made democracy possible on a scale larger than that of the Greek city-state. But its full impact was never felt by the majority of people. It remained largely a concept of the educated. It is possible that the United States, which has been the first country to do so many things, and was the first to bring material plenty to most of its people, is now the first country to face the consequences of the fact that widespread prosperity universalises the revolution of individualism. If that is the explanation of what is happening to America, the place could be almost ungovernable for a very long time: it could be living through the first onset of the war of all against all. The rest of us had better wave the Americans goodbye while we wait for the same cataclysm to hit us in our turn.

### The chances of recovery

That is one interpretation of the American crisis. But there is an alternative which does not depend on believing that something unique is taking place there. The more hopeful explanation merely assumes that the United States is suffering from a particularly vicious downturn in the normal cycle of expansionist self-confidence and inward-looking masochism that every country rides up and down on; and that sooner or later the normal corrective mechanism will send it back on the upswing.

If that is how it turns out—if history has not intervened this time with one of its secular twists of pattern—there is reason to hope that better times could be coming fairly soon. Three different things have contributed to the American disaffection of the past few years: the Vietnam war, the racial crisis and America's share of the pseudo-revolution of the young that exploded all over the western world in 1968. The American part in the Vietnam war will be almost over next year, and although the enemies of the war will continue to attack the residual American connection they may find the rest of the country increasingly reluctant to feel very strongly about it. By most of the measurable tests, the condition of the majority of America's blacks has improved markedly over the past decade. The gap in living standards that separates them from the whites has narrowed; the number of middle-class jobs open to them has increased; their children have a better chance of going to mixed schools. None of this will end racial antagonism, in America or anywhere else, but it may keep it off the streets. And the most telling fact of all is the failure of the would-be revolutionaries of 1968 to produce an ideology to justify their appeal to violence. That is why 1968 does not look like being another 1848. The upheaval of 1848 in Europe was followed by the formulation of marxism. The new left today has been able to produce very little more than warmed-over Marx.

Given the uncertainty involved in strategic forecasting it may be useful to develop alternative scenarios. Thus, the subsequent evaluative and creative processes may be based on different assessments of the future outlook. The final choice then awaits the last phase in the process when the strategic commitment has to be made.

# 6

# The resource audit

## RESOURCES ARE RELATIVE

THE TEMPTATION is great to begin the resource audit with an identification of a company's resources. Such an approach easily yields a long list of attributes. However, in terms of the strategic process this is putting the cart before the horse. Resources are relative. A company's strengths and weaknesses can only be appraised by relating them to its external environment and its strategic profile.

The environmental dimensions prevailing in its industry, and especially the competitive conditions, determine whether resources can be rated as strengths or weaknesses. In early 1967, American Motors ran a full-page advertisement containing an interview with its new president, Mr. Chapin. In it, the following conversation took place:

MR. CHAPIN: Our engines are the most modern on the road. They're one important result of the more than one-quarter billion dollars we've invested in recent years in plant and equipment and tooling.

INTERVIEWER: Over a quarter billion? That's more than most major companies are worth in total.

MR. CHAPIN: You're right. But when you talk about American Motors, you're talking about a company that outsells such major companies as National Cash Register and Campbell Soup, and has greater assets than General Mills and Armstrong Cork.

American Motors' size in sales and assets would be magnificent if the company were competing in either the soup or the cereal business. They

40

are of little comfort, however, in its existing business: automobiles. In 1967 Chrysler's assets were 10 times, Ford's 21 times, and General Motors' 35 times as large as those of American Motors. In spite of the large dollar figure of American Motors' sales and assets, it was—relative to its competitors—a dwarf in its particular business.

The management of a capital goods company saw its resources as perfectly adequate. New plants had been constructed to permit the firm to supply a growing market; a highly liquid financial situation was viewed as allowing great future flexibility. Profit margins were most satisfactory. However, major structural changes and a cyclical downtrend hit the industry. Severe excess capacity conditions made the expanded plant useless, creating heavy fixed expense burdens. Credit competition lengthened the average period outstanding for receivables from three to nine months, thereby absorbing the company's liquidity and forcing additional debt charges upon it. Price competition eroded profit margins, reducing the company's flexibility to incur marketing as well as research and development expenses to bolster its deteriorating market position.

Resources have to be related not only to the company's *current* but also to its *future* external conditions. It is essential to view them as relative not just in a static but also in a dynamic sense. A certificate of health in today's situation may turn into a fight for life under tomorrow's changed conditions. Henry Ford's single-model, single-color car was an outstanding product in an immature market; it was a liability in a more mature market which had shifted from utility and function to features and style. The same happened to Howard Head's metal ski.

Resources must be related to a company's strategic profile as well. Fashion skills are more critical to a company specializing in women's shoes than for one concentrating in ski boots. Broad distribution is more important to Piper selling low-priced aircraft than for Beech with its luxury planes. However, by changing its strategic profile to include a low-priced plane, Beech's selective distribution setup becomes a weakness. American Motors' limited resources may suffice if it concentrates on some narrow segments of the automobile market, but they may be disastrously weak if it tries to meet the Big Three on many fronts.

## THE RESOURCE DIMENSIONS

The resource audit encompasses a company's:

—operational dimension,
—financial dimension,
—management dimension.

The operational dimension will vary with the company's field of endeavor. In an industrial company it will typically consist of marketing, manufacturing, engineering, and research and development. In a publishing company, such as Bill Communications, the operational requirements will be editorial, circulation, and advertising, while in a mutual fund management company, such as Wellington, distribution, portfolio execution, and money management are involved. The financial dimension focuses on money as a strategic variable, while the management dimension analyzes a company's human resources.

### The operational dimension

In viewing the operational dimension, it is useful to begin by asking what it takes to succeed in a particular business. What are the key requirements for success? The strategist begins with the portrayal of the ingredients of both a successful and an unsuccessful company. What does it take to become a hero or a bum in a particular business? Another look at *Playboy* magazine exemplifies the successful strategy. Its content shielded the magazine against "me too" competition on one side and against television and regular entertainment on the other. The protection against "me too" competition came from a balanced content, which included several literary pieces by well-known and highly respected authors, with only a relatively small percentage of the pages allocated to pictorial sex. No printing expense was spared to give the magazine a high-class appearance. *Playboy* also was able to differentiate itself from other entertainment magazines, and especially from television, through those few pages on which it revealed its distinctive competence. Operationally, filling the content of the magazine according to this formula was a simple proposition. Professional authors submitted their material in the early sixties at the rate of about 100 manuscripts per week. Cartoons also largely originated on the outside, while photographers from all over the country were invited to submit film strips of prospective playmates. Printing, too, was subcontracted. The operational task of putting the magazine together was further facilitated by the fact that ( a ) the magazine appeared infrequently, that is, monthly, ( b ) its content was largely timeless, ( c ) it appealed to a large audience, and ( d ) its focus was extremely broad.

In terms of distribution, the formula was equally simple. Given its unique position, the magazine was sold at a high price, thereby avoiding the cost-price squeeze common to the industry. The high price furthermore gave the magazine great discretion in terms of its advertising policy: it did not have to rely on advertisers to make ends meet. Also, by relying primarily on newsstand sales, the company avoided the high circulation costs of obtaining and servicing subscribers. Mr. Hefner had simplified the operational requirements by adopting a strategy of relying to a large extent on outside help.

Yet, the same Mr. Hefner went through another lesser known and disastrous magazine experience when he launched *Show Business Illustrated* in 1961. In terms of content, *SBI* was much more demanding than *Playboy*; (*a*) it appeared more frequently, (*b*) its content was highly current, (*c*) it appealed to a specialized audience, and (*d*) its focus was predominantly local, depending on the entertainment offered in particular cities. Nor were outside contributors beating on the door with manuscripts and photographs. Competitively, the magazine was at a disadvantage in terms of timing vis-à-vis the daily newspapers or the weekly magazines. Nor did it have a distinctive competence to set it apart from other media. In terms of distribution, it was impractical to rely mainly on newsstand sales, and therefore it incurred heavy expenses in obtaining subscriptions. In addition, its high price, making it the most expensive semimonthly on the newsstand, proved to be a liability.

Within the context of the current and future environmental dimensions, the company's existing strategic profile, and the established success requirements, the strategist identifies and evaluates the firm's operational condition. By way of illustration, the Marlin Firearms Company is used here. Its research and development capabilities must be assessed. Do they permit the necessary product development? Does the company have the required skills to stay abreast of technological developments? Manufacturing also has to be analyzed. Is it capable of meeting the company's growth objectives? What happens to its cost structure if demand fluctuates, either upward or downward? Are its costs competitive, especially with imports from Europe and Japan? What future manufacturing investments are anticipated to meet the market and competitive requirements? Marketing is another function which must be scrutinized. Does Marlin have an appropriate distribution setup? Does its consumer franchise, and especially its brand name, provide protection against domestic and foreign competitors? Are its prices competitive? Does its product policy aim at the appropriate market segments?

Not only do the various operational elements have to be related to the external conditions, to the strategic profile, and to the success requirements of the particular business; these operational elements also have to be interrelated. The strategist thus has to build on his functional knowledge, in marketing, manufacturing, and research and development. A vast literature is available, particularly on the first two of these functional elements. The task of the strategist is to take the available expertise in all functional areas and integrate them with each other and with the above-mentioned aspects of the strategic equation. Furthermore, the operational dimension has to be related to the financial dimension.

## The financial dimension

Money often is an important strategic variable. A company's financial resources have to be related to its strategic requirements. In this connection, the strategist must have a clear notion of several aspects of the financial dimension, as will be illustrated by using Philip Morris, another of the companies included in this book. In simplified form, its balance sheet in 1969, a year in which several important investments were made, looked as follows (in millions):

| | | | |
|---|---:|---|---:|
| Receivables | $ 83 | Current and other liabilities | |
| Inventory | 447 | (excluding debt) | $130 |
| Net fixed assets | 147 | Current and long-term debt | 490 |
| Investments in subsidiaries | 228 | Equity | 356 |
| Other assets | 29 | | |
| Cash | 42 | | |
| | $976 | | $976 |

The first three categories of assets, totaling $677 million, were required in operations for both working capital and plant equipment. Netted against the $130 million in liabilities, this figure is reduced to $547 million, which was used to support $1,142 million in sales. In addition to the operational assets, Philip Morris carried $228 million in investments and $71 million in cash and other assets. To finance all these assets it relied on $490 million of debt and $356 million in equity. Its earnings before taxes in 1969 were $115 million; after taxes, $58 million. Its price-earnings ratio was approximately 12 times. One other item of interest was that $364 million of its inventory consisted of leaf tobacco.

The strategist is particularly interested in the following elements:

1. What are the asset requirements per dollar of sales? A quick analysis reveals the following:

$83/1,142$ = 7 cents for receivables
$447/$ "    39 cents for inventory, of which 32 cents was in leaf tobacco
$147/$ "    13 cents for net fixed assets
            59 cents for total operating assets
$130/1,142$ = 11 cents for liabilities
            48 cents for net operating assets

In other words, for each dollar of sales the company invests approximately one-half dollar in net operating assets.

2. What does the company earn? The figure is roughly 5 cents per dollar of sales, hence its return on its net operating assets is about 10%. Debt leverage increases this return on the basis of equity.

3.   How much cash is generated internally? Philip Morris, in addition to its $58 million profit after taxes, benefited from a $13.5 million depreciation cash flow but paid out about $23 million in dividends, leaving a net cash flow of a little under $50 million.

4.   How has the company committed its resources and where has the money come from? A 1968–69 funds flow shows (in millions):

| Uses | | Sources | |
|---|---|---|---|
| Working capital . . . . . | $   8 | Liabilities . . . . . . . . | $ 14 |
| Fixed assets . . . . . . . | 9 | Debt . . . . . . . . . . . | 135 |
| Investments . . . . . . . | 160 | Equity . . . . . . . . . . | 41 |
| Other assets . . . . . . . | 13 | | |
| | $190 | | $190 |

During this period sales increased by $122 million. Thus, Philip Morris was keeping its existing assets nearly constant (in spite of substantial growth) in order to use its retained earnings as well as substantial amounts of debt to diversify into other fields. In part, the company could keep its existing operating assets constant by virtue of the flexibility given to it by its large inventory in leaf tobacco and the alternative of relying on government tobacco stockpiles.

With the above elements in mind, a company's current performance can be appraised and its ability to grow as well as its ability to diversify can be analyzed. By having a feel for the asset requirements per dollar of sales (in terms of working capital and plant and equipment) the financial requirements of growth can be assessed. (Of course, average and incremental asset requirements per dollar of sales may differ and have to be analyzed in detail in the specific situation.) The ability to generate funds has to be related to these requirements: how much growth can be financed internally? Where borrowing is required, the company's debt capacity must be analyzed, as well as its vulnerability to debt. The company's flexibility to influence its asset requirements has to be explored, such as keeping its inventory constant, reducing inventory, or utilizing excess capacity. In this case, the strategist has to determine how long such an approach is feasible. The company's performance permits one to compare it with alternate opportunities. Will diversification improve or reduce profitability? Is it desirable to reduce operations in some segments of the business and use its currently committed resources elsewhere?

The financial dimension also has to be viewed dynamically. What is the impact of credit competition on working capital needs? What happens if service competition increases inventory requirements? What are the fixed asset requirements resulting from mechanization forced upon a company to keep its costs competitive? What happens to a firm's cash flow if competitive conditions force a reduction of its margins either through lower prices or through higher marketing and research and development expenses? What is the impact of rising interest costs? In other words, in relating a company's financial dimension to the future it may be necessary to construct different financial profiles based on growth or stagnation (if not decline) as well as on more or less severe competitive conditions.

### Management dimension

The management dimension is probably the most critical. To many a company the depth of its management resources constitutes its greatest strategic constraint. In many ways, and in contrast to the financial aspects, this dimension is the most difficult to assess. Some of the later chapters on corporate organization will focus more closely on this dimension. The following poem from an unknown author describes it nicely:

> Though your balance sheet is a model
> of what balance sheets should be
> Typed and ruled with great precision
> in a type that all can see.
> Though the grouping of the assets
> is commendable and clear
> And the details which are given
> more than usually appear.
> Though investments have been valued
> at the sale price of the day
> And the auditor's certificate shows
> everything O.K. . . . . .
> One asset is omitted—and its
> worth I want to know:
> That asset is the value
> of the men who run the show.

The capabilities of management, like the other resource dimensions, have to be related to the environmental requirements and the company's strategic profile. A watch company may have the world's best mechanical engineers, but they may prove of little help in developing an electronic watch. An insurance company may have salesmen who are outstanding in selling life insurance policies but ill-equipped and little motivated to sell mutual funds. A company's labor force may be highly skilled but unable to compete costwise with imports from the Far East. Management may be highly skilled in establishing and running movie houses, but can these skills be transferred to managing bottling plants?

Not only the abilities of management have to be assessed but also its depth. Some companies, particularly the smaller and rapidly growing ones, have barely enough talent to fill the necessary positions. Departure by one of the members of management, and especially the president, may leave a critical gap. In contrast, other companies may have several competent candidates available for each position. The organizational machinery, under these circumstances, continues to run smoothly even when key managers depart. In some instances, the capable specialist is critical. In others, however, specialists can be relatively easily replaced, and it is the generalist, the coordinator and integrator, who is a most vital and nearly irreplaceable member of management. In some cases, managers control the business they have helped to create: if they leave, as in the case of investment bankers, they frequently take their accounts with them.

One aspect of the managerial dimension which may have a critical impact on a company's strategic behavior is the nature and application of its control system. Lack of an efficient and clear control system can hinder strategic decision making. It is difficult to analyze and evaluate a situation if it is impossible to find out exactly what is going on. On the other extreme, too efficient a control system can be equally damaging. If results are measured frequently over short time spans, managerial responses will be geared to the system. When the paycheck is at stake, it is difficult to be a strategic statesman and favor the long run. Yet, responses which are keyed to a quarterly or annual profit and loss statement inevitably favor improvisation over long-haul strategy and foster a reluctance to commit investments and expenses which are reflected in the current statement but which are expected to yield results only in a future period. Short-term measurement may easily destroy the dynamic aspect of the strategic framework. Management plays it safe and aims for early results, which inevitably leads to a static approach. General Electric recently instituted a major effort in "strategic business planning." According to *Business Week*, GE's new president "thinks GE's new planning approach . . . reduces a manager's temptation to go for short-term results, sacrificing long-term gains—a criticism leveled at GE's decentralized structure. Performance of managers is now rated on adherence to their strategic plans rather than on short-term profits."[1]

---

[1] *Business Week*, July 8, 1972, p. 58.

# 7

# Strategic alternatives

## THE CREATIVE PROCESS

DEVELOPING strategic alternatives is a creative process. This creativity, however, takes place within the now well-defined framework of the external and internal dimensions, both in their current and future configurations. The strategist asks: given the prevailing environmental conditions and given the resources at a company's disposal, what strategic options are available? Does the strategic forecast suggest the opportunity for innovative strategies? Can existing or future resources be put to new or more desirable uses?

Combining the discipline of the strategy framework with the innovative strategic creativity has some important advantages. In established organizations, especially large ones, there is a tendency to hold back unconventional ideas. The reasons are simple: the mortality rate of such ideas is high, and no one wants to harm his track record. Also, unconventional ideas, creative as they may be, easily get labeled as crazy because the borderline between creative and crazy ideas is often very thin. A solid company man with balanced judgment, therefore, is likely to play it safe. The penalty of such an atmosphere is that sound but unconventional approaches never see the light of day. This need not be so, however. Within the strategic process unconventional or even crazy ideas are welcome. As long as they are cycled through the evaluative framework, there is a good chance that the bad ones will be weeded out and the occasional good ones retained for future exploration. Within the discipline of the strategic framework, it is possible to extend an open invitation to creativity.

Analysis of successful entrepreneurial strategies shows that they were frequently aided by two conditions: (1) the entrepreneur did not know that it could not be done and (2) he had nothing to lose and everything to gain. In developing strategic alternatives, the strategist should approach the creative process from the vantage point of these entrepreneurial conditions.

Product or strategy innovations, when they are introduced by entrepreneurs, are often laughed at by the established companies. The industry leaders, after all, are the experts, and their expertise tells them that what the entrepreneur is attempting cannot be done. Underwood, Royal, and Smith were the experts in the typewriter business, and they knew that the electric typewriter was neither feasible from a technical nor desirable from a marketing point of view. The Big Four in the liquor industry were attempting to build brand loyalty around drinks with a distinctive taste. Heublein's attempt to develop a brand franchise in vodka, both tasteless and odorless, appeared to them as destined for defeat. Howard Head, when he carried his early samples of metal skis into the snow country, was told by the professional skiers that wood was the only suitable material for a quality ski.

Expertise, indeed, can be a severe handicap in creatively developing strategic alternatives. Expertise, in fact, is often a result of an existing strategic profile. If the strategy is one of manufacturing a quality product with highly skilled labor and selling it through selective distribution channels by granting high retail margins and relying on dealer push, such a company is unlikely to consider mass-producing a lower quality product with unskilled labor and selling it through intensive distribution backed up by mass advertising to create customer pull. Likewise, to a Henry Ford who produced a low-cost utility vehicle for basic transportation, the General Motors strategy of model proliferation may have appeared as nonsensical.

The brake which expertise places on creativity is compounded by the opposite of the second entrepreneurial condition. While the entrepreneur or the challenger often has nothing to lose and everything to gain, the established company, in contrast, may have everything to lose and little to gain. To them a most painful aspect of the creative process is when certain appealing strategic options are developed which constitute threats to the existing strategy, sometimes to the point of making it obsolete. The natural reaction is to quickly close this Pandora's box. Yet any strategist who does so and closes his eyes to such options must be very sure that no one else thinks of them. In strategy formulation there is no monopoly on ideas. Regularly, companies which ignore options detrimental to their own strategy find that others, who may have nothing to lose, are less reluctant. When faced with the inevitable obsolescence of one's strategy, one may be better off in grasping that opportunity oneself rather than leaving it exclusively to others.

Developing a strategic alternative which calls into question the existing strategy is difficult not only because of the emotional and human reluctance to upset the traditional and often successful prevailing strategy but also because a novel strategic approach requires a shift in a company's resources. It may require building on weaknesses rather than on strengths. A company's existing commitment to selective distribution may make a shift to mass distribution difficult. Its reservoir of skilled manpower may make it reluctant to shift to mass production.

To advocate the creative process does not imply that the existing strategic profile will inevitably be superseded by an imaginative new strategy. The subsequent evaluative process will frequently result in the conclusion that the existing strategic posture is most appropriate. The purpose of developing strategic alternatives is to ensure that the strategist considers his existing strategy at this point only as one amongst many. There is a latent danger that the process of developing strategic alternatives becomes no more than the writing of variations on an established theme: that of the traditional strategy. Thus, the strategist should be cautioned not to consider his existing strategic profile as too much of a given.

The creative process, furthermore, is a powerful guarantee against a company blindly following industry or functional conventions. Just as a company may become a prisoner of its own strategy, it may also become a victim of industry practices or traditional approaches in terms of manufacturing, marketing, or finance.

Finally, the strategist should be cautioned that the exploration of strategic alternatives does not always lead to "either-or" choices. The issue is not necessarily between either the retention or the rejection of the existing strategy. The creative process which searches for options frequently leads to minor modifications and improvements in the existing strategy, which on balance emerges as the most desirable choice. However, retention and modification of the current strategic profile constitutes a more meaningful decision if it is made in full view of the various alternatives.

## TYPICAL STRATEGIC ALTERNATIVES

In developing strategic alternatives, the strategist typically faces a number of basic options which can be explored in somewhat more detail.

### The "do nothing" alternative

This one is the all-time favorite. Why not continue the existing strategy? While the recipe is simple, the reasons leading to it must be explored. Is retention of the status quo suggested on the basis of a thorough investigation? Or is it simply a matter of convenience or laziness? Is it a convenient way of sticking one's head into the sand?

There is a great temptation to put forth this strategic alternative. There may also be a great deal of justification for it. Innovation is risky, sometimes esoteric and possibly unwise. Thus, there is an opportunity to benefit from the mistakes of others. George Romney became a hero as champion of the compact car by sticking to his existing product line and by benefiting from the errors of the Big Three as they misread the trends in their industry. To draw on a football analogy, the fundamentals of strong blocking and tackling may be more crucial than the fancy pass patterns.

The do-nothing alternative, however, may also be a convenient escape from the uncomfortable pressures for change. Where the strategic forecast calls for a shift in strategy, action may be delayed by questioning the predictive judgment. Or a "wait and see" attitude may be adopted to await further evidence as to whether the predicted trends will indeed occur. Such reactions are especially convenient where the strategic response to new developments is either very risky or very costly. For example, major marketing or research and development investments may be required. Since most of these would have to be expensed in the current profit and loss statement, thereby reducing earnings per share or even resulting in losses, management may be reluctant to take such necessary strategic action. Instead, it may adopt the "do nothing" attitude by keeping these expenses within what it considers an acceptable level. The focus on the security analyst may overrule the strategic forecast.

## The liquidation alternative

While "do nothing" is the favorite, "liquidation" is the black sheep among the strategic alternatives. Yet, there are circumstances where this alternative may be best for all parties concerned. Too often, management holds on to an obsolete strategy or fights a constantly escalating war with inadequate and diminishing resources. Such a strategy may destroy managerial careers as well as the shareholders' equity and, in many instances, is also detrimental to the employees. Unfortunately, it is both difficult and painful to reach the verdict of liquidation. Management is unlikely to put itself out of work.

Liquidation is particularly difficult in the single-product company, where it entails terminating the corporate existence. In the diversified company, on the other hand, liquidation is a more common occurrence. Some of the newer conglomerates are particularly known not only for their acquisitions but also for their disinvestments. The older diversified enterprises, however, also follow this route. General Electric's new president in 1972 rose to fame through the successful sale of the computer business. During the week of his appointment, the company also sold off its television broadcasting equipment business. *Business Week*[1] commented that the new president, Reginald Jones, "was vaulted into GE's top spot largely because of his intimate identification with 'strategic business planning'—a technique that treats the company's vast array of ventures as an investment portfolio, sorting out the winners and losers through systematic analysis. The aim is to decide which ventures deserve the most investment capital and which should be dumped. TV broadcasting equipment turned out to be the loser."

## The alternative of specialization

During the boom years of the conglomerate it was not fashionable to stress the merits of a specialist strategy. Yet many companies owe their success to specialization. Of the subsequent cases, both Timex and Vlasic are eloquent examples. Indeed, the power of a single purpose can be substantial, particularly where competitors spread their energies and resources over a variety of activities. Thus, specialization may provide a competitive edge.

If one asks managers of the operating divisions of diversified companies who their most dangerous and difficult competitors are, they rarely cite other conglomerates. Instead, they usually mention much smaller specialized companies, which excell in a single product or service and which are able to react quickly and decisively.

In addition to providing a competitive edge, specialization also permits companies with limited resources to use them most effectively. Under George Romney, American Motors, with its limited resources vis-à-vis its giant competitors, aimed at one market segment: the compact car. Under Romney's successor, the company broadened its product scope with disastrous results. Vlasic, as a privately held company starting at a sales level of a few million dollars, has been able to compete successfully with the giant food processing companies.

A strategy of specialization permits a company to exploit particular market segments, sometimes resulting in spectacular performances even where the general industry conditions are stagnant. *Playboy's* success in the otherwise difficult magazine industry has already been mentioned. A large and well-known British shoe company more than quadrupled its sales during the fifties while the industry was virtually stagnant. It increased its market share in women's shoes from about 3% to over 8% and in children's shoes from 4% to nearly 12%, largely specializing in shoes for young children and older women. As such, it was able to compete and excell on the basis of comfort and reputation, thereby avoiding the vicissitudes of the fashion game.

---

[1] *Business Week*, July 8, 1972, p. 52.

Specialization also entails major risks. A company's fortunes are tied to a particular industry. If the industry declines, the company may be trapped. Changing market needs or major technological innovation may even put it out of business. Also, where a firm specializes in a cyclical industry, its fortunes may be subject to major swings. While management may accept such swings as a fact of life and prepare the company financially for it, the stock market may penalize it through a lower valuation of its shares. Another negative aspect is that specialization often creates a high level of expertise in a narrow area. This kind of expertise, as was pointed out earlier in this chapter, may be a hurdle to creatively developing strategic alternatives.

## The vertical integration alternative

A common strategic alternative, as was pointed out in Chapter 3, is to integrate backward in terms of one's supplies or to integrate forward into one's outlets. Vertical integration is a constant temptation because it permits a company to expand the scope of its activities and yet remain on relatively familiar ground. There are also powerful strategic reasons for integrating either backward or forward.

Backward integration may aim for a steady source of supplies, thus minimizing the risk of shortages in the merchant market. Backward integration may also seek to ensure a low-cost position, if not a cost advantage relative to one's competitors. Oil companies seek ample and low-cost crude oil sources to supply their refineries and market outlets. Steel companies want to be assured of sufficient supplies of iron ore at constant quality and reasonable cost.

Backward integration does not necessarily entail advantages. Given the usually high capital requirements it may place a heavy strain on a company's financial resources. Also, a company with its own sources of supply becomes more vulnerable to technological change. It is tied to a particular technology requiring existing plant and equipment. Where new products or processes are developed, the vertically integrated company either has to write off its supply investments and invest in the new innovations or be placed at a competitive disadvantage. Its competitors who have not integrated backward are flexible enough to switch to merchant suppliers who deliver the new products or utilize the new processes. The leader in the snowmobile industry, Bombardier, has integrated backward by acquiring its engine supplier. Its main challenger, Arctic, in contrast, purchases engines on a merchant basis, permitting it to feature a model with the Wankel engine.

Forward integration may be undertaken to secure outlets, thereby guaranteeing a steady volume. Such a move may make the company less vulnerable to pressures from its customers. Particularly, the guaranteed volume, even if it is sold internally at market prices, becomes most important during periods of excess capacity in highly capital intensive industries. The few extra percentages in plant utilization may make a substantial difference in profitability. Even if prices are depressed, the margins on incremental volume may be substantial where fixed costs are high and variable costs are low.

Forward integration also often helps a company to achieve greater product differentiation, thereby reducing the price sensitivity of its products. In the early phases of the vertical product flow, products usually are of a commodity nature: within the framework of technical specifications they are identical and hence extremely sensitive to price. At the end of the vertical product flow when they reach the ultimate consumer, products are often differentiated: marketing activities become more critical, price may prove to be less important, while brand loyalty provides the differentiated product with a secure market position. For example, the chemical intermediates used to make detergents are commodities highly sensitive to price, while the branded detergents are differentiated products, enjoying a more stable price and market position.

In addition to seeking a guaranteed volume and more stable prices, forward integration may also be pursued to achieve better margins. For commodities fixed assets are usually high and market expenses low, while for differentiated products the opposite is true. Greater price stability combined with lower asset requirements may become a tempting proposition. However, many a company integrating forward does not have the marketing know-how to succeed with differentiated products. To stay with the detergent example, Monsanto as a supplier was able to make a good detergent, but its efforts several years ago to market its own brand were a fiasco.

One common problem encountered in terms of both backward and forward integration is that of balance. The minimum efficient size at one part of the product flow may be substantially different from that at the other end. The iron ore mine may be too large an investment even for a good-sized steel company. The problem is sometimes compounded, especially in the chemical industry, by the necessity to dispose of various by-products.

While vertical integration may be tempting to some companies, others refrain from it as a matter of policy. Dansk Designs prefers to rely for the manufacture of its products on subcontractors. Vlasic is relying increasingly on outsiders to harvest the cucumbers needed for its pickles. General Cinema has no intention of integrating backward into movie production. Along the lines of the specialization alternative, these companies want to concentrate on their strengths. Other firms, however, may not have the freedom of choice. Of the companies described in this book, Hedblom, A. G. Brown, and Wellington are confronted with vertical integration developments in their competitive environments which require a strategic response from them.

## The diversification alternative

Of all the strategic alternatives, diversification is undoubtedly the most glamorous. Admittedly this glamour has paled somewhat as several well-known conglomerates have come upon hard times. Yet, whenever a company faces a strategic dilemma, diversification is immediately put forth as a quick and easy remedy. This is precisely what diversification should not be. It does not solve old problems. Nor is running away from one's problems through diversification the way to solve them. In fact, under these circumstances, diversification can be harmful by draining resources away from the problems which need to be solved. Opening a second front is not the way to solve a delicate situation on one's first front. Thus, diversification is not a solution to the problems encountered in one's existing business. These problems have to be faced separately and directly.

Diversification is an alternate way of committing one's resources. The strategist may decide that his existing business does not hold sufficient potential. He may wish to cut back or even liquidate it and commit his resources elsewhere. Alternatively, he may keep his existing activities at current levels or exploit their growth to their full potential but seek additional growth elsewhere. Thus growth through diversification may not always be a better utilization of existing resources but may aim at a better spreading of business risks or at achieving a growth rate which cannot be accomplished within a company's original given field of endeavor.

Diversification by moving into a more profitable and rapidly growing business and at the same time reducing one's commitment in a less profitable and stagnant business makes a great deal of sense. Unfortunately, many a strategist aims to do the former without the latter. Under these circumstances, the original business continues to deteriorate and drain company resources while also diverting management's attention from the more attractive diversification opportunities. These get short-changed in terms of management and money and therefore may fail to reach their full potential.

Diversification to achieve a more ambitious growth rate than is possible with the existing business creates other problems. This approach is frequently taken by companies which have achieved fame with a brilliant entrepreneurial strategy and which are eagerly looking for an "encore" to maintain their successful performance as well as the value of their shares. Unfortunately, success does not easily repeat itself, and a rapidly growing and highly profitable company finds it equally difficult to discover a counterpart which is for sale at a reasonable price. Faced by such a dilemma, many companies either reject one diversification proposal after another or acquire companies with lower growth and profitability rates, and often more problems, than their own.

When choosing between growth through the expansion of existing businesses and diversification, the strategist makes an intriguing tradeoff. With existing businesses he faces the uncertainty of future sales and profits but the certainty of knowing the industry. Diversification brings him the opposite: he may be able to add a certain amount in sales and profits but faces the uncertainty of a new and different business. Moving into an unknown business is the key variable in diversification. If company A which is in X business wants to acquire company B which is engaged in Y business, we know how A has performed in X and B in Y. The unknown and critical element of the equation, though, is how A will perform through B in Y. The same holds true where

a company develops by starting from scratch except that it does not have the experience, good or bad, in the new business that is secured with the acquired firm.

In assessing how a company may perform in a new industry, it is helpful to compare and contrast the success and competitive requirements in its own industry with those of the industry into which it plans to diversify. For example, when Heublein was contemplating diversifying into beer through the acquisition of Hamm, it would have been useful to compare and contrast the liquor and beer industries.

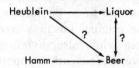

Such an analysis may save the diversifying company from a common error: that of applying its original and successful strategic recipe to the acquired company in a different industry. Diversification into another business often requires drastically different strategies. Yet it may be difficult for a company to follow one strategic approach in one industry and a totally different one in another industry. This danger applies especially to companies taking their first diversification steps. The highly diversified conglomerate, on the other hand, is forced, given the vast diversity of its units, to treat them separately and is, therefore, less tempted to transfer strategic responses.

This chapter describes diversification only as one of several strategic alternatives. It is not a guide for diversification decisions. In this respect, a vast literature is available detailing criteria and all the financial and negotiating elements. Obviously, the industry and company to be chosen as well as financial terms are important elements. Before these questions can be answered satisfactorily, however, it is necessary to place the diversification choice within a company's overall strategic context. The basic strategy has to be decided first before the details can be worked out. This is particularly important because diversification is not without risk. Errors here do not only affect the diversification move but they may backfire on the original strategic posture. A failure in diversification may entail the downfall of the entire company.

## The international alternative

Instead of product diversification a company may embark on a strategy of area diversification. In the former, the products are different but the country is the same, while in the latter the products are the same but the countries are different. The prospect of repeating a successful strategic formula elsewhere around the world is a tempting one. Of the companies discussed in this book, Timex and Philip Morris have done so successfully. The firms in the Capital International case see a major opportunity in such an alternative.

A critical question is whether foreign markets will be as receptive as the company's home market to both the products and the strategic formula. Will the strategy have to be adapted to different foreign conditions? Furthermore, what kind of competitive constellation will the strategist encounter overseas as he seeks to repeat his domestic success?

During the fifties international expansion was seen as a luxury, during the sixties as an opportunity, but during the seventies it may well become a necessity. Some industries have been international for years. Often this was the result of nature in that sources of supply, such as crude oil, were in different parts of the world from the major consuming areas. Companies in other industries, such as Nestlé, Unilever, Singer, and Colgate-Palmolive, have also been on the international scene for a long time. These companies essentially introduced successful products or applied effective strategies around the globe. Often, in spite of the international scope of these firms, the various national markets were largely separate entities harboring subsidiaries which were engaged in all facets of operations. The international connections were primarily in terms of ownership, dividends, or royalties rather than in terms of operations. Increasingly, however, competition is shifting from a national to an international scale. Worldwide sourcing supplants national sourcing. Companies borrow money all over the world. Research and development is geared to the needs of products and facilities sold and located in widely different contexts. Marketing confrontations occur in several markets simultaneously. Internationalization, where it provides major competitive strengths through worldwide rationalization, may become not just a matter of choice but one of necessity.

In viewing international alternatives it is useful to separate the developing from the industrialized countries. The former used to be supplied from central sources located in the latter. During the last several years, however, the developing nations have made great strides in terms of import substitution, a topic raised by the Central American cases in this book. Using the "infant industry" argument, these countries have typically closed their borders to imports. As a result, the developing world has increasingly been fragmented in separate and often small markets. The industrial world, on the other hand, after about a half a century of compartmentalization and protectionism is slowly moving to a freer interchange, sparked by developments such as the European Common Market. Also the predominance of the United States has dwindled, and in the early seventies at least three major industrial areas confront each other: Europe, Japan, and the United States. The Note on the Watch Industry portrays this phenomenon and permits an exploration of its implications.

# 8

# The test of consistency

THE TEST of consistency is the process by which a given strategy or strategic alternatives are evaluated. Strategies are tested for consistency with a company's external and internal dimensions, both in their identified current and in their predicted future scope. In simple terms, the strategist relates what a company is _able_ to do with respect to its resources to what is _possible_ in its external environment. The test of consistency seeks the most appropriate response by relating corporate strengths and weaknesses to environmental opportunities and threats.

Like most other aspects of the strategic process, this is more easily said than done. Conceptually, the test of consistency appears to be a logical and exact approach. Practically, however, it is a difficult and judgmental process. Three factors, especially, complicate the application of the test of consistency. First, the test involves the multiplicity of external and internal dimensions, resulting in a highly intricate network. Second, the multiplicity of these dimensions and hence the complexity of this network are further compounded by the dynamic nature of the test, in that both current conditions and future predictions are taken into account. Third, the various current and future dimensions which enter into the equation often lead to conflicting conclusions. As a result, the test of consistency does not always produce clear-cut answers. Instead, the general manager is often forced to make tradeoffs.

The need to consider a multiplicity of dimensions is evident from the earlier discussion of the environmental conditions and the company resources. The key challenge here is to give full consideration to all the elements involved. For example, companies in the watch industry have to contend with the full scope of environmental dimensions. Politically and economically they are affected by tariff policies, import restrictions, and variations in the foreign exchange rates of several currencies. In terms of the market dimension, they are confronted with changing distribution patterns and a role of lesser importance for the watch among consumer durables. Technological developments in the manufacture of better quality throwaway watches and highly advanced electronic watches are of great importance. With respect to competition, the success of Timex and the Japanese companies as major competitors as well as the possible emergence of the electronics firms are of vital importance to the established companies. In terms of resources, the competitive battle demands a full display of the operational dimensions. Marketing is critical in conquering a share of the hotly disputed market. Production is essential in maintaining competitive costs. Research and development has risen in importance as the pace of product development quickens. The financial dimension is also highly relevant as the stakes increase and larger and larger companies begin to dominate the industry. Needless to say, with the above challenges, the managerial dimension is also a critical variable.

In practice, it is easy to overlook several of the important dimensions. This results not only from the natural human tendency to simplify problems but also from the fact that some elements may overshadow others. A given resource may represent such an obvious weakness that it calls for urgent repair; or it may be such a tempting asset that its full utilization is irresistible. The same may be true for an environmental opportunity or threat. Yet, where a particularly squeaky wheel asks for oil, the other wheels are easily overlooked. In Marlin Firearms, the lack of productive capacity represented such a crying need. However, was the corporate response to this need consistent with the other environmental and internal dimensions? The test of consistency requires that all external and internal conditions be taken into account. As will be discussed subsequently, however, this does not mean that all dimensions are equally important.

The multiplicity of dimensions is further compounded by the need to consider both the identified current and the predicted future conditions. A strategic response must be tested under both today's and tomorrow's situations. Strategic decisions take time, and their impact is felt over a long time span. Therefore, the test of consistency must be a dynamic and not just a static one. Furthermore, since the predictive dimensions are necessarily judgmental in character, the test of consistency becomes judgmental as well. Under these circumstances, the strategist easily seeks refuge in the more certain current dimensions. Yet such an approach casts doubt on the validity of the test, especially where a number of dimensions are changing. As a result, if the test of consistency is to be dynamic, it must be judgmental. If the strategist demands certainty, he will only be able to perform a static test.

Where the strategic forecast predicts major change, the test of consistency may well expose the obsolescence of the established and hitherto proven strategic recipe. There is no need to repeat here the conditions described in earlier chapters which lead to such strategic obsolescence: changes in the political, social, and economic constellations; in the marketplace; in technology; or in competitive conditions. The critical challenge here is to anticipate this obsolescence, because when it actually occurs, it may be too late for meaningful corrective action. Unfortunately, anticipation means (1) abandonment of a still successful strategy and (2) doing so on the basis of uncertain judgmental predictions. Obviously, the tendency under these circumstances is to rely more heavily on today's consistent test than on tomorrow's prediction of inconsistency. In other words, it is a perfectly human reaction to refuse to apply the predictive level of consistency precisely in those situations where it is most needed.

Frequently, a given strategic response is consistent with certain of the internal and external conditions but inconsistent with others. When a multiplicity of dimensions enters into the equation, it is difficult to satisfy all of them. Inconsistencies may occur between a strategy and certain current dimensions, or different results may emerge when relating a strategy to both current and future conditions. Under these circumstances, the strategist has to make tradeoffs. As was pointed out earlier, it is important to take all dimensions into account. An intelligent choice can only be made if one knows what one is choosing from. However, postulating a complete analysis does not mean that all elements are of equal importance. (Here again, as earlier, urgency should not necessarily be equated with importance.) Where a strategy relates positively to some dimensions but negatively to others, it is not simply a question of offsetting pluses and minuses. Some inconsistencies may be critical, while others may prove to be minor. As a result, in making these inevitable tradeoffs the strategist again has to rely on his judgment.

The test of consistency in practice is both complex and judgmental. Yet not only is it often erroneously portrayed as a product of simple logic but also as a device permitting the strategist to obtain the best of all worlds. Through the test of consistency a strategy should attempt to maximize external opportunities and internal strengths and to minimize external threats and internal weaknesses. And, indeed, many a strategic plan postulates the vigorous pursuit of unexploited opportunities with the support of established and proven resources. Unfortunately, while it is common to aspire to a strategic equation which incorporates the best of all worlds, this is not always possible. Maximizing both opportunities and strengths and minimizing both risks and weaknesses may be inconsistent.

For example, in the farm equipment industry Deere sought to maximize its opportunities by entering the European markets, while Massey Ferguson attempted to increase its penetration in the United States. Each company thus confronted the other where it was weak and its competitor was strong. Not surprisingly, neither Deere nor Massey Ferguson's efforts were successful. By chasing what they considered unexploited opportunities, they were forced to attack from a position of weakness on a terrain where competition was firmly established. Instead of maximizing opportunities, both companies ended up by maximizing their weaknesses, with an adverse impact on the earnings of both companies. Luckily for each other, they both made the same mistake. A similar situation prevailed in the light aircraft industry, where Piper attempted to trade up and Beech to trade down.

Thus, maximization of opportunities often involves maximizing rather than minimizing one's weaknesses. It also may entail maximization of risks. Reliance on company strengths may involve closing one's eyes to new opportunities; and as a result, maximization of internal strengths may result in minimizing external opportunities. Thus, the test of consistency may confront the general manager with some basic strategic choices rather than with perfect answers. The resolution of these choices will be discussed in the next chapter.

# 9

# Strategic choice

## NECESSITY FOR STRATEGIC CHOICE

STRATEGIC decision making, in the final analysis, is a matter of choice. As stated by Zaleznik, "the essence of leadership is choice, a singularly individualistic act in which a man assumes responsibility for a commitment to direct an organization along a particular path."[1] Strategic choice thus becomes the capstone of the strategic process. It involves a number of key choices which periodically confront the general manager:

1. A tradeoff between maximizing opportunities and minimizing risks.
2. The timing of strategic moves based on anticipated changes.
3. An assessment of the potential competitive confrontation which may result from strategic action.

Not surprisingly, strategic choice is the most difficult step in the strategic process. Having established the framework and facts, having made predictive judgments, having scanned strategic alternatives, having applied the test of consistency, the general manager now must decide. This decision cannot be based solely on facts and analysis. It is also influenced by uncertain predictive judgments and qualitative tradeoffs among a multiplicity of dimensions. The strategist will need the nerve and courage to make major and often irrevocable commitments in the face of uncertainty and imperfect analysis. Under these circumstances,

[1] Abraham Zaleznik, "Management of Disappointment," *Harvard Business Review*, November–December 1967, p. 68.

strategic choice becomes a highly personal decision. As such, it will be shaped by the personality of the strategist, particularly by what he sees as (1) his individual goals and ambitions and (2) his obligations to society.

## KEY CHOICES

### The opportunity-risk tradeoff

As was pointed out in the previous chapter, it is not always possible to obtain the best of all worlds. Maximization of opportunities may involve simultaneously maximizing threats. Specialization and diversification involve a similar tradeoff. As was discussed in Chapter 7, specialization permits a company to fight its battle on familiar territory but also makes it totally dependent on the economic fortunes of its industry. Diversification makes a company less vulnerable to the business cycle and the ups and downs of a particular industry, but requires it to compete simultaneously in several businesses, in some of which management may not be entirely expert, possibly causing a dissipation of its resources and efforts.

These tradeoffs cannot be made on the basis of logic. The decision depends, in the final analysis, on the willingness of the strategist to shoulder risk. For example, if he is reluctant to do so, he is likely to elect a strategy which minimizes the external threats to which his company is exposed. At the same time, such a strategy will probably result in minimizing the company's opportunities. On the other hand, if the strategist is an eager risk taker, he will be ready to maximize opportunities even if it involves exposing the company to a great many external threats. Thus, before committing the company to a specific strategic plan, the strategist has to determine how much of a risk taker he really is. Where the decision process is a collective one, the board of directors or management committee has to make clear how much risk it is willing to shoulder.

Too often, these risk assessments are not made. They are avoided because the necessity for choice is not made explicit. Management saves itself from this painful confrontation by assuming that it can indeed obtain the best of two worlds: that opportunities can be maximized and threats minimized. This ostrich-like approach can simplify strategic decisions but it certainly does not enhance their quality.

### The timing dilemma

Where judgment accounts for a high proportion of the strategic process and where uncertainty is great, the tendency is to go slow and adopt a wait-and-see attitude. This is not always possible. Not all strategic decisions can be made in increments. At times it is necessary to make a commitment one way or another.

Even where a wait-and-see approach is feasible, it may not be desirable. Timing is a critical element. While the risk of early action is usually highest, so is the payoff. Furthermore, early action typically entails lower costs. Delays in action usually will be accompanied by risk reduction, payoff reduction, and cost increases. As opportunities become more certain and widely recognized, costs frequently become very high, accompanied by minimal payoffs.

Thus, timing entails a necessity to choose between a high-risk, high-reward strategy of moving early and the low-risk, low-reward attitude of wait and see. Sometimes, there is not even a choice because the wait-and-see approach may prove to be—in terms of results—a high-risk strategy. If a company does not move early, it may subsequently find itself totally outclassed by those who had the courage to do so. Early action, therefore, requires not only foresight but also a willingness to take risks.

### Assessing competitive confrontation

Strategic action usually is either a challenge or a response to existing strategies of competitors. The familiar questions asked in deciding on a strategy are whether (1) it is superior or at least equal to those strategies which it confronts, (2) it is innovative or imitative, and (3) it attacks competition squarely or attempts to avoid competitive confrontation. This analysis, however, has to be carried one step further. What will be the possible counterresponse to a new strategy? What counterattack may be expected? Thus, two interrelationships must be explored:

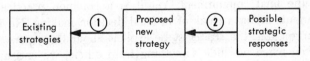

This way of viewing the competitive interplay focuses on an additional strategic choice. The strategist through his proposed new strategy is able to influence the possible strategic counterresponses by competitors. The nature of the attack greatly determines the likelihood and extent of a counterattack. Certain innovative strategies make it difficult and costly for the established companies to respond. Also, where the opposition feels that a new strategy is likely to fail, which is not uncommon with an unconventional new strategy, a quick and major response is less likely. In other instances, a competitive reaction follows immediately.

For example, technological innovation in steel processing gave new-comers a significant advantage over established companies. The old-timers, in turn, responded by building new facilities themselves, creating a great deal of excess capacity which left the entire industry worse off. Ideal are those situations, in contrast, where a preemptive strategy is possible, giving the early entrant a strong and durable hold over the market.

## THE STRATEGIST'S PERSONAL CHOICE

### Individual goals and ambitions

Strategic choice, as exemplified above, is tough and risky. How does the strategist resolve these choices? In the absence of a logical and compelling answer, strategic choices for the corporation often will be influenced by the chief executive's personal strategy. Strategic decision making inherently is a matter of personal choice. How bold does the strategist want to be? Is he willing to suffer the consequences of wrong judgments, both in terms of the company's strategic posture *and* in terms of his own career? As stated by Harry B. Henshel, President and Chief Executive Officer of Bulova Watch Company, Inc.:

The president's decision, if it is to have maximum effect, is bound to reflect his own attitudes, philosophy, and capabilities to a considerable extent. As a result, he may very well find himself standing alone behind his personal anal-ysis of a situation and his response to it. He may also find himself putting his job on the line as collateral for his judgment.[2]

The heavy dose of judgments and tradeoffs involved in the strategic process makes it inevitable that the personal attitudes of the strategist influence the final commitment. Yet it is a common practice to hide personal inputs under a cloak of rational decision making. Nevertheless, it is important that the strategist be explicit about these personal influ-ences. Often when we hide something from others, we end up fooling ourselves. Many an executive becomes the victim of his own rationalizations.

The strategist's attitude toward alternate courses of action, first of all, may be influenced by his ambitions. He may want to be known as the person who shaped the character of his company. Second, his attitude may be determined by the situation he has inherited. He may succeed a strong and well-known personality and be anxious to differen-tiate his regime from that of his predecessor by exploring totally new paths. Third, it may be a result of his background. For example, in

---

[2] Harry B. Henshel, "The President Stands Alone," *Harvard Business Review*, September–October 1971, p. 38.

making tradeoffs under the test of consistency a chief executive having risen through the sales route may place major, if not exclusive, emphasis on the environmental market dimension. Fourth, the strategist's attitude toward risk may be shaped by external pressures, for example, from the financial community. Fifth, it may be influenced by organizational pressures. This is particularly the case in divisionalized organizations, where the general managers of the operating divisions have to make strategic decisions but are also subject to a measurement and compensation system which may focus excessively on the short run. Also, where collective decisions have to be made, the strategist may avoid risks because by doing so it will be easier to arrive at a common denominator encompassing everybody's opinion and thereby facilitating consensus.

It is important to be explicit about the personal inputs which influence the strategist's attitude toward alternate actions because these elements, too, have to be submitted to the test of consistency. Is what the chief executive *wants* consistent with what *is possible* in the external environment and with what the company *is able* to do in terms of its internal resources? Management may not want to acquiesce in the union demands, but its limited resources and its weak competitive position may make it essential to avoid a strike. The division manager in a diversified company may not wish to incur marketing or research and development expenses which reduce his immediate profitability, but his division's position may make such expenditures imperative. Where, under these circumstances, a strategist follows his wishes, he may be courting disaster.

## Social responsiveness

The strategist is influenced in his choice not only by his own individual goals and ambitions but also by his attitude toward society and by what he sees as his own and his corporation's obligations.[3] Strategic choice is not solely an economic equation. It is also influenced by non-economic considerations, which are often encapsulated in an overworked phrase "corporate responsibility." Society has an impact on the strategic process in two ways. First, as described in Chapter 4, the political and social dimension is an important element of the environmental framework. It influences the strategic equation as an external force in much the same way as technology or competition. Second, perceived obligations to society cause managers to make strategic choices which obligate the corporation to social goals of a noneconomic nature, which, in some instances, may reduce economic performance. It is the latter which has

---

[3] For a comprehensive discussion of a company's social responsibilities, see Kenneth R. Andrews, *The Concept of Corporate Strategy* (Homewood, Ill.: Dow Jones–Irwin, Inc., 1971), chap. 5.

a direct bearing on the strategist's personal choice and thereby on the strategic posture of his corporation. In responding to these societal obligations, how are they to be incorporated into his strategic choice?

First, the corporate posture on these issues involves tradeoffs between performance as it has been traditionally measured and social benefits. Moreover, the penalties in terms of increased costs or lower revenues are generally more easily determined than the benefits, which are often intangible, long-term, or indirectly obtained. Second, the difficulty of the calculation does not absolve the strategist from the need to apply the same degree of rigor that he applies elsewhere to defining strategy in this area. To neglect analysis of both environmental and resource dimensions because such analysis is difficult or because the results may conflict with a philosophical conviction is to risk frivolity and ineffectiveness. Third, the strategy, if it is to be effective, requires a level of commitment to subsequent achievement at least as great as that for competitive responses. Before making statements about the intended performance of his company in equal employment, for instance, the chief executive should be sure of his willingness and ability to secure compliance from his organization. He must be ready to incur the costs and exert the leadership necessary to attain results or he may be justly criticized for merely reflecting a professional corporate piety.

## FROM STRATEGIST TO ORGANIZATION BUILDER

The strategic process described up to this point is largely intellectual in character. It is a process which the strategist can accomplish by himself, possibly using some staff or professional inputs. The many judgments and the ultimate strategic choice must be made by him and often by him alone. The job of the general manager does not end here, however. The strategy has to be implemented, requiring support and commitment from other people in the organization. The task of implementation involves not only ideas and facts but people as well. Therefore, it is not just intellectual but also administrative in character. The general manager must not only be a strategist but also an organization builder. Part II of this text focuses on that aspect of the general manager's job.

# Part II

# The general manager as organization builder

# 10

# Organizational diagnosis

## INTERRELATIONSHIP BETWEEN STRATEGY
## AND ORGANIZATION

IN MANY instances, business policy or general management courses, having covered the concept of corporate strategy and its application, will come to an end. Yet, from the general manager's point of view, it is like a baseball manager who posts his lineup and then calls the game. A general manager is not solely a paper strategist. It is his task to convert the intellectually formulated strategy through his organization into an operationally effective one.

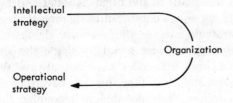

Intellectual strategy

Organization

Operational strategy

This task is compounded in the growing enterprise by the dynamics of change. First of all, growth entails a larger size, resulting in more people, more facilities, and, for everybody, more work. Is it possible to manage increasing size without losing the organizational and human strengths that made this growth possible? Second, growth often involves

71

a broader geographic dispersion, whether nationally or internationally, placing additional and sometimes different demands on the organization and its people. Third, growth may be based on diversification into different products, posing new challenges as dissimilar activities must be managed simultaneously. In sum, in a growing enterprise the general manager's job of converting an intellectual into an operational strategy is compounded by the fact that both tasks and people change significantly. The organizational challenge is similar to building a house on constantly shifting grounds.

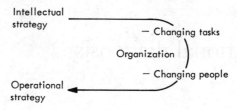

The general manager cannot evade this challenge. Continued growth requires a strong but frequently changing organization. Thus, if growth is to be more than ephemeral, the general manager must be not solely a successful strategist but a capable organization builder as well. Organizational change in support of a successful strategy will be a regular facet of the general manager's job in a dynamic enterprise.

Corporate organization and its people are not only the means through which strategy is implemented; they are also the major constraint. In fact, a significant hurdle to the successful execution of a strategy is the inability of the organization to carry it out. In these circumstances, it is convenient to place the blame on the organization. Yet how many strategic plans specifically take into account the fact that organizationally they entail changing tasks and people? The general manager as architect has to relate his plans to the organizational and human dimension.

Organization is not only a constraint in shaping strategy; it also greatly influences the strategic process. Suggestions, demands, and ambitions of organizational units or their members shape the strategic direction of the company. These influences may not always surface boldly or be recognized explicitly, but they prevail nevertheless. In several of the cases which follow, it is possible to recognize the organizational inputs which influence strategy.

The general manager, in summary, faces the task of (1) building and constantly adapting his organization to the demands of his strategy, (2) ensuring that his strategy takes into account organizational constraints, and (3) recognizing the organizational inputs which influence the strategic process.

This chapter deals with organizational diagnosis. It focuses (1) on the concept of organization by asking "what" the general manager manages and (2) on the test of organizational adequacy to determine whether the organization is sound. Both these questions are easier to pose than to answer. In fact, organizational diagnosis is one of the most difficult tasks confronting the general manager. The next chapter is devoted to organizational action. It describes (1) the tools of the general manager, that is, "how" he manages; (2) stages of corporate development identifying varying characteristics of different forms of organization; (3) the need to manage reality, which may involve compromises in terms of both decisiveness and clarity; (4) the need to manage time by giving specific attention to the timing and speed of organizational action; and (5) the risks confronting the general manager as he copes with his organizational challenges. Chapters 12 and 13 describe the management of organizational transition by highlighting two major and frequently occurring organizational shifts which are caused by growth: the process of institutionalization, when a company shifts from entrepreneurial to professional management, and the process of divisionalization, when a company moves away from a functional setup to one organized around business units. The shift to a divisional organization structure creates multiple levels of general management. Chapter 14 describes the divisional and Chapter 15 the corporate general management job. Chapter 16 concludes this text by focusing on the most important transition of a manager's career: the shift from specialist to generalist.

## CONCEPT OF ORGANIZATION

Organizational diagnosis requires definition. The general manager asks, "What am I managing?" and the student asks, "What am I analyzing?" This section proposes a way to view an organization. For this analysis the organization is seen as consisting of (1) a set of functional or divisional strategies, (2) a set of personal strategies, (3) a set of personal abilities, and (4) a set of relationships.

Organizational diagnosis begins with an identification of the various key activities which the general manager has to manage. In a specialized industrial company these will be functions such as manufacturing, marketing, engineering, research and development, finance, and control. A diversified industrial company, as will be discussed later, usually is divided into business units, each encompassing functional departments. Service companies will be organized around the activities peculiar to their businesses.

These activities should be viewed not as static stereotypes (that is, production, marketing) but in strategic terms (that is, the company's production strategy or its marketing strategy). Usually, each function, by virtue of its assigned responsibilities in the organization, has its own goals, ambitions, and plans. These various functional strategies should be identified. In the divisionalized company, identification focuses on the strategies of the various business units. For example, in the functionally organized Dansk Designs, marketing and design pursue different strategies, as do the project management and superintendent functions in Vappi. In the divisionally organized Carmen and Dynatech companies, each of the various divisions has quite different strategies.

The next step in organizational diagnosis is to identify the people. This task should not be confined to listing their names, titles, and job histories. Just as each function has its own goals, ambitions, and plans, so does each individual. Thus, an organization not only represents a group of people, it consists of a set of personal strategies. In Dansk Designs it is possible to attempt to identify the personal strategies of several of the key executives. In United Latex the five line and staff executives interviewed pursue quite different personal strategies.

Corporate, functional, and personal strategies, in the final analysis, are confined by the abilities of the people who carry them out. Hence, in identifying the people in the organization, it is necessary to look not only at their strategies but also at their abilities. Abilities, like corporate resources, must be viewed as relative to the demands placed upon them by the nature of the tasks to be performed. In National Franchise Management, Mr. Fisher has to assess the abilities of the manager of the Phone-A-Flower organization. The managing director of United Latex has to take into account the abilities of his managers in dealing with the issue of corporate-division relationships.

People as well as functions interrelate. As a result, each organization consists of a network of relationships. Beyond the formal links suggested by the organization chart or the flow of goods and services, there is inevitably an array of informal ties based on friendships, alliances, and background. Animosities or rivalries may also exist. In identifying the interconnections between the functions and between the people, it is important to do so again in strategic terms.

In a small packaged and branded foods company the marketing and manufacturing vice presidents were continuously locking horns. Yet, with a commonly accepted corporate strategy aimed at rapid and maximum market penetration, resulting in the allocation of every discretionary dollar to marketing, it was a foregone conclusion that marketing always won and manufacturing always lost. This pattern had been institutionalized and was accepted by both vice presidents. The marketing man saw his primary goal as sales growth, while the manufacturing man made a virtue of necessity, taking great pride in his ability to keep the plant running with an absolutely minimum budget. As a result, the interfunctional conflicts were largely mirror fights, conducted in a sense of good fun and fellowship. This pattern of relationships produced a cohesive organization and permitted rapid growth, albeit without significant profits since all discretionary money was channeled into marketing expenditures. The president then decided to focus more on profits; to implement this goal, he hired—at a salary significantly above that of the other two vice presidents—an administrative vice president. Conflicts immediately followed. The strategy of the marketing department which aimed at growth clashed with the strategy of the administrative department which focused on profits and hence on reduced marketing expenses. (Manufacturing expenses were already at minimal levels.) This clash between the strategies of the two departments was aggravated by a simultaneous conflict between the personal strategies of the marketing and administrative vice presidents. The former had always been the company's crown prince, but his position was now challenged by the new vice president who had a strong personal need for power and a desire to be next in line to the president. While the two old-timers questioned the new control system, the president had a blind faith in the ability and expertise of his new vice president. Relationships became marked by rivalry and hostility, and the company's performance declined. Instead of the hoped-for profits, losses occurred.

The functional and personal strategies and the resulting relationships create a multidimensional framework which the general manager must manage. These multiple dimensions must be identified since one cannot manage what one does not know. Furthermore, these strategies and relationships may involve conflicts, as the above description clearly demonstrates. Conflicts also are found in several of the subsequent cases, such as Vappi, Dansk Designs, or United Latex. In United Latex some division managers want to run their operations independently, while others are eagerly looking for help. The corporate staff managers, in turn, see their roles in divisional affairs differently. These conflicting divisional and personal strategies greatly influence the relationships in United Latex between the corporate staff and the operating units.

The framework of functional and personal strategies, abilities, and relationships is a dynamic one. People change, as do their attitudes, ambitions, and abilities. Functional opportunities and risks change. So do relationships. Organization is thus a dynamic concept. As a result, the general manager must constantly update the identification of his multidimensional organizational framework. Also, as organizational modifications are contemplated, their impact on this framework can be assessed. Thus, organizational diagnosis provides the general manager not only with the parameters within which he has to work but also with a framework to predict the implications of organizational change. The Vlasic Foods and Dansk Designs cases portray such dynamic situations, involving changes in several elements of the framework.

## TEST OF ORGANIZATIONAL ADEQUACY

Diagnostically, the general manager must not only identify his organizational framework but he must also evaluate its adequacy. The test of organizational adequacy determines whether a company's organization as defined in the previous section is able (1) to support its corporate strategy, (2) to meet the environmental threats, and (3) to discharge its key operational requirements. The test of organizational adequacy, therefore, relates the internal dimensions of functional or divisional strategies, personal strategies, personal abilities and relationships to external dimensions resulting from a company's strategy, the environmental threats confronting it, and its key operating requirements.

The first question to be tested is whether the organization is able to support the corporate strategy. Given the many possible strategic postures, it is impossible to generalize by developing an all-encompassing prescription. Some examples must suffice. Vlasic Foods is engaged in a strategy of continued and rapid growth through geographic expansion. Will its organization be able to support this growth strategy? Dansk Designs is contemplating entry into a different product line. Will its organization be able to satisfy the new and possibly more demanding requirements of this line? Is the Peace Corps organization adequate in view of its new strategy?

The second question focuses on the environmental threats which a company must face regardless of its strategic posture. The Strang company must cope with increased competitive pressures as well as a declining electronics market. Is its organization, hitherto geared to rapid expansion, able to meet these new challenges? Is the organization of Bill Communications as well as its underlying philosophy able to withstand the pressures of a few recession years?

The third question tests the organizational adequacy in terms of the industry's key operational requirements. Given the operating characteristics of the construction industry, how is Vappi's organization to be evaluated? How well is the Vlasic Foods organization able to cope with the critical coordination of farm and field, manufacturing and marketing, or the Dansk Designs organization with the balancing of the differing requirements of design, sourcing, and marketing?

In applying the test of consistency the general manager frequently meets three difficulties. First, as he attempts to relate organization to strategy, he may find the strategy unclear, emerging, or changing. How definite is, for example, Dynatech's strategy? If the answer to this question is uncertain, how does the general manager test the adequacy of his organization? Can National Franchise Management decide on an organizational response with respect to Phone-A-Flower until it has formulated a strategy for this new acquisition? Yet, it may have to make organizational decisions before the strategic choices can be sorted out.

A second difficulty results from the fact that symptoms of organizational malfunction are not always explicit. It is a common human tendency to cover up unpleasant things, and organizational situations are no exception. A malfunctioning machine will squeak or leak oil and alert the engineer; organizations do not so readily exhibit their malfunctions to the general manager. Hence, he has to be part detective to assess his organizational situation. Alternatively, members of the organization may exaggerate the symptoms. Are the complaints in Vappi serious or simply a manifestation of normal human discontent?

A third hurdle in applying the test of organizational adequacy is that symptoms often have multiple causes. If profits are down or new business is lost, is it because of uncontrollable external forces, because of an inadequate strategy, or because of a weak organization? Is a business recession to blame? Is the strategy at fault? Or is the organization the cause for unsatisfactory performance? This dilemma is faced by Vappi and Strang. If there are multiple possible causes, where does the blame lie? Given an uncertain diagnosis of the causes, how can the general manager evaluate the adequacy of his organization?

The test of organizational adequacy must be applied dynamically. How will the organization look some years hence? Will the functional and personal strategies change? Which people will contribute to the organization and what will be their abilities? What will happen to their relationships? Will a struggle be waged for the succession of the retiring chief executive? Will key people retire? Will it be possible to find enough new people with the same skills and commitment as the old-timers? How does one evaluate Dansk Designs without its chief designer? Will Vlasic Foods be able to find enough skilled people to support its rapid growth? What is the impact on Vappi of the departure of several project managers? Once the future scope and strength of the organization have been predicted, they have to be appraised as to how they will satisfy the requirements of the future. The general manager must constantly pose the question whether his strategy, emerging environmental threats, or changing operational requirements will outgrow his organization. Today's organization has to be related to tomorrow's strategy, risks, and tasks. As a result, future conditions have to be predicted. The test of organizational adequacy must be built on the strategic forecast. Thus, this chapter which began by stressing the interrelationships between strategy and organization ends on the same note, leading to a conclusion and a question. The conclusion is that the test of organizational adequacy, being dependent on the strategic forecast, is by necessity judgmental. The question is whether general managers give the same time to organizational prognosis that they give to environmental prognosis.

# 11

# Organizational action

## TOOLS OF THE GENERAL MANAGER

ORGANIZATIONAL diagnosis concerns itself with *what* the general manager manages; organizational action focuses on *how* he manages. Typically, the general manager uses three tools: (1) he acts as architect through the use of organizational structure; (2) he manages the various systems which have been designed, such as the budgeting or compensation system; and (3) he manages through his direct dealings with people. The general manager uses these three tools simultaneously. Thus, even though they will be described sequentially, they are in actual life closely and continuously interrelated. The choices which he makes in terms of these three tools greatly influence the organizational climate. They determine in large part the "way of life" of a particular company.

The design of the organizational structure is the general manager's most visible tool. The basic choice between a functional and a divisional organization will be discussed later. The latter is frequently a response to diversification, dictating a structure which (1) places the divisional manager in the best position to direct the business, (2) permits his success to be measured by observing the profits he produces, and (3) prevents the corporation, bent on further diversification, from burdening the divisional manager with the problems of new businesses. In addition, the divisional structure is often chosen as a deliberate tool to change management behavior. The United Latex case is one such example. Another example is a 120-year-old company producing a broad

78

and varied line of paper products. After years of stagnation, this company had changed from a "paternalistic, sleepy firm" to a "growth" company. Yet, its strategy had remained relatively constant. Management felt that its "new look" had resulted from changes in the organizational structure and in the bonus system. Its chairman of the board commented: "I am convinced that the biggest single factor in our recent success was the assignment of profit responsibility for the product line to a well-trained group of managers in a single operating unit. The second biggest factor was that we began paying management based on results."

Within the basic alternatives of a functional or divisional organization are a number of subordinate choices. The choices for the divisionalized company will be discussed in more detail in Chapter 13. In the functional firm, the general manager faces such questions as whether to assign the credit function to the financial staff or to the marketing manager, or the technical customer service activities to manufacturing or to sales. In a greeting card company, the president was wondering whether sales, merchandising, and product design, each under a separate vice president, should be combined into a single marketing department or whether sales and merchandising at least should be placed under a single vice president.

The design of the organization structure involves both task definition and allocation. In assigning responsibility to subordinates, the general manager must ensure that his structural design (1) relates effectively to the elements determining organizational adequacy, that is, corporate strategy, environmental threats, and key operating requirements; (2) relates the various tasks effectively to each other, permitting a cohesive and coordinated functioning of specialized activities; and (3) permits meaningful motivation and commitment, both of a monetary and non-monetary nature.

The general manager should not apply structural design mechanistically. It encompasses more than mere job descriptions and organization charts. In the consumer goods company example cited in the previous chapter, the president had used structural change, that is, the hiring of a new administrative vice president, to implement his goal of changing the corporate strategy from maximizing sales to enhancing profitability. Yet this change alone was not enough. The new strategy and structure had to be managed within the dynamic organizational context of functional and personal strategies, abilities, and relationships. A fancy title will not overcome a lack of ability, nor will a large corner office guarantee effective relationships. Organizational design must take place in a dynamic and strategic setting. In the earlier example, it resulted in a clash of both functional and personal strategies and destroyed hitherto effective relationships. The general manager as architect designs his organization structure not only around tasks but also around people and their relationships. As a result, he must take into account the operational as well as the political requirements. He must not only determine the most effective way of getting the goods out the door but also how to deal with power, influence, and personalities.

These comments raise the perennial dilemma of whether the organizational structure should be built around people or around tasks without regard to the existing members of the organization. In reality, however, this dilemma is a nonissue. The general manager must calibrate both requirements and must take into account and manage both tasks and people. Organizational design does not involve a choice between one or the other but the degree of balance and emphasis between the two. Even those who cling to structural purity feel the impact of the people dimension, particularly when one of the key executives departs, as happened, for example, in the Strang case in this book.

The general manager must be more than an architect who uses structural design as his only tool. He must also design and manage the many systems which focus on planning, resource allocation, budgeting, control, information, coordination and arbitration, compensation, as well as executive selection and development. These systems provide the general manager with tools through which he influences organizational behavior indirectly. Like structural design, they must (1) relate effectively to the elements determining organizational adequacy, (2) relate effectively to each other, and (3) permit meaningful motivation and commitment. In addition, the various systems must be congruent with the organizational structure, on one hand, and with the way in which the general manager utilizes them on the other. If a general manager evaluates his subordinates through a close and constant use of the control system and relates this system directly to the compensation system by basing the distribution of rewards (or sanctions), in the form of pay and promotions, on performance, then subordinates are likely to pay close attention to this control system. Where, in contrast, compensation and the control system are not interrelated, the latter is likely to be taken less seriously. Also, if performance measurement is determined by relating the control to the budgeting system, requiring managers to submit their own target estimates against which they are subsequently measured, and if the general manager does not permit his subordinates to reestimate their targets when results fall short, both systems will be taken very seriously. As a result, subordinates will submit their estimates carefully, possibly even conservatively, and where results are below target they will resort to early and vigorous action.

The cases in Part 2 of this book permit analysis of several systems and their use by the general manager. Compensation systems are described in Vlasic Foods, where the chief executive places a heavy reliance on a performance bonus versus a fixed salary, and in Vappi, where one group of managers is compensated on the basis of total company performance while another group, which has to coordinate closely with the former, receives a bonus based on the execution of a specific job. Both these companies have an intriguing system of achieving coordination through reliance on the team concept. In Dansk Designs a coordination system between the European and U.S. offices is being developed.

A third tool of the general manager is direct intervention. The leadership styles of the chief executives of Dansk Designs and Vlasic Foods, respectively, provide an interesting contrast between the relative influence of direct action and reliance on systems. The former manages largely through personal contact, providing critical inputs for new products as well as day-to-day coordination for existing ones. The latter, on the other hand, uses more formal planning, budgeting, control, and compensation systems in guiding his organization and stays away from daily operating activities. However, certain activities, such as the selection of key executives, require the personal input of the general manager. The chief executive of Dansk Designs wishes to retire but must first select his successor, while the Vlasic Foods chief executive must hire a new manufacturing vice president.

A critical question for the general manager is not just the extent to which he wishes to manage through direct intervention but also the consistency of his behavior. If he has chosen to rely largely on systems but on occasion chooses to intervene directly, he may well arrive at quick and decisive solutions for the specific problem at hand, but he may also be undercutting his subordinates, thereby making the resolution of future problems more difficult.

## STAGES OF CORPORATE DEVELOPMENT

The relative emphasis placed on the three tools varies depending on the stage of a company's development, which, in turn, is influenced by its strategic posture. In smaller organizations the importance of direct contact is usually greatest, whereas in larger companies the general manager relies more on structure and systems. Thus, the general management task is significantly different in each type of organization. These differences have led to the formulation of a model of stages of corporate development. Pioneered by Scott, inspired by Chandler's historical work,[1] and supported by Christensen, Salter, and others, it has resulted in a fruitful research effort.

The first stage of corporate development is a "small company with one or a few functions performed largely by one manager."[2] Its strategic

---

[1] Alfred D. Chandler, *Strategy and Structure* (Cambridge, Mass.: The M.I.T. Press, 1962).

[2] This and the following quotations are taken from Bruce R. Scott, "Stages of Corporate Development." (Copyright © 1971 by the President and Fellows of Harvard College.)

posture involves a single product sold through a uniform set of distribution channels. Through growth in volume, geographic expansion, or vertical integration a company moves to the second stage, which—even though the strategic single-product posture remains the same—involves a "multidepartmental enterprise, with specialized managerial departments based upon function." Diversification, leading to multiple product lines and multiple channels of distribution, leads to the third stage of the "multidivisional enterprise, with divisions based largely on product-market relationships." Scott singles out a number of characteristics for each stage in terms of research and development, performance measurement, rewards, control system, and strategic choices.

Research and development is essentially the province of the owner manager in stage 1; it becomes institutionalized in the second stage as a systematic search for product and process improvements; in stage 3 the search broadens to one for totally new and different products. Performance measurement in the stage 1 organization is by "personal contact and subjective criteria," becoming in stage 2 "increasingly impersonal using technical and/or cost criteria," and evolving in stage 3 into the impersonal use of such "market criteria" as return on investment. Rewards similarly move from being "unsystematic and often paternalistic" to "increasingly systematic with emphasis on stability and service" to "increasingly systematic with variability related to performance." Scott describes the control system of stage 1 as "personal control of both strategic and operating decisions," of stage 2 as "personal control of strategic decisions, with increasing delegation of operating decisions based on control by decision rules (policies)," and of stage 3 as "delegation of product-market decisions within existing businesses, with indirect control based on analysis of 'results.'" Strategic choices, finally, pit the needs of the owner against the needs of the firm in stage 1, while stage 2 involves choices in terms of degree of vertical integration, market share objectives, and breadth of product line. Stage 3 strategic choices concern "entry and exit from industries, allocation of resources by industry and rate of growth."

Scott concludes that this "cluster of characteristics suggests not just a form of organization but a 'way of managing' and to a considerable extent a 'way of life' within the enterprise. It is these clusters, their stability by stage, the problems of transition from one stage to another, the relative importance of each type of firm, and the historical trends by industry and by country which are of particular interest."

The cases on organization in this book are broken down into two sections, the first dealing with general management in the functional or stage 2 organization, and the second focusing on the divisional or stage 3 company. Several of the cases as well as Chapters 12 and 13 describe the management of transition from one stage to the next. Before discussing the process of transition, however, three aspects of organizational action must be emphasized: the need to manage within the realm of reality, the importance of timing, and the necessity to shoulder risks.

## THE CHALLENGE OF ORGANIZATIONAL ACTION

### Managing reality

Organizational action must be rooted in reality, sometimes requiring the general manager to abandon conventional organizational principles. Reality may force him to opt for conflict or confusion, even though theory may prescribe the pursuit of harmony or clarity. It is a common error to assume that all conflicts can be avoided through proper organizational design. Often, they are unavoidable elements of the organizational fabric. The challenge for the general manager is not to avoid them but to manage them properly. Lack of clarity is not necessarily undesirable, either. As organizational relationships emerge or as people prove themselves, it may be appropriate to let them earn their own way without making the assignment or authority explicit.

General managers may centralize activities and provide detailed operating guidance. Within such a setting, however, they may not always enforce the rules but rather permit selective violations of them. The general manager may consider these rules essential as guidance and support for his weaker or newer managers. The stronger and more experienced managers, on the other hand, may be unnecessarily confined by them and may be expected and even encouraged to take more independent action. While theoretically such an approach may appear inconsistent, it permits the general manager to set his rules on the basis of the lowest common denominator without constraining the scope of action of his stronger and more talented subordinates.

Another example of deliberate confusion is the so-called "psychological" decentralization. Here a subordinate is given more authority on paper than he exercises in reality. It happens where corporate staff managers are in a position to influence the scope of activities of operating line managers. Again, such a situation is not necessarily bad. First of all, staff executives may interfere only selectively. Second, the illusionary power may nevertheless be an important ceremonial attribute, providing some motivational benefits and establishing the authority of the operating manager among his own subordinates.

In terms of organizational action, conflicts and lack of clarity should not be summarily rejected and condemned without proper analysis. The key question is whether conflicts and confusion will lead to malfunction which may obstruct the strategy, expose the company to environmental threats, and prevent the proper execution of the key operational requirements. In a number of situations, conflicts and confusion may not lead to malfunction but will better satisfy the requirements of organizational adequacy than harmony and clarity.

Organizational action deliberately involving conflicts or lack of clarity may encounter resistance or misunderstanding. Under such circumstances members of the organization will typically blame the general manager for his inability to develop a structure without conflicts and for his indecisiveness in eliminating confusion. They will view harmony and clarity as desirable per se and will view their absence as evidence of the general manager's poor decision-making ability. Organizational action, like strategic choice, is often a lonely task, and the general manager may not always be able to achieve popularity and effectiveness simultaneously.

## Managing time

Time is even more critical in contemplating organizational action than in formulating strategy. It is easier to change plans than to change people. It is easier to expand a product line or a manufacturing plant than to train people. It is easier to predict rapid growth than to achieve it through organizational action. A strategist must be aware of the digestive capacity of his organization: how much can be done how fast?

Managing time also involves anticipating future needs and taking preventive organizational action. The decision to take preventive action, however, is not an easy one, and the action itself is often resisted by members of the organization. Rather, given the risk, pain, and cost involved, organizational change is often contemplated and accepted only when the symptoms of malfunction are so severe that the need is obvious. If delayed, organizational change frequently takes place in an atmosphere of crisis, adding a major handicap to an already difficult process. The alternative to taking preventive action, however, is not easy. Who wants to undergo preventive surgery when there is still hope that matters will not turn out so badly after all? Where there is hope, there is wishful thinking. As a result, it is much harder, when the existing organization is still reasonably successful, to convince its members that change is in order. Modifying behavior today in anticipation of future needs is a major challenge facing the general manager.

## Managing risks

The general manager as organization builder manages risks. It is common to associate risk taking exclusively with strategic responses to external forces such as products, technology, or competition. Yet the general manager faces great internal risks as well. Organizational change is often more difficult and riskier than strategic change. It involves shifts in people and relationships as well as in tasks. People and their behavior are not as easily changed as the organization chart or the strategic plan.

In deciding on organizational action the general manager must base his prescription on his organizational diagnosis. This diagnosis, however, may be uncertain, making it both difficult and dangerous for the general manager to be decisive. Unfortunately, the general manager frequently finds himself in this situation. In discussing the cases in the second part of this book, some observers may give a particular company a clean bill of health, others may diagnose a minor disease requiring a modest dose of medicine, while still others may call for major and immediate surgery. Situations eliciting such vastly different and conflicting diagnoses are not uncommon when several experts are consulted. If one wishes peace of mind by arriving at a clear-cut diagnosis, the only safe solution is to call in just one expert. Once faced with diverging diagnoses, however, what does the general manager do? He can wait and see. Or he can be decisive. But what if he sends a healthy patient to surgery? The risk of decisive action can be substantial. On the other hand, the wait-and-see attitude can be equally risky if the severely ill patient is sent home without treatment. Thus, where organizational diagnosis is uncertain, as it often is, organizational action is risky, and the organization builder inevitably has to manage risks.

Another risk results from the inevitable consequence of changing tasks and people: the breakup of old and hitherto successful patterns. In the process of instituting change, the general manager may be forced to destroy his home base. Once he has destroyed his base, he has no place to which to return in case of failure. Thus, organizational change is generally a one-way street. If it fails, the general manager faces an entirely new and usually more difficult beginning, requiring him to rebuild his organization anew.

Organizational change often involves total risk, not just incremental risk. Incremental risks in case of failure affect only the incremental decision. If a person buys a high-risk stock whose value subsequently declines to zero, the loss remains confined to the amount of the stock purchase and does not affect the person's entire net worth. Total risks, on the other hand, have ramifications far beyond the incremental decision. Failure, in such event, endangers the total situation. For example, some observers may argue that failure of Vlasic Foods to grow successfully by another $20 million or of Dansk Designs to launch the Gourmet line may jeopardize the existence of the entire company. Since the success of these strategic steps hinges to a large extent on the organizational underpinnings, the failure of the organizational changes contemplated in those companies might result in the downfall of the entire firm.

# 12

# Process of institutionalization

## SYMPTOMS OF MALFUNCTION

IT IS SUCCESS itself which necessitates the transition from entrepreneurship to professional management. Growth strains the existing organizational setup. The only way to relieve these strains is not to grow. If an entrepreneurship wants to retain its existing organization, the sole remedy is to avoid growth by not being successful.

Those entrepreneurships which succeed and which accept the consequences of growth will sooner or later outgrow their organizational setup. Usually this change occurs sooner because in an entrepreneurship all key activities and decisions are typically handled by a few key people, often primarily the president. The process is characterized by several symptoms:

—An overworked chief executive is involved in too many decisions and he has too many people reporting to him.
—The textbook remedy, that is, delegation, is not working.
—The combination of the overworked executive and the failure of delegation inevitably slows down the decision-making process.

There are several reasons why delegation is not effective. First, the chief executive bemoans the fact that his people are not capable of handling the additional responsibilities. His subordinates may have been hired during the earlier stages of the company's existence as operational

86

aides and not as managers. Thus, the size of the company may have outgrown their capabilities.

Second, in an entrepreneurship delegation is simply not a way of life. Normally, decisions are made in the process of daily and constant contact during which everyone checks with the boss. Letting someone run his own show independently is a rare exception. In this atmosphere, even when the chief executive assigns some of his tasks to others, it turns out to be in reality only pseudodelegation. The old habits continue to prevail in spite of written edicts to the contrary. Parenthetically, it is often the chief executive himself who is the prime offender.

Third, there is a simple pragmatic reason why delegation is difficult. In an entrepreneurship, the managers are usually jacks of all trades. Assignments are scattered and haphazard, largely influenced by the most urgent needs prevailing at each particular moment. In such a setting, it is difficult to assign specifically and consistently both authority and responsibility. In fact, most of the delegation may be of one-shot activities rather than defining and assigning a set of recurring tasks.

Fourth, in an entrepreneurship the chief executive may use "eye-balling" rather than formalized control in measuring performance. Where there is no scorecard, it is not unusual to receive no credit for the wins but nevertheless to get blamed for the losses. If assuming responsibility does not generate benefits on the upside but does involve penalties on the downside, one is more than likely to play it safe. When the boss bemoans the fact that his subordinates are unwilling to shoulder responsibility, he should first ask himself whether scorecards are being kept and whether on this basis he distributes the rewards as well as the penalties.

In the absence of delegation, decisions have to wait for the boss. Yet, as the company's size increases, the boss becomes less well informed. As a result, he must obtain more and more information from others. However, this information reaches him haphazardly and not in a standard or systematic fashion. Thus, more and more people are needed for the boss to make his decisions, and soon he will resort to committee management. This, in turn, will aggravate the phenomenon of being overworked as people sit around the table rather than doing their jobs. Also, it gets harder and harder to find times when everybody is available; hence, meetings are delayed, causing further decision slowdowns.

As the waiting time for decisions lengthens, people in the organization inevitably resort to self-help. Everybody begins to improvise in his own fashion. Rarely does this produce harmonious action. Rather, it frequently involves duplication, as people who do not get together do identical things. As everyone tries to do his best on his own, organizational cohesion suffers.

The above symptoms inevitably translate into a decline in performance and a rise in costs. The overworked chief executive then resorts to a typical cure of hiring an assistant or deputy to relieve him of some of his excessive workload. Unfortunately, this action often aggravates rather than remedies the symptoms. Instead of one overworked person there are now two. Both get involved in everything. Subordinates seek guidance from two bosses, and the bosses, in turn, have to coordinate among themselves. Thus, the available time for productive activity declines even further. The malfunction goes from bad to worse.

## THE GENERAL MANAGER'S RESPONSE

The organizational engine finally reaches the point where a few drops of oil are not enough to restore it to a smooth-running condition. Instead of the oilcan it needs a major overhaul. In medical terms, what is needed is surgery, not just medicine. Organizational surgery, however, like medical surgery, involves three elements: it is painful, it is risky, and it is costly.

Given the pain, risk, and cost, the general manager often delays organizational surgery. Moreover, the chief executive in this instance shares the privilege of being both the surgeon and the patient. As a patient, he has reason to ask for his own record as a surgeon, only to find that he has none. The successful entrepreneur is a proven obstetrician, but not necessarily a skillful surgeon.

In summary, the management of transition frequently takes place late; it is a painful, risky, and costly activity; and it is managed by someone with no prior experience. Fortunately, many manuals and textbooks stand ready to guide the general manager in this major challenge. The common operation prescribed for the above symptoms is specialization. Sometimes, expansion may take a company into vastly different product lines, as happened to the Carmen company in this book. In such an event, the transition may be directly to a divisional form of organization described in the next chapter.

## DESIGNING THE FUNCTIONAL ORGANIZATION

Specialization leading to a functional organization involves several elements:

1.  It attempts to combine related effort and to segregate unrelated effort. Thus, instead of having everybody do a little of everything, like activities are grouped together. People are able to do what they are best at, hence efficiency is expected to increase.

2.  Organizational tasks are defined and formalized, usually by function (such as manufacturing, marketing, engineering). Through this explicit codification, the general manager makes sure that all activities are properly covered.

3.  Authority required to discharge each task is delegated to the incumbent in each job. Thus, the general manager explicitly surrenders some of his decision-making power.

4.  With delegation goes control. A system of performance measurement is designed to evaluate the delegated activities. An explicit scorecard permits the general manager to determine how well the various tasks are being discharged. Likewise, these reports assist the managers in the conduct of their activities.

5.  Reporting relationships are established. Delegation is not always complete; and in certain instances, approval or guidance may be required. Generally, an attempt is made to minimize the number of reporting relationships for superiors and to have a subordinate report only to one boss.

6.  Coordination also has to be provided for, particularly horizontally among functions. In a number of instances, the specialized functions have to interrelate in terms of daily decision making or advance planning.

7.  Communication and information are essential for both the vertical reporting relationships and the horizontal coordination.

8.  Centralization, while the exception, may be necessary for certain activities. In some instances, specialization may be economically undesirable, or it may be necessary to use scarce management talent in a variety of activities.

9.  People have to be assigned to the various tasks in accordance with both their desires and abilities.

10.  As new people take on new assignments, their selection, training, and development have to be provided for. Often, this cannot be confined to the technical aspects of the job. As a plant superintendent moves to manufacturing vice president, the sales manager to marketing vice president, and the bookkeeper to controller, they shift more from operational to managerial activities. Thus, management development becomes increasingly important as the company grows and the organization becomes more complicated.

## IMPLICATIONS OF THE FUNCTIONAL ORGANIZATION

### A different general management job

The shift from the entrepreneurial "one-man show" to the specialized functional structure changes both the way of life of the organization and the job of the general manager. Under the previous structure, he was involved in day-to-day management, making specific decisions on current matters, resolving issues through direct intervention while dealing with individuals. This style of management typically is applied to both small and major decisions. Under the new structure, this style has to change.

Instead of dealing directly with specific issues on an "ad hoc" basis, the general manager will have to formulate broad policies encompassing sets of similar issues. Instead of poking his nose into everything, he has to categorize problems and develop guidelines for similar situations. Thus, compensation policies replace specific salary or bonus decisions for each individual. Such policies are necessary to maintain fairness in an increasingly larger organization and to permit meaningful delegation. The general manager's job shifts from direct intervention to delegation within a framework of policies and guidelines.

Instead of dealing with individuals, the chief executive now also manages functions. Again, the style of management shifts from direct action to indirect influence. By managing through guidelines and functional department heads, the chief executive's time horizon changes from a day-to-day orientation more towards the future. He must not only preside over the resolution of today's problems but also anticipate tomorrow's.

The general manager's job, as he withdraws from daily operations, becomes one of leadership through coordination and conflict resolution. Having functional managers reporting to him, he must manage specialists. His task is to mold these specialized functions into a cohesive corporate unit. The cases portraying functional organizations show that general managers use a number of different approaches in meeting this challenge.

### Need for adaptation

As a growing enterprise embarks upon the transition from entrepreneurial to functional management, two questions have to be answered affirmatively: first, is the organization able to change; and second, is the general manager able to change? The second question is often ignored. Corporate histories are full of examples of successful entrepreneurs who turned out to be unsuccessful organization builders. Chandler in his historical studies[1] of Du Pont and General Motors describes how both companies were created as large enterprises by entrepreneurs and empire builders, Coleman du Pont and William Durant, but that they were strengthened if not built organizationally by Pierre du Pont and Alfred Sloan. Thus a chief executive contemplating such a transition may wish to pause and reflect whether he has the qualifications to manage it by changing his leadership style. Alternatively, the

---

[1] Alfred D. Chandler, *Strategy and Structure* (Cambridge, Mass.: The M.I.T. Press, 1962).

entrepreneur may decide to withdraw, leaving the management of transition to a successor, who, even though he may not possess the same entrepreneurial drive, may be better equipped in terms of organizational talents.

The ability of the general manager to adapt is crucial. Yet, equally critical is the ability of the organization to move to a different way of life. Even if successfully implemented, however, a more formal and systematic organization may stifle the entrepreneurial spirit on which previous growth was based. This tradeoff must be recognized and managed.

The ability of an entrepreneurially based company to evolve toward a more formal functional organization should not be taken for granted. Organizational transition involves changes in tasks, in people, and in their interrelationships. Such change in established patterns of behavior is upsetting anad frequently resisted. Its implementation requires patience, guidance, and a great deal of teaching. An organization builder is in large part an educator.

### Risks of transition

Education is difficult. First of all, the organization builder must assess the digestive capacity of his people. Are they able to change to the new patterns of behavior required by increased formalization and are they able to discharge independently the tasks delegated to them? Just as a parent has to assess his child's driving ability before giving him the car keys, so must the general manager evaluate the ability of his organization. How much training and coaching are required to accomplish effective delegation?

Education is even more difficult where it is resisted. Such may be the case for organizational transition. It may take place against a background of success. Thus, the architect of organizational change in a growing company does not come to correct failure but to ensure continued success. Yet people resisting such a change may not see it this way. To them the argument of ensuring the future health of the organization is dwarfed by the argument that the existing setup has brought the company its proven success. Organizational surgery in this setting is like breaking up a winning team. To destroy the basis of previous success in order to ensure continued success in the future is often perceived as risky and perhaps unwarranted.

Thus, while the need and benefits of organizational transition are obvious to the general manager, they may be perceived differently by his people. The "new" life may seem less desirable than the "old" way of doing things. As Scott points out: "a company tends to lose some of its 'family like' nature as it grows, not just through the introduction of formal task specialization, but through the increased social 'distance' which separates people in a hierarchy."[2] Furthermore, newcomers have to be brought into the company. They may be seen as threats by the old-timers, who may resist their entry. Sometimes, newcomers bring expertise gathered through education, as in the case of Dansk Designs, or they contribute experience acquired through many years of work, as in the case of Vlasic Foods. Transition may require the hiring of new people with different skills and expertise. In these situations, the general manager must not confuse the organizational need for such people with the organizational acceptance of them by the old-timers in his company.

In managing organizational transition, the general manager must not only cope with the above difficulties and risks. Simultaneously, he has to continue his company's rapid growth pattern. To return to the surgery analogy, the patient has to return to work immediately after the operation and is given no time for rest and recuperation. While tasks, people, and relationships change, existing problems have to be solved, products have to be shipped, and capacity has to be expanded. The general manager cannot stop the world while he changes his organization.

[2] Bruce R. Scott, "Stages of Corporate Development," p. 29. (Copyright © 1971 by the President and Fellows of Harvard College.)

# 13

# Process of divisionalization

## SYMPTOMS OF MALFUNCTION

WHILE GROWTH forces an entrepreneurially organized company onto the path of institutionalization, growth through geographic expansion and product diversification necessitates the process of divisionalization. Both forms of expansion are a frequent phenomenon. Not only have companies achieved national coverage for their products or services, but many of them have expanded internationally as well. As they seek to adapt to special local conditions and to the many pitfalls of currency, trade, and tax regulations, the organization, hitherto geared exclusively to domestic operations, begins to show the strains. Likewise, diversification into different products has been a popular strategic response. Here, too, the organization with its activities originally aimed at a single product may find it difficult to cope simultaneously with a variety of dissimilar products. Demands imposed by internationalization and diversification are not limited to the giant companies. As shown by the Dynatech and Carmen organizations included in this book, the process of divisionalization affects smaller companies as well.

As in the case of institutionalization, the need for organizational transition resulting from internationalization and diversification manifests itself through certain symptoms of malfunction:

1. Interfunctional coordination and conflict resolution by necessity must be handled by top management, because beneath this level all managers are specialized by function. As top management gets further

and further removed from increasingly varying activities, its intimate operational knowledge declines to the point where it can no longer discharge this task effectively. The result under these circumstances is described as follows by the president of a large, functionally organized company engaged in several different product lines:

> It soon became apparent that for almost every decision, even the smallest, three to four people were needed, depending on how many functions were involved. Each man would enter the meeting having been briefed by his subordinates. However, in many cases, this information would not be the same. Yet, the top functional men usually were not sufficiently familiar with the details of the issue to resolve these discrepancies during the meeting. Hence it was often necessary to delay the decision and request further information and assistance from the lower echelons.

The breakdown of multifunctional coordination leads to organizational malfunction. In one company lack of direction by top management resulted in marketing, production, and engineering personnel not working together effectively, causing poor exploitation of opportunities for developing new products based on existing skills and markets. Also, managers in this company cited continual squabbles concerning improvements in manufacturing methods between process engineers and line production supervisors. Often, decisions by top management on these conflicts were postponed and the issues were never resolved. Under these circumstances, personal influence of certain managers rather than leadership from the top guided decisions on manufacturing improvements, production control, scheduling priorities, and research time allocations.

2. Even where decisions are reached by top management, it becomes increasingly difficult to have them understood and accepted by the company's lower echelons. A president contemplating divisionalization commented on this difficulty:

> The three or four people involved in a particular decision, agreement, or conflict could not bring their subordinates to the meeting, since this would have made the executive committee too cumbersome a body. Yet decisions made this way, in an exclusive circle, were not always understood by the people below, with a resulting decline in their commitment. We also felt this lack of participation by middle management to be a waste of our human resources.

3. Where functional managers at headquarters are far removed from operations but have to ensure coordination and conflict resolution—for example, in terms of resource allocation or transfer pricing—they are less likely to approach these matters pragmatically. Instead, these issues often become a matter of principle and prestige, leading to political maneuvering and power plays in which saving face becomes more important than reaching quick and reasonable decisions in the best interest

of the company. Thus, a dispute involving a few pennies in the internal transfer price of a product may delay production schedules or result in poor pricing decisions. Even though in theory the transfer price should have no impact on the total profits of the corporation, unresolved disputes may lead to behavior clearly detrimental to the corporation.

4. Compromise, rather than vigorous leadership, becomes a way of life in the company. In one large international company the president explained: "the members of the board are all specialists in their own sectors. It was only natural that in the final analysis each of them would defend his own sector and his own point of view during discussions." In addition, according to an observer outside this company, "the board members were too involved in day-to-day operational problems to devote the necessary time to planning or establishing an overall corporate mission. The result was that the president was not able to truly manage the company. He could only compromise among the managers at meetings."

5. Where overall corporate leadership is not forthcoming, the units will go their own and separate ways, resulting in *de facto* independence. Under these circumstances, it becomes difficult to formulate and implement an overall business policy for the corporation. Overlapping activities or even competition between the functional units may result.

6. Secrecy is another common symptom. Managers are familiar only with their own specialized activities. In the political atmosphere of a corporate environment they may be unwilling to share their data with other functions in the organization. Consequently, sales executives may have to make marketing decisions without having the cost structure of a product or the facts on plant capacity utilization.

7. The span of control of the chief executive frequently becomes unmanageable. As the corporation diversifies, new operating units are added, often resulting in new subordinates reporting to him. As this occurs, it becomes harder and harder for him to exercise effective leadership, especially where these reporting relationships involve him in a mass of minute details.

8. Finally and importantly, within the context of the above malfunctions it becomes very difficult to focus on profitability. Lines of accountability and responsibility become less clear, and with all the confusion and detail it may be virtually impossible to establish and maintain standards for measurement, evaluation, and reward. As in the process of institutionalization, where the scoreboard is out of order, the incentive to strive for exceptional performance diminishes. Managers are unable to obtain clear feedback on their achievements. Even where profit information is available, it may not relate to critical decisions or controllable items. In a functionally organized company it is usually only possible to measure profitability for the total organization. For each of the func-

tions, the measurement is normally on the basis of costs or quotas. Given the fact that all functions influence the total cost structure and that they are closely interrelated, it is always possible to pass the buck, blaming deficiencies in performance on lack of cooperation from another functional counterpart. This problem is compounded when operations involve different products or take place all over the world.

## THE GENERAL MANAGER'S RESPONSE

The general manager confronted with the above symptoms will be tempted to prefer prescribing medicine over performing surgery. Yet attempts to improve operating efficiency rarely resolve the fundamental structural problems resulting from internationalization and diversification. The impact of diverse product lines and of geography, especially as it extends across borders, requires a different organization structure. Such organizational surgery, however, has far-reaching implications in terms of tasks to be performed, relationships, and behavior of people. Such a break with established patterns involves risks similar to those described in the process of institutionalization. Surgery to reorganize the company along divisional lines is also painful, costly, and risky.

Nevertheless, divisionalization has become fashionable. Starting with Chandler,[1] the trend toward divisionalization has been documented in a number of studies. The vast majority of large U.S. companies have adopted a divisional structure during the last two decades, and a similar development is currently taking place in Europe. Interestingly, the first experimentation with such a structure took place in the early twenties at Du Pont. Chandler[2] renders a fascinating account of this transition which had its origins in Du Pont's World War I diversification into chemicals, paints and varnishes, celluloid, artificial leather, dyestuffs, and rayon. The organizational move, though, was triggered by losses in some of the new businesses, such as paints. The diagnosis of the organizational roots of these profit problems was facilitated by the fact that while Du Pont incurred losses, other smaller companies were making money in paints. A committee of junior executives analyzed the situation, concluding in March of 1920 that given the different sales requirements of the various businesses, the problem was not one of strategy but of organization. They proposed the realignment of management responsibilities around products rather than functions. Top management, however, rejected these recommendations, feeling—according to Chandler— that "the answer was not reorganization but better information and knowledge." Unofficial efforts toward *de facto* diversification, however,

---

[1] Alfred D. Chandler, *Strategy and Structure* (Cambridge, Mass.: The M.I.T. Press, 1962).

[2] Ibid., chap. 2.

continued to be made. They were disguised in reports dealing with profit improvements and statistical controls. A loss of close to $2.5 million during the first half of 1921 provided the final impetus, convincing top management to adopt in August of 1921 the organizational recommendations which had been made by the junior managers one-and-a-half years earlier.

Although in the years following the Du Pont experience a number of other organizations adopted a divisional structure, it took another three decades before this form of organization really took hold. In the fifties the best-known case of divisionalization was probably that of General Electric under Ralph Cordiner. So fashionable became the divisional organization that even companies which were not widely diversified adopted it. Divisionalization became prestige surgery, recommended as the instant answer for any company in trouble.

Indeed, divisionalization has certain temptations for general managers. The symptoms described earlier in this chapter may make him feel helpless. He recognizes that his company is not performing as it should—a declining profit picture may add a touch of urgency to his concern—but he does not quite know what to do about it. The problems have become too many and too vast, making it impossible to pinpoint and correct all the causes. Furthermore, as the company's scope expands geographically or productwise, the general manager becomes less and less expert on operating affairs. Where he lacks the necessary intimate knowledge, he is less capable of exerting a direct influence. As a result, he feels even more helpless. The divisional organization gives him a convenient way out of this dilemma because it permits him to delegate some of his general management tasks and, thereby, some of his problems.

## DESIGNING THE DIVISIONAL ORGANIZATION

### The divisional structure

The divisional organization is built around business units. Each unit has its own general manager who is responsible for the basic functions, such as manufacturing, engineering, and marketing. The performance of the unit is measured on the basis of its own profit and loss statement. In many ways a divisional organization consists of a number of relatively independent companies, with staff services provided either at the corporate or the divisional level or both (Exhibit 1). In large companies, divisionalization covers several levels (Exhibit 2). Staff services in such an organization may be located at either the corporate, group, divisional, or departmental level.

**EXHIBIT 1**

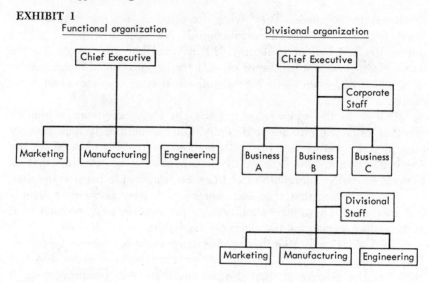

Functional organization                    Divisional organization

**EXHIBIT 2**

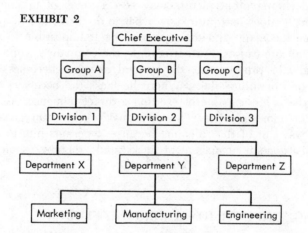

In designing a divisional organization a variety of alternatives is available. Some of the important and regularly occurring issues in terms of design are discussed below.

### Number of divisions

A first choice confronting the organization builder who contemplates divisionalization is how many divisions to create. On what basis are business units to be set up? Should the company be divided into a few large or several small divisions? The perennial problem here is the degree of overlap and the extent of interdependence which will be created between divisions. Minimizing overlap and interdependence means that only a few divisions can be created. The benefits of divisionalization, therefore, will be smaller than if a larger number of divisions is set up. A large number of divisions, on the other hand, makes overlap and interdependence unavoidable.

In one company a potential division sold raw materials both to outsiders and to another potential division. Should they be combined into one? If separately constituted, should the latter be permitted to have its own raw material facilities and, if not, should it be required to purchase its raw materials from the other division? If it is to rely on the other division for its sourcing, a complex problem of transfer pricing will be created. Also, do supplying divisions owe their counterparts any scheduling favors during periods of shortages? The decision on the number of divisions thus forces the organization builder to make tradeoffs. While costs and benefits of different organizational approaches can be analyzed, a general manager nevertheless has to rely to a large extent on his judgment because not all critical costs and benefits are objectively measurable.

The issue of the number of divisions arises in two ways. First, how many divisions immediately below the corporate level should be created? Second, should these divisions, in turn, be broken down into separate business units, thus carrying the principle of divisionalization deeper into the organization? Where this is done, several layers of general managers are created, and the organization builder must ponder what role the in-between general manager is to play.

Proponents of multilayer divisionalization cite several reasons for such an approach. In one company they stressed that it would (1) permit profit centers below the divisional manager level, (2) require the development of general management skills at lower organizational levels rather than retaining a specialized functional orientation up to the top of the division, (3) allow coordination of product or customer-centered plans below the division manager level, (4) give each business unit the flexibility of a small company and yet also provide the support and strength which goes with being part of a larger firm, and (5) result in an improved product and/or customer orientation, such as more appropriate technical services or more rapid introductions of new products.

Single-layer divisionalization with functionally organized divisions, on the other hand, avoids intensifying the problems of overlap and interdependence. For example, under a further breakdown into business units, different salesmen may call on the same customer, whereas a functional setup avoids such overlap as well as the problem of plant interdependencies. Use and allocation of joint services within the division may also prove simpler under a functional structure. In research and development, for example, activities can be centralized (1) to achieve the most efficient and balanced use of funds and (2) to avoid splitting the research effort into too many small teams.

## Corporate staff activities

Regardless of the degree of divisionalization, certain activities are likely to be centralized as part of a corporate staff. One company used the following criteria in deciding what to centralize:

1. To achieve economy in the use of specialized staffs: for example, personnel.
2. To consolidate tasks affecting the entire company: for example, legal work and insurance activities.
3. To achieve optimal use of scarce resources: for example, research and development and data processing.

Companies have taken vastly different approaches to the role of corporate staff activities. Berg in his research has documented that companies which have diversified by recent and often unrelated acquisitions generally have lean corporate staffs, while companies which have been diversified for a longer period of time and have entered into different product lines through internal expansion have opted for large corporate staffs. He refers to the former as "conglomerates," companies like Textron, Litton, or Gulf & Western, and to the latter as "diversified majors," like Bendix, Ingersoll-Rand, Westinghouse, or General Electric. Exhibit 3 gives intriguing data on some of the companies covered by the research, with sales in the $500 million to $2 billion range.

Centralization of certain activities into a corporate staff inevitably complicates reporting relationships. If there is a centralized controller's office or research and development staff, does the controller or R & D manager in the division report to the central staff directly (thereby reducing the authority of the divisional general manager), or through a so-called "dotted line" relationship, or not at all? The second or third alternatives are frequently followed, thereby giving the central staff merely an advisory role. The implications of such a situation for the central staff will be discussed in more detail in Chapter 15.

## Role of top management

When Du Pont pioneered the transition to the divisional organization in the early twenties, it faced the issue of whether top management should have operating responsibilities. In the old organization, the top-management committee consisted of the functional managers who were in charge of day-to-day operations. The architects of the new Du Pont

**EXHIBIT 3**
**Organizational data on companies**

| Companies | Diversified majors | | | | | | Conglomerates | | | | | | |
|---|---|---|---|---|---|---|---|---|---|---|---|---|---|
| | Company | | | | Four companies | | Company | | | | | Five companies | |
| Functions | A | B | C | X | Total | Avg. | F | G | H | I | J | Total | Avg. |
| General executives | 5 | 5 | 4 | 2 | 16 | 4 | 4 | 1 | 4 | 3 | 14 | 26 | 5 |
| Finance | 28 | 61 | 101 | 144 | 334 | 84 | 8 | 22 | 29 | 91 | 106 | 256 | 51 |
| (of which control) | (10) | (36) | (78) | (107) | (231) | (58) | (6) | (12) | (8) | (38) | (49) | (113) | (23) |
| Legal-secretarial | 4 | 10 | 22 | 42 | 78 | 20 | 1 | 7 | 5 | 6 | 66 | 85 | 17 |
| Personnel administration | 11 | 6 | 20 | 25 | 62 | 16 | 1 | 2 | 3 | 10 | 20 | 36 | 7 |
| Research and development | 54 | 130 | 139 | 232 | 555 | 139 | 0 | 0 | 0 | 0 | 0 | 0 | 0 |
| Marketing | 5 | 0 | 34 | 0 | 39 | 10 | 0 | 0 | 0 | 0 | 0 | 0 | 0 |
| Manufacturing | 5 | 1 | 0 | 5 | 11 | 3 | 0 | 0 | 0 | 0 | 0 | 0 | 0 |
| Public relations | 1 | 6 | 9 | 16 | 32 | 8 | 5 | 3 | 5 | 6 | 9 | 28 | 6 |
| Purchasing and traffic | 10 | 1 | 33 | 4 | 48 | 12 | 0 | 0 | 0 | 2 | 0 | 2 | 0 |
| Corporate planning | 3 | 3 | 2 | 6 | 14 | 5 | 5 | 4 | 1 | 7 | 9 | 26 | 5 |
| Totals | 126 | 223 | 364 | 476 | 1,189 | 297 | 24 | 39 | 47 | 125 | 224 | 459 | 92 |

Note: Numbers shown indicate professional personnel in corporate functions as determined from field research.
Source: Norman Berg, "Corporate Role in Diversified Companies" (Harvard Business School, Division of Research, Working Paper, 1971).

organization, however, felt that operating management could not be objectively critical and analytical and decided that the members of the executive committee should have no direct operating duties. Instead, they were—according to Chandler[3]—"to concentrate on overall planning, appraisal, and coordination." Also, "each was to help oversee one set of functional activities in all five of the new product divisions," but only "in an advisory way." The counter argument to this approach rests primarily on the fact that it adds additional overhead and that sufficient management resources may not be available to staff both nonoperating and operating tasks. The ideal solution may have to be watered down for practical reasons. A collective top-management group without direct operating responsibilities has grown in importance in recent years through the creation of the so-called "president's office."

Another important element of the top-management role is the degree of autonomy granted to the divisions. On one extreme, a strong top management may be constantly involved in divisional affairs, while on the other hand divisions may be allowed to operate independently, only being monitored through the control system. In the former, the job of divisional management will be narrow and the degree of decentralization reduced, while in the latter the organization takes on the characteristics of a holding company. The relationship between corporate and divisional management is a constantly evolving one, as illustrated by the United Latex case in this book. The resolution of this dilemma depends not so much on organizational theory as it does on the respective corporate and divisional strategies as well as on the abilities and ambitions of the corporate and divisional general managers.

## IMPLICATIONS OF THE DIVISIONAL TRANSITION

### Advantages of the divisional organization

Proponents of the divisional organization cite several advantages. First, by breaking the organization into smaller units, each with its own functions, the divisional organization is able to combine the advantages of a small company with the benefits of belonging to a large corporation. The small, relatively autonomous divisions under the command of a single general manager with coordination closer to the action permit better and quicker responses to market needs than the large centralized functional organization. Thus, the symptoms of malfunction arising in the overextended functional corporation are corrected. Yet in their strategic responses divisions can rely on the total resources of the corporation. Critical managerial talent can be transferred, money can be made

---

[3] Ibid., p. 106.

available, a strong research and development group can be of assistance, and so on.

Second, as will be discussed in more detail later, the availability of more general management positions facilitates management development and enhances career opportunities. Thus, the divisional organization may provide a better climate for attracting and motivating younger managers.

Third, divisionalization permits profit measurement at various organizational levels, enabling collection of control information on all the factors critically affecting profits of each business, with the result that unit and individual performance can be measured against goals and plans. Thus, divisionalization facilitates an action-oriented, future-centered management style. The functional organization, in contrast, prevents profit measurement below the top-management, total-company level; and consequently efforts at instituting administrative procedures and information systems must necessarily be limited to one function only. This forces control reports to focus on volume or costs. It is argued that cost-based management frequently becomes a breeding ground for comparisons against the past rather than against goals and plans and that such measurement results in a focus on cost minimization rather than on profit maximization. Also, stressing sales volume does not necessarily enhance profitability.

Fourth, divisionalization combined with profit-center reporting permits the assignment of authority and responsibility to a single person who can be given clear performance guidelines. In a functional organization, on the other hand, operating responsibilities are often shared among the functions, making it difficult to hold a particular person responsible for overall financial performance.

### Disadvantages of divisionalization

The divisional organization is not without drawbacks. First and foremost, it frequently entails higher costs. The additional levels of general managers add overhead. Especially when each division has full control over its line and staff activities, it is virtually impossible to avoid duplication. Different divisions may have similar but independent manufacturing facilities, which—if shared—could be run more efficiently. Market research staff and control departments have to be constituted for each division, thereby probably requiring more people and other costs than if they were handled by a functional corporatewide department. Thus, an organization contemplating divisionalization should carefully assess its ability to support such a costly structure.

Secondly, the divisional organization surrenders some of the functional expertise. Each division going its separate way may not generate the power and cohesion of a single, centrally coordinated effort. In the latter, responsiveness to changes within the functional area is increased and a broader base is provided for the collection and application of special know-how and other such intangibles.

Third, the corporation embracing divisionalization often faces an embarrassing lack of manpower. In the functional organization there was only one general manager. Suddenly a large number of general managers is required. From where in the organization will they come? How are potential candidates to be evaluated and trained? Also, the shift to divisionalization may be seen by some managers as involving a demotion. For example, plant managers report to a vice president of manufacturing. After divisionalization they report to a general manager who may be one or more layers away from the president. Hence, the plant manager may see his new boss as being of lesser stature (and also closer by) and thus view change as a personal demotion.

Fourth, divisionalization, while it permits clear-cut assignments of responsibility through the profit-center setup, also may produce an excessive focus on the short run by virtue of the stress placed on the current year's profit objective. This danger has already been alluded to in Chapter 6.

### A different "way of life"

In the functional organization, the general manager relates to specialists. In the divisional organization, in contrast, he manages general managers (Exhibit 4). As a result, the divisional organization has at least

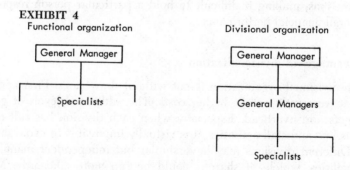

**EXHIBIT 4**

Functional organization

Divisional organization

General Manager

Specialists

General Manager

General Managers

Specialists

two levels of general managers, that is, at both the corporate and divisional level. Also, as a generalist the corporate general manager no longer relates to specialist managers but to other general managers. Thus, the divisional organization creates a larger number of general management slots than the functional organization. Having general managers as his subordinates permits the chief executive to delegate some of his troubles.

It changes his job significantly. In the functional organization, he must coordinate the functions through specific operating decisions, requiring detailed expertise on the issues at hand. In the divisional organization, he delegates this task to the divisional general manager who must provide the coordination and specific guidance. The chief executive is able to treat his divisions conceptually like independent companies, guiding them through abstract business plans and financial performance goals. Subsequent performance can be measured neatly and precisely on the basis of the division's profit and loss statement, permitting the chief executive to reward the winners and punish the losers.

Where interdependencies among divisions are minimal, it is possible to embrace the "every tub on its own bottom" theory. In allocating corporate resources, the chief executive can expand certain divisions while starving others. In the functional organization, in contrast, he is forced to balance functional demands given their interdependence.[4] Also, by treating divisions separately, it is possible to compartmentalize risks not just in terms of business risks but also in terms of the success or failure of the divisional general managers. Furthermore, within the divisional organization new divisions can be added or existing ones dropped with a minimum of disturbance to the other parts of the organization, providing the chief executive with an organizational vehicle which gives him great strategic flexibility.

Interdependencies and tradeoffs frequently prevent the creation of a "pure" divisional organization. Certain activities, such as research and development, sales offices, or manufacturing plants may have to be shared or centralized at the corporate level. It may be too costly or impractical to move all the way toward pure divisionalization. In one company, this dilemma was described as follows:

> One significant question here is how to organize the sales force. These men are highly skilled and quite expensive to employ—each salesman should enter commitments of at least $1 million yearly in order to justify his expenses. Since our customers are spread all over the country, it would appear economical to assign field salesmen by geographical areas each to sell all, or at least a number of, our products. Unfortunately, this system might take a good measure of the responsibility for the sales effort from the product group and place it at the level of centralized sales supervision. Our problem here is to leave sales responsibility at the product group level without having an undue duplication of field sales personnel.

Where compromises between divisionalization and centralization must be made, the chief executive and his managers face the issue of the degree of involvement and authority of the corporate vis-à-vis the divi-

---

[4] For a more detailed discussion, see John H. McArthur and Bruce R. Scott, *Industrial Planning in France* (Boston, Harvard Business School, Division of Research, 1969), p. 125.

sional level. This issue has become a perennial bone of contention in many divisional organizations.

In spite of the above impurities, the divisional organization is a much more performance-oriented institution than the functional company. As stated by Scott,[5] "This distinct 'way of life' is due in large measure to the internalization of market pressure for economic results, with upper levels of management typically applying more 'profit pressure' within the enterprise than is characteristic of the external environment. . . . This 'internalization' of the market mechanism is one of the crucial innovations of the divisionalized organization."

This form of organization not only changes life for the chief executive and changes his role but it also shapes the role of the divisional general manager who is subject to precise performance measurement. The scoreboard may compare divisions, leading to a highly competitive constellation among division managers. The market mechanism will have unpleasant career implications for the poor performer but it also will reward the "stars." The next chapter describes the job of the divisional general manager, while Chapter 15 focuses on the jobs of the corporate general manager and his corporate staff.

[5] Bruce R. Scott, "Stages of Corporate Development," p. 12. (Copyright © 1971 by the President and Fellows of Harvard College.)

# 14

# General management at the divisional level*

## JOB OF THE MIDDLE-LEVEL GENERAL MANAGER

OF THE SEVERAL levels of general managers in the divisional organization, this chapter focuses on the divisional general manager, the person who is in charge of one of the operating units of the company. Because organizations use different words to describe their business units, such as divisions or departments, the manager in charge will be referred to as middle-level general manager. The job of the middle-level general manager is discussed first because their number probably exceeds that of corporate general managers by a wide margin. Also, it is a job which is available to younger as well as older managers. General management in the divisional organization does not necessarily require many years of service. Therefore, a discussion of the middle-level general manager's job is of both actual and potential value to a large number of managers. Furthermore, and most importantly, while this job is of greater relevance to a larger number of people earlier in their careers than is the job of the corporate-level general manager, the literature has focused largely on the latter. One approach would be to refer to what is known about the top-level general manager. However, this knowledge is not necessarily applicable. The middle-level general management job is signifi-

---

* This chapter, in slightly revised form, appeared in the March–April 1972 issue of the *Harvard Business Review*, pp. 75–85, under the title "General Managers in the Middle."

cantly different. Furthermore, it is, in a number of respects, more difficult. It involves:

—managing multiple relationships,
—acting as "playing coach,"
—translating goals into action,
—translating action into measurement,
—assuming full responsibility while having limited authority,
—managing in a "political" environment.

## Managing multiple relationships

The middle-level general manager, like most managers, accomplishes his goals largely by managing relationships. There are few things which a manager can do alone; he must usually rely on the support, cooperation, or approval of a large number of people. As the textbooks say, "he gets things done through others."

Managing relationships at his level in the organization, however, is a threefold task requiring the middle-level general manager to act, at the same time, as subordinate, equal, and superior. Upward he relates to his boss as a subordinate; he takes orders. Downward he relates to his team as a superior; he gives orders. Laterally, he often relates to peers in the organization as an equal; for example, he may have to secure cooperation from a pooled sales force or solicit assistance from corporate staff services. Thus, the middle-level general manager wears three hats at the same time. In contrast, the top-level general manager acts primarily as a superior.

Managing this triple set of relationships is most demanding. It is difficult for any one person to excel in all three simultaneously. To be at once a decisive superior, a cooperative colleague, and a loyal subordinate is quite a challenge, similar to a baseball player having to excel simultaneously in hitting, fielding, and pitching. Not only does the middle-level general manager have to be good at all three; he also has to be able to shift quickly and frequently from one role to another.

In view of these conflicting and changing demands, it is often difficult for the middle-level general manager to arrive at a consistent pattern of behavior. Moreover, in the process of satisfying the requirements of one set of relationships, he may reduce his effectiveness in managing another. For instance, a middle manager who follows orders from headquarters to the letter may thereby, in the eyes of his subordinates, either weaken his authority or appear unreasonable and unresponsive. For one division, headquarters restricted its freedom to purchase from the outside; this order threatened to undermine the authority of the general manager. He was torn between the dilemma of asserting his authority with his subordinates by ignoring or fighting headquarters' orders, or weakening his image as a superior by following headquarters' directives. Being a good subordinate would have weakened him as a superior; yet, by being a strong superior, he would have been a disloyal subordinate. Also, prolonged negotiations with a peer in the pooled sales force to arrive at a mutually satisfactory solution made the general manager appear inconclusive and indecisive to his subordinates.

To successfully manage these multiple relationships with their often conflicting and changing demands, the middle-level general manager may want to—

1.  Make his network of relationships explicit. To whom does he have to relate? Which are the key relationships?
2.  Identify, in his specific situation, the triple set of requirements: What is expected of him as a good subordinate? What is required to be an effective colleague and equal? What does it take to provide leadership as a superior? This analysis forces the middle-level general manager to focus not only on his own goals and abilities but also on those of his "opposite numbers" at all three levels.
3.  Recognize the difficulty of achieving consistent behavior in view of the differing demands of the triple set of relationships and be willing to "wear three hats" simultaneously. To do so successfully involves balancing all three roles. Sometimes it requires tradeoffs. Under these complex circumstances, it helps to proceed explicitly.

Others in the organization who are relating to the middle-level general manager may, in turn, bear in mind that they are but one of the multiple relationships which he has to manage. Their expectations and responses should take this into account.

### Acting as "playing coach"

In managing multiple relationships, the middle-level general manager—at his particular level in the organization—may have to act in a dual role. In some respects, he is the leader of his unit who delegates, guides, and plans. In other respects, however, he has specific operating responsibilities and must "roll up his sleeves" to achieve output and to meet his targets. Therefore, he is both a delegator and a doer, both a strategist and an operator, or, to use the sports analogy, both a coach and a player. In contrast, his superiors are usually exclusively coaches and his subordinates are normally players.

This dual role requires a man to excel simultaneously at coaching and at playing. Continuing the analogy, sports experience indicates that it is easier to excel either as a coach or as a player and that the playing coach job is clearly the most difficult. The skills required to succeed as player are different from those of a successful coach, but the playing coach needs to possess the skills of both. Likewise, the dual role of a middle manager combines different skills and actions. On the one hand, he needs a broad overview, detachment, and a long-run perspective. On the other hand, he needs detailed knowledge and experience, the ability to involve himself directly and deeply, and a sense of urgency. The middle-level general manager must attempt to combine all these characteristics simultaneously.

Acting both as player and as coach, the middle-level general manager must constantly balance the two roles and sometimes make tradeoffs. Is he going to be too much of a player, too involved in operating details and in doing things himself? Or is he becoming too much of a coach by staying aloof, by delegating too much, by not getting sufficiently involved? It is easy to misperceive one's role, especially in regard to the latter. For example, top management of a large divisionalized corporation assigned a promising manager to a recent acquisition. Charged with enthusiasm for his new position, he saw himself as primarily a delegator, an organizational builder whose job was to oversee the installation of parent company procedures and guide the acquisition's integration with staff services of the parent. He had not considered becoming directly involved in operating details or concentrating attention on increasing sales, both of which his immediate superior, the former owner/manager, saw as primary responsibilities of the middle-management position.

This question of balance—of asking oneself, "To what extent do I get involved in actual operations and to what extent do I delegate?"—is most delicate. "To what extent do I try to be coach and to make the decisions, and to what extent do I try to be a player and wait for the coach upstairs to call the plays?" The balancing of the two roles is, of course, also influenced by the demands, expectations, and abilities of the middle-level general manager's superior and subordinates. The choice is not entirely free.

### Translating goals into action

The middle-level general manager usually receives abstract guidance from his superiors in the form of goals that he must translate into concrete action. If, for example, a company's chief executive sets the goal of a certain percentage increase in earnings per share (and mentions it to financial analysts, thereby making it an even stronger commitment), how does he go about achieving this goal? He will communicate it to his group vice president, who will salute and pass it on to his divisional general manager, who, in turn, will salute and pass it on to the middle-level general manager. The latter will salute, turn around, . . .

and find nobody to pass the goal on to. To use Harry Truman's famous dictum, this is where the buck stops.

The buck stops at the middle-level general manager, who must translate the abstract guidance of more earnings per share or meeting the budget into the concrete action required to achieve these goals. He has to translate the budgetary, financial, strategic language into operational language. He has to talk the general-manager language with his superiors and translate it into the functional-specialist language for his subordinates. His superiors, by contrast, are all general managers and are able to communicate in the same general management language. His subordinates, however, communicate in their common functional-specialist language. It is the middle-level general manager who must be bilingual and who must assume the job of translator: from abstract guidance handed down from above into concrete action to be followed below.

Often these abstract goals or financial budgets carry the label "difficult but achievable." While such labels may have a motivating purpose, they are basically a euphemism for the following proposition: Top management knows the results it wants to see, has no idea how to achieve them, and assigns to the middle-level general manager the twofold duty of figuring out how to perform the task and then getting it done. Orders from above are usually result-oriented and do not specify the means to be used to achieve these results. The boss tells what he wants, not how he wants it accomplished.

There are several reasons for the foregoing results-oriented procedure. One explanation is that the middle-level general manager is closest to the action; therefore, he has most of the data, and hence is in the best position to make the decisions relevant to translating goals into action. A second explanation states that it is a superior's privilege to push decision making down and let his subordinates sweat it out. Why should the boss stick his neck out when he has a subordinate to do it for him?

The implications of top management's approach, however, are more important than the explanations. First of all, the middle-level general manager is provided with a much broader *de facto* responsibility than is usually codified in job descriptions or organization charts. Consequently, he must often be more of a strategist than he realizes. It is important, therefore, that he go beyond the formalistic definition of his job, functioning broadly enough so that he deals explicitly with the full scope of his real responsibilities. A narrow definition of his job, by contrast, may cause him to ignore some critical tasks. He cannot assume a responsibility he does not recognize.

But, with responsibility goes risk, particularly where the goals are abstract and the charter is unclear. This risk is further compounded by the many constraints, external as well as organizational, within which the middle-level general manager operates. However, along with risk also goes opportunity. As Harry Truman put it, "If you can't stand the heat, get out of the kitchen." To be a strategist rather than just an order taker is exciting, even without the job's ceremonial attributes.

The opportunity to translate abstract goals into concrete action is in large part a strategic one. It requires the ability to develop plans. In doing so, the middle-level general manager must take into account external factors of an economic, political, marketing, technological, or competitive nature. Moreover, in line with his dual role, he must achieve congruence between the goals of subordinates (whose commitment is essential) and the goals imposed by superiors (whose approval he seeks).

This strategic task is both intellectual and administrative in nature. Furthermore, not only the development but also the communication of his plans is critical. Often, communication is most effectively accomplished not through proclamation but, rather, through "teaching" the general management point of view during day-to-day activities.

To translate goals into action the middle-level general manager must—

1. Define his job realistically and broadly.
2. Assume full responsibility for translating the abstract goals into concrete action through strategic decision making and planning, taking into account both external and organizational factors.
3. Effectively communicate his decisions and plans to both his superiors and subordinates.

### Translating action into measurement

Translation is required in both directions: not only from abstract guidance into concrete action but also from concrete action into abstract measurement. The boss measures success in terms of results; he is less interested in how it has been accomplished. Consequently, the middle-level general manager's performance is more often appraised by matching the abstract results of his actions with the abstract guidance that he has been given than by evaluating the quality of the specific action taken.

This fact of organizational life sometimes leads to misunderstanding. In one company, for instance, a middle-level general manager was unable to meet his goals and invoked his actions to show why. Top management, however, perceived the explanations as excuses. Concrete action was not part of its measurement system.

In terms of the total equation, there can be real problems when the signals from abstract measurement contradict those from abstract guidance. Where this occurs, the translation process frequently gets reversed. Instead of starting with the abstract guidance (goals) to develop specific action, the middle-level general manager starts with the abstract measurement (required results) and translates backward to his plan of action. For example, in one company, top management emphasized the need for its divisions to have ample productive capacity. In the measurement of performance, however, excess capacity was looked on unfavorably. As a result, division managers added capacity very cautiously, achieving high plant-utilization ratios at the expense of lost sales (which did not show up in the measurement system).

Translating action into measurement involves the same skills as translating goals into action. One language is operational and involves a variety of dimensions, whereas the other is abstract and is often in terms of a single dimension. The required ability is to relate these two different languages. And when measurement and goals are contradictory, the middle-level general manager must be able to tread a thin line between the two, sometimes making tradeoffs.

Furthermore, he must cope with an additional problem: the language of corporate measurement is sometimes inadequate for measuring and guiding the activities of his subordinates. While top management typically measures him on the basis of profit and loss, the middle-level general manager has to evaluate his subordinates in terms of different quantitative measures (such as costs, production and sales volume, number of rejects, and so on) as well as qualitative judgments (such as adequacy of the plant layout, effectiveness of the R & D effort, comprehensiveness of the marketing activities). These measures not only are different in kind and more numerous but also require greater expertise and more intimate knowledge of specifics.

## Assuming full responsibility and limited authority

The middle-level general manager typically assumes full responsibility for his unit and is evaluated on the results of his total operation. There is no way to shift the blame as might be done in a functionally organized setup, where marketing could claim that production did not deliver on time or where production could point the finger at marketing for not bringing in enough orders.

Like the chief executive, the middle-level general manager has to account for the performance of others. It is up to him to see that they work harmoniously and effectively toward the accomplishment of the required results. Unlike the chief executive, however, he has only limited authority in the pursuit of his goals. He often needs cooperation from equals, such as a pooled sales force or a centralized R & D department, and he receives solicited, or unsolicited, guidance from superiors. Thus, responsibility and authority do not overlap. The former exceeds the latter.

Textbooks state categorically that such an imbalance is wrong and that responsibility should be backed up with the necessary authority. Yet, this responsibility/authority discrepancy is an inevitable fact of life where divisionalization is carried far down into the organization. The choice is between few divisions with general managers who control almost everything and several divisions where the general manager has to rely on joint activities, such as a pooled sales force. Where the second alternative has been chosen, the middle-level general manager may become frustrated by the discrepancy between responsibility and authority. However, without this discrepancy his division would not exist and he would not have a general management job. From a career point of view, an imperfect general management job at age 32 may be preferable to a perfect one at age 57.

To function effectively in this imperfect world, the middle-level general manager must meet two requirements. First, in spite of the limited authority, he must be willing to accept full responsibility and take his action accordingly. At the same time, he should recognize that he cannot do everything himself, that he must cooperate and coordinate with others. The ability to manage multiple relationships is critical here.

Second, the middle-level general manager always has the opportunity to "go to court," to appeal to his superiors when cooperation from equals is not forthcoming. However, he should pick his fights wisely, carefully, and infrequently. By going to court, he asks somebody higher up to stick his neck out. The fact that this "somebody" has attained this higher position probably means that he is good at not sticking his neck out. A middle-level general manager often finds that taking a case to court does not necessarily resolve it and that the issue may be pushed down by his superior. As a result, this route should be relied on only as a last resort or where the issue is clear-cut. Otherwise, preventive settlements, even if they involve compromises, may be preferable.

## Managing in a "political" environment

The setup involving multiple relationships, playing-coach elements, translation from goals to action and back to results, and discrepancies between responsibility and authority necessarily results in a structure which requires coexistence among managers in an atmosphere inevitably political. There are different interests and interest groups, conflicting goals and ambitions, and positions of power and weakness. Organizationally, they are all tied together: the situation is one of coexistence.

This coexistence, moreover, is not always peaceful. The parties involved are not always neutral. Career objectives are at stake. Positions of power are created or reduced. Prestige may be an important factor. Tempers, feelings, and ambition may overrule analysis. In this environment the middle-level general manager is an easy, accessible, and often permissible target. The malcontent soldiers do not pick on the general directly; they go for his officers.

The general manager in the middle, furthermore, is in a vulnerable position. He needs cooperation and assistance and is therefore exposed to sabotage. Particularly, with a measurement system requiring immediate and frequent responses, his position is delicate. In a political sense, he is up for reelection continuously.

Thus, the middle-level general manager must possess political sensitivity as well as the constitution to stomach pressures and conflicts. He has to be aware of the configuration of the power structure and the direction of political winds. Unfortunately, in this potentially volatile atmosphere, managers often fail to ask an obvious but key question: "Who are my friends, and who are my enemies?"

## IMPLICATIONS OF THE MIDDLE-LEVEL GENERAL MANAGEMENT JOB

Some important implications can be drawn from the characteristics of the middle-level general management job. They affect not only the manager himself but his superiors as well.

One common pitfall is that superiors tend to judge middle-level managers in terms of their own jobs. They believe that middle-level general managers have the same opportunities, prerogatives, and power that they do and therefore should shoulder similar responsibility. The same belief is frequently shared by the middle-level general managers themselves. However, the above characteristics of the middle-level general management job make it quite different from that of the top-level general manager. These differences, as well as the resulting difficulties, should be recognized. The job itself is demanding enough. It should not be made more difficult by an incorrect understanding of its scope and characteristics.

Top management often fails to recognize that imperfection is a fact of life in the middle-level general management job. Furthermore, formal job descriptions frequently reflect sacred dogmas like overlapping authority and responsibility. Such ostrich-like attitudes create unrealistic expectations among all parties involved. Unrealistic expectations inevitably produce disenchantments and failures. Reality, even though it may not correspond to the demands of theoretical elegance, must be faced. If reality imposes imperfection, as it does, then imperfection must be recognized and accepted. Only by acknowledging imperfection rather than sweeping it under the rug will it be possible to manage its challenges.

## ADVANTAGES OF THE MIDDLE-LEVEL
## GENERAL MANAGEMENT JOB

The preceding description of the characteristics of the middle-level general management job portrays it as a major challenge, as indeed it is. Why would anyone want to accept such an ill-defined, open-ended, risky assignment? Yet, with risk goes opportunity and with open-endedness goes a job of considerably broader scope than what is stated on the formal job description. Why is it not possible, then, to design this job by including all the positive elements and eliminating all the drawbacks? The answer is that the drawbacks are inherent in the divisional organizational structure. They can be eliminated only by eliminating the structure itself.

A divisional structure is essential to the conduct of operations for a diverse range of products in a variety of countries. From the individual's point of view, it permits a large number of managers to assume general management responsibilities early in their careers, sometimes in their early or middle thirties after less than 10 years of business experience. In contrast, the functional organization usually offers an individual manager his first attempt at general management only during his middle fifties, after some 25 to 30 years of business experience. The choice, as indicated under the full responsibility/limited authority heading, is between having a broad opportunity to assume an imperfect general management job at an early age or having a very limited opportunity to hold a "perfect" general management job late in one's career. To put it in the context of Churchill's famous statement: early in a manager's career, the middle-level general management job is the worst assignment except for all the others.

The advantages of the middle-level general management job and the resulting opportunity of becoming a general manager early in one's career are many, both for the company and for its managers.

First, it is a major motivational factor. The opportunity to run one's "own show" at a young age, rather than having to wait for a quarter of a century, should make a business career more exciting. Also, by having a large number of general management slots in an organization, it is possible to attract and retain many capable managers rather than having an elimination contest for the company's single general management position.

Second, the shift of a manager from specialist to generalist early in his career is less perilous, and failure is less painful. If a manager has spent some 25 years as a specialist, he is apt to be firmly set in his ways and will find it difficult to make a major change. A younger manager, on the other hand, should still be flexible and able to adapt more easily to a different set of job requirements. Failure is easier to take—and to overcome—early in one's career than it is later on. Putting a 25-year track record on the line is a major risk and one that might well destroy an entire career.

Third, the early shift from specialist to generalist is also less risky from the company's viewpoint. When a manager who has been a specialist for a quarter of a century is selected for the president's job, the total conduct of the company is entrusted to someone with no record in general management. It is not at all certain that a successful engineering, marketing, manufacturing, or finance vice president will turn into a first-rate general manager. Yet, the entire fate of the corporation will have been placed in his hands. In the divisional organization, in contrast, the middle-level general manager typically manages one of several profit centers. Thus risk is greatly reduced by entrusting to an unproven general manager only a small segment of the total enterprise.

Fourth, a corporation with many middle-level general management jobs will develop a reservoir of general managers. They can be transferred and promoted as new opportunities arise. Since the scarcest resource of a company is usually competent management, a reservoir of middle-level general managers helps corporations overcome this hurdle and constitutes a major competitive advantage.

Fifth, the middle-level general management phenomenon is conducive to management development and training. A manager can start in a small profit center, establish a track record there, transfer to a larger unit, and so on. Thus, both the breadth and challenge of the general management job can be increased as a manager moves up in the ranks. His confidence and versatility will be increasingly enhanced, fostering personal career development as well as strengthening corporate competence.

Sixth, middle-level general managers are close to the action. Leadership and coordination, therefore, take place on the battlefield rather than from distant headquarters. Decisions can be made more quickly by better informed people who can more closely monitor an action's impact and ensure its proper implementation.

# 15

# General management at the corporate level

THE CREATION of middle-level general management positions in the divisionalized company forces a redefinition of the tasks and responsibilities retained at the corporate level. The implications for both the corporate staff and the top executives are significant. This chapter focuses first on the job of the staff manager and second on the critical functions of the chief executive. The point which has already been made for the chief executive, that is, that in the divisional organization he relates to general managers instead of to specialists, also applies to the corporate staff manager.

## THE JOB OF THE CORPORATE STAFF MANAGER

The job of the corporate staff manager will be explored through focus on the corporate planner.[1] While this job has much in common with other frequently encountered corporate staff activities such as personnel, control, and central engineering, it has been selected for emphasis here for two reasons. First, in many companies the job is a relatively new one that has been specifically created to help manage the diversified, divisionalized organization. Second, the planner is concerned with the formulation of corporate and divisional strategies which permits putting

---

[1] This section on the corporate staff manager is based on a paper, "The Role of the Corporate Planning Executive," prepared by Robert W. Ackerman for the Fifth Annual Conference for Planning Executives in 1972 held at the Harvard Business School.

the earlier chapters on the process of strategy in the context of the organizational structure.

## The illusionary power of the system

The most obvious, though perhaps the least useful, way of describing the planner's role is in terms of the tasks demanded of him by the system he manages. Executing the procedures required by the system defines the need for certain communications, relationships, and activities.

To those who take a professional's view of planning, these aspects of the job are of commanding importance. This view hinges on the assumption, however, that a well-designed system, professionally administered, will result in effective planning. Such, unfortunately, is not always the case. The system itself cannot dictate (1) either the contents of the plans or (2) the level of organizational commitment to using them as a basis for setting corporate strategy. Securing relevance for planning in the decision-making process may relate more to the planner's interpersonal competence than to his skills as a planner.

On the other hand, the corporate planner should be aware of the implications of the system for his job, especially when he is given the responsibility for initiating planning. In the start-up situation he frequently has the choice between installing a prepackaged system or developing one of his own. Ironically, interpersonal skills may be considerably more demanding in the former situation than in the latter. With the basic design questions decided beforehand (and without wide participation), the prepackaged system can be activated more rapidly. Relationships, which might otherwise evolve over time, must be managed under the strained conditions of a new but fully elaborated system.

## The illusion of neutrality

Corporate staff managers, as implementors of the system which they manage, may see themselves in a neutral role. They view their job as the scientific implementation of their discipline. They like to relate their role to that of the doctor, the psychologist, or the lawyer. However, the corporate staff manager frequently encounters situations where he is not considered neutral by others or where a neutral position is impossible. This may occur when the flow of resources is to be diverted from normal channels. For instance, in times of corporate crisis (or a national crisis, for that matter) chief executives frequently seek to reassert their authority over the affairs of operating units. If divisions are to be liquidated or divested, the chief executive may find it foolhardy to expect those involved to adopt corporatewide views. Similarly, planning for entry into a major new field and implementing that decision by accumulating the necessary resources from existing businesses may also be a task that cannot be delegated to middle-level general managers. Instead, the chief executive turns to his staff for support and guidance. In short, a neutral role for the corporate planner may rest on the assumption that the firm is functioning satisfactorily relative to its potential and that the chief executive does not see the need for intervention in the initiation of business plans and resource allocation proposals.

Furthermore, the needs and ambitions of other managers involved in planning constitute a major influence on the corporate planner. The power and attitudes of, for instance, the controller, the manager of the most profitable division, the executive who was passed over for the presidency, the executives who are vying for the top spot next, are all relevant concerns. The corporate planner must be aware of likely allies and likely enemies and the intensity and significance of their feelings. He is, after all, dealing with a process that affects the careers of the managers involved; it is natural that they calibrate its usefulness in personal terms.

### Managing relationships

Thus, like the middle-level general manager, the corporate staff manager must structure his relationships. In doing so, it is important to view these relationships from both sides. The corporate planner asks not only how he sees his job but also how others with whom he must interact see it. Likewise, the corporate planner must ask how the others see their own jobs. If the parties involved perceive their respective

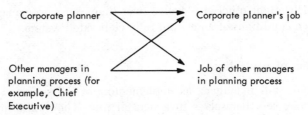

Corporate planner — Corporate planner's job

Other managers in planning process (for example, Chief Executive) — Job of other managers in planning process

jobs differently, misunderstandings or even conflicts may arise. Because multiple relationships must be managed, this analysis is required along a number of dimensions.

Frequently, the planner's principal client is the chief executive, whose respect and trust must be earned. If there is one basic truth in the lore of planning, it is that the exercise is futile unless it has the continuing, visible support of the chief executive. Without his dedication to the proposition that planning is useful and, more importantly, without his willingness to make commitments to his division managers on the basis of their planning activities, the function loses its effectiveness.

On an interpersonal level, the perceived relationship between the chief executive and the planner will, of course, have a major bearing on how the latter is viewed by the rest of the organization.

In relating to the chief executive, the corporate planner must consider at least two types of inquiry. The first relates to the personal needs of the chief executive and the pressures placed on his job. The new president brought into a crisis situation clearly has different concerns than his long-tenured counterpart in a successful company. The former may view planning as a mechanism for sorting out what is to be kept from what is to be liquidated, while the latter may hold planning to be one means of developing managers and insuring against unforeseen long-term consequences of environmental change. Their time horizons, mandates for change, and power in the organization may be radically different. Moreover, the nature of the relationships they must manage may vary, and this should be of great importance to their advisers. Most presidents have personal needs and goals that help to define what they expect from the planning function.

The second inquiry relates to the chief executive's management style and in particular the means he adopts to solve problems. For example, what is his tolerance for detail and how deeply does he tend to intervene in the decision-making process? Some chief executives place great reliance on delegated responsibilities and indirect methods of guiding decisions through performance appraisal and rewards; others are willing to share responsibility in exchange for the chance to influence the outcome directly. The emphasis has a great deal to do with how much the chief executive needs or wants to know about operating matters and where he looks for guidance.

The planning executive must also manage his relationships with division managers. It is naive for him to think that they will happily grasp the benefits of corporate planning. Their concerns have to do with the course of their careers as well as the chart they have plotted for their division. They are continually monitoring the opportunities for securing resources and are sensitive to the nuances of performance evaluation. The planner and his system represent elements at least partially beyond the operating manager's control and to that extent constitute a disruption and possibly a threat to previously existing decision processes.

Finally, the planning executive must relate to other staff functions, especially those responsible for financial controls. Unless he is to build a sizable analytical and clerical staff, the planner may have to depend on the controller's office for assistance. Without it, his efforts may be either hopelessly mired in detail or so far removed from the detail that his advice is not grounded in fact. There is, of course, a tension between planning and budgeting; to give precedence to one tends to lessen the influence of the other. It is not unusual that the planner and the controller find themselves in competition for the attention of both the chief executive and the operating managers. Given the importance frequently accorded the budget in the evaluation of executive performance and the greater bulk of the controller's task and organization, it is not surprising that the planning executive finds the odds untenable in the event of battle.

### Challenge of the corporate staff job

In the context of these relationships, none of them easy to manage, the corporate planner has a difficult task. He is generally expected to secure information from managers down the line regarding the nature of their activities and future plans. This information is to be forthright and truthful. More importantly, it is to be useful in guiding the future activities of the corporation. He is also expected to help the corporation develop objectives and goals and strategies for attaining them. One planner commented, "My job is to be the manager in charge of tomorrow." For him to be successful in measuring up to that responsibility, he will have to secure influence in the process through which strategic decisions are made. Unhappily for him, his office is rarely endowed with the power of position. His portfolio at the outset is thin and his mandate often superficial. In a head-to-head confrontation with divisional management, he will normally lose. With good reason, a strong chief executive will most likely sacrifice his staff advisers rather than disrupt reporting relationships with those responsible for operations.

Thus, even though the corporate staff is often referred to as the eyes and ears of the president, it rarely has his hands. It has to achieve action without power. Furthermore, it is difficult to measure its effectiveness. Its task usually is to assist others, to enhance their effectiveness, or to assess their competence. Where the assistance proves beneficial, it is difficult to separate how much is due to staff assistance. Would the operating manager have achieved identical (or even better) results without staff help? Where operating results are poor, it may be caused by operating management with the staff manager being an innocent bystander. Yet he may get blamed nevertheless. Thus, within the divisional structure, the job of the corporate staff manager is a highly delicate one. Unfortunately, many a staff executive fails to recognize these difficulties, or even aggravates them by relying primarily on the illusionary power of the system which he has been asked to manage.

Success hinges more on an ability to manage multiple relationships than on technical competence. A corporate staff manager in order to be effective must take a general management point of view. Taking into account his own objectives and capabilities, he must determine his role. Three basic options are available. On one extreme, the corporate staff manager may see himself as a neutral middleman, while on the other extreme, he may choose to play an independent and activist role. In between, he may see himself as a presidential emissary. While there may be some overlap, these roles are by and large distinct and will be described in more detail for the corporate planner.

### Possible roles of the corporate planner

*Planning broker.* In this role, the corporate planner struggles to maintain neutrality and impartiality in his relationships with other managers. He manages the long-range planning system, insures that the plans are comprehensive, and promotes the ideas and techniques of planning. However, he avoids taking positions whenever possible on the strategic issues confronting the corporation or its components. In a sense, he acts as a weather bureau by reflecting the chief executive's concerns to managers down the line and as a broker by giving advance exposure for their plans in corporate circles. He tends to view his career as a planner in professional terms and avoids getting caught in the cross-fire between operating managers on the same or different levels in the organization. He limits his exposure to criticism, keeping, as the current saying goes, a "low profile."

*Presidential adviser.* Alternatively, the corporate planner may see the president as his client and the president's needs as his concern. Rather than attempting to maintain neutrality, the planner may take advantage and make use of "the president's ear" to further his client's purposes. He ties his success and influence to the strength and resolve of the chief executive. While this position may seem extreme and dangerous for the planner, it is not necessarily so. It depends heavily on the relationships between the chief executive and his division managers. If the chief executive is a respected leader, the planner benefits from his close association. Moreover, the organization understands his point of view, knows how to approach him, and may in fact deal with him as the chief executive's stand-in.

*Strategic evaluator.* Finally, the planner may attempt to define a role which permits him to have his own position on strategic issues. In this case, he seeks independence rather than neutrality or subjugation to the chief executive. His client is the corporation, and his efforts are directed toward defining strategy that will be to its long-run advantage. In fulfilling this role, the planner must have freedom to evaluate plans and the influence to have his assessments taken seriously. To assess, however, is to judge the competence of the managers submitting plans, and to influence is to exert some control over the allocation of resources. In effect, the corporate planner adopts a position akin to that of a line manager. While clearly the most active role, it is also the most exposed. The stakes are higher, and the planner must decide whether the opportunities justify the risks.

A serious consideration of alternative roles forces the planning executive to diagnose his position in the organization. He should think through very carefully such questions as: (1) "Who is my client?" (2) "What distance should I maintain in my relationships with various other executives?" and (3) "What degree of independence do I want or need for my views on the substantive issues confronting the enterprise?" With an identification of his role or the role he would like to have, the planning executive can then begin to develop a strategy that will serve as a guide for future action. If planning is useful in managing the corporation, the planner has the responsibility for insuring that his office is managed in a fashion that insures that the benefit is obtained.

## THE JOB OF THE CORPORATE GENERAL MANAGER

Given the preceding description of the middle-level general manager's job and that of corporate staff managers, what job is left for the chief executive, the corporate general manager? An immediate answer usually given to this question is that he handles corporate relations with the outside, especially with the financial community and the government. If being "president in charge of public relations" were his only major task, then public relations would be by far the best-paid position in a firm. With the operating task delegated to middle-level general managers, the corporate general manager's job becomes one of managing managers. While the tools remain the same as those described in Chapter 11, that is, structure, systems, and personal intervention, the emphasis falls more heavily on the first two elements. The emphasis also shifts away from operational aspects to those which shape the scope and performance of the company: planning, resource allocation, performance measurement and compensation, and management selection and development.

Ralph Cordiner, the architect of General Electric's major move toward divisionalization in the early fifties, described the role of corporate general managers as follows: "They have been freed of operating responsibility and administrative details so that they can devote their time to long-range planning, appraisal of current performance, bringing divisional objectives and plans into a working pattern with over-all company needs, and making sure of the needed continuity of competent managerial and other personnel in the decentralized businesses."[2]

### Managing the strategic process

Among the tasks of the corporate general manager, planning is most frequently cited. Repeatedly, the statement is made that the chief execu-

---

[2] Ralph T. Cordiner, *New Frontiers for Professional Managers* (New York: McGraw-Hill, 1956), p. 68.

tive officer is now freed from operating details, being able to spend his time on policy. He is seen, by himself and others, as the corporation's chief strategist. His tools are the long-range plan and the resource allocation process. Bower, in his research on the management of the resource allocation process,[3] challenges this notion. In the large divisionalized corporation, given the vast array of different activities, the intimate knowledge of the businesses, their markets and technologies rests inevitably with divisional management. The critical link between strategic planning and action is the process through which resources are allocated. Bower has found that middle-level general managers provide what he calls the "definition" and "impetus" for specific projects. Definition is the process leading to the determination of the "technical and economic" characteristics of a proposal, while impetus is the willingness of the middle-level general manager to put "his reputation for good judgment on the line,"[4] by submitting and sponsoring the proposal to corporate general management. He obtains corporate approval in large part through securing their commitment to his strategic plan for the division and to him as a general manager capable of executing it.

Bower's findings lead him to the conclusion that the critical inputs to the resource allocation process are made at the stages of definition and impetus and that corporate general management acts largely as a ratifier. In fact, corporate general managers seldom have unbiased strategic alternatives presented to them by division executives for decision. Bower states: "That boards and appropriations committees in most companies recognize the extent to which they have delegated their capital appropriating power, is evidenced by the very low rate of project rejections which characterizes their actions."[5]

The role of corporate general management in planning and resource allocation encompasses several other aspects. First of all, financial and strategic goals have to be set. This process is not solely influenced by corporate or personal ambitions or by the demands and expectations of the financial community. It is also organizational in nature. Performance goals often result from a tug of war between corporate expectations and divisional forecasts, which occurs through the various phases of the formal planning and budgeting process. Corporate general management performs the delicate task of balancing its expectations of superior performance with what the divisions forecast as achievable goals. Sometimes, the challenge to forecast and deliver high-performance goals results not from corporate demands but from peer group pressure

---

[3] Joseph L. Bower, *Managing the Research Allocation Process: A Study of Corporate Planning and Investment* (Boston, Mass.: Harvard Business School, Division of Research, 1970).

[4] Ibid., p. 68.

[5] Ibid., p. 15.

as division managers all contend for the first-place spot in the corporate pennant race. In that event, the alleged disadvantage of bottoms-up goal setting, that is, that operating divisions will play it safe by submitting conservative estimates, is thus avoided.

Another aspect of the role of corporate general management is that of acting as catalyst, ensuring that divisional general management conducts its strategic planning. Berg[6] points out, on the basis of his research, that

many conglomerates make a determined effort to force the division manager to do more strategic planning for his division than was done for his company when it was independent. . . . A significant contribution of the conglomerate to the acquired company, therefore, can often be a new structure which *forces* more strategic planning.

The usual approach of conglomerates is to make small groups of line executives—not large committees and staff groups—directly responsible for planning the future of the business. The focus is on economic return and search for opportunity, rather than on commitment to a given product or way of doing business simply because "we have always done it this way."

A further important responsibility of corporate general management is to make decisions to embark on new business ventures, utilizing the financial resources generated by the existing divisions, as well as to divest existing businesses. The divisional organization, as has already been pointed out, provides greater freedom of action in this respect than the functionally organized company. Hence, corporate general management is able to focus explicitly and objectively on the full scope of available strategic alternatives. The chief executives of Dynatech and Carmen, although managing corporations much smaller than the giant conglomerates, face such strategic choices.

## Managing structure and systems

If corporate general management, lacking the intimate knowledge of its diverse activities, has delegated not only the operating but also to a large extent the strategic responsibility for its businesses to its middle-level general managers, how does it provide strategic leadership? Bower cites two sources of top-management influence in the planning and resource allocation process. One is called "context," described as "the set of organizational forces that influence the processes of definition and impetus."[7] Some of the forces mentioned are structure as well as information, control, and compensation systems. The other source of

---

[6] Norman A. Berg, "What's Different about Conglomerate Management?" *Harvard Business Review*, November–December 1969, p. 116.

[7] Bower, *Managing the Research Allocation Process*, p. 71.

influence is the use of abstract strategic guidance and measurement typically reflected by return on equity or rate of growth objectives.

The significant role of "context" in permitting corporate general management to influence the strategic process in the large divisionalized corporation underlines the close interconnection between strategy and organization as well as the strategic impact of the latter. The corporate general manager influences the strategic decision-making process indirectly through organizational structure and systems.

Such remote control vastly extends his range of influence, but it also removes him from the action. Use of the abstract strategic, financial, or budgetary language does not permit a portrayal of the richness of the actual operating data. Not every corporate general manager feels comfortable in relying exclusively on the abstract results (as communicated by the profit and loss statement) as evidence that actual divisional behavior is congruent with his intentions. To seek more information, however, is to assume more responsibility. Hence, the chief executive may be reluctant to violate his intentions of delegation.

Where corporate goals are primarily economic in nature, remote guidance through structure and systems can be measured relatively accurately and top management will feel comfortable that actual behavior is consistent with corporate policy. The worry here is largely whether the long term suffers by excessive focus on short-term results. However, where corporate goals are not solely economic, their measurement and hence the assurance of their implementation are much harder to determine. The profit and loss statement does not reveal whether divisional management is following corporate directives on equal opportunity employment or pollution control. In fact, the pressures generated by frequent abstract performance measurement may be critical obstacles to the successful implementation of noneconomic directives. Delegating the pursuit of noneconomic goals to divisional management poses an entirely new set of challenges to the chief executive in managing structure and systems.

## Managing relationships

Managing managers involves more than the use of structure and systems. Like the middle-level general manager and the corporate staff manager, the chief executive must manage relationships. One set of relationships involves the board of directors as a source of guidance and advice. The Vlasic Foods, Carmen, and Dynatech cases raise this issue. Does the chief executive seek objective guidance and evaluation or does he prefer a symbolic body to rubberstamp his decisions? Once the board has been committed to a certain course of action, does it retain its objectivity?

The chief executive furthermore must manage relationships with his division managers. The respective roles of corporate and divisional management must be defined. As witnessed by the BCI case, clashes in this connection are not infrequent. It is useful to ask these questions: (1) how does the corporate general manager see his own role; (2) how does the corporate general manager see the division general manager's role; (3) how does the division general manager see his own role; and (4) how does the division general manager see the corporate general manager's role:

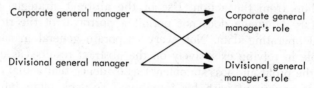

It is not unusual to find drastically different perceptions. Where these differences exist and are not made explicit, they can lead to major conflicts.

Relationships with his corporate staff also have to be managed. Corporate staff managers importantly assist the chief executive. As has already been described, they derive their effectiveness less from the systems and more from the multiple relationships which they manage. The chief executive faces the dilemma that strong support of his corporate staff may harm the latter's relationships with line managers. By putting all his weight behind his corporate staff managers, the chief executive may actually impair their effectiveness. Throwing his power around may be dangerous for his subordinates.

## Managing executive selection and development

In managing structure, systems, and relationships the corporate general manager, in the final analysis, must rely on the quality of his managers. Delegation of responsibility requires confidence in subordinates. Furthermore, success in leadership depends not only on the quality of the strategic choices, the organization and its people, but also on the ability of the chief executive to provide for his own succession. Many a prominent leader, whether in business or government, has failed on this score. Executive selection and management development are crucial tasks for the corporate general manager. The corporate and organizational climate are critical elements in attracting managers and helping them to develop. A chief executive must constantly ask: "Why do people want to work for my organization? Why do they want to upgrade their skills?"

# 16

# The transition to general management

Up to now, this text has dealt with both strategic and organizational transition. The general management task was viewed to a large extent within the context of dynamic situations requiring adaptations in terms of corporate strategy and organization. The final chapter focuses on transition from the job point of view: the shift from specialist into general management. It is probably the most critical point in a manager's career. The elements involved in this transition apply primarily to the manager who assumes a new and usually his first general management assignment. However, some of these elements have equal relevance to the experienced general manager.

**Major career transition**

General managers are usually promoted to this position on the basis of outstanding achievement as functional specialists. Hence, as general managers they operate on a new terrain to which their previous experience is not transferable. This new job represents a major transition. The shift from functional to general management often is considered to be the greatest challenge of a manager's entire career.

Indeed, the skills and activities which led to a functional manager's success—whether in marketing, manufacturing, engineering, R & D, control, or finance—are usually those of specialization, of deep involvement in a narrow area. The specialist knows more and more about less and less. In the medical and legal professions specialization is the usual route to excellence and eminence. The famous doctors and lawyers normally are authorities in special and narrow fields. The manager, too, during the early phases of his career, follows this pattern; he establishes his track record by excelling in a particular specialty. But, unlike the doctor and the lawyer, his career progression pattern is brutally shifted. Having earned his spurs as a specialist, the manager is given a new and drastically different challenge, that of excelling as a generalist. Instead of knowing more and more about less and less, he now shifts to knowing less and less about more and more. Different skills are required and different activities have to be undertaken. His job is not only new in terms of title but also in terms of substance. It represents a major career transition.

This transition, in turn, represents a major risk. The recently promoted general manager puts his track record in jeopardy on new and unfamiliar ground. Previously, each step up the functional specialization ladder led to familiar challenges which required proven skills. Now, the challenges are new and the skills unproven. Not all managers will be able to make this transition; not all will possess the required general management skills. In spite of earlier success, not all will successfully meet the new challenge.

### Resentment

In making this major and risky transition, the general manager does not always face a friendly working environment. Rather, his promotion to his new job may cause resentment. Not everybody will see his promotion positively. Some may ask themselves why they did not get the job. They may consider themselves better qualified, because of age or seniority, and they may view the general manager's promotion as undeserved and his capabilities and background as insufficient for the job. Others may resent the promoted individual because he represents an "educated elite."

Yet the general manager needs the cooperation and support of those very people who may resent his appointment. Their cooperation is essential, and he will face constant obstacles until he has it. In overcoming this possible handicap of resentment, administrative skills and experience are of utmost importance. Unfortunately, however, these skills are typically the new general manager's short suit; he is more often long on technical abilities and experience, which are obviously less relevant in coping with resentment. Thus, the skills most needed are often lacking.

## Newcomer

Sometimes a new general manager is brought in from the outside, or in the divisional organization he comes from another segment of the organization. As a newcomer, he will probably be unfamiliar with his unit's history, opportunities, and problems. Also, he will have no established relationships and will be dealing with a new set of people.

Obtaining facts or information to diagnose the situation in his new unit will not be easy for the newcomer. First, while the board of directors or corporate management may have assessed the unit's performance in terms of its abstract results, the general manager has to evaluate it in terms of concrete action. The latter is much harder to determine than the former. Second, the new general manager will have to acquaint himself not only with the "formal" organization of his unit but with its "informal" structure as well. While the formal structure can be found in the manuals and organization charts, the informal one has to be discovered through daily activities and interpersonal relationships. Third, "politics" may color the facts. Certain information may be deliberately withheld, while other aspects may be overemphasized. In summary, the newcomer's fact-finding mission is difficult and hazardous and he will be required to sift through information that is often contradictory, tough to evaluate, and not always obvious.

Establishing relationships is no easy task, either. It is a particularly difficult challenge to the manager who is not only undertaking his first general management job but is also possibly resented as a newcomer. Since relationships cannot be ordered from above, the new general manager will have to earn his own way. He will have to gain the confidence and respect of his counterparts not by virtue of the uniform he wears but instead by the quality of his daily activities.

Without essential facts and established relationships it is difficult for a newly appointed general manager to get off to a fast start. Yet, he often walks into a situation which requires quick and decisive action. In such an event, he will have to walk a tightrope between (1) an early commitment based on inadequate facts and nonexisting relationships or (2) indecision while he establishes his facts and relationships. The first course of action is often preferred since it establishes a manager's authority and image. He may also be responding to pressures which are pushing him in this direction. The risks, however, are great. Before he proceeds on such a path, it is worthwhile for him to pause and consider the long-run implications of action that precedes the establishment of facts and relationships. What, for example, are the chances of making major mistakes? While it is often argued that the wrong action is preferable to no action at all, it is important for the new general manager to get off to a good start, not just a fast one. Things that start badly usually get worse.

## Experimental leadership

A new general manager often functions as an agent of change. He may have received his assignment in order to bring about changes, or his own ambition may push him to develop new approaches. However, such change may have to be experimental. Obvious solutions may not be available. It may be necessary for him to learn through trial and error. In a divisional organization, the manager's unit may have been chosen as the experimental laboratory for the entire organization.

Experimentation, however, means vulnerability. Since an experiment is easier to defeat than a long-established policy, the forces of resistance may be encouraged to mount opposition, or even sabotage. Where the agent of change is an inexperienced newcomer, it is particularly easy to shift the blame to his shoulders.

Experimental leadership, furthermore, has an inherent weakness, especially for the inexperienced newcomer. It involves using trial and error as well as constant adjusting and testing, rarely permitting one to move ahead at great speed in a single direction. The slow testing and the occasional backtracking, however, may be viewed by subordinates as indecision and defeat. They may interpret experimental leadership as lack of leadership, withholding their respect and support and blaming their leader for inexperience and ignorance. Thus, experimental leadership may be perceived wrongly, especially where the general manager is unknown, inexperienced, and new to the job. Under this handicap it may be difficult for him to generate the necessary support, to obtain the required feedback, and to perform the inevitable education for a new course of action.

In the divisional organization, top management, under these circumstances, may not always come to the rescue. They may be watching rather than supporting the experiment. This is their privilege. From their vantage point, why should they stake their reputations, possibly their careers, on the uncertain outcome of an experiment? Thus, it is often unrealistic to expect rescue from above. More importantly, it is often wise for top management to remain neutral. Experiments are not always sound. Change is not a priori desirable. To judge the soundness and desirability of the experimental change, objective and neutral top management is needed. A neutral superior can act as a mutually acceptable arbiter where conflicts arise, as in situations of limited authority. The middle-level general manager may be better served in the long run by having such a neutral arbiter above him rather than a prejudiced ally. In the latter instance, resistance by others will go "underground," which obviously makes the task of obtaining cooperation and support more difficult. In the former instance, cooperation and support can be obtained through candid and open negotiation. The availability of an objective judge encourages reasonable attitudes by all parties concerned.

### Ratification

One important characteristic of the general manager's job is the need to obtain ratification for his actions. He can govern effectively only with the consent of those being governed. If this consent is withheld, it is exceedingly difficult to succeed. While the general manager formally is promoted or demoted by his board of directors or by his superior in the divisionalized organization, the jury usually consists of his subordinates and his peers. By giving or withholding their support, they greatly influence the general manager's career.

This need for ratification is easily overlooked or underestimated by the general manager. He may approach his job with supreme confidence in his own abilities, viewing his new appointment as evidence of his importance and talents. Where change is required, he may see himself as the new leader destined to bring order out of chaos and turn failure into success. At the same time, he may see his subordinates as old-timers who have failed in the past to meet the challenge. Hence, he may doubt their abilities and downgrade their importance. A general manager who approaches his job by overestimating his own importance and underestimating that of his subordinates is erecting a self-imposed barrier to ratification. He is creating the conditions for a self-fulfilling prophecy—with himself as the ultimate victim.

### Accommodation and compromise

Another important implication for the general manager is the necessity of finding his way in a maze of accommodation and compromise. He cannot always make quick decisions, take a straightforward course of action, or follow completely rational and logical solutions. The network is too complex, the parties involved are too many, and the interests affected too delicate. There is a constant need for accommodation and compromise to bring what he judges as necessary within the realm of what is possible.

Often, it is difficult to adjust to such a complex challenge. While he may have made his mark as a technical expert whose previous successes were based on purely rational solutions to technical problems, optimization may not be the most successful approach for the new general manager. He may have been the company's efficiency expert: logical, rational, decisive, hardnosed, constantly searching for the "best" answer.

Yet, the French saying, "le mieux est l'ennemi du bien" (the best is the enemy of the good) can be applied to him. Rarely do perfect solutions exist for the general manager. There are viable solutions, however, and they require constant accommodation and compromise.

## Job strategy

Given the difficulty and challenge of general management, the job should be approached as explicitly as possible. The general manager must identify the difficulties, challenges, opportunities, and risks. He must be explicit about the organizational structure of which he is part, about the relationships which he has to manage, and about the people to whom he has to relate. In terms of his job, he can identify his total organizational environment. He can match this with his own strengths and weaknesses as well as with his own personal goals and ambitions. Just as companies formulate their corporate strategy by matching their resources to their environment, so can the general manager formulate his own job strategy.

Looking at his job in strategic terms should help the general manager face his varied daily challenges, overcome frustrations, and develop a consistent pattern of behavior. Obviously, a job strategy should be not a ceremonial proclamation but, instead, a plan of action which the general manager "carries in his back pocket" to guide him in his daily actions. A managerial record, like a judicial one, is established through the cumulative impact of a series of decisions, many of which set precedents. If these decisions can be related not only to the specific demands of each separate issue but also to an overall philosophy and master plan, their internal consistency and cumulative impact will establish a strong and cohesive organizational fabric. This is the landmark of an effective and successful manager.

# CASES FOR PART I

## The general manager
## as strategist

# THE PROCESS OF
# CORPORATE STRATEGY

## *Arthur Keller**

ON MONDAY, March 13, 1967, Mr. Arthur Keller,[1] age 31, MBA 1965, entered the offices of Hedblom in Boxholm, Sweden, for the second time, having just been appointed its new managing director. Mr. Keller had first visited Hedblom, a company making ladies' dresses, in December 1966. As assistant to the president of Wientex A. G. from Vienna, Austria, a textile yarn producer and 50% shareholder in Hedblom, he had been sent to investigate Hedblom's deteriorating sales and profit performance. This investigation had led to bitter negotiations between Wientex and Hedblom's owner manager, who held the other 50% of the stock. As a result, Wientex had assumed full ownership on Friday, March 10. While Mr. Keller had been closely involved in the negotiations, he had not been able to participate in the final stages. He was informed of the acquisition on Sunday, March 12, and was asked to take the first possible plane for Sweden. It was during this trip that Mr. Keller, much to his surprise, was asked by Wientex's president to become Hedblom's managing director, this assignment being his first at the general management level.

Mr. Keller took control of a company which had suffered a severe decline in sales accompanied by mounting losses. (See Exhibits 1 and 2a and 2b for Hedblom's balance sheet since 1965 and its income statement since 1962.)

---

* Copyright 1968 by l'Institut pour l'Etude des Méthodes de Direction de l'Enterprise (IMEDE), Lausanne, Switzerland. Reproduced by permission.

[1] Names and figures have been disguised.

| | 1964-65 | 1965-66 | 1966-67 (6 months) |
|---|---|---|---|
| Sales (Skr million)* . . . . . . . | 16.2 | 11.5 | 4.0 |
| Profit (Skr million)† . . . . . . | (0.06) | (2.3) | (1.7) |

*Skr = 19.3 U.S. cents; $1 = Skr 5.17.
†Before depreciation on fixed assets.

The company had been continuously short of cash during the previous 12 to 18 months and on the verge of bankruptcy since the fall of 1966. From the middle of January 1967, its owner manager had given almost exclusive attention to his negotiations with Wientex, thereby neglecting operating decisions, which had been all the more serious given his highly centralized and authoritative leadership style. As a result, morale of the Hedblom managers had suffered greatly, while operations were often near a standstill and important decisions were left unmade. The general feeling of work force and town alike was that Hedblom would soon join the long list of defunct textile firms, a common occurrence in European textile towns like Boxholm during the middle 1960s.

### EXHIBIT 1

HEDBLOM
Balance Sheets,* June 1965–March 1967
(in thousands of Swedish kronor)

| | 6/30/65 | 6/30/66 | 3/31/67 |
|---|---|---|---|
| *Assets* | | | |
| Cash . . . . . . . . . . . . . . . . | 236 | 915 | 19 |
| Receivables . . . . . . . . . . . | 2,651 | 3,300 | 3,757 |
| Inventories. . . . . . . . . . . . | 6,562 | 4,074 | 4,302 |
| Net fixed assets . . . . . . . . . | 1,834 | 2,244 | 3,433 |
| Miscellaneous assets . . . . . . | 218 | 94 | 99 |
| Total assets . . . . . . . . | 11,501 | 10,627 | 11,610 |
| *Liabilities* | | | |
| Payables . . . . . . . . . . . . . | 5,276 | 5,187 | 7,881 |
| Loans . . . . . . . . . . . . . . | 2,926 | 4,391 | 5,271 |
| Capital . . . . . . . . . . . . . . | 3,299 | 1,049 | (1,542) |
| Total liabilities . . . . . . . | 11,501 | 10,627 | 11,610 |

*These balance sheets represent a consolidation and simplification of the original unaudited balance sheets given to Mr. Keller. Like the original statements from which these figures were derived, the inventory and capital accounts may not reconcile with the corresponding income statements.

On becoming managing director, Mr. Keller knew very little about Hedblom and its managers. While holding its 50% share, Wientex had exercised only a loose financial control, leaving operating decisions entirely to the owner manager. As a result, very little information on Hed-

**EXHIBIT 2a**

HEDBLOM
Income Statements, 1962–March 1967
(in thousands of Swedish kronor)

| | 1962 | 1/1/63 to 6/30/64 | 7/1/64 to 6/30/65 | 7/1/65 to 6/30/66 | 7/1/66 to 3/31/67 |
|---|---|---|---|---|---|
| Gross sales . . . . . . . . . . . . . . . . . | 10,196 | 23,739 | 16,196 | 11,529 | 7,723 |
| Sales taxes . . . . . . . . . . . . . . . . | 8 | 24 | 20 | 26 | 8 |
| Rebates . . . . . . . . . . . . . . . . | 301 | 665 | 414 | 321 | 146 |
| Net sales . . . . . . . . . . . . . . . | 9,887 | 23,050 | 15,762 | 11,182 | 7,569 |
| Cost of sales . . . . . . . . . . . . . . | 6,549 | 15,251 | 12,269 | 9,358 | 6,061 |
| Materials . . . . . . . . . . . . . . . | 3,461 | 8,203 | 7,397 | 5,109 | 3,028 |
| Wages . . . . . . . . . . . . . . | 1,979 | 4,435 | 3,683 | 3,455 | 1,882 |
| Payments to subcontractors . . . . . . | 902 | 2,148 | 912 | 563 | 954 |
| Utilities and maintenance . . . . . . . | 207 | 465 | 277 | 231 | 197 |
| Gross margin . . . . . . . . . . . . . | 3,338 | 7,799 | 3,493 | 1,824 | 1,508 |
| General and administrative costs . . . | 383 | 970 | 1,063 | 1,249 | 1,065 |
| Administrative salaries . . . . . . . . . | 611 | 1,019 | 732 | 796 | 631 |
| Sales commissions . . . . . . . . . . | 553 | 1,267 | 826 | 853 | 476 |
| Sales salaries . . . . . . . . . . . . . | 279 | 490 | 340 | 387 | 264 |
| Shipping . . . . . . . . . . . . . . . | 212 | 509 | 318 | 401 | 227 |
| Income from operations . . . . . . . . | 1,300 | 3,544 | 214 | (1,862) | (1,155) |
| Interest . . . . . . . . . . . . . . . | 69 | 186 | 285 | 378 | 479 |
| Other expenses (income) . . . . . . . | (2) | (9) | (6) | 11 | (14) |
| Net income . . . . . . . . . . . . . | 1,233 | 3,367 | (65) | (2,251) | (1,620) |
| Insurance and pensions . . . . . . . . | 105 | 127 | 143 | 143 | 107 |
| Depreciation . . . . . . . . . . . . . | 270 | 952 | 288 | . . . | 588 |
| Bad debts . . . . . . . . . . . . . | 21 | 40 | 31 | 41 | 19 |
| Inventory writedowns . . . . . . . . | 208 | 460 | 739 | 202 | 246 |
| Increase (decrease) in general reserves . . . . . . . . . . . . . . | 335 | 1,679 | (1,281) | (1,844) | . . . |
| Increase (decrease) in reserve for cyclical fluctuations . . . . . . . . | 135 | . . . | . . . | . . . | . . . |
| Increase (decrease) in pension reserve . . . . . . . . . . . . . . | . . . | 79 | 5 | . . . | . . . |
| Taxes other than income and sales . . . . . . . . . . . . . . . | 140 | 9 | 7 | 1 | 4 |
| Loss (gain) on sale of property . . . . . . . . . . . . . | (1) | (16) | (1) | (1) | (15) |
| Total income . . . . . . . . . . . . . | 20 | 37 | 4 | (791) | (2,569) |

Source: Company records.

blom was available at Wientex's headquarters. On Mr. Keller's first trip in December 1966, the owner manager had made only himself and his tight-lipped controller available for discussions. These, plus a quick plant tour, took up the whole four hours of the visit. During the subsequent negotiations, Hedblom's owner manager had formally forbidden his subordinates to maintain any contacts with Wientex, going so far as to stop all yarn purchases. The various managers at Hedblom, furthermore, were left in the dark regarding the negotiations. It was left to Mr. Keller to inform them of Wientex's complete takeover.

**EXHIBIT 2b**

HEDBLOM
Income Statements as a Percentage of Net Sales

|  | 1962 | 1/1/63 to 6/30/64 | 7/1/64 to 6/30/65 | 7/1/64 to 6/30/66 | 7/1/66 to 3/31/67 |
|---|---|---|---|---|---|
| Net sales . . . . . . . . . . . . . . . . . . | 100.0 | 100.0 | 100.0 | 100.0 | 100.0 |
| Cost of sales . . . . . . . . . . . . . . . | 66.2 | 66.2 | 77.8 | 83.7 | 80.1 |
| Materials . . . . . . . . . . . . . , . . . . . . | 35.0 | 35.6 | 47.0 | 45.7 | 40.0 |
| Wages . . . . . . . . . . . . . . . . . . | 20.0 | 19.3 | 23.3 | 30.9 | 24.9 |
| Payments to subcontractors . . . . . . | 9.1 | 9.3 | 5.8 | 5.0 | 12.6 |
| Utilities and maintenance . . . . . . . | 2.1 | 2.0 | 1.7 | 2.1 | 2.6 |
| Gross margin . . . . . . . . . . . . . . | 33.8 | 33.8 | 22.2 | 16.3 | 19.9 |
| General and administrative costs . . . | 3.9 | 4.2 | 6.7 | 11.2 | 14.1 |
| Administrative salaries . . . . . . . . . | 6.2 | 4.4 | 4.7 | 7.1 | 8.3 |
| Sales commissions . . . . . . . . . . . | 5.6 | 5.5 | 5.2 | 7.6 | 6.3 |
| Sales salaries . . . . . . . . . . . . . . | 2.8 | 2.1 | 2.2 | 3.5 | 3.5 |
| Shipping . . . . . . . . . . . . . . . . . | 2.1 | 2.2 | 2.0 | 3.6 | 3.0 |
| Income from operations . . . . . . . . . | 13.2 | 15.4 | 1.4 | (16.7) | (15.3) |
| Interest . . . . . . . . . . . . . . . . | 0.7 | 0.8 | 1.8 | 3.3 | 6.3 |
| Other expenses (income) . . . . . . . | * | * | * | 0.1 | (0.2) |
| Net income . . . . . . . . . . . . . . . | 12.5 | 14.6 | (0.4) | (20.1) | (21.4) |
| Insurance and pensions . . . . . . . . | 1.1 | 0.6 | 0.9 | 1.3 | 1.3 |
| Depreciation . . . . . . . . . . . . . . | 2.7 | 4.1 | 1.9 | . . . | 7.8 |
| Bad debts . . . . . . . . . . . . . . | 0.2 | 0.2 | 0.2 | 0.4 | 0.2 |
| Inventory writedowns . . . . . . . . . | 2.1 | 2.0 | 4.7 | 1.8 | 3.2 |
| Increase (decrease) in general reserves . . . . . . . . . . . . . . . | 3.4 | 7.3 | (8.1) | (16.5) | . . . |
| Increase (decrease) in cyclical fluctuations . . . . . . . . . . . . . . | 1.4 | . . . | . . . | . . . | . . . |
| Increase (decrease) in pension reserve . . . . . . . . . . . . . . . . . . | . . . | 0.3 | * | . . . | . . . |
| Taxes other than income and sales . . . . . . . . . . . . . . . . . . | 1.4 | * | * | * | 0.1 |
| Loss (gain) on sale of property . . . . | * | (0.1) | * | * | (0.2) |
| Total income . . . . . . . . . . . . . . | 0.2 | 0.2 | * | (7.1) | (33.9) |

*Less than .05%.

While Mr. Keller knew little about Hedblom, he knew even less about Sweden, which he had first visited during his December trip. He spoke hardly a word of Swedish and had to communicate with Hedblom's managers in English or German. Since the lower echelons and some of the managers were not fluent in these two languages, direct communication was impossible. Also, Mr. Keller was uncertain whether all the managers would be willing to stay. The previous owner manager, who was to withdraw immediately and completely, had asked his entire commercial staff to leave with him. During their first meeting, the commercial manager told Mr. Keller that he would stay for two to three months, since he felt that his immediate departure would be disastrous to the company, but that he was uncertain of his willingness to cooperate in the long run. Finally, Mr. Keller was able to devote only half his time to Hedblom, since he retained his earlier duties in Vienna as assistant to the Wientex president. These had involved him primarily in planning and implementing Wientex's forward integration from spinning and texturizing into knitting, weaving, dyeing, finishing, and, eventually, dressmaking.

In spite of the fact that he did not have any experience or know-how in either knitting or dressmaking, Mr. Keller, immediately after his arrival at Hedblom, was faced with some urgent operating decisions. The most critical was the introduction of the autumn line, which was already three weeks late and which had to be ready within 10 days if the company expected to write any sales for delivery during August and September. Also, before the middle of May, fabric selections were to be made and basic design issues settled for the 1968 spring collection, which would be introduced in early September 1967. The departure a few months earlier of one of the two directresses of design had left Hedblom short in design skills and required the immediate hiring of a new directress. Furthermore, during Mr. Keller's early days at Hedblom a delegation of workers came to him to complain that they lacked sufficient work; that production runs in sewing were too short; that too much sewing work, especially longer runs, was being subcontracted; and that certain working conditions left much to be desired.

It was against this background that Mr. Keller took charge of Hedblom and began to formulate his strategy. This case describes his activities through the end of April 1967, as he was learning about the company and its employees, making the necessary operating decisions, and beginning to develop plans which he hoped would restore Hedblom to profitability. Some basic background is provided on the textile industry, Wientex A.G., and Mr. Keller himself.

## TEXTILE INDUSTRY

"If you had told me when I was an MBA student that two years after graduation I would be working in the textile industry, I would have said you were crazy," stated Mr. Keller. "In fact, today when I meet classmates they think I am out of my mind in working for so old-fashioned and traditional an industry as textiles, especially in my field, the dressmaking business, which is called the ragtrade." He continued:

In fact, while the stereotypes of small family-owned companies, no innovation for over 100 years, poor profits, declining sales, fierce competition, and weak management apply to large sectors of this industry and to many companies, there are at the same time plenty of opportunities, a great deal of innovation, and an urgent need to apply modern management techniques. These opportunities and challenges have career implications. Since textile companies are short on management, young and relatively inexperienced people like myself are able to assume major responsibilities early in their careers, witness my job at Hedblom. On the other hand, both tradition and lack of management skills can make for fierce resistance to change, particularly to young newcomers like myself. Thus, we are continuously involved in arguments, and it is not always easy to keep a cool, analytical head amidst the politicking. At Harvard, we fight our battles in the classroom with guys who basically think alike, are the same age, and share similar ambitions. In the textile business, on the other hand, you are pretty much a lone wolf. However, I wouldn't want it any other way. I love the fights, the challenges, and particularly the responsibility. Less than two years after graduation I am sure that, among all my classmates, I have one of the most interesting jobs, permitting the maximum of personal growth. Where would I be two years out of school if I had joined an automobile or chemical company? Also, in my job I have true operating responsibility and I have to live with my decisions. I consider this quite a bit more exciting and challenging than if I had joined a management consulting outfit, going from job to job, certainly seeing and learning plenty of interesting things, but never having to stick my neck out and implement and live with my decisions.

The changes and innovations stressed by Mr. Keller affected all phases of the textile industry, from raw materials to cutting and sewing.

Changes in *raw materials* came through the increasing use and new developments of synthetics, especially acetates, nylon, and polyesters. In contrast to the natural fibers which were sold unbranded by many different producers, synthetic fibers were produced by only a few large chemical companies. These commonly branded their fibers and advertised them heavily. (For example, Dacron was Du Pont's and Terrylene and Crimplene were ICI's brand names for identical polyester fibers.) As a result, producers of synthetic fibers were in a much more powerful position vis-à-vis their customers than the suppliers of natural fiber. In fact, they were so powerful as to pose a threat of forward integration. Also, in terms of management, synthetic fiber producers were both sophisticated and powerful.

The traditional process in *yarn manufacturing* was spinning, whereby the fibers were given both the necessary length and thickness. In this complicated seven-stage process, both natural and synthetic fibers could be used. Synthetic fibers, however, permitted a new process called texturizing, which allowed yarn manufacturing to be done on faster machines and in one single operation, hence resulting in lower costs. During the early and middle 1960s, the entire growth of yarn manufacturing capacity was in texturizing. This expansion, in turn, resulted in severe competitive pressures for traditional spinners. Shortages in texturizing capacity had prevailed until the late 1960s, by which time continuous entry was creating a threat of excess capacity. The heavy capital requirements for texturizing and the rapid growth of this segment made manufacturers particularly vulnerable to forward integration by the large synthetic fiber producers. This threat led the yarn manufacturers to contemplate forward integration into fabric manufacturing as a step for reducing their vulnerability.

The traditional dominant process for *fabric manufacture* was weaving, a complicated and costly process which required four or five steps. Recently, the development of stronger and more standardized synthetic fibers had vastly broadened the application of the knitting process. Subsequent improvements in circular knitting machines (called Jacquards) by a handful of leading German machine manufacturers permitted the production of knitted goods which looked to the consumer identical to woven fabrics. These new machines allowed enormous flexibility in creating patterns. Knitting, a one-step operation, was also more economical than weaving. Hence, expansion of knitting capacity was rapid, being largely a function of the ability of the knitting machine manufacturers to deliver.

Traditionally, *finished clothes* were manufactured by large numbers of small companies (usually consisting of the family and few employees), by tailors, or by people at home. With the increased popularity of printed media and the changes in retail and mail-order distribution, larger and larger units began to supply finished clothes. These were often sold under a brand name which, in turn, was supported through advertising and promotion. Thus, the structure of the clothing manufacturing industries was changing from many small companies selling unbranded goods to fewer but larger companies selling branded goods. This development opened the opportunity for fabric manufacturers to integrate forward into finished clothes.

The combination of all these changes had revolutionary implications. The greater simplicity of the texturizing and knitting processes more than offset the higher cost of the raw materials. At the same time, improved styling possibilities plus, most importantly, new wash-and-wear characteristics endowed clothing made in the new way with greater consumer appeal, even without the benefit of a favorable price differential.

Besides changes in materials and processes, the textile industry was undergoing changes in its structure. On these Mr. Keller commented as follows:

One of the most interesting aspects of the textile business is that at the beginning of the vertical product flow we have the large, sophisticated, and professionally managed synthetic fiber producers like Du Pont or ICI, while at the end we have equally powerful and sophisticated large retailers like Sears and Macy's in the United States or Domus, Åhléns (Tempo), and Turitz (Epa) in Sweden. The Swedish retail chains are growing rapidly, accounting yearly for increasing segments of retail textile sales, having increased their market share from below 10% in the late 1950s to about 45% in 1967. In between, however, we have much smaller, and often poorly managed, companies.

Different phases of the textile industry had quite different characteristics. At the beginning of the vertical product flow, long life cycles for products and especially for capital equipment were required, while fashion imposed a very short life span on the end product. Synthetic fiber manufacture was highly capital-intensive, but also fabric manufacture required costly knitting machines. Moreover, it took production personnel about one year to familiarize themselves with these machines. In contrast, fabrics themselves had an 18-month life cycle (even shorter if subject to fashion), and dress fashions changed every six months.

The vertical product flow also made for long lead times, especially during the earlier steps. To be bought in the store in April–May, a spring dress had to be shipped during February–March, produced during October–January, and introduced to the trade during early September. Fabrics had to have been designed by early May of the previous year, or 12 months before the final purchase. Yarns used for the fabrics, if dyed, had to be presented six months earlier still. These lead times, combined with the inherent fashion risks, made timing critical: early production could result in gambling on the wrong yarns, fabrics, or dresses with the risk of severe inventory losses, while delays in manufacturing commitments could result in the producer's inability to deliver on time, usually resulting in cancellations given the short fashion life of the product.

As already indicated, forward and backward integration were constant possibilities in the textile industry. In the United States, large firms such as Burlington or Stevens had combined yarn and fabric manufacture but had not integrated forward into end products, such as dresses and suits. The situation in the United Kingdom was similar to that in the United States. On the Continent the industry had not integrated vertically, and separate companies usually limited their activities to one single step in the product flow. Industry observers, however, wondered whether increased vertical integration, especially among the larger and more dynamic firms, would not just be a matter of time.

## WIENTEX A. G.

Wientex A. G. was one of the leading yarn producers in Europe with manufacturing facilities in two countries belonging to the European Common Market[2] and two belonging to the European Free Trade Asso-

---

[2] European Economic Community (EEC), commonly referred to as European Common Market, comprised France, West Germany, Italy, and the three Benelux countries.

ciation.[3] Traditionally, Wientex had produced yarn by spinning, but with the advent of synthetic fibers it had started to use the texturizing process as well. While its spinning activities had been subject to fierce competition during the 1960s, its texturizing sales had grown rapidly and profitably, benefiting from the prevailing shortages of texturized yarn.

During December 1964, Wientex had purchased 50% of Hedblom, a Swedish knitter and dressmaker as well as the pioneer in Scandinavia of dresses made from the new synthetic fabrics. The reasons for the interest in Hedblom were (1) to acquire fabric and dress manufacture expertise which might pioneer new uses of Wientex's texturized yarns and thereby assist its sales efforts to other yarn customers, and (2) to secure a stable outlet for its yarns. Wientex management decided to leave most operating decisions with Hedblom's owner manager on the premise that (1) Wientex knew nothing about dressmaking and little about knitting, and (2) Hedblom's owner manager had proven highly competent and successful.

## ARTHUR KELLER

Arthur Keller had been graduated in 1959 as Diplom Ingenieur (Master of Engineering) from Vienna University, where he had specialized in civil engineering. Upon graduation he joined the production division of Chrysler International in Geneva, and had worked largely on setting up new assembly plants in developing countries. Mr. Keller commented on his Chrysler experience as follows:

> After one and one-half years as a trainee, doing everything and nothing and meeting a lot of people, I was one day put on a plane to Pakistan and had to assist our truck distributor in setting up a very small, very inexpensive assembly plant for trucks. I was in a foreign culture, with different values, away from home, and alone with no staff, no tools, no connections, and only 18th century materials and techniques to set up a 20th century plant. These factors quickly made me rely on common sense, gave me experience in adaptability, and taught me to take risks and responsibility. Similar assignments in the Philippines and Turkey contributed greatly to my personal growth before my business school training.

Married in 1962, Mr. Keller left Chrysler in 1963 to enter the MBA program at the Harvard Business School. After his MBA graduation, he joined a leading U.S. textile firm as assistant to the executive vice president. Here he worked on various short-run projects: investment policies and guidelines for the international division in Europe; market investigations for European textiles in the United States; and negotia-

---

[3] European Free Trade Association (EFTA) comprised the United Kingdom, the Scandinavian countries, Austria, Switzerland, and Portugal.

tions and investigations for plant sites in Europe. It was planned that after one to two years Mr. Keller would join this company's Austrian operation. For a variety of reasons this did not materialize, and in the fall of 1966 Mr. Keller was offered higher pay but a less exciting job. At the same time he met the president of Wientex. A job offer resulted, and Mr. Keller decided to accept. Looking back on his 17 months at the U.S. textile company, Mr. Keller reflected:

It was a very frustrating but useful experience. In one way, I didn't have responsibility and couldn't push anything myself. On the other hand, I gained tremendous experience and insight into the working relationships of top management and division management in a large corporation and what each one could and was supposed to do.

At Wientex in Vienna Mr. Keller assumed his duties on November 15, 1966, as assistant to the president. While initially assisting on regular daily activities, Mr. Keller's main responsibility soon crystallized around the issue of vertical integration: Should Wientex, as a yarn producer, integrate forward, and, if so, how should this policy be implemented? This responsibility resulted in his first visit to Hedblom in December 1966. Early that month Hedblom's balance sheet for June 30, 1966, had arrived, along with its income statement for the 1965–66 fiscal year. These statements indicated severe losses and a serious sales decline. Mr. Keller reviewed the previous financial statements and learned that control by Vienna had largely taken the form of social visits, given Wientex's policy of operating freedom for Hedblom. Once a young man from the controller's department had asked some highly pertinent questions, but this had resulted in a stormy protest to the Wientex board by the Hedblom owner manager, who forbade the young man ever to set foot in the Boxholm office again. After this high-level protest, younger staff members and even upper management from Vienna refrained from further investigation.

Mr. Keller described his own initiation into Hedblom, which occurred on his December 1966 visit. Arriving at the Stockholm airport at 8:00 A.M., he was met by the Hedblom chauffeur and driven the 150 miles to Boxholm in the company Rolls-Royce. On arrival, he was ushered into the owner manager's office where the following exchange took place:

KELLER:   Good morning. Are you Mr. Hedblom?
OWNER MANAGER:   Who the hell else would you expect to see here!

Afterwards, Mr. Keller commented on this incident as follows:

The owner manager's initial reaction was an outburst against management in Vienna, which, in his words, had really affronted him by hiring me for the verticalization strategy of the company. Afterwards, I did not see or learn anything. My plant tour lasted one-half hour without any figures, details, or questions answered.

Mr. Keller left with the suspicion that the situation at Hedblom had further and seriously deteriorated. On requesting the quarterly financial statements for September 30, he was told that they were not yet completed.

On his return to Vienna, Mr. Keller resumed his analysis of the available financial statements. Making projections, he predicted to the Wientex president that, on top of the already generous supplier credit given by Wientex, Hedblom would require Skr 1.5 million in fresh funds by January of 1967, or else face bankruptcy. His analysis met with disbelief in Vienna and was shrugged off with the comment that "things couldn't be that bad." However, on January 23, 1967, the December 31 quarterly financial statements arrived, together with a request for Skr 1.5 million in new funds. At that point, Wientex top management decided to move. Mr. Keller suggested that a Swedish lawyer be hired to assist in negotiations to assume complete ownership of Hedblom. His suggestion was accepted, and he went to Sweden. Several weeks of tough high-level negotiations ensued, resulting in the changes described at the beginning of this case.

## HEDBLOM

During his early weeks at Hedblom, Mr. Keller tried to learn about the company's history as well as the reasons for its successes and its recent failures. The following picture emerged: Hedblom had been founded in the 1880s as a wholesaling firm and had entered the knitting industry in 1919, when control passed to the second generation of owner managers. For the next 30 years, Hedblom specialized largely in warm knitted underwear, becoming one of the leading brands in Sweden. Large military orders during the war years led to very substantial profits. The line was expanded to include some knitted dresses and sweaters. These, too, were made from Hedblom's own fabrics, none of which were sold on a merchant basis.

In 1948 the next generation took over, and Hedblom's new owner manager was more interested in running a ladies' dress company than in spending his efforts on underwear. Thus he somewhat changed the company's emphasis, while retaining the same product line. This personal inclination was justified by subsequent changes in competition and customer requirements. The underwear market collapsed during the early 1950s as a result of (1) cheap foreign imports, (2) domestic excess capacity, and (3) fewer and different customer demands as houses were better heated and military orders disappeared. Hedblom responded by dropping its underwear line and by concentrating on ladies' dresses and sweaters. Its knitting capacity was used first for wool dresses and subsequently for mixed fabrics (such as 60% wool and 40% rayon). Hedblom dresses and two-piece suits were largely made of jersey. Jersey was the standard word in Europe for knitted fabrics with simple stitch, which could be used during three to four seasons. This heavy use of jersey reduced manufacturing and inventory problems.

The company's dresses derived their distinctive features from special trimmings, made on its flat knitting machines which had originally been purchased for its sweater line. With most competitors making dresses only and buying their fabrics, and with fabric suppliers not having these special machines and therefore not supplying trimmings, Hedblom acquired a unique position on the market. Competitors found it impossible to copy its models. Also, jersey materials were in short supply at that time. Thus, Hedblom during the late 1950s and early 1960s was able to base its strategy on (1) the advantage of having its dresses largely consist of standard jersey, which was not subject to fashion changes, and for which it had ample capacity while merchant supplies were insufficient; and (2) the advantage of giving its dresses distinctive features through trimmings which could not be copied by most competitors (only a few of whom had their own flat knitting machines). During these years, Hedblom began to support its brand name with modest press advertising.

The next major change started with the arrival of the Wientex salesman who attempted to interest the company in the brand-new texturized polyester yarns sold under the Crimplene brand. His major selling tool was a generous advertising allowance, the traditional approach of the synthetic fiber companies. Hedblom was willing to experiment and became the first company in Scandinavia to knit Crimplene yarn. Later, the commercial manager commented:

> Our technical expert was curious and interested, but the owner manager did not believe in it. Without the advertising allowance he probably would never have tried. We made some 2,000 Crimplene dresses in late 1962 and sold them as a specialty at the Göteborg dress fair. Our spring collection for 1963 was still entirely based on the traditional fabrics. During the early months of 1963, I got lots of calls from customers for those dresses they had bought at Göteborg with a name starting with "C." This is unheard of in the dress business. It happens once in your lifetime that customers spontaneously ask for things. As a result, when we were planning an interim collection between the spring 1963 and autumn 1963 collections, I suggested that it consist of Crimplene dresses. We sold 20,000 of them, which at that time was unbelievably high for an interim collection. We had struck gold. We were the first and only ones with a new product which had unique features in that it could be put in the washing machine and required no ironing.

As a result, Hedblom's sales increased rapidly, based on jersey and Crimplene dresses and also on sweaters. The company had become one of the largest dressmakers in Scandinavia. The commercial manager stated:

Hedblom alone was able to advertise Crimplene on a big scale and for several seasons. As introducer of Crimplene we got priority on the yarn quantities. Fabric manufacturers could not always execute the orders for Crimplene because of lack of yarn. The typical comment of the trade during these 1963 and 1964 years was, "Better a late delivery from Hedblom than no delivery at all." However, by 1965 times had changed. First of all, Hedblom was forced to drop the sweater line because of Italian and especially Far Eastern competition. Secondly, switches in fashion finally caught up with the jersey-trimmings combination, aggravated by the fact that Crimplene materials had replaced the wool or half-wool jerseys. Thirdly, Crimplene-based fabrics caught up with demand, and more and more Swedish dressmakers included Crimplene dresses in their collections. Both fabrics and dresses were predominantly of the cheaper variety. Also, cheap U.K. Crimplene dresses began to be sold aggressively in Scandinavia. These three changes reduced Hedblom's product line to Crimplene dresses only, which, in turn, were subject to increasing competition. It was just before these changes occurred that Wientex acquired its 50% share in Hedblom.

In spite of increased competition and a smaller product line, Hedblom remained late with its deliveries. But, whereas before we got away with it, the tolerance of our customers weakened as other supplies became available. Thus orders dropped, or were canceled when deliveries were late, or goods delivered late were returned. While our customers do not have a return privilege for goods which they can't sell, they are able to return merchandise which arrives after the promised date. Faced with stiffer competition, Hedblom increased its advertising expenditures and the number of models in its line. Of course, the latter move further aggravated our delivery problem. Our problem in not getting the goods out of the door on time also made for higher shipping costs: single dress shipments increased at the expense of bulk shipments because orders for a single customer could not be accumulated.

As to the reasons for the late deliveries, Mr. Keller learned that (1) the owner manager had the final say in all design decisions and often procrastinated, thus making Hedblom collections late; (2) fabric and dress manufacturing commitments were usually delayed until orders on the already late collection had been placed, resulting in production bottlenecks; and (3) manufacturing was the Cinderella in terms of top-executive attention, which went almost exclusively to merchandising. As a result, manufacturing considerations were ignored in style decisions; production scheduling was given low priority, resulting in hand-to-mouth operations; and expenditure and investment requests by manufacturing were often acted on only after considerable delays, if at all.

Losses started in 1965. They were aggravated in 1966 when the owner manager rented a brand new factory in Boxholm at the beginning of the year, into which he moved manufacturing during July. This building was located about a five-minute walk from the office building where the managing director, commercial manager, and controller were located, along with their respective departments. Until July 1966, production operations had been conducted in Sandvik, a small village about eight miles from Boxholm, where Hedblom had been one of the two employers. The move from Sandvik resulted from a disagreement between the owner manager and the town fathers concerning the extent of town support for the planned plant expansion.

After July 1966, the Sandvik plant stood idle, housing some obsolete machinery and inventory. Mr. Keller learned that this plant, while not modern, was still in decent shape and could possibly command a sales price of Skr 500,000. The Boxholm plant, in turn, had a maximum capacity of about 1.0 to 1.2 million meters of fabrics and between 500,000 and 600,000 dresses. At the average sales price of Skr 80 per dress, the plant could support a sales volume of over Skr 40 million. Yet several production executives, who had never been consulted concerning the move, commented that the plant was not ideal for fabric manufacturing. After the move, the owner manager threw out all the old piece rates and hired a consulting engineer to establish a new set. By March 1967, however, little progress had been made in this direction. The consulting engineer, hired at an annual expense of Skr 400,000, had also been charged with the installation of an IBM punch-card system for production scheduling and with the development of automatic materials handling systems.

Of great interest to Mr. Keller was the leadership style of his predecessor, whom he had only been able to observe across the bargaining table as a brilliant negotiator. The former owner manager was described as extremely authoritarian. Even the smallest detail required his approval. As the company grew in size and complexity, difficulties and delays resulted, according to several managers. Said one of them, "He wanted to hold everything in his hand, but his hand was getting too small." Delays were also caused by the owner manager's reluctance to make quick decisions; most issues were tossed back and forth before being decided. The implications of these delays in bringing out the collections (often as much as two months late) and for production have already been mentioned, as well as the owner manager's almost exclusive focus on merchandising and his neglect of manufacturing. Another factor mentioned was his great reliance on outside help: for example, the use of the consulting engineer in manufacturing and the use of an expensive Paris designer. Expense was never a hurdle, from the use of outside help to the company Rolls-Royce. In fact, the owner manager was described as quite a showman who had an impulsive tendency to be Number One wherever he went and to dominate his environment. Also, his working hours were unconventional, and he often kept his managers in the office far into the night, regardless of their prior social commitments. One manager commented:

Time had no meaning for him; life seemed a continuous improvisation, sometimes brilliant, sometimes less so, but never did we get the feeling that he went by a specific timetable. I think he considered himself to be an artist; aesthetics came first, and in fact his primary devotion went not to the business but to his private art collection.

Some incidents during the early weeks of Mr. Keller's management provided further indications on how Hedblom had been managed. Around the middle of April, Mr. Keller saw one of his top managers near the time clock. The following discussion followed:

KELLER:   Are you checking the time-clock cards?
MANAGER:   No, I am punching my own card.
KELLER:   What do you mean, punching your own card?
MANAGER:   Didn't you know that all of us here from the top down use the time clock?

During his first day, Mr. Keller found all the company's mail on his desk. Asking one of his managers why it had not been distributed, he was told, "But sir, the previous owner manager used to open and distribute the mail himself." Later that day Mr. Keller received the company checkbook with several checks made out but not signed. Again, he was told that the top executive himself signed all the checks. Likewise, all incoming orders passed Mr. Keller's desk before going to the sales department. Every day, he received a tabulation of orders from his secretary with the explanation that this, too, was company tradition. At the end of the month, Mr. Keller added these daily sheets and was shocked to find the figure so low. Immediately he called in the commercial manager and was told that his tabulation was incomplete since many orders came in by telephone and that these had never been included in the daily tabulation. If he wanted to know total orders for the month, he would have to ask the sales department.

## Manufacturing operations

One of the first tasks Mr. Keller set himself was to learn in detail about the company's manufacturing operations. These can be described by following the product flow through the factory.

The basement of the plant housed storage facilities for yarn. About 70% of this was white 150-denier Crimplene polyester supplied by Wientex for which Hedblom paid the same price as other Wientex customers. The remaining yarns covered a wide variety: they might be made of different materials (such as wool, Dacron-wool, or rayon-wool mixtures), or they might be colored. Dyed yarn was about 30% more expensive than white and was subject to fashion obsolescence. Obsolete dyed yarn commanded only about one third of the original price because the only way to use it was to knit it into fabrics which would be dyed darker.

The yarn moved by elevator to the first-floor knitting department. Producing entirely for in-house use, this department employed 20 men, all of them highly skilled in setting up machines and supervising operations. In spite of the sophisticated technology of the equipment, running the machines was still very much a craft. Up to 48 yarns were knitted simultaneously, and if only one broke the entire machine would stop. Errors or unevenness in the fabrics were not uncommon and would sometimes show up only after dyeing. As a result, constant and careful supervision was essential to ensure that faults be caught before too much yarn had been wasted. Because of the skill required, knitting machine operators were in short supply, even in a textile town like Boxholm which otherwise had a large labor surplus. As a result Hedblom had retained the skilled knitting operators and other scarce skilled workers from its Sandvik plant, and a special company bus shuttled the men back and forth between their homes in Sandvik and the plant in Boxholm.

In March 1967, the knitting department contained 59 machines: 36 flat knitting, 21 interlock, and 2 old Jacquard. Machines differed in terms of width of cloth produced, gauge of yarn handled, speed (with the Jacquards able to produce the widest variety of patterns). Annual capacity[4] on a three-shift basis amounted to 1.1 tons (or 3,300 meters) for a flat knitting and to 14 tons (or 42,000 meters) for an interlock or old Jacquard machine. Originally, the flat knits had been used for sweaters. Being obsolete for this purpose in 1967, they were used for knitted trimmings which could not be made on the circular interlock and Jacquard machines. To meet demand at 1967 levels, Hedblom needed on a one-shift basis only 8 to 12 flat knitting machines and 14 to 16 interlocks and old Jacquards.

Besides the existing machines, 10 new 24 "systems" (or sets of needles) Jacquards had been ordered by the previous management for delivery in June 1967 at a cost of Skr 100,000 each. Mr. Keller learned that these new machines were anxiously awaited and were expected to provide a significant competitive advantage through ability to knit special fabric designs that could not be handled on interlock machines.

---

[4] If continuously operated, machine capacity would be higher. The above figures take into account estimated downtime for setups and maintenance or because of breakdowns and also include use of machines in trying out new fabric designs.

Their annual three-shift capacity amounted to 10 tons of fabric per year, or 30,000 meters.

After knitting, fabrics not made of colored yarn were sent out for dyeing unless they were intended to remain white. Although dyeing accounted for a large share of production costs and although it could create a competitive advantage, it was subcontracted on the grounds that Hedblom did not produce enough fabrics to justify the large investment in dye facilities. Two weeks were typically required for fabrics to be dyed, to which one week of transit time had to be added.

The dyed fabrics were returned to Hedblom's third-floor cutting department, which comprised 10 men and 15 women. On a large table, 10 meters long by 2 meters wide, about 40 layers of fabric were laid out by a special machine. The pattern girl would then arrange the dress patterns, trying to cover as much cloth as possible. Subsequently, a net would be placed over the patterns and the whole would be sprayed with light red paint. The cloth covered with the patterns would be shielded, while the cloth painted red would have to be discarded. Arranging the patterns was a highly skilled and most crucial operation, since up to 20%–25% of the fabric could be lost in the cutting process. Also, defects in the fabric, about which the pattern girls complained frequently, made it even more difficult to achieve an efficient arrangement. With the red paint indicating how the cloth was to be cut, the actual cutting was done in two steps: rough cutting on the table, and finer cutting on special machines. The cut pieces were then assembled in batches to be sent to sewing.

Sewing employed 70 people, all women, and was located on the second floor. Operations were conducted pretty much the same way as around the turn of the century. There were two lines of 62 machines, with a conveyor line supplying and taking away boxes of dress parts. A lady dispatched these boxes, attempting to maximize long production runs.

On the same floor, 10 people in the pressing department prepared the dresses for shipping. Employing eight people, shipping was located on the ground floor. According to industry practice Hedblom assumed all freight costs to the customer. Hence it was important to accumulate all dresses ordered by a single account to permit cost-saving bulk shipments. Since shipping was viewed as part of customer relations, it reported to the commercial manager. Also reporting to this department was a third-floor unit where 15 people under a directress prepared dress patterns and produced sample dresses on a hand-cut, machine-sewn basis.

The top floor of the building stood empty. On seeing this floor, Mr. Keller inquired about converting part of it to offices and using the rest for storage. Estimates indicated that this would cost Skr 300,000 for fixed installations and Skr 100,000 for furniture. Mr. Keller also learned that Hedblom held a long-term lease on the office building which could not be canceled until 1972. Thus a possible move would not save any rent, since renegotiation of the lease appeared highly unlikely given the fact that several office buildings in Boxholm stood empty.

## Marketing operations

By March 1967 Hedblom specialized in ladies' dresses and two-piece suits, mostly but not entirely using Crimplene-based fabrics. Typically, a spring and autumn collection was presented, with a limited number of models. Hedblom catered largely to the 25- to 30-year age group, its price range being too high for younger customers. Dresses were sold on the basis of an image of atmosphere and quality. The line always included some high-fashion models, which were emphasized in Hedblom advertising, even though the bulk of sales occurred in the traditional models. Hedblom had also acquired a reputation for certain patterns, especially those using trimmings which it had been able to emphasize because of its flat knitting machines. All dresses were sold under the Hedblom brand except for end-of-season closeouts, which were sold unbranded.

Factory prices of Hedblom dresses averaged Skr 80 and ranged from Skr 50 to Skr 204. With retail markups amounting to 90% to 100% (sometimes 100% to 110% in Stockholm), retail prices averaged Skr 150 with a range of Skr 98 to Skr 395. Hedblom stamped its price on the label but did not enforce retail price maintenance. Because of its reputation, Hedblom commanded a 10% to 15% price premium for its dresses which were the only well-known branded ones in its price range. Most dresses in Sweden retailed for under Skr 100, although one other well-known brand retailed between Skr 300 and Skr 400. Competition came primarily from unbranded dresses made by small producers who purchased their fabrics. Entry of these firms into the industry was easy and high, as was their mortality rate. These companies always found it possible to pick up sales, especially with their low prices. Low-price imports, especially from the United Kingdom, also posed a competitive threat. Hedblom did not have data on the size of the Swedish dress market nor a breakdown in terms of prices and channels.

Hedblom followed a selective distribution policy, attempting to sell through the best dress retailer in town. Especially in the larger towns this exclusive policy was not pursued rigidly; however, Hedblom did not sell to the large department store chains or other mass merchandising outlets such as mail-order houses. The reasoning was that Hedblom's high price required a great deal of sales push, on which the company could not count in mass distribution channels. In department stores, also, a Skr 100 retail price was a limit which store buyers were reluctant to exceed. Hedblom had about 250 accounts in Sweden, of which 30 were in Stockholm. Five salesmen, of whom one took care of Stockholm alone, covered these accounts. They were paid a base salary and a 1% commission on sales. They placed their main sales emphasis on the introduction of the spring and autumn collections which they showed with mannequins to their customers in local hotels. They averaged about two to three customers a day when showing the collection.

Advertising was largely placed in local newspapers, often on a co-operative basis with Hedblom's better customers. Hedblom did not devote a fixed percentage of sales to advertising, the amount rather being a function of the advertising support received from the synthetic fiber companies. Expenditures in 1966 had amounted to Skr 400,000. In addition to its press advertising, Hedblom participated in fashion shows such as the Scandinavian Fashion Week in Copenhagen. Furthermore, the company employed a public relations adviser, a Mrs. Westman from Stockholm, who had been most successful in providing free publicity for Hedblom in newspaper accounts on fashions. In April 1967 Mr. Keller was faced with the decision on whether to spend Skr 40,000 as Hedblom's share of expenses for a trip by Mrs. Westman to South America, during which she would get the Hedblom collection photographed and write travel accounts which would provide the company with free publicity in the Swedish press as well as photographs of its collection in a unique setting.

Exports accounted for 20% of Hedblom's sales, with the bulk going to Denmark and Norway where the line was sold through independent agents who took a 10% commission. Advertising in export markets was paid for by Hedblom and amounted to Skr 50,000 in 1966. Hedblom also had sales offices in Germany and Switzerland. In Germany, which was not a member of EFTA, dresses paid an import duty of 30%. In Denmark, Norway, and Switzerland, which were members of EFTA, no import duties were levied. Freight costs to foreign markets were 30% to 40% higher than for domestic sales, but still only about 1% to 1½% of the cost of dresses.

Design was done in-house under a directress. The company also used the services of a Paris dress designer. Dress design involved travel by the directresses to gather inspiration for the models. Hedblom pretty much followed prevailing trends, and hence fashion risks were not very high. Timing in introducing dresses was critical, and it was just as dangerous—according to the commercial manager—to come out with some model too early, before the trend would catch on, as too late. Also, he indicated the need to synchronize design and selling to permit continuous feedback from the marketplace and quick responses to new market trends.

## Control and planning system

It was the absence rather than the existence of a control and planning system which struck Mr. Keller during his early investigations. The company lacked budgets, a standard cost system, and inventory control. Mr. Keller found no records to measure the efficiency and output of knitting, cutting, sewing, pressing, and shipments. He found only what he considered to be a complicated, unusable production report. Mr. Keller received two daily reports: the one on incoming orders has already been described; the other was a daily report on bank balances. A balance sheet and income statement was prepared yearly, but was ready only several weeks, if not months, after the closing date. At Wientex's request, some quarterly statements had been prepared in the past. Mr. Keller also noticed that all communications were centralized via the top executive. Managers did not have an information system to keep one another posted on important current events. Also, no system of copies of important letters or memos existed. In fact, the company had no memo forms.

## Departments and their managers

During his first weeks on the job, Mr. Keller tried to learn as much as possible about the company managers, operations, and problems. Talks on these aspects started the very first day, and from these and subsequent discussions he was able to construct the following picture.

The organization structure under the previous owner manager had five managers (in charge of control, purchasing, production, fabric design, and commercial) reporting to him as well as two directresses (in charge of dress designs). Mr. Jansson, age 44, had been controller since 1956. He had joined the company in 1950 and had previously held positions in the bookkeeping department. Mr. Keller recognized that for him the adjustment might be the most difficult. He had assisted the former owner manager during the negotiations with Wientex and hence had faced his new boss across the negotiating table. He had been the owner manager's confidant (his salary had been raised by 50% after Wientex took its 50% interest) and was the only manager who knew about the serious sales decline and disastrous losses. (The commercial manager, of course, knew the former and suspected the latter, but the other managers had no idea that the company situation was so grave.) Mr. Jansson's duties under the previous management had been confined to bookkeeping and his department had not been asked to provide the top executive with management control and planning reports. Hence Mr. Jansson had no expertise in these areas.

Purchasing was managed by Mr. Nilsson, age 40, who had joined Hedblom in 1948 as clerk and was promoted to his present position in 1952. Mr. Keller learned that Hedblom bought practically all its yarn from Wientex, particularly in recent months when supplier credit had become increasingly important. Mr. Nilsson's main problem was that, because of the late presentation of the Hedblom collections, he was forced to purchase on a hand-to-mouth basis. Also, he indicated that the company had a large excess inventory of fabrics and dresses, part of it three to four years old. This was not currently used and probably only worth one third of its book value of Skr 4.0 to Skr 4.5 million. Not counting the excess supplies, Mr. Nilsson estimated that Hedblom had supplies for about 10 to 12 weeks in storage. These supplies tied up about Skr 2.0 million at current output levels.

Production was managed by Mr. Lanner, age 40, who had joined the company as a time-study man in 1955. He took on his present job during the move in 1966. His main problem in the past had been the lack of attention to production and its subordination to the company's commercial activities. For example, the owner manager had only once set foot in the plant during the previous two months. Mr. Lanner also indicated that manufacturing was forced to operate in high gear when the collections were to be delivered, while operations were nearing a standstill during the intermediate periods. Also, special orders by sales frequently made long runs difficult. He stated that in terms of authority he had been subordinated to the consulting engineer. Also, because the lack of piece rates had resulted in maintaining people's previous Sandvik salaries, the decline in volume meant they were being overpaid. Furthermore, without piece-rate schedules, lower costs could not be realized by making layout or procedure more efficient. Mr. Lanner also stated that, much to his chagrin, the previous owner manager had unilaterally discarded the previous piece-rate schedule.

Production scheduling was managed by Mr. Carlsson, age 46, who had joined the company in 1956. On arrival at Hedblom, Mr. Keller did not know about Mr. Carlsson since he was not listed among the top managers. Toward the end of his first day, Mr. Keller was told by one of the managers that he might want to talk to Mr. Carlsson, who reported to both the manufacturing and commercial managers but who was described as one of the key men in plant operations. Mr. Carlsson mentioned the same problems as his purchasing and production colleagues. He had found it exceedingly difficult to do any forward planning, instead having to operate on a day-to-day basis. Particularly since the previous owner manager was unwilling to make advance fabric commitments (that is, to knit fabrics for certain dresses before orders had come in), production bottlenecks were inevitable. He also stressed the difficulties resulting from a complete lack of standardization, which made it necessary to juggle an excessive number of fabrics, dress models, and dress sizes. Finally, he questioned the appropriateness of the punch-card system which was being installed by the consulting engineer, stating that it was a standard system which the same man had installed for fabric companies but that it was inappropriate for a company making dresses. Also, he indicated that the system was overly complicated and that prior to its installation, planning and record keeping was done by hand.

The consulting engineer, age 60, was highly respected and well known in Boxholm. He was a specialist in the textile industry with wide connections. During their first meeting, the consulting engineer called Mr. Keller by his first name, and added:

I am an engineer like you, and surely you will appreciate my services and help. Mr. Hedblom previously gave me a free hand to make this the most automated, most modern textile company. I would like to continue this way, particularly having the production manager remaining my subordinate.

Mr. Sundman, age 58, who had joined Hedblom in 1931, was in charge of fabric design. He was recognized as an authority on knitting, and his expertise had in large part been responsible for Hedblom's strong fabric position. He also made the comments already described concerning the company's manufacturing problems. Mr. Sundman had one assistant and shared the knitting foreman with manufacturing in order to experiment with fabric designs. He also cooperated closely with the directresses in developing new fabric designs in tune with dress fashions.

Mr. Filipsson, age 42, had been commercial manager since 1963, having joined the company in 1955. He reiterated the great influence which the previous owner manager exercised over style decisions. He also voiced the opinion that with its two basic collections and its current product, price, and distribution policies, Hedblom would be able to sell at most 125,000 dresses a year, allowing sales of about Skr 10 million. He indicated that the desire of the manufacturing department for fewer models within the present assortment was impossible. Rather, Hedblom should have a wider range of models, especially if the bulk of sales were to be made in Scandinavia with only marginal sales elsewhere. His customers preferred to buy less in primary orders at collection time and more articles with short delivery times during the season. This pressure gave a competitive advantage to the flexible manufacturer. He explained that this trend stemmed from the reluctance of the dress stores to make large, firm commitments at the time collections were presented, or six months ahead of actual sales. The commercial manager finally expressed his disappointment on a recent experience with the most fashionable Swedish department store chain; it had placed a modest order for Hedblom dresses but had not reordered. He commented:

They simply used our dresses for the prestige and in their show windows and advertising, but they continued selling the cheaper dresses. It proves that department stores are only interested in the below Skr 100 range and are unable to sell the more expensive merchandise like ours. Also, this experience was with our high-class department store chain. I wouldn't even dare to sell Hedblom dresses to the other, lower price, department store chains or mail-order houses because of a real risk of losing sales to our regular clients as a result of such a move. Particularly, the mail-order houses are very unpopular with our customers.

# The Tax Man, Inc.

THE TAX MAN, INC., provided assistance to individuals and other clients in the preparation of tax returns through 25 owned offices in eastern Massachusetts and 6 franchised offices. In June 1970, Robert Murray, president, and Roger Servison, chairman, indicated that they believed The Tax Man was on the threshold of an exciting era of growth; they intended to make the company one of the leaders in its industry while at the same time seeking profitable fields for diversification. As results for the 1970 tax season were tallied, however, an unexpected loss of $89,000 on revenues of $183,000 appeared, creating the prospect of a severe near-term working capital problem. Securing additional financing, in management's judgment, depended in large part on their ability to define and articulate a means of developing the growth and profit potential in the business.

## THE TAX PREPARATION "INDUSTRY"

In 1913 the shortest amendment to the Constitution was passed, bringing into law 31 words which have since affected nearly every resident of the United States. Amendment XVI reads: "The Congress shall have the power to lay and collect taxes on income, from whatever source derived, without apportionment among the several states, and without regard to any census or enumeration."

In the years following the passage of this law, individuals wrestled annually with the preparation of their income tax returns. Assistance

160

was available initially from lawyers, aud:tors, bookkeepers, and even IRS agents who viewed tax preparation as a source of additional compensation. In the mid-1950s businesses devoted specifically to assisting large numbers of taxpayers were formed, most notably H&R Block, Inc. Nonetheless, the vast majority of federal tax returns continued to be computed either by the taxpayers themselves or by local part-time preparers such as real estate brokers, insurance agents, and assorted friends and relatives. One representative estimate of market segmentation in 1970, when approximately 77 million returns were filed, was the following:

**Tax preparation—1970***

|  | Returns (millions) | Percent |
|---|---|---|
| Self-prepared returns . . . . . . . . . . . . | 34.6 | 45 |
| Local part-time preparers . . . . . . . . . | 25.4 | 33 |
| Lawyers and accountants . . . . . . . . . | 9.3 | 12 |
| Income tax service business . . . . . . . . | 7.7 | 10 |
| Total. . . . . . . . . . . . . . . . | 77.0 | 100 |

* For a distribution of tax returns by adjusted gross income, see Exhibit 1.

Using an average fee of $11.50 per return, tax service businesses generated revenues of approximately $88 million in 1970; the total market potential was over $880 million.

**EXHIBIT 1**
**Number of federal tax returns by adjusted gross income categories—1968**

| Adjusted gross income | Returns (in thousands) | Percent |
|---|---|---|
| Less than $5,000 . . . . . . . . . . . . | 31,921 | 43.3 |
| $ 5,000–$ 10,000 . . . . . . . . . | 23,367 | 31.7 |
| 10,000– 15,000 . . . . . . . . . | 11,987 | 16.3 |
| 15,000– 20,000 . . . . . . . . . | 3,666 | 5.0 |
| 20,000– 25,000 . . . . . . . . . | 1,180 | 1.6 |
| 25,000– 30,000 . . . . . . . . . | 519 | 0.7 |
| 30,000– 50,000 . . . . . . . . . | 716 | 1.0 |
| 50,000– 100,000 . . . . . . . . . | 301 | 0.4 |
| 100,000– 200,000 . . . . . . . . | 62 | 0.1 |
| 200,000– 500,000 . . . . . . . . | 16 | . . . |
| 500,000– 1,000,000 . . . . . . . . | 3 | . . . |
| Over $1,000,000 . . . . . . . . . . . . | 1 | . . . |
| Total. . . . . . . . . . . . . . . | 73,739 | 100.0 |

Source: Internal Revenue Service, preliminary 1969 statistics on individual income tax returns.

By 1974 the number of tax returns was estimated to reach 87 million, an annual growth rate of roughly 3%. Furthermore, several recent developments suggested a substantial increase in the proportion of people seeking outside tax assistance. First, the federal income tax Form 1040 underwent a major revision in 1970 and the 1040A (short form) was eliminated altogether. The added complexities, real or imagined, of these changes received wide publicity. Moreover, during the next few years further modifications would be necessary to accommodate changes in the tax laws resulting from the federal tax legislation of 1969.

Second, the tax law revisions themselves involved important changes in the treatment accorded a wide variety of income and expense items, including both the standard deduction and the personal exemption. Virtually all taxpayers would be affected to some degree, further complicating the task of filing the typical return. As Henry Block, president of H&R Block, the leading tax service company, noted in a recent speech, "We have a saying in our business that if Congress simplifies taxes once more, even we won't understand it." He later added, "Another thing that has contributed to our success is what is referred to as the 'Martinsburg Monster' and that is the computer that checks every tax return. For it is the fear of the IRS that drives a lot of people to our door."[1]

Third, the aggregate number of returns has grown more rapidly than the number of taxpayers because states and cities have instituted income taxes in an effort to meet the enormously inflated costs of government at these levels. By 1969, 38 states and many cities had tax returns, each different from the other and each different to some degree from the federal return. Industry observers expected this trend to continue. The implications were further intensified in a society in which approximately 15% of the people moved every year.

Fourth, rising income levels in the United States created both an increased opportunity for tax savings and a demand for a greater variety of personal financial services. Indeed, some observers claimed that taxpayers with moderate incomes had, in percentage terms, the most to gain from the professional handling of their tax affairs, since many of the special deductions or exclusions were directed toward their needs.[2]

### Traditional competitors

Competitors for an anticipated larger percentage of an expanding market included independent operators, "professionals" such as accountants and lawyers, and a variety of new competitors in the form of tax preparation service companies.

---

[1] Speech to the Omaha-Lincoln Society of Financial Analysts, March 5, 1969.

[2] For instance, the dividend exclusion, the retirement credit, sick pay, child care, educational expenses, employment fees, and so forth.

*The independent operator.* A wide variety of individuals were engaged in part-time tax preparation, including real estate brokers, insurance agents, pawnshop operators, bookkeepers, and people who simply had gained a working knowledge of the tax laws. In some instances, the independent prepared only as many returns as he could personally handle during the tax season. He solicited clients by word of mouth or through customer contact established in the normal course of his business, perhaps supplemented by a sign in his office or on his storefront.

In other instances, the independent hired assistants and rented an office for the tax season. He often advertised on local radio, in the local newspapers and telephone book, and in general sought to establish a tax preparation business. While undoubtedly numerous, no estimates were available to suggest the number or average size of such establishments. They were characterized by industry sources as offering vastly differing degrees of technical competence and preparation quality as well as widely differing terms of performance guarantee, if any, and fee structures.

*The professional.* Frequently reluctant competitors for the individual tax return were the lawyers and the CPAs. In particular, the larger law and CPA firms tended to view such work as a goodwill gesture for their legal, trust, or audit clients and they exhibited little desire to expand these services beyond the levels required to satisfy client requests. In general, the professional dealt with individuals in relatively high income tax brackets who filed complex returns and who frequently relied on his professional guidance and services in other matters as well.

## New competitors

Beginning about 1955 with the formation of H&R Block, new competitors and forms of competition began to emerge which by 1970 had proliferated to the point that tax preparation companies, banks, finance companies, insurance companies, major retail chains, and computer service companies were all engaged in the tax field. However, so commanding was the H&R Block lead that this company was reputed to have retained over 85% of the market accounted for by income tax service businesses.

*H&R Block.* Henry and Richard Block in the early 1950s managed the largest bookkeeping service for small businesses in Kansas City, preparing tax returns on the side as a favor to clients. After first attempting to withdraw from the burden of tax work altogether, only to discover that their clients had nowhere else to go for assistance, they decided in 1955 to expand this service aggressively through advertising and promotion. Aided by an IRS decision that year to discontinue the "gratis" preparation of returns for taxpayers, volume expanded from $1,700 to

$25,000 and, as Henry Block put it, "We knew we had a good thing going for us."

In 1969, 3,286 H&R Block offices were spread throughout the United States and Canada; 5,300,000 individual returns were calculated, and tax preparation revenue for owned and franchised offices amounted to $56 million and net profits after taxes to $3.3 million. Moreover, growth continued at a rapid pace: total offices in 1969 increased 37%, tax preparation volume 46%, and net income 60% from 1968. Comparative figures for offices are indicated below, and summary financial data for H&R Block are provided in Exhibits 2 and 3.

| Offices | 1968 | 1969* | Increase |
|---|---|---|---|
| Company owned | 1,079 | 1,640 | 561 |
| Franchised | 689 | 845 | 156 |
| Satellite of owned office | 351 | 446 | 95 |
| Satellite of franchised office | 287 | 355 | 68 |
| | 2,406 | 3,286 | 880 |

* H&R Block had 162 offices, or about 5% of the total offices in the six New England states for the 1969 season: Connecticut, 46; Maine, 12; Massachusetts, 95; New Hampshire, 6; Rhode Island, 1; and Vermont, 2. The population of New England was roughly 11.5 million, or 5.8% of the national figure.

The company had consistently followed five policies over the years. The first was to expand the number of offices as rapidly as capable managers and financing permitted.[3] Recently, H&R Block management had begun to reserve large city locations for company-owned offices and had even repurchased some franchises. Second, the company was prepared to locate offices in towns with as few as 500 people through the use of satellites; in essence, these were individuals franchised to prepare returns under the H&R Block name. Third, the fee structure, which, as shown in Exhibit 4, was based on the complexity of the client's return, had remained unchanged since 1955, although the average charge per client had increased steadily. H&R Block management attributed this phenomenon to the growing size and diversity of client's sources and uses of funds.

Fourth, H&R Block stressed a high-quality, high-volume, low-cost operation directed primarily at the taxpayer with income in the $5,000 to $15,000 range. Quality was fostered by a tax preparation school, attended by 30,000–40,000 people annually at a fee of $60 per person. In addition to providing income for Block, the school was an excellent

[3] Mr. Block claimed, in his speech to the Omaha-Lincoln Society of Financial Analysts on March 5, 1969, that the number of offices opened during 1969 could have been 1,600 had the company wished to maximize growth.

**EXHIBIT 2**

### H&R BLOCK, INC.
#### Profit and Loss Statements
#### (highlights)

| | Year ended July 31 | | | | | Nine months ended April 30, 1966 | Year ended April 30 | | |
| --- | --- | --- | --- | --- | --- | --- | --- | --- | --- |
| | 1961 | 1962 | 1963 | 1964 | 1965 | | 1967 | 1968 | 1969 |
| **Volume** | | | | | | | | | |
| If owned offices | $715,034 | $1,114,226 | $1,834,586 | $2,876,707 | $5,010,412 | $7,702,447 | $12,907,125 | $19,785,785 | $29,543,635 |
| If franchised offices | 589,151 | 985,469 | 1,805,479 | 3,321,187 | 6,553,700 | 9,406,333 | 13,172,662 | 18,539,913 | 26,600,164 |
| Total volume | $1,304,185 | $2,099,695 | $3,640,065 | $6,197,894 | $11,564,112 | $17,108,780 | $26,079,787 | $38,325,698 | $56,143,799 |
| **Revenues*** | | | | | | | | | |
| Owned office volume | $715,034 | $1,114,226 | $1,834,586 | $2,876,707 | $5,010,412 | $7,702,447 | $12,907,125 | $19,785,785 | $29,543,635 |
| Franchise fees and other | 116,543 | 154,471 | 191,580 | 258,628 | 690,356 | 1,054,660 | 1,807,285 | 3,018,529 | 4,821,855 |
| Total revenues | $831,577 | $1,268,697 | $2,026,166 | $3,135,335 | $5,700,768 | $8,757,107 | $14,714,410 | $22,804,314 | $34,365,490 |
| **Earnings** | | | | | | | | | |
| Total revenues | $831,577 | $1,268,697 | $2,026,166 | $3,135,335 | $5,700,768 | $8,757,107 | $14,714,410 | $22,804,314 | $34,365,490 |
| Operating expenses | 658,639 | 995,618 | 1,667,226 | 2,528,204 | 4,487,431 | 6,785,583 | 11,701,891 | 18,248,645 | 26,722,916 |
| Earnings before taxes | $172,938 | $273,079 | $358,940 | $607,131 | $1,213,337 | $1,971,524 | $3,012,519 | $4,555,669 | $7,642,574 |
| Taxes on income | 82,694 | 124,076 | 170,564 | 296,506 | 559,775 | 910,330 | 1,421,500 | 2,509,320 | 4,363,000 |
| Net earnings | $90,244 | $149,003 | $188,376 | $310,625 | $653,562 | $1,061,194† | $1,591,019 | $2,046,349 | $3,279,574 |
| Earnings per share‡ | $.02 | $.03 | $.04 | $.06 | $.12 | $.20 | $.30 | $.39 | $.62 |
| Tax returns prepared (not including state tax returns) | 150,000 | 250,000 | 400,000 | 650,000 | 1,150,000 | 1,700,000 | 2,600,000 | 3,650,000 | 5,300,000 |
| Number of offices | 140 | 206 | 353 | 495 | 806 | 1,190 | 1,712 | 2,406 | 3,286 |

* For 1969, franchise fees and other revenues includes $586,771 of resident school tuition fees which were included in owned office volume for prior periods.

† The earnings for the nine-month period are not representative of those for a full fiscal year. Net earnings for the 12 months ended April 30, 1966 (unaudited) were $962,947 or $.18 a share on total revenues of $8,839,349.

‡ Based on shares outstanding at the end of each period retroactively adjusted for the five-for-four stock split in the form of a stock dividend declared May 2, 1969, for stock dividends in prior years, and for shares issued in connection with poolings of interest and the acquisition. As so adjusted there were at April 30, 1969, and 1968, 5,305,001 shares outstanding, and at the end of each prior period 5,277,512 shares outstanding.

Source: H&R Block 1969 Annual Report.

**EXHIBIT 3**

H&R BLOCK, INC.
Balance Sheet

|  | *April 30* | |
|---|---|---|
|  | *1968* | *1969* |
| *Assets* | | |
| Current assets | | |
| Cash . . . . . . . . . . . . . . . . . . . . . . . . . . | $ 2,876,134 | $ 3,011,690 |
| Marketable securities, at cost . . . . . . . . . . . . . . . . | 6,735,779 | 11,871,061 |
| Receivables, less allowance for doubtful accounts of | | |
| $40,000 . . . . . . . . . . . . . . . . . . . . . . . . . . | 446,576 | 545,766 |
| Prepaid expenses . . . . . . . . . . . . . . . . . . . . . | 308,519 | 334,279 |
| Total current assets . . . . . . . . . . . . . . . . . . | $10,367,008 | $15,762,796 |
| Equity in promotional joint venture . . . . . . . . . . . . | 41,844 | . . . |
| Property and equipment, at cost less accumulated deprecia- | | |
| tion and amortization . . . . . . . . . . . . . . . . . . | 1,027,060 | 1,325,723 |
| Franchises, at cost, and excess of cost of operating offices | | |
| over fair value of net assets acquired . . . . . . . . . . . | 919,107 | 1,217,531 |
| Total assets . . . . . . . . . . . . . . . . . . . . . . | $12,355,019 | $18,306,050 |
| *Liabilities and Stockholders' Equity* | | |
| Current liabilities | | |
| Accounts payable. . . . . . . . . . . . . . . . . . . . . | $ 667,597 | $ 679,602 |
| Payroll taxes and taxes withheld from employees . . . . . | 612,445 | 1,031,837 |
| Accrued managers' bonuses . . . . . . . . . . . . . . . . | 1,480,859 | 2,125,875 |
| Accrued salaries and wages . . . . . . . . . . . . . . . . | 429,414 | 715,542 |
| Deposits on franchise contracts. . . . . . . . . . . . . . | 193,664 | 271,279 |
| Federal and state taxes on income . . . . . . . . . . . . . | 3,848,860 | 6,151,460 |
| Current maturities on long-term debt . . . . . . . . . . . | 149,156 | 84,156 |
| Total current liabilities . . . . . . . . . . . . . . . . | $ 7,381,995 | $11,059,751 |
| Long-term debt, deferred income taxes . . . . . . . . . . . | 426,624 | 342,468 |
| Minority interest . . . . . . . . . . . . . . . . . . . . . | 81,947 | 104,700 |
| Commitments and contingencies . . . . . . . . . . . . . . | 16,500 | 6,101 |
| Stockholders' equity | | |
| Common stock, stated value $.01 a share—authorized, | | |
| 10,000,000 shares; issued and outstanding, 4,244,736 | | |
| and 5,305,001 shares, respectively . . . . . . . . . . . . | $ 42,447 | $ 53,050 |
| Paid-in capital. . . . . . . . . . . . . . . . . . . . . . | 352,632 | 352,632 |
| Retained earnings. . . . . . . . . . . . . . . . . . . . . | 4,052,874 | 6,387,348 |
| Total stockholders' equity . . . . . . . . . . . . . . . | $ 4,447,953 | $ 6,793,030 |
| Total liabilities and stockholders' equity . . . . . . . | $12,355,019 | $18,306,050 |

Source: H&R Block 1969 Annual Report.

recruiting ground for office managers. Increased volume was the objective of an extensive nationwide television advertising campaign each
year during the tax season in addition to ads placed in local print media.
Low costs were achieved through a minimum of overhead and office
frills, centralized purchasing of supplies and office services, and, in 1970,
experimentation with computer-assisted tax return preparation.

A fifth element in the H&R Block success formula was diversification.
Partly the thrust was geographical; by 1969, 166 offices had been located

**EXHIBIT 4**

H&R BLOCK, INC.
Tax Preparation Fees

$  5.00—Federal and local or adjacent state or city.
   Income from salaries only, not over three items.
   Deductions not itemized.
   1.00—Itemized deductions per section (over 1 item).
   2.50—Each additional local or adjacent foreign state or city return.
   2.50—Dividends and interest combined—not over four items.
   2.50—Pensions and annuities—per schedule.
   2.50—Rental income—per location.
   2.50—Capital gains and losses (D)—not over three items.
   2.50—Exchange of residence.
   2.50—Installment gain.
   2.50—S.E. without C. or F.
   2.50—Substitute wage and tax statement.
   2.50—Statement of dependency support.
   2.50—Casualty, education or alimony—per section.
   2.50—Retirement income credit (R).
   2.50—Foreign tax credit (1116).
   2.50—Sick pay (2440).
   2.50—Child care (2441).
   2.50—Investment credit (3468).
   2.50—Recapture of investment credit (4255).
   2.50—Moving expense (3903).
   2.50—Gas tax credit (4136).
   2.50—Tips (4137).
   2.50—Any other additional schedule.
   5.00—Return of client's dependent (federal short form only).
   5.00—Foreign state tax return (not local or adjacent).
   5.00—1040 NR (same as 1040).
   5.00—Auto, travel, and sales expense (optional method only—$2.50).
   5.00—Business income (C. & S.E.).
   5.00—Farm income (F. & S.E.).
   5.00—Exclusion of income earned abroad (2555).
   5.00—Application for loss carryback (1045).
  10.00—Hourly time charge for compiling tax information.
  10.00—Hourly time charge for W-2s in excess of three.
  10.00—Hourly time charge for dividends and interest in excess of four.
  10.00—Hourly time charge for capital gains and losses in excess of three.
  10.00—Redoing previously filed return not prepared by Block plus regular schedule of
       charges (amend or 1040X).
  10.00—Partnership (1065)—federal and state.
  15.00—Corporation (1120)—federal and state.
  20.00—Income averaging (G).
No charge—Miscellaneous income, not over one line.
No charge—Redoing completed Block tax return.
       (Extra charge for additional schedules.)
No charge—Estimates (1040ES).
No charge—Underpayment of estimates (2210).
No charge—Extra copies of return.
No charge—Refund due deceased taxpayer (1310).
No charge—Tax computation (T).
No charge—Intangible tax.

   The above figures are based upon client furnishing complete information itemized and totaled.

in Canada and others in Puerto Rico and New Zealand. The company had also enlarged the scope of its activities; for instance, in the education field a home-study course had been initiated. More important, prior to the 1970 tax season, a joint venture with the Pennsylvania Life Insurance Company was formed, called H&R Block Financial Services, to sell mutual funds and life insurance nationally. It was too early for industry observers to determine the success of this last activity, however.

***Other tax service companies.*** A number of smaller tax specialist companies were in operation during the 1970 tax season in addition to The Tax Man. Typical of the older, established companies was Weiss Tax Service, Inc., a family business with 16 owned offices in the greater Chicago area. Despite a spinoff in 1968 to accommodate certain members of the Weiss family, the company had attempted to expand by enlarging existing offices and opening new ones in nearby communities. At various times in the past, Weiss had been involved in merger negotiations with other tax companies, including H&R Block, but in each case it had been unable to reach an agreement. Summary operating data are noted below:

WEISS TAX SERVICE, INC.*

| Year ending December 31 | Revenues | Net profits | Offices |
|---|---|---|---|
| 1966 . . . . . . . . . . . . . . | $141,620 | $ (1,912) | 19 |
| 1967 . . . . . . . . . . . . . . | 197,216 | (1,863) | 15 |
| 1968 . . . . . . . . . . . . . . | 162,497 | 13,116 | 10 |
| 1969 (five months) . . . . . . | 247,381 | 16,743 | 16 |

* Disguised name.
Source: Weiss Tax Service annual reports.

A second company, located in New York City, was Witt Tax Centers, Inc., which had begun as a proprietorship in 1962. After raising nearly $500,000 in public and private equity placements in 1968, the company launched an acquisition and franchising program for the 1969 tax season, increasing the number of owned offices from 5 to 21 and the number of franchised offices from none to 20, including 10 which, immediately prior to the transaction, had been company owned. These policies were abruptly changed later in 1969. Witt management decided to own rather than franchise offices and to "establish a national network of financial service centers initially offering income tax preparation, mutual funds and life insurance."[4] Sixty-two tax centers were open for the 1970 season,

---

[4] 1969 Annual Report, Witt Tax Centers, Inc., February 18, 1970.

59 of them company owned. Financial results of late, however, were unfavorable:

WITT TAX CENTERS, INC.

| Year ending Sept. 30 | Revenues | Net profit |
|---|---|---|
| 1967 . . . . . . . . | $ 56,790 | $13,404 |
| 1968 . . . . . . . . | 88,383 | 26,986 |
| 1969 . . . . . . . . | 259,898 | (271,536) |

Source: Witt Tax Centers annual reports.

A third tax specialist organization was the Ben Franklin Income Tax Service Company, formed in 1969, financed by a private placement estimated by industry sources to be $2 to $2.5 million, and managed by a group of experienced executives formerly with Litton Industries and IBM. The company pursued a policy of rapid growth in both owned and franchised offices. By the beginning of the 1970 tax season, Ben Franklin reportedly owned as many as 100 offices in California and had embarked on an aggressive franchising program. The franchisee, under Ben Franklin terms, would pay $2,500 per office initially plus a fee of 20% of gross revenues; in addition, the company would have the option of repurchasing the franchise for cash or stock according to a formula based in part on historical earnings.

*Personal finance companies.* Several of the major personal finance companies offered tax services for the first time in 1970. Most significant among them was the Beneficial Finance Company which, through its newly formed Benevest subsidiary, opened 80 offices in California for the 1970 season and intended later to expand nationally. The Benevest offices were separate from the Beneficial Finance outlets,[5] the latter being subject to strict regulation under California small-loan statutes.

Benevest offered its clients an instant refund without interest[6] for tax overpayments, securing in return a pledge that the client would repay Benevest when he received his government check. Beneficial's motives were interpreted in *Business Week* as follows:

The refund ploy is, of course, expected to generate a large chunk of tax preparation business, but it is really a "kicker" to entice people to come in and sign up for a wide range of "family financial services"—especially mutual funds and life insurance—that Benevest's salesmen will peddle after the tax season closes. . . . For Beneficial, the nation's largest personal loan company, profit margins on sales of funds and insurance are likely to be higher than those on lending activities now being squeezed by rising interest

---

[5] Beneficial Finance had approximately 800 offices nationwide.

[6] The IRS has reported that 72.5% of returns filed claimed a refund.

rates. . . . Thus, the company will avoid the problem some fund-insurance sales organizations face of having to pay advances to salesmen until they can generate enough commission income to support themselves.[7]

Benevest was reported to expect revenues of $3 million to $5 million the first year, requiring an estimated $50 million in cash to support anticipated refunds. The average tax preparation charge per client of $25, however, was considerably above the industry average. A Benevest advertisement noted, however, that "not every taxpayer qualifies for an 'instant refund,' of course, but if you're a homeowner with an income of $12,000 or more, you probably qualify easily."

*Insurance companies.* At least one insurance group, the St. Paul Companies, Inc., had entered the tax preparation business directly. Through its subsidiary, Form 1040, Inc., St. Paul planned to open 46 offices in the Minneapolis–St. Paul area for the 1970 tax season. The company's 1968 annual report stated that while insurance was still the primary business, increasing competition for the public's investment funds and a cost-premium squeeze were forcing the company both to diversify its services and products and to find more aggressive ways to market insurance.

*Retail chains.* J. C. Penney, Sears, Roebuck, and Montgomery Ward offered tax preparation services during the 1970 tax season by placing booths in selected stores. In each case pricing and service was patterned after H&R Block. For Penney and Sears, the service was new and experimental; for Montgomery Ward, 1970 was the eleventh year. The size of these companies and some measure of their potential strength in the tax preparation industry are provided in the following statistics:

**Operating data for retail chains**

| | Sales (millions) | Stores | Estimated tax preparation centers in 1970 | Projected 1970 growth in stores |
|---|---|---|---|---|
| J. C. Penney | $3,756 | 1,646* | 24 | 35 |
| Sears, Roebuck | 8,863 | 826 | 88 | 28 |
| Montgomery Ward† | 2,715 | 468 | 135 | 22 |

*Includes 1,438 "soft line" stores.
†Now Marcor following a merger with Container Corporation.
Source: Annual reports and estimates by industry executives.

*Computer service companies.* A less easily defined, though potentially significant, factor in the industry was the computer service company which provided tax assistance either on a time-share basis or

[7] "Luring Clients with On-the-Spot Tax Refunds," *Business Week,* December 20, 1969, p. 80.

through a processing center. Such companies were of two types: those offering wholesale computer services to "professional" tax preparers and those offering assistance directly to the taxpayer. Typical of the former were Tax Computer Systems, Computax Systems, and Programmed Proprietary Systems. Skeptics noted several drawbacks in the use of such services, most notably the possibility of breakdown of overloading on and just prior to April 15 and the problem of accuracy. Other industry observers, however, pointed out that much of the time-consuming detail work in filling out a return could be eliminated. The ultimate effect might then be more competition for tax return preparation from (1) lawyers and CPAs who might then view the business as less time consuming and more profitable; (2) part-time preparers who would enjoy a substantially increased capacity; and (3) others such as banks, which might perceive tax work as a means of enlarging customer services. For instance, the National Bank of North America, Chase Manhattan, and The First National City Bank already provided tax services for their customers in 1970 on a limited basis.

Fiscal Systems, Inc., typical of computer service companies offering assistance directly to the taxpayer, distributed Tax-Pak through banks and department stores. For $2.50 the customer could buy a package of instructions and forms which included questions about his income and expenses. He received, about seven days after returning the forms to the company, a completed return ready for his signature. Sales of Tax-Pak were cut off on April 3 due to the processing and mailing time required prior to the April 15 filing deadline.

## Operating characteristics

The operations of tax preparation companies were influenced considerably by the seasonal nature of the demand for tax services. Typically, over 90% of a company's total income from this and related sources was received in the January-to-April period. An estimate by one industry spokesman of the level of activity during this period is provided below:

| Month | Percent of Revenues |
|---|---|
| January | 6 |
| February | 34 |
| March | 25 |
| April (through the 15th)* | 35 |
| | 100 |

*April 15th alone = 5%.

One impact of this operating pattern was financial. A tax preparation company which maintained a year-round central staff had administrative overhead costs to absorb in the "off season" as well as rent for individual offices. Moreover, funds were necessary for supplies and possibly for advertising and promotion prior to the next tax season. Securing long-term financing was complicated by the fact that the business and most of its tangible assets virtually disappeared for eight months of the year, to return only if management was successful in launching another tax-season effort.

A second, perhaps more fundamental, impact of seasonality related to the management of a geographically dispersed business depending on employees who were reasonably highly skilled. Roger Servison, chairman of The Tax Man, commented on this issue:

> One of the major problems confronting the income tax industry concerns the seasonal employment needs of the business. The heavy reliance on part-time, seasonal help makes it difficult to motivate and instill a sense of company pride and job responsibility in these employees. In addition, people who are readily available on a part-time basis are frequently people who for various reasons are not capable of holding a full-time job. Yet it is these people who must represent the company to the public. The impression created by a tax preparer is the only impression the customer receives, since none of the other employees have any personal contacts with the customers.
>
> This large demand for seasonal help during the tax season results in a high rate of turnover among employees and makes recruitment of personnel a major problem for tax companies.
>
> The high rate of employee turnover also has an adverse effect on the repeat business of a tax office. An office that is staffed by the same people year after year is able to develop a personal rapport with its clients that is more meaningful to the customer than the name of the company he is dealing with. Many people hesitate to divulge confidential information about their personal income to a new person each year.

Operations, in turn, responded to the technical requirements of the business. The preparation of tax returns was divided into three basic activities: client interview and preliminary tax computation, checking and processing the return, and handling subsequent audits and errors. The method of operation characteristic of H&R Block, but shared by most tax companies including The Tax Man, is described in the Appendix at the end of this case. The process for computer-based operations was mechanically different though conceptually the same.

The personnel requirements for a multioffice income tax business of the H&R Block type fell naturally into five categories, none of them, according to industry practice, requiring a college education. As one industry spokesman put it, "Any person with a high school education and an ability to work with numbers can be taught to compute income taxes with only eight to ten weeks of formal tax training." These positions are noted below in order of increasing skill and including the typical means of compensation:

1. *Tax return processors* made copies of completed income tax returns, compiled the various sheets in the proper order, and mailed the returns to the customer. This job was frequently performed on a part-time basis by high school students who were paid by the hour.

2. *Tax return checkers* reviewed all completed returns, a task which entailed verifying the appropriateness of tax law application, the mathematical accuracy of computations, and the completeness of the return. Normally checkers were also paid on an hourly basis. One checker was typically required for five preparers.

3. *Tax preparers* interviewed the client and prepared his tax return. Tax preparers were normally paid a commission of 20% to 25% of the gross amount of revenues derived from the returns they prepared. An experienced preparer could prepare about four returns of average complexity per hour.

4. *Office managers,* in addition to preparing returns themselves, were responsible for scheduling work, insuring that all cash was deposited promptly, submitting weekly reports on office performance, maintaining a proper inventory of supplies, and overseeing general office appearance. Office managers generally received a commission based on the total revenues of an office and were usually expected to work 55 hours a week during the tax season.

5. *Area managers* were responsible for recruiting and training personnel, equipping offices, checking on office performance, scheduling local advertising and promotions, and resolving operating problems. Area managers were typically responsible for approximately five offices and were paid a salary plus a percentage of the net profit of their operation. These men were frequently employed year-round to operate the tax schools and handle customer complaints during the period from May to January.

### Financial characteristics of an income tax office

Income tax offices were potentially high-margin operations. The variable costs associated with preparing a return were estimated by industry sources to be about $1.33, excluding the preparer's commission. With an average client charge of $11.50 per return, the contribution to overhead after commissions was about 61% of revenues, and the break-even volume for an office was roughly $6,200 (Exhibit 5). While The Tax Man management felt that the H&R Block break even might, if anything, be somewhat lower, the above figure was thought to be representative of the other tax specialist companies. Under these assumptions, the contribution from a large office was impressive.[8]

---

[8] H&R Block was reported to have some locations whose revenues exceeded $120,000.

**EXHIBIT 5**

THE TAX MAN, INC.
Typical* Income Tax Office Break-Even Calculations

| | | | |
|---|---|---|---|
| Average revenue per return . . . . . . . . . . . . . . . . . | | $11.50 | 100.0% |
| Variable costs (excluding preparer commission) | | | |
| Coffee . . . . . . . . . . . . . . . . . . . . . . . . . . . | $ .05 | | |
| Tax forms . . . . . . . . . . . . . . . . . . . . . . . . . | .09 | | |
| Copy paper (10 copies/return) . . . . . . . . . . . . | .08 | | |
| Copy developer . . . . . . . . . . . . . . . . . . . . . . | .03 | | |
| Checking and processing labor . . . . . . . . . . . . | .65 | | |
| Postage (optional) . . . . . . . . . . . . . . . . . . . . | .24 | | |
| Large envelopes. . . . . . . . . . . . . . . . . . . . . . | .05 | | |
| Client folders . . . . . . . . . . . . . . . . . . . . . . . | .05 | | |
| Government envelopes (2/return) . . . . . . . . . . . | .018 | | |
| Customer receipt . . . . . . . . . . . . . . . . . . . . . | .015 | | |
| Tax saver envelope . . . . . . . . . . . . . . . . . . . . | .047 | | |
| Check list . . . . . . . . . . . . . . . . . . . . . . . . . | .005 | | |
| Total variable costs . . . . . . . . . . . . . . . . . | | 1.33 | 11.5 |
| Average contribution per return before | | | |
| commission . . . . . . . . . . . . . . . . . . . . . . . | | $10.17 | 88.5% |
| Preparer commission . . . . . . . . . . . . . . . . . . . . | $ 2.88 | | |
| FICA tax. . . . . . . . . . . . . . . . . . . . . . . . . . . | .29 | 3.17 | 27.5 |
| | | $ 7.00 | 61.0% |
| Fixed costs | | | |
| Payroll. . . . . . . . . . . . . . . . . . . . . . . . . . . . | $2,700† | | |
| Rent (five months) . . . . . . . . . . . . . . . . . . . . | 800 | | |
| Advertising and promotion . . . . . . . . . . . . . . . | 1,370 | | |
| Repairs and maintenance . . . . . . . . . . . . . . . . | 200 | | |
| Utilities . . . . . . . . . . . . . . . . . . . . . . . . . . | 200 | | |
| Insurance . . . . . . . . . . . . . . . . . . . . . . . . . . | 25 | | |
| Miscellaneous . . . . . . . . . . . . . . . . . . . . . . . | 125 | | |
| Total fixed costs . . . . . . . . . . . . . . . . . . . | $5,420 | | |

Break-even
Volume:    $5,420 ÷ .885 = $6,200
Returns:    $6,200 ÷ 11.50 =    540

*Typical of operations patterned after H&R Block.
†The first $2,700 in commissions and FICA taxes is considered fixed since preparers are generally given advances approximating this amount in anticipation of commissions.
Source: Casewriter's notes based on Tax Man calculations.

## Marketing characteristics

A variety of competitive devices had historically been employed in marketing tax services. Location was one important factor in the success of an office. Since most tax companies relied heavily on walk-in business, the ideal location was a street-level storefront in a high-traffic shopping center. An office appealing to this clientele was thought to have an effective drawing radius of two to four miles and required a population of 15,000 to 20,000 households. Consequently, the tax company had to consider office density as well as location. Once a company had established itself in an area, however, it appeared that the number of offices per thousand households could be profitably increased.

Pricing was a second important element in marketing policy. Although the majority of tax companies advertised their prices as "$5 and up," the average charge per client in the industry was about $11.50. The average charge for small single-office companies was somewhat lower than the industry norm, while for companies offering instant refunds or computerized services it was considerably higher. Most companies based their prices on the complexity of the return. Thus, the basic fee for a nonitemized federal return was $5; additional schedules typically cost about $2.50 each. A few companies set fees by the amount they "saved" their clients. This practice had been criticized in the industry by those who contended that it encouraged the preparer to deduct questionable items on the client's return.

Providing guaranteed year-round service was a third method of attracting clients. The importance of continuing service and guaranteed accuracy was partially a result of the emphasis given to these factors by the IRS and the Better Business Bureau. Such organizations attempted to discourage the public from having their taxes computed by individuals who would not cosign the return or be available after the tax season to deal with client problems.

Finally, tax companies depended on client loyalty to generate a repeat business frequently as high as 75% to 80%. Thus, in January, tax companies generally sent a reminder to each of their former clients encouraging them to return. To this was often added an advertising program in newspapers and on local television.

## THE TAX MAN

The Tax Man, Inc., was organized by Mr. Joseph Rossi, a man in his mid-50s, on September 29, 1967, to purchase a single-office tax preparation proprietorship. The stated purpose of the corporation was "to assist individuals and others in the preparation and filing of tax returns of whatever nature and to license or franchise others to use the name of The Tax Man." During the 1968 tax season, eight offices were opened and approximately 4,600 returns were prepared, yielding $40,527 in gross revenue.

On November 18, 1968, the corporation filed a prospectus for a public offering in accordance with Regulation A of the Securities and Exchange Act for 39,500 shares at $2.50 per share. Approximately $60,000 of the proceeds was to be used in the establishment of 30 new offices. The prospectus stated that Mr. Rossi owned 12,000 shares and had options to purchase another 45,000 shares at $1 per share until July 31, 1971, and thereafter until July 31, 1975, at $5 per share, at which time the options would expire. Other members of management were stated to own 3,300 shares and to have options to purchase an additional 6,000 shares under similar terms. On November 13, 1968, the offering was made and a month later was fully subscribed.

On March 6, 1969, the U.S. District Court in Boston, on the basis of an affidavit filed by the SEC, temporarily enjoined The Tax Man from further sale of common stock under Regulation A. The injunction was made permanent on April 17, 1969. The principal complaints brought by the SEC against the corporation and the principal investors were inadequate or false disclosure of material facts in the registration statement and the prior and subsequent sale of unregistered shares to the public. The market price of The Tax Man stock fell from a high of $15 per share on March 6 to $2 in June of the same year.

During May and June of 1969 Messrs. Robert Murray and Roger Servison, both stockholders in the company and both in the process of obtaining a master's degree in business administration, began consulting for Mr. Rossi regarding plans for the 1970 tax season. During their study, they discovered that the company would report a large operating loss for the year ended July 31 and that additional financing would be required to reopen existing tax offices, then numbering 27, for the 1970 season.

A special meeting of the board of directors was held on July 12, at which time, among other actions, Messrs. Murray and Servison were elected to an expanded board, giving them, with one outside investor, a three-to-two majority. Subsequent events, including a still larger estimate of the operating loss and an absence of planning or progress in securing funds, prompted a second special meeting of the board on August 2. At that time Mr. Rossi was asked to resign as president and chairman of the board and, among other requests, to cancel approximately two thirds of his existing options.

### The new managers

Robert Murray and Roger Servison rationalized the risks involved in assuming the direction of The Tax Man by citing the fact that they were young (24), single, and able to start over again should the venture fail. Both men had a great deal of confidence, however, in their ability to turn the company into a successful growth business. They saw it as a means of gaining wide experience in general management and of ultimately obtaining some measure of financial independence, though in the beginning they were willing to work for very modest salaries. In terms of long-range career goals, they indicated a willingness to devote 8 to 10 years to operating the business, but then hoped to become more heavily involved in forward planning and administration.

Management tasks were divided as follows: Mr. Murray was to handle the legal and accounting functions while Mr. Servison was to concentrate on marketing and franchising. Responsibility for finance and personnel would be shared, and operations would be handled by dividing the offices geographically between the two men.

### New management's actions

The most immediate problem confronting the new management team was a financial crisis: as indicated by the balance sheet (Exhibit 6), current liabilities of $16,000 exceeded current assets by slightly more than $2,000 on July 31, 1969. Management's response was a private placement on October 6 of 200,000 shares at $.50 per share,[9] of which they each subscribed to 30,000 shares,[10] while the remainder was divided among a group of 10 investor friends. Mr. Servison indicated that the placement not only provided funds to sustain and expand the business but insured that voting control would be retained in friendly hands.

While the financial situation was being clarified, management also turned its attention to preparing for the 1970 tax season. During the next four months, action was taken along three dimensions. First, a tax school was opened in an effort to attract and train competent tax preparers and office managers. About 18 students were enrolled in the course at a fee of $50, of whom about half continued with The Tax Man as preparers or office managers.

Second, Mr. Frank Kelley, a former manager of H&R Block, was hired as operations manager with the hope that he would provide the day-to-day management expertise and training skills necessary for a multioffice operation. He had discussed the possibility of joining The Tax Man with the new principals prior to their assumption of control. Mr. Kelley subsequently hired two former associates as area managers.

Third, the new management sought to expand the number of offices through the sale of franchises and the acquisition of established tax practices. The former goal was implemented through the sale of one franchise in Massachusetts and another for Illinois, excluding Cook County, with the expectation that five offices would be opened in that state for the 1970 season. These transactions produced gross revenues of $22,150. The latter goal was implemented through five acquisitions encompassing eight offices in Massachusetts. The terms of the acquisitions are noted in the table on p. 179.

---

[9] The market price of the common stock fluctuated between $1 and $2 per share during this period.

[10] In addition, Mr. Servison and Mr. Murray each agreed to purchase an additional 30,000 shares over a five-year period at $1 per share.

**EXHIBIT 6**

THE TAX MAN, INC.
Balance Sheet

| | July 31 | | April 30 |
|---|---|---|---|
| *Assets* | *1968* | *1969* | *1970* |
| Current assets | | | |
| Cash | $ 3,239 | $ 6,722 | $ 7,660 |
| Note receivable | ... | 5,423 | 23,579* |
| Employee advances | ... | 400 | 300 |
| Prepaid expenses | ... | 782 | 3,110 |
| Total current assets | $ 3,239 | $13,327 | $ 34,649 |
| Fixed assets—at cost | | | |
| Land | ... | $30,835 | $ 30,835 |
| Buildings and improvements | ... | $16,480 | 15,714† |
| Office equipment | $ 4,660 | 16,391 | 44,070†‡ |
| Automobiles | ... | 2,000 | 2,000 |
| Total | $ 4,660 | $65,706 | $ 92,619 |
| Less: Accumulated depreciation | 583 | 2,697 | ... |
| Total fixed assets | $ 4,077 | $63,009 | $ 92,619 |
| Intangible assets§ | $11,592 | ... | $ 50,050 |
| Total assets | $18,908 | $76,336 | $177,318 |
| *Liabilities and Stockholders' Equity* | | | |
| Current liabilities | | | |
| Mortgage payable—current portion | ... | $ 1,400 | ... |
| Note payable | ... | 655 | $ 16,350 |
| Accounts payable | $ 257 | 4,061 | 51,958 |
| Accrued and withheld taxes | ... | 9,227 | 21,866 |
| Accrued payroll and commissions | ... | 200 | 6,396 |
| Total current liabilities | $ 257 | $15,543 | $ 96,570 |
| Long-term liabilities | | | |
| Mortgage payable—current portion shown above | ... | $30,297 | $ 30,961 |
| Notes payable | ... | ... | 6,250 |
| Total long-term liabilities | ... | $30,297 | $ 37,211 |
| Stockholders' equity | | | |
| Common stock, $1 | | | |
| Authorized 500,000 shares; issued and outstanding, 68,500 shares at 7/31/69, 339,286 at 4/30/70 | $15,000 | $68,500 | $169,643 |
| Capital surplus | ... | 57,375 | 58,228 |
| Retained earnings (deficit) | 3,651 | (95,379) | (184,334) |
| Total stockholders' equity | $18,651 | $30,496 | $ 43,537 |
| Total liabilities and stockholders' equity | $18,908 | $76,336 | $177,318 |

*Includes $14,000 in franchise initiation fees, $7,000 due in July 1970 and the remainder in July 1971.
†Net of depreciation.
‡Major items include copy machines and office signs.
§Reflects difference between purchase and book value on acquisitions.
Source: Company records.

**Acquisition terms**

| Acqui-sition | Number of offices | Revenues 1969 season | Method of acquisition | | |
|---|---|---|---|---|---|
| | | | Cash | Stock (shares) | Terms |
| A | 4 | $26,700 | $35,000 | 2,000 | $20,000 cash and 2,000 shares down, remainder over two years |
| B | 1 | 16,500 | 15,000 | ... | 50% down, 50% over a year |
| C | 1 | 6,700 | 2,150+ | 286 | $2,150 cash and 286 shares down, plus 125% of revenues from returning clients |
| D | 1 | 3,850 | 2,450+ | ... | Book value of office equipment plus $5 per returning client |
| E | 1 | 4,000 | 2,000 | ... | 25% down, remainder over two years |
| | 8 | $57,750 | $56,600 | 2,286 | |

With these steps taken and with sufficient funds remaining for supplies and working capital, management in the late fall of 1969 had looked forward to a tax season that would enable The Tax Man to break even financially in fiscal 1970 while also providing a solid base for future expansion and for securing bank loans to finance the 1971 tax season.

### The 1970 tax season

The 1970 tax season fell far short of expectations, and as of April 30 a loss of $89,000 had already been incurred for the current fiscal year (see Exhibit 7). Mr. Servison reviewed the shortcomings of the past five months as follows:

Our biggest problem, in retrospect, was our own lack of experience in the tax business. We made several costly mistakes, which hopefully can be avoided in the future.

Back in August 1969 we had no organization in the company. This, combined with our age and inexperience, created two kinds of problems. First, we had difficulty establishing our ideas. The operations manager and those men he brought with him had a concept for running the business that was different from ours. They wanted the kind of high-volume, low-cost operation that has made H&R Block successful. We, on the other hand, wanted to introduce new marketing techniques, upgrade the offices, and build a base for diversified services. Communications broke down. To keep these managers from resigning before the tax season began, we divided up the offices—one third using their methods and the others ours. Curiously, our offices turned out to yield better financial results, in part at least because we encouraged aggressive marketing. Anyway, that won't happen again since, as of April

# EXHIBIT 7

## THE TAX MAN, INC.
### Comparative Income Statements
### Years Ending July 31

| | 1967 | Percent | 1968 | Percent | 1969 | Percent | 1970 (9 months) | Percent |
|---|---|---|---|---|---|---|---|---|
| Gross revenues | | | | | | | | |
| Tax preparation | $3,360.00 | 100.0 | $40,527.00 | 100.0 | $ 83,786.50 | 95.5 | $153,665.54 | 83.7 |
| Franchise initiation fees and royalties | ... | ... | ... | ... | ... | ... | 22,145.50 | 12.1 |
| Miscellaneous | ... | ... | ... | ... | 3,960.00 | 4.5 | 7,567.07 | 4.2 |
| Total revenues | $3,360.00 | 100.0 | $40,527.00 | 100.0 | $ 87,746.50 | 100.0 | $183,378.11 | 100.0 |
| Operating expenses | | | | | | | | |
| Preparers' salaries | $2,300.00 | 68.5 | $15,640.26 | 38.5 | $ 69,237.34 | 78.8 | $102,216.26 | 55.7 |
| Office supplies and services | 220.60 | 6.7 | 3,546.17 | 8.7 | 20,393.08 | 23.3 | 40,835.53 | 22.3 |
| Advertising | 624.70 | 18.5 | 8,181.25 | 20.2 | 22,874.39 | 26.0 | 32,853.13 | 17.9 |
| Rent | 450.00 | 13.4 | 4,650.00 | 11.5 | 10,882.50 | 12.4 | 16,985.90 | 9.2 |
| Other operating costs | 272.02 | 8.1 | 4,275.08 | 10.5 | 24,448.79 | 27.9 | 28,602.04 | 15.6 |
| Total operating expenses | $3,867.32 | 115.2 | $36,292.76 | 89.4 | $147,836.10 | 168.4 | $221,492.86 | 120.7 |
| Operating profit (loss) | (507.32) | (15.2) | $ 4,234.24 | 10.6 | $(60,089.60) | (68.4) | $ (38,114.75) | (20.7) |
| Administrative costs | | | | | | | | |
| Salaries | ... | ... | ... | ... | $ 22,455.35* | 25.6 | $ 25,281.53 | 13.8 |
| Rent | ... | ... | ... | ... | ... | ... | 2,070.00 | 1.1 |
| Other administrative costs | ... | ... | $ 583.00 | 1.4 | 3,383.41 | 3.9 | 23,588.92 | 12.8 |
| Total administrative costs | ... | ... | $ 583.00 | 1.4 | $ 25,838.76 | 29.5 | $ 50,940.45 | 27.7 |
| Net profit (loss) | $ (507.32) | (15.2) | $ 3,651.24 | 9.2 | $(85,928.36) | (97.9) | $ (89,055.20) | (48.4) |

*Reflects the opening of a corporate office.
Note: Number of returns processed in 1970 was roughly 17,000, including 1,000 by the franchised offices.
Source: Company records.

15, we parted ways with Frank Kelley and the two area managers who came with him.

Second, we were critically short of good office managers. As a result, several of the offices had severe problems and one was not even able to open until March 21.

Cost control was another problem area. We didn't handle purchasing of supplies very well and costs in that area were excessive. With a better understanding of competitive bidding practices and better planning, I believe we could double volume next year and reduce supply costs $5,000 (about 12%). In addition, our bookkeeping department was not adequately staffed, with the result that we didn't have close control over labor costs. Many of our offices were overstaffed, and this, probably more than anything else, contributed to the operating loss.

Finally, we had some conditions left over from the prior year that turned out to have more serious implications than we expected. First, we had to relocate all but one of the original offices because leases for the 1969 season covered only a four-month period. The problems involved in finding suitable locations and getting supplies delivered caused the opening dates for most offices to be delayed until February 1, and unfortunately we were unable to relocate in Waltham and Salem at all. This probably meant at least $25,000 in lost revenues. More importantly, however, we discovered that less than 50% of last year's Tax Man customers returned this year, well below the normal industry average. This can be partially attributed to changed office locations, but we suspect that the service given in 1969 was inferior in many instances as well. Also, in three locations former employees went into competition with us, using our customer lists from the prior year.

The spring of 1970 was not, however, without its bright spots. Mr. Servison continued in this vein:

In other respects, 1970 was an encouraging year. We had about four offices that together accounted for over half of the operating loss. The better offices, on the other hand, showed very substantial volume increases which lifted several of them from break even to a solid profit. Here are the historical figures for our best managed office that shows this trend. The acquired offices in particular were strong performers. The return before taxes on gross investment was nearly 16%, which isn't bad for the first season, and it should improve considerably next year.

Management also felt that valuable experience had been gained in the conduct of the business. More specifically, progress was cited in the areas of procedures and control, marketing, and organization; however, particularly in the last instance, significant work remained to be done.

*Procedures and controls.* By the end of the tax season, data had been gathered for a comprehensive manual on policy and procedures which was to be made available for a management training session in January 1971. Mr. Murray hoped that the manual and the thought

"Best managed" office

| | 1967 | 1968 | 1969 | 1970 | 1970 |
|---|---|---|---|---|---|
| Revenues. . . . . . . . . . . . . . | $3,360 | $9,850 | $16,500 | $22,600 | 100.0% |
| Operating costs | | | | | |
| Payroll . . . . . . . . . . . . . . | $2,500 | $4,825 | $ 6,940 | $ 8,668 | 38.4% |
| Rent . . . . . . . . . . . . . . | 800 | 800 | 2,400 | 2,400 | 10.6 |
| Advertising . . . . . . . . . . | 650 | 800 | 1,000 | 1,000 | 4.6 |
| Supplies . . . . . . . . . . . . | 370 | 1,080 | 1,815 | 2,750 | 12.1 |
| Utilities . . . . . . . . . . . . | 100 | 100 | 300 | 300 | 1.3 |
| Insurance . . . . . . . . . . . | 10 | 10 | 10 | 10 | . . . |
| Telephone . . . . . . . . . . . | 100 | 100 | 600 | 600 | 2.6 |
| Total costs . . . . . . . . | $4,530 | $7,715 | $13,065 | $15,728 | 69.6% |
| Net profit (loss). . . . . . . . . | $(1,170) | $2,135 | $ 3,435 | $ 6,872 | 30.4 |

behind it would assist in consolidating the varied experiences of the office managers into a booklet of helpful advice on the efficient operation of a tax office.

Similarly, a cost control system comparable to that thought to be used by H&R Block was introduced during the tax season. With continuing refinements, Mr. Murray believed that it would be instrumental in achieving reductions in operating cost ratios on the order of 10% during the next tax season.

*Marketing.* Mr. Servison indicated that the results obtained from some of the marketing techniques introduced during the tax season had been very encouraging. For instance, an employee discount plan was marketed in some areas to companies employing 50 or more people as a special fringe benefit. Under this arrangement, the employer simply included a coupon with the wage and tax statement (W-2 form) mailed to employees each January which entitled them to a 10% discount on returns prepared by The Tax Man. In large part due to this effort, one new office opened with a volume well above the break-even point. Mr. Servison also felt that some companies might be willing to underwrite some or all of the service in future years, providing The Tax Man with temporary offices and in-plant promotion in exchange for reduced rates.

*Organization.* Progress in building an organization was viewed as mixed. Vacancies existed in three of the five area-manager positions, and although the remaining incumbents were seen as competent in this role, none was thought to be immediately able to assume the position formerly held by Mr. Kelley.

Messrs. Murray and Servison were, however, quite optimistic about the progress they had made in recruiting and training office managers. About half of the 25 company-owned offices were headed by what management considered to be capable managers who were likely to return to The Tax Man in 1971. These men promoted their offices aggressively and derived considerable satisfaction from directing an efficient operation.

Management also indicated that efforts to recruit competent part-time tax preparers had been very successful. Over 140 preparers had worked for the company in the course of the 1970 season, about 100 of whom were considered capable of performing this function at a satisfactory level. It was hoped that the existence of such a large number of experienced preparers would reduce the time and effort needed to recruit personnel in 1971. In addition, there was a possibility that some of them would be offered the position of office managers for the next season.

### Financial condition

One immediate problem confronting The Tax Man management was a shortage of working capital. The proceeds from the 1969 private stock placement had been expended and operations for the 1970 tax season had drained rather than replenished funds. Mr. Murray estimated that a minimum of $150,000 would be needed to support overhead (currently running at about $3,000 per month), to reduce accounts payable, and to finance start-up expenses for the 1971 tax season. An additional $150,000 would be necessary to undertake the acquisition, franchising, and diversification programs that management felt were important for the company's long-term growth.

Obtaining equity was complicated by the court injunction prohibiting the further sale of stock under Regulation A. To sell shares registered with the SEC, Mr. Murray felt that a full registration under the Securities and Exchange Act would be necessary. In view of The Tax Man's history, the legal expenses of such a registration would be high, requiring, in management's judgment, an issue of at least a million dollars to be economical. Alternatively, additional unregistered or "letter" stock could be sold privately to individuals. Mr. Murray thought the purchasers of the 1969 placement would be unwilling to invest sufficient additional funds, however, and he was concerned about the terms that would be demanded by a new investor group.

Messrs. Murray and Servison had initially approached several banks in an effort to secure a combination of term and seasonal financing. While the banks were sympathetic to the latter during the early months of the tax season, they were negatively disposed to the former, citing the absence of a profitable operating history, a weak balance sheet, and the relative inexperience of management.

More recently, management had contacted a number of venture capital organizations. The preliminary response in several instances had been favorable, although discussions had not progressed to the point of formulating a specific financing arrangement.

Included in the presentation to potential investors or lenders was a forecast of projected revenues for the 25 existing offices for the following three tax seasons. Taken together, the profit pattern below was estimated:

| | 1971 (000) | 1972 (000) | 1973 (000) |
|---|---|---|---|
| Revenues. . . . . . . . . . . . . . . . . . . . . . . . . . . . . . . | $278 | $372 | $492 |
| Break-even revenue @ $6,200 each . . . . . . . . . . . . | 155 | 155 | 155 |
| Revenues above break even . . . . . . . . . . . . . . . . | $123 | $217 | $337 |
| Contribution @ 61% . . . . . . . . . . . . . . . . . . . . . | 75 | 132 | 206 |
| Less: Area manager bonus @ 40%. . . . . . . . . . . . | 30 | 53 | 82 |
| Contribution to general overhead. . . . . . . . . . . . . | $ 45 | $ 79 | $124 |
| Less: General overhead. . . . . . . . . . . . . . . . . . . | 65 | 65 | 65 |
| Profit before taxes . . . . . . . . . . . . . . . . . . . . . . | $ (20) | $ 14 | $ 59 |

Mr. Servison indicated that 1973 revenues could easily be doubled by acquisitions and new offices.

### Alternatives for growth in income tax services

Management regarded growth in income tax services as both necessary and desirable. Mr. Servison reflected these views:

We have developed what we think to be a sound method of operation and are enthusiastic about opening new tax offices. Growth in this business is going to be exciting over the next few years as tax law changes drive some of the untapped market to professional tax preparers. In addition, we need greater volume to generate the contribution to support overhead in the off season and provide working capital for the next season.

Unfortunately, opening new offices ourselves presents some problems. One is money. A relatively modest office requires about $1,500 in furniture and equipment and another $2,000 in working capital to get started. Then we have to find a qualified manager. He and the preparers he has working for him are essential for the success of the office. Upgrading staff in existing offices has been a big job for us that isn't over yet. I doubt that we'll have men to spare for some time. Lastly, a new office typically doesn't show a profit for two to three years. With our financial status as it is, we are very much aware of the need for establishing a track record for our stockholders and potential sources of financing.

While not discounting entirely the possibility of opening company-owned offices, management was more inclined to pursue new office possibilities through franchising. The franchise arrangement included three important provisions. First, the franchisee would pay Tax Man $5,000 for exclusive rights to service a population center of 15,000 households. The fee would increase $500 for each additional 5,000 households. In return, The Tax Man would provide training and administrative services which, added to the expenses associated with selling the franchise, Mr. Murray estimated to cost about $2,500. Supplies and equipment were billed separately at cost (about $1,500). Second, the franchisee would pay The Tax Man 10% of gross revenues after the first tax season. While the initiation fee was thought to be among the highest in the industry, management felt the percentage of revenue was less than average.[11] Third, The Tax Man agreed to repurchase the franchise after five years at the option of the franchisee for 10 times the average profit after taxes, The Tax Man fee, and normal "owner's" salary for the previous two years payable in cash or marketable securities. The financial estimates provided with the franchise were predicated on opening a second office in the same population center in the third year, as shown in Exhibit 8.

Despite the opportunity for short-term gain, Mr. Servison had two reservations about mounting a major franchising program. He was concerned, first, by the initial expenses involved in assembling sales materials and procedure manuals, office design, travel, and so forth, which he estimated at about $20,000. Second, he was uncertain about the effect of possible legislation directed toward regulating franchise activities. Should future law require a registration of some kind for each franchise,[12] the added time and legal expenses involved would seriously diminish the attractiveness of franchising.

A final possibility for expanding geographically in tax services was the acquisition of established practices. Management was of the opinion that a sizable number of profitable practices could be purchased from owner managers who would be willing to continue as office managers. In fact, nine proprietors in eastern Massachusetts had already contacted The Tax Man offering to sell their practices. The number of returns and approximate revenues are shown in Exhibit 9.

Typically, the purchase price approximated the prior year's revenues, often with roughly half the amount payable immediately and the remainder after the tax season, the second payment sometimes based on a factor related to the percentage of returning clients. The Tax Man's financial condition posed a serious limitation to an acquisition program, however, since in management's view acquisitions would have to be made for cash rather than for stock.

---

[11] For instance, H&R Block received 15% of gross revenues from franchisees but required no initiation fee.

[12] "A Law Shapes Up on Franchising," *Business Week,* January 31, 1970. According to *Business Week,* the Senate Small Business subcommittee was considering full disclosure of franchise agreements, possibly through a registration statement and control over advertising statements by franchisers.

## EXHIBIT 8

### THE TAX MAN, INC.
#### Projections for Franchisees*

| | 1st year | 2nd year | 3rd year | 4th year | 5th year | 5th year summary |
|---|---|---|---|---|---|---|
| **Revenues** | | | | | | |
| 1st office | $5,000 | $10,000 | $17,500 | $22,000 | $25,000 | $ 79,500 |
| 2nd office | ... | ... | 5,000 | 7,500 | 10,000 | 22,500 |
| Total revenues | $5,000 | $10,000 | $22,500 | $29,500 | $35,000 | $102,000 |
| **Operating costs** | | | | | | |
| Payroll | $2,500 | $ 3,000 | $ 5,750 | $ 8,650 | $10,500 | $ 30,400 |
| Rent | 1,000 | 2,400 | 3,400 | 4,800 | 4,800 | 16,400 |
| Advertising and promotion | 800 | 800 | 1,000 | 1,000 | 1,000 | 4,600 |
| Supplies | 550 | 1,100 | 2,475 | 3,025 | 3,850 | 11,000 |
| Repair and maintenance | 200 | 200 | 300 | 200 | 200 | 1,100 |
| Sign rental | 200 | 200 | 400 | 400 | 400 | 1,600 |
| Utilities | 200 | 400 | 600 | 800 | 800 | 2,800 |
| Insurance | 100 | 100 | 200 | 200 | 200 | 800 |
| Contingency fund | ... | 100 | 225 | 295 | 350 | 970 |
| Miscellaneous | 50 | 50 | 100 | 100 | 100 | 400 |
| Total costs | $5,600 | $ 8,350 | $14,450 | $19,470 | $22,200 | $ 70,070 |
| Operating profit (loss) | $ (600) | $ 1,650 | $ 8,050 | $10,030 | $12,800 | $ 31,930 |
| Royalty fees | ... | 1,000 | 2,250 | 2,950 | 3,500 | 9,700 |
| Net profit (loss) | $ (600) | $ 650 | $ 5,800 | $ 7,080 | $ 9,300 | $ 22,230 |
| Owner's draw | 1,750 | 2,000 | 2,500 | 2,500 | 2,500 | 11,250 |
| Total owner proceeds | $1,150 | $ 2,650 | $ 8,300 | $ 9,580 | $11,800 | $ 33,480 |

*The figures are based on a market area of 12 square miles or less and a minimum of 15,000 households.
Source: Company records.

**EXHIBIT 9**

THE TAX MAN, INC.
Immediate Single-Office Acquisition Candidates

| City | Returns | Approximate revenues* |
|------|---------|-----------------------|
| A | 372 | $ 4,300 |
| B | 1,000 | 11,500 |
| C | 750 | 8,700 |
| D | 500 | 5,800 |
| E | 1,500 | 17,300 |
| F† | 1,000 | 11,500 |
| G | 225 | 2,600 |
| H† | 1,000 | 11,500 |
| I† | 1,000 | 11,500 |
| | 7,347 | $84,700 |

*At $11.50 per return.
†Could be consolidated with existing Tax Man office.
Source: Company records.

## Diversification

Management was also actively considering a number of alternatives for using The Tax Man capabilities to provide other services. Three types of businesses with widely differing characteristics were currently being evaluated: bookkeeping services, miscellaneous simple businesses, and personal financial services.

*Bookkeeping services.* Individuals with multiple income sources, proprietors, and small businessmen frequently needed part-time accounting services on a continuing basis. Tax Man bookkeepers could be assigned to several clients, providing the client with services and flexibility and the bookkeeper with full-time employment.

For The Tax Man there were several advantages to be gained from entering such a business. Overhead charges would be low, since personnel would work in client offices, and billings would not have dramatic seasonal fluctuations. At the same time, management felt that this type of service would be entirely consistent with the company's image and would probably result in new tax customers. Moreover, people qualified as bookkeepers could probably be trained to prepare tax returns with little difficulty.

The business also had certain drawbacks, identified by Mr. Murray as follows:

Not all of The Tax Man's present employees would be qualified to provide bookkeeping services. We would be confronted with another recruiting problem and possibly a training effort as well. In addition, bookkeeping services aren't seasonal, so we couldn't use them to offset tax work. It's possible that an entirely different staff would be needed, which might just aggravate our personnel problems.

Also, we, as management, don't have any particular expertise with this service, especially how to market it. We might find it necessary to hire an aggressive man to get it moving.

**Simple businesses.** With 25 office locations and a pool of reliable part-time employees, The Tax Man provided the basis for a variety of relatively uncomplicated businesses. Management had discussed using the offices as duplication centers or as driving schools during the off-season months. Alternatively, offices could be converted to the sale of real estate and casualty insurance. Sufficient data had not been gathered, however, to assess in detail the advantages and disadvantages of such ventures.

**Personal financial services.** Finally, personal financial services were being considered, including the sale of mutual funds and life insurance as part of a family budgeting and financial counseling service. Mr. Servison noted some of the reasons for his interest.

Depending on how The Tax Man is conceived of as a business, selling a broad range of financial services could be a natural extension of our existing business. Tax customers could be screened for sales potential, and the salesmen could capitalize on the rapport established during the tax-return preparation. Conversely, cold calls and continuing client contact would enhance the tax business.

Unlike the bookkeeping service, sales efforts for mutual funds and life insurance may be made seasonal so that some of the same people can prepare tax returns as well. Also, if the salesman begins work as a preparer or office manager during the tax season, he will build up a cash reserve as well as a customer list, which will reduce the need for us to provide him with working capital.

Mr. Servison felt that falling stock market prices and the financial difficulties experienced by numerous brokerage firms in the spring of 1970 would assist in recruiting securities salesmen. He was less sanguine, however, about finding men with this background who would also be interested in tax work.

At present, The Tax Man was exploring the possibility of selling the insurance and mutual fund product line of an established agent, thus avoiding the difficulties involved in registering a new program. With this arrangement, management believed that only its salesmen, as individuals, would need to be registered. The Tax Man would receive a share of the commissions and would provide certain administrative and accounting services. No investment would be required, however.

## RECENT EVENTS

In the first two weeks of June, The Tax Man management had begun to receive some indications of the performance of competing tax service companies during the 1970 season. The results were mixed. H&R Block had experienced another record-breaking year: revenues increased 43% and profits 83%, and approximately 1,100 new offices were opened.[13] On the other hand, many of the newer companies appeared to have had dismal results.

During this time The Tax Man received three tentative invitations to consider acquiring or merging with competing companies. While figures were not available, Mr. Servison had the impression that as of June 15 these companies could be characterized in the manner below:

| Company | Number of offices | Losses | Age of company (years) | Approximate unobligated cash* |
|---------|-------------------|--------|------------------------|-------------------------------|
| 1 . . . . . . . . . . | About 80 | About $500,000 | 1 | $400,000 |
| 2 . . . . . . . . . . | About 25 | Small | 6 | nil |
| 3 . . . . . . . . . . | 8 mobile units | About $100,000 | 1 | $ 50,000 |

*Remaining after payment of 1970 tax season expenses.

Mr. Servison was uncertain whether such opportunities should be pursued. Placing a value on The Tax Man was one difficulty,[14] accommodating his and Mr. Murray's personal desires another, and identifying the business benefits of a merger, acquisition, or sellout a third.

## APPENDIX
## TAX RETURN PREPARATION PROCESS

*Client interview and preliminary tax computation:* Usually the client visited a tax office where a preparer questioned him about sources of income and a wide variety of business and personal expenses that might be deductible for income tax purposes. Based on this information the preparer computed the client's tax return and told him what he owed or what his refund would be.

*Checking and processing:* The client's tax return was then sent to a processing center where it was thoroughly checked for completeness

---

[13] H&R Block stock, traded on the NYSE, closed at 46 on June 15, 1970 (the range in 1970 was 37 to 68). At this price the stock commanded a P/E ratio of about 40 based on 1970 earnings per share.

[14] As of June 15, Tax Man stock traded at $1 per share, indicating a market value of about $340,000, although the market for the stock was very thin.

and mathematical and legal accuracy. In the case of an error the return might be rerouted to the preparer for corrections and then sent back to the processing center. Two copies were then made of each tax return—one for the client's personal records and one for the tax company's files. The original and a copy of the completed return were mailed to the client, who signed the former and submitted it to the Internal Revenue Service.

The length of time between the date of the initial interview and the day the client received his completed return averaged about one week but could vary from a couple of days to as long as a month, depending on the company and the proximity to April 15th. Being able to promise rapid delivery was an important market advantage for an income tax company. During the final week of the tax season, processing centers were generally set up in each tax office so that one-day service could be given to the large number of customers who normally filed right before the April 15 deadline.

*Handling audits and correcting errors:* Tax companies that guaranteed their work also maintained a year-round staff of employees who were responsible for handling client complaints and helping them prepare for IRS audits. These people recomputed all returns that the IRS rejected or audited and usually went to the IRS office with the client for an audit.

# A. G. Brown and Son, Ltd.

A. G. BROWN AND SON of Halifax, Nova Scotia, was the largest food broker in the Canadian Maritimes, which included the provinces of New Brunswick, Prince Edward Island, Nova Scotia, and Newfoundland. Mr. Garnet Brown, president and majority owner,[1] maintained that the brokerage business was ideal for an entrepreneur since it required no inventory and little capital, and provided a continuing, valuable service to its clients. However, despite his considerable success in expanding revenues by over 125% from 1965 to 1969, Mr. Brown was disturbed by the steady decline in profits during this period, culminating in a small loss in 1969. At one point he mused:

Dad and I alone once sold $1,000,000 from our homes. Now it takes 14 salesmen and an office staff of five to sell $7,000,000. Of course, we wouldn't have the accounts if we didn't give the service. But one would think some of those added revenue dollars would reach the bottom line. I've been giving some thought to a couple of possibilities which might help, though—some having to do with the way we run the business and others having to do with how we might expand it.

## HISTORY

After graduating from high school in 1946, Mr. Brown left Halifax to play baseball for two years in the Brooklyn Dodgers farm system.

[1] Garnet Brown owned 89%, Donald Brown, a brother, 9%, and other members of the family 2%.

In 1948 he returned to Halifax and played ball with a local team for two more years. His athletic reputation then helped him obtain a job as an apprentice draftsman in a local shipyard.

In 1953 Mr. Brown's father, who had quit his job as a candy salesman to start a brokerage business in 1946, was offered the account of an expanding biscuit maker. Feeling that he had reached his capacity to provide service to the retailer, he arranged for his son to take the account. In 1970 it was the largest annual revenue producer for the company.

A. G. Brown and Son was formed as a partnership in 1956 and handled a retail sales volume of $500,000 that first year. Earle Hilchey, formerly a biscuit salesman for a national company, became the first nonfamily employee four years later; and in 1965, the year Mr. Brown's father passed away, responsibility for the New Brunswick territory was given to Donald Carlton. Then in 1968 the firm moved from a cramped, dimly lit two-room office of 800 square feet into a new 4,200-square-foot building constructed for the company and owned personally by Mr. Brown.

Financial statements are provided in Exhibits 1 and 2, and the growth in employees, revenues, and principals since 1962 is reflected in Exhibit 3.

## THE MARITIMES

The economy of the Maritimes had historically been dependent on farming, fishing, and commerce rather than industry, due in large part to the distance from major markets, their small population, rough topography, and a relative absence of industrially useful resources. The Canadian government, however, had recently begun a series of projects designed to speed economic development and increase the level of disposable income in the Maritimes, then among the lowest in the country. Unlike neighboring Quebec, the predominant language and ethnic background in these provinces was English rather than French. The population tended to be split evenly between towns and the countryside, with a few large cities such as metropolitan Halifax (population 200,000) containing most of those classified as urban in Exhibit 4. Many small food stores, listed as "others" in Exhibit 5, and a few chains served the people of the Maritimes and were at least partially dependent upon the information and services supplied by food brokers.

## FOOD BROKERS

In the United States and Canada, the food broker was an agent of one or more principals and was paid a commission of 3%–8% of sales to sell the principals' products and provide detail services to accounts and retailers. In Canada brokers did not normally obtain custody, pos-

**EXHIBIT 1**

## A. G. BROWN AND SON, LTD.
### Income Statements

| | 1965 | | 1966 | | 1967 | | 1968 | | 1969 | |
|---|---:|---:|---:|---:|---:|---:|---:|---:|---:|---:|
| Approximate yearly sales* | $2,782,720 | | $3,561,980 | | $4,813,420 | | $5,740,260 | | $6,267,600 | |
| Commission revenue | $ 139,136 | 100.0% | $ 178,099 | 100.0% | $ 240,671 | 100.0% | $ 287,013 | 100.0% | $ 313,380 | 100.0% |
| Expenses | | | | | | | | | | |
| Advertising and promotion | $ 5,223 | 3.8% | $ 6,826 | 3.8% | $ 6,938 | 2.9% | $ 10,136 | 3.5% | $ 7,795 | 2.5% |
| Association and club dues | 1,046 | 0.7 | 1,535 | 0.9 | 1,444 | 0.6 | 1,658 | 0.6 | 3,074 | 1.0 |
| Audit and legal fees | 1,088 | 0.8 | 2,817 | 1.6 | 4,404 | 1.8 | 4,880 | 1.7 | 8,304 | 2.7 |
| Interest | 2,183 | 1.6 | 2,554 | 1.4 | 4,943 | 2.0 | 6,573 | 2.3 | 7,171 | 2.3 |
| Car expense | 17,366 | 12.5 | 22,974 | 12.9 | 31,176 | 12.9 | 33,487 | 11.7 | 39,285 | 12.5 |
| Depreciation | 298 | 0.2 | 405 | 0.2 | 580 | 0.2 | 2,259 | 0.8 | 2,100 | 0.7 |
| Donations | 95 | 0.1 | 195 | 0.1 | 946 | 0.4 | 1,128 | 0.4 | 400 | 0.1 |
| Group insurance | 1,604 | 1.2 | 1,853 | 1.2 | 1,213 | 0.5 | 2,662 | 0.9 | 2,834 | 0.9 |
| Property expense | 1,531 | 1.1 | 2,450 | 1.1 | 1,491 | 0.6 | 1,126 | 0.4 | 1,710 | 0.6 |
| Insurance | 134 | 0.1 | 146 | 0.1 | 220 | 0.1 | 418 | 0.1 | 165 | 0.0 |
| Office supplies | 1,570 | 1.1 | 3,517 | 1.1 | 3,068 | 1.3 | 3,937 | 1.4 | 5,010 | 1.6 |
| Pension | 1,036 | 0.7 | 1,353 | 0.7 | 1,909 | 0.8 | 2,018 | 0.7 | 2,243 | 0.7 |
| Rent and storage | 480 | 0.3 | 620 | 0.3 | 1,839 | 0.8 | 11,265 | 3.9 | 13,709 | 4.4 |
| Salaries and bonuses | 55,179 | 39.7 | 68,526 | 39.7 | 114,441 | 47.6 | 153,457 | 53.5 | 162,131 | 51.7 |
| Sundry | 1,712 | 1.2 | 2,179 | 1.2 | 2,243 | 0.9 | 4,449 | 1.5 | 7,961 | 2.5 |
| Taxes | 30 | 0.0 | 48 | 0.0 | 104 | 0.0 | | 0.0 | 1,486 | 0.5 |
| Telephone | 2,968 | 2.1 | 3,759 | 2.1 | 4,819 | 2.0 | 6,429 | 2.2 | 7,563 | 2.4 |
| Travel | 18,047 | 13.0 | 24,900 | 13.0 | 34,115 | 14.2 | 38,312 | 13.4 | 40,428 | 12.9 |
| Unemployment insurance | 201 | 0.1 | 335 | 0.1 | 531 | 0.2 | 349 | 0.1 | 1,359 | 0.4 |
| Heat, light, water | | 0.0 | | 0.0 | | 0.0 | | 0.0 | 2,593 | 0.8 |
| Total expenses | $ 111,791 | 80.3% | $ 146,992 | 81.5% | $ 216,424 | 89.8% | $ 284,543 | 99.1% | $ 317,321 | 101.2% |
| Net profit from operations before taxes | 27,345 | 19.7 | 31,107 | 18.5 | 24,247 | 10.2 | 2,470 | 0.9 | (3,941) | (1.2) |

* Based on an average commission rate of 5%.
Source: Company records.

**EXHIBIT 2**

A. G. BROWN AND SON, LTD.
Balance Sheets
As of December 31

| | 1967 | 1968 | 1969 |
|---|---|---|---|
| *Assets* | | | |
| Cash | $ 2,003 | $ 11,791 | $ 5 |
| Accounts receivable | 35,072 | 50,900 | 39,555 |
| Stock subscriptions receivable | 4,996 | 3,888 | 3,888 |
| Loans to directors | 17,604 | 50,672 | 59,247 |
| Travel advances | 650 | 875 | 975 |
| Prepaid rent | ... | 13,500 | ... |
| Tax overpayment | ... | 1,157 | 585 |
| Fixed assets, net of depreciation | 7,738 | 14,149 | 13,181 |
| Cash value of life insurance | 7,163 | 13,154 | 21,885 |
| Investments at cost | 207,652 | 149,082 | 114,080 |
| Land | 12,995 | ... | ... |
| Total assets | $295,873 | $309,168 | $253,401 |
| *Liabilities* | | | |
| Bank loan | $ 61,961 | $ 86,028 | $ 69,011 |
| Accounts payable | 16,744 | 32,480 | 29,591 |
| Accounts payable to securities dealers | 47,679 | 36,811 | ... |
| Employees' tax deductions | 877 | 6,870 | 3,498 |
| Taxes payable | 4,853 | ... | 7,560 |
| Loans from directors | 2,032 | ... | ... |
| Capital stock | 10,000 | 10,000 | 10,000 |
| Surplus* | 151,727 | 136,979 | 133,741 |
| Total liabilities | $295,873 | $309,168 | $253,401 |

* Surplus account will not balance with income statement because corporate income taxes and losses on sales of investments are not reflected in the profit or loss figures in Exhibit 1.
Source: Company records.

session, or control of the actual product and did not have an interest in the buyer or the seller of the product.[2] The National Food Brokers Association[3] maintained as a policy that brokers should act as sales agents only and not speculate or purchase for their own accounts, reasoning that such actions would jeopardize the fundamental relationships of broker service to both principals and accounts.

*Principals* were generally manufacturers of a processed consumer food product, such as canned peas, although some dealt in fresh produce which was also sold to canners. *Accounts* were either wholesalers who distributed to independent retail grocers, affiliated retail groups such as IGA (Independent Grocers Association) which joined together to

---

[2] These activities were prohibited in the United States by the Robinson Patman Act which made the collection of brokerage fees on one's own purchases illegal. The purpose of this provision was to prevent large buyers from owning their own brokerage operation and thereby receiving an unfair price advantage over small buyers who could not support their own brokerage operation.

[3] The association represented brokers from Canada and the United States.

**EXHIBIT 3**

## A. G. BROWN AND SON, LTD.
### Business Statistics

| | 1962 | 1963 | 1964 | 1965 | 1966 | 1967 | 1968 | 1969 |
|---|---|---|---|---|---|---|---|---|
| Growth in revenue over previous year | ... | 34% | 15% | 14% | 35% | 35% | 19% | 9% |
| Profit/revenue | ... | ... | ... | +19.6% | +17.5% | +10.1% | +0.9% | -1.3% |
| **Trial accounts or accounts with commissions of less than $1,000** | | | | | | | | |
| Number added | ... | 4 | 7 | 4 | 6 | 5 | 8 | 9 |
| Number lost* | ... | 1 | 2 | 1 | 3 | 2 | 3 | 3 |
| Total accounts | 7 | 10 | 15 | 18 | 21 | 24 | 29 | 35 |
| **Accounts with commissions of over $1,000** | | | | | | | | |
| Number added | ... | 4 | 4 | 2 | 4 | 2 | 5 | 6 |
| Number lost* | ... | 0 | 1 | 0 | 0 | 0 | 2 | 2 |
| Total accounts | 4 | 8 | 11 | 13 | 17 | 19 | 22 | 26 |
| Revenue added† | | $ 13,900 | $ 23,700 | $ 5,500 | $ 25,800 | $ 9,100 | $ 12,800 | $ 27,600 |
| Revenue lost | | 300 | 1,100 | 100 | 800 | 900 | 3,100 | 13,700 |
| Revenue for year | | 99,188 | 114,094 | 139,136 | 178,099 | 240,671 | 287,013 | 313,380 |
| Total net change§ | | +25,242 | +14,906 | +25,042 | +38,963 | +62,572 | +46,342 | +26,367 |
| **Number of employees:** | | | | | | | | |
| Salesmen | 6 | 6 | 8 | 9 | 9 | 14 | 13 | 12 |
| Office staff | 2 | 3 | 3 | 3 | 3 | 4 | 4 | 4 |

* Accounts voluntarily lost or withdrawn by seller.
† Commissions in first full year with A. G. Brown.
‡ Commissions in last year with A. G. Brown.
§ Over previous year, including growth of old accounts.
Source: All figures based on casewriter's interpretation of company-supplied data.

**EXHIBIT 4**
The Atlantic provinces: Demographic data

|  | New Brunswick | Nova Scotia | Prince Edward Island | New-foundland |
|---|---|---|---|---|
| Population (in thousands)* | | | | |
| Urban† | 312 | 439 | 40 | 267 |
| Rural | 304 | 317 | 69 | 227 |
| Total | 616 | 756 | 109 | 494 |
| Ethnic background | | | | |
| British | 55% | 71% | 80% | 94% |
| French | 39 | 12 | 17 | 4 |
| German | 1 | 6 | 1 | ... |
| Dutch | 1 | 3 | 1 | ... |
| Other | 4 | 8 | 1 | 2 |
|  | 100% | 100% | 100% | 100% |

* 1966 census.
† Living in a town or city.
Source: *Market Data*, Survey of Markets 1969.

pool their buying and merchandising power, or chain supermarkets which owned many stores. *Retailers* were the individual consumer outlets for merchandise supplied by their buying organization.

The food broker acted as a sales representative for his principals at both account and retail levels. At the account level the broker dealt with buyers or buying committees. As new principals and products were added to his line, the broker sought to have his accounts accept the products by providing samples and market data. If a product was "listed," the broker's salesmen carried samples to the retail stores to introduce it to the owners or managers and solicit orders.

If the retailer was an independent, orders taken by the salesmen were usually relayed to the wholesaler who delivered the merchandise from his inventory. Orders could also be "drop shipped" directly from inventory maintained by the principal in a public warehouse, in which case the principal billed the wholesaler who in turn billed the retailer. Wholesalers also had salesmen, but they usually took orders for only those items which a retailer needed immediately or called specifically to obtain.

If the retailer was an affiliate or part of a chain, the headquarters staff determined which products were mandatory and which were op-tional for a store and stocked most of them in its own warehouse. Store managers then ordered their requirements from this warehouse, and headquarters reordered through the broker when their supply ran low.

In addition to order taking and inventory checking, the broker's sales-men communicated information on special allowances, planned promo-

**EXHIBIT 5**

Grocery market statistics

| | B.C. | Alta. | Sask. | Man. | Ont. | P.Q. | Total | N.B. | N.S. | P.E.I. | Nfld. |
|---|---|---|---|---|---|---|---|---|---|---|---|
| | | | | | | | Maritime provinces | | | | |
| **Sales (millions)** | | | | | | | | | | | |
| 1961 | $365 | $242 | $129 | $164 | $1,399 | $1,078 | $325 | $101 | $147 | $15 | $63 |
| 1968 | 613 | 363 | 176 | 257 | 2,100 | 1,707 | 455 | 151 | 190 | 20 | 93 |
| 1969 (est.) | 650 | 398 | 180 | 273 | 2,317 | 1,794 | 471 | 154 | 202 | 21 | 94 |
| Increase, 1969/1968 | 6.1% | 9.6% | 2.7% | 5.9% | 10.3% | 5.1% | 3.6% | 1.9% | 6.2% | 2.2% | 1.5% |
| **Chains' share of sales** | | | | | | | | | | | |
| 1961 | 48.3% | 50.4% | 35.6% | 40.1% | 60.2% | 33.8% | 29.1% | 28.8% | 30.4% | 15.7% | 15.7% |
| 1968 | 59.1 | 47.9 | 47.9 | 40.4 | 62.0 | 34.4 | 31.2 | 31.7 | 36.2 | 22.0 | 22.0 |
| 1969 | 55.7 | 47.5 | 47.5 | 42.5 | 64.6 | 35.6 | 33.9 | 32.2 | 36.4 | 31.6 | 31.6 |
| Sales as a percent of total Canadian market | 10.7% | 6.5% | 3.0% | 4.5% | 38.1% | 29.5% | 7.7% | 2.5% | 3.3% | 0.3% | 1.5% |
| **Food stores** | | | | | | | | | | | |
| Chains | 252 | 108 | 82 | 105 | 1,306 | 486 | 103 | ... | ... | ... | ... |
| Groups | 744 | 805 | 454 | 609 | 2,125 | 2,860 | 412 | ... | ... | ... | ... |
| Others | 928 | 466 | 697 | 611 | 2,761 | 6,083 | 4,219 | ... | ... | ... | ... |
| No. of chains | 6 | 8 | 8 | 8 | 19 | 10 | 4 | ... | ... | ... | ... |
| No. of groups | 10 | 22 | 22 | 22 | 18 | 63 | 13 | ... | ... | ... | ... |
| No. of wholesalers | 4 | 10 | 10 | 10 | 8 | 26 | 8 | ... | ... | ... | ... |
| Population increase, 1969/1966 | 10.3% | 6.7% | 0.4% | 1.7% | 7.1% | 3.5% | n.a. | 1.3% | 0.9% | 1.3% | 4.3% |
| **Per capita PDI*** | | | | | | | | | | | |
| 1963 | $1,805 | $1,617 | $1,742 | $1,541 | $1,824 | $1,382 | n.a. | $1,081 | $1,221 | $1,047 | $ 958 |
| 1968 | 2,370 | 2,260 | 2,060 | 2,290 | 2,520 | 2,050 | n.a. | 1,640 | 1,780 | 1,490 | 1,280 |
| 1969 | 2,460 | 2,365 | 2,160 | 2,395 | 2,625 | 2,150 | n.a. | 1,735 | 1,870 | 1,570 | 1,350 |
| **Per capita FSS†** | | | | | | | | | | | |
| 1963 | $235 | $190 | $145 | $193 | $238 | $223 | n.a. | $183 | $210 | $168 | $141 |
| 1968 | 305 | 238 | 183 | 265 | 287 | 288 | n.a. | 242 | 251 | 187 | 183 |
| 1969 | 308 | 255 | 188 | 278 | 311 | 300 | n.a. | 246 | 265 | 191 | 183 |

*Personal disposable income.
†Food store sales.
n.a. = not available.
Source: *Canadian Grocer*, February 1970.

tions, and new merchandising techniques. They also constructed displays to promote their principal's products and paid close attention to perishable or easily damaged items, calling attention to unsalable ones or removing them from the shelves. Since food stores typically stocked from 4,000 to 7,000 items, the broker traditionally assisted the retailer in merchandising his store and maintaining a balanced inventory.

Some of the functions of the food broker are summarized in Exhibit 6; major product groups, special services, and potential accounts other than wholesalers and chains are listed in Exhibit 7.

**EXHIBIT 6**
**Major functions of a food broker**

*Order and control*—taking orders from a retailer and transmitting them to the account serving the retailer; taking orders from the account and transmitting them to the manufacturer; following the progress of orders in the supply pipeline.

*Creative selling*—using marketing techniques to encourage the purchase and acceptance of products.

*Product introduction*—the process of first getting an account to stock a new item and then making certain that retailers know of its existence, purpose, and availability, encouraging an initial order, and checking to be certain that it reaches the shelf.

*Promotional follow-through*—informing accounts and retailers of coming promotions, encouraging participation and cooperation, and checking at the retail level to insure adequate preparation and stocks.

*Retail display*—advising retailers on the best means to display products and encouraging them to use special fixtures, end-of-aisle, or promotional displays.

*Local-level supervision*—educating retailers and accounts to new methods of selling, promoting, pricing, and displaying; checking to ascertain that adequate inventories are on hand, that damaged or overage products are removed from the shelves.

*Establish prestige*—helping create brand images for their principals' products with accounts and retailers.

*Clerical*—assembling information as required by the accounts and principals on cost, volumes, prices, etc.

*Field reporting*—apprising principals of competitive activity directed against their products and suggesting countermeasures.

Source: National Food Brokers Association *Handbook.*

## Competitive aspects

Since one broker's products often competed with those of another broker, it might be assumed that they viewed one another as competitors. However, because a broker was seldom permitted by the principals involved to represent competing products, and because most grocery stores stocked multiple brands of an item anyway, brokers felt that their main competition came from direct sales forces, on the one hand, and private brands, on the other. The threats were very different in nature.

**EXHIBIT 7**

**Product groups, special services, and nongrocer accounts**

*Product Groups*

1. Alcoholic beverages
2. Baby foods
*3. Candy and chewing gum
*4. Cereals
*5. Coffee and tea
*6. Condiments, olives, pickles, sauces, vinegar
*7. Crackers, biscuits, cookies
*8. Dairy products, cheese, margarine
*9. Dietetic (low calorie) and health-food specialties
10. Feed, hay, grain
*11. Fish, canned
*12. Fish, other than canned or frozen
*13. Flour—barreled, sacked, packaged
*14. Food products, miscellaneous
15. Frozen foods, consumer sizes
16. Frozen foods, food service (institutional) and industrial
*17. Fruits, vegetables, juices—canned
18. Fruit, dried
19. Gourmet foods
*20. Health and beauty aids, drug products
*21. Household supplies and equipment, such as cleaning supplies, insecticides, home canning supplies, wraps
22. Industrial equipment and supplies, such as cans, cartons, and caps
23. Ingredients for industrial users
*24. Jams, jellies, honey, spreads
*25. Laundry supplies, such as soaps, detergents, bleaches, starch, softeners
*26. Meat and poultry, canned
27. Meat and poultry products, other than canned or frozen
*28. Nonfood products, miscellaneous
29. Nuts
30. Paper products
*31. Pet foods and supplies
32. Prepared foods—canned, packaged
33. Produce, fresh fruits and vegetables
*34. Salad dressings, mayonnaise
35. Salt, seasonings, spices
*36. Shortenings—solid, liquid
37. Snack foods
38. Soft drinks
39. Soft goods, such as towels, hosiery, clothing
40. Store supplies, such as bags, trays, wraps
41. Sugar
42. Vegetables, dried, such as beans, rice, peas

*Special Services*

1. Exclusive sales agent—the broker acts for one or more sellers through other brokers
2. Exporting services
*3. Importing services
4. Industrial users—broker maintains special department for sale of products to industrial users
5. Food service (institutional)—broker maintains special department for sale of products for distribution to food-service users
6. Food service (institutional): end-user service—broker maintains sales personnel available for end-user merchandising, sales service, and detail work
*7. Merchandising service—broker maintains a force of salesmen available for retail merchandising, sales service, and detail work
*8. Private-label products

*Nongrocer Accounts*

*1. Bakery and dairy supply wholesalers
*2. Candy and tobacco wholesalers
*3. Drug trade
*4. Hardware trade
5. Industrial users (bakeries, dairies, meatpackers, bottlers, other manufacturers and processors)
6. Food-service (institutional) wholesalers
7. Janitor-supply wholesalers
8. Military installations
*9. Rack merchandisers
*10. Variety and/or department store trade

*Handled by, performed by, or sold to by A. G. Brown and Son, Ltd.
Source: National Food Brokers Association *Handbook.*

Manufacturers used brokers in large part to avoid the cost of a sales force and to gain distribution rapidly through established sales organizations. In the case of a small manufacturer with one or two products, the economics were perhaps obvious, since broad distribution could be accomplished internally only with many salesmen, whose time traveling between accounts and retailers would represent a sizable expense. However, for a large multiproduct manufacturer or a manufacturer who required significant amounts of service at the retail level, the economic advantage and perhaps the effectiveness of brokers were less apparent. Some manufacturers used both direct sales forces and brokers, although not in the same region.

Conversely, a grocery chain which had its own private brand usually established direct connections with a manufacturer, supervised all activities related to selling the products, and in doing so was able to offer the line at a lower price than comparable products. Further, it was not uncommon for a chain to restrict the number of competing brands or sizes in its retail stores to give the private brand an advantage.

Thus, both seller and buyer were evaluating the cost and effectiveness of the broker's services in the context of their own marketing and distribution strategies. Complicating the broker's task were a number of trends that appeared to be gathering force in food manufacturing and retailing in the United States and Canada.

First, the product lines of many manufacturers were expanding through the introduction of new products or the acquisition of other manufacturers. This tended to increase the frequency with which a broker experienced conflicts among the products of the companies he represented. To resolve the conflict, the broker frequently had to part with some or all of one principal's business, retaining the principal which provided the greater revenues. In addition to increasing the importance to the broker of a few conglomerate manufacturers, proliferating product lines hastened the point at which direct selling became economically feasible.

Second, as competition among manufacturers for market share intensified, promotions and deals to consumers, retailers, and wholesalers multiplied dramatically. This, coupled with the proliferation of processed foods, greatly increased the complexity of the salesman's job. Proper timing and accurate communication became increasingly important since buyers were limited in the number of promotions they could execute.

Third, grocery trade publications such as *Grocery Manufacturer* reported that supermarket growth appeared to have slowed as specialty stores[4] and fast-food operations captured more of the retail food market.

---

[4] Chains of small, neighborhood stores which carried only high-turnover items such as bread and milk, usually charged lower prices than supermarkets, and usually remained open when supermarkets closed.

Moreover, traditional segments of the supermarket business such as canned goods were decreasing in importance as frozen and precooked food and nonfood items gained acceptance. These trends not only slowed the growth of the traditional lines but also created a need for new distribution and selling techniques to cope with new and often more complex transportation, storage, and display requirements.

Fourth, many supermarket operators, caught in a web of rising costs, increasing retail competition, and consumer resistance to high prices, were experiencing increasing pressure on profit margins. One response was to reduce salary expenses at the store level. The broker's salesmen frequently attempted to fill the gap by performing the duties of stock clerks, such as shelf arrangement, stock taking, and display building. In some cases, union sentiment developed against this, forcing some chains to issue "hands-off" policies to brokers. A second response was to reduce inventory levels. In 1970, several chains in the United States were reportedly testing programs and equipment which would allocate shelf space by product profitability and volume and make reordering as simple as passing a hand-held reading device over a precoded card placed on the front of the shelf. This innovation could reduce inventories, making reorders more frequent and smaller in quantity, and hasten the delisting of less profitable products.

Confronted by these and other trends, the National Food Brokers Association underscored three areas of concern to its members. The first was inadequate compensation for services. Brokers felt that sales and commissions were rising but net income was declining as principals, accounts, and retailers demanded more service. Principals resisted brokerage rate increases, telling brokers to sell more if they needed more revenue. The second was a need for better field relations and closer ties with manufacturers to aid communications. An increasing turnover in the manufacturers' field supervisors sometimes resulted in misunderstandings and broker switching when a new supervisor was unfamiliar with a broker's market situation. Thirdly, increased broker switching and more dependence on large accounts caused brokers to desire more security in the form of longer term contracts with principals.

## COMPANY OPERATIONS

A. G. Brown and Son received commissions for brokering the products of approximately 35 principals. This figure is somewhat misleading, however, because a number of the principals had very limited product lines and sales in the Maritimes. More representative was the fact that the largest seven principals accounted for about 62% of the company's revenues. While most of the principals were food manufacturers, six were in nonfood businesses ranging from hockey sticks to beauty aids and

EXHIBIT 8

A. G. BROWN AND SON, LTD.
Products and Sales Rankings of Principals

| Product | No. of items | 1969 revenues | Percent of total* | Share of market rank† | Principal advertising expenditures: rank† |
|---|---|---|---|---|---|
| Cookies, cakes, hard candy . . . . . . | 74 | $ 61,569 | 19.6 | 1 | None‡ |
| Jams and marmalade . . . . . . . . . . | 15 | 30,626 | 9.8 | 1 | § |
| Chinese foods, sauces, pickles, olives, fruit drinks, frozen cocktail snacks . . . . . . . . . . . . | 167 | 29,080 | 9.3 | 4 | None |
| Canned fruits and vegetables. . . . . . | 75 | 20,184 | 6.4 | 3 | 3 |
| Cheeses. . . . . . . . . . . . . . . . | 42 | 19,578 | 6.2 | 2 | None‡ |
| Powdered milk . . . . . . . . . . . . | 12 | 17,249 | 5.5 | 2 | 3 |
| Margarines, shortenings, and oils . . . . . . . . . . . . . . . . . . | 18 | 16,310 | 5.2 | § | § |
| Pet foods. . . . . . . . . . . . . . . | 30 | 13,310 | 4.2 | 1 | 3 |
| Tea . . . . . . . . . . . . . . . . . . | 2 | 10,000 | 3.2 | 5 | 5 |
| Liquid detergents . . . . . . . . . . . | 4 | 9,045 | 2.9 | 2 | None‡ |
| Molasses . . . . . . . . . . . . . . . | 18 | 9,027 | 2.9 | 2 | None‡ |
| Flour . . . . . . . . . . . . . . . . . | 6 | 8,881 | 2.8 | 3 | 3 |
| Batteries . . . . . . . . . . . . . . . | 27 | 7,778 | 2.5 | 2 | 1 |
| Candy bars, cocoa. . . . . . . . . . . | 22 | 7,286 | 2.3 | 3-10 | None‡ |
| Canned tuna. . . . . . . . . . . . . . | 6 | 6,309 | 2.0 | 1 | 1 |
| Beauty aids . . . . . . . . . . . . . . | 61 | 5,766 | 1.8 | 5 | None‡ |
| Australian fruits. . . . . . . . . . . . | 10 | 4,639 | 1.5 | § | § |
| Canned clams . . . . . . . . . . . . . | 4 | 4,021 | 1.3 | 3 | None ‡ |
| Cereals, snacks, cake mixes, frostings . . . . . . . . . . . . . . . | 55 | 3,832 | 1.2 | 3 | 3 |
| Canned meats and fruit juices . . . . | 29 | 3,328 | 1.1 | § | 1 |
| Honey . . . . . . . . . . . . . . . . . | 14 | 3,275 | 1.0 | 1 | None |
| Canned chicken and turkey . . . . . . | 20 | 3,158 | 1.0 | § | § |
| Household cleansers . . . . . . . . . . | 10 | 3,036 | 1.0 | § | § |
| Coffeecake . . . . . . . . . . . . . . | 25 | 2,207 | 0.7 | 1 | 1 |
| Skin creams . . . . . . . . . . . . . . | 2 | 1,735 | 0.6 | § | § |
| Mothballs, aerosol insect sprays. . . . | 60 | 1,055 | 0.3 | § | § |
| Nine others, including spaghetti and macaroni products, baby foods, soup mixes, kosher meats and fish, and salt cod . . . . . . . . | 70 | 11,096 | 3.5 | | |
| Total. . . . . . . . . . . . . . . | 878 | $313,380 | 100 | | |

\* Rounded.
† Relative ranking in terms of sales volume and advertising expenditures according to Garnet Brown. The share of market for multiproduct principals may vary by product.
‡ Competing products were advertised.
§ No estimate given.
Source: Company records.

together accounted for roughly 10% of revenues. The largest nonfood account, a line of detergents, ranked tenth in commissions with $9,045 in 1969. A description of the principals is provided in Exhibit 8. By U.S. standards, A. G. Brown could be classified as a medium-size broker in terms of retail volume, as shown in Exhibit 9, although it was thought

**EXHIBIT 9**
Comparisons of broker size

|  | Small | Medium | Large | A. G. Brown |
|---|---|---|---|---|
| Sales volume. . . . . . . . . . . . . | Under $3,000,000 | $3-7,000,000 | Over $7,000,000 | $6,300,000 |
| Average number of principals represented . . . . . . . . . . | 21.1 | 23.4 | 26.0 | 35.0 |
| Average number of items sold. . . . . . . . . . . . . . | 513 | 532 | 738 | 880 |
| Average number of items per principal. . . . . . . . . . . . | 24 | 23 | 28 | 25 |
| Average number of accounts |  |  |  |  |
| Chain headquarters* . . . . . . . | 5.2 | 6.8 | 11.8 | 17 |
| Wholesale grocers . . . . . . . . . | 17.9 | 19.7 | 25.3 | 8 |
| Institutional accounts . . . . . . . | 9.5 | 14.1 | 26.6 | 0 |
| Industrial accounts . . . . . . . . | 7.6 | 16.9 | 24.5 | 0 |
| Average staffing |  |  |  |  |
| Managers. . . . . . . . . . . . . . | 1.1 | 1.3 | 2.5 | 2.5 |
| Salesmen . . . . . . . . . . . . . | 5.0 | 7.0 | 21.3 | 12.5 |
| Clerical. . . . . . . . . . . . . . | 1.5 | 2.3 | 5.9 | 4.0 |
| Other. . . . . . . . . . . . . . . | 0.1 | 0.1 | 0.3 | 0.0 |
| Total. . . . . . . . . . . . . | 7.7 | 10.7 | 30.0 | 19.0 |

*Includes affiliated groups.
Source: *Grocery Manufacturer*, December 1969.

to be as large as the next two companies in the Maritimes combined in terms of number of salesmen.

Brokerage commission rates averaged 5% but varied from 3% to 8%, depending in part on the service required and the expected volume. In practice they were negotiated, since very few brokers or principals really knew the costs of service per dollar of sales for specific products. Mr. Brown commented:

If I can determine the sales volume expected and the number of men needed as a direct sales force, I can apply some pressure. For instance, if a manufacturer who has $120,000 in sales with one salesman wants to use a broker, I know that his current selling expense is about $12,000 or 10%, so I'll shoot for 7%.

In some cases pressure was exerted by manufacturers for reduced commissions. For instance, large principals who converted part of their production to private brands for chain stores often requested reduced brokerage rates. The company might agree to accept one half to one third of the normal commission as a means of remaining involved at a reduced level of service. Small principals who private branded, however, were requested to pay the full commission or take all of their business elsewhere. On the other hand, rarely was it possible for

A. G. Brown to secure an increase in commission rates once they had been established.

The company serviced virtually all accounts and retail outlets in the Maritime Provinces which, as shown in Exhibit 5, numbered as follows:

| Accounts | Number | Retail outlets |
|---|---|---|
| Chains . . . . . . . . . . . . | 4 | 103 |
| Affiliated groups . . . . . . . . . . | 13 | 412 |
| Wholesalers . . . . . . . . | 8 | 4,219 |

Two chains and one affiliated group were estimated to account for 60% of the sales volume of the A. G. Brown line, and one wholesaler, representing roughly 1,000 independent retailers, another 20%.

The accounts were visited regularly by Don Brown and Don Carlton, both vice presidents. Their duties were to present new products for listing, take orders from accounts, and inform the buyers of deals and secure their participation in promotions and cooperative advertising. These men also called on certain large stores in Halifax and New Brunswick. The remainder of the detail work at the retail level was performed by 10 salesmen and 2 directors.

Since about 80% of the stores were small and geographically separated, the salesmen were assigned territories as shown in Exhibit 10. Salesmen were to visit all the stores in their territory on a regular basis, take orders, inform the retailer of promotions and deals being offered by principals, and encourage the use of available merchandising materials. In practice, larger stores required more time because they stocked more items and had a higher merchandise turnover than small stores. The salesmen might visit small retailers once every six weeks but would rarely let two weeks pass without a visit to a large chain or group account store.

In the independent stores the salesman wrote a separate order for each principal. These orders were mailed to Halifax daily, where clerks typed them onto the order form of the wholesaler who handled the pricing, billing, and delivery of the merchandise. Only orders for drop shipments were taken from the chain and group retail stores and sent to the Halifax office for processing. Principals calculated the commissions due the company on the basis of retail sales. While A. G. Brown did not maintain sales records to verify the accuracy of these calculations, spot-checks in the past had revealed only minor errors.

Salesmen received a fixed salary of from $5,000 to $10,000, a car, and expenses. Mr. Brown thought that most brokers paid their salesmen

**EXHIBIT 10**
Territories of A. G. Brown salesmen

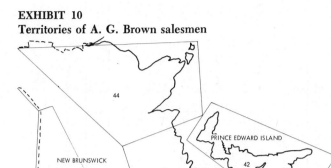

Note: Numbers refer to salesmen identified in Exhibit 13.
Source: Company records.

on commission but felt that this was an incentive to sell only the easiest lines or stores. Each salesman lived in or near his territory, visiting the Halifax office for special meetings involving large-scale promotions or the introduction of a new principal with a broad line of products.

Sales quotas, expense budgets, and revenue forecasts were not used because Mr. Brown felt that the vast differences in culture, geography, population, income, and size of stores among the territories, as well as the fact that most accounts purchased centrally but distributed widely, would make the data expensive to prepare and complicated to use. Instead, Mr. Brown used sales statistics on individual products which compared current year cumulative sales with the prior year as a means of control. The data were supplied monthly or quarterly by principals and were usually broken down by account as shown in Exhibit 11. If sales were lower than the previous year for the same period, the salesmen were asked to explain the difference and to augment their efforts. Salesmen also used these reports to encourage accounts to buy if they were lagging behind last year, or to congratulate them if they were ahead. Independent market share rating services were also used as a performance indicator.

EXHIBIT 11

## A. G. BROWN AND SON, LTD.
### Sales Summary from Principal*
Customer Sales Summary, Nine Fiscal Months to June 1970

| Wholesaler 611† product | Fiscal year to date | | | | | Current month | | | | |
|---|---|---|---|---|---|---|---|---|---|---|
| | Cases | | Percent change | Dollars | | Cases | | Percent change | Dollars | |
| | 1970 | 1969 | | 1970 | 1969 | 1970 | 1969 | | 1970 | 1969 |
| Apricot halves | 1 | | 100 | 5 | | 1 | | 100 | 5 | |
| Fruit cocktail | 98 | 83 | 18 | 587 | 492 | 9 | 8 | 13 | 72 | 67 |
| Peaches | 20 | 15 | 33 | 316 | 224 | 10 | | 100 | 77 | |
| Orange juice | 39 | 25 | 56 | 238 | 161 | 30 | | 100 | | |
| Pineapples—sliced | 200 | 195 | 3 | 2,835 | 2,845 | 30 | 53 | −43 | 393 | 861 |
| Prune nectar | 14 | 2 | 600 | 98 | 9 | | | | | |
| Peas—assorted | 150 | 135 | 11 | 981 | 796 | 30 | 25 | 30 | 201 | 163 |
| Zucchini | 5 | 5 | | 40 | 31 | | | | | |
| Spinach | 5 | 7 | −29 | 35 | 45 | 1 | 2 | −50 | 7 | 13 |
| Corn | 1 | | 100 | 4 | | 1 | | 100 | 4 | |
| Stewed tomatoes | | 5 | −100 | | 26 | | | | | |
| Customer Total | 533 | 472 | 13 | 5,139 | 4,629 | 82 | 88 | −8 | 759 | 1,104 |

*This report is typical of sales summaries received by A. G. Brown from its principals.
†Wholesaler refers to an account serviced by A. G. Brown. A. G. Brown received a similar report from the principal for each wholesaler.
Source: Company records.

## ORGANIZATION

Garnet Brown provided general supervision of all selling and administrative activities and regularly sampled the orders sent in by the salesmen. Routine supervision and training, however, were handled by the vice presidents or directors in the field. The four-man office staff reported to George Lauder. An organization chart is shown in Exhibit 12, and certain personal data on the company's employees are given in Exhibit 13.

Prior to 1965, Mr. Brown had traveled extensively in the provinces supervising salesmen and selling to accounts. That year Don Carlton and Earle Hilchey were promoted and assumed these functions for New Brunswick and Nova Scotia, respectively, and in 1966 Leo Deveaux was given the same responsibilities for Cape Breton and Newfoundland. Don Brown was promoted to vice president in 1967 and assumed the remainder of the account work in the Halifax area. Garnet Brown said:

Since 1965 my selling and travel activities have fallen off a lot, and my appearances at our accounts are mostly for public relations. Now I work most of the time with the problems of our principals and negotiate with prospective principals as they come along. Actually, I sometimes don't have enough of this work to keep me busy.

Accounts were divided among the vice presidents and directors, as Mr. Hilchey explained:

We used to communicate independently with all of the accounts. In several instances this caused mix-ups since no one knew what everyone else was doing. Now we meet regularly in the conference room to discuss new developments and keep everyone informed. In addition, our largest accounts have been put under the direct supervision of one of us.

In 1968, after several months of discussion among the management group, the decision was made to seek a general manager from outside to aid the organization in controlling its growth. His duties were to include the direct supervision of the salesmen and office staff. Caleb Benson, formerly the regional sales manager of a large U.S. food firm on the West Coast, was hired. He stayed with A. G. Brown 18 months and then left to form his own brokerage firm in Halifax. Garnet Brown described the relationship in these terms:

1967 was a very good year for our accounts, and 1968 looked as though it would be even better. We all felt that someone with experience in controlling a large sales force was needed. Everyone talked to Caleb when he was interviewed and agreed that he was the man, but somehow things got off on the wrong foot immediately after he was hired. He was a good salesman and should have been out in the territories assisting the men, but he put

**EXHIBIT 12**

A. G. BROWN AND SON, LTD.
Organization Chart

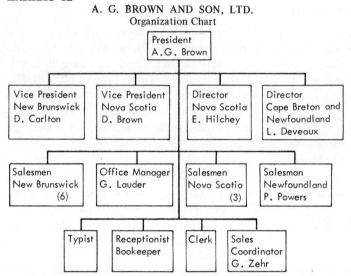

Note: Figures in parentheses refer to number of salesmen.
Source: Casewriter's notes.

his effort into building an empire here at the office. He did improve our office routines, but he wanted more responsibility, and his aggressive behavior seemed to be a source of irritation and conflict with the others.

Caleb seemed to feel superior and never really set a selling example. I backed him in what he was doing because I had brought him a long way and felt he deserved a chance. After several threats to leave, he finally quit. I think he might have been the right guy if we were in Toronto, but he was the wrong guy here.

Mr. Brown continued to feel that better field supervision was needed and was considering a new position of field supervisor to train new salesmen, monitor their performance, and insure good communications with the office. These tasks were now handled by the vice presidents and directors, but their selling activities consumed most of their time and their supervising functions tended to be a secondary concern. Mr. Carlton added:

A new salesman takes almost two years to train, with very close supervision the first six months to determine if the man can handle the job. A supervisor could increase sales by helping the salesmen learn the finer points of selling and by providing the additional knowledge which comes with experience.

Mr. Brown also agreed that a field supervisor could do much to improve sales, but he was unwilling to make an investment in the position until one or two more accounts with revenues sufficient to cover the added costs had been obtained.

**EXHIBIT 13**

## A. G. BROWN AND SON, LTD.
Personnel Data

| Name | Age | Year joined | Position | Years in present job | Previous job | Education | Salesman number* |
|---|---|---|---|---|---|---|---|
| A. Garnet Brown | 39 | 1956 | President | 5 | Salesman | High school | (39) |
| Donald Brown | 26 | 1964 | Vice president | 3 | Salesman | 1 yr. college | (52) |
| Earle Hilchey | 53 | 1960 | Director | 4 | Salesman, AGB | High school | (50) |
| Donald Carlton | 47 | 1961 | Vice president | 4 | Salesman, AGB | High school | (41) |
| Leo Deveaux | 40 | 1966 | Director | 4 | Salesman, AGB | High school | (46) |
| George Lauder | 50 | 1963 | Office manager | 5 | Salesman, AGB | Jr. high school | |
| | | | | | Royal Canadian Navy | | |
| Lorne Milburn | 29 | 1965 | Salesman | 5 | Tea salesman | High school | (45) |
| Austin Vye | 45 | 1966 | Salesman | 4 | Food salesman | High school | (42) |
| Al Reardon | 51 | 1967 | Salesman | 3 | Food sales supervisor | High school | (65) |
| Pat Powers | 44 | 1967 | Salesman | 3 | Shipyard storesman | High school | (63) |
| Wayne Devine | 30 | 1967 | Salesman | 3 | Canned milk salesman | High school | (66) |
| Bob Banks | 25 | 1969 | Salesman | 1 | Biscuit salesman | High school | (64) |
| Al Thomson | 42 | 1970 | Salesman | ½ | Biscuit salesman | High school | (44) |
| Chuck Craig | 26 | 1970 | Salesman | ½ | Floor salesman | High school | (100) |
| Keith Johnson | 59 | 1970 | Salesman | ½ | Floor salesman | High school | (53) |
| George Zehr | 40 | 1970 | Office staff | ½ | Office manager | High school | |

*To identify salesmen's territories as shown in Exhibit 10.
Source: Company records.

## GROWTH

Mr. Brown attributed the growth of the firm to several decisions he and his father had made in 1958.

Food brokerage used to be a telephone operation that ended when the owner retired or died. We also noticed that more and more large, chain-type markets which required increased service were opening. We decided to provide that service better than a manufacturer's sales force could. Since then we have put our profits into more men to upgrade our services. Our cheaper distribution is winning the battle against direct sales forces. Although advertising is being relied upon more and more to sell products to the consumer, nothing can replace a service which insures the manufacturer that his product is on the shelf.

We also decided to stay away from specialty items since the real money is in volume selling. Imports weren't attractive to us, either, since we couldn't be certain of continuing supplies. How could we tell what's going to happen to the mushroom crop in Taiwan next year or to tariff and import regulations?

As new principals were added or old principals acquired new products, salesmen had to spend more time servicing each store, thus reducing the number of stores they could cover without reducing the number of visits to each. In addition, new and larger stores were opening in many areas. Consequently, Mr. Brown continued to add new salesmen and reduce the territories of the old salesmen. He admitted, however, that measuring a salesman's capacity was difficult because of the diversity of stores and the number of products. He concluded:

Don and I try to visit the territories to sense what a man's load is and how he is performing, but we don't give this nearly enough attention. Salesmen are always complaining about something. When the complaints get loud enough, we reduce the size of the man's territory.

Mr. Brown indicated that growth beyond that of aggregate food sales meant taking principals from other brokers, displacing direct sales forces, or attracting new principals to the Maritimes. Considering the first alternative unethical, he relied on the company's reputation for performance to attract new principals. In part, Mr. Brown related the success of this policy and the ability of the company to retain principals to the business climate in the Maritimes.

We try to handle product duplications by giving the item of conflict to another broker while retaining the rest of the account. If the other broker then tries to steal the whole account from us, the manufacturer would think him a pig and probably remove the portion given to him. Business in the Maritimes isn't as cutthroat as it is in Toronto or the United States. If a manufacturer doesn't want his account split, then we have to choose who leaves.

We did lose one account because a new field manager convinced his company that he could double their current sales of $400,000 in the Maritimes by using a direct sales force. I tried to show them it would take more men than they expected, but they persisted. A year later their costs had doubled, their sales were still $400,000, and they had fired the field manager and the salesmen. They asked me to take them back, but I refused.

We also lost a big cheese manufacturer a while back because it merged with a company which had a direct sales force, but soon afterward another cheese company switched brokers to come to us.

On this last point, an A. G. Brown salesman commented that it was a little awkward to promote a new cheese as the best on the market when last month he had promoted a competitor's brand, but he felt that the stores were very appreciative of the service received from A. G. Brown. In fact, one chain delisted the principal which A. G. Brown had lost and listed the new one.

A. G. Brown stood willing to accept principals and service retail outlets without regard to size. Mr. Brown said:

We really haven't any average-type principals. Each has its own service needs. Biscuit code dates are very important, but canned goods are relatively trouble free. Our low-volume lines pay for our postage and bookkeeping. It's the overall picture that counts; we can sell all our lines at small stores and spread the cost.

On this point there was not total agreement in the company, however. Mr. Hilchey offered a rebuttal:

But small-volume lines take almost as much thought and trouble as big ones, in the sense that we are expected to do them justice. This is a distraction of a salesman's time. The same goes for stores that don't do a certain volume of business with our lines. You can go broke trying to service everybody. The mom and pop stores don't buy all of our lines anymore, and they only purchase a case at a time of what they do buy.

## RECENT OPERATING PROBLEMS

The decline in profitability had prompted Mr. Brown to seek ways of controlling expenses and holding back on expanding manpower until new principals had been secured. His efforts had been complicated in recent months by the loss of a large principal through merger and the addition of a comparably sized principal which wanted to switch from a direct sales force to a broker. To obtain the latter, however, A. G.

Brown agreed to hire three of the principal's salesmen. Garnet Brown summarized the problem as follows:

I don't know a lot about accounting, but I do know that our expenses are continually rising. Take car expense. I've tried leasing and owning, but both seem about as expensive to me. Our population has remained fixed while our principals want more service. We can't raise our brokerage percentage because of contracts, so we have to add new principals to keep up.

Another aspect of the problem was the increasing paperwork requested by manufacturers and accounts. For instance, Mr. Hilchey had recently been asked by an account to prepare a summary report on scheduled promotions and deals, including their timing and duration, costs, discounts, and cooperative allowances. The report took several hours to prepare and was supposedly a one-time affair, but Mr. Hilchey indicated that the account might now expect it routinely.

## OPPORTUNITIES

In addition to considering means of controlling costs, Mr. Brown was evaluating several opportunities for increasing revenues. The first involved the addition of a principal new to the Maritimes, whose only product, canned shrimp, was expected to reach $250,000 in volume. The commission was expected to be about 5%. Since the product did not conflict with any of the items currently represented by the company, accepting it appeared to present few difficulties.

The second opportunity was of greater significance. Mr. Brown had explored in a very preliminary way the possibility of representing a large, narrow-line manufacturer currently selling about $1,000,000 in the Maritimes through a direct sales force. He elaborated on this prospect:

From the number of men this company has in the field, I know they must be spending at least $100,000 distributing their line. And they aren't doing as well as they might, either. If they came with us, I think we could increase their sales by 20% because we have twice as many men in the field. What's more, our lines don't conflict. If they came with us, I would hire three new men and could then have two sales supervisors and another salesman.

Third, additional revenues could be sought from institutional or non-food lines. Mr. Brown was skeptical of the frozen foods and institutional areas because they involved troublesome aspects, such as refrigeration and time wasted chasing dietitians, but he was working to establish a split-representation system with a manufacturer of ethical and non-ethical drugs. The manufacturer had approached him with the proposition that A. G. Brown's salesmen service grocery stores with the nonethicals, such as cold syrups and cough drops, while the manufacturer's salesmen detailed the ethical drugs to doctors and pharmacies. A volume of about $100,000 with a 5% fee for brokerage was expected. Although he had not previously considered selling such items, Mr. Brown commented, "Until Berec approached me last year, I never considered selling batteries, either."

Manufacturing was a fourth area under consideration. Mr. Brown knew of a prominent local food manufacturer with a large market share in the Maritimes and sales and profits of roughly $2 million and $20,000, respectively. He felt that the company was overburdened with expenses and that, were he able to buy it, the salaries of the owner and three of the managers estimated to total about $60,000 could be saved. In addition, by disbanding the direct sales force in favor of A. G. Brown, he maintained that substantial reductions could also be achieved in selling costs, thought to be currently on the order of $125,000 a year. Mr. Brown had one important reservation in this case, however. A. G. Brown had begun representing a competing imported product recently introduced in the Maritimes. Sales had grown to nearly $200,000 which Mr. Brown attributed to a retail price about 4% lower and a package 20% larger in content than competing brands. He was uncertain whether the favorable response traditionally accorded local products could withstand this differential.

A final opportunity was private labeling. Although he did not like to be dependent on imports, Mr. Brown was negotiating with an English producer of jams and jellies from whom he could purchase a quality product at a price substantially below that of existing brands. He felt that the manufacturer would finance his inventory and that, perhaps through a separate corporation, he could net 5% on sales after all expenses. Should imports be cut off for some reason, he was confident that a source of preserves could be located in Canada. With the A. G. Brown reputation and access to the food markets, Mr. Brown estimated that $200,000 could be sold the first year.

## A PERSONAL ADDENDUM

The Brown family had been natives of Halifax for several generations. Having been a local sports personality and a successful businessman, Garnet Brown felt an obligation to the community and expressed a desire to devote some of his energy to civic affairs. Within the last five years he had become active in politics and had been elected in July 1969 to the Legislative Assembly of Nova Scotia as a Liberal member. He recounted his involvement:

I had always been in the organizational end of politics until last year. Elections were approaching then, and we didn't have a candidate. I ran because there wasn't anyone else. It takes some time, but I don't curl or belong to a home or school association, so I have no other outlets aside from the business. Being an opposition member makes it that much easier since we don't have executive or administrative responsibilities. We could very possibly win a majority in the next election, though: a change of only 4% in voting patterns could give us a landslide. Since I'm one of five opposition members in the legislature now, I suppose I would be considered for the cabinet in a Liberal government.

# The Marlin Firearms Company

THE MARLIN FIREARMS COMPANY, founded by New Haven gunsmith John Marlin in 1870, was nearly defunct when Frank Kenna purchased it at auction for $100 and the assumption of a $100,000 mortgage in 1924. From those precarious beginnings, the Kenna family had succeeded in revitalizing the company.

Sales for 1969 were $13.6 million, equal to nearly three times the 1959 sales volume. Since 1959, net income had increased by as much as 650% to $748,000 in 1967, but in 1969 a net income of only $269,000 was recorded, partially as a result of Marlin's recent move into a new plant in North Haven, Connecticut. The new facilities were designed to increase significantly Marlin's manufacturing capacity and thereby its sales and earnings potential. As evidence of this, sales for the first six months of 1970 were $8.8 million and profits after taxes of $340,000 were posted. (For financial data, see Exhibits 1, 2, and 3.)

Despite a new factory and the hope of continued growth, Marlin's corporate horizon was not cloudless. Imports which threatened Marlin's competitive position in the marketplace were one source of concern. Marlin had recently spent more than five years developing a centerfire, bolt-action, high-powered rifle designed to compete in the high-price end of the market. It was considered by management to be an excellent rifle, but in 1967 Mauser rifles from Spain, Argentina, Finland, and Sweden flooded U.S. markets. As a consequence, Marlin had postponed plans to sell the rifle until after July 1971 when a new pump-action shotgun was scheduled for introduction.

EXHIBIT 1

## THE MARLIN FIREARMS COMPANY
### Condensed Comparative Statements of Income
### For the Years Ended December 31

| | 1966 | 1967 | 1968 | 1969 | 6 mos. 1970* |
|---|---|---|---|---|---|
| Net sales | $11,334,318 | $12,558,056 | $14,563,346 | $13,578,915 | $8,758,839 |
| Less: Cost of goods sold | 7,523,710 | 8,295,897 | 9,808,448 | 9,354,900 | 6,007,005 |
| Gross profit | $ 3,810,608 | $ 4,262,159 | $ 4,754,898 | $ 4,224,015 | $2,751,834 |
| Less: Selling expenses | $ 1,625,318 | $ 1,762,560 | $ 1,925,401 | $ 1,904,775 | $1,135,480 |
| General and administrative expenses | 393,551 | 463,241 | 573,628 | 648,107 | 237,147 |
| Operating profit | $ 1,791,739 | $ 2,036,358 | $ 2,255,869 | $ 1,671,133 | $1,379,207 |
| Other income | | | | | |
| Miscellaneous | $ 28,122 | $ 11,431 | $ 20,106 | $ 8,694 | $ 15,286 |
| Gain on sale of equipment | ..... | 260 | ..... | ..... | 500 |
| Total other income | $ 28,122 | $ 11,691 | $ 20,106 | $ 8,694 | $ 15,786 |
| Other expenses | | | | | |
| Contributions | $ 14,436 | $ 12,140 | $ 9,975 | $ 21,693 | $ 1,548 |
| Sale of equipment—loss | $ 1,127 | ..... | 60 | ..... | ..... |
| Employees pension plan | 142,057 | 144,732 | 146,373 | 74,832 | 75,000 |
| Interest | 88,494 | 148,432 | 173,432 | 428,426 | 300,883 |
| Total other expenses | $ 246,114 | $ 305,304 | $ 329,840 | $ 524,951 | $ 377,431 |
| Profit before depreciation | $ 1,573,747 | $ 1,742,745 | $ 1,946,135 | $ 1,154,876 | $1,017,562 |
| Depreciation | 186,053 | 246,223 | 324,049 | 489,824 | 271,920 |
| Profit before prior years' expenses | $ 1,387,694 | $ 1,496,522 | $ 1,622,086 | $ 665,052 | $ 745,642 |
| Less: Prior years' sales commissions | ..... | ..... | 49,813 | ..... | ..... |
| Profit before taxes | $ 1,387,694 | $ 1,496,522 | $ 1,572,273 | $ 665,052 | $ 745,642 |
| Less: State and federal taxes | 670,736 | 748,144 | 850,254 | 151,505 | 405,735 |
| Income before extraordinary items | $ 716,958 | $ 748,378 | $ 722,019 | 513,547 | $ 339,907 |
| Extraordinary item—cost of relocation of plant facilities, net of federal income tax benefit of $273,851 | ..... | ..... | ..... | 244,807 | ..... |
| Net profit | $ 716,958 | $ 748,378 | $ 722,019 | $ 268,740 | 339,907 |

* Comparable figures not available for June 30, 1969.
Source: Company records.

**EXHIBIT 2**

## THE MARLIN FIREARMS COMPANY
### Condensed Comparative Balance Sheets

| Assets | For the years ended December 31 | | | | For six months ended June 30 | |
|---|---|---|---|---|---|---|
| | 1966 | 1967 | 1968 | 1969 | 1969 | 1970 |
| **Current assets** | | | | | | |
| Cash and equivalent | $1,612,778 | $1,226,981 | $ 775,426 | $ 330,099 | $ 1,087,331 | $ 274,889 |
| Accounts receivable (net) | 2,088,012 | 2,597,507 | 2,922,695 | 3,339,440 | 6,218,669 | 7,416,214 |
| Accounts receivable (U.S. gov't) | | | ...... | 482,587* | ...... | ...... |
| Inventories | 2,143,644 | 2,180,528 | 2,470,469 | 4,286,918 | 3,166,213 | 3,999,358 |
| Prepaid expenses | 25,333 | 28,366 | 93,835 | 136,421 | 108,033 | 114,332 |
| Total current assets | $5,869,767 | $6,033,382 | $ 6,262,425 | $ 8,575,465 | $10,580,246 | $11,804,793 |
| **Fixed assets** | $1,924,239 | $2,374,021 | $ 5,029,317 | $ 8,223,567 | $ 6,888,424 | $ 8,241,528 |
| Less: Reserve for depreciation | 817,252 | 1,017,335 | 1,110,833 | 1,271,703 | 1,366,872 | 1,347,289 |
| Net fixed assets | $1,106,987 | $1,356,686 | $ 3,918,484 | $ 6,951,864 | $ 5,521,552 | $ 6,894,239 |
| **Other assets** | | | | | | |
| Cash surrender value—life insurance | $ 65,727 | $ 97,300 | $ 132,091 | $ 145,084 | $ 131,227 | $ 163,770 |
| Accounts receivable—long term | 369,978 | 401,173 | 493,727 | 338,470 | 529,435 | 997,790 |
| Miscellaneous assets | 12,521 | 24,607 | 24,180 | 23,360 | 5,118 | 108,896 |
| Trademarks | 355 | 355 | 355 | 355 | 355 | 355 |
| Total other assets | $ 448,581 | $ 523,435 | $ 650,353 | $ 507,269 | $ 666,135 | $ 1,270,811 |
| Total assets | $7,425,335 | $7,913,503 | $10,831,262 | $16,034,598 | $16,767,933 | $19,969,843 |

**EXHIBIT 2** (continued)

|  | For the years ended December 31 | | | | For six months ended June 30 | |
|  | 1966 | 1967 | 1968 | 1969 | 1969 | 1970 |
|---|---|---|---|---|---|---|
| **Capital and Liabilities** | | | | | | |
| **Current liabilities** | | | | | | |
| Notes payable—bank | $ ..... | $ ..... | $ ..... | $ 1,980,000 | $ 4,300,000 | $ 4,880,000 |
| Notes payable—stockholders | 74,714 | 48,607 | 48,607 | 70,500 | 48,607 | 48,607 |
| Accounts payable | 686,993 | 656,646 | 1,642,609 | 1,693,129 | 934,207 | 1,915,755 |
| Accrued liabilities | 270,662 | 264,900 | 393,333 | 688,405 | 452,945 | 1,079,113 |
| Accrued taxes | 498,966 | 373,277 | 400,921 | 52,126 | 401,834 | 405,735 |
| Dividends payable | 5,985 | 5,977 | 5,919 | ..... | ..... | ..... |
| Total current liabilities | $1,537,320 | $1,349,407 | $ 2,491,389 | $ 4,484,160 | $ 6,137,593 | $ 8,329,210 |
| **Other liabilities** | | | | | | |
| Mortgage payable | $ ..... | $ ..... | $ 850,000 | $ 3,120,000 | $ 2,324,000 | $ 3,120,000 |
| Deferred income—contracts (net)† | 1,808,402 | 1,853,886 | 2,247,922 | 2,173,700 | 2,533,590 | 2,249,748 |
| Notes payable—stockholders | 231,460 | 208,960 | 110,957 | 37,048 | 83,244 | 27,808 |
| Loans—affiliated companies | 21,556 | ..... | ..... | ..... | ..... | ..... |
| Deferred income taxes | ..... | ..... | ..... | 590,909 | ..... | 271,324 |
| Total other liabilities | $2,061,418 | $2,062,846 | $ 3,208,879 | $ 5,921,657 | $ 4,940,834 | $ 5,668,880 |
| **Capital and surplus** | | | | | | |
| Preferred stock, 4%, $25 par | $ 172,375 | $ 172,375 | $ 172,375 | $ 172,375 | $ 172,375 | $ 172,375 |
| Common stock, 120,000 shares issued | 300,000 | 2,907,500 | 2,907,500 | 2,907,500 | 2,907,500 | 2,907,500 |
| Surplus | 3,415,865 | 1,690,143 | 2,320,512 | 2,592,749 | 2,653,474 | 2,937,520 |
| Less: Treasury stock, 4,000 shares | 61,643 | 268,768 | 269,393 | 43,843 | 43,843 | 45,642 |
| Net worth | $3,826,597 | $4,501,250 | $ 5,130,994 | $ 5,628,781 | $ 5,689,506 | $ 5,971,753 |
| Total capital and liabilities | $7,425,335 | $7,913,503 | $10,831,262 | $16,034,598 | $16,767,933 | $19,969,843 |

\* Investment credit and tax refunds.
† Marlin Industrial Division two-year contracts to be fulfilled.
Source: Company records.

**EXHIBIT 3**

THE MARLIN FIREARMS COMPANY
Other Financial Data

| | | | Year ended | | | First 6 months | |
|---|---|---|---|---|---|---|---|
| | | 1966 | 1967 | 1968 | 1969 | 1969 | 1970 |
| I. | *Financial ratios* | | | | | | |
| | A. Measures of profitability | | | | | | |
| |    1. Gross profit/sales | .336 | .340 | .327 | .311 | n.a. | .314 |
| |    2. Operating profit/sales | .158 | .160 | .155 | .124 | n.a. | .157 |
| |    3. Income before extraordinary | | | | | | |
| |      items/sales | .063 | .060 | .050 | .038 | n.a. | .039 |
| |    4. Return on net worth | .187 | .166 | .141 | .048 | n.a. | .057 |
| | B. Measures of current position | | | | | | |
| |    1. Current assets/current | | | | | | |
| |      liabilities | 3.800 | 4.500 | 2.500 | 1.800 | 1.700 | 1.400 |
| |    2. Accounts receivable/sales | .180 | .210 | .200 | .250 | n.a. | .840 |
| |    3. Inventories/sales | .190 | .170 | .170 | .320 | n.a. | .460 |
| II. | *Funds flow: 1966–69 (millions)* | | | | | | |

| Sources | | Uses | |
|---|---|---|---|
| Cash | $0.8 | Accounts receivable | $1.2 |
| Accounts payable | 1.0 | Inventories | 2.1 |
| Bank notes payable | 1.9 | Other | 0.1 |
| Long-term debt | 3.1 | Fixed assets | 5.9 |
| Contracts | 0.3 | Notes payable | 0.2 |
| Deferred taxes | 0.6 | | $9.5 |
| Retained earnings | 1.8 | | |
| | $9.5 | | |

n.a. = not available.
Source: Exhibits 1 and 2.

Recently Marlin had been confronted by a new threat from one of its old competitors, The Browning Arms Company. In 1967 Browning, long an importer of firearms sold under its own name, had introduced a .22-caliber, lever-action rifle made in Japan that competed directly with one of Marlin's best-selling rifles, the Model 39. By capitalizing on low manufacturing labor costs and marketing directly to retail gun dealers, Browning had been able to price the rifle at $75, compared to a list price of $94.95 for the Model 39. Marlin management was particularly concerned because they considered the Browning gun to be a high-quality product.

The issue of gun-control legislation had aroused additional concern. The "Commission Statement on Firearms and Violence" of July 28, 1969, written by the National Commission on the Causes and Prevention of Violence, stated:

After extensive study, we find that the availability of guns contributes substantially to violence in American society. Firearms, particularly handguns, facilitate the commission and increase the danger of the most violent crimes—assassination, murder, robbery, and assault. The widespread availability of guns can also increase the level of violence associated with civil disorder. Firearms accidents, while they account for only a small percentage of all accidents, cause thousands of deaths and injuries. . . .

The challenge for this Commission—and for the nation as a whole—is to find ways to cope with illegitimate uses of guns without at the same time placing undue restrictions on legitimate uses. We believe this is possible if both the advocates and the opponents of gun-control legislation will put aside their suspicions and preconceptions, accept the fact of a common danger without exaggerating its dimensions, and act for the common good.

It was clear to Marlin management that the Federal Gun Control Act of 1968 had not completely settled the issue of gun control. State and local gun-control legislation was anticipated across the country in a variety of forms. However, as only the fourth ranking manufacturer of long arms (rifles and shotguns) in the United States, Marlin did not feel it had the resources to lead any movement against gun-control legislation at either the federal, state, or local level.

Despite these problems, Marlin's president, Frank Kenna, Jr., was optimistic in July of 1970:

As far as the issue of gun-control legislation goes, I think it is just about over except in the pistol field. As a manufacturer of shoulder arms, Marlin has not been severely affected by gun-control legislation.

With regard to foreign competition, I think it is good for us. As yet, we don't really know how seriously the Japanese-made .22 rifle will affect our sales, but we have prepared a defensive move.

One thing the recessions of 1958, 1960, and now 1968–70 have shown me is that Marlin is nearly recession-proof. In 1966, when I saw we were nearly at capacity in our old plant, I decided to build a new one. We moved in June 1969 and now have the room to expand our production. Before, our sales were limited by capacity, but now sales should increase again. My objective is at least 10% growth in sales per year. You need at least that to keep even with inflation.

Actually, for the growth I foresee in the firearms industry, Marlin is probably undercapitalized; therefore we need to go public, and I would like to do it soon. This would be in the form of a primary rather than a secondary offering with the purpose being heavy acquisition of numerically controlled machines. Even though equity market conditions are currently poor, we've had our 1969 financial statements audited by one of the very best national auditing firms. This is all in preparation for going public.

## THE INDUSTRY

The firearms industry was one of the nation's oldest, dating back to 1798 when Eli Whitney first demonstrated the feasibility of mass production by developing interchangeable musket parts. The industry was characterized by a few major segments: handguns, long arms, ammunition, and accessories.

The Sporting Arms and Ammunition Manufacturers' Institute (SAAMI) reported that domestic wholesale shipments of nonmilitary arms and ammunition totaled $253 million in 1967 and $158 million in the first six months of 1968. Handgun sales accounted for about 8%; long arms, 45% (rifles, 25%, shotguns, 20%); and ammunition 47% of these totals.

Approximate figures for gun sales for 1967 are reflected below (value and units in millions):

| | Domestic shipments* | | Imports (units) | Total (units) |
|---|---|---|---|---|
| | *Value* | *Units* | | |
| Handguns . . . . . . . . | $ 19.5 | .45 | 1.20 | 1.65 |
| Rifles. . . . . . . . . . . | 63.2 | 1.52 | .26 | 1.78 |
| Shotguns. . . . . . . . . | 49.6 | .97 | .28 | 1.25 |
| | $132.3 | 2.94 | 1.74 | 4.68 |

\* Excludes shipments to government agencies. Industry observers felt this to be significant only in the case of handguns sold to law enforcement agencies.

In the long-arms segment, four manufacturers, three of them owned or controlled by larger companies, were thought by industry observers to account for roughly 80% of domestic sales.

| *Manufacturer* | *Parent company* | Approximate market share |
|---|---|---|
| Winchester-Western | Olin Corporation | 24% |
| Remington Arms | DuPont (owning 60%) | 24 |
| Savage Arms | Emhart Corporation | 17 |
| Marlin Firearms | . . . | 15 |

(Additional information on these and other long-arms manufacturers is provided in Exhibit 4.) In the handgun segment, the Colt Firearms Division of Colt Industries; Smith and Wesson, a division of Bangor Punta; and Sturm-Ruger were the acknowledged leaders in sales. Winchester-Western and Remington were thought to account for about 75% of ammunition sales.[1] At present, none of the large firearms manufacturers dealt heavily in government contracts for shoulder arms.

---

[1] Federal Cartridge Co. was in third place, specializing in private label ammunition for K-Mart, Montgomery Ward, Western Auto, and Sears, Roebuck.

**EXHIBIT 4**
Marlin's principal competitors in long-arms sales (in thousands)

| Manufacturer | 1968-69 sales | 1968-69 Net income | 1968-69 Total assets | Rimfire rifles | Centerfire rifles | Shotguns | Handguns | Telescopic sights, traps, accessories | Ammunition | Hunting clothing | Leisure time equipment | Tools, hardware | Other |
|---|---|---|---|---|---|---|---|---|---|---|---|---|---|
| Browning Arms Company | $ 42,621 | $ 1,262 | $ 34,712 | x | x | x | x | | | x | a | | |
| Emhart Corporation | 239,550 | 13,876 | 183,322 | x | x | x | | x | | | | | b |
| Savage Arms Division | n.a. | n.a. | n.a. | x | x | x | | | | | | | |
| Leisure Group, Inc. | 39,694 | 1,678 | 52,967 | | | | | | | | c | | |
| High Standard Division | n.a. | n.a. | n.a. | x | | | x | | | | | | |
| Marlin Firearms Company | 14,563 | 722 | 10,831 | x | x | x | | x | | | | | |
| O. F. Mossberg & Sons | n.a. | n.a. | n.a. | x | x | x | | | | | | | |
| Olin Mathieson | 1,156,896 | 50,342 | 1,078,108 | x | | | | | x | | | | |
| Winchester-Western Division | 238,200 | 11,400 | n.a. | x | x | x | | x | x | x | | d | e |
| Remington Arms Company | 129,499 | 12,834 | 11,281 | x | x | x | x | x | x | x | | f | |
| Sturm-Ruger | 9,068 | 1,401 | 8,803 | x | x | | x | | | | | g | |

a Archery equipment and boats.
b Employee Communication-Motivational Service.
c Camping equipment, skis.
d Cartridge-activated fastening tools.
e Hunting and fishing, travel agency services, safari lodges in East Africa, and high-quality books, art, films about outdoors.
f Chain saws, abrasive cutting tools, and powder-metal parts.
g Castings and winches.
n.a. = not available.
Source: Moody's Industrial Listings.

**Products**

Prices of firearms were dependent upon the quality of materials, product features, workmanship, styling, and accessories. Mass-produced guns ranged in price from $25 to $500, while at the extreme end of the spectrum the Ithaca Ejector Grade custom shotgun sold for $4,500. In the 1971 edition of *The Shooter's Bible,* handgun prices averaged $100, ranging from $38 for a six-shot .22-caliber pistol to $335 for a Browning Gold Medalist .22-caliber target pistol. Rimfire rifles[2] ranged in price from $25 to $335, with an average of $60. Centerfire, or "high-power" rifles,[3] requiring heavier materials and more machining, averaged $150, with prices ranging from $35 to $1,363. Shotguns were the most expensive sporting guns made. Although prices started as low as $34, most shotguns sold for about $200. (For price data by market segments see Exhibit 5.)

Remington was generally regarded as the leader in production engineering and product development. For example, nylon parts which were both durable and self-lubricating had been developed first by Remington. In 1956, they introduced a .22-caliber semiautomatic rifle with a nylon butt stock. After considerable consumer and dealer advertising, the rifle had become the best-selling .22 automatic on the market, according to industry sources. Remington also attempted to introduce plastic butt stocks on their bolt-action rifles, but poor market acceptance prompted a return to wooden stocks. Other companies had been less successful with new product innovations. Winchester, for instance, had attempted to popularize rifles with plastic sights and cast-metal actions instead of traditional machined actions. Although the economics of such construction were significant, the rifles never sold well and eventually were removed from Winchester's product line.

In part, product innovation was being forced on the industry by rising labor and material costs and the diminishing number of skilled gunsmiths in the country. Manufacturers were turning more and more to automated assembly lines and numerically controlled milling machines, routers, and wood carving machines.

Despite recent efforts to introduce new models and manufacturing innovations, gun making remained steeped in tradition. Patent infringement suits were almost nonexistent because gun mechanisms had remained virtually unchanged for many years. Those patents that were issued were generally very restricted. For example, Marlin's "time-honored" Model 39 was first designed in 1893. It had been modified

---

[2] Almost all rimfire rifles were .22-caliber arms suited mainly for target shooting and hunting small game.

[3] Although some centerfire rifles were .22 caliber, most were larger caliber; and centerfire cartridges, regardless of bullet size, typically had several times the power and range of rimfire ammunition.

**EXHIBIT 5**

**1970–71 Gun models by manufacturer**

| | Rifles | | | | | | | | Shotguns | | | | Handguns | | | | Total long arms | Total all guns |
|---|---|---|---|---|---|---|---|---|---|---|---|---|---|---|---|---|---|---|
| | Rimfire | | | | Centerfire | | | | | | | | | | | | | |
| Manufacturer | $0–$59.99 | $60–$149.99 | $150–$299.99 | $300+ | $0–$59.99 | $60–$149.99 | $150–$299.99 | $300+ | $0–$59.99 | $60–$149.99 | $150–$299.99 | $300+ | $0–$59.99 | $60–$149.99 | $150–$299.99 | $300+ | | |
| Armalite | 1 | | | | | | 1 | | | | | | | | | | 2 | 2 |
| Beretta | | | | | | | | | | | | | | 4 | | | .. | 4 |
| Bernardelli | | | | | | | | | | | 2 | 2 | | | | | 4 | 4 |
| Brescia | | | | | | | | | | | 1 | | | | | | 1 | 1 |
| Browning | | 6 | 1 | | | | 8 | 2 | | | 12 | 10 | | 5 | 1 | | 39 | 46 |
| Charter | | | | | | | | | | | | | | 2 | 7 | | .. | 9 |
| Colt | 2 | | | | | | | | | | | | | 22 | 7 | | 2 | 31 |
| Darne | | | | | | | | | | | | 3 | | | | | 3 | 3 |
| Davidson | | | | | | | | | | 2 | | | | | | | 2 | 2 |
| Franchi | 2 | | | | | | | | | | 11 | 17 | | | | | 30 | 30 |
| Galef-BSA | | | | | | 5 | | | | | | 1 | | | | | 9 | 9 |
| H & R | 4 | 1 | | | 1 | 1 | | | 2 | 3 | 3 | | 8 | 5 | | | 20 | 33 |
| High Standard | 2 | 1 | | | | | | | 4 | 9 | 5 | | 3 | 14 | | | 20 | 37 |
| Intercontinental | | | | | | | | | | 3 | | | | 3 | | | .. | 3 |
| Ithaca | 2 | | | | | 2 | | | 3 | 5 | 13 | 8 | | | | | 34 | 34 |
| Iver Johnson | | | | | | | | | | | | | 9 | | | | .. | 9 |
| Krieghoff | | | | | | | | | | | | 5 | | | | | 5 | 5 |
| Llama | | | | | | | | | | | | | | 7 | | | .. | 7 |
| Mannlicher | | | | | | | | | | | | | | | | | .. | .. |
| Schoenauer | | | | | | | 3 | | | | | | | | | | 3 | 3 |

| | | | | | | | | | | | | | | |
|---|---|---|---|---|---|---|---|---|---|---|---|---|---|---|
| Marlin* | 8 | 4 | 4 | | | | 1 | | 1 | | | 1 | | 15 | 15 |
| Mossberg | 13 | 4 | 1 | 7 | | 8 | | 13 | 5 | | 3 | 1 | | 42 | 42 |
| Remington | 9 | 10† | 6 | 9 | | 4 | 4 | 5 | | 1 | | | 10 | 54 | 55 |
| Ruger | 1 | 1 | 3 | 1 | | | 2 | | | 34 | | | | 14 | 26 |
| Savage/Anschutz | | 1 | 8 | 7 | | 2 | 6 | | | 1 | | | | 31 | 31 |
| Savage | 14 | 5 | | 2 | | | 2 | 2 | | 4 | | 5 | | 13 | 13 |
| Savage-Fox | | 6 | | | | | 1 | | | | | | | 17 | 17 |
| Savage & Stevens | | | | | | | | | | | | | | 4 | 4 |
| Dan Wesson | | | | | | | | | | | | | | · | 1 |
| Smith & Wesson | | | 5 | | | | | 1 | | | | | | 5 | 44 |
| Stallion | | | | | | | | | | | | | | · | 1 |
| Steyr-Mannlicher | | | 8 | | 4 | | | | | | | | | 12 | 12 |
| Stoeger | | | | | | | 1 | | | | | | | 1 | 5 |
| Tradewinds | | | | | | | | | | | | | | | |
| Husqvarna | | | 2 | 2 | | | | | | | | | | 2 | 2 |
| Universal | 3 | | 3 | | | | | | | | | | | 6 | 6 |
| Winslow | | | | 4 | | | | | | | | | | 4 | 4 |
| Weatherby | | 1 | 2 | | 2 | | | | | | | | | 5 | 5 |
| Winchester | 9 | 5 | 8 | 2 | 2 | 8 | | | | | | | | 61 | 61 |
| Total | 63 | 40 | 68 | 24 | 27 | 49 | 81 | 55 | 7 | 23 | 113 | 12 | 1 | 460 | 609 |

\* Glenfield models excluded.
† Includes two 5-millimeter models; otherwise, all rimfire rifles use .22-caliber ammunition.

Source: *1971 Shooter's Bible*, published by Stoeger Arms.

only slightly since then and was advertised as a "direct descendent of the Model 1891," Marlin's first .22 rifle made in 1891.

## Distribution

Most of the firearms manufacturers, including Marlin, sold guns through a two-tier distribution system. After paying an excise tax of 11%[4] on the factory price, the manufacturers sold to jobbers who, in turn, sold to retailers. Jobbers received a markup of 20% on wholesale price, and dealers typically received a markup of 25% on retail price. Direct sales to large department stores and discount chain stores were also made by the manufacturers, and private-label guns were produced for some large retail chains.

A few manufacturers such as Colt Firearms, Browning, and Ithaca Gun Company did not rely on jobbers. By "selling direct," the jobber's margin was eliminated and lower prices were possible, but the manufacturer then had to contend with a larger number of accounts. For instance, Browning had 4,000 retail dealer accounts and Colt had about 10,000 compared to 300 jobber accounts maintained by Marlin. Dealers were generally not large enough to stock significant inventories; as a result, in addition to the risk of dealer stockouts, gun orders were small and frequent, causing high freight charges per gun.

## Market growth

Some observers maintained that increasing urbanization would cause shotgun sales to grow faster than rifle sales. With shorter ranges than rifles, shotguns, they argued, would be more suitable for increasingly fewer and more crowded hunting areas. However, the fastest growing segment of the long-arms market had been centerfire rifles. Total unit production had increased 180% from 1960 to 1967, while rimfire production had increased 93% and shotgun production had risen only 90%. It was suggested by one executive that conservation funds and road-building programs were responsible for opening up and making accessible new hunting areas across the country. This, he pointed out, would cause an increased demand for both centerfire and rimfire rifles.

The National Commission on the Causes and Prevention of Violence estimated the number of firearms in civilian hands in the United States to be 90 million: 35 million rifles, 31 million shotguns, and 24 million

---

[4] The 11% excise tax (10% for handguns) had been imposed on the firearms industry to make funds available for conservation and game preservation. The money was turned over directly to the U.S. Wildlife Institute of Washington, D.C. Importers also paid the 11% "manufacturing tax" *after* a 20% import duty and $3.50 tax per gun had been paid on the landed price of a gun.

handguns. Most firearms owners were thought to own more than a single gun. According to Attorney Mark Benenson:

> Spot checks suggest that NRA club members may own an average of 12 rifles and shotguns, and that nonclub members may own an average of 6 rifles and shotguns. Hunters generally own at least three guns—a .22 rifle, a high-power rifle, and a shotgun. Other citizens also frequently have more than one firearm.[5]

## Gun-control legislation

The issue of gun controls was a sharply divisive one, polarizing nearly all participants; one was either *for* gun control or *against* it—there was no middle ground for most people. As a result, the recent debate over gun-control legislation had often been based on emotional rather than logical argument. In a May 1968 editorial, *Life* magazine contended that a gun law would be "a step toward sanity."

After Robert Kennedy was assassinated in June 1968, *Life* vigorously attacked the National Rifle Association (NRA) and called for stringent gun controls:

> . . . Congressmen and senators now find their mailboxes filled with a volume of letters to match the numbers that the taxfree National Rifle Association routinely produces for its own million members whenever the hint of regulation is in the air. The level of argument used by the gun lobby is evident in the remarks of NRA president, Harold Glassen: "We are witnessing an almost unbelievable phenomenon in America. We see Americans behaving like children, parroting nonsense, accepting unproved theory as fact and reacting as the German people did in the 1930s as the Goebbels propaganda mill drilled lies into their subconsciousness and dictated their every move."
>
> . . . We favor the registration of all firearms, long or short. The NRA has done a good job of persuading its members that registration is the first step toward confiscation of all weapons. Nonsense. Americans register, among other things, their autos, their dogs, and the births of their children. Yet confiscation of cars, cocker spaniels, or infants has never been a great problem.

Varying degrees of effectiveness were ascribed to gun-control laws. New York State's Sullivan Law, passed in 1911 and regarded as one of the strongest laws, made it illegal to purchase or own a handgun without a police permit. However, some observers pointed out that the law was rendered useless by the lack of similar controls in the bordering states of Connecticut and New Jersey. Meaningful action, they felt, was possible only at the federal level.

---

[5] Mark K. Benenson, "Statement Representing the New York Sporting Arms Association, Inc., before the Subcommittee on Firearms Control of the City Affairs Committee, New York City Council," August 25, 1967.

Two notable precedents of successfully implemented strict national controls were found in England and Japan. In England all firearms had to be registered with the police, certificates were granted only after an extensive check of the applicant, and, in effect, permission to possess a gun usually was granted only to supervised members of Britain's 4,500 gun clubs and farmers who needed firearms to control vermin. As a result, Britain had one of the lowest incidents of violent crime. In Japan, where firearm offenses were also low, the possession of handguns was limited to police, military personnel, Japan's 50 Olympic marksmen, and a few government research agencies. All long arms for hunting were licensed by Japan's Public Safety Commission.[6]

The Federal Gun Control Act, described by President Johnson as only a "halfway measure," became law on December 16, 1968. (For a brief summary of its provisions, see Appendix A.)

But the realization of lasting, effective controls even at the federal level was subject to question. By the end of November 1969, President Nixon had already signed an amendment to the Federal Gun Control Act of 1968 exempting shotgun shells and ammunition suitable for use only in rifles (excluding .22-caliber rifles) from record-keeping requirements. Nevertheless, a creeping antigun sentiment and public pressure continued to prompt a variety of proposals for further gun-control legislation at state and local levels.

## THE MARLIN FIREARMS COMPANY: HISTORY

The Marlin Firearms Company was founded in 1870 to sell pistols designed and manufactured by John Mahlon Marlin. The company continued making pistols until 1881, when it introduced its first repeating rifle to compete with the Winchester Model 1873, known as "The Gun That Won the West." Marlin continued to produce various caliber sporting rifles, and, in 1898, introduced a pump-action, 12-gauge shotgun.

While the Marlin family managed the business, emphasis had been placed on sporting guns. Then, in 1915, a syndicate headed by A. F. Rockwell bought the company for $1,500,000. Rockwell and his associates sought government contracts to produce military arms, and after the war the Rockwell Corporation turned to ball and roller bearings and let Marlin return to sporting rifles. The company struggled along until 1924 when financial difficulties beset it so severely that it went on the auction block. At that auction, Frank Kenna, Sr., bought it for $100.

Mr. Kenna, successful in a half-dozen enterprises, was able to rebuild Marlin: several defunct rifle and shotgun models were reintroduced, and new models were developed. To raise money in 1931, Mr. Kenna offered a Marlin rifle or shotgun free with the purchase of four

---

[6] *U.S. News & World Report,* June 24, 1968.

or more shares of preferred stock. Mr. Kenna began to diversify in 1936 by entering the razor blade business, and in 1940 added a new product-service area of employee "News Centers" and motivational communications.[7]

In 1947 Frank Kenna, Sr., died; his son Roger, who succeeded him, continued to improve the Marlin image and develop new gun models. When Roger died in 1959, his brother, Frank Kenna, Jr., stepped into the presidency.

### Ownership in 1970

In 1970 Marlin consisted of two operating divisions: the Marlin Firearms Division and the Marlin Industrial Division. In addition, the Marlin Realty Corporation was formed to lease the old plant. An organization chart is shown in Exhibit 6.

Of the 116,000 shares of common stock outstanding, the Kenna family as a group owned 39,550 shares directly and 75,440 additional shares were held by the Marlin Voting Trust, a 10-year trust expiring on December 31, 1971. Beneficiaries of the voting trust were various members of the Kenna family. The remaining 1,010 outstanding shares were owned by nonfamily members.

Frank Kenna, Jr., 47, had attended Yale University, served three years with the Marines during World War II, and completed his education at Clarkson College of Technology. He had started his career with Marlin in 1949 as an apprentice toolmaker and had worked his way up through the organizaton until he became president in 1959. Discussing his role in the organization, Mr. Kenna said, "I am involved in every phase of the business. I'm not yet a chairman-of-the-board type; I'm an operating man."

## MARLIN INDUSTRIAL DIVISION (MID)

The Marlin industrial division, owned 90% by the company and 10% by the Kenna family, accounted for about 20% of 1969 sales. Profit margins for the industrial division were described by one executive as "substantially higher than the firearms division—up to 50% higher." Motivational employee communication programs were supplied to industrial firms, hospitals, and transportation companies. The service consisted of a high-quality bulletin board, or "News Center," on which topical events and messages to employees were displayed. MID selected and produced

---

[7] The razor blade operation was discontinued in 1968 in the face of heavy competition and what management considered to be the unfavorable economic implications of the stainless-steel blade.

**EXHIBIT 6**

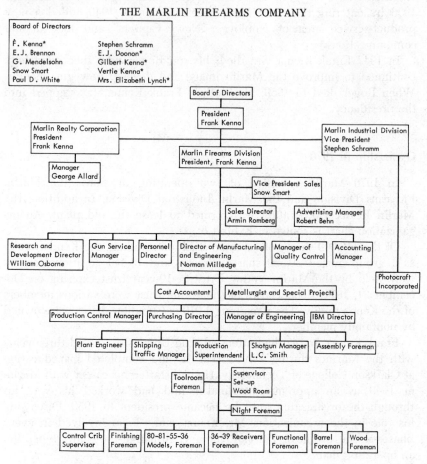

THE MARLIN FIREARMS COMPANY

* Members of the Kenna family.
Source: Company records.

the display literature and illustrated news and sports stories which were mailed out at least once a week to 8,000 clients.

The service was sold nationwide through a 30-man sales force. Typically the client signed a two-year contract, and division experience indicated about a 75% renewal rate. Clients included many of the nation's largest industrial firms, such as General Motors, Ford, Olin, and North American Rockwell.

Included in the industrial division was Photocraft, Incorporated, a wholly owned subsidiary specializing in the sale of advertising displays to banks and savings and loan associations. The display consisted of a cabinet containing an illuminated moving picture of an American flag.

Photocraft sold the units under two-year subscription leases, and in recent years annual sales had averaged $200,000.

Mr. Stephen Schramm, 57, had been vice president in charge of MID for six years and was a director of the parent company. He had come to Marlin in 1955 after several years of sales experience with Spiegel. According to Mr. Schramm, MID sales had tripled over the previous 10 years and were expected to at least double over the next 10 years. He said:

We are very optimistic about the future of the motivational communications business. It is a very exciting field because it is really so down-to-earth and simple. We have received enough inquiries from South America about our service that next year we plan to initiate a similar service in Spanish for South America. After that we may go to Europe.

Mr. Kenna noted one of the reasons for this success:

Advertising is unnecessary because of the strength of the Marlin name. Marlin is a good, strong name associated with the Marlin sailfish, our high-quality guns, and, until recently, razor blades. The name has also been used for cars, fishing tackle, swimming pool pumps, and a brand of cigarettes. Because of our image and masculine products, many top executives are interested in talking to our salesmen about an employee communication service.

## MARLIN FIREARMS DIVISION

The firearms division accounted for approximately 80% of total sales and employed the bulk of Marlin's 700 employees. It produced over 300,000 units per year, with prices ranging from $25 to several hundred dollars per gun.

### Product policy for firearms

Marlin sold rimfire rifles, centerfire rifles, and shotguns under the Marlin name. The company also marketed a lower price Glenfield line, the chief difference being that a less expensive birch stock was substituted for the traditional walnut stock. Some private-label selling was also done for national chain stores, such as Sears, Roebuck; Montgomery Ward; and Western Auto. The company believed its guns were generally of superior quality to comparably priced competing brands. The emphasis on quality was often described in terms of Frank Kenna's "walnut and steel" philosophy. Mr. Kenna noted that companies like Remington had recently tried without success to use plastic stocks and stamped metal parts for critical parts of rifle actions. In contrast to such cost-cutting methods, he felt that he owed customers reliable firearms in the best gun-making tradition.

In Marlin's 1970 centennial catalog, Mr. Kenna wrote:

And while our improved facilities and modern equipment will enable us. to achieve increased production volume, I assure you that Marlin will continue to make guns the right way. We know there is no substitute for solid steel forgings, American walnut, hand-fitted stocks and actions, and all the fine touches that make the name Marlin synonymous with traditional gun quality. As we begin a second century of American gun making, we remain dedicated to that goal.

A summary of the 1970 catalog including a description of each gun and its date of introduction is provided in Exhibit 7.

## Markets and customer profile

In a mid-1968 study summarized in Exhibit 8, the sales department estimated that Marlin accounted for approximately 13% of domestic long-arms sales: 28% in rimfire rifles, 11% in centerfire rifles, and 1% in shotguns. Marlin executives asserted that the company's inability to obtain a larger share of the centerfire rifle market was due, in part, to insufficient production capacity in the old plant.[8]

In the new facilities, Marlin expected to increase the production of higher priced guns with only a moderate increase in overall volume. For instance, by mid-1970 Marlin's production was within 1,000 units of comparable 1969 production figures, but revenues from gun sales were $800,000, or roughly 10% higher than 1969.

Marlin sold about 1% of its annual production abroad through Dodge and Seymour, a worldwide distributor. Although sporting-arms sales had recently picked up in West Germany, France, and Italy, restrictive gun laws abroad generally limited Marlin's export business. Many nations in Asia and Africa had banned or severely restricted the sale of firearms. In South America, some military governments had made the importation of sporting arms illegal.

On the basis of warranty cards returned on about 15% of unit sales, Snow Smart was confident that he had a profile of the average Marlin customer. Characterized as a young male factory worker, the "typical" Marlin customer was highly conscious of technical features and generally purchased a rifle for hunting or target practice. (For summary data covering a wide range of factors including the age and occupation of the purchaser, his reasons for selecting Marlin, his intended uses for the gun, and where and when he bought it, see Appendix B.)

Traditionally, retail gun sales were highest in July, August, September, and October when new rifles were purchased in preparation for the hunting season. Recently, however, a strong sales trend was discerned

---

[8] Maximum production in the old plant had been 300,000 units per year.

**EXHIBIT 7**
**Marlin 1970 models**

| Model | Caliber | Description | Price | Date model introduced | Comment |
|---|---|---|---|---|---|
| Rimfire | | | | | |
| Marlin 39CL........ | .22 | Lever-action repeater | $125.00 | 1970 | Commemorative—(originally introduced in 1922) |
| Marlin 49 ... | .22 | Automatic | 59.95 | 1968 | New model |
| Marlin 99 C/M.. | .22 | Automatic | 49.95 | 1957 | New model |
| Marlin 989. | .22 | Automatic | 49.95 | 1962 | New model |
| Marlin 980. | .22 | Bolt-action repeater | 49.95 | 1962 | Minor modifications |
| Marlin 81 | .22 | Bolt-action repeater | 46.95 | 1937 | New model |
| Marlin 80 | .22 | Bolt-action repeater | 44.95 | 1935 | New model |
| Glenfield 60 | .22 | Automatic | 43.95 | 1966 | Reproduction |
| Marlin 101. | .22 | Bolt-action single shot | 29.95 | 1959 | New model |
| Glenfield 10 | .22 | Bolt-action single shot | 26.95 | 1966 | Reproduction |
| Centerfire | | | | | |
| Marlin 444. | .444 | Lever-action repeater | 135.00 | 1964 | Minor modification |
| Marlin 1894. | .44 | Lever-action repeater | 105.00 | 1970 | Reproduction |
| Marlin 336 c/t.. | 30/30 | Lever-action repeater | 105.00 | 1947 | Minor modification |
| Glenfield 30 | 30/30 | Lever-action repeater | 99.95 | 1966 | Minor modification |
| Shotgun | | | | | |
| L.C. Smith Sidelock Double.... | 12 gauge | Sidelock double barrel | 300.00 | 1968 | Reproduction |
| Marlin 55 Goose. | 12 gauge | Bolt-action single shot | 59.95 | 1962 | Reproduction |
| Glenfield 50 | 12/20 gauge | Bolt-action single shot | 49.95 | 1966 | Reproduction |

Source: Company records.

**EXHIBIT 8**

Marlin's share of shoulder-arms market (January 1, 1960–June 30, 1968)

| | Rimfire | | | Centerfire | | | Shotguns | | |
|---|---|---|---|---|---|---|---|---|---|
| | Total (units) | Marlin (units) | Marlin (percentage) | Total (units) | Marlin (units) | Marlin (percentage) | Total (units) | Marlin (units) | Marlin (percentage) |
| 1960 . . . . . . . . | 461,000 | 112,000 | 24 | 224,000 | 29,000 | 13 | 517,000 | 23,000 | 4 |
| 1961 . . . . . . . . | 472,000 | 141,000 | 30 | 213,000 | 30,000 | 14 | 534,000 | 29,000 | 5 |
| 1962 . . . . . . . . | 517,000 | 138,000 | 27 | 270,000 | 39,000 | 14 | 552,000 | 31,000 | 6 |
| 1963 . . . . . . . . | 566,000 | 150,000 | 27 | 271,000 | 44,000 | 16 | 595,000 | 31,000 | 5 |
| 1964 . . . . . . . . | 695,000 | 168,000 | 24 | 342,000 | 55,000 | 16 | 687,000 | 27,000 | 4 |
| 1965 . . . . . . . . | 768,000 | 190,000 | 25 | 392,000 | 53,000 | 14 | 834,000 | 19,000 | 2 |
| 1966 . . . . . . . . | 826,000 | 201,000 | 24 | 562,000 | 76,000 | 14 | 913,000 | 13,000 | 1 |
| 1967 . . . . . . . . | 892,000 | 216,000 | 24 | 633,000 | 84,000 | 13 | 970,000 | 13,000 | 1 |
| 1968 (6 mos.). . . . | 539,000 | 151,000 | 28 | 420,000 | 45,000 | 11 | 547,000 | 7,000 | 1 |
| 7-yr. % increase (decrease) . . . . . . . . | 93% | 93% | .. | 183% | 190% | .. | 88% | (43%) | .. |

Source: Company records.

just prior to Christmas, indicating that guns were also a large gift item. As a consequence, more intensive promotion campaigns were slated by Marlin for the Christmas season. Other sales peaks had been identified around Father's Day and graduation time. Shipments to dealers tended to precede retail sales by about three months.

## Marketing policies

Marketing was headed by the vice president of sales, Snow Smart, 61, who had come to Marlin in 1951 after extensive hardgoods merchandising experience at Sears, Roebuck; Montgomery Ward; and Spiegel. Mr. Smart lived in Chicago to be near the headquarters of the larger retail chains. His office was equipped with a kitchen, pool table, and a large fireplace. On the walls were approximately 50 game heads he had collected on hunting trips around the world. Mr. Smart had a collection of about 40 sporting arms, many of them Marlins.

Mr. Smart visited the New Haven plant for one week each month to consult with production personnel and his sales director, Armin Romberg. Mr. Romberg, 53, had been with Marlin 34 years, 11 of them as sales director. In addition to supervising in-house marketing activities, he administered Marlin's credit policies.

Marlin firearms were sold by a combination of 20 sales representatives and five company regional salesmen. Salesmen were on commission, which averaged 4% on sales to jobbers. The company had over 300 active accounts, most of them jobbers who, in turn, sold to some 7,000 retail establishments. Marlin had not incurred a bad-debt loss since 1961, which Mr. Smart attributed to the company policy of accepting only those jobber accounts listed as AA or AAA by Dun & Bradstreet. In recent years the company had sold an increasing proportion of sales directly to certain large customers, including Montgomery Ward, Western Auto Supply, J. C. Penney, Spiegel, Aldens, Jewel Companies, K-Mart Sporting Goods, and Sears, Roebuck.

Prior to 1970 Marlin had not devoted a great deal of attention to the retail dealers, concentrating instead on securing financially stronger jobbers and providing them with better promotion aids and service. Recently, however, increased consideration was being given to the retailers. According to Snow Smart:

We have never made love to the dealers until this year. Actually, there are only about 5,000 good dealers in the country. This year for the first time we mailed kits containing catalogs, brochures, and sweepstakes contest information to 10,000 dealers. This was an attempt to generate interest among the dealers and make them more aware of Marlin.

The reason we are approaching the dealers directly is to prepare the way for bringing out a broader line of rifles and shotguns. Right now, we are only selling to about 40% of the sporting long-arms market; by expanding into shotguns, we can move into the other 60% of the market.

## Advertising and promotion

Media advertising was placed in sporting magazines such as *Outdoor Life, Sports Afield, Shooting Times, Field and Stream, The American Rifleman* (published by the National Rifle Association), and various trade journals. No cooperative advertising was done. The importance of tradition, craftsmanship, and quality was emphasized by Marlin's advertising and promotional literature.

Mr. Robert Behn, 29, had been director of advertising for seven months. Before coming to Marlin in the spring of 1969, he had worked in Remington's shaver advertising department. Mr. Behn discussed Marlin's advertising.

With 60% of our customers under age 30, we cater to the younger male, but we are not really in the youth market, such as the *Boy's Life* magazine audience. Given our present advertising and promotion budget, which is only about 5% of sales, such advertising still represents a luxury. However, as our budget allows, it will be important to cultivate these kids—particularly in the face of foreign imports. We need to stress the importance of high-quality, traditional American craftsmanship to educate the novice and first-time hunter.

To this Frank Kenna added:

Customers are generally very emotional about guns. There is a very manly feeling of deeply rooted Americana in owning a gun. This feeling actually extends to nearly everyone. A guy might buy one of our Model 39 Century Limited .22s just to put up on the wall of his den for a conversation piece, never intending to shoot it. The Model 39 is our "Cadillac" of the .22s, and its handsome workmanship, including a solid brass butt plate and octagonal barrel, makes it very decorative.

## New product development

The research and development department was responsible for working with sales and production to develop new models of rifles and shotguns. It was headed by 34-year-old William Osborne and consisted of four engineer-designers, three model-makers, and a technical and historical adviser. Mr. Osborne had been director of R & D for one year. Before coming to Marlin in 1966, he had worked as a project manager in Winchester's Ramset Tool Division.

Three to five years generally elapsed between the conception of a new rifle or shotgun and the development of an actual working prototype. For the rush design of a simple gun, two years could be expected. Typically, the new product idea was accompanied by performance, appearance, and cost objectives. R & D engineer-designers then made several preliminary sketches to define alternative design approaches to be reviewed by Bill Osborne, Snow Smart, and Frank Kenna.

The production department performed a thorough engineering job that encompassed specifying production methods and estimating costs. Norman Milledge, production manager, commented:

At $500,000 per major model change, such as we experienced on our new pump-action shotgun, we have to be careful in our approach to each new model proposed. Even minor modifications of existing models cost $50,000 to $100,000. Most new model ideas come from salespeople. We make up the prototypes and often make suggestions that help us in producing a more uniformly reproducible gun.

Of particular importance in any new product decision were Frank Kenna and Snow Smart, both of whom hunted extensively and were gun collectors. According to Mr. Osborne:

Market research comes from Snow Smart and Frank Kenna. They talk to their field people and their friends in the firearms industry. There are some internally generated ideas, too, but because firearms are very personal in such matters as a long or short stock, pistol grip or straight grip, etc., it is difficult to keep personal preferences separate from what the customer wants. The final say has to come from marketing.

Mr. Kenna discussed what made a good gun in these terms:

You can't do it by motivational research, as the Edsel fiasco proved. An intuitive feel is necessary, and all of Marlin's salesmen are gun men. One very important feature is quality, and that is stressed above all else.

We also offer new models, like the automobile industry. As with new cars, we don't change the basic "engine" but add new styling features. For example, we might change the shape of the stock, add some etching on the barrel, and so forth.

The new pump-action shotgun was presently in its third design cycle; a working prototype was expected to be available October 1. If the design was accepted for regular production at that time, the gun would probably be ready to market by July 1971. Temporarily shelved were production plans for a new bolt-action centerfire rifle; under the pressure of foreign imports, Marlin had postponed its introduction, although Mr. Osborne described management's attitude as "still positive" about the gun.

## Production

The firearms division had a work force of approximately 640 nonunion employees, 80% of whom were compensated on an incentive system related to piecework. Pay was competitive within the community and averaged about $3 per hour for the production workers. Production was conducted in one full eight-hour shift followed by a partial shift of only 60 people. The plant was closed for the first two weeks in August, and production was fairly even throughout the year because guns were produced for inventory during the slack selling seasons. In its new factory, Marlin was set up to produce 350,000 guns per year, but it was estimated that by going to two full shifts over 500,000 units per year could be turned out.

The manufacturing costs for one representative moderately priced gun were estimated by Mr. Milledge to be 18% materials, 25% direct labor, and overhead calculated at a rate of 230% of direct labor. In addition to occupancy costs—utilities, depreciation, etc.—major overhead expenses included the indirect costs associated with testing and engineering as well as indirect labor and fringe benefits.

### Foreign competition

Browning's introduction of the Japanese-made .22-caliber lever-action rifle was viewed with concern by Marlin management. In 1970 sales were expected to approach 6,000 units at a "fair-trade" price of $75. Marlin understood that delivery problems had limited volume to date but that these were now under control. Moreover, Browning had indicated to the trade that a higher caliber rifle would be introduced next, parts of which were made in Japan.

Marlin was reasonably sure that the combination of import duties and increased labor costs would force Browning's price on the .22-caliber rifle to $85 in 1971. Using this assumption and certain further assumptions concerning costs and margins, Marlin estimated that the price of the rifle in Japan was $30.16.

| | |
|---|---:|
| Retail price | $85.00 |
| Retailer's margin | 28.00 |
| Price to retailer ("wholesale" price) | $57.00 |
| Browning margin (15% of "wholesale") | 8.50 |
| Excise tax (11% of import price) | 4.80 |
| Import price | $43.70 |
| Per-gun tax | 3.50 |
| Import duty (20% of import price less per-gun tax) | 8.04 |
| Landed price | $32.16 |
| Transportation from Japan | 2.00 |
| Purchase price of gun in Japan | $30.16 |

For 1971 Marlin was contemplating a defensive move calling for the reintroduction of the Model 39 which had been withdrawn in 1970 in favor of the custom-engraved commemorative model. The gun was to be priced at $99.95 and designed especially for "competitive" selling.

The high quality of the Browning imports had made them competitive with several $100 American models, and in 1969 Marlin's Model 39, then priced at $94.95, had been discounted by many dealers. Armin Romberg explained that although Marlin guns were "fair-traded," the company was not as stringent as Browning in policing retail pricing, and only in the most flagrant cases of price cutting had Marlin requested that the jobber terminate a retail account. Actually, Marlin was counting on aggressive merchandising to maintain its market position. According to Mr. Kenna, K-Mart was one of the best gun merchandisers in the country because of its aggressive marketing techniques and computerized inventory system. By concentrating on the low-price, high-volume sales outlets like K-Mart, Mr. Kenna felt that Marlin could protect its market share in the face of low-price imports.

## MARLIN AND GUN-CONTROL LEGISLATION

Snow Smart thought that gun-control legislation had had its biggest impact on the sale of Marlin guns when the over-18 restriction on the sale of ammunition caused a slump in the sale of .22 automatic rifles in 1969. Sales had recovered in 1970, and he concluded:

Sales depend primarily on the economics of the country just like auto sales, and management must come up with new models. With the possible exception of some handgun legislation and some local gun-control laws, the gun-control legislation has pretty much passed. Guns, like automobiles, are so widely held by individuals in American society that it is unlikely they will be more stringently controlled.

Frank Kenna expressed his views about gun control in these terms:

I'm known as being sort of a maverick in the industry. Along with Mossberg, another manufacturer in town, we took a definite public stand on gun control during the controversy over the 1968 legislation and ran an advertisement to communicate our stand. (See Exhibit 9.)

I realized there was some kind of a problem, and I did something about it. During the civil disturbances, I cut some of our customers off. I just decided they were not creditable enough to handle Marlin products.

Marlin had formerly been a member of SAAMI but had felt itself to be relatively ineffectual in policy decisions compared to other larger members such as Remington and Winchester. Consequently, Marlin dropped its membership although it continued to support the activities of the association. It contributed regularly to organizations such as the National Shooting Sports Foundation, Ducks Unlimited, and the Connecticut Revolver Association.

EXHIBIT 9

Text of advertisement placed in *New Haven Register*

WE AS MANUFACTURERS OF SPORTING FIREARMS, THE PRIMARY PURPOSES OF WHICH ARE RECREATIONAL—FOR HUNTING AND TARGET SHOOTING; ARE OPPOSED TO REGISTRATION OF SPORTING RIFLES AND SHOTGUNS AT THE LOCAL, STATE, OR NATIONAL LEVEL BECAUSE:

1. Registration lists can be stolen or otherwise made available to unauthorized persons.
2. Registration information in the wrong hands can result in robbery of legitimate private collections of antique or modern arms.
3. The same data can pinpoint those homes without firearms protection, especially in rural or isolated areas far from municipal or state police surveillance.
4. Whereas confiscation of sporting arms may seem remote, it is well to remember that dictatorship fears an armed citizenry. That was why the Second Amendment of the U.S. Constitution was written. The Connecticut Constitution, Article 1, Section 17 says: "Every citizen has a right to bear arms in defense of himself and the state."
5. Obviously no criminal will register a firearm.
6. COMPLETE ENFORCEMENT of a firearms registration law would require the widespread use of every law enforcement officer of this country plus the armed forces of the United States.
7. Such action as would be required for COMPLETE ENFORCEMENT of a firearms registration law may conflict with both the Fourth and Fifth Amendments to the U.S. Constitution.
8. The cost of registration of 100 million firearms would be astronomical.

WE AS CITIZENS AND SPORTSMEN BELIEVE THAT CERTAIN PROPOSALS ARE WORTHY OF CONSIDERATION:

A. Three-day waiting periods for purchasing new firearms.
B. Prohibiting mail-order sales.
C. Sales by licensed dealers only.
D. Gun owners identification cards issued similarly to the method by which over 14 million hunting licenses are issued annually.

WE DO EMPHATICALLY DESIRE TO SEE ENFORCEABLE LAWS ENACTED THAT WILL EFFECTIVELY KEEP ALL TYPES OF FIREARMS AWAY FROM INCOMPETENT OR UNLAWFUL PERSONS:

O. F. MOSSBERG & SONS, INC.
North Haven, Connecticut

MARLIN FIREARMS CO.
New Haven, Connecticut

Source: Company records.

## PLANS FOR THE FUTURE

Mr. Kenna's chief objective was to expand Marlin's product line to a full line of shoulder arms. By introducing new models of centerfire rifles and shotguns, he indicated that the company could reach additional segments of the firearms market. He stated:

With our new facilities, I plan to go full line in shoulder firearms. Right now we make rimfire and centerfire rifles in a limited number of models, and only two models of shotgun. We have some heady plans for the future which include further expansion into the shotgun field with a new pump-action shotgun we are developing. As we get established in the plant, we will add more shotgun models and also introduce more models of our centerfire rifles.

These new models in production will require new machinery, of course, but we spent about $1,000,000 last year on equipment because of the new plant and expect to spend $500,000 annually in the future for new machinery. We are buying mostly numerically controlled machines, and they range in price from $40,000 to $130,000 per machine.

Some companies had sought broader markets through diversification as a hedge against potential future gun-control legislation. Olin's 1968 annual report said, "The Winchester-Western Division will look beyond sporting arms and ammunition to other products and services. . . ." In 1969 Winchester moved aggressively into the leisure and outdoor recreation markets by adding new products such as skis, tents, outdoor clothing, propane fueled camp accessories, and books and motion pictures oriented toward outdoor adventure.

Members of Marlin management took varying positions on the role of diversification in the company's future. Snow Smart said:

I think Marlin should diversify as fast as possible, preferably into something like fishing gear. The reason for going into fishing gear or any leisure-time activity, and even hardware, is that all these products are sold through the same jobbers.

Armin Romberg discussed diversification in these terms:

Frank feels we need a five-year plan because Marlin's problem has been in new product development. Although we have two new models in development now, the pump-action shotgun has been held up for three years because of design problems. Hopefully, the new shotgun will give us a start into a broader product line. With a complete line of shotguns as well as rifles, our sales will improve.

Further diversification does not appear feasible in the near future. We guessed wrong earlier when we were thinking of acquiring two companies. One made outboard motors and the other made fishing tackle. At the time, they did not look attractive, but since then they've grown very well. Unfortunately, we didn't see the opportunities in the outdoor sporting field.

With the gun business as seasonal as it is, fishing gear would be a logical choice to balance our seasonal sales. Whereas gun sales are heaviest in the fall, fishing gear sales are highest in the spring. Our customers would also be the same; 80% of our gun wholesalers are wholesalers for fishing gear, too.

As far as the ammunition business goes, I think the reason we don't get into it is because of restrictive legislation. Anyone who wants to go to the store to buy a 98¢ box of .22 ammunition has to fill out a cumbersome form. Many people find it inconvenient, and several retailers have discontinued selling ammunition because of the administrative headaches. We know that

Winchester let some of its .22-caliber ammunition workers go, and I understand that Remington's sales of .22-caliber ammunition are down 50% from last year. Moreover, that decline was thought to be a permanent loss of business.[9] At this time, ammunition certainly doesn't look like the right direction to go.

Looking toward the future, Frank Kenna said:

Unless an opportunity presents itself, I see no need to diversify from the firearms and employee-communications fields we're in right now. We do want to go full line in shoulder arms, but we don't contemplate, for example, going into the ammunition business.

I am open-minded about diversifying into some new field, but someone will have to make a pretty good case for it. Of course, when we go public, it will be a lot easier to diversify if we want to do it later.

## APPENDIX A
## SUMMARY OF THE FEDERAL GUN
## CONTROL ACT OF 1968

—Federal firearms business licenses would have to be obtained by all those connected with firearms transactions. This included manufacturers of "destructive devices" (grenades, rockets, etc.), firearms, and ammunition; importers, dealers, collectors, and pawnbrokers.

—A holder of a federal firearms license could not sell any firearms or ammunition to anyone under 18, nor handguns or handgun ammunition to anyone under 21. Records of all firearms and ammunition sales had to be maintained.

—A license holder could not sell any firearms or ammunition to anyone whom they knew to be under indictment or convicted of a crime punishable by more than a year's imprisonment, to be a fugitive from justice, a narcotics user or addict, or to be judged mentally defective or committed to a mental institution.

—A license holder could not, even under a contiguous state's laws, sell handguns to any unlicensed out-of-state resident.

—A license holder could not deliver any firearms over the counter to unlicensed persons from other states unless returning a firearm sent for repair or parts replacement.

---

[9] Other Marlin executives, however, speculated that this loss of business may have been temporary rather than permanent.

# APPENDIX B
## THE MARLIN FIREARMS COMPANY
### Warranty Card Report for Calendar Year 1969*

### I. *Model purchased*

| Model purchased | Caliber† | | Per-cent ‡ |
|---|---|---|---|
| Marlin 336 | .30 C | Lever-action repeater | 33 |
| Glenfield 60 | .22 R | Automatic | 10 |
| Marlin 39 | .22 R | Lever-action repeater | 9 |
| Glenfield 75§ | .22 R | Automatic | 9 |
| Glenfield 25§ | .22 R | Bolt-action repeater | 7 |
| Glenfield 30 | .30 C | Lever-action repeater | 7 |
| Marlin 99 | .22 R | Automatic | 7 |
| Marlin 989 | .22 R | Automatic | 3 |
| Glenfield 10 | .22 R | Bolt-action single shot | 3 |
| Marlin 55 Goose gun | 12-gauge SG | Bolt-action shotgun | 2 |
| Glenfield 50 | 12/20-gauge SG | Bolt-action shotgun | 2 |
| Marlin 49 | .22 R | Automatic | 1 |
| Glenfield 20 | .22 R | Bolt-action repeater | 1 |
| Marlin 444 | .444 C | Lever-action repeater | 1 |
| Marlin 57§ | .22 R | Lever-action repeater | 1 |
| Glenfield 70§ | .22 R | Automatic | 1 |
| Marlin 80 | .22 R | Bolt-action repeater | 1 |
| Marlin 101 | .22 R | Bolt-action single shot | 1 |
| Marlin 980 | .22 R | Bolt-action repeater | 1 |
| Marlin 81 | .22 R | Bolt-action repeater | – |
| Marlin 62§ | .30 C | Lever-action repeater | – |
| L.C. Smith 67 | 12-gauge SG | Side-lock double barreled | – |
| | | Total | 100 |

### II. *Age of person submitting warranty card*

| Age | Percent | Age | Percent |
|---|---|---|---|
| Less than 18 | 14 | 41 to 45 | 8 |
| 18 to 25 | 30 | 46 to 50 | 6 |
| 26 to 30 | 15 | 51 to 55 | 4 |
| 31 to 35 | 9 | 56 and over | 5 |
| 36 to 40 | 9 | Total | 100 |

### III. *Intended uses for gun (may be more than one use indicated)*

| Hunting | Percent ‡ | Other | Percent †‡ |
|---|---|---|---|
| Deer | 37 | Rifle matches | 4 |
| Rabbits | 21 | Practice | 29 |
| Ducks, geese | 2 | Skeet | – |
| Pheasants | 2 | Trap | – |
| Varmints | 15 | Self protection | 6 |
| Bears | – | Total | 116‖ |
| Other | – | | |

## APPENDIX B (continued)

IV. *Reason customer selected Marlin (may be more than one reason indicated)*

| Reason | Percent | Reason | Percent |
|---|---|---|---|
| Machined action | 11 | Liked its feel | 13 |
| Micro-groove barrel | 8 | Walnut stock | 5 |
| Fair price | 36 | Caliber | – |
| Adaptable to scope | 7 | Lever action | – |
| Safe, dependable | 11 | Side ejection | – |
| Looks and appearance | 17 | Magazine ad | – |
| Recommended by friend | 9 | Marlin name | – |
| Recommended by dealer | 6 | Total | 123‖ |

V. *Source of gift, if not purchased*

| Source | Percent | Source | Percent |
|---|---|---|---|
| Family | 26 | Graduation | – |
| Someone else | 3 | First rifle | 25 |
| Christmas | 20 | No response | 21 |
| Birthday | 5 | Total | 100 |

VI. *Date of sale*

| Month | Percent | Month | Percent |
|---|---|---|---|
| January | 3 | July | 4 |
| February | 2 | August | 7 |
| March | 2 | September | 11 |
| April | 1 | October | 20 |
| May | 3 | November | 20 |
| June | 4 | December | 23 |
|  |  | Total | 100 |

VII. *Sales outlet*

| Outlet | Percent | Outlet | Percent‡ |
|---|---|---|---|
| Montgomery Ward | 2 | Local dealer | 24 |
| J.C. Penney | 3 | K-Mart | 15 |
| Sears | 2 | Top Value | – |
| Western Auto | 1 | No response | 53 |
|  |  | Total | 100 |

VIII. *Customer's occupation*

| Occupation | Percent | Occupation | Percent |
|---|---|---|---|
| Office | 8 | Self-employed | 5 |
| Factory | 18 | Student | 17 |
| Ranch or farm | 4 | Laborer | – |
| Professional | 13 | Other | 28 |
| Executive | 3 | No response | 4 |
|  |  | Total | 100 |

\* Total number of cards processed was 34,690.
† C = Centerfire; R = Rimfire; SG = Shotgun.
‡ "–" denotes less than 1%.
§ Discontinued models.
‖ Total percentage exceeds 100% because of multiple responses.
Source: Company records.

# Cartridge Television Inc.

On July 13, 1971, Cartridge Television Inc. went public with a $22 million offering. The prospectus stated:[1]

The common stock of the Company offered hereby involves a high degree of risk. In evaluating these securities, a prospective investor should carefully consider the following factors:

1. The Company has been in existence only three years and has had no operating revenues since its inception.

2. Numerous firms, both in the United States and abroad, are engaged, or have announced their intention to engage, in the development of home video systems which are or would be competitive with the CARTRIVISION system. Most of these companies are substantially larger and possess greater resources and more extensive operating experience than the Company.

3. . . . . From its inception in 1968 to March 31, 1971, the Company incurred approximately $6,076,000 of research and preoperating costs in developing its CARTRIVISION system, and it estimates that at least an additional $7,509,000 of preoperating costs must be incurred before the first units can be sold. . . . The Company also estimates that approximately $8,640,000 will be spent to acquire additional capital equipment and tooling before the first units can be sold.

4. To date, commercial application of video tape systems manufactured by others has been limited primarily to industrial and business uses. In view of the novelty of the home video tape system developed by the Company, the substantial estimated retail prices of CARTRIVISION units and cartridges,

*6,076*
*7,509*
*8,640*
*22,225*

---

[1] Hornblower & Weeks-Hemphill, Noyes, *Cartridge Television Inc. Prospectus,* July 13, 1971.

245

and the difficulty of predicting public demand for the programming which will be available for use with the system, no assurance can be given that the CARTRIVISION system will meet with general public acceptance.

5.   As production and sale of the CARTRIVISION system have not yet commenced, the Company has no experience as to whether CARTRIVISION units manufactured in production quantities will operate satisfactorily under conditions of home use or whether they can be sold profitably.

6.   The Company does not have, nor does it presently plan to establish, its own plants to manufacture components of the CARTRIVISION system, other than its cartridge and video head manufacturing plant located in San Jose, California. The Company must depend on making satisfactory contractual arrangements with other manufacturers to assure adequate production and sales of its system.

7.   Failure by the Company to retain the services of its present key technical personnel or to attract additional qualified personnel, as required, could have an adverse effect on its operations.

8.   Published reports indicate that efforts are being made by various firms in the industry to standardize the technical characteristics of the tapes and cartridges used or to be used in home video tape systems. Since no tapes or cartridges other than those being developed by the Company are presently compatible with the CARTRIVISION system, industry standardization on a different type of tape or cartridge could have a seriously detrimental effect on the Company's prospects.

9.   Much of the earnings potential of the Company appears dependent upon its ability to offer customers pre-recorded tapes covering attractive subject matter. Keen competition is developing among the potential participants in this industry to conclude contractual arrangements covering a wide variety of popular programming. Because of its recent organization, small size and lack of demonstrated manufacturing and marketing abilities, the Company may be at a competitive disadvantage in obtaining satisfactory programming for the CARTRIVISION system.

10.   Although the Company has filed a number of patent applications pertaining to various aspects of the CARTRIVISION system, it does not expect to obtain fundamental patent protection for the basic concept or design of its system. No assurance can be given that patent infringement claims will not be asserted which may adversely affect the Company or that any valid patent protection will be obtained by the Company. The Company may be required to obtain patent licenses in order to produce and market the CARTRIVISION system, but no assurance can be given that such licenses can be obtained.

11.   Although the Company believes that the net proceeds of this offering will be sufficient to meet its long-term financing needs, no assurance can be given that unforeseen factors, such as problems in production or marketing, may not result in a need for additional financing. The Company anticipates, furthermore, that after production and sale of the system have commenced, it will require additional bank or commercial financing for its working capital needs. No assurance can be given, however, that any such financing can be obtained or, if obtained, as to the terms thereof.

12. The Company is not in a position to pay any cash dividends on its common stock, nor is it likely to be in such a position in the foreseeable future.

## HISTORY

On June 27, 1968, Ernest S. Alson, Victor Elmaleh, and Frank and Arthur Stanton organized Cartridge Television Inc. (CTI). Alson and Frank and Arthur Stanton were senior officers of World-Wide Volkswagen Corporation, the Volkswagen distributor for New York, New Jersey, and Connecticut, which had pioneered the introduction of the VW "beetle" in the late forties and early fifties and was rumored to be the largest VW distributor in the world. Elmaleh was president of Magna-Dolphin Inc., an automobile distributor. Elmaleh and Frank Stanton were also senior officers of Cragstan Industries, Inc., a toy manufacturer. The founders had obtained 218,100 shares of CTI for $7,270 at about $.03 per share, with 15,600 shares going to Alson and 67,500 each to the other three.

CTI acquired all the rights and interests of Playtape, Inc., pertaining to the invention, design, and development of a preliminary prototype home video tape recorder-playback system. Playtape was a wholly owned subsidiary of World-Wide Volkswagen Corporation, of whose stock CTI's four founders owned 92.1%. CTI's agreement with Playtape specified a basic purchase price of $120,000 and provided for annual royalties equal to the lesser of $500,000 or 2% of the income of CTI derived from the Cartrivision system before income taxes for each fiscal year in perpetuity commencing with the fiscal year beginning December 1, 1973. Also, CTI's principal executive offices, including furniture and equipment, were sublet at an annual rental of $42,000 under an agreement with Playtape which expired December 31, 1972.

Recognizing that their recorder-playback prototype required substantial further development before its commercial feasibility could be fully determined, the principal stockholders of CTI approached the large financial services and aerospace conglomerate, Avco. In May 1969 CTI and Avco executed contracts which provided for (1) the issuance and sale to Avco of 50.2% of CTI's outstanding shares for a cash purchase price of $500,000, (2) an agreement by Avco to lend CTI up to an additional $1,000,000 and to assist CTI in securing such further financing as might be required during the developmental stage, and (3) an agreement by Avco's electronics division to provide technical and engineering assistance in further developing the Cartrivision system. The latter agreement provided for future royalty payments by CTI to Avco in the same amounts and on the same terms as provided under the agreement with Playtape. Since May 1969 Avco had advanced CTI $7.5 million. Of this debt, $7.1 million was exchanged shortly before the public offering for 355,000 newly issued shares, increasing Avco's holdings to 670,000 shares, and 10-year stock purchase warrants for 12,500 shares at $20 per share.

The July 1971 public offering involved 1.1 million shares at $20 per share. After deducting underwriting discounts and commissions of $1,980,000 and expenses payable by the company of $170,000, CTI received $19,850,000. CTI planned to use its proceeds, according to the prospectus,

. . . to defray its additional preoperating costs (estimated at $7,509,000 as of March 31, 1971, of which approximately $1,173,000 will be used to reimburse Avco for startup expenses to be incurred in connection with production of CARTRIVISION recorder-playback units), to acquire additional capital equipment and tooling (estimated at $8,640,000 as of March 31, 1971, of which approximately $6,267,000 is expected to cover equipment and tooling to be located in Avco plants), to pay accrued interest and accounts payable (including amounts, $751,000 at March 31, 1971, payable to Avco), to repay $400,000 of short-term notes payable to Avco and any additional short-term borrowings which may be needed prior to the Company's receipt of the proceeds of this offering, and to provide funds to meet other operating needs of the Company. . . .

The underwriting also involved the issuance to the underwriter, Hornblower & Weeks-Hemphill, Noyes, of five-year warrants to purchase an aggregate of 50,000 shares of CTI's common stock at $24 per share. The following table from the prospectus shows the percentage of ownership of CTI's common shares before and after the refinancing of Avco's debt, after the public offering, and after Avco's and the underwriter's common stock purchase warrants of CTI have been fully exercised:

|  | Before refinancing | After refinancing | After offering | After exercise |
|---|---|---|---|---|
| Avco Corporation. . . . . . . . . . | 50.2% | 68.2% | 32.2% | 31.8% |
| Other present stockholders . . . . . | 49.8 | 31.8 | 15.0 | 14.6 |
| Public. . . . . . . . . . . . . . . . . | . . . | . . . | 52.8 | 51.3 |
| Hornblower & Weeks-Hemphill, Noyes . . . . . . . . . . . . . . . | . . . | . . . | . . . | 2.3 |

Total common stock outstanding after the offering, but before exercise of the warrants, was 2,082,750 shares. Exhibit 1 presents CTI's assets, intangibles, deferrals, and liabilities; while Exhibit 2 provides its statement of cash receipts and disbursements.

**EXHIBIT 1**

## CARTRIDGE TELEVISION INC.
Statement of Assets, Intangibles, Deferrals, and Liabilities
March 31, 1971
(pro forma and unaudited)

*Assets, Intangibles, Deferrals*

Current assets

| | |
|---|---:|
| Cash | $ 38,522 |
| Advances and prepaid expenses | 37,444 |
| Total current assets | $ 75,966 |
| Additional loan commitment from Avco Corporation* | 1,050,000 |
| Property, plant, and equipment, at cost | $2,373,782 |
| Less: Accumulated depreciation | (184,186) |
| Net property, plant, and equipment | $2,189,596 |

Intangibles and deferrals

| | |
|---|---:|
| Patent applications, at cost | 60,521 |
| Research and preoperating costs† | 6,075,700 |
| Total assets, intangibles, deferrals | $9,451,783 |

*Liabilities*

Current liabilities

| | |
|---|---:|
| Notes payable to Avco Corporation | $ 400,000 |
| Trade accounts payable, including $440,232 payable to Avco Corporation | 539,740 |
| Accrued interest payable to Avco Corporation | 311,074 |
| Accrued payroll and payroll taxes | 58,894 |
| Other accrued liabilities | 33,275 |
| Long-term debt due within one year | 130,200 |
| Total current liabilities | $1,473,183 |
| 8½% note payable | 368,100 |
| Commitments and contingencies‡ | ... |
| Total liabilities | $1,841,283 |

* A commitment by Avco Corporation as of March 31, 1971, to lend the Company an additional $1,050,000 (all of which has been received and substantially all of which has been used for research and preoperating costs and to purchase property, plant, and equipment) has been reflected in the above pro forma financial statement, as has the exchange by Avco on July 12, 1971, of $7,100,000 (including $650,000 of the foregoing $1,050,000) of the Company's then outstanding notes payable held by Avco for 355,000 shares of the Company's common stock and 10-year warrants exercisable at any time to purchase 12,500 shares of its common stock.

† The Company intends to continue deferring all costs incurred until sales of its products commence. The Company plans to amortize research and preoperating costs applicable to each product by charges to earnings based on units expected to be sold, subject to increased amortization if sales exceed projections, during the 36 months beginning with the first sales of the respective products.

‡ The Company has entered into agreements with the owners of certain film properties for the purpose of licensing the Company to use such properties with its video tape cartridges. The agreements are for varying periods of time, none of which extends beyond 1976. The agreements call for royalties to be paid by the Company at varying rates, based on sales and rentals of the video tape cartridges. Certain of these agreements call for minimum royalty payments aggregating $275,000.

The Company has entered into an engineering services agreement with Barger Corporation which obligates the Company to pay royalties up to an aggregate maximum of $300,000 based on future sales of certain products.

Source: Cartridge Television Inc. Prospectus, July 13, 1971.

**EXHIBIT 2**

CARTRIDGE TELEVISION INC.
Statement of Cash Receipts and Disbursements

| | June 27, 1968 (date of incorporation) to November 30, 1968 | Year ended November 30, 1969 | Year ended November 30, 1970 | Four months ended March 31, 1971 | Total |
|---|---|---|---|---|---|
| Cash receipts | | | | | |
| Sales of common stock............ | $ 10,000 | $515,000 | | | $ 525,000 |
| Proceeds of loans from Avco Corporation............... | | 200,000 | $4,900,000 | $1,350,000 | 6,450,000 |
| Total cash receipts........... | $ 10,000 | $715,000 | $4,900,000 | $1,350,000 | $6,975,000 |
| Disbursements (accrual basis) | | | | | |
| Research and preoperating costs* | | | | | |
| Salaries of officers and directors ................. | $ 15,000 | $ 162,369 | $ 79,416 | $ 256,785 |
| Other salaries and employee benefits ................ | | 256,556 | 1,414,233 | 625,312 | 2,296,101 |
| Materials and supplies .......... | | 29,990 | 573,384 | 147,471 | 750,845 |
| Travel ..................... | | 112,712 | 111,905 | 34,265 | 258,882 |
| Advertising, promotion and market surveys ............. | | 47,316 | 189,100 | 18,340 | 254,756 |
| Taxes ..................... | | 250 | 47,000 | 17,575 | 64,825 |
| Rent and utilities............. | | 23,098 | 146,433 | 62,977 | 232,508 |
| Industrial design ............. | | 804 | 102,982 | 17,765 | 121,551 |
| Engineering services and consulting fees ............. | | 54,550 | 260,816 | 33,015 | 348,381 |
| Interest (net of $9,673 interest income)................. | | (1,554) | 263,487 | 179,512 | 441,445 |
| Employment expenses.......... | | | 133,521 | 9,545 | 143,066 |
| Purchase of invention .......... | $120,000 | | | | 120,000 |
| Avco's production startup costs .... | | | | 393,779 | 393,779 |
| Other ................... | | 24,705 | 134,915 | 48,970 | 208,590 |
| | $120,000 | $563,427 | $3,540,145 | $1,667,942 | $5,891,514 |
| Property, plant, and equipment ..... | | 63,029 | 2,300,815 | 9,938 | 2,373,782 |
| Patent applications............. | | 31,098 | 23,604 | 5,819 | 60,521 |
| Principal payments on 8½% note ..... | | | | 151,700 | 151,700 |
| Other...................... | | 34,144 | 17,856 | 444 | 52,444 |
| Total disbursements (accrual basis) ................. | $120,000 | $691,698 | $5,882,420 | $1,835,843 | $8,529,961 |
| Accrual adjustments .......... | 115,000 | 214,734 | 781,060 | 482,689 | 1,593,483 |
| Total cash disbursements ...... | $ 5,000 | $476,964 | $5,101,360 | $1,353,154 | $6,936,478 |
| Net increase (decrease) in cash ....... | $ 5,000 | $238,036 | $ (201,360) | $ (3,154) | $ 38,522 |
| Cash at beginning of period ........ | | 5,000 | 243,036 | 41,676 | |
| Cash at end of period............. | $ 5,000 | $243,036 | $ 41,676 | $ 38,522 | $ 38,522 |

* Approximately $1,659,000 of research and preoperating costs (including interest of $385,000) have been charged to the Company by Avco Corporation.
Source: Cartridge Television Inc. Prospectus, July 13, 1971.

## THE CARTRIVISION SYSTEM

Cartridge Television Inc.'s system, identified by the registered trademark, "Cartrivision," consisted of a solid-state video recorder-playback unit which was integrated with a color television receiver. The system was designed (1) to play prerecorded cartridges in color or monochrome on the television receiver, (2) to record either color or monochrome television programs off the air for subsequent playback without processing, and (3) to play cartridges on which home movies with sound had been recorded with a special camera (initially available only in monochrome). The unit incorporated a timing device which permitted television programs to be automatically recorded off the air in the absence of the set owner, enabling the programs to be viewed later at the owner's convenience. Normal television viewing was available when the Cartrivision system was not in use or while programs were being recorded. CTI had begun development of an adaptor unit with recording and playback capabilities that could be adapted to a regular television receiver.

The tape used with the Cartrivision system was one-half inch wide iron oxide magnetic video tape which resembled the audio tape currently in general use. The tape came in different lengths and was wound in cartridges which permitted up to 114 minutes of continuous playing time, sufficient to display an average full-length motion picture without interruption. The tape could be erased and had an estimated life of more than 100 playings.

In the recording process, one of the system's three video heads placed on the tape a magnetic imprint which conformed to the electronic impulses derived from the picture. Separate audio heads recorded and reproduced the sound by the same method used by conventional audio stereo tape recorders. For playback, the three video heads scanned the video magnetic imprint sequentially, generating three picture fields from each one recorded. This technique, according to the prospectus, "increases by a factor of three the duration of program which can be recorded on a given length of tape, but produces a slightly less smooth image transition which could be perceptible to the trained eye under certain circumstances."

Prototype Cartrivision units had been exhibited publicly, but CTI did not expect production of the system and the cartridges to be sufficiently advanced to permit sales to consumers before mid-1972.

## OPERATING POLICIES

The prospectus stated:

### Marketing

Marketing plans for the CARTRIVISION system have not yet been finally determined. Initially, the Company will depend on sales of its system components to television receiver manufacturers who will market, for their own account, the completed CARTRIVISION system to consumers through distributors and retailers. Admiral Corporation[2] has agreed to purchase from the Company 10,000 recorder-playback units (with an option to purchase an additional 10,000 units), integrate the units with its own television receivers and sell the completed CARTRIVISION systems . . . In addition, Warwick Electronics Inc., a corporation associated with Sears, Roebuck and Co., has placed an order with the Company for 3,001 recorder-playback units to be delivered commencing in mid-1972 to cover the introduction of the CARTRIVISION system by Sears. The Company also intends to market, for its own account, CARTRIVISION units to commercial, industrial, and governmental customers.

The Company estimates that the retail price of the CARTRIVISION system, including the color television receiver, will be approximately $900–$1,000, although the Company may have no control over the price of certain elements of the system such as the receiver. The CARTRIVISION cartridges are expected to be offered for retail sale at prices ranging from approximately $10 to approximately $40, depending upon length (in the case of blank cartridges) and length, content, and artist (in the case of prerecorded cartridges). Distribution of cartridges is expected to be made initially through CARTRIVISION system dealers and selected music, record and audio cassette/cartridge distributors. Prerecorded cartridges will also be offered for rent at rentals starting at approximately $3 per use, and are expected to be available through a variety of retail outlets.

Arrangements have been made with United Artists Corporation and Time Life Video, a division of Time Incorporated, giving each company the right to purchase CARTRIVISION cartridges containing programming supplied by them at specified wholesale prices. The agreement with Time-Life Video also provides for certain mutual promotional efforts on a nonexclusive basis. No other arrangements have yet been made for distribution of the CARTRIVISION cartridges.

### Programming

Although blank cartridges will be offered for use in recording television programs off the air, or for making "home movies" with an auxiliary camera, much of the market appeal of home video systems is expected to revolve around the availability of prerecorded cartridges offering a broad range of subject matter. Accordingly, the Company is actively engaged in negotiating agreements making available to it movies, sporting events, musical and educational programs, "how-to" instruction, travel subjects, documentaries, cartoons, and dance and poetry performances for distribution on CARTRIVISION cartridges.

The Company has acquired nonexclusive license rights to more than 800 film presentations. These include 95 feature films from Avco Embassy Pictures Corp. (a subsidiary of Avco), 50 from United Artists Corporation, 28 from

---

[2] In addition to selling its own branded sets, Admiral produced TV sets for Montgomery Ward.

Lion International Films, and 15 from American International Pictures, Inc. Rights have also been negotiated for the use of National Football League films, a film series of well-known prize fights, instructional films dealing with a variety of participatory sports, and filmed classical music productions.

Substantially all of the Company's initial programming will consist of previously exhibited subject matter. The Company is seeking to obtain rights to original musical programs, including full-length symphonies, rock and pop concerts, country and western music, and opera and ballet productions. In this connection, the Company may participate in some production financing, but most of its programming is expected to be acquired from outside sources without Company participation.

The programming license agreements which are being negotiated give the Company the right to distribute the subject matter on CARTRIVISION cartridges for a specified period (normally at least three years) in return for royalties based upon the receipts derived by the Company from the sale or rental of the cartridges. Renewal rights for varying periods of time are customarily included, and minimum royalty guarantees are sometimes required. . . .

Keen competition is developing for home video programming rights, but since most of the subjects are being made available to potential competitors on a nonexclusive basis, the Company does not anticipate any major problems in securing rights to a broad range of material.

## Production

The Company has entered into agreements with two divisions of Avco providing for the production of 25,000 CARTRIVISION recorder-playback units in the presently agreed configuration, and for an option to purchase up to an additional 175,000 units. Using capital equipment and tooling owned and supplied by the Company, Avco's Electronics Division will produce electronic and mechanical components of the system at Huntsville, Alabama, and its Precision Products Division will manufacture and assemble the CARTRIVISION recorder-playback units at Richmond, Indiana. The Company has agreed to reimburse Avco for certain startup expenses aggregating approximately $1,567,000 incurred and to be incurred for the Company's account.

The agreements with Avco specify unit target costs and prices (including an 8% profit) based on delivery of a total of 200,000 units. If the Company does not exercise its option to acquire this entire quantity in accordance with the agreed delivery schedule, additional charges (estimated at a maximum of $2,900,000 if the Company does not exercise any part of its option) may be made by Avco based on its incurred costs, and equitable adjustments will be made in the target costs and prices based on any changes in the presently agreed configuration. On completion of delivery of 200,000 units, Avco's actual costs will be reviewed and cost savings or overruns from the agreed target cost will be shared equally by the Company and Avco, provided that the final price cannot exceed 116% of the adjusted target cost.

The Company does not intend to establish its own facilities for manufacturing the CARTRIVISION system but expects to contract with various domestic and foreign television receiver manufacturers to produce and market for their own account CARTRIVISION units on a nominal royalty or royalty-free basis. The Company has granted Admiral Corporation a five-year nonexclusive royalty-free license (renewable on certain conditions) permitting Admiral to manufacture and sell CARTRIVISION recorder-playback units.

The cartridge producing facility which the Company is equipping at San Jose, California, is expected to have the capability of producing more than 200,000 blank and prerecorded CARTRIVISION cartridges per month when fully operating on a single shift basis. If sufficient demand for its cartridges develops, the Company may establish additional cartridge manufacturing facilities or license other manufacturers to produce cartridges under the CARTRIVISION name on a royalty basis.

The Company recognizes the importance of quality control and continuous supply of video heads for its CARTRIVISION system, and has been conducting video head preoperating work with the intent of creating an internal source of supply. Prototype video heads are currently being produced at the San Jose facility, and the Company plans to install additional equipment at that location to enable it to establish a video head production capability. The Company also plans to purchase video heads from other sources.

Several sources of magnetic video tape are presently available to the Company, and the plastic material used in fabricating cartridges is available from a number of suppliers.

## Management

As of May 31, 1971, CTI had 136 full-time employees: 59 in technical operations; 33 in production, programming, and marketing; and 44 in administrative and clerical operations. The board of directors consisted of the four founders and four members of Avco management. Thor W. Kolle, Jr., a general partner of Hornblower & Weeks-Hemphill, Noyes, David L. Coffin, president of The Dexter Corporation, a producer of specialty chemicals and specialized long-fiber products, and George S. Trimble, president of The Bunker-Ramo Corporation, a diversified manufacturer and supplier of electronic components, information systems, and services and other products, were expected to be elected directors of CTI shortly after completion of the public offering. Mr. Frank Stanton, age 51, was president and was assisted by four vice presidents who had joined CTI between December 1969 and June 1970. Charles D. Brown, general manager of West Coast operations, had previously held management positions in the electronics division of Avco and had served as president of an electronics division of Textron. Samuel W. Gelfman, vice president of production and programming, had been vice president of the motion picture department of General Artists Corporation as well as assistant to the president of United Artists Corporation. Donald F. Johnston, vice president of marketing, had been a vice president of Philco-Ford Corporation. Denis B. Trelewicz, treasurer and secretary, had served in various staff positions with Avco and, prior to joining CTI, had been a Sloan Fellow at the Massachusetts Institute of Technology. The prospectus listed executive remuneration as follows:

| Name | Capacity in which remuneration is being received | Aggregate annual remuneration |
|---|---|---|
| Frank Stanton | President | $ 75,000 |
| Donald F. Johnston | Vice president | 65,000 |
| Samuel W. Gelfman | Vice president | 50,000 |
| All 12 officers and directors as a group | | 265,000 |

The prospectus continued:

The Company has adopted a Stock Option Plan, pursuant to which options to purchase a maximum of 175,000 authorized but unissued or treasury shares of the Company's stock may be granted to officers (including officers who are directors) and other key employees of the Company. . . .

*  *  *  *  *

The Company's Board of Directors has approved the grant of qualified options to acquire an aggregate of 41,500 common shares at the Price to Public, effective as of the date of this Prospectus, including 2,500 shares each to Messrs. Johnston and Gelfman and 10,000 shares to all officers and directors of the company as a group. The directors have also approved the grant to Frank Stanton of an option to acquire 50,000 common shares on similar terms. This option cannot be qualified due to the number of common shares owned by Mr. Stanton.

## Competition

The prospectus described CTI's competition as follows:

Various types of video tape recorders, different from the CARTRIVISION system, have been available and used for a number of years by the television industry, and a limited number are also being produced for the industrial and general consumer markets. However, the high price and operating complexities of these devices have prevented them from becoming mass market consumer items. Currently, a number of firms are devoting considerable research efforts to the development of lower cost home video systems.

To date, a number of different varieties of home video systems have been publicized. One is the magnetic tape cartridge system, of which the CARTRIVISION system is an example. Other magnetic tape systems are being developed by Sony Corporation of Japan, Ampex Corporation and Philips of Holland, among others.

A second approach is represented by Columbia Broadcasting System's Electronic Video Recording system which relies on miniaturized film coiled in a cartridge and run through a separate playback unit connected to a television set. Units incorporating this system are presently being produced by Motorola, Inc. Another proposed system is RCA Corporation's SelectaVision process based on holographic photography. Using a laser beam, RCA embosses an encoded picture on vinyl tape which is played through a module connected to a television set. Other approaches include the use of Super 8mm film in conjunction with a television set, and systems utilizing plastic discs on which the video images have been recorded in phonograph fashion.

Each of these home video systems presently being developed is incompatible with the others. In an effort to avoid the expense and consumer confusion inherent in the marketing of incompatible but competitive products, attempts are being made by certain electronics firms to standardize magnetic tape and cartridge configurations.

The foregoing information, which has been summarized from published reports and news articles, indicates that the major potential competitors of the Company and its CARTRIVISION system appear to be Sony, Ampex, Philips, CBS, and RCA. Each of these companies is substantially larger than the Company and has greater financial and other resources and more extensive operating experience in electronics. If general agreement is reached by a significant number of the Company's potential competitors on magnetic tape and cartridge standards incompatible with the CARTRIVISION system, the Company could be at a competitive marketing disadvantage.

The potential competitive clash thus was not only one among rival companies but also among technologies. Two more proven and established recording materials (magnetic tape and super 8mm film) were pitted against two drastically new techniques. CBS had introduced EVR, which used film but exposed it by a fine electron-beam scanner rather than by light, permitting the film to contain considerably more information and thereby reducing costs. Also, the EVR system was the only one which could be built directly into TV sets, avoiding duplication of player circuitry, which allowed further cost reduction. RCA's SelectaVision used a simple vinyl tape, combining a low-cost material with a highly advanced technology. Although the prototypes of both the CBS and RCA systems had not yet reached the quality of reproduction of the more established materials, they offered the prospect of major further advances both in terms of quality improvement and of cost reduction. The latter was a major questionmark for both magnetic tape and regular film. They used costly materials, and mass reproduction was both expensive and slow. The lowest cost product was the video disc. Like EVR and SelectaVision, however, it permitted playing only prerecorded programs. Magnetic tape, on the other hand, allowed its user to self-record

TV programs off the air and also use the system for immediate or delayed replay of home movies. However, the camera initially was limited to black and white, was bulky, and was therefore restricted in terms of mobility. Super 8 did not allow self-recording and handled only delayed (that is, after outside development) viewing of self-made movies. The playing time varied from a maximum of 15 minutes on video discs, to above 30 minutes for EVR, up to a maximum of 60 minutes for the other techniques. Cartrivision, however, by using its special technique had been able to reach 114 minutes of playing time. Also, Cartrivision used one-half inch tape compared with the three-quarter inch tape used by several other companies. As a result, it was expected that Cartrivision tape costs would be lower. Also, in terms of projected equipment prices, which were largely guesswork, Cartrivision was at the lower end of the scale. By and large it seemed that companies using magnetic tape or EVR (especially Motorola) would be among the early entrants. Most of these companies, such as Sony, were concentrating their initial efforts on the industrial market while Cartrivision aimed primarily at the consumer market. According to *Fortune:* "since none of the playbacks use any part of the public airwaves, all being confined to individual TV chassis, the Federal Communications Commission has no power—at least not yet—to regulate or impose standards on them."[3]

## MARKET ESTIMATES

Opinions on the outlook for video cassettes ranged from undisguised pessimism to strongly worded optimism. Some observers felt that video cassettes could never dislodge television, which was viewed an average of six to seven hours per day. *Broadcasting* in its April 26, 1971, issue stated:

Companies are spending millions of dollars a year wrestling with their various systems. But timetables for production and marketing keep getting pushed back. . . .

      ✿    ✿    ✿    ✿    ✿

. . . how much time is likely to pass before a significant proportion of the television audience acquires playing machines? The short answer, based on information, opinions and parallels on both sides of the dispute, is: at least five years and probably not in this decade.[4]

The article cited a number of reasons, including the slow initial growth of color television. It concluded:

---

[3] "Stand By for the Cartridge TV Explosion," *Fortune,* June 1971, p. 81. © 1971 Time Inc.

[4] "Cassette Revolution Slow a 'Borning," Special Report by Rufus Crater, *Broadcasting,* April 26, 1971, p. 60. © 1971 by Broadcasting Publications, Inc.

Where the prophecies of wholesale takeover by cassettes break down, in the opinion of many, is in the assumption that John Doe will want to spend the kind of money necessary to make the prophecies come true. In fact, it is pointed out, the average U.S. household's total expenditure for all box-office entertainment currently comes to less than $37 a year—a fraction of the money being talked about for cassette equipment and programs.[5]

On the other side, *Fortune* reported that "Peter Goldmark of CBS Laboratories, a major contributor to the new technology, has been talking about 'the greatest revolution in communications since the book.' "[6] Paul J. Caravatt, Jr., senior vice president of the Interpublic Group of Companies, predicted at a seminar for the American Association of Advertising Agencies that cassettes:

"Will ultimately seriously erode television network audience sizes" and "have revolutionary effects upon education, entertainment, public service, retailing and even religion."

Will provide a "mature market" for program material that at current retail prices could be as high as $11 billion a year.

"Represent a major breakthrough in human freedom," providing the individual for the first time with "a full spectrum of communication" and giving him "complete control over the output of his television set—to see and hear what he wants, when he wants, as long as he wants."[7]

CTI's Samuel Gelfman had also expressed optimism:

If you have ageless product . . . you don't have to make your money back right away. You make it over a period of years. Television and the theater have to be concerned with immediacy. Cartridge TV doesn't. If a program reaches a thousand homes a week, by the end of a year it's reached a good audience. By the end of 10 years, it's reached a hell of an audience.[8]

An Arthur D. Little study in 1971 had estimated the U.S. market as shown in the table at the top of page 259.

The Arthur D. Little study, noting that penetration of 44% of U.S. TV households through 1970 by color sets indicated a willingness to spend more than $300 for entertainment devices, also commented:

. . . The most significant new product of the early 1970s will be videoplayers; we forecast that factory sales of videoplayers, video-cassettes, and software will reach $0.9–1.5 billion worldwide in 1975. Growth in industry sales and profits will depend to a great extent on the willingness of manufacturers to standardize on videoplayers and cassettes and thereby permit full exploitation of this major potential market, while stimulating a substantial by-product demand for color TV sets, at present the industry's most important product. . . .

---

[5] Ibid., p. 64.

[6] Lessing, *Fortune*, p. 81.

[7] *Broadcasting*, April 26, 1971, p. 64.

[8] Ibid.

**Videoplayer market in the United States, 1972–80\* (factory sales in 1970 dollars)**

|  | 1972 | 1974 | 1976 | 1978 | 1980 |
|---|---|---|---|---|---|
| Estimated TV households (million), year-end | 64 | 66 | 70 | 75 | 80 |
| Videoplayer penetration (%), year-end | 0.3% | 2.6% | 5.6% | 9.3% | 14.0% |
| Videoplayer households (million), year-end | 0.2 | 1.7 | 3.9 | 7.0 | 11.2 |
| New videoplayer households for year shown (million) | 0.2 | 0.8 | 1.2 | 1.7 | 2.2 |
| | | | (in millions of dollars) | | |
| Consumer market: | | | | | |
| Hardware sales† | $ 53 | $213 | $319 | $451 | $ 584 |
| Software sales‡ | 11 | 51 | 93 | 152 | 223 |
| Software rentals§ | 11 | 51 | 93 | 152 | 223 |
| | $ 75 | $315 | $505 | $755 | $1,030 |
| Institutional and government market‖ | 90 | 125 | 150 | 175 | 200 |
| Total | $165 | $440 | $655 | $930 | $1,230 |

\*John P. Thompson, "International Outlook for Consumer Electronics," Arthur D. Little, Inc., April 1971.
 †Calculated at average factory price of $266 ($400 at retail).
 ‡Calculated at average factory sales of $50 × new videoplayer households (basic library) and $12.50 × old videoplayer households (additions to library). ($100 and $25 at retail, respectively.)
 §Estimated at same volume as sales.
 ‖Does not include software.

**Free world sales of consumer electronics products: 1969–75 (millions of U.S. dollars, at factory prices)**

| Products | 1969 | 1970 | 1975 Low | 1975 High |
|---|---|---|---|---|
| Videoplayers and prerecorded cassettes | $ 0 | $ 0 | $ 900 | $ 1,500 |
| Television sets | | | | |
| Black and white | 2,265 | 2,300 | 2,000 | 2,600 |
| Color | 3,900 | 4,100 | 6,200 | 7,500 |
| Audio tape equipment and software | | | | |
| Cassettes and cartridges | 372 | 585 | 1,475 | 2,235 |
| Players and recorder/players | 565 | 710 | 1,245 | 1,610 |
| Phonographs and hi-fi components | 1,400 | 1,475 | 1,300 | 1,775 |
| Radio | 1,370 | 1,425 | 1,555 | 1,990 |
| Cable television equipment | 100 | 135 | 435 | 575 |
| Interactive TV equipment | 0 | 0 | 55 | 235 |
| Home facsimile systems | 0 | 0 | 30 | 75 |
| Total (rounded) | $9,970 | $10,700 | $15,200 | $20,100 |

Source: Arthur D. Little, Inc. estimates.

# CORPORATE STRATEGY AND ENVIRONMENTAL CHANGE

## Note on the watch industries in Switzerland, Japan, and the United States

### AN OVERVIEW OF THE WORLD WATCH INDUSTRY IN 1970

As BEST as can be estimated, worldwide watch and watch movement production in 1970 reached the level of 175 million units. At manufacturers' selling prices this production had a value of about $1.3 billion. Pin-lever watches constituted slightly more than half of the total output; jeweled-lever watches made up the rest with the exception of 1%–2% of the total which belonged to a variety of electric and electronic models.[1]

Since the early 1950s, when worldwide watch production was at an annual rate of about 45 million units, the output of the industry had increased fourfold. In the 10 years leading up to 1970, worldwide output increased at annual rates that ranged between 7% and 11%. Talk about market saturation persisted among some watchmakers, yet as of 1970 the overall growth of the industry had not shown any noticeable sign of slowing down.

Table 1 shows the origins of the 1970 output.[2]

These figures in Table 1 illustrate several important points. The first is a well-known one: Switzerland is far and away the dominant watchmaking nation. In 1970 its production amounted to 42% of worldwide output.

---

[1] For a brief guide to watch technology, see Appendix A.

[2] The data presented in Tables 1 through 5 were calculated from information provided by the Federation of Swiss Watchmakers.

TABLE 1

Leading watchmaking nations—1970 (millions of watches and watch movements)

| Country | Production | Exports | Exports as percent of production |
|---------|------------|---------|----------------------------------|
| Switzerland | 73.7 | 71.4 | 97 |
| Japan | 23.8 | 13.7 | 58 |
| U.S.S.R. | 21.5* | 1.8 | 8 |
| United States | 20.0* | 0.2* | 1 |
| France | 11.0 | 4.1 | 37 |
| West Germany | 8.2 | 4.1 | 50 |
| Mainland China | 5.0* | ... | .. |
| East Germany | 3.5 | 1.8 | 51 |
| United Kingdom | 3.2 | 1.0 | 31 |
| Italy | 2.6* | 0.6 | 23 |
| Others | 2.0* | ... | .. |
| Total | 174.5 | 98.7 | |

*Estimated.

The second point is less well known: there is considerable production in countries currently outside the mainstream of Western commerce. In 1970 output in the U.S.S.R., East Germany, and mainland China represented about 17% of the world total. For the time being, at least, the bulk of this output stays within the Eastern bloc. Accordingly, the communist countries, and in particular the Soviet Union, will be excluded from this note's analysis of the struggle for the world watch market.

With the Eastern bloc out of the picture, the Swiss domination of watchmaking becomes all the more striking. In 1970 every other watch made in the noncommunist world came from a Swiss plant.

The third point has to do with how the watchmaking industries in Switzerland, Japan, and the United States are linked to world markets. In 1970 Swiss watchmakers exported virtually all of their output, Japanese firms exported slightly more than half of their output, and American companies exported almost none of their output. In the case of the United States, the largest watch market in the world, domestic production accounted for slightly less than half of its needs. Imports, some from foreign firms and some from U.S.-controlled plants sited overseas, filled the void.

While data on the production of watches by country are readily available, figures on market size by country are hard to come by. Still, rough estimates by major geographical areas are possible. In 1970 Europe in total represented a market about equal to that of the United States: watch purchases in both markets ran at an annual rate of around 45 million units. In the same year, Japan's home market was about a third of the size of those in Europe or the United States. And as for the rest of the world (excluding the communist countries), its market roughly matched that of Europe and of the United States.

The remainder of this note examines the three watchmaking industries that, as of the early 1970s, were the most active contenders for dominance in these markets. The Swiss, Japanese, and U.S. industries are discussed in the next three sections. The last section of this note discusses the recent technological advances that have turned the contest into competitive turmoil.

## THE SWISS WATCH INDUSTRY

> Watchmaking, long presumed the private preserve of Swiss interests, has in the last decade or so clearly become a field that's up for grabs. The Alpine republic's one-time international hegemony in the timekeeping business is now almost as full of holes as the country's justly famed cheese.
>
> 

*Value Line Selection and Opinion*

"Ridiculous!"

Executive Director, Watchmakers of Switzerland
Information Center

### Industry highlights in 1970

Watchmaking has always occupied an especially important place in the Swiss economy, and the year 1970 was no exception. Roughly 1,000 different firms and 80,000 employees were engaged in making $630 million of watch and watch-related products.[3] Watchmaking contributed almost 3% to the total Swiss GNP; in that year it was Switzerland's fourth largest industry and it employed close to 8% of all manufacturing workers.

Of necessity, the Swiss economy depends heavily on exports, and watches have routinely been one of the country's major foreign exchange earners. In 1970 about 97% of total watch production was shipped outside the Swiss borders. Valued at $610 million, these shipments represented 12% of total Swiss exports, making watches the country's third most important export product.

In 1970 watchmaking contributed to the Swiss economy in still another important, if intangible, way. As the Swiss Bank put it:

The long-standing repute of the Swiss watch industry also provides another free benefit to the Swiss economy. Being a typical symbol of quality and

---

[3] Unless otherwise indicated all data originally stated in Swiss francs have been converted into U.S. dollars at the 1970 exchange rate of 4.3 Swiss francs to one U.S. dollar.

reliability it acts as an advertising medium for other Swiss products. Swiss industry, due to the absence of low-cost natural resources, is often at a disadvantage, in terms of cost, when competing against other countries' products. Therefore, the reputation of the Swiss watch does help to publicize the quality of the "Swiss-made" brand and acts as a powerful sales argument.

Not only was the Swiss watchmaking industry important at home, it was important to the world. Excluding production in communist countries, every other watch made in the world in 1970 came from Switzerland. And three quarters of all watches exported from any country in 1970 came from Swiss plants.

Though the Swiss hold on the world market in 1970 was impressive, it was not so impressive as it had been several decades earlier. In the late 1940s the Swiss share of worldwide production was over 80% and the Swiss share of watch exports, from all sources, was around 95%. In response to those who talked about the weakness of the Swiss industry, pointing out that its share of the world market had been cut in half during the 1950s and 1960s, the Swiss answered by referring to the threefold growth in their watch production. Back in the late 1940s the Swiss industry produced around 25 million watches and watch movements each year; by the early 1970s the industry was producing annually at close to the 75-million-unit rate. Employment in the industry had actually increased slightly since the post–World War II years. In the Swiss view the dramatic growth in their watch output represented a considerable achievement and indicated that Switzerland would remain the dominant watch-producing nation for years to come.

### Swiss exports in 1970

Since, for all practical purposes, the Swiss export all the watches they make, it is necessary to look at the composition of exports in order to understand Switzerland's competitive position in foreign markets. By production category, the 1970 Swiss exports are shown in Table 2.

**TABLE 2**
**Swiss watch exports by stage of production—1970**

| Category | *Percent of exports in value terms* |
|---|---|
| Finished watches | 77.0 |
| Watch movements | 12.5 |
| Miscellaneous watch components (including a small amount of clock exports) | 10.5 |

The percentages in Table 2 were almost identical for jeweled-lever and pin-lever watches.

By type, Swiss exports of *finished* watches and movements are shown in Table 3.

**TABLE 3**
Swiss exports by type of watch—1970

|  | Units (millions) | Value (U.S. $ millions) | Average value per unit (U.S. $) |
|---|---|---|---|
| Jeweled-lever . . . . . . . . . . | 38.3 | 440 | 11.50 |
| Pin-lever . . . . . . . . . . . . . | 32.7 | 85 | 2.62 |
| Electric-electronic . . . . . . . | 0.3 | 8 | 26.00 |

Tables 2 and 3 make one point quite clear. In 1970 the export of finished jeweled-lever watches constituted the core activity of the Swiss watchmaking industry. Anything jeopardizing this segment could jeopardize the entire industry.

Table 4 shows, by major geographical region, where the Swiss exports went in 1960 and in 1970. Several points stand out. First of all, Swiss

**TABLE 4**
Swiss exports by major geographical regions—1960 and 1970
(for watches and watch movements combined)

|  | Percent of total exports in unit terms | | | |
|---|---|---|---|---|
|  | Jeweled-lever | | Pin-lever | |
|  | 1960 | 1970 | 1960 | 1970 |
| Europe . . . . . . . . . . . . . | 26.2 | 32.7 | 18.2 | 21.7 |
| Africa . . . . . . . . . . . . . | 3.9 | 4.9 | 10.7 | 5.7 |
| Middle East . . . . . . . . . . | 7.8 | 14.4 | 1.2 | 2.8 |
| Asia. . . . . . . . . . . . . . | 13.3 | 11.6 | 9.4 | 26.2 |
| USA–Canada . . . . . . . . . | 31.6 | 22.3 | 45.2 | 36.2 |
| Latin America . . . . . . . . . | 14.5 | 12.1 | 15.1 | 7.1 |
| Oceania . . . . . . . . . . . | 2.7 | 2.0 | 0.2 | 0.3 |

exports of jeweled-lever watches have been somewhat more dispersed than those of pin-lever watches. Second, during the 1960s, the U.S.–Canadian market declined in its relative importance to the Swiss while the European market became more important to them. And third, by 1970 Asia had become a major market for Swiss pin-lever watches. When looking at these figures, bear in mind that the value of jeweled-lever exports was almost five times that of pin-lever exports. Consequently, the shifts in market that took place with jeweled-lever watches had a far greater effect on the value of exports than did those that took place with pin-lever watches.

Table 5, which lists all the countries to which the Swiss shipped a million or more watches in 1970, rounds out the export picture.

**TABLE 5**
**Swiss exports of watches and movements to**
**major markets—1970 (for all types of watches)**

|  | Percent of total units | Percent of total value |
|---|---|---|
| United States . . . . . . . . . . | 27.4 | 20.2 |
| Hong Kong . . . . . . . . . . . | 14.2 | 10.0 |
| United Kingdom . . . . . . . . | 8.7 | 5.5 |
| Arabia . . . . . . . . . . . . . | 4.8 | 3.8 |
| West Germany. . . . . . . . . . | 4.1 | 5.7 |
| Italy . . . . . . . . . . . . . . | 3.7 | 6.5 |
| Spain . . . . . . . . . . . . . . | 3.6 | 3.8 |
| Argentina . . . . . . . . . . . | 2.2 | 2.2 |
| Brazil. . . . . . . . . . . . . . | 2.1 | 1.9 |
| Canada . . . . . . . . . . . . . | 1.9 | 1.5 |
| Mexico . . . . . . . . . . . . . | 1.6 | 2.0 |
| Japan . . . . . . . . . . . . . . | 1.4 | 3.7 |
| Total. . . . . . . . . . . | 75.7 | 66.8 |

As Table 5 indicates, 11 countries imported the bulk—three quarters in unit terms and two thirds in value terms—of Swiss watch production. As the world's largest watch market, the United States was, quite naturally, number one in importance to the Swiss. Yet, as suggested by Table 4, the Swiss share of the U.S. market has been eroding steadily. In fact, in 1950 99% of all watches imported into the United States were of Swiss origin; by 1970 this figure had dropped to around 70%. In the same period, the Swiss share of total watch consumption in the United States had declined from 50% to about 40%.

The number two export market for Switzerland in 1970, Hong Kong, was a recent arrival on the scene. One item largely accounted for the rapid emergence of Hong Kong as a Swiss customer. By 1970 almost 85% of all pin-lever movements (not finished pin-lever watches) made in Switzerland were destined for Hong Kong where they were cased and subsequently scattered over many Far Eastern markets. Determining who actually controlled what part of the Hong Kong trade in 1970 was an almost impossible task. Several Swiss pin-lever manufacturers had assembly plants in Hong Kong, yet local interests were also involved in the business. About all that could be said was that Hong Kong had become an important channel through which Swiss pin-lever watches reached many overseas markets.

One final point brought out in Table 5 needs mentioning. Note that Japan, the second largest watchmaker, was not a major market for the Swiss. This fact has certainly had a bearing on how the Swiss have viewed the competitive problems facing their industry. Whereas in any sort of contest among Swiss, Japanese, and U.S. watchmakers the Swiss could afford to give up their place in the Japanese market, they could not afford to see their hold on the U.S. market seriously jeopardized. As we shall see in a subsequent section, in 1970 the United States was also Japan's leading export market. It follows that if the 1970s were to see a struggle for leadership in the world watch industry, the battle would take place principally in the U.S. marketplace.

### Fragmentation: The Swiss industry's main problem

One fact, mentioned at the beginning of the preceding section, is the key to the number one problem that faced Swiss watchmakers in 1970. The industry, which included around 1,000 different enterprises, was far more fragmented than that in any other leading watchmaking nation. To understand why this was so calls for a brief review of the development of watchmaking in Switzerland.

### Early development

The Swiss did not invent the watch. Over 300 years ago the rudimentary techniques of watchmaking were brought to Switzerland by Huguenots fleeing religious persecution in France. At first they settled around Geneva; subsequently they spread throughout northwest Switzerland.

For better than a century and a half several factors combined to foster a very independent, family-oriented spirit among the early watchmakers. In part, watchmaking was a craft which depended on skills being passed on from one generation to the next. In part, where many of the watchmakers lived, in relative isolation in the mountains, prompted a very independent view. And in part, the fact that each family fabricated a few complete timepieces each year nourished a sense of a distinct family watchmaking tradition. By and large, the attitudes formed then, described by some as a stubborn individualism, persisted into recent times.

In the first half of the 1800s, in response to advances in mechanization, individual producers started to specialize: some families concentrated on making parts, others on assembling parts into finished watches. By the mid-1800s the industry had evolved into a two-tier manufacturing system with component manufacturing separate from watch assembling.

With few changes, the industry retained this characteristic up to the mid-1950s. Yet mechanization did not break down the small individual unit structure of the industry.

By 1900 watchmaking in Switzerland far outpaced that taking place anywhere else in the world. But the industry was made up of thousands of small family-owned firms. Though the Swiss dominated watchmaking on a worldwide scale and had established "Swiss made" as a symbol of quality in watches, they had done so with an industry ill equipped to cope with anything other than the most superficial economic difficulties. The crises of the 1920s and 1930s made this painfully apparent to the Swiss.

### The industry's and the government's response: 1920–30

In the early 1920s Swiss watchmakers saw sales collapsing and unemployment soaring. They set out to bring order out of the chaos by organizing themselves into a number of industry associations, each made up of firms engaged in the same type of manufacturing operations. The associations that sprang up in the period 1924–27 were:

1. The Federation Suisse de Fabricants d'Horlogerie (FH): those firms assembling watches from component parts supplied by others plus those few firms with integrated manufacturing operations. All of the output of member firms was of the jeweled-lever type. These were the firms that actually sold watches in the marketplace.
2. Ebauches SA: 17 manufacturers of ebauches grouped together into a trust.
3. The Union des Branches Annexes de l'Horlogerie (UBAH): the manufacturers of components other than ebauches.

The formation of these associations laid the foundation for industry cartelization. In 1928, in a series of restrictive private agreements among the three major associations, the manufacturing, pricing, and exporting policies of member firms were brought under industry control.

No sooner had the watchmakers taken these steps when the depression of the 1930s got underway. Deteriorating conditions in the industry forced the Swiss government to come to its aid. As a first step, the government, in 1931, invested in a super holding company, the Société Générale de l'Horlogerie Suisse SA (ASUAG), which, in turn, acquired the majority of the shares of Ebauches SA and of several of the leading components manufacturers. This move eased the financial woes of a number of the watchmakers and made the government a direct partner in industry affairs. Then, in 1934, a federal statute ratified the web of the industry's private controls and imposed new ones; thereafter, watch manufacturing and exporting were permitted only with government approval. From 1934 through 1965, the structure of the Swiss watchmaking industry and the makeup of the many restrictive covenants under which it operated remained almost unchanged. A list of the principal government-sanctioned rules of the industry includes the following:

1.  The members of Ebauches SA and UBAH agreed to sell components only to the members of FH.
2.  In turn, the members of FH agreed, with one exception, to buy components only from member firms of Ebauches SA and UBAH. The firms in FH did reserve the right to buy foreign-made components, but they also agreed not to buy such components unless they were priced more than 20% under the Swiss level.
3.  In addition, the members of FH agreed to fix their selling prices in accord with a complex interassociation pricing system and a markup formula. Ebauches SA and UBAH supplied the components at specified prices, subject to change only after interassociation negotiation. And the watch assemblers and integrated manufacturers established their prices using a standard markup above association-determined manufacturing costs.
4.  Finally, FH members agreed to limit their guarantees on finished watches to one year.
5.  As regards government rules, firms could only engage in watchmaking after obtaining authorization from a federal department. The federal legislation effectively froze the structure of the industry: firms could not expand, move, sell out, acquire others, or change the nature of their operations without government approval.
6.  In addition, the government rules regulated the Swiss industry's links with the rest of the world. To preserve order in overseas markets, firms were required to obtain permits to export finished watches, movements, and components. More importantly, to insure that new foreign competitors would not spring up and that existing foreign competitors would not benefit from advances in Swiss technology, government approval was required for the export of tools and dies, engineering drawings, and watchmaking machinery.

This elaborate system, designed to protect the status quo in a highly fragmented industry, persisted for almost 40 years. Yet by the late 1950s events in the marketplace were making it obvious that something had to change.

### The breakdown of the watch cartel

Discontent with the cartel arose first among the member firms of FH, for they were the ones who had to meet competition face to face.

Despite the Swiss attempt to pen up watchmaking technology, during the 1950s foreign rivals expanded production and began to make inroads into Swiss sales. On the continent, French and German watchmakers cut into the Swiss market share; in the United States, Timex imperiled at least a portion of Swiss exports; and in the Far East, where the threat was still in the offing, markets were ripe for an obviously impending Japanese invasion.

The malcontents in the FH claimed that the cartel rules protected the marginal assembling firms and fostered inefficiency among the component manufacturers. They also pointed out that, in the face of mounting price competition in overseas markets, the cartel promoted a type of conduct on the part of some watchmakers that jeopardized the quality image of the whole Swiss industry. Whereas the efficient producers were able to meet price competition, with sufficient residual profits to improve their manufacturing efficiency and the quality of their output still further, the marginal firms, in order to survive, had turned to producing low-quality watches which they dumped at giveaway prices in foreign markets.

After several years of negotiations within the industry, the malcontents won the first round of concessions. The industry agreements were revised to provide for greater leeway in the pricing of components to the FH members and in the application of the pricing formula for finished watches.

Then in 1961 the government bowed to the obvious necessity of bringing the industry up to date. It rescinded, effective as of January 1, 1966, the requirement for manufacturing permits. After that date firms were free to expand, contract, merge, sell out to foreign companies, or buy foreign companies. Thus the government move opened the way for industry concentration. As part of the same legislative package, the government established a watch standards commission to put an end to the debasement of the watches by the small producers. And finally, the government decreed that the requirement for export permits would expire in 1971. After that date there would be no official impediments to the transfer overseas of watchmaking technology.

The 1961 legislation sounded the death knell for the Swiss watch cartel. It finally died in 1966 when the industry associations abolished all the remnants of the fixed-price system.

The death of the watch cartel did not, however, spell the end for the important industry associations, which have continued to serve as spokesmen for the various sectors of the industry. Exhibit 1, which shows the composition of the industry as of 1970, demonstrates that its structure remained defined by the associations. Nor did the death of the watch cartel mean the end to joint actions among Swiss watchmakers. To the contrary, the associations have continued to be the backbone of a collec-

EXHIBIT 1

**Structure of the Swiss watch industry—1970**

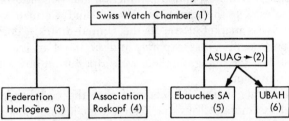

(1)  The association that represents the entire industry in govern-
     mental and foreign trade matters.
(2)  The holding company, 38 % controlled by the Swiss government,
     that owns a majority interest of Ebauches SA and of three of the
     largest component manufacturers.
(3)  The association of jeweled-lever watch manufacturers. In 1970 it
     had 486 members.
(4)  The association of pin-lever watch manufacturers. In 1970 it had
     over 50 members.
(5)  A trust composed of 17 subsidiaries producing ebauches.
(6)  The association of component manufacturers. It includes hundreds
     of small firms among its members as well as four large component
     producing firms or groups of firms. The four are:
     *a)*  Fabriques d'Assortiments Réunies (escapements).
     *b)*  Fabriques de Balanciers SA (balance wheels).
     *c)*  Groupement des Fabricants Suisses de Spiraux (hairsprings).
     *d)*  Pierres Holding SA (jewels).

tive approach to industry activities, especially in promotional programs
and R & D projects. These collective activities will be discussed shortly,
but first it is necessary to look at the steps the Swiss have taken to
cope with the problem of fragmentation.

### Industry concentration

In the early 1960s about 2,000 separate enterprises were engaged
in one facet or another of watchmaking in Switzerland. Roughly speaking, these 2,000 firms fell into the following categories:

*Finished watch manufacturers*
1.  About 500 firms solely assembling jeweled-lever watches.
2.  About 60 integrated manufacturers of jeweled-lever watches.
3.  About 70 integrated manufacturers of pin-lever watches.
*Component manufacturers*
4.  Seventeen manufacturers of ebauches, all members of Ebauches
    SA.
5.  About 650 manufacturers of separate parts.
6.  Around 500 other firms performing miscellaneous functions.

Though these figures accurately reflect the extent of fragmentation
that existed among finished watch manufacturers, they misrepresent the
situation that existed among component manufacturers. Three organiza-

tions, originally trusts composed of many small companies, dominated individual parts manufacturing. They were:

Fabriques d'Assortiments Réunies SA (the major supplier of escapement mechanisms).
Fabriques de Balanciers SA (the major supplier of balance wheels).
Groupement des Fabricants Suisses de Spiraux (the major supplier of hairsprings).

Together with Ebauches SA, these three groups supplied about three quarters of the Swiss industry's requirements for ebauches and separate parts.[4] Since they accounted for such a large share of component production, it is obvious that the hundreds of other firms in the component sector either fulfilled highly specialized roles or were quite marginal firms.

As we have seen a decade later, the number of firms in the Swiss watch industry was down to around 1,000. Since 1966, when the Swiss government's restrictions on the sale or acquisition of watch companies lapsed, the industry experienced a crescendo of mergers. The Swiss were hurriedly—some observers said frantically—trying to create watchmaking firms matching the size and competitive clout of the major foreign rivals. Why the industry was caught up in the mergers' wave and where it was heading was summed up by one leading Swiss watchmaker in these terms:

For many years far-sighted representatives of the watch industry stubbornly tried to introduce new methods, to overcome outmoded structures, to eliminate the compartmentalization typical of Swiss watch production, to channel the interest of technically-minded Swiss watchmakers more into modern marketing, to overcome difficulties rooted in outmoded protectionist ideas and to surmount assorted similar problems. With few exceptions, however, they had to wait until very recently before there were any visible signs of a trend toward industry cooperation and corporate concentration.

This development is irreversible and will doubtless accelerate in the future. It is already quite conceivable that, under the growing pressure of competition from *within and without* the watch industry, there will soon be a considerable increase in the number of medium-size companies (rather than hundreds of small ones). The only product lines likely to escape this trend will be a few specialty items and exclusive products, the success of which does not depend on mass turnover.

Under these circumstances we do not think it overly bold to predict that, aside from the few exceptions mentioned, in five years there may be only about ten watch producing enterprises operating in this country.[5]

---

[4] In 1968 another holding-company-type arrangement was established within the components sector. A number of the small watch jewel manufacturers became members of Pierres Holding SA. Altogether, the members of this new group supplied about 60% of the total Swiss jewel production.

[5] Robert Brandt, "The Position of the Watch Industry," *Credit Suisse Bulletin,* December 1970. Emphasis added.

As of 1972 there was, at least on paper, ample evidence that the Swiss were succeeding at consolidating the industry. Whether the Swiss were also succeeding at converting the many newly formed companies into operationally effective organizations was still an open question. The world received a fairly steady stream of reports about mergers and plans for mergers; it did not hear much of what went on within the board rooms and corporate offices of the Swiss companies. Undoubtedly, the pains and problems of transition were taxing the managerial skills of many Swiss executives.

Still, progress looked impressive. Both horizontal and vertical mergers were changing the industry profoundly. For instance, as the result of a series of horizontal mergers, the Swiss finally had one watch company that could match the size of large foreign rivals. Founded in 1930, the Société Suisse de l'Industrie Horlogère (SSIH), the manufacturer of such famous brands as Omega and Tissot, had always been a leader in the watchmaking industry. In the early 1960s it controlled about 9% of total Swiss watch exports. But even with that share of exports, SSIH was small compared to the leading Japanese and U.S. watchmakers. Then, after 1966, SSIH broadened its activities and, in 1971, merged with Economic Swiss Time Holding (ESTH). This second group, composed of a number of pin-lever manufacturers, accounted for 20%–25% of total Swiss pin-lever output. By the end of 1971, the enlarged SSIH controlled over 20% of Swiss watch exports and had an annual turnover of close to $130 million.

ASUAG, the "supertrust" controlling a majority interest in Ebauches SA and in the three largest component manufacturers, gave birth to another large horizontal group when, in 1971, it combined the assembling firms selling seven different brands into the General Watch Holding Company. This move forged important new financial and managerial links between the component manufacturing and assembling sectors of the watch industry.

Meanwhile, Ebauches SA entered into another set of arrangements with both horizontal and vertical merger characteristics. In 1970 the Longines-Record Watch Company and the Rotary Watch Company joined to form Holdings Longines SA. Then, in 1971, Ebauches became a major partner in this new venture. As in the case with ASUAG, the Swiss joined together companies whose fundamental activities were assembling and marketing watches and simultaneously linked the amalgamation to the component manufacturing sector.

The upshot of these mergers, and dozens more, has been the creation of a partially concentrated industry. *By 1971 almost three quarters of all Swiss watch exports were accounted for by eight watchmaking groups.* But the industry structure was still lopsided. A residue of several hundred small firms contributed the other quarter of Swiss exports. Thus there was a growing gap between the big watchmaking combinations and the little independent producers. Under these circumstances, it seemed fairly certain that only one of two different futures faced most of the small companies: absorption by the big holding groups or collapse.

As for the large watch companies, the mere fact that most of them had multiplied their size through a series of mergers did not guarantee that they would enjoy the benefits of size. They still had to tackle such tasks as eliminating duplicate product lines, combining production facilities, streamlining management systems, and so on. As suggested above, in the early 1970s the evidence of progress along these lines was still sparse.

### Swiss investment in the U.S. watch industry

The Swiss effort to bolster the competitive position of their industry was two-pronged. At the same time that they were concentrating it at home, they were protecting it by investing in U.S. watchmaking firms. In the second half of the 1960s they made the following moves:

1. Iseca SA, a consortium of Swiss watch manufacturers, acquired 100% of the Waltham Watch Company.
2. Sopinter SA, a Swiss holding company, acquired a 16% interest in Elgin.
3. Chronos Holding SA, a financial company set up for the express purpose of promoting amalgamation within the Swiss industry, purchased 20% of Gruen.

And in 1971 the Swiss took another step which could ultimately give them control of one of the most famous names in American watchmaking, the Hamilton Watch Company. Apart from its proud tradition in conventional watchmaking, Hamilton had been on the technological forefront on more than one occasion. In 1957 it had been the first U.S. firm to market an electric watch. In 1971, with its "Pulsar" (which used light-emitting diodes), it was the first U.S. firm to market a digital watch. Still, Hamilton came upon hard times.

The history of the Swiss move to take over Hamilton started in 1970 when Bush Universal, Inc., a diversified firm that leased piers and buildings in Brooklyn, New York, bought 50.2% of the almost bankrupt Hamilton company. Subsequently, after Hamilton's losses deepened further, Bush spun off the watch business into a new subsidiary and sold 17% of it to Aetos SA, itself a subsidiary of the leader in the Swiss industry, SSIH. Aetos, as part of the deal, also accepted a note from Hamilton which, if converted after three years, would increase the Swiss company's interest in Hamilton to 51%. Hamilton seemed destined to become a member of the Swiss camp.

The basic motivation for all these investments was fairly clear. Though the second tier of U.S. watchmakers, those that had not attained the size of Bulova and Timex, were barely able to meet the mounting competition within the industry, they all possessed one valuable asset: established trade names. To the Swiss, control of the names, in part or in whole, opened the door to increased penetration of the U.S. market. There was some evidence that the Swiss intended to fight the electronic watch battle in the United States with trade names which American consumers would assume were those of fine old U.S. watchmakers.

What else were the Swiss doing to insure the continued prosperity of their watchmaking industry?

### Promotional practices

Up until the late 1960s Swiss watchmakers relied mainly on an institutional approach to promotion. They channeled a high proportion of their promotional expenditures through industrywide organizations, like the Federation of Swiss Watchmakers, into collective campaigns in overseas markets. The campaigns stressed the quality and reputation of "Swiss-made" watches rather than specific brands. Of course, a few of the larger Swiss watchmakers supplemented the industry's activities by promoting their own brands. Names like Rolex and Omega became world-renowned. Still, the sale of watches bearing established brand names constituted a small fraction of total Swiss exports. This was particularly true in the case of watches falling in the low- and medium-price categories.

As of the early 1970s this all started to change. The 1971 Annual Report of the Federation of Swiss Watchmakers (FH) described the new approach:

During 1971, the FH continued on the new course adopted after the turning point in its promotional activities in 1970, i.e., that of henceforth concentrating on designing, carrying out, and financing promotional activities with fuller cooperation from the brands involved. This change in the FH's approach to promotion consisted in a shift away from collective promotion mainly benefiting the industry as a whole in favor of programmes integrating the brands involved in every way. . . .

Even though Swiss watchmakers reallocated more and more of their promotional funds from industry to company campaigns, they still continued to support the industry's many long-standing technical programs. Since World War II, the Swiss sponsored watch-repair training schools in many countries. They established technical centers and after-sales service centers in a number of foreign markets. They frequently held seminars, in Switzerland and overseas, on a wide range of subjects related to the watch industry. And they conducted a variety of training programs covering the management, marketing, and distribution aspects of the watch business. Almost all of these efforts were collective undertakings. By and large they were regarded as essential to the success of the industry. And there were no signs that Swiss efforts along these lines would diminish in the 1970s.

## Research and development

As with promotional activities, the Swiss watchmakers have tended to approach R & D from an industry rather than from an individual-firm standpoint. The two major Swiss R & D programs begun in the 1960s, both related to the development of the electronic watch, highlight this point.

In 1962 Ebauches SA, the other main component manufacturers, and a number of the watch assembling firms joined together to establish the Centre Electronique Horloger (CEH). The initial goal of the electronic watch center was to develop a new time-determining device to compete with Bulova's tuning-fork mechanism. Later, the CEH also took on the task of developing a quartz crystal watch movement. The role of the CEH was defined as extending beyond the laboratory. It was chartered to produce prototypes of new watches for the purpose of test marketing them. Once the prototypes proved themselves in the marketplace, the clients of CEH would pick them up for full-scale manufacturing and marketing.

Whether the first decade of operation of the CEH was regarded as a success or not seemed to depend on who was making the assessment. American watchmakers pointed out that the CEH failed at developing a tuning-fork device that did not violate Bulova's patents. The Swiss claimed that the CEH had come up with an acceptable alternative. Still, in 1968 Ebauches SA entered into a license agreement with Bulova to manufacture and sell watches based on Bulova's tuning-fork movement. As for research on the quartz crystal watch, the Swiss stressed that the CEH had perfected a commercial model before anyone else. Yet when the Swiss introduced their first quartz watches in 1971, American watchmakers noted that they contained integrated circuits made by U.S. firms. The Swiss had hoped to avoid this turn of events. In fact, this hope had prompted their second major R & D effort of the 1960s.

In 1966 the Federation of Watch Manufacturers (FH), two Swiss companies (Brown Boveri and Landis & Gyr), and Philips of the Netherlands formed FASEC, a laboratory for joint research in the fields of semiconductors, integrated circuits, and lasers. The purpose of the project was clear enough: to make sure that the Swiss watchmaking industry would not be dependent on U.S. electronics manufacturers.

Yet some observers interpreted the formation of FASEC as an indication of the weakness of the Swiss watchmaking industry, for it had to turn to a foreign company, Philips, for advanced electronics technology. As of 1972 there was no way for outsiders to measure what FASEC had accomplished, since Swiss electronic watches still contained American-made circuitry and the Swiss were reticent about describing FASEC's research output.

How much has the Swiss industry spent on developing the electronic watch? Unfortunately, the figures are not available to answer the question with any precision. What follows, therefore, is based on the crudest of estimates. According to some reports, the Swiss have spent around $2.5 million per year on CEH's research activities. If the Swiss industry has backed up FASEC to the same extent, the industry has been putting about $5 million a year into R & D related to the electronic watch. This figure looks respectable until it is compared to total industry turnover; it amounts to about 0.8% of industry sales. Suppose, and this is rather unlikely, that individual Swiss firms have matched the R & D expenditures of the industry-sponsored programs. Total outlays, even then, would have added up to not much more than the 1½% of industry sales.

If these figures describe, even in rough terms, the level of R & D commitment of the Swiss industry in the late 1960s and early 1970s, they raise the question of whether that commitment was high enough. It's safe to assume that the Swiss were asking themselves that same critical question.

## Diversification

Throughout the last decade Swiss watchmakers have talked at length about the advantages of diversification. Yet it is fair to say that as of the early 1970s no Swiss watchmaker, big or small, was in any sense diversified. True, some produced items other than watches and clocks, but almost without exception these other goods were intimately related to the technology of timekeeping.

In the case of the many small firms, the reasons why they held fast to their narrow product lines were fairly obvious. A close family orientation, 30 years of protection under cartel rules, and a perception of their businesses in specific technical terms did not foster among the small watchmakers the inclination or the bases for diversification. And in the case of the large firms, they had been so preoccupied since the mid-1960s making and digesting mergers that it is unlikely they had either the time or the resources to pursue diversification seriously. Whatever the causes, the Swiss watchmakers faced the problems of the 1970s from a very narrowly defined business base.

## THE JAPANESE WATCH INDUSTRY

A Swiss watch manufacturer was asked if the Russians posed a threat in his business.

"The Russians!" he laughed. "They always seem to be ten years behind."

"And the Japanese? How far behind are they?"

"About three weeks. . . ."

*Jewelers' Circular-Keystone*

### Early development

Watchmaking started in Japan in the 1880s. For the next 50 years Japanese watchmakers concentrated almost exclusively on supplying their home market and on making jeweled-lever watches. They stressed jeweled-lever production because they wanted to emulate the best in western watchmaking. Yet, by most standards, the quality of the timepieces made in Japan in the industry's early days was inferior to that of timepieces made in the West. And, in fact, the Swiss dominated the premium end of the market, supplying about 90% of Japanese imports.

By the late 1930s Japanese production of watches and watch movements had reached the level of around 5 million units per year. One firm had emerged as the industry leader; alone it accounted for almost one half of Japanese production. Then World War II and its aftermath postponed further growth of the industry for almost 20 years. Japanese watchmakers did not produce at the five-million-unit level again until the 1958–59 period. By then, however, the industry had fully recouped from the war, had completely retooled, and had significantly upgraded the quality of its product. The Japanese were ready to make their presence known as a full-fledged member of the world watch industry.

### The expansion of the industry in the 1960s

In 1960 Japanese production of watches and watch movements hit the seven-million-unit level, equivalent to slightly more than 7% of worldwide watch output. Still, almost all the Japanese production was absorbed at home; the industry exported only 200,000 watches and movements that year.

Then during the 1960s Japanese watch production more than trebled in unit terms. In 1970 the industry poured forth almost 24 million watches and movements, about 14% of worldwide watch output. And by 1970 over one half of this production was destined for overseas markets. Or, to put the development in perspective, the industry exported almost twice as many watches and movements in 1970 as it had produced for total home consumption in 1960.

In part, the Japanese had pushed themselves into foreign markets; in part, they had been pulled into foreign markets. As the 1960s rolled on, the Japanese watchmakers could see that their home market was becoming increasingly saturated. Consequently, they looked overseas. They aggressively invaded the Southeast Asian market, long the private domain of the Swiss. In a somewhat more halting fashion, they started to move into Western European markets and into the United States. But in the case of the United States, the Japanese were also pulled into the market by U.S. watchmakers who imported large quantities of inexpensive Japanese movements and parts for assembly here or in the Virgin Islands. By the late 1960s the Japanese export push began to take on a clear pattern. Almost two thirds of all Japanese watch and watch-movement exports were destined for two markets: the United States or Hong Kong.

The growth of the industry and the success of its surge overseas was particularly remarkable because it involved so few firms.

### Industry structure

In sharp contrast to the situation in Switzerland and to the state of the U.S. industry until recent years, the Japanese watch industry has always been highly concentrated. Over the years, four firms have accounted for almost all Japanese watch production. More strikingly, two firms have accounted for almost 90% of the production. As of 1970, the industry structure was as shown in Table 6.

Obviously, K. Hattori & Co. is the General Motors of the Japanese watch industry. To understand the industry, therefore, one has to know something about this dominant leader. How did the company operate in 1970? Actually, K. Hattori was only the sales arm of a cluster of firms known as the Seiko Group. Two subsidiaries in the group, Daini

**TABLE 6**
**Japanese watch production, 1970**

| Firm | Estimated share of Japanese production | Estimated production of watches and movements (millions of units) | Exports as a percent of production* |
|---|---|---|---|
| K. Hattori & Co. . . . . . . . . . . | 60% | 14 | 20 |
| Citizen Watch . . . . . . . . . . . . | 28 | 7 | 45 |
| Orient Watch . . . . . . . . . . . . | 9 | 2 | 60 |
| Ricoh Watch . . . . . . . . . . . . | 3 | 0.8 | n.a. |

*In terms of value.
n.a. = not available.

Seikosha and Suwa Seikosha, produced watches, movements, and components. Another subsidiary produced clocks. Still other subsidiaries manufactured products outside the timepiece field. K. Hattori managed all the sales activities for the group, marketing its products worldwide under the Seiko trade name.

By the mid-1960s the Seiko Group had become the world's largest producer of jeweled-lever watches. The reasons for Seiko's success are spelled out in the sections that follow. Bear in mind that even though the discussion focuses on the entire industry, what Seiko has done has been the key to what the industry has accomplished.

### The industry's product and market strategy

Though there have been minor differences in approach among the four Japanese watchmakers, in the last two decades they all adopted more or less the same product and market strategy. As mentioned previously, the industry started out making only jeweled-lever watches. By and large, the industry has continued that practice into the 1970s. The Japanese have left pin-lever production to others.

Just because the Japanese have not made pin-lever watches does not mean that they have not competed in the low-price end of the market. To the contrary, at home and in Asian countries the Japanese have marketed a complete line of jeweled-lever watches ranging in price from the cheapest to the most expensive. Yet the main thrust of their marketing attack has been in the medium-price category. They have matched their competitors, mainly the Swiss, in terms of quality and feature of watches but have undercut them in terms of price.

In penetrating the U.S. and European markets, the Japanese have taken a somewhat different tack. They have avoided selling their own watches at either end of the market. In particular, they have let others fight it out at the bottom of the market. More so than in the Far East, they have focused their selling efforts on watches in the medium-price category. This means, for instance, that in the United States the Japanese have concentrated on marketing watches retailing in the $30–$100 range. Yet, within this segment of the market, the Japanese have relied on their usual price strategy: more watch for the same price or a comparable watch for less money.

Several reasons have kept the Japanese out of the luxury end of the watch market in the United States and in Europe. First, a few firms have dominated the luxury watch business for many years; they have created an entrenched position for themselves as prestige watchmakers. Allied to this is the fact that the luxury watch business is as much one of selling jewelry as it is one of selling watches. To penetrate the top end of the watch market, the Japanese would have had to invest heavily in building up a prestige image and in developing new marketing skills. And even if they had been successful, their sales would have been limited in unit terms. Thus, the very nature of the luxury business was contrary to a key feature of the Japanese watch strategy: mass production.

The situation at the low-price end of the market has been quite a different matter. The Japanese watchmakers have not taken on the pin-lever manufacturers, like Timex, directly. But indirectly they have been very much involved in the competitive battle, particularly the one in the United States, between the pin-lever and the jeweled-lever manufacturers.

In the late 1950s the Japanese watchmakers, especially Seiko and Citizen, became major suppliers of watch movements and components to the U.S. industry. Some American jeweled-lever manufacturers imported inexpensive movements from Japan, put the movements into their own cases, and marketed the watches at prices comparable to those for the Timex line of watches. Others imported Japanese movements and parts into the Virgin Islands, finished the watches there in company-owned assembly plants, and shipped the watches, duty-free, into the United States. Firms like Benrus and Elgin got their movements and parts from Seiko. Bulova, from 1960 on, got its movements and parts from Citizen. Generally speaking, arrangements like these have continued up through the early 1970s.

How successful have the Japanese been at penetrating overseas markets? Reliable data relating to their market share in Asia and in a number of Western European countries do not exist. Regarding the United States, official data relating to the year 1968 make it possible to arrive at a rough answer to the question. In 1968 about 5% of the watches imported directly into the United States came from Japan and about half of all the components imported into the Virgin Islands in that year also came from Japan. Adding together direct and indirect imports, the Japanese supplied about 8% of the U.S. market at that time.

Obviously, with only about 14% of worldwide sales and 8% of U.S. sales under their control in 1970, the Japanese watchmakers had a good distance to go to catch up with the Swiss. Yet the Japanese reached this point in not much more than a decade, and what worked in the past could well work in the future. Without doubt, what worked in the past most successfully for the Japanese watchmakers was related to their manufacturing capabilities.

## Manufacturing

A combination of four factors has made it possible for the Japanese to be remarkably efficient low-cost watch producers. These factors have been:

1. A ready supply of disciplined, zealous workers at low wage rates;
2. Advanced mechanized and automated production techniques;
3. Vertical integration; and
4. Mass production of standardized movements and watch models.


By putting these together, the Japanese manufacturers attained economies of scale unmatched anywhere else in the world watch industry.

The labor factor is, of course, the first that immediately comes to
the outsider's mind. And there is no doubt that the Japanese have had
a significant edge over other producers in this respect. This has been
especially true in the case of jeweled-lever watches since the labor content
associated with their production is relatively high. For example, as late
as 1965 the workers assembling jeweled-lever movements in Japan were
earning about one fifth of what their counterparts were earning in the
United States. By the late 1960s, however, rapidly rising wage rates
in Japan were eroding the industry's labor-cost advantage.

The response of the industry to mounting wages highlighted its determination to preserve its competitive advantage. Japanese watchmakers
were not content to stay at home seeing their costs spiraling upwards.
Instead, they were prepared to shift production, or at least some of
it, to new low-wage countries. By 1970 both Seiko and Citizen had
established manufacturing facilities in Hong Kong. Thus, the watchmakers, like many other Japanese manufacturers, had few qualms about
pursuing low-wage labor wherever it could be found. Moreover, because
their overall sales were still expanding, they did not have to face the
problem of protecting employment at home.

Still, Japan's labor-cost advantage should not be overemphasized. It
has been only part of the total manufacturing picture. The Japanese
watchmakers have also stressed the use of the most advanced produc-
tion-line techniques. According to industry legend, this all came about
as the result of a visit to the United States by engineers of K. Hattori
& Co. After World War II they studied the production techniques used
by a number of U.S. watchmakers and also visited the auto-assembly
plants in Detroit. Apparently they were not especially impressed by
what they saw in the watch industry but were struck by what they
saw in the automobile industry. In any case, by the mid-1950s K. Hattori
& Co. had adapted its watchmaking to a conveyor-belt assembly-line
operation. With this type of production Hattori could use not only cheap
labor but also unskilled labor. The rest of the Japanese industry soon
followed Hattori's lead.

The industry took all the other steps necessary to foster low-cost
production. It integrated backward into the manufacture of components,
jewels, even watchmaking machinery. And it standardized production
whenever and wherever it could. The result of combining all these fea-

tures of manufacturing has been a total mass-production approach to watchmaking.

Comparing the Swiss industry to the Japanese industry dramatizes the difference in their approach to manufacturing. In Switzerland, as we have seen, around 1,000 firms were involved in producing, largely through a two-tier system, about 74 million watches in 1970. In the same year two Japanese firms, Seiko and Citizen, produced in-house the equivalent of 30% of the total Swiss output.

What did this difference mean in terms of actual production costs? As might be expected, the watchmakers were reluctant to give out specific figures. One has to rely on indirect measures to get at the answer. Table 7 provides at least a clue.

### TABLE 7
### Per-unit value of watch movements imported into the United States* (calculated from 1970 data)

| Movements | From Switzerland | From Japan |
|---|---|---|
| 0 to 1 jewel............ | $ 2.08 | $ 1.15 |
| 2 to 7 jewels ......... | 3.65 | 3.06 |
| 8 to 15 jewels†......... | 12.55 | 10.85 |
| 16 to 17 jewels ......... | 7.50 | 4.23 |
| Over 17 jewels‡ ......... | 28.80 | 6.63 |

*Valued at f.o.b. the exporting country.
†Imports of movements in this category were well below those in the 16 to 17 jewels category, which explains the high per-unit price.
‡Comparison of prices for watches in this category is probably invalid since the imports from Switzerland include a high proportion of luxury models.

Are these figures a valid guide to the production cost differential between Switzerland and Japan? Undoubtedly the Swiss would say no, claiming that the Japanese figures represent only marginal prices. Perhaps this is true, but even so the figures pinpoint an advantage that the Japanese have had over the Swiss. With a large home market, the Japanese have been able to absorb all fixed costs over their domestic production. They could, therefore, afford to sell at or near marginal costs in foreign markets. With practically no home market, the Swiss could pursue the same pricing strategy only with great difficulty. Whether the figures in Table 7 reflect production costs or pricing policies or a combination of the two, they show that the Japanese had the ability to undercut Swiss prices anywhere from 15% to 45% in the largest watch market in the world.

## Other factors in the industry's growth

Of course Seiko and the other Japanese watchmakers did not achieve their success all on their own. They had a number of things going for them, such as a large home market fairly well protected from foreign competition. In the decades of the fifties and sixties only expensive watches were imported into the country. In unit terms these imports seldom amounted to more than 5% of Japanese production, although, because of the price factor, they did amount to as much as 20% of the market in value terms.

Government policy helped as well. To forestall the proliferation of marginal watch producers and to minimize the drain on foreign reserves caused by the importation of watchmaking machinery, the government encouraged the highly concentrated industry structure. Consequently, the leaders in the industry did not have to waste time or resources contending with new competitors.

And then there was the dramatic growth of the Japanese economy. Its expansion at a rate about two and a half times as great as that for the other advanced countries certainly prompted Japanese watchmakers to enlarge and upgrade their production facilities. The buoyant home economy undoubtedly induced Japanese watchmakers to take investment risks that competitors elsewhere shied away from.

Regarding the future, it seems likely that factors such as those listed above will play a somewhat less important role as ingredients of success. At least over the next decade or so the winners in the world watch industry will be those firms most adroit at mastering an array of new technologies and meshing the technologies with the marketplace. The Japanese watchmakers have armed themselves for the battle in their own way.

## Nonwatch production: The source of new technology

Over the years the "big two" in the industry have moved into the manufacture of products outside the timepiece field. By 1970 Seiko was producing desk-top electronic calculators, high-speed printers for use with computers, miniature industrial robots, machine tools, electronic displays of various types, and information equipment. By then, Citizen Watch was producing mechanical and electronic calculators, office equipment, and machine tools. To be sure, in neither case did the sales of these items represent a major part of the firm's total revenue. But the manufacture of these nontimepiece product lines did expose the firms to technologies that were incorporated in the new types of watches under development.

And the two smaller watchmakers developed their own means for tapping new technology. Ricoh Watch, for instance, became a part of an industrial combine producing copiers, cameras, meters, clocks, and related items. Thus even these firms acquired a sort of in-house access to the skills and knowledge needed to support R & D activities for the new generation of watches.

By the early 1970s it was still too early to determine how successful the Japanese would be at transplanting the latest phases of electronic technology into watchmaking. Yet there were signs that the Japanese were not about to be outplayed. In 1970 Seiko became the first watchmaker in the world to introduce a watch employing the quartz crystal technology. Subsequently, Seiko had to withdraw the watch from the market to sort out technical problems. But within the year Seiko was back on the market with an improved quartz watch—one boasting "a special temperature compensating device designed to make the crystal's vibration as perfect as possible in order to provide extra accuracy." Clearly, Seiko was not about to give up its claim to a share of the electronic watch market.

One American, comparing the overall strategies of the Swiss and the Japanese watchmaking industries, summed up the situation in the following way:

For years the Swiss ruled the world watch market with a regiment. The Japanese are countering now with several giants. A lot of the troops in the regiment aren't going to make it in a battle with giants. Besides, the industry can't hold very many giants. How the U.S. watchmakers will come out of this, in between the Swiss and the Japanese trading punches, isn't at all clear.

## THE U.S. WATCH INDUSTRY

> We've been able to beat foreign competition simply because we *are* foreign competition.
>
> Harry B. Henshel, president,
> Bulova Watch

### Highlights as of 1970

In 1970 U.S. consumers spent approximately $1 billion to purchase about 45 million wristwatches, of which roughly 40%, or about 18 million, had been manufactured at home, while the remaining 60% had been imported from foreign countries or from the Virgin Islands.[6] At the same time, U.S. watch exports, as they had been for many years, were nil. Thus in 1970 the United States was both the world's largest watch market and the world's largest net importer of watches. However, as

---

[6] Since imports constituted such a high proportion of U.S. watch consumption, tariffs were obviously a factor that could not be overlooked by U.S. and foreign watchmakers. Appendix B briefly discusses the tariff issue.

we shall see shortly, these figures do not mean that foreign watchmakers supplied 60% of the U.S. market.

Although the United States was the world's largest watch market, watchmaking represented an insignificant part of U.S. manufacturing industry. Workers engaged in watchmaking constituted only one tenth of 1% of total manufacturing employment. In fact, only two U.S. watch companies, Bulova and Timex, were involved in any domestic watch production. This point is crucial. To understand anything about the U.S. watch industry as it moved into the 1970s, it is first imperative to distinguish between those watchmakers that were both U.S. manufacturing and selling enterprises and those that were merely U.S. marketing organizations. Making that distinction calls for some history.

### The post–World War II shift in watch production

Since the beginning, U.S. companies have struggled to cope with the labor requirements of watchmaking. Manufacturing watches by traditional techniques has always been labor intensive; beyond that it has called for its own brand of skilled labor. Neither of these requirements has ever been easily met in the United States. Some U.S. watch sellers never tried; from the start they imported finished watches or alternatively imported movements and simply put them in watch cases here. Other firms tackled the problem by locating at least part of their production overseas. Bulova and Gruen, for example, established their own manufacturing plants in Switzerland in the early years of the 1900s. Still other companies located all their manufacturing capacity in the United States, counting on mechanization to offset foreign producers' labor advantages.

After World War II most of the big names in the U.S. watch industry had the better part of their output manufactured in the United States, though a few did obtain a significant share of their needs from their own Swiss plants. And after the war jeweled-lever watches dominated the U.S. market. Then during the 1950s and early 1960s the situation changed drastically. Timex first stormed the low-price end of the watch market and later moved up into the middle price range. At the same time marginal Swiss producers flooded the U.S. market with inexpensive pin-lever and jeweled-lever watches making price competition all the more severe. And by the early 1960s the Japanese began to carve out their piece of the U.S. market. On top of this, the mass-merchandising revolution of the 1950s threw the traditional watch distribution system, sales through jewelers and fine department stores, into chaos. To survive in a market dominated by price competition, one after another U.S. watch company gave up on domestic watch manufacturing until, as pointed out above, by 1970 there were only two survivors.

Some of those who shifted to foreign supply acquired their own over-seas plants, resulting in an increase in the number of U.S.-controlled plants in Switzerland. According to one estimate, in the second half of the 1960s about 45% of the jeweled-lever watches imported into the United States from Switzerland were made in plants owned by American firms. Other U.S. companies, however, found independent Swiss or Japanese firms which supplied them with watches, which they then sold in the United States under their own familiar trade names. In addition, many of the U.S. watchmakers turned for at least part of their needs to manufacturing and assembly in the Virgin Islands. (See Appendix C.)

The upshot of all this shifting was that during the 1950–70 period a number of the well-known names in the U.S. watch industry became little more than marketing organizations. Their control of manufacturing operations, if indeed they engaged in manufacturing at all, became secondary. They survived largely by exploiting the trademarks that they had established over the years in the United States. By the early 1970s, however, it was becoming questionable whether these watch marketers could survive.

### Industry structure

Even though market-share data are not publicly available, it is clear that two companies ruled the U.S. watch market in the early 1970s. Probably somewhere between two thirds and three quarters of all watches sold in the United States were made by either Bulova or Timex. Another half-dozen U.S. watch companies and a throng of foreign watch-makers scrambled for the rest of the U.S. market.

Exhibit 2 presents some of the basic facts about the firms traditionally considered to be part of the U.S. watch industry. Three points stand out in the exhibit. First, most of the companies did not manufacture in the United States. Second, most were losing money in the early 1970s. And third, several had sold out to larger U.S. companies or to Swiss interests. If Exhibit 2 included balance sheet data, it would also show that a number of the companies were heavily in debt. Apart from Bulova and Timex, the once proud U.S. watch industry was in a fairly sorry state as of the early 1970s. What had Bulova and Timex done right to separate themselves from the others?

### Bulova

During the 1960s Bulova's management pursued four main goals:

1. Marketing a line of watches covering all price and user segments,
2. Creating a worldwide production base,
3. Expanding its international operations,
4. Exploiting to the fullest its tuning-fork innovation.

**EXHIBIT 2**
Leading names in the U.S. watch industry

| Company or division | Ownership | Recent performance statistics | | | Watch production base |
|---|---|---|---|---|---|
| | | Fiscal year | Sales | Net income (loss) | |
| Benrus | U.S. | 1971* | $25 million | ($4.5 million) Operating at break even or loss since 1968 | Manufacturing and assembly in Switzerland and Virgin Islands |
| Bulova | U.S. | 1972† | $147 million | $3.9 million | Twenty plants around the world including several in the U.S. |
| Elgin National Industries | Largely U.S.; Swiss own about 5% | 1971 | $130 million (about 25% in watches) | ($13.2 million) | Manufacturing and assembly in Switzerland and Virgin Islands |
| Gruen Industries | 80% U.S.; 20% Swiss | 1971† | $9.6 million | ($100,000) | Manufacturing and assembly in Switzerland, Canada, and U.S. |
| Hamilton | Since 1970, a 50%-owned marketing subsidiary of Bush Universal; Swiss own 17%, with option to buy 51% in 1974 | 1972* | $47 million | ($2.4 million) | Leases manufacturing and assembly plants in Switzerland and Virgin Islands |
| Longines-Wittnauer | Since 1970, a division of Westinghouse | n.a. | n.a. | n.a. | Manufacturing and assembly in Switzerland |
| Sheffield | U.S. | 1971 | $15 million | As of 1972, in bankruptcy proceedings | Manufacturing and assembly in Switzerland, New York, Virgin Islands, and Guam |
| Timex | Privately owned, U.S. | 1971 | $200 million (estimated) | n.a. | Twenty plants around the world including several in the U.S. |
| Waltham | Since 1968, the U.S. distribution subsidiary of a Swiss watchmaking consortium | n.a. | n.a. | n.a. | Manufacturing and assembly in Switzerland and, for its electronic watch, in the U.S. |

* For fiscal year ended January 31.
† For fiscal year ended March 31.
n.a. = not available.

How Bulova tackled the U.S. marketplace is indicative of the product strategy the company implemented around the world. Throughout the 1960s and into the 1970s Bulova sold a line of watches in each of the three major market segments, low-, medium-, and high-price, and equaled or outpaced competition in each segment.

At the bottom of the market, in the price range of around $30 and under, Bulova offered its "Caravelle" line. In 1961, in response to Timex, Bulova had countered with this line which, though priced competitively with Timex's pin-lever watches, consisted solely of watches containing jeweled-lever movements. Bulova was able to challenge Timex because it had turned to a Japanese supplier, Citizen Watch, for inexpensive jeweled-lever movements. By the mid-1960s Bulova claimed that it was the leader in the jeweled-lever part of the inexpensive watch market. Parenthetically, it should be noted here that Bulova's success with the Caravelle line probably explains why Citizen, Japan's second largest watchmaker, has never moved into the U.S. market on its own.

The middle of the market, consisting principally of jeweled-lever watches selling in the $30 to $100 price range, had always been Bulova's stronghold. The company marketed literally hundreds of models under the "Bulova" name, and within this segment of the market remained price competitive by manufacturing the watch movements in its own Swiss plants. In fact, supplying the U.S. market made Bulova the largest single manufacturer in Switzerland.

At the top of the market, Bulova's tuning-fork watch, the "Accutron," was in a class of its own. Why this was so calls for a little history. Clocks based on the tuning-fork principle dated from the turn of the century. In 1952 a young Swiss engineer, working at the Bulova plant in Switzerland, got management approval to develop a miniaturized tuning-fork movement. By the mid-1950s he had partially succeeded. Bulova brought his prototypes to the United States and miniaturized them further by applying advanced electronics and metallurgical techniques. After patenting the device, Bulova put it on the market in 1960 as the Accutron watch.

Though the Accutron did not compete head-on with luxury mechanical watches, those sold more as jewelry than as timepieces, it soon grabbed the lion's share of watch purchases in the over-$100 price category. Moreover, Bulova swept the market with a watch designed solely for men; for technical reasons, "mini Accutrons" for women were not put on the market until 1971.

Whereas Accutron's uniqueness undoubtedly accounted for much of Bulova's success within the high-price segment of the watch market, uniqueness of product could not account for Bulova's success in the other two segments of the market. Instead, Bulova relied on aggressive marketing. Advertising and distribution support, for years Bulova's forte, were the two critical marketing factors.

By the second half of the sixties, Bulova was spending as much as $4 million at a crack on its seasonal advertising campaigns. By the beginning of the seventies it was spending half of all watch advertising dollars in the United States. It maintained the largest sales force within the industry and provided the distributors, particularly jewelers, with dozens of different selling and service programs. In short, Bulova, which came out of World War II somewhat larger than its rivals, increased the gap by pouring funds into marketing at a rate unparalleled in the industry.

Meanwhile, Bulova management built the manufacturing base that insured the success of its marketing strategy. It expanded the company's manufacturing operations until, by 1970, it had 20 plants scattered around the world. As suggested by the quotation at the beginning of this section, Bulova's management saw its worldwide production system as its key competitive strength. With this system Bulova could pick the time and place for producing a particular watch. For instance, it concentrated U.S. production on the Accutron, which required a low labor input but sophisticated technology.

Furthermore, as it broadened its manufacturing base, Bulova became capable of conducting R & D and market testing at more than one site. It developed its mini Accutron for women in Switzerland and first put it on the market in France.

As production spread around the world, so, too, did sales. Whereas in 1960 international business accounted for not much more than 5% of Bulova's consumer sales (these exclude defense and industrial sales), a decade later the percentage was in the 20% range. Part of this surge could be attributed to the Accutron, which Bulova introduced, with success, in a number of overseas markets. Thus, by carrying competition into its foreign rivals' own backyards, Bulova diluted somewhat the efforts they could bring to bear on the U.S. marketplace.

At the same time that Bulova was pushing out its sales base, it was also shoring up its worldwide dominance in the field of tuning-fork technology. In 1968, Swiss manufacturers, unable to develop a version of the tuning-fork movement that did not conflict with the Bulova patent, agreed to enter into a licensing agreement with Bulova. Consequently, by the early 1970s several Swiss producers, Bulova's licensees, were making and selling their own versions of the tuning-fork watch. And on the other side of the globe, the Citizen Watch Company, Japan's second largest watchmaker and a minority partner with Bulova in a joint manufacturing venture, was making and selling Accutrons under another license agreement with Bulova.

The combination of all these factors turned Bulova into the world's largest jeweled-movement watch seller, in dollar terms.

## Timex[7]

Coming out of nowhere in 1950, Timex carved out a major place for itself in the U.S. watch market in the 1950s and in foreign markets in the 1960s. On almost every count Timex's product and market strategy differed from that of the traditional watchmakers. Timex did not build its reputation on the jeweled-lever watch. Instead, it took a pin-lever movement, simplified it even further so that it could be mass-produced with automated techniques, put it in simple but tasteful cases, and marketed its first watch line to retail at $6.95 to $7.95. Then Timex went outside the conventional distribution system, first selling most of its watches through drugstores and subsequently through a number of mass merchandisers. Next Timex drummed up sales through intensive advertising. Like Bulova, Timex spent far more for its advertising than was customary in the industry at the time. But unlike Bulova or any other rival, Timex promoted its line in ways that were unorthodox and, according to critics, somewhat garish. One example of Timex's off-key advertising approach, its "torture tests," became a standard of network TV in the late 1950s.

By the early 1960s Timex could claim that it was selling one out of every three watches in the United States. It then broadened its product line with electric watches and some jeweled-lever models. Consequently, by the late 1960s Timex could claim that it was selling every other watch in the United States.

While Timex was strengthening its hold on the market, it was also, like Bulova, building up a worldwide manufacturing system. By 1970, it, too, had 20 plants scattered around the world. Thus both giants in the U.S. watch industry had manufacturing bases more widely dispersed than any of their U.S. rivals or, for that matter, than any of their foreign rivals.

### Lessons from Bulova and Timex

The success of Bulova and Timex calls attention to several important points, which, although they relate basically to the U.S. marketplace, may apply elsewhere as well.

1. By the end of the 1960s watchmakers could no longer base their marketing strategies almost exclusively on the push of the conventional distribution system. Both Bulova and Timex marketed their products

---

[7] For a complete description of this firm, see the case entitled "The Timex Corporation."

directly to consumers and made their brand names, not the jeweler's recommendation, the key to watch sales. In part, this switch in marketing emphasis was a natural consequence of the sweeping changes that affected the distribution and retailing of many consumer goods. In part, it was associated with the slow but steady disappearance in the United States of an important source of consumer information: the watch repairman. It was also related to consumer confusion over quality. In the 1950s and 1960s the industry baffled the consumer with literally thousands of watch models and recurrent price cutting. Unable to determine what was a good watch at a fair price, the consumer naturally turned to the one or two brands with which he or she was most familiar.

2. Unexploited niches were a thing of the past in the U.S. watch market. Bulova was very explicit about its strategy in this regard. Note this comment in its 1970 annual report:

Bulova's market researchers have sought to identify the particular needs of segmented consumer groups. That we have succeeded in this crucial phase of our operations is evidenced by the record number of more than 800 different watch models offered to the United States markets.

The report went on to note that Bulova sold watches in the price range of $10.95 to $11,000. And, of course, Timex completely blanketed the low-price field and part of the mid-price field. The rest of competition, the other U.S. watchmakers and dozens of foreign manufacturers, offered hundreds of additional models. By 1970, the chance that a watchmaker would find a niche unnoticed by competition was, for all practical purposes, nil.

3. Finally, the U.S. watch company with a strictly domestic orientation was an anachronism. During the 1960s Bulova and Timex redefined themselves as multinational firms; their outlook on markets and production became worldwide. Over time they internationalized their marketing, production, and R & D skills and competed successfully because they exploited advantages regardless of where the advantages were located. It is questionable if either firm, or any other major watchmaker, for that matter, could survive in the 1970s if it limited its operations to a single country.

What about some of the other factors that would determine the competitive ability of U.S. watchmakers in the 1970s?

## Research and development

Government-supported R & D work and defense-oriented production expanded the technological base of the leading U.S. watchmakers in a way not open to the watchmakers in Switzerland and Japan. Moreover, unlike the Swiss but like the Japanese, the U.S. companies concentrated on acquiring advanced technical skills within their own organizations.

For some of the U.S. companies, the skills they accumulated, largely at government expense, added up to an impressive list. Take Bulova, for instance. During the 1950s and 1960s Bulova developed and produced a whole array of intricate electromechanical devices for missiles and was a major supplier of parts for conventional munitions. Commenting on its technical capabilities outside the watchmaking field, Bulova's 1968 annual report had stated:

The products made in the company's four non-consumer areas have, as a common denominator, watch-making technology and miniature electronics threading through the production of artillery and mortar fuses, micro-circuit automation equipment, test instrumentation, crystals, oscillators, and servo-mechanisms, and production of millions of pin-head sized synthetic jewels.

The report went on to emphasize the advantages inherent in these activities:

The esoteric-sounding inventory of principal products of the non-consumer units—fuses, safe and arm devices, micro-bonders, crystal filters, optical choppers, tuning-fork oscillators, laser beam choppers—seem remote from watch-design and manufacture but they represent an in-house technological base whose impact can be company-wide with consumer or non-consumer involvement.

Other watchmakers engaged in similar activities. Timex developed and manufactured gyroscopes and timing devices. Benrus supplied high-precision components for missiles, power-supply systems for naval vessels, and electronic instrumentation for satellites. Elgin made flight instruments.

To be sure, not all of the U.S. watchmakers retained the technical knowledge and expertise they acquired in the course of meeting defense needs. Those that had to sell out to other companies or that had experienced especially hard times at the end of the 1960s more than likely saw their reservoir of knowledge and skills dwindling away or becoming obsolescent. In the early 1970s the smaller U.S. watch companies showed no striking evidence that they had a technological lead over Swiss and Japanese companies. Bulova and Timex were a different matter, however. They had prospered throughout the 1960s. They, therefore, had the opportunity to build up their reservoirs of skills. In the early 1970s they were in the technological vanguard, and as the decade rolled on their accumulated technical capabilities might well turn out to be their most important competitive edge over Swiss and Japanese rivals.

## Diversification

At one time or another in the fifties and sixties almost all the U.S. watchmakers experimented with diversification. Generally speaking, none of the experiments was successful. Several firms did develop lines of industrial products like precision parts or electromechanical components, but the sale of these lines never became a major part of their operations. And as for consumer goods, the watchmakers demonstrated a fairly consistent inability to market successfully a second consumer line.

Some industry observers attributed this weakness to the watchmakers' unique but specific set of marketing skills. Others claimed that the watchmakers had so many problems to deal with that they never had the chance nor the resources to pursue diversification seriously. And the cynics suggested that it was simply another case of an industry with a fixation on one technology and on one product. Whatever the cause, as the industry moved into the 1970s there was little evidence that its members could regard diversification as a readily available means for meeting adversity or for stimulating growth.

## U.S. investment in the Swiss industry

The expiration, at the end of 1965, of the Swiss government's prohibition against the acquisition or sale of watchmaking companies was followed by a flurry of U.S. investments in the Swiss industry. As soon as the barriers dropped, Hamilton and Benrus each purchased Swiss watchmakers in order to obtain manufacturing sites in Switzerland. The next year, 1967, Bulova bought out Universal Geneve, a maker of quality high-priced watches. According to reports, Bulova's motive differed from that of the two other U.S. investors. Bulova had its eye on Universal Geneve's worldwide distribution system. Other U.S. watchmakers might have invested in Swiss companies as well had not the Swiss gone on the offensive and started to invest in U.S. companies.

An outsider made the next major move into the Swiss watch industry in 1971 when the American firm Zenith acquired a majority interest of the Movado-Zenith-Mondia Holding Company, Switzerland's fourth largest watchmaker.[8] The merged companies announced their intention to parlay Zenith's electronics expertise with the Swiss group's watchmaking skills to compete in the electronic watch market.

Predicting whether cross-country investment (U.S. companies in Swiss firms and vice versa) would keep up its pace throughout the rest of the 1970s was complicated by two opposing factors. On the one hand, the opportunities for this type of investment were declining. In Switzerland, the wave of horizontal and vertical mergers lessened the number of candidates for acquisition by U.S. companies. And in the United States almost all of the watch companies, with the exception of Bulova and Timex, had come under partial or complete Swiss control.

---

[8] Prior to the merger Zenith of the United States was not related in any way to the Zenith part of the Swiss watchmaking group.

On the other hand, further investment in each other's industries might be the best way for U.S. and Swiss watch companies to cope with the instability arising out of the electronic watch battle. For example, in an article entitled "Swiss Watchmakers Plan More American Mergers," the director of the Federation of Swiss Watchmakers, Mr. Retornaz, predicted more Swiss acquisitions of American watch importers. Reporters noted that he stressed one theme: "Retornaz returned again and again to a central thought with the Swiss vis-à-vis the United States: stability."[9] If U.S. and Swiss watchmakers continued to forge new links between the two industries, the quest to bring order out of potential chaos would almost assuredly be a root cause.

## THE ELECTRONIC WATCH BATTLE

> It all shapes up as an intriguing struggle that can be safely watched by most investors from the security of the sidelines.
>
> *Value Line Selection and Opinion*

### Marketplace developments: The opening shots

By the second half of the 1960s watchmakers in Switzerland, the United States, and Japan had joined in earnest the race to be first on the market with a quartz crystal electronic watch. And it was inevitable that the race would be run in the world's largest watch market: the United States. American consumers could well afford the new type watches; each firm's best chance at attaining mass-production economies rode on penetrating the large U.S. market; and the center of the new technology was the United States.

Seiko temporarily claimed the crown when in 1970 it introduced its analog version in the United States. But product difficulties forced Seiko to recall the watch shortly after it had been put on the market. Then Bulova launched its analog Accuquartz in a luxury version retailing at $1,350. The year 1971 saw other manufacturers announcing the introduction of their own expensive versions of quartz watches. Piaget, for example, brought out one retailing at $2,900. Toward the end of the year Hamilton launched its digital Pulsar at a retail price of $2,100. Clearly, the industry was first trying to skim the cream off the market by packaging luxury cases around the new technology. But the cream did not last long.

At the end of 1971 Bulova brought out an improved version of the Accuquartz bearing a retail price of $395. Seiko returned to the marketplace with a quartz line retailing in the $450–$475 range. Then in April 1972 the Swiss, through Ebauches SA, announced a full line of quartz

---

[9] *National Jeweler*, May 1972.

crystal watches, both of the analog and digital variety, to retail at prices of $300 and under. Hardly had the Swiss sprung their news when Timex announced that it was about to introduce an analog quartz crystal watch to retail at $125. In the midst of all this activity, jewelers were complaining that new product announcements were flowing out of corporate headquarters a lot faster than the new marvel watches were flowing off assembly lines.[10] Industry rivals were in a sort of frenzy to be the latest with the newest. Still, the U.S. watch market did settle down to a full two months of tranquility.

### Mid-1972: The skirmishing is over

Readers of the July issues of the various jewelry trade magazines published in the United States came across a number of eye stoppers. For example, one two-page advertisement carried this copy:[11]

*Benrus Defies*
*Omega, Bulova, Seiko, Timex!*

---

THE NEW BENRUS SOLID STATE TECHNIQUARTZ
WATCH IS UNEQUALLED IN PERFORMANCE STANDARDS
. . . . AND PRICE!

---

Benrus thus challenged the industry with the introduction of its analog version of a quartz watch, a timepiece which was to carry a suggested retail price of $99. Furthermore, Benrus let it be known that it intended to market the watch through all available distribution channels, including mass merchandisers. Up to that point all the watchmakers, including Timex, had restricted distribution of the new watches to the jewelry trade. Benrus' management had apparently decided to use a page out of the Timex marketing manual.

But the Benrus advertisement was almost back to back with others showing that the solid-state watch was about to become a reality in the U.S. marketplace. The Waltham Watch Company, a division of the Swiss Société des Garde-Temps, announced that it would soon have available a quartz crystal, completely solid-state, liquid crystal display watch. Priced at under $200 retail, the watch would come on the market at less than half the price for the first few watches of this type. As

---

[10] Privately, many jewelers greeted the introduction of the electronic watch with dismay, for they did not understand its technology. Consequently, the electronic watch jeopardized their traditional functions as advisers to consumers and as repairmen.

[11] *Jewelers' Circular-Keystone*, July 1972.

important as its price was the fact that it was an "all-American developed *and manufactured* product."

At the very same time, Gruen announced that it was about to introduce its Teletime, a watch comparable to Waltham's. The retail price tag on the Gruen watch was to be $150.

All these announcements represented news enough, but the trade press contained another tidbit that may have been more important than everything else. Microma Universal of Mountain View, California, one of the principal suppliers of integrated circuits and liquid crystal displays to watchmakers, disclosed its intention to sell watches under its own name. Microma said it planned to market an analog quartz watch at a retail price of $79.50 and a digital solid-state watch at a retail price of $149.50. Microma also said that it had agreed to make a quartz watch for Sears, Roebuck. Thus the first of the electronics manufacturers, albeit a small one, was about to invade the watchmakers' domain. Subsequently, another interesting aspect of Microma's venture was brought to light in a trade press article which revealed that Ebauches SA would supply Microma with the mechanical parts required for its analog watch.

### The role of the electronics manufacturers

As of mid-1972 all quartz watches, including those put out by Swiss and Japanese watchmakers, contained integrated circuits made by U.S. electronics manufacturers. Whereas Microma had decided to move forward into watch marketing, what the rest of the U.S. electronics manufacturers would decide to do was still an open question. Texas Instruments, for example, supplied Ebauches SA, the spearhead of the Swiss move into quartz watches, with integrated circuitry. But T.I. said nothing about becoming a watch marketer itself. Yet it had recently decided to shift its role in the electronic calculator business. Until 1972 T.I. had simply supplied large-scale integrated circuits to others for assembly into inexpensive electronic calculators. Then T.I. brought out a calculator under its own label. The parallel possibility with watches was all too obvious.

Another company, Motorola, had resolutely declared in early 1972 its intention to remain a component supplier. Six months later the watchmaking trade press was full of rumors that Motorola was not so resolute anymore.

Other electronics manufacturers with a toe in the door included RCA, Intersil (the supplier of Seiko), Solid State Devices, and Optel. Several of these were relatively new companies set up to participate in the evolving electronic watch business. Predicting what their long-term role would be was complicated by a rapidly developing set of ties between them and watchmakers.

The case of Optel, Inc., of Princeton, N.J., illustrates this point. In 1969, five scientists and engineers, formerly with RCA, established the company to develop and sell liquid crystal displays. Two years later Swiss interests helped finance Optel by purchasing, for $700,000, its entire issue of class B cumulative convertible preferred stock and by loaning the firm $900,000. As part of the financial package, Optel agreed to give "members of the Swiss Group the right to request certain priorities from Optel in connection with development orders and purchase of optoelectronic products."[12] By mid-1972 Optel was in full swing, producing components for digital solid-state watches. Its entire output was destined for Switzerland.

## Technical factors relating to the electronic watch

As of 1972, it seemed fairly certain that the following technical and production considerations would hold true for the electronic watch:

1. Manufacturing the electronic watch would call for very low labor inputs. Some observers predicted that labor costs might eventually amount to no more than 10% of total manufacturing costs. In contrast labor costs could run as high as 70% of total manufacturing costs for fine mechanical watches.
2. Unlike the situation with the tuning-fork watch, when Bulova controlled the technology through patents, no firm was likely to build up any sort of patent wall with the electronic watch. The relevant technology was widely held, in large part, by firms outside the watchmaking field.
3. Unlike the case with mechanical watches, cost reductions for the electronic watch would not come at the expense of quality. Even if the prices for it did fall to very low levels, the electronic watch, when completely perfected, would not be a junk watch. Instead, it would have the quality associated with the most expensive mechanical watches.
4. The cost of the innards of the electronic watch would be determined by the cost-volume relationships connected with the manufacture of electronics components. Consequently, the cost advantages of volume for the electronic watch might well exceed those for the mechanical watch.
5. And finally, the electronic watch would undergo important improvements in the next five years. As of 1972, it was still far from being a completely perfected product. Neither of the two key technical components, the quartz crystal and the liquid crystal display, was free from shortcomings. In fact, several leading watchmakers cau-

---

[12] *Optel Corporation*, prospectus issued by Philips, Appel, and Walden, Inc., June 21, 1972.

tioned the industry against extolling too strongly the merits of the quartz watches then on the market. The Bulova Watch Company, for instance, issued a statement in July 1972 which listed the following limitations to quartz cyrstals: (*a*) they are all subject to aging and, accordingly, subject to some change in their vibration frequency; (*b*) they are particularly sensitive to shock; and (*c*) they are quite sensitive to temperature. Bulova warned that guarantees of accuracy of within a minute-a-year, which some firms offered, were unrealistic. Bulova's statement went on to say that it would not yet market watches using liquid crystal displays because the clarity of the devices then available was inadequate and because their effective lifetime was still to be established.

### Assessing the impact of the electronic watch

Uncertainties, such as those related to the ultimate role of the electronics manufacturers and those related to the remaining product deficiencies, put large question marks after all predictions of the future for the electronic watch. Still, this didn't stem the tide of prognostications concerning what the electronic watch would do to the watch industry.

The president of one U.S. electronics company made the prediction that received the most attention: "The solid-state watch will put 50,000 Swiss out of work."[13] Other executives in U.S. industry echoed the same theme. The head of another U.S. electronics firm put it this way: "The time has come for an American company to become the Ebauches." And the president of Benrus saw the future like this: "All evidence points to the emergence of an American watch industry and to the submergence of the Swiss and non-American watch manufacturers."

These forecasts depended, of course, on assessments of the share of the market that the electronic watch would capture from the mechanical watch. Many Americans and Japanese, particularly those relatively unconcerned by the technical uncertainties surrounding the quartz watch, took a dim view of the future for all mechanical watches. The president of Benrus, for example, predicted that electronic watches would soon capture 20% of the watch market; and he added that he could foresee a time when they would control 90% of the market. Executives in the U.S. electronics industry prophesized, quite naturally, that the death of the mechanical watch was imminent.

Undoubtedly the main reason why the electronics industry held such high hopes for the new generation of watches was the long-range price prospect. Those best acquainted with the costs involved in making the electronic components predicted continuing price declines. For instance,

---

[13] Put in perspective for the American reader, this prediction would compare with a forecast of putting 1.3 million Americans out of work.

the head of Motorola's quartz timepiece electronics division said in August 1972 that he looked for quartz watch prices to slide to $50 by 1974. Long term, he saw no reason why their retail prices could not be brought down to $10.

Japanese watchmakers seemed to avoid the price issue but talked about the electronic watch capturing 50% of the total market. Moreover, they suggested that the Swiss would be the most affected by the electronic watch. They predicted that Swiss watchmakers would be forced to turn increasingly to the production of decorative watches.

To nobody's surprise, the Swiss saw the situation in a different light. Responding to a prediction that the electronic watch spelled the end for the conventional watch, a vice president for Ebauches SA had this to say:

We have thoroughly examined this matter on both the technical and the marketing level, and we are convinced that if a happy future is in store for the electronic watch, the mechanical watch, in its simple or automatic version, also has brilliant possibilities. In 1980, the consumption of watches will be approximately 300 million units (as against 180 million in 1972). The most optimistic forecasts fix the share of electronic watches at one-third, with the balance, at least 200 million pieces, being mechanical watches.[14]

Another spokesman for the Swiss industry emphasized that its watchmakers were as well prepared as any to fight it out in the electronic watch battle:

Henry Altorfer, executive director of the Watchmakers of Switzerland, underlines how Ebauches SA has laid a permanent foundation for watch progress and how back in July 1967, long before the Japanese or anybody else had it, the Swiss had Beta-21, the prototype of the quartz watch. By 1969 . . . the Swiss were ready to produce the quartz watch in volume.

"We have been and will continue to be world leaders in watch production and technology," Altorfer assured.[15]

## APPENDIX A
## A BRIEF GUIDE TO HOW WATCHES WORK AND TO THEIR PRINCIPAL TYPES

Wristwatches come in innumerable sizes, shapes, designs, and price ranges. Yet until the last decade most of the differences among watches were superficial matters of styling and extra features. The basic running mechanisms of watches were classed into a few general categories. All watches were mechanical and of the spring-powered type. And by tradition they were put into only one or the other of two categories: jeweled-

---

[14] *Business Week*, June 10, 1972.

[15] *National Jeweler*, August 1972.

lever or pin-lever. These terms will be explained later. But with the advent in the late 1950s of the electric watch and the subsequent introduction of several types of electronic watches, the problem of describing how watches work and classifying them grew in complexity.

Still, if matters are simplified considerably, it is possible to acquire without much difficulty a working familiarity with watch technology. That is the aim of this guide. It begins by describing the traditional spring-powered watch, a timepiece little changed in over 300 years, and then traces the major innovations that have so dramatically changed the nature of wristwatches in the last two decades.

## THE STANDARD SPRING-POWERED WATCH

The traditional mechanical watch consists of two distinct parts: the *exterior visible elements* (the case, crystal, dial, and hands) and the *interior movement*. What happens on the outside of a watch is obvious; what goes on inside is a mystery to many. The *movement* normally consists of a hundred or more parts which form three major groups:

1.  The *ebauche*, or movement blank, which accounts for more than three fifths of all parts. It comprises the framework of the watch (the plates and bridges), the gear train (the wheels and pinions), and the winding and setting mechanism. In a rough way, the ebauche can be thought of as the chassis and engine of an automobile.
2.  The regulating components (the *escapement*, balance wheel, and hairspring), which make the movement work at the correct rate. Roughly, these can be thought of as the transmission of an automobile.
3.  Other miscellaneous parts which cannot be classed under any generic heading.

When these hundred or so parts are assembled, how do they work? Winding a watch tightens the spiral of its mainspring. As the spring unwinds, it drives a series of gears to which the hands of the watch are attached. But the unwinding of the mainspring has to be restrained and precisely controlled to provide the right increments of time. This requirement is what makes a watch movement complex.

The task of releasing energy from the mainspring in a precise way is carried out by the regulating components, the heart of which is the *escapement mechanism*. A gear called the escapement wheel is attached to the main gear train. The escapement wheel is restrained from rotating freely, thereby blocking the unwinding of the mainspring, by two teeth in a part called the anchor fork. The anchor fork rocks back and forth releasing one tooth and immediately thereafter engaging the other tooth in the escapement wheel. This alternate release and engagement of the escapement wheel permits it to advance by tiny increments, and these increments of rotation are converted by the other gears into the second, minute, and hour movements of the watch hands.

But what makes the anchor fork move? It is connected to a balance wheel which rotates back and forth, and the balance wheel is, in turn, connected to a hairspring which coils and uncoils to keep the balance wheel in motion. As each tooth on the anchor fork disengages from the escapement wheel (the tooth actually slides away from the wheel), it transmits enough power through the anchor fork and balance wheel to the hairspring to coil it slightly. As the hairspring uncoils, it rotates the balance wheel in the opposite direction, which, in turn, rocks the anchor fork in the opposite direction starting the next cycle in the regulating mechanism. This whole complex set of movements goes on about 300 times a minute and produces the familiar ticking in the spring-powered watch.

Even though all mechanical watch movements operate according to the principle just described, not all movements are of the same quality. The quality of a movement is determined, in part, by the precision with which the many tiny parts are made and, in part, by the care that goes into adjusting the functioning of the components. For example, Swiss manufacturers of premium watches have traditionally employed master watchmakers to make all the many and time-consuming adjustments needed to produce a highly accurate movement.

Then there is the whole matter of jewels. Since watch movements consist of many tiny parts, it is obvious that friction and wear must be minimized if watches are to be accurate and long lasting. In many watches, though in far from all of them, this is accomplished by putting jewels at all the critical pivot and contact points in the movement. One standard Swiss movement, for example, contains 15 jewels. Very high-quality movements may contain as many as 30 jewels. While the purpose of jewels in watch movements is generally well understood, the contribution that they make to the cost and quality of watches is often misunderstood.

Many people assume that watches containing 15 or more jewels are expensive because the jewels are expensive. Moreover, they assume that the number of jewels in a watch movement indicates the quality of the watch. The second of these assumptions is not necessarily true; the first is just plain false. With rare exceptions all jewels used in watchmaking—excluding, of course, those used on the outside of a watch for decorative purposes—are synthetic and quite inexpensive. Thus the number of jewels in a movement has little to do with the price of a watch. As regards the issue of quality, most movements containing 15 or more jewels are produced with the precision and care required to make a fine timepiece. Yet some less scrupulous watchmakers, knowing that consumers erroneously equate the number of jewels with quality, have gouged the public by putting out expensive but crude timepieces containing many jewels. It follows that establishing the true quality of the standard spring-powered watch is not an easy matter for the average consumer.

The issue is further complicated by the fact that there are two different types of spring-powered watches.

## The distinction between jeweled-lever and pin-lever watches

As a rule all mechanical watches are regarded as being either of the jeweled-lever or the pin-lever variety. Although the distinction is based on specific technical differences, many watchmakers and jewelers contend that the distinction is an indication of overall watch quality. Manufacturers of jeweled-lever watches consider pin-lever watches inferior in many respects. They characterize the pin-lever watch as a crude timepiece, poorly made with low-grade materials, which will not last and which will not keep accurate time. They concede that pin-lever watches are inexpensive (they prefer to use the word cheap), but they claim that the customer is getting just what he or she pays for. As the ultimate insult, they refer to pin-lever watches as "throwaways."

As might be expected, manufacturers of pin-lever watches have a different point of view. They contend that their watches do a perfectly adequate job, that their watches are durable, and that consumers do not have to pay exorbitant prices to own reliable timepieces. They also point out that there are inferior (they use words like "schlock") jeweled-lever watches.

But leaving aside all the claims and counterclaims that competing watchmakers have hurled at one another's products, what is the technical difference between the two types of watches? It relates to whether a watch movement contains jewels in its escapement mechanism. In pin-lever watches, metal pins replace the jewel-tipped teeth in the anchor fork; this accounts for the name "pin-lever." Other parts of the escapement mechanism are also simplified, further eliminating the need for jewels. Simplification, more so than elimination of the jewels, makes it possible to produce pin-lever movements at costs below those for jeweled-lever movements. Indeed, the inventor of the pin-lever movement, a man called Roskopf, had as his goal the development of a movement so simple that watches could be made for the common man. His contribution has not passed unnoticed, for even today watchmakers often refer to pin-lever movements as Roskopf movements.

Even though the distinction between jeweled-lever and pin-lever watches relates specifically to the type of escapement mechanism, the difference commonly extends to other parts of the watch. For example, pin-lever watches usually contain few or no jewels in their entire movements. And notwithstanding what many pin-lever manufacturers claim, most pin-lever watches are made to looser tolerances than those found in jeweled-lever watches. Furthermore, the materials used in pin-lever watches, and their overall styling, are often not up to the standards of the jeweled-lever watch.

## The subtypes of spring-powered watches

The many ways in which mechanical watches, either jeweled-lever or pin-lever, are modified to produce a variety of subtypes can be passed over quickly. In the 1970s a number of the special features are taken for granted. By and large everybody understands what is involved when a watch is described as being shockproof, waterproof, antimagnetic, self-winding, etc. Calendar watches, those showing the day and month on the face, are common. So, too, are chronographs, watches with start-and-stop mechanisms to measure elapsed time. The important point is this: All these subtypes call for some added complexity in their manufacture, yet none represents a radical departure from the characteristics of the standard mechanical watch.

## THE NEW GENERATION OF WATCHES

### The electric watch

Development of miniaturized batteries and electric motors, largely the result of World War II R & D efforts, made possible the first major advance in timekeeping: the electric watch. Commercially available for the first time in the United States in 1957, the electric watch was marketed worldwide by many manufacturers in the early 1960s.

As regards its technology, the electric watch represents only a partial step away from the spring-powered watch. It does not contain a mainspring nor many of the components usually found in escapement mechanisms. Instead, current from a battery drives a tiny balance-wheel motor, which, in turn, is connected through a gear train to the hands of the watch. Yet the watch is conventional in the sense that it still depends on the oscillation of moving mechanical parts to determine time increments. For this reason the accuracy of most electric watches is not strikingly better than that of good spring-powered watches. Consequently, electric watches, though moderately successful in the marketplace throughout the 1960s, did not capture the lion's share of the medium- and high-price watch market. And the innovations that followed the electric watch severely clouded its long-run commercial future.

## The tuning-fork watch

Although the electric watch represented the first break with 300 years of watchmaking tradition, its impact on the watch industry was far less than the second major innovation in watch technology, the development of the tuning-fork watch. With it, the whole principle of determining time was changed. Greatly simplified, the tuning-fork watch works in the following way. Electric current from a small battery flows through coils surrounding a tuning fork. The flow of current stimulates the tuning fork to vibrate at 360 cycles per second. A tiny strip of metal connected to the tuning fork transmits its vibrations to a set of gears, which, as in the conventional watch, convert the time increments into the sweep of the hands on the watch face. Because the time-determining element is a tuning fork which vibrates over 31 million times per day, the accuracy of the watch surpasses that of even the most finely manufactured spring-powered watches. Tuning-fork watches, if properly adjusted, should be accurate to within one minute per month.

Until 1971, all tuning-fork watches sold were men's models. Then, after further miniaturization of the tuning-fork movement was finally accomplished, models for women became available.

## The quartz crystal watch

By the end of the 1960s another major innovation in watchmaking appeared in the marketplace. This newest innovation, the use of quartz crystals as the time-determining device in watch movements, could, at some point in the future, improve the accuracy of watches to unheard-of levels, and it also opened the door to the completely solid-state watch. In fact, a number of different types of watches were developed around the new technology. They all were based, however, on the same operating principle.

When electric current is passed through a quartz crystal, it can be stimulated to vibrate at a very high frequency. This oscillation can be converted into very precise time increments. Microcircuitry subdivides the crystal's frequency into electric pulses which then drive the watch in one of several different ways. In some quartz crystal watches, the pulses operate a tiny electric stepping motor which, in turn, is connected through a gear train to the hands of a watch with a conventional face. In other quartz crystal watches the pulses are used to excite a tuning-fork device. From that point on, the operation of this type of watch is identical to that of the existing tuning-fork watches. In still others, the pulses are fed into mini-computers—really integrated circuits—that convert the pulses into the usual minute and second time increments. In the case of this last type of watch, which incorporates no moving parts, the conventional face and hands of the watch are replaced by new methods of displaying time. These developments are discussed in the following section.

### Changes in the face of the watch

Until 1972 all the dramatic advances in watch technology remained unseen miracles to those who in the last decade or so purchased one of the newer watches. The works inside were different, but the familiar face and hands were still there. In 1972, though, innovation became visible. Watches with completely different faces, with tiny displays resembling those of a digital clock or of an electronic calculator, appeared on the market for the first time.[16] The new faces incorporated one or the other of two different devices which were the product of quite recent technical advances: liquid crystal displays and light emitting diodes.

The devices work on two different principles. A liquid crystal display consists of two pieces of glass with a thin coating of an electrically sensitive chemical between them. When current is passed through the chemical, it changes its crystalline structure. The altered crystals reflect ambient light, that is, they reflect light coming from an outside source. The advantage of the liquid crystal display is that it requires a very low level of current to operate since it is not actually generating light. Its disadvantages are twofold. First, the quality of the image it presents, the brightness and precision of the numbers, depends on the brightness of external illumination. Second, its durability and its stability under extreme temperatures are open to question. At least, as of 1972, the device had yet to be completely debugged.

As for the other device, light-emitting diodes, they are, crudely put, semiconductors that glow. In the early 1970s they found their greatest use in the displays of small electronic calculators. Whereas they give off a brighter and more precise image than liquid crystal displays, they have the disadvantage of requiring more current to operate them than liquid crystal displays. Because the diodes require so much power, no watch-size battery can keep them illuminated at all times. As of 1972 only one watchmaker had marketed a timepiece containing this device. To read the time, the wearer had to press a button which illuminated the otherwise blank face of the watch.

Both display devices were seen as raising another problem. Industry experts seriously questioned whether consumers would accept such a drastic change in the appearance of wristwatches. For this reason, and

---

[16] Manufacturers now refer to electronic watches with conventional faces—that is, with hands—as *analog* models and to those with numerical displays as *digital* models.

because of the technical shortcomings discussed above, the firms introducing watches with the new faces did so in a tentative way. Only limited quantities of the watches trickled into the marketplace in 1970 and 1971. Some manufacturers, including leading U.S. and non-U.S. firms, remained out of the race to get a digital watch on the market. Instead, they preferred to wait until the technical and marketplace dust had settled before committing themselves to the "new look" in watches.

## APPENDIX B
## THE U.S. TARIFF SITUATION

The duties on watches and watch components imported into the United States were initially established by the Tariff Act of 1930.[17] Since then, Executive Orders have modified the level of duties on several occasions. In 1936, as part of a reciprocal trade agreement with Switzerland, the U.S. government reduced by one third the duties levied on movements containing 1 to 17 jewels. These concessions lasted until the post–World War II years. In 1951 U.S. watchmakers applied for relief (i.e., a hike in duties) under the escape-clause provisions of the Trade Agreement Extension Act of that year. Three years later the President, responding to the U.S. manufacturers' complaints and to the Tariff Commission's findings, raised by 50% the duties on movements in the 1-to-17-jewel category.

Throughout the 1950s the U.S. watch industry pressed unsuccessfully for additional protection by pleading the "defense essentiality" argument.

The escape-clause rates, set in 1954, were terminated in January 1967 by Presidential Proclamation: once again the duties on movements in the 1-to-17-jewel category dropped by a third. At the same time, as part of the Kennedy round GATT negotiations, the U.S. government granted the first concessions on movements containing more than 17 jewels. Beginning January 1, 1968, the duty on such movements was to be reduced, in five annual stages, by a total of 50%. The rates applicable to movements with 17 jewels or less were left untouched by the Kennedy round.

As of the early 1970s, the tariff situation was as shown in Exhibit 3.

Over the years the U.S. watch industry's increasing reliance on overseas production has prompted the industry to change its stance on the issue of tariffs. Before World War II and in the decade immediately following it, U.S. watch manufacturers, though not U.S. watch importers, lobbied hard for tariff protection. But as the industry increased its dependence on foreign sources of supply, it started to sing a different tune. The companies with overseas plants and those importing from

---

[17] Rates of duty are provided separately for the individual components of watches, that is, the movement and the case. Duties are assessed on each component.

**EXHIBIT 3**

**U.S. rates of duty applicable to imports of watch movements and cases**

| Item | Rate as of Dec. 31, 1967 | Rate pursuant to concessions granted in 1964-67 trade conference | |
|---|---|---|---|
| | | Second stage effective Jan. 1, 1969 | Final stage effective Jan. 1, 1972 |
| Watch movements, unadjusted, not self-winding | | | |
| 1. Having over 17 jewels | $10.75 each | $8.60 each | $5.37 each |
| 2. Having no jewels or 1 jewel | $.75–$.90 each depending on width | No change | No change |
| 3. Having over 1 jewel but not over 7 jewels | $.90–$1.80 each depending on width | No change | No change |
| 4. Having over 7 but not over 17 jewels | $.90–$1.80 each depending on width | No change | No change |
| Additional duties on watches with 17 jewels or less | | | |
| For each jewel in excess of 7 | $.09 | No change | No change |
| For each adjustment | $.50 | No change | No change |
| Self-winding | $.50 | No change | No change |
| Watch cases | $.75 each plus 30% ad valorem | $.60 each plus 24% ad valorem | $.37 each plus 15% ad valorem |

Source: U.S. Tariff Commission, *Summaries of Trade and Tariff Information (1970)*.

foreign producers defected from the industry's protectionist position. By the mid-1960s the industry was divided into two camps.

The events of 1967, the termination of the escape-clause rates, and the Kennedy round concessions prodded the few firms with jeweled-lever production in the United States to transfer it abroad. By the late 1960s, when all production was either foreign-based or part of Bulova's and Timex's worldwide manufacturing systems, the industry had adopted what could be regarded as a low-key free trade position.

## APPENDIX C
## WATCH ASSEMBLY IN THE U.S. INSULAR POSSESSIONS[18]

Because of a loophole in the U.S. tariff law, in the late 1950s many U.S. firms turned to watch assembling in the Virgin Islands. The loophole hinged upon the stipulation that watches could be imported duty free

---

[18] The U.S. insular possessions include the Virgin Islands, Guam, and American Samoa.

into the United States from its insular possessions provided that no article contained foreign materials valued at more than 50% of the total value of the article. With labor costs such a high proportion of total watch manufacturing costs, it was not difficult to meet this criterion.

Watches assembled in the Virgin Islands from foreign parts first started to flow into the United States in 1959. Within a decade 15 different companies had assembly plants there. About half of the parts, by value, used in the Virgin Islands operations came from Japan; another quarter came from Germany. The Swiss, restricted by law until 1971 from exporting parts, never gained a foothold.

By 1968 almost 15% of total U.S. watch imports came into this country via the Virgin Islands route. By then a trickle of imports had also started to come in from Guam. In order to limit this blossoming circumvention of tariff duties, the U.S. government had, in the previous year, put a quota on imports from the insular possessions limiting them to one ninth of U.S. consumption in the prior year. Several firms, citing the quota as one reason for their decisions, shut down their Virgin Islands plants. Yet most watchmakers continued their Virgin Islands operations into the 1970s.

# Timex Corporation

### From industry upstart to industry leader

In 1950 the United States Time Corporation of Middlebury, Connecticut, introduced its line of inexpensive Timex watches into the U.S. marketplace. Neither American nor foreign manufacturers took much notice of the new competitor. After all, in the eyes of the traditional manufacturers, the Timex line consisted of nothing more than cheap pin-lever watches destined, at best, to meet the needs of a minor part of the U.S. market.

Twenty years later the same firm, renamed now after its world-famous Timex brand,[1] had sales in the range of $200 million, plants scattered all over the world, 17,000 employees, and rival manufacturers taking notice of its every move. In fact, Timex had become such a potent factor in the world watch industry that the Federation of Swiss Watchmakers, having studied its rival in minute detail, published a monograph entitled "The Timex Formula."

Timex had grown to be the world's largest manufacturer of pin-lever watches and a principal manufacturer of other types of watches. With its inexpensive watches it had stormed the U.S. market and so fixed the name Timex in the American consumer's mind that by 1970 every other watch bought in the United States was a Timex. And starting in the early 1960s, Timex had marched into one after another foreign

---

[1] In 1969 the firm changed its corporate name from United States Time Corporation to Timex Corporation.

market to the point where it became almost as major a factor in the watch industry overseas as in the United States.

How did Timex do it? How did Timex first reshape the watch industry in the United States and then reshape the watch industry on a worldwide basis? How have other manufacturers responded to the Timex challenge? And where does Timex go from here? These are the questions that are taken up in the pages that follow.

## THE EARLY DAYS OF TIMEX

### The company's founder

Since its inception, Timex has been guided by Mr. Joakim Lehmkuhl. Born in 1895 in Norway, Mr. Lehmkuhl had studied engineering in the United States, receiving degrees from Harvard and M.I.T. in 1918 and 1919, respectively, and then had returned to Norway to direct a small shipbuilding firm and eventually to publish a political newspaper. In 1940, in advance of the German invaders, he fled with his family to England. Shortly thereafter, he was sent by the Norwegian government in exile to New York to take charge of the wartime Norwegian Shipping Center. Recognizing that his assignment was temporary, Mr. Lehmkuhl soon set about looking for another opportunity to use his talents.

### The birth of Timex

In 1942 Mr. Lehmkuhl found his opportunity. Seeing the need for fuse timers for bombs and artillery shells, he and a group of businessmen acquired a majority interest in the virtually bankrupt Waterbury Clock Company in order to convert the firm to fuse production. Prior to the war, the Waterbury Clock Company had manufactured the $1 Ingersoll pocket watch. Very quickly, with Mr. Lehmkuhl as its president, the firm became the largest producer of fuses in the United States.

After the war, as disappearing defense orders emptied its shop, Waterbury's total sales dropped from $70,000,000 to $300,000. Mr. Lehmkuhl reconverted his company from wartime production to watch production "because it seemed the only thing to do." But the days of the $1 Ingersoll watch were over. The U.S. market for such a watch had largely disappeared, and what market did exist was being flooded by cheap Swiss imports. On top of this, inflated costs prevented his or any firm from producing a watch to retail at $1.

Still, Mr. Lehmkuhl was convinced that a good, inexpensive watch could be produced by combining the precision tooling techniques used in making fuse timers with a high degree of mechanization. He gave Waterbury's engineers the task of designing a quality watch that could be truly mass-produced. By 1949 they had succeeded in upgrading the simple mechanism used in children's watches into the prototype of the Timex watch. It had one feature of particular importance. Picking up a development that came out of the World War II research effort, the engineers substituted new hard alloy (Armalloy) bearings for jewels in the movement. According to the company, this feature made the watch the equal of many jeweled-lever models and better than the other pin-lever models then available.

In the meantime, Mr. Lehmkuhl dropped the tarnished Ingersoll name, changed the company's name to U.S. Time, and adopted the brand "Timex" for the new product line.

## TIMEX THROUGH THE FIFTIES

### Product policy

The Timexes put on the market in 1950 were men's watches designed to retail at $6.95 to $7.95. Their simple, tasteful styling and modernistic lines represented an innovation in the low-price field. Gradually, the company added watches with more features and slightly higher prices. First came Timexes with sweep second hands. Then the firm introduced models that were shockproof, waterproof, and antimagnetic. In 1954 Timex brought out a line to retail at $12.95. Calendar and self-winding models soon followed. All of the Timex models, regardless of features, carried a one-year guarantee.

In 1958 Timex introduced its first line of women's watches. Promotion of the line was keyed to the idea that a woman could buy an entire wardrobe of watches—one for dress, one for sports, one for general use—for less than $50. The company claimed that by the early 1960s it had attained more than 36% of the under-$50 women's watch market.

Mr. Robert Mohr, who was vice president of sales at the time, discussed Timex's early product policy in the following terms:

People wonder how we make a watch and sell it for as little as we do. That's all to the good. We promote the idea that the watch is not just a gift season item—something you buy for the June graduate, or at Christmas time, Father's Day or Mother's Day.

Basically, we promote the watch as something for everyday use, that people don't have to worry about because the cost is low.

It works out in our favor, because when you sell more watches than anyone else, you can do more.[2]

---

[2] "New TV Commercials Will Give It Even Harder to Those Hardy Timexes," *Advertising Age*, December 10, 1962.

## Distribution policy

Mass distribution was the keystone to Timex's marketing strategy. At the outset, because it lacked the funds for extensive promotion of its line, the company set out to get widespread retailer support for its watches. Timex initially approached jewelers, the traditional outlet for watches. But many jewelers were reluctant to handle the Timex line. Their reluctance was based on various reasons: some downgraded the Timex line because of its price range or because of its simple pin-lever movements, others objected to the fact that they would only make a 30% margin on the retail price with the Timex line as contrasted to the 50% margin they usually made on their other lines.

Rebuffed in general by the jewelry trade, Timex tried other channels of distribution. As a result, the company started to market its watches directly through 20,000 retail accounts, the bulk of which were drug-stores. In the early days almost 80% of Timex's sales were made by drugstores. Over the years, Timex constantly increased both the number and type of retail outlets through which it sold its watches. At its high point Timex had almost 250,000 retail accounts on its books.

In its approach to retailers, Timex routinely emphasized the importance of stock turnover. It also stressed retail price maintenance even though its suggested retail prices and markups were well below those traditional in the jewelry trade. Mr. Mohr described the distribution strategy:

> We taught jewelers that markups don't mean a thing if you don't have the turnover. That was our story, and we preached it hard. Jewelry stores have a 1.5 average watch turnover per year. That wasn't enough for us. We put watches into drugstores, hardware and tobacco stores. Today Timex watches are sold in 80,000 of these stores. We don't sell discount, and we maintain a fair trade price, enforcing it wherever possible. We have a low price to begin with, so why cut it more?[3]

Timex management claimed that its retailers' average turnover was six times per year.

"Timex's sales approach"—according to *Tide*—"was based completely on showmanship unheard of in the conservative watch business." Timex salesmen visiting retailers slammed the watches against walls and dunked them into buckets of water to illustrate their shockproof and waterproof qualities. In 1954 the company designed a showcase for point-of-purchase display with levers which could dunk a Timex in water and smash it against an anvil. According to Mr. Lehmkuhl, these promotional tactics largely accounted for the rapid rise in sales in the early 1950s. Then in the mid-1950s Timex turned to television.

---

[3] Ibid.

## Advertising policy

Prior to 1956 Timex's advertising had been on a small scale and limited mainly to magazines. In 1956 it began intensive advertising on network television. It was estimated that Timex's annual advertising budget grew from about $200,000 for the year 1952 to around $3 million for the years at the end of the decade. About 85% of the advertising budget was allocated to television.

Timex's commercials hammered home the themes of product durability and low cost. The company became renowned, first at home and then abroad, for its so-called "torture test." Its commercials featured news commentator John Cameron Swazey showing a Timex which, under varying circumstances, "took a licking and kept on ticking." In one of the early torture tests, done live, a Timex was fastened to an outboard engine propeller. In the water, the Timex inadvertently slipped off the spinning propeller. It was recovered, running, and Timex ended up with yet another highly favorable bit of publicity for its watches. One torture test followed another. The watches were shown ticking away after being fastened to the hooves of galloping horses, after surviving 135-foot dives at Acapulco, and after being attached to surfboards and amphibian airplanes.

For critics of the unorthodox advertising campaign, the company had its answer: "Timex is a watch designed for active people; then why not show it undergoing rugged tests?"[4]

## Manufacturing policy

Timex could sell its watches the right way because it could make them the right way. Manufacturing in Timex was characterized by mass production with relatively unskilled labor and by constant management attention to production efficiency and to quality control. *Business Week* described the company's manufacturing operations in the following terms: "The entire operation adds up to an almost textbook example of how to run a taut ship."[5] The "simple but strict" production formula was based on: (1) rigid standardization, with full interchangeability of parts; (2) maximum mechanization to reduce human error and to minimize labor costs; and (3) centralized quality control. According to Mr. George Gelgauda, technical director, "Parts fit together whether they are made here in Middlebury, Connecticut, or in Germany." To insure standardization and the most advanced mechanization possible, the company employed 500 toolmakers who designed almost all of the

---

[4] "Rigors of Hawaii Are Setting for New Timex Tests," *Advertising Age*, October 21, 1963.

[5] "A Time Bomb for Watchmakers," *Business Week*, November 16, 1963.

firm's production equipment. Control was centralized even to the point of keeping the records on all its tools at the U.S. headquarters.

Keeping the product simple was another key element in Timex's manufacturing policy. For example, the frame of the basic Timex watch went through six manufacturing operations as contrasted with 100 for an imported watch. The Timex movement had 98 parts held between two plates, whereas foreign movements frequently had 120 parts held together by a series of five plates. The Timex had four screws; other watches had as many as 31. Of course, industry rivals tried to turn this simplicity against Timex. For instance, they pointed out that the cases of the Timex watches were riveted together, making repairs impossible. The American consumer, as will become apparent, paid little attention to these criticisms.

Another example illustrates how management achieved low-cost production. As many operations as possible were mechanized so that the end product needed little adjustment. According to Mr. William J. O'Connell, an assistant division manager:

> When we put a watch together with relatively unskilled labor, it must be able to run accurately the minute the last wheel is put in place. We can't afford the petty, troublesome adjustments that are found in the handmade watch industry.[6]

More than one observer, after seeing the Timex manufacturing operations, was prone to describe Mr. Lehmkuhl as the Henry Ford of the American watchmaking industry.

Timex managed its inventories as strictly as it managed its production operations. Sales forecasting and inventory control were centralized. Sales were pinpointed through warranty cards, and estimates were constantly revised at a data processing center at Middlebury. Parts and work-in-process inventories were updated daily at headquarters. Finished-goods inventories were kept at rock bottom.

By the end of the decade Timex employed about 7,000 people in its home office and in its three U.S. and six European plants. Stateside, in addition to its main plant in Middlebury, Connecticut, it had factories in Little Rock, Arkansas, and Abilene, Texas. Overseas, it had plants in England, Scotland, West Germany, and France. Its French plant, in Besançon only 27 miles from the Swiss border, was located in a region rich in the tradition of watchmaking.

Though the company had not actively sought diversification, the firm became also an important supplier of parts for the Polaroid Land Camera. Furthermore, Timex moved into defense business. It maintained a $1 million research laboratory in Irvington-on-Hudson, New York, which featured "the cleanest room in the world" for the manufacture of gyroscopes and for the testing of timing devices.

---

[6] Ibid.

### Competitive reaction: Too little or too late

Of course, competition did not stand absolutely still as Timex carved up the U.S. watch market throughout the 1950s. Yet many of Timex's rivals continued to focus most of their energies on their traditional market segments—watches in the $30 to $100 range. And when they did try to defend against Timex by adding lines of inexpensive watches, they seldom could take on Timex in head-to-head competition. Some tried, like Benrus, and eventually gave up. They lacked both Timex's manufacturing and mass distribution capabilities. Lacking these, it made no sense for them to match Timex's intensive advertising campaigns.

The other major American watchmaker, Bulova, did try to answer the Timex threat with its own Caravelle line, jeweled-lever watches retailing in the $10 to $30 range. But even though Bulova started to gear up for this counteroffensive in the late 1950s, it did not attain national distribution of the Caravelle line until 1963, 13 years after Timex hit the U.S. market.

By and large, therefore, Timex stood alone in its segment of the U.S. marketplace throughout the 1950s. Its performance statistics as it moved into the early years of the next decade reflected this fact.

### Sales and financial results

The first Timex watch was put on the U.S. market in 1950. A decade later, the company was selling around 7,000,000 watches annually. In 1962 an Alfred Politz research study indicated that one watch out of every three sold in the United States carried the company's trade name of "Timex." Though Timex did not publish its financial data, its 1961 sales and after-tax income were reported by *Advertising Age* as being $71,200,000 and $2,900,000, respectively. The company, according to President Lehmkuhl, was completely free of debt, had financed all recent expansions out of earnings, and intended to continue to do so. Clearly, the Timex strategy had paid off in terms of dollars and cents.

## TIMEX THROUGH THE SIXTIES

### Upgrading the product line

Having established a strong foothold in the low-price segment of the U.S. market, Timex took a number of important steps in the 1960s to broaden its product line. Its first move in this program had actually taken place in 1957 when Timex introduced a line of 17-jewel watches designed to retail at $17.95. Despite predictions that Timex could not sell watches at this price level through outlets such as drugstores, the line was a success.

Then in 1962 Timex followed with a 21-jewel watch line priced at $21.95. These watches, in part because they carried a higher markup than usual for Timex, were reported to have eased the entry of the firm into distribution through the jewelry trade. Slowly Timex won over jewelers' begrudging acceptance.

Timex's next step was a response to the competitive threat posed by the electric watch. The first of these had appeared in the U.S. market in 1957, and by the early 1960s many different models were available. While the electric watch did not represent a significant technical improvement over conventional watches, it did endanger the sales growth of those firms completely committed to mechanical watches. Timex responded in typical fashion. In 1963 it introduced a line of electric watches retailing at $39.95, about half the price of its nearest competitor. *Consumer's Bulletin* had this to say about the electric Timex:

Although the Timex is very low in price for an electric watch, it was found to keep surprisingly accurate time during the first three months of operation, up to the time this issue of the *Bulletin* went to press. . . . While the case and the flexible bracelet were of lower quality than found on more expensive watches, they were judged to be satisfactory and gave a good appearance.[7]

After selling about 200,000 men's electric watches at $39.95 in 1964, Timex introduced a women's electric watch and a men's electric calendar watch, both at $45, in 1965. With the higher priced additions to the line, Timex began to run "prestige" advertising in national magazines.

Some industry observers suggested that Timex was headed for trouble by moving up out of its traditional low-price market niche. Mr. Lehmkuhl didn't see it that way. Interviewed in 1968, he had this to say about the matter:

REPORTER:   Do you face any risk in moving into higher price watches?
MR. LEHMUHL:   No, no. We are already the largest producers of electric watches at a higher price. That just built up the name for the lower price watches, too.[8]

Swiss watchmakers, too, didn't see Timex headed for trouble by following this policy. To the contrary, they saw it as a threat to their market position in the United States. The 1969 annual report of the Swiss Watchmakers Association, discussing mounting competition in the United States, posed the problem in these terms:

---

[7] "Timex Electric Watch," *Consumer's Bulletin*, March 1964.
[8] "Making the Most of Time," *Nation's Business*, September 1968.

As to marketing, we must take into consideration a new fact, the selling-up policy started by Timex, by adding to its range of products a certain number of more costly articles, either because they are made with higher quality movements, or because they are of a different technical construction. This new factor could possibly lead to profound changes in the market as was the case in 1950.

## Going international

At the same time that Timex was upgrading its product line, it was also spreading out into foreign markets. Timex first established operations in Canada and in England. Promptly, it transplanted its marketing techniques to these new markets. Even though Timex's sales figures were not broken down for domestic and overseas markets, it was estimated that by 1965 its market share in these countries was comparable to its share in the United States. Regardless of where it was used, Timex's "torture test" advertising campaign captured the fancy of local consumers. For example, in South Africa Timex was an unknown brand in 1962. Timex launched its campaign, and in the month of December 1963 alone Timex sold 10,000 watches in that market. Timex then entered the French market, selling its line under the "Kelton" trade name, and by the mid-1960s Timex was ready to knock over the large West German market.

The West German story highlights how effective Timex had become as an international marketer. The company applied the same marketing formula, modified in several important ways, that had been successful in over 30 countries. As in many other markets, the manufacturers selling in West Germany concentrated on watches in the medium and upper price ranges, ignoring the lower price range. A Timex executive described the situation in these terms:

They were trying to sell West German customers on the idea that expensive wristwatches added to the owner's prestige. We set out to fill the vacuum in the lower price watch market and convince buyers that good watches don't have to be expensive.[9]

But first the company had to surmount a distribution hurdle. The company knew it had to distribute through large department stores and mail-order houses to build volume. Yet over 75% of watch sales in West Germany moved through jewelers and specialty watch stores. If these outlets were antagonized, they could jeopardize all Timex's plans. Accordingly, the company set out to win their allegiance.

---

[9] "How Timex Hit German Markets with Top Quality, Durability—and the Hard Sell," *Business Abroad*, February 5, 1968.

Timex developed a three-pronged approach to convince jewelers that its business would be too good to pass up:

1.  An intensive institutional campaign describing Timex and its plans for West Germany was directed at jewelers and other retailers.
2.  Inducements to handle the Timex line, including margins comparable to those on other watch lines, were offered the jewelry trade. In addition, they were encouraged to send malfunctioning Timexes to its French plant for repair by granting them a 25% handling commission.
3.  Sales success of the line was almost guaranteed to the trade by Timex. The company outlined its plans for its usual aggressive, imaginative advertising campaign which would fully support the trade's effort to sell the watches.

As the clincher, Timex invested almost $1 million to test-market its line and its marketing formula in one of West Germany's most populous regions. The test marketing was a success, jewelers and other retailers alike were convinced, and Timex went national in January 1967. In less than two years, Timex had captured 10% of the West German watch market with over 70% of its sales going through jewelry stores. In 1967 it sold approximately 500,000 low-price watches; estimates of its sales for 1968 ran in the range of 600,000 to 750,000 watches. By 1969 the Swiss Watchmakers Association, in its annual report, openly acknowledged that Timex was hurting Swiss export sales into Germany. The report noted that keen competition from Timex was driving down the average value of watches shipped to Germany.

Meanwhile, Timex had turned its attention to the Far East. And as in the past, Timex did not do things in the conventional way. Its venture into Japan prompted observations like the following:

> Foreign watchmakers do not always use existing sales routes. Timex of the United States, for example, has gone into a tie-up with Maruman, a leading cigarette lighter manufacturer, and is engrossed in blazing new sales routes.[10]

Elsewhere in the Far East Timex was on the move, and again the Swiss singled out Timex as a cause of some of their woes. Commenting on a downturn in exports to the Far East, the 1971 annual report of the Swiss Watchmakers Association had this to say:

> The most obvious factors which seem to have influenced our trade in this area are, broadly speaking, a major Russian commercial offensive on the Hong Kong market and aggressive Timex policies in the Far East.

---

[10] *Oriental Economist*, November 1971.

The Japanese, too, had comments about Timex's moves in the late 1960s. They didn't hesitate to point out that Timex was taking on formidable competitors. As one executive of Seiko emphasized:

. . . while Timex advertises itself as "the world's largest manufacturer," this is for pin levers. When it comes to jeweled-lever watches, Seiko occupies first place.[11]

## TIMEX IN THE EARLY SEVENTIES

As the decade of the 1970s opened, quartz watches created a technological revolution in watchmaking. First introduced in early 1970 as luxury models priced above $1,000, quartz watches in early 1972 were being sold by leading Japanese, Swiss, and U.S. companies at $400 and up. In April 1972 Timex announced its entry:

"With a quartz watch priced at $125," Robert Mohr, executive vice president of the company, announced in mid-April, "we're 60% under the least expensive watch already on the market."[12] When Mohr was asked how Timex could put a quartz watch on the market at such a price, he replied:

Timex Corporation has a solid background of experience in essentials like the design and manufacture of miniaturized parts. In addition, the company has a technology geared to vast production. In making millions of watches annually, we have developed watchmaking production techniques unmatched anywhere in the world.[13]

Mr. Mohr added that Timex was so confident that its quartz watch would be a leader that the company intended to support it with a full-scale advertising and promotion campaign. The leading jeweler's news magazine noted that the Timex announcement had "stirred" the trade.

Timex's low-price leadership, however, was immediately challenged. Ebauches, the major Swiss component manufacturer, announced a line of quartz watches to retail at $30 to $300. Benrus and Gruen announced retail prices of $99 and $150, respectively, while Microma Universal, one of the watchmakers' principal suppliers of integrated circuits and liquid crystal displays, planned to sell a quartz watch under its own name for $79.50. While all the above announcements related to analog quartz watches, digital solid-state watches were also announced at price levels ranging from $149.50 to $200.

In late 1971, in spite of the impending technological and competitive changes, Mr. Lehmkuhl was optimistic about Timex's future. Sales in

---

[11] *National Jeweler,* May 1972.

[12] Ibid.

[13] Ibid.

1971 were comfortably over $200 million and up 10% from the prior year. A *New York Times* article quoted Mr. Lehmkuhl:

"We'll try to find items to fill out our line of watches," he said, "such as modern clocks, and even quartz clocks."

And Timex, which already is a major world factor in timepieces with 20 factories abroad, still doesn't think it has enough of the world market. More foreign plants are being planned.

"Volume," he adds with a faint smile, "is the oxygen of our business."[14]

[14] *New York Times,* December 5, 1971.

# Introductory note on Central America

LINKING the two great continents of the New World is an isthmus commonly known as Central America. Although the land area is only 200,000 square miles (slightly larger than California) and the population somewhat less than 14 million, the isthmus is divided into six nations, among them Guatemala, El Salvador, Honduras, Nicaragua, and Costa Rica. Panama, the sixth country, has chosen over the years to remain apart for numerous political and economic reasons and consequently will be referred to only tangentially in this note.

Industrialization was slowly gathering force in Central America in the 1950s, sparked in part by the hope that in the future a common market would be formed to provide local manufacturers with wider opportunities. This note provides a brief description of the area and some of the factors which might influence the decision to invest in it in the mid-1950s. (See map in Exhibit 1.)

## EARLY HISTORY

The Maya civilization, which had flourished in the Yucatan Peninsula in what is now Guatemala and Honduras, had substantially disintegrated in the century prior to 1502 when Columbus explored the coast in his last attempt to find the passage to the East. Balboa and Pizarro followed Columbus in search of gold and power, bringing the Catholic Church with them. Political control was eventually consolidated from 1523 to 1539 by Alvarado, one of Cortes' lieutenants, in Antigua (Guatemala).

321

**EXHIBIT 1**
**Central America**

When Spanish rule was peacefully cast off in 1821, a brief union with Mexico and several, often bloody, attempts at confederation ensued in the next two decades. However, each province developed separately under its own leadership, and the possibility of political union was overshadowed by a strong sense of national identity that has persisted to the present day.

## DEMOGRAPHIC AND SOCIOECONOMIC CHARACTERISTICS

Some indication of population density is given in Table 1. Population statistics should be viewed with caution, however, especially those for Guatemala in which over half of the population were Indians who lived essentially outside the money economy. In El Salvador, Honduras, and Nicaragua more than 90% of the people were of mixed blood with little social discrimination. On the other hand, the population of Costa Rica was almost entirely of European stock. Central America had one of the highest population growth rates in the world (3.5%) which resulted in a "young" population (in Honduras 60% of the population was 19 years of age or younger).

TABLE 1
Central American population statistics

| Country | Square miles | Population (in thousands) | Population/ square mile |
|---------|-------------|--------------------------|-------------------------|
| Guatemala . . . . . | 42,642 | 4,420 | 105 |
| El Salvador . . . . . | 8,164 | 2,850 | 348 |
| Honduras . . . . . | 43,277 | 2,135 | 49 |
| Nicaragua . . . . . | 57,143 | 1,655 | 29 |
| Costa Rica . . . . . | 19,575 | 1,425 | 74 |
| Panama . . . . . . | 28,576 | 1,160 | 41 |
| | 199,377 | 13,645 | 68 |

The capital city was by far the dominant urban center in each country in terms of population, wealth, commerce, and industry (see Table 2).[1] Each supported several newspapers and radio stations. The capitals, aside from Tegucigalpa, were connected by good roads or railroads to seaports which historically constituted for the agriculturists an outlet to world markets and for mercantile interests a means of securing manufactured goods for local consumption. In recent years the Pan American Highway had been built through Central America, linking the six countries as shown in Exhibit 1. The highway spurred the construction of subsidiary roads which had the effect of opening portions of the interior to increased traffic and commerce, though a considerable amount of it, especially on the Caribbean coast, remained isolated. Concurrent with this trend was a rapid increase in the number of automobiles and slow but steady progress in rural electrification.

Although the distribution of wealth was uneven throughout Central America, there were differences among countries. Exhibit 2 provides

TABLE 2
Population of capital cities

| Country | Capital city | Approximate population |
|---------|-------------|------------------------|
| Guatemala | Guatemala City | 480,000 |
| El Salvador | San Salvador | 280,000 |
| Honduras | Tegucigalpa | 125,000 |
| Nicaragua | Managua | 200,000 |
| Costa Rica | San Jose | 150,000 |

---

[1] With the exception of Honduras, in which San Pedro Sula in the north rivals Tegucigalpa in significance.

# EXHIBIT 2
## Socioeconomic characteristics of Central America

| Country | Total No. of households | Urban households (percent) | Rural households (percent) | Socioeconomic class* | | | Literacy rate | Average income per capita (1961) (U.S. $) | Average income per household (1961) (U.S. $) |
|---|---|---|---|---|---|---|---|---|---|
| | | | | Class A-B | Class C | Class D | | | |
| Guatemala . . . . . . | 764,000 | 35 | 65 | 10% | 35% | 55% | 25% | $176 | $ 985 |
| El Salvador. . . . . . | 502,000 | 39 | 61 | 10 | 30 | 60 | 47 | 220 | 1,100 |
| Honduras. . . . . . . | 367,000 | 23 | 77 | 5 | 30 | 65 | 47 | 207 | 1,180 |
| Nicaragua . . . . . . | 258,000 | 41 | 59 | 5 | 25 | 70 | 38 | 213 | 1,300 |
| Costa Rica . . . . . . | 243,000 | 34 | 66 | 10 | 40 | 50 | 88 | 344 | 2,000 |

* Approximate incomes in each class: Class A–B: More than $300/month.
Class C: $100–$300/month.
Class D: Less than $100/month.

Source: Compiled from industry records and from information contained in *Proposed Mutual Defense and Assistance Programs FY 1964*, Agency for International Development (Washington, D.C.: U.S. Government Printing Office, 1963).

some data on this and other socioeconomic indicators for the area. Some English was spoken along the Atlantic Coast but otherwise the language was Spanish. Literacy ranged from less than 30% in Guatemala to 88% in Costa Rica.

## ECONOMIC CONDITIONS

The Central American economy depended heavily on agriculture to provide employment (two thirds of the work force were engaged in agriculture) and generate the foreign exchange necessary to finance imports and consequently was very sensitive to world commodity prices. The crop varied from country to country, although coffee tended to be the dominant one, and the top two generally accounted for 70% to 90% of the total. In all cases, the United States was the principal trading partner in the mid-1950s, followed by Germany (see Exhibit 3).

**EXHIBIT 3**
**Foreign trade in Central America in the mid-1950s**

| | Principal exports | Percent | Percentage of total accounted for by U.S. * | |
|---|---|---|---|---|
| | | | Exports | Imports |
| Guatemala | Coffee | 75 | 65 | 60 |
| | Bananas | 12 | | |
| El Salvador | Coffee | 79 | 40 | 48 |
| | Cotton | 11 | | |
| Honduras | Bananas | 58 | 52 | 60 |
| | Coffee | 17 | | |
| Nicaragua | Cotton, raw | 36 | 37 | 55 |
| | Coffee | 17 | | |
| Costa Rica | Coffee | 52 | 51 | 50 |
| | Bananas | 41 | | |

* The second largest trading partner was generally Germany.
Source: *The South American Handbook* (New York: John T. Clark & Son, 1961).

The economies of Central American countries exhibited two character-istics which were unusual in much of Latin America. First, inflation was relatively minor, averaging from 1% to 3% a year. Second, the dollar exchange rate for local currencies, with the exception of Costa Rica, had been unchanged for many years, dating back to 1898 in the case of the Guatemalan quetzal. In Costa Rica, the colón had fluctuated in value relative to the dollar, but the net deterioration in the rate of exchange had been slight. Moreover, there had been a relative absence of currency controls; that is, funds could generally be converted into foreign currencies and removed from the country.

Tariff duties on most manufactured imports were substantial. As a means of attracting investment in industry, however, all governments employed tax incentives. For instance, it was common for investors to be granted an import duty exemption for all materials and equipment necessary to set up a factory and possibly for raw materials that could not be supplied locally. The investor might also secure an income tax exemption for a number of years. Finally, he might request, with a lower probability of success, that the tariffs on competing imports be raised to put him in a more favorable competitive position.

In the postwar years a gradual shift was occurring in Central America away from a complete dependence on agriculture and toward limited degrees of industrialization. This trend was typically manifested by the substitution of locally made goods for imports. However, there was little trade among Central American countries. Imports from other Central American countries had to surmount the same high tariffs as those from the United States and Europe.[2] Also, there was a strong consumer feeling that locally manufactured goods were inferior to U.S. and European products. As a result, markets continued to be dominated by importer-distributors who held the exclusive rights on high-quality U.S. and European merchandise.

The importer-distributor, consequently, occupied a position of considerable power in the Central American distribution system. One observer noted:

In El Salvador, for instance, less than 50 such importer-distributors handle the bulk of all Salvadoran imports, while at the same time performing the major part of the wholesaling activities in the country as well as selling at retail. Typically, these importer-distributors required an exclusive national franchise before they would agree to handle the products of any given manufacturer and tended to make a high markup (typically 10% to 20% when selling to wholesalers and retailers, but in some instances ranging up to 100%) for their services. This was true in spite of the fact that in most cases they carried overextended product lines and provided spotty coverage of retail outlets (very often not bothering at all to sell outside the capital city) and generally unaggressive marketing support. The position of power of these importer-distributors was reinforced by the fact that they tended to be the only firms within the distribution system that were strong enough financially to carry substantial inventories or to extend all-important credit to undercapitalized wholesalers and retailers.

At the retail level, prices of manufactured goods tended to be relatively high. On the theory that the uneven distribution of wealth pre-

---

[2] During the mid-1950s, there was some talk among the various Central American countries of the possible formation of a common market, which might lead to the ultimate elimination of tariffs between member countries and the establishment of common external tariffs. However, the outcome of these exploratory talks was still extremely uncertain.

vented the development of mass markets for most consumer goods, retailers preferred a "high margin–low volume" pricing policy and carried
a large, thin inventory.[3] The only exceptions to this pattern were one
or two relatively low markup food or department stores in the capital
cities. In addition, the central market, consisting of many stalls, sometimes out-of-doors, continued to be an important center of trade in towns
and cities.

## POLITICS: DOMESTIC AND INTERNATIONAL

The political system in Costa Rica varied from that of the other
Central American republics in that Costa Rica supported a vocal, active
democracy. That is not to say that the others were harsh dictatorships.
Rather, they were for the most part run by strongmen, generally duly
elected and supported by the wealthy and in large measure by the
"campesinos" (rural dwellers) as well. There were no guerrillas of consequence which posed a threat to the stability of the government. For
brief periods in the postwar decade, both Costa Rica and Guatemala
were governed by coalitions including Communists but both were over-
thrown by conservative elements.

Despite the fact that the United States had intervened in Central
American politics on numerous occasions, including the presence of
marines in Nicaragua on peace-keeping duty from 1912 to 1933, relations
with the "Colossus of the North" were by and large very cordial. There
was comparatively little openly expressed hostile sentiment toward North
Americans or toward other foreigners for that matter. In business, various
kinds of working arrangements including licensing agreements and joint
ventures were common. There were no laws requiring local ownership
in industrial ventures, though it was not unusual for a well-placed private
investor to be sought as a means of securing entry to the market.

---

[3] Bank credit for working capital was available, although not always easy to
obtain. Interest rates were 12% per annum or higher.

# The Central American Paint Market (A)

## INDUSTRY STRUCTURE

DURING the early 1950s only imported paints were sold in Central America.[1] For the most part, these imported paints came from the United States, although there were a few minor imports from Europe. As of the early 1950s, the leading brands on the paint market were those of the following companies in estimated order of importance:

1. Hathaway Paint Company[2] (U.S.).
2. Du Pont (U.S.).
3. Excello, Inc.[2] (U.S.).
4. Standard Paint Company[2] (U.S.).
5. California Paint Company[2] (U.S.).

These companies all sold their paint in Central America through what were known as "distributors." Typically in each country there were 10 to 15 of these distributors, each of whom held the rights to import and market a given brand of paint in that country. These distributors typically carried a variety of products, some of which might be related to paint (e.g., building materials and supplies, hardware, wallpaper) and some of which might be completely unrelated (e.g., whiskey, typewriters). Distributors operated one or more retail outlets of their own through which they made the bulk (80% to 90%) of their sales. At the

---

[1] Guatemala, El Salvador, Honduras, Nicaragua, Costa Rica.

[2] Some company names and financial figures have been disguised.

same time, they also functioned as wholesalers, reselling paint to a few hardware and variety stores located in or about the capital city but at substantial distances from their own retail outlets.

Sales through these "subdealers" were usually quite small and almost never accounted for more than 10% to 20% of a given distributor's total volume. Only in rare instances did distributors maintain outside salesmen to sell to subdealers, and almost never did they attempt to obtain sub-dealers outside the capital city. Thus, they tended to be "distributors" more in name than in fact. Rather, they might better be thought of as large retail dealers who imported paint directly from manufacturers in the United States and Europe.

Almost without exception distributors and subdealers restricted themselves to carrying the brands of only one paint manufacturer. In part this was because carrying the brands of a second manufacturer would have required tying up too much money and space in inventories; in part it was also due to the fact that most manufacturers objected to having local dealers carry competing brands.

Most of the imported paints were of high quality and were relatively expensive, retailing from $7.50 to $8.50 per gallon. Of this amount, import duties represented about $1.50 to $1.75.[3] When selling direct to the painters or the public, the distributor's margin ranged from 30% to 35% of the retail selling price. Distributors took 5% to 10% of the retail price as margin when selling to subdealers, who, in turn, received 25% of the retail selling price. The distributors were important sources of credit to both the subdealers and painters, often carrying their accounts for 60 to 180 days.

Most of the initiative for expanding the market came from local distributors rather than the U.S. paint companies. Generally speaking, the U.S. company managements considered the Central American countries to be too little and too fragmented to warrant major attention. Several of the U.S. companies, having originally been sought out by the agents in Central America, had never bothered to send a sales representative to visit the area.

## PAINT MARKETING

Paint tended to be an infrequently purchased product. Moreover, its purchase was often regarded by consumers as part of a major invest-ment which also included paying for the services of a painter. According to industry executives, "professionals" were used for most home painting jobs, while the "do-it-yourself" market was extremely limited.

---

[3] Import duties varied somewhat from country to country from year to year but tended to average out at about $.20/gross kilo plus 15% ad valorem. (A gallon of prepared paint weighs approximately five kilos.)

There was general agreement within the paint industry that in choosing a particular brand and type of paint, consumers tended to rely
heavily on the advice of the painter or of a paint dealer.[4] In fact, in
many cases the person whose home was being painted left the final
decision up to the painter.

Typically, the first step taken by a person interested in having painting
done around his house would be to engage an independent painter
or a paint contracting company. The two parties would then discuss
the nature of the job, the type, quality, color, and brand of paint to
be used, and the price to be charged. In some cases, the price quoted
by the painter or contracting company included the cost of the paint
itself, while in other cases only labor was included. In the latter case,
the homeowner either bought the paint from the dealer himself or else
the painter bought the paint and presented the dealer's bill to the homeowner, who then made payment directly to the store.

Regardless of how the paint was obtained, the painter or contracting
company usually tended to recommend strongly the brand of paint sold
by his "favorite" dealer. In deciding which dealer's paint to recommend,
the painter was typically motivated by several factors.

First, the paint sold by the dealer had to be of "acceptable" quality.
However, since the paint handled by all dealers in Central America
met this criterion, the final choice usually depended on other factors.
The most important of these were, in rough order of importance:

1.  The size of the discount offered by the dealer to the painter.
2.  The amount of credit which the dealer was willing to offer the
    painter, not only on the paint itself but on other paint supplies.
3.  The warmth of the personal relationship between the painter and
    the dealer.
4.  The services offered by the dealer, including color mixing, advice
    on difficult paint problems, delivery, etc.
5.  The breadth of the product line offered by the dealer in terms of
    price-quality levels, types of paint, and colors.
6.  The convenience of the dealer's location for the painter.

The first of these factors, the discount to the painter, requires some
explanation. In all the Central American countries it was a common
practice for independent painters and paint contractors to ask for and
be given a special "discount" by paint dealers. The size of the discount
was typically 5% to 10% for independent painters and 10% to 20% for
large paint contractors. Painters and contractors expected to be given
this discount regardless of whether they purchased the paint on behalf
of their clients or whether the client himself purchased the paint from
the dealer. In the latter case, the payment of the discount was usually

---

[4] "Dealer" refers to either the paint outlet of the distributor or the "subdealer."

arranged after the fact between the painter and the dealer and without the knowledge of the painter's client. Once having established a satisfactory relationship with a given paint dealer, the painter usually tended to remain fairly loyal unless a major falling out occurred.

According to industry spokesmen, painters and paint contractors had a variety of ways to insure that their clients followed their advice to use the paint sold by a particular dealer. As one person in the industry put it:

If the painter's client insisted on using a brand of paint sold by a different dealer than the one recommended by the painter, then the painter might water down the unwelcome paint before applying it. Then when the client later points out that the paint job doesn't look very good, the painter will tell him it is the fault of the inferior paint which the client has insisted on using. Since the word of this sort of thing gets around pretty quickly, homeowners are usually inclined to go along with the painter's recommendations.

During the middle 1950s the size of the Central American household paint market amounted to somewhat less than one million gallons. Costa Rica, El Salvador, and Guatemala each accounted for about one quarter of the total, with one eighth going to Honduras and one eighth to Nicaragua. Most sales were made to the household market. Automotive and industrial sales were negligible.

Sales to the government, on the other hand, typically accounted for a stable 10% of the market in most Central American countries. Large consumers of paint within the governments included housing ministries, government-owned utilities, transportation ministries, local municipalities, etc.

Bids for government business were submitted by the company's distributor in each country, who, in most instances, operated a "captive" paint contracting service and hence was able to bid on the total paint job.

## PAINT MANUFACTURING

From a technical point of view, the making of household paints was quite simple. Basically, it involved the following steps:

1. Mixing a white or colored pigment in powdered form with a liquid vehicle (e.g., linseed oil and turpentine or synthetic resins) to form a stiff paste.
2. Grinding the paste in a roller mill, or some other grinding machine, until it had reached a specific consistency.
3. Thinning the mixture with turpentine or some other thinner and tinting it to the proper shade with additional pigment.
4. Putting the paint in cans and attaching a label.

The technology required was readily available from many independent suppliers of paint-making equipment and raw materials. In specialty paints—such as automotive lacquers, anticorrosive paints, and industrial paints—technical know-how was more important and more difficult to obtain.

The minimum capacity for an efficient and flexible plant was 600,000 gallons per year, for which the required investment in land, building, and equipment was estimated at $300,000. It was possible to construct less efficient and flexible plants of smaller size. However, the investment required for land, building, and equipment would not decrease proportionately to size. For example, it was estimated that a 150,000-gallon-per-year facility would require an investment of $150,000. Fixed costs were estimated at $100,000 per year, covering manufacturing overhead (such as maintenance, utilities, insurance, etc.) as well as a minimum labor force to run the plant. Above a 150,000-gallon output labor costs were expected to increase by approximately 30 cents per gallon. Raw material costs were estimated between $1.50 and $2.50 per gallon depending on the quality of the paint. In addition, selling and administrative expenses as well as financing charges would have to be covered.

# The Central American Paint Market (B)

In 1956, Pincor (Pinturas de Costa Rica S.A.), a locally owned company, entered the Costa Rican paint market through the construction of a plant with a capacity of 600,000 gallons. Pincor adopted the following policies.

## PRICING AND PRODUCT POLICY

Pincor priced its paints at ¢27.50[1] per gallon compared to ¢50 to ¢60 for imported brands from the United States. In its pricing policy, Pincor as a local manufacturer, having secured permission to import raw materials duty-free, did not have to pass on to the consumer any Costa Rican import duties.[2]

Also, the price differential was further facilitated by the fact that the imported paints were the premium or top-of-the-line brands of the U.S. companies. Pincor, on the other hand, decided to produce more standard paints which, although they were of acceptable quality, were not of the premium variety.

## DISTRIBUTION

Unlike the manufacturers of imported brands, Pincor decided not to rely on distributors (who also acted as importers) to secure its outlets.

---

[1] U.S. $1 = Costa Rican ¢6.62 (colones); ¢1 = $.15.

[2] Amounting to ¢1.32 per kilogram plus 20% ad valorem, which, based on a CIF price of ¢23 per gallon, amounted to about 50% of imported value. (A gallon of prepared paint weighs approximately five kilos.)

Rather, in selling to paint dealers it employed a direct sales force. Salesmen were paid a salary of about ¢1,000 a month ($150) plus an average monthly bonus of ¢500 ($75). The job of these salesmen consisted not only of selling to dealers but also providing technical advice and service with respect to customer problems encountered by dealers.

To supplement the efforts of its regular dealers, Pincor also opened one retail outlet of its own located in the same building which housed its administrative offices. Furthermore, in order to participate in institutional-type jobs (government contracts, public buildings, and large construction jobs) Pincor engaged four paint contractors.

Pincor's direct sales effort was aimed at establishing dealers not only in San Jose, where all the Costa Rican distributors of imported paint had traditionally concentrated their efforts, but also in the other parts of Costa Rica.

## ADVERTISING

To convince the paint trade and the public that its paint brand, Superior, was reputable and reliable, Pincor planned to make heavy use of advertising, allocating up to 10% of sales. Pincor management felt that they had to overcome a widely held feeling in Costa Rica that locally manufactured products were inferior to imported ones.

The main theme planned for Superior was an "evidence campaign." Pictures of local houses and buildings which had been painted with Superior paint were to be shown in newspaper and TV advertising as "evidence" of its quality and durability. In each case the owner of the house or building, as well as the painter, would be identified.

## MARGINS AND CREDIT

Pincor decided to grant retailers a margin of 20% off retail list price. This compared with the 35% discount off list granted to the importer-distributors and 25% granted to their subdealers. Pincor's credit terms for its dealers were 30 days. The importer-distributors, on the other hand, granted significantly longer credit terms.

# The Central American Paint
# Market (C)

IN 1957, one year after Pincor had formulated a new strategy, a second local company, Punto Blanco, established operations in Guatemala. Punto Blanco limited itself to a basic line of medium-quality oil paints which were sold exclusively in Guatemala at prices significantly under those of imported paints. The company distributed its paints through three newly created company-operated retail outlets in Guatemala City as well as through a number of small subdealers, most of which were hardware stores and were typically given a 20% margin off retail. Punto Blanco spent proportionately more on advertising than importers, stressing the theme: Punto Blanco paints—high quality at low prices.

In 1958 Sr. Cortez, export sales manager of California Paints, one of the largest U.S. paint companies, concluded that Central American manufacturing should be started. In that year California only sold $375,000, or 90,000 gallons. However, Sr. Cortez was influenced by (1) serious talks about the possible creation of a Central American Common Market; (2) import duty reductions and (3) tax incentives giving the first locally established plant a competitive advantage; and (4) the fact that locally manufactured products were finding a ready market for their modestly priced products.

His enthusiasm was shared by Sr. Goya, California's Salvadoran distributor, and his brother, who had been California's Central American sales representative since 1954. However, members of California's top management in San Francisco were somewhat reluctant to make direct investments in Latin America, partly because of political and economic risks and partly because of a number of pressing organizational and competitive problems in the United States.

Nevertheless, Sr. Cortez and the Goya brothers felt so strongly that they declared themselves willing to provide much of the needed capital. This proposal was sufficiently attractive to California that a new joint-venture company, Industria Centroamericana de Pinturas S.A. (INCEP), owned in equal thirds by California, the Goya brothers, and Sr. Cortez, with each partner contributing $115,000 in equity, was formed in early 1959. California agreed to provide INCEP with its paint formulae and with technical assistance and to permit INCEP to use its brand names, in return for which INCEP paid a 4% license fee. A 600,000-gallon annual one-shift capacity plant costing $270,000 (including land) was constructed in El Salvador. Sr. Cortez, who resigned from California, became "gerente" (general manager) of INCEP, and Sr. Goya sales manager.

Both men developed INCEP's strategy, given California management's belief that the paint markets in Central America and the United States were sufficiently different that the former could best be exploited by someone who was actually on the scene and in close touch with the local situation. Moreover, since Sr. Cortez was formerly California's export sales manager, it was felt that he would know when to call on the U.S. company for help.

## PRODUCT POLICY AND PRICING

INCEP's product line included the same premium paints previously imported by California, including not only the basic oil, latex, and vinyl paints but also a variety of specialty enamels, varnishes, lacquers, anticorrosive paints, and industrial finishes. The import duty saving was passed on to the consumer, resulting in a price reduction from $7.50–$8.50 a gallon to $6.10–$6.50 a gallon.

## DISTRIBUTION

California's distribution setup in 1959 consisted of one exclusive distributor (usually a large hardware supply house) per country. These distributors typically did not have an outside sales force to line up and work with subdealers, largely relying on sales through their own retail outlet.

INCEP was planning to adopt a more flexible policy, aiming at the enthusiastic support of as many distributors and dealers as possible. Thus, management was planning to sign up additional distributors in all Central American countries. Also, a captive four-man sales force (at $250 per man monthly plus traveling expenses) was organized to cover the "interior" of El Salvador.

## ADVERTISING AND PROMOTION

Main emphasis would be placed on educating consumers concerning the protective qualities of paint in general and California paint in particular. In developing its advertising, INCEP had received only limited help from California. It consisted of the same advertising materials as California sent to its dealers in the United States. In the opinion of INCEP's management, however, these materials were of little or no value inasmuch as they not only were almost all in English, but they also stressed themes that were not appropriate for Central America. For example, California's U.S. advertising was directed mainly at the do-it-yourself market; in Central America this market was practically nonexistent.

In addition to its media advertising, INCEP was planning to invest in several special promotions directed at painters. Although the company had not undertaken any formal market research, both Sr. Cortez and Sr. Goya believed that painters were a key factor in the paint market. If a company could win the loyalty of a large number of painters, then these painters could, in turn, exert a strong influence on the paint purchasing decisions of their home-owning clients.

INCEP was considering the following:

1. A series of free training programs for Salvadoran painters, consisting of three hours of training a week for six weeks;
2. A program whereby a painter and his family would be offered free medical care for a month if during the preceding month he purchased at least $30 worth of INCEP paint; and
3. A continuing program whereby complimentary overalls and hats bearing the California name would be given away to painters.

## MARGINS AND CREDIT

INCEP management had decided to grant generous margins and credit terms to obtain the active support of good distributors and dealers. Distributors were to be granted a 30% discount from the retail list price, while dealers (a retailer who purchased directly from an INCEP salesman) and subdealers (a retailer who purchased from a distributor) were given discounts of 20% to 25% depending on their size. Some competitors, on the other hand, granted their distributors a 25% discount and their dealers a 20% discount. Distributors and dealers, in turn, would be authorized by INCEP to grant their customers (the public and painters) up to 10% in discounts whenever necessary.

Sr. Cortez also firmly believed in the use of lenient credit terms as a means of building up dealer support. Consequently, although INCEP's credit terms were officially 60 days with a 2% discount for cash payment, the company was planning to grant distributors and dealers up to 180 days to pay their bills, providing they signed a promissory note. This was 60 to 90 days longer than the credit granted by most competing paint firms. This practice of granting generous credit terms would enable distributors and dealers, in turn, to extend liberal credit to their customers, particularly to painters who often were extremely short of ready cash.

# The Central American Paint Market (D)

## SUBSEQUENT DEVELOPMENTS AT INCEP

### Product policy and pricing

FACED WITH the success of local competitors in Costa Rica and in Guatemala which sold liquid paints in the $3.50–$4.50 price range and powdered paints for $1.50–$1.75/equivalent gallon, INCEP's product line was broadened in 1960 to include both medium- and low-price paints. Formulae for the new lines were provided by California through its Cuban affiliate. The offerings in the medium- and low-price categories, on the other hand, were limited to a fairly narrow line of basic paints and varnishes.

### Brand policy

INCEP introduced the medium- and low-price paints under different brand names (Perfecta and Economica, respectively). The California brand was used exclusively for the premium paints, partly from a desire to avoid confusing the paint trade and the consumer and partly from the unwillingness of the California company to have its brand name associated with any but the highest quality paints.

In addition, in 1962, INCEP had brought out a set of parallel brands (Inspector for premium and Moderna for medium quality) in an attempt to obtain a more extensive distribution network.

Finally, INCEP had agreed to produce "private label" paints for certain large distributors, who sold under their own brands.

The fee payable to California was 2% for the INCEP-created new brands, compared to the 4% for California-brand paints.

### Distribution

In El Salvador, INCEP had added four new distributors in the capital city, as widely dispersed as possible, thus ensuring that each had an area which was exclusively "his." The four-man sales force in the "interior" had signed up 180 dealers.

In Guatemala, Honduras, and Nicaragua, INCEP still relied fairly heavily on its original exclusive distributors, although it had signed up one additional distributor in each country, located either in a different city (in Honduras) or in a different part of the capital city. Although this geographic dispersion helped to dispel the original distributors' resistance to the loss of their national exclusivity, in one or two cases INCEP had found it necessary to grant them a special 1% or 2% commission on all sales made through the newly added distributors.

The introduction of the parallel brands permitted the addition of an exclusive distributor in El Salvador, Guatemala, and Nicaragua.

### Advertising and promotion

After the introduction of the additional brands, management's strategy had been to concentrate INCEP's advertising efforts primarily on the California brand and to leave the promotion and sale of all other brands in the hands of distributors and dealers. The idea was to build up the California reputation for quality in the minds of consumers and to motivate them to visit a California dealer whenever they needed paint. Once the consumer was inside a store carrying the California brand, the dealer would then be able to offer him not only the premium quality California line but also the lower priced Perfecta and Economica lines. Distributors and dealers of the Inspector/Moderna brands in a few cases had been granted a 2% or 3% "advertising allowance" to encourage them to advertise, but very few of them had actually used this allowance for advertising purposes.

### Costa Rican activities

Because of a series of bilateral treaties, INCEP was able until 1961 to export to all the other Central American countries at duties considerably lower than those paid on paints imported from outside Central America. This was true in spite of the fact that not all the countries (notably Costa Rica) had yet decided to join the Central American Common Market.[1] Then in 1961, when it began to appear as though Costa Rica might never join, the bilateral treaty between El Salvador and Costa Rica covering paints was suspended. The Costa Rican duty on paint imports from El Salvador then went up to the same level as that on paint imports from outside Central America. Rather than risk losing out in the Costa Rican market, INCEP's management, together with the INCEP distributor in Costa Rica, decided to build a paint factory in Costa Rica. A new company, Industrias Costarricense de Colores S.A. (INCOLOR), was formed with a total capitalization of $270,000, and ownership divided 50% for INCEP, 40% for the Costa Rican distributor, and 10% for the Goya brothers. Day-to-day management of INCOLOR was to rest in the hands of the Costa Rican distributor. In addition, an agreement was worked out whereby California extended the same licensing arrangements to INCOLOR as to INCEP. The new INCOLOR plant, which had an annual capacity of about 200,000 gallons, was completed in April 1962 and was subsequently used to supply Costa Rica. By 1964, INCOLOR sold through a five-man sales force to 95 dealers.

---

[1] In December 1960, discussions which had been going on for several years culminated with Guatemala, El Salvador, Nicaragua, and Honduras signing a treaty creating the Central American Common Market. The treaty called for the elimination of the internal tariffs and the establishment of common external tariffs on most products over a five-year period.

# The Central American Paint Market (E)

## OVERALL SITUATION IN 1964

EXHIBIT 1 shows the overall size of the 1963 paint market in Central America in terms of value (at manufacturers' prices) and gallonage, as well as a breakdown of sales among different paint companies. The percentage market share of each company is shown in Exhibit 2. Inasmuch as no exact industrywide records were kept, it should be pointed out that the figures are based on informed estimates by various industry executives. These same executives also estimated that the total paint market in Central America (in terms of gallonage) had been growing at the rate of 10% per year over the past several years.

## INCEP'S SITUATION IN 1964

### Sales and performance

Exhibit 3 gives INCEP's sales and profits from 1959 through 1964. Exhibits 4, 4a, 5, and 5a provide balance sheet and income statements as of August 31, 1963. These figures do not include INCOLOR's operations. Of Salvadoran sales, which accounted for well over half of INCEP's total, about 40% were made in the "interior," 5%–7% to the government, and the remainder in the capital city. The sales breakdown by

342

**EXHIBIT 1**

Estimated size and breakdown of the Central American paint market (value at manufacturers' prices and gallons; in thousands of dollars and gallons, 1963)

| | Totals | | El Salvador | | Guatemala | | Honduras | | Nicaragua | | Costa Rica | |
|---|---|---|---|---|---|---|---|---|---|---|---|---|
| | $ | Gal. | $ | Gal. | $ | Gal. | $ | Gal. | $ | Gal. | $ | Gal. |
| INCEP | 1,500 | 450 | 900 | 270 | 240 | 72 | 195 | 63 | 165 | 45 | | |
| INCOLOR | 530 | 140 | | | | | | | | | 530 | 140 |
| Hathaway* | 1,465 | 408 | 276 | 73 | 803 | 227 | 242 | 69 | 129 | 34 | 15 | 5 |
| Standard† | 486 | 150 | 390 | 120 | 33 | 10 | 32 | 10 | 16 | 5 | 15 | 5 |
| Kativo S.A. | 1,440 | 360 | | | | | 75 | 25 | | | 1,440 | 360 |
| Kativo (Nic.) | 775 | 175 | | | | | 28 | 12 | 700 | 150 | | |
| Punto Blanco | 540 | 202 | 142 | 52 | 370 | 138 | | | | | | |
| Represas‡ | 90 | 25 | | | | | | | 90 | 25 | | |
| Cubremas§ | 135 | 45 | | | | | 135 | 45 | | | | |
| Others | 500 | 130 | 80 | 25 | 70 | 20 | 70 | 20 | 80 | 20 | 200 | 45 |
| Total | 7,461 | 2,085 | 1,788 | 540 | 1,516 | 467 | 777 | 244 | 1,180 | 279 | 2,200 | 555 |

* Licensee of the Hathaway Paint Co. but 100% owned by the agents who formerly imported Hathaway paints from the United States. Of these agents, one (Sanchez & Cia. in Guatemala) owned 58% of Hathaway de C.A.; the remaining 42% was spread among agents located throughout Central America.

† Originally (1962–63) joint venture with ownership split as follows: Standard Paint Co. (U.S.), 48%: Salvadoran interests, 52%. In 1963 Standard Paint Co. sold out to its Salvadoran partner. However, the local company retained its old name and continued to produce Standard paints as licensee of the Standard Paint Co. (U.S.).

‡ 100% locally owned. The last remaining Central American distributor of the Excello Co., a large U.S. paint firm. As of 1964 the Represas brothers had a small paint processing facility and were dickering with Excello to form a joint venture with expanded manufacturing facilities.

§ Wholly owned by the Gulf Paint Co., a small U.S. firm located in Florida.

Source: Estimates of company executives.

EXHIBIT 2

Market share percentages—Central American paint industry (based on
estimated gallon sales, 1963)

| | *El Salvador* | *Guatemala* | *Honduras* | *Nicaragua* | *Costa Rica* | *Total Central America* |
|---|---|---|---|---|---|---|
| INCEP . . . . . . . . . | 50% | 16% | 26% | 16% | | 22% |
| INCOLOR . . . . . . . | | | | | 24% | 7 |
| Hathaway . . . . . . . | 14 | 49 | 28 | 12 | 1 | 20 |
| Standard . . . . . . . . | 22 | 2 | 4 | 2 | 1 | 7 |
| Kativo S.A. . . . . . . | | | | | 65 | 17 |
| Kativo (Nic.). . . . . . | | | 10 | 54 | | 8 |
| Punto Blanco . . . . . | 9 | 29 | 5 | | | 10 |
| Represas . . . . . . . . | | | | 9 | | 1 |
| Cubremas . . . . . . . | | | 19 | | | 2 |
| Others . . . . . . . . . | 5 | 4 | 8 | 7 | 9 | 6 |
| Total . . . . . . . . . . | 100% | 100% | 100% | 100% | 100% | 100% |

Source: Estimates of company executives.

price categories was estimated as follows for the year ending August
31, 1963:

| | Unit sales | | Dollar sales | |
|---|---|---|---|---|
| | Gallons | Percent | Dollars | Percent |
| High-price paints ($6–$8) . . . . . . . . . . | 138,000 | 30 | 645,000 | 43 |
| Medium-price paints ($3–$5) . . . . . . . . | 253,000 | 55 | 780,000 | 52 |
| Low-price paints ($1.50)* . . . . . . . . . | 69,000 | 15 | 75,000 | 5 |
| | 460,000 | 100 | 1,500,000 | 100 |

\* The low-price paints were in powdered form and were sold in five-pound packets. One five-pound packet was equivalent to one gallon of liquid paint.

In 1964 sales of paints in the medium- and low-price categories continued to outpace sales in the high-price category. This was a matter
of some concern to management inasmuch as the gross profit on the
medium- and low-price lines was only about 37% of sales while that
on the high-price line was about 43%. This concern was heightened by
the belief that the overall market for paint in Central America was
settling into the following pattern:

| | |
|---|---|
| High-price paints . . . . . . . . . . | 20% |
| Medium-price paints . . . . . . . . | 75 |
| Low-price paints . . . . . . . . . . | 5 |

A rough breakdown of INCEP's 1963–64 gallon sales by brand is shown below:

| | |
|---|---|
| Perfecta | 45% |
| California | 25 |
| Economica | 15 |
| Moderna | 8 |
| Inspector | 5 |
| Private brands | 2 |
| | 100% |

In view of the disappointing sales growth of the Inspector and Moderna brands, management had concluded that further proliferation of brands probably would not be worthwhile.

**EXHIBIT 3**

INCEP
Annual Sales*

| Year | Sales in gallons | Sales in dollars | Percentage increase over preceding year | Total profits† |
|---|---|---|---|---|
| 1959–60 | n.a. | 940,000 | | $ 99,000 |
| 1960–61 | n.a. | 1,500,000 | 62 | 200,000 |
| 1961–62 | 445,000 | 1,400,000 | (8) | 60,000 |
| 1962–63 | 460,000 | 1,480,000 | 6 | 181,000 |
| 1963–64‡ | 525,000 | 1,650,000 | 12 | n.a. |

\* Disguised data.
† "Operating profit" plus "other income."
‡ Preliminary estimates.
n.a. = not available.
Source: Company records.

## Promotion

Another disappointment had been the painter-oriented promotions. Established painters showed little interest in the free training programs, feeling that they did not require further training. Attendance, totaling about 200, had been mainly by 14- to 17-year-old apprentices who as yet had little impact on paint purchases. The free medical care program, in which several thousand dollars had been invested, turned out to be a failure. On the basis of its experience, management had concluded that it was more effective to offer painters tangible rewards for loyalty (such as rebates on purchases, liberal credit, or free overalls) than to offer them intangible incentives (such as training or free medical care).

During 1963 and 1964, INCEP had spent approximately 6.5% of sales

**EXHIBIT 4**

## INCEP
### Balance Sheet
### As of August 31, 1963*

| Assets | | |
|---|---|---|
| **Current assets** | | |
| Cash | $ | 12,000 |
| Accounts receivable | | 370,000 |
| Notes receivable | | 282,000 |
| Raw material inventory | | 166,000 |
| Packaging material inventory | | 34,000 |
| Goods in process | | 4,000 |
| Finished goods | | 228,000 |
| Materials in transit | | 18,000 |
| Total current assets | | $1,114,000 |
| **Fixed assets** | | |
| Land | $ | 33,000 |
| Buildings | | 116,000 |
| Machinery and equipment | | 178,000 |
| Vehicles | | 10,000 |
| Furniture | | 52,000 |
| Other | | 8,000 |
| Less: Depreciation | | (71,000) |
| Net fixed assets | $ | 326,000 |
| Intangible assets | | 62,000 |
| Deferred charges | | 68,000 |
| Other assets: Deposits | | 11,000 |
| Receivables in suspense | | 39,000 |
| Total assets | | $1,620,000 |

| Liabilities | | |
|---|---|---|
| **Current liabilities** | | |
| Accounts payable | $ | 175,000 |
| Notes payable | | 74,000 |
| Discounted notes receivable | | 258,000 |
| Accrued expenses | | 33,000 |
| Other | | 1,000 |
| Total current liabilities | | $ 541,000 |
| **Fixed liabilities** | | |
| Long-term debt | $ | 158,000 |
| Other long-term obligations | | 37,000 |
| | | $ 195,000 |
| **Net worth** | | |
| Authorized and paid-in capital | $ | 345,000 |
| Legal reserve | | 27,000 |
| Other reserves | | 22,000 |
| Retained earnings | | 490,000 |
| Total net worth | | $ 884,000 |
| Total liabilities | | $1,620,000 |

* Disguised data.
Source: Company records.

**EXHIBIT 4a**

INCEP
Percentage Breakdown
Gross Assets and Liabilities
August 31, 1963

| *Assets* | | *Liabilities* | |
|---|---|---|---|
| Cash . . . . . . . . . . . . . . . . . | 0.7% | Trade credit . . . . . . . . . . . . | 10.3% |
| Receivables . . . . . . . . . . . . | 38.6 | Gross bank credit . . . . . . . . . | 19.6 |
| Raw materials and work in | | Other credit . . . . . . . . . . . . | 2.0 |
| process . . . . . . . . . . . . . . | 13.1 | Long-term debt . . . . . . . . . . | 9.4 |
| Finished goods . . . . . . . . . . | 13.5 | Other long-term obligations . . . . | 2.2 |
| Gross fixed assets . . . . . . . . . | 23.5 | Depreciation . . . . . . . . . . . . | 4.2 |
| Other . . . . . . . . . . . . . . . . | 10.6 | Total net worth . . . . . . . . . . | 52.3 |
| | | Paid-in capital . . . . . . . . . . | 20.4 |
| | | Retained earnings . . . . . . . . | 31.9 |
| Total gross assets . . . . . . . | 100.0% | Total gross liabilities . . . . . | 100.0% |

Percentage Breakdown
Net Assets and Liabilities

| *Assets* | | *Liabilities* | |
|---|---|---|---|
| Cash . . . . . . . . . . . . . . . . . | 0.9% | Trade credit . . . . . . . . . . . . | 12.9% |
| Receivables—net . . . . . . . . . . | 28.9 | Net bank credit . . . . . . . . . . | 5.4 |
| Raw materials and work in | | Other credit . . . . . . . . . . . . | 2.5 |
| process . . . . . . . . . . . . . . | 16.3 | Long-term debt . . . . . . . . . . | 11.6 |
| Finished goods . . . . . . . . . . | 16.8 | Other long-term obligations . . . . | 2.7 |
| Net fixed assets . . . . . . . . . . | 23.9 | Total net worth . . . . . . . . . . | 64.9 |
| Other . . . . . . . . . . . . . . . . | 13.2 | Paid-in capital . . . . . . . . . . | 25.3 |
| | | Retained earnings . . . . . . . . | 39.6 |
| Total net assets . . . . . . . . | 100.0% | Total net liabilities . . . . . . | 100.0% |

**EXHIBIT 5**

INCEP
Income Statement
For Year Ending August 31, 1963*

Net sales: 460,000 gallons

| | | |
|---|---|---|
| Total sales . . . . . . . . . . . . . . . . . . . . . . . | $1,480,000 | |
| Less returns . . . . . . . . . . . . . . . . . . . . . | 42,800 | |
| Net sales . . . . . . . . . . . . . . . . . . . . . . . | $1,437,200 | 100.0% |
| Manufacturing costs | | |
| Raw materials . . . . . . . . . . . . . . . . . . . | $ 692,000 | 48.1% |
| Other direct costs . . . . . . . . . . . . . . . . | 129,000 | 9.0 |
| Factory overheads . . . . . . . . . . . . . . . . | 41,400 | 2.9 |
| Cost of goods sold . . . . . . . . . . . . . . . . . . | $ 862,400 | 60.0% |
| Gross profit . . . . . . . . . . . . . . . . . . . . . . | $ 574,800 | 40.0% |
| Selling, administrative, and general expenses | | |
| Selling expense . . . . . . . . . . . . . . . . . . . | $ 172,500 | 12.0% |
| Advertising expense . . . . . . . . . . . . . . . . | 100,000 | 6.9 |
| Administrative expense . . . . . . . . . . . . . . | 140,000 | 9.8 |
| Financial charges . . . . . . . . . . . . . . . . . . | 48,500 | 3.4 |
| Subtotal . . . . . . . . . . . . . . . . . . . . | $ 461,000 | 32.1% |
| Operating profit . . . . . . . . . . . . . . . . . . . | $ 113,800 | 7.9 |
| Other income . . . . . . . . . . . . . . . . . . . . | 67,200 | 4.7 |
| Total profit . . . . . . . . . . . . . . . . . . . | $ 181,000 | 12.6% |

* Disguised data.
Source: Company records.

**EXHIBIT 5a**

INCEP

Key Ratios Expressed as Percentages of Net Sales*

August 31, 1963

Receivables
| | |
|---|---|
| Notes receivable . . . . . . . . . . . . . . . . | 19.6% |
| Accounts receivable . . . . . . . . . . . . . . | 25.8 |
| Total receivables . . . . . . . . . . . . . . | 45.4% |

Inventories
| | |
|---|---|
| Finished goods . . . . . . . . . . . . . . . . . | 15.9% |
| Raw materials and work in process. . . . . . | 15.4 |
| Total inventories. . . . . . . . . . . . . . | 31.3% |

| | |
|---|---|
| Total fixed assets. . . . . . . . . . . . . . . . . | 27.6% |
| Net fixed assets. . . . . . . . . . . . . . . . . | 22.7 |
| Gross assets . . . . . . . . . . . . . . . . . . . | 117.7 |
| Net assets . . . . . . . . . . . . . . . . . . . . | 94.8 |
| Debt (bank credit and long-term debt). . . . . . | 34.1 |

Net profit as a percentage of—
| | |
|---|---|
| Gross assets . . . . . . . . . . . . . . . . . . . | 10.7% |
| Net assets . . . . . . . . . . . . . . . . . . . | 13.3 |
| Net worth. . . . . . . . . . . . . . . . . . . . | 20.5 |

* Net sales (U.S. dollars in thousands) $1,437.

on advertising and promotion. This was broken down approximately as follows:

| | |
|---|---|
| 25% | Radio spots |
| 25 | Television (one half-hour show per week) |
| 10 | Newspapers |
| 20 | Direct mail and point-of-sale |
| 20 | Painter promotions |
| 100% | |

Of the amount invested in media advertising, approximately 75% was spent in El Salvador and 25% in the other three countries served by INCEP.

## Finance and ownership

During the entire 1959–64 period, one of the most serious problems faced by INCEP was a shortage of working capital. Even though all profits were retained for use in the company and only stock dividends were issued, management still was unable to finance its receivables and its inventory requirements from internal sources, from normal suppliers' credit, and through rediscounting customers' notes with local banks. Consequently, it became necessary for INCEP to seek help from California in the form of a special open-account line of credit for the purchase of raw materials plus an additional 8% medium-term loan. At one point California had as much as $300,000 in credit and loans outstanding to INCEP. Feeling that this was too much, California management finally arranged in 1963 to buy out INCEP's share in INCOLOR at book value.[1] At the same time INCEP negotiated a $150,000 long-term 8% loan with the Central American Bank for Economic Integration (CABEI). These two actions, coupled with the policy of retaining all earnings, permitted INCEP to pay off the medium-term loan which it had received from California and reduce sharply its dependence on its open-account purchasing arrangement with California. Nevertheless, the problem of financing receivables still remained. Consequently, one of the questions which management felt should be examined was whether INCEP's traditional system of liberal credit terms should be revised.

In 1964 Sr. Cortez, who was an entrepreneur by nature, had learned of an excellent opportunity to start another new business in Central America and had decided to leave INCEP and sell out his share of ownership. Upon learning of Sr. Cortez's desire, California's management, which in the years since 1959 had become more open to the idea of foreign direct investment and which felt that INCEP was now on a firm footing and offered continued growth potential, purchased Sr. Cortez's stock. By so doing, California increased its share in INCEP from $33\frac{1}{3}$% to a controlling interest of $66\frac{2}{3}$%. Sr. Goya was named as INCEP's new general manager.

Management was concerned that INCEP's market share had remained fairly constant since 1962. In part, they attributed this to the marked increase in competition from other companies such as Hathaway (the Guatemalan-based licensee of a large American paint firm), Standard (the Salvadoran-based licensee of a second American paint firm), and Kativo, all of which now had local manufacturing facilities. At the same time, however, they wondered whether the slowdown in INCEP's growth might not also be due to the strategy which the company was pursuing.

## KATIVO CHEMICAL INDUSTRIES, LTD.

Originally conceived as a paint firm, Kativo had been manufacturing and selling paints in Costa Rica ever since 1949. Until 1956, however, the company's sales of paint never rose above $70,000. In that year the company was recapitalized and the capacity of its paint factory was expanded to 600,000 gallons a year. At the same time, Dr. Jirik, president of Kativo, engaged Sr. Kissling to supervise marketing activities.

The first task which Sr. Kissling undertook was to build up the company's distribution network, initially in Costa Rica and subsequently in other Central American countries. In discussing this period in the company's development, Sr. Kissling later spoke as follows:

---

[1] California later also purchased the 10% share in the ownership of INCOLOR which had formerly been held by the Goya family.

Prior to 1956, there were only a handful of dealers in Costa Rica who carried Protecto, the paint made by Kativo. Following recapitalization of the company, however, we began to recognize that if we wanted to grow in the Central American paint business it was absolutely critical that we build a stronger dealer organization. Unfortunately, doing this was no simple matter. The biggest problem was that we were still relatively unknown and many potential dealers assumed that because Protecto was locally manufactured it was probably no good. Moreover, all of the really important established paint distributors and retailers both here in Costa Rica and in the rest of Central America were already committed to selling various imported brands of paint on an exclusive basis. This meant that in order to obtain good dealers for Protecto we had to be able to offer them something that they couldn't obtain from the foreign firms who manufactured imported paints.

In this situation, the two unique things which we were able to capitalize on were our lower prices and our ability to provide the dealers with direct service from the manufacturer. At the same time, to reassure both the dealers and the public about the quality of Protecto paints, we embarked upon a relatively ambitious advertising campaign. By combining all of these factors with hard work and a lot of aggressive selling using our own sales force, we were gradually able to bring more and more dealers into the fold. As a result, by 1960, the network of dealers which we had been able to put together for Protecto in Costa Rica was stronger than that enjoyed by any of the imported brands of paint. Thus, Protecto became by far the largest selling single brand in Costa Rica.

Unfortunately, we did not meet with the same success outside of Costa Rica—at least not initially. This was because we were even less well known in the other Central American countries than we were in Costa Rica and we just didn't have the necessary manpower or resources to mount an ambitious marketing campaign in these other countries. Eventually, however, we hit upon a new approach for introducing our paints in these markets. Instead of trying to sign up traditional paint distributors, we began to enter into joint ventures with ambitious local businessmen who, though lacking experience in paints, had some capital and were eager to grow. So far, we have entered into three such ventures: one each in Nicaragua, Panama, and Honduras. The first two, which have involved the construction of additional paint factories, have been highly successful. For instance, our joint venture in Nicaragua accounts for between 60% and 70% of the Nicaraguan paint market. The third, which has been confined to setting up a marketing company in Honduras, has run into personnel problems and has been a disappointment. In the remaining two Central American countries, El Salvador and Guatemala, we have not yet been able to do much of anything with regard to the distribution of our paints.

## Multiple brands

Sr. Jorge Arce, a Costa Rican with seven years' marketing experience with Pepsi Cola and Max Factor, who had come to Kativo as paint marketing manager in April 1963, commented that Kativo's marketing strategy had changed somewhat between 1960 and 1964:

Originally, all marketing activities centered around the Protecto brand. With time, however, it began to become evident that one brand could only grow so big. For one thing, once we had about 150 Protecto dealers it became increasingly difficult to add new dealers without having them located almost on top of present dealers. Then, too, it also became evident that there was room for market segmentation, both in terms of price levels and in terms of new types of specialty paints, such as automotive lacquers.

As a result, Kativo—

1. Introduced a low-price line of paints under the Duratex brand name, to be sold by the same dealers who handled Protecto, at ¢23.50 per gallon. Three percent of net sales were allocated for advertising which stressed economy as its main theme.

2. Added both medium- and low-price paints under a license arrangement with a U.S. firm, the Sapolin Paint Company, covering the manufacture of two of its paint brands: Sapolin and Excelsior, which had formerly enjoyed limited sales in Costa Rica on an import basis. The agreement called for Kativo to sell the two brands in Costa Rica through the same three distributors who had formerly handled them on an import basis and who supplied about 50 dealers. Advertising and promotion was to be handled by these distributors.

3. Obtained the rights to manufacture a line of high-price paints and automotive lacquers under a license agreement with Du Pont. Kativo was authorized to manufacture certain Du Pont paints in its Costa Rican and Nicaraguan plants, in return for paying Du Pont a royalty on sales which varied according to the particular type of paint. The marketing of the Du Pont paints would remain with the exclusive importer-distributors which Du Pont already had in each country and with a Central American sales representative who was a Du Pont employee and who made his headquarters in Guatemala. Kativo, however, was to have an advisory voice in matters of advertising and pricing.

4. Manufactured and sold paints in Costa Rica under still another brand name: Nacar. The Nacar line was roughly equal in quality, variety, and price to the Protecto line, but was sold through an exclusive distributor to entirely different dealers. Six percent of net sales was allocated to advertising which stressed "coverage" and durability.

## KATIVO'S SITUATION IN 1964

### Manufacturing problems

In December 1963, Kativo suffered an unforeseen setback when its Costa Rican paint production facilities including inventories were largely destroyed by a volcano flood of mud and rock. By erecting a temporary paint plant using salvaged equipment and by shifting part of its production to subsidiaries in Nicaragua and Panama, Kativo was able to survive the catastrophe with only a temporary decline in sales due to inventory shortages. On the other hand, the temporary production arrangements caused an increase in production costs: cost of goods sold in 1964 was averaging 54% of sales as compared to 49% in 1963.

As of the summer of 1964, the company was well on its way toward completing a new paint plant in Costa Rica with an annual capacity of 700,000 gallons. This plant was being financed mainly through the use of additional long-term debt which the company had been able to raise through local Costa Rican banks.

## Competitive pressures

By 1964 Kativo was facing increasingly aggressive competition in its home market from the Central American affiliates of two large U.S. firms: The California Paint Company and the Hathaway Paint Company. Competition from INCEP had begun in 1960, at a time when Protecto had become the leading paint brand in Costa Rica with an estimated 70% of the market. In 1961, in order to protect its 10%–15% market share, INCEP created a local affiliate INCOLOR, which commenced operations in 1962. Subsequently, efforts to promote and sell California and Perfecta paints were increased with the result that by 1964 these two brands had raised their share of the Costa Rican market to over 20%. According to Kativo executives, the Perfecta line, with prices identical to Protecto's, rather than the California line, had been responsible for the major share of this increase.

Just after the flood occurred, another major competitor made a bid to break into the Costa Rican paint market. This was Hathaway de Centroamerica, the Guatemala-based licensee of the Hathaway Paint Company, one of the largest paint firms in the United States. Since Costa Rica had joined the Central American Common Market in late 1963, Hathaway was able to export from Guatemala. Working through an exclusive distributor in Costa Rica, Hathaway was currently making a concerted effort to capture a significant share of the Costa Rican market, with both high- and medium-price paints, sold under different brands. In the aftermath of the Kativo flood, the Hathaway distributor had tried to convince a number of Kativo paint dealers that in view of Kativo's uncertain financial situation they would be well advised to drop the Kativo line and carry the Hathaway brand instead. Even though this tactic proved to be relatively ineffective in that only five dealers switched, the Hathaway distributor was stepping up his marketing efforts in other ways as well, including increased expenditures on advertising and a particularly aggressive effort to win large government and institutional contracts through the submission of below-cost bids. In spite of these efforts, Kativo executives estimated that sales of Hathaway paints still accounted for less than 5% of the total Costa Rican market as of the summer of 1964.

## Margins and credit

Nevertheless, even though almost all dealers had remained loyal to Kativo, some of them were beginning to agitate for higher margins and longer credit terms. Whereas the dealer margins on all of the Kativo lines were 20% off retail list price, INCOLOR and Hathaway granted dealers 25%. Moreover, Kativo executives believed that INCOLOR and Hathaway were authorizing dealers to give their customers as much as a 10% discount. Of this 10%, 5% usually went to the homeowner and 5% to the painter. Kativo, by contrast, only authorized its dealers to pass on a 5% discount to their customers. In most cases management believed that this 5% went to the homeowner rather than the painter.

As far as credit terms were concerned, Kativo granted its dealers 30 days' credit. Enforcing this limit, however, was extremely difficult

**EXHIBIT 6**

KATIVO COSTA RICAN PAINT OPERATIONS*
Profit and Loss Statement
(in thousands of colones and dollars)

| | Fiscal year ending Sept. 30, 1963 | | | 1st 10 months of fiscal year ending Sept. 30, 1964 | | |
|---|---|---|---|---|---|---|
| | ¢ | U.S. | Percent | ¢ | U.S. | Percent |
| Net sales (gallons) . . . . . | 360,000 | | | 310,000 | | |
| Net sales. . . . . . . . . . | ¢9,550 | $1,440 | 100.0 | ¢8,200 | $1,240 | 100.0 |
| Manufacturing costs | | | | | | |
| Direct costs . . . . . . . . | ¢4,730 | $ 712 | 49.5 | ¢4,447 | $ 672 | 54.2 |
| Factory overheads . . . . | 990 | 150 | 10.4 | 770 | 116 | 9.4 |
| Cost of goods sold . . . . . | ¢5,720 | $ 862 | 59.9 | ¢5,217 | $ 788 | 63.6 |
| Gross profit . . . . . . . . | ¢3,830 | $ 578 | 40.1 | ¢2,983 | $ 452 | 36.4 |
| Selling, administrative, and general expense | | | | | | |
| Selling costs† . . . . . . . | ¢ 964 | $ 145 | 10.1 | ¢ 885 | $ 134 | 10.8 |
| Advertising . . . . . . . . | 430 | 65 | 4.5 | 410 | 62 | 5.0 |
| Administrative . . . . . . | 496 | 75 | 5.2 | 550 | 83 | 6.7 |
| Financial charges . . . . . | 420 | 64 | 4.4 | 565 | 86 | 6.9 |
| Subtotal . . . . . . . . . | ¢2,310 | $ 349 | 24.2 | ¢2,410 | $ 365 | 29.4 |
| Operating profit. . . . . . | ¢1,520 | $ 229 | 15.9 | ¢ 573 | $ 87 | 7.0 |

\* Disguised data.
† Selling costs include salesman and contractor compensation as well as related social charges, company store, traveling and transportation expenses, and overhead related to all these activities.
Note: Estimated sales for 1963-64 were (in thousands) $1,486, broken down as follows: Protecto, $1,138; Duratex, $90; Nacar, $172; Sapolin, $56; and Excelsior, $30. Manufacturing of Du Pont paints had just been started.
Source: Company records.

**EXHIBIT 7**
**Kativo consumer survey data, 1964**

A. *Breakdown of residences according to type of occupancy*

| | | Socioeconomic level | | |
| | | --- | --- | --- |
| Type | Total | High | Medium | Low |
| Owner . . . . . . . | 65.2% | 69.0% | 70.5% | 58.1% |
| Renter . . . . . . . | 34.8 | 31.0 | 29.5 | 41.9 |
| | 100.0% | 100.0% | 100.0% | 100.0% |

B. *Breakdown of residences according to construction material used for exterior walls*

| | | Socioeconomic level | | |
| | | --- | --- | --- |
| Material | Total | High | Medium | Low |
| Wood . . . . . . . . | 54.8% | 27.4% | 52.0% | 71.9% |
| Cement. . . . . . . | 45.2 | 72.6 | 48.0 | 28.1 |
| | 100.0% | 100.0% | 100.0% | 100.0% |

C. *Breakdown of residences according to the time elapsed since the last painting job*

| | Totals | | | Socioeconomic level | | |
| | --- | --- | --- | --- | --- | --- |
| Time | Total | Owners | Renters | High | Medium | Low |
| Less than 3 mos. . . . . . . . . . . | 9.5% | 2.8% | 6.7% | 13.1% | 9.0% | 8.1% |
| 3 mos.–1 yr. . . . . . . . . . . . . . | 29.3 | 9.0 | 20.3 | 25.0 | 34.6 | 26.3 |
| More than 1 yr. . . . . . . . . . . . | 53.9 | 17.7 | 36.2 | 57.1 | 48.7 | 57.4 |
| Never painted . . . . . . . . . . . | 3.3 | 1.8 | 1.5 | . . . | 1.9 | 6.3 |
| Don't know . . . . . . . . . . . . . | 4.0 | 3.5 | 0.5 | 4.8 | 5.8 | 1.9 |
| | 100.0% | 34.8% | 65.2% | 100.0% | 100.0% | 100.0% |

D. *Percentages of respondents who stated they had obtained a discount when purchasing paint*

| Obtained | | Socioeconomic level | | |
| a discount | Total | --- | --- | --- |
| | | High | Medium | Low |
| No . . . . . . . . . . . | 51.6% | 42.8% | 59.5% | 48.7% |
| Don't know . . . . . . | 34.6 | 39.3 | 33.3 | 33.3 |
| Yes . . . . . . . . . . | 13.8 | 17.9 | 7.2 | 18.0 |
| | 100.0% | 100.0% | 100.0% | 100.0% |

**EXHIBIT 7** (*continued*)

E.  *Breakdown of residences according to brand of paint used*

| Brand | Totals | | | Socioeconomic level | | |
|---|---|---|---|---|---|---|
| | Total | Renters | Owners | High | Medium | Low |
| Protecto . . . . . . . . . . . . . | 48.6% | 12.2% | 36.4% | 34.8% | 49.4% | 55.0% |
| Perfecta . . . . . . . . . . . . . | 5.2 | . . . | 5.2 | 2.2 | 7.2 | 4.9 |
| Hathaway . . . . . . . . . . . . | 4.9 | 0.2 | 4.7 | 7.6 | 6.0 | 2.5 |
| California . . . . . . . . . . . . | 4.0 | 0.3 | 3.7 | 10.9 | 2.4 | 1.8 |
| Nacar . . . . . . . . . . . . . . | 3.6 | 1.0 | 2.6 | 3.3 | 4.8 | 2.5 |
| DuPont. . . . . . . . . . . . . . | 3.3 | 1.4 | 1.9 | 9.6 | 1.8 | 1.9 |
| Duratex . . . . . . . . . . . . . | 1.6 | 0.7 | 0.9 | 1.1 | 1.8 | 1.8 |
| Excelsior . . . . . . . . . . . . . | 0.5 | . . . | 0.5 | . . . | . . . | . . . |
| Sapolin . . . . . . . . . . . . . . | 0.2 | . . . | 0.2 | . . . | 0.6 | 1.2 |
| Others . . . . . . . . . . . . . | 1.4 | 0.7 | 0.7 | 4.4 | 0.6 | 0.6 |
| Don't know . . . . . . . . . . . | 26.7 | 17.0 | 9.7 | 27.1 | 25.4 | 27.8 |
| Total . . . . . . . . . . . . | 100.0% | 33.5% | 66.5% | 100.0% | 100.0% | 100.0% |

F.  *Breakdown of residences according to type of paint last used*

| Type | Totals | | | Socioeconomic level | | |
|---|---|---|---|---|---|---|
| | Total | Renters | Owners | High | Medium | Low |
| Oil . . . . . . . . . . . . . . . . . | 38.9% | 11.3% | 27.6% | 20.7% | 36.1% | 51.2% |
| Vinyl . . . . . . . . . . . . . . . | 19.2 | 3.8 | 15.4 | 21.7 | 20.5 | 16.7 |
| Powder . . . . . . . . . . . . . . | 3.6 | 1.9 | 1.7 | 2.2 | 3.0 | 4.9 |
| Latex . . . . . . . . . . . . . . | 2.7 | 0.5 | 2.2 | 4.4 | 1.2 | 3.1 |
| Varnish . . . . . . . . . . . . . | 1.2 | 0.5 | 0.7 | . . . | 3.0 | . . . |
| Enamel . . . . . . . . . . . . . . | 0.9 | . . . | 0.9 | 3.3 | 0.6 | . . . |
| Don't know . . . . . . . . . . . | 33.5 | 15.5 | 18.0 | 47.7 | 35.6 | 24.1 |
| Total . . . . . . . . . . . . | 100.0% | 33.5% | 66.5% | 100.0% | 100.0% | 100.0% |

inasmuch as most dealers had very limited working capital. Consequently, as of August 1964, Kativo's outstanding accounts receivable represented about 60 to 75 days' sales. Management believed that competitors granted even longer credit privileges, ranging from four months all the way up to consignment sales in the case of some customers. However, management felt that granting more generous credit terms was out of the question at this particular time, in view of Kativo's presently limited financial resources and low profit margins. In fact, they believed that, if anything, the company should try to decrease its accounts receivable. On the other hand, they wondered whether there might not be merit in the idea of raising dealer margins, as well as the limit on the size of the discounts which dealers were authorized to give their customers.

**EXHIBIT 7** (continued)

G. Breakdown of residences according to the reasons stated for using a given brand

| Reasons given | Total | Protecto | Perfecta | Hathaway | California | Nacar | Du Pont | Duratex | Others | Don't know |
|---|---|---|---|---|---|---|---|---|---|---|
| Don't know | 35.7% | 6.2% | ... | 0.5% | 0.9% | 0.8% | 0.1% | 0.9% | 0.5% | 25.8% |
| Good quality | 28.8 | 19.9 | 1.6% | 3.0 | 0.9 | 1.0 | 1.8 | 0.2 | 0.2 | 0.2 |
| Was recommended | 12.8 | 7.4 | 1.0 | 0.5 | 1.2 | 0.9 | 0.7 | 0.2 | 0.2 | 0.7 |
| Better than others | 9.5 | 5.5 | 0.9 | 0.7 | 1.0 | 0.2 | 0.7 | ... | 0.5 | ... |
| Was good and cheap | 7.5 | 5.6 | 1.0 | ... | ... | 0.2 | ... | ... | 0.7 | ... |
| Because of advertising | 2.0 | 2.0 | ... | ... | ... | ... | ... | ... | ... | ... |
| Other reasons | 3.7 | 2.0 | 0.7 | 0.2 | ... | 0.5 | ... | 0.3 | ... | ... |
| | 100.0% | 48.6% | 5.2% | 4.9% | 4.0% | 3.6% | 3.3% | 1.6% | 2.1% | 26.7% |

**EXHIBIT 7** (*continued*)

H. *Breakdown of residences according to who the respondent said made the final decision as to the brand of paint to be used*

| Who selected the brand | Totals | | | Socioeconomic level | | |
|---|---|---|---|---|---|---|
| | Total | Renters | Owners | High | Medium | Low |
| Husband . . . . . . . . . . . . . | 38.6% | 5.0% | 33.6% | 31.0% | 33.3% | 48.1% |
| Independent painter . . . . . . . | 18.5 | 4.9 | 13.6 | 10.6 | 30.7 | 10.6 |
| Owner of house . . . . . . . . . | 14.6 | 14.6 | . . . | 7.1 | 11.8 | 21.3 |
| Construction company. . . . . . | 7.4 | 1.5 | 5.9 | 22.6 | 4.0 | 2.7 |
| Wife . . . . . . . . . . . . . . | 4.7 | 0.8 | 3.9 | 8.4 | 0.6 | 6.7 |
| Paint contractor. . . . . . . . . | 4.0 | 0.5 | 3.5 | 9.5 | 3.9 | 1.3 |
| Son . . . . . . . . . . . . . . . | 1.8 | 0.5 | 1.3 | 1.2 | 3.4 | 0.7 |
| Relative . . . . . . . . . . . . | 1.5 | . . . | 1.5 | 2.4 | 1.3 | 1.3 |
| Husband and wife. . . . . . . . | 0.8 | . . . | 0.8 | 1.2 | 1.3 | . . . |
| Other. . . . . . . . . . . . . . | 0.8 | . . . | 0.8 | . . . | 0.6 | . . . |
| Don't know . . . . . . . . . . . | 7.3 | 6.5 | 0.8 | 6.0 | 9.1 | 6.0 |
| | 100.0% | 34.3% | 65.7% | 100.0% | 100.0% | 100.0% |

I. *Among the residences which had been painted who actually did the painting?*

| Person who did painting | Totals | | | Socioeconomic level | | |
|---|---|---|---|---|---|---|
| | Total | Renters | Owners | High | Medium | Low |
| Independent painter . . . . . . . . | 53% | 18% | 35% | 43% | 54% | 51% |
| Paint contracting company. . . . . . . . . . . . . | 7 | 2 | 5 | 21 | 4 | 3 |
| Construction company . . . . . . . | 7 | 1 | 6 | 21 | 6 | 1 |
| Family member . . . . . . . . . . | 24 | 5 | 19 | 8 | 20 | 37 |
| Don't know or other . . . . . . . . | 9 | 8 | 1 | 6 | 12 | 8 |
| | 100% | 34% | 66% | 100% | 100% | 100% |

Among all of those who said they did not do painting themselves, the average amount of money reported to have been spent per job on paint as opposed to labor was as follows:

| | | |
|---|---|---|
| Cost of paint. . . . . . . | ¢282 | 35% |
| Cost of labor. . . . . . . | 530 | 65 |
| Total. . . . . . . . . | ¢812 | 100% |

Kativo management felt that competitive pressures would continue to increase, especially since both competitors were beginning to step up their efforts to obtain distribution outside the capital city. As of 1964, whereas only 50% of Kativo's paint sales were in San Jose, management estimated that 80% to 90% of both INCOLOR'S and Hathaway's sales were concentrated in the capital city.

**EXHIBIT 7** (*continued*)

J. *Breakdown of residences according to who decided the colors to be used*

| Who decided the color | Totals | | | Socioeconomic level | | |
|---|---|---|---|---|---|---|
| | Total | Renters | Owners | High | Medium | Low |
| Husband . . . . . . . . . . . . . . | 34.3% | 6.1% | 28.2% | 27.4% | 28.1% | 44.0% |
| Wife . . . . . . . . . . . . . . | 22.7 | 3.6 | 19.1 | 11.8 | 31.4 | 19.9 |
| Owner . . . . . . . . . . . . . . | 13.8 | 13.8 | . . . | 8.3 | 11.8 | 18.7 |
| Husband and wife. . . . . . . . | 9.7 | 1.3 | 8.4 | 17.9 | 10.5 | 4.6 |
| Construction company . . . . . . | 3.8 | 1.0 | 2.8 | 15.5 | 0.6 | 0.7 |
| Ex-owner . . . . . . . . . . . . | 2.8 | . . . | 2.8 | 5.9 | 3.9 | . . . |
| Painter . . . . . . . . . . . . . | 1.7 | 0.7 | 1.0 | 2.4 | 1.9 | 1.3 |
| Children . . . . . . . . . . . . . | 1.6 | 0.3 | 1.3 | 1.2 | 2.0 | 1.3 |
| Domestic. . . . . . . . . . . . . | 1.6 | . . . | 1.6 | 1.2 | 1.3 | 2.1 |
| Paint contractor. . . . . . . . . | 1.0 | 0.5 | 0.5 | 3.6 | 0.6 | . . . |
| Don't know . . . . . . . . . . . | 7.0 | 7.0 | . . . | 4.8 | 7.9 | 7.4 |
| | 100.0% | 34.3% | 65.7% | 100.0% | 100.0% | 100.0% |

K. *Percentage of residences classified according to which paint brands they considered to be most expensive*

| Which gallon costs the most | Totals | | | Socioeconomic levels | | |
|---|---|---|---|---|---|---|
| | Total | Renters | Owners | High | Medium | Low |
| Protecto . . . . . . . . . . . . | 46.6% | 22.5% | 24.1% | 40.7% | 50.5% | 45.8% |
| Perfecta . . . . . . . . . . . . | 39.9 | 12.5 | 27.4 | 44.5 | 38.9 | 38.3 |
| Equal. . . . . . . . . . . . . . | 13.5 | 3.3 | 10.2 | 14.8 | 10.6 | 15.9 |
| California . . . . . . . . . . . | 64.4% | 25.1% | 39.3% | 78.8% | 61.1% | 60.0% |
| Protecto . . . . . . . . . . . . | 33.6 | 13.9 | 19.7 | 19.3 | 37.0 | 37.8 |
| Equal. . . . . . . . . . . . . . | 2.0 | . . . | 2.0 | 1.9 | 1.9 | 2.2 |
| Hathaway . . . . . . . . . . . | 64.5% | 23.0% | 41.5% | 80.7% | 65.8% | 54.9% |
| Protecto . . . . . . . . . . . . | 27.6 | 12.5 | 15.1 | 17.5 | 25.9 | 34.4 |
| Equal. . . . . . . . . . . . . . | 7.9 | 2.6 | 5.3 | 1.8 | 8.3 | 10.7 |
| Hathaway . . . . . . . . . . . | 54.5% | 19.9% | 34.6% | 49.2% | 55.1% | 56.7% |
| California . . . . . . . . . . . | 44.4 | 18.1 | 26.3 | 47.4 | 43.9 | 43.3 |
| Equal. . . . . . . . . . . . . . | 1.1 | . . . | 1.1 | 3.4 | 1.0 | . . . |

## Market survey

Faced with these competitive pressures, Kativo management decided at the beginning of 1964 to commission a local market research organization to conduct a survey into paint purchasing habits on the part of Costa Rican consumers. Up to that time, Kativo had done very little formal market research into the paint end of its business. The resulting study, which was conducted in the metropolitan San Jose area, covered a stratified sample of 390 residences broken down according to socio-

**EXHIBIT 7** (*continued*)

L. *Brand of paint considered to cost the least*

| Brand | Totals | | | Socioeconomic level | | |
|---|---|---|---|---|---|---|
| | Total | Renters | Owners | High | Medium | Low |
| Protecto . . . . . . . . . . . . . | 34.4% | 29.0% | 37.4% | 37.1% | 26.1% | 41.3% |
| Perfecta . . . . . . . . . . . . . | 26.7 | 26.0 | 27.1 | 29.1 | 29.6 | 22.6 |
| Nacar . . . . . . . . . . . . . . . | 13.2 | 16.8 | 11.2 | 11.4 | 16.2 | 11.3 |
| California . . . . . . . . . . . . | 10.2 | 9.2 | 10.8 | 7.2 | 10.8 | 11.3 |
| Sapolin . . . . . . . . . . . . . . | 4.7 | 7.5 | 3.1 | 5.6 | 5.8 | 3.0 |
| Du Pont . . . . . . . . . . . . . | 3.0 | 3.1 | 3.0 | 2.4 | 5.0 | 1.5 |
| Hathaway . . . . . . . . . . . . | 2.8 | 3.1 | 2.6 | 1.6 | 2.5 | 3.8 |
| Duratex . . . . . . . . . . . . . | 1.8 | 1.1 | 2.2 | 1.6 | 0.5 | 3.0 |
| Others . . . . . . . . . . . . . . | 3.2 | 4.2 | 2.6 | 4.0 | 3.5 | 2.2 |
| | 100.0% | 100.0% | 100.0% | 100.0% | 100.0% 1 | 100.0% |

M. *Brand of paint considered to be of the best quality*

| Brand | Totals | | | Socioeconomic level | | |
|---|---|---|---|---|---|---|
| | Total | Renters | Owners | High | Medium | Low |
| Protecto . . . . . . . . . . . . . | 41.0% | 35.1% | 44.1% | 36.1% | 41.0% | 43.7% |
| Hathaway . . . . . . . . . . . . | 19.2 | 19.4 | 19.1 | 15.3 | 21.8 | 18.7 |
| California . . . . . . . . . . . . | 18.9 | 22.3 | 17.1 | 19.4 | 22.9 | 14.9 |
| Du Pont . . . . . . . . . . . . . | 7.9 | 8.1 | 7.8 | 15.9 | 3.9 | 7.3 |
| Perfecta . . . . . . . . . . . . . | 6.6 | 7.8 | 6.0 | 2.1 | 6.1 | 9.1 |
| Nacar . . . . . . . . . . . . . . . | 2.2 | 2.9 | 1.8 | 1.4 | 2.1 | 2.7 |
| Duratex . . . . . . . . . . . . . | 0.7 | 0.6 | 0.8 | 0.7 | . . . | 1.2 |
| Others . . . . . . . . . . . . . . | 3.5 | 3.8 | 3.3 | 9.1 | 2.2 | 2.4 |
| | 100.0% | 100.0% | 100.0% | 100.0% | 100.0% | 100.0% |

Source: Company-financed market survey.

economic class in roughly the same proportions as the population as a whole. Kativo management hoped that these findings would prove to be useful to them in their efforts to formulate future marketing strategy. Particularly, they hoped to answer the question whether they had reached the optimal variety of products in terms of brands and price levels.

## Pricing

In view of the rise in production costs which the company had experienced since the loss of the Costa Rican factory, and the relatively low gross margins on the Protecto oil paint, in which its sales were heavily concentrated, management was giving serious thought to the possibility of certain price and product changes. A new Protecto "professional" paint with slightly upgraded ingredients and completely modernized label designs would be introduced at ¢35 compared with ¢27.50 for the regular Protecto paints. The Duratex price would be raised from ¢23.50 to ¢24.50. Management believed that a certain number of consumers would "trade up" from the regular Protecto oil paint to the "professional" quality oil paint, particularly since a recently conducted market research study had revealed that the Protecto brand already had the highest quality image of any paint brand in Costa Rica (see Exhibit 7, Part M). If the response to this change were sufficiently enthusiastic, management believed it might then prove possible at a later date to increase the retail price of regular Protecto oil paint as well, perhaps to ¢29.50 or ¢30.00.

Exhibit 6 gives operating statements on Kativo's Costa Rican paint operations. Exhibit 7, Parts A–M, summarizes some of the more pertinent findings of the market survey.

# *A note on the mutual fund industry*

WHAT IS a mutual fund? Answering this question for the neophyte, the Investment Company Institute (ICI) pointed out that a fund combined investment resources from many individuals, which were then channeled into varied securities under the continuous supervision of professional investment managers,[1] who were nearly always organized as a separate management company. Mutual funds were also "open end," that is, the number of shares could be indefinitely expanded, and a customer's shares would be redeemed by the fund at any time for a price tied to the net asset value of the underlying investments. These two characteristics—indefinite expansibility and redeemability—distinguished open-end from closed-end funds. The latter had a finite number of shares which were traded on the market like any other security at a price determined by supply and demand.

Compared with other types of institutions and financial intermediaries, mutual funds enjoyed strong growth in the postwar years. From less than $500 million in 1940, assets rose to $17 billion by the end of 1960 and to more than $48 billion by the end of 1969.[2] Thus, within nine years mutual fund assets almost tripled, while assets for financial institutions as a group only approximately doubled, from about $700 billion to about $1.6 trillion. (See Exhibits 1 and 2 for data on the relationship of mutual funds to other financial assets.)

---

[1] Investment Company Institute, *Mutual Fund Fact Book,* 1970, p. 5.

[2] Ibid., p. 16. These ICI figures cover institute members only and tend to run 4%–5% below figures for all publicly available funds.

Strong as this showing was, mutual funds had looked even stronger in November 1968 when assets had peaked at $54.9 billion. And funds were to look more vigorous again in April 1971 when the previous all-time record was broken by an asset total of $55.9 billion. On the other hand, funds had looked much weaker as recently as June 1970 when

**EXHIBIT 1**
**Assets of major institutions and financial intermediaries**

| | 1960 (in billions) | 1970 (in billions) | Percent change | Percent of 1970 total |
|---|---|---|---|---|
| Savings institutions | | | | |
| Commercial banks . . . . . . . . . . . . . . | $257.6 | $ 576.7 | 124 | 35 |
| Credit unions . . . . . . . . . . . . . . . . | 5.7 | 17.9 | 214 | 1 |
| Mutual savings banks . . . . . . . . . . . . | 40.6 | 79.0 | 95 | 5 |
| Savings and loan associations . . . . . . . | 71.5 | 176.2 | 146 | 11 |
| | $375.3 | $ 849.8 | 126 | 52 |
| Insurance | | | | |
| Fire and casualty (excluding mutuals) . . . | $ 22.8 | $ 51.8 | 127 | 3 |
| Life. . . . . . . . . . . . . . . . . . . . . . | 119.6 | 207.3 | 73 | 12 |
| | $142.4 | $ 259.1 | 82 | 15 |
| Investment institutions | | | | |
| Bank-administered personal trusts . . . . . | n.a. | $ 288.5 | n.a. | 17 |
| Closed-end investment companies . . . . . | $ 1.8 | 3.0 | 67 | 0 |
| Mutual funds . . . . . . . . . . . . . . . | 17.0 | 47.6 | 180 | 3 |
| | $ 18.8. | $ 339.1 | n.a. | 20 |
| Pension funds | | | | |
| Corporate noninsured (book value). . . . . | $ 33.1 | $ 97.0 | 193 | 6 |
| Government (book value) . . . . . . . . . . | 56.3 | 123.5 | 119 | 7 |
| | $ 89.4 | $ 220.5 | 147 | 13 |
| Total. . . . . . . . . . . . . . . . . . | $625.8* | $1,668.5 | . . . | 100 |

* Understated owing to the unavailability of a reliable 1960 estimate for bank-administered personal trusts. (In 1970 this figure had been put at $62.3 billion, with no estimates supplied for 1968 or 1969.)
n.a. = not available.
Source: Investment Company Institute, *Mutual Fund Fact Book*, 1970, p. 7; 1971, p. 7; 1972, p. 4.

assets had sunk to only $38.5 billion[3] during a slump on the stock exchange. Just where assets would stand at any time depended on two determining factors: net sales of fund shares to the public and the state of the market for common stocks, since it was in common that most fund assets were invested. Of these two determinants, it was the latter that sometimes drove fund assets down; the former had exerted a con-

[3] Wiesenberger Financial Services, *Mutual Affairs*, May 1971, p. 6 (ICI data).

**EXHIBIT 2**
Household acquisition of assets, 1970 (in billions of dollars)

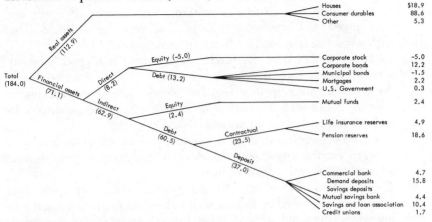

| | |
|---|---|
| Houses | $18.9 |
| Consumer durables | 88.6 |
| Other | 5.3 |
| Corporate stock | -5.0 |
| Corporate bonds | 12.2 |
| Municipal bonds | -1.5 |
| Mortgages | 2.2 |
| U.S. Government | 0.3 |
| Mutual funds | 2.4 |
| Life insurance reserves | 4.9 |
| Pension reserves | 18.6 |
| Commercial bank Demand deposits | 4.7 |
| Savings deposits | 15.8 |
| Mutual savings bank | 4.4 |
| Savings and loan association | 10.4 |
| Credit unions | 1.7 |

Source: Board of Governors of the Federal Reserve System, *Flow of Funds, Seasonally Adjusted,* 2nd Quarter, 1971.

tinuing upward pressure throughout the postwar era, at least to 1971. When in May and June of that year fund share sales fell below redemptions for the first time in decades, the possible meaning of this reversal became a topic of lively debate.

## HISTORY AND TRENDS

After their emergence in 1924–25,[4] mutual funds went through a long evolution, many phases of which left their mark on 1970. Besides the growth already discussed, these developments included the following:

1.  A relatively slow start for mutual versus closed-end funds during the booming 1920s, followed by disaster for the closed-ends when the stock market crashed in 1929.
2.  A subsequent decade of reassessment, during which investigation of flaws (mainly in closed-end funds) by the Securities and Exchange Commission (SEC) guaranteed that the whole U.S. fund industry would be subject to federal regulation.
3.  A later forging ahead by open-end funds under the impetus of such factors as the introduction of monthly payment plans in the 1930s and a growing consumer acceptance of stocks as values soared in the postwar boom, more than keeping pace with rising inflation.

---

[4] The first fund was Massachusetts Investors Trust (MIT); the second, Incorporated Investors, which was later taken over by Putnam Management Co. In 1970 Putnam was merged with Marlennan Corp., a large insurance broker.

4. The relative unattractiveness of bonds as an alternative investment medium (see Exhibit 3), at least until the later 1960s.

5. Persistence of two structural patterns, with nearly all funds and their investment managers organized as separate companies but with a few funds guided by "internal management."

6. Early segmentation of the fund industry into "load" and "no-load" sectors, the first of which actively pursued the consumer while the second, much smaller segment slowly gained momentum by offering consumers the option of buying shares accompanied by no sales push—and by no associated 8.5% sales fee.

7. The further segmentation of the industry as funds were developed to serve varying investment objectives by assigning varying degrees of emphasis to risk versus return.

8. The evolution of fund rating organizations[5] which, for a fee, kept subscribers informed as to how well individual funds were performing when compared with all other funds having similar investment objectives.

9. The evolution of "fund complexes" as companies managing investments for one fund added other funds with different goals.

10. A rapid increase not only in the number of funds but in the number and types of fund sponsors, with brokerage houses and insurance companies showing a particular interest in acquiring or creating fund management companies.

11. Further acceleration of the trend toward what the SEC was to call "integrated, multipurpose enterprise,"[6] as fund management companies sought for membership on the stock exchanges or looked for investment advisory business from institutions and other clients wishing to invest in media other than publicly available mutual funds.

12. A growing appeal of mutual funds for institutions (Exhibit 4) and for other large investors, encouraged in part by quantity discounts from the normal sales fee as well as by the privilege of switching at nominal cost from one fund in a complex to another.

13. Starting in the later 1950s, a general shift of buyer interest away from funds with conservative objectives and toward highly aggressive funds, often oriented toward capital gains, since these funds by and large showed a yeastier performance during the bull market into 1968.

14. Reflecting this trend, an "increased willingness by most major

---

[5] Among fund rating organizations were Wiesenberger Financial Services, Fundscope, Inc., United Business Services' *Mutual Fund Selector*, and Arthur Lipper, Inc.

[6] SEC, *Institutional Investor Study Report* (Washington, D.C., 1971), Vol. 1, p. xii.

**EXHIBIT 3**
Selected market indicators

| | Yearly highs and lows, Dow-Jones average industrials | | Yield of the Standard & Poor's daily stock price indexes industrials* | Stock earnings/ price | Yield to maturity high-grade corporate bonds industrials |
|---|---|---|---|---|---|
| Year | High | Low | | | |
| 1952 . . . . . | 292.00 | 256.35 | 5.88% | 9.55% | 2.87% |
| 1955 . . . . . | 488.40 | 388.20 | 3.97 | 8.69 | 2.97 |
| 1960 . . . . . | 685.47 | 566.05 | 3.36 | 5.85 | 4.26 |
| 1961 . . . . . | 734.91 | 610.25 | 2.90 | 4.75 | 4.20 |
| 1962 . . . . . | 726.01 | 535.76 | 3.32 | 6.00 | 4.18 |
| 1963 . . . . . | 767.21 | 646.79 | 3.12 | 5.68 | 4.12 |
| 1964 . . . . . | 891.71 | 766.08 | 2.96 | 5.53 | 4.26 |
| 1965 . . . . . | 969.26 | 840.59 | 2.94 | 5.85 | 4.39 |
| 1966 . . . . . | 995.15 | 744.32 | 3.32 | 6.70 | 5.09 |
| 1967 . . . . . | 943.08 | 786.41 | 3.07 | 5.71 | 5.47 |
| 1968 . . . . . | 985.21 | 825.13 | 2.91 | 5.84 | 6.12 |
| 1969 . . . . . | 968.85 | 769.93 | 3.07 | 6.05 | 6.92 |
| 1970 . . . . . | 842.00 | 631.16 | 3.21–4.12 | . . . | 7.10–8.20 |

* Aggregate cash dividends divided by aggregate market value.
   Source: Cols. 1 and 2, Wiesenberger Financial Services, *Investment Companies*, 1971 ed., p. 53; Col. 4, "Economic Report of the President, 1970," cited SEC, *Institutional Investor Study Report*, p. 84; Cols. 3 and 5, Standard & Poor's *Trade and Securities*, 1970 ed., Security Price Index Record.

WEEK ENDED JUNE 5, 1971

## New York Times Weekly Combined Averages

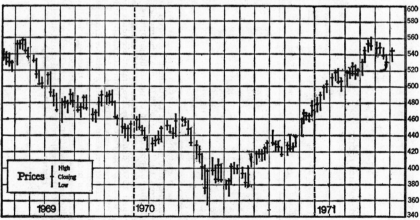

Source: *The New York Times*, June 6, 1971.

### Stock and Bond Yields

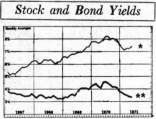

* Bonds.   ** Stocks.

   Average yield on *Barron's* 10 highest grade bonds and average yield on stocks in the Dow-Jones Industrial Average.
   Source: *The Wall Street Journal*, June 21, 1971.

# EXHIBIT 4
## Selected market data on mutual funds

| Year | Total assets (millions) | Total sales[a] (billions) | Net new money[b] (billions) | Total No. of accounts[c] (thousands) | Reported institutional accounts[d] Number (thousands) | Reported institutional accounts[d] Value (millions) | Fiduciaries[e] Number | Fiduciaries[e] Value | Business[f] Number | Business[f] Value | Institutions[g] Number | Institutions[g] Value | Other Number | Other Value |
|---|---|---|---|---|---|---|---|---|---|---|---|---|---|---|
| 1957 | $ 8,714.1 | $1.4 | $1.0 | 3,110 | 90 | $ 624.5 | 69 | $ 341.0 | 7 | $ 122.2 | 11 | $110.9 | 3 | $ 50.5 |
| 1960 | 17,025.7 | 2.1 | 1.3 | 4,898 | 220 | 1,171.0 | 190 | 680.3 | 12 | 246.9 | 12 | 160.9 | 5 | 83.8 |
| 1964 | 29,116.2 | 3.4 | 1.5 | 6,302 | 428 | 2,603.3 | 378 | 1,488.9 | 24 | 680.6 | 17 | 248.8 | 9 | 184.9 |
| 1965 | 35,220.2 | 4.4 | 2.4 | 6,709 | | | | | | | | | | |
| 1966 | 34,829.4 | 4.7 | 2.7 | 7,702 | 708 | 3,984.0 | 638 | 2,420.5 | 33 | 994.6 | 21 | 275.7 | 17 | 293.1 |
| 1967 | 44,701.3 | 4.7 | 1.9 | 7,904 | | | | | | | | | | |
| 1968 | 52,677.2 | 6.8 | 3.0 | 9,080 | 879 | 5,859.4 | 745 | 3,290.5 | 92 | 1,737.4 | 23 | 311.6 | 20 | 520.0 |
| 1969 | 48,290.7 | 6.7 | 3.1 | 10,391 | | | | | | | | | | |
| 1970 | 47,618.1 | 4.6 | 1.6 | 11,019 | 1,071 | 6,174.0 | 810 | 3,106.4 | 168[h] | 2,320.0 | 18 | 271.9 | 74 | 475.7 |

a Includes sale of shares due to customers' reinvested dividends. From $85.5 million in 1956, these rose to $785.0 million in 1970. Excluded from sales were customers' reinvested capital gains. (In 1970 these were over 80% of $922 million disbursed in this way.)

b Sales less redemptions. From 1941 through 1970, net new money totaled about $28.5 billion. The remaining increase in industry assets (about $19.5 billion) was principally due to appreciation of portfolio securities.

c Three main classes of accounts accounted for about 95% of the total: regular, accumulation (both contractual and voluntary), and dividend reinvestments. From 1956 through 1970, dividend reinvestment accounts increased from 10.4% to 28.1% of the total; accumulation plans (the great bulk of which also reinvested all distributions) increased from 18.0% to 40.3%. The remaining types of plans were contractual single payment and regular withdrawal types, the latter of interest mainly to retirees.

d Separate reporting of institutional accounts was available from companies accounting for 65%–80% of total fund assets (69% in 1970). For reporting companies, the institutional asset share rose steadily from 9.4% in 1963 to 18.9% in 1970.

e Fiduciaries include banks and individuals serving as trustees, guardians, and administrators.

f Business investors include corporations, employee pension and profit-sharing plans, unions, and other financial institutions.

g Institutional investors include foundations, churches, schools and colleges, hospitals, fraternal organizations, etc.

h An increase of almost 78,000 in employee pension and profit-sharing plans more than offset declines in business and union plans.

Source: Investment Company Institute, Mutual Fund Fact Book, 1971 ed., pp. 18, 22, 48, 54, 55.

classes of institutional investors . . . to adopt more aggressive investment strategies and trading practices."[7]

15. Pushing the "cult of performance" still further, the evolution of what the SEC was to call some "relatively exotic . . . investment vehicles,"[8] including funds with frankly speculative objectives, "hedge" funds, and—not a part of the U.S. industry—"offshore" funds.[9]

16. Some reappraisal of investment objectives and a possible shift in emphasis following the market slump of 1969–70, which brought especially disastrous results for the most aggressive or "go-go" funds.

17. A new regulatory climate both domestic and overseas, with foreign legislation emphasizing such fundamental goals as protecting the unwary investor and keeping investment capital at home, and U.S. legislation in 1970 making relatively minor changes in what was regarded as a basically sound existing law.

18. Pressure, mainly from the SEC, on the New York Stock Exchange to alter some of its practices and fees, with potentially major implications for the pattern of important relationships between mutual funds and brokerage houses.

19. A mandate for the SEC to investigate the economic impact of all kinds of institutional investors.

20. Anxiety among fund management companies about maintaining their record of growth in the fast-changing era that seemed to lie ahead, and a related interest in diversification.

## Numbers of funds and extent of industry concentration

From 1948 through 1970, the number of funds available to the general public increased from about 100 to 586. Classified by investment emphasis (Exhibit 5), these included common stock funds, bond and preferred funds, balanced funds investing in all three types of securities, and others. Of these categories the first was by far the largest, holding almost 85% of total assets. Classified by asset size (Exhibit 6), funds ranged from a few hundred thousand dollars to more than $2.6 billion in 1970,

---

[7] Ibid.

[8] Ibid.

[9] Many hedge funds escaped regulation through being organized as limited partnerships, while offshores escaped through setting up in a tax haven and selling only to foreign nationals. Speculative policies included hedging or buying short, buying new issues of unproven companies, buying letter stock at a discount and putting it on the books at full value, rapid turnover, etc. Offshores at first achieved spectacular success by emphasizing performance and by aggressive direct selling at a time when European competitors did neither. Unwise, not to say questionable, investments by the largest offshores including Investors Overseas Services (IOS) helped build their "bizarre" reputation.

**EXHIBIT 5**
Mutual funds classified by type (December 31, 1968, 1970)

| Type of fund | Number of funds 1968 | Number of funds 1970 | Combined assets (billions) 1968 | Combined assets (billions) 1970 | Asset shares 1968 | Asset shares 1970 |
|---|---|---|---|---|---|---|
| Common stock | | | | | | |
| Maximum capital gain . . . . | 120 | 189 | $ 7.9 | $ 7.0 | 14.0% | 13.9% |
| Growth . . . . . . . . . . . | 100 | 168 | 15.5 | 16.4 | 27.0 | 32.4 |
| Growth, income. . . . . . . | 81 | 118 | 20.2 | 17.1 | 35.5 | 33.8 |
| Specialized . . . . . . . . . | 27 | 17 | 1.6 | 0.3 | 2.7 | 0.5 |
| Balanced . . . . . . . . . . . . | 31 | 30 | 7.7 | 6.3 | 13.6 | 12.5 |
| Income . . . . . . . . . . . . . | 27 | 26 | 2.1 | 2.0 | 3.7 | 3.9 |
| Tax-free exchange . . . . . . | 30 | 28 | 1.6 | 1.1 | 2.8 | 2.3 |
| Bond and preferred . . . . . . | 8 | 10 | 0.3 | 0.3 | 0.5 | 0.7 |
| Total . . . . . . . . . . . . | 424 | 586 | $57.0 | $50.7 | 100.0% | 100.0% |

Source: Wiesenberger Financial Services, *Investment Companies*, 1969 ed., p. 44; 1970 ed., p. 44.

**EXHIBIT 6**
Mutual funds classified by size (December 31, 1968, 1970)

| Size of fund (millions) | Number of funds 1968 | Number of funds 1970 | Combined assets (billions) 1968 | Combined assets (billions) 1970 | Asset shares 1968 | Asset shares 1970 |
|---|---|---|---|---|---|---|
| Over $1,000 . . . . . | 13 | 10 | $22.6 | $16.5 | 39.7% | 32.7% |
| $500–$1,000. . . . . | 14 | 14 | 9.9 | 9.9 | 17.4 | 19.5 |
| 300–   500. . . . . | 18 | 13 | 6.9 | 5.2 | 12.2 | 10.2 |
| 100–   300. . . . . | 61 | 59 | 9.9 | 10.1 | 17.4 | 19.9 |
| 50–   100. . . . . | 58 | 56 | 4.2 | 4.1 | 7.4 | 8.0 |
| 10–    50. . . . . | 117 | 169 | 2.8 | 4.1 | 4.9 | 8.1 |
| 1–    10. . . . . | 116 | 188 | 0.5 | 0.8 | 0.9 | 1.5 |
| Under $1. . . . . . . | 27 | 77 | 0.1 | 0.3 | 0.1 | 0.1 |
| Total . . . . . . | 424 | 586 | $57.0 | $50.7 | 100.0% | 100.0% |

Note: Failure of dollar figures to add is due to rounding. Table includes all publicly available funds (a larger number than covered by Investment Company Institute).
Source: Wiesenberger Financial Services, *Investment Companies*, 1969 ed., p. 44; 1970 ed., p. 44.

with those in the billion-and-up class accounting for about one third of the industry's assets.

As previously noted, two or more funds with different objectives might form a complex under a single management company. According to the ICI's *Annual Reports*, there were 98 such complexes by 1968; according to *The Wall Street Journal's* fund price data, most complexes had

# EXHIBIT 7

## Selected large management companies, mutual fund industry (years to December 31,[a] dollars in millions)

| | Dreyfus Corporation | | Investors Diversified Services, Inc. | | ISI Corporation | | Keystone Custodian Funds, Inc. | | National Securities & Research Corp. | | Vance, Sanders & Co., Inc.[b] | | Wellington Mgt. Company | |
|---|---|---|---|---|---|---|---|---|---|---|---|---|---|---|
| | 1968 | 1970 | 1968 | 1970 | 1968 | 1970 | 1968 | 1970 | 1968 | 1970 | 1968 | 1970 | 1968 | 1970 |
| Assets managed | $2,666.4 | $2,440.2[c] | $7,892.6[d] | $7,750.8 | $998.0[e] | $614.0[e] | $1,881.2 | $1,547.2 | $1,023.1 | $834.0 | $700.0 | $518.5 | $2,657.2 | $2,200.0 |
| Gross revenue | 15.2 | 36.3 | 179.7 | 229.9 | 7.7 | 25.0 | 17.8 | 16.0 | 6.7 | 4.8 | 7.0 | 6.4 | 13.0 | 12.6 |
| Net operating income | | | 23.3 | 28.4 | | −0.01 | | | | | | | | |
| Net after taxes | 3.9 | 3.9 | 26.2 | 28.2 | 0.96 | −4.4 | 2.8 | 0.4 | 1.6 | 0.9 | 1.8 | 1.1 | 2.5 | 1.4 |
| Fund sales | 423.7 | 221.2 | 503.0 | 276.0 | 60.7 | n.a. | 445.1 | 358.3 | 128.5 | 60.0 | 179.0 | 139.2 | 291.7 | 190.0 |
| Net unpaid balance on contractual sales | 488.8 | 402.0 | n.a. | n.a. | 144.3[f] | 25.2[f] | 217.3 | 317.4 | 26.7 | 24.2 | ... | ... | 119.0 | n.a. |
| Market capitalization | 100.7 | 76.5 | 351.4 | 249.6 | R135.0[f] | | 49.9 | 15.2 | 22.5 | 12.1 | 25.2 | 13.3 | 42.5 | 25.0 |
| Price/earnings ratio (R) | R25.9 | R17.9 | R13.4 | R9.7 | 0.03% | | R17.5 | R40.6 | R13.3 | R12.8 | R14.0 | R11.7 | R17.3 | R16.2 |
| Yield (percent) | 2.0% | 3.8% | 3.4% | 4.9% | | | 2.7% | 2.3% | 4.9% | 7.4% | 5.3% | 8.0% | 4.1% | 5.2% |
| Gross revenue (percents) | | | | | | | | | | | | | | |
| Management fee | 80.0% | 27.0% | 14.0%[g] | 9.4%[g] | 74.0% | 16.5% | 49.5% | 48.7% | 61.0% | 71.0% | 44.0% | 43.0% | 72.0% | 79.0% |
| Net distribution | 5.0 | 5.2 | 25.3 | 15.0 | 24.0 | 5.1 | 35.1 | 26.2 | 33.0 | 23.0 | 56.0 | 57.0 | 26.0 | 18.0 |
| Other | 15.0 | 67.8 | 60.7 | 75.6 | 2.0 | 78.4 | 14.4 | 25.1 | 6.0 | 6.0 | 0.0 | 0.0 | 2.0 | 3.0 |

a Except ISI for 1968 (June 30), Vance, Sanders and Wellington (October 31), market capitalization, P/E, and yield figures are all year-end.

b Vance, Sanders was primarily a distributor of mutual funds, including some (e.g., MIT) that it did not advise.

c After 1968, Dreyfus moved from a single fund to a complex, added activities in the U.S. and foreign investment company field, made a major entry into housing, joined a second regional stock exchange, and formed a joint venture with a bank to manage large investment accounts.

d Although mutual funds accounted for $6.6 billion out of $7.9 billion of IDS assets in 1968, funds accounted for only 28% of net operating income, the rest coming from insurance, financial, and miscellaneous. In 1969, fund assets were $6.0 billion, and fund contribution to net operating income was 6.6%.

e Assets for mutual funds only.

f Year-end figures. During 1968, ISI expanded by moving from a single fund to a multifund complex, spreading operations beyond California, and adding property and casualty coverage to its existing life insurance business.

g Includes fund-related brokerage income.

n.a. = not available.

Source: Wiesenberger Financial Services, Investment Companies, 1969 ed., pp. 356–66; 1971 ed., pp. 382–90.

only two or three mutual funds, although four and five were also common, while the highest number listed was eleven. Of the management companies controlling complexes, by far the largest was Investors Diversified Services, Inc. (IDS) with assets over $6 billion at the end of 1970, of which some $5.18 billion was in mutual funds. (See Exhibit 7.)

In discussing whether the fund industry should be regarded as "concentrated," the SEC concluded that it should, based on a finding that in 1968 the top five advisory firms advised 34.6% of mutual fund assets; the top 25, 75.4%; and the top 50, 90.0%.[10] The ICI, however, took a different view. In 1966 it told a Congressional committee: "By any structural test . . . the mutual fund industry is effectively competitive. Concentration at all levels is low and has declined during the period of maximum industry growth." In support of this contention, the institute proffered, among other points, the following statistics on shares of total industry assets controlled by the four and the eight largest firms:

| Year | Asset share of mutual funds | | Asset share of fund management companies | |
|---|---|---|---|---|
| | Four largest | Eight largest | Four largest | Eight largest |
| 1952 . . . . . | 37% | 50% | 40% | 59% |
| 1965 . . . . . | 25 | 39 | 35 | 52 |

Source: U.S. House of Representatives, Committee on Interstate and Foreign Commerce, *Investment Company Act Amendment of 1967, Hearings* (Washington, D.C., 1968), p. 257.

## COMPANY AND INDUSTRY STRUCTURE

Writing in 1966, the SEC observed that the "most striking feature" of the organization of mutual funds was the extent to which companies in the industry "contract out their principal functions to other organizations that work for them on a fee basis."[11] In elaboration, the agency noted that carrying on the work of a fund usually involved (1) a separate fund company, (2) a separate management company, and (3) a group of separate brokerage houses or independent broker dealers.

Functions undertaken by the fund company itself were often little more than light housekeeping: maintaining records, making routine transactions, communicating with shareholders, etc. Functions undertaken by the management company included (1) creating the fund (at a cost of $50,000 to $250,000), (2) managing the investment portfolio,

---

[10] SEC, *Institutional Investor Study Report*, p. 143.

[11] SEC, *Public Policy Implications of Investment Company Growth* (Washington, D.C., 1966), p. 45.

and (3) acting as "principal underwriter" or distributing fund shares at least as far as the wholesale level.[12] Functions undertaken by broker dealers included (1) executing orders for the purchase or sale of fund securities, (2) sometimes giving investment advice, and (3) in a majority of cases retailing fund shares to the public through a pool of "registered reps" and "associated persons" licensed to sell by the National Association of Securities Dealers (NASD). Early in 1970 this selling pool contained some 175,000 members, of whom 80,000 were believed to specialize in funds while some 50,000 others were insurance salesmen who had obtained their NASD license. (By the end of 1970, reflecting the woes of the brokerage industry, this pool had shrunk somewhat, but only by about 3%.)

Traditionally, about twice as much retail business was handled through independent broker dealers as through captive sales forces. The latter, being expensive to maintain, tended to be associated with large investment complexes having both fund and nonfund business, as, for example, IDS.[13] Some small funds also sold this way, and for 1969 the SEC reported that having an in-house sales force was regarded as "very important" by 10 of 14 small management companies, but by only 5 of 26 large ones (assets over $100 million). Twelve large companies in the sample said they never used the method; nine implied a combined approach.[14]

Not all funds used any active sales push at all, since some were sold on a no-load basis, thus saving the investor an 8.5% sales charge. Such funds were generously small, however, 43 of 95 having assets under $5 million early in 1970. Still, they were growing relatively fast: from 8% of industry assets in 1969 they rose to 10% by the end of 1970, having tripled their shareholder accounts over the previous three years to just short of 1.2 million. In the first six months of 1971, they astonished observers by taking 40% of the industry's net sales (which were reported as $331 million). This success caused *Forbes* to headline the query, "Is the Ugly Duckling Turning into a Swan?" These gains were not

---

[12] As pointed out by the SEC, "The underwriting of mutual fund shares is quite different . . . from the underwriting of conventional securities," and is more akin to ordinary distribution than to underwriting as commonly understood. Whereas the conventional underwriter "is concerned with raising a specific amount of money within a limited time," the job of the fund underwriter is "to channel as great a *continuous* flow of new capital into the fund as it possibly can." Moreover, the conventional underwriter is associated with the issuer only through a temporary contract, but the "fund underwriter is also the [fund's] investment adviser or closely affiliated to the adviser." Thus he stands to gain in more than one capacity from sales of fund shares. See SEC, *Public Policy Implications of Investment Company Growth*, pp. 9, 54, and 55.

[13] Besides having five mutual funds, the IDS captive sales force of some 4,350 men handled insurance and face-amount certificates. (Paying a fixed amount at maturity, these were often sold on installments.)

[14] SEC, *Institutional Investor Study Report*, p. 204.

broadly distributed, however, since about $111 million net went to the biggest no-load company (T. Rowe Price), whose largest fund in 1970 had year-end assets of $655 million.[15]

The relationship between a fund company and its management adviser was a contractual one, except in rare cases where the fund was "internally managed" and was not a separate concern (e.g., MIT prior to 1969). Since the SEC saw some risk that an unscrupulous management company might take advantage of a separate fund, the Investment Company Act of 1940 had limited contracts to a year's duration, after which the fund board had to vote on whether or not to renew. Terminations were so rare, however, that management companies with little besides their organization and this annual contract to sell might fetch many millions of dollars. For example, the stock of the Dreyfus Corporation, management company of the Dreyfus Fund, brought its owners $42 million when some 82% of it was sold to the public in 1965.

When a management company went public, a question could be raised as to which stockholders—the fund's or the adviser's—its directors should act as fiduciaries for. Early in 1971, the financial community awoke to the discovery that a less theoretical though cognate legal issue had been raised as to why the owners of a management company rather than the owners of its associated fund should benefit when an adviser was sold. Under the aegis of Mr. Abe Pomerantz (a lawyer known as the Ralph Nader of the fund industry), two test cases had been brought—one involving the Dreyfus Corporation and the other involving Lazard Frères. Reviewing the latter, a three-judge panel of an appeals court had delivered a bombshell to the management companies in the shape of a decision for the challengers. Whatever its ultimate disposition, this presaged many similar cases and a long period of litigation. Dilating on his legal arguments to *Forbes*, Pomerantz asked, "Why should a fiduciary be permitted to sell his fiduciary office?" Moreover, when a management company goes up for sale, why should not the fund's independent directors regard it as their duty to consider bids from outside money managers?[16] Should the Pomerantz view prevail, claims against management companies which had sold their equity might reach $500 million.[17]

Relationships between the management company and the brokerage houses used to buy and sell securities and/or to retail shares in the fund could be simply contractual—or closer. While remaining separate

---

[15] As rated by *Forbes*, this fund earned a "B" for performance in both up-and-down markets; that is, in both types of market it was ranked in the second quartile, among 258 rated funds. See *Forbes*, "Mutual Funds 1971," August 15, 1971, cover and pp. 49–74. For net sales figures of the industry, see Wiesenberger Financial Services, *Mutual Affairs*, February–July 1971.

[16] "The Bomb Thrower," *Forbes*, July 15, 1971, pp. 63, 64.

[17] "New Ruling Perils Fund Management Deals," *Boston Globe*, July 13, 1971.

legal entities, advisers and brokers might (with some limitations) acquire one another, create a new subsidiary in the other's field, or be acquired by a common parent. As noted in the following section, the trend in the late 1960s was toward a growing number of combinations.

## Multipurpose aggregates

When the SEC in 1971 spoke of an accelerating trend toward "integrated multipurpose aggregates," it had reference to the combination of firms in areas that were formerly distinct, such as brokerage, insurance, and investment management—for both funds and other types of clients (Exhibit 8).[18]

**EXHIBIT 8**
**Affiliations of advisory firms obtaining at least one third of their assets from funds\* (1968)**

| Asset size of adviser | Number of firms | Broker dealer | Life ins. co. | Non-life ins. co. | Bank or trust co. | Other investment adviser | Investment partnership | Others |
|---|---|---|---|---|---|---|---|---|
| | | | | Percentage of responses indicating affiliation with following entities | | | | |
| Over $100 million | 27 | 56% | 30% | 26% | 15% | 33% | 15% | 44% |
| Under $100 million | 14 | 64 | 7 | 0 | 0 | 35 | 21 | 21 |
| Total | 41 | 59 | 22 | 17 | 10 | 34 | 17 | 37 |

\* Registered investment companies, open-end and closed-end.
Source: SEC, *Institutional Investor Study Report*, p. 162.

The interest of insurers in the fund industry was due in part to a precipitously falling share in savings and a relatively slow asset growth (under 75% from the end of 1960 through 1969, versus 184% for funds). Another motive was to give the approximately 450,000 insurance agents a chance to sell an investment whose goal could be identified as "growth" or "growth and income" rather than "fixed return." Diversification into funds also lent support to the industry's claim that its agents were capable of serving as all-round financial planners for their clients.

---

[18] Banks, too, had sought to enter the fund industry but had proved unable either to get Congress to write authorizing legislation or to get the Supreme Court to agree that bank charters already gave them the right (*ICI* vs. *First National City Bank of New York*, 1971). Banks could, however, be associated with funds, as through a common parent.

Insurance companies moved into funds only in the late 1960s, but by March 31, 1971, they owned almost 17% of fund assets. Affiliations initiated by one side or the other brought another 27% into the insurance orbit:

| Category of relationship | Number of funds (March 31, 1971) | Assets (billions) |
|---|---|---|
| Insurer organized and managed . . . . . . . . . | 80 | $ 0.8 |
| Insurer owned, traditionally managed . . . . . | 86 | 7.8 |
| Insurer affiliated, not controlled . . . . . . . . | 53 | 15.1 |
| Total. . . . . . . . . . . . . . . . . . . . . | 219 | $23.7 |

Source: Wiesenberger Financial Services, *Mutual Affairs*, May 1971, pp. 1, 2.

The entrance of brokerage houses into funds was seen as controversial, inasmuch as the traditional pattern was for members of these two industries to bring each other business rather than to invade each other's territories. Thus, institutions as a group had helped to push the brokerage commissions of NYSE members from $900 million in 1962 to $3.2 billion in 1968, largely by increasing institutional transactions. Between 1960 and 1969 these rose 548%, or from about a quarter of NYSE volume to about a half. Banks and mutual funds alone increased their share from 18% to 34%. Profits, too, were relatively high on this business. In 1968 "the median pretax profit was $824,000 for all NYSE firms, $672,000 for primarily retail firms, and $2.4 million for primarily institutional firms."[19]

Especially controversial was the entrance into funds of broker members of the NYSE, since the NYSE, unlike the regional stock exchanges, would not let institutions, including funds, acquire membership in their organization. Yet by February 1971, approximately 60 mutual funds representing some $3 billion in assets were under the aegis of Big Board members.[20]

Although the Big Board's policy against "institutional access" could be defended as making for a sounder market, it could also be interpreted as a selfish stratagem for protecting the brokerage commissions of existing Big Board firms. Also, it tended to impair the functioning of the major stock exchange by driving large transactions to other markets

[19] SEC, *Institutional Investor Study Report*, Summary Volume, pp. 101–2.

[20] Wiesenberger Financial Services, *Mutual Affairs*, February 1971, p. 1. The size of a Big Board member's fund had to conform to a NYSE ruling that said no member firm (or parent having more than 25% control) could derive more than half its income from sources other than securities brokership or dealership.

where they would be handled more cheaply. Under these circumstances, the SEC had pressed the NYSE to offer institutions not access but negotiated rates on transactions over $500,000. In spite of this change, which was arranged late in 1970 for 1971 introduction, and in spite of the fact that the floor might be dropped from $500,000 to $100,000, some fund sponsors were arguing that sauce for the goose was sauce for the gander, and that if NYSE member firms were to be allowed to create funds, then funds should be allowed to buy seats on the NYSE. Funds not depending on broker dealers to do their retail selling had argued this way for a long time. A more recent convert was the large Dreyfus Corporation (assets $2.7 billion at the end of 1970), already a member of a regional exchange. In 1971 Dreyfus' chairman, Mr. Howard Stein, wrote to the NYSE stating that although he was opposed to institutional membership in theory, he did not want his company left out in the competitive cold. In the absence of a "uniform and inclusive" prohibition of institutional access, he said, "our directors and officers believe that our responsibility to our stockholders requires us to seek membership with all the resources at our command. . . ."[21] As of mid-1971, the Dreyfus application (already joined by others) was still being taken under advisement.

Since the movement of insurers and NYSE members into funds was proceeding with a rush, although relatively recent, everyone in the fund industry was eager to know how well the newcomers were doing. For example, special interest was attached to the success of the fund created in 1970 by Allstate, Sears, Roebuck's insurance arm. This fund was to operate as a no-load during its first four months, and plans were made to have 7,400 agents selling it by 1971. The fund would not, however, receive their chief emphasis but would rather round out their line. Allstate's president was quoted as saying, "We're in mutual funds primarily to sell life insurance; our life insurance profits are much greater."[22] The Allstate Fund reportedly reached $125 million in asset size during its no-load period but added only about $10 million over its next year.

Taken all together, insurance-related funds expanded their assets a little over 12% during the first quarter of 1971, a period during which the stock market rose 7.8% as measured by the Dow-Jones 30. By categories, insurer-owned and operated funds gained 16.9%, insurer-owned funds under traditional management gained 12.2%, and insurer-affiliated funds gained 12%.[23]

In a more comprehensive though less recent rundown on relative

---

[21] Ibid., p. 3.

[22] John C. Bogle (president of Wellington Management Company), "The Member Firm and Mutual Fund Complex: A Marketing Parternship," speech before the NYSE Marketing Conference, New York, N.Y., June 19, 1970.

[23] Wiesenberger, May 1971, pp. 1, 2.

market shares, the president of traditionally organized Wellington Management Company reported as follows:

We move into the 1970s burdened with some important misinterpretations about the present decade . . . the generally-held view that the marketing patterns of our industry have changed radically . . . is plainly and simply a myth. In fact, the past decade saw incredibly little change both in *who* distributes mutual fund shares and in *how* they are distributed.

—As to "who," the industry is still dominated by the established management companies. In total, more than 90% of industry assets are represented by 49 major ($100,000,000 plus) complexes, 45 of which were formed prior to 1950. . . .

—As to "how," there have been only nominal variations in distribution patterns. As 1970 began, the relationship between funds distributed by independent broker dealers (67% of industry assets) and controlled sales forces (24%) was *identical* with 1960. Both groups, in turn, had given up what must be regarded as a remarkably small market share to the no-load funds (up from 5% to 7% of industry assets) and to two new groups of funds—those formed by insurance companies and by brokerage firms—each of which has attained a market share of slightly below 1%.[24]

The condition of the brokerage industry in early 1971, however, was a cause of concern for those fund managers who relied on independent broker dealers for their retail distribution.

The brokerage industry has been, and in many ways still is, out of control. Hit broadside this year by the tail of the 1969–70 bear market, it has now left adrift some of the customers to whom it once seemed almost to guarantee protection. It has lost two of its largest firms and a raft of smaller ones, and many of the survivors are severely crippled by operating and capital losses. The industry ends the year committed to salvage projects that may eventually cost it many millions of dollars. And it still cannot be said to be out of the woods. The industry has lost respect in the eyes of all of its audiences: its customers, its contributors of capital, the Securities and Exchange Commission, and Congress. . . .

Some aggregate figures compiled by the New York Stock Exchange indicate the range of the disaster. Included in the Exchange's sample were seventy-five firms, among them the fifty largest, and the information produced was pretax monthly profit-and-loss figures on the firms' over-all business (including realized, and in some cases also unrealized, capital gains and losses on the firms' own portfolios). In the last quarter of 1969, a period that was none too glorious itself, these firms had average monthly profits of more than $29 million. In the first quarter of 1970, the profits averaged $4,200,000, and then the roof really caved in. April's *losses* were an astronomical $31 million, and May's losses were $22 million.[25]

---

[24] John C. Bogle, cited in *Institutional Investor*, June 1970, p. 33.

[25] Carol J. Loomis, "Wall Street on the Ropes," *Fortune*, December 1970, pp. 62, 64.

## FEES AND CHARGES

Even if part of a "multipurpose aggregate," a fund company purchased key services from other legal entities and thus made substantial payments to outsiders. Estimating 1970 totals, *Forbes* suggested that funds generated $250 million in brokerage commissions, $200 million in management fees, and $265 million in selling charges, for a total of over $700 million.[26] Of these amounts, management companies separate from the fund got the management fees and a percentage of the distribution income; broker dealers and their salesmen got the rest.

Traditional base fee rates for the largest number of funds and proposed 1971 brokerage charges are indicated below.

### Fees paid by the largest number of funds

| Fee | Traditional prevailing rate | Traditional normal range of rates | Rate base |
|---|---|---|---|
| Management fee | | | |
| (per year) . . . . . . . . . . . . . | 0.50%* | 0.25%-0.75% | Average assets |
| Sales charge . . . . . . . . . . . . | 8.50† | 7.50  -8.85‡ | ⎰Purchase |
| Wholesale . . . . . . . . . . . . | 2.00 | 0.50  -2.50 | ⎱price of |
| Retail . . . . . . . . . . . . . | 6.50 | 6.00  -8.00 | shares |
| Brokerage (buy and sell commissions) (1971 proposals) | | | |
| Orders under $2,500 . . . . . . . | | 1.30% ÷ $ 12 | Value of order |
| $ 2,500-$ 19,999 . . . . . . . . | | 0.90  +   22 | "    "    " |
| $20,000-$ 29,999 . . . . . . . . | | 0.60  +   82 | "    "    " |
| $30,000-$499,999 . . . . . . . . | | 0.40  +  142 | "    "    " |
| $500,000 and up . . . . . . . . | | Negotiated | "    "    " |

* Basic rate, sometimes keyed to assets on a sliding scale or subject to performance premiums and penalties.
† Basic rate, subject to quantity discounts. Equivalent to 9.3% of amount invested. Not charged on reinvested capital gains and usually not charged on reinvested dividends.
‡ Except no-loads, where no sales charge is made.
Source: SEC, *Public Policy Implications of Investment Company Growth*, 1966, pp. 94–99; *The Wall Street Journal*, July 13, 1971. For later trends in management fees and sales charges, see text.

As the ICI was quick to point out, percentages reflecting base fees for the largest number of funds provided an inflated picture of the average fund charges footed by investors. Distortion was ascribed to the failure of majority figures to reflect the dominance of a relatively few large funds, some with a relatively low base fee and most with a schedule of fees that declined as assets or order size increased. Weighted for dollar volume, ICI cost figures showed management ad-

---

[26] "Mutual Funds 1971," *Forbes*, p. 64.

visory fees only 0.35% of assets by 1968 and generally trending downward; sales commissions (excluding no-load funds altogether) were down to less than 5.4% of gross sales (Exhibit 9).

**EXHIBIT 9**
**Trends in mutual fund sales commissions as a percent of gross sales and in operating ratios and management company advisory fees as a percent of assets managed**

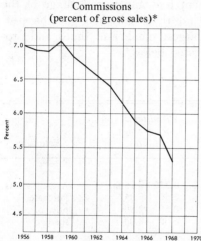

Commissions
(percent of gross sales)*

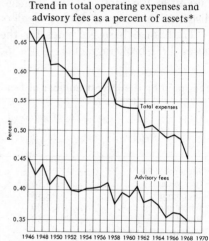

Trend in total operating expenses and advisory fees as a percent of assets*

* No-load funds and exchange funds not included. Conversions, capital gains reinvested and single-payment contractual redeposit activity not included. Based on a sample comprising approximatley 85% of industry sales.

* Yearly expenses are based on the average of assets at beginning and end of year for each company. Estimates are based on a sample group representing more than 90% of assets of ICI members.

Source: U.S. Cong., House Committee on Interstate and Foreign Commerce, *Mutual Fund Amendments, Hearings*, 1970, pp. 433, 435 (ICI testimony).

By 1968 the fund fee structure already reflected to some extent the influence of outside pressures, and these were to continue, if not accelerate. Thus, the falling ratio of management fees to assets reflected in part litigation of the early 1960s, when Abe Pomerantz brought a series of suits aimed at forcing management companies to pass on some economies of scale to fund holders. (In 1971 Pomerantz claimed these suits had already saved investors $60 million.)[27]

Like management fees, the fees paid to brokers for securities transactions were also subject to outside pressure, especially from the SEC.

---

[27] "Mutual Funds 1971," *Forbes*, p. 63. Besides these suits, also influential was the so-called "Wharton Report" on mutual funds, commissioned in 1958 by the SEC and published in 1962.

One SEC approach, tried on Dreyfus, was to insist informally that the management company join a regional stock exchange and pass on resultant brokerage income to fund shareholders by using it to offset management fees.[28] Another approach of wider impact was the SEC's ruling that by 1971 brokers on the NYSE must substitute negotiated charges for fixed minimum commissions on portions of transactions over $500,000. This ceiling, moreover, might go lower in the future. Assessing the impact of the change to date, the president of Wellington Management Company stated in early 1971, "The prevailing brokerage fee rate was probably running about $\frac{5}{10}$ of 1%; as of today, it looks as though it will run about $\frac{3}{10}$ of 1% under the 'competitive' schedule."

Both brokerage fees and the distribution of rewards to brokers for retailing fund shares were affected by the SEC's attack on "give-ups," which climaxed in December 1968 when a Commission ruling outlawed this practice. Under the give-up system, a fund would use a single broker to execute a large transaction but would ask him to give up a portion of his fee, often 60% to 70%. Recipients of the give-up were nearly always other broker dealers whom the fund management company wanted to reward, beyond the normal fee, for retailing fund shares.[29] As the SEC saw it, however, if give-ups were recoverable at all, they should be recovered by the fund shareholders, not assigned to brokers for selling new shares at no demonstrable gain to the present owners of the fund. As might be expected, the same investor-oriented argument already formed the basis for a Pomerantz suit, with 50 more likely to follow a mid-1971 appeals court success.[30]

Besides attacking the use of give-ups to reward retailing efforts, Pomerantz had it in mind to attack "interpositioning" used for the same purpose.[31] This practice involved using brokers to execute transactions which could be done more cheaply some other way: over-the-counter, by direct exchange, or through an off-board service like "Instinet," which claimed to save its customers 50%–75% by using computers to execute block trades. Since the SEC had found that funds made less use of these low-cost methods than other institutional investors,[32] the issue of interpositioning could conceivably be headed for a lively legal future.

---

[28] In 1970 Dreyfus brokerage income was $1.3 million.

[29] Since the NYSE prohibited give-ups to nonmembers, funds had some incentive to use the regional exchanges if they wished to reward all their broker-dealers, most of whom belonged to no exchange at all. NYSE member firms, however, accounted for 39% of fund sales in 1969, up from 22% in 1962. See SEC, *Institutional Investor Study Report*, Summary Volume, p. 110.

[30] The suit on which an initial victory had been won was against the management of Boston's "Fidelity Group," second largest complex in the fund industry. "Mutual Funds 1971," *Forbes*, p. 63.

[31] Ibid., p. 64.

[32] SEC, *Implications of Investment Company Growth*, p. 17.

In still another move aimed at the structure rather than the size of the distribution fee, the SEC got Congress in 1970 to restrict the old practice of front-end loading. Used when shares were sold through a "contractual plan" (i.e., when a buyer bound himself to purchase under a long-term installment-type arrangement), front-end loading simply meant that half the sales fee on all the money to be spent was deducted from the buyer's first several payments. Thus a buyer who dropped his plan early might well bring a loss upon himself. Viewing this result as undesirable, the Investment Company Act of 1970 gave funds their choice of modifying front-end loading in two ways: either the distributor could collect no more than 20% of the full commission charge in each of the first three contract years, or he had to make refunds of the sales charge to buyers who dropped out of the plan early: all of it to buyers who dropped out within 45 days, 85% to buyers who dropped out within 18 months. During the hearings of this proposal, the most strenuous opposition came from a spokesman who said he represented 50 contractual plan sponsor companies, "hundreds of small independent broker dealers across the country," and customers with $7 billion of assets. His argument was that qualified salesmen could only be attracted and held if compensated promptly, that insurance companies had long used front-end loading for this purpose, and that funds should be permitted to use it too.

Although the attack on distribution fees had so far hit their structure rather than their size, their size was also under review. Provisions in the Investment Company Act of 1970 required NASD, as the industry's principal self-regulating body, to study the level of distribution charges with a view to their possible reduction in the interest of fund owners and buyers. Should the NASD suggestions, when they came, prove unacceptable to the SEC, the latter would be able to act on its own.

By 1970 attacks on the fee structure seemed to be showing some result. Whereas management companies in 1965 had made an average base charge of about 2% of the fund share price for their wholesaling function, by 1970 this percentage, though scattered, tended to be lower, with 1.75% very common and 1.5% the most popular figure.[33] The overall distribution fee was, however, still described as being 8.5%.

Whereas the average or prevailing management fee had been 0.5% of assets in 1965, the SEC reported that in 1968 it was 0.45% for all fund advisers in its study and 0.44% for large ones (assets $100 million and up). The more significant dollar-weighted figure was 0.39%. Even so, average management advisory fees for funds in the large-fund category were higher than the average advisory fees quoted by advisers to other large clients:

---

[33] Wiesenberger Financial Services, *Investment Companies*, 1971 ed., pp. 100–110.

**Advisers' average fee rates per class of account, 1968**

| Size range of account (in millions) | Funds | Institutions and corporations | Individuals and personal trusts |
|---|---|---|---|
| $0–$0.25 . . . . . . . . . | 0.85% | 0.64% | 0.55% |
| $0.25–$1 . . . . . . . . . | 0.78 | 0.42 | 0.38 |
| $1–$10 . . . . . . . . . . | 0.40 | 0.26 | 0.19 |
| $10–$100 . . . . . . . . . | 0.47 | 0.12 | 0.06 |
| $100 up . . . . . . . . . | 0.44* | 0.03† | 0.02‡ |

* Based on 94 companies with an average size of approximately $450 million.
† Based on 41 accounts with an average size of approximately $250 million. Included accounts of nonregistered investment companies, employee benefit plans, insurance companies, nonprofit institutions, etc.
‡ Based on five accounts with average size of $150 million.
Source: SEC *Institutional Investor Study Report*, pp. 208–10.

## FUND COSTS AND MANAGEMENT COMPANY FINANCES

With funds buying most of their services outside, their in-house costs might be relatively low. These costs plus the management fee were known as the fund's "expense ratio." Early in 1971, the president of Wellington Management Company believed that a reasonable rule of thumb would be about 50 cents of in-house costs for every dollar of management fee. Wiesenberger Services reported the great majority of expense ratios was under 1% of average fund assets, but more than 1% was not uncommon and even 6% was not the top figure in exceptional cases.[34]

Of greater interest than the in-house costs of funds was the financial picture of management companies. The two main sources of revenue for them were investment advisory services and broker-dealer functions, including both securities transactions and net underwriting (or distribution income net of dealer discounts). For a sample of 41 management companies obtaining at least one third of their assets from funds, the SEC reported that in 1968 advisory services accounted for 38.1% of gross revenues and broker-dealer functions for 34.0%. The breakdown, however, differed substantially between large management companies (assets $100 million and over) and small:

| Companies | Number | 1968 Advisory revenue/total | 1968 Broker-dealer revenue/total |
|---|---|---|---|
| Large . . . . . . . . . | 27 | 43.44% | 19.44% |
| Small . . . . . . . . . | 14 | 27.86 | 62.07 |

Source: SEC, *Institutional Investor Study Report*, pp. 142, 149, 162.

[34] Ibid.

The largest contribution to management company costs arising from fund-related activities was the cost of compensation—about 70% of the total in 1964 and 60% in 1968. Over the years, average total fund-related costs had risen 17% from about $900,000 to about $1.2 million for companies able to provide a breakdown (Exhibit 10).[35]

**EXHIBIT 10**
**Operating expense breakdown for advisory firms advising assets of $100 million and up**

| Expense | 1964 (29 respondents) | 1968 (34 respondents) |
|---|---|---|
| Account supervisors, counselors, portfolio managers | 12.0% | 12.3% |
| Research staff | 5.8 | 6.6 |
| Sales personnel | 34.4 | 17.6 |
| Professional traders, clerical, other | 11.1 | 15.5 |
| Executives (not included above) | 6.1 | 8.0 |
| Total compensation | 69.4% | 60.0% |
| Administrative services for clients | 6.2 | 6.7 |
| Advertising and other customer solicitation | 3.6 | 5.2 |
| Subscriptions, communications, equipment expense | 5.0 | 8.1 |
| Other (rent depreciation, travel, etc.) | 15.8 | 20.0 |
| Average ($ millions) | $ 1.77 | $ 2.14 |

Source: SEC, *Institutional Investor Study Report*, pp. 227, 238.

The largest contribution to fund management company profit came from advisory rather than from distribution functions. Indeed, the latter were sometimes carried on at a loss. In a study based on figures for 1960, the Wharton School of Finance had found that 16 out of 37 management companies had lost money on their "underwriting" function. In a study based on 1961–64, the SEC had found 3 of 10 companies incurring a loss on their distribution. Even where distribution did yield a profit, "profit margins generally were much lower than those on fund advisory operations." Thus, as a percentage of gross revenues arising out of each activity, median advisory profits were 45.6% while median distribution profits were 8.7%. The SEC concluded, "To a significant extent mutual fund advisers use the profits from advisory fees . . . to subsidize underwriting activities."[36]

Whatever the profit—or loss—from underwriting, in good years management companies enjoyed a high overall ratio of profit to gross income, and the profit ratio on fund business sometimes outpaced that from

[35] SEC, *Institutional Investor Study Report*, pp. 227, 238.
[36] SEC, *Implications of Investment Company Growth*, pp. 121–125.

# EXHIBIT 11
Profit by source—advisory firms with fund* and other clients, 1964, 1968 (dollars in millions)

| Asset size of adviser | No. of firms | Asset source | | Revenue source | | Expense source | | Profit source | | Profit/assets | |
|---|---|---|---|---|---|---|---|---|---|---|---|
| | | Fund | Other | Fund | Other | Fund | Other | Fund | Other | Fund | Other |
| *1964* | | | | | | | | | | | |
| $750+ | 7 | $6,219.9 | $3,216.9 | $55.61 | $6.15 | $29.76 | $5.41 | $25.76 | $0.75 | 0.414% | 0.0233% |
| $100–$750 | 13 | 2,930.6 | 963.3 | 16.62 | 2.25 | 8.99 | 1.30 | 7.63 | 0.95 | 0.260 | 0.0986 |
| Less than $100 | 7 | 176.9 | 90.3 | 1.24 | 0.24 | 0.79 | 0.41 | 0.46 | -0.17 | 0.260 | -0.1883 |
| Total | 27 | $9,327.4 | $4,270.4 | $73.47 | $8.64 | $39.51 | $7.12 | $33.66 | $1.53 | 0.361 | 0.0358 |
| *1968* | | | | | | | | | | | |
| $750+ | 11 | $12,599.4 | $8,701.6 | $75.88 | $13.55 | $46.28 | $9.96 | $29.60 | $3.59 | 0.235% | 0.0413% |
| $100–750 | 17 | 4,770.7 | 1,870.0 | 23.95 | 15.60 | 15.15 | 7.75 | 8.81 | 7.85 | 0.185 | 0.4198 |
| Less than $100 | 10 | 192.0 | 114.4 | 1.28 | 0.44 | 2.20 | 0.47 | -0.92 | -0.19 | -0.479 | -0.1661 |
| Total | 38 | $17,562.1 | $10,686.0 | $101.11 | $29.59 | $63.63 | $18.18 | $37.49 | $11.25 | 0.2135 | 0.1053 |

*Registered investment companies, open-end and closed-end.
Source: SEC, *Institutional Investor Study Report*, pp. 229, 244.

other clients. Thus, for management companies where such a breakdown could be made, the SEC reported profits on fund business were 45.8% of revenues in 1964 and 37.1% in 1968. On other business the parallel percentages were 17.6% and 38.0%. (See Exhibit 11.) Since even 1968 was a prosperous year for funds, these ratios undoubtedly were high in relation to profits for the next two years.

## FUND PERFORMANCE AND OTHER SALES APPEALS

To sweeten fund-associated fees and charges, an investor received in return diversification of his portfolio, professional money management, automatic reinvestment of dividends and/or capital gains if desired, switching privileges within a complex, a Keogh Act (self-employed retirement) plan if needed, or a fixed dollar withdrawal program, plus news of his fund's progress in the daily stock reports. Rating services were also available to give him comparative news for a fee. (Under SEC regulations dating back to 1940, funds could not themselves use these kinds of data in their own advertising.)

Thus the news quickly spread when some funds with "growth" and/or "maximum capital gains" as their objective started chalking up exceptionally strong records in the postwar market through 1968. Large numbers of new funds were formed within this category, while some other categories actually shrank. Sales of performance funds expanded fast, too: whereas they captured only 10% of sales in 1962, they got almost 50% four years later. And, although fund-to-fund performance spreads were increasing, the growth categories overall did far better than the more conservative types in the decade to 1968.[37]

With the market slide of 1969–70, performance funds slid even further than the rest, however (Exhibit 12). During 1970 alone, for example, 22% of the smaller growth funds lost more than 25% of their net asset share value, while the group as a whole lost 17.7%.

What the downturn meant for the future was still not clear as of mid-1971. Investors for the first time in decades were moving out of funds by increasing redemptions over sales. The SEC was saying that one proven need was to have a measure of risk in a fund that would be as precise as the measure of performance. To fill this need, the SEC was thinking of a measure based on volatility.[38] In addition, to help

---

[37] In an effort to identify more precisely what factors correlated with performance, the SEC made regression analyses covering nine likely variables. It found that "even jointly" these had "little ability to explain variations." Thus, no significant relationship was found between performance and fund or complex asset size, net sales, cash inflow, performance fees, sales load, etc. On the other hand, "a significantly negative relationship" was found between "portfolio turnover and performance." SEC, *Institutional Investor,* Summary Volume, pp. 30, 31.

[38] Ibid., pp. xii–xiv.

**EXHIBIT 12**

Approximate percentage change in net assets per share with capital gains reinvested and dividend income taken in cash (years through December 31)

| Fund category | Number of funds 1968 | Number of funds 1970 | Number with 10-year records 1970 | Percent change in assets per share 1959–68 | Percent change in assets per share 1961–70 | Percent change in assets per share 1968–70 |
|---|---|---|---|---|---|---|
| Growth funds | | | | | | |
| Large | 22 | 17 | 15 | +239.5% | +127.1% | −15.4% |
| Small (assets under $300 million) | | | | | | |
| Maximum capital gain* | 70 | 110 | 31 | +261.6 | +105.1 | −31.8 |
| Long-term growth of capital and income† | 39 | 40 | 25 | +170.9 | +100.4 | −14.8 |
| Other diversified common stock funds | | | | | | |
| Growth and current income‡ | 34 | 36 | 31 | +140.0 | + 97.0 | −11.6 |
| Growth and current income with relative stability§ | 21 | 19 | 18 | +143.4 | +109.7 | − 8.8 |
| Balanced funds | 27 | 23 | 23 | +116.6 | + 77.6 | − 8.2 |
| Income funds | 19 | 25 | 21 | +122.5 | + 96.7 | −11.4 |
| Tax-free exchange funds | 28 | 28 | 0 | ... | | −12.6 |
| Stock market averages‖ | | | | | | |
| Dow-Jones Industrial | | | | +107.1 | + 83.0 | |
| Standard & Poor's 500 | | | | +132.1 | +104.7 | |

*Volatility generally high.
†Volatility moderately above average.
‡Volatility average.
§Volatility below average.
‖Percent changes adjusted to include dividends paid in the same manner as for the individual companies. Unadjusted declines for 1968–70 were −11.3% (D-J) and −11.4% (S&P).
Note: Specialized funds (concentrating on insurance, utilities, and other industries) not included.

Sources: U.S. Cong., House Committee on Interstate and Foreign Commerce, Mutual Fund Amendments, Hearings, (1970), p. 436; Wiesenberger Financial Services, Investment Companies, 1969 ed., pp. 122–29; Management Results to December 31, 1970; Investment Companies, 1971 ed., pp. 118–27.

prevent fund managers from pursuing performance at unnoted cost to safety, the SEC wanted to improve the "symmetry" in management's incentive compensation. Already the 1970 law had decreed that premiums for strong performance must be matched by penalties for weak, but the SEC believed that management performance should be measured against a yardstick that would take risk or volatility into account. That is, the adviser of a high-risk fund should not earn a premium just for outperforming Poor's 500, for example.[39]

Within the fund industry itself, much thinking was done about ways, other than performance, to go on building sales. An often repeated axiom was that whereas the decade of the 1960s had been the decade of the investment manager, the decade of the 1970s would be the decade of the marketer. Attention was directed to such issues as new services, new kinds of clients, new channels, and new ways of competing with other kinds of savings institutions and advisers.

Broker dealers, too, could be expected to have some ideas. Interested to know what a major fund retailing house would say, *Forbes* went to a forum run by Merrill Lynch "who had held off until 1969 before deciding to thunder after mutual fund business." This house had picked out a "select group" of not necessarily related funds, representative of various types. Among them, for example, was a large, old, growth-and-income fund (whose 10-year performance record was average for its Wiesenberger category) and a small, aggressive fund (close to but not at the top of its group in each of the last two years). Asked how Merrill Lynch evaluated funds, the company's spokesman replied, "Quality and depth of management . . . that's the most important thing. If Johnny Hot-Shot leaves the fund, we don't want your money left to the second string."[40]

## REGULATION

Even in the course of pressuring Congress for new legislation on investment companies, the SEC conceded in 1966 that the industry needed no major overhaul: "On the whole, the investment company industry reflects diligent management by competent persons. The flagrant abuses which prevailed prior to 1940 . . . have to a significant extent been eliminated."[41]

The year that marked the watershed between a sound and an unsound industry—1940—was the year in which the first Investment Company Act was passed. The abuses this act curbed, mainly seen in early closed-ends, were summarized by the SEC as follows:

---

[39] Ibid. Also, Vol. II, pp. 254–66.

[40] "Forum," *Forbes*, July 1, 1971, p. 57.

[41] SEC, *Public Policy Implications of Investment Company Growth*, p. 1.

(1) Outright dishonesty; (2) transactions in securities and other types of property with, and loans to, controlling persons; (3) unsound [complicated or debt-heavy] capital structures; and (4) the virtually complete immunity of many well-entrenched, self-perpetuating managements from liability to the companies and from any semblance of shareholder control as well as the ease with which such controlling positions could be transferred.[42]

No other major act affecting funds went into force until 1970. Of its main provisions several have been mentioned already: the modification of front-end loading, the NASD study of sales charges looking to their eventual reduction, and the progress toward symmetry in incentive payments. In addition, the shareholders and the SEC were given a new legal standing in the courts if they wished to sue about management fees. Whereas formerly fees would only be scaled down if shown to be "unconscionable," henceforth the test to be applied was "breach of fiduciary trust or duty."

As a fast changing industry, however, funds and their management companies could anticipate changing regulations. By 1970 the SEC was already engaged on a major study of institutional investors (including but not limited to funds and their advisers). After reviewing background data and appraising institutions as investment managers (Parts I and II of the report), the study went on to examine the impact of institutional investors on the securities market and on corporate issuers (Parts III and IV). Many facts and some suggestions emerged, and some issues were identified as less ripe for action than for continued study. Among the latter was the trend toward multipurpose aggregates, which were seen as posing both competitive and regulatory problems. Thus the "bundling" of various kinds of service was seen as inhibiting free competition in the efficient performance of each, while performance of various kinds of service for numerous accounts or customer classes was seen as productive of conflicts of interest. For example, where several different portfolios were managed, how was it determined which ones would receive a short supply of a promising stock, or which ones would first be cleared of securities slated for a gradual liquidation? Did advisers with a brokerage connection tend to "churn" portfolio stocks? Questionnaires from the SEC were designed to shed light on such areas of conflict. Also to be watched were the artificial constraints—some imposed by business but some imposed by the government itself—that might be influential in promoting aggregates. Aggregates might be legitimate enough, but only if formed to improve efficiency.

Even where aggregates were not a factor, conflicts of interest could occur, especially where services were purchased from outsiders on the basis of reciprocity. In reciprocal arrangements it was said to be all

---

[42] Ibid., p. 66.

too easy for awards to be made for a service to the manager rather than his client.

Whereas the study of institutions as investment advisers held many caveats, the study of institutional impact on markets and on issuers tended to quiet at least some fears. Based on the number of trading markets less costly than the NYSE, the SEC had wondered how far the central market function was impaired by large institutional trades done elsewhere, but this suspicion received no emphasis in the detailed findings. Based on the size of institutional trades and on the widely held belief that institutions moved together on a stock, the SEC had wondered about the impact of institutional trading on stock prices. Quite explicitly, the detailed findings downplayed this concern: while impact was discernible and required watching, by far the most important changes in stock prices were due to factors other than a "net imbalance" in institutional positions on a stock. Based on the growth of institutional holdings in the 1950s, some observers had questioned whether institutions would soon control most listed equities, but the SEC discovered that their share of *holdings* (as opposed to *trading*) had risen little during the past decade and that individuals still controlled some 70% of NYSE stocks. Based on the amount of money institutions had to invest, some observers had worried about their impact on the allocation of the nation's resources, but the SEC discovered that most of their investment consisted of trading in outstanding, relatively high-price stocks issued by large, established companies; institutions also provided some risk capital by taking new issues from small new concerns. Based on the size of combined institutional holdings in some big companies, concern had been expressed about concentration of economic power in institutional hands, but the SEC study confirmed the widely reported belief that institutions almost never interfere in management decisions— apart from merger fights. If dissatisfied with a management, institutions simply pull out. Should an institution intend to follow some other policy—for example, voting its stock against management on social or environmental issues—the SEC suggested it make this stand clear. Moreover, a fund's own proxy statement could not refuse space to stockholder resolutions seeking other owners' support for such a stand.

## NEW HORIZONS

Besides confronting many alternatives for organizing and competing in their own industry—both in the United States and abroad—fund management companies were moving outside it by 1970. In a rundown covering only publicly held management companies, *Barron's* reported as follows on this trend:

Finally, the publicly held managers . . . have branched out into *other lines.* At least three besides Vance-Sanders offer oil drilling funds: IDS, Putnam Management and Equity Funding. Real estate development or construction has attracted several, notably Dreyfus, Shareholders Capital, IDS and Equity Funding. . . . This summer, Dreyfus teamed up with Marine Midland Banks to form an investment advisory service for large institutional accounts.

Among others offering investment advisory service are National Securities & Research, Wellington Management Company, Putnam and Supervised Investors Services. Last year, IDS bought two broker-dealer firms. . . . Magnavest arranges private financing for various companies, while Equity Funding owns a cattle-breeding concern, Ankony Angus.[43]

---

[43] "Turn for the Better? Mutual Fund Management Companies Have Nowhere to Go But Up," November 30, 1970, p. 16.

# Wellington Management Company

FROM A HIGH OF $3.0 billion in 1968, mutual fund and other assets supervised by the Wellington Management Company (WMC) had dropped to a low of $2.3 billion as the stock market bottomed in May 1970. But by October 31, the end of the company's fiscal year, the figure had climbed back to $2.9 billion, further rising to $3.3 billion on January 31, 1971. Commenting on the plunge and the subsequent recovery, Mr. John C. Bogle, president and chief executive officer of WMC, explained this volatility and discussed its implications for the company as follows:

Our operations are particularly affected by wide swings in securities prices, because the value of assets under management bears directly on investment advisory fees, our largest source of income. Implicit in our changing earnings results over the past year is a profound fact about the kind of business we are in—expenses tend to be relatively stable over the short term; revenues, on the other hand, may fluctuate dramatically. In a word, our company's operating results have "leverage."[1]

The company's essential challenge, he added, was not only to cope with volatile markets but to deal with changes in the investment community, to meet high performance standards, and to compete effectively, with a view toward assuring WMC's future growth and independence.

## HISTORY

In a brick Colonial townhouse a block off Philadelphia's fashionable Rittenhouse Square, Wellington Management's offices have an easy, country gentle-

---

[1] First Quarter Report to WMC Stockholders, January 31, 1971.

men air and abound with prints and momentos of the era of the first Duke of Wellington. The man responsible for the Wellington style is twinkling, snowy-haired Walter Morgan, long a student of the Iron Duke's battles against Napoleon.[2]

WMC had been founded in 1928 by Mr. Walter L. Morgan, widely considered the "dean" of the mutual fund industry. Three years earlier, he had started his own accounting firm and had become impressed with the ineptitude of his clients' stock market adventures. Believing that he could advise them much better, he obtained $75,000 from accounting clients, put in $25,000 of his own, and teamed with an investment banker to start his own fund. The name "Wellington" was adopted in 1934.

Leery of the "get-rich-quick" closed-end trusts then trading at twice their net worth, Mr. Morgan chose an open-end fund and emphasized investment in bonds and preferreds. This emphasis placed the new fund firmly in the "balanced" category and gave Mr. Morgan the cachet of being the major founder of the type.

When Mr. Morgan reduced his fund's common stock position from 75% of assets to 40% prior to the crash of 1929, his conservative portfolio gave him a relatively good performance record during the depression. Even so, fund assets grew slowly until 1935, when initiation of the first monthly purchase program increased sales from 10,000 to 100,000 shares per year. At 10-year intervals, assets of the fund grew and changed as follows:

| Year | Assets managed (millions) | Percentage of assets invested | | |
|------|------|------|------|------|
| | | Cash, bonds | Preferred | Common |
| 1935 . . . . . . | $    1.1 | 41 | 14 | 45 |
| 1945 . . . . . . | 26.9 | 32 | 20 | 48 |
| 1955 . . . . . . | 495.6 | 21 | 12 | 67 |
| 1965 . . . . . . | 2,047.6 | 32 | 4 | 64 |

Source: Company records.

Commenting on the philosophy of the fund in 1965, Mr. Morgan said: "A sound financial institution must retain its basic character and be more durable than the individuals who direct its affairs; in Wellington Fund this meant a continued dedication to truly conservative investment principles, no matter how tempting the lure to abandon them in search of even larger rewards." Mr. Morgan felt that his fund had performed at a time when good performance was most needed. "I'm sure we have

[2] "Buying a Younger Generation," *Business Week*, November 19, 1966, p. 150.

done a better job for the investor than he could have done for himself," he said.

- The conservative, balanced policy worked well until late in the 1950s. Responding to the changing investment climate in 1958, WMC created a second fund, the Windsor, in the "growth and income" (G&I) category. By the mid-1960s, however, the long bull market had attracted many investors to the so-called "performance" funds—that is, those that showed the greatest yearly gains in per-share assets. By 1962 performance funds were accounting for 10% of fund sales, and by 1966 for nearly 50%. At this point, Mr. Morgan decided that WMC needed an infusion of investment talent, a new investment head, and some management assistance to help Mr. Bogle, then executive vice president and "heir apparent," manage the company.

Acting on these ideas, Mr. Bogle developed the idea of a merger with an aggressive performance fund manager in order to modify the company image and to provide a product line more attuned to public wants. In November 1966, WMC reached an understanding with Ivest, Inc., the manager of the "high flying" Ivest Fund.

## THE IVEST MERGER

### Ivest history

Ivest Fund had been started in Boston in 1959 when four young investment analysts, working with different firms, decided to pool $2,000 each to see how it would fare in the market. By 1960 their portfolio, with the addition of monies from other clients, had grown to $150,000 and the four decided to found their own firm: Thorndike, Doran, Paine & Lewis, Inc. (TDP&L). Although all were under 30, they felt their impressive record and their individual contacts would provide steady business. Since none of the four was interested in supervising a sales organization and since the initial asset size of the fund was too small for the fees to support an overhead, the Ivest Fund was initially offered as a no-load, and investment counseling for nonfund clients was chosen as the major activity of the firm.

TDP&L's counseling business expanded rapidly and by 1966 had accounts totaling $154 million. The Ivest Fund, however, showed a disappointing rate of growth, even though in 1963 it led the industry in performance and even though it also dropped the no-load feature in favor of an 8.5% sales charge designed to stimulate push by salesmen. Ivest's first five-year performance record (172% gain) immediately preceding the merger was second only to that of Fidelity Trend; however,

Fidelity, organized one year earlier than Ivest, had assets of $636 million in 1965 compared to Ivest's $37 million. According to *Business Week,* Ivest had been held back by a "mediocre" sales effort, but by joining with Wellington it gained access to a sales team that was "one of the best" in the business.[3]

The *Institutional Investor* described the Ivest management in the following terms:

> Born in Boston, as were his three Ivest partners, he [Doran] went to Yale and the Harvard Business School. But even before college, he and his prep school friend Nick Thorndike "always had in the backs of our minds to do something together." At one time it was going to be real estate, but after both worked as analysts, the Ivest thing took shape. Doran is chairman of the company policy group on investments.
>
> Thorndike, whose principal area of responsibility is administration of the Ivest Fund, is a Lowell and a Harvard man. Before Ivest, he worked as an analyst for the Fidelity Fund management company, and got an inside look at Jerry Tsai and some high-performance funds before he helped found his own.
>
> The Ivest art collection is Steve Paine's doing. Stricken with polio years ago, Paine became a connoisseur and collector of modern painting and sculpture. Paine also worked as an analyst for a counseling firm and now he focuses on Ivest's research group, selecting, developing, and evaluating the talent.
>
> Personnel and office management are the principal responsibilities of George Lewis. A member of the Saltonstall family, he worked as an account manager and analyst for Tucker Anthony & R. L. Day before he and his partners put Ivest together.[4]

## Merger terms

Initiated in 1966, the merger of WMC with Ivest and TDP&L was formally completed in 1967. All the stock of the two companies was acquired in exchange for 148,000 shares (15.4%) of WMC's Class A common traded on the over-the-counter market and having a value of $4 million. At the same time 9,500 out of 10,000 shares of Class B stock owned by Mr. Morgan and Mr. Joseph E. Welch, then president of WMC, were placed in a voting trust to be controlled by Messrs. Morgan, Welch, and Bogle until April 30, 1971. Unlike the Class A shares, each of which had one vote, each Class B share had 250 votes.

With the expiration of the trust, total voting power (Class A plus Class B) would be divided as follows: Mr. Bogle, 28%; Messrs. Thorndike, Doran, Paine, and Lewis, 10% each; Mr. Cabot (a Boston executive

---

[3] Ibid.

[4] "The Whiz Kids Take Over at Wellington," *Institutional Investor,* January 1968, p. 64.

in charge of fund investments), 3%; company employee stock plans, 3%; and other investors, 26%. Commenting on these arrangements, *Business Week* said: "These curious terms and, indeed, the merger itself intrigues the rest of the industry no end. . . . Some Wall Streeters feel Wellington is paying too much; others talk of the 'mouse swallowing the elephant.'" Others pointed out, however, that other, similar deals were "in the works."[5]

Apart from the voting and the financial terms of the merger, another informal stipulation provided that Ivest and TDP&L, although becoming subsidiaries of WMC in Philadelphia, would continue basing their activities in Boston.

## A GROWING PRODUCT LINE

### The multifund concept

Besides adding the Windsor Fund and acquiring Ivest, WMC took other steps to increase the number of funds it offered. The purpose of these moves was articulated in the annual report for 1968:

> The bulk of our revenues continue to come from mutual fund operations. We now manage 11 separate mutual funds, including four that were formed in 1967, and an additional three in 1968. This multifund concept is reflected in our marketing theme: *"No One Mutual Fund Can Be All Things to All People."*

> .  .  .  .  .

> This diversification is part of a carefully conceived corporate strategy: to provide a multiplicity of financial services. The strategy has as its objectives:

> 1. To increase our growth potential, and broaden our opportunities;
> 2. To minimize variations in the flow of investor capital under our management, in varying market and economic conditions;
> 3. To enhance our investment management capabilities, making it possible to attract, motivate, and retain top professional analysts and money managers.

Of the funds created in the latter 1960s for the WMC complex, the first three were tax-free exchange funds (TFEs), all designed to take advantage of a special temporary law permitting large investors to exchange securities in their own portfolios for shares in a fund without paying a capital gains tax or other taxes on the transaction. All sold under the name Exeter, these three funds received stock valued at $136 million in exchange for their shares in 1966 and early 1967.

---

[5] "Buying a Younger Generation," *Business Week*, p. 150.

WMC's fourth new fund, called Gemini, was a pioneering fund that with three others inaugurated the "dual purpose" market: in this type of fund, "income shares" received all the net income of the fund, and "capital shares" received any capital appreciation on the fund's entire portfolio. With initial assets of $35 million, Gemini was a closed-end investment company listed on the New York Stock Exchange. (Six other management companies ultimately sponsored dual funds in 1967; their combined assets were $300 million.)

The Exeters and Gemini were all initiated before the completion of the Ivest merger. After Ivest, the next fund to be added was Explorer. The goal here was that of seeking maximum long-term growth of capital by investing in "relatively small unseasoned or embryonic companies." Since Explorer was designed for substantial investors who could afford higher than average risks, the minimum initial investment was set at $25,000.

Following Explorer—and, like Explorer, managed by WMC not directly but through the new Ivest subsidiary—came three more funds, all conceived during fiscal 1968. These were Trustees' Equity, Technivest, and the W. L. Morgan Growth Fund. Trustees' Equity was established for institutional investors who had tax-exempt status and were willing to make relatively high-risk investments. Technivest, which began operations early in December following an initial underwriting of $87 million, was aimed at seeking maximum capital growth "through aggressive use of investment management techniques emphasizing technical analysis." The W. L. Morgan Growth Fund, also a December entrant, initially made its shares available exclusively, through exchange or purchase, to holders of the Wellington Fund who wanted a more "venturesome" investment program seeking "possible long-term growth of capital." Later, W. L. Morgan was opened to the general public.

After about a one-year hiatus, in 1970 WMC set up a twelfth fund with a strictly income orientation. Started on the base of a small acquired fund which was renamed the Wellesley Income Fund, this venture responded to then existing market conditions by investing primarily in bonds.

Selected data on these 12 funds are summarized in Table 1; historical data on the assets, sales and liquidations, and industry share of the WMC complex are summarized in Exhibit 1. Data on the funds' performance relative to others in the same categories are summarized in Exhibit 2.

Although the Wellesley Income Fund, with assets of only $200,000 when put on the market in mid-1970, was the smallest fund in the company complex, the decision to create it had been reached only after long consideration. The initial suggestion for such a fund was advanced by Mr. Bogle himself in May 1969. Arguing that bond yields were at

**TABLE 1**

| Name | Year founded | Wiesen- berger category | Assets (millions) 12/31/69 | Assets (millions) 1/31/71 | Manage- ment fee* | Expense ratio, fiscal 1970† |
|------|-------------|------------------------|----------|---------|------------|------------|
| Wellington . . . . . . . . | 1928 | Bal. ‡ | $1,422 | $1,405 | 0.27% | 0.41% |
| Windsor . . . . . . . . . | 1958 | G&I § | 306 | 472 | 0.425±0.075 | 0.70 |
| Ivest . . . . . . . . . . | 1959 | MCG§ | 297 | 306 | 0.50 ±0.125 | 0.81 |
| Exeters (3)‖ . . . . . . . | 1966–67 | TFE § | 110 | 93 | 0.50 | 0.70 |
| Gemini‖ . . . . . . . . . | 1967 | Dual | 45 | 51 | 0.50 | 0.83 |
| Explorer . . . . . . . . . | 1967 | MCG | 46 | 31 | 0.625 | 0.89 |
| Trustees' Equity . . . . . | 1968 | MCG | 5 | 12 | 0.50 ±0.125 | 1.00 |
| Technivest ‖ . . . . . . . | 1968 | MCG | 61 | 55 | 0.50 ±0.125 | 0.71 |
| W. L. Morgan . . . . . . | 1968 | MCG | 21 | 45 | 0.50 ±0.125 | 1.00 |
| Wellesley . . . . . . . . . | 1970 | Income | . . . | 40 | 0.50 | 0.80 |

*The ± percentage refers to an incentive portion of the fee.

†Includes management fee and other expenses usually assumed by the fund rather than by the management company, as percent of average assets.

‡On January 31, 1971, Wellington's balanced portfolio was made up of common stock, 72.5%; bonds and reserves, 25.1%; convertibles, 1.1%; and preferred, 1.3%.

§G&I = growth and income: MCG = maximum capital gain; TFE = tax-free exchange.

‖New shares no longer being offered.

Source: Company records and Wiesenberger Financial Services, Supplement to *Investment Companies 1970*, January 1971.

historic highs and that a fund based mainly on bonds would balance the product line, Mr. Bogle maintained that the new fund would also enhance the company's image:

> Perhaps most important of all—a Wellington Management Company bond fund would mark us with leadership quality. It would reflect our independent judgment, and our willingness to depart from "the crowd" in an industry all too filled with opportunists. Properly handled, and under today's conditions, it could be a dramatic public relations masterstroke. A Wellington bond fund would add real substance to our claim that "No One Mutual Fund Can Be All Things to All People."

The WMC board of directors disagreed, however, as did the major brokerage houses through which WMC distributed. Mr. Bogle's proposal was turned down on a seven-to-two vote of the board, after such negative arguments as the following:

> There is virtually no desirability in starting a bond fund at this time. Our organization is common stock oriented, and the idea goes directly counter to this. It will be bad for our public image because bonds have been a bad investment medium. The general public is uninterested in bonds. Not only would the fund fail to mark us with leadership quality (as suggested), but I cannot for the life of me understand how anyone can equate bonds and leadership in the public marketplace.

**EXHIBIT 1**

WELLINGTON MANAGEMENT COMPANY
Fund Assets, Sales, and Redemptions
(dollars in millions)

| Calendar years to Dec. 31 | Assets | | | Gross sales* | | | Redemptions* | | |
|---|---|---|---|---|---|---|---|---|---|
| | All WMC funds | WMC percent of total industry | Wellington Fund | All WMC funds | WMC percent of total industry | Wellington Fund | All WMC funds | WMC percent of total industry | Wellington Fund |
| 1955 | $ 497 | 6.3 | $ 497 | $ 67 | 5.9 | $ 67 | $ 20 | 4.5 | $ 20 |
| 1956 | 578 | 6.4 | 578 | 101 | 8.0 | 101 | 15 | 3.5 | 15 |
| 1957 | 605 | 6.9 | 605 | 96 | 7.5 | 96 | 15 | 3.7 | 15 |
| 1958 | 897 | 6.8 | 859 | 120 | 8.0 | 109 | 17 | 3.3 | 17 |
| 1959 | 1,060 | 6.7 | 1,017 | 137 | 6.5 | 134 | 26 | 3.3 | 26 |
| 1960 | 1,184 | 7.0 | 1,133 | 125 | 6.6 | 115 | 32 | 3.8 | 27 |
| 1961 | 1,504 | 6.6 | 1,419 | 157 | 5.7 | 130 | 40 | 3.4 | 35 |
| 1962 | 1,486 | 7.0 | 1,413 | 149 | 6.1 | 136 | 37 | 3.3 | 32 |
| 1963 | 1,718 | 6.8 | 1,642 | 139 | 6.4 | 133 | 50 | 3.3 | 40 |
| 1964 | 1,957 | 6.7 | 1,883 | 178 | 5.9 | 152 | 64 | 3.4 | 53 |
| 1965 | 2,139 | 6.1 | 2,047 | 155 | 3.9 | 155 | 63 | 3.2 | 58 |
| 1966 | 2,042 | 5.9 | 1,867 | 124 | 3.0 | 81 | 94 | 4.7 | 84 |
| 1967 | 2,447 | 5.5 | 1,856 | 216 | 5.2 | 36 | 156 | 5.7 | 135 |
| 1968 | 2,657 | 5.0 | 1,754 | 244 | 3.9 | 21 | 225 | 5.9 | 179 |
| 1969 | 2,189 | 4.5 | 1,416 | 128 | 2.1 | 13 | 207 | 5.7 | 123 |
| 1970 | 2,413 | 5.1 | 1,377 | 203 | 5.3 | 9 | 124 | 4.1 | 69 |

*Sales and redemptions do not include dividend reinvestments or exchanges within fund groups. Company estimated that $136 million was exchanged from Wellington Fund into other Wellington Management Company Funds in 1967–70.
Source: WMC figures from company records. Percentages reflect share of industry, based on Investment Company Institute tabulations.

**EXHIBIT 2**

Management results for WMC mutual funds (approximate percentage change in net assets per share with capital gains reinvested plus income dividends received in cash)

| Category* and name of fund | 1970 | 1969 | Periods to December 31, 1969 | | | | |
|---|---|---|---|---|---|---|---|
| | | | Two years | Three years | Four years | Five years | Ten years |
| **Smaller growth funds (1)** | *Objective: Maximum capital gain (volatility, generally high)* | | | | | | |
| WMC's participants | | | | | | | |
| Explorer | −25.7% | −11.7% | + 3.3% | ... | ... | ... | ... |
| Ivest | − 4.5 | − 7.9 | − 9.9 | +32.8% | +29.8% | +83.3% | † |
| Morgan (W. L.) | − 5.2 | + 3.3 | ... | ... | ... | ... | ... |
| Technivest | − 2.1 | −11.5 | ... | ... | ... | ... | ... |
| Trustees' Equity | −12.9 | + 5.0 | +36.6 | ... | ... | ... | ... |
| Average for group | −17.7 | −16.3 | + 6.9 | +49.6 | +44.5 | +91.4 | +144.3% |
| **Smaller growth funds (2)** | *Objective: Long-term growth of capital and income (volatility, moderately above average)* | | | | | | |
| WMC's Windsor‡ | + 6.0% | − 3.7% | +16.7% | +53.0% | +47.1% | +89.1% | +154.7% |
| Average for group | − 4.1 | −10.7 | +23.6 | +33.4 | +26.9 | +53.4 | +112.4 |
| **Balanced funds** | | | | | | | |
| WMC's Wellington‡ | + 6.0% | − 7.7% | − 0.3% | + 7.8% | + 0.4% | + 5.8% | + 50.4% |
| Average for group | + 3.5 | −11.3 | + 1.8 | +21.3 | +14.4 | +25.7 | + 80.0 |
| **Tax-free exchange funds** | *Objective: Growth* | | | | | | |
| WMC's complex | | | | | | | |
| Exeter 1 | − 6.1% | −12.5% | − 5.9% | +26.0% | ... | ... | ... |
| Exeter 2 | −11.4 | −14.6 | − 9.2 | ... | ... | ... | ... |
| Exeter 3 | −14.2 | −15.0 | − 7.7 | ... | ... | ... | ... |
| Average for group | − 5.0 | − 9.6 | + 2.9 | + 4.1 | +31.8% | +60.3% | ... |

* In 1970 the number of funds in these categories was as follows: smaller growth funds (1), 107; smaller growth funds (2), 40; balanced funds, 23; tax-free exchange funds, 29.

† Figures omitted because the fund, though in existence, was not readily available for the public or because a complete change of policy made the figures not meaningful.

‡For the decade through 1970, Windsor gained 143.4 versus a group average of 102.1; Wellington gained 51.1 versus 77.4.

Note: The indicated objectives represent the judgment of the source editors as the most appropriate category for each fund and may or may not be the same as the stated objectives of any specific fund.

Source: Weisenberger Financial Services, *Investment Companies 1970,* pp. 122–31; and "Management Results, Mutual Funds and Closed-End Investment Companies to December 31, 1970" (Supplement to *Investment Companies 1970*), January 1971.

As an alternative to a bond fund, splitting the original Wellington Fund into two components was considered, with one based on bonds and the other on common. This idea, too, met with no enthusiasm. Meanwhile, stock prices declined further and bond yields rose still higher. As a result, the board and the distributors changed their minds by the spring of 1970 and endorsed Bogle's proposal to acquire an already registered income fund in order to move as quickly as possible. This acquired fund was renamed "Wellesley."

One important purpose of having a wide variety of funds was to offer buyers the service of easy transfer from one fund to another as customer objectives or the climate for investments changed. Thus, the W. L. Morgan Fund had been primarily created to allow customers to move from the balanced and conservative Wellington Fund to something with a greater potential for capital gains. In 1969 the exchange privilege was made more general: holdings in any one of WMC's funds could be exchanged for equal asset values in any of the seven company funds for which shares were still in continuous issue (namely, Wellington, Windsor, Ivest, Explorer, Trustees' Equity, Morgan, and—by 1970—Wellesley). The only fee was a nominal service charge of $5 per transaction.

In explaining this right of exchange to shareholders, the company added the following caution:

Before making an exchange, shareholders must consider the differences among the funds as to income, growth, market risks, and expense ratios, and that any profit in the shares being exchanged will be taxable as a capital gain. Any of these exchange privileges may be suspended by the directors if in their judgment it is operating to the detriment of the fund.

It was hoped that redeeming shareholders could be encouraged to reinvest in another WMC fund when they wanted to change their invest-. ment objectives. Mr. Bogle commented:

Of course, we'd like to keep all redemptions in the Wellington family. However, since the Wellington Fund's management fee was set years ago at an extremely low rate of 0.27% and the basic fee on our other funds is 0.4% to 0.5%, we only have to retain about half of Wellington Fund's redemptions in order to maintain the same level of advisory fee income. While we're not yet at that goal—the present retention runs about 30% of redemptions—we are moving toward it.

## The investment counseling business

Besides offering a variety of funds, WMC had entered the investment counseling business in 1967 with its acquisition of TDP&L at the time of the Ivest merger. Since acquisition, both the assets managed and the gross revenues of this business had continued the uninterrupted growth which had marked their earlier years:

|  | *Fiscal year (in millions of dollars)* | | | | | |
|---|---|---|---|---|---|---|
|  | *1961* | *1966* | *1967* | *1968* | *1969* | *1970* |
| Assets. . . . . . . . | $10 | $154 | $277 | $453 | $463 | $750 |
| Revenues. . . . . . | 0.046 | 0.471 | 0.726 | 1.290 | 1.774 | 2.173 |

Source: Company records.

David Ogden, president of TDP&L, compared his operations to the fund business as follows in mid-1970:

> Our customers are pension funds, large corporations, or wealthy individuals. It's a very identifiable, fast-growing market and requires a much lower investment in administration and distribution than the fund business.
>
> We recently reduced our expenses overall in the company and, of course, TDP&L had to share this expense cut. Now my people see little reason why they should share an expense cut when the counseling business has been growing at such a rapid rate. On the other hand, I try to tell them, "Look, if we get the whole ball of wax successful, the company must be better off for it." And also two years from now I'm not sure that the fund business won't be better than the investment counseling business. You see, in a good market anybody can make money and the motivation for hiring investment counsel declines somewhat. It is in bad markets when the people are dissatisfied with their own investment abilities that they seek professional investment counsel.

### A short experience with computer services

A further but short-lived diversification of WMC activities occurred between Feburary and November 1969, when the company purchased and later sold Financial Dynamics, Inc., of Denver, Colorado. WMC's annual report described this acquisition as follows:

> This company is a rapidly growing financial service organization applying advanced computer technology to sophisticated investment concepts. It provides institutional investors with a computerized statistical research service called "Financial Dynamics." In addition, it has developed one of the largest financial data banks in the country, and is engaged in custom programming for the business and investment community. We believe Financial Dynamics, Inc., can assist us in three significant ways:
>
> 1. Enhancing our investment capability through more intensive use of computer techniques,

2. Providing additional investment management talent,
3. Aiding our potential earnings growth.

Having purchased Financial Dynamics for 120,000 Class A shares in February 1969, WMC sold out at a small ($123,000) net book loss in November of the same year for about $4.4 million in cash. Mr. Bogle explained the reasons as follows:

A few years ago we thought we had to be all things in the investment industry. Our mistakes were:

1. We never really had an understanding of the company, and no set of financial controls to aid us with it.
2. We had no management to provide to the company.
3. We did not have sufficient working capital to make available to the company.

As it turned out, our sale was a fortunate one, for in the difficult past year, FDI suffered a significant earnings decline.

## THE WMC MANAGEMENT STRUCTURE

With the Ivest-TDP&L merger, Messrs. Morgan and Welch began to withdraw from active management of WMC, and in November 1967 the presidency passed to Mr. Bogle, who had been with Wellington since 1951. A 1968 article in *Institutional Investor* described Mr. Bogle as follows:

An intense, articulate man, Bogle affects a relaxed manner. Six years ago, when he was only 32, he had a heart attack, and he gave up tennis for golf and hardly smokes or drinks at all. But if he has slowed down in any other way, it is not apparent to an outsider. Like his boss [Walter Morgan], Bogle is a Princeton man. A native of Montclair, New Jersey, he attracted Morgan's attention in 1951 with a paper he wrote on mutual funds for an economics course [in college]. Morgan hired him, and Bogle worked his way into and up the organization. Despite his illness and the fact that he is a bit older—say two years—than the Boston people, his crew haircut and angular frame give him the look of a boy playing hard-driving executive.[6]

By his own admission, Mr. Bogle's areas of expertise did not include investment analysis. Both as head of the company and as a board member on all the WMC funds (except Ivest), he brought to bear skills which lay, he felt, mainly in marketing and administration, including government regulation, finance, and the analysis of statistics. In line with these areas of interest, the marketing and administrative activities

---

[6] "The Whiz Kids Take Over at Wellington," *Institutional Investor*, p. 64.

of the company continued to be handled from Philadelphia where Mr. Bogle had his offices. During 1969–70 Mr. Bogle was also active as chairman of the Investment Company Institute (ICI), a trade association whose members accounted for 90% of the fund industry's assets. An articulate speaker, Mr. Bogle frequently made major addresses at industry gatherings.

Under Mr. Bogle as president of WMC were two executive vice presidents, both TDP&L men, who continued to work as they had before the merger in Boston. Boston was also the location at which most of the supervision of the investment advisory services was centered, not only for most of the funds' assets but also for the investment counseling business of the TDP&L subsidiary. (See Exhibit 3 for an organization chart.)

### Mutual fund management

Management activities for mutual funds were headed by Mr. Walter Cabot in Boston. Reporting to him, among others, were the portfolio managers for the 12 mutual funds. Although most of the funds had one manager each, one fund, Ivest, had two managers, and two funds, Windsor and Gemini, shared a single manager, Mr. Neff (the only fund manager to be located in Philadelphia). A single manager also handled the three Exeter tax-free exchange funds.

Assisting the fund managers was a pool of investment analysts. At one time, most members of this pool had worked for particular funds or groups of funds rather than for the complex as a whole. Although this situation had largely changed, specialization by fund remained a factor, especially with the analysts reporting to Mr. Neff. For the most part, however, analysts were specialized not around particular funds but around one or a few of the many industries in which assets might be invested.

Portfolio managers for the funds received both salary and incentive pay, with salaries ranging from $25,000 to $50,000 in 1969. The amount of the incentive pay depended on the relative performance of each fund as measured against that of a group of other, comparable funds selected by management, and on the incentive fees earned by the fund. In addition, a corporate profit-sharing plan could provide up to 15% of total salary plus incentives. Thus, theoretically, compensation had no upper limit. In 1970, owing to his two bonuses, one of the WMC fund managers was the highest paid individual in the company.

While acknowledging that capable portfolio managers were critical to the investment business, Mr. Cabot felt that the days of the "Hollywood portfolio manager" were gone. To his mind, communications were the key to the investment business and he felt that WMC possessed

**EXHIBIT 3**
WMC organization—December 1970

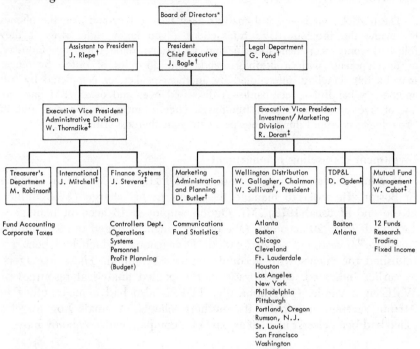

* The board consisted of J. Welch, chairman (formerly president of WMC), Jack Bogle, Walter Cabot, Robert Doran, George Lewis, Walter Morgan, Stephen Paine, W. Nicholas Thorndike, Andrew Young (general counsel).
† Located in Philadelphia.
‡ Located in Boston.
Source: Company records.

an extraordinary system, one which enabled it to take advantage of all the expertise of its analysts in all locations, whether working for the funds or the counseling business. Using a high-fidelity telephone system between operations in Boston, Philadelphia, and Atlanta, a meeting was held between 9:10 and 9:50 each morning. The previous day's transactions for each fund were read off during the first 10 minutes, and purchases were challenged and defended. The next 20 minutes were devoted to research reports from each of the three locations. It was during this time that the analyst could alert fund and account managers to developments they were currently investigating, report on recent contacts or visits to companies, or present complete recommendations to the group. Reports lasted about 90 seconds and generated questions and comment from any of the 60 people (fund and counseling) who participated in the mandatory meeting. The final 10 minutes were open for discussion of any topic.

A description in the *Institutional Investor* for January 1968 provided the flavor of a typical meeting:

The portfolio managers and analysts meet face to face and over the phones to review the previous day's transactions ("you know right away if they followed your recommendations") and to discuss some company, industry, or development, with a flexible agenda and no rules of order. Sentences may be left dangling, interrupted by another speaker, or completed by still another. A handful of companies is discussed over and over: IBM one day out of five. . . . Under such free-for-all circumstances, as one man put it, "You don't say stupid things. Your peers are your sharpest critics."[7]

### Investment counseling management

Heading the counseling subsidiary, TDP&L, was Mr. David Ogden in Boston. In order to manage the assets in his charge ($750 million at the end of fiscal 1970), Mr. Ogden employed 15 account managers, each with 15 to 20 accounts. One of these men managed the $10 million "in-house" investment service called "Dimensions," which had been established for clients with accounts under $1 million. These managers, as earlier indicated, could draw on the pooled analytical resources of WMC as a whole. Geographically, TDP&L also had a major office in Atlanta serving principally its southern clients. A small Los Angeles office had been closed in 1970 as part of a companywide economy move.

### U.S. distribution of mutual funds

To wholesale the seven mutual funds being offered on a continuous basis, WMC employed 17 district representatives, nine of whom had been with the company for two years or more. These men serviced more than 500 brokerage firms that retailed WMC funds, almost invariably along with those of other sponsors.

In 1969 sales by region had broken down as follows:

|  | *Percentage of WMC 1969 sales* | *Percentage of industry 1969 sales* |
|---|---|---|
| New England | 5 | 8 |
| Mid-Atlantic | 43 | 22 |
| Midwest | 22 | 26 |
| South | 16 | 12 |
| Southwest | 3 | 5 |
| Northwest | 2 | 6 |
| Far West | 9 | 21 |

Source: Company records.

---

[7] Ibid., pp. 27, 62.

During 1970, only 10 brokerage firms accounted for 40% of WMC's fund sales and 20 firms accounted for 60%. According to Mr. Bogle, this breakdown reflected company "concentration" strategy, which chose to place major reliance on relatively few but large retailing houses. Indeed, one firm with a large network of branches accounted for more than 15% of sales, up from under 3% the previous year. This concentration caused the senior executives of Wellington Distributors (a wholly owned subsidiary) some concern, since the house in question was about to underwrite a new mutual fund for one of WMC's principal competitors. Mr. Bogle pointed out, however, that the retailing service of this broker would still be available to WMC and others.

## INCOME AND EXPENSES

Like most fund management companies, WMC had a gross income from funds that was made up of two main components: (1) the management fee for the investment advisory service, and (2) that portion of the sales charge not passed on in payment for the retailing function. As indicated in Table 1, fees on the 12 Wellington funds varied from 0.27% of yearly average assets (the original Wellington Fund) up to 0.625% (Explorer), with 0.5% being the most widely used figure. On several of the funds, but not on Wellington, fees were subject to incentive adjustments (usually ± 0.125%).

Besides the advisory fee from its funds, starting in 1967 WMC earned an advisory fee from the counseling activities of TDP&L. Combined advisory fees and net sales commissions contributed to gross earnings as follows for years ending October 31 (in millions of dollars):

|  | 1966* | 1967* | 1968 | 1969 | 1970 |
|---|---|---|---|---|---|
| Fees . . . . . . . . . . . . . | $6.05 | $ 7.39 | $ 9.33 | $10.28 | $ 9.75 |
| Commissions (net) . . . . . . | 1.91 | 2.82 | 3.44 | 1.81 | 2.26 |
| Total† . . . . . . . . . . . | $8.14 | $10.37 | $13.04 | $12.43 | $12.57 |

\* Includes Ivest and TDP&L.
† Includes other income (under $600,000 for each of these periods).
Source: Company records.

Mr. Bogle indicated that WMC, like most other fund management companies, carried very little of its income from selling onto the final profit line, since selling expenses tended to devour income realized from this source. Thus the management fee was the principal source of WMC's net income. He emphasized, too, that profits from selling activities were particularly difficult to earn in years when sales were at relatively low levels, since most sales costs did not vary substantially with sales volume.

In reviewing the company's total expenses in all areas, Mr. Bogle called attention to the quantum rise that had taken place from 1966 to 1969 as well as to the financial controls that had enabled the company to bring this trend under control in 1970. Both factors were, he said, illustrated in the following table for fiscal years ending October 31 (in millions of dollars):

|  | 1966* | 1967* | 1968 | 1969 | 1970 |
|---|---|---|---|---|---|
| Operating expenses . . . . . . | $4.34 | $5.92 | $7.76 | $9.53 | $9.66 |

\* Includes Ivest and TDP&L.

Mr. Bogle also pointed to the high cost of the company's transition from essentially a single-product company to a multifund investment advisory complex. "It is simply much more expensive to manage, market, and administer a dozen funds and an investment advisory organization than it is to perform these functions for a single fund," he said. He also emphasized the difficulty of accurately establishing a "break-even point" for assets, at which an individual mutual fund generated sufficient revenues to be profitable for the manager, since a relatively small fraction (he guessed one third) of costs could be considered "direct." Nevertheless, he speculated that $50–$75 million of assets was probably necessary for a mutual fund to generate sufficient revenues to cover direct expenses, direct overhead, and indirect overhead costs. (For financial statements, see Exhibits 4 and 5.)

## FUTURE PLANS

The shape of WMC's future strategy was only partly settled in early 1971. The company had definitely planned more vigorous participation in the foreign market, and executives had firm if not unalterable views on vertical integration. They were also eager to keep WMC as an independent company. Decisions about how large the fund complex should be and whether to emphasize funds or investment counseling were, however, topics still under internal debate.

### Mutual fund distribution overseas

In the spring of 1970 Wellington decided to establish an international operation. This activity, which was to be managed by one man in Boston and one in Paris, was described in an investment journal as follows:

Wellington Management is teaming up with two leading French institutions to organize Inter-Europe Management. Its partners are Société Générale,

**EXHIBIT 4**

WELLINGTON MANAGEMENT COMPANY
Income Statements for Years Ending October 31
(dollars in millions, except per-share figures)

| | *1966* | *1967* | *1968* | *1969* | *1970* |
|---|---|---|---|---|---|
| Gross sales @ offering price | $145.0 | $189.0 | $291.7 | $130.5 | $190.0 |
| Total management fees and sales commissions | | | | | |
| Wellington | $ 6.5 | $ 5.4 | $ 4.8 | $ 4.4 | $ 3.5 |
| Windsor | 0.6 | 0.7 | 0.9 | 1.8 | 2.9 |
| Ivest | 0.4 | 2.8 | 4.0 | 2.3 | 1.7 |
| Exeters (3) | ... | 0.5 | 0.8 | 0.7 | 0.5 |
| Gemini | ... | 0.1 | 0.2 | 0.2 | 0.2 |
| Explorer | ... | ... | 0.6 | 0.4 | 0.2 |
| Trustees' Equity | ... | ... | ... | ... | 0.1 |
| Technivest | ... | ... | ... | 0.4 | 0.2 |
| W. L. Morgan Growth | ... | ... | ... | 0.1 | 0.4 |
| Wellesley | ... | ... | ... | ... | 0.1 |
| Total funds | $ 7.5 (92%) | $ 9.5 (91%) | $ 11.5 (88%) | $ 10.3 (83%) | $ 9.8 (78%) |
| Investment counseling fees | 0.5 (6%) | 0.7 (7%) | 1.3 (10%) | 1.8 (14%) | 2.2 (17%) |
| Other income | 0.1 (2%) | 0.2 (2%) | 0.2 (2%) | 0.3 (3%) | 0.6 (5%) |
| Total revenue | $ 8.1 | $ 10.4 | $ 13.0 | $ 12.4 | $ 12.6 |
| Expenses | | | | | |
| Compensation and related expenses | $ 2.8 | $ 3.6 | $ 4.6 | $ 5.7 | $ 6.0 |
| Marketing and promotional expenses | 0.7 | 1.3 | 1.4 | 1.5 | 1.4 |
| General and administrative expenses | 0.8 | 1.1 | 1.7 | 2.3 | 2.3 |
| Total expenses | $ 4.3 | $ 6.0 | $ 7.7 | $ 9.5 | $ 9.7 |
| Net income | $ 3.8 | $ 4.4 | $ 5.3 | $ 2.9 | $ 2.9 |
| Taxes | 1.8 | 2.2 | 2.8 | 1.5 | 1.5 |
| After-tax income | 2.0* | 2.2 | 2.5 | 1.4 | 1.4 |
| Earnings per share (operations) | $ 1.88* | $ 2.34 | $ 2.52 | $ 1.33 | $ 1.31 |
| Earnings per share (after extraordinary items) | 1.88 | 2.34 | 2.52 | 1.08 | 1.31 |
| Dividends per share | 1.75 | 1.80 | 1.80 | 1.40 | 1.10 |
| Stock prices: | | | | | |
| High | 44¾ | 40¼ | 50 | 44½ | 23¾ |
| Low | 22 | 24¼ | 35½ | 21 | 10 |
| Close | 25¼ | 30¼ | 43¾ | 21¼ | 21¼ |

*** Prior to adjustment to reflect the Ivest merger, net was $1.86 million and EPS was $2.09.**
**Note: Figures may not add owing to rounding.**
**Source: Company records.**

**EXHIBIT 5**

WELLINGTON MANAGEMENT COMPANY
Balance Sheet as of October 31
(in thousands of dollars)

| | 1966 | 1967 | 1968 | 1969 | 1970 |
|---|---|---|---|---|---|
| *Assets* | | | | | |
| Current assets | | | | | |
| Cash . . . . . . . . . . . . . . . . . | $ 609 | $ 503 | $ 1,944 | $ 3,167 | $ 2,233 |
| Short-term investments | | | | | |
| at cost . . . . . . . . . . . . . . . | . . . | . . . | . . . | . . . | 5,135 |
| Receivables | | | | | |
| Shares sold. . . . . . . . . . . . | 1,851 | 6,578 | 4,698 | 6,311 | 4,266 |
| Advisory fees . . . . . . . . . . . | 876 | 1,300 | 1,376 | 1,524 | 1,841 |
| Sale of subsidiary. . . . . . . . . | . . . | . . . | . . . | 3,814 | . . . |
| Total current assets. . . . . . . | $3,336 | $ 8,381 | $ 8,018 | $14,816 | $13,475 |
| Marketable securities at cost. . . . . | 2,562 | 1,600 | 3,053 | 1,407 | 1,395 |
| Other. . . . . . . . . . . . . . . . . | 276 | 467 | 841 | 890 | 389 |
| Property and equipment (net). . . . | 486 | 535 | 785 | 1,208 | 1,212 |
| Total assets . . . . . . . . . . | $6,660 | $10,983 | $12,697 | $18,321 | $16,471 |
| *Liabilities* | | | | | |
| Current liabilities | | | | | |
| Payables | | | | | |
| Notes . . . . . . . . . . . . . . . . | . . . | $ 400 | . . . | . . . | $ 100 |
| Shares sold. . . . . . . . . . . | $1,467 | 5,212 | $ 6,353 | $ 8,474 | 6,385 |
| Accrued taxes. . . . . . . . . . . | 787 | 921 | 697 | 362 | 1,259 |
| Other payables accrued . . . . . . | 405 | 1,178 | 1,608 | 1,913 | 2,100 |
| Reserve in dividends . . . . . . . . | 614 | 731 | 733 | 384 | . . . |
| Total current liabilities . . . . | $3,273 | $ 8,442 | $ 9,391 | $11,133 | $ 9,844 |
| Deferred taxes . . . . . . . . . . . . | . . . | . . . | . . . | 1,029 | 65 |
| Long-term debt . . . . . . . . . . . | 430 | 430 | 430 | 430 | 330 |
| Capital | | | | | |
| Common stock (par 10¢) . . . . . | $ 91 | $ 105 | $ 105 | $ 118 | $ 118 |
| Surplus . . . . . . . . . . . . . . . | 972 | 1,042 | 1,105 | 4,339 | 4,339 |
| Retained earnings. . . . . . . . . | 2,416 | 2,986 | 3,688 | 3,294 | 3,797 |
| Treasury shares (at cost). . . . . . | (522) | (2,022) | (2,022) | (2,022) | (2,022) |
| Total capital . . . . . . . . . . . | $2,957 | $ 2,111 | $ 2,876 | $ 5,729 | $ 6,232 |
| Total liabilities . . . . . . . . | $6,660 | $10,983 | $12,697 | $18,321 | $16,471 |

Source: Company records.

France's third biggest bank, and Union des Assurances de Paris, the country's largest insurance firm.

Prior to this new venture, Wellington's principal link to the overseas market has been through investment counseling to European institutions (including one of the largest Swiss banks).

The fund will be sold door-to-door, which will mark the first time Wellington will be involved in direct retail distribution.[8]

## Vertical integration

With more funds moving toward an in-house sales force, and more brokers and insurance companies moving toward selling funds (either

---
[8] *Securities,* June 1970, pp. 12, 14.

their own or a subsidiary's), companies like WMC, which had not yet integrated forward into the retail function, had frequent occasion to review this policy. Mr. Bogle noted that while these developments had so far produced "incredibly little change both in *who* distributes mutual fund shares and in *how* they are distributed," yet "past stability" might well be the "harbinger of future upheaval."[9]

In another mid-1970 statement, this time before a group of brokers, Mr. Bogle returned to the integration issue with the following observations:

> We recognize that many NYSE firms have already taken steps to directly integrate money management capability with their marketing ability. We also recognize the reasons for these steps. And we do not doubt that those who enter the mutual fund field with the formation of "in-house" funds (there are some 50 of these at this time) recognize two major risks of this step:
>
> 1.  That it in fact provides, in principle, the "institutional access" that it seems in all of our interests to resist.
> 2.  That, if a groundswell develops in this area, it may well force the money management firms to move toward both direct retail distribution and portfolio execution capability.
>
> We believe, however, that our company's prime commitment is to the effective management of money. This is a full-time job, and we do not seek to lose this focus by engaging either in the direct retail distribution of mutual fund shares or in the execution of our fund brokerage transactions. In short, we prefer, as a matter of corporate strategy, to avoid competing with you. Not only do we presently lack the skills involved in those two areas, but we wonder whether in the long run our interests—in the broadest sense—are furthered. I am speaking particularly of the possible adverse effects on the investment community and the individual investor if institutional access to the marketplace should develop—and its further impairment of market liquidity.[10]

## Independence

Both Mr. Bogle and Mr. Robert W. Doran, executive vice president for investment and marketing (through whom both the funds and the TDP&L counseling subsidiary reported), agreed that preserving independence was a key corporate goal. Mr. Bogle expressed himself as follows:

> . . . Perhaps [our] most important goal of all . . . is our desire to remain independent—to remain a relatively small, professionally oriented organization

---

[9] From a speech to the 1970 National Mutual Fund Conference sponsored by *Institutional Investor*. See *Institutional Investor*, June 1970, p. 33.

[10] "The Member Firm and the Mutual Fund Complex: A Marketing Partnership," a speech delivered before the NYSE Marketing Conference, New York City, June 19, 1970.

where we can enjoy working together. Remaining independent is no small order for a firm like this—especially when you realize that in recent years, 15 of our 43 major competitors (fund assets of $250,000,000 or more) have been acquired by outside interests, reducing by more than one third the majors in the "independent sector," and there surely are more acquisitions in the wings.

There are, of course, compelling reasons *not* to be independent. Many acquisitions have taken place with a view toward providing direct channels of retail distribution for fund shares, based on the commonly held view that the days are numbered for the system of distribution through independent dealers. One does not have to draw many branches out on a "decision tree" to realize that the *corporate cost of acquiring a controlled distribution channel is all too likely to be our independence;* and to realize further that the firms that have the courage to remain in the independent sector may end up with a competitive advantage through their very uniqueness.

Corporate acquisitions often take place because the financial terms are so overwhelmingly favorable that they compel management acquiescence as a duty to the public stockholders. Our management's position may be a bit different than that of the typical corporation, however, for we are responsible to *both* the management company stockholders *and* the fund shareholders. If a merger were to cost us the services of key personnel, for example, the game might not be worth the candle. And retaining our key people in an entrepreneurial environment is vital, although perhaps the consequences described a few months ago in *The New York Times* overstated the case against acquisition by an outside firm: An executive in the acquired company is reported to have said that he and his associates were given "the mushroom treatment"—

"Right after the acquisition, we were kept in the dark. Then they covered us with manure. Then they cultivated us. After that, they let us stew for awhile. And, finally, they canned us."[11]

Mr. Doran, who was described as a "driving force" behind the Boston group and as being, like Mr. Bogle, a "hard working, imaginative, strong executive who enjoyed positions of leadership," agreed:

The happiness level in this company is very important. We are not here just to make money—it's essential that our work be fun and enjoyable. I feel we should go to great lengths to accommodate individual needs and desires.

I would think that size as a corporate goal is not an important consideration. What we really want to do is to be able to manage money best. We want to be recognized as the outstanding money managers in the country. And if we do this well, this impacts on our profit and our sales. Also, remaining independent in spite of an industry trend towards merging to obtain distribution systems . . . I don't think that we want to be the largest firm in the business but we would certainly like to act as the spokesman for the industry.

[11] Annual Report to WMC Employees, 1969.

**Emphasis**

While agreeing that WMC should strive for excellence and independence, Mr. Bogle and Mr. Doran expressed different views about what activities WMC should chiefly emphasize in order to realize these two overriding objectives. As he pointed out in his 1969 Annual Report to Employees, Mr. Bogle believed in the primacy of the fund complex:

Since some 85% of our revenues are based on mutual fund management fees and sales commissions, it seems clear that we must continue to improve our mutual fund operations. We must concentrate our corporate efforts on even better investment performance, on greater marketing thrust, and on "spit-and-polish" efficiency in our administrative operations. This is not to say that our investment counsel arm, TDP&L, is unimportant—indeed its success may be critical to the achievement of our long-term earnings growth—but rather that the requisite nearby quantum earnings improvement can *only* come if we learn how to run more effectively our major business—mutual funds. A possible conclusion from this primary objective is that we should limit any corporate acquisitions to those in which we can make a meaningful management contribution, rather than those in which our present skills might be either ineffective or diluted.

Compelling advantages make the creation of a full line of mutual funds to suit a variety of investor needs a second clear goal. As I pointed out in my report to you a year ago, this "multifund" strategy, if properly carried out, should help to broaden our opportunities for success by reducing our dependence on a single product, minimize the obvious risks to our distribution system, stabilize capital flow, enhance our management capability, and increase our growth potential. Implicit in this strategy are these assumptions: (a) that we can maintain Wellington Fund assets through improved performance and a healthier sales/liquidation mix, (b) that Ivest and Windsor Fund assets can be built up to a far larger extent, and (c) that the Explorer, Morgan Growth, Trustees' Equity and Technivest Funds of today can provide us with five-year asset growth (into 1974, say) that compares with the growth of Windsor and Ivest over the past five years (from $80 million to $550 million in aggregate).[12]

Elaborating on this idea to the casewriter, Mr. Bogle developed his argument as follows:

I'm not sure we can reduce our product line in this business even if we want to do so. In other industries you merely cease production and customers purchase a new line. In this business we're not really sure what the implications of this action would be, since those who own the product may well still have confidence in it. Legally we could merge the fund into something else or perhaps sell it if we could get the fund's board to approve; but the uncertainty of the public reaction and the possible disastrous results if confidence in WMC were undermined seem to discourage this course of action.

---

[12] Ibid.

While there may be some near-term economies in eliminating a fund, we really don't know how much a fund costs. It would fly in the face of what we've done. Though I know I'm known as "Mr. Product Proliferation," I think we have to look at the potential. We've got to be prepared to take advantage of a tremendous trend in our modern society: that of product specialization. (When there are 25,000 different versions of a single make of car available, we realize that the era of industrialization has not ended up in standardization.) We've got to be ready and able to create any type of fund that meets a sound investor need.

Mr. Doran expressed special optimism about the potential of the investment counseling business:

The counseling area is the one in which we have had our most dynamic growth, and I believe that this growth will continue to be dynamic. We are presently in a very extraordinary position. We are now attracting the kind of capital that we want and we have the right type of accounts. In other words, we have relatively few accounts with a relatively large amount of money in each account. Our clients include 18 of *Fortune's* top 500 industrial companies, one of the nation's top retailers, a large utility, a major foundation, and many educational institutions. I forsee that we will increase our share of the market and increase our profits significantly.

On the other hand, I have some questions on the advisability or the future success of the "financial supermarket." I think you can get hung up trying to offer everything to everyone, and I don't feel that the individual to whom we cater (with a large amount of money in his account) is likely to seek the services of a financial supermarket when purchasing money management. I think the extent to which we have proliferated products in the past was questionable and proved expensive. We don't have the resources to cover adequately both the conservative stocks and the embryonic, small venture companies. I think we may have to face the question of reducing the product line sooner than we think.

# Note on the commercial broadcasting industry

THE COMMERCIAL broadcasting industry is composed of two major segments, television and radio, which together generated about $4 billion in revenues in 1970. This note develops the structural characteristics of these industry segments and some of the economic, political, and social forces at work in them.

## TELEVISION

### Structure and performance

There were 862 television stations in the United States at year-end 1970, an increase of 303 or 54% from the 559 stations on the air in 1960. The highest percentage of increases, as shown in Exhibit 1 and in Table 1, had been in UHF rather than VHF channel allocations[1] and in educational rather than commercial stations.

Both UHF and educational television enjoyed the strong support of the Federal Communications Commission, which was responsible for granting and renewing licenses. Conversely, with the VHF frequency bands already crowded, only two new VHF commercial stations had been authorized from 1967 to 1970. The FCC had demonstrated its interest in UHF by increasing the allowable power of UHF transmission,

---

[1] UHF (ultra high frequency), channels 14–83, operate at 470–890 megacycles and VHF (very high frequency), channels 2–13, operate at 174–216 megacycles.

**EXHIBIT 1**
Television stations on the air (1945–70)

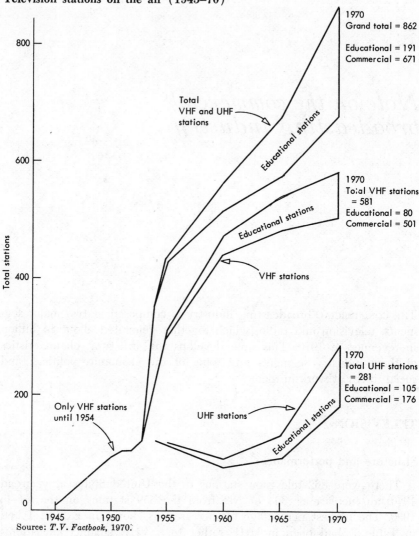

Source: *T.V. Factbook*, 1970.

**TABLE 1**

|  | VHF | | UHF | | |
|---|---|---|---|---|---|
|  | Commercial | Educational | Commercial | Educational | Total |
| 1960 . . . . . . . . | 440 | 34 | 75 | 10 | 559 |
| 1970 . . . . . . . . | 501 | 80 | 176 | 105 | 862 |
| Increase . . . . . . | 61 | 46 | 101 | 95 | 303 |
| Percent. . . . . . . | 14% | 135% | 135% | 950% | 54% |

thus expanding the broadcast range to be more competitive with VHF, increasing the UHF license allocations, making some areas all UHF, and requiring, after 1964, that television set manufacturers install UHF receiving capability on all new sets.[2]

The three television networks (ABC, CBS, and NBC) entered into affiliation agreements with local stations, about 530 in total, across the country. Each network originated programs, produced in-house or secured from independent studios, including national and international news, public affairs features, and sporting events. The networks sold advertising on the show or event to national accounts, remitting a portion of the proceeds as "station payments" to affiliates which broadcast the program. While affiliates relied on the networks to cover most of their prime time, they produced or acquired much of the daytime programming themselves, purchased their own movie rights, and, of course, were responsible for local news. Stations also had sales representatives who sold "national spot" advertising (time sold independently of the program) to national accounts on a commission basis.

The networks and their 15 owned and operating stations (O&Os)[3] were dominant factors in the profitability of the industry (see Exhibit 2). Network activities accounted for 41% of 1969 total television broadcast revenues of $2.8 billion and 17% of total pretax profit of $554 million. Their O&Os, representing about 2% of the nation's stations, had another 12% of total revenues and 24% of pretax profits.

Looking beyond ABC, CBS, and NBC, performance among TV broadcasters could be categorized in four ways. First, the largest metropolitan markets generated a very large share of television revenues, as shown in Exhibit 3. Many of the important stations in these markets were part of broadcast groups owned by companies such as Westinghouse, Metromedia, Cox Broadcasting, and RKO General. Second, profitability appeared to increase significantly with size for both VHF and UHF stations, as shown in Exhibit 4. Third, despite FCC support, a substantial majority of UHF stations continued to be both small and unprofitable. One explanation for this phenomenon was the fact that UHFs were frequently latecomers to the market and faced competition from entrenched stations with network affiliations. Finally, affiliates, as one would suspect, were mostly VHFs and were substantially more profitable than nonaffiliates, as reflected in the FCC sample shown in Table 2.

Industry observers pointed to several competitive reasons for the superior performance of network affiliates. For instance, expensive programming and special events which were beyond the financial means of independents were obtained from the networks. Moreover, media

---

[2] According to the FCC, 68% of TV homes were able to receive UHF channels.

[3] Each network had five VHF stations in the top 10 markets, the maximum number of VHFs allowed by the FCC to any single owner.

**EXHIBIT 2**

**1969 broadcasting industry revenues, expenses, and income**

| | Broadcast revenues | | Broadcast expenses | | Broadcast income before taxes | |
|---|---|---|---|---|---|---|
| | Dollars (millions) | Percent of industry | Dollars (millions) | Percent of industry | Dollars (millions) | Percent of industry |
| **Television** | | | | | | |
| 3 networks*...... | 1,144.1 | 41 | 1,051.3 | 47 | 92.7 | 17 |
| 15 network stations*....... | 323.3 | 12 | 189.9 | 8 | 133.4 | 24 |
| All other stations | | | | | | |
| 489 VHF ...... | 1,214.9 | 43 | 844.2 | 38 | 370.7 | 67 |
| 169 UHF ...... | 114.0 | 4 | 157.2 | 7 | (43.2) | (8) |
| Total television industry..... | 2,796.2 | 100 | 2,242.6 | 100 | 553.6 | 100 |
| **Radio** | | | | | | |
| 3 networks ...... | 44.1 | 4 | 50.4 | 5 | (6.3) | (6) |
| 20 network stations ....... | 48.8 | 4 | 43.0 | 5 | 5.8 | 6 |
| 4,174 other stations reporting to the FCC ........ | 955.8 | 92 | 844.1 | 90 | 111.7 | 100 |
| Total radio industry..... | 1,048.7 | 100 | 937.5 | 100 | 111.2 | 100 |

*The percentage share of the $1,467,400 ($1,144,100 + $323,300) held by each major network was as follows: CBS (38.4); NBC (35.4); ABC (26.2).

Note: To avoid double counting, station payments of $254 million and $10 million have been excluded from network revenues and expenses for television and radio, respectively.

Source: FCC Annual Report, 1970.

buyers found it simpler and safer to allocate advertising budgets to network programming or national spot salesmen who could offer packages on proven stations covering many markets.

As a network, CBS had generally been the leader in prime-time ratings by a narrow margin over NBC, with ABC in third place. The CBS lead in total national advertising revenue had dwindled in recent years and in 1970 stood at CBS, 34.5%; NBC, 34.5%; ABC, 27.3%.[4] It was not unusual, however, for the order of finish to change depending on the success of the prime-time program lineup. For local stations, the specific affiliation was not necessarily a good indication of relative market share. In other words, competition at the local level encompassed many factors relating the station to the community of which network programming was only one.

---

[4] *T.V. Factbook,* 1970.

TABLE 2

| | Network affiliated | | Independents | | Total | |
|---|---|---|---|---|---|---|
| | VHF | UHF | VHF | UHF | VHF | UHF |
| Number of stations reporting. . . . . . . | 422 | 94 | 34 | 48 | 456 | 142 |
| Number reporting profits . . . . . . . . . | 357 | 48 | 21 | 2 | 378 | 50 |
| Percent profitable. . . . | 85% | 51% | 62% | 4% | 83% | 35% |

Source: Federal Communications Commission.

EXHIBIT 3
**1969 revenues of commercial television and radio stations in metropolitan markets (thousands of dollars)**

| | Number of stations | Network payments | National spot advertising | Local adver- tising | Total revenues | Percent of total |
|---|---|---|---|---|---|---|
| TV stations in— | | | | | | |
| 10 largest markets . | 68 | $ 65,300 | $ 555,700 | $153,500 | $ 773,500 | 41.0 |
| 15 next largest markets . . . . . . | 66 | 39,000 | 209,350 | 95,600 | 353,950 | 19.8 |
| 264 smaller markets . . . . . . | 549 | 149,800 | 343,050 | 269,850 | 753,700 | 39.2 |
| All metropolitan markets . . . . . . | 683 | $254,100 | $1,108,100 | $518,950 | $1,881,150* | 100.0 |
| Radio stations in— | | | | | | |
| 10 largest markets . . . . . | 229 | $ 2,550 | $ 154,950 | $151,000 | $ 308,500 | 35.7 |
| 15 next largest markets . . . . . . | 208 | 1,900 | 51,050 | 86,400 | 139,350 | 16.3 |
| 333 smaller markets . . . . . . | 1,618 | 4,150 | 98,250 | 307,000 | 409,400 | 48.0 |
| All metropolitan markets . . . . . . | 2,055 | $ 8,600 | $ 304,250 | $544,400 | $ 857,250* | 100.0 |

*These figures do not represent total TV and radio industry revenues of $2.8 billion and $1.05 billion, respectively, because networks retained a substantial portion of their advertising revenues and made network payments to stations carrying network advertising.
Source: Compiled from *FCC News*, No. 53051, July 24, 1970, Table 17; and *FCC News*, December 14, 1970.

## Television advertising

Broadcast media, particularly television, had increased its share of total advertising expenditures in the 1960s at the expense of print and other media (see Table 3). Significantly, 64 of the top 100 advertisers spent more than 50% of their media dollars on TV. Television's "big

**EXHIBIT 4**
Profitability of VHF and UHF television stations by total broadcast
revenues, 1969

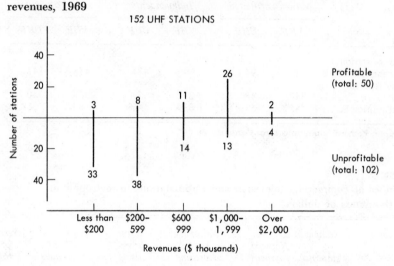

152 UHF STATIONS

Number of stations

Profitable
(total: 50)

Unprofitable
(total: 102)

Revenues ($ thousands)

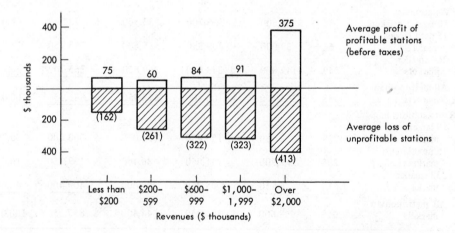

$ thousands

Average profit of
profitable stations
(before taxes)

Average loss of
unprofitable stations

Revenues ($ thousands)

spenders" in 1970 included foods and beverages (20%); toiletries (17%);
drugs (12%); transportation (11%); household products, chiefly soap
(11%); tobacco products (10%); other consumer goods (14%); utilities
and trade associations (5%).

Contributing to revenue growth were a modest rise in the number
of commercial minutes per day (from 145 in 1964 to 162 minutes in
1969, according to one survey of the top 75 markets)[5] and increases
in advertising rates averaging 6.6% per year for the top 10 markets and

[5] *Advertising Age*, November 2, 1970, p. 2. The NAB code permitted 10 minutes
per hour.

**EXHIBIT 4** (*continued*)

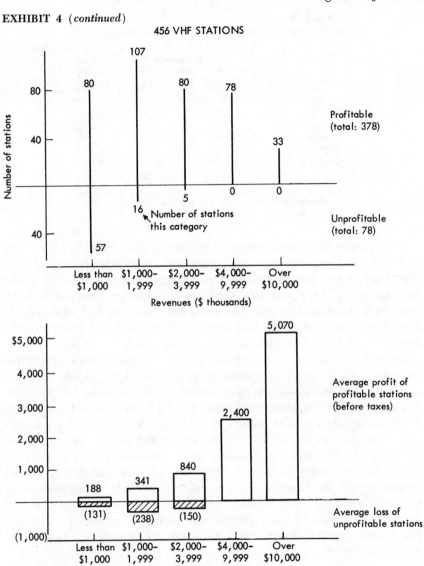

456 VHF STATIONS

Source: FCC Annual Report, 1970.

3.4% for the next 40 markets during the 1960s.[6] Since expanding the number of minutes devoted to commercials was subject to public criticism for "cluttering" and advertiser criticism for downgrading message retention, revenue growth was dependent primarily on how rapidly rates could be increased.

[6] Ibid.

TABLE 3

| | Share of expenditures | | Annual growth rate |
|---|---|---|---|
| | *1960* | *1969* | |
| Television . . . . . . . | 13.4% | 18.3% | 9.3% |
| Radio. . . . . . . . . . | 5.8 | 6.5 | 6.9 |
| Newspapers . . . . . . | 31.1 | 29.8 | 5.2 |
| Magazines . . . . . . . | 7.9 | 7.0 | 4.3 |
| Other . . . . . . . . . . | 41.8 | 38.4 | 4.1 |
| | 100.0% | 100.0% | 5.7% |

Source: *T.V. Factbook*, 1970, p. 58a.

Broadcasters had been successful in raising advertising rates for several reasons. First, although the proportion of households with a television set topped 90% in 1962, the penetration of color into 37% of the households by 1970 and the surge in multiple-set households were thought to increase the attention given television. In fact, the average TV viewing per household had leveled off at about five hours in 1965 but then rose to six hours and nine minutes in 1969.

Second, broadcasters had argued that it was possible for advertisers to target their messages at specific geographic or demographic audience segments, thus increasing the efficiency of the expenditure. For instance, in February 1970, the major networks signed a contract with the National Football League for $184 million to broadcast NFL games for the next four seasons on radio and TV, an increase of $76 million over the previous four-year contract. In February 1971, networks signed a one-year pact with the major baseball leagues for $40 million. Having signed contracts with the leagues, the networks then sought sponsors desiring to reach a highly concentrated male audience. Advertising was sold at prime-time rates (about $60,000 per minute) or higher ($200,000 per minute for the Super Bowl, $100,000 per minute for the World Series).

## Revenue-cost relationships and trends

Despite the ability to secure rate increases, the networks were confronted with a number of difficulties in 1971. It should be noted, of course, that with the supply of advertising minutes essentially fixed, the networks had good reason to be concerned about their rate cards. Their concern was heightened by the fact that programming costs accounted for about 80% of total network expenses after station payments in 1969. Such costs were largely fixed in the short run and bore no direct relationship to the program ratings which determined audience size and hence influenced advertising rates. Moreover, network programming costs had been increasing at a rate of 9.7% during the 1960s, somewhat in excess of network revenue growth of 8.5%. The networks had protected their margins by reducing the proportion of revenues remitted to affiliates as station payments.[7]

A major problem for the networks was the drop in ratings for their programs which almost exactly balanced the increase in the number of TV households.[8] This in turn was a reflection of two further adverse factors. First, the market shares of affiliates in many cases were being fragmented by the intrusion of new stations and CATV into their broadcast areas. Second, as local broadcasters assessed the implications of lower station payments, some of them began to substitute local programming for network shows and sold the program time themselves to local advertisers. Consequently, it was becoming more difficult for the networks to deliver the full affiliate lineup to national advertisers, which necessitated rebates in the short run and over the longer term encouraged advertisers to consider buying national spots rather than network program time.

## Prime-time access rule

In 1971 the FCC adopted a rule designed to encourage nonnetwork programming in prime time, that is, generally 7:00 P.M. until 11:00 P.M. The rule limited network programming to not more than three hours per day (down from three and one-half hours), which had the effect of increasing program costs to the local station and reducing network revenue. On the other hand, the decrease in network time available seemed to firm up network rates, which had sagged about 10% following the January 1971 ban on cigarette advertising. Cigarettes had accounted for about $210 million in revenue, most of it in prime time.[9]

For television station operators, trends of major significance were shifts in the sources of revenue and increasing programming costs evident in Table 4.

---

[7] Station payments declined from 25% of total network revenues in 1960 to 18% in 1969.

[8] For instance, the Nielsen rating for the top-rated show dropped from 42.4 in 1960 to 31.1 in 1970. As a result, despite the increase in TV hours, the number of homes reached by this program dropped from 18.9 million to 18.2 million. *Advertising Age*, November 2, 1970, p. 66.

[9] CBS estimated this would reduce the network's pretax profits by $5 to $15 million in 1971. *Advertising Age*, November 2, 1970.

TABLE 4

| | (In millions) | | Five-year growth rate |
|---|---|---|---|
| Revenues | 1964 | 1969 | |
| Network station payments......... | $ 214 | $ 254 | 3.5% |
| National spot ................ | 711 | 1,108 | 9.3 |
| Local..................... | 276 | 519 | 13.5 |
| Total broadcast revenue (net)* ..... | $1,081 | $1,652 | 8.9% |
| Total broadcast expenses ........ | 725 | 1,191 | 10.4 |
| Total pretax profit ............ | $ 355 | $ 461 | 5.3% |

*Total sales plus miscellaneous revenue less commissions to advertising agencies, representatives, and brokers.
Source: *Broadcasting*, March 22, 1971.

## CATV

Community antenna television was regarded by some as the most noteworthy development in broadcasting in the sixties. CATV companies erected towers capable of picking up signals of television stations from 60 to 100 miles away from the communities they served. Microwave relays could be used to bring in programs from even more distant stations. The signals received were then fed to homes of subscribers by means of coaxial cables. Subscribers usually paid about $20 for initial installation of the cable plus a monthly fee ranging from $5 to $7. Originally, CATV companies confined their efforts to small communities having limited TV coverage. Starting in 1964, however, CATV systems were set up in a number of major markets in which the nature of the terrain or the number of tall buildings interfered with reception of the signals of local TV stations.

Growing at a compound annual rate of 20% since 1960, 2,800 CATV systems served 4.5 million subscribers or about 6% of U.S. households in 1970. The seven largest systems accounted for 25% of total subscribers. CATV revenues totaled approximately $400 million in 1970. One source forecast that 28 million homes would be served by 4,400 systems in 1980.[10]

Since a typical system carried 6 to 12 channels, a viewer was offered the potential for increasing by two to four times the number of available channels. Most systems had excess channel capacity, and entrepreneurs in CATV looked to the day when these channels might be used commercially for such services as "TV shopping-at-home," information retrieval, and newspaper facsimile. In 1971 excess channels were often devoted to weather, stock market, and wire-service news reports and limited program origination.

[10] *Advertising Age*, November 2, 1970, p. 98.

In 1969 the FCC ruled that CATV systems would not be permitted to carry distant signals into the top 100 markets. CATV operators were required to delete commercials, with priority going to nonaffiliated UHF stations. However, a directive scheduled to become effective in March 1972 would allow two distant signals to be imported into the top 100 markets.

CATV operators were not permitted to import network programs if they duplicated the broadcast of a local network affiliate. Nevertheless, the impact on ratings, especially for nonaffiliates and those stations which depended heavily on local advertising, could be severe. One survey of three market areas in which 50% of the homes were CATV subscribers revealed that local stations suffered an audience loss ranging from 14% to 25%. Indignant station owners argued that CATV operators got a "free ride" by not paying for programming, on the one hand, and collecting fees from subscribers on the other.

## RADIO

### Structure and performance

Radio stations on the air in the United States numbered 6,991 in 1970, up 2,673 or 60% from the 4,368 stations in operation in 1960, as shown in Exhibit 5. FM accounted for 1,838, or about 70% of the station additions.[11] Since 1968, the FCC had virtually stopped issuing licenses for AM broadcasting, due primarily to growing congestion in the AM frequency band which was having the effect of reducing the effective range of broadcast signals. Approximately 76% of FM radio stations were part of AM/FM combinations, though the FCC had a long-term goal of separate ownership.

Unlike television, the radio networks and their 20 owned and operated stations were relatively minor factors in this segment of the industry. Network and O&O revenues of $44.1 million and $48.8 million, respectively, were together only 8% of the 1969 radio total of $1,048.7 million, as shown in Exhibit 2. Moreover, network pretax losses of $6.3 million more than offset O&O profits of $5.8 million. Nonnetwork stations, by contrast, had pretax profits of $111.7 million.

Prior to the advent of television, the networks had been powerful forces in radio. However, centralized programming proved less effective in holding diverse audiences than locally produced shows, and gradually the networks' role was reduced to news, public affairs, and an occasional

---

[11] FM had the advantages over AM of higher fidelity characteristics and relative freedom from static, fading, and background overlapping of other stations' programs.

**EXHIBIT 5**
**Radio stations on the air  (1945–69)**

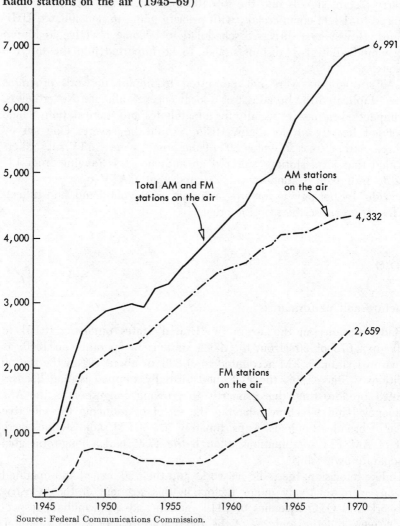

Source: Federal Communications Commission.

holdover such as "The Arthur Godfrey Show."[12] In addition, the number of stations in individual markets steadily increased (for instance, there were 34 stations in New York City) and were supported by independent news services.

Like television, profitability could be categorized in several ways. One indicator was size; the bigger the station, the more likely it was

---

[12] The Arthur Godfrey Show, produced by CBS, was scheduled to go off the air in 1972.

to be profitable (see Exhibit 6). Second, FM stations, at least those which were not part of an AM/FM combination, generally were loss operations, as shown in Table 5.

TABLE 5
1969 FM radio financial performance

| | Stations reporting | FM revenues (millions) | FM pretax profits (millions) |
|---|---|---|---|
| AM/FM combinations | | | |
| No FM revenues . . . . . . . . . . . | 387 | . . . | . . . |
| FM profits not reported . . . . . . . | 953 | $21.9 | n.a. |
| FM profits reported . . . . . . . . . | 179 | 12.1 | $(4.8)* |
| FM independents . . . . . . . . . . . | 442 | 33.4 | (5.5)† |

*45 reported profits averaging $18,929; 134 reported losses averaging $42,114.
†136 reported profits averaging $16,674; 306 reported losses averaging $25,541.
Source: FCC AM/FM Broadcast Financial Data, 1969.

While the number of independent FM stations rose from 218 in 1960 to 442 in 1969 and revenues from $5.8 million to $33.4 million, losses increased from $2.4 million to $5.5 million. Growth had been limited by the fact that until the mid-1960s few radios were produced with FM receiving capability. This situation was rapidly changing, as illustrated in Exhibit 7.

## Cost and revenue trends

As indicated above, radio had increased its share of total advertising expenditures in the United States during the 1960s. Many radio station owners maintained that the medium was in a favorable position for continued growth. They pointed to the fact that there were about 303 million radios in the United States in 1969, almost five on the average per household, and the figure had been growing at a rate of 10% to 15% per year. Opportunities for market segmentation through programming policy were thereby enhanced. The peak listening period occurred between 6:00 and 10:00 A.M.; to the extent that this was a result of commuters (75 million of the radios were in automobiles), station owners argued that the quality of the audience during these hours was higher than normally obtainable.

The future growth of radio was, of course, by no means assured. Population migrations to the suburbs and beyond were tending to shrink and reduce the affluence of metropolitan markets. With the limited range

**EXHIBIT 6**

**Profitability of commercial radio stations by total broadcast revenues, 1969***

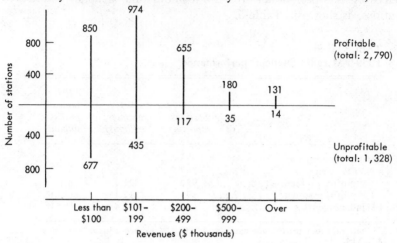

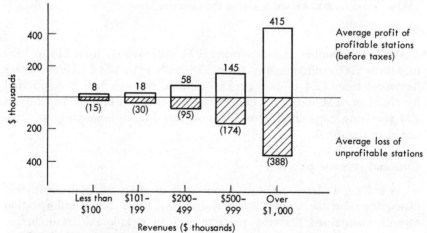

Revenues ($ thousands)

* Includes AM and FM stations.
Source: *FCC News*, December 14, 1970.

of most radio signals, this meant larger potential audiences for outlying stations. The commuter market was also undergoing change as industry moved from the cities and more emphasis was placed on mass transit. Furthermore, the impact of audio cassettes in automobiles or miniature television sets was as yet unknown.

One factor was clear to most radio station operators: local advertising was becoming steadily more dominant among their sources of revenue, as shown in Table 6.

**EXHIBIT 7**
**U.S. sales of radio sets***

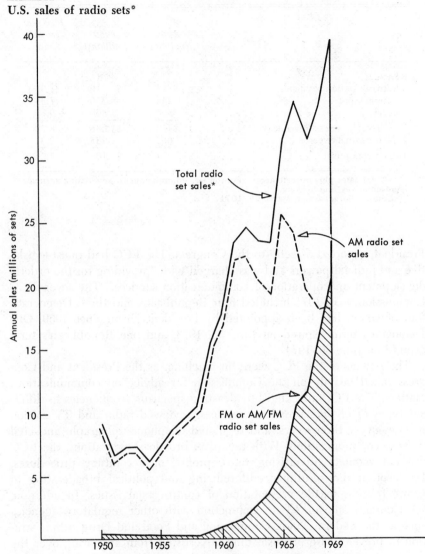

* Does not include automobile radios.
Source: Electronics Industries of America, *Market Data Book* 1970.

## THE FEDERAL COMMUNICATIONS COMMISSION

The Federal Communications Commission, created by Congress in 1934, was an independent federal agency charged with regulating interstate and foreign communication (radio, TV, telephone, cable, and satellite). Its seven commissioners, appointed for seven-year terms by the

TABLE 6

|  | 1964<br>(millions) | 1969<br>(millions) | Five-year<br>growth<br>rate |
|---|---|---|---|
| Revenues |  |  |  |
| Network station payments . . . . . . . . . . . . | $ 11 | $ 10 | (1.9%) |
| National spot . . . . . . . . . . . . . . . . . . | 244 | 350 | 7.5 |
| Local. . . . . . . . . . . . . . . . . . . . . . . | 504 | 800 | 9.7 |
| Total broadcast revenue (net)*. . . . . . . | $732 | $1,086 | 8.2% |
| Total broadcast expense . . . . . . . . . . . . | 661 | 985 | 8.3 |
| Total pretax profit . . . . . . . . . . . . . . . | 71 | $ 101 | 7.3% |

*Total sales plus miscellaneous revenue less commissions to advertising agencies,
representatives, and brokers.
Source: *Broadcasting*, March 22, 1971.

President, reported directly to the Congress. The FCC had quasi-legisla-
tive and judicial powers and was charged with "providing for the orderly
development and operation of communication services." The seven FCC
Commissioners in 1971 included four Republicans and three Democrats,
four of whom had been appointed by President Nixon since 1969. One
Democrat's term expired on June 30, 1973, and one Republican's term
expired on June 30, 1974.

The powers of the FCC were far-reaching, as the President and Congress relied heavily on the Commission for advice on communications
matters. The FCC allocated broadcasting spectrum frequencies to different types of civilian broadcast services, reviewed radio and TV station
licenses every three years, and regulated telephone, telegraph, and civil
defense communications. With regard to broadcasting stations, the FCC
did not regulate advertising rates, profits, or accounting procedures.
However, it did scrutinize editorializing and political broadcasting to
insure fairness in the presentation of controversial issues. In addition,
the Commission worked in conjunction with other regulatory agencies
such as the Federal Trade Commission and Food and Drug Administration to prevent false or misleading advertising from appearing over the
air.

### Renewing licenses

Until the late sixties, few stations encountered problems in renewing
their broadcasting licenses every three years. However, beginning with
a pact between black groups in Texarkana, Texas, and KTAL-TV in
June 1969, citizens' groups had been bargaining for minority group programming in return for withdrawing (not filing) petitions with the FCC

to deny a station's renewal license. Many of these attempts had been successful in getting station owners to present more programming relevant to minority groups and to hire black and Spanish-surnamed Americans.

The FCC had recently proposed that all commercial TV stations be required to file detailed annual reports on their programming. In addition, the same proposal would require stations to make announcements at specified intervals throughout their license period, inviting comments on their service to the community. The president of the NAB complained that "these proposals, if adopted, would produce a jumpy, responsive, subservient broadcasting system . . . stations will become the sounding boards for a cacophony of narrow interests."[13]

## Major FCC issues and rulings

*Multiple ownership of media.* In March 1970, the FCC proposed a rule prohibiting commonly owned broadcasting stations (radio and TV) and newspapers from operating in the same market (as defined by the Commission). In addition, the Commission set a limit on the number of stations a single owner could control of seven AM, seven FM, and seven TV stations.[14] Present licensees were given five years to reduce their holdings.[15] In February 1971, the rule was relaxed somewhat to allow AM/FM combinations and to permit joint ownership of radio and UHF–TV stations in the same city. In June 1971, the Commission was reviewing the comments received on the ruling prior to issuing a final statement.

*The "fairness doctrine."* In 1967 the FCC enunciated its famous fairness doctrine: "Licensees must give adequate coverage to public issues . . . and coverage must be fair in that it accurately reflects the opposing views."

In 1970 the fairness doctrine was strengthened by a ruling that "licensees must *actively seek* individuals whose opinions differ from those of the station management."

*Public complaints.* Private interest groups had petitioned the FCC with increasing frequency to enact rules with regard to advertising and public affairs coverage. In 1970 the Commission received petitions from Action for Children's Television (ACT) and Termination of Unfair Broadcasting Excess (TUBE). The ACT group proposed (1) no com-

---

[13] *Broadcasting*, April 5, 1971, p. 55. Statement by Vincent T. Wasilewski.

[14] Of the seven TV stations, no more than five of them could be VHF stations.

[15] *Broadcasting* (April 5, 1971, p. 48) noted 600 broadcast combinations of TV and radio stations in the same market areas. The article also mentioned that 14% of all TV stations were controlled by individuals or companies which also owned a newspaper.

mercials on children's programs and (2) a requirement that each TV station provide daily programming for children (14 hours per week minimum) during specified hours. TUBE asked the Commission to adopt more stringent rules to prevent deceptive advertising. Although the FCC had not made judgments involving these petitions by June 1971, public hearings had been scheduled for September 1971 to determine the real effects of ads directed at children.

## BROADCASTING AND OTHER PUBLIC AGENCIES

### Congress

Congressional action was necessary to effect regulation of rates and the admissibility of advertising subject matter. Two recent examples of Congressional action were the 1970 ban on cigarette advertising and a 1968 law requiring radio and TV stations to sell time to all candidates for federal, state, and local offices at the lowest rate charged to commercial advertisers with long-term contracts.

### Federal Trade Commission

The FTC worked in conjunction with the FCC to identify "false, misleading, and deceptive advertising." Commercials for headache remedies, gasoline additives, and automobiles were among the products which had been questioned by the FTC in recent years. For instance, in 1970, the FTC charged that Standard Oil (Chevron) had misrepresented its product by claiming that its gasoline "reduced air pollution." Chevron was forced to devote 25% of its print advertising (for a specified period of time) to a publication of FTC findings. In a similar vein, the manufacturer of Wonder Bread was told to prove that its product "helps build strong bodies 12 ways" or submit to the 25% "corrective" penalty.

### Justice Department and federal courts

In 1971 the Justice Department's antitrust division ordered CBS to divest itself of a CATV subsidiary, Viacom International. The federal court system provided appellate review of FCC decisions. For example, in June 1969, a U.S. Court of Appeals overturned an FCC decision to renew the license of a Jackson, Mississippi, television station. The court ruled that the station had not served the needs, tastes, and interests of the substantial black population in its area and that, in programming on the racial issue, it had presented only a segregationist viewpoint.

## CRITICISM OF THE NETWORKS

### Comments by Vice President Agnew

On several occasions, Vice President Spiro Agnew had lashed out at news media for what he termed "irresponsibility." In a speech delivered in Des Moines, Iowa, on November 18, 1969, the Vice President said:

. . . According to Harris polls and other studies . . . for millions of Americans the [TV] networks are the sole source of national and world news. . . . Now how is this network news determined? A small group of men . . . settle upon the 20 minutes or so of film and commentary that's to reach the public. This selection is made from the 90 to 120 minutes that may be available. Their powers of choice are wide. They decide what 40 million Americans will learn of the day's events in the nation and in the world. . . . These men can create national issues overnight.

. . . We do know that to a man these commentators and producers live and work in the geographical and intellectual confines of Washington, D.C. or New York. . . . We can deduce that these men read the same newspapers. They draw their political and social views from the same sources. Worse, they talk constantly to one another, thereby providing artificial reinforcement to their shared viewpoints.

. . . Is it not fair and relevant to question the concentration [of power] in the hands of a tiny, enclosed fraternity of privileged men elected by no one and enjoying a monopoly sanctioned and licensed by the government? The views of the majority of this fraternity do not—and I repeat, *not*—represent the views of America.[16]

Dr. Frank Stanton, President of CBS, reflected the sentiments of the networks toward the charges levied by Mr. Agnew:

. . . The public, according to opinion polls, has indicated again and again that it has more confidence in the credibility of television news than in that of any other medium. Our newsmen have many times earned commendations for their enterprise and for their adherence to the highest professional standards. Since human beings are not infallible, there are bound to be occasions when their judgment is questioned.

Whatever their deficiencies, they are minor compared to those of a press which would be subservient to the executive power of government.

### "The Selling of the Pentagon"

Immediately following the broadcast of the CBS documentary "The Selling of the Pentagon" in April 1971, the question of broadcaster responsibility and "truthfulness" was aired in the public forum through

---

[16] *New York Times*, November 24, 1969.

a heated exchange of views between the news media, on one hand, and disgruntled congressmen, senators, and Defense Department officials on the other. The latter questioned both the factual accuracy and editorial tone of the documentary. CBS, while refusing to release all of the film used to produce the documentary, claimed that it had acted in the public interest by directing viewers' attention to an important aspect of national defense policy.

As it had done during the Agnew controversy, the FCC elected not to intervene, expressing its collective opinion as follows:

It would be unwise and probably impossible for the Commission to lay down some precise line of factual accuracy—dependent always on journalistic judgment—across which broadcasters must not stray. Any attempt to do so would be inconsistent with the national commitment to wide-open debate of public issues and would involve the FCC deeply and improperly in the journalistic functions of broadcasters.

# Arkana Broadcasting Company*

In June 1971, Mr. James E. Pickett, president of Arkana Broadcasting Company, headquartered in Nashville, Tennessee, was evaluating the prospects for his company. Although Arkana had grown steadily since its founding in 1964, several events had increased the uncertainties associated with the broadcasting business.

First, the Federal Communications Commission had proposed a ruling that would have the effect of prohibiting multimedia ownership in the same market of VHF television stations and radio stations or newspapers. Comments on the ruling had been solicited and received by the FCC; should it be put into effect, five years would be granted for compliance. Arkana owned AM/FM radio as well as VHF television stations in both Nashville, Tennessee, and Greensboro, North Carolina. In addition, the organization that owned Arkana also controlled the largest newspaper in Nashville.

Second, the previous two years had been characterized by a lively debate among public interest groups, broadcasters, and government officials over the nature of the public interest to be served by the media, in particular television. Recently, the controversy over the CBS documentary, "The Selling of the Pentagon," followed by the *New York Times*' disclosure of secret government documents on the Vietnam war, had sharpened the focus of the public on the role of news media in the United States. When WLRA–TV sought to renew its license in 1970,

---

* Names, locations, and certain financial information have been disguised.

Arkana had been subjected to criticism from a Nashville resident who filed a complaint with the FCC alleging that the station had failed to program for the entire community and had presented programming favoring its own viewpoint. After considering the matter for several months, the FCC renewed the license.

Third, CATV (community antenna television) had grown rapidly in the past decade and had steadily increased its penetration into Arkana's markets. Mr. Pickett believed that CATV posed a major competitive threat to free "over-the-air" television stations by fragmenting audiences and thereby endangering advertising revenues. Coupled with increasing costs of TV programming, it posed a potential threat to Arkana's profits.

It was in this context that Mr. Pickett had decided to review Arkana's situation in relation to the complex factors which affected operations and future plans. Although a large part of the company's profits were derived from its two TV stations, Mr. Pickett had negotiated the acquisition of several FM radio stations in recent years, including one in Chicago, and was convinced that as the number of radios in use with FM receiving capability increased, the profits and value of these stations would increase as well. He was uncertain, however, whether to seek expansion in radio or television or, in the event Arkana was required to divest one or the other in its major markets, which one to retain.

## HISTORY

Arkana Broadcasting was incorporated in 1964 as a subsidiary of the Arkana Investment Company (AIC), which in turn was owned by five long-time friends and associates, several of whom had worked together in state and local political and civic affairs. Through another corporation, AIC operated the *Nashville Post,* the largest paper in the city in terms of circulation and advertising revenues. Revenues were comparable to those for WLRA, although profits were lower. The newspaper, however, had been the initial investment of AIC and several of the directors had helped to build it in earlier years. When AIC had been formed its initial purpose was to serve and invest in the Nashville community. This remained an important consideration for individual board members, although activities by 1971 extended beyond the confines of Nashville.

Mr. Pickett, 56, a native of Nashville, had been a career officer in the U.S. Army Signal Corps and had attained the rank of Colonel. He had retired in 1962 to join the National Association of Broadcasters in Washington, D.C., remaining there until 1964 when he was recruited to serve as president of the newly formed Arkana Broadcasting Company. Mr. Pickett had been the architect of Arkana's expansion program. He had made recommendations to Arkana's board of directors and had personally taken the lead in consummating subsequent acquisitions and in selecting management for the acquired stations.

Arkana Broadcasting had been formed with the primary objective of becoming an effective instrument for service in communities where its facilities would be located, as well as for returning a reasonable profit. The company immediately assumed ownership of WLRA AM/FM/TV in Nashville, stations long operated by AIC, and subsequently acquired several broadcast facilities, most of them in southeastern cities. In 1971 the company owned two VHF television, three AM radio, and six FM radio stations. Financial data on Arkana are contained in Exhibits 1, 2, and 3.

## ARKANA MANAGEMENT AND BOARD OF DIRECTORS

Working with Mr. Pickett at Arkana's headquarters were two staff vice presidents (finance and special affairs), a corporate secretary, and an assistant to the president. The Nashville and Greensboro AM/FM/TV stations were each headed by a vice president and general manager. All other units had general managers. The nine-man board of directors consisted of Mr. Pickett, four vice presidents, the corporate secretary, and three members of the AIC board. The latter three men, none of whom had operating experience in the broadcasting industry, also served on the board of directors of Arkana Investment Corporation. Information on the officers and directors of Arkana Broadcasting is presented in Exhibit 4. An organization chart is contained in Exhibit 5.[1]

Mr. Pickett reviewed some of the major decisions he had made in acquiring new stations:

When I was given the opportunity of managing and developing Arkana, I looked for big-city stations where we could reach the greatest number of people. In the past seven years, we have acquired at least one metropolitan radio or TV station in each of six states. Basically, the stations have been turn-around situations which could be bought for cash. My policy has been to build up a first-rate reputation in each of our areas.

In 1968 we decided to buy an FM radio station in Chicago, even though it was run-down and had little audience. However, the station had great potential and is now a leading good music station in the city. Some of our directors felt we should run very conservative programs and take strong positions on national issues, as they had done at times with the newspaper. I had to convince them that under the Communications Act and FCC regulations we had to serve the whole community and furnish fair and objective programming.

---

[1] In keeping with the objective of community service, each station had a board of directors comprised of prominent local figures. These directors are not listed in Exhibit 5.

**EXHIBIT 1**

## ARKANA BROADCASTING COMPANY
### Income Statement for Year Ended December 31, 1970
(thousands of dollars)

| | Television | | Radio | | | | | | Total |
| | Nashville | Greens-boro | Nashville (AM/FM) | Tulsa (AM/FM) | Greens-boro (AM/FM) | Houston (FM) | Chicago (FM) | Monroe, La. (FM) | Total Arkana |
|---|---|---|---|---|---|---|---|---|---|
| Sales | | | | | | | | | |
| Network payments | $ 665 | $ 630 | $ 25 | $ 8 | $ 11 | $ 0 | $ 0 | $ 0 | $ 1,339 |
| National spot revenues | 1,432 | 1,320 | 400 | 290 | 289 | 98 | 508 | 24 | 4,361 |
| Local advertisers | 1,390 | 1,290 | 425 | 328 | 510 | 188 | 901 | 140 | 5,172 |
| Total sales | $3,487 | $3,240 | $850 | $626 | $810 | $286 | $1,409 | $164 | $10,872 |
| Expenses | | | | | | | | | |
| Technical | $ 198 | $ 201 | $ 84 | $ 64 | $ 98 | $ 55 | $ 106 | $ 50 | $ 856 |
| Program | 1,232 | 1,148 | 276 | 186 | 225 | 107 | 391 | 62 | 3,627 |
| Selling | 425 | 340 | 151 | 88 | 162 | 70 | 200 | 38 | 1,474 |
| General and administrative | 955 | 851 | 279 | 172 | 211 | 150 | 348 | 68 | 3,034 |
| Total expenses | $2,810 | $2,540 | $790 | $510 | $696 | $382 | $1,045 | $218 | $ 8,991 |
| Profit before taxes | $ 677 | $ 700 | $ 60 | $116 | $114 | $ (96) | $ 364 | $ (54) | $ 1,881 |

Source: Company records.

EXHIBIT 2

## ARKANA BROADCASTING COMPANY
### Summary Financial Data 1967–70
(in thousands of dollars)

| | Television | | Radio | | | | | | Total |
|---|---|---|---|---|---|---|---|---|---|
| | Nashville | Greens-boro | Nashville (AM/FM) | Greens-boro (AM/FM) | Tulsa (AM/FM) | Houston (FM) | Chicago (FM) | Monroe, La. (FM) | |
| **Revenues** | | | | | | | | | |
| 1967 | $3,081 | $2,562 | $793 | $606 | $447 | ... | ... | ... | $ 7,489 |
| 1968 | 3,356 | 3,095 | 841 | 687 | 520 | $222 | $1,016 | ... | 9,737 |
| 1969 | 3,489 | 3,121 | 834 | 763 | 540 | 245 | 1,321 | $137 | 10,450 |
| 1970 | 3,487 | 3,240 | 850 | 810 | 626 | 286 | 1,409 | 164 | 10,872 |
| **Pretax profit** | | | | | | | | | |
| 1967 | 960 | 503 | 55 | 49 | 23 | ... | ... | ... | 1,590 |
| 1968 | 1,022 | 647 | 73 | 61 | 63 | (127) | 249 | ... | 1,988 |
| 1969 | 916 | 778 | 62 | 86 | 51 | (117) | 369 | (67) | 2,078 |
| 1970 | 677 | 700 | 60 | 114 | 116 | (96) | 364 | (54) | 1,881 |
| Year acquired | 1964 | 1967 | 1964 | 1967 | 1965 | 1968 | 1968 | 1969 | |

Note: Figures restated to include the full year's results in the year of acquisition.
Source: Company records.

**EXHIBIT 3**

## ARKANA BROADCASTING COMPANY
### Consolidated Balance Sheet, December 31, 1969 and 1970

### Assets

| | 1969 | 1970 |
|---|---|---|
| Current assets | | |
| Cash and cash items | $ 1,647,380 | $ 1,064,163 |
| Marketable securities—at cost | 278,890 | 147,397 |
| Trade accounts receivable | $ 1,878,810 | $ 2,701,784 |
| Accounts receivable—other | 629,888 | 496,479 |
| Total accounts receivable | $ 2,508,698 | $ 3,198,263 |
| Note receivable | | $ 64,770 |
| Broadcasting films—current portion | $ 707,000 | 717,000 |
| Prepaid expenses (TV tubes, insurance, travel, etc.) | $ 129,806 | $ 117,157 |
| Total current assets | $ 5,271,774 | $ 5,308,750 |
| Real estate contract receivable (interest at 7¼% due monthly; principal balance due on or before May 21, 1973) | $ 320,636 | $ 100,100 |
| Investments—at cost | | $ 295,698 |
| Property—land, buildings, equipment, leasehold improvements, etc.—at cost (less accumulated depreciation and amortization) | $ 7,345,232 | $ 8,572,457 |
| Other assets | | |
| Network contract—at cost | $ 4,535,329 | $ 4,535,329 |
| Licenses—at cost | 1,968,919 | 1,968,919 |
| Other intangibles—at cost less amortization | 1,414,586 | 1,412,142 |
| Broadcasting films—less current portion | 1,258,703 | 714,378 |
| Excess of cost over net equity in consolidated subsidiaries | 394,742 | 418,363 |
| Other | 88,313 | 111,895 |
| Total other assets | $ 9,660,592 | $ 9,161,026 |
| Total assets | $22,598,234 | $23,438,031 |

### Liabilities

| | 1969 | 1970 |
|---|---|---|
| Current liabilities | | |
| Notes payable to banks—current portion | $ 359,370 | $ 240,000 |
| Film contracts payable—current portion | 1,033,504 | 533,687 |
| Trade accounts payable | 433,445 | 427,813 |
| Advertising services due | 261,487 | 425,332 |
| Accrued liabilities | 479,514 | 550,610 |
| Income taxes due | | 41,000 |
| Total current liabilities | $ 2,567,320 | $ 2,218,442 |
| Long-term debt | | |
| Notes payable to bank | $ 3,500,000 | $ 4,760,000 |
| Mortgage note payable | 138,108 | |
| Film contracts payable | 403,672 | 226,171 |
| Total long-term debt | $ 4,041,780 | $ 4,986,171 |
| Minority interest in subsidiaries | $ 65,068 | $ 57,559 |
| Stockholders' equity | | |
| Common stock—no par value, authorized 500,000 shares; issued and outstanding, 350,000 shares | $11,075,168 | $11,075,168 |
| Additional paid-in capital | 4,357,043 | 4,357,043 |
| Retained earnings | 491,855 | 743,648 |
| Stockholders' equity—net | $15,924,066 | $16,175,859 |
| Total liabilities | $22,598,234 | $23,438,031 |

Source: Company records.

**EXHIBIT 4**

ARKANA BROADCASTING COMPANY
Officers and Directors
June 1971

| Name | Title | Age | Background |
|------|-------|-----|------------|
| James E. Pickett | President | 56 | See text of case |
| Samuel Caruthers | VP finance | 44 | BA degree<br>15 years with General Electric finance department<br>4 years as controller for WLRA<br>VP since 1968 |
| Larry R. Crawford | VP special affairs | 50 | BA, LLB degrees<br>10 years in CBS legal department<br>12 years as Congressional liaison for National Association of Broadcasters<br>VP since 1965 |
| Billy Ray White | VP and general manager | 48 | BA degree<br>25 years in radio and TV<br>Sales manager, then VP and general manager of WLRA AM/FM/TV, Nashville<br>VP since 1966 |
| Judd A. Shipley | VP and general manager | 47 | BA degree<br>22 years in radio and TV<br>VP and general manager of Greensboro station since 1967 |
| Cyrus Lawton | Secretary | 53 | BA, LLB degrees<br>Partner in Nashville law firm<br>Secretary and director since 1946 |
| J. Robert Simpson | Director | 74 | BA degree<br>Banker. Director, Arkana Investment Co. |
| Robert Lee Jones | Director | 72 | BA degree<br>Chairman, small manufacturing enterprise. Director, Arkana Investment Company |
| C. Jefferson Davis | Director | 70 | BA degree<br>Cotton farmer. Director, Arkana Investment Company |

Source: Company records.

Mr. Pickett himself was active in the community. He had served as president of the Rotary Club and of the Chamber of Commerce, had been on several state committees, and had assumed positions of increasing responsibility in his church. He was also a respected spokesman in the broadcasting industry.

## COMPETITIVE POSITION

Arkana management had guided the company's television stations, both CBS affiliates, to leadership positions in their markets. In Nashville,

**EXHIBIT 5**

### ARKANA BROADCASTING COMPANY
Organization Chart

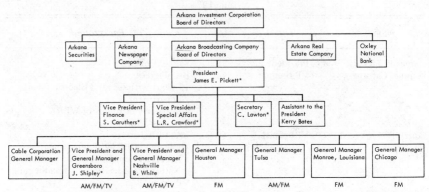

*Officer and director of Arkana Broadcasting Company.
Source: Company records.

ranked 30th nationally in the number of TV homes, Arkana had increased its share of advertising dramatically from 1964 to 1967, particularly advertising from local accounts. More recently, however, the station had lost some ground, which was attributed to several factors in the market. First, competition from the other network affiliates had stiffened in response to Arkana's aggressive community action programming and through new program formats at key hours. They were successful in narrowing the gap in daytime and nonprime-time ratings. Second, in August 1968 a UHF station went on the air. Although the signal from this new competitor reached less than 30% of the homes receiving signals from the major stations, it nonetheless siphoned off some advertising dollars and proved unsettling in the market. A VHF noncommercial education channel had also entered the market in the early 1960s and appeared to be attracting more attention as the quality of child and adult programming improved.

Finally, CATV had come to town attracted by the mountainous terrain in the area surrounding Nashville. Should the FCC permit the importation of distant signals, the effect could be a general dip in ratings for the local broadcasters. Particularly upsetting to Mr. Pickett was the difficulty he had encountered in securing permission from the FCC to build translators, essentially microwave relay towers, which would enable him to improve the clarity of his station's signal. The Commission took the position that the translators would allow Arkana to increase its broadcasting range, thereby infringing on the territory of stations in contiguous markets.

Arkana also owned the leading television station in the Greensboro-Winston-Salem-High Point area, the 49th-ranked market in terms of TV homes. The market was shared by three network affiliates and had not, at least as yet, attracted independent stations or been seriously affected by CATV. Competitive and market data are provided in Exhibits 6 and 7.

In radio Arkana was also the leader in Nashville and Greensboro in terms of advertising revenues. The same was true of the AM/FM combination in Tulsa and the FM station in Monroe, Louisiana. While the Houston station was considerably smaller than several in its 18-station market, it was nonetheless thought to be the Number 2 FM broadcaster and was making steady progress in increasing market share and reducing losses. Finally, Arkana's station was among the largest overall in the Chicago area and was the leading FM station. The Nashville, Greensboro, and Tulsa stations were affiliated with CBS; the remainder were independents.

**EXHIBIT 6**

ARKANA BROADCASTING COMPANY
Market Statistics

I. *Television competition*

| | Advertising rates* | | Circulation† | | TV† homes (000) |
|---|---|---|---|---|---|
| *Station* | *Prime-time prog./hr.* | *Daytime spot/30 sec.* | *Daily (000)* | *Weekly (000)* | |
| *Nashville*—Number of stations: 3 VHF, 1 UHF, 1 education (VHF) | | | | | |
| ABC Affil. (VHF)........ | $1,000 | $ 33 | 233 | 408 | 635 |
| NBC Affil. (VHF)........ | 1,200 | 45–90 | 325 | 477 | 680 |
| CBS Affil. (VHF)‡ ....... | 1,180 | 70–180 | 347 | 474 | 652 |
| Independent (UHF)§...... | 250 | n.a. | 5 | 21 | 186 |
| *Greensboro—Winston-Salem—High Point*—Number of stations: 3 VHF | | | | | |
| ABC Affil. (VHF)........ | $1,000 | $40 | 253 | 444 | 876 |
| NBC Affil. (VHF)........ | 1,000 | 41 | 207 | 361 | 616 |
| CBS Affil. (VHF)‡....... | 1,000 | 65 | 270 | 416 | 798 |

II. *Market characteristics*

| | TV homes (thousands) | National rank | | |
|---|---|---|---|---|
| | | *TV homes* | *Consumer spending* | *TV advertising* |
| Nashville...... | 474 | 30 | 38 | 40 |
| Greensboro..... | 327 | 49 | 52 | 50 |
| Tulsa........ | 340 | 52 | 60 | 55 |
| Houston...... | 705 | 14 | 16 | 14 |
| Chicago ...... | 2,508 | 3 | 3 | 3 |
| Monroe....... | 138 | 104 | 119 | n.a. |

**Exhibit 6** (*continued*)

III.  *Consumer buying indices* ‖

|  | Nashville | Greensboro | Tulsa | Chicago | Monroe |
|---|---|---|---|---|---|
| Beer. . . . . . . . . . . . . | 37 | 31 | 54 | 131 | n.a. |
| Coffee (instant) . . . . . . . | 97 | 128 | 67 | 74 | n.a. |
| Coffee (regular) . . . . . . . | 73 | 83 | 108 | 104 | n.a. |
| Deodorants . . . . . . . . . | 99 | 103 | 97 | 94 | n.a. |
| Dog food. . . . . . . . . . . | 120 | 123 | 142 | 75 | n.a. |
| Gas . . . . . . . . . . . . . | 106 | 114 | 105 | 95 | n.a. |
| Hair coloring . . . . . . . . | 108 | 69 | 124 | 103 | n.a. |
| Headache remedies . . . . . | 101 | 102 | 90 | 108 | n.a. |
| New cars . . . . . . . . . . | 94 | 101 | 91 | 105 | n.a. |
| Soft drinks. . . . . . . . . . | 114 | 157 | 108 | 106 | n.a. |
| Supermarkets . . . . . . . . | 85 | 88 | 87 | 109 | n.a. |
| Wash loads . . . . . . . . . . | 93 | 89 | 99 | 94 | n.a. |

\* Rate charged by the network to advertisers. The station received a share as a station payment.
† Circulation refers to the number of TV homes expected to view the station daily and weekly. TV homes reflects the number of homes reached by the station's signal.
‡ Arkana station.
§ Went on the air August 1968.
‖ Relative to national average of 100.
n.a. = not available.
Source: I and II, *TV Factbook*, 1971; III, American Research Bureau Survey, 1971.

## COMPANY POLICIES

### Programming

Arkana management felt that success in achieving strong positions in radio as in television was due to programming and marketing policies. In FM, the basic programming format was music suitable for background and for comfortable listening.

Mr. Pickett commented on the programming philosophy he encouraged at Arkana:

The first objective for Arkana is public service, to be an effective instrument for responsible action in the community. Each of our managers is required to select the 10 most pressing problems in his community—pollution, school busing, drugs, transportation, etc.—and design programs which will provide the public with various points of view on these problems. We give free air time to get the issues discussed.

We are also not afraid to say and do what we think is right. For instance, people get excited about Vietnam and LSD, but alcohol kills 28,000 on the highway each year. Thirty-five times that many are injured. In one case we succeeded in getting the highway patrol, the Med Center, and the Bar Association to conduct tests to determine if the permissible alcohol content was safe. We demonstrated that with a much lower alcohol content subjects were drunk, and we produced a film on the disaster caused by drunk driving. We succeeded in getting the legislature to pass a law tightening the criterion for drunk driving.

EXHIBIT 7

## ARKANA BROADCASTING COMPANY
### Summary Financial Data for Arkana Markets
(dollars in thousands)

| | Television | | | | Radio | | | |
|---|---|---|---|---|---|---|---|---|
| | Nashville | Greensboro | Nashville | Greensboro | Tulsa | Houston | Chicago | Monroe |
| **Revenues (total market)** | | | | | | | | |
| 1968 | $7,259 | $6,092 | $4,381 | $2,937 | $2,280 | $ 8,199 | $31,100 | $484 |
| 1969 | 8,371 | 6,571 | 4,909 | 3,608 | 2,730 | 9,702 | 36,370 | 561 |
| 1970 | 9,587 | 7,328 | 5,467 | 3,758 | 2,912 | 10,617 | 35,576 | 529 |
| **Station income (total market)** | | | | | | | | |
| 1968 | 1,813 | 1,311 | 821 | 393 | 114 | 1,961 | 6,405 | (1) |
| 1969 | 2,095 | 1,655 | 779 | 592 | 264 | 2,168 | 9,882 | 49 |
| 1970 | 1,787 | 1,790 | 917 | 594 | 279 | 2,075 | 8,882 | 63 |
| **Percent of 1970 revenues for the total market accounted for by—** | | | | | | | | |
| Network | 16% | 19% | 2% | 1% | 1% | 1% | 3% | ... |
| National/regional spot | 46 | 46 | 37 | 20 | 34 | 51 | 51 | 24% |
| Local | 38 | 35 | 61 | 79 | 65 | 48 | 46 | 76 |
| Total | 100% | 100% | 100% | 100% | 100% | 100% | 100% | 100% |
| **Arkana share of market—1970** | | | | | | | | |
| Network | 43% | 45% | 33% | 32% | 40% | 0% | 0% | 0% |
| National/regional spot | 32 | 39 | 19 | 38 | 29 | 2 | 2 | 18 |
| Local | 36 | 50 | 13 | 17 | 17 | 4 | 5 | 32 |
| Share of total market | 36% | 44% | 16% | 22% | 21% | 3% | 3% | 26% |
| Number of stations | 5 | 3 | 12 | 12 | 9 | 18 | 32 | 4 |

Source: *Statistical Trends in Broadcasting*, John Blair & Co., 1971.

In another case, one of our managers discovered that millions of dollars of state funds were lying fallow in no-interest bank accounts. We waded in with both feet, criticizing the state for not earning interest on taxpayers' money. We succeeded in persuading the state to put the money in certificates of deposit. The banks retaliated for awhile by switching their advertising to competing stations.

Mr. Pickett was particularly concerned with the development of strong managers able to deal effectively as individuals with the needs of their communities. Station managers reported that the freedom granted them to respond to community needs contributed significantly to the enthusiasm which they brought to their work and to their sense of professional pride. Mr. Kerry Bates, assistant to the president, described Mr. Pickett's management style in the following anecdote:

It's not his style to ride herd on his managers. During the November elections, he was appalled at our news coverage, and he watched other channels. Our manager got cheerleaders from the university to post election returns. The girls wore miniskirts. The station's switchboard was flooded with calls. The station manager, however, let them continue. Mr. Pickett voiced his displeasure but didn't try to discipline the manager.

The newscasters are in "show biz." They're hard to fire because they're stars. Mr. Pickett is almost too humane. He works through the "rub-off method." He wants to develop managers who are independent, and I must say he's succeeding. Those managers effectively set the policy for their stations.

Mr. Larry Crawford, vice president for special affairs, commented further on Arkana's programming:

We believe that good news coverage is a major ingredient for success in broadcasting. That's why we have more of it than most of our competitors and pay attention to what our audience says about our news coverage, right down to comments about the kind of tie the sportscaster wears! Another important thing about news is that advertisers want to identify with *strong,* public-minded stations. It's a fact that most stations which rank first in audience ratings at news time also lead the market overall.

In FM, we're selling music and news all day long. AM radio is more complex because the critical period is "drive time" [7:00 to 9:00 A.M. and 4:00 to 6:00 P.M.]. An AM station must have a good disc jockey for those two time periods. Having a good sportscaster is also a big plus for coverage of local sports which aren't televised. Since our AM stations usually concentrate on the over-25 audience, we're not as concerned with the top 20 rock-and-roll tunes. Two of our AM stations have been successful with a late evening show called "Take a Stand," which features advocates representing opposing views on a significant public issue supplemented with phone calls from the audience.

In television we carry practically all of the network programs. With TV, of course, the opportunities for impact from public affairs broadcasting is greater than with radio, and we have tried to exploit that. Our objective is to serve the whole community. We don't believe in pushing our opinions on others.

## Marketing

Mr. Caruthers, vice president of finance, described Arkana's approach to marketing:

The underpinning of our success lies in market analysis. In determining what is needed to build and hold market share, we look at our markets to determine what population segments aren't fully exploited. We utilize a university professor's research team and various rating services to give us a detailed profile of those segments and what they desire in the way of TV and radio programming. Once we think we have the "target audience" analyzed, we tailor programming and advertising to suit its needs. Most of our competitors do only a cursory job of this, which gives us a big advantage.

As shown in Exhibit 6, advertising rates for Arkana's TV stations were more or less the same as those for the other network affiliates for prime-time programs but were substantially higher for daytime spots. The company had also been successful in increasing rates in radio as audience surveys portrayed increasing market shares.

Mr. Bates commented on matters of advertising subject matter:

There is some feeling among our board members that beer and pills should not be advertised on television. However, we have said that, if we eliminated these ads, we would be charged with being "self-serving," imposing our values on the community.

Anticipating the ban on cigarette advertising, Arkana was among the first broadcasters to decline such ads—before the law cleared Congress. Several agency media buyers were reportedly upset by this, and some revenue was lost as a result. On a wider issue, Mr. Bates expressed some concern over the impact of consumerism on television advertising:

The media are going to be in trouble in 10 years because of exaggerated product claims. My seven-year-old son was watching TV the other night, and during a commercial he turned to me and said, "That isn't true, is it, Dad?" The advertisers are building cynicism among viewers. They're prostituting themselves for a buck. Pretty soon viewers won't believe any advertising message.

## Public affairs

Mr. Pickett was active in promoting the interests of local broadcasters before legislative and other groups. In particular, he sought more comprehensive regulation of CATV and greater latitude for VHF stations to construct translators.

TV should be a local medium, and CATV threatens local broadcasting with extinction because it fragments the audience. By bringing in distant signals it can make the market more oriented to the large population centers and large national events than to the local markets and occurrences in the locality. But let's face it, CATV is here to stay. Our objective is to have it put under common carrier regulations, since all it does is carry signals. This would prohibit cable operators from substituting advertising and from programming in competition with local stations.

Indirectly, the importance of local stations is being reinforced by attacks on network news coverage. Much of what Vice President Agnew has said is justified. We have a top-flight Washington correspondent. After one speech in which Mr. Agnew attacked the "news establishment," our correspondent sent me a Gallup poll of college students which showed that in every region except the Northeast better than half of those interviewed supported what Mr. Agnew had said. In the Northeast, however, 65% of the students interviewed reacted negatively to the Vice President's remark. It is our correspondent's opinion that the networks are trapped by being located in the liberal Northeast. They tend to look down on the rest of the country. Since these news executives are located in New York, for the most part, they are continually subjected to liberal philosophies.

## THE FUTURE

The course to be followed by Arkana in the future was not altogether clear to Mr. Pickett. Originally, it had appeared logical for Arkana to acquire additional broadcast properties in both radio and television up to the limit allowed by the Commission. In total, Arkana could add one radio and five television stations, no more than three of which could be VHF.[2] Moreover, it was possible to "trade up" by selling stations and buying others in larger markets. Such a course would address Mr. Pickett's second and third objectives for the company: increasing revenues and profits.

The recent FCC proposals on multimedia ownership, the turmoil in television broadcasting and the competitive threats of CATV and market fragmentation had caused Mr. Pickett to reevaluate the company's position. It was possible that a divestment of either the radio or television stations in Nashville and Greensboro would be required. Should the company keep the more profitable television franchises or keep those in radio and embark on a major development of that medium?

Mr. Pickett remained enthusiastic about the pattern of success Arkana had had in serving its communities. However, while there appeared to be no lack of commitment from the board to the broadcasting industry, it was clear that under most circumstances growth would have to be financed internally. Indeed, it was possible that Arkana Investment

---

[2] Broadcasting stations typically sold for 15 to 25 times after-tax earnings.

Corporation would look to Arkana Broadcasting as a source of funds, particularly in the event that cash generated in the business remained unused. Yet he commented:

We have demonstrated that we can take lackluster stations and make them profitable. On the other hand, our problems have never been greater. In this business, you face all the drama of an afternoon soap opera—outside interference, threats, and two-timing. We are caught up in so many problems, I don't know where to begin. Sometimes I think I shouldn't sleep at night.

# STRATEGIC ALTERNATIVES AND CORPORATE CHOICE

# *Kativo Chemical Industries, Ltd.*[*]
# *Detergents*

## COMPANY ACTIVITIES

In 1962 Kativo Chemical Industries, Ltd., with operating headquarters in San Jose, Costa Rica, manufactured and sold mainly paints. Sales in fiscal 1962 exceeded $1 million. (See Exhibits 1 and 2 for financial data.) This represented about 65%–70% of the total Costa Rican paint market. Kativo had managed to maintain this market share in spite of rigorous competition from the local affiliates of two large U.S. paint companies.

In addition to paints, Kativo also engaged in a number of smaller activities. Since 1955 Kativo had produced polyester corrugated sheets reinforced with fiberglas under the brand name Skylite for use in skylights, roofs, and similar applications. Production of these sheets was basically a hand operation. Sales of about 15,000 sheets were predicted during 1962. These sheets were distributed on an exclusive basis through the same stores which carried Kativo paints.

In 1958 the company had begun to manufacture acrylic plastic under the brand name Acrylite. This was an expensive form of plastic, but it provided an aesthetically pleasing, high-strength material for making signs. Original capacity was 10 sheets per day, but addition of a second oven expanded the rate to 20 sheets per day by 1962.

For a time Kativo also produced plastic chairs and boats, but these were not successful and were subsequently discontinued. Markets for

---

[*] Certain financial data in this case have been disguised.

448

both products were small and adequately served by cheaper products made of other materials.

In 1959, following a policy decision to begin operations in the entire Central American Common Market (even though Costa Rica had not yet joined), Kativo commenced exporting paint to Nicaragua. A combination of high duties and stiff competition from other brands encouraged Kativo, with local Nicaraguan partners,[1] to form a company, Kativo

**EXHIBIT 1**

### KATIVO CHEMICAL INDUSTRIES, LTD.
Consolidated Balance Sheet as of September 30, 1962
(in thousands of U.S. dollars)

*Assets*

| | |
|---|---:|
| Current assets | |
| Cash | $ 113 |
| Marketable securities | 31 |
| Receivables | |
| Notes receivable | . . . |
| Accounts receivable–trade | 216 |
| Accounts receivable–nonconsolidated affiliated companies | 44 |
| Accounts receivable–other | 52 |
| Less: Allowance for doubtful receivables | (7) |
| Net receivables | $ 305 |
| Inventories | |
| Finished products | $ 219 |
| Work in process | 8 |
| Raw materials | 391 |
| Raw materials in transit | 64 |
| Total inventories | $ 682 |
| Prepaid expenses | 18 |
| Total current assets | $1,149 |
| Long-term notes receivable | |
| Nonconsolidated affiliated companies | . . . |
| Other | . . . |
| Investments in nonconsolidated affiliated companies* | 231 |
| Property, plant, and equipment | |
| Construction in process | $ 214 |
| Land | 62 |
| Buildings | 85 |
| Machinery, equipment, furniture | 318 |
| Total property, plant, and equipment | $ 679 |
| Less: Allowance for depreciation | (81) |
| Net property, plant, and equipment | $ 598 |
| Research and development expenses | 126 |
| Other assets and deferred charges | 56 |
| Total assets | $2,160 |

---

[1] Kativo's Nicaraguan partners were two young and aggressive brothers, Laonides and Fabio Abaunza. Prior to joining forces with Kativo, the Abaunza family had for four years owned and operated a Nicaraguan importing and distributing company which sold a wide line of products, including electronic equipment, movie films, and paper products.

**EXHIBIT 1** (*continued*)

*Liabilities*

Current liabilities
  Notes and drafts payable
    Banks ........................................ $    42
    Trade. ....................................... 100
    Other ........................................ . . .
  Accounts payable
    Trade. ....................................... 67
    Other ........................................ 52
    Estimated Costa Rican income taxes. ................. 19

        Total current liabilities ........................ $  280
Advances from customers ............................. 28

Long-term debt
  Notes payable
    Banks ........................................ $     9
    Other. ....................................... 47
    12% bonds payable in 10 equal annual installments beginning
      April 1, 1965 ............................... 200
    12% bonds payable in 10 equal annual installments beginning
      July 1, 1965 ............................... 19
    9% convertible notes payable January 16, 1966 ............ 663

        Total long-term debt. ........................ $  938

Stockholders' equity
  Common stock at par value ......................... $  752
  Capital paid in excess of par value of shares issued ........... 56
  Retained earnings
    Appropriated for legal reserve ..................... 14
    Unappropriated. ............................. 92

        Total stockholders' equity ..................... $  914

        Total liabilities and net worth .................. $2,160

\* Kativo de Nicaragua S.A., Kativo de Panama S.A.
Source: Company records.

de Nicaragua S.A., and to build a paint plant shortly after entering the Nicaraguan market. The plant had a capacity of 180,000 gallons per year (one-shift production). In its first year of operation, sales were raised from a level of $16,000 to $200,000. This success was credited mainly to the effort and ability of Laonides Abaunza, part owner and general manager of Kativo's Nicaragua operations.

In 1962 Kativo found an excellent manager in Panama who became Kativo's partner in a joint venture set up for the production of plastic sheets. The presence of good management encouraged the company to commence paint production. Kativo was fortunate to buy a plant from a U.S. company that wished to liquidate its investment in Panama. Within nine months, sales of paint were raised from $15,000 to $40,000 per month. At the same time the labor force was reduced from 20 people to 10.

During the same year the company realized that its purchasing was inefficient, since each plant was obtaining raw materials separately in small lots. To increase the efficiency of purchasing, a company was

**EXHIBIT 2**

KATIVO CHEMICAL INDUSTRIES, LTD.
Statement of Consolidated Earnings* for Year Ended September 30, 1962
(in thousands of U.S. dollars)

| | | |
|---|---:|---:|
| Net sales . . . . . . . . . . . . . . . . . . . . . . . . . . . . . . . . . . | $1,215 | 100.0% |
| Cost of goods sold . . . . . . . . . . . . . . . . . . . . . . . . . . . | 659 | 54.2 |
| Gross profit . . . . . . . . . . . . . . . . . . . . . . . . . . . . . . . | $ 556 | 45.8% |
| Selling, administrative, and general expenses | | |
| Selling . . . . . . . . . . . . . . . . . . . . . . . . . . . . . . . . . | $ 190 | 15.6% |
| Administrative and general . . . . . . . . . . . . . . . . . . . . . | 105 | 8.6 |
| Interest. . . . . . . . . . . . . . . . . . . . . . . . . . . . . . . . | 96 | 7.9 |
| Research and development . . . . . . . . . . . . . . . . . . . . | 188 | 15.5 |
| Bad debt . . . . . . . . . . . . . . . . . . . . . . . . . . . . . . . | 13 | 1.1 |
| Discount on Costa Rican government bonds . . . . . . . . . . . . | 19 | 1.6 |
| Total selling, administrative, and general expenses . . . . . . . | $ 611 | 50.3% |
| Operating loss. . . . . . . . . . . . . . . . . . . . . . . . . . . | (55) | (4.5) |
| Other income | | |
| From nonconsolidated affiliated companies | | |
| Royalties . . . . . . . . . . . . . . . . . . . . . . . . . . . . . . . | $ 41 | 3.4% |
| Dividends . . . . . . . . . . . . . . . . . . . . . . . . . . . . . . . | . . . | . . . |
| Interest . . . . . . . . . . . . . . . . . . . . . . . . . . . . . . . . | 16 | 1.3 |
| Rebates of duties on raw materials imported . . . . . . . . . . . | 14 | 1.1 |
| Miscellaneous . . . . . . . . . . . . . . . . . . . . . . . . . . . . . | 8 | 0.7 |
| Total other income. . . . . . . . . . . . . . . . . . . . . . . | $ 79 | 6.5% |
| Earnings before Costa Rican income taxes . . . . . . . . . . . . | $ 24 | 2.0% |
| Estimated Costa Rican income taxes . . . . . . . . . . . . . . . . . | 5 | 0.4 |
| Net earnings . . . . . . . . . . . . . . . . . . . . . . . . . . . . . . . | $ 19 | 1.6% |

*This income statement includes only the operations of Kativo Chemical Industries, Ltd.
and its *wholly owned* subsidiaries. The operations of *partly owned* subsidiaries were not
consolidated into the income statement of the parent company.
Source: Company records.

set up in the Colon Free Zone of Panama to act as a central purchasing
and warehousing service. The ability to purchase in larger lots was
expected to supply a strong bargaining position from which Kativo could
negotiate better prices and other credit terms on raw material purchases.

Also in 1962 Kativo established a marketing company, Kativo of Honduras S.A., as a joint venture with local Honduran interests to sell paints
to be supplied from the Nicaraguan plant because high duties kept
Costa Rican products out. However, lack of good management held
sales well below the initial quota of 70,000 kilos per year.

## MANAGEMENT PHILOSOPHY

Both Dr. Frank Jirik,[2] president, and Sr. Walter Kissling,[3] executive
vice president, were concerned with the social and ethical impact of

[2] Dr. Frank Jirik, who had founded Kativo in 1949, was a Ph.D. in chemistry
from the University of Kansas who had emigrated from the United States.

[3] Sr. Walter Kissling, a Costa Rican of European parentage, previously worked
in Central America for a U.S. drug firm and had joined Kativo in 1956.

Kativo's decisions in Central America. Both men felt that the company was an integral part of each country in which it operated and was responsible both to its own employees and to its customers for operating as a dependable and farsighted economic force.

In their personal approaches to the business, however, each man differed substantially from the other. Dr. Jirik was regarded by many who knew him as a combination of research scientist and entrepreneur. He obtained his satisfactions as much from the pleasure of doing research as from the act of doing business. In fact, once the initial challenge of setting up a new enterprise had worn off, he found the day-to-day operation of a going concern to be rather tedious. He realized, however, that profitable, well-managed, going concerns were absolutely essential in order to have sufficient financial resources to support the creative research in which he was interested.

Dr. Jirik dreamed of a Kativo that would operate worldwide in the developing countries, based on a sound, technical research staff. He was of the opinion that simplified technologies would be the foundation of Kativo's growth. He did not consider that lack of knowledge of a market was a barrier to entry. He felt that in entering a new industry it was not enough to buy a ready-made plant and then push a switch to make it work. He believed in learning enough to do the job alone, or not going into it. Thus, Kativo designed and built its own plants, which was a source of great pleasure to Dr. Jirik.

Sr. Kissling started in marketing but proved himself an able administrator and rose quickly to his present position. In recent years, Sr. Kissling had been involved more deeply than Dr. Jirik in the daily operating decisions of the business. His special sphere of influence had tended to be in the areas of marketing, legal matters, and accounting. Dr. Jirik, on the other hand, continued to maintain control over production. Unlike Dr. Jirik, Sr. Kissling believed that knowledge should be bought when it was already available. Thus, Sr. Kissling had in certain instances supported the idea of manufacturing agreements with foreign companies. He had also argued that Kativo did not have the research staff or the funds to develop all the products it needed to make full use of its distribution network. Thus, he foresaw joint ventures with large American concerns to supply the products missing from Kativo's line.

In spite of the shortage of administrative, sales, and technical people, they felt that Kativo differed favorably from many other Central American firms through its use of professional administrators in key positions. They considered that a basic problem in Central America was the fact that many businesses, being family held, had not recognized that the economic changes taking place in recent years put a premium on professional administration as a determinant of continued progress. Thus Kativo devoted much time and effort in training potential administrative people in the techniques of modern management and in company procedures. The company also attempted to overcome a shortage of skilled mechanics by in-company training, particularly since the manufacturing processes required mostly workers with medium and high skill levels. Furthermore, Kativo's labor policies included higher than average wages and a special savings plan. This plan, under which a 5% salary contribution by the worker was matched threefold by the company, was run by a board of directors elected by the employees with Dr. Jirik serving as president. Workers were entitled immediately to their own and one third of the company contribution, and after 15 years to the entire sum. Kativo management felt that these labor policies had helped in keeping turnover of personnel low.

## THE DETERGENT DIVERSIFICATION

In late 1959 Kativo executives had begun to consider the possibility of a major diversification. Even though paint sales were developing nicely, management felt that they would begin to level off in the next few years and that in order to continue to grow Kativo would have to consider new product areas. It was decided to seek out industries which met the following criteria:

1. A *basic* industry.
2. An industry with high growth potential.
3. An industry in which Kativo's chemical technology and experience would be applicable.
4. An industry with high import duties in which little or no local manufacture existed as yet and to which the government would be willing to offer investment incentives and protection during the early stages.

Synthetic detergents seemed to meet these criteria perfectly. They filled a basic type of need: laundry washing. They offered considerable growth potential: although imported detergents had already gained a foothold in Central America, there was still a large segment of the population which either had not yet begun to use them or else used them only on a limited basis. Their manufacture involved a type of chemical technology which was quite similar to that required for the manufacture of paints. Finally, there were as of 1959 no detergent plants in Costa Rica (and only one in all of Central America, located in Guatemala), and duties on imported detergents were relatively high. In Costa Rica, for example, the duty was $.30/kg. plus 25% ad valorem. Since the CIF price of detergents was roughly $.40/kg., this meant that the total tariff ($.30 + $.10 ad valorem = $.40) amounted to 100% of imported value. Moreover, preliminary soundings indicated that if a company were willing to establish local manufacture, there was a good possibility that the Costa Rican government would, on the one hand, raise import duties still higher and, on the other, offer the local company significant investment incentives, including complete tax exemption for 10 years and duty-free imports of raw materials, machinery, and construction materials, also for 10 years.

### The development of the local detergent industry

Until the 1950s, Central Americans washed their clothes almost exclusively with hard brown laundry soap which was sold in the form of either bars or balls. This hard soap was essentially a commodity item. In most cases it came in unwrapped, unbranded form, though in some instances the manufacturer would stamp his name on the bar itself. In each of the five Central American countries there were typically two or three companies producing these hard laundry soaps. Though actual statistics were not available, it was estimated that total hard-soap consumption for the five Central American countries during the early 1950s was in the neighborhood of 50 million kilos/year, or $10 million at wholesale prices. This consumption figure, however, represented not only the hard soap used for laundry purposes but also that used for all other purposes, including dishwashing and bathing.

In the middle 1950s, imported synthetic detergent powder[4] began to dribble into the various Central American countries for the first time. For the most part, these imports came from the United States and represented the brands of two large American firms: Colgate-Palmolive (Fab) and Procter & Gamble (Ace[5] and Tide). At first these imports were insignificant. Within a very short time, however, imports began to increase rapidly in all five countries.

In exporting detergents to Central America, Colgate-Palmolive and Procter & Gamble used different approaches. Colgate worked through as many as 20 small importer distributors in each market who, in turn, sold the Colgate line along with other brands of products to many hundreds of tiny grocery and drug retailers. To oversee its activities in Central America, Colgate had a full-time sales manager who was located in El Salvador but who reported to Colgate-Palmolive International in New York. This man had working for him one or two "missionary"

---

[4] "Synthetic detergent" is a term applied rather loosely to water soluble, surface substances with pronounced ability to wash and clean but differing from the true soaps in their chemical composition and in the important respect of not forming a scum in hard water.

[5] Ace was a brand name which P&G had used in other Latin American countries but not in the United States. It was, however, derived from the company's U.S. brand Duz. The word "does" in Spanish is "hace" (pronounced ah-say)—hence the decision was made to use Ace (which was also pronounced ah-say).

salesmen in each Central American country. Part of the time these sales-men traveled with the wholesaler's salesmen and part of the time they operated on their own, buying Colgate merchandise from various whole-salers and reselling it to retailers.

Procter & Gamble, on the other hand, handled its Central American sales through its Cuban subsidiary. The management of the Cuban com-pany worked with one exclusive importer wholesaler in each Central American country. These exclusive agents imported Procter & Gamble products and resold them to retailers. Periodically, the Cuban company would send representatives to solicit orders from the exclusive importer wholesalers, work with their salesmen, and arrange promotions.

Though at first no attempt was made to compile specific market-share figures, Procter & Gamble's sales of imported detergent in Central America were reportedly slightly higher than Colgate's during the early years. Toward the end of the 1950s, however, Colgate began to edge ahead of Procter & Gamble so that by 1960 its brand, Fab, held the leading position in most of the local markets. At that time Colgate estab-lished local marketing companies in each of the Central American coun-tries. The primary task of these companies was to take over the selling and marketing functions which had previously been performed by im-porter distributors. Each company typically consisted of a general man-ager, a six-man sales force, and a small administrative staff.

Meanwhile, the success of the imported detergents began to attract the attention of a few local Central American businessmen. Among them was a Sr. Rios, a Guatemalan with two grown sons, one of whom had studied chemical engineering in the United States. Having seen how important laundry detergents had become in the United States and feel-ing that there was a significant long-run potential for detergents in Guatemala, Sr. Rios and his sons decided to set up a detergent plant to serve the local Guatemalan market. Consequently, with an investment of approximately $200,000, they established a company named Industria Quimica and built Central America's first local detergent factory. The plant, which opened in 1956, had an annual one-shift capacity of about 1,200,000 kilos. The new detergent was called Superdet and was intro-duced on the Guatemalan market at a retail price approximately 5% lower than that of the leading imported brands. In spite of initial resis-tance on the part of the Guatemalan consumers to the idea of a locally manufactured detergent, Superdet soon captured 30%–35% of the local market, a share which it held for several years. Industria Quimica also acted as contract supplier for Procter & Gamble. In 1961 another local company, Kong Hermanos, was started in Guatemala, also with an an-nual capacity of 1.2 million kilos. It sold its own brand, Terso, and in addition was the contract supplier for Colgate-Palmolive for all Cen-tral American countries except Costa Rica.

## THE NATURE OF THE MARKET FOR DETERGENTS IN CENTRAL AMERICA

Laundry washing practices and detergent consumption patterns tended to vary in Central America as a function of socioeconomic class and location of household (urban or rural). Country-to-country variations were also discernible.

Generally speaking, poor families (especially those living in rural areas) washed their laundry at public wells or in nearby streams; middle-class families did their washing at home in sinks with scrub boards and cold water; and upper-class families had their laundry done by domestic help using hot water and, in some cases, electric washing machines.

As was mentioned earlier, the traditional cleaning agent used for clothes washing throughout Central America was hard soap in the form of bars or balls. By 1962, however, hard soap had already begun to be widely replaced or supplemented by powder detergents, particularly in urban areas. For example, it was reported that the percentage of urban families using detergents varied as follows:

| | |
|---|---|
| Guatemala | 74% |
| El Salvador | 89 |
| Honduras | 90 |
| Nicaragua | 62 |
| Costa Rica | 79 |

While no similar studies had been made for rural families, industry executives generally believed that the use of detergents dropped off sharply outside the cities due to poor distribution facilities and the fact that a large percentage of the "campesinos" (country dwellers) lived outside the money economy.

Another fact which industry executives felt was significant was that many housewives who had begun to use detergent did so mainly to supplement, rather than replace, hard soaps. These housewives would employ detergents to loosen particularly difficult dirt (e.g., that found on shirt collars and cuffs or on work clothes), but would then scrub the rest of the garment with regular hard soap. It was felt that this practice was particularly widespread among the middle- and low-income classes, regardless of country.

### Channels of distribution

At the retail level detergents were sold mainly through food stores, though in some cases they could also be found in other types of outlets such as pharmacies, department stores, and hardware stores. In the early

1960s the estimated number of food stores in each of the Central American countries was:

| | Number of stores | Number of households | Households per store |
|---|---|---|---|
| Guatemala | 7,000 | 764,000 | 109 |
| El Salvador | 3,600 | 502,000 | 139 |
| Honduras | 2,400 | 367,000 | 153 |
| Nicaragua | 4,000 | 258,000 | 65 |
| Costa Rica | 6,000 | 243,000 | 40 |
| Total | 23,000 | 2,134,000 | 93 |
| U.S.A. | 231,000 | 54,600,000 | 237 |

In each country, by far the greatest majority of stores were very small outlets called "pulperias" which were operated by one family and which sold a relatively narrow line of food products. Only recently had a few self-service stores and supermarkets begun to appear in Central America.

In most of the five countries detergents tended to be carried on a regular basis by about 50% of the potential food store outlets. The remaining 50% were either too small or too remote to be reached by either the detergent companies' salesmen or by wholesalers. Depending on the country, the brand, and the quantities ordered, the retailers' margins on detergents tended to vary between 15% and 20%.

To sell to the retailers, detergent importers used either a sales force of their own or an exclusive distributor in each country. These, in turn, would sell direct to the largest retailers in the country. In an effort to reach the remaining retail outlets they would also sell to some small wholesalers who provided limited coverage of the tiny pulperias. In many cases these wholesalers also operated their own retail shops.

Exclusive distributors, when they were used, usually operated on a 10%–15% margin (based on list price to final consumers). Wholesalers, on the other hand, were given a 2.5%–5% margin. Trade terms to retailers normally included a 2%–3% cash discount or 30 days' credit.

## Pricing

At the manufacturers' level all the detergent companies attempted to avoid direct price competition, feeling that once started it might lead to ruinous price wars which would be disastrous for everyone involved. Instead they preferred to rely on indirect competitive pricing tactics such as offering retailers better credit facilities, larger cash discounts, free promotional merchandise, or changing the size of the detergent containers.

## Advertising and promotion

The detergent companies were among the heaviest advertisers in Central America. Advertising and promotion budgets typically ran between 8% and 15% of net sales, with expenditures rising even higher during the introduction stage of a new detergent.

The relative emphasis placed on advertising versus promotion[6] varied from country to country. In this respect Costa Rica and El Salvador represented the extremes. In Costa Rica almost all forms of consumer promotions were prohibited by the government; consequently, emphasis lay almost entirely on media advertising. By contrast, El Salvador which had no similar restrictions was the scene of tremendous promotional activity, including everything from "self-liquidating" premium offers (the customer sends in a box top plus a nominal amount of money and receives some type of premium in return) to give-away contests and sampling campaigns.

In the remaining three countries most forms of advertising and promotion were permitted and were used extensively by the detergent companies. However, in Guatemala and Nicaragua all artwork was required by law to be done locally. Consequently, it was not possible for a company operating internationally to import finished detergent ads, pretaped radio commercials, or prefilmed TV commercials into these countries.

In planning and executing advertising and promotional campaigns, the detergent companies had to take into consideration the high level of illiteracy which existed in most Central American countries. This factor led to relatively heavy reliance on nonprint media such as radio and to the use of special channels of communication such as sound trucks.

## THE MANUFACTURING PROCESS

The manufacturing process involved in the production of powdered detergents was relatively uncomplicated from a technical point of view. In its simplest form, the process comprised the following basic steps:

1. The mixing of the "basic active ingredient" (sodium sulfonate) with several other chemical substances known as "builders and fillers" and with water to form a watery mixture called a "built slurry."
2. The spraying of the slurry under pressure through one or more

---

[6] "Advertising" refers specifically to media advertising (i.e., newspapers, magazines, radio, TV, and billboards); "promotion" refers to such activities as special price offers, giving away or selling premiums, consumer contests, sampling campaigns, combination packs, etc.

fixed nozzles into the top of a tall spray tower where the liquid particles were met by a stream of hot air which removed the moisture and caused the particles to fluff and form a dry powder by the time they fell to the bottom of the tower.

3.  The packaging of the synthetic detergent powder in cartons or envelopes, using either automatic or semiautomatic packaging machines.

The cost of a spray-tower detergent plant in Central America (including land, buildings, and equipment) tended to run from about $200,000 for a facility with annual capacity of 1,200,000 kg. to $300,000 for a facility with a capacity of 3,000,000 kg. Predesigned equipment could readily be purchased in a complete package from any one of several manufacturers in the United States or Europe. As part of the purchase arrangement, the equipment supplier usually provided an on-the-scene technician who would supervise installation and initial start-up of the plant.

Manufacturing costs were typically broken down as follows:

| | |
|---|---|
| Raw materials . . . . . . . . . . . . . . . . . | 50%–55% |
| Packaging materials . . . . . . . . . . . . . | 25  –30 |
| Direct labor . . . . . . . . . . . . . . . . . | 3  – 5 |
| Factory overheads . . . . . . . . . . . . . | 7  –15 |
| Total manufacturing costs . . . . . . . . | 100% |

The two most frequently encountered production problems in Central America were (1) obtaining a detergent powder of the proper density and (2) regulating the moisture content of the powder. The density problem was critical in that if the detergent powder were too heavy and compact relative to its volume, a greater quantity was necessary to fill the cartons up to the top. This, of course, could increase production costs. The moisture problem arose mainly during Central America's rainy season when the detergent powder tended to absorb moisture from the humid air. This sometimes caused the detergent either to cake or to ooze out of its package.

Usually it was possible to resolve these difficulties through careful control measures or through slight variations in the ingredients used.

## THE ENTRY DECISION

Having decided that synthetic detergents offered interesting possibilities, management contacted first Colgate-Palmolive and then Procter & Gamble to see if either would be interested in having Kativo act as a contract supplier for detergents in Central America. Colgate (which at the time held 75% of the Costa Rican detergent market) replied that although it respected Kativo as a paint maker, it did not feel that Kativo had sufficient know-how[7] or financial backing to be a good detergent maker. Consequently, it indicated that it was not interested and suggested that it might be wiser if Kativo reconsidered its determination to get into the detergent business. Procter & Gamble was not interested, either, mainly because at the time it was concentrating on other parts of the world.

Kativo's executives then decided that if they wanted to break into the detergent industry they would have to get into the marketing as well as the production of detergents and be willing to bring out a brand of their own. After spending a number of months studying what this would involve and evaluating their own capabilities, they decided to proceed with plans to enter the industry. The company's research team then designed and built its own detergent plant with a single-shift capacity of 3 million pounds per annum.

In November 1962, Kativo entered the Costa Rican detergent market. Dr. Jirik and Sr. Kissling had formulated the following competitive strategy:

1. During the early stages, benefit to the maximum extent possible from the protection offered to potential local manufacturers by the Costa Rican government. In particular, as the first local manufacturer, take advantage of the high duties on imported detergents and offer the consumer a locally made detergent at a significant price saving. However, be ready to stop competing on the basis of price if and when the international companies establish local manufacturing facilities.
2. In developing a suitable product, use the presently imported brands as a model. More specifically, insure that the new detergent is at least equal to the imported detergents in quality and composition.
3. Design own detergent plant rather than buying one of the pre-packaged plants available for export from the United States or Europe.
4. Concentrate initially on the Costa Rican market, but later expand into all the other Central American countries. (This policy was based on the belief that with the coming of the Central American Common

---

[7] In approaching Colgate-Palmolive, Kativo executives indicated that they were planning to design their own detergent plant rather than to buy a "turn-key" plant from a U.S. or European equipment manufacturer. This plan was a result of Dr. Jirik's deep personal conviction that the development of *local* technical know-how was an essential prerequisite for healthy economic growth in areas such as Central America. Furthermore, as a Ph.D. in chemistry, he believed that the design and development of one's own plant was extremely important in order really to understand the basic manufacturing process involved. He also believed that the existing prepackaged plants were overpriced and were too large and inflexible for the needs of developing areas.

Market it would be imperative to sell on a CACM-wide basis in order to survive competitively in a consumer goods industry such as detergents.)

5. Use nationalism to good advantage and exploit management's first-hand knowledge of the workings of the Costa Rican market and the behavior of the Costa Rican consumer in formulating a specific marketing plan. In so doing, however, do not be afraid to borrow applicable ideas from the international companies and to rely on the advice of a local advertising agency.

6. Work hard, learn fast, use young and hungry people, and try to be more flexible than the international giants.

## KATIVO'S INITIAL MARKETING PLAN

To implement these plans, a marketing manager, Sr. Ronald Rees, was hired. Sr. Rees was a young Costa Rican in his thirties with university training in the United States (Boston University) who had previously worked in the Costa Rican insurance business. While Sr. Rees had little actual marketing experience (there was an acute shortage of trained Costa Rican marketing executives), he was considered by management to be extremely bright and dynamic and to be fully capable of developing into a competent marketing manager.

Working in close cooperation with Sr. Kissling and with a local advertising agency, Sr. Rees formulated Kativo's marketing plan to enter the detergent business. He was able to use a survey of consumer buying habits commissioned by Kativo and conducted by a local market research firm in 1961, covering 400 housewives in the greater San Jose area. Some of the major findings of this study are given in Exhibit 3.

### Channels of distribution

According to Sr. Rees, the most crucial marketing decision which management had to make was whether to rely on wholesalers for the distribution of the new detergent or to develop a company-owned sales force. After considerable discussion, management decided on the latter course of action.

The critical factor in this decision was management's conviction that Costa Rican wholesalers, though representing a cheaper form of distribution, could not provide adequate support for a new brand of detergents. At the time there were about 15 grocery wholesalers in Costa Rica. All of these, however, tended to handle very broad product lines and to provide only limited coverage of available retail outlets. Moreover, their salesmen tended to be poorly trained and spent more time taking orders than actually selling. As Sr. Kissling put it:

Wholesalers are fine in Costa Rica for a brand which already has an established consumer demand. For a new product, however, they would be hopelessly inadequate. With so many products to handle, their salesmen just wouldn't be able to do the selling job or in-store promotional work necessary to get a new brand firmly accepted at the retail level. With a new product such as a powdered detergent, the most we could hope for would be permanent coverage of 10%–15% of the potential retail outlets.

Management realized that the alternative course of action, setting up a company-owned sales force, would be extremely expensive, espe-

**EXHIBIT 3**

KATIVO CHEMICAL INDUSTRIES, LTD.
Market Survey Data, September 1961

A. *Percentage of households which use detergents according to socioeconomic class*

|  | Total | Socioeconomic class | | |
|---|---|---|---|---|
|  |  | Upper | Middle | Low |
| Use detergents. . . . . . . . . . . . . . . . | 92.9 | 94.1 | 95.3 | 90.8 |
| Do *not* use detergents . . . . . . . . . . . | 7.1 | 5.9 | 4.7 | 9.2 |
|  | 100.0 | 100.0 | 100.0 | 100.0 |
| Number of households interviewed . . . . . | 400 | 119 | 129 | 152 |

B. *Percentage of households which use soap in bars or balls according to socioeconomic class*

|  | Total | Socioeconomic class | | |
|---|---|---|---|---|
|  |  | Upper | Middle | Low |
| Use soap in bars or balls . . . . . . . . . . | 89.3 | 76.5 | 84.5 | 95.4 |
| Do *not* use soap in bars or balls . . . . . . | 10.7 | 23.5 | 15.5 | 4.6 |
|  | 100.0 | 100.0 | 100.0 | 100.0 |

C. *Percentage of families which stated they used electric washing machines for laundry purposes*

|  | Total | Socioeconomic class | | |
|---|---|---|---|---|
|  |  | Upper | Middle | Low |
| Use electric washing machines. . . . . . . | 32.6 | 81.2 | 48.8 | 11.3 |
| Do *not* use electric washing machines . . . | 67.4 | 18.8 | 51.2 | 88.7 |
|  | 100.0 | 100.0 | 100.0 | 100.0 |
| Number of respondents . . . . . . . . . . . | 393 | 119 | 127 | 149 |

**EXHIBIT 3** (*continued*)

D. *Percentage of households using various types of cleaning products for various types of washing jobs*

| Cleaning product used | Sheets and linens | Work clothes | Nylon and fine fabrics | Shirts and other clothes | Dish wash-ing |
|---|---|---|---|---|---|
| Detergents alone . . . . . . . . . . . . . . . | 45.6 | 32.1 | 53.0 | 38.8 | 43.3 |
| Detergent and bar or ball soap. . . . . . . . | 34.6 | 42.4 | 16.7 | 36.8 | 9.0 |
| Detergent, bar or ball soap, and soap powder. . . . . . . . . . . . . . . . . . . | 0.9 | 1.1 | 0.9 | 1.2 | . . . |
| Detergent and liquid cleaners . . . . . . . . | . . . | . . . | . . . | . . . | 0.6 |
| Detergent and scouring powder . . . . . . . | . . . | . . . | . . . | . . . | 1.7 |
| Bar or ball soap alone . . . . . . . . . . . . | 14.2 | 18.9 | 13.4 | 19.0 | 35.4 |
| Bar or ball soap and soap powder . . . . . . | 1.1 | 2.7 | 0.8 | 1.1 | . . . |
| Soap powder alone . . . . . . . . . . . . . . | 2.2 | 1.0 | 1.2 | 1.2 | 2.0 |
| Other soaps . . . . . . . . . . . . . . . . . . | . . . | . . . | 13.1 | 0.5 | .4 |
| Liquid cleaners . . . . . . . . . . . . . . . . | . . . | . . . | . . . | . . . | 7.0 |
| Send laundry out of house. . . . . . . . . . | 1.1 | 1.8 | 0.9 | 1.4 | . . . |
| Don't have these clothes . . . . . . . . . . . | 0.3 | . . . | . . . | . . . | . . . |
| Ashes . . . . . . . . . . . . . . . . . . . . . | . . . | . . . | . . . | . . . | 0.6 |
| Total. . . . . . . . . . . . . . . . . . . | 100.0 | 100.0 | 100.0 | 100.0 | 100.0 |
| Number of respondents . . . . . . . . . . . | 398 | 399 | 397 | 399 | 398 |

E. *Reasons given for using both detergents and bar or ball soap by the housewives who said they follow that practice*

| Reasons given | Percent of households |
|---|---|
| "Like to loosen dirt with detergent, then rub each garment with bar soap" . . . . . . . . . . . . . | 35.3 |
| "Habit" . . . . . . . . . . . . . . . . . . . . . . . . . | 13.5 |
| "More economical". . . . . . . . . . . . . . . . . . . . | 5.3 |
| "The washing machine doesn't get the clothes clean. Have to use bar soap afterwards" . . . . . . . | 0.7 |
| "Other reasons"* . . . . . . . . . . . . . . . . . . . . . | 45.2 |
| | 100.0 |
| Number of respondents . . . . . . . . . . . . . . . . . | 127 |

*"Other reasons" included gets the clothes whiter, less damaging to the clothes, gets the dirt out better, washes cleaner, etc.

cially since only one product was involved. Nevertheless, executives believed that if Kativo's detergent really were to succeed and compete effectively against Colgate-Palmolive (which already had a six-man sales force), there was little choice but to choose this latter alternative.

Having reached this conclusion, the company made a census of Costa Rican grocery retailers, decided which stores to visit (3,000 out of 6,000), established possible selling routes, and determined how many salesmen would be required to provide the desired coverage. As a result of this

**EXHIBIT 3** (*continued*)

F. *Percentage of attributes mentioned as being most important in a detergent*

| Quality | Total | Socioeconomic class | | |
|---|---|---|---|---|
| | | Upper | Middle | Low |
| Able to get clothes really white . . . . . . . | 64.4 | 63.6 | 66.1 | 63.2 |
| Not too harsh for the hands . . . . . . . . . . | 45.2 | 44.9 | 44.6 | 45.8 |
| Washes rapidly . . . . . . . . . . . . . . . | 28.7 | 21.2 | 26.4 | 31.9 |
| Strong enough to wash well . . . . . . . . . | 20.6 | 6.8 | 20.7 | 22.9 |
| Not too perfumed . . . . . . . . . . . . . | 20.4 | 10.2 | 23.1 | 20.1 |
| Pleasantly perfumed . . . . . . . . . . . . | 16.4 | 6.8 | 17.4 | 17.4 |
| Makes plenty of suds . . . . . . . . . . . . | 5.5 | 2.5 | 8.3 | 3.5 |
| Is white in color. . . . . . . . . . . . . . | 3.6 | 2.5 | 6.6 | 1.4 |
| Other . . . . . . . . . . . . . . . . . . . | 5.1 | 6.8 | 4.1 | 5.6 |
| Total* . . . . . . . . . . . . . . . . . | 209.9 | 165.3 | 217.3 | 211.8 |
| Number of respondents . . . . . . . . . . | 383 | 118 | 121 | 144 |

*Totals add up to more than 100% due to multiple responses.

G. *Percentage distribution of households according to the detergent package size which they usually purchased*

| Package size | Total | Socioeconomic class | | |
|---|---|---|---|---|
| | | Upper | Middle | Low |
| Envelopes (50 gr.) . . . . . . . . . . . . . | 12.1 | . . . | 3.2 | 21.1 |
| Small (215 gr.) . . . . . . . . . . . . . . | 50.8 | 26.4 | 48.4 | 57.1 |
| Large (567 gr.) . . . . . . . . . . . . . . | 28.4 | 53.6 | 35.5 | 18.3 |
| Giant (1,400 gr.) . . . . . . . . . . . . . | 6.8 | 13.6 | 12.1 | 1.4 |
| King (2,375 gr.) . . . . . . . . . . . . . . | 0.6 | 6.4 | . . . | . . . |
| Indifferent . . . . . . . . . . . . . . . . | 1.3 | . . . | 0.8 | 2.1 |
| Total . . . . . . . . . . . . . . . . . | 100.0 | 100.0 | 100.0 | 100.0 |
| Number of respondents (interviewees who used detergents) . . . . . . . . . . . . . . . . | 374 | 112 | 123 | 139 |

H. *Percentage of preferred brand of detergent among detergent using families*

| Brand preferred | Total | Socioeconomic class | | |
|---|---|---|---|---|
| | | Upper | Middle | Low |
| Fab (Colgate). . . . . . . . . . . . . . | 75.2 | 74.5 | 77.8 | 73.2 |
| Tide . . . . . . . . . . . . . . . . . . | 26.7 | 30.9 | 21.4 | 30.2 |
| Ace . . . . . . . . . . . . . . . . . . | 5.2 | 4.5 | 3.9 | 6.3 |
| Others . . . . . . . . . . . . . . . . . | 7.4 | . . . | 0.7 | 14.0 |
| Indifferent . . . . . . . . . . . . . . . | 2.8 | 2.7 | 4.7 | 1.4 |
| Total* . . . . . . . . . . . . . . . | 117.3 | 112.6 | 108.5 | 125.1 |
| Number of respondents . . . . . . . . | 374 | 112 | 123 | 139 |

*Totals add up to more than 100% due to multiple responses.
Source: Agency survey for Kativo.

analysis, a sales manager, five salemen, and four sales "assistants" were hired. Annual sales-force costs were estimated at approximately $60,000, consisting of $24,000 in salaries, $8,000 in social charges, $20,000 in transportation and traveling expenses, and $7,000 in overhead. Salesmen were to be paid about $2,700/year. It was expected that 65% of this amount would be in the form of salary, 30% in the form of commissions, and 5% in the form of performance prizes. Initially the sales force would handle only one product, Kativo's new detergent. In the long run, however, management hoped that it might be possible to use the detergent sales force for the distribution of a limited number of other companies' products on a commission basis and thus decrease the relative selling costs which the new detergent would have to bear. Until that time, management felt that one way to cut selling costs would be to have salesmen drive trucks, instead of cars, and make immediate deliveries on retailer orders.

### Product policy

Top management had decided that from a technical point of view the new detergent powder should be closely modeled after the imported brands. These brands seemed to have achieved fairly good acceptance in Costa Rica as well as in other parts of the world. Since Kativo was somewhat limited in its research and development capability as well as in its experience with detergents, management believed that the safest course of action would be to aim for a product which was similar to existing brands in composition, carton sizes, and quality. This last was particularly important, since management wanted at all costs to avoid the low-quality stigma which was often attached to locally manufactured products in the minds of Costa Rican consumers.

### Pricing

Price was considered an extremely critical area. As long as import duties remained high and Kativo was the only company with local manufacturing facilities, a low consumer price was considered Kativo's best weapon for breaking into the Costa Rican market. On the other hand, management did not want to set the price so low as to endanger its profit objectives of a 20%–25% return on net equity investment. Nor did they want to make the product so cheap as to give consumers the impression that it was inferior. Finally, they wanted to be prepared for the day when the international manufacturers themselves might either have local manufacturing facilities or be able to import from other CACM countries on a duty-free basis.[8] Indeed there were rumors that Colgate-Palmolive, being now convinced that Kativo would actually go ahead with plans to enter the detergent market, was already thinking of putting up a factory of its own in Costa Rica. If this were to happen, Kativo executives did not feel that they could afford to get into a price war with Colgate, since in the long run such a war would be more disastrous for a small company like Kativo than for an international company like Colgate with its huge financial resources.

With these considerations in mind, management set the suggested consumer price of its detergent an average of 17% below that of the leading imported brands. Kativo also provided the retailers with larger margins on most of its package sizes. Comparative price lists are shown in Exhibit 4.

Meanwhile, Kativo had applied for and obtained a special increase in tariff rates on powdered detergents, to go into effect as soon as Kativo opened its local plant. Under the new tariff schedule the ad valorem rate would be raised from 25% of CIF value to 100%, while the specific duty of $.30/kg. would remain unchanged. This meant that a kilogram of imported detergent powder whose CIF value was $.40 would henceforth be subject to $.70 of duties ($.30/kg. + $.40 ad valorem), thus raising the total cost to the importer from $.80/kg. to $1.10/kg. In addition, under its investment incentive program, the government had granted Kativo a 10-year exemption from income taxes on detergent earnings plus permission to import construction materials, machinery, and raw materials on a duty-free basis during the same period.

### Brand policy

After soliciting consumer suggestions on a product name and finding that the name most frequently proposed was already taken, Kativo finally chose the name Prim. This derived not from the market survey but from an advertising slogan which the company and its advertising agency contemplated using: "El Primero Nacional" (the *first national* brand of detergents). Given this slogan, Prim seemed to be a natural choice. It was short, it had favorable implications, and it could be used in connection with words such as "primero" and "primoroso" (exquisite).

A major issue in the brand area was whether to associate Prim with its parent company, Kativo. Management believed that over a period of years Kativo had gradually built up a good reputation among Costa Rican

---

[8] In 1962 Costa Rica had not yet ratified the CACM treaty. Consequently, imports of detergents from other Central American countries were subject to the same tariffs as those from outside the area. Nevertheless, it was expected that Costa Rica would soon ratify the treaty, thus opening the way for eventual duty-free imports from any place within the CACM.

**EXHIBIT 4**
**1962 detergent prices**

*Price of detergent to retailers*

| Size | Fab–Ace–Tide | | | Prim | | | Difference | | |
|---|---|---|---|---|---|---|---|---|---|
| | Weight | ¢ | $ | Weight | ¢ | $ | ¢ | $ | % |
| King | 2,408 gr. | 17.50 | 2.64 | 2,380 gr. | 13.83 | 2.08 | 3.67 | 0.56 | 21 |
| Giant | 1,416 | 10.50 | 1.59 | 1,400 | 8.30 | 1.25 | 2.20 | 0.34 | 21 |
| Large | 567 | 4.38 | 0.66 | 567 | 3.46 | 0.52 | 0.92 | 0.14 | 21 |
| Small | 208 | 1.75 | 0.26 | 205 | 1.42 | 0.21 | 0.33 | 0.05 | 19 |
| Envelope | 50 | 0.50 | 0.075 | 49 | 0.42 | 0.063 | 0.08 | 0.012 | 16 |

*Price of detergent to consumers*

| Size | Fab–Ace–Tide | | | Prim | | | Difference | | |
|---|---|---|---|---|---|---|---|---|---|
| | Weight | ¢ | $ | Weight | ¢ | $ | ¢ | $ | % |
| King | 2,408 gr. | 18.00 | 2.72 | 2,380 gr. | 15.85 | 2.40 | 2.15 | 0.32 | 12 |
| Giant | 1,416 | 11.00 | 1.66 | 1,400 | 9.50 | 1.43 | 1.50 | 0.23 | 14 |
| Large | 567 | 4.75 | 0.72 | 567 | 3.95 | 0.60 | 0.80 | 0.12 | 17 |
| Small | 208 | 2.00 | 0.30 | 205 | 1.65 | 0.25 | 0.35 | 0.05 | 18 |
| Envelope | 50 | 0.60 | 0.09 | 49 | 0.50 | 0.075 | 0.10 | 0.015 | 17 |

$1.00 = ¢6.62 (colones).
Source: Company records and observations.

consumers as a quality paint maker. Consequently, it was felt that a strong initial advertising tie-in with the Kativo name might help to overcome some of the Costa Rican's traditional resistance to any locally made products. Later, as Prim began to achieve acceptance on its own, the support of the Kativo name would be of less importance and could be withdrawn.

## Package design

In choosing a package color, management decided to break with the U.S. tradition of using bright primary colors with strong shelf impact. Having discovered through their market survey that local housewives were a little afraid of detergents on the grounds that they were strong and thus hard on the hands, management decided on pastel package shades. It further decided to give housewives a choice of pastel pink or pastel blue, with the idea that the pink carton, which had slightly strong connotations, would appeal to housewives who wanted a heavy-duty detergent, while the light-blue carton, which had delicate connotations, would appeal to housewives who were looking for a gentle detergent that would not injure the hands. Management also believed that by bringing out cartons in two different colors they would be able to obtain more space on the retailers' shelves for the new detergent.

Kativo executives added another original twist of their own: a measuring spoon in each package. This was done in the belief that the Costa Rican housewife was more economy-minded than her U.S. counterpart and would welcome a means of insuring that none of the detergent was wasted.

## Advertising

In developing an appropriate advertising theme for the new detergent, management worked very closely with a local advertising agency. After considering a wide variety of ideas, the company-agency team narrowed down the final choice to one of three possible themes:

1.  Appealing to national loyalty: "Prim . . . El Primero Nacional." (Prim . . . the first national brand.)
2.  Emphasizing that Prim offered consumers a better choice: "El rosado para lavado corriente; el celeste para la ropa mas fina." (The pink box for normal laundry needs; the blue box for delicate clothes.)
3.  Stressing that Prim was more economical than other brands: "Mida, mida, mida . . . no desperdicie! Haga su Buchaca." (Measure, measure, measure . . . no waste! Save for your piggy bank.)

After weighing the pros and cons of these themes, management decided to make the third the primary focus for the introductory advertising campaign but to retain the first two as subsidiary themes.

By stressing the "savings" theme, management felt that the Prim advertising would be communicating to cost-conscious Costa Rican housewives the fact that Kativo was on "their side." Hopefully, housewives would begin to feel that every time they used Prim they were making a saving. Management believed that this type of campaign would be more effective than one based on extravagant superlatives and claims of "better washing power," even though the latter type campaign seemed to be the kind most frequently used by the international companies.

The first-year advertising budget was fixed at ¢240,000 ($36,000). This was to be spent on various media as follows:

| | |
|---|---|
| Newspapers | 23% |
| Radio | 40 |
| TV | 16 |
| Cinema | 3 |
| Point of sale | 4 |
| Outdoor | 4 |
| Production costs | 4 |
| Agency fees* | 4 |
| Other | 2 |
| | 100% |

*This was in addition to the normal 15% commission which the agency received from the media.

The money spent in the newspapers was to be primarily for full-page advertisements. The expenditures on radio and TV, on the other hand, were to be mainly for the sponsorship of a series of religious programs. Originally, both the agency executives and Kativo's management had hoped to be able to sponsor programs of the "soap opera" type on both radio and TV. However, they soon found that it was extremely difficult to obtain such programs, mainly due to the fact that the rights to most of the Spanish language "soap operas" which had been produced in Latin America had already been purchased by the large international companies, most notably Colgate-Palmolive. The decision to sponsor religious programs instead was based on the belief that they would appeal to Costa Rica's highly religious population.

Since almost all forms of consumer promotions were illegal in Costa Rica, management was not able to engage in such activities as sampling, premium offers, consumer contests, etc.—all of which were widely used for the sale of powdered detergents in most other countries.

## Sales targets and projected costs

As part of the planning process, Kativo executives also made an attempt to set sales targets for Prim and to draw up budgets covering the first two years. These are shown in Exhibit 5.

The sales target of 600,000 pounds for the first year was considered to be the minimum required to break even. This amount represented 20% of production capacity. Management hoped, of course, that sales

**EXHIBIT 5**
**Operating budget for Prim for first two years**

|  | *1st year* | | | *2d year* | | |
|---|---|---|---|---|---|---|
| Sales objective......... | 600,000 lbs. | | | 1,200,000 lbs. | | |
| Net sales ............ | ¢1,904,000 | $290,000 | 100.0% | ¢3,808,000 | $575,000 | 100.0% |
| Manufacturing costs |  |  |  |  |  |  |
| Raw materials........ | ¢ 485,000 | $ 73,200 | 25.5% | ¢ 970,000 | $146,500 | 25.4% |
| Packages........... | 232,000 | 35,000 | 12.2 | 450,000 | 69,000 | 11.8 |
| Direct labor ........ | 40,000 | 6,000 | 2.1 | 40,000 | 6,000 | 1.1 |
| Factory overheads ..... | 200,000 | 30,200 | 10.5 | 250,000 | 37,800 | 6.6 |
| Cost of goods sold ..... | ¢ 957,000 | $144,400 | 50.3% | ¢1,710,000 | $259,300 | 44.9% |
| Gross profit ......... | ¢ 947,000 | $145,600 | 49.7% | ¢2,098,000 | $315,700 | 55.1% |
| Selling, administrative, and general expense |  |  |  |  |  |  |
| Sales force.......... | ¢ 383,000 | $ 57,800 | 20.1% | ¢ 506,000 | $ 76,500 | 13.3% |
| Advertising ......... | 240,000 | 36,200 | 12.6 | 240,000 | 36,200 | 6.3 |
| Administration ....... | 100,000 | 15,100 | 5.2 | 160,000 | 24,200 | 4.2 |
| Financial charges ..... | 190,000 | 28,700 | 10.0 | 270,000 | 40,800 | 7.1 |
| Subtotal ............ | ¢ 913,000 | $137,800 | 47.9% | ¢1,176,000 | $177,700 | 30.9% |
| Operating profit....... | ¢ 34,000 | $ 7,800 | 1.8% | ¢ 922,000 | $138,000 | 24.2% |

Source: Company records.

**EXHIBIT 6**
**Estimates on the Costa Rican detergent market**

*Costa Rican imports of detergents in the preceding five years*

| Year | Kilograms | Pounds |
|---|---|---|
| 1957 ...... | 853,038 | 1,880,000 |
| 1958 ...... | 818,984 | 1,802,000 |
| 1959 ...... | 976,411 | 2,150,000 |
| 1960 ...... | 1,221,880 | 2,695,000 |
| 1961 ...... | 1,237,645 | 2,712,000 |

*Forecast sales of detergents in the coming five years\**

| Year | Kilograms | Pounds |
|---|---|---|
| 1962 ...... | 1,316,854 | 2,857,573 |
| 1963 ...... | 1,401,133 | 3,040,459 |
| 1964 ...... | 1,490,805 | 3,235,047 |
| 1965 ...... | 1,586,217 | 3,442,091 |
| 1966 ...... | 1,687,735 | 3,662,385 |

*The elasticity of demand for detergents was estimated to be 1.6 as a function of changes in GNP. GNP was forecasted to rise at the rate of 4.1% per year. Thus the annual increase in the demand for detergents was assumed to be 1.6 × 4.1% or 6.5% per year.
Source: Industry records.

would be even higher. In trying to see what market share 600,000 pounds would represent, management drew up a five-year market forecast, based partly on past sales and partly on the estimated growth in GNP (see Exhibit 6). Based on this forecast, 600,000 pounds would represent approximately 20% of the total 1963 detergent market.

In the second year, management hoped to double sales to 1.2 million pounds. By so doing, they felt it would be possible to raise operating profits from $8,800 (1.8% of sales) to $138,000 (23.8% of sales).

# Colgate-Palmolive International
## Costa Rican detergent operations

## ENTRY DECISION

When it became evident to Colgate management that Kativo was constructing a detergent plant and was planning to launch its own brand, it faced the choice of continuing to import or to set up local manufacturing.

After considerable discussion, a joint decision was reached at the local and headquarters levels of the Colgate organization to meet the Kativo challenge by building a detergent plant in Costa Rica. The decision was based on three main considerations:

1. Management believed that even such a well-known brand as Fab would find it almost impossible to compete with a locally manufactured brand after the new tariff went into effect.
2. The outcome of the Costa Rican CACM negotiations was still uncertain. Even if Costa Rica *did* join, the decision could be so delayed that Fab might completely lose its Costa Rican consumer franchise in the interim.
3. Colgate's international headquarters in New York had recently been experimenting with a new type of detergent plant which had the virtues of being small, flexible, and comparatively inexpensive. The new plant (called "Chem-Serve") had been designed with the developing countries in mind, and management was currently looking for a small market in which to try it. Costa Rica seemed ideally suited for the experiment.

Having made the decision to build in Costa Rica, management's first task was to obtain a government permit. First inquiries indicated there might be reluctance to authorize a large international company like Colgate-Palmolive to build a plant whose products would compete directly with those of Kativo, a local firm. The situation was aggravated by the fact that the government had already granted a permit to a second local company, Punto Rojo (a maker of bar laundry and toilet soaps). Punto Rojo, however, had not yet begun constructing its detergent plant. Colgate's problem was solved when Punto Rojo agreed to transfer its construction permit to Colgate, provided Colgate would act as a contract supplier for Punto Rojo when and if the latter decided to launch a powdered detergent of its own. Punto Rojo, in turn, was already acting as a contract supplier of Palmolive toilet soap for Colgate. The terms of the Punto Rojo permit were identical to Kativo's, except that they did not carry income tax exemptions.

## THE INTRODUCTION OF PRIM

By November of 1962, Kativo's new plant was ready to begin production and marketing of Prim got underway. The initial reaction on the part of grocery retailers was quite positive, and within a very short time Kativo salesmen were able to get Prim onto the shelves of over 2,500 stores. Supplementary sales through wholesalers brought the total number of retail stores stocking Prim up to about 3,500 (out of a total of 6,000 grocery retailers in Costa Rica). The public's reaction to Prim was also positive, although resistance was encountered on the part of some consumers who felt that a locally made detergent could not possibly be as good as the imported brands. Nevertheless, aided by a 17% price advantage over imported brands, Prim soon began to move off retailers' shelves.

Colgate meanwhile, as an interim defensive measure against Kativo, had imported abnormally large shipments of Fab from the United States immediately prior to the opening of the Kativo plant (when import duties had been increased). For the next three months (November 1962–January 1963) Fab continued to be sold at the same price as previously. However, the stock which Colgate had imported under the pre-Kativo tariff ran out at the end of January. Rather than importing more Fab at the new high rate, Colgate stopped selling its detergent entirely, pending the opening of the new plant. This led to a large increase in the sales of Prim during February through April. It was estimated that if Kativo could continue to sell this volume it would succeed in capturing 50% or more of the local detergent market. In April, however, the new Colgate plant was ready and the first locally manufactured Fab was introduced to Costa Rican consumers.

## COLGATE'S MARKETING POLICY FOR FAB

The new locally manufactured Fab was to resemble the imported product as closely as possible and to be sold under the same brand. Management felt that any significant change might be interpreted by consumers as an indication that the locally made Fab was inferior. In the early months, however, the locally made powder tended to exhibit relatively high density, plus moisture and caking problems. While the product as such performed very well, its appearance required improvement. Moreover, the density problem could have been serious, since it meant that filling up the cartons would require a greater weight of powder. This, in turn, would increase costs.

The moisture problem was also irksome, inasmuch as Kativo began to call the attention of the public and the trade to the fact that Fab "caked." Kativo conducted demonstrations in some of the larger stores, comparing the caking characteristics of Fab to those of Prim.

As a result of these problems, the team of American technicians who had originally come to Costa Rica to set up the new Colgate plant was recalled. Following a number of adjustments to the plant and a change in the original formula, the density and moisture problems were solved in the early fall of 1963.

### Packaging

When Kativo introduced Prim, it used essentially the same sizes as the imported brands. With the advent of locally produced Fab, however, Colgate's management decided to change the weight, size, and shape of the cartons being used. The new cartons all were thinner but had a relatively larger face surface than the old ones. The large face surface not only permitted better "shelf facings" in retail stores but also gave the cartons the appearance of being quite large. This was part of an area standardization program.

Two months after the introduction of the locally produced Fab, Kativo's management followed suit, reducing the powder density of Prim (thereby giving it more volume) and using carton sizes which were optically even larger than those being used by Fab, though by weight the new Prim cartons contained about the same amount of powder as the Fab cartons.

### Pricing

Mr. Waldron, Colgate-Palmolive's general manager in Costa Rica, commented on his pricing policy for Fab as follows:

In Costa Rica, as in all other countries, it has been our policy to avoid cutthroat price wars with the competition. Although there is little doubt that in a price war Colgate-Palmolive would probably be able to outlast a local company, we feel that, in the long run, price wars benefit no one. Instead, we try to price our products to satisfy the consumer price-quality compromise: low enough so that they will be reasonable from the consumer's point of view but not so low as to require reduced quality to maintain a healthy profit stature.

The retail prices of locally manufactured Fab were comparable or slightly lower than those for Prim. On the larger sizes the markup granted by Colgate to the retailer was higher than those allowed by Kativo.

The trade terms offered to retailers by Colgate-Palmolive included a 3% cash discount plus a 2% quantity discount on orders of ¢3,500 ($530) and more. To obtain this quantity discount, retailers could combine purchases of Fab with purchases of Colgate-Palmolive's other products.

Thirty-day credit was offered to retailers who did not elect to take a cash discount. Although Colgate tried to enforce this 30-day limit fairly rigidly, competitive pressure occasionally resulted in larger than desired receivables.

## Channels of distribution

In all, there were about 6,000 potential grocery outlets for the sale of detergents in Costa Rica. Of these, Colgate management considered that less than 3,500 were large enough to warrant being visited by a company salesman. Wholesalers provided limited coverage of the remaining 2,500.

Mr. Waldron believed that one of Colgate-Palmolive's greatest competitive strengths lay in the fact that its well-trained six-man sales force was able to provide a strong, steady selling effort at a reasonable cost. Because the sales force handled over 20 different Colgate products, total sales-force costs for an individual product were relatively low. Salesmen divided their selling time among various products roughly as follows:

Detergents . . . . . . . . . . . . . .  30%
Toilet soaps . . . . . . . . . . . . .  25
Dental cream  . . . . . . . . . . . .  20
Other products . . . . . . . . . . .  25

Sales-force costs, however, were allocated to various products on the basis of sales volume.

The supervisor of the sales force, Sr. L. Gutierrez, a Costa Rican who had worked for Colgate-Palmolive ever since the Costa Rican company had been formed in 1960, spent most of his time traveling with salesmen, training them, and handling relations with large customers.

He made every effort to instill a spirit of competition among the salesmen through the use of sales contests[1] and incentive compensation plans.

Since the introduction of locally produced Fab in 1963, all salesmen had stepped up their efforts to sell Fab to the grocery trade, to insure that it was advantageously displayed in every store, and to assure retailers that it was the best detergent on the market and should be recommended to consumers in preference to any other brand. Both Mr. Waldron and Sr. Gutierrez believed that steady sales-force pressure was a critical factor in determining the competitive success or failure of Fab.

### Advertising

In reviewing Colgate-Palmolive's advertising efforts for Fab, Mr. Waldron commented as follows:

Advertising is an area where we, as an international company, have more resources available to us than most companies. In radio, for example, which is an especially important medium in Central America, we are able to draw on a pool of programs and commercials which Colgate-Palmolive has created in other Latin American countries. Television and press advertising material is, of course, also available from outside sources and is particularly important, as you would probably expect, in television production. Many advertising campaigns from other locations are not perfectly suited to our local needs, and these we adapt at more reasonable costs than original productions.

Another advantage which we have is that we are able to take advantage of special advertising volume discount rates on local media when available, due to the number of products that we have and our obviously large advertising expenditure.

During the period when Fab was still being imported into Costa Rica, its advertising budget had tended to average less than 5% of sales. Following the introduction of locally produced Fab, however, the amount spent was increased significantly.

Although Colgate-Palmolive used a local advertising agency in Costa Rica in purchasing media time and space, most of the actual creative work was still done outside Costa Rica, either at Colgate's Central American area headquarters in Guatemala or in one of the other Latin American markets in which Colgate operated.

### Results

Exhibit 1 charts Fab's competitive progress from 1958 through 1963, based on market-share figures obtained in a series of consumer usage surveys conducted by the company.

---

[1] The top salesman in 1964 would win a trip to Mexico City with his wife.

**EXHIBIT 1**
**Brand-share percentages of detergents in Costa Rica***

| Brand name | 1958 | 1959 | 1961 Feb./Mar. | 1961 Nov./Dec. | 1962 Apr./May | 1963 April | 1963 Aug. | 1963 Sept. |
|---|---|---|---|---|---|---|---|---|
| Fab | 60.8 | 63.5 | 69.7 | 75.3 | 74.1 | 41.4 | 46.5 | 44.9 |
| Prim | ... | ... | ... | ... | ... | 36.6 | 33.6 | 39.4 |
| Ace | 11.2 | 6.6 | 4.9 | 1.5 | 2.1 | 0.8 | 1.3 | 0.2 |
| Tide | 26.9 | 26.0 | 21.6 | 17.6 | 13.7 | 6.0 | 6.9 | 4.4 |
| Punto Rojo | ... | ... | 3.2 | 4.5 | 5.9 | 11.6 | 8.8 | 8.7 |
| Others | 1.1 | 3.9 | 1.9 | 1.1 | 4.2 | 3.6 | 2.9 | 2.4 |
| | 100.0 | 100.0 | 100.0 | 100.0 | 100.0 | 100.0 | 100.0 | 100.0 |
| Nonusers | n.a. | n.a. | n.a. | n.a. | 26.9 | 24.9 | 22.3 | 34.3 |
| | | 1960: Colgate-Palmolive established local Costa Rican company | | | Nov. 1962: Prim introduced by Kativo | | April 1963: Locally produced Fab introduced | |

*These figures are based on a check of roughly 1,280 homes in the major cities and towns in Costa Rica. At each home the housewife was asked whether she used laundry detergents and, if so, what brand she currently had on hand. In each survey an effort was made to obtain the same proportion of upper, middle, and lower class homes as existed in the country as a whole. Different homes and sometimes even different cities and towns were included in each survey.
n.a. = not available.
Source: Market survey.

# Kativo Chemical Industries Ltd. Supplement

THE COLGATE decision to build a local plant was a blow to Kativo executives, who had expected that Colgate might eventually put up a local plant but had not felt it would happen so soon. In April, when the new Colgate plant was ready and the first locally manufactured Fab was introduced to Costa Rican consumers, Kativo management observed the event by running full-page press ads welcoming the new Fab to the local market (Exhibit 1). The purpose of these ads was both to show that Kativo was a good sport and to make sure that Costa Rican consumers were apprised of the fact that the new lower priced Fab on the market was a *locally produced* detergent. This latter was to dispel any misconceptions that Fab was still imported and therefore of better quality than Prim.

In spite of having known that Fab was to go into local production, Kativo executives were caught by surprise when they learned that Colgate had changed carton sizes and had priced the new sizes in such a way that they appeared cheaper than the corresponding Prim sizes. (See Exhibit 2 for price lists.) Since none of the cartons was marked with its weight and since the new Fab cartons had large face surfaces (at the expense of thickness), they gave the illusion of being bigger than they actually were and hence seemed like bargains compared to Prim. Kativo management was quite concerned about this situation, especially since it quickly became evident that Prim's sales in the larger sizes were being hard hit by the new locally produced Fab. Consequently, after a week's deliberation, management decided to change

478

**EXHIBIT 1**
Kativo's advertisement greeting Fab

**"EL PRIMER DETERGENTE NACIONAL"**

SE COMPLACE EN DAR SU
BIENVENIDA A

# FAB

**AHORA FABRICADO EN COSTA RICA**

La sana competencia estimula la superación en productos y servicios, la cual beneficia directamente al consumidor.

**CONSUMA Y USE LO QUE EL PAIS PRODUCE**

Source: Company records.

**EXHIBIT 2**
Detergent prices in the Costa Rican market

|  | Price to retailer | Price to consumer |
|---|---|---|
| **Prim old sizes** | | |
| King (2,380 gr.) . . . . . . . . | $2.08 | $2.40 |
| Giant (1,400 gr.) . . . . . . . . . | 1.25 | 1.43 |
| Large (567 gr.) . . . . . . . . . . | .52 | .60 |
| Medium (205 gr.). . . . . . . . . | .21 | .25 |
| Envelope (49 gr.) . . . . . . . . . | .063 | .075 |
| **Fab new sizes** | | |
| King (2,000 gr.). . . . . . . . . . | $1.51 | $1.81 |
| Giant (1,000 gr.) . . . . . . . . . | .82 | .98 |
| Large (500 gr.) . . . . . . . . . . | .44 | .53 |
| Medium (215 gr.). . . . . . . . . | .22 | .26 |
| Envelope (50 gr.) . . . . . . . . . | .063 | .076 |
| **Prim new sizes** | | |
| King (1,760 gr.). . . . . . . . . . | $1.58 | $1.90 |
| Giant (964 gr.) . . . . . . . . . . | .87 | 1.04 |
| Large (482 gr.) . . . . . . . . . . | .44 | .53 |
| Medium (205 gr.). . . . . . . . . | .21 | .26 |
| Envelope (49 gr.) . . . . . . . . . | .063 | .076 |
| Primito (28.3 gr.) . . . . . . . . . | .045 | .053 |

Source: Company records and observations.

the contents and prices of certain of the Prim carton sizes (Exhibit 2).

Sr. Kissling commented as follows on the decision to make the above change:

This was one case when we were glad to be a local company, since we were able to move fast in order to meet a competitive problem. In a similar situation, the international companies probably would have haggled back and forth between their head office and their local management for months before coming to a decision. By contrast, we were able to reach a decision in a week's time. Of course, the subsequent implementation required about two months. But even this was faster than the international companies could have done it.

Before the new carton sizes were actually on the market, Prim sales dropped off sharply, only to rise again in August once the packaging and pricing changes had been made (see Exhibit 3).

Aside from the foregoing packaging and pricing changes, Kativo management made one other significant change in its marketing program during Prim's initial year. This was to introduce a new advertising theme and to shift the major media emphasis to TV. The new advertising theme was built around a well-known local saying in Costa Rica, "con toda la pata," which literally translated meant "with the whole duck"

EXHIBIT 3
Monthly sales of Prim in Costa Rica (November 1962–
September 1963)

| 1st fiscal year | Dollars | Cases | Lbs. |
|---|---|---|---|
| 1962 | | | |
| October . . . . . . . . . . . | . . . | . . . | . . . |
| November . . . . . . . . . . | $ 26,200 | 2,137 | 60,000 |
| December . . . . . . . . . . | 19,400 | 1,531 | 43,000 |
| 1963 | | | |
| January . . . . . . . . . . | 40,000 | 3,378 | 85,000 |
| February. . . . . . . . . . . | 49,700 | 4,725 | 115,000 |
| March . . . . . . . . . . . . | 46,600 | 4,071 | 101,000 |
| April . . . . . . . . . . . . . | 45,400 | 3,978 | 100,000 |
| May . . . . . . . . . . . . . | 28,100 | 2,535 | 60,000 |
| June . . . . . . . . . . . . . | 32,100 | 3,254 | 79,000 |
| July . . . . . . . . . . . . . | 34,900 | 3,305 | 78,000 |
| August . . . . . . . . . . . . | 51,200 | 4,718 | 117,000 |
| September . . . . . . . . . . | 52,200 | 4,916 | 119,000 |
| Totals . . . . . . . . . | $425,800 | 38,548 | 957,000 |

Source: Company records.

or "with the whole leg," but which figuratively meant "something very good" in local slang. Thus the new advertising theme embodied the expression "Prim esta con toda la pata" and made use of a cartoon duck as an advertising symbol. Kativo management felt that this theme would strike a particularly sympathetic chord with Costa Rican consumers because of its uniquely local flavor.

The shift to TV came after Kativo was offered a unique opportunity to sponsor a series of rerun movies in Spanish at a very favorable price. Two movies were to be run each weekday under the sole sponsorship of Prim. Sponsorship of this series meant that TV's share of Prim's advertising budget went up from 16% to 40%, while the share of newspapers and radio went down commensurately.

Given the foregoing changes in the marketing program, Prim's first-year operating results were better than originally anticipated (see Exhibit 4). Actual sales were 957,000 pounds or ₡2,825,000 ($427,000), which represented about 150% of budget. Operating profit was ₡201,500 ($30,400) or 7.2% of sales, also better than budget.

## NICARAGUAN OPERATIONS

Shortly after Prim had been launched in Costa Rica in November 1962, Kativo's management had begun to consider the possibilities of

EXHIBIT 4
Profit and loss statement for Prim (November 1962–
September 1963)

| Net sales (lbs.) | | 957,000 lbs. | |
|---|---|---|---|
| Net sales (money). . . . . . . . . . | ₡2,824,600 | $427,000 | 100.0% |
| Manufacturing costs | | | |
| Direct costs . . . . . . . . . . . . | ₡1,117,700 | $169,000 | 39.5% |
| Factory overheads . . . . . . . . | 352,600 | 53,000 | 12.5 |
| Cost of goods sold . . . . . . . . . | ₡1,470,300 | $222,000 | 52.0% |
| Gross profit . . . . . . . . . . . . . | ₡1,354,300 | $205,000 | 48.0% |
| Selling, administrative, and general expense | | | |
| Selling costs . . . . . . . . . . . . . | ₡ 556,000 | $ 84,900 | 19.7% |
| Advertising . . . . . . . . . . . . | 253,800 | 38,400 | 9.0 |
| Administration . . . . . . . . . . | 167,000 | 25,200 | 5.9 |
| Financial charges . . . . . . . . . | 176,000 | 26,100 | 6.2 |
| Subtotal . . . . . . . . . . . . . . | ₡1,152,800 | $174,600 | 40.8% |
| Operating profit (loss) . . . . . . . | ₡ 201,500 | $ 30,400 | 7.2% |

Source: Company records.

introducing the new detergent in other Central American countries, particularly in Nicaragua where Kativo's joint venture had been very successful in paints. One barrier to exporting Prim from Costa Rica to Nicaragua, however, was that detergent tariffs between the two countries were still relatively high. Consequently, on an export basis, Kativo would have no special advantages over Colgate-Palmolive and Procter & Gamble who were already exporting their detergents into Nicaragua. However, Kativo heard of a Nicaraguan group which had obtained a government industry concession to build a detergent plant in Nicaragua. The group was planning to buy a plant in Mexico, but Kativo offered to build a plant for them. Subsequently, the group's lack of experience in making detergents, running a plant, and marketing a consumer product led them to pass control of the operation to Kativo. A new company called DENISA (Detergentes de Nicaragua S.A.) was formed with a 1,000,000 cordoba ($143,000) capitalization and with the following ownership structure:

| | |
|---|---|
| Kativo S.A. (Costa Rica). . . . . . . . . . . | 34.5% |
| Kativo de Nicaragua S.A. . . . . . . . . . . | 26 |
| Local Nicaraguan group . . . . . . . . . . . | 39.5 |

The new Nicaraguan detergent plant began production in the middle of 1963 with a one-shift capacity of 1,000,000 kilograms of powder. It was designed by Kativo S.A. engineers who, having benefited from the experience of building the Costa Rican plant, were able to keep construction and equipment costs down to a total of $80,000.

Overall management of DENISA was placed in the hands of Laonides Abaunza, the "gerente" (or general manager) of Kativo de Nicaragua S.A., who was to work closely with Kativo headquarters in Costa Rica. Prim's marketing strategy in Nicaragua was similar to that used in Costa Rica with one exception: whereas in Costa Rica Kativo had entered the market by setting the consumer price of Prim an average of 17% below that of imported detergents, it introduced Prim in Nicaragua at the same retail price as imported brands. The reaction of consumers and of the grocery trade to Prim was excellent. Within a very short period, Prim managed to capture and maintain an estimated 50% share of the Nicaraguan detergent market.

# Colgate-Palmolive International Supplement

MR. WALDRON noted that, while battling Prim, Colgate had managed to increase sales of other products at an even faster rate. This meant that the company as a whole was becoming less dependent on the detergent end of its business for its continued livelihood. However, Mr. Waldron was concerned about some recent developments which foretold a significant change in the competitive complexion of the Costa Rican detergent business. The first of these was the stepped-up activity of Procter & Gamble in Costa Rica. In February 1964, following Costa Rica's adherence to the CACM, Procter & Gamble had begun to import its two brands of detergents, Tide and Ace, on a duty-free basis from a new contract supplier located in Honduras and to sell these brands to retailers in Costa Rica at prices up to 5% lower than those of Fab; so far, this move had only slightly increased these brands' market share. Mr. Waldron thought that the increase had not been greater because Procter & Gamble was still selling its products through a local distributor who handled many other products and was not equipped to devote a strong steady sales push to Procter & Gamble's products.

Meanwhile, a second formidable competitor, Unilever, had also entered the Central American market through a joint venture with local interests in El Salvador. Unisola (as the new joint-venture company was called) had recently completed a new detergent factory in El Salvador and in August 1964 had launched its detergent (Rinso) on the Salvadoran market. Since the new plant had enough capacity to service the entire Central American market, Mr. Waldron felt it would only be a matter of time before Unisola would introduce Rinso in Costa Rica.

Thus, looking ahead, Mr. Waldron foresaw a situation where three large international companies and one active local company would all be competing vigorously for the Costa Rican detergent market. He viewed this prospect as follows:

Facing tough competition is nothing new to Colgate-Palmolive. Neither are the expected competitors. In fact, in almost every major market in the world Colgate, Procter & Gamble, and Unilever are battling it out with one another. Consequently, we really aren't too dismayed about the competitive struggle which we now see shaping up here in Costa Rica. As a matter of fact, the prospect of increased competition has a very positive side: in creating market expansion at a faster rate than it would if there were only one detergent company in Costa Rica. This is an important consideration, since the detergent market here is still relatively small compared to the laundry soap market.

Then, too, increased competition will keep us on our toes and insure that we run the most efficient and effective operation possible. Without such competition there is sometimes a tendency to become complacent.

Our objective now is to make sure that we continue to retain the initiative in the market even after Procter & Gamble and Unilever get their Costa Rican marketing activities into high gear. To do this will require a careful

**EXHIBIT 1**
**Detergent plants in Central America**

| Brand name. | Date plant opened | Company | Location | Estimated annual one-shift capacity (millions of kilograms) |
|---|---|---|---|---|
| Superdet | 1956 | Industria Quimica* | Guatemala | 1.2 |
| Terso | 1961 | Kong Hermanos† | Guatemala | 1.2 |
| Prim | 1962 | Kativo S.A. | Costa Rica | 1.3 |
| Fab | 1963 | Colgate-Palmolive ‡ | Costa Rica | 0.9 |
| Prim | 1963 | DENISA (Kativo subsidiary) | Nicaragua | 1.0 |
| Tide, Ace | 1963 | Quimicas Dinant § | Honduras | 3.0 |
| Rinso | 1964 | Unisola | El Salvador | 2.0 |

* Industria Quimica manufactured and sold its own brand, Superdet. During 1961 and 1962 Industria Quimica also acted as the contract supplier for Procter & Gamble. However, this contract was lost in 1963.

† In addition to manufacturing and selling its own brand, Terso, Kong also was the contract supplier for Colgate-Palmolive. Under this contract Kong supplied Colgate-Palmolive's detergent needs to all CACM countries but Costa Rica.

‡ This plant made detergents under a new process (called Chem-Serve) which did not require a spray tower. It produced only for the Costa Rican market.

§ From September 1963 onward, Quimicas Dinant was Procter & Gamble's exclusive contract supplier in the CACM. Under this contract Quimicas Dinant manufactured Ace and Tide.

Source: Industry records.

**EXHIBIT 2**
**Estimated 1964 sales of laundry detergents, Central American Common Market**

| Country | Unit sales (thousands of kilos) | Percent of total unit sales | Dollar sales @ wholesale (thousands of U.S. dollars) | Percent of total dollar sales |
|---|---|---|---|---|
| Guatemala . . . . . . . . . | 1,310 | 30.1 | 1,080 | 27.4 |
| El Salvador. . . . . . . . . | 725 | 16.7 | 600 | 15.2 |
| Honduras . . . . . . . . | 385 | 8.9 | 335 | 8.5 |
| Nicaragua . . . . . . . . | 405 | 9.3 | 535 | 13.6 |
| Costa Rica . . . . . . . . | 1,525 | 35.0 | 1,390 | 35.3 |
| Total CACM. . . . . . | 4,350 | 100.0 | 3,940 | 100.0 |

Source: Industry records.

**EXHIBIT 3**
**The Central American market shares of detergent brands (based on the urban in-home incidence of various brands)** *

| Company and brand | Guatemala July 1964 | El Salvador June 1964 | Honduras May 1964 | Nicaragua July 1964 | Costa Rica June 1964 | Total Central American |
|---|---|---|---|---|---|---|
| **User homes** | | | | | | |
| Colgate-Palmolive | | | | | | |
| Fab White . . . . . . | 69.1% | 60.0% | 57.0% | 36.0% | 45.4% | 54.0% |
| Fab Blue. . . . . . . | 6.7 | 6.3 | 3.9 | 3.4 | . . . | 3.6 |
| Procter & Gamble | | | | | | |
| Ace. . . . . . . . . . | 2.2 | 26.2 | 30.2 | 9.2 | 1.9 | 9.0 |
| Tide . . . . . . . . . | . . . | 0.4 | 8.4 | 0.6 | 8.8 | 3.9 |
| Kativo | | | | | | |
| Prim . . . . . . . . . | . . . | 6.8 | 0.1 | 49.9 | 30.7 | 18.7 |
| Industria Quimica | | | | | | |
| Superdet. . . . . . . | 17.0 | . . . | . . . | . . . | . . . | 4.6 |
| Kong Hermanos | | | | | | |
| Terso. . . . . . . . . | 1.9 | . . . | . . . | . . . | . . . | 0.5 |
| Punto Rojo | | | | | | |
| Punto Rojo† . . . . . | . . . | . . . | . . . | . . . | 10.1 | 3.6 |
| Others . . . . . . . . . | 3.1 | 0.3 | 0.4 | 0.9 | 3.1 | 2.1 |
| Total. . . . . . . . | 100.0% | 100.0% | 100.0% | 100.0% | 100.0% | 100.0% |
| Nonuser homes as a percent of all homes . . . . . . | 26.5% | 10.7% | 10.1% | 37.8% | 20.8% | |

* These figures are based on a check of roughly 1,250 homes in the major cities of each country. At each home the housewife was asked whether she used laundry detergents and, if so, what brand she currently had on hand. In each sample an effort was made to obtain the same proportion of A, B, and C/D socioeconomic class homes as existed in each country as a whole. This particular market research study was one of a continuing series of similar studies conducted at regular three-month intervals by one of the companies in the industry. Different homes and sometimes even different cities were included in each study.
† Punto Rojo was actually a soap powder rather than a detergent powder.
Source: Private company market survey.

reexamination of our present strategy in view of the expected change in competitive conditions.

Exhibit 1 lists the detergent plants in Central America as of August 1964, Exhibit 2 provides estimated 1964 sales of laundry detergents in the Central American Common Market countries, while Exhibit 3 gives market-share data based on the urban in-home incidence of various brands.

# General Cinema Corporation

IN JUNE 1971, General Cinema Corporation, owner of one of the largest movie-theater circuits in the United States, was well on its way to completing a 10th year of increasing sales, profits, and earnings per share. From 1961 to 1970, aided by the acquisition of several soft-drink bottling companies,[1] sales had increased from $10.4 million to $159.4 million, and earnings per share from $.23 to $2.11, as shown in Exhibits 1 and 2. The theater division continued to provide 44% of total revenues and 78% of net income, having exhibited a growth rate of nearly 20% during the 1960s. In contrast, gross receipts for theater exhibitors as a whole increased at a rate of about 2% during that period.

Richard Smith, chairman and president, reflected on his concerns for the future:

> Our management group has put together an extraordinary record over the past 10 years. We have worked hard for the acceptance we enjoy today; our stock carries a price-earnings ratio of over 20, and nearly a third of it is held by financial institutions. I don't want to sacrifice that record.
>
> One of our goals is to have half of our income secured from outside the theater business. That is difficult to do, however, when theater operations keep growing as they have recently. How can one accumulate enough capital to finance the mass required to match the growth in movies? Only this year we realized that we couldn't find enough reasonably priced soft-drink properties to absorb our cash flow. We could always become a conglomerate, but

---

[1] The company had become the second largest Pepsi-Cola bottler in the United States.

we've learned by watching them for the past several years that managing such a corporation isn't easy. Most of them try to do too many things they don't know enough about.

We would like to find one large opportunity. I would be particularly intrigued by a mature industry that is poised for change, comparable to the movie business 10 years ago. Our balance sheet includes a substantial amount of debt now, which relieves me of the need to act for a little while, but then the loans will be worked down to the point that I will be under pressure to make a move.

## THE THEATER EXHIBITION INDUSTRY

### Depression

The motion picture business passed through a traumatic period in the years following the end of World War II, prompted, on the one hand, by changing competitive conditions and, on the other, by a major alteration in the structure of the industry.

The American public, which spent almost 20% of its recreation dollar on movies in 1946, became enamored with other ways of using leisure time in the postwar years. Television in particular offered an alternative form of entertainment, evidenced by the explosion in the percentage of households with TV sets—to 74% in 1954 from only 3% in 1948. The exodus to the suburbs was accompanied by enormous increases in expenditures of time and money on participative sports, gardening, automobiles, and so forth.

Motion picture exhibitors were beset by other problems as well. Population shifts left many theaters, especially those in metropolitan areas, increasingly removed from their potential audiences. Moreover, while unprofitable theaters closed and attendance declined, the number of feature films produced in the United States declined as well—from over 400 a year in the 1940s to 200–250 in the mid-1950s. Thus the neighborhood theater with a policy of three program changes a week and a few double features had to secure most of the pictures made each year or resort to older films.

Producers, aware that "B" and "C" grade pictures were most susceptible to competition from television, initiated fewer but increasingly more expensive films. Higher production costs were passed on to the exhibitors through higher film rentals. The practice also developed of putting extravaganzas "on the road," which meant negotiating with a limited number of large downtown theaters for premiere runs at premium prices to skim the cream off the market.

**EXHIBIT 1**

GENERAL CINEMA CORPORATION
Balance Sheet – Years Ended October 31
(in thousands of dollars)

| Assets | 1960 | 1963 | 1966 | 1967 | 1968 | 1969 | 1970 |
|---|---|---|---|---|---|---|---|
| Current assets | | | | | | | |
| Cash and short-term investments | $2,720 | $2,887 | $5,279 | $6,320 | $8,803 | $12,050 | $12,562 |
| Notes and accounts receivable | ... | ... | | | 1,477 | 3,891 | 4,683 |
| Sundry deposits and receivables | 103 | 137 | 637 | 323 | 511 | 893 | 1,465 |
| Inventories | 65 | 121 | 188 | 220 | 1,850 | 3,902 | 4,788 |
| Other current assets | 166 | 366 | 293 | 299 | 387 | 860 | 1,206 |
| Total current assets | $3,054 | $3,511 | $6,397 | $7,162 | $13,028 | $21,596 | $24,704 |
| Investments and advances | | | | | | | |
| Unconsolidated affiliates | $679 | $471 | $369 | $227 | $171 | $484 | $942 |
| Other | 101 | 100 | 233 | 166 | 152 | 1,408* | 2,153* |
| Property, plant, and equipment | | | | | | | |
| Cost | n.a. | $15,598 | $23,535 | $26,365 | $49,477 | $60,633 | $73,976 |
| Less depreciation | n.a. | (4,127) | (5,663) | (6,595) | (8,912) | (17,037) | (23,174) |
| | $4,743 | $11,471 | $17,872 | $19,770 | $40,565 | $43,596 | $50,802 |
| Other assets | $610 | $1,969 | $2,036 | $2,257 | $3,550 | $7,421 | $12,669† |
| Franchises, trademarks, and goodwill | ... | 134 | 244 | 244 | 5,006 | 21,453 | 22,174 |
| Total assets | $9,187 | $17,656 | $27,151 | $29,876 | $62,472 | $95,958 | $113,444 |

*Liabilities*

| | | | | | | | |
|---|---:|---:|---:|---:|---:|---:|---:|
| **Current liabilities** | | | | | | | |
| Debt due within one year | $ 294 | 771 | $ 588 | $ 570 | $ 1,063 | $ 3,398 | $ 3,629 |
| Accounts payable | 418 | 1,271 | 2,754 | 3,732 | 6,462 | 11,519 | 13,065 |
| Taxes payable | 568 | 681 | 1,599 | 1,722 | 4,487 | 3,987 | 4,679 |
| Total current liabilities | $1,280 | $ 2,723 | $ 4,941 | $ 6,024 | $12,012 | $18,904 | $ 21,373 |
| Deferred income tax | | 179 | 235 | 282 | 481 | 929 | 1,169 |
| Long-term debt | 1,021 | 5,626 | 9,691 | 9,510 | 31,287 | 48,175 | 58,086 |
| Other | 208 | 319 | ... | ... | ... | 152 | ... |
| **Stockholders' equity** | | | | | | | |
| Common stock (par value $1) | $1,186 | $ 2,255 | $ 3,530 | $ 3,725 | $ 3,860 | $ 4,556 | $ 3,351‡ |
| Paid-in capital | 10 | 10 | 83 | 83 | 83 | 3,199§ | 4,441 |
| Retained earnings | 5,493 | 6,557 | 8,671 | 10,252 | 14,749 | 20,043 | 26,252 |
| Treasury stock | (13) | (13) | ... | ... | ... | ... | (1,228) |
| Total | $6,676 | $ 8,809 | $12,284 | $14,060 | $18,692 | $27,798 | $ 32,816 |
| Total liabilities | $9,187 | $17,656 | $27,151 | $29,876 | $62,472 | $95,958 | $113,444 |

\* Principally investment in Coral Television Corp.

† Principally unamortized leasehold expense and debt discount and expense.

‡ Common stock converted from no par to $1 par value.

§ Increase largely due to proceeds from sale of 150,000 warrants issued for $20 per share in connection with debt placement.

n.a. = not available.

Source: Annual reports.

# EXHIBIT 2

## GENERAL CINEMA CORPORATION
### Profit and Loss Statements—Years Ended October 31
(in thousands of dollars)

| | 1960 | 1961 | 1962 | 1963 | 1964 | 1965 | 1966 | 1967 | 1968 | 1969 | 1970 |
|---|---|---|---|---|---|---|---|---|---|---|---|
| Revenues | $8,140 | $10,423 | $12,799 | $15,637 | $20,815 | $25,163 | $33,672 | $42,386 | $71,671 | $129,534 | $159,408 |
| Costs and expenses | | | | | | | | | | | |
| Film, cost of sales | $4,035 | $ 5,392 | $ 6,569 | $ 8,042 | $10,642 | $13,174 | $18,294 | $23,464 | $40,102 | $ 75,421 | $ 94,233 |
| Operating and administration | 2,529 | 3,475 | 4,144 | 5,172 | 6,762 | 7,943 | 10,633 | 13,484 | 16,501 | 20,262 | 23,166 |
| Selling and distribution | | | | | | | | | 3,080 | 14,201 | 18,759 |
| Interest | | | 134 | 120 | 217 | 341 | 350 | 418 | 1,223 | 3,381 | 3,991 |
| Depreciation | 400 | 516 | 699 | 821 | 1,034 | 1,203 | 1,345 | 1,529 | 2,669 | 5,654 | 6,759 |
| Total | $6,964 | $ 9,383 | $11,546 | $14,155 | $18,655 | $22,661 | $30,622 | $38,895 | $63,575 | $118,919 | $146,908 |
| Operating income | $1,176 | $ 1,040 | $ 1,253 | $ 1,482 | $ 2,160 | $ 2,502 | $ 3,050 | $ 3,491 | $ 8,096 | $ 10,615 | $ 12,500 |
| Capital gains | 92 | 88 | 34 | 57 | 48 | 131 | 8 | 39 | 50 | 9 | 54 |
| Total | $1,268 | $ 1,128 | $ 1,287 | $ 1,539 | $ 2,208 | $ 2,633 | $ 3,058 | $ 3,530 | $ 8,146 | $ 10,624 | $ 12,554 |
| Income tax | 486 | 427 | 516 | 620 | 891 | 1,119 | 1,248 | 1,537 | 3,810 | 4,837 | 5,718 |
| | $ 782 | $ 701 | $ 771 | $ 919 | $ 1,317 | $ 1,514 | $ 1,810 | $ 1,993 | $ 4,336 | $ 5,787 | $ 6,836 |
| Equity in net income of unconsolidated subsidiaries and minority interests | 88 | 26 | | (16) | 30 | 80 | 205 | 197 | 257 | 169 | 279 |
| Net income before extraordinary items | $ 870 | $ 727 | $ 771 | $ 903 | $ 1,347 | $ 1,594 | $ 2,015 | $ 2,190 | $ 4,593 | $ 5,956 | $ 7,115 |
| Extraordinary items | | | | | 90 | 51 | (33) | 96 | 395 | 194 | 226 |
| Net income | $ 870 | $ 727 | $ 771 | $ 903 | $ 1,437 | $ 1,645 | $ 1,982 | $ 2,286 | $ 4,988 | $ 6,150 | $ 7,341 |
| Shares outstanding (avg.)* | 2,983 | 3,155 | 3,158 | 3,162 | 3,162 | 3,170 | 3,175 | 3,227 | 3,246 | 3,346 | 3,371 |
| Earnings per share | | | | | | | | | | | |
| Before extraordinary items | $ .34 | $ .23 | $ .24 | $ .27 | .41 | .50 | .63 | .68 | 1.42 | 1.80 | $ 2.11 |
| After extraordinary items | .34 | .23 | .24 | .27 | .44 | .52 | .62 | .71 | 1.54 | 1.85 | 2.18 |
| Dividends per share | .06 | .14 | .15 | .15 | .15 | .16 | .18 | .22 | .15 | .26 | .34 |

* Adjusted for stock splits: 2½ for 1 in 1967, 5 for 4 in 1965, and a 10% stock dividend in 1964.
Stock price, June 30, 1971 = 54¾ per share.

**EXHIBIT 2** (*continued*)

| | Theater Division | | | Beverage Division | | |
|---|---|---|---|---|---|---|
| | *1968* | *1969* | *1970* | *1968* | *1969* | *1970* |
| Revenues | $54,108 | $57,698 | $69,591 | $17,563 | $71,836 | $89,817 |
| Costs and expenses | | | | | | |
| Film, cost of sales | $29,919 | $31,263 | $38,497 | $10,183 | $44,158 | $55,736 |
| Operating and administrative | 15,645 | 16,668 | 18,975 | 856 | 3,594 | 4,191 |
| Selling and distribution | .... | .... | .... | 3,080 | 14,201 | 18,759 |
| Interest | 246 | 287 | 701 | 977 | 3,094 | 3,290 |
| Depreciation | 1,654 | 1,800 | 1,905 | 1,015 | 3,854 | 4,854 |
| Total costs and expenses | $47,464 | $50,018 | $60,078 | $16,111 | $68,901 | $86,830 |
| Operating income | $ 6,644 | $ 7,680 | $ 9,513 | $ 1,452 | $ 2,935 | $ 2,987 |
| Capital gains | 9 | (13) | (3) | 41 | 22 | 57 |
| Total | $ 6,653 | $ 7,667 | $ 9,510 | $ 1,493 | $ 2,957 | $ 3,044 |
| Income tax | $ 3,129 | 3,507 | 4,233 | 681 | 1,330 | 1,485 |
| | $ 3,524 | $ 4,160 | $ 5,277 | $ 812 | $ 1,627 | $ 1,559 |
| Equity in net income of unconsolidated subsidiaries | 257 | 218 | 279 | .... | .... | .... |
| Minority interest | .... | .... | .... | .... | (49) | .... |
| Income before extraordinary items | $ 3,781 | $ 4,378 | $ 5,556 | $ 812 | $ 1,578 | $ 1,559 |

Source: **Annual reports.**

The results for the theater exhibition industry during this period were dismal, as shown by the following table:

|  | 1946 | 1948 | 1954 | 1958 | 1963 |
|---|---|---|---|---|---|
| Percent of U.S. recreational expenditures | 19.8% | 15.5% | 9.4% | 6.3% | 4.1% |
| Percent of U.S. spectator amusement expenditures | 81.9% | 78.5% | 73.4% | 64.5% | 53.4% |
| Admissions receipts (millions) | $1,692 | $1,506 | $1,228 | $992 | $904 |
| Number of theaters | n.a. | 18,631 | 18,491 | 16,354 | 12,652 |

n.a. = not available.
Source: U.S. Department of Commerce.

Prior to 1949, the motion picture industry was dominated by the "Big Five" (Paramount, Twentieth-Century Fox, Warner Bros., Loew's, and RKO), each firm possessing production, distribution, and exhibition facilities. Approximately 80% of all feature films and a significantly higher percentage of box office successes were released by these companies.

Although the Big Five controlled only 17% of the nation's theaters in 1945, they accounted for 45% of domestic film rentals. In particular they were the dominant factor in downtown theater districts, as they operated more than 70% of the first-run movie houses in cities with populations exceeding 100,000. As much as 80% of the profits reported by integrated companies were thought to come from the exhibition activities.[2]

After a decade of litigation the U.S. Department of Justice secured consent decrees from the Big Five in 1949 and 1952 which provided that: (a) each picture was to be rented on a picture-by-picture, theater-by-theater basis, without regard for other pictures, exhibitor affiliations, or other theaters; (b) each existing company was to be divided into a theater company vested with all wholly owned domestic theaters and a production-distribution company which was to assume title to studios and film exchanges; and (c) certain pooled theaters and others which represented the "fruits of conspiracy" were to be divested.[3]

During the next two decades the theater portions of the Big Five led extraordinarily varied existences and by 1971 had changed almost beyond recognition. In each instance for which data were available, theater revenues declined until 1962 in line with industry experience. The number of theaters reached low points for Paramount, National

---

[2] William F. Hellmuth, Jr., in Walter Adams (ed.), *The Motion Picture Industry in the Structure of American Industry* (New York: The Macmillan Co., 1961), p. 405.

[3] For the five companies, the divestitures amounted to about 1,200 theaters, the last of which were disposed of in 1958.

Theaters, and Loew's during 1965, and for the remaining two circuits were still falling in 1970.

**Number of theaters**

|  | 1948 | 1958 | 1965 | 1970 |
|---|---|---|---|---|
| Paramount (ABC) . . . . . . . . . . . . . . | 1,424 | 511 | 399 | 434 |
| National Theaters (National General) . . . | 588 | 290 | 215 | 301 |
| Loew's Theaters (Loew's Inc.) . . . . . . . | 188 | 104* | 59 | 117 |
| Stanley Warner (Cinerama) . . . . . . . . . | 441 | 253 | 195 | {132 |
| RKO Theaters (Cinerama) . . . . . . . . . . | 124 | 65 | 55 | |
|  | 2,765 | 1,223 | 923 | 984 |

*1959 figure.
Note: Names in parentheses were parent companies in 1971.

The Paramount, National, and Loew's theater circuits formed the nucleus for three large corporations, each with sales in excess of $500 million in 1970, of which movie exhibition revenues constituted less than 15%. The RKO and Stanley Warner theaters were acquired by Glen Alden in 1956 and 1967, respectively, and what was left of them was sold in 1971 by the $1.3 million conglomerate to deficit-ridden Cinerama, Inc. (1970 sales, $39.9 million; loss, $8.6 million). Ironically, Stanley Warner had owned 90% of Cinerama in the early 1950s in an unsuccessful attempt to reverse the slide in movie attendance by exhibiting films made with the three-dimensional Cinerama process. Brief historical sketches of the Big Five are provided in the Appendix.

## Rejuvenation

From a nadir in 1962, the movie exhibition business staged a comeback reflected in the statistics in Exhibits 3 and 4. Behind the increasing admission receipts and number of theaters were several factors frequently mentioned by those familiar with the industry. Mr. Smith stressed some of them in the comments below:

The myth of the fifties that movies catered primarily to a limited, declining, nonsophisticated segment of the population has been exploded in the sixties by the success of multiple-auditorium theater complexes simultaneously offering up to eight different films with the widest variety of audience appeal. Areas that only a few years ago were considered marginal for a satisfactory return on the investment required for a single theater now are capable of supporting a multiple-auditorium complex. The most fundamental change in the sixties has been in the audience profile. Today's audiences are, for the most part, younger, better educated, more affluent—many from the academic

**EXHIBIT 3**
Statistics on the motion picture industry

| | Admission receipts (millions) | Admission price index (1957–59 = 100) | Percent of U.S. recreational expenditures | Percent of U.S. spectator amusement expenditures | Number of feature films* |
|---|---|---|---|---|---|
| 1960 . . . . . . . | $  951 | 110 | 5.2 | 59.2 | 155† |
| 1961 . . . . . . . | 921 | 115 | 4.7 | 56.7 | 185† |
| 1962 . . . . . . . | 903 | 121 | 4.4 | 54.9 | 145 |
| 1963 . . . . . . . | 904 | 125 | 4.1 | 53.4 | 150 |
| 1964 . . . . . . . | 913 | 135 | 3.7 | 51.8 | 150 |
| 1965 . . . . . . . | 927 | 146 | 3.5 | 51.2 | 165 |
| 1966 . . . . . . . | 964 | 158 | 3.3 | 50.1 | 168 |
| 1967 . . . . . . . | 989 | 169 | 3.2 | 47.7 | 215 |
| 1968 . . . . . . . | 1,045 | 185 | 3.1 | 49.1 | 230 |
| 1969 . . . . . . . | 1,097 | 201 | 3.0 | 48.5 | 325 |
| 1970 . . . . . . . | 1,175 | 218 | n.a. | n.a. | n.a. |

*Approved by Code Administration.
†Estimated.
n.a. = not available.
Source: U.S. Department of Commerce.

community and more of the "white-collar" rather than "blue-collar" group. They are critical, involved in the issues of the day, and shun the make-believe world that used to pass for "real life" in the movies that enchanted millions a mere 10 or 15 years ago. . . . [See Exhibit 5.]

No longer is moviegoing a pure escapism for the masses. The return of the screen to reality has created the opportunity for movie makers to be the greatest artists of our times as they work with relevant themes unfettered by overly restrictive production codes. This new freedom of expression has not arrived without attendant problems and the theater operator's public relations have never been more sensitive, but the net gain from the involvement of an entire new generation in the business of film making and moviegoing is impossible to overestimate.[4]

While total receipts were increasing at 5% to 6% a year in the late 1960s, attendance was growing only 2% and the traditional, 2,000–3,000-seat downtown "movie palace" continued to lose audiences. Industry observers credited the decline of the downtown theater to a constellation of factors: urban decay, crime on the streets, insufficient parking, deteriorating facilities due to age and lack of investment, and a "fragmentation" in consumer tastes which made it difficult to fill a large theater consistently for long runs. Only in New York City, Boston, Minneapolis–St. Paul, San Francisco, and a few other cities were downtown theater districts thought by General Cinema to be vibrant.

---

[4] *Cinemas for the Seventies*, Richard A. Smith, president, General Cinema Corporation, February 26, 1970.

**EXHIBIT 4**
**Statistics on motion picture theaters**

| | 1963 | 1964 | 1965 | 1966 | 1967 | 1968 | 1969 | 1970 |
|---|---|---|---|---|---|---|---|---|
| **I. Estimated theater population** | | | | | | | | |
| Indoor (four-wall) | 9,150 | 9,340 | 9,560 | 9,750 | 9,930 | 10,080 | 10,320 | 10,550 |
| Drive-in | 3,502 | 3,560 | 3,630 | 3,690 | 3,720 | 3,740 | 3,780 | 3,800 |
| Total | 12,652 | 12,900 | 13,190 | 13,440 | 13,650 | 13,820 | 14,100 | 14,350 |
| **II. Theater construction** | | | | | | | | |
| A. Opened | | | | | | | | |
| Shopping centers | 46 | 74 | 100 | 103 | 98 | 90 | 92 | 96 |
| Other indoor | 47 | 44 | 61 | 65 | 83 | 81 | 156 | 155 |
| Drive-in | 34 | 35 | 47 | 55 | 31 | 20 | 39 | 24 |
| Total | 127 | 153 | 208 | 223 | 212 | 191 | 287 | 275* |
| Investment (millions) | ... | ... | ... | $ 75.8 | $ 70.8 | $ 61.3 | $ 94.8 | $108.5 |
| Investment/theater (thousands) | ... | ... | ... | 339.9 | 334.0 | 320.9 | 330.3 | 394.5 |
| B. Announced or announced and construction started | | | | | | | | |
| Shopping centers | 97 | 147 | 138 | 101 | 92 | 108 | 133 | 84 |
| Other indoor | 50 | 84 | 53 | 76 | 103 | 113 | 152 | 167 |
| Drive-in | 46 | 66 | 55 | 44 | 40 | 59 | 59 | 27 |
| Total | 193 | 297 | 246 | 221 | 235 | 280 | 344 | 278 |

*251 were four-wall theaters. Of these, 155 were single-auditorium theaters and 96 were multiauditorium complexes accounting for 211 auditoriums. There were about 51 single-auditorium theaters with 400 seats or less and about 63 multiauditorium complexes accounting for 143 auditoriums with 400 seats or less.

Source: Motion Picture Association of America.

**EXHIBIT 5**
Yearly movie admissions by age

| | Percent of total yearly admissions | | Percent of population |
|---|---|---|---|
| | *1969* | *1970* | *1969–70* |
| Total public, age 12 and over . . . . . . . 100 | 100 | 100 | |
| Age | | | |
| 12–15 years . . . . . . . . . . . . . . . . 18 | 16 | 10 | |
| 16–20 years . . . . . . . . . . . . . . . . 31 | 27 | 12 | |
| 21–24 years . . . . . . . . . . . . . . . . 16 | 16 | 8 | |
| 25–29 years . . . . . . . . . . . . . . . . 12 | 13 | 9 | |
| 30–39 years . . . . . . . . . . . . . . . . 10 | 12 | 14 | |
| 40–49 years . . . . . . . . . . . . . . . . 6 | 8 | 16 | |
| 50–59 years . . . . . . . . . . . . . . . . 3 | 6 | 13 | |
| 60 years and over . . . . . . . . . . . . 4 | 2 | 18 | |

Source: Survey prepared by the Opinion Research Corporation of Princeton, New Jersey, for the Motion Picture Association of America.

The effect of the decline of the downtown theater and its neighborhood satellites was felt in the competition for film exhibition rights. Exhibitors negotiated with film distributors, often in competition with other exhibitors, for the right to show films. The type of contract varied considerably, depending on the projected success of the movie and the bargaining ability of the parties involved. At one extreme was a "flat" deal whereby the exhibitor paid the distributor a fixed amount for the right to show a film for some specified length of time. Typically, older movies—for instance, a 1948 Bogart picture—were handled in this way. At the other extreme, the distributor might seek a "four-wall" deal whereby he would rent the theater for a fixed amount and retain all the admission receipts. Most of the arrangements were between these extremes and involved some form of revenue sharing. For a "hot" picture the distributor might seek a "90/10" deal; he would pay the exhibitor's normal expenses and 10% of the receipts and keep the rest. Should a picture fail to meet expectations, the exhibitor could negotiate with the distributor for the right to withdraw it prematurely. The annual cost of film rights was typically 35%–40% of gross receipts. (See Exhibit 6.) Herb Hurwitz, vice president, theaters, at General Cinema, noted:

The exhibitor is really selling his ability to fill seats when he negotiates for a picture. For that particular movie he must convince the distributor that the share of receipts he offers will yield more revenue to the distributor than the arrangements offered by the competition. In some respects the "A" grade pictures are easier to assess because you can bet they will do well

**EXHIBIT 6**

**Theater operating costs**

| | |
|---|---|
| THE HOUSE, including rent or the equivalent; mortgage payments; depreciation of building and equipment; heat, light, power, telephone, and any other costs incurred as owner or tenant . . . . . . . . . . . . . . . . . . . | 24.5% |
| THE STAFF, including all salary and wage payments to regular and part-time employees; also, cost of uniforms, etc. . . . . . . . . . . . . . . . . . . . . . . | 26.6 |
| THE SHOW, including all film rentals, cost of stage shows if any, and cost of film handling . . . . . . . . . . . . . . . . . . . . . . . . . . . . . . . . . . . . | 36.4 |
| SALES APPROACH, including all advertising, publicity, exploitation, and promotion; poster rentals, trailers, accessories, and displays; newspaper advertising, including pro-rata share of cooperative advertising . . . . . . . . . | 9.0 |
| OPERATING PROFIT, before state and federal taxes . . . . . . . . . . . . . . . | 3.5 |
| TOTAL . . . . . . . . . . . . . . . . . . . . . . . . . . . . . . . . . . . . . . . | 100.0% |

Source: The Motion Picture Herald Institute of Industry Opinion.

for everyone. However, the "B" and "C" films are really the critical ones for the success of a theater. Of course, the distributor has to worry about his total lineup. He won't look favorably on the exhibitor who is willing to bid high on the "hot" pictures and expects a bargain on the rest.

As shopping centers and new suburban theaters commanded a greater share of movie audiences and were often able to obtain higher ticket prices, they broke the dominance of downtown theaters in securing first-run movies. "Perimeter runs" (auditioning a film in the suburbs of a city) became common. Agreements on "clearance" (providing a theater with exclusive rights in a drawing area for a specified time period) became less restrictive. "Showcasing" (releasing a film simultaneously in a number of theaters in an area) became more common, and the number of road show films diminished. Partially as a result of these factors, first-run movies were available for longer periods of time in the new theaters than had been customary in the past. All these factors contributed to the profitability of the new theaters.

### Film production, distribution, and promotion

Theater owners depended heavily on the quantity and audience appeal of movie productions. The major film producers had been plagued in the late 1960s by excess inventories of high-budget films, resulting in massive write-offs estimated by one source at $250 million.[5] MGM and Twentieth-Century Fox had both experienced severe losses in recent years. The new management of MGM acted in 1969 to cancel 15 pictures which would have cost some $55 million to produce and subsequently adopted a policy limiting investments per film to about $2 million.[6] Twentieth-Century Fox indicated that it planned no film starts at all

---

[5] *Variety*, May 12, 1971.

[6] *Value Line*, January 1, 1971, p. 1439.

for the first half of 1970.[7] A list of the top box office successes in 1970 is provided in Exhibit 7.

The large, old-line producing-distributing companies, a number of them having become subsidiaries of large diversified firms, continued to dominate film releases. The leading nine distributors received about 77% of all film rentals according to one 1970 survey. However, an increasing number of new companies had appeared, most of them distributing low-budget undertakings frequently produced by newcomers and featuring young actors. Low-cost films could be immensely profitable; for instance, "The Graduate," produced by Avco Embassy, the 12th ranking distributor, for less than $3 million, yielded well over $40 million in admission receipts. Exhibitors were counting on rising receipts to provide incentives for producers. In fact, some films such as "The Godfather" were so much in demand that producers were able to secure substantial advance payments from exhibitors for their pictures even before filming was completed.

The industry had been plagued recently by controversy over pornography and the alleged inadequacy of the Motion Picture Association's rating scheme. *Variety* commented:

MPAA President said, "The ratings are becoming more difficult because the (film making) creative people are dealing with subjects they never touched before." What this amounts to, of course, is the producers' anxiety to exploit once taboo matters including wide-open sex, perversion, violence, drug addiction, and indiscriminate rebellion against the establishment.

Highly placed sources in the film industry say that what is really happening among showmen is, finally, recognition of a rebellious mid-America public.[8]

In May 1971, Protestant and Catholic church groups spoke out strongly against both the quality of the ratings and the industry's willingness to enforce the code. That same month, 25 newspapers announced that they would not accept advertisements for "X" rated films,[9] a matter of some concern to exhibitors, for newspapers had been the industry's chief advertising medium.

### Competition

While the Big Five had reacted slowly and modestly to the turnaround in the industry, a number of new participants had moved aggres-

---

[7] Ibid., p. 1445.

[8] *Variety*, May 12, 1971.

[9] Films were rated "G" (acceptable for general audiences), "GP" (general audiences, parental discretion advised), "R" (restricted—under 16 years of age must be accompanied by an adult), and "X" (no one under 17 admitted).

sively into the field. Among them were franchisers who noted the increasing popularity of movies and the fact that theater management required comparatively little experience.[10] Network Cinema, formed in 1969 and partially owned and promoted by Jerry Lewis, sold franchises for $15,000 plus $40,000 in equipment (the franchisee had to select and purchase his own site). While only six Network Cinema theaters were reportedly operating in May 1971, over 1,500 franchises had been sold. This company and many of the other recent entrants concentrated on "mini" theaters having 350 or fewer seats per auditorium.

In addition to competition from traditional leisure-time activities, theater owners were confronted by alternative means of dispensing movies. Since recent box office successes were not generally available to television and inventories of older films were being rapidly depleted, each of the television networks had begun the production of feature-length pictures for original release. Lurking in the background was the prospect of pay TV, which conceivably could offer competitive rental fees to conventional film distributors for first-run pictures. A third possibility was the video cassette. The viewer would buy or rent a film on video tape and replay it at his convenience on a recorder incorporated in his television set. United Artists, Twentieth-Century Fox, and Avco Embassy Pictures announced plans to put films on cartridges and sell them for about the price of admission to a first-run movie. RCA and Sony had developed recorders to be available in 1972 for about $400.

Mr. Melvin Wintman, executive vice president of General Cinema, indicated that in his opinion these new sources of competition would not have a serious impact on theater operators:

The economics of the business work against other means of exhibition. A feature-length picture can be shown on television once or maybe twice during prime time, no matter how good it is, while we can offer guarantees of 10–15 weeks for a picture like "Love Story." As a result, television can afford perhaps $500,000 to $600,000 per picture, about the equivalent of a double-length regular hour TV program. That is a million or so less than the cost of a good low-budget film. In fact, we support the networks: the more films produced, the better. If they strike a good one, they may bring it to theaters first, or, if not, we are always interested in less expensive fillers.

Pay TV, on the other hand, could be a problem if a large-enough audience could be attracted. However, the public hasn't accepted the pay-TV concept.[11] We also suspect that the moviegoer really wants to get out of the house, especially the woman, to see a show. For this reason, I bet, except for pornography, cassettes won't generate much of a market for recreational films either, though they may be great for educational purposes.

---

[10] Projectionists were readily available from the projectionists' union, and films could be secured through a booking agency.

[11] A December 1970 survey by Sindlinger & Co. indicated that for various reasons only 12% of Americans were interested in paying for television programs.

**EXHIBIT 7**
**Box office statistics**°

| Rank | Title | Dist. | Playing weeks | Gross Receipts |
|------|-------|-------|---------------|----------------|
| 1 | Airport . . . . . . . . . . . | U | 629 | $12,378,259 |
| 2 | Mash . . . . . . . . . . . . | FOX | 932 | 12,186,906 |
| 3 | Patton . . . . . . . . . . . | FOX | 832 | 9,327,636 |
| 4 | Hello Dolly . . . . . . . . | FOX | 739 | 9,078,338 |
| 5 | Z . . . . . . . . . . . . . . | C5 | 928 | 7,919,478 |
| 6 | Bob, Carol, Ted, Alice . . | COL | 748 | 7,160,506 |
| 7 | Woodstock . . . . . . . . . | WB | 536 | 7,108,600 |
| 8 | Catch 22 . . . . . . . . . | PAR | 391 | 5,982,490 |
| 9 | Cactus Flower . . . . . . . | COL | 486 | 5,167,043 |
| 10 | Lovers & Strangers . . . . | CRC | 478 | 4,496,608 |
| 11 | Cotton Comes Harlem . . | UA | 303 | 4,458,401 |
| 12 | Butch Cassidy & Kid . . . | FOX | 717 | 4,413,816 |
| 13 | Out-of-Towners . . . . . . | PAR | 286 | 4,411,683 |
| 14 | They Shoot Horses . . . . | CRC | 468 | 4,317,835 |
| 15 | Getting Straight . . . . . . | COL | 451 | 4,298,712 |
| 16 | Midnight Cowboy . . . . . | UA | 551 | 4,036,491 |
| 17 | Paint Your Wagon . . . . | PAR | 444 | 3,919,143 |
| 18 | Beneath Planet Apes . . . | FOX | 331 | 3,822,161 |
| 19 | Funny Girl . . . . . . . . . | COL | 343 | 3,800,202 |
| 20 | Clear Day See F'ver . . . . | PAR | 336 | 3,737,760 |
| 21 | Joe . . . . . . . . . . . . . | CAN | 371 | 3,553,283 |
| 22 | Marooned . . . . . . . . . | COL | 327 | 3,370,833 |
| 23 | Adventurers . . . . . . . . | PAR | 338 | 3,292,310 |
| 24 | Darling Lil . . . . . . . . . | PAR | 184 | 3,226,802 |
| 25 | Boys in the Band . . . . . | NGP | 436 | 3,216,380 |
| 26 | Scrooge . . . . . . . . . | NGP | 216 | 3,158,909 |
| 27 | Anne of Thousand Days . | U | 343 | 2,957,516 |
| 28 | A Man Called Horse . . . | NGP | 350 | 2,873,710 |
| 29 | Beyond Valley Dolls . . . | FOX | 276 | 2,777,371 |
| 30 | Easy Rider . . . . . . . . . | COL | 602 | 2,713,808 |
| 31 | Five Easy Pieces . . . . . . | COL | 255 | 2,678,790 |
| 32 | The Reivers . . . . . . . . | NGP | 381 | 2,637,657 |
| 33 | Majesty's Secret Serv. . . | UA | 369 | 2,541,515 |
| 34 | Tora Tora Tora . . . . . . | FOX | 128 | 2,491,823 |
| 35 | Call Me Mr. Tibbs . . . . . | UA | 234 | 2,438,690 |
| 36 | What Say Naked Lady . . | UA | 351 | 2,435,197 |
| 37 | Myra Breckinridge . . . . | FOX | 24 | 2,410,036 |
| 38 | Boy Named C. Brown . . | NGP | 238 | 2,341,565 |
| 39 | 2001 Space Odyssey . . . | MGM | 302 | 2,276,688 |
| 40 | B. Cassidy/Jean Brodie . . | FOX | 298 | 2,237,115 |
| 41 | Without A Stitch . . . . . | VIP | 244 | 2,225,685 |
| 42 | Diary Mad Housewife . . | U | 214 | 2,132,963 |
| 43 | Bird Crystal Plumage . . . | UMC | 313 | 2,108,068 |
| 44 | Sex. Freedom Denmark . | AFI | 105 | 1,902,403 |
| 45 | Secret Santa Vittoria . . . | UA | 274 | 1,877,292 |
| 46 | John and Mary . . . . . . | FOX | 296 | 1,769,059 |
| 47 | Topaz . . . . . . . . . . . | U | 231 | 1,750,280 |
| 48 | Satyricon . . . . . . . . . | UA | 217 | 1,733,178 |
| 49 | Chisum . . . . . . . . . . . | WB | 215 | 1,707,852 |
| 50 | Sunflower . . . . . . . . . | AVE | 137 | 1,707,479 |
| 51 | Boatniks . . . . . . . . . . | BV | 232 | 1,651,406 |
| 52 | Goodbye Mr. Chips . . . . | MGM | 272 | 1,597,649 |
| 53 | Two Mules Sister Sara . . | U | 219 | 1,591,238 |
| 54 | Tick Tick Tick . . . . . . . | MGM | 145 | 1,586,850 |
| 55 | The Landlord . . . . . . . | UA | 165 | 1,580,898 |
| 56 | Watermelon Man . . . . . | COL | 147 | 1,568,315 |
| 57 | Oliver . . . . . . . . . . . . | COL | 240 | 1,562,765 |
| 58 | Women In Love . . . . . . | UA | 196 | 1,512,818 |
| 59 | Kelly's Heroes . . . . . . . | MGM | 185 | 1,488,685 |

**EXHIBIT 7** (*continued*)

| Rank | Title | Dist. | Playing weeks | Gross Receipts |
|------|-------|-------|---------------|----------------|
| 60 | Putney Swope . . . . . . . | C5 | 301 | 1,483,000 |
| 61 | It's a Mad Mad World . . . | UA | 213 | 1,439,826 |
| 62 | The Damned . . . . . . . . | WB | 223 | 1,437,725 |
| 63 | C C & Company . . . . . . | AVE | 252 | 1,398,624 |
| 64 | Liberation of L B Jones . | COL | 136 | 1,392,080 |
| 65 | Sicilian Clan . . . . . . . . | FOX | 220 | 1,381,602 |
| 66 | Pornography Denmark . . | SPX | 127 | 1,346,463 |
| 67 | The Grasshopper . . . . . | NGP | 221 | 1,339,738 |
| 68 | The Hawaiians . . . . . . . | UA | 172 | 1,305,524 |
| 69 | Fantasia . . . . . . . . . . | BV | 138 | 1,297,350 |
| 70 | Jenny . . . . . . . . . . . | CRC | 213 | 1,282,290 |
| 71 | Owl and Pussycat . . . . . | COL | 62 | 1,238,795 |
| 72 | Cherry Harry Raquel . . . | EVE | 155 | 1,209,900 |
| 73 | Willie Boy Is Here . . . . . | U | 181 | 1,175,404 |
| 74 | Bloody Mama . . . . . . . | AIP | 159 | 1,167,390 |
| 75 | Magic Christian . . . . . . | CUE | 183 | 1,166,380 |
| 76 | Sterile Cuckoo . . . . . . . | PAR | 209 | 1,122,226 |
| 77 | He and She . . . . . . . . . | AQU | 162 | 1,118,684 |
| 78 | Little Fauss & Halsy . . . | PAR | 127 | 1,110,921 |
| 79 | The Arrangement . . . . . | WB | 213 | 1,110,070 |
| 80 | Let It Be . . . . . . . . . . | UA | 191 | 1,109,919 |
| 81 | Love Story . . . . . . . . . | PAR | 22 | 1,108,170 |
| 82 | Virgin and Gypsy . . . . . | CHE | 162 | 1,096,173 |
| 83 | Cheyenne Social Club . . | NGP | 194 | 1,078,630 |
| 84 | Zabriskie Point . . . . . . | MGM | 220 | 1,072,518 |
| 85 | Soldier Blue . . . . . . . . | AVE | 130 | 1,060,065 |
| 86 | Only Game in Town . . . | FOX | 179 | 1,039,690 |
| 87 | Monte Walsh . . . . . . . . | NGP | 136 | 1,000,384 |

Total films in sample . . . . . . . . . . . . . . . . . . . . 1,350
Total films grossing over $100,000 . . . . . . . . . 330
Total gross receipts in sample . . . . . . . . . . . . $340,927,000
% of $, top 25 films . . . . . . . . . . . . . . . . 41
% of $, those over $1 million in gross receipts. . . . 75

| | Distributor symbols | Ranking in revenues |
|------|---------------------|---------------------|
| AIP | American International Pictures | 13 |
| AQU | Aquarius | 23 |
| AFI | Art Films International | 21 |
| AVE | Avco Embassy | 12 |
| BV | Buena Vista | 11 |
| CAN | Cannon | 15 |
| CHE | Chevron | 20 |
| C5 | Cinema 5 | 10 |
| CMA | Cinemation | 16 |
| CRC | Cinema Releasing Corporation | 9 |
| COL | Columbia Pictures | 2 |
| CUE | Commonwealth United | 19 |
| FOX | 20th-Century Fox | 1 |
| MGM | Metro-Goldwyn-Mayer | 8 |
| NGP | National General Pictures | 6 |
| PAR | Paramount | 4 |
| SPX | Silver Screen | n.a. |
| UMC | U-M Film Distributors | n.a. |
| UA | United Artists | 3 |
| U | Universal | 5 |
| VIP | VIP | 18 |
| WB | Warner Bros. | 7 |

\* Statistics taken from a 1970 survey of 850 large city theaters representing about 33% of total box office receipts. Playing weeks refer to the aggregate number of weeks the film was shown in these 850 theaters.
n.a. = not available.
Source: *Variety*, May 12, 1971.

## GENERAL CINEMA

General Cinema was an outgrowth of a company organized in 1922 by Mr. Philip Smith to build and operate movie theaters. In 1935 Mr. Smith was credited with constructing and opening the first successful open-air theater. He subsequently was a leader in adapting talking pictures to drive-in theaters and in developing and promoting innovations in the concession business. Although the company remained small, it nonetheless was one of the largest and most successful entrants in the open-air segment of the industry in the years prior to World War II.

Mr. Richard Smith, who became president in 1961 upon his father's death, commented on the years after World War II:

> While the rest of the industry enjoyed great prosperity during the war, we just barely survived the effects of gas rationing and daylight savings time. After the war, however, the situation was reversed.[12] Television was devastating to the indoor theater operator and the large chains were beset with legal problems. On the other hand, we found that we attracted a different kind of audience—families and young people—and benefited from laws which lowered driving ages, just as downtown theaters were penalized by inadequate parking facilities. New projection techniques were developed which permitted viewing earlier in the evening, and this company was among the first to lengthen the playing season by introducing heaters to keep cars warm in the wintertime. Desirable land parcels of 25 to 35 acres were available in those days close to population centers at reasonable prices, and we expanded by building modern facilities equipped with playgrounds and amusement areas. As our position improved we began competing for first-run movies.

By 1959, Midwest Drive-In (the name was ultimately changed to General Cinema in 1964) owned 19 open-air theaters and was one of the three largest competitors in this segment of the industry. However, as land availability declined and values increased sharply, new locations became difficult to secure and growth leveled off in the late 1950s at about $5.5 million in sales and $600,000 in after-tax profits.

### 1960, a year of decision

In 1960 Midwest Drive-In acquired the Smith Theater Company (1959 sales of $2.1 million and profits of $136,000), owner of 14 indoor theaters in suburban and resort locations and one drive-in. Both companies were controlled by two families[13] and managed by the Smith

---

[12] While the number of indoor theaters declined from 17,811 in 1948 to 14,714 in 1954, the number of drive-ins increased from 820 to 3,775.

[13] Prior to the public offering, the Smith family owned or controlled 45.3% and the Stoneman family 25.4% of the outstanding stock of the combined companies. These amounts were reduced to 34.9% and 20.0% following the offering. Mr. Richard

Management Company.[14] The public was then offered 180,000 shares of the combined company (renamed General Drive-In) at $12.50 per share, the proceeds from 130,000 shares accruing to certain selling shareholders and the remainder to the company. The company's share of the proceeds were to be used for expansion of shopping-center theaters and diversification into tenpins bowling.

Among the properties acquired with the Smith Theater Company was a theater in the Framingham Shopping Center. The shopping center, thought to be the first of its kind in the United States, had caught Philip Smith's imagination in 1951, and the promoter persuaded him to put a theater in it. Initially, the theater lost money and the shopping center itself, for over a decade, experienced periodic financial difficulties. By 1959, however, admission receipts were twice the initial level, and the shopping-center theater was contributing the largest profits in the theater group by a wide margin. A second shopping-center theater had been acquired in 1955, there being at that time, according to management, about four such shopping centers in the entire country.

In the late 1950s Richard Smith, who had assumed responsibility for developing new theater locations, noticed that the number of shopping centers under consideration was increasing rapidly. However, he found promoters, whom he asked to invest two thirds or more of the $300,000 required for a 1,200-seat theater, reluctant to take the risk in a troubled industry in conjunction with a small private company. The 1960 merger and public offering were conceived to ease the financial impediments to growth. In the prospectus accompanying the offering plans were announced for seven shopping-center theaters, four of which were to be in operation within the year.

The company also indicated that it planned to enter the tenpins bowling business through the immediate construction of three bowling centers in New England having a total of 104 lanes. The proprietors noted: "After the company has had the benefit of its experience in this area, it may expand its original goal of 300 to 400 lanes and undertake the establishment of bowling alleys . . . in metropolitan areas outside of New England." It was management's intention to proceed in bowling as it had in open-air theaters. Centers were to be "first-class," complete with restaurants and lounges and geared for use by families and young people. Tenpins bowling was enjoying a rapid rise in popularity in the United States in all parts of the country except the Northeast, which had traditionally been the province of candlepin bowling. According to the American Bowling Congress, the number of tenpins lanes in-

---

Smith was not among the selling shareholders. In 1971 these percentages were approximately 25.9% and 12.4%, the reduction due largely to a secondary issue in 1968.

[14] It was common in the theater industry for individual theaters to be operated by a management company in return for a management fee.

creased 87% from 1955 to 1960 and individual memberships in the Congress jumped 111%.

The management group considered bowling to be a particularly appropriate opportunity for the company; it was a leisure-time business thought to appeal to the type of person who enjoyed an evening at the movies. In addition, automatic pinsetters appeared to make tenpins bowling the most attractive variety of the sport for the participant. Moreover, General Drive-In was experienced in securing sites, constructing facilities, and managing a multiple-location business. In some respects growth in bowling seemed more attainable than in theaters; locations were not so difficult to find, since they were not tied to shopping centers, and credit and marketing assistance were readily available from AMF and Brunswick Corporation, the dominant pinsetter manufacturers.

## Theater operations

General Cinema enjoyed rapid growth in theater operations in the 1960s. The number of theaters grew from 39 in 1960 to 203 in 1970, most of them added in shopping-center locations, as indicated in Exhibit 8.

**EXHIBIT 8**

GENERAL CINEMA CORPORATION
Theater Operations

| October 31 | Drive-in | Shopping center* | Suburban and resort | Down-town | Total | Proposed and under construction |
|---|---|---|---|---|---|---|
| 1960 . . . . . | 20 | 4 (4) | 15 | .. | 39 | 11 |
| 1961 . . . . . | 26 | 8 (8) | 19 | .. | 53 | 10 |
| 1962 . . . . . | 26 | 10 (10) | 18 | .. | 54 | 17 |
| 1963 . . . . . | 32† | 20 (23) | 20† | .. | 72 | 17 |
| 1964 . . . . . | 34 | 25 (31) | 15 | .. | 74 | 31 |
| 1965 . . . . . | 36 | 46 (62) | 14 | .. | 96 | 33 |
| 1966 . . . . . | 46‡ | 69 (89) | 13 | 1 | 129 | 32 |
| 1967 . . . . . | 47 | 89 (114) | 10 | 1 | 147 | 36 |
| 1968 . . . . . | 48 | 103 (132) | 8 | 1 | 160 | 42 |
| 1969 . . . . . | 47 | 114 (149) | 8 | 1 | 170 | 37 |
| 1970 . . . . . | 48 | 137 (206) | 4 | 14§ | 203 | 39 |

* Number in parentheses indicates number of auditoriums; the 1970 total includes one triple and one quadruple cinema complex.
† Includes acquisition of six drive-in and two suburban theaters.
‡ Includes acquisition of 10 drive-in theaters.
§ Includes acquisition of a 15-theater chain in Minneapolis–St. Paul, 13 of the theaters located downtown.
Source: Annual reports.

The company at first found it difficult to procure first-run movies for its new shopping-center theaters. In several instances the company had to "buy its way" into markets by bidding aggressively on top pictures until its reputation was established in the community and among film distributors. Through clean, modern facilities and tasteful programming, stress was placed on creating an image of sophisticated entertainment that would attract family interest. Although some "X" rated films were exhibited, the company refused to show productions it considered pornographic, such as "I Am Curious-Yellow." It was also the largest customer for Walt Disney films in the country.

Beginning in 1963, General Cinema experimented with Cinema I and II theaters, two 500–1,000-seat auditoriums under one roof instead of one 1,200–1,400-seat auditorium. The test proved successful on several counts. First, there were some operating cost savings in personnel, advertising, and maintenance. Second, the twin auditoriums provided a means of dampening the effect of increasing construction costs while at the same time increasing revenues. The company's investment in a shopping-center twin approximated $100,000 to $150,000 as compared with $75,000 to $125,000 for a single auditorium; the average revenue per location was 50% to 80% higher. Although a few auditoriums had been built with as few as 400 seats, the company had not pursued "mini" theaters.

Location was considered to be crucial in determining a theater's success. In addition to the market research performed by the leading retailers in a new shopping center, management was particularly concerned about the economics of film procurement. The existence of several first-run theaters in an area could provide the distributor with leverage to drive a harder bargain and the moviegoer with competitive alternatives. Having a reliable knowledge of operating and construction costs, the company worked with the three remaining variables—ticket price, attendance, and film rental fees—to determine whether there was an opportunity for a 20% return on initial investment after taxes.

Mr. Wintman, executive vice president, touched on the philosophy which guided the division:

I am fundamentally conservative. Dick Smith asked me, "What would you do if business were to fall off 25%?" I don't want to wait for that. Good or bad, we should operate on the lowest possible base. We haven't grown up with Hollywood ideas the way the other big chains have—corporate jets, lunch at "21," and all that.[15] Every theater should stand on its own here, even though we're "fat" at the moment. We think we have the best theaters in the business and we don't spare the expense to keep them that way. We build *functional* not *lavish* theaters. However, once a theater is built, comparatively little reinvestment is needed to maintain it at that level relative to the cash flow it generates. This provides us with a source of funds for expansion.

---

[15] The General Cinema management group frequently, in groups or singly, had sandwiches delivered to the office for lunch.

Interest rates and reduced residential construction in the suburbs had slowed the growth in shopping-center development during the late 1960s. Mr. Smith indicated that only 50 such projects were underway in major or regional centers of interest to General Cinema in 1970, compared to 300 in 1966. However, in the first months of 1971, the pace of construction appeared to be picking up again. Attention was also being given to developing the "after market," existing shopping centers not having a theater. Should the opportunities become available, Mr. Smith felt that the company possessed the financial and management capability to triple the 15 to 20 shopping-center theaters opened annually in recent years.

In August 1970, General Cinema purchased Mann Theaters for $5.75 million in cash and notes. Mann operated 15 theaters in Minneapolis–St. Paul, 13 of them in downtown locations, and had sales of about $5.6 million. Mr. Smith explained the apparent departure from company policy of limiting theater additions to shopping centers:

We made an exception with Mann's, and if another one came along like it, I'd do it again. Minneapolis has done a nice job in resolving its urban problems; the downtown area has a lot of life in it. We had only one theater in Minnesota and had just missed a couple of shopping-center deals, which had been upsetting. The Mann Theaters were in good shape and could form the nucleus of a new region. We've since added several shopping-center cinemas in the area.

## Bowling operations

The number of bowling centers operated by General Cinema grew rapidly to 15 having 494 lanes in 1963 and accounting for about 10% of corporate sales. However, difficulties were encountered from the outset, and as early as 1962 thoughts of a major expansion into bowling were put aside. The centers never quite reached the break-even point. Five of them were either sold or converted into cinemas between 1965 and 1967, and in late 1968 long-term leases with purchase options were issued to Consolidated Bowling Corporation for the remaining facilities for a fee which approximated General Cinema's annual expenses.

However disheartening the bowling interlude had been, Mr. Smith expressed the view that the experience had been a healthy one for the management group:

We made some mistakes in entering the bowling business. For one, we misjudged our market. Rather than depending on families and the casual player, the bowling alley relies on blue-collar men's leagues in the evening and daytime bowling by women's groups—frequently the blue-collar workers' wives. The work force in New England is less blue-collar heavy industry than in the Midwest and is a lot more difficult to organize this way. We started to uncover the difficulty when we opened three centers outside of New England as part of our program to learn the business.

To attract leagues you should also be able to sell beer on the lanes. We found we weren't very good at securing liquor licenses. We understimated the competitive response from the candlepin operators in New England.

Withdrawing wasn't easy. The pinsetter manufacturers were competing with one another for good locations and putting pressure on operators to keep up. More importantly, we had a publicly stated goal of 400 to 500 lanes,[16] and I felt an obligation to meet that commitment. However, the operation was taking time away from theater expansion, and we began to discuss what ought to be done with it. Some of the group didn't want to accept a reverse and were in favor of trying to make it work. I thought we had given the business sufficient effort and was in favor of letting it go. After a lot of discussion, my point of view finally prevailed.

### Soft-drink bottling operations

In March 1968, General Cinema acquired the American Beverage Corporation for $18.1 million in cash, thereby obtaining Pepsi-Cola franchises in Miami, Florida; in Akron, Dayton, and Youngstown, Ohio; and a Schweppes franchise and a private-label brand in Houston. Through a sale-and-lease-back agreement, $12 million was raised to apply against purchase price. In November 1968, Pepsi-Cola Allied Bottlers, having franchises in northern Florida, West Virginia, Virginia, and Indiana, was acquired for $8.4 million in cash. The Pepsi-Cola franchise in Cleveland was purchased in January 1969 for $4.9 million in cash. These three companies formed the nucleus of the soft-drink beverage business, to which was added during 1969, for $5.5 million in cash, three additional companies holding Pepsi-Cola, 7-Up, and Dr. Pepper franchises in the Southeast, the largest in Atlanta. By year-end, 1970 profits after taxes from soft drinks were $1.56 million on sales of $89.8 million.

Franchised bottlers paid the franchiser for the concentrate to make the drink and were charged a fee to cover a portion of the franchiser's national advertising expenditures. In return, bottlers received exclusive rights to produce and market the product in a specified territory, an advertising allowance for a portion of their local advertising, some technical services in marketing and manufacturing, and various types of assistance in packaging, including the development of new containers. Bottlers had final responsibility for pricing, packaging, local advertising, and merchandising, although the franchisers attempted to encourage certain uniform policies.

The soft-drink industry, with estimated wholesale sales of $4.6 billion in 1970, had been growing at about 7% per year during the 1960s, as

---

[16] The figure in the prospectus was raised by a hundred lanes in the 1961 and 1962 annual reports.

reflected in Exhibit 9. Rising demand was attributed in particular to increases in the under-30 population which consumed nearly half of the soft drinks sold. Although the 10–29 group, as a percentage of the total population, was expected to peak around 1975, many observers anticipated that growth for the next decade would continue more or less in line with the experience of the recent past.

Coca-Cola, Inc., had 42.2% of the market in 1970 and had been increasing its nationwide market share at the expense of Pepsico (16.6%), Royal Crown (6.6%), and Canada Dry (3.3%), as shown in Exhibit 10. Coca-Cola was particularly strong in the on-premise and "cold drink" markets (vending machines, etc.),[17] although it also held the lead in food stores. However, participation varied considerably among markets; for instance, in Dayton, Ohio, Pepsi-Cola outsold Coke by almost 3 to 1, according to a recent survey, while in Atlanta the ratio was reversed. General Cinema managers attributed such variations, in large part, to the length of time the bottler had been in the market, the quality of his routeman training and supervision, and the amount of advertising and "price-off" money he was prepared to spend.

A number of trends were discernible in the soft-drink industry. First, private labels had captured an increasing share of the take-home market (from 3.8% in 1962 to 11.4% in 1969), especially that portion of it sold by chain stores (from 8.9% in 1962 to 22.1% in 1969). Second, the number of bottlers had fallen from a peak of about 8,000 in 1960 to about 3,500 in 1970, of which 450 had more than two thirds of the volume.[18]

A major reason for the demise of small competitors was the market acceptance of nonreturnable (NR) bottles and cans, which sharply increased packaging costs and permitted larger bottlers, who were able to effect lower production costs and lower delivery expense, to compete more aggressively on price promotions. This trend had also resulted in smaller margins for the industry as a whole. There was, however, growing pressure from environmentalists to limit the use of one-way containers, representing 55% to 60% of soft-drink packaging in 1970. In numerous states laws were pending to ban or tax NR bottles and cans. Those thought to be most severely affected by such laws were private-brand producers and large franchisers who had spent heavily for plant and equipment to automate NR filling operations. Both Coca-Cola and Pepsico were also test marketing disposable plastic bottles and, together with can and bottle manufacturers, were experimenting with recycling plants.

The industry was also confronted by a challenge from the FTC, which

---

[17] Roughly 45%–50% of soft drinks were sold through food stores, 35%–40% through vending machines and other outlets for "cold drinks," and the remainder as syrup for on-premise consumption.

[18] *Business Week*, April 25, 1970, p. 70.

**EXHIBIT 9**
**Soft-drink market statistics**

*I. Soft-drink consumption*

| Year | Millions of cases | Gallons per capita |
|------|-------------------|--------------------|
| 1963 . . . . . . . . | 2,550 | 20.4 |
| 1964 . . . . . . . . | 2,750 | 21.7 |
| 1965 . . . . . . . . | 2,960 | 23.1 |
| 1966 . . . . . . . . | 3,300 | 25.5 |
| 1967 . . . . . . . . | 3,500 | 26.5 |
| 1968 . . . . . . . . | 3,830 | 28.6 |
| 1969 . . . . . . . . | 4,090 | 30.2 |
| 1970 . . . . . . . . | 4,400 | 32.2 |

Source: John C. Maxwell, Jr., *The Soft Drink Industry* (Oppenheimer & Co.), June 18, 1971.

*II. Consumption by age*

| Age group | Percent of population 13 and older | Percent of consumption | Consumption index |
|-----------|-----------------------------------|------------------------|-------------------|
| 13–17. . . . . . . . | 11 | 16 | 145 |
| 18–24. . . . . . . . | 12 | 19 | 158 |
| 25–34. . . . . . . . | 16 | 19 | 119 |
| 35–49. . . . . . . . | 29 | 24 | 83 |
| 50 and over . . . . . | 32 | 22 | 69 |

Source: Company records.

*III. Population age-mix trends*

| Year* | 10–29 year age group | | All other age groups | | Percent 10–29 year age group to total population |
|-------|----------------------|----------------|----------------------|----------------|--------------------------------------------------|
| | Millions | Percent increase† | Millions | Percent increase† | |
| 1950 . . . . . . . | 45.8 | n.a. | 105.9 | 13.0 | 30.2 |
| 1955 . . . . . . . | 47.1 | 2.8 | 118.2 | 11.6 | 28.5 |
| 1960 . . . . . . . | 52.4 | 11.2 | 128.3 | 8.5 | 29.0 |
| 1965 . . . . . . . | 61.0 | 16.4 | 133.6 | 4.1 | 31.4 |
| 1970p . . . . . . | 70.9 | 16.2 | 135.1 | 1.1 | 34.4 |
| 1975p . . . . . . | 78.3 | 10.4 | 141.1 | 4.5 | 35.7 |
| 1980p . . . . . . | 80.4 | 2.7 | 154.8 | 9.7 | 34.2 |
| 1985p . . . . . . | 82.9 | 3.1 | 170.0 | 9.8 | 32.8 |

* p = projection.
† By five-year periods.
Source: U.S. Bureau of the Census, Series C.

**EXHIBIT 10**
Soft-drink market shares

| | 1966 | 1967 | 1968 | 1969 | 1970 | Percent increase (decrease) in cases sold 1966–70 |
|---|---|---|---|---|---|---|
| Coca-Cola Company | 37.6% | 39.4% | 40.7% | 41.3% | 42.2% | 51 |
| Coca-Cola . . . . . . . . . . | 30.3 | 31.4 | 32.6 | 34.0 | 34.8 | 53 |
| Other. . . . . . . . . . . . . | 7.3 | 8.0 | 8.1 | 7.3 | 7.4 | 41 |
| Pepsico Inc. | 18.0 | 17.7 | 17.5 | 16.9 | 16.6 | 22 |
| Pepsi-Cola . . . . . . . . . | 14.2 | 14.3 | 14.3 | 14.1 | 14.2 | 33 |
| Other. . . . . . . . . . . . | 3.8 | 3.4 | 3.2 | 2.8 | 2.4 | (18) |
| Royal Crown Cola Company. . . . . . . . . . | 7.9 | 7.7 | 7.6 | 7.1 | 6.6 | (10) |
| Seven-Up Company. . . . . . | 6.1 | 5.7 | 5.9 | 6.1 | 6.1 | 34 |
| Canada Dry Corporation . . . | 3.9 | 3.7 | 3.3 | 3.2 | 3.3 | 10 |
| Dr. Pepper Company . . . . . | 2.6 | 2.9 | 3.1 | 3.1 | 3.5 | 77 |
| Beverages International*. . . | 2.4 | 2.7 | 3.0 | 3.3 | 3.4 | 89 |
| Cott Corporation . . . . . . . | 1.5 | 2.0 | 2.2 | 2.5 | 2.4 | 68 |
| Other companies . . . . . . . | 20.0 | 18.2 | 16.7 | 16.5 | 15.9 | 12 |
| Total. . . . . . . . . . | 100.0% | 100.0% | 100.0% | 100.0% | 100.0% | 33 |

\* Hires, Crush, Sun Drop, CR.
Source: John C. Maxwell Jr., *The Soft Drink Industry.*

had initiated a study in 1970 to determine if the exclusive sales territories franchised to bottlers represented a restraint of trade. As of May 1971 the study had not been completed and no legislation at the federal level had yet been proposed.[19]

General Cinema operated 17 bottling plants and 19 distribution warehouses in seven states. Products were principally distributed in trucks operated by route salesmen to retail outlets and, in some instances, to distributors. The company also owned or leased coolers and vending machines to dispense products in factories, schools, service stations, and other locations. In most of these markets serviced by the company, Pepsico had strong market positions relative to Coca-Cola.

Profit margins had been adversely affected in recent years by the trend toward one-way containers. In 1971 about 45% of the company's sales were packaged in this way. As a major Pepsico bottler, General Cinema was among the first to initiate tests with a new resalable, returnable bottle. On the other hand, the ban on cyclamates in 1969 had affected directly only 7% of soft-drink sales (against 10% for the industry), and its impact was thought to have run its course. Management was

---

[19] The FTC filed suit in August 1971.

hopeful that Pepsico would move to reestablish itself in the sugar-free segment of the market.

In his 1970 letter to General Cinema shareholders, Mr. Smith revealed the investment policy to be pursued in the beverage division:

Capital expenditures in the beverage division for the purpose of modernizing equipment, upgrading production lines, and adding new marketing equipment totaled about $6 million in 1970. To further this program the 1971 budget is $2.5 million. We intend to limit capital outlays in the future so that they will not exceed depreciation, leaving net profit for the retirement of debt.

### Organization

Until 1966, three functional managers reported to Mr. Smith, all of whom had been with the company from the late 1940s: Mr. Wintman (theater operations), Mr. Lane (controller), and Mr. Seletsky (film purchasing).[20] In 1966 Mr. Wintman was placed in charge of all theater activities, including real estate, which had formerly been managed by Mr. Smith, and Mr. Hurwitz was promoted to vice president of theaters. A regional organization was also developed in both film procurement and operations. As the number of cinemas grew, a level of assistant vice presidents was created in 1970 for theater operations, film, real estate, and construction. When the real estate man left the company in late 1970, the department was staffed by three new, young managers. An organization chart, as the researcher understood it, is provided in Exhibit 11, there being no official document.

The acquisition of the beverage companies required further modification in the organization structure. Mr. Smith established the Beverage Operating Committee, composed of the men who managed the three operating companies, two of their subordinates, Mr. Brian Veasy, Mr. Lane, Mr. Zellen (corporate controller), and himself, to act as a sort of board of directors for the beverage business. Mr. Veasy, a recent MBA, was added to the corporate staff as the liaison between Boston and the field units. Mr. Smith explained why the committee had been formed.

Soft-drink bottling is essentially a local business and we bought a group of family-dominated companies. The older generation has more or less retired, and a younger generation has assumed responsibility for operations. Other than consolidating some of the smaller acquisitions into the three large ones, we have left the organizations about as they were.

I have resisted putting a single man in charge of beverages for a couple of reasons. First, I can't be sure whether there is a man in the organization ready for the job yet. I would rather see how things go for a while before

---

[20] Mr. Wintman and Mr. Lane were made vice president and treasurer, respectively, in 1962, and Mr. Seletsky a vice president in 1963. Mr. Seletsky died in 1968.

**EXHIBIT 11**

GENERAL CINEMA CORPORATION
Organization Chart

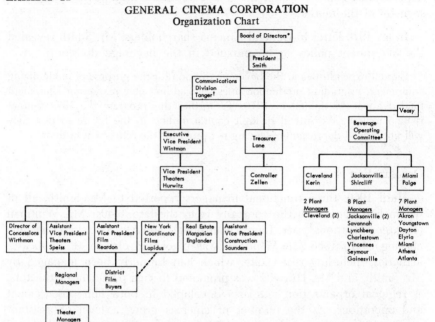

* Richard A. Smith, chairman of the board; S. Sidney Stoneman, vice chairman of the board; Julius Darsky, president, American Beverage Division; J. Atwood Ives, general partner, Paine, Webber, Jackson & Curtis; Emmanuel Kurland, corporate general counsel; Edward E. Lane, treasurer; David I. Margolis, president, Colt Industries, Inc.; Charles L. Moore, senior vice president, The First National Bank of Boston; Robert T. Shircliff, president, Pepsi-Cola Allied Beverage Division; Melvin R. Wintman, executive vice president.

† Mr. Tanger was a special consultant to Mr. Smith and was responsible for looking after the company's radio and television interests.

‡ Smith, Lane, Shircliff, Paige, Kerin, Veasy, Bliss (Dayton plant manager), and Dean (assistant to Shircliff).

Source: Casewriter's notes.

deciding who the man ought to be. Second, we didn't know much about the business when we made the acquisitions. Having a man between us and the market might have restricted the amount of information flowing up here. As it is, I keep in contact with Pepsico and have the controllers in the three regions report to Bill Zellen as well as to the manager there. However, other than putting in financial controls, evaluating capital requests, and discussing the timing of price increases, we haven't done much to interfere.

Mr. Smith also reflected on the application of a management philosophy that he felt had been successful at General Cinema:

The corporation should supply them (the three operating managers in the beverage "division") with good supporting managers and not try to make them something they aren't. They should be encouraged to do whatever they can do well. For instance, one of them has a flair for marketing. We should make use of this talent and assign him a good financial manager to help him in that area. Rather than expect him to be able to do everything, I would rather reward him for his special skills. The theater business has been managed in this fashion. John D. Rockefeller, Sr., once made the comment that "The essence of management is to get an extraordinary job out of ordinary people." That is my hope here. Of course, in return for increased efficiency, there is always the problem of replacing a highly skilled man, and the burden is undoubtedly greater at the top. But those are disadvantages I am prepared to live with.

One of the junior members of the management team provided a further indication of the decision-making process:

I can't speak for bottling, but in theaters there is one man who makes the important decisions—Mr. Smith. That includes each new theater location though we have a real estate committee[21] that meets to review proposed sites.

## Management and diversification

Messrs. Smith (46), Wintman (53), and Lane (59) had worked closely together for over 20 years in the development of General Cinema. Mr. Smith commented on certain aspects of the diversification issue:

After the bowling venture I didn't think seriously about diversification until our cash-flow picture started to change in 1966 and it became clear that we were going to have money to invest. We weren't afraid to think big. In 1967 we almost bought a $100 million vending machine company which in many ways complemented our theater business. However, our P/E was only 10 then and the dilution would have been substantial because a considerable amount of stock would have had to be used. Everyone here was bullish about theaters as well and didn't want to risk a conflict of interest situation with other vendor operators.

We will soon be in the position again of having funds available for investment. I am interested in developing just one additional opportunity. When the company was smaller it was O.K. to think about starting in a field from scratch, but that isn't as appropriate now as the purchase of an existing business. It should be big enough to have an immediate impact on earnings. It should have a capable management, good growth prospects, and a continuing need for investment. At the same time, General Cinema must be able to bring its competence to bear on the new business. I don't want to be dependent on the specialized skills of a few individuals. For that reason highly technical or stylized or even manufacturing businesses are not really of interest.

Unfortunately, some of the most logical areas for General Cinema present serious accounting problems. For instance, real estate development would

---

[21] The real estate committee included Messrs. Wintman, Hurwitz, Saunders, Smith, the real estate group, and sometimes Messrs. Carl Reardon (for film advice) and Ed Lane (for financial advice).

be a natural business for us. However, we can't figure out a way to avoid the heavy depreciation write-offs in the early years. We know about discounted cash flow, but it would be 15 to 20 years before the benefit would be reflected in earnings, and we're not that patient.

CATV is another business that has growth potential and is entering a new phase of development by penetrating urban areas and initiating programming. It depends on entertainment marketing and decentralized controls; we'd be good at it.[22] However, it also suffers from the high investment, long-term earnings-payout phenomenon. The dilemma for me is that by doing nothing our earnings will increase at 20% or so for the next several years. Our stock has been selling at 20 to 30 times earnings on the strength of our record, and a decision that looked as though it might jeopardize that could hurt our reputation.

Mr. Wintman was a lawyer by training and as a major in the Army had taken part in the Nuremberg trials at the end of World War II. He had joined the Smith Management Company in 1949 as a concession manager in a drive-in theater following his release from the armed services. He remained directly involved in the field supervision of theater operations until 1966, writing at one point a comprehensive manual for the company's drive-in managers. He stressed certain additional concerns related to diversification:

I would like to continue in service businesses where we have some expertise. We should learn to be as proficient as those already in whatever business we enter. Rather than becoming dependent on an acquired management I would feel more comfortable if we could do their job as well as they do if the need arose.

Mr. Lane had become permanently associated with the Smith Management Company as the financial manager in 1949. He had previously worked in accounting capacities for several retail chains, spent the war years as a lieutenant in the Navy, and for several months prior to joining the company was with a public accounting firm. He reflected on some of the reasons for General Cinema's success:

We have a tremendous pride in the accomplishments of General Cinema. Our executive group has been able to make quick decisions that have been essential in nailing down theater sites and making acquisitions. Our batting average has been pretty good so far. Dick Smith has a great deal of self-confidence and optimism that has given us the spirit to take controversial locations and make them work.

The beverage business looked like it might have been the solution to our diversification problems. We had found another noncyclical growth business that could be leveraged to the benefit of our shareholders. However, there just aren't any more good franchises around at the right price, and if we

---

[22] In 1969 General Cinema invested in three FM radio stations for $1,475,000 and invested $2 million in convertible debentures of a Miami television station which would convert, subject to FCC approval, into 70% of the then outstanding common stock. The television station was operating close to the break-even point.

bought one for cash, the new accounting rules for goodwill could hurt us.[23] The business is now self-sustaining and we are looking again. . . . We are reluctant to consider film production, though I suppose we would do it if we felt we had to.

As a means of internal communication and a guide for evaluating diversification opportunities, Mr. Lane summarized his understanding of the criteria to be applied in a memorandum reproduced in Exhibit 12.

**EXHIBIT 12**

GENERAL CINEMA CORPORATION
Acquisition Objectives

We are presently engaged in two main areas: THEATRES and SOFT DRINKS. We are not interested in becoming a conglomerate; we are interested in a third major division to absorb our increasing cash flow rather than use it to pay off debt.

Describing the third division in general terms is simple; in specific terms, difficult. It should be leisure-time-oriented, consumer-oriented, perhaps service-oriented and youth-oriented. It must have good potential for expansion to keep pace with our overall corporate growth rate of 15%–20% or better, with perhaps $2,000,000–$3,000,000 earnings. If smaller, it must be able to absorb infusions of capital for accelerated growth. In other words, it must provide a base for a third large division. Further, it should be a field in which it is possible to achieve a return on investment of at least 20% before taxes.

It is also fairly simple to rule out what we don't want: research and development, complicated manufacturing processes, involved or unique technology, cyclical or stylized characteristics; cash flow rather than earnings.

Possible fields—and these are by no means intended to be all-inclusive or exclusive—are:

| | |
|---|---|
| BEVERAGES . . . . . . . . . . . | Soft drinks (major Pepsi-Cola franchises, other national brands to complement the areas in which we now operate; no private-label brands) |
| HOUSEHOLD FURNISHINGS | |
| COMMUNICATIONS. . . . . . . | (*earnings,* not just cash flow) |
| EDUCATION | |
| DIRECT MAIL MARKETING | |
| ENTERTAINMENT . . . . . . . . | Motion pictures, musical |
| REAL ESTATE. . . . . . . . . . | Development services (earnings, not just cash flow) |
| OTHER SERVICES . . . . . . . . | Household, business, parking lots, vending |
| SPECIALTY RETAILING. . . . . | Gifts, novelties, greeting cards, crafts, games, sewing, hobbies |

Source: Company memorandum.

Mr. Smith described the process he was employing to search for opportunities:

I am doing most of the worrying about diversification myself. The process is time-consuming; it took 15 months to work out the first soft-drink acquisition. We don't have a planning or corporate development office at General Cinema. It doesn't make much sense when we're looking for only one opportunity. Nor have I asked consultants to prepare a study for us. However,

---

[23] Goodwill (the excess of purchase price over net taxable assets) created by acquisitions accounted for as a purchase had to be amortized over not more than 40 years, according to a 1970 opinion of the Accounting Principals Board.

I have put the word out through our Board and the bank that we want something, and am getting a number of inquiries.

## APPENDIX
## HISTORICAL SKETCHES OF THE BIG FIVE THEATER EXHIBITION COMPANIES (1949–71)

*Paramount Theaters (1949); American Broadcasting Company (1971):* The largest of the exhibitors, Paramount, was obligated to divest roughly half of the 1,298 theaters it held in 1949, a task it completed in 1955. In 1953 the company, then with sales of $121 million and profits of $5.6 million, merged with the American Broadcasting Company, which had sales of about $50 million and was operating at a slight loss. While television revenues grew, the company continued to close theaters throughout the 1950s and 1960s. In 1964 ABC embarked on a theater expansion program that resulted in new facilities by 1970. Theater revenues, which hit a low of $76 million in 1962, had rebounded to $100 million in 1970, or 13% of total ABC sales of $748 million.

*National Theaters (1954); National General (1971):* In the 1950s National Theaters, the exhibition part of Twentieth-Century Fox, experimented with Cinemiracle, a film-making process, and attempted to diversify by acquiring television and radio stations, CATV systems, and a distributor of television programs. All of these ventures were subsequently sold. After entering and withdrawing from the real estate and mobile homes businesses in the early 1950s, National, in 1963, began to build new theaters and to produce feature films. In 1966 for the first time the number of theaters opened in a year exceeded the number closed as the company announced plans to add properties at the rate of 30 to 35 a year.

In 1968 National acquired Grosset and Dunlap, paperback book publishers, and the following year added the far larger Great American Insurance Group (1970 sales were $347 million). In 1970 theater revenues were $72 million, $3 million above those in 1969, representing 14% of the corporate total of $523 million. The construction of new theaters appeared to have slowed and the film production division, which operated at a loss on $40 million in sales, was not initiating new pictures.

*Loew's Theaters (1959); Loew's Inc. (1971):* Within a year after becoming an independent company, Loew's entered the hotel business and subsequently real estate development, which within six years contributed more revenue than theaters. In 1964 the company began to construct theaters in shopping centers, adding them at a rate of about 10 per year. Loew's acquired Lorillard, the fifth largest domestic cigarette manufacturer, in 1969 and embarked on a major home-building joint venture (the $100 million development of Staten Island). Theaters had become a relatively minor part of 1970 sales of $699 million.

*Stanley Warner (1954); Cinerama (1971):* Through a 90% interest acquired in Cinerama in 1953, Stanley Warner first attempted to produce and exhibit films made with the Cinerama process. This proved unprofitable, and in 1958 Stanley Warner sold its stock in Cinerama to the public. In 1954 the company had merged with International Latex, an undergarment producer, and in subsequent years added other consumer goods manufacturers.

By 1967, when the company was acquired by Glen Alden, sales were $242 million, of which theaters contributed $39 million. While a few new theaters were constructed beginning in 1964, the total continued to fall until the merger. Glen Alden combined Stanley Warner with the previously acquired RKO circuit and instituted a major cost-cutting program in the new division. Then in January 1971, the RKO-Stanley Warner division was sold to Cinerama at roughly book value for $21.5 million. Cinerama since 1958 had gone through several reorganizations and, while still struggling to develop the Cinerama process, had moved into real estate through the purchase in 1969 of three hotels in Hawaii. Losses were incurred in 1970 of $8.6 million on sales of $39.9 million.

*RKO Theaters (1950); Cinerama (1971):* RKO sales fell from $37 million in 1950 to $29 million in 1956 when control of the company was secured by Cleveland Arcade, a small manufacturer of woolens and worsteds, and the name changed to List Industries. The following year, List merged with Glen Alden, primarily a coal mining company at the time. Control of Glen Alden was secured by Meshulan Riklis in 1964, who proceeded to add companies to it, including Stanley Warner in 1967. Prior to the acquisition little had been done to bolster the growth of the RKO theater business. In 1970, before divesting the RKO-Stanley Warner Division, Glen Alden sales were $1,316 million, of which theaters represented less than $40 million.

# Philip Morris Incorporated

IN APRIL 1971 Philip Morris Incorporated was riding the crest of 17 years of uninterrupted growth in sales and net earnings. In 1970 Philip Morris' sales ($1.5 billion) and earnings ($77 million) were 296% and 369%, respectively, of the 1960 results. The company's earnings per share had grown at a compound annual rate of 13% since 1960 and 23% since 1965. In addition, Philip Morris had increased its share of the U.S. cigarette market from 9% to 16% in the decade of the sixties. In the international market (free world only), the company's market share had spurted from 1% in 1960 to 6% in 1970. Philip Morris was the third largest privately owned cigarette manufacturer in the world market, ranking behind the British-American Tobacco Company and R. J. Reynolds Industries, the leading U.S. manufacturer.

The corporation's growth had come in the face of adversities which were a continuing source of concern for the industry. Foremost among these was the decline in per-capita cigarette consumption in the United States. While total consumption had grown approximately 13% from 1960 to 1970, per-capita consumption among the over-18 population had declined 5% during the same period. Second, the debate over the relationship between cigarette smoking and health continued, with the anti-cigarette forces winning Congressional approval of a ban on TV and radio advertising of cigarettes effective January 2, 1971. Excise taxes posed a third problem. While the federal excise tax had remained constant at 8¢ per pack, state and local taxes had grown from an average of 4.8¢ in 1960 to 10.7¢ in 1970.[1] In New York City the total tax on cigarettes was 30¢ per pack and the retail price had soared to over 50¢.

## THE AMERICAN CIGARETTE INDUSTRY

### History

In the last two decades of the 19th century when cigarettes represented less than 5% of expenditures for tobacco, James B. Duke assembled what became known as the "Tobacco Trust." By securing exclusive rights to a newly developed cigarette machine which halved production costs and permitted greatly expanded operations, Duke was able to finance large advertising expenditures and engage in ruthless price competition. So successful were his tactics that the trust garnered 85% to 95% of the domestic market, some of it gained through amalgamations with other firms which chose to merge rather than face extinction.

In 1911 the trust was held in violation of the Sherman Act and its assets divided among some 16 successor companies, the major domestic ones being R. J. Reynolds, Liggett & Myers, P. Lorillard, and American Tobacco (in 1969 renamed American Brands).[2] The cigarette brands marketed in the United States by the trust, numbering over 100, were assigned to the latter three companies; R. J. Reynolds produced only plug and smoking tobacco.

In 1913 Reynolds introduced the Camel which in just four years captured 35% of the market. Its popularity was attributed to a new blend of tobaccos, a packaging innovation,[3] and a shift in advertising from coupons and prizes to print media.[4] Liggett & Myers and American Tobacco followed suit with Chesterfield and Lucky Strike in 1913 and 1916, respectively, and together these three brands by 1925 had amassed over 82% of the market at the expense of the many brands inherited from the trust. Lorillard successfully introduced a competitive cigarette, Old Gold, in 1926, though it never grew to rival the "big three."

The depression years witnessed the rise of two new competitors. In 1929, Brown and Williamson, which had been acquired by British-American Tobacco in 1927, introduced Raleigh using the redeemable coupon

---

[1] U.S. Department of Agriculture, Bureau of Economic Research, *Tobacco Situation*, December 1970.

[2] In addition, the British American Tobacco Company assumed direction of the trust's overseas activities.

[3] Camels were the first cigarette, aside from a few expensive blends, to be sold in a soft package of 20 rather than a cardboard slide and shell box.

[4] Walter Adams, *The Structure of American Industry* (New York: The Macmillan Co., 1961).

as a merchandising device. Buoyed by the success of the venture, B & W in the next several years brought out the filter-tipped Viceroy and the mentholated Kool, which together provided the company with just over 19% of the market by 1942. Philip Morris, a small independent producer, introduced a new Philip Morris cigarette in 1932, at a retail price of 15¢ per pack, 3¢ over the price maintained for the dominant brands.[5] Philip Morris kept one penny to finance an advertising campaign and used the other two cents to secure distribution and dealer interest. Within six years Philip Morris became the country's fourth largest brand with 6.1% of the market.

Following the war, the number of brands proliferated substantially

**EXHIBIT 1**
**Cigarette consumption and price trends**

I. *Consumption*

| Year | Total unit output* (billions) | Domestic unit consumption (billions) | Nonfilter production percent of total | Filter-tip production percent of total | Over-18 years, consumption per capita (units) |
|---|---|---|---|---|---|
| Average | | | | | |
| 1955–59 | 447.8 | 428.4 | 63.6 | 37.4 | 3,884 |
| 1960 | 506.9 | 470.1 | 49.1 | 40.9 | 4,172 |
| 1965 | 556.8 | 528.7 | 35.6 | 64.4 | 4,258 |
| 1966 | 576.3 | 541.2 | 31.8 | 68.2 | 4,287 |
| 1967 | 576.2 | 549.2 | 27.6 | 72.4 | 4,280 |
| 1968 | 579.5 | 545.7 | 25.1 | 74.9 | 4,186 |
| 1969 | 557.6 | 528.9 | 22.5 | 77.5 | 3,993 |
| 1970 | 575.0 | 542.0 | 21.6 | 78.4 | 3,960 |

* Differences between consumption and output accounted for by exports and net inventory fluctuations.
  Source: U.S. Department of Agriculture, Economic Research Service, *Tobacco Situation*, various issues.

II. *Percent of disposable income and prices*

| Year | Disposable income per capita* (millions) | All tobacco expenditures per capita† | Percent of disposable income | Consumer price index‡ All items | Tobacco | Wholesale price index for tobacco‡ |
|---|---|---|---|---|---|---|
| 1960 | $1,937 | $67.60 | 3.5 | 103.1 | 107.1 | 102.9 |
| 1965 | 2,432 | 69.50 | 2.9 | 109.9 | 120.2 | 119.8 |
| 1970 | 3,330 | 77.40 | 2.3 | 135.2 | 159.0 | 140.3 |

* Based on total population.
† Over-18 population only.
‡ 1957–59 = 100.
Source: U.S. Department of Agriculture, *Tobacco Situation*, March 1971, pp. 6 and 37.

[5] The Philip Morris brand had formerly been an expensive Turkish blend.

**EXHIBIT 1** (*continued*)

III. *Cigarette smokers in the population, by age and sex*

| | 1955 | | 1965 | | | 1968 | | |
|---|---|---|---|---|---|---|---|---|
| Age | Non-smoker | Smoker | Never smoked | Former smoker | Smoker | Never smoked | Former smoker | Smoker |
| *Male* | | | | | | | | |
| 17–24* ...... | 40.7% | 59.3% | 45.1% | 6.6% | 48.3% | 51.0% | 6.7% | 42.3% |
| 25–44 ....... | 31.2 | 68.8 | 22.7 | 17.7 | 59.6 | 26.2 | 18.2 | 55.6 |
| 45–64 ....... | 41.8 | 58.2 | 23.9 | 24.0 | 52.1 | 26.6 | 24.5 | 48.9 |
| Over 65 ...... | 70.5 | 29.5 | 43.3 | 28.0 | 28.7 | 45.0 | 29.7 | 25.3 |
| *Female* | | | | | | | | |
| 17–24* ...... | 62.3 | 37.7 | 59.6 | 5.5 | 34.9 | 64.6 | 5.4 | 30.0 |
| 25–44 ....... | 71.7 | 28.3 | 46.5 | 9.6 | 43.9 | 49.0 | 10.0 | 41.0 |
| 45-64 ....... | 75.9 | 24.1 | 59.4 | 8.6 | 32.0 | 59.7 | 9.0 | 31.3 |
| Over 65 ...... | 91.9 | 8.1 | 85.2 | 4.5 | 10.3 | 85.1 | 5.1 | 9.8 |

* 1955 figures are for ages 18–24.
Source: Calculated from U.S. Department of Health, Education and Welfare, *Vital and Health Statistics.* Data based on survey of 40,000–50,000 households.

as the big three share of the market shrank to 54% in 1953. American Brands, betting heavily on king-size (Pall Mall and Tareyton), took the lead from R. J. Reynolds, which did not abandon its policy of exclusive concentration on one brand until the king-size Cavalier in 1949. After the first major cancer scare in 1953, however, the increasing penetration of king-size brands was arrested and filter-tip cigarettes gained rapidly in popularity. Reynolds (Winston), Lorillard (Kent), and Philip Morris (Marlboro) joined Brown and Williamson (Viceroy) in securing important market shares for filter brands, Winston helping to propel Reynolds to overall industry leadership in sales.

Hardly had the filter cigarette firmly established itself when the menthol filter took hold (1956), led again by Reynolds (Salem) and followed by Brown and Williamson (Kool) and Lorillard (Newport). In succeeding years, new waves of products came on the market—charcoal filters, complex filters, and 100 millimeters—represented by new brands and adaptations of existing brands. By 1970, when cigarettes accounted for more than 90% of tobacco expenditures, over 40 brands comprising nearly 100 sizes, types, and packages were sold by the six leading companies, the largest, Winston, having a share of 15.2%.

## Structure

In 1970 American consumers spent $9.4 billion for 542 billion cigarettes. Data reflecting recent trends in cigarette consumption and prices are provided in Exhibit 1. The quantity of cigars, smoking tobacco, and snuff consumed per capita had declined slightly since 1950; retail sales of these products in 1970 approximated $1 billion.

The six major cigarette producers held 99.8% of the domestic market in 1970. In recent years Philip Morris and, to a lesser extent, Brown and Williamson had increased their market shares. Exhibits 2, 3, and 4 reflect market trends by brand and type of cigarette. Shown below are 1970 sales and profits and growth trends for the major producers:

|  | *1970* | | | | *Growth: 1966–70* | |
|  | *Sales (millions)* | *Domestic cigarette unit sales (billions)* | *Sales in tobacco*\* | *Net profits/ sales* | *Sales* | *Profit* |
| --- | --- | --- | --- | --- | --- | --- |
| *Company* | | | | | | |
| R. J. Reynolds . . . . . . . | $2,485 | 1.67 | 73% | 7.7% | 40.0% | 38.3% |
| American Brands . . . . . . | 2,674 | 1.03 | 77 | 4.1 | 87.3 | 25.6 |
| Philip Morris. . . . . . . . . | 1,510 | 0.88 | 87 | 5.1 | 94.9 | 126.1 |
| Brown & Williamson . . . . | 890 | 0.88 | 99 | 4.5 | 63.1 | 51.2 |
| P. Lorillard† . . . . . . . . . | 500 | 0.45 | 100 | 5.0 | 12.7 | (14.7) |
| Liggett & Myers . . . . . . . | 697 | 0.34 | 53 | 4.2 | 20.6 | 29.9 |

\* Includes other tobacco products and cigarette sales of consolidated foreign subsidiaries.

† P. Lorillard was purchased by Loew's Theatres in 1968.

Source: Annual reports of companies listed and parent companies. Domestic cigarette sales calculated from John C. Maxwell, Jr., "Historical Trends in the Tobacco Industry," Oppenheimer & Co., 1970.

The policies with regard to diversification and overseas operations varied considerably among these companies as the brief sketches below (excluding Philip Morris) illustrate.

**R. J. Reynolds.** Reynolds had capitalized on the growth of its two principal brands, Winston and Salem, while initiating a major program of diversification in 1963 which moved the company into containerized shipping, packaging, and food products. Reynolds had introduced only four new brands in the sixties, two of which were still sold in 1970 (Vantage and Doral) accounting for about 1.4% of the market. The company had also aggressively attacked overseas cigarette markets in the 1960s and had built manufacturing facilities in Europe and Puerto Rico.

**American brands.** In the 1960s American Brands introduced 10 filter brands to offset declining sales of its nonfilter "flagship" brands, Pall Mall and Lucky Strike. However, in 1970 the six surviving entries (Silva Thins, Carlton, Montclair, Maryland Menthol 100s, Half and Half, and Bull Durham) accounted for only 1.4% of the domestic market. Beginning in 1966 American Brands began to diversify, acquiring a liquor company

(Beam Distilling) and two food companies (Sunshine Biscuits and Duffy-Mott) which by 1970, augmented by subsequent acquisitions, contributed over 20% of net sales. Early in the company's history, British-American Tobacco had secured rights to sell American Brands' domestic labels overseas. Consequently, American had virtually no participation in the international market until a two-thirds interest in Gallaher Ltd., a British tobacco company with sales of roughly $1 billion, was acquired in 1968.

**Brown and Williamson.**  The U.S. subsidiary of the British-American Tobacco Company had remained almost exclusively (99%) in tobacco products throughout the sixties. It had marketed nine new filter brands and one nonfilter, but none of its new brands had been successful with the exception of Belair. The company's growth had been largely due to the increased market share of Kool. In 1969 Brown and Williamson introduced Laredo, a roll-your-own cigarette with a filter which the consumer could "manufacture" himself for 20¢ a pack.

**Liggett & Myers.**  As L & M and Chesterfield continued to lose ground, Liggett & Myers in 1964 began a program of diversification which resulted in 43% of its 1970 sales coming from nontobacco enterprises, chiefly liquor and pet foods. Liggett & Myers introduced seven new brands from 1960 to 1970, but only one, Lark, with a 1.4% share, remained on the market at the end of this period.

**P. Lorillard.**  Also remaining almost exclusively in the domestic tobacco business, P. Lorillard had introduced four new brands in the 1960s. Only one, True, had gained as much as 1% of the market. In 1968 the company was purchased by Loew's Theatres, becoming the principal subsidiary of a $700 million corporation.

In the sixties, after-tax profits of tobacco companies had averaged 5.5% on sales and approximately 13.5% on equity, although the performance varied substantially among the six major firms. The companies also differed in their choices of financial policies (amount of debt and dividend payout) as shown in Exhibit 5, which compares the four publicly held corporations.

## Characteristics

*Manufacturing.*  Manufacturing firms bought cured "green" leaf at tobacco auctions, then stored and aged it for two or more years. In the factory the first steps in the manufacturing process were to remove the leaf stems and blend the tobacco. Each manufacturer had its own special blends which were closely guarded secrets. The blends were formed from domestic and imported (Turkish) tobaccos of varying crop years. In order to obtain blending on a consistent basis, companies used computers to insure that variables such as geographic location, type

**EXHIBIT 2**

Market share of major companies by type and brand of cigarette, 1952–70

| Company and brand | Type* | 1952 | 1961 | 1966 | 1967 | 1968 | 1969 | 1970 |
|---|---|---|---|---|---|---|---|---|
| **R. J. Reynolds** | | | | | | | | |
| †Winston | PF | ··· | 12.0% | 14.5% | 15.0% | 15.4% | 15.3% | 15.2% |
| Winston Menthol 100s | MF | ··· | ··· | ··· | 0.5 | 0.5 | 0.3 | 0.4 |
| †Salem | MF | ··· | 8.4 | 8.7 | 8.4 | 8.5 | 8.3 | 8.5 |
| Doral | PF | ··· | ··· | ··· | ··· | ··· | 0.4 | 0.8 |
| Doral Menthol | MF | ··· | ··· | ··· | ··· | ··· | 0.2 | 0.4 |
| Camel | PF | ··· | ··· | ··· | 0.7 | 0.6 | 0.7 | 0.8 |
| Vantage | PF | ··· | ··· | ··· | ··· | ··· | 0.3 | 0.2 |
| Tempo | CF | ··· | ··· | 0.2 | 0.2 | 0.1 | ··· | ··· |
| Camel | NFR | 25.7% | 13.6 | 8.7 | 7.8 | 6.3 | 6.3 | 5.4 |
| Cavalier | NFK | 0.5 | ··· | ··· | ··· | ··· | ··· | ··· |
| Total market share | | 26.2% | 34.0% | 32.1% | 32.6% | 31.4% | 31.8% | 31.7% |
| **American brands** | | | | | | | | |
| †Tareyton | CF | ··· | 2.2% | 3.6% | 3.6% | 4.0% | 4.1% | 4.0% |
| Pall Mall 100 mm | PF | ··· | ··· | 1.4 | 1.8 | 1.7 | 1.9 | 2.0 |
| Pall Mall Menthol 100 mm | MF | ··· | ··· | 0.2 | 0.4 | 0.4 | 0.4 | 0.4 |
| Silva Thins 100 mm | PF | ··· | ··· | ··· | 0.1 | 0.5 | 0.6 | 0.6 |
| Silva Thins Menthol 100 mm | MF | ··· | ··· | ··· | ··· | 0.2 | 0.3 | 0.3 |
| Montclair | PF | ··· | ··· | 0.2 | 0.2 | 0.1 | 0.1 | 0.1 |
| Carleton | CF | ··· | ··· | 0.2 | 0.2 | 0.2 | 0.2 | 0.2 |
| †Lucky Strike | PF | ··· | ··· | 0.8 | 0.5 | 0.3 | 0.2 | 0.2 |
| Maryland Menthol 100s | MF | ··· | ··· | ··· | ··· | ··· | ··· | 0.1 |
| Other Filter | | ··· | ··· | ··· | 0.2 | 0.2 | 0.1 | 0.1 |
| Pall Mall | NFK | 10.4% | 14.6% | 12.2 | 11.1 | 10.6 | 9.6 | 8.6 |
| Lucky Strike | NFR | 18.7 | 8.5 | 4.4 | 3.9 | 3.8 | 3.5 | 3.0 |
| Tareyton | NFK | 3.2 | 0.3 | 0.2 | 0.2 | 0.2 | 0.2 | 0.1 |
| Total market share | | 32.3% | 25.6% | 23.2% | 22.2% | 22.2% | 21.2% | 19.7% |
| **Brown and Williamson** | | | | | | | | |
| †Kool | MF | ··· | 2.2% | 4.5% | 4.9% | 5.8% | 6.7% | 7.7% |
| †Viceroy | PF | 0.6% | 3.7 | 3.9 | 3.7 | 3.8 | 3.8 | 3.7 |
| †Raleigh | PF | ··· | 1.4 | 2.7 | 2.7 | 2.8 | 2.8 | 2.7 |
| †Belair | MF | ··· | 0.1 | 1.7 | 1.7 | 1.7 | 1.7 | 1.8 |
| Other Filters | | ··· | 0.1 | 0.1 | 0.1 | 0 | 0 | 0 |
| Raleigh | NFK | 2.5 | 0.8 | 0.8 | 0.7 | 0.6 | 0.5 | 0.5 |
| Kool | NFR | 2.6 | 0.9 | 0.7 | 0.6 | 0.5 | 0.4 | 0.3 |
| Wings and Avalon | NFK | 0.2 | 0.1 | ··· | ··· | ··· | ··· | ··· |
| Total market share | | 5.9% | 9.3% | 14.4% | 14.4% | 15.2% | 15.9% | 16.7% |
| **Philip Morris** | | | | | | | | |
| †Marlboro | PF | ··· | 5.0% | 5.8% | 6.4% | 7.5% | 8.6% | 9.7% |
| Marlboro Menthol | MF | ··· | ··· | 0.3 | 0.2 | 0.1 | 0.1 | 0.1 |
| B & H 100s | PF | ··· | ··· | 0.4 | 1.8 | 1.8 | 1.8 | 2.0 |
| B & H Menthol 100s | MF | ··· | ··· | 0.1 | 0.6 | 0.7 | 0.8 | 0.9 |
| †Parliament | PF | 0.4%‡ | 2.0 | 2.0 | 1.7 | 1.7 | 1.6 | 1.6 |
| Virginia Slims 100s | PF | ··· | ··· | ··· | ··· | 0.1 | 0.5 | 0.6 |
| Virginia Slims Menthol 100s | MF | ··· | ··· | ··· | ··· | ··· | 0.3 | 0.4 |
| Philip Morris | CF | ··· | ··· | 0.7 | 0.6 | 0.5 | ··· | ··· |
| Philip Morris Menthol | MF | ··· | ··· | 0.3 | 0.1 | 0.1 | ··· | ··· |

**EXHIBIT 2** (*continued*)

| Company and brand | Type* | 1952 | 1961 | 1966 | 1967 | 1968 | 1969 | 1970 |
|---|---|---|---|---|---|---|---|---|
| Multi-Filter | CF | ... | ... | ... | ... | ... | 0.1 | 0.4 |
| Multi-Filter Menthol | CF | ... | ... | ... | ... | ... | 0.1 | 0.1 |
| Alpine | MF | ... | 0.3 | 0.6 | 0.5 | 0.5 | 0.4 | 0.4 |
| Other Filter | | ... | 0.1 | 0.1 | 0.1 | 0 | 0 | 0 |
| Philip Morris | NFK and NFR | 9.1 | 1.8 | 0.9 | 0.9 | 0.8 | 0.6 | 0.5 |
| Dunhill | NFK | 0.1 | ... | ... | ... | ... | ... | ... |
| Marlboro | NFR | 0.1 | ... | ... | ... | ... | ... | ... |
| Total market share | | 9.7% | 9.2% | 11.2% | 12.9% | 13.8% | 15.2% | 16.7% |
| *P. Lorillard* | | | | | | | | |
| †Kent | PF | 0.2% | 7.2% | 5.8% | 5.8% | 5.8% | 5.3% | 5.0% |
| Kent Menthol 100s | MF | ... | ... | ... | ... | ... | ... | 0.1 |
| True | PF | ... | ... | 0.5 | 1.0 | 1.2 | 1.0 | 0.9 |
| True Menthol | MF | ... | ... | ... | 0.5 | 0.6 | 0.5 | 0.6 |
| †Old Gold | PF | ... | 1.0 | 0.8 | 0.8 | 0.9 | 1.0 | 0.9 |
| †Newport | MF | ... | 1.5 | 1.6 | 1.4 | 1.4 | 1.0 | 0.8 |
| Spring 100 mm | MF | ... | 0.1 | 0.3 | 0.2 | 0.2 | 0.1 | 0.1 |
| Old Gold | NFK and NFR | 5.4% | 0.7 | 0.4 | 0.3 | 0.2 | 0.1 | 0.1 |
| Total market share | | 5.6% | 10.5% | 9.4% | 10.0% | 10.1% | 9.0% | 8.5% |
| *Liggett & Myers* | | | | | | | | |
| †L & M | PF | ... | 5.5% | 3.8% | 3.4% | 3.2% | 3.1% | 2.9% |
| L & M Menthol 100s | MF | | ... | ... | 0.2 | 0.2 | 0.1 | 0.1 |
| Lark | CF | | ... | 1.6 | 1.5 | 1.5 | 1.3 | 1.4 |
| †Chesterfield | PF | | ... | 0.3 | 0.3 | 0.2 | 0.2 | 0.3 |
| Chesterfield | NFK and NFR | 16.9% | 5.3 | 2.8 | 2.3 | 2.1 | 2.0 | 1.8 |
| Fatima | NFK | 0.9 | ... | ... | ... | ... | ... | ... |
| Total market share | | 17.8% | 10.8% | 8.5% | 7.7% | 7.2% | 6.7% | 6.5% |
| All other companies | | 2.5% | 0.6% | 1.2% | 0.2% | 0.1% | 0.2% | 0.2% |
| Total industry | | 100.0% | 100.0% | 100.0% | 100.0% | 100.0% | 100.0% | 100.0% |

*Key to abbreviations:
PF = Plain Filter        NFK = Nonfilter King
MF = Menthol Filter      NFR = Nonfilter Regular
CF = Charcoal Filter
†Includes both 85 mm and 100 mm brands.
‡Parliament owned by Benson & Hedges Company, purchased by Philip Morris in 1954.
Source: Calculated from John C. Maxwell, Jr., "Historical Trends in the Tobacco Industry," Oppenheimer & Co., 1970.

of tobacco, and crop years were combined to produce a cigarette with a consistent taste and quality.

The technology of cigarette manufacturing based on cigarette rolling and packaging machines had not changed radically over the years. While machine speeds had increased and operations had become more capital

**EXHIBIT 3**
**Market share by type of cigarette, 1966 and 1970**

| Type of cigarette | 1966 | | | | | | | 1970 | | | | | | |
|---|---|---|---|---|---|---|---|---|---|---|---|---|---|---|
| | R. J. Reynolds | American brands | Brown & Williamson | Philip Morris | Lorillard | Liggett & Myers | 1966 industry total—this type | R. J. Reynolds | American brands | Brown & Williamson | Philip Morris | Lorillard | Liggett & Myers | 1970 industry total—this type |
| Plain filter | 14.5% | 2.4% | 6.7% | 8.3% | 7.1% | 4.1% | 43.1% | 17.0% | 3.0% | 6.4% | 13.9% | 6.8% | 3.2% | 50.3% |
| Menthol filter | 8.7 | 0.2 | 6.2 | 1.3 | 1.9 | | 18.3 | 9.3 | 0.8 | 9.5 | 1.8 | 1.6 | 0.1 | 23.1 |
| Charcoal filter | 0.2 | 3.8 | — | 0.7 | — | 1.6 | 6.3 | — | 4.2 | — | 0.5 | — | 1.4 | 6.1 |
| Total filter | 23.4% | 6.4% | 12.9% | 10.3% | 9.0% | 5.7% | 67.7% | 26.3% | 8.0% | 15.9% | 16.2% | 8.4% | 4.7% | 79.5% |
| Nonfilter king size | | 12.4% | 0.8% | 0.6% | 0.3% | 1.8% | 15.9% | | 8.7% | 0.5% | 0.4% | 0.1% | 1.3% | 11.0% |
| Nonfilter regular | 8.7 | 4.4 | 0.7 | 0.3 | 0.1 | 1.0 | 15.2 | 5.4 | 3.0 | 0.3 | 0.1 | — | 0.5 | 9.3 |
| Total nonfilter | 8.7% | 16.8% | 1.5% | 0.9% | 0.4% | 2.8% | 31.1% | 5.4% | 11.7% | 0.8% | 0.5% | 0.1% | 1.8% | 20.3% |
| Total company % of market | 32.1% | 23.2% | 14.4% | 11.2% | 9.4% | 8.5% | 98.8%* | 31.7% | 19.7% | 16.7% | 16.7% | 8.5% | 6.5% | 99.8%* |

* Totals do not include "other" companies which accounted for 1.2% and 0.2% in 1966 and 1970, respectively.
Source: Calculated from John C. Maxwell, Jr., "Historical Trends in the Tobacco Industry," Oppenheimer & Co., 1970.

# EXHIBIT 4
## Estimated share of domestic industry by category and Philip Morris brand, 1966–70

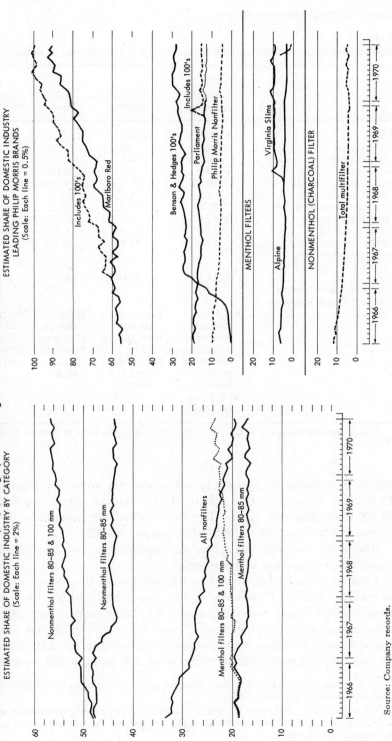

ESTIMATED SHARE OF DOMESTIC INDUSTRY BY CATEGORY
(Scale: Each line = 2%)

ESTIMATED SHARE OF DOMESTIC INDUSTRY
LEADING PHILIP MORRIS BRANDS
(Scale: Each line = 0.5%)

Source: Company records.

**EXHIBIT 5**
Comparison of major tobacco manufacturers, 1970 (in millions of dollars)

|  | R. J. Reynolds Industries | American Brands | Philip Morris | Liggett & Myers |
|---|---|---|---|---|
| Sales . . . . . . . . . . . . . . . . . | $2,485 | $2,674 | $1,510 | $ 697 |
| Net income . . . . . . . . . . . . . | 202 | 108 | 78 | 29 |
| Long-term debt . . . . . . . . . . . | 300 | 448 | 370 | 90 |
| Net worth . . . . . . . . . . . . . . | 980 | 785 | 453 | 220 |
| Percent debt/net worth . . . . . . | 30.6% | 57.2% | 81.8% | 40.9% |
| Percent earnings/sales . . . . . . . | 8.1 | 4.1 | 5.2 | 4.2 |
| Percent earnings/net worth . . . . | 20.6 | 13.8 | 17.2 | 13.2 |
| Earnings per share . . . . . . . . . | $ 4.56 | $ 4.01 | $ 3.36 | $3.80 |
| Dividend payout . . . . . . . . . . | 2.40 | 2.10 | 1.05 | 2.50 |
| Dividend payout percent. . . . . . | 52.6% | 52.4% | 31.2% | 65.9% |
| Price/earnings multiple (April 1971 price/1970 eps). . . . . . . . . . . . . . . . | 14.5 | 12.0 | 19.5 | 14.5 |
| Percent of sales in tobacco. . . . . | 73% | 77% | 87% | 53% |
| Other activities or companies owned . . . . . . . . . . . . . . | McLean Industries (container-ized shipping) Various food products companies W. R. Grace (shipping) | Sunshine Biscuits Beam Dis-tilling Duffy-Mott (food pro-ducts) | Miller Brewing Clark gum Personna razor blades | Pet foods J & B Scotch Other liquor |

Source: Arnold Bernhard & Co., Inc., *The Value Line*, Investment Survey, March 5, 1971.

intensive, economies of scale in manufacturing were not significant. Production workers in the industry had remained almost constant at 32,000 throughout the sixties. The value added per production worker increased 33% from 1960 to 1966, while wages rose 30%.[6]

The table on page 531 gives an approximate cost breakdown of cigarettes per thousand and per pack.[7]

Companies could borrow up to roughly 80% of the money required to purchase leaf for themselves, or they could wait and bid for govern-ment-stockpiled leaf two years later. The latter method was cheaper since government "carrying charges" were less than the interest on bor-rowed money. However, most companies preferred to purchase the bulk of their requirements initially rather than risk losing a bid on govern-

---

[6] U.S. Department of Commerce, Bureau of Defense Services Administration, Food and Tobacco Statistics, 1967.

[7] Manufacturing costs were thought to be roughly comparable in overseas opera-tions. The end cost to the consumer usually hinged on the amount of tax added by various governments.

| Item | Per thousand | Per pack |
|------|-------------|----------|
| Raw materials, chiefly leaf tobacco. . . . . | $   2.00 | $   .04 |
| Labor and factory overhead . . . . . . . . | 1.50 | .03 |
| Marketing and distribution . . . . . . . . | 1.00 | .02 |
| General administrative expenses . . . . . . | .35 | .007 |
| Manufacturer's profit before taxes . . . . . | 1.00 | .02 |
| Federal excise tax. . . . . . . . . . . . . | 4.00 | .08 |
| Total price to wholesaler . . . . . . . . | 9.85 | .197 |
| Wholesale margin . . . . . . . . . . . . . . | .40 | .008 |
| State excise tax . . . . . . . . . . . . . . | 1.00– 9.00 | .02 –.18 |
| Total price to retailer . . . . . . . . . . | $11.25–19.25 | $.225–.385 |
| Retail margin . . . . . . . . . . . . . . . | 1.00– 3.00 | .02 –.06 |
| State and city sales taxes. . . . . . . . . . | 0– 4.00 | 0 –.08 |
| Total price to consumer . . . . . . . . . | $12.25–26.25 | $.245–.525 |

*10 –.26*

*.10 –.34*

Source: Casewriter's discussion with various industry experts.

ment leaf two years later. In the event that a company's sales fell below the anticipated level, it could reduce its purchases for the coming two-year period, thus reducing its leaf inventory.

*Advertising and distribution.* Manufacturers directed their marketing toward establishing a "brand image" for their products. Once established, media advertising reinforced the image by emphasizing features of the cigarette which appealed to certain segments of the market. New variations of a successful brand such as changes in the filter, the length of the cigarette, or packaging were introduced to expand the brand's market appeal. The basic theme of media advertising might also be changed in an effort to build or maintain market share. For example, Marlboro's early advertising theme emphasized "filter, flavor, flip-top box." In 1960 the famous tattooed "Marlboro man" appeared. In 1967 the tattoo disappeared from prominence as the Marlboro man appeared on horseback in a distinctive outdoor environment, "Marlboro Country."

According to industry observers, advertising as a percentage of sales averaged approximately 6%, or $.60 per thousand cigarettes. Prior to 1971 approximately 75% of all cigarette advertising had been placed on TV. Spending on individual brands varied considerably; for instance, in 1970 the TV outlay for Winston ($800 million in sales) was $26 million, or 3.3% of sales. The same company (R. J. Reynolds) spent $6.3 million on TV for its Vantage brand ($10 million in sales) for an advertising-to-sales ratio of 63%. It was common for companies to spend $5 million or more to underwrite development, test-market, and promotion costs for new brands such as Vantage. Conversely, advertising expenditures on a declining brand were often cut drastically, thus increasing profit on a per-unit basis. Exhibit 6 summarizes the 1969 media expenditures of the six major producers. Exhibit 7 compares TV advertising

**EXHIBIT 6**
1970 media expenditures of major tobacco companies* (in thousands of dollars)

| Company | Total expenditure | Magazines | Newspapers | Television | Radio | Outdoor | Total company sales* | Advertising percent to sales |
|---|---|---|---|---|---|---|---|---|
| R. J. Reynolds | $ 77,844 | $ 9,986 | ... | $ 66,807 | $ 805 | $ 246 | $2,485,000 | 3.14 |
| Philip Morris | 63,598 | 13,746 | 8 | 48,177 | 834 | 833 | 1,510,000 | 4.22 |
| American Brands | 49,691 | 15,444 | 67 | 33,457 | 16 | 707 | 2,674,000 | 1.86 |
| Brown & Williamson (British-American) | 47,302 | 12,249 | 1,500 | 30,962 | ... | 2,591 | 890,000 | 5.31 |
| P. Lorillard (Loew's Theatres) | 41,482 | 5,365 | 1,969 | 31,440 | 1,128 | 1,580 | 500,000 | 8.26 |
| Liggett & Myers | 32,815 | 12,204 | 935 | 17,800 | 247 | 1,629 | 697,000 | 4.71 |
| Industry total | $312,732 | $68,994 | $4,479 | $228,643 | $3,030 | $7,586 | $8,756,000 | 3.57 |

* Sales include nontobacco products and international; advertising expenditures are for domestic tobacco and nontobacco products only.
Source: *Advertising Age*, May 17, 1971, p. 32.

**EXHIBIT 7**
Television advertising of selected brands

| Brand | Com-pany* | Date intro-duced | 1970 sales dollars (millions) | 1970 TV adver-tising dollars (millions) | TV adver-tising percent to sales |
|---|---|---|---|---|---|
| *The top five brands* | | | | | |
| Winston . . . . . . . . . . . | RJR | 1953 | 820 | 27.1 | 3.3 |
| Pall Mall . . . . . . . . . . | AB | 1946 | 580 | 9.4 | 1.6 |
| Marlboro. . . . . . . . . . . | PM | 1954 | 510 | 18.7 | 3.7 |
| Salem . . . . . . . . . . . . | RJR | 1954 | 440 | 18.7 | 4.2 |
| Kool . . . . . . . . . . . . . | B & W | 1955 | 400 | 13.9 | 3.5 |
| *New brands introduced* | | | | | |
| *since 1969* | | | | | |
| *(in chronological order)* | | | | | |
| Doral. . . . . . . . . . . . | RJR | June 1969 | 65 | 10.4 | 16.0 |
| Maryland | | | | | |
|   Menthol 100s . . . . . . . | AB | Sept. 1970 | 4 | 0 | 0 |
| Flair . . . . . . . . . . . . | B & W | Oct. 1970 | 0.5 | 0 | 0 |
| New Leaf . . . . . . . . . | PM | Oct. 1970 | 3 | 1.8 | 60.0 |
| Vantage . . . . . . . . . | RJR | Oct. 1970 | 10 | 6.3 | 63.0 |
| Eve. . . . . . . . . . . . . | L & M | Nov. 1970 | 4 | 0 | 0 |
| Hallmark. . . . . . . . . . | B & W | Nov. 1970 | 0.2 | 0 | 0 |

\* Company symbols as follows: RJR (R. J. Reynolds); AB (American Brands); PM (Philip Morris); B & W (Brown & Williamson); L & M (Liggett & Myers).
Source: *Broadcast Advertisers Reports* and casewriter's estimate of sales for individual brands based on the Maxwell report for 1970.

expenditures of the five leading brands with brands introduced since 1969.

The distribution of cigarettes had undergone a substantial change in the postwar years. Wholesalers at one time handled virtually all cigarette distribution, but by 1970 they had relinquished roughly half the market to chain stores and vending machine operators who purchased directly from the manufacturers, the latter accounting for about 20% of cigarette sales. Because cigarettes generated a high dollar volume per square foot of shelf space, obtaining distribution among the 1,500,000 retail outlets selling cigarettes was not inordinately difficult for a "promising brand." Even the selection offered by vending machines, which initially had been limited to six or eight per machine, had grown to 25 or more. Manufacturers' sales were generally made on a cash basis.

Each company maintained a sales force which augmented the wholesalers' efforts by coordinating promotion of new brands with the wholesaler and checking on the placement of the company's brands in individual outlets, especially large supermarkets. Rotating stock to insure freshness was hardly ever necessary since the shelf life of cigarettes was four to six months. However, a lively competition existed in the execution of in-store promotion such as the placement of display racks and posters.

## Prices and taxes

Since the introduction of Philip Morris in 1932, price differentials among comparable cigarettes had been virtually nonexistent. Price cutting at the manufacturer's level was rare, because companies had discovered that price cuts were merely absorbed by wholesalers or retailers as extra profit and were not passed on to the consumer. Price increases, on the other hand, were usually initiated by R. J. Reynolds or American Brands and followed by the other companies. Manufacturers' prices had been increased three times since 1967 in this fashion in response to higher wages, storage, transportation, and marketing costs.

Retail prices were also influenced by taxes. While the federal excise tax had remained constant at 8¢ per pack, aggregate state taxes had increased sevenfold since 1950.[8] In 1971 there was speculation that the federal government might increase the federal excise tax. In addition, counties and cities were beginning to follow state governments in imposing excise taxes (ranging from 1¢ to 7¢ per pack). Mayor Lindsay of New York proposed that the city's excise tax be revised to levy a heavier tax (4¢ per pack) on "high nicotine" brands and a lower tax (2¢) for "safer" brands. The attacks on smoking added to the financial hardships encountered by all levels of government suggested that additional "sin taxes" on cigarettes might be substantial in the seventies.

Together, these factors had caused cigarette prices to rise faster than the Consumer Price Index. Opinions among industry executives concerning the effect of higher prices varied. One experienced marketing executive commented:

We don't like to see our prices driven up by higher taxes, but, on the other hand, it hasn't affected our sales very much. People who enjoy smoking will pay the cost, just as they do for liquor. In Europe where our cigarettes retail at 75¢ to $1 per pack, our sales are going up, up, up.

On the other hand, a senior vice president of R. J. Reynolds pointed to the fact that in 14 states which increased taxes in 1970, cigarette smoking dipped 3.3%. In states which did not hike taxes, there was a 2.6% increase in sales.

Higher taxation had spawned increased bootlegging and hijacking, both of which were a concern to the cigarette manufacturers. New York City distributors maintained that approximately 20% of the cigarettes

---

[8] U.S. Department of Agriculture, *Tobacco Situation*, March 1970, p. 48.

sold in the city were bootlegged from other states. Since the retail value of a truckload of cigarettes was nearly $150,000, bootlegging and hijacking had become more commonplace. One manufacturer, Liggett & Myers, had put guards on some of its trucks.

## Smoking and health

The health issue occupied second place behind social objections to cigarette smoking until after World War II. In 1953, the first major cancer scare in connection with smoking occurred. A scientist from the Sloan-Kettering Institute for Cancer Research announced that he had induced cancer among laboratory mice by painting them with cigarette smoke tars. Cigarette output and consumption dropped slightly in 1953 and 1954, but the upward trend resumed again in 1955 as cigarette manufacturers offered filtered brands.

The possible relationship between cigarettes and diseases continued throughout the fifties and sixties to be a subject of scientific controversy. In January 1964 the U.S. Surgeon General's Advisory Committee on Smoking and Health issued a 350-page report in which it argued that there was no doubt about the role of cigarette smoking in lung cancer and several other diseases. It stated, "Cigarette smoking is a health hazard of sufficient importance in the United States to warrant appropriate remedial action." Brief excerpts from the summary and conclusions of the report are shown in Exhibit 8.

The Tobacco Institute, representing the industry, took the position that the data on which these conclusions were based were inconclusive. Subsequent efforts on the part of scientists to link cigarettes with disease were also found wanting by the institute. In fact, some industry executives expressed the view that as a scientific matter the prospects for a clean bill of health for cigarettes appeared brighter in 1970 than in 1964. Representative of the industry's position is the following excerpt from *The Cigarette Controversy: Eight questions and answers*, published by the Tobacco Institute.

For many adults, cigarette smoking is one of life's pleasures. Does it cause illness—even death? No one knows. The case against smoking is based almost entirely on inferences drawn from statistics and no causal relationship has actually been established. Many respected scientists find that cigarette smoking has not been shown to cause any human disease. . . . Do statistics prove that cigarette smoking is a cause of lung cancer, heart disease, emphysema, bronchitis, and other diseases? It is a cardinal principle that statistics alone cannot prove the cause of any disease. Has any new evidence that actually convicts cigarettes been reported in recent years? No. Interestingly, some of the most suggestive new evidence has implicated factors other than cigarettes. . . . The role of emotional stress in disease, for instance.

## Government regulation

Almost immediately after the Surgeon General's report was issued in January 1964, the Federal Trade Commission began to hold hearings pursuant to establishing rules under which the public would be made aware of the hazards of cigarette smoking. The Tobacco Institute testified that it could police itself and that mandatory trade regulation rules were not in accord with the FTC's authority under the FTC Act. In April 1964, the leading cigarette manufacturers announced the adoption of a cigarette advertising code to be enforced by an independent administrator. The code set forth certain advertising appeals which were not to be used, for example, social prominence, sexual attraction, appeals to persons under 18, advertising on campuses and in comic books. The code did not specify separate rules for broadcasting on television or radio.

## EXHIBIT 8

### Excerpts from the 1964 Surgeon General's Report on Smoking and Health

The Committee examined the seven prospective studies separately as well as their combined results. Considerable weight was attached to the consistency of findings among the several studies. However, to simplify presentation, only the combined results are highlighted here.

Of the 1,123,000 men who entered the seven prospective studies and who provided usable histories of smoking habits (and other characteristics such as age), 37,391 men died during the subsequent months or years of the studies. No analyses of data for females from prospective studies are presently available.

To permit ready comparison of the mortality experience of smokers and non-smokers, two concepts are widely used in the studies—excess deaths of smokers compared with non-smokers, and mortality ratio. After adjustments for differences in age and the number of cigarette smokers and non-smokers, an expected number of deaths of smokers is derived on the basis of deaths among non-smokers. Excess deaths are thus the number of actual (observed) deaths among smokers in excess of the number expected. If the age-adjusted death rates are the same, the mortality ratio will be 1.0; if the death rates of smokers are double those of non-smokers, the mortality ratio will be 2.0. (Expressed as a percentage, this example would be equivalent to a 100 percent increase.)

Table 2 presents the accumulated and combined data on 14 disease categories for which the mortality ratio of cigarette smokers to non-smokers was 1.5 or greater.

The mortality ratio for male cigarette smokers compared with non-smokers, for all causes of death taken together, is 1.68, representing a total death rate nearly 70 percent higher than for non-smokers. (This ratio includes death rates for diseases not listed in the table as well as for the 14 disease categories shown.)

In the combined results from the seven studies, the mortality ratio of cigarette smokers over non-smokers was particularly high for a number of diseases: cancer of the lung (10.8), bronchitis and emphysema (6.1), cancer of the larynx (5.4), oral cancer (4.1), cancer of the esophagus (3.4), peptic ulcer (2.8), and the group of other circulatory diseases (2.6). For coronary artery disease the mortality ratio was 1.7.

Expressed in percentage-form, this is equivalent to a statement that for coronary artery disease, the leading cause of death in this country, the death rate is 70 percent higher for cigarette smokers. For chronic bronchitis and emphysema, which are among the leading causes of severe disability, the death rate for cigarette smokers is 500 percent higher than for non-smokers. For lung cancer, the most frequent site of cancer in men, the death rate is nearly 1,000 percent higher.

**EXHIBIT 8** (*continued*)

Table 2.[1] *—Expected and observed deaths for smokers of cigarettes only and mortality ratios in seven prospective studies*

| Underlying cause of death | Expected deaths | Observed deaths | Mortality ratio |
|---|---|---|---|
| Cancer of lung (162-3)[2] ..................... | 170.3 | 1,833 | 10.8 |
| Bronchitis and emphysema (502, 521.1)........... | 89.5 | 546 | 6.1 |
| Cancer of larynx (161)..................... | 14.0 | 75 | 5.4 |
| Oral cancer (140-8)...................... | 37.0 | 152 | 4.1 |
| Cancer of esophagus (150).................. | 33.7 | 113 | 3.4 |
| Stomach and duodenal ulcers (540, 541) ......... | 105.1 | 294 | 2.8 |
| Other circulatory diseases (451-68).............. | 254.0 | 649 | 2.6 |
| Cirrhosis of liver (581)..................... | 169.2 | 379 | 2.2 |
| Cancer of bladder (181) .................... | 111.6 | 216 | 1.9 |
| Coronary artery disease (420)................. | 6,430.7 | 11,177 | 1.7 |
| Other heart diseases (421-2, 430-4)............. | 526.0 | 868 | 1.7 |
| Hypertensive heart (440-3) ................. | 409.2 | 631 | 1.5 |
| General arteriosclerosis (450) ................ | 210.7 | 310 | 1.5 |
| Cancer of kidney (180) ................... | 79.0 | 120 | 1.5 |
| All causes[3]............................ | 15,653.9 | 23,223 | 1.68 |

[1] Abridged from Table 26, Chapter 8, Mortality.
[2] International Statistical Classification numbers in parentheses.
[3] Includes all other causes of death as well as those listed above.

### Other Findings of the Prospective Studies

In general, the greater the number of cigarettes smoked daily, the higher the death rate. For men who smoke fewer than 10 cigarettes a day, according to the seven prospective studies, the death rate from all causes is about 40 percent higher than for non-smokers. For those who smoke from 10 to 19 cigarettes a day, it is about 70 percent higher than for non-smokers; for those who smoke 20 to 39 a day, 90 percent higher; and for those who smoke 40 or more, it is 120 percent higher.

Cigarette smokers who stopped smoking before enrolling in the seven studies have a death rate about 40 percent higher than non-smokers, as against 70 percent higher for current cigarette smokers. Men who began smoking before age 20 have a substantially higher death rate than those who began after age 25. Compared with non-smokers, the mortality risk of cigarette smokers, after adjustments for differences in age, increases with duration of smoking (number of years), and is higher in those who stopped after age 55 than for those who stopped at an earlier age.

In two studies which recorded the degree of inhalation, the mortality ratio for a given amount of smoking was greater for inhalers than for non-inhalers.

The ratio of the death rates of smokers to that of non-smokers is highest at the earlier ages (40–50) represented in these studies, and declines with increasing age.

Possible relationships of death rates and other forms of tobacco use were also investigated in the seven studies. The death rates for men smoking less than 5 cigars a day are about the same as for non-smokers. For men smoking more than 5 cigars daily, death rates are slightly higher. There is some indication that these higher death rates occur primarily in men who have been smoking more than 30 years and who inhale the smoke to some degree. The death rates for pipe smokers are little if at all higher than for non-smokers, even for men who smoke 10 or more pipefuls a day and for men who have smoked pipes more than 30 years.

Source: U.S. Department of Health, Education, and Welfare, *Smoking and Health: Report of the Advisory Committee to the Surgeon General of the Public Health Service*, chap. 4, pp. 28–29.

The FTC, for its part, issued the "Trade Regulation Rule for the Prevention of Unfair or Deceptive Advertising and Labeling of Cigarettes in Relation to the Health Hazards of Smoking." An Act of Congress provided that from January 1, 1966, manufacturers would be required to affix the warning: "Caution: Cigarette Smoking May Be Hazardous To Your Health" to all cigarette packages.

In 1967 the FCC ordered radio and TV stations to allow time for antismoking advertisements. Thus, stations running cigarette ads had to make available a significant amount of free time for antismoking commercials: one antismoking for every three smoking commercials. Then in April 1970 concern over public health and pressure from various anticigarette groups culminated in Congressional passage of legislation which revised the health warning on cigarette packages and banned all TV and radio advertising of cigarettes after January 2, 1971.[9] Moreover, beginning in November 1970, all cigarette packages were required to have the following words printed on them: "Warning: The Surgeon General Has Determined That Cigarette Smoking Is Dangerous To Your Health." This was more definitive than the previous admonition, "Caution: Cigarette Smoking May Be Hazardous To Your Health."

The FTC was empowered to enforce the ban on broadcast advertising and was armed with the prerogative of unleashing an even stronger warning label in the event that manufacturers did not comply with the spirit and letter of the law. The law also stated that the FTC could require, six months after notifying Congress, the health warning in print media after July 1, 1971, or sooner if the FTC determined that manufacturers were substantially expanding advertising in newspapers, magazines, and billboards.

## The international market

The international market for cigarettes was not as concentrated as the U.S. market, although several large companies and government monopolies accounted for a sizable portion of total world production of 3 trillion units in 1968. British-American Tobacco accounted for 450 billion units, excluding its Brown and Williamson subsidiary. R. J. Reynolds and Philip Morris, the second and third largest publicly held

---

[9] Despite the withdrawal of cigarette advertising from television and radio, anticigarette commercials continued after January 2, 1971. On December 15, 1970, the FCC issued a rule that broadcasters no longer had a definite obligation to carry free antismoking messages but were expected to do so in the time they devoted to matters of public concern. At the same time, the FCC ruling indicated that broadcasters were free to decide whether the issue of smoking and health was controversial enough to warrant allowing the cigarette industry to answer attacks upon it.

firms in the international market, sold an estimated 110 and 90 billion units, respectively. According to industry observers, another large international firm, the Rothman Group, a consortium of privately and publicly held firms, sold nearly 300 billion units worldwide. Government-controlled monopolies in Japan, Korea, and Taiwan controlled another 250 billion units in total.

| Region | 1968 population* (millions) | 1968 output† (billions) | Cigarettes per capita | Percent increase in output† 1964–68 |
|---|---|---|---|---|
| North & Central America | 285 | 699.2 | 2,450 | 11.8 |
| South America | 204 | 145.2 | 710 | 19.9 |
| Western Europe | 353 | 569.5 | 1,610 | 25.0 |
| Eastern Europe & USSR | 340 | 485.7 | 1,430 | 22.0 |
| Africa | 336 | 84.2 | 250 | 22.7 |
| Asia | 1,946 | 953.8 | 490 | 38.4 |
| Oceania | 19 | 29.4 | 1,540 | 28.4 |
| World Total | 3,483 | 2,967.0 | 855 | 24.5 |

* United Nations, *Demographic Yearbook*, 1969, p. 115.
† U.S. Department of Agriculture, Foreign Agricultural Service, "World Cigarette Output," FT 4-70, September 1970.

The problems of overseas operations were numerous and complex. First, American companies faced stiff competition in some areas such as Europe, and they anticipated increased competition in less-developed areas as the better local firms became more sophisticated. Second, nationalism was not expected to diminish in the seventies, and some industry executives believed that their companies, being highly visible, could not count on maintaining 100%-owned subsidiaries. Third, trademark laws were less stringent outside the United States; hence, American companies had to work diligently to prevent foreign firms from taking a U.S. brand and marketing it themselves.

On the other hand, factors in foreign markets such as growing affluence, craving for American brands, and less-active antismoking campaigns were responsible for the 4% annual growth rate in the overseas consumption of cigarettes. Moreover, the market share held by international companies was increasing in many areas in response to aggressive marketing techniques, new products, and the use of American brand names. Furthermore, the proportion of the free world market (excluding the United States) held by filter cigarettes had grown from about 20% in 1961 to nearly 60% in 1970, a trend thought to favor the international companies.

## PHILIP MORRIS INCORPORATED

### History

In 1847, Philip Morris, Esq. opened a tobacco shop on Bond Street in London. Noting the uniqueness of a product introduced to England by soldiers returning from the Crimean War, Mr. Morris began to produce tobacco rolled in paper. The product, called "paparose" by the Russians, was renamed "cigarette" by Mr. Morris in 1853. Mr. Morris introduced several brand names (Philip Morris, Oxford Blues, and Cambridge "English" Ovals) and soon began exporting cigarettes to the colonies.

In 1902 Philip Morris Incorporated was established in the United States to import and sell the English brands. In 1919 a group of U.S. investors purchased Philip Morris, Inc. Over the next decade or more, the company changed hands a number of times but remained a small importer without domestic brands or manufacturing facilities.

Then in 1933 with only $3 million in sales, in the midst of the depression, the company introduced its first American brand. Mr. George Weissman, president, reflected on this event which he felt set an important precedent for the subsequent management of the company.

More than a hundred companies have tried to break into the "Club" over the years but only Philip Morris has succeeded. It happened in 1933 when Alfred Lyon, vice president of marketing and later president, decided to market the premium-priced Philip Morris "brown pack" as a "popular brand."[10] The company needed manufacturing facilities, but that was a minor problem compared to securing distribution and creating consumer awareness. We just didn't have the money to compete with the big five.

On the other hand, the big five were still acting like the old trust: create demand through advertising and cut wholesaler and retailer margins to the bone. When Philip Morris was introduced with the same manufacturer's price but a higher retail price, the trade got a break. It was a hand-to-mouth operation financed in part by the sale of stock in the company to wholesalers and retailers; receipts for one day's shipment were used to pay the excise tax on those for the next day. There was little money for radio advertising at first. However, before the other companies reacted and prices stabilized again, we were firmly established with 5% to 6% of the market.

That experience continues to be meaningful for Philip Morris. Our relationships with the trade have continued to be close and our sense for people very keen. Perhaps as a result, we were the first to recognize the importance of supermarkets and chain drugstores in the 1950s. Moreover, we have never felt inhibited by the traditions of the big five. We've felt we could buck the industry and succeed. We've also figured Philip Morris could never com-

---

[10] At that time, the popular brands were Camel, Lucky Strike, Chesterfield, Old Gold, and Raleigh.

pete dollar for dollar with Reynolds and American; we've had to innovate, to accept the risk of higher costs and lower margins that accompany the introduction of many new products in our businesses.

The company's share of the cigarette market fluctuated in a range of 7% to 10% from the late 1930s until 1965, when it began a steep ascent. The intervening years were, however, not uneventful. Noting the rapid acceptance of filter-tip brands such as Winston, Viceroy, Kent, and L&M and the corresponding threat to the nonfilter Philip Morris brand, the company began actively to consider the introduction of its own filter cigarette. Before this could be done, Mr. O. Parker McComas, a former banker and then president of Philip Morris, negotiated the purchase of Benson & Hedges, makers of Parliament filter cigarettes, for $22 million in 1954. The principal owners of Benson & Hedges were members of the Cullman family who were later to assume important leadership positions in the combined company.

The next year Philip Morris introduced a filter brand: Marlboro.[11] The product was unique in that it came in a flip-top box. Marlboro was an immediate success,[12] so much so that Philip Morris agreed to purchase the next two years' production of the patented packaging machinery from the manufacturer.

## Domestic cigarette operations

Cigarettes represented about 95% of the sales of the Philip Morris U.S.A. division, the remainder coming from shaving products, chewing gum, and hospital supplies. Despite the success of Marlboro, the company had entered the 1960s with the smallest market share among the six major producers. By 1971, however, management claimed that Philip Morris had moved into third place and was rapidly closing the gap on American Brands. Much of the growth had occurred since 1965.

*Brands.* The competitive position of the company's principal domestic brands is noted in Exhibits 2 and 3. Mr. Weissman outlined some of the policies that guided Philip Morris' marketing policy.

We have not often been first with a new cigarette. For example, others introduced king-sized, filters, menthols, and even 100-millimeter brands before we did. Yet, we have been successful in making our products unique. Marlboro came out in a flip-top box. We put a plastic package around Multi-Filter, our charcoal-filter brand. Virginia Slims was a "first" for us since it was the first cigarette to be directed specifically at women. We were also unique in taking a corporate name, Benson & Hedges, and putting it on a premium

---

[11] The Marlboro name had actually been introduced at the turn of the century by Philip Morris for an expensive lady's cigarette.

[12] Some company executives indicated that Marlboro captured 10% of the New York City market in the first 30 days.

cigarette, Benson & Hedges 100s. We want to give the consumer a high-quality cigarette that is distinctive.

Another essential element in our success is our ability to react rapidly to changes in market or competitive conditions. We have a corporate products committee which regularly reviews the progress on individual brands. The chairman and I are personally involved with the formulation of marketing policy for our major brands. Moreover, if we have a good product idea, we can get top-management commitment in a hurry.

Mr. Ross Millhiser, president of Philip Morris U.S.A. and former Marlboro brand manager, explained certain further dimensions of the marketing task:

We want our products to have charisma, and this requires attention to packaging and advertising. When we think we have the optimal combination of product quality and consumer appeal for a certain segment of the market, we test the brand for several months. If it gets 1% of the market, we consider launching it nationwide. I don't really need market surveys to tell me how a new brand is doing. We can get some idea in a few weeks from the repurchase pattern whether it is taking hold.

**Advertising.**  Philip Morris spent roughly 80% of its $60 million 1970 advertising budget on broadcast media. The company had been highly successful in the use of creative advertising for its products. The campaigns for Marlboro and Benson & Hedges 100s had been widely acclaimed in advertising circles for their sophisticated consumer appeal.

In April 1971, company officials were assessing the impact of losing the opportunity to advertise on television. They generally agreed that television had been the most efficient means of disseminating the advertising message for cigarettes and that its prohibition was unlikely to diminish competition for consumer loyalty. On the other hand, it was not altogether clear that the long-run effects on the industry in general and Philip Morris in particular would be serious.

For one thing, company officials noted that cigarette consumption had been rising steadily long before television came into existence. Second, in the United Kingdom, where cigarette commercials had been banned in all media since 1967, consumption had risen almost 3% per year. Television advertising had never been allowed in France, yet unit sales had increased at an annual rate of 5.8% from 1964 through 1969. Philip Morris found solace in the fact that another consumer products industry, distilled spirits, had experienced sales increases of 4.5% per year without the use of broadcast advertising. Finally, the company believed that since it had well-established quality brands in the growth segments of the industry, it stood to lose least among major manufacturers.

**Distribution.**  From the company's factories in Richmond, Virginia, and Louisville, Kentucky, products were shipped by rail, truck, or plane to 60 warehouses located near major market areas. The warehouses, in turn, supplied wholesalers, major retail accounts such as food and drug chains, and large vending machine owners. The company maintained a sales force numbering several hundred who performed a detail function typical in the industry.

## Policy on public health

The stated policy of Philip Morris on cigarettes and health, expressed in its 1970 annual report, was as follows:

Our position remains the same—more and better research is needed to answer the questions that have been raised by statistical associations that themselves are wide open to questioning.

To this end, the tobacco industry is spending more money than the combined forces of all the voluntary health agencies on research in smoking and health.

. . . We welcome all serious and responsible opportunities to cooperate with the government and other agencies in the field of smoking and health.

From 1964 to 1970, Philip Morris and other tobacco companies had contributed $18 million to the American Medical Association's Education and Research Foundation for the purpose of studying the relationship between tobacco and health. Philip Morris had worked with the Federal Trade Commission to set up "tar and nicotine" testing laboratories. Mr. Cullman personally served as chairman of the Tobacco Institute's executive committee and frequently gave speeches around the country concerning the company's position on the health question.

Since 1953, when the first cancer scare had occurred, Philip Morris researchers had succeeded in developing filters which reduced the tar and nicotine delivery in the average cigarette by 46%. The company was capable of producing a cigarette virtually free of tar and nicotine, but such "high filtration" cigarettes had not been popular with cigarette smokers in general. The most popular brands, including Marlboro, were relatively high in nicotine content.

## Philip Morris International

In addition to acquiring Benson & Hedges, a second important event occurred in 1954: the company established its first foreign subsidiary, Philip Morris (Australia) Ltd. Mr. Weissman discussed the "quirks of fate" which had prompted Philip Morris' involvement in international operations:

Being a British company in the days of the Empire, the Philip Morris name had been established around the world; it was in a sense an international company from the outset. Unlike some of our competitors, our domestic brand names belonged to us overseas as well. This is another instance in which not being a member of the old "Club" has given us more flexibility and the opportunity to be more aggressive.

Then in 1954, one of our distributors in Australia came to New York and asked us if we would be interested in starting a company down there to take advantage of the demand for U.S. cigarettes following the war. We decided to do it and sent him back with a pledge to buy 71% of the equity. We got into the Latin American market by another quirk of fate. In 1956, the Venezuelan government wanted local manufacture of items which had been imported, so we bought our distributor and got into the manufacture of cigarettes in Latin America.

My involvement in the international division came in 1960, when Joe Cullman came into my office one day and said, "Why don't you head up the international division?" He gave me only one guideline: "Expand your sales with no diminution of earnings." Since I was running the entire domestic cigarette business at the time, I wasn't sure whether it was a promotion or a convenient way of setting me aside.

From its founding in 1954, Philip Morris International's sales grew from 5% of the corporate total to 28% in 1970. Since 1961, sales had increased at a compound rate of 33% per year, reaching $425 million in 1970.[13] In the international market, Philip Morris was the fastest growing U.S. company, and its products were available to consumers in more than 150 nations and territories, including all the major world markets except the United Kingdom, Indonesia, and mainland China.

Philip Morris International was organized in four regions: Canada, Latin America, Asia/Pacific, and Europe, each having a regional vice president who had responsibility for profits, market share, and unit volume. Manufacturing facilities in 20 countries produced the company's U.S. brands and a wide variety of local brands tailored to the tastes of individual countries.

Philip Morris had emphasized several policies in regard to foreign operations. Mr. Hugh Cullman, president of Philip Morris International, discussed some of these policies:

We don't "wave the flag" in foreign countries. Outside the British Commonwealth where the name Philip Morris is widely known, we use indigenous names for our subsidiaries. We recognize that value systems are different in these countries, and our operations and products are designed to be consistent with these values.

We aim to develop brands which compete in the premium-priced segment of the market. Overseas, there are different price categories of cigarettes, unlike the United States. Our managers are responsible for sales and profits, but when a decision affects one of our U.S. brands such as Marlboro, the

---

[13] $425 million was the total for consolidated subsidiaries, all of which were wholly owned. In addition, there was another $280 million in sales of unconsolidated subsidiaries, many of them partially owned.

manager of a foreign subsidiary must check back with New York. Also, Joe (Cullman) and George (Weissman) like to inspect personally the progress of overseas operating units.

## 1957: Early diversification

In 1957 Philip Morris became, in management's view, the first tobacco company actively to entertain diversification. Management's reasons for seeking nontobacco enterprises at that time were threefold. First, there was a desire to move away from dependence on one product. Second, there was interest in applying the company's marketing expertise in other fields. Third, should the cigarette business, or Philip Morris' share of it, level off, a sizable cash flow would be available for investment.

In July 1957 a flexible packaging company, Milprint, Inc., was acquired for 385,000 common shares (worth approximately $16.8 million). Milprint owned Nicolet Paper Company, a producer of glassine and specialty papers. After these two acquisitions were made, the company formed the industrial division, Milprint and Nicolet accounting for 90% of the division's sales. The remaining 10% was supplied by Polymer Industries, acquired in 1958, which manufactured adhesives and textile chemicals, and Koch Convertograph, acquired in 1968, which produced bottle and other labels. While most of Philip Morris' cigarette packaging and printing was done by outside firms, management felt that having in-house packaging capability kept their outside suppliers' prices down. The industrial division's annual growth rate had averaged 3.4% since 1961.

Subsequently, three consumer products companies were acquired in the areas described below. As part of Philip Morris U.S.A. division, these companies accounted for $40 million in sales in 1970.

**Shaving products.** American Safety Razor Company, acquired in 1960, was the third largest manufacturer of shaving products. Its razor blade, trademarked "Personna," accounted for 12% of the domestic market in 1970 as compared with 5% in 1960.[14] Burma-Vita Company, manufacturer of Burma Shave products, was acquired in 1963.

**Chewing gum.** Clark Brothers Chewing Gum Company, purchased in 1963, produced a variety of chewing gums. It held 6% of the domestic chewing gum market in 1970, as compared with less than 1% when acquired.[15]

**Hospital supply.** The medical products' division was composed of several hospital supply companies acquired in 1967. Products included surgical blades, sutures, and sterile disposable hospital kits. The division was sold in 1971.

---

[14] Gillette, the dominant producer of razors and blades, was estimated to have 60% of the market.

[15] Wrigley's, the leading gum producer, held roughly 45% of the market.

### 1969: Major diversification in premium beer and land development

In 1969 Philip Morris had once again concerned itself with diversification. One senior finance executive commented:

Inevitably, our domestic cigarette business will level off as our market share increases and growth in consumption stabilizes around 1% to 2% per year. Our cash flow will increase dramatically at that time and we need growth businesses in which to invest this cash flow. Our historic growth in the cigarette business can't go on forever, especially in the domestic market.

Mr. Millhiser added a further dimension:

Some of our competitors have lost faith in the cigarette industry. Whenever you see a large increase in profits on a small increase in sales, it probably means the company is exploiting the business. I don't believe the growth in cigarette sales will end. By the same token, it's hard to find another business that is as good as this one. We looked at the confectionary industry for about three years but decided it was too parochial to tolerate the product innovation and too dominated by nonfranchised distributors. Beer probably comes closest to matching our skills with a market opportunity.

*Miller Brewing Company.* In June 1969 Philip Morris purchased 53% of the stock of Miller Brewing Company from W. R. Grace and Company for $130 million in cash. One year later, the remaining 47% was acquired for $97 million in cash from the De Rance Foundation, a charitable organization controlled by a descendant of the Miller family. The total purchase price of $227 million was approximately 25 times Miller's earnings in 1967 and 1968. Approximately $150 million of the purchase price was cost in excess of book value.

Miller produced Miller High Life beer, one of three nationally distributed premium-priced beers in the United States (the other two were Budweiser and Schlitz). Since 1960, beer consumption in the United States had been growing at a rate of 3.2% per year, but the premium-priced segment had grown at 8.5%. By 1980 total beer consumption was estimated to reach 150 million barrels, of which premium beer was expected to be 40%.

The company had three breweries, located in Milwaukee (4 million barrels), Azusa, California, and Fort Worth, Texas (1 million barrels each). Miller's output of 5 million barrels in 1969 represented 4.4% of the industry total and 16% of the premium-priced segment, as shown in Exhibit 9. Philip Morris officials viewed Miller as a stable company with a "Cadillac" reputation which marketed its products in a growth segment of a consumer-oriented industry. Philip Morris tobacco and Miller beer were sold in many of the same retail outlets.

One of the most important factors influencing Miller's 1970 results

**EXHIBIT 9**

PHILIP MORRIS INCORPORATED
Miller Brewing Company

*I. Financial reports*

| Year to 12/21 | Sales (incl. excise taxes) (millions) | Operating income (millions) | Operating margin | Net income (thousands) |
|---|---|---|---|---|
| 1965 . . . . . . | $137.6 | $14.6 | 10.5% | $7,215 |
| 1966 . . . . . . | 154.8 | 15.9 | 10.5 | 8,346 |
| 1967 . . . . . . | 173.0 | 18.6 | 10.5 | 9,586 |
| 1968 . . . . . . | 184.4 | 18.1 | 9.8 | 9,035 |
| 1969 . . . . . . | 196.3 | 15.3 | 7.8 | 8,202 |
| 1970 . . . . . . | 198.5 | 11.4 | 5.8 | 7,400* |

\* Estimated.
Source: Company records.

*II. Miller's sales compared with industry sales*

| Year | Thousands of barrels | | | Miller percent of industry | Miller percent of premium segment |
|---|---|---|---|---|---|
| | Industry | Premium segment | Miller | | |
| 1965 . . . . . . . . | 100,411 | 22,200 | 3,667 | 3.7 | 16.4 |
| 1966 . . . . . . . . | 104,262 | 24,200 | 4,146 | 4.0 | 17.0 |
| 1967 . . . . . . . . | 106,974 | 26,300 | 4,584 | 4.3 | 17.4 |
| 1968 . . . . . . . . | 111,415 | 28,500 | 4,847 | 4.4 | 16.9 |
| 1969 . . . . . . . . | 116,270 | 31,000 | 5,080 | 4.4 | 16.3 |
| 1970 . . . . . . . . | 120,100 | 33,700 | 5,113 | 4.4 | 15.8 |
| Increase, 1965–69 . . . . . . | 15.8% | 39.6% | 38.5% | | |

Source: U.S. Treasury Department, Bureau of Internal Revenue; company data.

had been the continuing adverse effect of a 1969 strike in Milwaukee which affected 80% of the company's capacity. This resulted in a considerable loss of distribution, shelf space, and on-premises availability for Miller which was only partially regained in 1970. Nonetheless, the company took steps to enlarge the capacity of its Fort Worth plant by 300,000 barrels and to plan an eastern brewery (capacity, 2,000,000 barrels) in Newark, Delaware. The estimated cost of these improvements was expected to be approximately $90 million.

*Mission Viejo Company.* In January 1970 Philip Morris purchased convertible debentures and options in Mission Viejo Company, a land development and home construction company in Orange County, California, for $20 million. Under terms of the agreement, Philip Morris maintained temporary control of Mission Viejo until 1973. Between 1973 and 1975, for an additional $13 million Philip Morris could exercise an option enabling the company to control 52% of Mission Viejo on a permanent basis. If Philip Morris did not exercise this option and convert its debentures by December 31, 1975, it would retain straight debentures and own a fractional amount of equity in Mission Viejo.

Founded in 1966, Mission Viejo was a new town located on 11,000 acres of land midway between Los Angeles and San Diego. By 1970, 3,000 acres had been developed and the city's population was 14,000. It was estimated that the population of Mission Viejo would reach 100,000 by 1990.

Mr. John Cookman, senior vice president, finance, believed that the Mission Viejo venture complemented the corporation's operations, since the high cash flow generated by its cigarette sales could be applied to the heavy initial cost of community development. In addition, he noted that the growth potential in real estate and the demand for competent management were considerations which beckoned to Philip Morris.

Nationally, the home-building industry was severely affected by the 1970 economic downturn. The rate of housing starts (approximately 2 million per year) dropped to 1 million in January 1970 as mortgage interest rates, housing costs, and unemployment increased. The southern California economy was particularly hard hit as layoffs in aerospace and defense industries raised unemployment in that area well above the national level. Mission Viejo, however, recorded the highest total home sales of any home builder in Orange County. A total of 765 homes were sold in 1970 for $20 million. The president of Mission Viejo Company estimated that 1971 sales would be 800–1,000 homes for a total of $30 million. In January 1971 housing starts had increased to a seasonally adjusted annual rate of 1.7 million units.

## Organization

Prior to the 1969 and 1970 diversification, Philip Morris was organized into three divisions supported by a small corporate staff devoted primarily to finance, planning, and legal matters. The divisions themselves were structured differently; domestic by functional specialty (aside from the small nontobacco units), international by area, and industrial by product. Miller and Mission Viejo were simply added as new operating divisions as shown in Exhibit 10.

The task of monitoring and providing guidance to the new divisions was assumed personally by members of the top-management group. Mr. Weissman, in particular, devoted a considerable amount of time to the development of Miller. Mr. Cookman, who had been one of the early proponents of Mission Viejo, continued to pay close attention to its progress.

**EXHIBIT 10**

PHILIP MORRIS INCORPORATED
Organization Chart

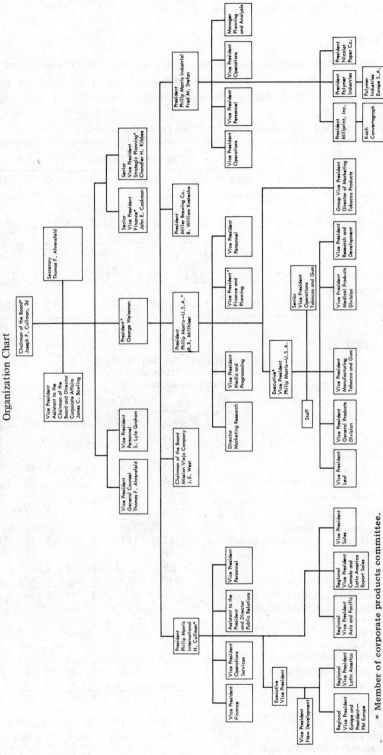

* Member of corporate products committee.
Source: Company records.

## Finance

From 1960 to 1970, long-term debt rose from $67.4 million to $370 million due largely to the acquisition of Miller. The dividend payout ratio had declined during the same period from 66% to 31%. On the

**Cash flow and capital expenditures, 1963–70 (millions of dollars)**

|  | Years ended December 31 | | | | | | | |
|---|---|---|---|---|---|---|---|---|
|  | *1963* | *1964* | *1965* | *1966* | *1967* | *1968* | *1969* | *1970* |
| Retained earnings . . . . . . . | $ 8.2 | $ 8.8 | $12.7 | $18.2 | $27.5 | $29.2 | $35.7 | $52.2 |
| Depreciation . . . . . . | 6.8 | 8.3 | 8.9 | 9.5 | 10.9 | 12.1 | 13.5 | 17.7 |
| Total . . . . . . . . | $15.0 | $17.1 | $21.7 | $27.7 | $38.4 | $41.3 | $49.2 | $69.9 |
| Capital expenditures . . . . | 26.2 | 19.4 | 12.1 | 17.1 | 25.7 | 26.4 | 23.6 | 39.6 |
| Excess of funds over expenditures . . . . | ($11.2) | $( 2.3) | $ 9.6 | $10.6 | $12.7 | $14.9 | $25.6 | $30.3 |

### EXHIBIT 11

PHILIP MORRIS INCORPORATED
Consolidated Income Statements, 1966–70
(in millions of dollars)

|  | Year ended December 31 | | | | |
|---|---|---|---|---|---|
|  | *1966* | *1967* | *1968* | *1969* | *1970* |
| Sales . . . . . . . . . . . . . . . . . . . . . | $772 | $905 | $1,020 | $1,142 | $1,510 |
| Cost of sales | | | | | |
| Cost of products sold . . . . . . . . . . . | $303 | $354 | $ 400 | $ 455 | $ 577 |
| U.S. and foreign excise tax . . . . . . . . | 265 | 311 | 338 | 373 | 519 |
| Total cost of sales . . . . . . . . . . . | $568 | $665 | $ 738 | $ 828 | $1,096 |
| Gross profit . . . . . . . . . . . . . . . . . | $204 | $240 | $ 282 | $ 314 | $ 414 |
| Nonoperating expenses | | | | | |
| Selling, research and development . . . . | $122 | $139 | $ 159 | $ 166 | $ 220 |
| Corporate expense . . . . . . . . . . . . . | 10 | 11 | 12 | 13 | 15 |
| Interest . . . . . . . . . . . . . . . . . . | 8 | 10 | 16 | 29 | 35 |
| Total nonoperating expenses . . . . . . | $140 | $160 | $ 187 | $ 208 | $ 270 |
| Consolidated earnings before taxes . . . . . | $ 64 | $ 80 | $ 95 | $ 106 | $ 144 |
| Earnings from unconsolidated subsidiaries . . . . . . . . . . . . . . . . | | | | | |
| Domestic . . . . . . . . . . . . . . . . . . | 0 | 0 | 0 | 3 | 3 |
| Foreign . . . . . . . . . . . . . . . . . . | 3 | 3 | 3 | 2 | 7 |
| Other income (expense) . . . . . . . . . . | (1) | (2) | 1 | 4 | (3) |
| Earnings before income taxes . . . . . . . . | $ 66 | $ 81 | $ 99 | $ 115 | $ 151 |
| Income taxes . . . . . . . . . . . . . . . . . | 32 | 38 | 50 | 57 | 73 |
| Net earnings . . . . . . . . . . . . . . . . . . | $ 34 | $ 43 | $ 49 | $ 58 | $ 78 |
| Earnings per share | | | | | |
| Primary . . . . . . . . . . . . . . . . . | $1.54 | $1.97 | $2.18 | $2.58 | $3.36 |
| Fully diluted . . . . . . . . . . . . . . . | 1.54 | 1.94 | 2.14 | 2.40 | 2.85 |

Source: Company records.

**EXHIBIT 12**

PHILIP MORRIS INCORPORATED
Consolidated Balance Sheets, 1966–70
(in millions of dollars)

| | 1966 | 1967 | 1968 | 1969 | 1970 |
|---|---|---|---|---|---|
| *Assets* | | | | | |
| Current assets | | | | | |
| Cash . . . . . . . . . . . . . . . . . . . . . | $ 27 | $ 38 | $ 37 | $ 42 | $ 52 |
| Accounts receivable . . . . . . . . . . . . | 46 | 59 | 70 | 83 | 102 |
| Inventories | | | | | |
| Leaf tobacco . . . . . . . . . . . . . | 238 | 327 | 366 | 364 | 444 |
| Other inventory . . . . . . . . . . . . | 60 | 60 | 86 | 83 | 124 |
| Total inventory. . . . . . . . . . . . | $298 | $387 | $452 | $447 | $ 568 |
| Prepaid expenses . . . . . . . . . . . . . | 2 | 2 | 3 | 3 | 7 |
| Total current assets . . . . . . . . . | $373 | $486 | $562 | $575 | $ 729 |
| Investments in unconsolidated subsidiaries | | | | | |
| Domestic . . . . . . . . . . . . . . . . . | $ 0 | $ 0 | $ 0 | $132 | $ 22 |
| Foreign . . . . . . . . . . . . . . . . . | 18 | 24 | 68 | 96 | 68 |
| Total investments . . . . . . . . . . . | $ 18 | $ 24 | $ 68 | $228 | $ 90 |
| Fixed assets | | | | | |
| Land . . . . . . . . . . . . . . . . . . . . . | $ 5 | $ 5 | $ 6 | $ 7 | $ 12 |
| Buildings . . . . . . . . . . . . . . . . . | 45 | 47 | 50 | 57 | 107 |
| Machinery, equipment . . . . . . . . . . . | 123 | 142 | 163 | 173 | 274 |
| Fixed assets before depreciation . . . . . | $173 | $194 | $219 | $237 | $ 393 |
| Less: Accumulated depreciation . . . . | 63 | 70 | 81 | 90 | 156 |
| Total fixed assets. . . . . . . . . . . . | $110 | $124 | $139 | $147 | $ 237 |
| Other assets . . . . . . . . . . . . . . . . | 3 | 6 | 6 | 13 | 15 |
| Brands, trademarks, goodwill . . . . . . . | 9 | 9 | 12 | 13 | 168 |
| Total assets . . . . . . . . . . . . . . | $513 | $649 | $787 | $976 | $1,239 |
| *Liabilities and equity* | | | | | |
| Current liabilities | | | | | |
| Notes payable. . . . . . . . . . . . . . . . | $ 32 | $ 85 | $155 | $158 | $ 187 |
| Accounts payable. . . . . . . . . . . . . . | 68 | 75 | 76 | 78 | 148 |
| Taxes payable . . . . . . . . . . . . . . . | 16 | 16 | 13 | 17 | 39 |
| Dividends payable . . . . . . . . . . . . . | 4 | 4 | 5 | 6 | 7 |
| Total current liabilities . . . . . . . | $120 | $180 | $249 | $259 | $ 381 |
| Long-term debt | | | | | |
| Senior . . . . . . . . . . . . . . . . . . . | $129 | $171 | $176 | $168 | $ 178 |
| Subordinated . . . . . . . . . . . . . . . | 0 | 0 | 24 | 164 | 192 |
| Total long-term debt. . . . . . . . . . | $129 | $171 | $200 | $332 | $ 370 |
| Deferred income taxes . . . . . . . . . . . | 10 | 11 | 15 | 18 | 20 |
| Reserve applicable to international operations. . . . . . . . . . . . . . . | 1 | 4 | 4 | 5 | 9 |
| Other liabilities . . . . . . . . . . . . . . | 3 | 3 | 3 | 6 | 7 |
| Total liabilities . . . . . . . . . . . . . | $263 | $369 | $472 | $620 | $ 787 |
| Preferred stock . . . . . . . . . . . . . . | $ 27 | $ 26 | $ 26 | $ 26 | $ 25 |
| Common stock . . . . . . . . . . . . . . . | 23 | 23 | 23 | 23 | 24 |
| Capital surplus . . . . . . . . . . . . . . | 46 | 49 | 54 | 59 | 95 |
| Retained earnings . . . . . . . . . . . . . | 170 | 197 | 227 | 262 | 315 |
| Less: Treasury stock . . . . . . . . . . . | (16) | (15) | (15) | (14) | (6) |
| Total equity . . . . . . . . . . . . . | $250 | $280 | $315 | $356 | $ 453 |
| Total liabilities and equity . . . . . | $513 | $649 | $787 | $976 | $1,239 |

Source: Company records.

other hand, cash flow relative to capital expenditures had increased steadily in the latter part of the decade.

Mr. Cookman discussed Philip Morris' capital expansion plans for 1971–75:

We're going to invest $400 million in our existing businesses. First, we're building what we believe is the world's largest cigarette factory in Richmond. This will cost $80 million. We are planning a new 2 million barrel brewery in Newark, Delaware. The total investment there will be $90 million. In Europe, our plans call for $80 million for expansion of our operations there. Finally, we've planned $150 million for updating our existing facilities. Our program calls for a fairly even stream of investment each year . . . around $80 million. Our new cigarette factory will be in operation by the end of 1973.

## EXHIBIT 13

### PHILIP MORRIS INCORPORATED
Selected Financial Data, 1960–70
(in thousands of dollars)

|  | 1960 | 1961 | 1962 | 1963 |
|---|---|---|---|---|
| Operating revenues | $509,332 | $529,127 | $550,624 | $585,059 |
| Federal excise taxes | 175,947 | 184,146 | 187,133 | 193,768 |
| Foreign excise taxes | ... | ... | 3,785 | 8,276 |
| Earnings before income taxes | 44,578 | 45,985 | 47,464 | 46,729 |
| Pretax profit margins | 8.8% | 8.7% | 8.6% | 8.0% |
| Net earnings | $ 20,984 | $ 21,511 | $ 21,946 | $ 22,052 |
| Dividends declared: common | 13,085 | 13,212 | 13,046 | 12,855 |
| Dividends declared: preferred | 1,011 | 970 | 953 | 953 |
| Net earnings reinvested | 6,888 | 7,329 | 7,947 | 8,244 |
| Percent of net earnings reinvested | 32.8% | 34.1% | 36.2% | 37.4% |
| Capital expenditures | $ 7,300 | $ 8,733 | $ 11,843 | $ 26,243 |
| Annual depreciation | 5,362 | 5,638 | 6,293 | 6,765 |
| Property, plant, and equipment (gross) | 93,641 | 99,066 | 110,204 | 139,595 |
| Property, plant, and equipment (net) | 59,960 | 61,560 | 68,664 | 93,150 |
| Inventories | 209,326 | 232,541 | 228,088 | 235,375 |
| Current assets | 249,819 | 277,350 | 279,068 | 297,295 |
| Working capital | 190,423 | 190,859 | 179,222 | 190,982 |
| Total assets | 321,717 | 351,018 | 365,024 | 412,543 |
| Short-term debt | 21,000 | 45,200 | 57,400 | 53,800 |
| Senior long-term debt | 67,400 | 65,400 | 63,400 | 91,400 |
| Subordinated long-term debt | ... | ... | ... | ... |
| Total debt | 88,400 | 110,600 | 120,800 | 145,200 |
| Stockholders' equity | 195,956 | 199,685 | 201,720 | 208,711 |
| No. of common shares—actual | 22,029,792 | 21,972,954 | 21,526,428 | 21,429,444 |
| No. of common shares—weighted average | ... | ... | ... | ... |
| Primary earnings per common share | $ .91 | $ .94 | $ .98 | $ .99 |
| Fully diluted earnings per common share | .91 | .94 | .98 | .99 |
| Dividend declared per common share | .60 | .60 | .60 | .60 |
| Book value per common share | 7.74 | 7.99 | 8.25 | 8.62 |
| Market price of common share high-low | 13½–10 | 20⅞–13 | 18¾–10⅛ | 15–11⅛ |
| Closing price 12/31* | 13⅜ | 18⅜ | 12¼ | 12⅜ |

*Closing price April 30, 1971 = 66⅜.
Source: 1970 Annual Report.

The company's stock, traded on the New York Stock Exchange, had been a favorite of financial institutions. Nearly one third of Philip Morris' common stock was owned by institutional accounts, compared to less than 10% for such other institutional favorites as IBM, Xerox, and Eastman Kodak. Financial data on the company are contained in Exhibits 11–14.

## Philip Morris in the seventies

Mr. Joseph F. Cullman 3rd, chairman of the board, commented on his view of where the corporation was headed:

. . . I don't want this company to become overstimulated, to go wild. All managements are under pressure to do this . . . to pump up their earnings. We have been a disciplined company, and it has paid off. My task is to

**EXHIBIT 13** (*continued*)

| 1964 | 1965 | 1966 | 1967 | 1968 | 1969 | 1970 |
|---|---|---|---|---|---|---|
| $641,439 | $704,544 | $771,975 | $904,841 | $1,019,846 | $1,142,373 | $1,509,540 |
| 194,312 | 214,128 | 234,975 | 271,073 | 295,903 | 319,086 | 372,092 |
| 22,462 | 27,780 | 30,057 | 39,658 | 41,841 | 54,247 | 147,124 |
| 44,466 | 52,423 | 65,144 | 81,317 | 100,107 | 115,613 | 150,008 |
| 6.9% | 7.4% | 8.4% | 9.0% | 9.8% | 10.1% | 9.9% |
| $ 22,614 | $ 26,509 | $ 34,183 | $ 43,601 | $ 48,866 | $ 58,340 | $ 77,498 |
| 12,867 | 12,896 | 15,101 | 15,226 | 18,755 | 21,794 | 24,452 |
| 953 | 943 | 923 | 922 | 922 | 887 | 870 |
| 8,794 | 12,670 | 18,159 | 27,453 | 29,189 | 35,659 | 52,176 |
| 38.9% | 47.8% | 53.1% | 63.0% | 60.0% | 61.1% | 67.3% |
| $ 19,366 | $ 12,078 | $ 17,089 | $ 25,688 | $ 26,373 | $ 23,636 | $ 39,595 |
| 8,316 | 8,857 | 9,532 | 10,903 | 12,139 | 13,512 | 17,658 |
| 153,224 | 159,759 | 172,593 | 193,656 | 219,346 | 236,962 | 394,088 |
| 102,417 | 104,044 | 110,157 | 123,555 | 138,704 | 147,354 | 236,697 |
| 257,256 | 271,823 | 297,761 | 386,576 | 451,922 | 447,319 | 568,428 |
| 318,978 | 339,082 | 372,895 | 485,908 | 561,685 | 574,988 | 728,837 |
| 202,810 | 213,826 | 253,257 | 306,172 | 312,406 | 315,871 | 347,682 |
| 443,438 | 466,277 | 512,549 | 648,994 | 786,578 | 976,489 | 1,239,424 |
| 56,700 | 57,300 | 27,200 | 82,600 | 153,800 | 158,100 | 187,100 |
| 102,300 | 100,800 | 133,800 | 173,800 | 176,000 | 168,700 | 178,500 |
| . . . | . . . | . . . | . . . | 25,000 | 163,600 | 192,100 |
| 159,000 | 158,100 | 161,000 | 256,400 | 354,800 | 490,400 | 557,700 |
| 217,783 | 230,677 | 249,821 | 280,186 | 314,496 | 355,808 | 452,849 |
| 21,458,478 | 21,521,730 | 21,613,344 | 21,830,874 | 22,200,308 | 22,565,334 | 24,158,840 |
| . . . | . . . | . . . | 21,674,884 | 21,928,890 | 22,269,461 | 22,806,598 |
| $1.01 | $1.19 | $ 1.54 | $ 1.97 | $ 2.18 | $ 2.58 | $ 3.36 |
| 1.01 | 1.19 | 1.54 | 1.94 | 2.14 | 2.40 | 2.85 |
| .60 | .60 | .70 | .70 | .85 | .98 | 1.05 |
| 9.03 | 9.63 | 10.48 | 11.77 | 13.12 | 14.78 | 17.87 |
| $14\frac{1}{8}$–$11\frac{1}{4}$ | $16\frac{1}{8}$–$12\frac{1}{8}$ | $17\frac{7}{8}$–$12\frac{1}{4}$ | $28\frac{3}{4}$–$15\frac{3}{4}$ | $34\frac{1}{4}$–22 | $36\frac{3}{8}$–$25\frac{1}{8}$ | $50\frac{1}{4}$–28 |
| $12\frac{1}{4}$ | $14\frac{3}{4}$ | 17 | $22\frac{1}{4}$ | 32 | $35\frac{3}{4}$ | $49\frac{1}{2}$ |

**EXHIBIT 14**

PHILIP MORRIS INCORPORATED
Financial Highlights for Individual Divisions, 1961–70

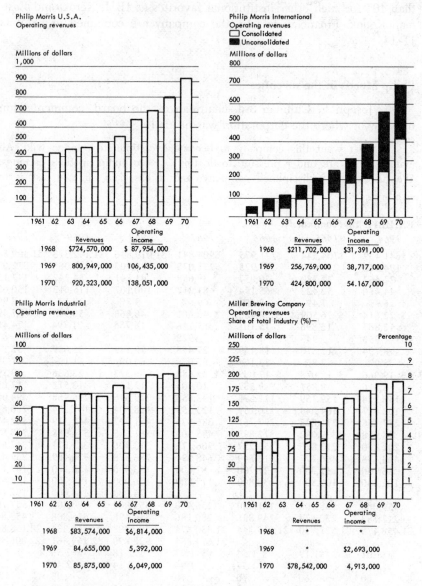

Philip Morris U.S.A.
Operating revenues

Millions of dollars

|      | Revenues      | Operating income |
|------|---------------|------------------|
| 1968 | $724,570,000  | $ 87,954,000     |
| 1969 | 800,949,000   | 106,435,000      |
| 1970 | 920,323,000   | 138,051,000      |

Philip Morris International
Operating revenues
☐ Consolidated
■ Unconsolidated

Millions of dollars

|      | Revenues      | Operating income |
|------|---------------|------------------|
| 1968 | $211,702,000  | $31,391,000      |
| 1969 | 256,769,000   | 38,717,000       |
| 1970 | 424,800,000   | 54.167,000       |

Philip Morris Industrial
Operating revenues

Millions of dollars

|      | Revenues     | Operating income |
|------|--------------|------------------|
| 1968 | $83,574,000  | $6,814,000       |
| 1969 | 84,655,000   | 5,392,000        |
| 1970 | 85,875,000   | 6,049,000        |

Miller Brewing Company
Operating revenues
Share of total industry (%)—

Millions of dollars                    Percentage

|      | Revenues    | Operating income |
|------|-------------|------------------|
| 1968 | *           | *                |
| 1969 | *           | $2,693,000       |
| 1970 | $78,542,000 | 4,913,000        |

\* Miller operating revenues only from August 1, 1970. Philip Morris equity of 53% in Miller net income for 1969 and 100% for 1970.
Source: 1970 Annual Report.

keep our sales and profit momentum going. Now that we have Miller and the possibility of expanding our participation in Mission Viejo, I don't foresee a pressing need for moving off into further new directions.

We are going to devote more effort and resources to matters of corporate responsibility, especially in the areas of minority hiring and controlling pollution. Americans are becoming aware of things beyond material possessions. And American industry, which is responsible for our high economic standards, must address itself to the problems which confront our society.

# Note on the international bulk-shipping industry

In 1968 the international bulk-shipping business represented one of the world's few remaining examples of near perfect or classical competition. The size of the industry in dollar terms is not easily gauged, owing to the elusive and dispersed nature of the statistics and the absence of any effective central pool of intelligence, such as might have been offered by a truly industrywide trade association. A rough measure for 1968 would be about 150 million deadweight tons, tankers and bulk carriers included, valued at an average cost of $140 per DWT, or a gross asset value of $21 billion. Upon this the industry, during the boom of 1968, might be expected to generate $.35 to $.40 in revenues per dollar of assets at cost, for total revenues of some $7.4 to $8.4 billion. Of this sum, independents could be expected to earn about two thirds (about $5 billion), with the remainder going to captive fleets.

The term "international" is intended to differentiate this segment of the shipping industry from the American shipping business, and the term "bulk" is used to contrast it with the general-cargo or liner business. Somewhat simplified, a bulk ship transports a full cargo of a single commodity, such as oil, coal, or grain, and is specifically designed for that purpose. A typical bulk ship would be an oil tanker or an ore carrier; as such, it would generally be of larger size, would require fewer crew members, and could be turned around in less time than a typical general-cargo vessel, which might be required to carry anything from cases of whiskey to umbrellas. Moreover, bulk vessels are usually operated in "tramp" trades as opposed to liners, which maintain regular routes. In other words, bulk cargoes determine the ports of call rather than the converse.

## BULK MARKETS

Shipping space was traded daily via brokers in three principal markets: New York, London, and Tokyo. The demand side was represented by anyone having a shipment to move—an oil company, a coal importer or exporter, or a shipowner having a short position. Similarly, the supply side consisted of independent shipowners or user companies with captive tonnage in excess of their requirements.

In general the U.S. bulk-shipping industry did not participate in the international market, since U.S. construction and operating costs excluded American ships from competition. In recognition of this disadvantage, U.S. law[1] excluded foreign-flag ships from American trades, that is, from any trade in which cargoes were both loaded and discharged at U.S. ports.

The market could be further broken down in terms of demand for two basic types of vessels: tankers and bulk carriers. Traditionally, a tanker could handle only petroleum products (usually crude oil) and, in some cases, a few other specialized liquid cargoes. Bulk carriers, on the other hand, could handle only dry-bulk commodities. Historically, the markets for these two basic types of bulk vessels had been isolated from each other. More recently, however, the two markets had developed strong cross-elasticities owing primarily to (1) the increasing use, through a specialized technique, of tankers in the grain trades; and (2) the emergence in 1965 of a new design of vessel known as the "OBO" (oil-bulk-ore), which was equipped to handle a full load of either liquid or dry cargoes, although only one at a time.

### The tanker market

As of 1968 the tanker business had been a well-organized commodity-type market for a long time. For ease in trading, the industry employed an index of basic flat rates per ton of oil, specified for any pair of load/discharge ports desired, and variable mainly as a function of the distance between them. With the use of this rate index (called "Intascale") as a common denominator, the market price for tanker space could be determined for any pair of ports in the world, in terms of the going percentage discount from, or premium over, the flat rate. Historically, the market low had been established for one unfortunate vessel, for one voyage, during the summer of 1965 at Intascale minus 80%, at which rate even the largest, most efficient ship of the time could

---

[1] The Jones Act.

hardly be expected to cover its direct variable costs. Correspondingly, the recent historical highs had occurred at two points in time: first, during the 1956–57 Suez Canal closure when rates exceeded Intascale plus 100%, and then subsequent to the 1967 June war when rates again approached the plus 100% mark. As of February 1968 they had fallen to about Intascale flat, which was still substantially higher than the 1965–66 annual average of about Intascale minus 40%–50%.

## The bulk-carrier market

For a variety of reasons, rate levels in the bulk-carrier market were not as easily ascertainable as in the tanker market. First, there was no basic index of rates to which percentages could simply be applied. Second, economies of bulk shipment had only recently been realized in a number of commodities, such as potash, phosphate rock, coal, and salt; thus, there were a number of relative newcomers (i.e., potential cargoes) to the trade. Third, owing to the increasing number of different commodities in the market, all moving to and from different ports, the market was much more heterogeneous than the tanker market. As a result, it seemed doubtful that a basic index of rates *could* be established, even if someone were to attempt it. Further, turnaround times varied with the loading and discharge capacities of the port involved, whereas in oil these were fairly standard worldwide. Finally, there was more product differentiation among the ships themselves (size, cubic capacity, draft, cargo-handling gear on board, etc.) than with tankers which, apart from size, were relatively homogeneous. Nevertheless, certain staple trades existed (such as coal from Norfolk to Japan or iron ore from Seven Islands to Baltimore) where market rates per ton were established, and these in large measure provided a base to which all other trades could be adjusted.

In both markets—tankers and bulk carriers—the key rates were "spot" rates, that is, rates for a single voyage to commence at some time in the near future (for example, anywhere from two weeks to two months from "fixing" date). Occasionally, lead times were shaved even closer, as in the case of a "spot prompt" tanker lying at anchor in the Persian Gulf awaiting cargo. Such ships were virtually at the mercy of the demand side of the market and acted in most cases as depressants upon market rates.

## Long-term business

Strongly dependent on the spot-rate structure and market expectations about the future were the rates obtainable in the various types of long-term business. Term business in bulk shipping could be roughly compared to the operation of the futures market in commodities, with all the refinements such as hedging, shorts, etc. Lead times varied widely, and contracts might run for many years. (For example, a time charterer might agree today to a 10-year charter to commence one year hence.) If the spot voyage rates were high today, the period time-charter rate, translated into a single voyage equivalent, could be expected to be lower, *if* it was the general belief of the market that a decline was forthcoming.

Types of term business generally conformed to one of the following categories:

1. *Time charter:* The charterer leased the cargo-carrying capacity of the ship at a fixed dollar rate per deadweight[2] ton per month for a fixed period of time (e.g., 3 to 15 years).
2. *Bare-boat charter:* Like a time charter, except that the charterer undertook to operate the ship at his own expense (crew, maintenance, repairs, etc.), whereas under a time charter the owner absorbed these expenses, leaving the charterer only those expenses associated with the voyage itself (fuel, port charges, canal charges, etc.).
3. *Contract of affreightment:* Here the owner undertook to transport, using any ship he desired within given size limits, a certain quantity of a given commodity per annum between two or more specific points. Remuneration was set at a fixed dollar amount per ton transported. Contracts might vary in duration from 1 year to 10.
4. *Consecutive voyages:* The owner undertook to provide a specific ship (sometimes with substitution options) for consecutive voyages at a given rate per ton of cargo transported. In tankers, the rate was usually stated in terms of Intascale plus or minus a percentage. Duration of the contract might be stated in terms of a number of voyages or years, with the owner undertaking to maintain a certain average speed in transit.

## SHIPYARDS, CHARTERERS, AND BROKERS

Besides the independent owners, other important factors in the bulk-shipping industry were (1) the shipyards, (2) the charterers, and (3) the brokers, whose services might be needed to bring the other principals together.

1. *Shipyards* constructed ships to owners' specifications, based on a prior order. In general, lead time between the signing of a construction contract and delivery of a vessel was two or three years. During periods of peak demand, however, such as 1957 or 1967, lead times could reach five years. Shipyards competed on the basis of price, delivery, maximum size of ship which they could physically handle, quality of workmanship,

---

[2] The "deadweight" of a ship is defined as the full cargo capacity, including water, fuel, and stores—in short, all but the hull, machinery, and fixtures.

and credit terms. One of the Japanese yards' most significant competitive advantages over European builders, aside from price, was their ability to offer the owners (through government assistance) favorable financing terms—specifically, 80% of the cost of the vessel over eight years at 5½% interest, secured by a first mortgage on the ship. These terms had been maintained without interruption for 10 years or more, despite varying credit availability elsewhere and generally rising interest rates.

2.   *Charterers,* as implied earlier, were the users of bulk transportation services. They consisted mainly of the oil companies in the tanker business and the steel companies, coal exporters, and grain houses in the bulk-carrier business. Particularly in tankers, the charterers were also owners, maintaining as a rule of thumb an owned fleet equal to 35% to 40% of their requirements. Often the independent owners also acted as charterers when, for example, they found themselves short of tonnage under a contract of affreightment.

3.   *Brokers* were intermediaries; as such, they performed a variety of services. Many large brokers dealt in both tanker and bulk-carrier markets, as well as in the new-building market (bringing owner and yard together) and in the secondhand tonnage markets where ships were bought and sold. The brokers' major function was to disseminate information on transactions concluded, spot or term, and on requirements overhanging the market. The majority of brokers were found in the major markets—New York, London, and Tokyo—and in other locations where a number of owners resided, such as Greece or Scandinavia. Generally, communications with owners, charterers, and other brokers proceeded via telephone, telex, or written circulars.

## OWNERS

A typical owner pursued his business in the following manner: he assessed the future market and decided on the size and type of ship likely to be in demand. If lucky, he might be able to reach agreement with a charterer before committing himself to a shipyard. More often than not, however, he first contracted for the ship with the yard and then attempted, before the first significant payment on the ship was due, to obtain a long-term charter or contract with a reputable user. Then, on the strength of that charter (which was really on the strength of the charterer's credit) he obtained long-term financing, if not from the yard (which in turn was financed by someone else—for example, in Japan's case, by the Export-Import Bank), then typically from a commercial bank, life insurance company, or pension fund. With a long-term takeout in hand, he could then obtain the necessary interim, or construction financing, which might amount to 15%–25% of the total delivered cost of the ship (or approximately the usual equity left over after term financing).

Once he had obtained a vessel, the independent owner marketed its space in one or more of the ways previously described, in most cases with one or two brokers acting as intermediaries. A large majority of owners maintained their own operating staffs and had fully owned management companies. In some cases operation of a ship was subcontracted to a management specialist.

In 1968 shipowners were spread throughout the world. Leading groups, however, were centered in Scandinavia, Greece, Hong Kong, and Great Britain. Their ships generally flew the flags of the countries

**EXHIBIT 1**
Relative sizes of tankers presently in use

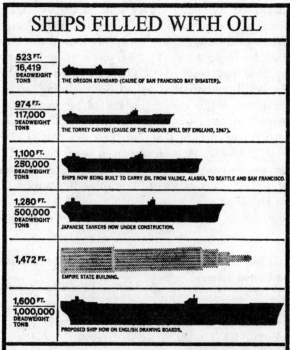

**SHIPS FILLED WITH OIL**

| | |
|---|---|
| **523 FT.** **16,419** DEADWEIGHT TONS | THE OREGON STANDARD (CAUSE OF SAN FRANCISCO BAY DISASTER). |
| **974 FT.** **117,000** DEADWEIGHT TONS | THE TORREY CANYON (CAUSE OF THE FAMOUS SPILL OFF ENGLAND, 1967). |
| **1,100 FT.** **250,000** DEADWEIGHT TONS | SHIPS NOW BEING BUILT TO CARRY OIL FROM VALDEZ, ALASKA, TO SEATTLE AND SAN FRANCISCO. |
| **1,280 FT.** **500,000** DEADWEIGHT TONS | JAPANESE TANKERS NOW UNDER CONSTRUCTION. |
| **1,472 FT.** | EMPIRE STATE BUILDING. |
| **1,600 FT.** **1,000,000** DEADWEIGHT TONS | PROPOSED SHIP NOW ON ENGLISH DRAWING BOARDS. |

The chart gives you the relative sizes of presently in-use tankers such as the Oregon Standard (which recently crashed in San Francisco Bay) and the Torrey Canyon which crashed off England in 1967. Please note that the Oregon Standard is only one-fifteenth the size (in carrying capacity) of the ships which would bring oil down the coast from Valdez, Alaska, to San Francisco, and a sixtieth the size of a ship being proposed by the English. Most of the ships will carry oil cargoes that would nearly fill the Empire State building to overflowing. And in case you think something about their being *bigger* makes them *safer*, consider this: If the captain of one of those 250,000 tonners from Alaska sees trouble ahead while going full speed, it will take him a *half hour* to stop the thing!

Source: Friends of the Earth advertisement, *New York Times*, February 17, 1971.

mentioned, or alternatively the very popular "flags of convenience"—Panama, Liberia, or Honduras—which involved no taxation.

## RECENT DEVELOPMENTS

During the decade preceding 1968, two major developments in the industry were noteworthy: a dramatic increase in the size of ships and rationalization of shipyard production methods.

### The size revolution

The increase in the size of bulk ships, as best exemplified in tankers, can be demonstrated by changes over time in the average deadweight tonnage of ships under construction: whereas in 1956 projected new additions to the free-world tanker fleet (excluding that of the United States) averaged 29,000 deadweight tons, by 1966 this average had risen to 62,100 DWT and by 1967 had reached 135,000 DWT. The quantum jump in 1967 could be attributed to the second Suez closing in 10 years and to the determination of oil companies *not* to be burned a third time. They thus leaped to sizes which could economically avoid the canal, compensating by economies of scale for the extra cost of circumnavigating the cape. By 1968 the decision was even more clear. Of 52.6 million tons on order for delivery between 1969 and 1973, no less than 84% were ships of 150,000 tons or more. A graphic illustration of this trend is provided in Exhibit 1.

The average size of tankers in use remained, of course, considerably

**EXHIBIT 2**

Changes in total and per-tanker tonnage for the free-world tanker fleet (excluding the United States)

|  | 1956 | 1959 | 1961 | 1964 | 1967 |
|---|---|---|---|---|---|
| Fleet total (in millions of DWT) | 33.7 | 49.2 | 60.0 | 72.5 | 107.0 |
| Average size of tankers in operation (in thousands of DWT) | 16.2 | n.a. | 21.2 | 25.3 | 35.0 |
| Percent of fleet by size class (in thousands of DWT) |  |  |  |  |  |
| 10 to 25 | 75.4 | 59.9 | 48.6 | 34.8 | 21.9 |
| 25 to 35 | 14.5 | 31.6 | 34.0 | 29.4 | 15.0 |
| 35 to 45 | 10.1 | 5.5 | 9.4 | 11.7 | 11.9 |
| 45 to 75 | ... | 3.0 | 8.0 | 19.7 | 35.8 |
| 75 and over | ... | ... | ... | 4.4 | 15.4 |
|  | 100.0 | 100.0 | 100.0 | 100.0 | 100.0 |
| Average size of tankers under construction (in thousands of DWT) | 29.0 | n.a. | 44.7 | 53.3 | 135.0 |

n.a. = not available.
Source: Anglo Norness Shipping Company, Ltd., records.

lower than the average size of tankers on order (see Exhibit 2). And within the international fleet as a whole, almost 50% of the tankers in use remained below the 35,000-ton figure which was the average for 1967.

The general trend toward larger sizes was the result of economies of both *construction* and *operation*. In 1968 the shipyard price for a 25,000-ton tanker was about $150–$200 per DWT, whereas for a tanker in excess of 150,000 tons the price was $70–$80 per DWT. In addition, the variable costs of operating a tanker—exclusive of depreciation, administration, or financing charges—showed substantial economies of scale. A typical Liberian-flag 32,000-ton tanker in 1968 might be operated for about $40,000 per month, not including voyage costs such as fuel, port charges, and canal dues. By comparison, a vessel of 150,000 tons, with five times the former's capacity, might operate for $55,000–$60,000 per month, with a crew of approximately the same size. (For a sample calculation of tanker profitability on a 95,000-ton ship, see Exhibit 3.)

**EXHIBIT 3**
**Sample calculation of tanker profitability**

Vessel:      Tanker 95,000 deadweight tons
Built:        1961, Japan
Cost:        $12.4 million ($130 per DWT)
Financed:   80% over 8 years @ 5½% interest reducing
Use (1968): 15-year time charter @ $2 per DWT per month

|  | Thousands of dollars | Percent |
|---|---|---|
| Net revenues (95,000 × $2.00 × 11.5*) | 2,200 | 100.0 |
| Operating costs† (maintenance and repairs, insurance, personnel, administration) | (500) | (22.6) |
| Gross operating income | 1,700 | 77.4 |
| Fixed costs |  |  |
| Depreciation (20 years straight line to 5% residual) | (590) | (26.8) |
| Interest (on 7th-year loan balance in 1968) | (140) | (6.4) |
| Net income | 970 | 44.2 |
| Add back: Depreciation | 590 | 26.8 |
| Less: Loan amortization | (1,250) | (57.0) |
| Net cash flow | 310 | 14.0 |

    * Typically, downtime for repairs, etc., ran about two weeks a year.
    † Voyage costs (fuel, port charges, etc.) excluded, since under time charter these are for charterer's account.
    Source: Anglo Norness Shipping Company, Ltd., records.

Exhibit 4 reveals one oil company's estimate of the behavior of these economies of scale, including all costs, on its own fleet. The shape of the curve clearly demonstrates diminishing returns to scale, but even at 500,000 tons, which was about the limit of anyone's thinking in 1968, the curve does not appear to have flattened completely. By far the greatest cost uncertainty built into these calculations was insurance. Most estimates merely extrapolated past insurance-cost experience with

**EXHIBIT 4**
Economies of scale in tanker transportation

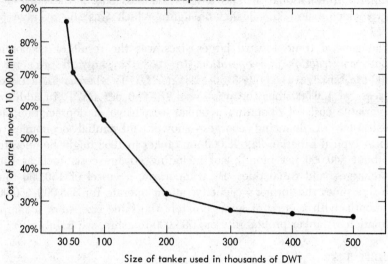

Size of tanker used in thousands of DWT

Source: Major oil company (name withheld by request).

smaller vessels. Yet a disaster like that of the Torrey Canyon, which in 1967 fouled beaches in both England and France, suggested that concentration of the world's tanker fleet into fewer and larger units would seem to increase the risk of high dollar amounts in losses. By 1968, however, the effect of this episode seemed to have dissipated. Nevertheless, repetition of a similar disaster was a possibility that the industry showed no signs of having fully appreciated.

Like tankers, bulk carriers had also undergone a size revolution, although to a lesser degree. Owing to the heterogeneous nature of the commodities moved in this market, no traffic existed in the volume necessary to justify units greater than 150,000 tons. In addition, port development, cargo handling, and storage were much greater problems with dry-bulk commodities than with liquid ones, which can be pumped through pipelines extending many miles out to offshore installations. However, as of 1968, coal and iron ore particularly were being transported in lots of 70,000 to 85,000 tons, and one example existed of salt moving in ships of 150,000 tons. By contrast, as late as 1961 bulk carriers of greater than 20,000 tons were very rare.

### Rationalization of the shipyards

The second major development during the decade was the success of the world's leading shipyards in reducing production costs and increasing capacity through improved techniques in fabrication. By constructing ships in large sections and utilizing the building berths (the former bottleneck) merely for welding the completed sections together, berth time for a typical large ship was reduced from a year to about two months. The effect was a dramatic decrease in unit construction costs, over and above the effects of building larger ships, as well as a greatly increased capacity at nominal incremental investment. It was difficult to separate the effects of these two developments; suffice it to say that the combined effect was dramatic, particularly on the obsolescence of existing fleets.

In general, market rates were determined by the lowest cost unit, that is, the largest and newest tanker. Users were flexible to some extent in their size requirements and might place a bid in the spot market for a ship of anywhere from 35,000 to 60,000 tons, thus putting the two sizes in competition with each other and forcing the smaller ship to live with a rate established by the larger, probably newer, and lower cost ship. Finally, as replacement costs decreased and as market rates adjusted to the newer, larger vessels, the secondhand market followed suit, greatly depressing secondhand tonnage resale values during the decade between the Suez Canal closures.

## SUPPLY AND DEMAND RELATIONSHIPS

*Demand* for shipping space is a function of demand for the commodity shipped or of its production, whichever is lower, adjusted for the duration of the voyage. *Supply* at any given time is a function of the size of the existing fleet plus additions through new construction and minus both vessels scrapped or lost and net layups for any purpose.

In theory, supply should adjust to demand, or at least to some expectation of demand, and rates should be a function of the balance between them. In shipping, the evidence would indicate a particularly erratic market behavior. One of the principal sources of disequilibrium lies in the tax structure of certain leading shipping nations, particularly in Scandinavia. Here, liberal accelerated depreciation allowances, coupled with high marginal tax brackets, both personal and corporate (up to 60%), are designed to encourage constant expansion of the national shipping fleets—an important source of foreign exchange. Norwegian owners, for example, are permitted to charge against current income an amount up to 25% of the cost of a new vessel during the tax year in which a new-building contract is signed. This would probably be two to four years before delivery, at which time the owner would have paid in equity only the initial installment of 5% of the contract cost.

In 1957 and again in 1968, shipyard backlogs worldwide were approaching five years under the impetus of Suez-inflated rates. Such a situation might be interpreted as indicating shortsightedness on the part of shipowners, rushing to secure new tonnage many years ahead on the assumption that current high rates would continue. In some cases, this interpretation might be valid. The main reason, however, was that in years of high profits from existing ships, taxable owners had to generate tax shields by ordering new ones. The fact that overbuilding might result in future net losses did not deter the owners, given the time value of money and their intuitive understanding of present-value theory.

Another distortion stemmed from the lack among shipowners of accurate, comprehensive statistics on developments on both sides of the marketplace. A few brokers assembled annual figures on the supply side, but little attempt was made to project demand in a rigorous fashion. Most shipowners maintained minimal staffs comprised of shipping specialists who were fully occupied with daily operations. Hence it was up to the boss himself to do the long-range strategic planning, and this he generally did by intuition. Although comprehensive statistics were very much in existence, they were all in the hands of the *users* of tonnage, who kept them to themselves.

This situation was symptomatic of a third major source of distortion— namely, the marked difference in industry structure between the supply and the demand sides of the market. On the supply side, ownership was highly fragmented and dispersed worldwide. The 10 largest independent tanker owners in 1968, for example, accounted for perhaps 15 million tons, or an estimated 15% of the world tanker fleet. The supply side was, by contrast, concentrated—dominated by a few large users. In the tanker business, demand meant the major international oil companies, of which there were nine, plus a few others—the Japanese, French, Germans, Italians, and, very recently, the Russians. Except for unusual periods such as the two Suez closings, the majors were in an ideal position to control their markets. Large operations-research staffs, using computer-aided analysis, generated and evaluated the data. As large shipowners themselves, directly owning about one third of the world's tonnage, the oil companies were intimately familiar with the independents' costs and therefore with their rates of return at any given level of freights. Through swapping tonnage among themselves across the market, they could set rates directly. Finally, there was some evidence that at least during the depressed winter of 1966–67, the oil companies were sequentially coordinating their respective entries into the spot market and thus avoiding the appearance of a marked increase in demand.

As a result of these peculiarities, plus the two major technological developments described above, the decade between the Suez crises showed a general trend toward declining rates and narrowing profit margins for shipowners. Exhibit 5 plots the bellwether indicator in the

**EXHIBIT 5**
Spot tanker rate composite (Intascale)

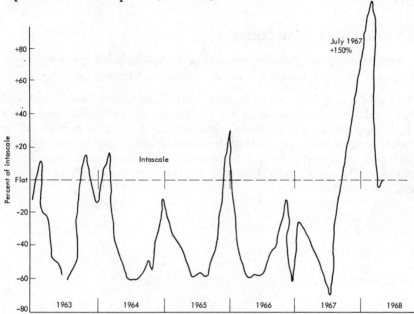

Source: Anglo Norness Shipping Company, Ltd., records.

tanker business—the spot-rate market—for the latter half of the decade. It can be noted that besides being cyclical the business is highly seasonal, with the magnitude of its swings unlikely to be matched by any other industry. Reasons for this seasonality are essentially twofold: (1) in the winter consumption of oil is higher (heating needs, etc.); and (2) winter weather slows down ships, producing in effect a curtailed supply. In an industry characterized by high fixed costs and substantial debt leverage, a year-to-year variation in the strength of the winter market could produce a much more than proportionate swing in industry profits.

A curve of the annual average rates, if superimposed on the seasonal fluctuations, would show a negative slope, bottoming in early 1967, when virtually no appreciable winter market materialized. During that period, most tankers of average size and age operating in the spot market would have shown losses, since their annual average income could well have slipped below Intascale minus 40%–50%, which might be taken as their break-even point. Without Suez, and with a continuing down trend, average rates for 1967 and 1968 would probably have reached levels where a number of owners, unable to cover the variable costs of operations, would have laid up their ships, as they did during the summer of 1963.

## ENVIRONMENT SUMMARIZED

Summarizing the industry environment in which his company operated, one shipping company executive expressed himself as follows:

The bulk-shipping industry can be characterized as a Monte Carlo "crapshoot," highly volatile, where customers are highly rational and well-informed, but where suppliers are tax-motivated, unanalytic, and given to impulse—all in a world of rapid obsolescence. Most shipowners readily recognize the inequities existing in their marketplace, but when anyone refers to the bargaining advantage of the users a typical reaction is, "Don't worry—something will happen; it always has!"

# Anglo Norness Shipping Company, Limited (A)

In 1968, after a stormy five years, the Anglo Norness Shipping Company was enjoying the most dramatic bonanza in its 22-year history mainly as a result of the Arab-Israeli June war of 1967 and the increased requirements for transport which followed the closing of the Suez Canal. Profits for the year to end on June 30 were projected to exceed $15 million, or $1.58 per share, up from only $400,000, or $.05 per share for the previous year. The company's stock price had risen on the London Exchange to a recent high of about $3.15, up from its historical low of less than $1 the previous year. Even so, its market value represented a very reasonable multiple of current earnings and was well below book value, which was projected to reach about $5.50 per share by year end, including about $2.25 in cash.

As a result of this much improved position, Mr. Erling Naess and his elder son, Michael, as the controlling stockholders of Anglo Norness, were facing a critical strategic decision. Should they use their greatly increased resources to expand in any phase of the bulk-shipping business to which the company was presently committed? Should they diversify? Should they seek—or sell out to—a merger partner, inasmuch as suitors seemed bound to be attracted by the company's strong cash position and its relatively low price/earnings ratio? If so, by what criteria should possible merger offers be judged?

At the time when these choices had to be considered (February 1968), Mr. Naess, aged 65, was chairman of the company. Michael, aged 28, was vice president of one of the principal operating subsidiaries but was on leave of absence to attend the Harvard Business School, where he was halfway through his first year.

## THE FLEET

In the banner year of 1968 (see Exhibit 1 for selected historical financial statistics), Anglo Norness was one of the 10 largest independent bulk shipping carriers in the world. Its fleet of 40 vessels accounted for almost 1.8 million DWT. Of this tonnage, just over half was in tankers, while the rest was divided among bulk carriers, OBOs,[1] and specialized chemical sulphur vessels (see Exhibit 2). This fleet profile represented a continuing trend toward increased diversification, for as recently as 1961 some 90% of the company's tonnage had been allocated to tankers.

As suggested by comparative figures on the average size of tankers in operation (54,000 DWT for Anglo Norness versus 35,000 worldwide), the company had been a leader in the trend toward larger and larger ships. Both the trend toward increased diversification and the trend toward larger sizes had been accelerated in 1967–68 as the company took advantage of good times to sell off some of its smaller, older tankers and to arrange for the conversion of two others to more highly specialized uses.

Of the total Anglo Norness tonnage, some 27% was not company-owned but rather leased or chartered. Leasing, like debt, was widely used as a way to finance operations in so capital-intensive an industry as shipping.

## ORGANIZATIONAL STRUCTURE

A number of changes had occurred over the years in the Anglo Norness organization, but as of 1968 the company consisted of three main functional groups, each in a different location: finance and accounting and the company's official domicile were in Bermuda, chartering (sales) had its principal offices in New York, and operations were spread throughout the world depending on the nationality of the vessels and crews.

Direction of the company was in the hands of two principal individuals: Mr. Erling Naess acted as chairman; another individual, who had joined the company in 1966, was chairman of the recently created executive committee, of which the other members were Mr. Naess and two outside directors. Mr. Naess, a Norwegian citizen resident in Bermuda, maintained his principal base in New York. The chairman of the executive committee maintained a separate office in New York, one

---

[1] Oil-bulk-ore carriers.

**EXHIBIT 1**

## ANGLO NORNESS SHIPPING COMPANY LIMITED (A)

### Selected Financial Data

(dollars in millions except per-share figures)

| Year to June 30 | 1958 | 1959 | 1960 | 1961 | 1962 | 1963 | 1964 | 1965 | 1966 | 1967 | 1968* |
|---|---|---|---|---|---|---|---|---|---|---|---|
| Total assets | $61.3 | $78.7 | $117.6 | $156.2 | $168.0 | $185.1 | $193.2 | $172.5 | $136.6 | $124.2 | $125.2 |
| Vessels in operation | | | | | | | | | | | |
| –at cost | 43.3 | 43.7 | 73.1 | 136.6 | 151.2 | 184.0 | 192.4 | 173.1 | 169.9 | 174.9 | 168.9 |
| –after depreciation | 41.2 | 40.0 | 66.6 | 124.3 | 131.3 | 152.9 | 151.8 | 130.3 | 102.4† | 96.2† | 83.6† |
| Investments | 10.1 | 16.2 | 17.1 | 15.1 | 18.8 | 17.9 | 19.0 | 20.2 | 13.8† | 12.7† | 11.8† |
| Net fixed assets | 59.1 | 74.2 | 112.3 | 147.6 | 159.9 | 173.6 | 173.9 | 156.5 | 120.3 | 108.9 | 95.6 |
| Long-term loans | 43.4 | 55.4 | 88.2 | 114.2 | 116.8 | 115.4 | 116.5 | 99.9 | 93.5 | 81.6 | 60.7 |
| Equity | 14.0 | 18.8 | 24.6 | 33.9 | 43.1 | 54.9 | 61.9 | 57.9 | 35.2† | 35.2† | 52.8† |
| Equivalent number of shares in issue | 5,969,600 | 6,174,600 | 7,183,577 | 7,844,310 | 8,800,419 | 9,300,419‡ | 9,512,346 | 9,513,097 | 9,513,097 | 9,513,097 | 9,513,097 |
| Equity value per share | $2.32 | $3.04 | $3.45 | $4.20 | $4.92 | $5.94 | $6.50 | $6.08 | $3.69 | $3.70 | $5.55 |
| Gross freights | n.a. | n.a. | 17.6 | 26.3 | 36.4 | 41.4 | 51.5 | 56.3 | 58.1 | 57.2 | 74.1 |
| Operating profit | 6.2 | 6.4 | 9.2 | 15.7 | 18.2 | 21.0 | 23.2 | 18.5 | 20.2 | 16.1 | 33.5 |
| Depreciation | 1.4 | 2.2 | 3.1 | 5.9 | 7.6 | 8.4 | 9.5 | 9.5 | 10.7 | 11.7 | 11.1 |
| Net interest payable | 1.1 | 1.4 | 2.2 | 4.5 | 5.6 | 5.9 | 5.8 | 5.0 | 4.4 | 4.1 | 2.8 |
| Group profit, after minority interests | 3.6 | 3.4 | 4.2 | 5.3 | 4.8 | 6.7† | 8.1 | 2.8 | 3.8 | .05 | 16.4 |
| Earnings per share | $.62 | $.52 | $.60 | $.66 | $.56 | $.78§ | $.85 | $.29 | $.40 | $.05 | $1.72 |
| Gross freight/gross vessels | …. | 24% | 24% | 19% | 24% | 22% | 27% | 33% | 34% | 33% | 44% |
| Operating profit/gross freight | …. | …. | 52% | 60% | 51% | 51% | 45% | 33% | 35% | 28% | 45% |
| Percent return on net fixed assets | …. | 4.6% | 3.7% | 3.6% | 3.0% | 3.9% | 4.7% | 1.8% | 3.2% | 0.4% | 16.4% |
| Long-term debt/book equity | …. | 3.0% | 3.6% | 3.3% | 2.7% | 2.1% | 1.9% | 1.7% | 2.6% | 2.3% | 1.2% |
| Percent return on average book equity | 21.0% | 21.0% | 20.0% | 18.2% | 12.5% | 14.0% | 13.8% | 4.7% | 8.2% | 1.1% | 37.3% |

* Estimate for the full fiscal year.
† After revaluation of assets.
‡ Including 500,000 shares issued for the acquisition of British Oil Shipping (now in voluntary liquidation).
§ Excluding the profits earned by British Oil Shipping and the shares issued for that company's acquisition.
n.a. = not available
Source: Company records.

**EXHIBIT 2**

## ANGLO NORNESS SHIPPING COMPANY, LIMITED (A)
### Composition of the Company Fleet and Relative Size of Its Tankers
### (tonnage in thousands of DWT)

| Year | Anglo Norness number of ships | | | Anglo Norness total deadweight tonnage | | | Anglo Norness | | Average tonnage of tankers in worldwide operation† |
|---|---|---|---|---|---|---|---|---|---|
| | Tanker | Other* | Total | Tanker | Other | Total | Tanker tonnage/total tonnage (% of total) | Average tanker tonnage | |
| 1960 | 15 | 3 | 18 | 448.5 | 56.6 | 505.1 = | 90% | 30 | 20.3 |
| 1961 | 22 | 4 | 26 | 820.5 | 84.3 | 904.8 = | 91 | 37.4 | 21.2 |
| 1962 | 22 | 11 | 33 | 820.5 | 318.4 | 1,138.9 = | 79 | 37.4 | 22.1 |
| 1963 | 22 | 16 | 38 | 909.0 | 786.4 | 1,695.4 = | 54 | 41.5 | 23.2 |
| 1964 | 27 | 19 | 46 | 1,125.9 | 900.2 | 2,026.1 = | 56 | 41.7 | 25.3 |
| 1965 } 1966 | 30 | 19 | 49 | 1,315.5 | 900.2 | 2,215.7 = | 59 | 43.8 | 27.1 / 29.2 |
| 1967 } 1968 | 17 | 23 | 40 | 917.3 | 871.5 | 1,788.8‡ | 51 | 54.0 | 35.0 |

*As of February 1968 the nontanker components of the fleet were divided as follows:*

| | Bulk-carrier | Oil-bulk-ore | Chemical-sulphur | Total |
|---|---|---|---|---|
| Number of ships................. | 17 | 2 | 4 | 23 |
| Tonnage | | | | |
| Thousands of DWT........... | 655.5 | 113.1 | 102.9 | 871.5 |
| Percentage of fleet total........ | 37% | 6% | 6% | 49% |

* Excluding the United States.

‡ Including 27% leased tonnage, made up of 32% leased tanker tonnage and 29% leased bulk carrier tonnage.

Source: Exhibit 2 of the "Note on the International Bulk-Shipping Industry" and company annual reports.

floor above Mr. Naess, where he was assisted by a staff of three persons.

In total the organization consisted of 31 different ship-owning companies and another 7 management or operating companies. Two major consulting reports submitted to the company within the previous five years had strongly recommended simplification of this structure and centralization of control in New York, Bermuda, or London. Two main factors made this difficult, however. First, the multiplicity of owning companies had originally been created to accommodate different minority interests in individual ships or groups of ships, some of which were still outstanding in 1968. Second, the company's tax-free status might be threatened if operations and management were centralized in either the United States or the United Kingdom. As it was, the subsidiaries located in those countries were officially merely "agency" companies. Centralization in Bermuda raised the question of communications and the availability of sufficient qualified staff.

## COMPANY HISTORY

A Norwegian by birth and an economist by training, Mr. Erling Naess had had a brief career in British banking before turning to whaling and then permanently to shipping. In the years before World War II, he had built up a seven-vessel fleet of different types, and during the war he had emigrated to the United States to become deputy director of the agency established to manage the Norwegian fleet during the German occupation. After the war, with most of his own fleet sunk, Mr. Naess founded the Norness Shipping Company of Nassau (predecessor of Anglo Norness), in partnership with friends representing two leading Wall Street investment banking organizations.

The Norness fleet developed steadily, primarily in tankers, until 1956–57, when Norness, like most of its competitors, was inspired by the first Suez closing to embark on an unprecedented expansion. In 1958 the company had 17 ships in operation totaling 500,000 tons and another 22 ships on order totaling 1,142,000 tons, some with delivery dates six years away.

Financing such growth posed a major problem, to which three basic solutions were found: (1) obtaining prior long-term charters for as many of the ships as possible, which increased the security that could be offered to lenders; (2) ordering some ships on a lease rather than a purchase basis, which gave Norness access to assets with no equity investment at all; and (3) raising money on the capital market.

Leasing terms on the ships, which were all owned and managed from Scandinavia, were essentially as follows: Norness would use the tonnage for 15 years, during which it would pay all operating costs plus amortization on a straight-line basis, plus 5.5% to 6% interest, plus

50% of any profit. Losses, if any, would be carried forward against future profit with no interest charges, and at the end of the 15 years the ships would revert to the owners. (Some years later these terms were to come under fire from the outside investors brought into the picture when Norness sought funds on the capital market.)

To minimize the possibility that the U.S. maritime unions or the U.S. Internal Revenue Service would try to treat Norness as a U.S. company, new equity capital was raised in London, not New York. A separate corporation was formed in 1959 (Anglo American Shipping Company of Bermuda), to which Norness transferred one existing ship and four under construction, among which were two of the largest tankers then on order in the world (90,000 DWT). All five ships were tied to long-term, high-rate contracts, and when all became operational, they would earn over $2 million a year. The Norness company kept 69% of the new firm's common stock, and Norness management took over its direction.

The remaining 788,000 common shares of Anglo American were sold to the public at $2.80, along with $12.5 million in 7% "loan stock" (like preferred). The low ratio of price to projected earnings (3.5) was accounted for by the fact that several of the ships would not be "on stream" for two to three years. That the initial price was regarded as favorable was attested to by the fact that in the aftermarket the shares opened at $5.75.

As head of both a public and closely held company, Erling Naess formed a policy that "gilt-edged" long-term business would be allocated to the former and more speculative business to the latter. A question arose, however, about the allocation of a new bulk-carrier business which Mr. Naess pioneered at this time by convincing the Japanese that coal for their steel mills could be carried more economically if it were transported in larger ships. With contracts of affreightment secured, 35,000-ton carriers on order, and some "backhaul" business arranged to reduce shipping time in ballast, prospects looked so bright that the British directors of the publicly held company argued that the Naess management would lay itself open to charges of conflict of interest if the public firm were excluded from this business.

Although Mr. Naess did not feel that Anglo American should return to the capital markets so soon, he yielded to this British argument, and a merger of the two firms was arranged, the successor to be named Anglo Norness. Based on a two-year projection of the closely held company's earnings through fiscal 1964 (a projection that turned out 99% correct), each Norness Shipping share was exchanged for 820 shares of the new firm, and, on the date of its debut (December 15, 1962) the latter saw its common stock close at $6.50.[2] Shares subsequently

---

[2] After the merger, the Naess family held approximately 35% of the shares.

peaked at about $11 during fiscal 1963, but fiscal 1964 turned out to be the last good year for some time.

## FINANCIAL PROBLEMS

The troubles that befell the company after 1964 show up clearly in the financial record (Exhibit 1). Problems included expiration of several of the company's high-rate time charters, delivery of the high-cost new ships that had been ordered several years earlier during boom conditions, similar deliveries to many other owners resulting in an oversupply of tonnage which weakened the spot-market rate, and Norness' obligation to amortize the cost of several new leased ships over 15 years instead of the more customary 20. The effect was a steep downturn in earnings (off 65% from fiscal 1964 to fiscal 1965) and rising stockholder discontent, the latter provoked by a relatively optimistic dividend forecast which had unfortunately been permitted to circulate via the annual report issued at the end of 1964.

The financial debacle of 1965 provoked a series of unpleasant events, among them a public meeting in London (unfavorably written up in the press), wherein management was closely questioned about such factors as the 820-to-1 exchange rate on the Norness Shipping-Anglo Norness stock, the adequacy of the financial reporting, and the propriety of having privately owned Naess family companies serve the publicly held merged company as agents on a commission basis. As a result, over the next two years the following changes occurred:

1. An executive committee of the board was created to "strengthen management and policy-making," and a new executive was imported to serve as chairman of that committee.
2. All agency companies controlled by the Naess family were acquired by Anglo Norness.
3. The entire fleet was revalued, based on an outside appraisal, resulting in an immediate charge to retained earnings of $22 million and an acceleration of depreciation with respect to certain vessels nearing expiration of their time charters.

## SUEZ—1967

These changes contributed little to restoring the profit picture. Earnings were helped somewhat by a strong winter market in 1966, but then declined to an historic low with a weak winter market in 1967. Just at the end of the latter fiscal year, however, the June Arab-Israeli war broke out; Suez was closed; several Middle East pipelines were shut down; and the alternative tanker haul around the cape effectively doubled the length of the trip and halved the volume of shipping space available. Spot tanker rates responded by jumping in one month from Intascale[3] minus 70% to Intascale plus 100%, and although rates subsequently eased, they remained at Intascale flat or higher for the rest of the calendar year.

With this turn of events, Anglo Norness' controversial policy, set in 1964, of maintaining charter-free ships in the open market rather than committing them to long-term break-even business paid off royally. At the outbreak of the war Anglo Norness had no less than 15 tankers or OBOs available for spot-market oil cargoes. After the first round or two of frenzied fixtures, the company settled down to take full advantage of the situation.

Since no one knew how long the crisis would last, it became management's objective to prolong the bonanza as long as possible. Intermediate-term business was available, representing one- to three-year contracts at rates which, though certainly below spot rates, were nevertheless well above recent levels. The company took as much of this business as it could. In addition, the secondhand market had firmed up, permitting the company to dispose of a number of marginally efficient, older tankers at a book profit. Finally, a few of the owners of the troublesome leased tankers, attracted by the prospects of receiving 100% of their current operating profits, agreed to cancel the leases for nominal compensation.

On the rising tide of new-found success the troubles of 1965–66 faded. The relieved board subsided into silence. The executive committee ceased to exercise any significant function. Erling Naess reestablished his authority as the chief executive officer. The new "imported" chairman of the executive committee, his support within the board having dissipated along with the company's problems, adjusted himself and took his position as top operating man under Erling Naess.

For the first time in several years, Anglo Norness could afford the luxury of some long-term strategic thinking.

---

[3] An index of basic rates per ton of oil, specified for any pair of load/discharge ports desired, and variable mainly as a function of the distance between them.

# Anglo Norness Shipping Company, Limited (B)

As THE MANAGEMENT of Anglo Norness evaluated the range of alternatives available to the company in early 1968,[1] two serious merger offers were presented to them. One came from a large oil company and the other from a small but fast-growing conglomerate with interests in various phases of what it called the "ocean industry."

## THE ACQUISITION OFFERS

The oil company suitor, Occidental Petroleum, had assets of $779 million as of the end of 1967 (see Exhibits 1 and 2 for financial data). It had recently brought on stream substantial wells developed in the Libyan Desert and was accordingly seeking a way of quickly developing its own tanker fleet. What it asked for was a three-week option on the Naess family stock (35% of the Anglo Norness total), plus another major block (15.8%) held by principals of a major Wall Street firm. Should the option be exercised, Occidental would then tender for the rest. The option price would be $4.50 per share in cash.

The other suitor, Zapata Off-Shore Company, had assets of $81.1 million at the end of its fiscal year, September 30, 1967. Like Occidental, Zapata sought agreement with the two controlling blocks. Also like Occidental, it wanted Mr. Erling Naess, Anglo's chairman and founder, to continue as chief executive officer. In addition, Zapata would guarantee

[1] See Anglo Norness Shipping Company, Limited (A).

577

**EXHIBIT 1**

OCCIDENTAL PETROLEUM CORPORATION
Balance Sheet as of December 31, 1967 *
(in millions of dollars)

| *Assets* | | *Liabilities* | |
|---|---|---|---|
| Current assets | | Current liabilities | |
| Cash . . . . . . . . . . . . . . . . . | $120.7 | Notes and debt due . . . . . . . . . | $ 17.7 |
| Marketable securities . . . . . . . | 8.8 | Accounts and accruals . . . . . . . | 109.7 |
| Receivables (net) . . . . . . . . . . | 136.7 | Dividends payable . . . . . . . . . | 2.9 |
| Inventories. . . . . . . . . . . . . | 35.9 | Accrued taxes. . . . . . . . . . . . | 3.9 |
| Prepayments . . . . . . . . . . . . | 5.1 | Total current liabilities . . . . | $134.2 |
| Total current assets . . . . . . | $307.1 | Senior long-term debt . . . . . . . | 165.6 |
| Long-term notes receivable . . . . . | 22.4 | Deferred revenue on future | |
| Investments and advances to | | production . . . . . . . . . . . | 52.2 |
| subsidiaries, affiliates . . . . . . | 55.6 | Deferred federal income taxes. . . . | 3.8 |
| Property, plant, equipment . . . . . | $503.8 | Other deferred credits . . . . . . . | 1.9 |
| Reserve for depreciation, | | Minority equity . . . . . . . . . . . | 12.4 |
| depletion, etc. . . . . . . . . . . | 131.6 | Preferred stock ($1) . . . . . . . . | $ 1.5 |
| Net property, plant, | | Common stock ($.20) . . . . . . . . | 8.8 |
| equipment . . . . . . . . . . | $372.2 | Warrants . . . . . . . . . . . . . . . | (under 0.1) |
| Other assets . . . . . . . . . . . . . | 21.8 | Capital surplus. . . . . . . . . . . | 279.2 |
| | | Retained earnings . . . . . . . . . . | 119.6 |
| Total assets . . . . . . . . . | $779.1 | Total equity . . . . . . . . . | $409.1 |
| | | Total liabilities . . . . . . . . | $779.1 |

*Includes companies merged in a pooling-of-interest basis through January 1968.
Note: Failure of figures to add is due to rounding.
Source: Moody's *Industrial Manual,* 1968.

a seat on its board to Mr. Naess and would change its name to incorporate "Norness" in its title.

Zapata's purchase offer was $5 per share in 4¾% debentures, convertible at $53 into Zapata common. Following a recent stock split, this common was currently priced on the American Stock Exchange at about $40. By March 1968 it would be listed on the New York Stock Exchange.

With some 9.5 million shares of Norness stock outstanding, Occidental's cash offer came to approximately $42.7 million. Owing to the conversion feature, the value of Zapata's offer would vary, depending on the company's prospects as reflected in the price of its stock.

## Occidental Petroleum

Under the leadership of Dr. Armand Hammer, Occidental Petroleum had grown rapidly during the 1960s. A partial account of this growth is recorded in the following excerpt from a *Fortune* article in 1968:[2]

When Dr. Hammer (he trained as an M.D. but never practiced) took command in 1957, Oxy was an obscure and profitless little California oil and gas producer with total operating revenues (as recently as 1959) of less than $800,000. He turned it into a natural resource and fertilizer con-

[2] Stanley H. Brown, "Dr. Hammer's Magic Tingle," *Fortune,* July 1968. © 1968 Time Inc.

**EXHIBIT 2**

OCCIDENTAL PETROLEUM CORPORATION
Comparative Consolidated Income Account and Statistical Record
Years Ended December 31
(in millions)

| | 1963 | 1964 | 1965 | 1966 | 1967 |
|---|---|---|---|---|---|
| *Income account* | | | | | |
| Oil, gas sales and revenues . . . . . | | | | $506.8 | $514.9 |
| Sulphur, agricultural chemicals sales . . . . . . . . . . . . . . | | | | 159.5 | 171.4 |
| Coal sales. . . . . . . . . . . . . . | | | | 135.6 | 139.4 |
| Gross revenues . . . . . . . . . | $514.2 | $678.9 | $718.5 | $802.0 | $825.7 |
| Interest, dividends . . . . . . . . . | 1.3 | 0.8 | 1.3 | 2.7 | 5.3 |
| Total income . . . . . . . . . . | $515.5 | $679.7 | $719.8 | $804.7 | $831.0 |
| Cost of sales* . . . . . . . . . . . . | 462.2 | 618.1 | 651.2 | 722.7 | 731.9 |
| Selling, general, administrative expense . . . . . . . . . . . . . | 33.5 | 38.2 | 41.6 | 47.1 | 55.3 |
| Interest. . . . . . . . . . . . . . . | 2.2 | 3.4 | 4.5 | 8.4 | 10.0 |
| Balance . . . . . . . . . . . . | $ 17.7 | $ 20.0 | $ 22.5 | $ 26.5 | $ 33.8 |
| Federal income tax† . . . . . . . . | 5.5 | 4.8 | 3.7 | 1.0 | . . . |
| Minority interest . . . . . . . . . | 0.5 | 0.5 | 0.8 | 1.0 | 1.7 |
| Equity in income of noncon-solidated subsidiaries . . . . . . | 1.3 | 3.7 | 6.2 | 0.2 | 0.6 |
| Net income before extra-ordinary items . . . . . . . | $ 13.0 | $ 18.5 | $ 24.3 | $ 24.7 | $ 32.7 |
| Extraordinary items‡ . . . . . . . . | 5.6 | 4.3 | 4.1 | 5.7 | 12.9§ |
| Net income to surplus . . . . . | $ 18.6 | $ 22.7 | $ 28 4 | $ 30.4 | $ 45.5 |

| | 1963 | 1964 | 1965 | 1966 | 1967 |
|---|---|---|---|---|---|
| *Statistical record* | | | | | |
| Earnings per common share ‖ | | | | | |
| Before extraordinary items . . . | $ 0.74 | $1.22 | $1.64 | $1.63 | $2.04 |
| After extraordinary items . . . . | 1.30 | 1.64 | 2.00 | 2.13 | 3.03 |
| Dividends per common share . . . | 0.50 | 0.50 | 0.55 | 0.70 | 0.80 |
| Price range: common . . . . . . . | 34¾– 19⅝ | 35– 23½ | 35½– 21 | 57¾– 26 | 122¼– 40⅝ |
| Fixed charges earned | | | | | |
| Before income taxes . . . . . . . | 11.88 | 9.19 | 8.18 | 4.76 | 5.54 |
| After income taxes . . . . . . . . | 9.41 | 7.76 | 7.36 | 4.64 | 5.54 |
| Number of shares outstanding. . . | . . . | . . . | . . . | 11,182,274 | 14,688,763 |

*Including depreciation, amortization, and depletion of $18 million in 1966 and $22.4 million in 1967. Other years not stated.
†Represents federal income taxes of subsidiaries prior to dates of becoming subsidiaries.
‡Includes gain on sale of property, plant, and equipment; tax benefits on loss carry-overs and losses on investments; income from sale of gas, production payments, etc.
§Includes net gain of $12.8 million on sale of Kern County Land Company.
‖Includes companies merged in a pooling-of-interest basis through January 1968.
Source: Moody's *Industrial Manual*, 1968.

glomerate that earned $45,548,000 on a gross of $825,740,000 in 1967 and will crack the billion mark in sales this year. As he has assiduously sought to tell the world, he did it by finding more gas and oil in California and then by moving Oxy in several other directions: fertilizer, sulphur, petrochemicals, petroleum transportation, California real-estate development, coal mining, Libya, and petroleum refining and distribution in Western Europe. Along the way, he thought briefly about making a move to acquire Pure Oil and did make a highly profitable if unsuccessful bid to get Kern County Land

Co. And right now Occidental is involved in the acquisition of Hooker Chemical Corp. for an exchange of stock. Both Oxy's and Hooker's shareholders will vote on the deal this month, and if they approve it, Oxy will add a diversified chemical producer that last year netted $24 million after taxes on sales of $341 million. The consolidated revenues of the expanded Occidental could exceed $1.5 billion this year and net might run well over $100 million.

### After 1970, what?

Occidental, which sold for 20 cents a share when Dr. Hammer first heard of it twelve years ago, lately traded around $50 after a three-for-one split. The recent performance of the stock has given rise to criticisms that the company is overzealous in promoting itself, and last year the New York Stock Exchange eliminated margin trading in Oxy stock because of its "volatility." It doesn't seem to bother investors that for all its diversity, Oxy derives much of its internal growth potential and nearly all of its recent glamour from one product in one place: oil in Libya. "It's just another oil company," one oilman says, "and should be selling for ten to fifteen times earnings."

A lot of oil companies do sell in that range, but Hammer had obviously persuaded investors that Oxy is anything but a typical oil company. Without Hooker, some analysts have been predicting 1968 earnings of $1.75 to $2 a share, putting Oxy's price-earnings ratio well above 20. But such projections are conservative in *Fortune*'s view: $2 to $2.25 a share this year seems more likely. And without any major new discoveries or acquisitions, internal growth, especially from Libyan production, can boost earnings to at least $4 a year by 1970. But that is when Libyan earnings are expected to peak. What happens then depends on Hammer's ability to solve several problems including the concentration of earning power in Libya, the absence of an apparent successor to the energetic but aging doctor, and the pressure on world oil prices as new discoveries in areas such as the Persian Gulf, Nigeria, Alaska, and the North Sea bring enormous quantities of crude oil into the market.

The essence of the doctor's success is not oil but "the deal." A man who works closely with him described appreciatively the way Armand Hammer "gets all tingly" as he begins to close one. "They call me a closer," Hammer reflected. "There's nothing worse than a deal that wasn't closed."

A further description of Dr. Hammer and the Occidental organization is provided in Exhibit 3.

### Zapata Off-Shore Company

Zapata had grown, in part, as the result of a vigorous acquisition program which had carried the company into cognate industries. According to public information contained in Zapata's annual report for 1967, revenues of $36.3 million and income of about $5 million (in about the same proportions) came from the following businesses:

Offshore contract drilling of oil and gas wells for the petroleum
industry . . . . . . . . . . . . . . . . . . . . . . . . . . . . . . . . . . . 57%
Fishing and conversion of fish into high-protein meal used mainly
for chicken feed and, to a lesser extent, conversion into fish oil
with multiple uses . . . . . . . . . . . . . . . . . . . . . . . . . . . . 17%
Service boats for servicing offshore drilling rigs . . . . . . . . . . . . . . 14%
Dredging . . . . . . . . . . . . . . . . . . . . . . . . . . . . . . . . . . . . 9%
Marine construction . . . . . . . . . . . . . . . . . . . . . . . . . . . . . . 3%
Exploring for oil and gas through a syndicate in which the company
held a 27% interest and to which its commitment was $300,000
yearly for three years . . . . . . . . . . . . . . . . . . . . . . . . . . . <u>. . .</u>
100%

Financial statements and a record of Zapata common stock performance
are contained in Exhibits 4, 5, and 6.

Since Zapata had an active acquisitions program, longer run and even
immediate prospects obviously would not depend on trends in its present
businesses alone. The company's acquisition strategy had been outlined
in great detail by Mr. Robert H. Gow, executive vice president, at a
meeting of securities analysts in 1967:

I very much dislike the distinction between internal earnings growth and
acquired earnings growth. In Zapata's case, it is virtually impossible to make
such a distinction. This is because the vast majority of Zapata's growth in
earnings per share has come from what would normally be described as
internal growth, that is, from the addition of new equipment to our various

**EXHIBIT 3**
**Excerpts from "Dr. Hammer's Magic Tingle"***

**Occidental Petroleum's chairman
has a sixth sense about deals—
whether in pencils, czarist memorabilia,
or whiskey. Right now the dealing's
lifting Oxy toward the majors.**

*by Stanley H. Brown*

**His own thing**
The doctor has never come to terms with corporate bureaucracy.
Instead, he has built a headquarters organization to serve his particular needs and style. "Unstructured," says Dorman Commons, fifty,
Oxy's uncommonly able financial vice president. A "skinny, hard-
running group," says another headquarters man. The company's home
office consists of about a dozen key men plus staff on one and a half
floors in a Los Angeles office building a few blocks from Hammer's
house.
The front part of Armand Hammer is an accessible, often charming man, full of anecdotes, an easy smiler. But the back part is usually

* Stanley H. Brown, "Dr. Hammer's Magic Tingle," *Fortune*, July 1968. © 1968
Time Inc.

**EXHIBIT 3** (*continued*)

working to conserve Hammer's time and energy. The man's schedule is wildly fluid, changing constantly, because he goes where he thinks he can serve the most productive purpose. He will think nothing of bypassing an operating executive because he can't reach the man and going direct to a subordinate. When a bypassed executive complained, Hammer apologized sincerely, and then did the same thing next day, explaining that he was only trying to help the executive. It's as though he were offering himself to the highest bidder in terms of business priority for his time and the most efficient application of his energy. That makes him extremely difficult to work with, because Hammer assumes that everyone can make as forceful and effective use of himself as he does.

Hammer describes his function at Occidental as that of "the leader of the orchestra." And like some well-known band leaders who can't read a note, Hammer has little interest in operating details. The Occidental man who said, "Dr. Hammer wouldn't know a barrel of oil if he fell into it," was not being critical at all, just a little hyperbolic. Hammer makes it a point to have able men around who know what he doesn't want to know. He gives them a free hand and pays them generously in stock options (more than 500 Oxy people are on the option list and a score are Oxy millionaires).

But the doctor guards jealously his prerogatives as chief executive officer. He surprises his staff with his decisions, sometimes based on information they didn't even know about. "He has his own sources," one high executive observes. Long before he passed his seventieth birthday last May, Hammer had already made clear that despite any indication he had given that that might have been his retirement date, he has no intention of stepping down at any time.

Hammer has put his stamp on Occidental indelibly, though he is probably no more indispensable to its future than Royal Little proved to be at Textron. There is no shortage of talented staff or operating men in the company, but neither is there an obvious successor at this point. Walter Davis, head of Permian at Midland, Texas, functions part time as head of operations at Los Angeles headquarters. "But the doctor doesn't like anyone else calling the shots," says an Oxy executive. To the question of whether there is a No. 2 man, Hammer replies with a smile, "No, but there are several contenders."

**EXHIBIT 4**

**Price behavior of Zapata stock, 1962–67 (fiscal years ended September 30)**

| Year | Closing price | Percent change | Annual lows | Percent change | Annual highs | Percent change | High-low spread | Spread as a percent of close |
|------|------|------|------|------|------|------|------|------|
| 1962 . . . . | $ 2.35 | . . . | $ 1.75 | . . . | $ 3.85 | . . . | $ 2.10 | 90 |
| 1963 . . . . | 4.63 | 97 | 2.37 | 35 | 5.37 | 40 | 3.00 | 65 |
| 1964 . . . . | 7.63 | 65 | 4.75 | 100 | 8.50 | 59 | 3.75 | 49 |
| 1965 . . . . | 8.63 | 13 | 7.63 | 61 | 11.63 | 38 | 4.00 | 46 |
| 1966 . . . . | 16.25 | 88 | 8.25 | 8 | 27.37 | 134 | 19.12 | 117 |
| 1967 . . . . | 49.12 | 203 | 15.00 | 82 | 49.12 | 80 | 34.12 | 70 |
| Average. . . | | 93 | | 57 | | 71 | | 87 |

Source: Zapata Off-Shore Company *Prospectus,* July 1968.

**EXHIBIT 5**

ZAPATA OFF-SHORE COMPANY
Consolidated Balance Sheet as of September 30, 1967
(in millions of dollars)

| *Assets* | | *Liabilities and Equity* | |
|---|---|---|---|
| Current assets | | Current liabilities | |
| Cash | $ 4.20 | Current maturities on long-term debt | $ 6.31 |
| Notes and accounts receivable | 10.10 | Accounts payable and accrued liabilities | 5.51 |
| Inventories | 2.14 | Income taxes payable | 2.54 |
| Prepaid expenses | .55 | Total current liabilities | $14.36 |
| Total current assets | $16.99 | Long-term debt† | 29.65 |
| Property and equipment, net* | 61.02 | Reserve for deferred taxes | 4.81 |
| Deferred charges, etc. | 3.11 | Minority investment | 1.27 |
| Total assets | $81.12 | Stockholders' investment | |
| | | Preferred | $ 8.77 |
| | | Common‡ | .55 |
| | | Warrants§ | .93 |
| | | Capital in excess of par | 10.15 |
| | | Reinvested earnings‖ | 10.62 |
| | | Total equity | $31.02 |
| | | Total liabilities and equity | $81.12 |

*37.*

*Property and equipment at cost by end use changed as follows from 1966 to 1967:

| Use | 1966 | 1967 |
|---|---|---|
| Offshore drilling | $39.24 | $53.57 |
| Other vessels | 7.96 | 20.15 |
| Protein production | 0 | 3.45 |
| Oil, gas | .14 | .43 |
| Total | $47.34 | $77.61 |
| Less: Reserves for amortization and depreciation | 12.14 | 16.59 |
| Total | $35.20 | $61.02 |

†Includes $19.23 million in senior long-term debt (net of current maturities of $5.30 million), mainly composed of a 6¾% mortgage note. Also includes $1.32 million long-term debt of a subsidiary, mainly a 7% note to a supplier, not guaranteed by the parent. Also includes subordinated debt:

| 6% | debentures due 1975 = | $1.37 million |
|---|---|---|
| 6% | notes due 1982 = | 1.71 |
| 6½% | debentures due 1977 = | 6.02 |
| | | $9.10 million |

‡Par $.50 per share; authorized 5 million shares; issued 1,524,987 shares. This stock was subsequently split two for one.
§Consists of warrants to buy 232,053 shares of common at $30 per share.
‖All reinvested earnings were restricted as to payment of cash dividends on common.
Source: Zapata Off-Shore Company, 1967 Annual Report.

fleets of rigs, workboats, fishing facilities, etc. In general, what the acquisitions of the past three years have done for us is give us the asset base or the entry into the activity which made the internal growth possible. On the other hand, since this growth would not have taken place if Zapata had not made the acquisitions, it could quite correctly be viewed as "growth by acquisition." I would prefer to describe it as growth through the application of financial or corporate strategy.

## EXHIBIT 6

ZAPATA OFF-SHORE COMPANY
Summary of Consolidated Earnings for Fiscal Years Ended September 30
(dollars in millions, except earnings per share)

|  | 1963 | 1964 | 1965 | 1966 | 1967 |
|---|---|---|---|---|---|
| Revenues. | $11.27 | $13.23 | $14.92 | $16.48 | $36.33 |
| Direct costs and expenses | 6.53 | 6.51 | 6.91 | 8.34 | 20.83 |
| Depreciation. | 2.10 | 2.18 | 1.92 | 1.52 | 3.35 |
| General administrative expense | .93 | 1.18 | 1.54 | 1.87 | 2.87 |
| Operating profit. | $ 1.72 | $ 3.36 | $ 4.55 | $ 4.75 | $ 9.29 |
| Other income (expense)* | (.24) | (.22) | (.15) | (.59) | (2.10) |
| Profits before taxes and extraordinary items | $ 1.48 | $ 3.14 | $ 4.40 | $ 4.16 | $ 7.18 |
| Provision for income taxes |  |  |  |  |  |
| Current | .20 | .42 | 1.08 | .89 | 1.00 |
| Deferred | .52 | 1.03 | .98 | .45 | 1.20 |
| Profit before extraordinary items. | $ .76 | $ 1.69 | $ 2.34 | $ 2.83 | $ 4.98 |
| Extraordinary items |  |  |  |  |  |
| Gain on sale of marketable securities | | | | | .21 |
| Write-off investments† | | | | (3.21) | |
| Gain on sale of physical assets. | | .12 | | 1.26 | |
| Total. | | $   .12 | | $ (1.95) | $   .21 |
| Net profit | $   .76 | $ 1.81 | $ 2.34 | $   .88 | $ 5.19 |
| Preferred dividends | .07 | .07 | .07 | .04 | .17 |
| Common dividend | 0 | 0 | 0‡ | 0‡ | 0 |
| Earnings per common share§ |  |  |  |  |  |
| Before extraordinary items. | .025 | .059 | .82 | 1.00 | 1.67 |
| After extraordinary items | .025 | .063 | .82 | .30 | 1.74 |

*Mainly interest owed ($2.17 million in 1967).
†Write-off of investments in Westec, Amata Gas, and Zapata Lining Corporations.
‡A 4% stock dividend was declared in 1965 and 1966.
§Based on average shares outstanding after giving effect to a two-for-one stock split effective January 15, 1968, and assuming conversion of the cumulative convertible preferred and 6% convertible subordinated notes.
Source: Zapata Off-Shore Company *Prospectus*, August 1968.

Mr. Gow then went on to define the five principles which he saw as having guided Zapata's behavior to date:

1. To concentrate on those areas of commercial activity where it is always possible to invest an unlimited amount of money, that is, where capital expansion can take place unhindered by a strict limit to the marketplace. Return on total investment need not be particularly high when extensive use of the second principle is made.
2. To apply, to the maximum extent possible, other people's money and credit.
3. To use listed securities primarily to acquire assets which then serve as the credit base necessary to make the down payments on some other credit-financed acquisition or investment. Here the company has adopted the phraseology "Type I–Type II" in referring to its acquisitions. Type

I is defined as the asset-type company, acquired to strengthen the balance sheet and to expand the company's credit base without contributing necessarily to earnings in the first round, but without diluting them either. Type II is an earnings acquisition. The two types are alternated sequentially, and hopefully the stock will go up and fewer shares can then be exchanged for the equivalent amount of assets acquired in the next Type I.

4. Not to hesitate to acquire so-called "cyclical" earnings if the overall trend of these earnings is upward and if the cycles have at least a minimal correlation with the company's existing business.

5. To avoid areas where management is unique, that is, areas where management can "blackmail" you through your fear of their quitting. Management, good operating management, is terribly important in the dredging business or the drilling business, for example. But you can find replacement. The situation is quite different from, for example, the conditions that would exist if we acquired a small computer company. There a team of five experts could leave you and your growth could stop altogether. A corporate strategy like Zapata's requires maximum compounding of equity cash flow. Let me repeat that because in a way it sums up all the principles: our stress is on the overall rate at which cash equity can be made to compound. This implies that the cash flows from all the divisions be invested in the one which is showing at any moment the greatest opportunity to absorb cash. The ruthlessness with which this objective of compounding return on equity cash must be followed requires that there be few if any indispensable management groups within the corporate structure.

Zapata's acquisition policy was assessed by Smith, Barney as follows:

Management's objective is to develop increased earning power through expansion of the company's present activities and by making additional acquisitions. The plan is to expand Zapata's earning power by alternately acquiring companies with strong financial positions and then purchasing companies which are less strong financially but which offer good prospects for earnings growth. Negotiations are in progress with one or more companies almost continuously. Companies of special interest are those engaged in activities related to the ocean. We are impressed particularly with the thoroughness with which potential acquisitions are studied and with the careful way in which they are integrated into the Zapata corporate structure.

As its overall view, the Smith, Barney report had added: "In our opinion the stock is an excellent long-term investment and purchase is recommended."

## ANALYSIS OF THE ACQUISITION POSSIBILITIES

### Michael Naess' analysis

In view of the capital appreciation opportunity contained in the Zapata offer, Michael Naess set about to analyze this proposal in detail.

A visit to the company's headquarters in Houston, Texas; annual reports; stock price records; and investment house appraisals added to his knowledge of the situation. A description of his study is contained in the Appendix at the end of this case. Assuming the Zapata shares continued to sell at 25 times earnings after the merger and assuming profits for 1968 of $8.5 million for Zapata ($1 million less than Zapata's pro-forma statements included) and $5 million for Anglo Norness, Michael Naess estimated that the debentures would sell for $126, or $6.30 per Anglo Norness share. Based on his financial analysis, he concluded that the Zapata offer was superior to that of Occidental.

A few other qualitative considerations reinforced his preference. The general area of ocean enterprise intrigued him with its promise of future growth. Zapata seemed well on its way to becoming the leading "ocean conglomerate." In addition, the offshore drilling industry had encountered two cyclical setbacks in the last 10 years, 1957 and 1967, precisely the years of shipping's greatest boom. The apparent existence, therefore, of a negative coefficient of correlation between Zapata and Anglo Norness' earnings appealed to him. Also, there appeared to be some potential synergies in the similarities between the two companies, that is, in the customers, in the use of debt to finance capital-intensive activities, and in the technologies of operating and maintaining heavy equipment at sea. Finally, the closing of the Suez Canal for the second time in a decade seemed likely to force the oil companies to seek new sources of supply in order to reduce their dependence on the Persian Gulf. This seemed to indicate strengthened demand for offshore concessions and drilling equipment.

Michael therefore decided to use whatever influence he could muster to persuade his father and the other individuals concerned to accept the Zapata offer.

## The generation gap

While Michael Naess had been gradually deciding in favor of Zapata, his father, Erling Naess, had been leaning in the other direction. The latter described his reactions in a letter to his son:

> You will, on your own, study the Zapata figures. It is astonishing to me that the shares of Zapata, with a net asset value of less than $7.50 per share, can sell in the market at around $50 per share. I am afraid that it illustrates the hectic nature of the market in "glamour stocks." You will note the "tight" financial situation, with current assets barely exceeding current liabilities. Also, the large number of loans, with options to purchase common stock of Zapata. I cannot help getting a feeling that the Zapata situation is one of "wheeling and dealing." Anglo Norness' position is incomparably stronger, financially.
>
> I trust you will contact me as soon as you have studied the Zapata material.

By early February, the Wall Street principals, having studied both situations, indicated that they had a slight preference for the Occidental cash offer but would go along with whatever the Naess block decided. It was thus up to the two Naesses to decide the fate of the company.

Here Michael Naess faced a dilemma. It had become increasingly obvious that his father, age 66, opposed the Zapata offer, fearing that it was too risky. Erling Naess had been through rough times during the 1965–66 Anglo Norness troubles, and he now seemed to want security. In addition, there was the security of his four daughters, his teen-age younger son, and his grandchildren—all of whom held, either directly or in trust, large amounts of Anglo Norness stock—to think of. Michael Naess, on the other hand, found it difficult to impose his father's apparent risk aversion onto the rough probability analysis which he had done. He was too firmly rooted to his own rather neutral attitude toward risk. Hence he was concerned not only with the issue of the comparative merits of the two offers but also with the subsidiary issue of how far to push his own decision, once made. What right did he have to be contentious? His father had created the company, and although Michael had made some contribution, most of the value represented by his own Anglo Norness shares came to him by way of gifts from his father. These considerations made him extremely uneasy about his position. He resolved, nevertheless, to debate the issue up to whatever point seemed reasonable.

A series of telephone conversations followed between Erling and Michael Naess, during the course of which each became successively more entrenched in his own position. Relations became strained and then outwardly hostile. Communications had broken down. No new information or logic was being added. Erling Naess accused his son of "wheeler-dealer," unrealistic pipe dreaming. Michael thought his father afflicted with a "1929 syndrome."

At length both Zapata and Occidental applied pressure. In mid-February Occidental asked that the decision be made within 10 days. At about the same time, Zapata informed Erling Naess that its offer would be withdrawn by the end of the month.

On February 15, attempting to restore reason to the debate, Michael Naess wrote a long letter to his father, presenting the financial analysis which he had worked out and summarizing his arguments:

On balance, and in summary, our choice must rest upon an evaluation of the risk inherent in the Zapata debentures. The above analysis is conservative, in my opinion, and the near-term risk factor seems moderate. Longer term risks might be greater, and I would therefore recommend that if we were to take the Zapata route, we would sell some proportion of our Zapata stock, say, within a few months of consummating the deal, at a price between $104 and $114 per $100 face. Zapata management has offered to assist us by sponsoring a secondary offering. They have, however, made it clear that they would be disappointed if Naess family members active in the management were to dispose of a large proportion of their holding.

*Nonfinancial considerations.* Under this category, by necessity, analysis becomes much more subjective. Our objective, as we established it in broad terms several weeks ago, is to diversify Anglo Norness, which to me implies *both* a diversification of our investment for reasons of financial security *and* a diversification of our managerial efforts for reasons of job satisfaction. We both foresee diminishing returns in shipping during the next few years. In diversifying, we are therefore seeking to expand into areas which permit greater creativity.

Zapata's expanding position in the broad field of "oceanics" appeals to me as one of great potential creativity. Both their intentions to place you on the board and their offer to engage me as part of the "acquisitions" team satisfy me that we would both play significant roles in the creative effort.

The Occidental deal strikes me *not* as a diversification step but rather as an outright absorption. Mere size of the absorbing entity, I suppose, governs this impression. Anglo Norness' contribution to total EPS in the Zapata case is measurable in dollars, whereas in the Occidental case it amounts to cents. For me, at least, in a motivational sense, this is an important difference. In terms of our significance to the absorbing company, the difference becomes even more dramatic when you consider that within Zapata our contact had been with the two top executives, whereas, to my knowledge, you have yet to meet the chief executive of Occidental, despite two visits culminating in agreement upon the formal document of sale which, though unsigned as yet, nevertheless shows that things have gone rather far.

On the other hand, Anglo Norness fits much more readily into the Occidental picture. This might be beneficial in the sense that it offers an added guarantee for the utilization of the Anglo Norness tonnage. But it also locks us in, as managers, to the shipping business, which I thought we had agreed was not a highly creative area.

Occidental has led you to believe that, after merger, Anglo Norness would continue to operate as an autonomous entity. But the very reasons underlying the "better fit" of the Occidental deal seem to preclude autonomy. After the Signal merger, which links Signal's refining and marketing with Occidental's production, the result will be an integrated oil company *except* for one gap, transportation, which we would fill. Clearly, Anglo would have to be carefully integrated with production schedules, on the one side, and refinery runs on the other. Occidental requirements would have first preference on Anglo tonnage. Under modern management-control philosophy, Anglo would probably represent a separate profit center, and its services would be billed internally to the other divisions *at* market rates, and we have both agreed, I think, that the medium- and long-term outlook for the market, particularly tankers, is dismal. Hence, as a profit center, Anglo would probably show losses. Our investment would be safe, of course, due to the original cash exchange, and you might argue that Anglo's losses *would* be the other divisions' gain, such that if, on balance, the result was a favorable contribution to profits per share, and we owned Occidental shares, we would be helping ourselves. But the process is rather too indirect, I fear, to be of strong significance as a motivating force, or as a source of creative satisfaction. This perhaps explains why so many of the oil company executives with whom we deal, the marine VPs, have struck me as rather apathetic and not terribly enthused with their work. And I fear that the Occidental deal would place you (and later, perhaps, me if I followed you) in the same category as these gentlemen.

*Conclusion.* There are many other areas worthy of discussion which this memo has ignored. But it has not been my purpose to produce a definitive report. You have been astounded and perplexed at my inability immediately to perceive the vast superiority of the Occidental deal, of which you tell me you are so convinced. This memo purports to clarify some of my thinking.

A few days later, having digested Michael's letter, Erling Naess summarized *his* arguments:

The cost to Zapata of 9,500,000 Anglo Norness shares at $5 per share would be $47,500,000 in $4\frac{3}{4}\%$ subordinated debentures. Adding to this $47,500,000 the debentures already issued by Zapata in connection with prior acquisitions, including Paramount, the resulting capital structure would be about 85% debt and only about 10% equity (the difference of 5% being preferred stock).

Keeping carefully in mind my responsibility towards the close to 1,000 shareholders of Anglo Norness (not only the Naess family but the "grey mass" of outside shareholders, some of whom probably have an important part of their savings invested in Anglo Norness), I am unable to muster the necessary insouciance about debt to swallow this extremely top-heavy capital structure, seeing that the alternative "route," that is, Occidental, would give the shareholders CASH or the close equivalent to cash, which would completely relieve me of any further responsibility.

There hardly can be any doubt that the top-heavy capital structure of Zapata would give rise to critical comment in the financial press around the world, particularly in London. On the other hand, a cash offer of $4.50 from Occidental would go far to restore the Naess name to its glory of 1962 and 1963. At my age, and with a desire to take it more easy in the years to come, can you really blame me for not wishing to expose myself to new blasts of newspaper criticism?

In your memorandum, you yourself have conceded that "Anglo Norness fits much more readily into the Occidental picture." The fact is that Anglo Norness fits into the Occidental picture like a hand fits into a glove.

On the other hand, Anglo Norness merged into Zapata will make Zapata even more of a conglomerate than it already is. Zapata already controls subsidiaries in such different industries as

Offshore drilling
Construction (dams, etc.)
Fishing
Dredging

One or two of Anglo Norness' smaller tankers may conceivably be converted to drilling ships, but this is the only "commercial contact" between Norness and Zapata which I can discover.

You state, in your memorandum, that Zapata's expanding position in the broad field of "oceanics" appeals to you as one of great potential creativity. I agree with you. I can also understand and sympathize with your appreciation of the offer made you, personally, by Zapata, to engage you as part of the "acquisition team."

However, let us look at the offers made by Occidental in this area. Their ideas are as follows:

a) Anglo Norness will continue to function as a completely autonomous, decentralized company, only subject to their overall centralized financial control.

b) I will join the board of Occidental, apart from being the chairman and chief executive officer of Anglo Norness.

c) If you are interested, an important position in Occidental, not only in Anglo Norness, will be offered YOU. In my estimation, this is an even greater challenge and chance of "potential creativity" than the one offered you by Zapata, for the simple reason that Occidental has far greater resources to apply in "creative effort."

d) I have the feeling that Occidental is in just as great need as Zapata is of the international know-how of the Naess tribe, and that, supported by a large-investment in Occidental, the Naess tribe has a tremendous future in Occidental. The opportunity is knocking on the door. You have merely to open the door.

The Zapata offer is subject to SEC registration of the $4\frac{3}{4}\%$ subordinated debentures. I am told that the granting of this registration would probably take about three months and that in the event the registration was refused, Zapata would be unable to go through with the "deal" and would be free of their commitment. In other words, we would not know for sure for three months that we have a "deal."

On the other hand, Occidental will not require SEC registration. They will pay cash in full to all the hundreds of small holders of Anglo Norness shares, thus reducing the number of persons who will receive four-year notes below the figure which compels registration to be made.[3]

Your evaluation of the attraction of Zapata's offer is based upon certain assumptions regarding Wall Street's reaction to the Zapata-Anglo Norness merger. All this assumes that the financial community in New York will believe in the future of Zapata as an "oceanic conglomerate." Only provided this belief continues STRONG will Zapata's shares be given the high market standing, that is, the P/E multiple of 25, which they are now enjoying.

One of the major reasons for my skepticism is the belief that the "conglomerate honeymoon" ended when the Litton Industries "myth" exploded and the Litton stock plunged from about $115 per share to $65. When I say that the "myth" exploded, I refer to the claim of the leading U.S. conglomerates that their use of advanced management techniques and abilities can be applied successfully to any type of business and that, therefore, a small "scientific management team" can improve the earnings of any company

---

[3] To ease the tax burden on certain of the large selling stockholders, Occidental had made available the option of four-year serial notes, which would qualify under the IRS code as an installment sale.

in any industry and, consequently, justify a much higher P/E ratio than the company had before.

When Litton Industries announced a profits drop of 30% due to "management problems," the whole house of cards collapsed.

You and I know perfectly well that to maintain Anglo Norness' earnings in the years to come will require grueling hard work and demand great skill and experience of a kind that Zapata cannot possibly supply. Managerial ability, as demonstrated in the offshore drilling business and other enterprises absorbed by Zapata, *cannot* be transferred to the business of Anglo Norness. It would still be up to you and to me to make Anglo Norness fulfill the $5 million per annum expectation upon which your evaluation of the Zapata stock is based.

The P/E multiple of 25 applied to Zapata stock is based upon the expectation of "growth." It is my belief that the headlong scramble for "growth" indulged in by the leading U.S. conglomerates has come to a sad end and that companies like Zapata will have to submit to an enforced pause in their acquisition programs. When this is realized by the financial community, it is logical to expect that the P/E multiple will drop to the more realistic one of about 15. If at the same time Anglo Norness should have a poor year and only break even, the stock of Zapata would fall to about $28—being 15 times earnings of about $1.90 per share, diluted. The 4¾% subordinated convertible debentures would probably fall to about 60, equal to about $3 per share of Anglo Norness, compared with the $4.50 cash offered by Occidental.

Except for visions of "growth," why should Zapata stock sell at a higher multiple than the shares of immensely strong companies like Standard Oil of New Jersey, Royal Dutch, etc.? It would be easy to present arguments why the Zapata shares should sell at a LOWER, not higher, multiple than these seasoned, strong companies.

Even if this letter leaves you unconvinced, I am at least hoping that you appreciate that I have studied your memorandum of February 15 carefully, weighing your arguments.

## A third view

Despite the emphasis given to the merger alternatives, at least one member of the top-executive team continued to feel that Anglo Norness might have greater opportunities as an independent company. Thus, the chairman of the Anglo Norness executive committee wrote as follows to Michael Naess at the Harvard Business School:

My purpose in writing is to let you know that I believe the failure of all the current [merger] negotiations, should this occur, would not necessarily be a disaster in my opinion. There is every reason to expect that by June 1969 Anglo could have a cash availability in the order of 20 million dollars. While probably sounding exceedingly optimistic, it is more and more looking to me as if we should be the ones doing the acquiring, rather than rushing to sell out. Perhaps everyone is being overly influenced by the problems of the past, rather than looking coldly at the present as well as the near-term future.

## APPENDIX
## MICHAEL NAESS' STUDY OF ZAPATA OFF-SHORE COMPANY

*Stock performance record.* After his two-day trip to Houston, where Zapata management answered his questions and disclosed to him its forecasts, Michael Naess turned to an analysis of the past performance record of Zapata's stock. Looking at the closing annual prices from 1962 through 1967 (as adjusted for splits), he found a rise from $2.35 to $49.12, for an average yearly gain of 93%, noncompounded. Year-to-year gains, however, varied widely, and the overall average was greatly strengthened by a jump of 203% in 1967.

Michael wondered, therefore, whether the high closing price of 1967 represented a "technical climax" and whether accepting Zapata's offer would mean that Anglo would be "getting in at the top." He also noted a great volatility, as measured by the yearly high-low spreads which averaged 87%. In order to get some measure of growth besides that based on year-end changes, Michael tabulated the yearly lows and highs and figured the annual percentage change in each. From these calculations he found that the yearly growth reflected by the lows averaged 57%; as reflected by the highs it averaged 71%. Michael felt that the average of these two figures—64%—was a better yardstick of past stock price performance than the 93% computed from the year-end closes, since there seemed to be no reason to attach any special importance to the latter.

The question of whether accepting Zapata's offer meant getting in at the top could only be answered by a comparative evaluation of Zapata before and after the Norness acquisition. Accordingly, Michael Naess examined the past financial statements, especially the operating ratios, the equity structure, and the earnings per share. He appraised earnings prospects within Norness, and he went as far as he could in calculating the difference the Norness acquisition would make in this picture.

*Finances.* Studying Zapata's financial statements, Michael noted in particular the tight current picture with a current ratio at September 30, 1967, of slightly less than 1.2/1. He also observed the high degree of leverage in the capital structure. Adding deferred taxes and minority interest to book equity, he noted that there was about $37 million in equity against $30 million in long-term debt. He also knew, however, that since drilling rigs represented the major part of the company's assets, a high degree of leverage could be expected. Drilling rigs were normally financed in much the same way as Anglo Norness' ships. On the strength of a long-term drilling contract with an oil company, the owner could borrow heavily for the construction of a rig, in effect taking advantage of the customer's credit rating.

Turning to the equity structure, he noted that on a split basis there were 3,100,000 common shares outstanding. Potential conversion was as follows: preferred stock into 502,000; warrants, 516,000; options, 176,000; and conversion of the 6% note due in 1982, possibly 114,000. Total potential shares out were, therefore, about 4.4 million. Pro-forma earnings on this basis, assuming conversions at date of issue during 1967 and using the average number outstanding, were $1.58 per share, as opposed to the $1.76 reported. At $40, therefore, the stock was selling at about 25 times fully diluted 1967 earnings.

*Outlook.* Michael Naess next examined the earnings outlook for 1968. While in Houston, Zapata management had shown him their latest pro-forma income statement, which showed 1968 net income of $9.5 million, or about $3.05 per share undiluted. This projection included contribution from the purchase in January of Paramount Pacific, Inc., a heavy construction firm based in Los Angeles, for $16.7 million in convertible debentures identical in terms to those offered to Anglo Norness, plus a cash payment of $5 million to be made contingent upon future earnings.

Even apart from the Paramount or other acquisitions, Michael learned that the financial community was optimistic on Zapata's near-term earnings. Thus, one brokerage house (Smith, Barney & Co.) forecast that per-share earnings would rise, undiluted, in the neighborhood of 40% in 1968 over 1967. In support of this view, the Smith, Barney report pointed out that earnings from offshore drilling—the largest money-maker—should be improved by a full year's return on a major investment made in 1967. Earnings from the fishing fleet—the second largest source of income—should be improved by absence of the start-up costs that had accompanied acquisition of this business early in the 1967 fishing season. Earnings of the service-boat fleet, the third largest sales and income producer, would be increased by a full year's operation of four new boats, which raised the total number to 21. Earnings from dredging and marine construction should also increase, reflecting operations of a subsidiary owned for only part of the previous year.

So far as longer term prospects were concerned, the broker's report pointed out that the future of offshore drilling work looked good, based on the oil industry's prediction that crude from offshore wells would increase its share of the free-world total from 16% of all production in 1966 to 40% within the next 10 years. With demand also rising at a compound rate of 6% a year, offshore production should increase five-fold. Fishing-fleet prospects, too, appeared secure, since Zapata's break-even price for fish meal (the principal end product) was only $90 a ton, much lower than the current market price of $130, and also lower than the break-even price of the principal competition, which came from smaller, older boats owned in Peru. In addition, Zapata might prove successful in projected efforts to expand its fishing season beyond the customary six months a year.

*Zapata plus Norness.* Before trying to determine how a combined Anglo Norness-Zapata would look, Michael Naess decided that to be conservative he would arbitrarily reduce Zapata's 1968 earnings forecast of $9.5 million to $8.5 million. To this he attempted to add the effects of the Anglo Norness acquisition.

At $5 per share for Anglo's 9.5 million shares, the company would cost Zapata about $47.5 million. With over $20 million in Norness cash projected by June, Michael decided to call $10 million "redundant." The net cost was thus $37.5 million. In terms of current profits of $16 million, Zapata was paying a ridiculous 2.4 times earnings. His best estimates of Anglo's earnings for 1969 and 1970, however, were about $5 million in each year, and on this basis the price was 7.5 times earnings.

Assuming the company would be purchased for 20% cash,[4] the amount of convertible debentures to be issued would be $38 million. Convertible at $53, dilution would be 720,000 shares, and contribution to Zapata's consolidated earnings would be $7 per incremental share issued, fully diluted. The deal, at this point, looked too good for Zapata. On the other hand, given Anglo's current price in London of $2.60, Zapata was already paying a premium of better than 90%.

An attempt to estimate pro-forma consolidated earnings specifically for 1968 proved to be fruitless. As a purchase, Anglo could only contribute to Zapata's earnings from the effective date of the deal, and it was impossible to predict what that date would be, given the need for proxy statements, registration, permission of the Office of Direct Foreign Investment, etc. Michael therefore assumed that it was the rate of annualized earnings, rather than the earnings reported for a particular fiscal year, that was important in predicting equity values.

Hence, he argued, at some point during 1968 Zapata would be earning at the rate of $8.5 million plus $5 million from Anglo Norness, or $13.5 million per annum, less interest on the new debentures, after tax of $900,000, or net $12.6 million. Not counting dilution, this would be $4.06 per share on 3.1 million shares. Adding conversions of 1.1 million from

---

[4] Due to Bank of England restrictions during the post-devaluation period, as well as to Department of Commerce regulations on direct foreign investment, it appeared that Zapata would not be able to offer its debentures to foreign stockholders, particularly those resident in the United Kingdom. As a result, these individuals would be offered $5 per share in cash. It was difficult to determine exactly what percentage of the company's stock was still held abroad. The stock had been traded actively since the June war, and the company's registry was known to be well behind the times. Most of the activity had been traced, however, to American buying. Accordingly, it was estimated that Zapata would end up purchasing only about 20% of the company for cash and 80% for convertibles.

the Paramount Pacific and Anglo Norness debentures to the 4.4 million previously computed, fully converted shares outstanding would be 5.5 million. Earnings in this case, however, would be unencumbered by the interest on the debentures or the preferred dividend and would presumably be bolstered by some return from the proceeds of the warrants and options. A reasonable estimate would be $14.5 million, which on 5.5 million shares would amount to fully diluted earnings of $2.65 per share.

If the combined company could maintain its former multiple of 25 times fully diluted earnings, which would in turn depend on maintenance of its growth rate, the stock would move to $67 near term. On this basis, the debentures, assuming no premium over conversion value, would sell at $126 per $100 face value. This, Michael concluded, would be equivalent to $6.30 per share of Anglo Norness. If he added back the $1 million which he had lopped off Zapata's earnings projection for 1968, earnings went to $2.80, the stock to $70, and the bonds to $132, which was $6.60 per Anglo share. Finally, slightly further out, Zapata had projected $12 million internally for 1969, based on rig contracts coming in later during 1968. On this basis, earnings would be $3.10 fully diluted, the stock $78, and the bonds $148, equal to $7.40 per Anglo share.

Finally, Michael calculated that for the Zapata offer to equate with the Occidental offer of $4.50, the bonds would have to sell at $90 per $100 face. On this basis, the stock would be at $47½, again assuming no premium. For this to happen, the multiple would have to fall to 18 times the conservative estimate, 17 times Zapata's projected EPS, and 15 times the 1969 expectation. Given the multiples applied to the rest of the offshore industry, he considered it unlikely that even with the addition of the speculative Anglo Norness to the portfolio, Zapata's multiple would fall much below 20 times fully diluted earnings.

Expressed in a different way, if the $4.50 Occidental offer was compared with $6.30 as Zapata's offer, for the latter to be equal to or worse than the former there would have to be a joint probability of only 70% that both the earnings and the multiple would turn out as expected. The earnings estimate appeared to be about 95% certain, given the 10% adjustment of Zapata's projection. The multiple was less sure. If the market valued Anglo's contribution at 10 times earnings, then the weighted average attached to the combined company should be about 19.5 times. This was still higher than the break even of 18 times derived above.

# Capital International S.A.*

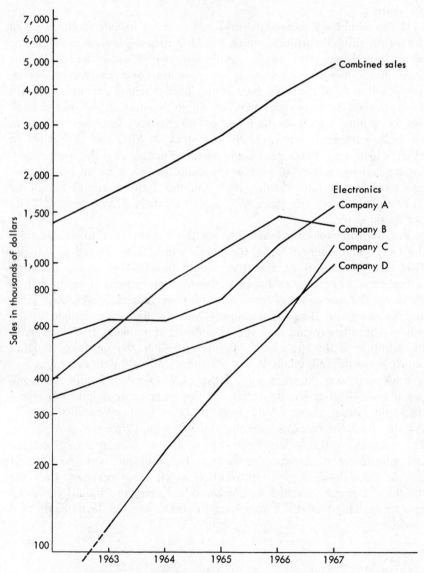

THIS CHART shows the sales performance during the last five years of four small specialized electronics companies, all from different European countries. We may have a possible opportunity of merging these four companies into one larger multinational corporation. I would like to discuss this proposition. During the next few weeks, we should reach a decision on whether or not to proceed, and, if so, how? Also, I should like to use our discussions for a consideration of mergers and the so-called merger movement in Europe. Particularly, I should like to discuss whether the concept on which the current proposition is based is viable, not just in this specific instance, but also for other European companies and industries.

With this statement, Mr. Ken Mathysen-Gerst opened a meeting of the Capital International S.A. (CI-SA) staff on August 25, 1967. Several subsequent staff meetings were devoted to this merger proposition. Mr. Mathysen-Gerst visited all four companies to discuss his plans with them. Their reactions ranged from moderate to great enthusiasm. All four were willing to explore the proposition and cooperate with a survey by CI-SA. Until the completion of this survey, the identity of no participant would be disclosed to the others. Afterwards, however, the survey would be made available to all, and this study plus reciprocal visits would permit a decision to be reached on the feasibility of the proposition. Exhibit 1, which was also presented during the initial staff meeting, provides some basic data on the four companies.

Mr. Mathysen-Gerst, age 39, a tall, lean American, formerly of Dutch citizenship, who spoke with precise sentences couched in quiet tones, was managing director of Capital International S.A., Geneva. Upon graduating from the Harvard Business School in 1959, he had joined the Capital Research and Management Company in Los Angeles. Here he had become increasingly involved in the management of European investments, and in 1962 he was asked to open a Geneva office.

CI-SA was a Swiss subsidiary of the Capital Group, Inc., a U.S. financial holding company whose principal operating subsidiary, the Capital Research and Management Company, managed four U.S. mutual funds with assets in excess of $1 billion. At one time it had managed an international fund, which, following the imposition of the U.S. interest equalization tax, was merged into one of the other funds because the tax destroyed the necessary investment flexibility. In 1967 CI-SA was providing a variety of services, including financial consulting related to mergers and acquisitions on behalf of European and U.S. corporate clients.

## ORIGIN OF THE MERGER PROPOSITION

During early 1967, CI-SA had been retained by a U.S. client to conduct an acquisitions search in the European electronics industry. During this search, CI-SA had contacted 420 smaller companies, 80 of which

**EXHIBIT 1**
**Information on the four electronics companies**$^*$

| Company | A | B | C | D | Pro forma consolidated |
|---|---|---|---|---|---|
| *Location* | Germany | Sweden | Italy | Belgium | EEC-EFTA |
| Exports as a percentage of sales............... | 25% | 20% | 15% | 10% | n.a. |
| Market share at home......... | 70% | 45% | 55% | 90%† | n.a. |
| *1967 forecasts* (in thousands of dollars) | | | | | |
| Sales ................. | $1,530 | $1,320 | $1,100 | $1,000 | $4,950 |
| Net earnings............ | 170 | 75 | 30 | 35 | 310 |
| Cash earnings ........... | 225 | 155 | 50 | 60 | 490 |
| *Financial condition* (in thousands of dollars) | | | | | |
| Long-term debt........... | ... | $ 320 | $ 165 | ... | $ 485 |
| Net worth ............. | $1,375 | 453 | 175 | $ 155 | 2,148 |
| Total............... | $1,375 | $ 773 | $ 340 | $ 155 | $2,633 |

*Product information*

Company A had three product lines, with closed-circuit TV accounting for the major part of sales. The core of certain process controls, made and supplied to a leading industrial equipment manufacturer, and parts for telemetry systems rounded out its $1.5 million sales total.

Company B had achieved sales of $1.3 million on one product line, that is, motor controls mostly for industrial uses. The recent dip in sales had been due to the recent completion of a major one-time defense contract. Throughout 1966–67 commercial sales continued to increase. An upswing in the sales trend was predicted for the future. The company had a manufacturing and sales subsidiary in the Netherlands.

Company C specialized exclusively in machine tool controls with sales of $1.1 million. It had recently obtained an important contract from a major German machine tool manufacturer.

Company D produced three product lines but had most of its strength in hospital intercom systems. Closely related general intercom systems and a later addition, language labs, accounted for the remainder of its $1 million sales. It had obtained some major orders for 1968 delivery to German and French hospitals.

*Product lines have been disguised. Percentages have been rounded.
†For hospital intercom systems.
n.a. = not available
Source: CI-SA internal memorandum.

had warranted more thorough study. After this search had been completed, the U.S. client in the summer of 1967 had entered into negotiations with a Belgian company having sales of approximately $15 million. The client had decided to give priority to acquisition candidates with more than $10 million in sales.

In conducting the search, Mr. Mathysen-Gerst had been surprised by the large number of successful companies in the European electronics industry. These companies, he said, were characterized by excellent technology, specialization in a single product or product line, strong entrepreneurial owner managers (but weak second-line management and lack of control systems), rapid growth, and a predominantly national focus. On the basis of his investigations, Mr. Mathysen-Gerst became even more convinced that the much talked-about technology gap between Europe and the United States was vastly exaggerated. If any gap was revealed by the CI-SA search, it was in terms of management depth, organizational structure, and control systems.

Many of the companies investigated appeared to have excellent opportunities for growth. Most had already grown from small, garage-type operations to $1 million companies—still, however, run by their owner managers as one-man shows. Further growth was expected to take these companies into the $10 million range, at which point a larger and more formally structured organization would be required. Among these companies, some saw their future growth as going beyond their present policy of selling, in essence, a single product to their own national market. These companies were anxious to sell in other European countries as well and thus to capitalize more fully on their technological leadership. In addition, a number of firms contemplated diversifying at home, thereby reducing the risk of reliance on a single product.

Mr. Mathysen-Gerst identified the major hurdles to continued rapid expansion of these small, successful electronics companies as follows: (1) a shortage of financial resources, (2) a shortage of qualified management, and (3) the difficulty of repeating their success in different countries or product segments. One means of overcoming these hurdles was merger with a larger company. Mr. Mathysen-Gerst had argued this point in generating interest in a takeover by his U.S. corporate client. He had discovered, however, that a number of companies were not interested in takeover by a corporate giant but would consider joining forces with companies of similar size. This discovery led Mr. Mathysen-Gerst to his merger proposition.

## EUROPEAN ELECTRONICS INDUSTRY

In 1967 sales of the electronics industry in Europe were estimated at about $9.5 billion, compared with $22 billion in the United States. Giants like Philips or Siemens were operating side by side with literally hundreds of small companies, some of which were successful while others were barely surviving. The large number of companies was in part a result of the marked segmentation of the industry. This, in turn, was caused by the tremendous breadth of technology employed. For example, cores for magnets were as much a part of this industry as circuits printed directly on cardboard. Each market segment, ranging from $500,000 to some $200 million, was served by from 1 to 50 companies with sales between $500,000 and $30 million. A sales breakdown by country for eight major product categories is provided in Exhibit 2; within these categories were 82 segments, 28 of which were components.

In addition to product segmentation, there was also segmentation

**EXHIBIT 2**
Five-country electronics markets—1967 (in millions of dollars)

| | Belgium | Nether-lands | Italy | Sweden | Ger-many | Total | Europe total* |
|---|---|---|---|---|---|---|---|
| 1. Consumer products . . . | 46.8 | 46.3 | 257.0 | 55.5 | 462.2 | 867.8 | 1,642.8 |
| 2. Medical equipment . . . . | 9.6 | 8.3 | 5.8 | 7.5 | 46.8 | 78.0 | 144.9 |
| 3. Communications, of which . . . . . . . . . . | 67.2 | 72.8 | 108.8 | 63.9 | 453.0 | 765.7 | 1,552.8 |
| *a*) Closed-circuit TV . . | 0.7 | 0.6 | 2.0 | 0.4 | 4.8 | 8.5 | 19.6 |
| *b*) Intercom and sound systems . . . . . . : . . | 3.2 | 5.0 | 6.6 | 3.9 | 24.9 | 43.6 | 123.9 |
| 4. Computer and related† . . . . . . . . . . | 43.1 | 50.1 | 127.0 | 42.3 | 291.1 | 553.6 | 1,121.7 |
| 5. Nuclear . . . . . . . . . | 9.0 | 10.7 | 9.3 | 7.0 | 21.1 | 57.1 | 103.4 |
| 6. Industrial equipment, of which . . . . . . . . . . | 79.9 | 76.1 | 86.3 | 67.5 | 296.9 | 606.7 | 1,096.6 |
| *a*) Machine tool controls . . . . . . . . | 8.2 | 9.5 | 11.3 | 10.0 | 33.0 | 72.0 | 133.4 |
| *b*) Motor controls . . . . | 8.5 | 8.0 | 5.5 | 5.8 | 25.8 | 53.6 | 88.0 |
| *c*) Power supplies . . . . | 11.3 | 11.0 | 10.5 | 10.1 | 22.7 | 65.6 | 119.4 |
| *d*) Process controls . . . | 35.0 | 34.0 | 38.0 | 31.0 | 110.0 | 248.0 | 460.5 |
| 7. Test and measuring instruments . . . . . . . . | 38.4 | 51.4 | 49.8 | 37.5 | 125.2 | 302.3 | 532.0 |
| 8. Components . . . . . . . | 95.7 | 154.7 | 194.8 | 103.2 | 679.5 | 1,227.9 | 2,498.7 |
| Total . . . . . . . . . . . | 389.7 | 470.4 | 838.8 | 384.4 | 2,375.8 | 4,459.1 | 8,692.9 |

*Does not include the "smaller European electronics markets" of Austria, Ireland, Greece, etc., which totaled about $814 million, giving a "total Europe" figure of $9,506 million.
†Not including process control systems.
Source: *Electronics*, December 26, 1966.

by countries. Most companies confined their activities to their national market. This policy was due, at least in part, to the producers' substantial dependence on sales to their governments and other public authorities. In some instances, "relationships" were essential to making these sales. Even in arm's length situations, special skills and experience were required for submitting a standard government bid. Compounded by problems of language and culture, these factors made it difficult to market in other countries, even for companies with product leadership.

During the late 1950s and the 1960s, the electronics industry had grown rapidly, doubling in size every four or five years. Growth was highly uneven, however, from one product segment to another. Annual gains ranged from 2%–4% on some consumer products, such as radios, to 35% for highly sophisticated systems and control equipment. For 1967, *Electronics*[1] magazine predicted an industry growth of 8%, or twice the rate of the GNP, with the rates for different segments ranging from —1.5% in consumer products to +27% in industrial controls. Besides

---

[1] By the end of 1967, the total industry growth rate had slowed from the peak of the early 1960s.

varying among product segments, growth rates also varied among countries, as suggested by the following figures for 1966–67:

| Country | Electronics industry | Components sector | Nuclear equipment sector |
|---|---|---|---|
| Germany . . . . . . | +8% | +15% | +1% |
| Italy . . . . . . . . | +15%–20% | +9% | –10% |

The differences in growth rates among both product segments and countries resulted primarily from different rates of technological change and different product life cycles. Government programs and policies, for example, in defense or health also helped to account for varying patterns among countries.

## THE MERGER CONCEPT

Mr. Mathysen-Gerst's merger concept, which he referred to as "project synergistics," was based on five criteria. First, the participating companies were to be of equal size. This requirement ran counter to what appeared to be the trend in mergers, whereby larger companies absorbed smaller ones. The reason for this criterion was that no single partner should dominate or control the merged unit during its initial stages.

Second, all participating companies would have to be healthy. This requirement, too, appeared contrary to common merger practice. In many instances, companies in trouble seemed to be the most eager to find partners or the most likely to be regarded as a possible candidate for merger. For project synergistics, on the other hand, the members were to be leaders in their segment of the electronics industry. They had to be profitable and in good financial standing, and they had to offer the prospect of continued rapid growth. The reasons for this requirement were that the merger had to be forward-looking—oriented toward attacking new opportunities than toward correcting old mistakes. Also, rapid growth would facilitate digestion of the inevitable merger adjustments, inasmuch as a growth situation would provide opportunities for all parties concerned. Further, rapid growth would permit the newly merged unit to establish its new identity early. Growth would require major adjustments and changes by the participating companies anyway, and therefore these adjustments might as well occur within the framework of the merger. Finally, a growing company was seen as a major attraction in obtaining the manpower needed to meet future opportunities.

Third, the member companies had to be small. In these it was felt that the synergistic effects would be strongest. Also, small companies would have to change, at any rate in terms of management organization, if they were to digest further growth. If, instead of moving from domi-nation by the owner manager to a functional setup, they moved directly to a divisional organization, the problems of adjustment would perhaps be no more grave. In fact, such problems might be less severe, since, with a divisional structure, the conduct and organization of the operating units could be geared to the personalities involved. Also, such a structure might facilitate attracting and training the manpower needed to cope with future growth opportunities, particularly those involving product diversification or establishment of operations in different countries.

Fourth, the participating companies had to be engaged in different product segments. This requirement, again, appeared contrary to the current trend, which featured mergers among companies in identical lines. Spreading of risk was one argument for this criterion, since the resulting company would be less vulnerable to technological change. Moreover, the varying growth patterns of each segment would possibly average out, thus giving the merged company a less cyclical pattern of its own. Furthermore, with participants active in different product lines, the turmoil resulting from a merger would be reduced. For exam-ple, if four companies making, say, transformers, should be merged, the manufacturing, marketing, and R & D activities of each of the four would have to be integrated and coordinated in order to reduce unneces-sary overlap and benefit from possible economies of scale. Such moves would have major implications, sometimes negative, for the people in-volved. Such action would not be required for companies in different product lines. Mr. Mathysen-Gerst was skeptical, in any case, of the alleged positive results of merging companies in the same line, especially of alleged economies of scale. Given the small size, even when combined, of the companies he was considering, he believed economies of scale would be negligible.

Fifth, the participating companies would have to be from different countries. Again, this requirement was different from the prevailing trend. Except for Agfa-Gevaert,[2] few examples of mergers across national boundaries were known. The purpose of this requirement was to achieve area as well as product diversification. Also, having partners in different countries would create a beachhead in each of them. With each par-ticipating company remaining a national unit while also belonging to the merged parent, government sales, not just of the products of the

---

[2] In 1964 Agfa and Gevaert, German and Belgian companies, respectively, merged their photographic interests, allegedly to compete more effectively with Kodak. However, both companies maintained separate corporate headquarters, and as of 1967 the operations of the two companies were far from fully integrated. Also, without a European corporation law, the merger raised complicated legal questions.

local company but of those of the other partners as well, might be facilitated.

## MERGER PROCEDURE

In the area of merger procedures, Mr. Mathysen-Gerst identified five issues about which he was especially concerned. First, he wanted to determine what critical questions should be investigated in the CI-SA survey. In this connection, he had already begun work on a questionnaire to be used as a basis of the investigations he would have to conduct in each company before a decision could be reached on the operational feasibility of the merger negotiations. Among the points to be particularly investigated was how well each proposed participant measured up in terms of the criterion of health. Mr. Mathysen-Gerst had already defined health in terms of technological excellence and product leadership, profitability and financial strength, as well as rapid growth. In addition, he felt that no company should have a severely retarded functional capability in marketing, manufacturing, or R & D. He realized, however, that these conditions required further elaboration. Also, he was wondering whether this evaluation should not be made by an independent firm possessing the necessary technical expertise.

A second issue was the formula by which each partner's share in the merged venture would be determined. Should shares be based exclusively on earnings? If so, it might penalize those partners who had invested more heavily in R & D and marketing, both possibly key factors for future success. In addition to earnings, what other elements should be included in the formula? And what time span should be used? Also, to what extent should past performance determine each company's share as against projected future performance? For example, some companies might argue that they had new developments just around the corner which would greatly increase their future relative contribution. As one way to resolve their particular dilemma, Mr. Mathysen-Gerst was considering a "55% now—45% later" exchange of stock procedure. That is, 55% of the shares of the separate units would be exchanged immediately for shares of the merged company, with the formula applied on past performance. The remaining 45% would be exchanged in three to five years, with the formula applying to the results of this additional period.

A third issue related to the raising of additional funds. Mr. Mathysen-Gerst expected to find four to six additional shareholders who would be able to contribute between $1 million and $1.5 million to the merged unit. This outside money would provide additional funds to take advantage of growth opportunities. Also, the new shareholders could contribute potential contacts for obtaining new business and could permit easier debt financing. With this purpose in mind, Mr. Mathysen-Gerst had already approached a few potentially active shareholders, such as some European banks and individuals willing to invest venture capital. Their initial response had been encouraging.

A fourth issue was the compensation arrangement for CI-SA. In a number of instances, CI-SA proceeded on the basis of a fixed *per diem* compensation, while in others its compensation had been contingent upon the success of its search and related to the price of the acquisition. In the interest of project synergistics, Mr. Mathysen-Gerst was thinking of taking CI-SA's compensation in the form of stock in the merged unit. Thus, CI-SA would see a return for its extensive efforts only if the venture succeeded. However, Mr. Mathysen-Gerst hoped to develop a stock-option plan which would give CI-SA a very handsome return in case of success. In addition, he expected to request some "earnest" money from the participating firms. Even though this sum would be only a minor contribution to expenses, it would provide an early indication as to the seriousness of the participants. Given the small size of the companies involved, the payment of even a small amount of earnest money was expected to make the owner managers pause to consider whether they really wanted to proceed.

Fifth, Mr. Mathysen-Gerst wanted to proceed on the basis of a definite timetable. He was inclined to move rapidly, on the premise that speed allowed him to test the sincerity of the parties involved and would prevent tying up CI-SA's resources for an extended period. Exhibit 3

**EXHIBIT 3**
**Capital International's timetable for project synergistics**

| | |
|---|---|
| September 22 | Deliver in person detailed survey questionnaire to four participants requiring complete disclosure of all relevant data and information. |
| October 4 | Return questionnaires to CI-SA. |
| October 9–14 | Review and clarify each questionnaire through personal meetings. |
| October 18 | Send to all participants copies of all completed and clarified questionnaires plus consolidation of all relevant financial and operational data. |
| October 23 | Joint visit to Company A in Germany. |
| 24 | Joint visit to Company B in Sweden. |
| 25 | Joint visit to Company D in Belgium. |
| 26 | Joint visit to Company C in Italy. |
| 27 | Joint review.* |
| November 3 | *Go/no go decision* regarding operational feasibility of project synergistics. |
| November 5 | Companies pay $2,000 into joint pool to cover legal/organizational costs of project. |
| November 25 | Capital International S.A. mails detailed financial proposal to all participants. |
| December 1–4 | Capital International S.A. reviews financial proposal with each participant individually. |
| December 9 | Geneva conference. Joint examination of financial proposals; reexamination of operational and management aspects. |
| December 15 | *Final go/no go decision,* involving firm commitment to project synergistics. |
| February 15 | Complete legal organization. |
| March 1 | Start. |

* These formally organized reviews will be followed during November by individually organized visits of each participant to the others.
Source: CI-SA internal memorandum.

provides a tentative timetable which he planned to submit to the managers of the four companies.

## SYNERGISTIC EXPECTATIONS

Mr. Mathysen-Gerst did not expect that project synergistics would benefit from the traditional synergistic effects commonly attributed to mergers in textbooks: for example, economies of scale in manufacturing, R & D, and possibly marketing. Rather, he expected synergistic benefits in terms of organization, internationalization, and finance—all relatively weak areas in small electronics companies. In terms of organization, he hoped for one thing to create a base big enough to support planning and control capabilities. Bringing together four healthy companies with relatively strong functional capacities would help to achieve this objective. (Mr. Mathysen-Gerst's tentative evaluation of the functional capabilities of the merger candidates, as presented to the August 25 staff meeting, is presented in Exhibit 4.) Another organizational gain was expected to arise from the ability of the merged company, especially if successful, to attract qualified management personnel.

In terms of internationalization, the synergistic benefit would come through the assistance which each member could provide the others in his own home market. Such help would permit the partners to become international more rapidly than if each were to proceed independently.

In terms of finance, the merged units were expected to have easier access to capital markets, thus removing lack of funds as a major constraint on future growth. Another financial benefit was seen in the possibility that the merged unit might create "paper" for future acquisitions. Moreover, through the merger, marketability of the stock currently held by the owner managers in their own firms would be greatly facilitated. Finally, CI-SA's continued involvement in the merged unit was also expected to contribute to the financial synergistic benefits.

## OUTLOOK

In a memo prepared for a September 5 staff meeting, Mr. Mathysen-Gerst stated the objectives, goals, and philosophy of project synergistics as follows:

### Objective

To create a successful multinational enterprise. Success to be measured by:

  *a)*  Rapid growth in sales (at least 30% per year over the next three years) and increase in the share of the market.

*b*)    Return on investment sufficient to finance internal growth and produce rapid growth in earnings per share (commensurate with sales growth).
*c*)    Assured long-term continuity and viability (measured by management in depth, job satisfactions, new product flow, etc.).

### Specific medium-term goal

Attainment of a profitable sales volume of $100 million in 1978, half through internal growth and half through acquisitions (the latter to accelerate growth in earnings per share).

### EXHIBIT 4
### Capabilities of the four companies and expected synergy flow

| Company<br>Location | | A<br>Germany | B<br>Sweden | C<br>Italy | D<br>Belgium |
|---|---|---|---|---|---|
| *Tentative ranking of*<br>  *functional capabilities*\* | | | | | |
| R & D . . . . . . . . . . . . . . | | 2 | 1 | 1 | 4 |
| Manufacturing. . . . . . . . . . | | 1 | 3 | 2 | 2 |
| Marketing . . . . . . . . . . . . | | 3 | 4 | 3 | 1 |
| Control. . . . . . . . . . . . . | | 4 | 2 | 4 | 3 |

| | To | SYNERGY FLOW | | | |
|---|---|---|---|---|---|
| | | (7)<br>A | (6)<br>B | (8)<br>C | (11)<br>D |
| From<br>A<br>(10) | R & D | | + | ++ | ++ |
| | Manufacturing | | + | + | + |
| | Marketing | | 0 | + | + |
| B<br>(8) | R & D | + | | + | + |
| | Manufacturing | + | | + | + |
| | Marketing | 0 | | + | + |
| C<br>(9) | R & D | ++ | + | | + |
| | Manufacturing | 0 | 0 | | + |
| | Marketing | + | ++ | | ++ |
| D<br>(4) | R & D | + | 0 | 0 | |
| | Manufacturing | 0 | 0 | 0 | |
| | Marketing | +· | + | + | |
| Controller | Cost acctg.<br>Mgt. info. system | +++ | +++ | +++ | +++ |
| Board of<br>management | Policy: strategy | +++ | +++ | +++ | +++ |

+++    Extremely high synergy.
++    High synergy.
+    Some synergy.
0    Little, if any, synergy.

Other plus factors not shown: CI-SA's continuing involvement in: (*a*) acquisition/search program, (*b*) external financing, (*c*) U.S. and Japanese connections.
    \* Rankings went from a top figure of 1 down to 4.

**EXHIBIT 4** (*continued*)

*Comments:*

The four companies have been selected from a group of 35 potential candidates. They have been chosen not only because of their product leadership in their home markets but also in view of the apparent high caliber of the owner managers. Aged respectively 37, 45, 47, and 50, the latter have all founded their own companies with very limited financial resources: the Belgian company about 15 years ago, although its major product line is only about five years old; the German company about 10 years ago; and the Swedish and Italian companies approximately five years ago. Three of the owner managers have advanced engineering degrees, while two of them have worked in the United States with well-known and leading electronics companies. Three of them are proficient in English, while the fourth understands that language. In addition to English and their national language, some of them speak other languages as well. One of the owner managers flies his own plane. My preliminary investigation indicates that they are self-starters and open-minded, as well as aggressive and resourceful entrepreneurs.

These companies are quite dependent on their owner managers. Such companies are usually strongest in the area where the one man has strength; and although these companies show a better than average development of supporting management, given that they are one-man shows, the loss of the owner manager would be a severe enough blow to necessitate exclusion from further negotiations. There are holes in second-line management and certainly a lack of competent successors. There is little delegation, and hence little attention has been given to formal systems in three key areas: reporting, controlling, and planning.

The German and Belgian companies have developed especially good relations and high sales to the public authorities. However, overall, the Belgian company is strongest in marketing in my tentative ranking of functional abilities. In R & D both the Swedish and the Italian companies are strong, while the German R & D effort is second only to its excellent manufacturing capabilities. The control function is rather less well developed, with only the Swedish company showing much strength. On the whole, the overall marketing function shows the inherent weaknesses expected in a technically oriented industry where manufacturing and R & D claim primary importance.

Source: CI-SA internal memorandum.

## Underlying business policy

1.  Products to have a satisfactory price-value relationship and to be designed to meet a definite and useful market need.
2.  Business to be managed in accordance with high ethical standards relative to customers, dealers, suppliers, employees, the public (thus assume full tax burden), and shareholders.
3.  Modest internal R & D to be heavily supplemented by obtaining university support, outside R & D contracts, and licensing—all to insure an adequate flow of new products, without committing a disproportionate share of total resources to R & D.
4.  The companies' interests to be interwoven firmly and irrevocably to insure that owner managers will work toward common objectives.

The working paper, while setting a goal of $100 million in sales by 1978, also included a first target of $10 million by 1970. During the staff discussions, the question arose whether this was a realistic expectation. Some staff members argued that it was too ambitious, others that it was too modest. If internationalization really were achieved, companies might be able at a maximum to duplicate their national performance in the other countries covered by project synergistics. For example, since the four-nation market served by the group was 10 times as big as the home market of the Swedish member, the latter would be able to increase its size 10 times if it could repeat its past local performance elsewhere. Even though no one at CI-SA argued this optimistically, some did feel that a member firm could achieve a market share in its partners' countries of one third to one half of its market share at home. If so, the growth rate of the merged company would clearly exceed the target set in the working paper. As a result, the question was raised whether the target was not too modest, particularly in terms of the $1 to $1.5 million which Mr. Mathysen-Gerst was planning to raise.

A further question raised about the potential growth of the merged unit was that of future balance. Should equality among the units be maintained, or should it be possible for one division to dominate the others as a result of more rapid growth? This issue was viewed as particularly relevant for as long as the last 45% of the shares was still to be distributed.

The working paper stated the organizational plans as follows:

1.  Engage a controller-treasurer to develop and implement an appropriate cost accounting system and a high-speed (EDP) management information system.
2.  Constitute a board of management, to consist of four company managers plus a controller (the latter to act in part as a lubricant to smooth management relations and in part, if necessary, as an action expediter). This board should meet (a) regularly twice a month for one day on a rotating country basis; (b) irregularly, whenever special action was required.
3.  Constitute a board of directors composed of four individual company owner managers, plus Mathysen-Gerst as *administrateur délégué*[3] until 1970, plus four outside investors.

    Note: a)   Shareholders to have right of cumulative voting (at least for the next five years).

    b)   Shareholders to elect board of directors.

    c)   Directors to elect board of management.

    d)   Owner managers to be assured of a seat on the board of directors through the cumulative voting, but not necessarily on the top board of management.
4.  In 1970, sales should have reached $10 million, the management information system should be operative, and the evolution from confederate to federate management structure should be about two-thirds completed. Action: Take over the remaining 45% of the shares, and the board of directors elect the president of the board of managers.

Several issues concerning the organization of the merged unit were raised during the staff meetings. Organizational plans had been based on the following premises: (1) that rapid growth would result in upward mobility to jobs created as they become needed, (2) that management would thus have to develop replacements, and (3) that the company would as a result find it easier to attract capable manpower. However, would it be possible for successful entrepreneurs to grow into skillful general managers? Would previously independent owners be able to work with and take advantage of a controller? And would the collegial

---

[3] Member of the board of directors and president of board of management.

management setup work? Also, was the assumption on the development of a chief executive a sound one, namely, that he would emerge through the process of natural selection? The fear was expressed that healthy motivation might degenerate into destructive competition. Also, would it be possible for the four one-man shows to make the transition to a divisional structure? Particularly, would it be possible for the units to organize for cooperation and coordination?

In reviewing the outlook of the merger proposal with his staff, Mr. Mathysen-Gerst stressed his enthusiasm for the merger concept but also indicated that many obstacles would have to be surmounted in its implementation. Hence he assigned a high risk of failure to the project. However, he hoped that his time input could be limited to 20 days prior to the "go/no go" decision on the project. On this basis, he felt that even if a no-go decision should result, the experience gained in working with small companies and with the various elements involved in merging European firms across their national boundaries would prove beneficial. More importantly, Mr. Mathysen-Gerst believed that meaningful economic integration in Europe would inevitably require the creation of multinational European companies. For some time he had seen a major opportunity for CI-SA in contributing to this development. During the last few years he had been deeply involved in several attempts to merge major and well-known European companies from different countries. On the basis of this experience, Mr. Mathysen-Gerst was very much aware of the numerous obstacles. One seemingly insurmountable hurdle had been the difficulty of changing the national scope and outlook of large, well-established, tradition-bound organizations. In view of these difficulties, he was anxious to explore the potential of merging small, dynamic companies across national boundaries—companies whose organizational structure and physical facilities were still evolving. If this merger concept were to prove promising, Mr. Mathysen-Gerst envisaged that CI-SA's activities could be broadened to include merger assistance to smaller companies in capitalizing on the business opportunities provided by European economic integration.

# CASES FOR PART II

## The general manager as organization builder

# GENERAL MANAGEMENT IN THE
# FUNCTIONAL ORGANIZATION

## *Vlasic Foods Inc.*

VLASIC FOODS INC. processed and marketed a broad line of pickles supplemented by relishes, peppers, sauerkraut, and related items. Sales had grown rapidly from $1.7 million in 1962 to over $20 million in 1969, and profits had increased accordingly. Despite the fact that Vlasic products in 1970 were available to only about 50% of U.S. consumers, management maintained that the company had at least as large a market share in the industry as its giant competition, the H. J. Heinz Co.

The success of Vlasic Foods had increased considerably the value of the 49% interest in the company owned by Vlasic & Co., a family partnership through which Robert Vlasic, 44, kept track of a number of enterprises from his three-room suite in the Fisher Building in Detroit. Mr. Vlasic, also chairman of the board of Vlasic Foods, was instrumental in the formation of corporate policy for the company, particularly in the areas of financing, capital investment, management controls, and executive compensation. While maintaining an intensive awareness of operating results, he had encouraged his senior managers to assume the tasks of market planning and day-to-day administration. His charge to Russell Post, president of Vlasic Foods, was simply, "to grow as fast as you want, as long as you keep that 5% [net income to net sales] on the bottom line."

In August 1970 Mr. Vlasic was attempting to anticipate the consequences of continued growth. The latest plan, based on the assumption that manufacturing capacity and financing would not be limiting factors, indicated sales of over $55 million in existing product lines by 1974–75, as shown in the following table:

|  | 1970–71 | 1971–72 | 1972–73 | 1973–74 | 1974–75 |
|---|---|---|---|---|---|
| Case production (thousands) . . . . . . . | 6,700 | 8,040 | 9,648 | 11,580 | 13,900 |
| Dollar sales (net) (thousands) . . . . . . . | $26,700 | $32,000 | $38,400 | $46,100 | $55,500 |

Mr. Vlasic commented on the implications of the plan:

The numbers may seem unrealistic except that each time we draw up a plan, Russ Post and Al Dubin[1] come in with what seems like an unattainable forecast and then exceed it. I have just put together a report comparing our actual sales with those forecast in earlier five-year plans. In each case the volume estimated for a particular year increased as the year approached and still proved conservative. Assuming we are able to produce revenues of $55 million and finance it somehow, I am sure that managing a company of that size will be considerably different than it is for the one we have today. We are running very hard—I don't want us to stumble.

## THE PICKLE INDUSTRY

Pickles were among the most popular vegetables in the United States. According to Pickle Packers International (PPI), the industry's trade association, pickles had passed corn, peas, snap beans, whole tomatoes, and vegetable juices in per-capita consumption from 1954 to 1967 and enjoyed a growth rate considerably higher than canned fruits and vegetables as a whole (see Exhibit 1). Some feeling for the magnitude of this growth is provided in the following table:

| Year | Consumption (tons) | Per-capita consumption (pounds) |
|---|---|---|
| 1930 . . . . . . . . | 107.7 | 2.35 |
| 1940 . . . . . . . . | 141.7 | 2.88 |
| 1950 . . . . . . . . | 261.2 | 4.62 |
| 1960 . . . . . . . . | 347.6 | 5.19 |
| 1968 . . . . . . . . | 542.5 | 7.16 |

Source: U.S. Department of Agriculture, Statistical Reporting Source.

Placing a value on this consumption was difficult because aggregate

[1] Treasurer and former president of Vlasic Foods.

statistics were not available on manufacturers' or retailers' sales. However, PPI published the following estimate for chain stores:

| | Tons | Retail sales (millions) | Average margin | Wholesale sales* (millions) |
|---|---|---|---|---|
| Pickles . . . . . . . . . . . . | 114.5 | $168.2 | 24.7% | $126.2 |
| Pickle specialties† . . . . . . | 81.0 | 67.4 | 26.7 | 49.4 |
| Total . . . . . . . . . . . | 195.5 | $235.6 | 25.3% | $175.6 |

\* Derived.
† Includes relish, peppers, pimentos.

**EXHIBIT 1**
**Growth trends of pickles, vegetables, and fruit**

| | 1952-54 average | 1969 | Percent change |
|---|---|---|---|
| Pickles, U.S. consumption . . . . . | 590 | 1,108 | 87.8 |
| Canned vegetables . . . . . . . . | 6,660 | 9,259 | 39.0 |
| Canned fruit . . . . . . . . . . . . | 3,300 | 5,023 | 52.2 |

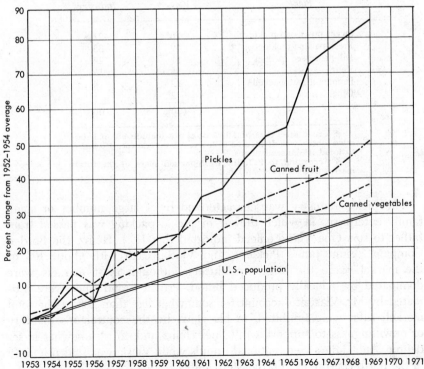

Benchmark data: Consumption, millions of pounds.
Source: U.S. Department of Agriculture.

Vlasic management estimated that total wholesale sales approximated $250 million.

Pickle products were divided into two broad categories, processed and fresh-packed. Processed pickles were manufactured by first fermenting the fresh cucumber in large open vats of brine for up to six months until they were completely cured. This brine-cured pickle was then further processed by desalting and adding sweet or dill liquors and spices to obtain the desired varieties. Additional products were obtained by cutting the cured pickles into various shapes, chopping them up to make relish, or adding other processed vegetables such as cauliflower, onions, and peppers.

Fresh-packed pickles were processed by bottling the fresh, green cucumber with sweet or dill liquor and pasteurizing. The result was a milder pickle, the most common being "bread and butter" sweet pickles and kosher-style dills. The market share accounted for by fresh-packed pickles had grown substantially during the 1960s. Vlasic had been one of the leaders in popularizing this product segment and continued to rely on it for over 50% of sales.

**Percentage of sales (1969–70)**

| Pickle | Vlasic* | Industry |
|---|---|---|
| Sweet processed pickles . . . . . . | 10% | 21% |
| Fresh-packed pickles† . . . . . . . | 49 | 35 |
| Dill-processed pickles . . . . . . . | 11 | 24 |
| Relish . . . . . . . . . . . . . . . | 16 | 15 |
| Peppers (fresh-packed) . . . . . . | 12 | 4 |
| Other . . . . . . . . . . . . . . . . | 2 | 1 |
| | 100% | 100% |

\* Vlasic sales base of 100% does not include 9% of total sales which was divided as follows: 4% sauerkraut, 4% institutional, 1% miscellaneous.

† According to PPI, the fresh-packed share of the total market had been 19% in 1966.

The pickle industry was characterized by a large number of small family enterprises in which the art of pickle packing was passed from father to son. One Vlasic official indicated that H. J. Heinz, the Borden Company (Aunt Jane's Pickles), and Vlasic, each with about 10% of the market, were the largest producers, although most markets were dominated by a locally produced brand. Private-brand sales were estimated by Mr. Vlasic to account for somewhat less than 20% of the total market; sales were inhibited, in his view, by the contractor's inability or unwillingness to support a full line. Heinz and, to a somewhat lesser degree, Aunt Jane's were national brands while Vlasic was sold primarily in the north-central and northeastern states.

Several larger food-processing companies, including Libby, McNeill & Libby, Stokely, and Consolidated Foods, had been attracted to the industry but had later withdrawn. Mr. Vernon Filek of PPI provided one view of what had happened:

Some large companies tried to let people with experience in other areas manage their pickle operations. These people did not understand the problems of pickle manufacturing and often got a bad product. In some instances when a pickle company was acquired, the experienced pickle packers would clash with "corporate" management procedures and resign.

## VLASIC FOODS

### History

In 1922 Joseph Vlasic, Robert Vlasic's father, started a milk distribution business in Detroit. As the business grew, eventually becoming the largest in Michigan, the elder Vlasic found that his rapport with store owners afforded an opportunity to form a new business, Vlasic Foods, to distribute other food products. Then, in 1937, he was approached by a man who wanted the company to distribute his new "home style" fresh-packed pickles. Joseph Vlasic agreed to buy and market the pickles but only if he could control the brand name. The first Vlasic pickles were directed at the Polish community in Detroit and, in fact, the first label was written entirely in Polish.

For many years, Vlasic bought all its pickles from independent packers. However, as the business grew, it became difficult to find larger quality packers willing to pack for a private label. Moreover, it was felt a "showplace" plant was needed to convince customers that Vlasic was indeed a pickle company. For these reasons, Robert Vlasic acquired a small pickle company in Imlay City near Detroit in 1958. Unfortunately, it turned out that most of the facilities were designed for making sauerkraut instead of pickles and in large part had to be rebuilt. In 1962 Albert Dubin, one of Joseph Vlasic's first employees and later a 25% owner in each of the Vlasic enterprises, was put in charge of the pickle venture. Mr. Dubin recalled, "We learned the pickle-packing business the hard way. Those first few years were very costly."

In 1960 Russell Post was transferred from the distribution company to become sales manager. Robert Vlasic attributed most of the subsequent success of the company to the Dubin-Post team: "Russ Post is a good salesman. He and Al Dubin have worked very well together. Russ would use almost any amount of promotion to get a sale, while Al watches expenses and costs like a hawk."

## Acquisitions

In 1965 Vlasic acquired the Crown Foods Company, a Detroit pickle company somewhat smaller than Vlasic, having a branded product, two plants, and three managers who had grown up in the pickle industry. The acquisition was made for stock, and the Raznick brothers, Fred, Herman, and Maurice, joined Vlasic as vice presidents.[2]

In 1968 Vlasic acquired the Shupak Pickle Company in Philadelphia, also for stock, to secure a marketing foothold in the East. In the next two years, the Shupak label was discontinued and a substantial portion of the manufacturing facilities were abandoned because of their inherent inefficiency. In 1970 Vlasic invested $700,000 in a new manufacturing facility to process deli-style kosher dills in Philadelphia and the old plant was sold. Two managers were added with the Shupak acquisition: Jerry Shupak, 33, became a vice president with the title of eastern sales manager, and his father, Morris Shupak, who was to retire in October 1970, was made vice president in charge of the Philadelphia operation.

## Marketing

Russell Post commented on the role of marketing at Vlasic:

We are a marketing company. We are selling pickles while most of the other family-held businesses concentrate on making them. In fact, our major problem is getting enough products to sell. Vlasic isn't moving into any new markets in 1970 because existing accounts are absorbing all of our increased production.

The distribution of Vlasic pickle products had expanded gradually from Michigan primarily to the Midwest and East. Exhibit 2 shows sales by market. The company sought to be number one in the markets that it served rather than attempt to secure volume through nonintensive national distribution. Thus, company officials estimated that Vlasic had over 50% of the Michigan market, nearly 30% in Cleveland and northern Ohio, and approaching 20% in Chicago and Boston. The Vlasic product line of 73 items, almost equally divided between fresh-packed and processed varieties, was thought by management to be the broadest in the business. Mr. Post indicated how he approached new markets:

When we go into a new market, we know we'll be number one within two years. We get the best broker in town and convince him we can do it. When we first approach a customer, he usually says he needs another pickle item like a hole in the head. He can't believe that anyone would try to sell him 45 new items, let alone refuse to sell him any unless he agreed to take at least 15. But we start our marketing program and our

---

[2] Mr. Herman Raznick was killed in an automobile accident in 1969.

**EXHIBIT 2**
Vlasic's retail sales by markets

| Market | Percentage of total market for year ended June 30 | |
| --- | --- | --- |
| | *1969* | *1970* |
| Michigan . . . . . . . . . . . . . . . . . | 30.9 | 28.1 |
| Ohio and West Virginia . . . . . . . . | 21.2 | 18.6 |
| East Coast . . . . . . . . . . . . . . . | 12.4 | 14.3 |
| New England . . . . . . . . . . . . . | 7.3 | 10.0 |
| Illinois and St. Louis . . . . . . . . . | 7.8 | 9.6 |
| Pennsylvania less Philadelphia . . . . . | 5.6 | 4.9 |
| New York less New York City. . . . . | 3.8 | 4.8 |
| Indiana and Louisville . . . . . . . . . | 4.6 | 3.9 |
| South. . . . . . . . . . . . . . . . . . | 2.8 | 3.3 |
| West . . . . . . . . . . . . . . . . . . | 1.7 | 1.7 |
| Other. . . . . . . . . . . . . . . . . . | 1.9 | 0.8 |
| Total retail sales . . . . . . . . . | 100.0 | 100.0 |

Source: Vlasic sales report.

salesman keeps calling. Eventually the customer realizes it's only a matter of time before he lets us in. If he takes 15 items, we come back the next week and try to sell him 30 more. Sooner or later we will.

Vlasic was alone among pickle manufacturers in using extensive advertising promotion. Mr. Post estimated that the company spent over half a million dollars in selected markets for animated cartoon television commercials in 1970. Mr. Post maintained that pickles were essentially purchased on impulse, and consequently volume was influenced strongly by exposure both in-store and in the media. Thus, Mr. Vlasic in 1966 commissioned a prominent designer for a substantial fee to rework the company's labeling and packaging designs. On the other hand, Vlasic rarely engaged in competition through price reductions.

**Distribution**

After retail accounts had purchased Vlasic products, considerable effort was devoted to enlarging the shelf space devoted to them. Mr. Post commented on the nature of the competition at this level:

A chain store typically carries only two lines of pickles and relishes. Since six key items may account for 30% of sales, the chain account may carry a narrow private-brand line. In any event, we are normally in the position of replacing a smaller line with ours, which is much broader and therefore requires more shelf space. Obtaining the additional shelf space is most difficult. Sometimes our people have to rearrange an entire grocery aisle to pick up a few more feet for pickles. But we are absolutely convinced that attractive shelf displays supplemented by special floor displays will generate additional sales without retail price reductions.

In addition to their regional sales managers, Vlasic had a staff of detail men who worked with retailers arranging for displays, checking on product rotation, and training the food broker's salesmen. The broker's men actually serviced the customer by taking the weekly order and following up on shipments, etc., but the Vlasic man was held responsible for getting the items authorized by the retail account and supervising the market's development.

### Entry into New England

Vlasic's success in entering the New England market in 1968 provided an illustration of this marketing philosophy in action. Mr. Jerry Souza of Food Enterprises, the brokerage company selected by Vlasic, commented:

The pickle market in New England in 1968 was asleep. One reason was that pickles had been price imaged. When one chain in an area price images an item, the others are forced to follow. As a result of this heavy price competition, very little profit was being made on pickles in New England. The market was dominated by one local company with 45%; Heinz had 14%; and two others had about 20% between them, with the rest scattered.

The dominant company didn't advertise or offer promotions to the retailers. Heinz had spotty distribution in the area. There was general dissatisfaction with pickle marketing among retailers. Prices were low; lines were small; there were no promotion or advertising campaigns. Pickles were drab, unexciting products.

We and Vlasic offered the retailers a whole new concept, a completely new approach to their pickle departments. We gave them the opportunity to get away from image pricing. Vlasic offered the same cost per case but a higher suggested retail price. Vlasic had a good product and a wider line with well-designed packaging. It was also willing to promote and advertise. We weren't selling pickle items, we were selling an entirely new pickle department.

By August 1970 Vlasic's market share had grown to 18% and Mr. Souza was confident he would be representing the number one pickle company by the end of the year. He emphasized that the support he got from the company would keep market share.

The people at Vlasic really keep the pressure on. Russ Post accepts nothing but exceptional performance. He is also prepared to move a lot more quickly than his competition. We get a very fast response to changes in local conditions.

# Farm and field

Each year the farm and field department, supervised by Mr. Leo Jokel, a veteran of 22 years with the Vlasic enterprises, contracted for the cucumbers grown on thousands of acres from Florida to Michigan.[3] Cucumbers in one location tended to mature at the same time. By purchasing over a large geographical area, Mr. Jokel was able to even out the flow of produce to the processing plants. The shortage of processing capacity and the emphasis on fresh-packed pickles increased the importance of cucumber procurement policies considerably. The matter was further complicated by uncertainties surrounding the total acres planted in the nation, the yield per acre under contract to Vlasic, and, of course, the price. To encourage loyalty during years when cucumbers were in short supply, Vlasic at times bought produce above the quantities agreed upon when yields were higher than anticipated. For 1971, Mr. Jokel intended to extend his purchases into Alabama to fill in the gap between the harvests in Florida and North Carolina.

In the South, Vlasic contracted with individual farmers for a specified acreage of cucumbers which was typically related to the amount of picking labor (e.g., the size of his family) that the farmer had available. Virtually all produce from the South was handpicked, and Vlasic supplied the seed. Farmers brought the cucumbers daily to receiving stations (Vlasic had 42 in North Carolina) and received payment; in fact, two checks were often made out because many farmers were sharecroppers who divided the proceeds with the landowner.

In Michigan and Ohio, Vlasic traditionally contracted with large growers to plant and harvest the crop. Until recently the company had supplied migrant laborers to pick the harvest and maintained extensive housing facilities for them and their families. In 1969 the company decided to discontinue furnishing the labor. Instead, subcontractors were hired who, in turn, contracted for acreage and supplied their own migrant workers. These subcontractors sold their entire output to Vlasic.

The farm and field activities were on the verge of significant change because of several external forces. In the first place, the law permitting the importation of Mexican labor was allowed to expire in 1965, and by 1970 the supply of domestic migrant labor was threatened. Cesar Chavez had successfully organized the grape pickers in California and was actively engaged in organizing workers in other agricultural sectors. Also, the increasing national concern over the plight of migrant workers was beginning to find expression in the courts. In July 1970, for instance, a Michigan apple farmer was taken to court because he did not provide adequate housing.

[3] Roughly 50% of Vlasic's cucumbers came from Florida, North Carolina, and Virginia, and the other 50% from Michigan and Ohio.

Secondly, the pickle industry was beginning to use mechanical harvesters to pick the cucumber crop. Vlasic owned five harvesters which were used successfully to pick about 10% of the 1970 harvest. These machines, costing over $20,000 apiece, were more effective than any developed in past years, and Mr. Jokel planned to purchase five more for 1971. Eventually he hoped that growers would buy their own machines. Currently, other large pickle companies were thought to employ mechanical harvesters more extensively than Vlasic. Mr. Jokel estimated that 12% of the total 1970 harvest was picked by machine.

## Manufacturing

Cucumbers were trucked to the three Vlasic processing plants within hours after they were picked. Those to be fresh packed were sorted by size, washed, cut to the desired shape, and packed in glass jars with a sweet or dill liquor. In the harvest seasons, which extended from May through August, Vlasic processed all the fresh-packed pickles for the ensuing year; consequently, the plants operated two nine-hour shifts six days a week during this period. Cucumbers received in excess of packing capacity were placed in large open vats of brine to be packaged as processed pickles during the winter months when the plants operated on one shift five days per week.

The plants in Imlay City and Bridgeport, Michigan, were automated although hand labor was required to "top out" the jars by adding the last two or three pickles to each jar. The Memphis, Michigan, plant was a hand-packing operation for peppers and spear-shaped pickles which could not be packed by machine. According to Mr. Blum, vice president of manufacturing, all Vlasic plants were operating above capacity in 1970. While the Memphis plant was being expanded by about 30% for the 1971 season, he stated that it would be very difficult to expand the other plants because all available land on the existing sites had been used and the acquisition of contiguous space was doubtful. Exhibit 3 provides production figures for each location.

Vlasic hired women and high school students during the fresh-pack season to complement a cadre of permanent employees. Since working in a pickle plant required very little skill, wage rates were much lower than for jobs in other Detroit industries. As a result, the company experienced difficulty finding labor when employment levels in the area were high. In addition, working conditions were at times arduous.

The plants were located in three small towns near Detroit. It was possible for Mr. Blum to visit each of them in a day if he devoted about half the time to driving. Some feeling for the pace and style of the plant managers is provided in the description of a visit with one of them recounted in the Appendix.

# EXHIBIT 3

## VLASIC FOODS INC.
### Summary Financial and Production Statistics

| | | | | | Twelve months ended | | | | |
|---|---|---|---|---|---|---|---|---|---|
| | 6/30/62 | 6/30/63 | 6/30/64 | 6/30/65 | 3/30/66* | 3/30/67 | 3/30/68 | 3/30/69 | 3/30/70 |
| Net sales (thousands) | $1,739 | $2,657 | $3,802 | $5,170 | $5,602 | $9,801 | $12,724 | $17,186 | $20,992 |
| Net income (thousands) | 63 | 104 | 155 | 266 | 332 | 471 | 627 | 838 | 1,018† |
| Net income/net sales | 3.6% | 3.9% | 4.1% | 5.1% | 5.9% | 4.8% | 4.9% | 4.9% | 4.9% |
| Earnings per share | $.15 | $.25 | $.31 | $.40 | $.50 | $.69 | $.91 | $1.12 | $1.24 |
| Production (in thousands of cases) | | | | | | | | | |
| Imlay City | 700 | 950 | 1,270 | 1,721 | 1,213 | 1,666 | 1,851 | 2,311 | 2,627 |
| Bridgeport | | | | | 575 | 895 | 859 | 1,739 | 2,157 |
| Memphis | | | | | 341 | 522 | 594 | 633 | 974 |
| Philadelphia | | | | | | | | 296 | 115 |
| Total | 700 | 950 | 1,270 | 1,721 | 2,129 | 3,083 | 3,304 | 4,979 | 5,873 |

* Nine months only.
† After extraordinary charge of $14,000.
Source: Casewriter's summary of Vlasic Foods reports.

Pollution control was a continuing matter of concern to the industry because pickle plants generated a large amount of liquid waste from the washing and brine operations. Private sewer lines had been constructed at two of the plants to feed the waste into holding ponds, where it was treated and held until the state allowed it to be pumped into local rivers. In the past, Vlasic had received complaints from farmers near the holding ponds and had responded by placing aerators in the ponds, which successfully eliminated most of the odors.

### Robert Vlasic

Mr. Vlasic spent approximately 50% of his time on Vlasic Foods, the remainder being consumed by a number of other businesses, including a food brokerage firm, an auto leasing company, a nursing home, and real estate developments. He explained his role in these terms:

Most of the time I spend on the pickle company is devoted to personnel planning and financial matters. For instance, I have handled our relationships with the banks and have negotiated the acquisitions we've made in the past. At the moment I've assumed responsibility for building a new plant on the East Coast, and when we go public I will assume the investor relations function as well. My theory is that the operating people have a full-time job running the business. My job should be to insulate them from outside influences so that their efforts will not be diluted. I'm also probably better qualified to handle most of these functions, too. On the other hand, I don't meddle in operations and may visit the plants only two or three times a year.

Mr. Vlasic did not receive a salary nor did he maintain an office at Vlasic Foods. Instead, he collected a management fee based on a small percentage of gross operating income from this and other ventures which he used to defray the operating expenses of Vlasic & Co. However, he maintained a very close awareness of the activities of his enterprises through a control system which he had designed.

I have a rule that one—and only one—piece of paper is to be submitted weekly to me from each business [see Exhibit 4 for an example from Vlasic Foods]. I am very concerned with the reporting forms which are used; in fact, so much so that I design them all myself. I do so partially because this type of communication is critical and partially because I enjoy it. A good deal of my time is devoted to studying the information and preparing special reports which we discuss at our board meetings.[4] [Note: Mr. Vlasic had large file cabinets behind his desk from which he could immediately produce neatly typed detailed information on any aspect of the business.]

---

[4] In addition to the weekly activity reports, Mr. Vlasic received (*a*) monthly printouts of sales in cases by product, broker, and customer; (*b*) monthly summaries of sales promotions and major sales expense items; and (*c*) quarterly financial closings by subaccount.

**EXHIBIT 4**

## VLASIC FOODS INC.
### Weekly Activity Report for Week Ending 7-24-70

| SALES | $ Total | %GP |
|---|---|---|
| F.P. Pickles | 203,334 | * |
| Proc Pickles | 125,732 | * |
| Relishes | 34,004 | * |
| Peppers | 56,213 | * |
| Kraut | 13,641 | * |
| Institutional | 32,028 | * |
| Shupak | 17,313 | * |
| Government | | |
| Miscellaneous (Olives) | 627 | * |
| TOTALS | 482,892 | * |

| QTR/DATE | | |
|---|---|---|
| $ Sales | 1,903,109 | |
| Bal Proj | 3,7.96,891 | |
| Bal Weeks | 9 | |

| CASES SHIPPED | This Week | Quarter To Date |
|---|---|---|
| Imlay | 49,767 | 204,184 |
| Bridgeport | 50,572 | 191,195 |
| Philadelphia | 3,790 | 11,800 |
| Storage | 2,997 | 14,191 |
| TOTALS | 107,126 | 421,370 |

| | PLANTS | Bridgeport | Imlay | Memphis | Phil. | Total |
|---|---|---|---|---|---|---|
| PRODUCTION THIS WEEK | $ Value | 354,480 | 393,036 | 366,098 | 16,278 | 1,129,892 |
| | Cases | 73,202 | 91,019 | 74,832 | 2,332 | 241,385 |
| PRODUCTION QUARTER TO DATE | $ Value | 1,824,775 | 1,966,777 | 1,388,033 | 59,565 | 5,239,150 |
| | Bal Proj | 3,225,225 | 3,283,223 | 2,206,967 | 115,435 | 8,830,850 |
| | Cases | 390,627 | 435,618 | 268,950 | 8,302 | 1,103,497 |
| | Bal Proj | 709,373 | 764,382 | 561,050 | 21,698 | 2,056,503 |
| LABOR THIS WEEK | $ Actual | 9,572 | 12,308 | 39,424 | 2,432 | 63,736 |
| | Standard | 14,006 | 13,482 | 40,266 | 1,153 | 68,907 |
| | FAV (UN) | 4,434 | 1,174 | 842 | (1,279) | 5,171 |
| PACKING QTR/DATE | $ Actual | 58,820 | 58,738 | 123,430 | 6,757 | 247,745 |
| | Standard | 67,363 | 67,489 | 146,659 | 4,146 | 285,657 |
| | FAV (UN) | 8,543 | 8,751 | 23,229 | (2,611) | 37,912 |

| EMPLOYEES | Admin | Sales | F&F | Bridg | Imlay | Memp | Shupak | Total |
|---|---|---|---|---|---|---|---|---|
| Number | 53 | 18 | 21 | 295 | 314 | 634 | 34 | 1,369 |
| Reg. Hrs | | | 742 | 9,732 | 10,462 | 23,659 | 1,676 | 46,271 |
| O.T. Hrs | | | 3 | 368 | 488 | 653 | 145 | 1,657 |

\* Data withheld by company.
Source: Robert Vlasic.

Major policy decisions were made by the executive committee, composed of Messrs. Vlasic, Post, and Dubin, which met twice a month in Mr. Vlasic's offices. The agenda for one meeting in July, designed and distributed by Mr. Vlasic, is shown below:

| *Agenda* | *Comment\** |
|---|---|
| 1. Acquisition possibility | Mr. Vlasic indicated reasons for deciding against buying a particular pickle company on the East Coast |
| 2. Pollution control | Discussion of a consultant's proposal to study pollution problems for the company |
| 3. Capital expenditures | Discussion of requests for 1970–71 |
| 4. Accounting format changes | Mr. Vlasic presented plans for increasing the clarity of financial data presentation |
| 5. New corporate image | Presentation by Mr. Vlasic of the design for a new corporate logo |
| 6. Case sales by market | Review of sales for June |

\* Provided by Mr. Vlasic and corroborated by Messrs. Post and Dubin.

Mr. Vlasic had also devised a formal planning system for the company. Each manager made detailed one- and five-year projections which were summarized to provide a financial forecast for Vlasic Foods. The projections were submitted to Mr. Vlasic, who approved or returned them after careful study. The first-year figures were revised quarterly, and those for subsequent years annually. Historically, sales estimates had always been low, although Mr. Vlasic commented: "In the beginning I was always adjusting their sights upwards, trying to get them to reach. Now I find myself on the other side of the table talking about restraints and getting overextended." Financial data are provided in Exhibits 3 and 5.

### Ownership and compensation

On August 1, 1970, Vlasic & Co. owned 49% of Vlasic Foods, assuming conversion of certain debentures and exercise of stock options. The remainder of the ownership interests were spread among 23 individuals, 17 of whom were employees. Mr. Vlasic explained a policy he felt had contributed to the company's success over the years:

My father felt very strongly that a man works harder if he owns a piece of the business. Al Dubin was given the opportunity to become a very sizable stockholder for that reason. We have continued that policy in several ways.

First, our acquisitions have been for stock—the seller is encouraged to integrate his operation with ours and see his career tied to the success of Vlasic.

Second, we have given stock options to key men in management and recently have extended options to some men at supervisory levels.[5] I have developed a formula to set the option price: book value plus the earnings per share for the previous three years.[6] This is considered quite a bargain.

Although there was no ready market for Vlasic shares, Mr. Vlasic had always repurchased any shares offered at the current option price.

Compensation policy for top management was also based on a strong belief in incentives. Mr. Vlasic summed it up by saying, "We have a philosophy that it's best to pay a man a modest salary and give him the rest in bonus if he and the company both perform well." Although bonus determination was theoretically one of the tasks of the compensation committee,[7] Mr. Vlasic indicated that he made the final decision based on the internal reports and his subjective evaluation of the man's performance. While bonuses were paid each May for the prior year,

---

[5] Options had been granted to all men at the vice-presidential level, four men at the next level, and four more among the supervisors.

[6] Vlasic had a "qualified stock option plan" and as a result, provided certain conditions were met, the recipients did not realize income for tax purposes upon receipt or exercise of the option. Under one of these conditions, a qualified stock option could not be granted to an employee who held over 5% of the shares (which for Vlasic included Messrs. Dubin, Post, Blum, and the Raznick brothers).

[7] Composed of Robert Vlasic, Joseph Vlasic, and Al Dubin.

# EXHIBIT 5

## VLASIC FOODS INC.
### Balance Sheets—March 30, 1969, and March 29, 1970

| Assets | 1969 | 1970 |
|---|---|---|
| Current assets | | |
| Cash | $ 546,591 | $ 814,055 |
| Accounts receivable (less allowance for doubtful accounts of $12,764 in 1969 and $23,000 in 1970) | 1,178,243 | 1,146,997 |
| Inventories, at the lower of cost (first-in, first-out) or market | | |
| Produce | $ 953,578 | $ 1,137,268 |
| Containers and supplies | 358,247 | 336,881 |
| Finished goods | 5,588,501 | 6,875,928 |
| Total inventories | $ 6,900,326 | $ 8,350,077 |
| Prepaid expenses | 38,088 | 62,664 |
| Total current assets | $ 8,663,248 | $10,373,793 |
| Property, plant, and equipment at cost | | |
| Land and buildings | $ 366,904 | $ 604,126 |
| Machinery, equipment, and fixtures | 2,544,125 | 2,908,279 |
| Leasehold improvements | 1,277,489 | 1,357,249 |
| Total property, plant, and equipment | $ 4,188,518 | $ 4,869,654 |
| Less: Reserves for depreciation and amortization | 2,309,592 | 2,715,754 |
| Net property | $ 1,878,926 | $ 2,153,900 |
| Other assets | 80,300 | 47,800 |
| Total assets | $10,622,474 | $12,575,493 |

| Liabilities | 1969 | 1970 |
|---|---|---|
| Current liabilities | | |
| Unsecured notes payable to bank | $ 975,000 | $ 2,000,000 |
| Current portion of long-term debt | 304,867 | 315,752 |
| Accounts payable | 1,266,255 | 1,243,514 |
| Accrued liabilities | 478,262 | 438,200 |
| Accrued income taxes | 390,892 | 306,874 |
| Total current liabilities | $ 3,415,276 | $ 4,304,340 |
| Long-term debt, less current portion included above | 2,948,500 | 3,171,508 |
| Shareholders' equity | | |
| Common stock, $1 par value; authorized 800,000 shares in 1969 and 1,000,000 in 1970; outstanding, 735,000 shares in 1969 and 719,000 shares in 1970* | $ 735,000 | $ 719,000 |
| Paid-in surplus | 271,550 | 110,450 |
| Retained earnings* | 3,252,148 | 4,270,195 |
| Total shareholders' equity | $ 4,258,698 | $ 5,099,645 |
| Total liabilities | $10,622,474 | $12,575,493 |

* Difference accounted for by the redemption of 30,000 shares for $254,700 and the exercise of options for 14,000 shares at various prices aggregating $77,600.

the managers were given some feeling for what they would be if the profit projections for the year were attained. Mr. Vlasic had concluded in 1968 that the percentage of total compensation for top management paid in cash bonuses ought to be cut back, salaries increased, and a formal profit-sharing plan introduced for all nonunion employees. In 1969, 6% of employee earnings were contributed to the profit-sharing fund, and it was hoped that eventually this percentage could be increased to 10%. Nonetheless, for the seven top-paid managers (Post, Dubin, Blum, Jerry Shupak, Maurice and Fred Raznick, and Jokel), the bonuses were substantial in relation to salary and, in Mr. Vlasic's judgment, were likely to remain an important part of the compensation package for senior management.

| Year | Compensation index | Percentage of compensation | | | |
|---|---|---|---|---|---|
| | | Salary | Bonus | PSF | Total |
| Top seven managers | | | | | |
| 1968 . . . . . . . . . . . | 100 | 53 | 47 | .. | 100 |
| 1969 . . . . . . . . . . . | 112 | 52 | 45 | 3 | 100 |
| 1970 . . . . . . . . . . . | 115 | 59 | 35 | 6 | 100 |
| Three middle managers* | | | | | |
| 1968 . . . . . . . . . . . | 100 | 83 | 17 | .. | 100 |
| 1969 . . . . . . . . . . . | 110 | 80 | 16 | 4 | 100 |
| 1970 . . . . . . . . . . . | 123 | 82 | 13 | 5 | 100 |

* A regional sales manager, the institutional sales manager, and a farm and field supervisor. In 1968 the average compensation of these men was 40% that of the top seven managers.

## Organization

The formal organization structure and assignment of responsibilities was a subject of continuing discussion at Vlasic. Each time a modification was made or a new man added, the organization chart was carefully redesigned by Mr. Vlasic to incorporate the change. The most recent chart of May 1970, reproduced in Exhibit 6, was drawn up when Russell Post assumed the presidency. Mr. Vlasic commented on this event:

Al Dubin has worked terrifically hard over the past 40-odd years and is now a wealthy man. He has talked about retiring several times to enjoy the fruits of his labor and I wouldn't be surprised if he does in a couple of years. Russell has agreed to become president and assume responsibility for manufacturing, which had previously reported to Dubin. Al is continuing to look after the control function and farm and field, though in time he may relinquish the latter as well.

When Mr. Post moved up to president, Ed VerLee was made national sales manager with the entire field sales force reporting to him, including

**EXHIBIT 6**

VLASIC FOODS INC.
Organization Chart
May 1970

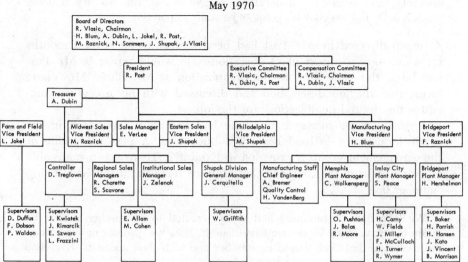

Maurice Raznick and Jerry Shupak, both vice presidents. Mr. Post retained control over marketing policy and the allocation of advertising and promotion funds. He was currently considering the addition of a high-level staff man to assist him with the merchandising function.

The three processing plants in Michigan reported to Herman Blum.[8] He described his job as follows:

> Pickle packing is a tough business, especially when you are continually pushed by sales for more production than the plants are supposed to be able to deliver. We pack over half of our annual production in four months, which means a lot of 18-hour days during the summer for our supervisors and plant managers. We have a pretty tired lot by August. A good deal of my time is devoted to touring plants, listening to problems, and helping the plant managers break bottlenecks. Meeting the production quotas is of utmost importance in the fresh-pack season because volume lost can't be regained.
>
> Developing managers is an important part of what I do. Vlasic has a more conscientious crew than any of its competitors. We've been able to hire people who are willing to get their hands dirty and work long hours. I tell them that's what it is going to be like and that we expect it. Our top management sets a good example and everyone else follows.

Mr. Blum, however, was soon to assume a new position in the company. He continued:

---

[8] At present the small deli-pickle operation in Philadelphia was directed by a general manager responsible directly to Russell Post.

Bob Vlasic has suggested that I relinquish responsibility for production and plant operations. I would keep manufacturing processes and layout, quality assurance, and research and development. No one in the industry is doing much R & D, and someday it's going to be really important.

A search directed by Mr. Post had been underway for several months for a manager to direct plant operations. He would report to Mr. Post and be at the same level in the organization as Mr. Blum. Mr. Vlasic formulated the job description and discussed with his executive committee the desired qualifications for the job.

Virtually every manager at Vlasic had had long experience in the pickle industry or in food brokerage businesses. A personal profile of the management group is provided in Exhibit 7. There was a noticeable esprit de corps in the company that Maurice Raznick attributed to being "number one":

We [the Raznick brothers] had always wanted to be number one in the pickle industry. With Vlasic, we have done it. Now we give our new salesmen the challenge that they should be number one with their accounts. Everyone here is committed to being the best.

### Expansion

To fulfill the sales forecasts for the next several years, Vlasic was confronted with a need for considerable additional capacity. For a variety of reasons, particularly proximity to markets and growing areas, it was best to locate plants in different parts of the country. The Vlasic plan called for a plant in the East immediately and another in the West within five years. Mr. Vlasic described the situation as follows:

We have been looking for a company to buy on the East Coast for a year now; the ideal candidate would have a good physical plant with poor brand identification and low profits. I don't suppose we would be willing to pay for a really profitable company unless it had surplus production capacity, because that is what we are looking for. An acquisition hasn't worked out, so I'm now searching for a plant site.

The cost of this first plant was estimated at $3.5 to $4 million, and two years were thought to be necessary to have it on line at full capacity (3 million cases), during which time it would probably sustain losses.

Financing the coming expansion created certain difficulties. All the existing facilities were owned by Vlasic & Co. and Mr. Dubin and leased to Vlasic Foods. The money for this purpose had been raised through the sale of other Vlasic companies, notably the milk and food distribution businesses. Now, as Mr. Vlasic put it, "There is no more money in the barrel." His tentative plan called for a bond issue to finance the

**EXHIBIT 7**

VLASIC FOODS INC.
Management Profile

| Executive | Position | Years with Vlasic* | Age | Previous experience | Education |
|---|---|---|---|---|---|
| R. Vlasic | Chairman | | 44 | . . . | B.S. industrial engineering |
| R. Post | President | 13 | 46 | Family-owned distribution business bought by Vlasic | B.A. economics |
| A. Dubin | Treasurer | 42 | 57 | . . . | B.A. accounting |
| H. Blum | V.P. manufacturing | 11 | 51 | Manager pickle plants since 1946 | M.S. biochemistry |
| L. Jokel | V.P. farm and field | 22 | 53 | 30 years in food business in various capacities | High school |
| M. Raznick | V.P. midwest sales | 5 | 60 | Family-owned pickle co. acquired by Vlasic | High school |
| E. VerLee | Sales manager | 6 | 41 | Food brokerage co.; wholesale grocery co. | 2 years college |
| J. Shupak | V.P. eastern sales | 2 | 35 | Family-owned pickle co. acquired by Vlasic | BBA |
| M. Shupak | V.P. Philadelphia | 2 | 58 | Family-owned pickle co. acquired by Vlasic | n.a. |
| F. Raznick | V.P. Bridgeport | 5 | 48 | Family-owned pickle co. acquired by Vlasic | n.a. |
| D. Treglown | Controller | 7 | 34 | CPA firm | BBA |
| R. Charette | Regional sales manager | 5 | 42 | Came to Vlasic with acquired Crown Co. | 1 year college |
| S. Scavone | Regional sales manager | 2 | 34 | Food brokerage co. | 1 year college |
| J. Zelenak | Inst. sales manager | 16 | 44 | Retail and institutional distribution co. | 1 year college |
| J. Cerquitella | Shupak division general manager | 1 | 40 | 13 years, food distribution companies | BBA |
| A. Bremer | Chief engineer | 2 | 58 | Plant engineer for large pickle co. 20 years | High school |
| H. VandenBerg | Quality control | 2 | 56 | 20 years in pickle bus. | B.S. education |
| K. Wolkensperg | Plant manager | 1 | 30 | Experience with another pickle company | 3 years college in chemistry |
| S. Peace | Plant manager | 8 | 44 | 15 years in pickle plants | High school |
| H. Hershelman | Plant manager | 3 | 43 | 20 years in pickle plants | High school |

* Years with Vlasic includes time with any Vlasic business.
n.a. = not available.
Source: Casewriter's notes.

new plant, with the possibility at some point in the future of a public offering of Vlasic stock.

The organizational consequences of expansion were also of concern to the management group. Combined with the new roles in prospect for Russ Post and Herman Blum, they posed the need for additional operating managers and possibly a new organization structure. Already Mr. Post was devoting a portion of his time to traveling to and from Philadelphia in an effort to improve the performance of the new deli plant there (see Exhibit 4).

Mr. Vlasic had also begun to consider major changes in the function and composition of the board of directors, which currently was composed of:

| | |
|---|---|
| Robert Vlasic | Chairman |
| Russell Post | President |
| Albert Dubin | Treasurer |
| Herman Blum | Vice president, manufacturing |
| Leo Jokel | Vice president, farm and field |
| Maurice Raznick | Vice president, midwest sales |
| Jerry Shupak | Vice president, eastern sales |
| Norman Sommers | Attorney |
| Joseph Vlasic | Director |

Meetings, held quarterly, had served as occasions to discuss operating results and had been viewed by the line managers as an indication of their success in business. Though he recognized it would not be received favorably, Mr. Vlasic was disposed to replace the four vice presidents with outside directors who would be in a position to offer advice and counsel on the problems likely to confront the company in the future.

## APPENDIX
## VISIT WITH A PLANT MANAGER

In July 1970 the researcher visited the hand-packing plant in Memphis, Michigan, with Herman Blum, vice president of manufacturing, on one of his frequent field trips.[9] The two men passed through the front office, occupied by five girls who were busy with payroll and other clerical tasks, to another office opening out into the packing area. There they were greeted by the plant manager, Mr. K. A. Wolkensperg, dressed in a sports shirt, who had just walked in from the plant.

After the researcher had been introduced, Mr. Blum and Mr. Wolkensperg discussed production quotas and operating problems for several minutes. Mr. Wolkensperg indicated that one of his problems

---

[9] Mr. Blum visited the plants about three times a week during the fresh-pack season.

had been a shortage of labor. The conversation was concluded when Mr. Blum said that he would pay a visit that afternoon to the employment agency in [the largest neighboring town about 20 miles away] to see what could be done. Mr. Wolkensperg then offered to show the researcher the plant, commenting as they left the office:

Packing pickles is a hard business. Our people work long hours, and the jobs aren't too pleasant. But we are here to get pickles packed—not to be sociologists. We aren't like a big operation, such as General Foods which has to have a nurse in every plant. Things happen very fast during the harvest season, and we have to be able to make quick decisions. We couldn't function with a big corporate bureaucracy which had to approve every decision. I don't get to the main offices much. Most of my time is spent out here on the floor.

The work force, largely women, were returning from a coffee break, and the floor supervisors were shouting for them to come along. Mr. Wolkensperg picked up a pickle that the researcher almost stepped on and took it over to one of the cleanup crew, cautioning him to be more careful. Passing by a cucumber cutter, he told the operators to keep the chatter to a minimum. A few seconds later, a supervisor hurried up to say that one of the processing machines had broken down. Evidently Mr. Wolkensperg had pieced it together earlier with "scotch tape and bailing wire." With the assistance of a maintenance man, he proceeded to get it started again. No sooner had this been finished than several yards away one of the labeling machines jammed and bottles began to pile up in front of the machine. Mr. Wolkensperg turned his attention to this new situation, offering advice to the lead operator which resulted in a solution to the problem.

As the three men returned to the office, Mr. Wolkensperg observed:

We don't have time to overhaul our machines now. That will have to wait until fall. My job is to keep this place moving without sacrificing quality. What you've just seen is pretty typical. It would sure help if we had some more good people in the plant, though.

Walking back through the parking lot, Mr. Blum expressed his satisfaction with the way the Memphis plant was being managed. Although Mr. Wolkensperg had been with Vlasic for only a year, Mr. Blum indicated that he was viewed as "a comer" in the organization.

# *Vappi & Company Inc.*

I SUPPOSE a consultant would consider our organization[1] a little weird in that each project has essentially two bosses—the project manager and the superintendent. In practice, I think that this arrangement may result in better decisions; there are two inputs instead of one. It is hard for just one person to consider all the factors; with two, there are more ideas and more possibilities. In this business, there are many ways of getting something done, and having two heads thinking about it seems better than one.

On the other hand, I suppose having one man in charge would give more control on project costs and schedules. There are occasional conflicts, but I think, in general, that the man in whose area of competence the crux of the decisions lies tends to take the dominant role in the decision-making process. For example, if it's a problem concerning the architect, the project manager's opinion is likely to prevail. If the problem concerns the work force, the superintendent's opinion is most important. The nature of the problem determines who is most influential. My vice presidents work well together. Each defers to the other's special area of competence. They complement each other. I think their personalities are the key to this structure.

Vincent Vappi, president of the Vappi construction company, was explaining his firm's organization in 1970. Each project was managed by both a superintendent and a project manager. These men reported to different superiors who, in turn, reported to Vappi. Under this arrangement the firm had grown from $10 million in sales in 1962 to $40 million in 1969. (See Exhibits 2 and 3 for financial data.) Yet

---

[1] See Exhibit 1 for an organization chart.

**EXHIBIT 1**

VAPPI & COMPANY INC.
Organization Chart—June 1970

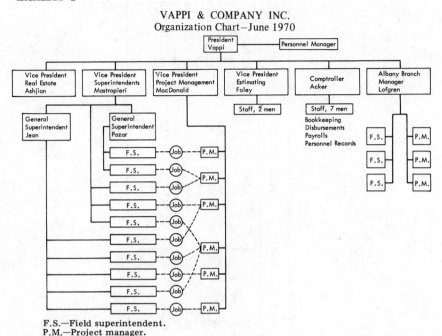

F.S.—Field superintendent.
P.M.—Project manager.

operating losses in 1969, the firm's planned entry into the real estate business, and the recent loss of three out of eight project managers[2] raised some questions as to the structure's future viability.

## VINCENT VAPPI

The article was titled "How to make a million: three American success stories," the magazine was *U.S. News & World Report* for December 15, 1969. One of the three millionaires was Vincent Vappi.

For C. Vincent Vappi, an urbane 42-year-old builder from Boston, the road to a million dollars took longer to travel. The construction firm he controls—Vappi & Company—has grown steadily, and his personal fortune, now more than 2 million dollars, has risen accordingly.

Mr. Vappi's father, a brickmason, from Italy, started the business in 1927. For many years, it was a small operation—a few warehouses, small additions to plants, subcontracting work.

By 1948, when Mr. Vappi graduated from Massachusetts Institute of Technology, the company was worth $250,000. He joined it as a field supervisor

---

[2] One project manager left for health reasons. The two others went to work in firms where they felt the opportunities were greater.

**EXHIBIT 2**
Vappi performance versus industry median

| | | 1962 | 1963 | 1964 | 1965 | 1966 | 1967 | 1968 | 1969 |
|---|---|---|---|---|---|---|---|---|---|
| Profit/billings . . . . . . . . . | Vappi | 0.6% | 0.2% | 0.6% | 1.4% | 0.4% | 0.5% | 0.05% | ( 0.7%) |
| | Industry | n.a. | 1.5 | 1.3 | 1.4 | 1.4 | 1.4 | n.a. | n.a. |
| Profit/net worth . . . . . . . . | Vappi | 8.9 | 3.0 | 8.3 | 23.6 | 8.0 | 9.0 | 1.2 | (14.0 ) |
| | Industry | n.a. | 11.5 | 8.5 | 9.7 | 12.4 | 9.9 | n.a. | n.a. |
| Profit/working capital . . . . | Vappi | 8.8 | 2.5 | 5.2 | 14.7 | 6.1 | 5.9 | 0.9 | ( 7.2 ) |
| | Industry | n.a. | 18.8 | 14.7 | 16.7 | 19.1 | 16.3 | n.a. | n.a. |
| Billing/working capital . . . . | Vappi | 14.9 | 14.0 | 8.8 | 10.0 | 14.9 | 12.2 | 17.4 | 10.7 |
| | Industry | n.a. | 12.6 | 11.1 | 11.1 | 11.5 | 12.2 | n.a. | n.a. |
| Billing/net worth . . . . . . . | Vappi | 14.8 | 15.0 | 13.8 | 16.8 | 20.0 | 22.5 | 16.5 | 24.1 |
| | Industry | n.a. | 7.8 | 6.7 | 6.7 | 9.0 | 7.3 | n.a. | n.a. |

n.a. = not available.

**EXHIBIT 3**
Vappi contract activity, 1962–70

| Year | Value of new contracts (millions) | New contracts negotiated (%) | Value of completed contracts (millions) | Value of work done during year (millions) | Net profit (loss) (after tax) (thousands) |
|---|---|---|---|---|---|
| | *Total company contract activity* | | | | |
| 1962 . . . . . . . . . | n.a. | n.a. | $ 8.5 | $10.3 | $ 61 |
| 1963 . . . . . . . . . | n.a. | n.a. | 5.4 | 13.0 | 24 |
| 1964 . . . . . . . . . | $ 19.5 | n.a. | 17.2 | 12.2 | 72 |
| 1965 . . . . . . . . | 26.8 | n.a. | 16.3 | 19.9 | 286 |
| 1966 . . . . . . . . | 26.0 | n.a. | 23.4 | 29.3 | 121 |
| 1967 . . . . . . . . | 51.0 | 21 | 26.7 | 31.7 | 153 |
| 1968 . . . . . . . . | 25.2 | 40 | 31.4 | 43.4 | 22 |
| 1969 . . . . . . . . | 110.6 | 12 | 44.2 | 37.5 | (253) |
| 1970*. . . . . . . . | 27.7 | 0 | 36.5† | n.a. | n.a. |
| | *Contract activity for Albany alone* | | | | |
| 1965 . . . . . . . . . | n.a. | 0 | $ 1.02 | | |
| 1966 . . . . . . . . | n.a. | 0 | 4.68 | | |
| 1967 . . . . . . . . | $ 6.6 | 0 | 3.15 | | |
| 1968 . . . . . . . . | 2.0 | 0 | 5.4 | | |
| 1969 . . . . . . . . | 23.8‡ | 0 | 3.6 | | |
| 1970 . . . . . . . . | 11.0‡ | 0 | n.a. | | |

*To September 15, 1970.
†Projected.
‡The Albany office had four contracts in September 1970. The two largest were with IBM, one for a $10-million building and the other for a $20-million building.
n.a. = not available.

at $90 a week. Shares in the firm his father had given him were then worth less than $20,000.

In 1952, he became a vice president at $12,000 a year, then managing vice president in 1955 at $28,000. It was then that his father first became ill, and the younger Vappi began to change the nature of the business. He explains:

"It seemed to me that universities would mushroom. So we began bidding for campus jobs. A 2.5 million dollar dormitory for Boston University came first. One project led to another.

"The key events were getting the next big job—to show we could handle bigger or more complex buildings, or do big jobs in a hurry. There was a 6-million-dollar law-education building for Boston University, then a 9-million-dollar apartment house for married students at Harvard."

Business grew in volume from 6 million dollars in 1955 to 10 million in 1962. This year, Vappi & Company will put up 40 million dollars in new construction, including hospitals, libraries, government buildings.

*A clash in viewpoints.* Along the way, Mr. Vappi's ideas conflicted with those of his father.

"His idea was to make all the decisions, and seek higher profits on fewer jobs. I wanted more volume, even if it meant less profit at first. I wanted to adopt modern-management concepts and parcel out more responsibility to others.

"When my father said, 'Give me back more management responsibility or buy me out,' I bought him out. I paid $150,000 for his interest in 1962—$5,000 down, the rest to be paid off at $12,000 a year, interest free."

That gave Mr. Vappi 55 percent of the voting stock, then worth $337,500. He also owned part of a realty trust, valued at $100,000, that he had set up with four brothers and sisters.

Late in 1965, his holdings in the building firm and realty trust passed the million-dollar mark. At last accounting, his net worth was 2.36 millions.

His present 70 percent interest in the construction company, valued at 2 million dollars, accounts for most of his assets. The realty trust, which developed an industrial park in a Boston suburb, is being liquidated this year. Mr. Vappi expects to wind up with a gain on that deal of $600,000 after taxes.

The whopping gain will make a bulge in income this year. In recent years, Mr. Vappi's earnings had run around $100,000—$81,000 in salary as president of Vappi & Company, $12,000 salary as head of the realty trust, the rest in capital gains.

But Mr. Vappi decided to cash in the realty trust this year, rather than wait, to avoid higher rates on capital gains that he expects Congress to vote.

The $600,000 of profits—"the first significant free money I have had"—are being invested in Treasury Notes, temporarily, and in stocks. "With credit tight," he says, "this is a tough time to invest in real estate. The tax-reform bill may also make real estate less attractive an investment."

If he doesn't invest in real estate, Mr. Vappi will put money in tax-free bonds as "an anchor to windward." Still, over the long run, "you have to invest in growth stocks or real estate to keep ahead of inflation and taxes.

"I don't feel like a millionaire," Mr. Vappi comments. "I feel more like a well-off member of the middle class. We live comfortably, but not like the jet set. We have a little more of everything, but our living style hasn't changed, basically, over the years."

In 1948, Mr. Vappi and his wife lived in a fourth-floor walk-up in Cambridge. Now they own two $100,000 homes—one in Milton, Mass., and a summer place along the Massachusetts shore at Marion—three cars, and a 34-foot sloop. College for a daughter and private school for another daughter and son cost up to $12,000 a year.

Mr. Vappi spends more and more of his time on community activities, as a trustee of a hospital, private school, college and an aquarium. These outside activities "keep me up with the problems of our time, and they are also a low-key way of keeping our company's name before the community."

Though day-to-day operations of the company have been turned over to others, Mr. Vappi still visits each job site. One day, while Mr. Vappi was walking through a mental-health center his firm is building, a friend said:

"Money isn't the big thing with Vince. He gets a sense of accomplishment, going around Boston and seeing the buildings he has put up, buildings that will be around long after he has gone."[3]

Vappi's goals for the construction company were to double sales by 1980. These objectives were motivated by a desire to create more positions in the management structure for bright young men—to challenge these men so that they would stay with the firm. On the other hand, he felt a balance was needed. Vappi expressed the feeling that the extraordinary rate of growth experienced by the firm in the 1960s might have overchallenged many of his personnel. Bob MacDonald, vice president of project management, commented on this point.

The field force and the project managers are very young. The company has grown so fast that many of them have questions about their ability in their present positions. The expansion was so dramatic we've been running to catch up. We've also had problems with the blacks, unions, and even the architectural firms which have been growing so fast that their plans have suffered. Recently I lost three of my eight project managers, and as a result I am heavily engaged in projects trying to pick up the slack until our new managers learn their jobs.

Having concentrated solely on growth in the past, Vappi wanted to "fine tune" his operation so that sales growth would be accompanied by a gross income of 5% of sales and a general overhead of less than 2½% of sales. (See Exhibits 2 and 3 for financial performance from 1962 to 1969.)

Vappi was also concerned about planning for orderly management succession. "I have an emotional investment in the firm, and I naturally don't want to see it disintegrate. I might leave active management of the firm fairly soon, to pursue extracurricular activities—or fairly late, to retire. The time range, therefore, is very broad." The two principal candidates for Vappi's position as president were Bob MacDonald, the vice president of project management, and Frank Mastropieri, vice president of superintendents. Both men had been with the company since the mid-1950s and had always been treated as equals. Each man was under 45 and had an excellent reputation in the industry. (See Exhibit 4 for personal data on key managers.)

## VAPPI & COMPANY INC.

Vappi & Company was considered by architects, owners, and subcontractors to be an excellent building contractor. The firm specialized in

**EXHIBIT 4**
Vappi top management

| Name | Age | Year joined Vappi | Positions at Vappi | Formal education |
|---|---|---|---|---|
| Vappi. . . . . . . . . . | 43 | 1948 | President | B.S., MIT 1948 |
| MacDonald . . . . . . | 38 | 1957 | V.P. of project management, 1962; project manager, 1957 | B.S., MIT 1953; M.B.A., HBS 1957 |
| Mastropieri . . . . . . . | 44 | 1952 | V.P. of superintendents, 1964; superintendent, 1954; engineer, 1952 | B.S., Northeastern 1946 |
| Foley. . . . . . . . . . | 50 | 1954 | V.P. of estimating, 1958; estimator, 1954 | B.S., MIT 1948 |
| Ashjian . . . . . . . . . | 38 | 1958 | V.P. of real estate, 1969; project manager, 1958 | B.S., Northeastern 1954; M.S., MIT 1958 |
| Acker. . . . . . . . . . | 55 | 1955 | Comptroller, 1955 | None |
| Lofgren . . . . . . . . | 35 | 1960 | Albany branch manager, 1965; assistant super-intendent, 1963; engineer, 1960 | n.a. |
| Jean . . . . . . . . . . | 39 | 1954 | General superintendent, 1968; superintendent, 1960; engineer, 1955 | Associate, Wentworth College 1952 |
| Pazar . . . . . . . . . . | 41 | 1953 | General superintendent, 1969; superintendent, 1955; engineer, 1953 | B.S., MIT 1954 |

n.a. = not available

nonresidential buildings and was a leader in poured concrete technology. In 1969 Vappi had $111 million in new contracts, which placed it 55th among the 400 largest contractors in the United States. During the same year, Vappi *completed* work on projects worth $40 million (see Exhibit 3).

Construction jobs were acquired in two basic ways. Using the traditional method, an owner had an architect complete all plans and specifications and then invited contractors to bid on the project. Architects thus frequently influenced the selection of the contractors. An increasingly used method of acquiring jobs in the industry involved the owner's selection of a reputable contractor in the early planning stages and inviting him to negotiate an overall cost and fee. This procedure allowed the contractor to influence significantly the design and specifications.

Upon securing a job, the general contractor immediately let subcontracts varying from 60% to 90% of the total dollar volume of construction to subcontractors in as many as 23 different trade functions. For example, Vappi was directly responsible for all concrete work (forming and pouring) and some masonry and carpentry. All other work was subcontracted.

"Subs," as they were called in the trade, were completely independent. They dealt separately with their own unions, had scheduling problems of their own, and, in general, belonged to organizations over which the general contractor had little influence or control. "Reputation" occasionally exceeded "bid price" as a determinant in selection of the "sub." Subcontracts were all fixed price, with the general contractor protected by a performance bond against subcontractor default on contract terms.

All Vappi's bids and some contract negotiations[4] were handled by John Foley and his two-man staff. Foley based his estimates on subcontractor bids as well as on an analysis of the architect's plans and an assessment of future material and labor costs. Since Vappi's average project had high architectural content, required several years to complete, involved year-round work in all weather, and was often delayed by strikes, the most difficult part of the estimating task was predicting labor productivity on the aspects of the job for which Vappi was directly responsible.

The history of the Employment Security Building contract illustrates many of the problems associated with construction projects:

| | |
|---|---|
| August 1966: | Bids solicited, plans distributed. |
| September 1966: | Vappi's bid, $11,000,000; low bid, $9,900,000. |
| November 1966: | All bids rejected, bidders invited to resubmit. |
| December 1966: | Foley estimates a cost of $11,600,000. Final Vappi bid, $10,745,000. |
| January 1967: | Vappi awarded contract. Next lowest bid, $11,100,000. LaPlante assigned as project manager, Pazar as superintendent. |
| April 1967: | Vappi's attempt to change foundation design for purpose of saving money denied. Officials felt a possibility of suits from other bidders. |
| May 1967: | Inadequate rock formation increases foundation costs and delays concrete operations. |
| August 1967: | Labor shortage in Boston area becomes acute. The most skilled craftsmen drift towards jobs paying the most overtime. Vappi hampered by inexperienced laborers. |
| June 1968: | Ironworkers strike (they place reinforcing bar inside concrete forms). Concrete work and many other trades delayed until September 15. |
| May 1969: | Carpenter workers strike. Most construction delayed three months. Pazar promoted to general superintendent. |
| January 1970: | Partial occupancy. |
| March 1970: | Full occupancy. |
| June 1970: | All work completed. (Exhibit 5 contains a photograph of the building.) |

---

[4] Foley usually made the technical estimates for negotiated contracts and either Vappi or MacDonald handled the actual negotiations with the owners and architects.

**EXHIBIT 5**
Employment Security building

The number of different projects managed by Vappi at any one time varied considerably. The average number during 1968–69 was 17. In July 1970 the company was managing 11 projects with values ranging from $1.6 million to $23 million. (See Exhibit 6 for a typical portfolio of projects.)

### A branch office

In 1964, perceiving that construction for colleges and universities in the Albany-Schenectady-Troy area might allow him to commence operations there in a manner similar to the Boston area, Vappi opened a branch office in Albany. In 1970 the office was staffed with a branch manager, three project managers, three superintendents, and an office manager. These men managed projects ranging in value from $1 million to $20 million. Except for periodic financial reports, New York operations were completely separated from those in Boston.

Of the top-management staff, only Vappi himself made regular trips to Albany. Vappi viewed branch offices as primarily an "overflow outlet" for his young, aggressive engineers who might otherwise leave the firm in search of higher positions. Vappi was not anxious to open another branch office soon. He explained: "I'd like to see this one ripen and mature; I'd like to get some confidence in them so I don't have to put out brush fires; I'd like to see them show profits before I consider another one."

**EXHIBIT 6**

## VAPPI & COMPANY INC.
### Jobs under Construction: October 1968

| | Original contract amount | Revised contract amount | Original estimate of profit | Current estimate of profit | Percent completed |
|---|---|---|---|---|---|
| B.U. instructional . . . . . | $ 5,225,000 | $ 6,986,777 | $ 96,300 | $ 275,000 | 88 |
| Maine Medical . . . . . . . | 6,647,580 | 7,644,920 | 429,774 | 365,358 | 90 |
| Rouse Co. . . . . . . . . . | 3,740,000 | 4,015,000 | 150,000 | 215,000 | 100 |
| Quincy Market, Gloucester . . . . . . . | 2,300,000 | 1,815,000 | 100,000 | 100,000 | 100 |
| Employment Security . . . . . . . . . | 10,745,000 | 11,073,397 | 400,000 | −557,032 | 48 |
| Burlington site. . . . . . . | 1,341,000 | 1,339,000 | 30,200 | − 7,000 | 100 |
| Filene's, Burlington . . . . | 1,922,009 | 1,685,103 | 65,000 | − 14,728 | 100 |
| Mental Health . . . . . . . | 10,935,400 | 10,936,484 | 1,000,000 | 12,997 | 44 |
| Sears, Burlington . . . . . | 2,046,422 | 3,693,020 | 47,492 | 47,000 | 100 |
| Paul Revere . . . . . . . . | 4,777,000 | 5,356,766 | 145,000 | − 53,000 | 85 |
| Technical Operations . . . | 834,000 | 832,000 | 47,000 | 47,000 | 100 |
| WNAC . . . . . . . . . . . | 3,594,000 | 3,658,062 | 150,000 | 150,000 | 84 |
| University Hospital . . . . | 348,800 | 348,600 | 19,000 | 25,500 | 99 |
| Gillette, Andover . . . . . | 6,695,000 | 6,806,557 | 175,000 | 245,022 | 70 |
| Quincy Market, South Bay . . . . . . . | 3,500,000 | 3,500,000 | 140,000 | 140,000 | 22 |
| Radcliffe, new house . . . | 6,227,400 | 6,227,400 | 225,000 | 255,000 | 1 |
| Gillette office . . . . . . . | 1,931,913 | 1,227,400 | 100,000 | 100,000 | 1 |
| Harvard Law . . . . . . . . | 3,547,000 | 3,547,000 | 82,500 | 100,500 | 23 |
| | $76,357,624 | $81,396,999 | $3,402,266 | $1,457,873 | |

## Real estate

In 1969 Vappi decided to reenter the real estate development business. (Between 1955 and 1962, the firm had been involved with real estate development on a small scale.) Peter Ashjian, previously a project manager, was given the position of vice president of real estate. In July 1970 Ashjian was studying real estate literature while phasing out the projects he was managing.

Vappi planned to enter joint ventures with real estate management firms to develop industrial parks and sell or lease buildings. He wanted to complete one project before starting another until his staff became more experienced. While profit margins in real estate were greater than in construction, Vappi felt that his reputation and skills as a professional, respectable community builder would be maintained best by keeping real estate to less than one third of the firm's sales.

## Organization structure

Two key individuals, having equal status and authority, supervised each project: the project manager and superintendent. The project manager officially represented Vappi to the owner and architect and was responsible for all coordination among the three of them; he purchased all materials and negotiated the subcontracts. A project manager could have from one to three projects, depending on their complexity. The superintendent supervised, directed, and coordinated all "on-site" activities, which included determination and scheduling of manpower requirements. The remainder of the company was organized to support and control these two critical jobs. (See Exhibit 1.)

As Vappi's comments at the beginning of this case indicate, one of the questions facing Vappi and his firm in 1970 was the long-term viability of this way of organizing the company's activities. Frank Mastropieri, vice president of superintendents, commented:

I've been plugging a long time for having one man in overall charge of each project. On big projects which require a full-time project manager, the project manager should be based on the job—he should have his office on site instead of at headquarters; this would allow us to appoint a "head man" who could then give the project tighter control, keep costs down, and insure schedules were met.

Manny Pazar, one of the two general superintendents, illustrated the problem:

You've got to realize that the easy decisions each will try to solve—everybody takes shots at the easy ones; the hard ones everyone shuns. I think we drop some of the important decisions because no one has been assigned to take care of them. For example, a project manager ordered the reinforcing bar for a tightly confined project, not realizing that the superintendent didn't have enough room to store it. He would have had to move it five times if it had arrived when ordered. I think these functions (project manager and superintendent) should be combined into one position. We are getting further and further apart.

It seems there is an overlap of effort due to this nondelineation of duties. It bothers me not to know what my job is—I think I'm more valuable if I know what is expected of me, where I'm going. I don't know where my authority starts and where it ends. There should be more coordination, more meeting of the minds. The project manager, the superintendent, and the general superintendent all have their place—but the overlap confuses the superintendent. The general superintendent might tell a superintendent something in the morning only to have it reversed in the afternoon by the project manager.

A project manager, however, was more optimistic than Pazar. He agreed with Vappi that the present structure provided a good system of checks and balances.

As it is now, there is a system of checks and balances. I ask the super if he has been doing this and that, and he asks me if I let this subcontract and what I included in it. Other contractors have a project manager right on the job, and that is nothing more than a glorified super.

Now I have to purchase the job and give the owner the contract. If we were under a single system, the project manager would spend a lot more time coordinating and scheduling and the super would spend more time actually supervising the job. Anyway, I am sure that working out a good personal relationship can overcome this "ball dropping" that some think can happen.

Generally the supers are the guys pushing for single responsibility. They like to run the job and are used to giving orders and having things done their own way. Supers don't have any feeling for the administrative and coordination problems, however. They don't display an awareness of the administrative aspects and they don't think in terms of protecting themselves or the owner. Supers have come up through the ranks, having worked on jobs as engineers for 10 years before being made the super of their own job.

## Compensation system

The potential coordination problems caused by the dual responsibility structure were being compounded in some people's eyes by the company's evaluation and reward system. Pazar commented:

How can they really evaluate me when they won't tell me exactly what I'm supposed to do? I was so frustrated by my lack of job description as a superintendent and not knowing who was supposed to do what, that I asked to be made a project manager. When they told me I was going to be a general superintendent instead, I agreed only on the condition that they spell out exactly what I was responsible for. It's been four months now, and they still haven't told me.

MacDonald indicated that he had no specific criteria for evaluating a project manager. He based his evaluation on how well he thought the project manager handled architect relations and the subcontractors working for him and how well he coordinated with the superintendents. Mastropieri said he gave some weight to the labor-cost variance figures but that he generally evaluated his subordinates on "how well they controlled the job," their initiative, and their ability to plan ahead and see problems coming. Although Vappi had no explicit criteria for evaluating his subordinates, he felt that his daily contact with them sufficiently enabled him to determine their compensation.

Compensation was the source of much dissatisfaction among project managers and superintendents, however. Bonuses were paid to supers at the completion of a profitable project. The size of these bonuses was determined by Vappi, Mastropieri, and MacDonald and varied according to an assessment of the quality of the work and the amount of profit realized. Bonuses were paid to project managers at the end of the calendar year if the company had made a profit. Vappi devised a rough plan under which 10% of the profit before taxes and contribution to pension and profit sharing was distributed, two thirds to the vice presidents and one third to the project managers. One project manager summarized his objection to the system: "After three years, my project showed a $100,000 profit where we planned for only $50,000. Yet the superintendent who had an unfavorable labor variance of $40,000 got a $1,500 bonus, while I got nothing because the company didn't make a profit that year." (See Exhibit 7.)

**EXHIBIT 7**
**Compensation of Vappi management**

|  | 1965 | 1966 | 1967 | 1968 | 1969 | 1970 |
|---|---|---|---|---|---|---|
| Vice presidents |  |  |  |  |  |  |
| Median salary . . . . . . . . | $20,000 | $22,000 | $23,000 | $25,000 | $28,000 | $33,000 |
| Bonuses . . . . . . . . . . . | 3,000 | 7,000 | 0 | 4,000 | 0 | * |
| Project managers |  |  |  |  |  |  |
| Median salary . . . . . . . . | 12,700 | 13,500 | 14,400 | 15,100 | 16,600 | 20,100 |
| Bonuses—High. . . . . . . . | 1,500 | 3,000 | 0 | 2,000 | 0 | * |
| Median . . . . . . | 700 | 2,500 | 0 | 1,300 | 0 | * |
| Low . . . . . . . | 0 | 2,000 | 0 | 800 | 0 | * |
| Superintendents† |  |  |  |  |  |  |
| Median salary . . . . . . . . | 10,519 | 11,799 | 12,925 | 15,127 | 17,579 | 19,630 |
| Bonuses—High . . . . . . . | 720 | 2,500 | 1,500 | 2,000 | 667 | 2,000‡ |
| Median . . . . . . | 720 | 2,500 | 715 | 1,300 | 450 | 1,750‡ |
| Low . . . . . . . | 200 | 2,500 | 500 | 750 | 333 | 1,500‡ |

\* Awarded at year-end.
†The two general superintendents were paid at the high end of the superintendents' salary range.
‡To date, September 15, 1970.

Career progression was also a cause of concern to some employees. One project manager claimed the position of project manager was a dead-end job. Having once attained that role, there was nowhere else to go. Inasmuch as the firm had young men at all levels, vacancies were likely to occur only when someone left the firm or if a branch office were to open. Some superintendents, perceiving the project manager position as a prestige job, had become project managers. One who had made the move said, however: "As project manager, I like the variety of work, the hours, and the contacts with the other project managers. But if I'd stayed as a superintendent, I could have been further along in the company and made more money."

Most members of the firm felt that Vappi's salaries were comparable to the industry averages, but many felt that because Vappi had such good people the salaries should be significantly above average. For example, MacDonald said that many project managers were capable of running their own companies and periodically received tempting offers.

# Strang Corporation

In the first week of March 1970, Michael H. Strang, 34, president of the Strang Corporation, was wondering what action he should take in light of a disturbing decline in sales that had persisted throughout January and February. Over these two months, sales of Strang products—sockets and carriers for the semiconductor industry—had been about half of what had been forecast the previous summer. The decline was particularly perplexing since Strang's sales for the first half of the fiscal year, July through December 1969, had been 101% of forecast and had set a record of $2,641,000 in spite of economic developments interpreted by some observers as the first signs of a recession in the electronics industry.

Mr. Strang was concerned whether the sales lag was likely to be temporary or lasting. Would sales pick up again in early summer after the company's customers had depleted the substantial inventories they held? Had the company overestimated the potential of its markets, or were emerging competitors stronger than the company had anticipated? These questions were of immediate concern because Mr. Strang was depending on a sixth consecutive year of rapid growth in sales and earnings to provide the basis for financing continued expansion. Furthermore, a prolonged decline in sales would necessitate cutting back recently hired technical personnel and postponing plans for the development of new products. Such actions would severely compromise Mr. Strang's growth objectives for the company.

## COMPANY HISTORY

The Strang Corporation had been founded in 1948 by Michael Strang's father, Robert H. Strang, to do consulting engineering and build special equipment for the electronics and optical industries. It was located in a suburb of Chicago. In the late 1950s and early 1960s the major product of the company was custom-engineered proprietary test equipment for electronic components manufacturers.

In the early 1960s transistor sockets that were suitable for use in Strang's test equipment were not commercially available. As a result, the company had had to design and manufacture its own sockets. Meanwhile, semiconductor users increasingly began to develop their own test equipment. As test-equipment business became harder to find, Robert Strang and his son decided to offer their sockets as a component part and thereby tap the expanding market that they had not been able to reach with customized equipment. A few test-socket[1] designs for transistors and integrated circuits were introduced and quickly accepted by the industry because of their excellent ability to withstand repeated insertions and removals.

Semiconductor manufacturers were then confronted with a related difficulty. The integrated-circuit devices, which typically had 14 or more pins, were extremely delicate to insert and handle. Therefore, the major semiconductor manufacturers developed their own carriers of a proprietary nature, hoping that they would become standard. According to Strang, the "not invented here" syndrome caused a lack of cross-fertilization. When Strang introduced a nonproprietary carrier line available to all manufacturers, it was eagerly received by users who wished to have standard means of receiving their integrated circuits. Strang, of course, also manufactured a line of test sockets which were compatible with the new carriers.

Thus Strang became virtually the sole supplier to the industry in two market segments: test sockets and IC carriers. In 1965 the test equipment line was sold off in order to concentrate on the socket and carrier lines, and in 1966 Michael Strang became president.[2]

---

[1] A test socket was used by component manufacturers to make connection with the semiconductor while it was tested or aged by applying an electrical current. This use differed from that of production sockets which were installed in a manufacturer's product to allow replacement of defective semiconductors at the device level. This latter type of socket was finding more applications as use of integrated circuits grew. One integrated circuit could replace a printed circuit-card assembly which consisted of resistors, capacitors, and transistors soldered together on the card.

[2] Although Robert Strang held the title of chairman of the board, his interests were primarily in technical areas. As a result, his son Michael, who had majored in economics and had done graduate work in that field, had full operating responsibility for the company.

Sales and earnings increased rapidly as demand for these products mushroomed. In May of 1968, 100,000 shares of common stock were offered to the public at $8 per share.[3] The price of the stock quickly jumped to $14 and climbed to over $24 in late 1968 and early 1969. By January 1970, the price of the stock had stabilized in the $19–$22 range. For the fiscal year ended June 30, 1969, sales had increased from $498,000 in 1965 to $4,300,000—an average annual growth rate in excess of 70%. In the same five years, earnings had grown from $.10 per share to $.72, or 66% per year (see Exhibits 1 and 2 for financial data).

**EXHIBIT 1**

STRANG CORPORATION
Income Statement Summary
(dollar figures in thousands)

| | *Fiscal year ended June 30* | | | | |
|---|---|---|---|---|---|
| | *1965* | *1966* | *1967* | *1968* | *1969* |
| Net sales . . . . . . . . . . . . . . . . . | $498 | $1,123 | $1,825 | $2,746 | $4,333 |
| Cost of sales . . . . . . . . . . . . . . . | 247 | 568 | 960 | 1,392 | 2,270 |
| Gross income . . . . . . . . . . . . . . | $251 | $ 555 | $ 865 | $1,354 | $2,063 |
| Selling, G & A expense . . . . . . . . . . | 193 | 370 | 552 | 828 | 1,308 |
| Operating income (loss) . . . . . . . . . | $ 58 | $ 185 | $ 313 | $ 526 | $ 755 |
| Other income (expense) . . . . . . . . . | (1) | (1) | (1) | (1) | . . . |
| Net income before taxes . . . . . . . . . | $ 57 | $ 184 | $ 312 | $ 525 | $ 755 |
| Provision for income taxes. . . . . . . . | 19 | 83 | 145 | 253 | 394 |
| Net income . . . . . . . . . . . . . . . | $ 38 | $ 101 | $ 167 | $ 272 | $ 361 |
| Net income per share . . . . . . . . . . . | $.10 | $.26 | $.40 | $.64 | $.72 |
| Shares outstanding* (average). . . . . . | 373,980 | 384,430 | 396,200 | 429,280 | 505,280 |

*Adjusted for 10-for-1 stock split in January 1968.
Source: Company records.

It was in this context of a history of rapid growth and expectations of additional future growth that Mr. Strang pondered the impact of a decline in sales volume on the future course of his company.

## PRODUCT LINE

Strang's product line consisted of three major groups:

1. *Carriers:* plastic parts used to hold delicate integrated circuits during the process of aging, burn-in, shipment to the user, final test, and final installation.
2. *Test sockets:* special long-life sockets which both producers and users installed in a variety of aging and test facilities in their plants.

---

[3] The remaining 400,000 shares of outstanding stock were held, almost in their entirety, by members of the Strang family.

**EXHIBIT 2**

STRANG CORPORATION
Balance Sheet Summary
(dollar figures in thousands)

| | June 30, 1967 | June 30, 1968 | June 30, 1969 | Dec. 31, 1969 | Feb. 28, 1970 |
|---|---|---|---|---|---|
| *Assets* | | | | | |
| Current assets | | | | | |
| Cash . . . . . . . . . . . . . . . . . . . . | $ 76 | $ 563 | $ 47 | $ 102 | $ 29 |
| Accounts receivable, net . . . . . . . . . | 246 | 361 | 878 | 1,206 | 871 |
| Inventories . . . . . . . . . . . . . . . | 193 | 379 | 665 | 1,111 | 1,261 |
| Prepaid expenses . . . . . . . . . . . . | 7 | 20 | 12 | 19 | 17 |
| Total current assets . . . . . . . . | $522 | $1,323 | $1,602 | $2,438 | $2,178 |
| Property, plant, and equipment | | | | | |
| Land, building, and improvements . . . | . . . | . . . | $ 271 | $ 456 | $ 466 |
| Machinery, tools, and equipment . . . . | $282 | $ 796 | 1,304 | 1,744 | 1,886 |
| Leasehold improvements . . . . . . . . | . . . | 90 | 139 | 169 | 170 |
| | $282 | $ 886 | $1,714 | $2,369 | $2,522 |
| Less: Accumulated depreciation . . . | 95 | 236 | 515 | 695 | 773 |
| | $187 | $ 650 | $1,199 | $1,674 | $1,749 |
| Other assets . . . . . . . . . . . . . . . . | $ 5 | $ 6 | $ 49 | $ 50 | $ 53 |
| Total assets . . . . . . . . . . . . | $714 | $1,979 | $2,850 | $4,162 | $3,980 |
| *Liabilities* | | | | | |
| Current liabilities | | | | | |
| Demand note payable to bank . . . . . | . . . | . . . | $ 120 | $ 600 | $ 600 |
| Current portion of long-term debt . . . | . . . | $ 44 | 85 | 82 | 82 |
| Accounts payable. . . . . . . . . . . . . | $101 | 113 | 251 | 688 | 750 |
| Accrued income taxes . . . . . . . . . . | 149 | 211 | 238 | 230 | 125 |
| Accrued expenses . . . . . . . . . . . | 113 | 136 | 217 | 173 | 150 |
| Total current liabilities . . . . . . . | $363 | $ 504 | $ 911 | $1,773 | $1,707 |
| Long-term debt . . . . . . . . . . . . . . | $ . . . | $ 118 | $ 186 | $ 456 | $ 424 |
| Deferred income taxes . . . . . . . . . . | $ . . . | $ 23 | $ 58 | $ 59 | $ 59 |
| Stockholders investment | | | | | |
| Common stock . . . . . . . . . . . . . . | $ 48 | $ 61 | $ 61 | $ 61 | $ 61 |
| Paid-in surplus . . . . . . . . . . . . . . | 5 | 703 | 703 | 703 | 702 |
| Retained earnings. . . . . . . . . . . . . | 298 | 570 | 931 | 1,110 | 1,027 |
| | $351 | $1,334 | $1,695 | $1,874 | $1,790 |
| Total liabilities . . . . . . . . . . | $714 | $1,979 | $2,850 | $4,162 | $3,980 |

Source: Company records.

3. *Production sockets:* component items installed in many types of computer and military electronics products which consumed the bulk of integrated-circuit production.

The design of these products called for a great deal of technical sophistication to meet the rigid mechanical and electrical requirements imposed by the customer. Furthermore, the rapid pace of technological change in the semiconductor industry necessitated constant product improvement and change. Management estimated that the product line "turned over" about every three years as current products became obsolete and new ones were added.

A technical staff of two engineers and six technicians and designers was responsible for product development. The group was headed by Tom Bensen, 30, who had worked with Strang since graduation from engineering school. There were 1,540 items in the line, 100 of them accounting for 68% of sales. Of the remaining 1,440 items, 1,328 contributing 16% of sales were obsolete or special items carried as a special service for specific customers. These items were by and large test sockets used for replacement purposes in existing installations. Strang management outlined the major competitive and economic parameters of the three product groups as follows:

*Carriers* made up about 20% of Strang's sales in 1969. Management estimated that the company had about 50% of the carrier market. The carrier was an intricately molded plastic part about an inch square. It was considered an expendable intermediate product in the electronic manufacturing process and was usually thrown away after use. Hence the number of carriers sold was directly linked to unit volume in the semiconductor industry; moreover, automated handling of ICs had greatly increased the number of carriers used. Unit volumes of carriers were in the millions, and prices were a few cents a unit. Most of the semiconductor suppliers carried substantial inventories of carriers in order not to risk holding up shipment of their product. Furthermore, Strang had tried to maintain the price of carriers in the face of generally declining unit prices available to the semiconductor manufacturers for their IC/carrier package. At the same time, the manufacturers had encouraged competitive bidding from other existing or potential carrier suppliers.

While carrier designs were frequently complex to engineer, they could often be copied by a manufacturer with precision plastic molding capability. Even though Strang had patients on numerous items, the protection offered was limited in some instances by the ease of developing closely similar products. Therefore, it was possible for a specialty molding house with moderate design and sales overhead to bid competitively, and on several high-volume items in recent months Strang had been forced to cut prices to meet competition. This price erosion, loss of sales to competitors, and user inventory adjustments were thought to have played a substantial part in the lastest drop in sales.

To develop a stronger market position through multiple suppliers, Mr. Strang, in 1968 and 1969, had licensed two specialty producers to manufacture the Strang carriers on a royalty basis. Others in the company felt that this move was a mistake because it "gave away sales to the competition"; clever tooling and better service, they maintained, could provide the needed competitive edge.

*Test sockets* were the major group in Strang's line and accounted for 50% of the dollar volume and a somewhat greater share of the gross margin. Mr. Strang estimated that the company had a 65% share of this market. The sockets were used in a wide variety of capital equipment applications. The manufacturing process entailed the production and assembly of intricate molded plastic parts and tiny metal contacts. Order sizes ranged from hundreds of units to tens of thousands of units, and unit prices started at $.60. As a result of the lower volume and the specialized nature of the product, competition in this area was not so intense as it was with carriers. However, sales were linked to capital spending plans and therefore were affected by the economic climate. The higher than normal proportion of replacement-type orders which had materialized in recent months Mr. Strang attributed to the "postponability" of capital equipment purchases.

*Production sockets* amounted to about 25% of Strang's volume. However, the company held only a few share points in a market which was dominated by such large companies as AMP, Inc., and ELCO. Unit prices ranged from $.20 to $1.25, and order volumes went as high as hundreds of thousands of units. Management felt that this market held great potential as the minimum replaceable unit moved from the printed circuit-card, or subassembly, level, to the integrated-circuit or device level. However, the rate of technological obsolescence was high, and large investments in engineering time and production equipment were needed to enter the field on a competitive basis.

## MARKETING

Strang had no direct sales force. Instead, the company followed the usual industry practice of engaging manufacturers' representatives who typically represented several component manufacturers and contracted to provide sales assistance to customers in a given territory. In return they were paid a 10% commission on all direct sales in the territory. Large orders were shipped directly from Strang to the customer upon receipt of his purchase order. Often blanket contracts for annual requirements with periodic inventory releases during the year were entered into with large customers. As a result, it was possible for Strang to carry a large backlog of bookings but not to realize sales if the customer held back on releases against his order.

In addition to ordering direct from Strang, the customer could also buy from a local franchised distributor. Typically, distributor orders were for prototype quantities or to fill an initial run on long-term production when there was not time for direct shipment. The distributor took title to any merchandise he bought from Strang and, in general, was speculating on its resalability. The distributors reported their sales to

Strang, who in turn paid the representative in the territory where the sale was made a 7% commission. About one third of Strang's sales in 1969 were to distributors.

Geographically, sales to Strang's customers were concentrated heavily in California and along the East Coast. Within these areas of concentration, Strang depended heavily on a few key accounts from among the several hundred distributors and end-use customers serviced in 1970. Furthermore, the larger customers had several buying locations and often bought through a distributor; there were 650 locations in all. As a result, sales to six or ten "locations" could often be traced to one customer. This concentration of buying power was particularly important since, in 1969, only 35 locations bought 76% of Strang's total dollar volume.

The sales department was under the general supervision of Mr. Karl See, vice president of operations. Mr. See, 37, had been with the company since 1965 and was named sales manager to replace Mr. Strang when the latter became president in 1966. When Mr. See was made vice president of operations, Mr. Robert Hart, 34, was promoted to sales manager. Nevertheless, Mr. Strang continued to establish overall marketing policy.

In March 1970 there were 18 people in the sales department. Four regional sales managers kept in contact with representatives and customers, supported by four sales administrators and six clerical employees. The remaining four employees were responsible for customer service, catalogs, and advertising and promotion.

## MANUFACTURING

Since 1969, Mr. See had also been responsible for manufacturing, which had become a major area of concern as sales volume rapidly increased. Mr. See had expanded both the plastic molding and toolmaking operation (located on leased premises about five miles from Strang's storefront offices) and the assembly operation in Chicago. He hired a general foreman for the plastic molding department, a materials manager, and had an additional 10 molding machines installed. By January the assembly plant had been painstakingly put on a three-shift basis, and total company employment had grown to 280 people, about 180 of them hourly employees in production. At this point, Mr. Strang felt that they were approaching capacity: "We could turn out perhaps $8 million if pushed to the walls."

The rapid acceptance of Strang's products and the subsequent growth of the company had placed the burdens of success on management during the past year. Customers were pressing for more and different products. The financial community was interested in expansion and increasing earnings. In response, two major kinds of opportunities were considered in 1969: extensions and additions to the existing product line and acquisition or merger.

## NEW PRODUCTS

Two areas for new product development were outlined. One was interconnection systems keyed to the anticipated growth in mini-computer sales. Strang currently supplied the sockets for the integrated circuits used in these systems. However, since most small computer companies were thought to concentrate on design and final assembly but not on the production of subassemblies or components, connected socket systems were viewed as a logical outgrowth of Strang's existing capability. Mr. Strang was enthusiastic about this project, seeing it as a challenge offering excellent growth potential. He estimated that several million dollars and three to five years' time would be required to develop the necessary engineering staff and production capability.

A second area of interest to Mr. Strang was an improved IC package to be developed in conjunction with another noncompetitive manufacturer. Here Strang's expertise in electromechanical connection systems would be vital. Both of these projects fit Mr. Strang's theory of "ever widening concentric circles" of market development, and he felt that by 1974 they would represent sales as large as those budgeted for the entire company in 1970 as shown in the projections in Exhibit 3.

## ACQUISITION AND MERGER

Since the company stock had gone on the market, over 100 acquisitions had been considered. In September 1968, Strang announced an agreement in principle to acquire a manufacturer of semiconductor test equipment in California. This move toward vertical integration was later canceled when the final asking price was too high. In the summer of 1969, merger discussions were held with the Morrell Corporation, a large supplier of electronic connectors. Mr. Strang felt that the product lines were compatible and that the Morrell international marketing organization would be beneficial to Strang. When Morrell announced its plans to acquire Strang, the price of Strang stock dropped substantially; the negotiations were finally terminated when the principals could not agree upon a mutually satisfactory price. An investment analyst commented in November 1969:

The Strang Corporation has again been courted in the merger market. Last spring the Morrell Corporation initiated merger discussions but they were later broken off. Then a few weeks ago, Stuart-Grant Industries, listed on the American Stock Exchange, sought control of Strang but negotiations were quickly terminated.

**EXHIBIT 3**

STRANG CORPORATION
Five-Year Projection
(dollar amounts in thousands)

*Fiscal year ended June 30*

| | 1970 | 1971 | 1972 | 1973 | 1974 |
|---|---|---|---|---|---|
| *Sales by Product Line* | | | | | |
| Carriers | $1,260 | $2,040 | $ 2,760 | $ 3,360 | $ 4,500 |
| Test sockets | 3,300 | 4,110 | 5,270 | 6,220 | 7,100 |
| Production sockets | 1,200 | 2,400 | 3,460 | 4,820 | 5,920 |
| Interconnection, packaging | 240 | 450 | 1,110 | 3,000 | 6,480 |
| | $6,000 | $9,000 | $12,600 | $17,400 | $24,000 |
| *Income Statement* | | | | | |
| Sales | $6,000 | $9,000 | $12,600 | $17,400 | $24,000 |
| Cost of sales | 3,114 | 4,636 | 6,426 | 9,048 | 12,240 |
| Gross income | $2,886 | $4,364 | $ 6,174 | $ 8,352 | $11,760 |
| Selling, G & A expense | 1,740 | 2,430 | 3,402 | 4,612 | 6,000 |
| R & D expense* | 84 | 270 | 504 | 522 | 720 |
| Operating income | $1,062 | $1,664 | $ 2,268 | $ 3,218 | $ 5,040 |
| Other income (expense)† | (12) | (146) | (281) | (438) | (618) |
| Income before taxes | $1,050 | $1,518 | $ 1,987 | $ 2,780 | $ 4,422 |
| Provision for taxes | 572 | 820 | 1,073 | 1,500 | 2,388 |
| Net income | $ 478 | $ 698 | $ 914 | 1,280 | 2,034 |
| Earnings per share | $.96 | $1.34 | $1.75 | $2.44 | $4.02 |
| Number of shares | 505,280 | 515,280 | 520,280 | 525,280 | 530,280 |
| *Cash Flow* | | | | | |
| Beginning cash balance | $ 48 | $ 529 | $ 442 | $ 350 | $ 413 |
| Add: | | | | | |
| Net income-operations | $ 478 | $ 698 | $ 914 | $ 1,280 | $ 2,034 |
| Depreciation | 472 | 732 | 1,013 | 1,295 | 1,531 |
| Increase in accounts payable | 240 | 316 | 430 | 524 | 638 |
| Additional financing needed | 960 | 1,920 | ... | 2,640 | (1,200) |
| Increase in accrued expenses | 48 | 48 | 120 | 60 | 60 |
| Increase in accrued taxes | 168 | 300 | 90 | 60 | 120 |
| Increase in deferred taxes | 84 | 144 | 234 | 276 | 390 |
| Cash generated | $2,450 | $4,158 | $ 2,801 | $ 6,135 | $ 3,573 |
| Deduct: | | | | | |
| Additions to plant and equipment | $1,080 | $3,240 | $ 1,608 | $ 4,440 | $ 1,284 |
| Increase in receivables | 480 | 450 | 540 | 720 | 990 |
| Increase in inventory | 348 | 600 | 720 | 876 | 1,068 |
| Increase in prepaid expenses | ... | 16 | 30 | 37 | 46 |
| Cash applied | $1,908 | $4,306 | $ 2,898 | $ 6,073 | $ 3,388 |
| Ending cash balance | $ 590 | $ 381 | $ 345 | $ 412 | $ 598 |

* Expense associated with new product development over and above current engineering staff.
† Royalty and rental income less interest expense.
Source: Company Five-Year Plan, dated August 1969.

The market for integrated circuits—though still only a small segment of the electronic components field—has since its inception experienced uncommonly impressive growth. For at least the next few years, annual gains of 50% appear likely. Strang Corporation, whose future is closely tied to the expansion of the integrated circuits market, is expected to grow even more rapidly. The company, a producer of sockets, connectors, and protective carriers for integrated circuits, has enjoyed average annual earnings improvement of better than 150% for the last five years. Over the next several years, Strang's growth rate ought to be at least 50% per year—and possibly as high as 100%. Figured conservatively on this basis, earnings per share of about $2.50 are estimated for 1972 suggesting a stock price of roughly $50 at the current price-earnings ratio. The stock is recommended as a businessman's risk for risk-oriented accounts stressing above-average capital growth.

## FISCAL 1970 BUDGET

The Morrell negotiations did, however, serve to focus the attention of management on the need for more explicit planning and budgeting.

**EXHIBIT 4**

STRANG CORPORATION

---

M E M O R A N D U M

*To:*      Dave Marshall, D. R. Marshall Sales Corporation

*From:*   Robert Hart, Sales Manager*

*Date:*    July 30, 1969

Dear Dave:

We at Strang Corporation would like to congratulate you and your organization and express our appreciation for the tremendous job you did with the Strang Corporation during the last year.

We have attached a separate sheet where we have broken down this total performance into direct bookings and distributor sales at the cost price.

A most significant factor we feel has been the work of Royal Sales, and this, of course, reflects the fine cooperation between your staff and this distributor.

We are, of course, looking to continued growth in your area during fiscal 1970 and feel that your organization has both the talent and the market to reach our new forecast of $1,440,000 for northern California. We do, however, feel that this will require a tremendous amount of support from the factory, and we shall certainly make every endeavor to see that this support is forthcoming.

We would say that basically we have to strengthen our new product introduction so that we can not only meet the requirements of our older customers but also offer products to you that will increase our potential in the user market. We also feel that we will need a radical improvement in the performance of P. R. Warren Company, and we definitely want to discuss this with you during NORBIT.

This 1970 forecast of $1,440,000 is a 40% increase over your actual performance in 1969 and so the figure may not really be as optimistic as you may feel at first glance.

Dave, I'd appreciate very much if we could have your formal comments on what you feel you'll need to meet this forecast, and we will certainly do everything possible to be of assistance to you.

---

* Roger Hart reported at this time to Mr. See, vice president of operations.

Fiscal 1969 had been highly successful, and there had been inquiries from both Morrell management and financial analysts regarding the future growth plans of the Strang Corporation.

During July and August of 1969, a five-year forecast of sales, earnings, and cash flow was developed by Mr. Strang, Mr. See, and Steve Hodgekins, the company controller who had joined Strang in early 1969. These projections called for an annual sales growth of 40% based on existing product expansion and the development of the interconnection and packaging projects. Sales volume figures were derived primarily from management estimates of future market potential and the extrapolation of past growth rates. Regional breakdowns were furnished to all sales representatives. (A typical example is shown in Exhibit 4.) Adoption of this budget committed Strang to maintaining a sales level of over $120,000 per week during 1970 and required the addition of more factory personnel, managers, and capital equipment. Additional financing of $1,000,000 in 1970 and $1,900,000 in 1971 was required (see Exhibit 3).

By January of 1970 Mr. Strang believed that his goals for 1970 would be met. Results for the first six months had met or exceeded goals, as shown in Exhibit 5. A $600,000 loan had been obtained, and plans were underway for a stock issue to secure the funds needed in 1971

**EXHIBIT 4** (*continued*)

### D. R. MARSHALL SALES CORPORATION
*Fiscal Year 1969*

| | |
|---|---:|
| Direct bookings . . . . . . . . . . . . . . . . . . . . . . . . . . . . . . . . . . . . . . | $ 666,448.45 |
| Distributor sales (at cost) | |
| Royal. . . . . . . . . . . . . . . . . . . . . . . . . . . . . . . . . . . . . . . . . . . | 304,993.63 |
| P. R. Warren. . . . . . . . . . . . . . . . . . . . . . . . . . . . . . . . . . . . . . | 53,079.54 |
| | $1,024,521.62 |
| Forecast–fiscal year 1969 . . . . . . . . . . . . . . . . . . . . . . . . . . . . . | $ 840,000.00 |
| Percentage over forecast . . . . . . . . . . . . . . . . . . . . . . . . . . . . . . | 20% |
| Percentage of total in distributor sales (at cost). . . . . . . . . . . . . . . . . | 35% |

*Forecast for Fiscal Year 1970*

| | |
|---|---:|
| Direct bookings . . . . . . . . . . . . . . . . . . . . . . . . . . . . . . . . . . . . | $ 864,000.00 |
| Distributor sales (at cost) | |
| Royal. . . . . . . . . . . . . . . . . . . . . . . . . . . . . . . . . . . . . . . . . . | 420,000.00 |
| P. R. Warren. . . . . . . . . . . . . . . . . . . · . . . . . . . . . . . . . . . . . . | 156,000.00 |
| | $1,440,000.00 |
| Percentage increase over fiscal 1969 (forecast) . . . . . . . . . . . . . . . . . | 71% |
| Percentage increase over fiscal 1969 (actual) . . . . . . . . . . . . . . . . . . | 40% |
| Percentage of forecast in distributor sales (at cost) . . . . . . . . . . . . . . . | 40% |

*Forecast by Quarters–Fiscal Year 1970*

| | 1st Qtr. | 2nd Qtr. | 3rd Qtr. | 4th Qtr. | Total |
|---|---:|---:|---:|---:|---:|
| Direct bookings . . . . . | $190,100 | $207,400 | $224,600 | $241,900 | $ 864,000 |
| Distributor sales | | | | | |
| (at cost) . . . . . . . . | 126,700 | 138,200 | 149,800 | 161,300 | 576,000 |
| Total. . . . . . . . . | $316,800 | $345,600 | $374,400 | $403,200 | $1,440,000 |

Source: Company records.

EXHIBIT 5

STRANG CORPORATION
Income Statement Summary
(dollar figures in thousands)

| | Six months ended Dec. 31, 1969 | | Month ended Jan. 31, 1970 | | Month ended Feb. 28, 1970 | | Year to date | | Remaining budget period | | |
|---|---|---|---|---|---|---|---|---|---|---|---|
| | Budget | Actual | Budget | Actual | Budget | Actual | Budget | Actual | March | 4th qtr. | Year |
| Net sales | $2,634 | $2,641 | $570 | $348 | $593 | $295 | $3,797 | $3,284 | $769 | $2,154 | $6,720 |
| Cost of sales | | | | | | | | | | | |
| Material | 421 | 422 | 91 | 55 | 95 | 52 | 607 | 529 | 124 | 343 | 1,075 |
| Direct labor | 288 | 286 | 56 | 49 | 56 | 43 | 401 | 378 | 71 | 186 | 656 |
| Overhead | 890 | 864 | 164 | 192 | 163 | 152 | 1,218 | 1,210 | 180 | 521 | 1,919 |
| Overhead capitalized | ... | (67) | ... | (8) | ... | (7) | ... | (83) | ... | ... | ... |
| Total cost of sales | $1,599 | $1,505 | $311 | $288 | $314 | $240 | $2,226 | $2,034 | $375 | $1,050 | $3,650 |
| Gross income | $1,035 | $1,136 | $259 | $ 60 | $279 | $ 55 | $1,571 | $1,250 | $394 | $1,104 | $3,070 |
| Selling, G & A expense | | | | | | | | | | | |
| Selling expense | $ 248 | $ 193 | $ 35 | $ 53 | $ 37 | $ 43 | $ 320 | $ 289 | $ 38 | $ 136 | $ 493 |
| G & A expense | 407 | 360 | 76 | 89 | 79 | 67 | 563 | 516 | 76 | 229 | 868 |
| Commission expense | 235 | 197 | 52 | 24 | 53 | 25 | 340 | 246 | 70 | 194 | 605 |
| Total selling, G & A | $ 890 | $ 750 | $163 | $166 | $169 | $135 | $1,223 | $1,051 | $184 | $ 559 | $1,966 |
| Operating income (loss) | $ 145 | $ 386 | $ 96 | $(106) | $110 | $(80) | $ 348 | $ 199 | $210 | $ 545 | $1,104 |
| Other income (expense) | $ ... | $ 8 | $ ... | $ ... | $ ... | $ ... | $ ... | $ 7 | $... | $ ... | $ ... |
| Net income before taxes | $ 145 | $ 394 | $ 96 | $(106) | $110 | $(80) | $ 348 | $ 206 | $210 | $ 545 | $1,104 |
| Provision for income taxes | 74 | 215 | 54 | (61) | 60 | (47) | 188 | 109 | 116 | 300 | 605 |
| Net income | $ 71 | $ 179 | $ 42 | $ (45) | $ 50 | $(33) | $ 160 | $ 97 | $ 94 | $ 245 | $ 499 |
| Net income per share* | $.14 | $.35 | $.08 | $(.09) | $.10 | $(.07) | $.32 | $.19 | $.19 | $.48 | $.99 |

* Average shares outstanding: 505,280.
Source: Company records.

**EXHIBIT 6**

STRANG CORPORATION

MEMORANDUM

*To:*    Mike Strang                                              March 3, 1970

*From:*    Dave Marshall

*Subject:*    Market Climate

As the result of our conversation today I have set down my thoughts on "what's going on in California." Offhand, I would say that about two thirds of our sales decline is due to general economic conditions and one third to competitive conditions.

1. The industry in California is "running scared." Everybody is nervous about cuts in defense spending. Nobody knows what is going to happen, but right now the major contractors are just not getting much new business. Consequently, they are working off their carrier inventories and only buying as needed. Obviously they will have to start buying again, but who knows when or at what rate.

2. Capital expenditure plans are also being canceled. As a result we can expect only replacement-type orders for test sockets—at least for the next few months until the air clears. If the decline persists, we are in real trouble here.

3. Something has got to be done about carrier pricing. You can justify a 20% higher price on test sockets to a purchasing agent on the basis of superior performance. Not so with carriers; they buy those by the bushel, and ours are just as good as the next guy's to them. Along this same line, some customers are complaining about premature product releases, missed deliveries, technical failures, and general nonresponsiveness from Chicago. They say Strang has been having more than its share lately. If you need convincing on this point, let me take you on a short swing around the Peninsula.

4. On the more positive side, I see no reason that we can't move all the items on the inventory list you showed me when the market picks up. Nor do I have any doubts about the abilities of the coast firms to cover their payables to us—though they're going to stretch them as far as they can.

Source: Casewriter's notes.

**EXHIBIT 7**

STRANG CORPORATION

MEMORANDUM

*To:*    Mike Strang

*From:*    Steve Hodgekins

*Subject:*    Projections for balance of FY 70 (March–June)

Per your request today I have run out a pro forma assuming that sales continue at 50% of budget. Attachment 1 shows the result—a loss of $209,000 in the last four months of the fiscal year.

With regard to "how far *could* we cut?" I have done some quick break evens as shown in Attachment 2. At $2.5 million per year *all* the "fat" would be out, but this would be a pretty quiet place.

It is pretty clear to me that if sales says things are going to stay bad, we had better cut back our production force by at least 100 people and play out the inventory that we had built up to cover the spring upturn. Where we go from there vis-à-vis S, G & A is going to be a tough one.

**EXHIBIT 7** (*continued*)

*Attachment 1*

Income Statement, March 1, 1970–June 30, 1970

*(thousands)*

| | |
|---|---:|
| Sales . . . . . . . . . . . . . . . . . . . . . . . . . . | $1,461 |
| Cost of sales | |
| Material (16% of sales). . . . . . . . . . . . . . . | 234 |
| Direct labor (11% of sales) . . . . . . . . . . . . . | 161 |
| Variable overhead (10% of sales) . . . . . . . . . . | 146* |
| Fixed overhead . . . . . . . . . . . . . . . . . . . . | 416* |
| Total cost of sales . . . . . . . . . . . . . . . . | $ 957 |
| Gross income . . . . . . . . . . . . . . . . . . . . . | $ 504 |
| Selling, G & A expense | |
| Selling expense (as budgeted) . . . . . . . . . . . . | $ 174 |
| G & A expense (as budgeted) . . . . . . . . . . . . . | 305 |
| Commission (8% of sales) . . . . . . . . . . . . . . | 234 |
| Total selling, G & A . . . . . . . . . . . . . . . . | $ 713 |
| Operating income (loss) . . . . . . . . . . . . . . . | $ (209) |

* Variable overhead is assumed to be 10% of sales and fixed overhead at the rate of about $104,000/month. Overhead is therefore about 35% variable, and the 1969–70 budget of $1,919,000 breaks down into $672,000 variable and $1,247,000 fixed.

*Attachment 2*

Break-Even Calculation

*Basis*

| | |
|---|---:|
| Sales . . . . . . . . . . . . . . . . . | 100% |
| Variable portion of sales | |
| Material . . . . . . . . . . . . . . . | 16 |
| Labor. . . . . . . . . . . . . . . . . | 11 |
| Overhead . . . . . . . . . . . . . . | 10 |
| Commission . . . . . . . . . . . . . | 8 |
| Total variable portion . . . . . . | 45% |
| Contribution. . . . . . . . . . . . . | 55% |

*Current fixed costs (12-month basis)*

*(thousands)*

| | | |
|---|---:|---|
| Overhead. . . . . . | $1,248 | (12 × $104,000) |
| Selling . . . . . . | 445 | (current 8-month figure annualized) |
| G & A . . . . . . . | 774 | (current 8-month figure annualized) |
| Total . . . . . . . | $2,467 | |

*Break-even sales levels for different levels of fixed costs**

*(in thousands of dollars)*

| | | | | | |
|---|---:|---:|---:|---:|---:|
| Annual sales . . . . . . . . . . . . . . . . . . | $4,500 | $4,000 | $3,500 | $3,000 | $2,500 |
| Fixed costs to break even . . . . . . . . . . | 2,467 | 2,200 | 1,930 | 1,650 | 1,370 |
| Amount below present level of fixed costs . . . . . . . . . . . . . . . . . . | 0 | 267 | 537 | 817 | 1,097 |

* Based on contribution rate of 55%.

Source: Casewriter's notes and company documents.

to enter the interconnection market. Additional employees had been added in the plant, and discussions were underway with technical people to bolster the development staff. Mr. See had convinced Dave Marshall, Strang's representative in California, to sell his business and join Strang to assist him in administering the expanded marketing program.[4] Strang stock was holding up well in spite of investor disenchantment in the electronics industry.

Other troubles began to appear during January 1970, however. Bookings did not pick up after Christmas as expected, and customers attempted to reduce inventory commitments. Returns for faulty merchandise and for readjustment in distributor inventories, which normally ran about 4% of sales, jumped to 9%. Shortly after Mr. Marshall arrived in February, Mr. See announced that he would be leaving in May to set up his own distributorship to handle Strang and other electronic manufacturers' products.

The sales decline continued into February. The financial results for January and February were disappointing: both months showed a loss. The inventory that had been built up in anticipation of advancing sales was rising at an even greater rate as sales declined. Declines in all segments of the electronics industry were reported in various trade journals. On the other hand, long-run growth prospects for the computer industry continued to be excellent, and with U.S. participation in the war in Southeast Asia winding down there was considerable speculation that increased budget allocations for more sophisticated weapons systems would be forthcoming.

With these facts in mind, and two memoranda that he had just received (see Exhibits 6 and 7), Mr. Strang sat down to ponder what action, if any, he should propose to the board of directors and his management group.

---

[4] Mr. Marshall had sold his business to several of his former employees on an earn-out basis, agreeing as part of the deal not to enter into competition with his former associates in northern California for a period of five years.

# Dansk Designs Ltd.

FOUNDED IN 1955 to market a line of stainless steel flatware, Dansk Designs' sales grew from $100,000 in its first year of operation to over $10,000,000 in 1970. The firm's 1970 product catalog listed 600 items for the "top of the table" in product categories such as china, glass, table linens, wooden accessories, flatware, and cookware that could be used for serving.

Dansk was not content, moreover, to rest on past accomplishments. Ted Nierenberg, founder, president, and sole owner of Dansk, wanted the firm to maintain a 20% growth rate per year in profits. In order to do this, he planned to enter a new market area: housewares. Whereas Dansk's existing product line consisted of eight product categories, Nierenberg expected the new housewares line eventually to have three times that number.[1]

In response to Dansk's past growth and in anticipation of its future expansion, the company's organization was changing. In the 1950s and early 1960s, Dansk had consisted of Ted Nierenberg, Jens Quistgaard, and Ed Lubell.[2] Nierenberg provided marketing insights and located manufacturing sources, Quistgaard designed all the products, and Lubell was in charge of general administration and finance and administered manufacturing. As the size of Dansk's business grew, however, these men required help. Therefore additional designers were added, a number

---

[1] See Exhibit 1 for information on the housewares line.
[2] See Exhibit 2 for information on Dansk's personnel.

**EXHIBIT 1**

## DANSK GOURMET DESIGNS LTD.

I. *Maria Wazeter's description of the housewares line*

There has always been a tremendous gap between Dansk's products—with heavy inputs of museum-caliber design, expensive raw materials, and skilled craftsmanship (hand finishing) in the manufacturing process—and mass-produced housewares, which have usually been designed to be manufactured as cheaply as possible.

In the Gourmet collection, Dansk will be bringing the same design standards to mass production, modifying manufacturing techniques to retain the handcrafted look which has been its hallmark. The Gourmet collection has been a corporate umbrella where Dansk is developing such concepts as:

*New materials:* acrylic, pyroceram, ceramic crucible material, and coquille aluminum, where present design is weak and the creative potential large.
*Basic, "classic" materials:* for example, cast iron, copper, and automatic glass, where both functionality and style can be improved.
*New processes:* for example, "coquille" aluminum, where a very prosaic and utilitarian metal is given a sheen resembling hammered pewter.

These innovations alone give Dansk enough raw material to develop a marketing strategy for at least 15 years out.

Gourmet is actually something of a misnomer, for while the lines might be designed to meet a gourmet's specifications, they are intended for a much wider group, larger than the circle of Dansk's present customers. A great many people identify with the gourmet concept, even if they only heat up frozen "spinach souffle" or "green beans with almonds" instead of the traditional TV dinners. Brides, career girls, mothers of school-age children with increasing leisure time—these are some of the consumer groups whose new-found interest in cooking and corollary need for information and reassurance have spawned cooking schools, cookbook guilds, and specialty retail outlets (like The Pot Shop in Harvard Square).

From the marketing angle, the potential is enormous. First, while Dansk has always sold at a premium, Gourmet will market Dansk style at a competitive price. Dansk products have always had a "fragile-handle-with-care" stamp about them; the new Gourmet lines, on the other hand, fairly exude durability—engineered for everyday use and a more mobile population. Also, Dansk's appeal will be wider, including not only the "classic to contemporary" group of customers who buy traditional materials like wood and crystal but the younger, more avant-garde group who are willing to buy good design and acrylic.

The major issue which Dansk must resolve is the rate at which the Gourmet collections will reach the market to maximize the impact of each collection. Introducing the maximum feasible number at one time would underline the style coordination and systems advantages and, in addition, make possible the creation of a Dansk "shop" within each store (with all items or lines assembled rather than spread out in several departments).

The second alternative, which might create equal impact over the long run, would be successive waves of product introductions on a quarterly basis. Some balance must be struck between maximum impact and minimum risk. What criteria should be used to assign priorities to the various lines?

Along with the potential, of course, the pitfalls are greater. Just a few examples:

1. In the past, size and production efficiency of some of the Dansk-contracted European factories has set *maximum* sales limits on such products as Flamestone and Orecast. Many of the newer products, such as automatic glass, will have minimum sales levels to be economically feasible, which may be 3, 5, 10 or more times average volume for Dansk's regular lines.

2. As a corollary, Dansk has based its merchandising on selective distribution, usually one to three department stores in each city. While with Gourmet Dansk will be moving out of isolated departments like china and crystal into new, higher traffic areas, will this, in itself, generate enough volume?

3. The distribution problem is more acute, given that absolute dollar margins will be smaller even if percentage-wise the contribution stays the same. Or *should* it stay the same?

4. Advertising: Traditionally Dansk has spent roughly 5% of sales on advertising, in

**EXHIBIT 1** (*continued*)

print media oriented toward a reasonably narrow band of customers—high income, well-educated readers of general publications and shelter magazines. With a larger budget, (e.g., based on doubled sales volume), TV, educational films, and/or pamphlets, newspaper advertising—all the more expensive media become feasible. How can we best reach that mass market?

5. Mistakes: If a current piece doesn't sell, or if Dansk occasionally has to indulge a designer by manufacturing and selling one of his favorite "museum pieces," the item can be "specialed" out of inventory. But how do you bury 25,000 white elephants? Or, more accurately, how can you abort them while ensuring that your designers feel appreciated and satisfied professionally?

II.  *"For Dansk, New Line and New Image"**

### By RITA REIF

Dansk Designs Ltd., a tablewares producer that has been synonymous with prestigious, high-priced modern wares for cooking and serving, is working on a new, second image.

"We think there is a terrific market for mass-produced silverplate in this country, silverplated flatware in traditional styling," said Ted Nierenberg, founder of the 15-year-old concern based in Mount Kisco, N.Y.

The statement had a startling ring coming from the president of the concern that made Scandinavian modern a style to dine by in the nineteen fifties and sixties. Retail sales in this period rose to more than $10-million annually.

The proposed plan is to produce silverplated flatware, ovenproof china, glassware, plastic-handled cutlery and three collections of cookware in cast aluminum, cast iron and enameled aluminum—all at moderate prices. The designs, to make their debut in the spring of 1972, will be marketed under a new label, Dansk Gourmet Designs Ltd.

### Bruised but Shiny

"This is exactly the kind of mottled, glittering finish we're going to put on our silverplated flatware," the 47-year-old executive said during a luncheon at Sardi's earlier this week. He was holding up a bruised but shiny fork that he had picked up from the table. "We'll make it, dents and all, and in Louis XV styling."

Mr. Nierenberg said he has spent more than a year developing the collections. He worked with Gunnar Cyrén, formerly chief designer at Orrefors, the Swedish glassworks, in developing the shapes for all of the designs. Ritva Puotila of Finland, who designs Dansk's linens, is the colorist for the collections.

"Gunnar and I spent almost a month last summer touring French restaurants and hotels," Mr. Nierenberg continued. They were checking not only the materials that chefs claim are best in cookwares and the type of tablewares that stand up under continued use in commercial establishments, but they were doing design research. And, from the look of the advance sketches, Mr. Nierenberg and his cohorts also became aware of the popularity of the wares in Bonniers and in Georg Jensen's basement as well as those in the Carrier Cook Shops.

The pair decided on a return to traditional shapes for most of the wares. Molds will be fashioned to resemble fruits or baskets and the knobs and handles on pots and casseroles will be shaped like fish, bound asparagus, mushrooms, pineapples, fruits and a horse's head.

---

* *New York Times*, December 24, 1970. © 1970 by The New York Times Company. Reprinted by permission.

**EXHIBIT 1** (*continued*)

"I think we can make six well-designed glasses to sell for the price of one glass—about $8," Mr. Nierenberg said. And with the glasses purchasers will get a rack that is part of the plastic packaging but which has been designed so that it can be used to store the wares.

"The collection may make the pegboard obsolete," he continued, producing a sketch of knives that have notched blades so that they can be hung on hooks on a rack that comes packaged with the knives.

The knife blades will be handmade in Japan, Mr. Nierenberg said, but he still hasn't decided where the plastic handles for these designs and the bistro-styled flatware (knives, forks and spoons) in the same collection will be made. He is currently checking on factories in France, Italy, Scandinavia and this country.

of MBAs were hired to assist Lubell, and Nierenberg delegated much of the marketing activity.

Nierenberg viewed these organizational changes as part of Dansk's transition from entrepreneurial to professional management. He felt that the successful accomplishment of this transition was critical if he were to realize his personal goal of withdrawing as chief executive officer by 1973.

## DANSK'S BUSINESS

### Products

Nierenberg described his product-market policy as anything for the "top of the table." Dansk designed and marketed flatware, china, linen, glass, decorator cookware, and wooden bowls and trays. Its products were of high quality and were priced accordingly. The firm was described by a competitor as follows:

Dansk's greatest strength is marketing and product development. They set their goals and they follow them: the "top of the table," good design, good taste, and good advertising. They are in a very good secure spot and a remarkable position today.

Because Dansk defined its market as products for the top of the dining room table, the firm competed with a broad range of companies: Lenox China, International Silver, Georg Jensen Silver and Steel, Baccarat Crystal, etc. Dansk's 1970 sales exceeded $10,000,000, and its profit after taxes was in the neighborhood of $750,000. Exhibits 3 and 4 itemize Dansk's products: their designers, manufacturers, and contribution to Dansk's overall sales.

**EXHIBIT 2**
Biographical summary of key Dansk people

| Name | Age | Year* | Affiliation in 1970 | Location | Background |
|------|-----|-------|---------------------|----------|------------|
| Ted Nierenberg | 47 | 1955 | President | Mt. Kisco | B.S., mechanical engineering, Carnegie Tech; engineering officer, Army Air Force; Epco (5 years); Small Business Administration, 1968. |
| Ed Lubell | 47 | 1956 | Executive V.P. | Mt. Kisco | B.S., business administration, Hofstra University; M.S., industrial engineering, Columbia University; AMP, Harvard Business School; bombardier navigator, Army Air Force; plant manager, Epco (9 years). |
| Burt Klapper | 44 | 1960 | V.P. marketing | Mt. Kisco | B.B.A., marketing, University of Miami; PMD, Harvard Business School; manager, store operation, AMC. |
| Keld Rosager-Hansen | 31 | 1970 | V.P. overseas operations | Denmark | B.S. and M.S., chemical engineering, Denmark; MBA, Harvard University; industrial engineer, corporate secretary, Colgate-Palmolive (Europe). |
| Sy Baxter | 40 | 1958 | Sales manager | Mt. Kisco | B.A., journalism, New York University; graduate studies, sales management, New York University; sales, Bulova Watch Co. |
| Barry Ginsburg | 33 | 1966 | Asst. V.P. | Mt. Kisco | B.A., history, Colby College; MBA, Cornell University; personnel officer, Air Force; systems analyst, Bell Telephone Labs. |
| Jerry Lieberg | 26 | 1969 | Controller | Mt. Kisco | B.A., political science, Yale University; MBA, University of Wisconsin; government representative, ALCOA. |
| Maria Wazeter | 29 | 1970 | Product strategy manager | Mt. Kisco | B.A., Wellesley College; MBA, Harvard University. |
| Jens Quistgaard | 51 | 1955 | Designer | Denmark | Silversmith apprenticeship; chief designer, Just Anderson; ceramic designer. |
| Gunnar Cyren | 39 | 1970 | Designer | Sweden | Graduate, Konstfack Art School, Sweden; goldsmith-silversmith; chief designer, Orrefors Glass, Sweden. |
| Niels Refsgaard | 36 | 1965 | Designer | Denmark | Graduate, Copenhagen School of Decorative Arts; potter. |

**EXHIBIT 2** (*continued*)

| Name | Age | Year* | Affiliation in 1970 | Location | Background |
|------|-----|-------|---------------------|----------|------------|
| Ritva Puotila | 35 | 1960 | Designer | Finland | Decorative Arts, Athenaeum, Helsinki, Finland; textile designer and colorist. |
| Richard Nissen | 41 | 1957 | Supplier, wood products | Denmark | Wood production and machine design (23 years); owner-manager, Richard Nissen |
| Alf Rimer | 35 | 1959 | Independent model maker | Denmark | n.a. |

\* Indicates the year in which the individual became affiliated with Dansk.
n.a. = not available.

## Marketing

The starting point for all Dansk products was response to a perceived market opportunity. Keld Rosager-Hansen, vice president of overseas operations, commented:

Ted and others in the company have a certain ability to perceive a market need and match it with a winning design. They can see when a good design is also a marketable design. You can contrast this to selling detergent. There you can walk down the street and ring doorbells to see if people like your product. You can't do that here because the market segment is so small. How do you get at such a diffuse group? You have to rely a lot on personal judgment.

Dansk had a strong following of consumers. Nierenberg referred to them as "Dansk club members." For example, in 1970 almost 50,000 people wrote to Dansk requesting brochures or information about products, or making suggestions, etc. On the other hand, Dansk did not know very much about these customers. No market polling, panels, or research had ever been attempted.

In 1970 Dansk marketing activities were directed by Burt Klapper, 44, who had joined Dansk in 1960 as a salesman. In 1965 he was promoted to general sales manager and in 1968, upon returning from the four-month PMD program at the Harvard Business School, was named to the newly created position of vice president of marketing. Sy Baxter replaced Klapper as sales manager.

The third member of the marketing team was Maria Wazeter who had joined Dansk in June 1970 after graduating from the Harvard MBA Program. Her title was product strategy manager. Both Klapper and Nierenberg hoped that she would be able to generate some useful information about Dansk's market.

**EXHIBIT 3**
**Product line summary of Dansk designs**

| Product line | Patterns | Pieces* | 1st pattern intro- duced | Designers† | Country of manufacture |
|---|---|---|---|---|---|
| **I** | | | | | |
| Stainless steel flatware . . . . . | 8 | 12–15 | 1955 | Q | Germany, Finland France |
| Salt and pepper shakers . . . . | 1 | 2 | 1960 | Q | Denmark |
| **II** | | | | | |
| Enameled steel cookware (Kobenstyle) . . . . . . . . | 1 | 18 | 1957 | Q | Denmark, Finland, Sweden, France, Holland |
| Copperware (discontinued) . . . . . . . | 1 | 12 | 1962 | Q | Denmark |
| **III** | | | | | |
| Woodenware. . . . . . . . . . | 1 | 50 | 1957 | Q | Denmark |
| **IV** | | | | | |
| China dinnerware (Flamestone) . . . . . . . . | 2 | 18 | 1957 | Q | Denmark |
| Stoneware dinnerware (Generation) . . . . . . . . | 10 | 20 | 1966 | R | Denmark |
| Fine china (Epoch) . . . . . . . | 5 | 16 | 1969 | R | Norway |
| **V** | | | | | |
| Cast-iron candlesticks . . . . . | 1 | 12 | 1963 | Q | Denmark |
| Silver-plated candlesticks . . . | 1 | 3 | 1968 | Q | Finland |
| **VI** | | | | | |
| Textiles . . . . . . . . . . . . . | 1 | 50 | 1964 | P | Finland, Belgium |
| **VII** | | | | | |
| Bar and stemware . . . . . . . . | 22 | 4–5 | 1967 | Q | Finland, Belgium, France |
| **VIII** | | | | | |
| Cast-iron cookware (orecast) . . . . . . . . . . . | 1 | 14 | 1969 | Q | Finland, Belgium |

*Indicates number of pieces per pattern.
†Q = Quistgaard, R = Refsgaard, P = Puotila.

Two distinctive features of Dansk's marketing strategy were the use of advertising (5% of sales) to create a strong brand image and a captive sales force (consisting of 22 men organized on a territorial basis) to offer the retailer, in Klapper's words, "far greater than normal service, greater inventory turns, and fewer markdowns."[3] Klapper touched on both these areas in the following comments:

To me Dansk advertising is one of the cornerstones upon which the company was built. There is a very special "feel" and consistency of distinctive creative elegance to it. To the retailer, it is known as the "hallmark of quality"

[3] On the other hand, Dansk had withdrawn from trade shows in 1965 and did not maintain showrooms, as was the custom in the industry.

**EXHIBIT 4**
Dansk product line statement

| Product line | Percentage of gross profit | | Sales by product line as a percentage of total sales | | | | | | |
|---|---|---|---|---|---|---|---|---|---|
| | 1969 | 1970 | 1964 | 1965 | 1966 | 1967 | 1968 | 1969 | 1970 |
| Kobenstyle . . . . . . . . | 18.4 | 18.3 | 12.6 | 9.9 | 12.4 | 13.9 | 20.8 | 17.5 | 16.0 |
| Stainless steel flatware . . . . . . . . . | 19.4 | 18.1 | 22.8 | 18.4 | 17.7 | 15.7 | 18.0 | 18.6 | 16.7 |
| Wood . . . . . . . . . . . . | 19.2 | 17.0 | 24.2 | 32.8 | 20.6 | 17.9 | 17.1 | 20.2 | 21.0 |
| Generation/Epoch . . . . | 11.5 | 14.1 | . . . | . . . | 2.9 | 7.5 | 9.1 | 12.0 | 13.0 |
| Designs with light . . . . . | 11.2 | 8.5 | 17.4 | 28.1 | 22.9 | 19.3 | 15.1 | 11.3 | 8.0 |
| Orecast . . . . . . . . . . . | 2.0 | 5.1 | . . . | . . . | . . . | . . . | . . . | 2.1 | 4.0 |
| Flamestone . . . . . . . . | 5.2 | 6.8 | 7.3 | 7.0 | 8.0 | 7.4 | 6.0 | 5.4 | 6.0 |
| Barware . . . . . . . . . . | 4.9 | 4.2 | . . . | . . . | 0.7 | 2.0 | 3.7 | 5.1 | 5.0 |
| Silver plate . . . . . . . . | 3.6 | 3.6 | 4.1 | 3.5 | 4.0 | 4.8 | 3.7 | 3.7 | 4.6 |
| Stemware . . . . . . . . | 2.1 | 3.0 | . . . | . . . | . . . | 1.8 | 2.4 | 2.2 | 3.0 |
| Textiles . . . . . . . . . | 1.8 | 1.6 | 11.6 | 6.3 | 5.6 | 4.5 | 2.7 | 1.7 | 2.0 |
| Miscellaneous . . . . . . . | . . . | . . . | . . . | . . . | 1.1 | 4.4 | 0.9 | 0.2 | . . . |

of our industry. To consumers, it connotes the very best in taste and presentation. Nobody counts, but the number of award-winning ads are many.

We've always sold the concept—the Dansk brand. We're always selling Dansk—not an ice bucket or a salad bowl. It's undignified to discuss how much a store buyer wants of each line. I say "buy it all." That's a two-way street, though. In return for their buying the full line, they get a *real* brand name which is backed by a tightly controlled, limited distributorship (less than 500 retail outlets).

We've been leaders. We're not worried about being liked—leaders lead, they don't win popularity contests. Hence, many retailers wait for us to stumble. We are that firm in our attitudes and sales policies. The retailer has a real responsibility when he represents Dansk. I'm most comfortable with these policies.

## Design

Design activity at Dansk was dominated by Jens Quistgaard. Quistgaard-designed products accounted for 75% of Dansk's dollar sales in 1970. It was generally agreed by those who knew him that Quistgaard was a most talented and temperamental artist, and he looked and played that role to its fullest. Wearing a full beard and knickers, Quistgaard, who was 51 years old, lived on an island four miles off the coast of Denmark. His comments illustrated his philosophy of design and life:

As long as there are people living here, there will always be a certain classic way of life that will not change. A certain group of intellect, a certain wish to own something that is beautiful. As a philosophy of life, it will always be so that a home will not be a garage or clinic. You will have a lot of *impractical* things around. Therefore, we will always have people that will want things that are beautiful, that are forged, that are made the classic way. People will appreciate woodenware and things that have a similarity to the human body and to movement. You will never go around with empty hands. You will want to enjoy yourself by using these beautiful things. Silk, wool, all the classic materials will never be replaced by paper or plastic.

We are having rockets, speed, hospitals, and all this kind of modern thing. When we come back to our private home, we will have fewer things, but much, much more beautiful, more artistic, and longer lasting. For the security of your inside feelings you need poetry now more than ever to combat the harsh, cold, vinegar look of the offices and factories. You will not live for your work. You will live for your private home and the classic appeal of that. All intellectual people will have it that way. You will still have paintings and a lot of things which will have changing fashions and style, but which will have the same major Gestalt. I think that's so important.

Dansk's second major designer was Niels Refsgaard. Refsgaard had joined Dansk in 1965; his china patterns accounted for 15% of Dansk's 1970 dollar sales. Like Quistgaard, Refsgaard was a Dane, although he thought of himself more as a potter than a designer:

I have been a potter for many years. When I have an idea, I only dream of a shape. Then I make many samples, and I pick the one that comes closest to that dream. You see, I come from 10 generations of blacksmiths, and, as forging is to a blacksmith, potting is a simple feeling of good proportion. It takes much hard work, but finally you have something that you can look at and feel and say, "that is right—that is what I want."

The third major designer was Gunnar Cyren, a Swede, who joined Dansk early in 1970. His primary responsibility was the new housewares line to be known as Dansk Gourmet Designs Ltd. Prior to coming to Dansk, Cyren had been chief designer at the Orrefors Glass Company in Sweden. The following comments reflect his approach to design:

It is my habit to work from 8 till 4:30 every day. In school you do it always, and then when you have been working for 10 years as an apprentice—that's ordinary work. The creativeness is only part of it. I'm not creative all the time. Even if it's not routine work, it's handicraft work. Many things have to be designed to accurate drawings. Many things are just a matter of keeping order. It is essential to have order on the table, order in your mind. From order comes good design, or design is order—a form of order.

Nierenberg compared Cyren and Quistgaard as follows:

I think Gunnar is a versatile designer and may develop to be as good or better than Jens. The temperament of these two men is very different. We are making industrially oriented (in a production sense) products. It's a combination of handcraftsmanship and mechanization. The mechanization is naturally gaining and this imposes constraints. Jens bristles with the constraints—he constantly wants the factories to design new and special machinery. Gunnar is challenged by the constraints. He wants to maximize the originality within these constraints.

As of the end of 1970, these three men, along with Ritva Puotila, a Finn, who designed Dansk's easy-care table linens and was responsible for all the firm's color decisions, and Alf Rimer, Dansk's model maker, made up Dansk's design activity. Quistgaard had the greatest experience and broadest range of talents. He had designed in wood, glass, china, cast iron, stainless steel, and silver. Refsgaard had only designed in china, and while he professed a desire to work in other materials, he had yet to do so. Cyren was considered to be an artist of considerable talent, even though his experience had been exclusively in glass and silver. It was Lubell's opinion that for the next two or three years Dansk would have to rely on Quistgaard for most of its new designs in wood, stainless steel, flatware, enamel on steel, and cast iron.

Dansk designers were paid on a royalty basis and were reputed to be paid very well. For example, Quistgaard, who had a guaranteed minimum royalty income of $50,000 a year until he was 65, had royalty income in 1969 and 1970 considerably in excess of the minimum. Dansk designers were prohibited from designing products which competed with Dansk's line. If this were to happen, Dansk could stop paying all royalties.

## Manufacturing

Dansk had no manufacturing operations of its own; all its products were produced by contract manufacturers, with Dansk providing the designs and tooling. The need to provide profitability to contract manufacturers and sufficient contribution to cover Dansk's high cost of doing business[4] placed a premium on finding and developing special low-cost production techniques or competences to keep the cost of Dansk products competitive. For example, Dansk marketed glass products that looked like cut glass but actually were produced by a new injection process developed in France.

Dansk had about 30 different suppliers who were located in Denmark, Norway, Sweden, Finland, France, and Germany. Production in the Far East was being contemplated. Most suppliers were small or medium-sized and were generally under individual or family ownership. The degree of Dansk involvement ranged from situations where Dansk brought

---

[4] Maintaining a modeling shop in Copenhagen of four very skilled men; high tooling costs; high marketing expenses, including advertising and a sales force that not only sold and serviced but performed detail work as well.

only a small percentage of a supplier's volume to those where it bought 100%. In 1970 Dansk found sales of many of its products constrained by the capacity of the contract manufacturer. These suppliers were either unwilling or unable to expand production for Dansk.

The relationship between Dansk and its suppliers was an informal one: the suppliers agreed to produce a particular product for Dansk at an agreed-upon price and Dansk agreed to purchase a certain amount. The arrangements were closed by handshakes and could be terminated by either side. Dansk protected its designs by patents and copyrights and had a reputation for defending its position, having taken some imitators to litigation. As a result, in the last two or three years it had experienced little difficulty of this nature.

Richard Nissen, principal supplier of Dansk's wood products, was a good example of a Dansk contract manufacturer. He too was a Dane and prided himself on the extent to which he and Dansk had been able to preserve the handcrafted nature of the products while manufacturing on semiautomatic machinery. He commented:

By being inventive, we think we can make machinery that will do better than the craftsman himself. It might take a slight transforming of the artist's idea. It might have a curve which we cannot produce. Then we have to compromise. It can be done.

As his business expanded, Nissen had gotten more and more into management and further away from tooling and production. As a result, there had been considerable difficulty with a line of rosewood trays that Quistgaard had designed. Nissen explained:

I forgot there were very few people in the factory left that could do the work. As a matter of fact, there was only me who had the experience. Last year, the last very good craftsman died of a heart attack. So, you know: new people, a new design concept—they were not used to it. Well, I knew afterwards that they felt scared to death. They would promise you anything. The more the Dansk Copenhagen office[5] called, the more scared they were. Especially when they were threatened with competition! You know, Dansk could always send the job to another supplier.

With regard to the future, Nissen commented:

My goals are not to expand for any price. I don't want to be big in volume. I would like to be large in quality. It's not the volume that counts. In the woodworking business there will be room for quality in the future. Quantity products will be made in plastic. It's a goal that I am setting to go along with the products I know. I also know these products are of such a special nature that they will be too expensive for the consumer's need unless one

---

[5] The Copenhagen office handled Dansk's day-to-day operating relationships with contract manufacturers. In addition, office personnel participated in product-feasibility studies directed from Dansk's headquarters.

can make the feelings and emotions go along with them. That's what the artist does—what Jens understands. Volume, no; quality and some expansion, yes. If I have a good thing to produce, that's my job in society. If I can fulfill this job in society, in the needs of today or tomorrow, it is my motivation. If I can do this for Dansk, I will, but I want the name "Nissen" brought in a little, too.

Dansk's manufacturing and other internal operations were the responsibility of Ed Lubell, executive vice president. Up until 1966 Lubell had handled the firm's administration, inventory management, ordering, distribution, finance, and supervision of the people Dansk employed in the Copenhagen office. In 1966 Dansk opened a Paris production-supervision office as its manufacturing facilities widened beyond Scandinavia. In the same year, Barry Ginsburg was hired as controller, with particular emphasis on inventory management and factory ordering procedures. In 1969 Jerry Lieberg was hired to assume Ginsburg's activities; Nierenberg wanted Ginsburg to take on more new product-feasibility studies[6] and be the only person communicating with the production offices on all but broad policy matters.

Another important organizational change involved the overseas operations. In May 1970, Keld Rosager-Hansen joined Dansk as vice president of overseas operations. Rosager-Hansen was a Dane with an MBA degree from Harvard. He had worked for six years with Colgate-Palmolive in Europe, where he had established Colgate's first industrial engineering department and had then gone through the general-management rotation program. Rosager-Hansen was hired by Dansk with the idea of his taking over the Paris production-supervision office as well as the Copenhagen office. In the past, both offices had reported to Lubell (on new product feasibility) and to Ginsburg (ongoing production). It was felt that much work was being duplicated, whereas a single strong European manager could exercise judgment in selecting the best supplier with whom to make product-feasibility studies. After two months on the job, Rosager-Hansen assessed the situation in Europe as follows:

Although there are not very many people in Dansk, they are very much apart geographically. The communication problems that are caused by that kind of distance are much larger than you expect till you've been in them. So one of the problems we've got to get solved is how the proper communications with Mt. Kisco ought to be established.

At present there is a flurry of small little slips going back and forth. The telex bills are astronomical. I believe we send a couple of yards of telexes every day. We can't go on like that forever. The people here spend

---

[6] Two feasibility gates had to be passed before Dansk would commit to a new product, one technical and one economic. Could the product be manufactured as designed? If so, did the economics (investment in tooling and product costs) make sense given Dansk's assessment of the market?

most of their time writing letters to Mt. Kisco or answering letters from them. People's time is taken up by the wrong things. Because of the communications problem, everybody's attention is really turned in the direction of Mt. Kisco. Instead, we should be looking out for the problems which are really between us here and the suppliers.

Rosager-Hansen met with Ed Lubell in Copenhagen to discuss these problems. The general conclusion of the meeting was that some standard operating procedures were needed in Dansk. Excerpts from Rosager-Hansen's minutes of the meeting are included as Exhibit 5.

## Ownership

Nierenberg owned all the equity in Dansk. He was planning, however, to give part of that equity to other managers. As of the end of 1970, Lubell and Klapper were the first to receive stock in Dansk. Nierenberg explained the reasoning behind this action:

I've now completed the plan to give away stock. I don't want options or conditions. When I see some of the people here doing exactly what I would have done when it meant real personal hardship to me or my family in order to make the goal, they're not acting like owners, they are owners. So this year Burt and Ed own some of the company. And I hope it will be more and more. My responsibility is greater, but their contribution is proportionately much larger. I now see things with numbers, and yet each number represents a lot of people. And I hope it will be more people.

A public offering was also being contemplated by Nierenberg:[7]

No company that's growing 15% or 20% a year can stay private. People who do are just building a kingdom—a little fairyland where you have a king, a crown prince, and many people-in-waiting. These companies tend to be dominated by a single strong individual, and other people in the company just execute his orders. Ed Lubell has been this particular kind of executive. That's why I sent Burt off to PMD and Ed to AMP at Harvard. I wanted them to see what a manager's responsibilities were all about.

Before they went, they may have felt the gap between my contribution to the company and theirs was narrowing, and now they feel it's widening. They're beginning to become managers. They just never realized the alternatives I considered. I want to spread the responsibility, the motivation, and the ownership.

We'll either get acquired or go public. But the longer we can grow internally and keep better internal controls before we need outside financing, the greater is the equity to all of us. I don't want to go public as anything but a first-class company. I've watched a lot of people try to bail themselves out by going public—that's not for me.

---

[7] As a result, there are no detailed financial data in the case study. For the purpose of analysis, however, it can be reasonably assumed that finances were not a problem.

**EXHIBIT 5**

# DANSK DESIGNS LTD

PRODUCTION: NYE KONGENSGADE 15, DK-1472 COPENHAGEN K TELEPHONE: *14 42 44 TELEX: 9018 CABLE: DANSIGN COPENHAGEN
HOME OFFICE:  MOUNT KISCO,  NEW YORK 10549 U.S.A.   TELEPHONE: (914) 666-2121  TELEX: 13 74 98  CABLE: DANSKIMP MTCO

Minutes of Meeting in Copenhagen
Thursday, September 10, 1970          Copenhagen,      c.c.   TN, BK
                                                             BG, JL
                                                             CA*, SP*

Present:  E. S. Lubell, K. Rosager-Hansen

1) Initiation of projects to be carried out by the Copenhagen group.
   At present projects are started in Copenhagen mostly through one-way
   communication by a letter being received from somebody in Mount
   Kisco.  The lack of dialogue or a feedback to the U.S. had sometimes
   caused misunderstandings in relation to unfilled expectations.  In view
   of this it was decided that any major project to be initiated in
   Copenhagen as a general rule shall be agreed upon with KRH at a
   face-to-face meeting in Copenhagen, Mount Kisco, or elsewhere.  In
   special cases a request for work can be submitted to KRH, who will
   evaluate the feasibility and the amount of time involved.  The request
   will then be returned with a likely day of completion or with comments
   indicating why a project cannot be undertaken as is.  In the latter case
   the project can be reconsidered at the first following face-to-face meeting.

   The above procedure does not concern routine operations, e.g., discussions
   of product quality and delivery times as well as price requests from established
   suppliers on basically traditional product types.  However, any project
   involving new suppliers or new types of products is covered by the above
   procedure.

2) Modus Operandi.
   Basically it is the responsibility of Mount Kisco to define the problems and
   the Copenhagen group is to identify and carry out the solutions.  As the
   objective is to obtain the results that are most favourable for the company as
   a whole, the origin of the right solution to a given problem is of little importance.  Therefore the Copenhagen group will always review any suggestion
   as to how to solve a problem presented by MK.  On the other hand,
   Copenhagen has no obligation to follow such proposals, and feedback on the
   proposals will not necessarily take place except when clarification is
   desired by the Development Manager.*  In view of this it will be most adequate
   that said proposals are presented as straightforward statements rather than as
   questions that suggest the necessity of an answer (e.g., "Perhaps it is an idea
   also to get quotes from "X" RATHER THAN "Please also get quotes from X; when
   can we expect?").

---

* Development managers reporting to Rosager-Hansen. Organized by materials (i.e., wood and
china), these men expedited Dansk's orders.

## Management

Two important aspects of Dansk management must be emphasized: delegation and style. While the firm began as a one-man show, Nierenberg consciously tried to develop managers that could assume an increasing amount of the day-to-day operation of the firm. The following comment by Barry Ginsburg reflected Nierenberg's move toward delegation:

In the last few years there has been real delegation of authority from the top down. Ted used to do everything: labels, names, new products. I'm sure he even did the doorknobs in the building. Now I do the doorknobs. Maybe they aren't as good, but that's not his job. He has become more of a chairman than president now. He piles it on Burt and Ed. As a result, they can't do what they used to, so they pile some of it on me. I think it's great—the way it should be. Maybe it should have happened earlier. This is all new since I've been here. He used to look at the new orders every morning. You know—what do you mean so and so only ordered six ice buckets? We can no longer trot in to him. We have to figure it out ourselves. This is the only way to have ongoing entity which will transcend individuals.

The second characteristic of Dansk management was its style. The high-quality, highly designed image of the firm's products carried over into the firm's operations. The headquarters building in Mt. Kisco, New York, was a striking structure placed on six acres of garden and woods. The interior decor was a blend of modern and antique.

This corporate character, moreover, went beyond the physical surroundings. Guests were taken to lunch in the finest restaurants, and there was a conscious attempt to run the firm in a first-class manner.

Another aspect of Dansk's style was its informality. Everyone at Dansk was on a first-name basis. There was no organizational chart. The atmosphere was an open one where people felt free to say what was on their minds.

## THE REVENUE GAP

Nierenberg's growth goals for Dansk were ambitious ones:

The exciting thing for me is, can we keep Dansk growing at 15% to 20% a year? What other things can we do without cutting back on our Dansk line? Can we generate the same kind of growth in other areas? If we can go to $40 million on an internal basis, rather than by acquisition, we can begin to say we've got something that would be damned exciting for the people in it. You just don't see it that often. That's the kernel of the challenge.

Based on their assessment of the market, Dansk management did not feel that their existing product line would provide sufficient growth to meet Nierenberg's objectives. To fill this gap, Dansk was planning to introduce a line of houseware products to be called Dansk Gourmet Designs Ltd. (see Exhibit 1). Maria Wazeter described Gourmet:

Dansk Gourmet has developed 35–40 new product categories or product concepts, pinpointing virtually every cooking and serving function. Some may be technologically impossible at present; some may be infeasible at present; some may be infeasible for the next five years. For a few categories, the market may not be large enough to justify the design, tooling, and administrative expense.

Yet, even after these products are winnowed out, the number of categories reaching the marketplace still should at least triple what Dansk has at present. If Dansk now has close to 600 items in eight categories, the numbers involved in 24 or more new collections are staggering. In short, I can see the present Dansk line still growing yet becoming the "minor" portion of Dansk's overall sales volume within the next 5 or 10 years.

These growth goals and new product plans had significant implications for all aspects of Dansk's operations. The remainder of the case study will examine one of the most critical: new product development. The need for a steady stream of new products was apparent. Sales of some existing products were already constrained by supplier capacity; growth in these areas would mean new products and new suppliers. Gourmet represented a corporate commitment to increase the number of products that Dansk was selling by 300% in the course of 5 to 10 years.

## THE DEVELOPMENT PROCESS

In Dansk's early years, the development activities were performed by Nierenberg and Quistgaard. Nierenberg's description of staved teak is a good illustration:

I had been intrigued by Danish teakwood furniture. It was beginning to be very fashionable. Teak had a magical quality. To Americans it connoted fancy yachts and boats. There were some lovely teak salad bowls in a few stores in Denmark that were expensive and made from a single solid piece of wood. I told Jens [Quistgaard] that I thought there might be a market for teak accessories such as trays and ice buckets and salad bowls because food could be placed directly on the teak and it was easy to wash off and reoil to replenish the finish if it dulled.

Jens designed some bowls and trays, but when I priced out these items with some wood turners, it meant that a bowl would have to retail for $100 and a simple tray for $30 or $40. When I analyzed the cost, it was obvious that if this product line was to come to fruition, we would have to economize drastically on the material.

I then asked Jens about the possibilities of manufacturing from staves, as in barrel production, which led to visiting barrel factories, which led to

Richard (Nissen) and the creation of staved teak. There were a few days never to be forgotten.

Jens wanted the staves bent and thought they could be bent with steam. The steam would bend them all right, but they didn't stay bent. Richard came up with the idea of cutting the staves in compound curves to form a bowl. We tried gluing together the first bowl made from staves. We were upstairs in a cruddy attic of an equipment garage. Richard, Jens, myself, and a foreman—there were 16 staves and four pairs of hands, and every time one pair of hands reached for the clamps, the bowl fell apart. Suddenly, there was another pair of hands with the clamps at the right time and the right place. It was Hans (Richard's father) who had come back late at night to see what we were doing. Jens made some designs, Richard made some calculations, and when he gave me the first prices, I knew we were on the right track.

By 1970, however, the number of participants in the development process had grown. Lubell commented:

Until recently, Ted [Nierenberg] had been the sole contact with the designers. He could not continue to be and still develop Gourmet. The logical step was to pair up Burt [Klapper] with the most important and most difficult designer, Jens [Quistgaard]. We decided to start Burt in wood, where Jens was most secure and the production parameters most clearly defined.

Furthermore, Ted was getting into the Dansk product development cycle at every step. Now Burt is conceiving the product strategy, reviewing sketches and designs, and editing. Burt's and Jens' record together on wood the last 18 months is excellent. Now they are working together on designs with light, flatware, and cookware. Maria [Wazeter] is developing product strategy for glass and china and linens.

The transition was not without its problems, particularly in the design area. After a fast and successful beginning, Dansk experienced a period of stagnation in the early 1960s. Sales growth slowed. Problems with contract manufacturers appeared. Salesmen were lost. Profits declined. The situation came to a head in 1965. Klapper commented:

It became clear that the J.H.Q.[8] china design dream was just that—a dream. Jens did not complete the job. Ted's belief in Jens' ability to "make a market" for Dansk in china was being eroded. By this time we were in a "survival strategy"—selling tremendous amounts of unproven items—clogging retail pipelines—forcing markdowns, etc. We were choking ourselves and the retailers with often undesirable inventory—trying to make our figures.

Nierenberg also commented on this situation:

Ed [Lubell] and Burt [Klapper] and I believed in our ability to execute the total top-of-the-table strategy. We were committed to a new location and warehouse in Mt. Kisco, and it was no small commitment. If I went off to Denmark, worked with Jens and saw it (the china design) through, I would have been

---

[8] Quistgaard's signature.

repeating the same annual crisis experience for the 11th time since 1955. I did not want to spend half of my life in Denmark. I also realized our survival depended on Jens—we had no depth of design resources.

Nierenberg traveled to Denmark to tell Quistgaard that Dansk would hire other designers for the first time. Quistgaard threatened to quit. Nierenberg offered him a guaranteed $50,000 a year minimum income until his 65th birthday. (Quistgaard was making about $35,000 a year at the time.) Quistgaard finally accepted the arrangement but refused to design in china ever again.

Niels Refsgaard was hired to design for Dansk and came up with the very successful "Generation" pattern. Klapper saw significance in the decision to hire Refsgaard:

"Generation" was the beginning of the real implementation of a strategy that was "top of the table": rejecting the "survival strategy" and going for a concept. As if axiomatically came the next major change: the restructuring of the Dansk-factory relationship. No more "loans and advances" to Nissen, etc. No "captive" factories—no paternalistic relationships with factories. Factories were to become sources, professionally shopped and compared. We would stand on our own two feet—so would those factories with whom we could contract and build a healthy relationship, hopefully long-term. But, realistically, profitable for both parties.

Nierenberg was not satisfied with just two designers, however. He continued to search for new design talent and in 1968 met Gunnar Cyren. The courtship of Cyren lasted two years, during which time (in 1969) Cyren was promoted to chief designer at Orrefors. Even though the promotion placed Cyren in charge of five designers, many of whom were older and more established than himself, Cyren decided to join Dansk in the spring of 1970:

The big hook for me in Ted's [Nierenberg] program was that I was responsible for the whole new collection called Gourmet. I'm not taking part of another collection. I have a whole area for myself. That's a very nice point. I don't know how much it is politics for Ted, so that he can get beside the problem with Jens. I don't think Jens wants any competitors. One way to get around that might be a new collection, and then call it Gourmet. In any case, I will be working directly with Ted. There will be no one between us, and I trust him to the utmost extent. . . . I am satisfied with that.

Quistgaard's reaction to these new designers was decidedly negative:

It is like a man who has been an opera star for many years. Then all of a sudden the owner, because of a crisis, decides to bring in a little competition to push the singer into another success. This is absolutely wrong. You cannot tell a person how he must sing and act in a role. If he could do that, he would be a superman. You can't press a man into a mold. If you do, you are trying the wrong way. If you try to press artists into a team when their styles do not go together, it will be a disaster.

From Quistgaard's point of view, Nierenberg's delegation of design selection to Burt Klapper compounded the problem. Nierenberg commented on the situation:

For the good of the company, I cannot work with Jens [Quistgaard] anymore. If we are to be a dynamic company, we must plan ahead—maximize alternatives—conduct feasibility studies—unfortunately, discard good designs that can't meet profitability criteria or duplicate a market need. We must work on a two-year development cycle. Jens always knew that when he was late with a design, I'd show up and bail him and the company out. He knew that I knew shortcuts nobody else knew. That's an expertise I don't want anybody else in the company to acquire.

Quistgaard expressed his opinion of the new approach as follows:

I want to be in on choosing the designs myself. I want to have my voice there. Too much of my valuable work is going into the wastebasket. That I cannot stand, either as an artist businessman or as a human being. It's so humiliating. All the decisions are made over my head. They are not skilled enough to criticize this sort of thing. They don't have the talent to choose all that well. If they don't have me in on the design, then they are doing themselves more bad than good.

Burt's [Klapper] letters are as sweet as can be, but he has so much to learn about design, style, coordination, and such. I also know from experience that he is a very clever guy. He won't make the same mistake twice, but he is too scientific in his approach.

Ted [Nierenberg] and I are so close that if you change the pattern too much and give it to other people, no matter how nice they are, if they don't have the tact and respect for me, they will take out their power too much. I am very afraid of the future because of too much other designing, too much delegating to people who don't have the skill. They can perhaps gain that, little by little. I hope they will take me in and ask my opinion and not just make a calculation about the price, or something like that.

Refsgaard was also dissatisfied with the extent to which his work was criticized:

They should believe more in each other as people and in us as designers. It is not funny to have people interpret your design for you. Like Burt [Klapper], who is suddenly acting as new designer for Dansk. He is telling me that something would be a good design if I took 3 millimeters off here and smoothed this curve. Jens has had the same problems. Sometimes I feel they are trying to wring me like a sponge—get the last drop out. For example, last Christmas I did some patterns for decorating the white porcelain, Epoch. They were good designs. I sent them to Mt. Kisco, and for three months they made me change and develop new patterns. Now they have finally gone back and chosen my first design. Why do I waste my time so? I should just tell them that this is my design and do something else.

At the end of 1970, Nierenberg made the following comments:

The year 1970 was very gratifying. The country has been in a slump—some of our competition was hit very hard. We have had a very good year. Gunnar Cyren looks like somebody with whom we can build. Jens is a loner! He's jealous and resentful. It's showing. Some of his resentment is carrying over to Niels—it's a little like "my enemy's enemy is my friend." I feel Keld's skills are helping us.

I've been very demanding of everybody. I guess a lot more than I used to be and more than everybody has come to expect. Sometimes I have the feeling when I'm bearing down hard on somebody in their office that they welcome a phone or intercom ringing—it takes the pressure off for a moment. Everybody is comfortable in the safe zones. Burt in sales and existing product marketing. Ed in feasibility criteria and execution of my policies. Barry where Jerry now is. Jens in wood. Niels with Generation. I have the feeling that everybody wants to hide under the table when they know I'm about to ask about alternatives for selling Gourmet—or should we continue a production-supervision office in Paris—or the source alternatives for products we've never made before—or what will be our sales compensation plan in three years? I don't want anybody to drown, but if you don't swallow a little water, you never learn how cruel that ocean can really be!

# GENERAL MANAGEMENT IN THE DIVISIONALIZED ORGANIZATION

# BCI Ltd.*

"In today's world, we do not think that our subsidiary companies can expand to their full potential without some help from central advisory services provided by our headquarters staffs," stated Mr. Henry Lampton, one of BCI's executives and a leading contender to succeed the BCI managing director, who would retire within one year. British Commercial Investments Ltd. (BCI), a London-based industrial holding company, comprised 16 subsidiary companies, with operations ranging from the manufacture of oil drilling equipment to electrical components and from special steel fabrication to the construction of agricultural buildings. Originally, the company had been involved solely with Malayan rubber plantations, but in the fifties it was decided to diversify entirely out of these politically risky activities through acquisition of small- to medium-size private companies, mainly in the United Kingdom. During the preceding seven years, partly through acquisition and partly through internal growth, gross tangible assets had risen from £9 million to £31 million and pretax profits from £900,000 to £3.4 million. A recent shift in emphasis had occurred, however. According to one executive:

Our present investment effort is directed mainly towards internal expansion by existing subsidiaries and the acquisition of no new subsidiaries unless they complement technologically those we already have. These two efforts, growth from within and acquisition of *related* companies, is what will produce the

* This case was written by Professor C. E. Summer. Copyright 1972 by l'Institut pour l'Étude des Méthodes de Direction de l'Enterprise (IMEDE), Lausanne, Switzerland. Reproduced by permission.

kind of profit we are interested in. Also, we have instituted what we call the BCI Three-Year Forecast, which involves much forward thinking-in-detail. This kind of planning is accepted as essential in modern company planning, but, even if it wasn't, something very similar would be needed to ensure the continued strength of BCI.

## PARENT-SUBSIDIARY RELATIONSHIPS

The shift in emphasis in corporate objectives as well as the increased attention to formal planning had also led to changes in the relationships between BCI and its subsidiaries. According to Mr. Lampton, who had been instrumental in bringing about these changes:

We have been trying recently to provide additional help to our subsidiary companies. Until very recently, however, we were rather diffident about providing these services to give specialized advice in particular fields; it would be fatal to try and force them on unwilling subsidiary managements. But recently the success of our operations research group, the welcome accorded to the monthly economic bulletins of our chief economist, and the demand for the services of our BCI marketing adviser all attest to the need felt by subsidiary managers. Only in the last three weeks a computer adviser has joined our staff and has begun to familiarize himself with existing EDP installations and projects. We have been too slow in recognizing the part which EDP techniques will play in the future. We hope to provide companies individually too small to justify their own EDP units with access to facilities, and to reduce costs for all by organizing a coordinated network available on a BCI-wide basis.

It is, however, a part of our philosophy that our underlying principal subsidiaries (or, if you like, divisions) should be of a size that they can support their own local functional staff of a high caliber. We are not suffering under the delusion that we can operate a large central services team capable of resolving the local problems of such a diverse organization. Our advisory staff are used as catalysts.

Finally, I would like to say something about the services rendered to subsidiary operating companies by our BCI nominee director. We like to think that the personalities, experience, and sometimes wider contacts which our directors have are an important source of help to managements of BCI subsidiary companies.

Another executive elaborated:

BCI maintains a (nonexecutive) director on the board of each of its subsidiaries, usually as chairman. Although nonexecutive, the BCI nominee normally visits each of his two or three companies about once a week, or twice every three weeks. The BCI nominee typically has had considerable industrial experience before joining our organization, either with a firm of accountants or management consultants, or with some other industrial corporation in an executive capacity. Many of them have university education and have also attended advanced management programs such as the Administrative Staff College at Henley, Harvard Business School, Stanford Business School, or IMEDE in Lausanne.

Mr. Lampton continued:

The position of a BCI nominee director involves a rather heavy responsibility. We are not bankers, interested only in the financial aspects of the business. We are not there to take a normal dividend and let it go at that. In some financial holding companies, the local managements have the idea that they are entirely self-sufficient, except for dividends. At the same time, the directors nominated by the parent company to the boards of those subsidiaries create the impression that they are banker types—somewhat superior to getting into real operating problems. I personally believe that in some such holding companies the subsidiary managers are being supine; they sit there with talent which could add to operations, but which they abdicate. Specifically, I am certain that in this day of complex technology and society, the director has a moral responsibility to help his managers—to encourage them to do planning for the future, to aid them in selecting and staffing their operations, and to give advice where the director has talent or knowledge.

I can give you one example. Most recently, BCI acquired the L. M. Trowbridge Company from the Trowbridge family. This company specializes in construction projects using asphalt products—parking lots, tennis courts, large industrial asphalt areas. It is to the benefit of everyone—BCI, Harrogate [another subsidiary which produces asphalt materials] and Trowbridge managers, and employees of both companies—to merge the operations of the two companies. In this way, both will be more profitable, enjoy more growth, and stand a much better chance of survival in the British economy. Next year we plan to form a company to hold both Harrogate and Trowbridge in the interest of better all-round operations. The move was, inevitably, initiated by the BCI nominee chairman; the managers of Harrogate and Trowbridge don't have the same chance of standing back and taking an overall view of their operations. Without our BCI man, the merger would never have been initiated.

This shows how far we have moved from our position when BCI was still mainly involved in Malayan plantations and when our United Kingdom subsidiaries were regarded merely as diversified investments to be bought and sold, managerial responsibilities resting wholly with the underlying unit. Gradually we have come to acknowledge that this is an untenable position and have taken on full responsibility for the underlying units while allowing them a very wide degree of local autonomy in the main areas of their businesses.

## THE ACQUISITION OF HARROGATE

Seven years ago, Mr. Jack Stanley, a man of 82 and the owner of a number of family companies including Harrogate Asphalt, wanted to put his estate in order so that it could be passed on to his heirs.

His brother approached a member of BCI management in London with the idea that BCI might be interested in acquiring Harrogate Asphalt. Mr. Lampton, then 31 years old and living in Birmingham as the BCI Midlands representative, was assigned the job of doing a management evaluation of the Harrogate company, which was located in Frampton, a small town in Yorkshire near Harrogate.

Lampton's general conclusion was that Harrogate represented an excellent investment. He based this on a thorough analysis of finances, management, marketing, production, and raw material procurement. He also found that the Harrogate management had sold a less profitable coal business some years earlier, had concentrated on the more profitable asphalt operations, had introduced a revolutionary technological process in the late fifties, and had expanded production and sales. He found that the company was in sound financial condition and that profits had increased at a fast pace.

Mr. Lampton's management evaluation report described Mr. Paul Denham, Harrogate's managing director and secretary, as follows:

Mr. Denham is 48 years old. He has spent the last 25 years with Mr. Stanley and has grown up with the business. He has been the prime mover in the expansion of Harrogate over the past several years. Despite Harrogate's rapid growth, the company is still relatively easy to administer and Denham has a tight personal control over it. He has a very pleasant personality. He is a strict disciplinarian and is respected for it. As the company is in a rural area and there is a very low labor turnover, Denham regards the employees with Edwardian paternalism. He has three sons at public school; the eldest (at 16) works in the company during vacations. Denham hopes one of the three will join him in the business later.

The works, transport, and sales managers were seen by Lampton as capable but "only one is likely to grow to sufficient stature."

Lampton pointed out that the workers in the plant earned very good wages compared to general conditions in British industry. The wages were exceptionally high in relation to the surrounding agricultural area. Wages of between £30 and £40 per week were due to the fact that when the new revolutionary production machinery was purchased, neither the manufacturer of the machinery nor the Harrogate management knew that it would be so productive. Piece rates were established based on what the machines were estimated to produce, but these were "grossly wrong."

Lampton continued:

The company (in the event, wisely) did not change these rates but reserved the undisputed right to trim all production units to a bare minimum of labor. As the company has constantly expanded, no surplus labor has been laid off but merely transferred to new units.

Needless to say, at these rates competition for jobs at Harrogate is very high. There was an intensely "brisk" air about the whole place. It is nonunion labor. There is no pension scheme. Hours worked are long (normally 07:30 to 18:30) and annual holidays are split, a week in the summer and another in the winter. The work is arduous and in the winter conditions are not good by the very nature of the business. As the rates are all fixed by team output, there is no room for individual slacking. Relations with management appear to be good. Total labor force has risen rapidly in the past year to around 100.

Lampton concluded his report:

The reason for the company's success is probably due to its geographical position (both for raw materials and markets), the fact that it invested early in a revolutionary production machinery (outside engineers reckon that Harrogate has more of these than anyone else, but Denham has no proof of this), very efficient management (mainly by Denham), and because it is supplying a material in increasing demand over the past decade.

As a result of this report, BCI made an offer to Mr. Jack Stanley for his company. This was accepted, and Harrogate became a subsidiary of the London holding company. At the time of acquisition, Jack Stanley, with his wife, daughters, and grandchildren, owned 90% of Harrogate, and Paul Denham and his wife owned 10%. This latter represented an interest which Stanley had permitted Denham to buy. During the first three years of BCI ownership, Denham retained his minority ownership, but this was subsequently sold to BCI on recommendation of his own financial adviser.

Because the future of the company's sales and profits looked so good, Stanley had proposed that Denham receive £4,000 net salary per year, and 2½% of net profits over £100,000. Previously, he had received a lower salary (£2,000) plus 5% of total net profits. Lampton stated that Denham agreed with this, and that at the time it meant a total take-home of £5,000. His total earnings had risen consistently over the years, culminating in £17,000. This was considered by the casewriter to be a relatively high remuneration in British industry.

### The first five years of operation

During the first year, the board of directors of Harrogate consisted of Jack Stanely, Paul Denham, and Gerald Kemp, a full-time executive of BCI who was assigned as the parent-company representative.

During those years, Mr. Henry Lampton was serving as BCI representative in the Midlands and as nominee director of two BCI subsidiaries located near Birmingham. Nevertheless, Mr. Lampton recalled certain things which he knew went on during the first five years.

In that period, the new equipment installed from Mason & Grant gave Harrogate an overwhelming competitive advantage in a business mainly served by fairly small companies, with the result that profits, sales, and return on new capital increased dramatically. Here is a company whose return on net worth was among the highest of any BCI company. Nevertheless, in my judgment, there were definite signs of trouble. Stanley died at the end of the second year. This left the BCI director and Paul Denham. About a year later, these two directors recommended as the third director Roger Sample, a young man who was hired by Denham in the second year of our ownership. I'll have more to say about him later, but I acknowledged Roger from the first time I met him to be a capable chap, though his experience in Harrogate was limited.

The board meetings of those days consisted of a rather formal, cut-and-dried reporting of figures, once a month.

At this point, the casewriter asked: "Was Paul Denham making the policy decisions?" Mr. Lampton responded: "If there were any policy decisions being made—though I doubt there were."

Lampton continued:

Also, in about the second year, Harrogate suddenly found itself with a strike on its hands. Denham was at loggerheads with the union and he was at a loss as to what to do. The BCI director had to go up there and deal with the union, and a settlement was reached. As I recall, Denham simply gave up and said that he could not deal with them.

Also, Denham operated by turning up at 8 A.M., opening the mail, then sitting in the sales (internal) office for two hours, returning to his own office where he would incarcerate himself and merely look at figures of past performance. He rarely went to see customers off site or saw customers when they came in.

## Recent events

About two years ago, while some other changes were being made in the BCI organization, Mr. Lampton, at age 36, returned from Birmingham to the BCI London head office as a director of BCI; at the same time he was also assigned to the board of the Harrogate subsidiary. Mr. Lampton commented on his new Harrogate assignment as follows:

I arrived on the scene of this highly successful company (60% on net worth is remarkable by any criteria) full of youthful bounce and asking why they don't look at the situation in the building products industries for growth. I knew that the company was doing no real forward planning, and that with the addition of a lot of hard work along this line the company could do much better. I also had a certain amount of good will and ambition—and the knowledge that I would have a delicate time with Paul Denham.

But I soon found that it was an unusual company. I saw a managing director making £15,000 a year but no other men of responsibility. His four top men, including Roger Sample, were making £ 3,000 or under. This came as a surprise. Here was an outstandingly successful company, profit-wise, with no staff in depth. In fact, in addition to Roger Sample, the only talent I could see was a good production assistant who had just given notice of his termination.

First let me say that I am not adverse to local autonomy—I believe it is best—but not for one local autocrat. Let me also say that my relationship with Denham was a good relationship, personally speaking, but when I tried to bring some things up for improvement around the board table (I had instituted more frequent board meetings and insisted that we discuss company policy problems rather than just review figures of past performance) he did not want to discuss them. Instead, he would say, "This is not a matter for formal board—why don't you come around to my office and let's talk about them informally." Nevertheless, I thought that all three board members (including Sample) should be in on important matters, and that there should be formal board meetings, with the board having the responsibility for making decisions.

Let me give you an example. Our operators in the plant were getting very high piece rates, but it was physically very hard work, 58 hours a week, and two one-and-a-half-week holidays that had to be split, one-and-a-half weeks in summer and one-and-a-half in winter: anyone absent without a doctor's note got instant dismissal. When Denham asked me not to bring this up in the board but to come to his office, I said, "No, this is a board matter." I could see that these conditions would mean trouble, and Roger Sample was telling me—not as a moral issue at all, but as a practical issue—we couldn't keep things this way. For my own part, I regarded it as a practical issue *and* a moral issue. In a way, we were blackmailing the workers with high pay and not providing opportunity for recreation. They were spending money in considerable amounts in gambling and drinking (this seemed to be a problem in the town). So I proposed that we allow them to take their two one-and-a-half weeks together, thus affording more of a real holiday and rest away from the job.

As I persisted in placing this matter before the board, Denham finally said: "I don't want any part of this discussion. If you want to make board policy, do it." Notice that he wasn't saying, "I am the managing director, I will think and be responsible about this." Instead, he was abdicating the managing directorship to us.

I mentioned Roger Sample. Denham had hired him some years ago from a local construction firm, and he subsequently became production manager. While he had rather narrow experience working locally up there in Yorkshire, he is a man of talent. He knew I thought highly of him, but he was reticent with me at first because he didn't know what kind of game I was playing. He did not have much confidence in pushing his ideas, because when Denham resisted he did not know if I would back him. Gradually, however, we established a relationship of trust. It came about through situations like the following. On my side, I could see great need for looking beyond the narrow confines of present products and processes. The company needed market research and research on new technology. On Roger's side, he had been reading magazines of the industry and had become aware of some new processes which were being developed in Sweden. He wanted to go there to investigate but had been forbidden by the managing director. Later, I raised this at the board table, but Denham's reaction was, "Don't let's meddle outside the company now. We have a system which is producing high profit." Why he took this attitude I don't know. I suspect that the real trouble lay in the fact that Denham had been outgrown by the company he managed, and he was afraid that anything new might put him still further out of his depth. Harrogate's very success was against him.

Some time later, the accountant for the plant quit. I think it was because he was mistreated by Denham. At this point, I tried to get Denham to go out and find a really top-flight managerial accountant, one who could think and plan rather than simply be an audit clerk. As things proceeded, I could see that Denham just wasn't capable of doing this, so I persuaded him that we should go out and hire an outside firm of consultants to do the recruiting. The consultants presented four candidates for our approval. I was party to interviewing them. We rejected two immediately, and there were two left, in my opinion, who were suitable. About this time I left to attend the 13-week Advanced Management Program of Harvard University in the United States. When I returned, I found to my amazement that he had rejected both of them and instead had hired a local accountant at £ 1,800 a year rather than the £ 4,000 man I had envisaged.

About this time I recognized that Paul Denham was a man who was going to reject any sort of idea, and any sort of talent, that he was not familiar with. I was utterly disenchanted with what he was doing. When I got back from Harvard, Paul Denham also recognized that I was a chap who was going to stick to his guns. I could see trouble ahead and was determined to do something about it, even though the company's profit record continued to be outstanding.

### Mr. Lampton continued:

At the second board meeting after I returned, Roger Sample brought up a subject which I had encouraged him to study. (I had encouraged him to look at all facets of the business.) Our office staff had very high turnover. The staff was working on Saturday mornings, but there was no need, no work, for this. When Roger proposed it, Paul again said he wanted no part of it. He wasn't even fighting it. I suspect it was because he knew it was going to be put into effect anyway.

At any rate, I was intent on pursuing this to some sort of conclusion. The meeting became heated and intense. Denham said: "Hell, why do we waste our time on these matters; go out and find out what the order position is and let's get down to work." At this point, and in front of Roger, I blew my top. "This is real business," I said, "and if we don't pursue it, we have a real crisis."

### One BCI executive commented that during this time,

Lampton was very conscious that the company's success was in some measure due to the tremendous pace which Denham had set for the company in earlier years. Indeed, the competitive edge which Harrogate had gained came largely from the fact that the company utilized its machines so intensively—the credit for which, at any rate initially, was Denham's.

( See Exhibit 1 for Harrogate's sales and profit performance. )

**EXHIBIT 1**

HARROGATE ASPHALT PRODUCTS LTD.
Selected Financial and Operating Results

| Year | Sales | Profits before taxes |
|---|---|---|
| −14 . . . . . . . . £ | 31,000 | n.a. |
| −13 . . . . . . . . | 55,000 | £ 22,000 |
| −12 . . . . . . . . | 83,000 | 28,000 |
| −11 . . . . . . . . | 110,000 | 39,000 |
| −10 . . . . . . . . | 178,000 | 62,000 |
| − 9 . . . . . . . . | 224,000 | 87,000 |
| − 8 . . . . . . . . | 361,000 | 136,000 |
| − 7 . . . . . . . . | 520,000 | 150,000 |
| − 6 . . . . . . . . | 867,000 | 260,000 |
| − 5 . . . . . . . . | 1,053,000 | 310,000 |
| − 4 . . . . . . . . | 1,096,000 | 300,000 |
| − 3 . . . . . . . . | 1,638,000 | 450,000 |
| − 2 . . . . . . . . | 1,922,000 | 595,000 |
| − 1 . . . . . . . . | 2,050,000 | 600,000 |
| Current year . . . . . | 2,500,000 | 750,000 (estimated) |

Figures are rounded to nearest £1,000.
n.a. = not available.
Source: Company records.

After the above incident, Mr. Lampton upon returning to London wrote Denham a letter stating:

I have given myself some cooling time since our last meeting to consider its implications. I believe that it is most important that you and I meet away from Harrogate to discuss both the future of the business and the way in which you and I can operate together constructively for its good.

The letter then requested Denham to come to London for a meeting. According to Lampton:

I felt that it was stupid to keep this up and that we must resolve it somehow. Anyway, Denham had not once been to London in all the years we owned the company. I always invited him to the annual dinner we hold for subsidiary managing directors, but he always accepted and then sent a last-minute excuse.

The night before the meeting was to take place here at the head office, Paul Denham telephoned to say that he was not feeling well. He had shut himself off and did not realize that someone else owns the company and that he was not, as he thought, master of his own domain. I drove all the way to Yorkshire the next day. He was surprised to see me. I said that it is intolerable to go on this way and that we must cooperate if the company is going to progress. I told him also that we must educate Roger Sample in a wider sphere, that we must move him out of the production manager position and give him experience on the commercial side. He agreed to this, and to promote Roger's assistant to production manager.

On his return from Yorkshire, Mr. Lampton also sent to Denham the letter which appears as Exhibit 2. He continued:

During this entire period I had been getting close to Roger Sample, but at this point I got very close. He said, "I don't want to be disloyal to the managing director. You are moving me from an area where I know the work and feel secure to an area where I do not. But I am going to be of no use to anybody if I go on not being allowed to be in contact with customers. I wonder if Paul, who is 54, knows that, at 38, I am cornered?"

**EXHIBIT 2**

BCI LTD.

Mr. Paul Denham, Managing Director
Harrogate Asphalt Products Company
Frampton, Yorkshire

Dear Paul:

Although I was disappointed that you did not feel fit enough to come down here yesterday, I am glad that we had our discussion about the future, and I hope that you now understand and sympathize with our determination to strengthen the management at Harrogate so that it can be in a position to maintain its leadership in its own field and to exploit other opportunities in allied fields. I am sure that our decision to put Roger in full charge of sales is sound.

At the same time I hope that you understood that the BCI management is insisting that the individual subsidiaries institute, this year, a formal approach towards three-year planning and forecasting (the majority of the companies did this last year, of course). This is not an academic exercise but, in our opinion, an essential step both for the operating companies and for BCI. The preparation of such a report must essentially be a team effort that has your full backing, and as it is sometimes difficult to start viewing the future in this way I have, as I told you, arranged for James Kemp, our management accountant and planning specialist, to be free for a week (or more, if necessary) at the end of this month or in September to give you any help you may need. I sincerely hope that I have managed to persuade you that one is not just looking for a "figure pledge" that you would consider you had broken were it not achieved. When you look at the framework around which such a report is constructed, you will see that it requires the participation of the whole management team.

Naturally, I am anxious about your health and I do hope that you can soon discover what is wrong with your arm. What you said about overworking and the need for a really worthwhile break of two months or more seems to me not only desirable but necessary if you are going to be able to maintain your energies in the future. You have our complete backing for this, and I hope you can manage this as soon as possible.

Yours,

H. Lampton

Source: Company records.

Mr. Lampton said that he then offered Sample a service agreement (contract) to insure that he would not be summarily fired. Sample responded, according to Lampton, "No, that is not what I want. I will give you a pledge to stay three years, but I will leave if there aren't some changes in the way the company is running."

Mr. Lampton continued:

Naturally, I did not put it to Denham that way. I told him it would be a good thing to send Roger to a three-week marketing course I knew about at the University of Glasgow. He said that this is not productive for the company, but that if Roger wants it and I approve, he would go along.

On the very day that Roger left, Paul Denham took sick. Roger phoned from Glasgow (Paul had phoned him) and wanted to know if he should go back to Frampton.

# National Franchise
# Management, Inc.

NATIONAL FRANCHISE MANAGEMENT, INC. (NFM) was originally formed in Houston, Texas, to provide professional management services for restaurant owners who wished to franchise their restaurants. During the company's first year of operation, food franchising fell strongly out of public favor. In March 1970 Mr. Jim Fisher, the president and founder of NFM, arranged for NFM to buy Phone-A-Flower, Inc., of Tiptonville, Tennessee, an international flowers-by-wire company which served almost 9,000 subscribing florists. The retail value of the flower orders which were cleared through the Phone-A-Flower system in fiscal 1970 was $10,805,000. The company's gross revenues were $1,861,000.

In June 1970 Mr. Fisher was faced with the problem of making changes in the Phone-A-Flower organization so that it would fit into his plans for NFM. He planned to acquire other companies with NFM stock in order to achieve a size large enough for a public stock offering. At that time he was actively involved in bargaining for another company even larger than Phone-A-Flower and had approached a third whose stock was already publicly traded.

## JIM FISHER

Mr. Fisher had been in the acquisition business since 1959. In that year he and two other Harvard Business School graduates had formed Equidyne Industries, Inc., to buy and develop smaller industrial companies. By offering their management training, these three men were able to buy a manufacturing concern which made satellite tracking antennas. This venture, however, met with near disaster when the company was underbid on 85 consecutive government contracts. After a change of product line, Equidyne Industries was able to sell the company without incurring heavy losses.

Jim Fisher then decided to buy the Houston Bottling Co., which bottled and distributed Coca Cola. He was able to acquire this company with only a minor investment. The company prospered; sales grew from $1.8 million in 1960 to $10.0 million in 1968. During this period the bottling company also acquired several other related companies in the Houston region. In 1968 Mr. Fisher sold his bottling company stock for a substantial financial gain. Although he retained his position as chairman of the board, he withdrew from active management of the company and began looking for another type of business venture.

Mr. Fisher's personal goals had changed with the success of the bottling company. He explained: "I enjoyed building small companies, and I learned what can be done with them. But now I want to run a large, publicly held corporation. I've made my money. I want to see what can be done with the public vehicle."

During this period Mr. Fisher became involved in political and civic affairs in Houston; one of his long-range goals was to hold an elective or appointive government office. He also served on the boards of several corporations. His extensive travel, for both business and pleasure, led one of his associates to comment: "Jim Fisher is a very hard man to catch."

In the spring of 1969, Mr. Fisher formed National Franchise Management, Inc. The company's only asset at the time was its right to franchise, in Texas and Oklahoma, Tasty Burger Restaurants, a recently formed restaurant chain based in Florida. Mr. Fisher hired Bob Trumbull, who had previously worked for the Houston Bottling Co., to be general manager. Mr. Fisher and Mr. Trumbull were shortly joined by Jim Barrett, a successful Houston restaurateur. In exchange for 30% of NFM, Mr. Barrett turned over his Big Jim's Restaurant and the franchise rights to the name. Big Jim's Restaurant was located in Houston and served higher priced lunches and dinners. NFM also bought three small Top Dog restaurants in Houston and the franchise rights to this name. These restaurants served frankfurters from drive-in windows and had only small seating capacities.

By September 1969 Mr. Fisher believed that the growth potential for the food franchising industry had become severely limited. Several food franchising companies had gone bankrupt, and many others had been accused of accounting manipulation. For these reasons, franchising stocks were out of favor with the investing public and with potential franchise buyers. (See Exhibit 1 for NFM's balance sheet at the end of 1969.)

**EXHIBIT 1**

NATIONAL FRANCHISE MANAGEMENT, INC.
Balance Sheet as of December 31, 1969

*Assets*

Current assets

| | | |
|---|---|---|
| Cash | | $ 3,293 |
| Prepaid rent | | 90 |
| Total current assets | | $ 3,383 |

Investments and other assets

| | | |
|---|---|---|
| Investment in and advances to subsidiaries | $98,536 | |
| Other investment, at cost | 60,000 | |
| Deferred expense—note | 30,574 | |
| Deposits | 60 | 189,170 |
| Furniture and fixtures | | 1,576 |
| Total assets | | $194,129 |

*Liabilities and Stockholders' Equity*

Current liabilities

| | | |
|---|---|---|
| Accounts payable | | $ 3,617 |
| Accrued liabilities | | 370 |
| Rental—purchase contracts payable | | 1,202 |
| Total current liabilities | | $ 5,189 |

Other liabilities

| | | |
|---|---|---|
| Loans from stockholder | $11,296 | |
| Subordinated debentures, 9½%, due January 1, 1975 | 30,000 | |
| Debentures and capital stock subscribed | | 50,868 |
| Less: Uncollected subscriptions ($72,464) | 9,572 | |

Stockholders' equity

| | | |
|---|---|---|
| Common stock, $.12 par value; 1,500,000 shares authorized; 725,000 shares issued and outstanding | 87,000 | |
| Capital in excess of par value | 51,072 | 138,072 |
| Total liabilities and stockholders' equity | | $194,129 |

Note: The company considered itself a nonoperating company as of December 31, 1969, and all expenses incurred to that date have been deferred. During the period from December 31, 1969, to March 31, 1970, the company sold $202,800 in stock and debentures to investors.
Source: Company records.

During this period, while Mr. Fisher was looking for another direction in which to take the company, he was contacted by Mr. Don Carty, a Houston businessman who found potential acquisitions for a fee. Mr. Carty suggested Phone-A-Flower as an attractive possibility for NFM. Shortly thereafter, Mr. Fisher made his initial contact with the president of Phone-A-Flower, Richard Zalisk.[1]

## ACQUISITION OF PHONE-A-FLOWER

On March 31, 1970, National Franchise Management purchased Phone-A-Flower, Inc., for 350,000 shares of convertible preferred voting

---

[1] In December 1969 Mr. Zalisk decided to hire Don Carty as marketing manager of Phone-A-Flower.

stock. Included in the agreement were provisions for two smaller companies, Northwest Data Processing Company and Tiptonville Printing Company. NFM received all the outstanding stock of the former, an in-house computer facility which served Phone-A-Flower and two very small outside customers, and it paid $60,000 in cash for an option to purchase the Tiptonville Printing Company for an additional cash payment of $240,000. The printing company was located in the same building as Phone-A-Flower and was owned by the same three stockholders. It derived 85% of its business from Phone-A-Flower.

The 350,000 shares of preferred voting stock of NFM that went to the former Phone-A-Flower owners had a par value of $6 and a $.60 noncumulative dividend preference. Six percent of this preferred stock could be converted into common stock each year on a share-for-share basis. At the option of Mr. Zalisk, 20,000 shares of the preferred stock were to be redeemed at par value by NFM each year starting May 1, 1971. The $.60 dividend preference, Jim Fisher explained, was not really part of the selling price of the company but was a way of assuring Mr. Zalisk that NFM would not drain cash from Phone-A-Flower. According to Mr. Fisher, both parties realized that the dividend would never be paid.

Each of the three stockholders in Phone-A-Flower also received 10-year management contracts with NFM. Richard Zalisk, the president of Phone-A-Flower, was to receive $35,000 per year; his wife, Mrs. Jackie Zalisk, $25,000 as executive vice president; and Joe Deichman, $25,000 as senior vice president of administration. There was an unwritten agreement between NFM and Mr. and Mrs. Zalisk that the business would remain in Tiptonville.

Following NFM's purchase of Phone-A-Flower in April 1970, Jim Fisher owned 30% of NFM, Jim Barrett owned 20%, and Mr. Trumbull, Mr. and Mrs. Zalisk, and about 20 other investors owned the remaining 50%. As part of the sale agreement, NFM transferred $120,000 in working capital to Phone-A-Flower, and Jim Fisher was elected chairman of the board.

Phone-A-Flower, Inc., one of three wire-service organizations in the United States sharing the market for flowers wired to out-of-town recipients, had subscribers in the United States, Canada, Mexico, as well as overseas affiliates. A subscribing florist was able to transfer a flower order to a distant location to be prepared and delivered by another Phone-A-Flower subscriber. The company guaranteed payment to the florist who prepared and delivered the flowers (the receiver); it also served as a clearing house to collect from the florist who had placed the order (the sender).

Phone-A-Flower furnished each subscribing florist with the basic supplies and forms needed to transact his order. In addition, the subscriber received a monthly publication, *Florist News,* which contained both editorial and news articles of current interest to florists and a list of subscribers in good standing. Phone-A-Flower's initial subscription fee was $120, which included $50 for a refundable deposit, $50 for the salesman's commission, and $20 for the cost of a credit check. The monthly charge was $2.50.

A floral order was usually communicated from one florist to another via telephone. Phone-A-Flower furnished members with a communications system by which a florist could call the communications center in Tiptonville and send orders to several places for less than the cost of phone calls to the individual florists. However, it was estimated that the communications center, consisting of eight toll-free telephone lines, had only 50 regular users.

The florist who originated an order collected from the customer and was billed for these outgoing transactions by Phone-A-Flower at the rate of 85% of the retail value of the order. The florist who delivered an order could immediately draw a draft on Phone-A-Flower for 75% of the retail value as compensation for delivery of the order. In this way the delivering florist immediately received payment for the inventory and delivery costs plus profit. The drafts were drawn on the Phone-A-Flower bank accounts in Dyersburg, Tennessee, at either the Farmers Bank and Trust Company or the First National Bank.

When the drafts had cleared the Phone-A-Flower bank accounts in Dyersburg, they were processed by Phone-A-Flower's computer system. Twice each month the orders so processed were billed to the florists who had originated them. The difference between the income or billing at 85% of the retail value and the cost of the draft at 75% of the retail value represented the company's proceeds for handling the transaction. Approximately 60% of Phone-A-Flower's gross income was derived from this source. The monthly charge of $2.50 for subscription renewal dues provided 15% of Phone-A-Flower's gross revenue. The advertising space purchased by florists in the monthly *Florist News* publication contributed another 15%; service charges to customers accounted for 6%; and other miscellaneous items contributed the remaining 4%.

## THE RETAIL FLORIST TRADE

The U.S. retail florist trade included approximately 22,000 independent florists whose sales had been growing at an annual rate of about 5% since 1950 and equaled $1.2 billion in 1969. The florists' share of the total floral market, however, was being increasingly threatened by a number of nonflorist retail outlets, such as supermarkets, whose sales had reached $600 million in 1969.

The typical retail florist shop was a small proprietorship managed by the owner, 75% of whose sales were taken over the telephone on a credit basis. Consequently, the majority of the customers never saw their purchases, and the florist had to decide quickly whether to extend credit and accept the order. In spite of this method of order taking, however, only minor bad-debt losses were reported.

One characteristic of the independent dealers seemed to be a chronic need for increased operating capital. Since most of their inventory was perishable, there was little collateral to offer in obtaining loans. In addition, retail florists for the most part tended to consider themselves artists rather than businessmen and often failed to handle their business matters with the same skill with which they designed their floral arrangements.

### Wire services

The annual value of the telegraphed flower orders of the three wire-service organizations in the United States approximated $160 million. According to a 1965 U.S. Department of Agriculture survey, 85% of the retail florists belonged to a wire service and one fourth of those with wire-service membership belonged to two or even three services. All three services published monthly magazines listing names, addresses, and phone numbers of all members in good standing. A recent edition of Phone-A-Flower's *Florist News* magazine, containing 400 pages, resembled a large telephone directory.

People in the florist industry, according to Mr. Zalisk, president of Phone-A-Flower, tended to be clannish, fostering many strong friendship ties. Most florists, for example, had developed standard correspondents in other cities. For most florists, as well, reciprocity was an important factor in determining which wire service to use and which florist shop to call when wiring an order. When one florist received an order from another whom he did not know, he often tried to return the favor. He tended, also, to use the same wire service through which the first order had been sent. The economics of the situation did not appear to dictate his choice. One florist commented: "I really don't know which wire service is cheaper. They all have different ways of figuring the cost. I've never really given much thought to it."

Most U.S. florists charged their customers $.50 extra for a wired order, sometimes adding as well the cost of the telephone call to the wire-service communications center or to a member florist in another city. These extra charges were not included in the gross retail value which was used to determine wire service margins.

By far the largest of the wire-service organizations was Florist Transworld Delivery (FTD), a cooperative organization of florists founded in 1892. It was located in Detroit and had, among florists, a reputation for high quality. The total number of orders sent through its system had increased steadily at an annual rate of about 6% during the period 1950 to 1969. In 1969 its almost 12,000 members sent $125 million worth of orders through the system. FTD members paid an initial fee of $386.50 and approximately $4.50 monthly. Membership was limited to retail florists, and only the most successful shops in a city could meet FTD's high standards. Under the FTD system the charge to a sending florist approximated 83% of the retail value of the order. Although an FTD customer could take advantage of FTD agreements with Diners Club and other credit card companies and charge his flower order by signing the standard credit card form, this system was not extensively used.

From 1961 to 1969 FTD had experienced strong competition from the other two organizations, Phone-A-Flower and Teleflora Delivery Service, Inc. According to an FTD official, one reason for this competition was the FTD system of variable discounts which made it cheaper for florists to send orders of under $7.50 in value through one of FTD's competitors. In 1970, however, FTD changed this discount rate, thereby becoming competitive in the lower price range. The average wire order for all three organizations in the industry was approximately $10.

Teleflora Delivery Service, Inc., was headquartered in El Segundo, California. It had over 8,000 members and had handled $20 million worth of orders in 1969. Its initial subscription fee was $139 and its monthly charge was $4. Although Teleflora did not compute its charge to a sending florist on the same basis as its two competitors, the cost to the sending florist averaged about the same as under the FTD system. The company charged 81% of the retail value of the order plus $.25 per order; the receiving florist was paid 79% less $.25 per order.

## PHONE-A-FLOWER

Phone-A-Flower had been started in 1961 by Mr. Richard Zalisk, who got the idea for the company while selling subscriptions to his *Florist Yearbook.* This directory, which had been published since 1955 and was recognized as the authority in the industry, contained 20,000 listings of florists along with their addresses and phone numbers. Mr. Zalisk, age 62, retained ownership of the directory when he sold Phone-A-Flower to NFM in 1970.

Mr. Zalisk came from a small town in Arkansas. After receiving a diploma from Tech High School in Chicago, he became a tool and die apprentice and finally a quality control supervisor in a Westinghouse plant. At that point, according to Mr. Zalisk, "I decided that I wanted to get out of the city and never live in one again."

After leaving Chicago, Mr. Zalisk became a traveling salesman for an embalming supply company. One of the towns in his territory was Tiptonville, Tennessee, where he got to know many of the local business-men. According to one merchant:

Those were hard times for everybody—Richard Zalisk included. People in town did him a lot of favors. There were always checks down at the bank being held for payment until Richard came back through town. Why, once I sold him a set of tires for his old Nash on credit. He would pay me a dollar on them every time he came through. That old Nash would always stall at the red light in the center of town, and I would give him a push in my truck.

Mr. Zalisk decided to settle in Tiptonville and open a florist shop. But, as he explained it:

Tiptonville is a small town. It was very hard for me to make a living for my wife and six kids. I tried opening another shop in a nearby town but just couldn't make a go of it. I decided to try to put together a florist directory.

I didn't want to make a lot of money—just a good living for my family. I wanted the kids to have a good education. I also wanted to build a service that everyone had faith in. You know, today I have a friend in almost every florist shop in the country.

While he was traveling for the *Florist Yearbook,* Mr. Zalisk heard many complaints about the existing wire services. Several of his florist friends suggested that he might start a wire service himself. Mr. Zalisk began asking florists what they wanted in a wire service:

They told me that they resented a wire service telling them how to run their shops, setting prices, etc. What they wanted was a way to get payment from a wired order quickly and safely. After thinking about this problem, I came up with the draft system. I went to the Federal Reserve Bank and had this draft specially designed so that it would go through as a cash item. This draft has been the cornerstone of our company, the thing which makes us different from the others.

According to Mr. Haig Mardikian, who worked closely with Mr. Zalisk in managing Phone-A-Flower, "Mr. Zalisk based his new business on a basic trust in people and especially on the honesty of members of the floral industry. Each subscriber was furnished with a checkbook with which he could write checks to himself on the Phone-A-Flower bank account as payment for wired orders which he had received." Mr. Mardikian proudly told the casewriter: "Phone-A-Flower has not had a single fraudulent draft in its entire nine-year history."

This same basic trust in people was evident in the company's credit policy. According to one manager:

The emphasis during the growth of the company was on getting new subscriptions and generally building the name of the company. Almost no credit checks were made on new subscribers, and little time was devoted to collection of accounts receivable. Often no attempt was made to collect past-due accounts. Some of these accounts were held by Mr. Zalisk's old friends who had experienced financial difficulties. During some years, as much as 10% of the accounts receivable were written off as bad debts.

A summary of accounts receivable data is shown in Exhibit 2.

**EXHIBIT 2**
**Phone-A-Flower's extended aged accounts receivable (in thousands of dollars)**

| Date | Total | Current (less than 15 days) | 15–30 days | 30–45 days | 45–60 days | Over 60 days |
|---|---|---|---|---|---|---|
| 12/05/69 | $ 917 | $338 | $228 | $119 | $ 64 | $168 |
| 12/20/69 | 915 | 428 | 173 | 106 | 62 | 176 |
| 1/05/70 | 822 | 251 | 260 | 91 | 66 | 154 |
| 1/20/70 | 1,115 | 731 | 113 | 97 | 32 | 142 |
| 2/05/70 | 1,207 | 562 | 390 | 54 | 55 | 146 |
| 2/20/70 | 1,098 | 419 | 318 | 193 | 26 | 142 |
| 3/05/70 | 1,148 | 451 | 268 | 156 | 101 | 172 |
| 3/20/70 | 1,064 | 448 | 242 | 122 | 70 | 182 |
| 4/05/70 | 1,042 | 453 | 236 | 113 | 61 | 179 |
| 4/20/70 | 1,140 | 559 | 235 | 112 | 46 | 188 |
| 5/05/70 | 1,235 | 486 | 356 | 126 | 68 | 199 |
| 5/20/70 | 1,151 | 484 | 258 | 151 | 52 | 206 |
| 6/05/70 | 1,517 | 780 | 304 | 125 | 79 | 229 |
| 6/20/70 | 1,351 | 486 | 452 | 131 | 64 | 218 |

## Growth of the company

Since its incorporation in 1961 with 180 subscribers, Phone-A-Flower had experienced dramatic growth:

| Year | Total subscribers |
|---|---|
| 1961 | 180 |
| 1962 | 450 |
| 1963 | 1,832 |
| 1964 | 3,575 |
| 1965 | 5,214 |
| 1966 | 5,423 |
| 1967 | 6,367 |
| 1968 | 7,528 |
| 1969 | 8,444 |
| 1970 | 8,984 |

From the beginning, Mr. and Mrs. Zalisk had been assisted by Mr. Joe Deichman who became a 31% owner of the business. Deichman, a native of Tiptonville, had been the local undertaker before joining the company. In 1970 he was 45 years old.

In 1966 Mr. Haig Mardikian, then age 61, was hired as general manager. Mr. Mardikian had been a San Francisco florist with a national reputation in the industry. He continued to be very active in industry associations and remained in constant demand for speaking engagements. His articles in *Florist News* and his speeches were usually directed toward urging florists to upgrade their business techniques and to adopt innovative marketing ideas.

In the same year, the Phone-A-Flower family expanded further to include Denis and Leslie Bovin, highly respected designers and commentators who spent approximately 70% of their time at industry conventions and design schools. Phone-A-Flower management considered this creative husband-and-wife team a significant asset to the business. Because of their importance to the company, the Bovins were always on equal footing with the other members of the informal management group. Both held the title of vice president of public relations.

Phone-A-Flower stimulated the growth of two other companies financed by the same three stockholders. The Phone-A-Flower billing department evolved into the Northwest Tennessee Data Processing Company, while the printing shop for the monthly *Florist News* magazine and the yearly *Florists Yearbook* became Tiptonville Printing Company. Joe Deichman owned a 20% share in the printing company and 33% of the data processing firm; Mr. and Mrs. Zalisk owned the remaining shares. According to one manager:

> There are really no clear lines drawn between these companies. Employees are swapped from one to the other during rush periods. After all, they are all owned by the same three people and are all still in the same building. We don't have a transfer pricing system. It all seems to even out. For example, during the Mother's Day period Mrs. Stone, the head bookkeeper, works on Phone-A-Flower business. During slack periods, however, she also keeps books for Tiptonville Printing and does some work for *Florist Yearbook*.

The same informality existed in purchasing supplies. Any employee could make purchases in the company's name. According to one manager, "People just went out and bought what they needed."

In 1970 Phone-A-Flower had almost 9,000 subscribers and 90 full-time employees. In fiscal 1970, the company's billings to sending florists had reached $9.1 million. Financial statements for Phone-A-Flower are presented in Exhibits 3 and 4. Tiptonville Printing Company, with modern equipment in good condition, had total assets of $144,000. Northwest Tennessee Data Processing, the computer facility located in one room

EXHIBIT 3

PHONE-A-FLOWER, INC.
Statement of Earnings
(in thousands of dollars)

| | Year ended March 31 | | |
|---|---|---|---|
| | *1968* | *1969* | *1970* |
| Gross orders transmitted . . . . . . . . . . . . . . . . . | $8,053.3 | $10,241.5 | $10,805.0 |
| Amount due to Phone-A-Flower on orders . . . . . . | 6,845.4 | 8,705.6 | 9,184.3 |
| Less: Amount paid Phone-A-Flower florists. . . . . | 6,040.0 | 7,681.4 | 8,103.8 |
| Commissions . . . . . . . . . . . . . . . . . . . . . . . | $ 805.4 | $ 1,024.2 | $ 1,080.5 |
| Other revenue . . . . . . . . . . . . . . . . . . . . . . . | 464.2 | 513.7 | 780.5 |
| Gross revenues . . . . . . . . . . . . . . . . . . . . . | $1,269.6 | $ 1,537.9 | $ 1,861.0 |
| Expenses | | | |
| Publication cost. . . . . . . . . . . . . . . . . . . . . | $ 167.5 | $ 201.1 | $ 210.5 |
| Salaries and commissions . . . . . . . . . . . . . . | 320.8 | 337.6 | 440.2 |
| Officers' salaries . . . . . . . . . . . . . . . . . . . | 69.5 | 151.0 | 160.2 |
| Bad debts . . . . . . . . . . . . . . . . . . . . . . . . | 103.8 | 170.2 | 114.2 |
| Taxes. . . . . . . . . . . . . . . . . . . . . . . . . . . | 16.7 | 20.8 | 27.8 |
| Interest . . . . . . . . . . . . . . . . . . . . . . . . . | . . . | 17.9 | 101.2 |
| Depreciation and amortization*. . . . . . . . . . . | 12.1 | 19.3 | 36.7 |
| Advertising . . . . . . . . . . . . . . . . . . . . . . . | 53.2 | 71.5 | 65.3 |
| Office supplies . . . . . . . . . . . . . . . . . . . . . | 37.0 | 22.3 | 61.4 |
| Postage and mailing . . . . . . . . . . . . . . . . . | 39.8 | 57.4 | 62.5 |
| Telephone and telegraph. . . . . . . . . . . . . . . | 19.4 | 30.1 | 109.0 |
| Credit and collection. . . . . . . . . . . . . . . . . | 12.5 | 48.8 | 34.7 |
| Convention expense . . . . . . . . . . . . . . . . . | 27.2 | 32.6 | 40.8 |
| Bank charges and exchange . . . . . . . . . . . . . | 8.0 | 14.8 | 10.6 |
| Travel . . . . . . . . . . . . . . . . . . . . . . . . . . | 87.5 | 50.2 | 56.9 |
| Equipment lease . . . . . . . . . . . . . . . . . . . . | 44.8 | 70.0 | 45.6 |
| Building lease* . . . . . . . . . . . . . . . . . . . . . | 13.6 | 15.5 | . . . |
| Art work. . . . . . . . . . . . . . . . . . . . . . . . . | 12.7 | 8.9 | 5.9 |
| Miscellaneous . . . . . . . . . . . . . . . . . . . . . | 63.5 | 97.8 | 139.0 |
| Total expenses . . . . . . . . . . . . . . . . . . . | $1,109.6 | $ 1,437.8 | $ 1,722.5 |
| Net earnings before income taxes. . . . . . . . . . . . | $ 160.0 | $ 100.1 | $ 138.5 |
| Income taxes . . . . . . . . . . . . . . . . . . . . . . . | 72.1 | 34.0 | 61.6 |
| Net income . . . . . . . . . . . . . . . . . . . . . . . | $ 87.9 | $ 66.1 | $ 76.9 |

*The building lease was capitalized in 1970 and was being depreciated.
Source: Company records.

of the Phone-A-Flower building, operated on a break-even basis with net assets of $130,800 as of March 31, 1970.

## Community relations

Phone-A-Flower and its related companies occupied an attractive modern building in Tiptonville, Tennessee (population 1,600). The Phone-A-Flower building had been built for the company in 1963 by the city of Tiptonville and was occupied on a long-term lease, of which 16 years remained in 1970. Phone-A-Flower and its employees purchased most of the municipal bonds which the city issued for the building

EXHIBIT 4

## PHONE-A-FLOWER, INC.
### Consolidated Balance Sheet
(in thousands of dollars)

| | *Year ended March 31* | | |
| --- | --- | --- | --- |
| | *1968* | *1969* | *1970* |
| *Assets* | | | |
| Current assets | | | |
| Cash | $ 64.3 | $ 126.6 | $ 28.2 |
| Certificates of deposit | 63.4 | 87.0 | 101.5 |
| Net accounts and notes receivable | 508.4 | 1,055.6 | 1,399.1 |
| Prepaid expenses | 1.8 | 3.4 | ... |
| Total current assets | $637.9 | $1,272.6 | $1,528.8 |
| Property and equipment | | | |
| Office furniture, fixtures, and computer equipment* | $ 63.6 | $ 79.1 | $ 249.8 |
| Leasehold improvements and equity† | 14.6 | 27.2 | 267.2 |
| Automobiles‡ | 53.4 | ... | ... |
| Total property and equipment | $131.6 | $ 106.3 | $ 517.0 |
| Less: Accumulated depreciation | 36.2 | 42.7 | 103.7 |
| | $ 95.4 | $ 63.6 | $ 413.3 |
| Investments and other assets | | | |
| Tax credit | ... | ... | $ 46.6 |
| Investments | $ 99.6 | $ 77.5 | 11.5 |
| Total investments and other assets | $ 99.6 | $ 77.5 | $ 58.1 |
| Total assets | $832.9 | $1,413.7 | $2,000.2 |
| *Liabilities and Stockholders' Equity* | | | |
| Current liabilities | | | |
| Accounts payable | $ 54.5 | $ 40.4 | $ 82.2 |
| Accrued expenses | 12.2 | 18.4 | 32.6 |
| Federal and state taxes | 71.6 | 8.9 | 52.9 |
| Notes payable, banks | 14.4 | 604.1 | 635.5 |
| Advances from NFM | ... | ... | 24.0 |
| Bonds payable, City of Tiptonville | ... | ... | 7.9 |
| Total current liabilities | $152.7 | $ 671.8 | $ 835.1 |
| Deferred liabilities | | | |
| Subscription deposits | $411.6 | $ 443.3 | $ 480.7 |
| Notes payable, banks | 12.0 | ... | 39.6 |
| Advances from NFM | ... | ... | 96.0 |
| Bonds payable, City of Tiptonville | ... | ... | 140.4 |
| Total deferred liabilities | $423.6 | $ 443.3 | $ 756.7 |
| Stockholders' equity | | | |
| Common stock§ | $ 1.2 | $ 1.2 | $ 180.0 |
| Retained earnings | 255.4 | 297.4 | 228.4 |
| Total stockholders' equity | $256.6 | $ 298.6 | $ 408.4 |
| Total liabilities and stockholders' equity | $832.9 | $1,413.7 | $2,000.2 |

* Includes Northwest Tennessee Data Processing in 1970 only. No computer facilities were owned by Phone-A-Flower, Inc., in 1968 or 1969.

† The lease agreement with the City of Tiptonville was capitalized in 1970. The municipal bonds owned by the company were netted against those bonds which the company was obligated to buy. The liability shown on the books was the net amount of the outstanding bonds, the company-owned bonds, and funds in the hands of the trustees.

‡ Automobiles were leased after the year ended March 31, 1968, rather than being owned by the company.

§ During the current year the capitalization of the company was changed from 1,000 shares of no-par value stock authorized (and issued at a stated value of $1.20 per share) to 150,000 shares of $1.20 par value authorized. At the time of this change a stock dividend was declared to the effect that the outstanding shares were increased to 135,000 shares with a transfer from retained earnings of $160,800. On January 20, 1970, the company acquired all the outstanding stock of NWT Data Processing Co., Inc., in exchange for 15,000 shares of its common stock.

Source: The financial statements of the period ended March 31, 1970, were prepared by NFM's accounting firm. The statements for the years ended March 31, 1968, and March 31, 1969, were prepared by the casewriter from the records of Phone-A-Flower's Jackson, Tennessee, accounting firm. In all three years, the casewriter has simplified the statements for the purpose of case analysis.

construction. The lease payments of $1,800 per month were used by the city to pay principal and interest on the bonds.

The physical prominence of the Phone-A-Flower building within the town of Tiptonville was representative of the financial influence and prestige of the company within the farming community. Not only did Phone-A-Flower merge with the community on a personal level—Mr. Haig Mardikian, for example, was president of the Tiptonville Chamber of Commerce—but it provided a new means of support to the area at a time when the profitability of farming was declining.

The Phone-A-Flower business influenced considerably the character of the town. The modern Tiptonville Post Office was, in fact, the product of the large volume of mail which Phone-A-Flower sent out each month. In 1961, the year in which the company was incorporated, a 12-room motel had been built next door to the present Phone-A-Flower building. The only one in town, the motel thrived on the comings and goings of people on Phone-A-Flower related business trips. Although the motel owner's recent business had been good as a result of the additional traffic from Houston, he was alarmed by the sale of Phone-A-Flower and feared that the company might be moved out of Tiptonville.

While perhaps the most tangible, economic benefits were only one aspect of Phone-A-Flower's contribution to the community. Several Tiptonville businessmen with whom the casewriter conversed conveyed a strong sense of pride in the fact that a local business had achieved national prominence. "The Phone-A-Flower people are all local boys, and they are every bit as good as anything in Boston," commented a Tiptonville dry cleaner.

Richard Zalisk did his share to foster this close relationship between the company and the community. Page one of the 1970 edition of the *Florist Yearbook* displayed pictures of the Tiptonville High School, the Post Office, and the town's several churches (see Exhibit 5).

### Marketing

"Phone-A-Flower's marketing approach in 1970 is basically the same as it was in 1961," explained Joe Rogers, manager of the 12 salesmen. "Our salesmen try to sell florists on the idea that they can have their money immediately after they receive a wire order from another florist." According to Rogers, this marketing approach was especially appealing to small florists who were short of operating cash:

The florist gets his money immediately and may not have to pay for almost a month. Phone-A-Flower is helping him to finance his business. The small florist becomes a member to finance his business—to receive orders rather than to send them. Phone-A-Flower's 85% billing rate to the sending florist is

**EXHIBIT 5**

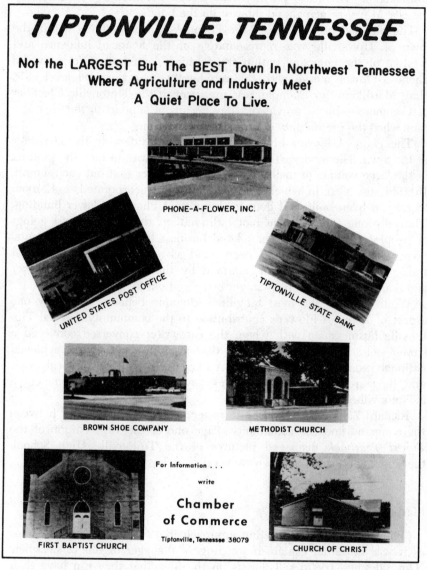

# *TIPTONVILLE, TENNESSEE*

## Not the LARGEST But The BEST Town In Northwest Tennessee
## Where Agriculture and Industry Meet
## A Quiet Place To Live.

PHONE-A-FLOWER, INC.

UNITED STATES POST OFFICE

TIPTONVILLE STATE BANK

BROWN SHOE COMPANY

METHODIST CHURCH

FIRST BAPTIST CHURCH

For Information . . .

write

**Chamber
of Commerce**

Tiptonville, Tennessee 38079

CHURCH OF CHRIST

the highest in the industry. The other two competitors have rates of approximately 83%.

Phone-A-Flower salesmen were paid a $100-per-week base salary plus $50 for every subscription sale and $6 for making a customer relations call on an existing member. Each salesman was asked to make 20 customer relations calls and 10 new subscription sales calls per week. A new car was furnished by the company each year, but the salesman had to bear all other expenses himself. In 1969 Phone-A-Flower salesmen made from $6,000 to $25,000 before deducting expenses and taxes.

Mr. Rogers commented: "One of the main problems is that salesmen have such large territories that they are lucky if they visit each florist in their territory once each year." He pointed out that one salesman, for example, "has all of the New England states plus West Virginia, while his home is in Tiptonville."

Each year Phone-A-Flower held a national convention for subscribing florists, as did its two competitors. In 1970 the company's budget allocated $50,000 for the convention, which was to be held at the Royal Orleans Hotel in New Orleans during August. It was estimated that approximately 300 subscribing florists plus all Phone-A-Flower salesmen and officers would attend. Florists looked upon a national convention as a vacation and a time for old friends to get together; the mood was always highly festive.

### Billing procedures

The distinguishing feature of Phone-A-Flower's wire service was its draft system. The processing of the bank drafts into accounts receivable and eventually into bills mailed to sending florists was handled by an automated data processing center which employed a Univac 9300 computer. Jim Babcock, director of data processing, commented: "Our computer capacity is enough to handle twice as much business. We might possibly have to buy some extra auxiliary equipment, but it wouldn't be too expensive. Right now, we are running at about 66% capacity working one shift per day."

The computer was legally a separate company, although it occupied a room in the same building and had its bookkeeping done by Mrs. Stone of Phone-A-Flower. Mr. Babcock noted that Northwest Tennessee Data Processing could not really compete with the special computer service companies for outside jobs, such as handling the bookkeeping for small local banks and insurance companies.

In November 1968, a billing change was made. Previously, each florist had filled out a weekly report of the orders he had sent through the system. This report, along with a check for 85% of the retail value of the orders, was forwarded to Phone-A-Flower. In November 1968, these weekly reports were eliminated. Accounts receivable information was obtained from the bank drafts which the banks returned to the company. The receiving florist wrote the name and address of the sending florist on the draft; from this information the sending florist was billed twice monthly for 85% of the orders which he had sent. According to Mr. Deichman, Phone-A-Flower management wanted to simplify the bookkeeping job of the sending florist who used the Phone-A-Flower system.

### Financial requirements

The new system, however, caused serious problems. Previously the company had often received the 85% payment from the sending florist before the draft of the receiving florist had been deducted from the company bank account. Phone-A-Flower had actually been making interest income on this float. Under the new system, the draft had to be received before Phone-A-Flower even knew which florist to bill, and it was a week later before the average bill was mailed. With this development, a large amount of capital was needed to finance accounts receivable.

Due to the above circumstances, Phone-A-Flower in December 1968 obtained a line of credit from the Merchants National Bank of St. Louis, Missouri. This loan was secured by accounts receivable and carried an interest rate of 10%. A record of the loan balances is shown in Exhibit 6.

**EXHIBIT 6**

PHONE-A-FLOWER, INC.
Merchants National Bank of St. Louis
Loan Account Analysis
(in thousands of dollars)

| | High daily loan balance | Low daily loan balance | Average daily loan balance | Total bankable A/R billing | | Total interest expense |
|---|---|---|---|---|---|---|
| | | | | High | Low | |
| *1969* | | | | | | |
| January . . . . . | $692 | $371 | $575 | $1,048 | $ 755 | $4.7 |
| February . . . . . | 692 | 521 | 590 | 1,067 | 893 | 4.6 |
| March . . . . . . | 620 | 509 | 571 | 990 | 841 | 4.8 |
| April . . . . . . . | 731 | 497 | 608 | 934 | 836 | 5.0 |
| May . . . . . . . . | 906 | 641 | 749 | 1,057 | 856 | 6.4 |
| June . . . . . . . | 961 | 787 | 877 | 1,360 | 888 | 7.2 |
| July . . . . . . . . | 832 | 485 | 584 | 1,178 | 864 | 6.1 |
| August . . . . . . | 554 | 478 | 509 | 943 | 842 | 5.0 |
| September . . . . | 532 | 444 | 493 | 924 | 792 | 4.8 |
| October . . . . . | 576 | 444 | 530 | 925 | 794 | 5.3 |
| November . . . . | 642 | 541 | 602 | 955 | 864 | 5.5 |
| December . . . . | 683 | 565 | 624 | 1,019 | 912 | 6.1 |
| *1970* | | | | | | |
| January . . . . . | 953 | 664 | 860 | 1,262 | 824 | 8.4 |
| February . . . . . | 941 | 738 | 862 | 1,186 | 1,085 | 7.7 |
| March . . . . . . | 828 | 691 | 754 | 1,094 | 1,045 | 7.6 |
| April . . . . . . . | 802 | 610 | 716 | 1,123 | 1,038 | 7.1 |

During 1969 the bank became increasingly concerned about the line of credit. One reason for this concern was that the State of Tennessee prohibited charging interest rates higher than 10%. This 10% included fees, service charges, and other expenses associated with the loan. The only way to get around this law was with some sort of compensating balance arrangement. However, under the bank's accounts receivable formula, Phone-A-Flower did not have the debt capacity to borrow to pay its debts and to keep a compensating balance as well. Joe Deichman stated that in his opinion the bank had been losing money on the loan because of the increased interest rates on the bank's own borrowings. "When the loan was made, no one thought that interest rates might rise as high as they did," was Mr. Deichman's explanation.[2]

Due to the above situation and the increasing size of Phone-A-Flower's capital needs, the bank requested that additional cash of $240,000 be invested in the business in November 1969. It also requested that an additional $480,000 in collateral be pledged to offset the $50 deposit of each Phone-A-Flower subscribing florist. These deposits had to be refunded if the individual florists canceled their subscriptions and returned their supplies.

At this time, Mr. Zalisk began to seek a source of capital for the company. First, he considered a public offering of stock. The stock market was in a downturn, however, so this alternative was rejected. During this period Mr. Don Carty, acquisition "finder," approached Jim Fisher about the situation.

## DEVELOPMENTS AT NATIONAL FRANCHISE

Throughout the fall of 1969 and the early spring of 1970, Jim Fisher was involved in bargaining with Mr. Zalisk on the Phone-A-Flower acquisition. In April 1970 Mr. John Gartley, a previous investor in NFM, was persuaded to join NFM as financial vice president. Gartley, age 32, was a Certified Public Accountant with seven years' experience with an international public accounting firm. After leaving the accounting firm in 1966, Gartley as an executive vice president had financially guided a medium-size industrial firm through a period of very rapid growth. Simultaneously, he had started and managed two other small manufacturing companies.

In June 1970 Jim Barrett decided to withdraw from NFM. In exchange for his 20% ownership he was given the existing Big Jim's Restaurant and the rights to franchise the name. His stock was put into the treasury.

Things had also changed in Tiptonville. Steve Hyde of Dallas had been hired from U.S. Steel and installed as Phone-A-Flower's financial vice president in April. As of June 1970, he was the only new manager who had been brought to Tiptonville as a result of the acquisition. Mr. Hyde, who was 37 years old in 1970, had worked in the credit

---

[2] Yields on short-term U.S. government bonds rose from 5.23% in November of 1968 to 7.85% in 1969.

departments of both Texaco and U.S. Steel. His authority at Tiptonville was more extensive than his title indicated; most employees, in fact, considered him the spokesman for the new owners. Although Mr. Hyde had always lived in cities, he got along well with the people in Tiptonville. An invitation to join the Chamber of Commerce and his family's invitation to join a local church exemplified their acceptance by the community. Jim Fisher had also asked Steve Hyde to take flying lessons so that he could pilot a proposed company airplane between Tiptonville and Houston.

In another management change, Don Carty tendered his resignation because of a personality clash with Richard Zalisk. According to one manager at Phone-A-Flower, Carty had expected to be given considerable authority because of his role in arranging the acquisition. When it was decided that Zalisk would remain as president of Phone-A-Flower, Carty resigned in frustration. Bob Trumbull, general manager of NFM, was named marketing manager to replace Carty.

Although Mr. Zalisk remained as president and continued to occupy the very large and well-appointed office which he had built for himself in the Phone-A-Flower building, a newly formed executive committee had final authority over all important management decisions. Joe Deichman had been made chairman of the executive committee, which was composed of Richard Zalisk, John Gartley, Bob Trumbull, and Steve Hyde. Organization charts of Phone-A-Flower before and after the acquisition are shown in Exhibits 7 and 8.

An extension of the line of credit with the Merchants National Bank of St. Louis had been secured until July 31, 1970, and Mr. Hyde had already started to overhaul the credit department. Nevertheless, the accounts receivable were still growing. Mr. Fisher approached the Citizens National Bank of Houston and made arrangements for a $900,000 line of credit beginning August 1, 1970. He felt that this would be sufficient since business at Phone-A-Flower had been historically low during the last half of the year. (See Exhibit 6.)

## FUTURE GOALS

Phone-A-Flower was the principal asset of NFM. Mr. Fisher wanted the retail value of flowers sent through Phone-A-Flower to reach $40 million by 1975. He stated that he wanted at least one third of the $18 million estimated annual growth in the flowers-by-wire market. He considered Phone-A-Flower a good base for a publicly held corporation and hoped that the company's almost 9,000 subscribing florists would be a market for NFM stock.

A primary concern of Mr. Fisher was what changes to make in marketing. If Phone-A-Flower were to grow as he projected, the company

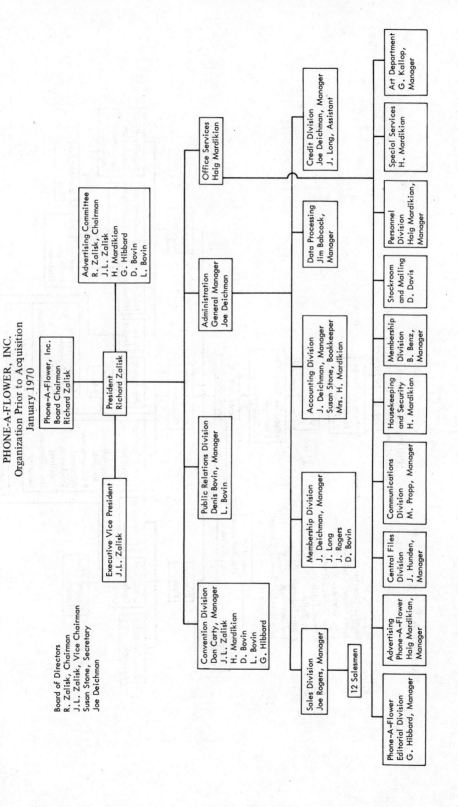

**EXHIBIT 7**

PHONE-A-FLOWER, INC.
Organization Prior to Acquisition
January 1970

Board of Directors
R. Zalisk, Chairman
J.L. Zalisk, Vice Chairman
Susan Stone, Secretary
Joe Deichman

Phone-A-Flower, Inc.
Board Chairman
Richard Zalisk

President
Richard Zalisk

Advertising Committee
R. Zalisk, Chairman
J.L. Zalisk
H. Mardikian
G. Hibbard
D. Bovin
L. Bovin

Executive Vice President
J.L. Zalisk

Administration
General Manager
Joe Deichman

Office Services
Haig Mardikian

Public Relations Division
Denis Bovin, Manager
L. Bovin

Convention Division
Don Carty, Manager
J.L. Zalisk
H. Mardikian
D. Bovin
L. Bovin
G. Hibbard

Membership Division
J. Deichman, Manager
J. Long
J. Rogers
D. Bovin

Accounting Division
J. Deichman, Manager
Susan Stone, Bookkeeper
Mrs. H. Mardikian

Data Processing
Jim Babcock,
Manager

Credit Division
Joe Deichman, Manager
J. Long, Assistant

Sales Division
Joe Rogers, Manager

Central Files
Division
J. Hunden,
Manager

Communications
Division
M. Propp, Manager

Housekeeping
and Security
H. Mardikian

Membership
Division
B. Benz,
Manager

Stockroom
and Mailing
D. Davis

Personnel
Division
Haig Mardikian,
Manager

Special Services
H. Mardikian

Art Department
G. Kallop,
Manager

12 Salesmen

Advertising
Phone-A-Flower
Haig Mardikian,
Manager

Phone-A-Flower
Editorial Division
G. Hibbard, Manager

**EXHIBIT 8**

**PHONE-A-FLOWER, INC.**
Organization after Acquisition by NFM
June 12, 1970

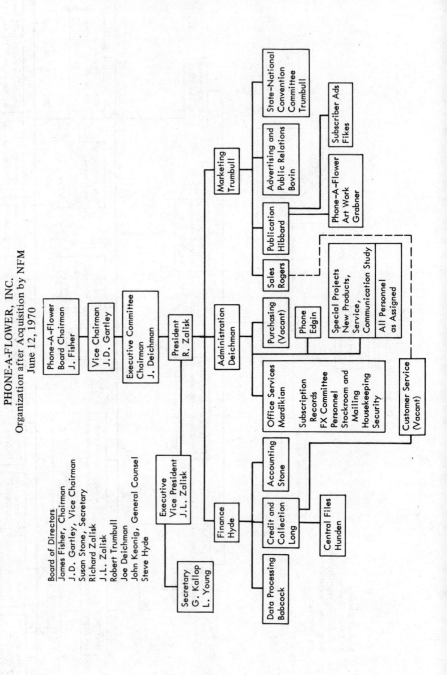

Board of Directors
James Fisher, Chairman
J.D. Gartley, Vice Chairman
Susan Stone, Secretary
Richard Zalisk
J.L. Zalisk
Robert Trumbull
Joe Deichman
John Keonig, General Counsel
Steve Hyde

would have to get the wire business of the larger shops which handled the majority of the flowers-by-wire orders. Nearly all of these shops were heavy users of FTD. By and large, Phone-A-Flower subscribers were smaller florists, many located in small towns. The southeastern states represented the company's area of strength.

On the afternoon of June 12, 1970, Joe Deichman presented his own proposal for changes at Phone-A-Flower to Fisher and John Gartley. He had not informed Mr. Zalisk of his proposal. (See Exhibit 9 for a summary of the plan.)

**EXHIBIT 9**
**Summary of proposed changes in Phone-A-Flower procedure**

Joe Deichman
June 12, 1970

1. The draft system will be eliminated. Receiving florists will send a list each week listing orders received. Their accounts will be credited for 75% of order value.
2. From the list received from receiving florists, the accounts of sending florists are debited at 82% of the order instead of the present 85%.
3. Monthly renewal fee will be raised from $2.50 to $3.50.
4. On the third or fourth day of the month statements of accounts will be sent both to florists with debit balances and those with credit balances. Payment of debit balances should be received at Phone-A-Flower before the 25th. Checks for credit balances will be mailed on the 20th of the month.
5. Salesmen's compensation will no longer be based on the number of new subscriptions sold. Instead, it will be based on the dollar amount of billings coming from each account in the salesman's territory.
6. Phone-A-Flower will stop accepting any florist who applies for a subscription. A strict credit-rating policy will be enforced. We will concentrate on dollar billings rather than number of members.
7. The listing of all Phone-A-Flower members will not be included in the monthly *Florist News* publication. Instead we will print a yearly *Handy-Book* with this listing. Each monthly *Florist News* magazine will contain a supplemental list of changes in the *Handy-Book*. This change will eliminate 30% of the pages in the monthly *Florist News* magazine.

Mr. Deichman explained his ideas:

These proposed changes will eliminate the need for cash to finance the accounts receivable. Our checks to florists with credit balances should reach our bank at about the same time as the checks from florists with debit balances. Therefore, financing will only be needed for overdue accounts.

Changing the billing to sending florists from 85% to 82% will make us cheaper than our competition. This will give our salesmen something with which to approach the large florists. I worked this idea out with Joe Rogers [the sales manager]. He and the salesmen are very enthusiastic. This along with the change in salesman's compensation will change our entire marketing program. We will no longer be going after large numbers of small florists but a more select group of larger florists. Phone-A-Flower now has all the geographical coverage that it needs.

Mr. Deichman went on to explain that less than $1,200,000 in additional yearly clearings would be needed to finance his proposed changes. (See Exhibit 10 for his supporting statement.) Mr. Deichman stated

**EXHIBIT 10**

PHONE-A-FLOWER, INC.
Deichman Proposal
Cost Comparison Based on 7,500 Subscribers,
$10 Million Annual Gross Clearing
(only items which would be affected, income or expense)

|  | Present | Proposed | Difference |  |
|---|---|---|---|---|
| Income |  |  |  |  |
| Commissions earned . . . . . . | $1,000,000 | $ 700,000 | –$300,000 |  |
| Renewal fees . . . . . . . . . . | 225,000 | 315,000 | 90,000 |  |
| Total income . . . . . . . . | $1,225,000 | $1,015,000 | –$210,000 |  |
| Net decrease in income to overcome. . . . . . . . . . . . . . . . . . |  |  |  | –$210,000 |

① (Need increase gross clearing of $3,000,000 to offset $210,000 loss of income.)

| Expenses |  |  |  |  |
|---|---|---|---|---|
| Phone-A-Flower drafts* . . . . . | $ 24,000 | 0 | $ 24,000 |  |
| Bank service charges . . . . . . | 12,000 | 0 | 12,000 |  |
| Interest. . . . . . . . . . . . . | 65,000 | $12,000 | 53,000 |  |
| Bad debt–net . . . . . . . . . . | 75,000 | 45,000 | 30,000 |  |
| Credit and collection . . . . . . | 45,000 | 25,000 | 20,000 |  |
| Statements† . . . . . . . . . . . | 20,000 | 10,000 | 10,000 |  |
| Clerks–2 @ $4,000 each . . . . . | 8,000 | 0 | 8,000 |  |
| Total. . . . . . . . . . . . | $249,000 | $92,000 | $157,000 |  |
| Decrease service charge income . . |  |  | – 40,000 |  |
|  |  |  | $117,000 | 117,000 |
| Net difference in income and expense to overcome . . . . . . . . . . . |  |  |  | –$ 93,000 |

② (Need increase gross clearing of $1,330,000 to offset $93,000 loss.)

Phone-A-Flower publication
Print annual *Reference Book.* Update *Reference Book* quarterly by insert
in *Florist News.* Figures reflect only printing cost. Would have additional
savings on preparation each month.

|  |  |  |  |  |
|---|---|---|---|---|
| $43,558 net savings . . . . . . . . . . . . . . . . . . . . . . . . . . . . . . . . . |  |  |  | 43,558 |
|  |  |  |  | –$ 49,442 |

③ (Need increase gross clearing of $710,000 to offset $49,442 loss.)

\* Supplies given to each florist: drafts, receipts, etc.
† 8,144 subscribers × 25¢ cost per statement × 24 billing periods.
Source: This exhibit was prepared by Mr. Deichman to support his proposal.

that Mr. Rogers and the salesmen believed that the needed additional orders to be sent through the Phone-A-Flower system could be achieved within six months after the marketing change.

Deichman also explained that his proposal avoided the earlier Phone-A-Flower system of weekly reports by the sending florist.

We want to make the Phone-A-Flower system as easy as possible for the sending florist. My proposal puts the incentive where it should be—with the sending florist. In the past, small florists have subscribed to receive Phone-

A-Flower orders. Now larger florists will use our system to send orders. The sending florist is the one who makes the decision of which wire service to use.

Jim Fisher was also concerned about the location of Phone-A-Flower's operations. The clearing of drafts and checks was to be moved to the Citizens National Bank of Houston. After this move occurred, the information would have to be mailed daily to Tiptonville to be run through the bookkeeping system, which would cause an unnecessary delay. Bob Trumbull also wanted to transfer the marketing function of the company to Houston, as his family did not want to move to Tiptonville. Jim Rogers wanted to resign as sales manager in order to go back to his original job as Phone-A-Flower salesman. In addition, neither Fisher nor Gartley had any intention of moving to Tiptonville.

# Hedblom (A)*

ON OCTOBER 31, 1967, Mr. Arthur Keller,[1] managing director of Hedblom, a ladies' dress company located in Boxholm, Sweden, welcomed members of the press to the company premises to show them the plant, the new offices, and the 1968 spring collection. More importantly, as he privately explained, he wanted to convey the image of the "new Hedblom":

> During my first few months on this job,[2] I had to develop a strategy to ensure survival and subsequent profitability and growth. By the middle of the summer the strategy had been pretty well formulated and we are now busy implementing it. These are the crucial months during which all our decisions will be put to the test: our new collections are out, additional activities are starting, and internal changes have been made. Now we must produce the anticipated results. At the same time, we are ready to present our new image to the outside world, hence our press visit today.

Mr. Keller described the process of formulating a strategy for Hedblom as follows:

> The basic strategy which I decided on during my first weeks at Hedblom had to be viable for at least two or three years. It might, of course, have

---

[1] Names and figures have been disguised.

[2] Mr. Keller became managing director on March 13, 1967. Events leading up to this appointment and Mr. Keller's early weeks on the job are described in the Arthur Keller case.

to be modified owing to unforeseen changes, especially with respect to competition. Nevertheless, I wanted to settle on a long-term plan which basically would avoid a zigzag course of action. However, at the same time, given the company's desperate position, I had to produce immediate results. My most critical decision was the fundamental choice between expansion or reduction of company activities. Under my predecessor the company had overexpanded: plant capacity was about four times our actual sales volume of less than Skr 10 million, while fixed expenses amounted to over Skr 6 million. With a contribution of about 35 cents on the sales dollar, to break even we almost needed to double sales or to halve our overhead expenses. While we could expect to improve our contribution by improving production, we feared that five percentage points would probably be the maximum, given our high inputs of raw materials and labor. As a result, modest measures would not restore profitability: we needed either an enormous sales effort to expand volume, or major surgery to cut fixed expenses. I decided for the first alternative.

This inevitably led us to an analysis of possible product-market relationships. Our first investigation was whether sales of Hedblom-brand dresses could be increased, and if so whether changes were required in our marketing strategy. Our second investigation related to possible sale of dresses not under the Hedblom brand. We were particularly anxious to explore ways of reaching the important and rapidly growing distribution channels, such as department store chains, which our selective policy had hitherto ignored. The third step in exploring avenues for increased sales was to look beyond ladies' dresses, considering other ladies' clothes, men's clothes, articles for the teen-age group, coats, sportswear, or fabrics. Finally, the fourth opportunity for larger sales was in markets outside Sweden or even Scandinavia. We decided to move in all four directions.

Our expanded activities on the marketplace resulted in several internal changes. The main tasks here were to improve manufacturing efficiency, and particularly to overcome our late delivery problem, as well as to make sure that our new activities would receive sufficient systematic attention. As a result, I changed the organization structure, moved all offices into the plant building, and worked on streamlining the manufacturing and control activities.

Two other aspects received my constant attention. First, I made a concerted effort to rebuild morale both inside and outside the company. Second, the relationship between the managing director and his top managers needed to be changed, and I tried to be aware of my leadership style: what signals it would convey to my men and what responses it would bring about.

A more detailed description of these changes follows.

## PRODUCT LINES

### The Hedblom line

After long discussions during April and May of 1967, it was decided not to change the Hedblom line in terms of distribution channels, price, styling, and image. Selective distribution accompanied by the necessary retail sales push appeared the best approach, given the price of Hedblom dresses. Price reductions of a modest scale were ruled out because (1) price elasticity at above Skr 100 was felt to be low, and (2) the company could not afford to risk a reduction in gross margin. Major price cuts would have meant a complete change in marketing strategy and would have resulted in abandoning the company's distinctive competence. Styling and image had permitted Hedblom to charge a 10% to 15% price premium, and this capability was to be reinforced, not weakened. Thus, changes in the Hedblom line would be in the direction of more collections and better services.

The first collection for which Mr. Keller would be solely responsible was that for spring 1968, and it was to receive his major attention. During April and May 1967, fabrics were to be selected and models designed for showing on September 1; thereafter the sales organization would solicit orders and production would begin manufacture so that deliveries could begin in February–March 1968. In April–May, the consumer would finally give her market verdict on efforts started 12 months earlier. The collection would include 65 to 70 dresses to be sold at an average factory price of Skr 80. A sales target of 40,000 pieces was set, and initial orders were deemed encouraging.

In addition to this "head collection," as it was called, two intermediate spring collections were also planned. A sportswear collection, with showings in early November and deliveries in April, was to include 25 to 30 dresses and suits at an average factory price of Skr 125 (with a range of Skr 83 to Skr 204). On these the sales target was set at 15,000–20,000 pieces. A "high-summer collection" was to be shown in February for delivery in May. It would include 20 dresses of which about 15,000 were to be sold at an average factory price of Skr 80.

The same approach was to be followed for the autumn of 1968. The head collection would be shown in March 1968, with August and September deliveries; a more elegant cocktail dress collection would come in May and a Christmas collection in August. Deliveries for the two interim collections were planned for October and early December. Number of models and price ranges for the three autumn collections paralleled those for the spring, except that autumn dresses were typically priced Skr 10 higher.

Mr. Keller was convinced that the increased number of collections would expand sales rather than simply shift orders. Also, he felt that adding collections was the best response to the retailers' increasing reluctance to make large and firm commitments twice a year several months ahead of sales. Finally, he expected that the extra collections would reduce the retailers' need to reorder. Mr. Keller also commented:

As long as we had only two collections, it was almost impossible to avoid large fluctuations in sales between the first and second as well as the third and fourth quarter of each year. With the above plan we not only expect to spread sales more evenly but also to assure more even utilization of the design, sales, production, and shipping departments.

As for better services, the main emphasis was on deliveries. On-time delivery was target Number One, and Mr. Keller decided to risk advance manufacturing commitments of both fabrics and dresses to ensure that goods would leave the factory on the promised date. Furthermore, for the spring 1968 head collection a catalog would be printed of the seven best selling dresses (of which only the best selling sizes and colors would be included) on which immediate delivery from stock would be provided. Special merchandising, such as labels attached to the dresses, was to emphasize Hedblom's new delivery policy.

Mr. Keller viewed advertising as another aspect of service in that it would support the sales efforts of Hedblom retailers. Special arrangements with synthetic fiber companies were investigated, and for the second 1968 spring collection Mr. Keller was able to obtain support of Skr 250,000 from one of the large synthetic fiber producers because this collection pioneered the use of its synthetic fiber for sportswear. Also, Mr. Keller shifted the emphasis from newspapers to magazines. He stated:

> I insisted that all our advertising plans be completely ready when we introduced a collection. In this way we could give the salesman all information about advertising when he started selling and this should help him in getting orders. It also forces us to plan our advertising thoroughly and thoughtfully, instead of buying space in daily newspapers at the last minute, as we did before.

Two changes were effected in the Hedblom organization. First, in-house design efforts were strengthened by hiring a new directress and the expensive Paris designer was dropped. Second, the sales organization was analyzed, with Mr. Keller going over all the accounts. As a result, the number of outside salesmen was reduced from five to four by shifting one man to an inside sales job, the aim of which was to strengthen customer services. Also, sales quotas were established.

### Dress sales without the Hedblom brand

For September 1967, the introduction of a second dress collection was planned. This line was to be sold, either under the "Karin" name or unbranded, with initial efforts in Scandinavia but ultimately all over EFTA.[3] It was different from the Hedblom line in that it was (1) priced lower, to retail at Skr 90; (2) included fewer models and used less

---

[3] European Free Trade Association comprised the United Kingdom, the Scandinavian countries, Austria, Switzerland, and Portugal.

fancy fabrics and patterns, while remaining of high quality; (3) aimed at different customers, such as big chains and mail-order houses; (4) sold through a separate sales organization, composed initially of two new salesmen; (5) promoted by distinctive sales inducements, such as immediate delivery from stock or special styles for customers placing large orders; and (6) supported by little or no advertising and no public relations activities.

To get this line ready for September the decision had been made in April, and a new directress, exclusively responsible for this line, had been hired to report to work on May 17.

### Fabric sales

Mr. Keller decided to expand the product line beyond dresses. One possibility considered was adding other outerwear, such as ladies' clothes other than dresses, men's clothes, articles for the teen-age group, coats, or sportswear. However, (1) it would have required a new marketing setup; (2) it would have posed entirely new problems for manufacturing; and (3) it would have taken a long time to establish a market position. Fabric sales, in contrast, appeared a more logical approach in that (1) this required only minimal marketing efforts; (2) Hedblom had both the manufacturing skills and excess knitting capacity; (3) sales would materialize immediately, particularly through aggressive pricing; and (4) Hedblom had an outstanding fabric designer, giving the company a strong competitive advantage.

Fabric sales began in the fall of 1967. A cover-up organization in Denmark was used to protect the parent company, whose Scandinavian sales manager feared losing yarn sales were Hedblom to compete openly with his customers. This company, primarily a dyer and finisher, dyed the Hedblom fabrics and sold them in Denmark through its own organization and in the rest of EFTA and the EEC[4] through its foreign agents. For this purpose a special fabric collection had been created containing seven different types of cloth, each of which came in different colors. Selling prices averaged Skr 17 per meter or Skr 51 per kilo.

### FOREIGN MARKETS

Mr. Keller commented on his policies for penetrating foreign markets as follows:

One of my early decisions was to close the German sales office. The reason was that I did not believe that I could bank on anything like De Gaulle's accepting Great Britain or the other EFTA countries into the European Com-

---

[4] European Economic Community, commonly referred to as European Common Market, comprised France, West Germany, Italy, and the three Benelux countries.

mon Market. So I just forgot about the potential of markets such as Germany or France, where the duty on dresses of 30% simply makes it impossible for us to compete effectively. On the other hand, I placed major emphasis on the other EFTA markets, establishing sales offices in Austria, Switzerland, and Great Britain; hiring an agent in Finland; and placing increased pressure on our agents in Denmark and Norway. Also, this fall, I appointed an agent in the United States where the dress duty is about 25%. Dresses are sold to our overseas sales offices or agents at regular factory prices with freight paid by us.

# CHANGES INTRODUCED BY MR. KELLER

## Organizational changes

Besides reviewing and revising policies, Mr. Keller revised company structure:

My policy from the outset was to use everybody at Hedblom, but also to realign some of the tasks. In May of 1967, I announced a revised organization structure. The changes, compared to the previous organization, were as follows:

—Purchasing and shipping were added to production planning, and all were assigned under Carlsson.
—Merchandising would focus on the design, sales, and advertising of Hedblom dresses, with a much freer hand than before in style decisions. This area was put under Mr. Filipsson, to whom shipping had previously reported.
—Design and sales for the second dress line as well as sales of fabrics were placed under Mr. Nilsson, who previously managed purchasing.
—Production would remain under Mr. Lanner, who would be responsible for manufacturing fabrics and Hedblom dresses, as well as the second dress line.
—Fabric design for all three activities (hence on a vastly enlarged basis) would remain under Mr. Sundman.
—Bookkeeping would be enlarged to include management control and planning under Mr. Jansson.

Mr. Keller explained some of the thinking back of his decision:

The main issue which was difficult to resolve in creating the new organization was whether to place the second line of dresses under Hedblom merchandising as a separate section, or to make it an independent activity. I decided for the latter, in that one man could give his full attention to the new line without being distracted or worried by the Hedblom line. Thus, I wanted to give one man full control and responsibility for a line. At the same time, I hoped to motivate both men by having them compete with each other both outside and inside the company.

## Move of offices

Late in April 1967, it was decided to convert half the top floor of the factory building into offices and the remainder into storage rooms. Costing Skr 400,000, this move occurred in August 1967. Mr. Keller decided on this change in order to permit better coordination among his top managers, closer supervision by himself, and also for symbolic reasons.

## New fabric developments

As a result of the extra collections for the Hedblom line, plus the addition of the second line as well as fabric sales, fabric-design activities were increased significantly. Also, greater emphasis was placed on innovation. Hedblom pioneered a fabric made of a new 110-denier yarn produced by Wientex. It also experimented successfully with cross-dyed Dacron fabrics. There were three types of Dacron which looked alike when white but which yielded different colors if placed in the same dye. By knitting these yarns together, it was possible to obtain patterns which previously had required colored yarns. Even though some start-up problems occurred and the color flexibility was limited, use of Dacron cross-dyed fabrics promised to facilitate manufacturing and to reduce inventory. Also, Hedblom expected major advertising support from the fiber manufacturer in introducing its Dacron cross-dyed dresses.

## Changes in manufacturing

*General policies.* As already indicated, Mr. Keller decided against contracting Hedblom's operations. This would have involved leasing some of the manufacturing space and selling several of the machines. He felt that such a move would have had a disastrous impact on employee morale and company image. Instead, a policy of filling up the plant was pursued, thereby spreading the high overhead. At the same time Mr. Keller attempted to cut costs and to speed deliveries. In attempting to achieve these goals, he relied entirely on his own people and refrained from bringing in outside help.

*Additions.* Mr. Keller installed three quality-control posts: one inspecting knitted goods, one inspecting goods returned from dyeing, and one inspecting completed dresses. The purpose was to make the organization more quality conscious and to discover errors early, thus reducing waste of fabrics. Constant attention to machine operations was particularly critical in knitting since an early discovery of errors could mean significant savings of otherwise wasted yarn.

By October 1967 the 10 new Jacquard knitting machines, which had been ordered prior to Mr. Keller's arrival, had been delivered and were operating. Even though total knitting capacity was far in excess of Hedblom's needs, Jacquard capacity, permitting finer and more varied fabrics and patterns, had been in short supply. Use of Jacquard machines allowed the company to specialize in so-called "knitter's dress models" which were difficult for dressmakers using merchant fabrics to copy.

Also new was an emphasis on long-term production planning, with a focus on obtaining the best prices, the best utilization of productive capacity, and improved shipping, rather than, as previously, planning only day-to-day operations.

*Eliminations.* Mr. Keller relieved the consulting engineer of his duties. While costing a yearly Skr 400,000, results had been meager. New piece-rate standards had not been established. The punch-card system for production control had not provided the necessary data and had to be replaced by a manual system. Finally, the materials handling system was totally unnecessary, given the size and simplicity of Hedblom's operations.

*Production changes.* Changes in production operations included (1) a willingness to make advance commitments on fabrics and dress manufacturing; (2) a resulting ability to spread production volume evenly over the year, thus avoiding the previous peaks and valleys; (3) a policy of maximizing long runs in sewing and minimizing subcontracting, which would be confined to short runs (during his early days at Hedblom, Mr. Keller established a policy of doing at least 90% of the sewing in-house and of personally approving any outside contracting); (4) changes in plant layout to facilitate product flow and reduce costs; (5) a focus on cutting operations to reduce the high fabric losses; (6) use of transparent thread in sewing, which permitted the use of only two threads (light and dark), thereby facilitating sewing operations and minimizing thread inventories; and (7) achievement of bulk shipments by accumulating dresses ordered by a single customer. Mr. Keller emphasized constant attention to costs in all aspects of manufacturing.

## Changes in the control function

On the changes in the Hedblom control and planning functions, Mr. Keller commented as follows:

First of all, I told my people to forget about the traditional one-year time span for reports and to focus rather on three months' performance. Second, we immediately but slowly began to work with budgets. While admittedly crude (for example, for lack of standard costs we had to guess historical costs), these were total operating budgets, focusing on profits and not just on costs. We prepared the first one for May through July, which we immediately compared with actual results during the first 10 days of August. On this basis we were able to improve the next budget. Third, we began to develop a new standard cost system with a cost book consisting of new cost sheets. For this work we used a first-year student from HBS during the summer. Fourth, in terms of operations, I receive (1) a weekly sales report broken down by the various lines, by salesmen, and by area; (2) a weekly quality-control report; (3) a weekly cutting and sewing schedule; and (4) a weekly report on indirect labor. Fifth, we started to establish controls and planning for investments and major expenses and to develop source-and-use-of-funds projections for the next six months and for shorter periods whenever necessary.

Currently, we have just introduced a very comprehensive budget-control report, prepared by Carlsson and analyzed by Jansson. This report compares to the budget the quantities bought, produced, shipped, etc. We hope to simplify it in the future, making it my basic weekly report. This report, together with a three-month budget and variance analysis, should be sufficient for me to control Hedblom's activities.

As far as the controls used by my managers are concerned, I refrained on purpose from meddling with these. I gave each man freedom, leaving it up to him to design his own controls, while stressing the need for improved reports. My managers are in a better position to judge what is critical and how best to control it. Of course, they must be able to answer my questions. In this way, I check whether or not my managers have their own effective control system. Also, some of the reports I receive I do not read regularly. I just have them sent to me to make sure that people plan ahead in some of the crucial areas—for example, cutting and sewing schedules. The danger is to develop too many figures. As a result, I do not want data on the total number of workers, feeling that direct labor can best be controlled by my subordinates and that results will clearly show in the output-per-man figures. However, the indirect labor I like to watch as an overhead item.

Working on the control and planning system was no easy job. Also, I feel we still have a long way to go.

## Other steps

In addition to the above steps, the obsolete inventory was liquidated. Entered on the books at Skr 4 to Skr 4.5 million, it was sold for Skr 1.5 million. The Sandvik plant was not sold, however. Mr. Keller had initially planned to do this until his managers pointed out that a sale to another textile firm would probably mean the loss of the Hedblom skilled workers who still lived in Sandvik. Potential purchasers among nontextile firms could not be found. The company Rolls-Royce, on the other hand, was sold immediately, much to the chagrin of the commercial department which considered it an excellent public relations tool.

As a source of extra, although marginal, revenue Mr. Keller entered into a licensing arrangement with a South African firm. With seasons there occurring six months later, this arrangement created little extra expense for Hedblom and resulted in a minimum annual royalty of Skr 20,000, expected to increase to Skr 100,000.

## Morale building

Mr. Keller gave his constant and systematic attention to morale both inside and outside the company. He was planning an "open house" for employees and their families, during which plant tours would be organized and the entire dress collection would be modeled. Other steps to improve internal morale were (1) the creation of more work; (2) Mr. Keller's willingness to listen to employee complaints and follow up on them; (3) close cooperation with the workers' council (which told Mr. Keller after three months that he was ineffective because he had not brought more work to the plant); (4) regular plant visits by Mr. Keller, who took a detailed interest in all operations. With his managers Mr. Keller was able to move away from the previous stringent working conditions, encouraging initiative and permitting much more operating freedom.

In terms of building outside morale, Mr. Keller made the customer king, guaranteeing on-time deliveries, taking back unwanted goods, and stressing Hedblom quality. He improved bank relations, getting the prime rate with assistance of the parent company. As mentioned above, a plant visit and a showing of the collection was arranged for the press, and another one was planned for town and county officials. It was hoped that both visits would generate a great deal of publicity and goodwill. A similar purpose justified a trip by the company's public relations adviser to South America. Mr. Keller felt that Hedblom's outside image had suffered prior to the takeover and that restoration of a good image was critical for both selling and recruiting of scarce skilled knitting and sewing personnel.

## MANAGEMENT STYLE

Mr. Keller commented on his management style as follows:

My main task at the beginning was to gather information and to get cooperation. Basically, I knew nothing about the dress business and little about Hedblom. I therefore conducted a detailed and systematic investigation of all aspects of company operations. Given the uneven attention paid by my predecessor to the different segments of the company, I was particularly anxious to focus on all areas. Every time I visit Boxholm, I walk around the building, meet the people, talk to them as best I can in my broken Swedish, and particularly ask questions, questions, questions. In a way, knowing very little when you start is an advantage because it allows you to ask even the most stupid questions, and by asking about so many things you are bound to discover problems and focus on critical issues. You simply take nothing for granted. By having people explain and justify what they have been doing for years as a matter of unquestioned routine you often discover what needs to be investigated and appraised. Also, in this way you learn a lot about your own people. In my questioning I usually try to get into details; only in this way do you really find out what is going on and build a platform for future action. Of course, policy and long-term planning are part of my job as general manager, but details are just as important.

With my managers I practice an open-door policy and, as a result, I see each man practically every day. Usually, our meetings last between 30 minutes and one hour, and they almost always relate to a specific operating problem. About twice a month I meet with all six managers together, but these meetings are largely to convey information: on policies, on results, etc. I do not believe in committees for decision making and coordination. Particularly at Hedblom we are still small enough so that these things can take place on a daily and informal basis. At the beginning I was more meeting-oriented. To get to know the managers better and to facilitate coordination, I scheduled regular luncheon meetings. After several weeks, however, I learned that lunch was a sacred time for one of my managers who used to go home during this time for a nap. Incidentally, this man rarely leaves before 8:00 P.M. in the evening and his siesta is more than justified. After I learned about this, we stopped our luncheon meetings and nothing formal or regular took their place. Also, I often have dinner with the managers since I am usually alone in Boxholm, but this is mostly on an individual basis.

My policy is to delegate. Because of my language handicap, I am in fact forced to do so, and this is a good thing. I have also tried to encourage initiative by the managers and even arguments. This is not easy, given the leadership style under which they had worked previously. Also, I am trying to make everybody cost-conscious. Watching costs is critical in our business, and cost reduction is imperative to restore Hedblom to profitability. Yet there is really nothing dramatic that you can do to cut costs: no shortcuts, no labor-saving machinery, and no great economies of scale. Thus, it is very necessary to watch every step and every penny. In a recent meeting the production manager mentioned that his direct-labor-per-kilo-of-fabric-knitted ratio would go up because he had hired extra people in view of a large fabric order which was subsequently canceled. This concern about costs and awareness about his department's efficiency is quite a change from a few months ago.

My job naturally is to think ahead. Hence I try to focus the attention of my managers not only on today's problems but also on what we might be facing in six months or one year. This is especially important given the lead times in our business. Another job I have is that of arbiter. Fortunately, there is not too much conflict around here, and so this role is not a very active one. Sometimes I try to avoid conflicts by making the decisions myself. For example, I anticipated conflicts in allocating fabrics among our three basic activities. Every line (Hedblom, Karin, and fabrics) of course would want the best cloth, so I allocated fabrics to each of them.

# Hedblom (B)*

ON WEDNESDAY, March 13, 1968, Mr. Arthur Keller,[1] age 32, managing director of Hedblom, a ladies' dress company located in Boxholm, Sweden, entered his office to find a big bouquet of flowers with a card from his six top managers expressing their gratitude and conveying their best wishes. "Yes," Mr. Keller remarked, "today is my anniversary here.[2] It has been an exciting and rewarding year, and we look forward to the future with confidence. Our goal is to make Hedblom into one of the leading dress companies, not just in Sweden, but in all of EFTA."

In looking back at the results of the past year, Mr. Keller stressed the full cooperation and complete devotion of his associates. "If, during the remainder of my career, I get the same support from my associates as I have received here during the past year, I will be very fortunate," he said.

The feeling was mutual. One of the managers said, "Since Mr. Keller has been here I feel several years younger." Another manager commented that he now was able to work more freely, to make his own decisions, and to use initiative. A third manager liked the open-door policy and the attention he received. He also appreciated being informed

---

[1] Names and figures have been disguised.

[2] Mr. Keller became managing director of Hedblom on March 13, 1967. Events leading up to this appointment and Mr. Keller's early weeks on the job are described in the Arthur Keller case. The strategy which Mr. Keller decided upon during his first months on the job is described in the Hedblom (A) case.

about what went on in the entire company, and he liked the high degree of delegation. Finally, he was delighted that Mr. Keller took a keen interest in the company, and especially that he took walks through the plant.

In appraising the results of his actions during the past year and in assessing the future outlook for Hedblom, Mr. Keller commented as follows:

Our three 1968 spring collections of Hedblom dresses sold well, and results exceeded our targets. The initial results of our 1968 autumn collection are most encouraging, especially since autumn was typically Hedblom's weak collection. Our style reputation has increased during the past year and our on-time deliveries have enhanced trade goodwill. Our advertising has become more effective and should support even larger sales. We expect to sell between Skr 12 and Skr 14 million of Hedblom dresses. Also I feel that we now have a basis for profitable long-term growth with Hedblom dresses in Sweden, averaging about 10%–15% per year.

Initial results with our second [Karin] line and with our fabric sales have been encouraging, but some major issues have to be resolved before we can achieve our true potential. In 1968 we expect to get Skr 2 to Skr 4 million in sales revenues from our second line and Skr 2 to Skr 4 million from fabric sales, but with more and better efforts we should be able to reach, respectively, Skr 10 to Skr 12 million and Skr 4 to Skr 6 million. We expect yearly growth rates of 10% to 15% for our second line of dresses and of 15% to 20% for fabrics.

Foreign markets are also still mostly potential, although we have made good progress during the past year. Our potential could be fantastic. Sweden's GNP is 13.5% of the EFTA total (excluding Portugal), and if we were to do equally well elsewhere in EFTA as in Sweden, we could expect 7½ times as much sales as now, or up to Skr 100 million. Of course, it is unlikely that we will achieve the same market penetration as in Sweden, at least in the near future, but nevertheless this is our target. Before we get that far, some issues here, too, have to be settled.

Our organization seems to have digested the change and growth very well. The office move worked out perfectly, as did the changes in organization structure. There is only one issue which comes back all the time: whether the second dress line should be independent, or organizationally part of merchandising.

Fabric design has been doing a tremendous job, but I begin to get complaints that with our three lines too many demands are placed on our designer. Manufacturing has also made great improvements, but here, too, some of the strains of our broader product line are being felt. In the management control area we still have to make most of our progress, but, after all, this is the area where we really started from scratch.

All in all, I am most happy about the past year and confident about the future. In 1967 we closed with a loss, but very much reduced from previous years. During 1968 we expect to make a decent profit, and all indications point to a profitable first quarter. [See Exhibit 1 for recent financial

**EXHIBIT 1**

HEDBLOM
Abbreviated Operating Statement
(in millions of Swedish kronor)*

|  | 7/1/66 to 6/30/67 | 7/1/67 to 12/31/67 | 1/1/68 to 6/30/68 (budget) |
|---|---|---|---|
| Net sales† | 10.3 | 4.8 | 9.3 |
| Gross margin | 1.1 | 1.5 | 2.5 |
| Selling and administrative expense | 3.6 | 1.7 | 1.6 |
| Income from operations | (2.5) | (0.2) | 0.9 |

*Skr = 19.3 U.S. cents; $1 = Skr 5.17.
†Net sales = gross sales minus sales taxes, rebates, and shipping.

Tentative Breakdown of Manufacturing Expenses
Developed during the Summer and Fall of 1967
(in percentages)

| | | |
|---|---|---|
| Yarn | | 45.1 |
| Accessories | | 3.9 |
| Knitting | | |
| Labor | 2.5 | |
| Overhead | 6.0 | 8.5 |
| Cutting | | |
| Labor | 2.8 | |
| Overhead | 1.5 | 4.3 |
| Sewing | | |
| Labor | 16.0 | |
| Overhead | 4.8 | 20.8 |
| Dyeing | | 5.8 |
| Development and samples | | 5.8 |
| Other costs | | |
| Variable | 4.0 | |
| Overhead | 1.8 | 5.8 |
| | | 100.0 |

Source: Company records.

data.] For the future there are two more issues that occupy me: Hedblom's relations with its parent company, which is also its major supplier; and our distinctive competence, especially whether it will ensure sufficient long-term profitability.

In his appraisal of past results and future outlook for Hedblom, Mr. Keller mentioned nine issues which he had to face in March of 1968. These are described in more detail below.

## THE RETAIL REVOLUTION

The crux of this issue, as Mr. Keller described it, was that (1) Hedblom's selective distribution ruled out certain large and growing dress distribution channels, and (2) these channels wanted to retail dresses at below Skr 100—in other words, at much lower prices than Hedblom's. Could Hedblom cater to this market segment without damage to its bread-and-butter line? Particularly, how would its traditional channels, the small dress shops, respond if Hedblom dresses were sold in the mass merchandising outlets? Also, could Hedblom continue to command high prices if under the same brand dresses at half that price were sold? The company had looked at four basic alternatives: (1) continue to ignore these growing channels; (2) make sales to these channels at lower prices but use unbranded merchandise or else the store's own brand; (3) sell through these outlets, but use a second, different company brand; or (4) try to make sales to these outlets under a different parallel brand, but at the same prices as Hedblom dresses.

With the Karin brand the company had opted for the third alternative, but the issue was far from settled. Initially, the plan was to sell Karin dresses to every potential client, but when the time came the company proceeded very carefully and slowly for fear that an aggressive approach might jeopardize sales of Hedblom dresses. The commercial manager estimated potential losses in Hedblom dress sales at 50% of current volume. As a result, Karin dresses were sold in Sweden to only six large department stores and three mail-order houses. The commercial manager kept pushing for the alternative of supplying the mass retail outlets with unbranded, low-price dresses. He argued that unbranded sales, rather than use of a second brand, offered protection to the Hedblom line, thus permitting aggressive sales. Also, he felt there was no future in department stores for dresses over Skr 100, and therefore he did not believe in a parallel high-price brand.

## ORGANIZING PARALLEL ACTIVITIES IN DRESSES

Early in 1968 Mr. Keller was faced with increasing pressure from the commercial manager, Mr. Filipsson, to make Karin sales his responsibility. His reasoning was that Karin styling and sales greatly influenced the market position of Hedblom dresses. Hence it was essential to assure close and continuous coordination of the merchandising of both lines. This could be done better, Mr. Filipsson argued, if the Karin directress and the two salesmen were to report directly to him.

Mr. Nilsson, to whom the Karin line was currently assigned, did not have strong feelings about the issue. He regretted that he had not been able to pursue a more aggressive sales policy, and, lacking this, he wondered whether all his troubles had been worthwhile. He had encountered difficulties in getting the fabrics he wanted, with the Hedblom dress manager using a preemptive strategy in asking for his fabrics. There had also been some conflicts on dress models, with the Hedblom dress people arguing that the Karin models too closely resembled the Hedblom ones. All in all, Mr. Nilsson indicated, Karin was treated pretty much like a stepchild. Operating problems, on the other hand, had been few.

Most important, he had been able to deliver his Karin dresses on time, with the manufacturing department always meeting its promises.

## FABRIC SALES

We started fabric sales with great enthusiasm to fill up the plant, but now some people are beginning to have second thoughts. By selling fabrics to makers-up you help your own competitors in a way. But the biggest resistance to our fabric sales has come from our parent company, Wientex.

With these words Mr. Keller described his main issue in regard to selling fabrics. The parent company's argument was that this activity put Hedblom into competition with companies that were Wientex's yarn customers. These customers, Wientex's Scandinavian sales manager feared, might retaliate by not buying from him. He was particularly afraid of this retaliation if Hedblom were to force its way into the fabric business through a low-price strategy. He cited Wientex's strong position in Scandinavia, where it had a 60% market share in texturized yarns.

On Hedblom's side the argument was that Wientex would lose customers anyway because two yarn producers in Finland and Norway had established texturizing facilities and would definitely take market share away from Wientex. At any rate, intense price competition in texturized yarns was predicted for Scandinavia, and this would make fabric sales preferable to yarn sales. The latter were entirely price sensitive, and since yarn was a commodity, customer loyalty was nil. With fabrics, on the other hand, it was possible to achieve some product differentiation, especially through excellence in designs. Furthermore, Hedblom management cited the U.S. integration of yarn and fabric facilities and predicted such a trend for Europe. Finally, Hedblom's managers cited the example of a British yarn producer which had a subsidiary selling fabrics. This subsidiary had sold Crimplene-based fabrics in Scandinavia without provoking retaliation from the British company's customers. On balance, Hedblom management felt that the gains on fabric sales far outweighed possible losses on yarns.

The above issue, however, had prevented Mr. Nilsson from pushing fabric sales aggressively. He had to rely exclusively on the Danish cover-up organization, which he considered to be (1) too costly, (2) too complicated, (3) poor in terms of its sales organization, (4) wholly dependent on small customers, and (5) unable to reach large accounts. Mr. Nilsson felt that if fabric sales could be made under the Hedblom name, the company's reputation plus aggressive selling would enable him to move up to 100 tons of fabrics per year in EFTA instead of the currently expected annual sales of between 40 and 80 tons. He did not see much long-term potential in the European Common Market, given its high import duties of about 14%. Some temporary sales could, however, be made in Germany, where yarn prices higher than in Sweden allowed absorption of the import duty. He expected yarn prices to drop in Germany, at which point Swedish fabric sales would be priced out of the market.

## FOREIGN MARKETS

Mr. Keller identified his chief issue in this area as follows:

The only way to make real headway in foreign markets is to have your own sales organization which is well qualified and dedicated. We have made a great deal of progress, but the road ahead appears both long and strenuous. However, we feel that the sales potential in EFTA is worth the trouble and money. At this point, however, foreign sales amount to 20% to 30% of the total, but this includes fabric sales through Denmark.

The foreign markets are giving us more problems than we anticipated. Each country has different demands, and the timing of introductions of dress collections also varies. Furthermore, we did not give our distribution setup enough thought. Should we rely on agents who get a 10% commission and who carry other lines? Or should we hire our own exclusive salesmen? In this case, should their compensation be through straight salary or through commissions, or, if both, in what proportions? Motivation, compensation, and control of our foreign sales activities is still an unresolved issue. In Norway and Austria results have been fine, while in Switzerland and Denmark they have been below expectations.

## PARENT COMPANY SUPPLIER REGULATIONS

In contrast to the hitherto prevailing product shortages, Hedblom management predicted excess capacity for texturized yarns and therefore expected severe price competition. Price pressures on yarns, of course, would be beneficial to Hedblom as a purchaser. However, relations with the parent company had to be considered. One of the reasons for the Hedblom purchase by Wientex had been the desire to secure a stable outlet. By March 1968 Hedblom absorbed about 15% to 20% of the output of Wientex's Austrian texturized yarn plant and thus was an important factor in this plant's profitability. Within this setting, would Hedblom be able to shop around freely for yarn bargains? Would it be able to demand lower prices from its parent?

Related to the above issues was the question whether Hedblom should continue to purchase, and emphasize in its merchandising, the Crimplene branded texturized polyesters. Wientex sold Crimplene branded yarn, passing on a Skr 1.50 advertising allowance per kilo received from its raw materials supplier. Other texturizers also sold mostly branded polyesters. With the possibility of excess capacity, yarn producers might attempt selective price cutting by reducing prices on unbranded polyesters while maintaining them on branded sales. It was rumored that some companies were already doing this, allowing price cuts up to 15% (or about twice the usual advertising allowance which, of course, would not be granted for unbranded sales). The possibility of a dual market raised implications for Hedblom, which had always emphasized Crimplene in its dress sales. Should Hedblom continue this emphasis, particularly in view of the increasing brand proliferation of synthetics and the resulting consumer confusion? Also, the aggressive sale of cheap U.K. Crimplene dresses in Scandinavia might weaken the prestige of Crimplene for Hedblom. The question was raised among Hedblom managers whether there would not be, particularly in the long term, greater security in the Hedblom brand than in the Crimplene brand.

## STYLING DEMANDS

In March 1968 Mr. Sundman, fabric design manager, commented on styling issues as follows:

With our new activities, the demand on my department has increased greatly. Last year we developed more fabrics than in the previous four to five years together. In fact, for 1968's high-summer and autumn dress collections, along with fabric sales, 63 qualities in all have been developed. [See Exhibit 2.] And that only covers half a year. At this rate we have to develop

**EXHIBIT 2**
**Fabric qualities for 1968**

| Brand | Purpose | Qualities developed | Qualities on Jacquards |
|---|---|---|---|
| Hedblom . . . . . | High-summer collection | 6 | 3 |
| Hedblom . . . . . | Autumn head collection | 17 | 11 |
| Hedblom . . . . . | Autumn cocktail collection | 12 | 11 |
| Karin . . . . . . . | Autumn collection | 21 | 11 |
| Fabric. . . . . . . | Sales | 7 | 2 |

about 125 qualities yearly, which amounts to one design every second working day. Up to now, we have been able to produce this many designs because we had some ideas in reserve from previous years, but these will soon be exhausted. Also, we can reintroduce some fabrics of earlier years, but that will not get us far either. Thus, I frankly cannot see how we can continue to satisfy the enormous demands of our product line. My department consists of only myself and an assistant. Furthermore, fabric designs have to be tried on the machines, and this too imposes some restrictions and costs.

## MANUFACTURING DEMANDS

Mr. Lanner, production manager, discussed manufacturing problems as follows:

I think we have too many collections. Also, manufacturing does not have enough influence on dress choices. As a result, our efficiency is reduced.

Mr. Carlsson, manager for production scheduling, purchasing, and shipping, added the following points:

Changing style trends make it necessary to purchase more and more colored yarn. Earlier, close to 80% of our purchases were of white yarn, but if the present trend continues it may soon be only 50%. This change makes our purchases more costly and increases wastage as well as risk of obsolescence. We are doing our best in purchasing to reduce the percentage of dyed yarns, but there is only so much you can do.

## MEASUREMENT CONTROL

Mr. Keller discussed what he saw as a key issue here as follows:

I am supposed to make long-run decisions, and yet I am measured on the basis of Hedblom's quarterly results. Also, I am measured on the basis of the bottom line: profit and loss. But I cannot measure any of my subordinates on this same basis. I cannot measure fabric design on profit or loss, or manufacturing or merchandising. If I were to try to do so, they would blame one another: merchandising would say that manufacturing made the wrong dresses, made them poorly, or delivered late. Manufacturing would accuse merchandising of placing all sorts of special orders, of not selling enough, etc. Yet, my boss doesn't care about any of these excuses; he simply points at me. Under these conditions how can I design a control system which focuses on the criterion by which I am measured, and yet is meaningful to my subordinates, particularly in guiding them to make profit-oriented decisions? This is currently my biggest problem in the area of internal management and organization.

## LONG-TERM OUTLOOK FOR HEDBLOM

Mr. Keller continued:

Is this business attractive long term, and how can we profitably beat competition? In purchasing we have no advantages: everybody can buy yarn at the same price and we face no shortages. In knitting we have a certain advantage with our Jacquard machines; these permit us to use our design skills and to achieve great pattern flexibility which gives us an edge over the makers-up. In cutting we have no advantage; all still hinges on the pattern girl. I have been talking to one of the computer companies to see whether something can be done to minimize fabric losses, but this does not look immediately feasible. In sewing we do not have an advantage, just more sewing machines. I see no way to gain an advantage here except through radically different techniques such as using adhesives, possibly with other materials—for example, paper. In shipping we do not have an advantage either, except that, given our size, we can possibly ship more in bulk. Thus, in manufacturing we do not have much of an edge.

Merchandising is different. Through our advertising and public relations we have achieved quite an image, and I think we are on the way to achieving a customer franchise. Still we are not sure how far advertising will carry us, how much we will have to spend continuously, and how durable the impact will be for ladies' dresses. Also, we have two types of competition: the small makers-up of which there are many, given the ease of entry into the dress business, and the large sophisticated retail outlets like the department store chains. What long-term threats do these two types of competition pose for a company like Hedblom? Furthermore, the economics of our business should be considered, especially in terms of variable costs and working capital requirements. Given these conditions, what are the implications both in terms of size and in terms of growth?

I think that we have rescued Hedblom, and all our attention up to this point was focused on this task. Now, as we used to say at the B-School, we can start thinking about whether this is the business we should be in.

# Hedblom (C)*

ON JUNE 19, 1968, while reviewing the Hedblom (B) case for release, Mr. Keller commented: "The nine issues which I faced back in March are accurately portrayed. However, some major new developments have occurred in the meantime, particularly in terms of the Hedblom product line and fabric sales." Mr. Keller continued as follows:[1]

As part of our Hedblom intermediate spring sportsclothes collection, which we started selling in early November 1967 for delivery in April 1968, we included ladies' slacks to retail at Skr 59. Initial orders through the sales force totaled 3,000 pieces, while orders written for the whole collection amounted to 16,000. Since April, reorders by telephone have been for 8,000 pieces. This success and some market studies indicate that there must be a market for high-priced wash-and-wear slacks and other types of sportswear, for both women and men. We do not think, however, that European men will buy polyester wash-and-wear suits, even though only the expert eye can tell the difference between our knitted and the traditional woven fabrics. Slacks of knitted polyester, on the other hand, appear to have a great potential. Clothes care for them is different, and the European housewife, who has been putting her dresses in the washing machine for some years, may like to do this for her husband's slacks as well. Also keep in mind that permapress is less useful in Europe because most households do not have tumble dryers.

We are now considering hiring another directress to concentrate entirely on

[1] Names and figures have been disguised.

736

the trouser business and possibly even a special salesman to sell trousers on a year-round basis.

In fabric sales we face a much greater opportunity. When put in charge of Hedblom, I also retained my earlier duties as assistant to the president of Wientex, our Austrian parent company; here my work primarily involved planning and implementing Wientex's forward integration from spinning and texturizing into knitting, weaving, possibly dyeing and finishing, and, eventually, dressmaking. In this part of my job I looked at several companies as possible acquisitions and also investigated some projects which we could start from scratch. I rejected all these except two. One was the potential acquisition of a $10 million fabric company in the European Common Market, on which negotiations are proceeding slowly. The other project, to be started by us, involved making circular double-knits at a company to be located in Germany but set up to supply the entire European Common Market with fabrics. I finished preparations for this project by September of 1967, and it was approved by the Wientex board of directors. Permission was granted to purchase knitting machines, to hire people, to open sales offices, and to build a new plant. The only restriction was that the company would not be involved in dyeing and finishing. Deliveries were to start during the early part of 1969. On this basis I proceeded with preparations. Support within the company was strong, since the texturizing division saw the German project as a large captive account and outlet.

Less than a month ago the board reversed its decision, and the German project was canceled. The same pressures against forward integration as described in the "B" case led to this decision: our yard-goods people were afraid of losing some of their customers if we competed with them in fabrics. By last month, however, we had 23 circular knitting machines on order for a total purchase price of $544,000. We had hired two sales managers (for France and Germany, respectively), two fabric designers, two knitting technicians, and two secretaries. Up to now I have not succeeded in convincing top management to revive the German project. Hence I face the decision of what to do with the people I have hired and the machines on order.

At the same time, we are reaching the conclusion that the Danish cover-up organization which sells our Hedblom fabrics under another name is not performing satisfactorily. They do not sell enough, have no important customers, and simply are not in touch with the market. Yet we see a tremendous demand for knitted fabrics, and we believe that with our reputation and skills we should succeed.

The cancellation of the German project now provides us with the following opportunities at Hedblom. Our expected rise in dress sales necessitates, in any event, an additional seven Jacquard circular knitting machines. Instead of taking seven of the 23 machines on order for Germany, why not gamble and take all of them? If so, the time appears ripe to negotiate, as a *quid pro quo*, for permission from the parent company to sell fabrics under our own name, thus doing away with the cover-up restrictions. With the pressure of the 23 machines on order, I feel that I have a good chance to persuade top management. Incidentally, these machines are scheduled for delivery at a rate of four per month, starting in about four weeks. Thus, a decision to take delivery or to cancel has to be made immediately. Also, if at Hedblom we move into fabrics in a major way, we can employ most of the people I have hired for the German project.

The additional 16 machines, costing about Skr 2 million, would add an incremental fabric capacity of between 240 and 250 tons a year and could produce about Skr 12 million in fabric sales. For 1968, in contrast, we expect fabric sales of between 40 and 80 tons, or Skr 2 to 4 million. Also, our total current knitting output, serving dresses and other finished clothes as well as fabric sales, now amounts to about 250 tons yearly. A ton of fabric sales is expected to yield profits before taxes of between Skr 5,000 and Skr 6,000, or $1,000–$1,200 per ton, or about 10% on sales.

Of course, in the short run, this move would create excess capacity again, but this time of the most modern types, involving high-production 36 "systems" machines with fine gauge and excellent styling capabilities which could provide us with further competitive advantages.

# Dynatech Corporation

In June 1970, Mr. Jay Barger, president of Dynatech Corporation, was preparing for a corporate strategy meeting to be held at the end of July. Scheduled to attend the meeting in addition to Mr. Barger were the following executives:

Kenneth Roberts, vice president and treasurer of Dynatech;
Thomas Shukay, general manager of the Cryomedical division;
Paul Hall, vice president of Dynatech and president of the Cooke Engineering Division;
James Turner, vice president of Dynatech and president of the R & D division; and
Richard Cass, president of the Bacon Industries Division.

The purpose of the meeting was to reassess Dynatech's goals and objectives, and, if necessary, to make new plans to achieve those objectives. Mr. Barger was particularly interested in discussing the issue of a separate medical sales division to market Dynatech's medical products. He explained:

Today, medical products account for about one third of our sales, but by 1975 I expect them to account for two thirds of sales. Concurrently, I hope to achieve a corporate growth rate in sales of 40% per year, although 20% is probably a more realistic projection.

To achieve our growth and product-mix objectives, I am now considering the advisability of creating a medical products sales division. Then the laboratory-equipment line of our Cooke Engineering Division and the cryosurgical instruments of our Dynatech Cryomedical Products Division could be marketed by one organization. It may make sense to do that, particularly in light of our plans to develop international markets and introduce new products.

Presently, each of these divisions is operating through its own combination of distributors, manufacturers' representatives, house sales, and direct sales force.

Dynatech manufactured and marketed several high-technology products, which included microbiology laboratory equipment, cryosurgical instruments, electrical connections used in communications, and special adhesives such as premixed frozen epoxies. The company also performed research and development contract services for the government and industry, largely in the fields of thermal engineering and fluid mechanics.

Sales had grown steadily from $1.8 million in 1966 to $4.6 million in 1969 before leveling off in 1970. Earnings had experienced uneven growth from $44,000 in 1966 to $126,000 in 1970. (For financial data, see Exhibits 1 and 2.)

**EXHIBIT 1**

DYNATECH CORPORATION
Consolidated Income Statements
For the Years Ended March 31

|  | 1967 | 1968 | 1969 | 1970 |
|---|---|---|---|---|
| Net sales . . . . . . . . . . | $2,649,311 | $3,394,097 | $4,647,688 | $4,616,736 |
| Earnings (loss) before income tax and nonrecurring items . . . . . . | 213,497 | (194,449) | 142,832 | 187,119 |
| Federal income tax . . . . . | 81,652 | (28,154) | 73,130 | 86,800 |
| Nonrecurring items . . . . . |  |  | (44,531) | 25,200 |
| Earnings (loss) after tax . . . . . . . . . . . . | $ 131,845 | $ (166,295) | $ 25,171 | $ 125,519 |
| Earnings (loss) per share . . . . . . . . . . . | .45 | (.40) | .05 | .25 |
| Stockholders' equity . . . . | 699,543 | 797,081 | 1,183,524 | 1,311,420 |
| Number of employees at years end . . . . . . . . | 140 | 220 | 225 | 219 |

Note: The figures in this table have been adjusted for the five-for-one stock split of November 1968 but not for subsequent poolings of interest. Net income per share is based on the average number of shares outstanding each year. On the basis of including operations of the pooled companies prior to the years of acquisition, results for 1967 would be as follows: sales, $2,899,766; earnings after tax, $147,671; earnings per share, $.47.

Source: Annual reports.

## HISTORY

Dynatech had grown out of a consulting relationship between Professor Warren Rohsenow, professor of mechanical engineering at M.I.T., and Mr. Jay Barger, an assistant professor of mechanical engineering at M.I.T. The original objective of the company, which had been started in 1954 as a partnership under the name of Microtech, was to handle some of the large consulting jobs available to Professor Rohsenow. In 1958 Microtech landed its first large government defense contract; in

**EXHIBIT 2**

DYNATECH CORPORATION
Consolidated Balance Sheets
As of March 31

|  | 1967 | 1968 | 1969 | 1970 |
|---|---|---|---|---|
| *Assets* | | | | |
| Current assets | | | | |
| Cash and marketable securities . . . . . . . | $ 246,547 | $ 497,145 | $ 549,702 | $ 294,279 |
| Accounts receivable, net of allowance for doubtful accounts . . . . . . . . . . . . . | 715,002 | 949,517 | 819,776 | 1,120,324 |
| Inventories at lower of average cost or market . . . . . . . . . . . . . . . . . . . | 293,529 | 653,798 | 560,052 | 808,917 |
| Other current assets . . . . . . . . . . . | 275,764 | 297,224 | 249,807 | 200,942 |
| Total current assets . . . . . . . . . . | $1,530,842 | $2,397,684 | $2,179,337 | $2,424,462 |
| Fixed assets, less accumulated depreciation and amortization . . . . . . . . . . . . . . | 286,716 | 333,562 | 379,234 | 389,469 |
| Capitalized research and development . . . . . | | 43,600 | 183,111 | 339,259 |
| Goodwill . . . . . . . . . . . . . . . . . . | | 529,795 | 728,203 | 757,738 |
| Other assets . . . . . . . . . . . . . . . . | 112,324 | 165,296 | 173,089 | 167,152 |
| Total assets . . . . . . . . . . . . . . | $1,929,882 | $3,469,937 | $3,642,974 | $4,078,080 |
| *Liabilities* | | | | |
| Current liabilities | | | | |
| Notes payable and current installment of long-term debt . . . . . . . . . . . . . | $ 365,653 | $ 76,736 | $ 145,630 | $ 349,776 |
| Accounts payable . . . . . . . . . . . . . | 273,568 | 182,485 | 183,819 | 232,903 |
| Other accrued liabilities . . . . . . . . . . | 202,358 | 400,127 | 277,541 | 274,657 |
| Total current liabilities . . . . . . . . . | $ 841,579 | $ 659,348 | $ 606,990 | $ 857,336 |
| Long-term debt | | | | |
| 7% registered notes, $40,000 due annually commencing January 1, 1973 . . | | 400,000 | 400,000 | 400,000 |
| 6% convertible subordinated notes, due January 31, 1978 . . . . . . . . . . . | 251,166 | 1,375,000 | 1,375,000 | 1,375,000 |
| Other long-term debt, less current installment . . . . . . . . . . . . . . . | | 124,418 | 77,460 | 53,084 |
| Minority interest in subsidiary . . . . . . . . | | 114,090 | | |
| Deferred federal income taxes . . . . . . . . . | | | | 81,240 |
| Stockholders' equity | | | | |
| Common stock, par value $.20 per share, authorized 1,500,000 shares, issued and outstanding—1967, 430,360; 1968, 538,200; 1969, 555,133; 1970, 555,133. Less shares in treasury at cost—1967, 13,175; 1968, 52,875; 1969, 51,485; 1970, 51,485 . . . . . . . . | $ 75,566 | $ 95,836 | $ 99,533 | $ 99,629 |
| Additional paid-in capital . . . . . . . . . . | 366,680 | 530,385 | 887,960 | 890,241 |
| Retained earnings . . . . . . . . . . . . . . | 394,891 | 170,860 | 196,031 | 321,550 |
| Total stockholders' equity . . . . . . . . | $ 837,137 | $ 797,081 | $1,183,524 | $1,311,420 |
| Total liabilities and stockholders' equity . . . . . . . . . . . . . . . . | $1,929,882 | $3,469,937 | $3,642,974 | $4,078,080 |

Source: Corporate records.

1960 the company name was changed to Dynatech. From 1960 to 1962 annual sales grew at 100% per year, from $400,000 to $1,500,000.

Despite the short-term success of research and development contract work, the growth potential of R & D services in terms of earnings was thought to be limited. To improve the company's earnings, it was decided to try to hold the line with R & D services and make Dynatech into a diversified products-oriented company. Initially, products were developed internally, but a series of abortive product efforts between 1962 and 1964 convinced Mr. Barger that an aggressive acquisition program was needed. In 1965, therefore, the company launched a program of diversification. Subsequently, sales tripled, from $1.5 million in 1965 to over $4.5 million in 1969.

By June 1970, after extensive product diversification, Mr. Barger expressed his belief that of their many products the greatest potential growth in earnings was represented by Dynatech's medical products:

In a recent memo to the board of directors [June 4, 1970], I have indicated that our primary objective at present should be to strive for internal product development in our medical product lines. I have also proposed that the R & D division work on developing or acquiring a new medical product line.

## FINANCE

Dynatech's stock, held by approximately 350 shareholders, was traded over the counter with prices in June 1970 in the neighborhood of 7 bid, 8½ asked.[1] Dr. Rohsenow and Mr. Barger owned 40% of the stock. Originally, they had controlled 67% of Dynatech's stock, and at one point nearly 80%, but their stockholdings had been diluted both by acquisitions and by some private placements of the company's stock.

Dynatech's vice president and treasurer, Mr. Kenneth Roberts, a 1955 graduate of Harvard Business School, had hoped that Dynatech could "go public" in early 1970. He commented:

We're actually in a position where we can grow more rapidly than we can provide the necessary capital. Even though decently capitalized for up to 50% more business, I think Dynatech could grow at a rate of about 20% a year to achieve a sales level of $15 million in 1975. Most of this growth would be in the form of medical products, which probably should account for $8–$12 million sales by 1975.

Because we are near the limit in debt capital, the logical alternative is equity. But before we can raise any equity capital, we have to improve

---

[1] The stock had begun to be traded—although unregistered with the SEC—in 1969, as some shares had been in the hands of stockholders for many years. Dynatech expected to comply with the Securities Act of 1934, which required registration within a certain time interval after a total of 500 stockholders had been reached.

our earnings record or the stock market has to improve considerably—particularly the over-the-counter market.[2]

## ORGANIZATION

Dynatech divisions were organized in what Mr. Barger called a "free form" structure, with each operating as a separate profit center. The only centralized function was finance (see Exhibit 3). All corporate

**EXHIBIT 3**

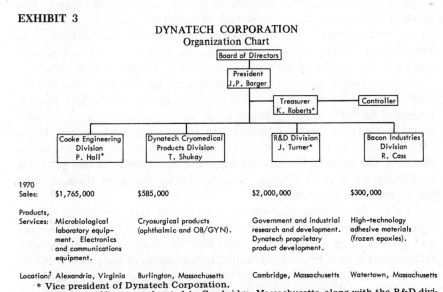

DYNATECH CORPORATION
Organization Chart

* Vice president of Dynatech Corporation.
† Executive offices were located in Cambridge, Massachusetts, along with the R&D division and were approximately four miles from the Bacon Industries Division in Watertown and about 15 miles from the Cryomedical division in Burlington.
Source: Casewriter's notes based on interview data.

operating officers and division heads were salaried and eligible for stock options. In addition, Mr. Hall, president of Cooke Engineering Division, and Mr. Cass, president of Bacon Industries Division, were on a bonus plan which resulted in the payment of an additional percentage of their salaries based upon their divisions' ROI performance. (Return on investment was calculated by dividing a division's net income by its "net worth" at the beginning of the bonus year.)

## DYNATECH CRYOMEDICAL PRODUCTS DIVISION

Under a 1966 licensing agreement, the Cryomedical division manufactured and marketed the Amoils Cryosurgical System. Invented by Dr. Amoils of South Africa, the system, which sold for $1,900, consisted

---

[2] During the period from late 1968 to June 1970, U.S. shareholders sustained paper losses in the stock market approaching $300 billion; in the first six months of 1970 alone, the Dow-Jones Industrial Average fell from 811.31 to 631.16.

of a surgical probe and a control unit which maintained the probe tip at —60° centigrade. The cold probe tip replaced some of a surgeon's previous instruments. The first application for the system was in ophthalmology, where the probes had been used for cataract removal, retinal repair, the removal of foreign objects from the eye, as well as treatment of some glaucoma conditions.

In 1968 the Cryomedical division had sustained a loss of $323,000 on sales of $340,000. This was due in part to large investments in two nonmedical product lines which had subsequently proved unprofitable. In an effort to improve the division's performance, Mr. Barger brought in Mr. Thomas Shukay as division manager in February 1969. Mr. Shukay had formerly been a project manager at Hughes Aircraft Company.

Given a charter to turn the Cryomedical division around, Mr. Shukay made several drastic changes: indirect expenses were slashed from a budgeted $436,200 to $272,200 and 23 of the 50 employees were released to make room for better qualified and more competent people. Upon Mr. Shukay's recommendation, Mr. Barger authorized the liquidation of one of the unprofitable product lines and the transfer of two products to Dynatech's R & D division, leaving the Cryomedical division with just cryosurgical instruments.

In 1969 the Cryomedical division developed and introduced a general-purpose console and probe which could be used by obstetricians and gynecologists (OB/GYN). The OB/GYN doctors used Dynatech's cryosurgical system to treat cervicitis (inflammation of the cervix). Previously, this mild disease (thought to be contracted at some time by up to 95% of all women) had been treated by electrocauterization, a painful and unpopular technique.

The division's 1969 sales were $651,000 and its losses $61,000. During 1970 the division almost broke even with sales of $585,000.

### Ophthalmic product distribution

Cryomedical's opthalmic instruments were distributed in the United States exclusively by Keeler Optical Company, a national distributor of eye-care products and medical supplies. Keeler received a discount of 33⅓%. It placed a large annual order in the fall preceding its sales year and generally took two-thirds delivery from the Cryomedical division by March 31. Its order for 1970 amounted to $360,000. Said Mr. Shukay of Keeler:

We like to work with Keeler because we get together about once a year and he commits himself to an annual order. It helps us plan production, and we do not need to expend a great deal of management time on the arrangement. We think he does a pretty good job for us. But, of course, with this arrangement we don't get all the needed feedback from end users.

Mr. Shukay described the ophthalmic market in terms of the 8,000 registered ophthalmologists in the United States. Some 1,500–2,000 of them did cataract removal and retina repair work, thereby representing potential customers for the Cryomedical division. By June 1970, Keeler had placed approximately 1,000 units; Frigitronics, Dynatech's major competitor in the cryomedical field, had also placed 1,000 units.

## OB/GYN product distribution

In 1969 the Cryomedical division had established a direct sales force to introduce the new general-purpose cryosurgical system. The sales force, which was composed of a sales manager and two salesmen, worked closely with professional groups like the American College of Gynecologists to establish Dynatech's name in OB/GYN cryosurgery. As of June 1970 the sales force had made 250 sales or field placements; placements were made at the rate of about 20 per month.[3] Frigitronics had sold or placed 200 units.

One Dynatech executive commented:

Selling to obstetricians and gynecologists is far different from selling to opthalmologists. The ophthalmologist typically has in his office a great deal of equipment. He is conditioned to the idea of securing a large array of complex, expensive instruments, perhaps $50,000 worth, which will have to be paid off over several years. The OB/GYN man, on the other hand, has relatively less equipment in his office so that our cryode represents a relatively high-ticket item for him.

Further, the ophthalmic units are used in hospital operating rooms, while the OB/GYN units are used primarily in OB/GYN doctors' offices.

Yet another difference is found in the respective "after-markets" found in each field. The ophthalmologist has an appreciable aftermarket in lenses, frames, etc., whereas the OB/GYN man has virtually no aftermarket. This difference between the two medical fields explains some of the differences in our distribution policies. With ophthalmic cryosurgical equipment, there already existed national distributors like Keeler catering to the ophthalmologists. On the other hand, with few equipment needs and no aftermarket, the OB/GYN men have no distributors specializing in or even concentrating on them. This was, in part, why we introduced the cryosurgical unit with our own direct sales force.

In March 1970 Cryomedical started semiprivate label selling by distributing its OB/GYN units through the Medical Instrument Division

---

[3] A unit was "placed" when left with a doctor on a trial basis. Within a 90-day trial period, a "sale" was made if the doctor accepted the unit.

of Syntex, a national distributor of drugs and medical supplies with $80 million in annual sales. Syntex had trained salesmen to sell the cryosurgical units, and their sales and placement rate was expected to equal that of the Cryomedical division. Syntex was guaranteed a maximum of 50 units within a period of 30 consecutive days. The rest of the OB/GYN production was available for Dynatech's sales force.

Cryomedical's sales manager noted that distribution through Syntex had not caused any reduction in the placement rate of the Cryomedical division. He felt, however, that some improvements could be made in the distributor-Dynatech relationship: "All of our distributors could be more effective if our salesmen could supervise them regionally; that way our personnel could devote more time to obtaining feedback from the field and developing new products."

The Cryomedical division also had nonexclusive agreements with two sales representatives, one located in Montreal and the other in Atlanta. The Montreal rep had been chosen for his bilingual abilities and his familiarity with Canadian markets. The Atlanta rep was considered important in providing Dynatech with adequate representation in the "capital of the southern sphere."[4] (See Exhibit 4 for the sales organization of the Cryomedical division.)

Shukay viewed the OB/GYN market as composed of 18,500 doctors of whom 12,500 were primarily gynecologists; gynecology was, for the rest, a secondary specialty. Recognizing that the gynecological unit product life cycle had been estimated to be about five years, peaking at the third year, Mr. Shukay made the following analysis of OB/GYN cryode sales. He projected that one third of the active gynecologists would eventually use cryosurgery. He further assumed that many of these 4,000 gynecologists might be in joint practice in hospitals or clinics so that the number might be reduced by 50%, leaving 2,000 possible sales. If competition left Dynatech with only a 50% share of market, this number would be reduced to a sales volume of 1,000 units or about $2 million in sales over a period of about five years for an annual sales volume of about $400,000. With less competition, sales approaching $4 million over five years could be anticipated.

---

[4] The "southern sphere," in medical sales parlance, was recognition of the excellent market acceptance of new medical technology in the southern United States. Only a few cryosurgical systems had been placed and successfully sold in the Northeast. Cryomedical division personnel interpreted this situation as a reflection on the new technology they were selling. In general, they found that many of the younger, more progressive doctors in large metropolitan centers like Atlanta, Houston, and Los Angeles (thus, "southern sphere") were eager to try improved surgical techniques. While by no means "backwards," the eastern doctors tended to be more conservative and traditional in their approach to medicine. Consequently, Cryomedical's major marketing efforts were geared to the "southern sphere" market.

**EXHIBIT 4**

### DYNATECH CORPORATION
Dynatech Medical Products Marketing Organizations

Dynatech Cryomedical Products Division

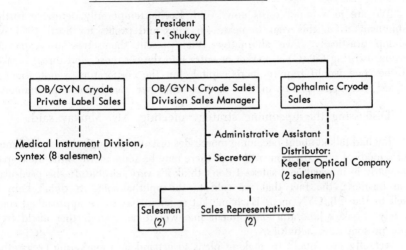

Cooke Engineering Division

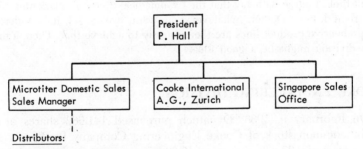

Note: Dashed lines indicate relationships outside Dynatech organizations.
Source: Casewriter's notes based on interview data.

## June 1970

Of immediate concern to Mr. Shukay was the status of existing distributor relationships. Keeler had informed the Cryomedical division in February that most of the 1970 order would not be accepted. Due to Dynatech's aggressive negotiations, Keeler was overstocked and was trying to reduce its inventories before accepting any more shipments. No further orders would be forthcoming for at least nine months. Mr. Shukay commented:

We are in a minor crisis now. With Keeler temporarily deferring further shipments from this year to next, our sales and profits for fiscal 1971 will slump drastically. Two alternatives that present themselves are expansion of our existing OB/GYN market or entry into the ear, nose, and throat market. Either one would require more capital, but the corporation is not about to invest one more penny in this division until we can become profitable.

Discussing the upcoming strategy meeting, Mr. Shukay said:

Jay had talked about becoming more sales-oriented through the establishment of a medical sales division. Although there may be some merit to the idea—particularly in international sales—I don't think it's very feasible. In this cryosurgical business, the fact that we sold to the ophthalmologists didn't help us sell to the OB/GYN men. Each market segment has to be approached separately. Cooke's laboratory-instrument line would be even farther afield from our present sales activities.

Actually, we should be making plans to expand into marketing areas other than cryosurgery. The cryosurgery markets are limited and will not be big for all time. I agree with Jay that the Cryomedical division's marketing philosophy should be: "Doctor, whatever you want, we've got it." Wider, more comprehensive product lines are the only way to achieve that. Then, a medical sales division might be a good idea.

## COOKE ENGINEERING DIVISION

On February 9, 1968, Dynatech purchased 141,662 shares or 80.7% of the common stock of Cooke Engineering Company for $8 per share. The remaining 33,853 shares or 19.3% of common stock were obtained in a statutory merger in the spring of 1969.

Basically, Cooke's sales fell into two categories: government and commercial. Government work included the planning of military communications systems, electronic system assembly to specifications, and the design and manufacture of radar data distribution systems.

Cooke's two commercial products were in the communications and medical fields. Coaxial jacks, marketed under the name of COJAX, were electrical connection devices that had been developed for the military but were used extensively in TV studio installations as well. Cooke also made the Microtiter, a system used in performing serial microtitrations in biological and hospital laboratories. Used in blood tests to measure resistance to viruses such as polio and German measles, the system consisted of an assortment of permanent equipment plus disposables such as plastic trays. The retail prices of Microtiter components ranged from $1,000 for some equipment to a few cents for a disposable tray.

Sales for Cooke in 1970 had been $1.8 million, with a net income of $131,000. In 1969 net income had been $113,000 on sales of $1.5 million. The Microtiter alone had accounted for $688,000 in sales in 1970, and forecasted sales for Cooke in 1971 were $2.1 million, of which about 50% would be Microtiter sales.

## Microtiter

Since its introduction by Cooke in 1961, Microtiter sales had increased by about 20% per year and Microtiter contributed profits of 25% of sales before taxes.

Four distributors accounted for 60% of Microtiter sales. They received 25% to $33\frac{1}{3}$% discount on list price. House sales, or direct orders, accounted for approximately 21% of Microtiter sales, and foreign orders from Cooke International, A.G. in Zurich represented 19% of 1970 sales. The lab products (Microtiter) sales manager talked about Cooke's distributor setup.

Of the four distributors, the two small ones turn out to be the best distributors from a technical knowledge standpoint. That is, they have competence in the areas of microbiology and can speak with great knowledge about the advantages and uses of a Microtiter system. The two large distributors, although providing wide distribution, are not very aggressive in the sale of Microtiter systems. Typically, they will have catalogs containing up to 50,000 different items, none of which can be consistently pushed by their salesmen. These large distributor salesmen are besieged by as many as 200 different companies vying for their attention just so they will push specific products for the companies.

A direct sales force was in the planning stages, with the first man tentatively slated for the West Coast with headquarters in California. There was a direct sales force currently functioning successfully at the international level: the Zurich sales office had made a profit of $30,000 before taxes on sales of $140,000 in fiscal 1970. Planned for September of 1970 was the opening of a Singapore sales office to handle distribution of the Microtiter systems in Japan, and a competitive Japanese manufacturer of Microtiter-type equipment was being approached as a possible production source for Cooke in the Far East. (See Exhibit 4 for Cooke's marketing organization.) The Latin American market was also being studied with a view toward establishing a sales company in that territory.

In the United States, Microtiter experienced only fringe-type competition. Overseas, in what appeared to be very lucrative markets, Cooke had initially no significant competition. Microtiter sales were considered by Cooke marketing managers to be directly related to the population of an area; a recent market survey of the Far East showed a potential sales volume of $27 million.

## Cooke Engineering Division's future

Looking ahead to the July strategy meetings, Mr. Paul Hall, president, said:

I would like to follow the field of microbiology by completely automating the Microtiter system. This would include readout and printout of all test results. To do that would take several hundred thousand dollars, but I don't anticipate any problem in funding.

I see no reason why we can't continue to grow at 20% a year in Microtiter sales. With some of our new product ideas, we may be able to grow even faster by broadening our medical products. By 1975 about 70% of our sales should be in the laboratory instrument or medical products areas. The net result would be $5 million sales for Cooke within five years, according to the plan which we have started. In about three years we may split Cooke into two parts: one to deal in microbiology and one to deal in communications and electronics.

On the subject of a medical sales division, Mr. Hall said:

I don't think it makes much sense to form a medical sales division for our present product lines. The Cryomedical division and Cooke sell to very different customers. If we both had broad lines of overlapping products, such a sales division would be a good idea. However, no firm decision has been made to make Dynatech a medical products company. We don't want to give up our work in the areas of adhesives and pollution control. On the other hand, we may want to spin the companies off, just as we are contemplating spinning off the electronics part of Cooke.

## R & D DIVISION

The research and development division was composed of four technical consulting service departments in the following areas: chemical engineering, mechanical engineering, thermal and fluid engineering, and machine design. There was also the Thermatest department which specialized in technical products and data services and which manufactured and sold heat-measuring instruments and thermocouple welder units.

The R & D division's primary role was that of providing research and engineering services to industry and government. However, through its acquisition of technology-based companies, Dynatech had expanded its R & D knowledge and capabilities. To capitalize on the acquired technologies, Dynatech in 1969 chartered the R & D division to serve also as a technology center for the corporate family of companies and subsidiaries.

Mr. James Turner, president of the R & D division, had joined Dynatech in 1960 after several years with Ingersoll-Rand Company. He discussed the R & D division and its future:

In this business you live by your wits and run hard. R & D is very cyclical, with about 30% of our business coming from the government. With the present economic slump we're particularly hard-pressed even in industrial work.

Addressing the subject of the upcoming meeting in July, Mr. Turner said:

I think that medical products will dominate the discussions, but Dynatech will not get rid of any profitable operations. As a service company, we take little investment, and we could be helpful in developing new products. What we need, really, is to get in on something at the front end or product definition stage and not be relegated to putting out fires when some projects run into technical problems.

As far as specific goals for the meeting, I would like to see us continue funding our engine antipollution device. We are only spending a fraction of what Cooke and Cryomedical are sinking into new medical products. Although the auto industry is proving tough to crack, we have patents on the device, and there is a tremendous potential return, even if at a low probability.

## BACON INDUSTRIES DIVISION

A small division of about $300,000 in annual sales, Bacon specialized in bonding agents, adhesives, and coating compounds for metals. The division did all its own research and chemical engineering development. On the horizon was a potentially profitable market in frozen epoxy adhesives, forecasted to reach $2 million by 1975. With only one competitor presently in the field and many large companies seeking a second-source supplier, the probability of a successful market penetration seemed high.

Mr. Richard Cass, president of Bacon Industries, discussed the July strategy meetings:

My immediate objective at Bacon is to expand our marketing efforts—particularly for the introduction of our frozen epoxy product line. I expect to present my plans at the meeting, and I hope to get valuable feedback from the other division heads.

The bulk of the meeting will probably center around Dynatech's medical products. Jay is promoting medical products hard, and we will be looking for new product ideas in the medical area.

Psychologically, it must be a very difficult problem to shift to medical products because R & D has been the first love of most Dynatech people. I personally am not that concerned about Bacon Industries not fitting the medical products image. I think that profits and growth talk more than image.

## BOARD OF DIRECTORS

Of Dynatech's eight directors, only Mr. Barger was an operating officer of the company. The other directors were:

| | |
|---|---|
| Dr. Warren M. Rohsenow (chairman) | Professor, mechanical engineering department, M.I.T. |
| James B. Hangstefer | President, Science Business Ventures |
| J. Keith Louden | Trustee and corporate director |
| Richard Love | Vice president, James Capel, Inc. |
| Marshall Simonds | Partner, Goodwin, Procter & Hoar |
| Philip A. Singleton | Chairman of the board. Hoodfoam Industries, Inc. |
| Charles C. Withers | Former president, Towle Manufacturing Company |

The board, through regular quarterly and frequent special meetings, played a moderately active part in determining future plans. In light of the company's uneven past growth, several directors felt that it was time to reassess Dynatech's plans.

The board chairman, Professor Warren Rohsenow, stressed the importance of interrelated activities:

Everything really had its basis in the R & D division. The original idea was for the R & D division to develop proprietary products through patents or advanced technologies. Too many product companies do not have this adequate technical backup. As a result of our structure, there is a valuable interaction between the R & D service division and our acquired divisions. We are not a conglomerate but rather a company with interrelated technologies in the areas of heat transfer, stress analysis, and vibrations.

We have established a high-quality image in the mechanical and chemical engineering fields, and our diversity allows us flexibility. To specialize in any one field at this time could be a long-range liability. Of course, there is pressure from some of the other board members to do that now in medical products.

Mr. Marshall Simonds talked about the company's medical products and a need for increased emphasis on marketing.

As for the future direction of Dynatech, I think we have no choice but to go into medical products; they are presently the brightest spot in our corporate picture. The Microtiter and to a lesser degree the cryosurgical probes have been literally the salvation of this company during the past year or two. The R & D division and Bacon Industries are just treading water at this point.

With medical products now the "in" thing for the investment community, they would help Dynatech's image in preparation for a public stock offering. Presently one of our biggest limitations is capital.

In a broader sense, Dynatech's real problem has been an historical weakness in the marketing and selling end of its effort to become product-oriented. Because of our origin as an R & D company, we are relatively inexperienced in bringing products to market. We have not yet demonstrated a consistent ability to market and sell new products successfully.

One suggestion has been a medical sales division, but I'm not so sure that is the answer. To establish such an in-house organization would mean abandoning our present distributors. Given our inexperience in marketing, I don't think we have the necessary expertise yet.

## LOOKING AHEAD TO THE JULY STRATEGY MEETING

Vice President and Treasurer Kenneth Roberts saw the July meeting as an important instrument for coordinating Dynatech's future plans:

We have been running under a decentralized form of organization—kind of like a conglomerate. However, we've never been successful in making long-range plans. As a consequence, we've been a reactive company and very volatile in our performance.

The issue of greater centralization must be faced. The independent divisions want to stay independent, but there are real advantages to consolidating space, personnel policies, and perhaps even sales.

# The Carmen Company

BEFORE 1969, our only decision was whether to open a new shoe store or a leased shoe department. Then we began an acquisition program, a decision which has begun to strain our organization and financial resources.

As Dr. Boris Carmen, chairman of the board of The Carmen Company, reflected on the condition of the company in June 1970, a number of concerns competed for his attention. After healthy increases for several years, profits in 1969 were down 70% to $183,000 even though sales rose 29% to $21.5 million, and results for the first quarter of 1970 indicated a loss of $189,000 compared with a loss of $112,000 the previous year. In spite of operating developments in several divisions, Dr. Carmen had pressed ahead with the organizational change initiated in 1967, having as its basis the creation of semiautonomous operating units. On the one hand, he and others on the board of directors were evaluating how well the organization was functioning, and, on the other, attempting to define the future direction of the company.

## HISTORY

Dr. Carmen's father had opened a name-brand cancellation shoe store in St. Louis, Missouri, in 1910. The business prospered, and by 1947 he owned and operated a very large store in St. Louis and several smaller, satellite stores in towns scattered around Missouri. In 1947 Boris Carmen assumed the ownership of the satellite stores, securing at the same time an operating manager, Mr. Sidney Wiess, who had been employed by the elder Carmen since 1932.

The stores originally specialized in cancellation footwear, but Dr. Carmen experimented with juvenile shoe stores and high-fashion women's shoe stores. In 1957, responding to the rapid growth of discount stores, Dr. Carmen opened a leased shoe department in a small midwestern discount store. Encouraged by the immediate success of this venture, he sold his other stores and in 1962 went public to raise capital for a large-scale expansion into leased shoe departments.

In 1965 Carmen acquired the Able Shoe Company, a chain of nine "free-standing"[1] budget self-service shoe stores in Louisiana. In 1967 Carmen purchased for a modest price Orlin Shoes, Inc., an operator of nine conventional[2] shoe stores in Michigan, Illinois, and Indiana, with the intention of improving Orlin's poor profit record. In September 1968, Carmen stock was listed on the American Stock Exchange.

During 1969, an imported shoe operation (Yorkshire Shoes, Ltd.), a group of extended-care medical facilities (Carmed), and a toy retailing chain (Playtime, Inc.) were added to the company, and the company's name was changed from Carmen's Shoe Stores, Inc., to The Carmen Company. Also in 1969, Carmen sold the Orlin stores, because the invest-

**EXHIBIT 1**

THE CARMEN COMPANY
Organization Prior to 1962

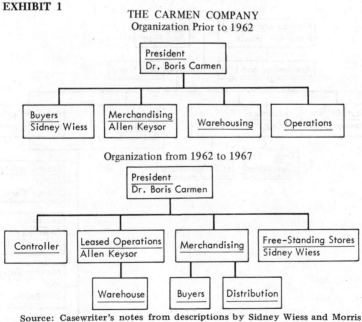

Organization from 1962 to 1967

Source: Casewriter's notes from descriptions by Sidney Wiess and Morris Furman.

---

[1] Not located in another store.

[2] Offering a broad range of styles and prices with attendant fitting services.

ment required to turn the operation around appeared to outweigh any future benefits, and purchased six self-service budget shoe stores in St. Paul.

Prior to 1967, Carmen had been organized along functional lines with managers for merchandising, leased departments, and free-standing shoe stores reporting to Dr. Carmen as chairman and president. In 1967 Paul Platt was hired as president, a position which, at the time, was defined to include direct supervision of all shoe operations. A divisionalized organization evolved over the next two years with the addition of Carmed, Playtime, and Yorkshire Shoes. Then in May 1970, Morris Furman was promoted to division manager for retail shoes, freeing Mr. Platt of much direct responsibility for shoe operations. This organizational transition is reflected in Exhibits 1 and 2.

Despite the recent diversification, the company's primary business

**EXHIBIT 2**

THE CARMEN COMPANY
Organization as of June 1970

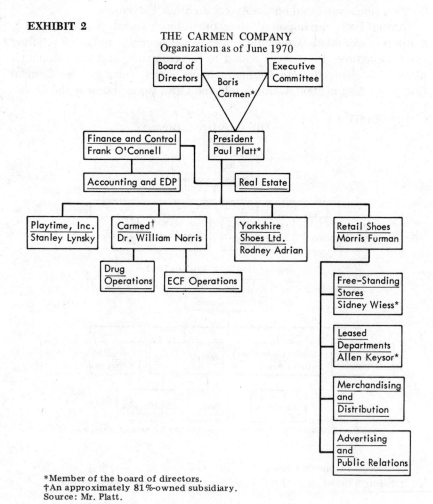

*Member of the board of directors.
†An approximately 81%-owned subsidiary.
Source: Mr. Platt.

continued to be shoe retailing, which in 1969 accounted for 87% of revenues and 46% of profits. A brief description of each operating division is provided below, and financial statements are presented in Exhibits 3, 4, and 5.

## OPERATING DIVISIONS

### Shoe retailing

Carmen was thought to rank among the top 20 in retail shoe sales in the United States. The company owned 33 free-standing stores and operated 99 leased departments, with the latter accounting for approximately 80% of the division's revenues. The growth in shoe sales reflected in Exhibit 6 had resulted largely from an increasing number of both stores and leased departments. In both instances, the company stressed self-service, low prices, and a broad line of shoes supplemented by handbags and hosiery, the latter items accounting for 5% of the division's sales. Compared with the largest retail shoe chains, however, Carmen's sales per outlet were significantly lower.

| Company | Sales (millions) | Outlets | Sales/outlet (thousands) |
|---------|-----------------:|--------:|-------------------------:|
| Melville Shoe Corp. | $293 | $1,200 | $244 |
| Edison Brothers | 240 | 658 | 365 |
| Morse Shoe Company | 138 | 575 | 240 |
| Carmen Company | 17 | 114 | 146 |

Source: 1968 annual reports.

The leased shoe departments were located in discount stores. The discounter provided space, housekeeping functions, cashiering, and advertising and promotion and was relied upon to build traffic for the various departments. To some extent growth in shoe sales had been forced by the rapid expansion of two discount chains; Carmen opened a department in each new store. Currently about 40% of the division's sales were obtained from departments in these two chains.

### Health-care facilities

The Carmen Company, through an 81% interest in Carmed,[3] operated extended-care facilities which treated patients under the direction of

---

[3] The remaining 19% was divided among Carmed management and former owners. The company acquired its interest in Carmed in April 1969 for 13,000 shares valued at $208,000 and $43,750 in cash. Carmed was used as a vehicle for acquiring the Franklin Nursing Homes.

**EXHIBIT 3**

## THE CARMEN COMPANY
### Sales Revenue and Profits by Division

| | Shoes | Health-care facilities* | Toys† | Total |
|---|---|---|---|---|
| **1967** | | | | |
| Sales or revenues . . . . . . . . . . . | $13,326,196 | 100% | ... | $13,326,196 |
| Income before income taxes and extraordinary | | | | |
| items . . . . . . . . . . . | 537,056 | 100 | ... | 537,056 |
| Return on sales . . . . . . . . . . . | 4.0% | | | 4.0% |
| **1968** | | | | |
| Sales or revenues . . . . . . . . . . . | 16,666,786 | 100 | ... | 16,666,786 |
| Income before income taxes and extraordinary | | | | |
| items . . . . . . . . . . . | 842,544 | 100 | ... | 842,544 |
| Return on sales . . . . . . . . . . . | 5.1% | | | 5.1% |
| **1969** | | | | |
| Sales or revenues . . . . . . . . . . . | 18,727,480‡ | 87.3 | $2,302,221 | 10.7% | $431,707 | 2.0% | 21,461,408 |
| Income before income taxes and extraordinary | | | | |
| items . . . . . . . . . . . | 204,653 | 46.4 | 169,245 | 38.3 | 67,676 | 15.3 | 441,574 |
| Return on sales . . . . . . . . . . . | 1.2% | | 7.4% | | 15.7% | | 2.1% |

*From date of acquisition, April 3, 1969, sales and profits for all of 1969 were $2,868,012 and $189,601, respectively.
†From date of acquisition, November 20, 1969, sales and profits for the year ending August 31, 1969, were $837,477 and $12,781, respectively.
‡Includes Yorkshire Shoes, Ltd.
Source: April 1970 Prospectus.

**EXHIBIT 4**

## THE CARMEN COMPANY AND SUBSIDIARIES
Consolidated Statement of Income

| | Fiscal year ended | | | | |
|---|---|---|---|---|---|
| | Dec. 25, 1965 | Dec. 31, 1966 (53 weeks) | Dec. 30, 1967 | Dec. 28, 1968 | Dec. 27, 1969 |
| **Sales and revenues** | | | | | |
| Sales | $10,003,999 | $12,296,758 | $13,326,196 | $16,666,786 | $19,159,187 |
| Operating revenues—Carmed | | | | | 2,302,221 |
| Total sales and revenues | $10,003,999 | $12,296,758 | $13,326,196 | $16,666,786 | $21,461,408 |
| **Deductions** | | | | | |
| Cost of sales | $ 6,443,558 | $ 7,817,372 | $ 8,449,687 | $10,203,623 | $11,686,099 |
| Cost of operations—Carmed | | | | | 1,502,175 |
| Depreciation and amortization | 69,124 | 92,362 | 78,270 | 84,558 | 139,501 |
| Rent | 1,005,053 | 1,333,327 | 1,287,669 | 1,617,143 | 2,220,267 |
| Interest | 84,642 | 124,755 | 103,530 | 76,266 | 260,014 |
| Amortization of debenture expenses | 6,805 | 10,635 | 10,635 | 10,635 | 10,635 |
| Other selling, general and administrative expenses | 2,110,587 | 2,522,213 | 2,859,349 | 3,832,017 | 5,201,143 |
| Total deductions | $ 9,719,769 | $11,900,664 | $12,789,140 | $15,824,242 | $21,019,834 |
| Income before income taxes and extraordinary items | $ 284,230 | $ 396,094 | $ 537,056 | $ 842,544 | $ 441,574 |
| Income taxes | $ 77,491 | $ 130,300 | $ 156,700 | $ 279,734 | $ 217,604 |
| Income after income taxes | $ 206,739 | $ 265,794 | $ 380,356 | $ 562,810 | $ 223,970 |
| Minority interest | | | | | 17,375 |
| Income before extraordinary items | $ 206,739 | $ 265,794 | $ 380,356 | $ 562,810 | $ 206,595 |
| Extraordinary items | (21,176) | (76,231) | | 40,250 | (22,757) |
| Net income | $ 185,563 | $ 189,563 | $ 380,356 | $ 603,060 | $ 183,838 |
| Per-share net income | $.46 | $.47 | $.81 | $.86 | $.24 |

Source: April 1970 Prospectus.

**EXHIBIT 5**

THE CARMEN COMPANY AND SUBSIDIARIES
Consolidated Balance Sheets

|  | Dec. 31 1966 | Dec. 30 1967 | Dec. 28 1968 | Dec. 27 1969 |
|---|---|---|---|---|
| *Assets* | | | | |
| Current assets | | | | |
| Cash and marketable securities . . . . . . . . | $ 646,132 | $1,186,457 | $1,251,083 | $ 2,149,322 |
| Accounts receivable (net) . . . . . . . . . . . | 150,829 | 316,444 | 529,693 | 1,317,516 |
| Merchandise inventory . . . . . . . . . . . . . | 3,292,129 | 3,373,244 | 5,198,106 | 6,749,435 |
| Prepaid expenses and supplies . . . . . . . . | 39,909 | 40,748 | 56,278 | 240,945 |
| Total current assets . . . . . . . . . . . | $4,128,999 | $4,916,893 | $7,035,160 | $10,457,218 |
| Other assets . . . . . . . . . . . . . . . . . . . . | $ 308,038 | $ 294,979 | $ 255,535 | $ 675,098 |
| Goodwill . . . . . . . . . . . . . . . . . . . . . . | | | | 656,022 |
| Property and equipment, at cost | | | | |
| Building . . . . . . . . . . . . . . . . . . . . . | $ 107,333 | $ 107,333 | $ 107,333 | $ 107,333 |
| Equipment . . . . . . . . . . . . . . . . . . | 247,834 | 323,042 | 533,387 | 1,406,516 |
| Leasehold improvements . . . . . . . . . . | 74,600 | 135,935 | 162,909 | 231,170 |
| | $ 429,767 | $ 566,310 | $ 803,629 | $ 1,745,019 |
| Less: Accumulated depreciation and amortization . . . . . . . . . . . . . . . | 149,724 | 263,258 | 322,936 | 400,241 |
| | $ 280,043 | $ 303,052 | $ 480,693 | $ 1,344,778 |
| Land . . . . . . . . . . . . . . . . . . . . . . . | 21,298 | 21,298 | 21,298 | 21,298 |
| Total property and equipment . . . . . . | $ 301,341 | $ 324,350 | $ 501,991 | $ 1,366,076 |
| Total assets . . . . . . . . . . . . . . . | $4,738,378 | $5,536,222 | $7,792,686 | $13,154,414 |
| *Liabilities* | | | | |
| Current liabilities | | | | |
| Notes payable . . . . . . . . . . . . . . . . . . | $ 100,000 | | $ 400,000 | $ 1,625,000 |
| Accounts payable . . . . . . . . . . . . . . . . | 915,958 | $1,060,933 | 1,574,521 | $ 2,153,319 |
| Accrued expenses . . . . . . . . . . . . . . | 268,934 | 338,859 | 428,706 | 725,244 |
| Federal income taxes . . . . . . . . . . . . . | 137,222 | 163,579 | 246,402 | 134,705 |
| Current installments on term debt . . . . . | 257,549 | 79,649 | 79,935 | 214,712 |
| Total current liabilities . . . . . . . . . | $1,679,663 | $1,643,020 | $2,729,564 | $ 4,852,980 |
| Term debt, net of current installments* . . . . | $1,635,754 | $ 856,273 | $1,276,337 | $ 3,290,104 |
| Deferred federal and state income taxes . . . . | | | | $ 34,436 |
| Minority interest . . . . . . . . . . . . . . . . . | | | | $ 84,885 |
| Shareholders' equity | | | | |
| Preferred stock . . . . . . . . . . . . . . . . | $ 385,250 | $ 298,200 | | |
| Class A and Common Stock (741,639 shares outstanding at 12/31/69) . . . . . . | 506,397 | 845,667 | $1,607,168 | $ 741,639 |
| Capital surplus . . . . . . . . . . . . . . . . | | 1,170,709 | 1,164,196 | 3,215,046 |
| Retained earnings . . . . . . . . . . . . . . . | 531,314 | 722,353 | 1,015,421 | 935,324† |
| Total shareholders' equity . . . . . . . | $1,422,961 | $3,036,929 | $3,786,785 | $ 4,892,009 |
| Total liabilities . . . . . . . . . . . . . | $4,738,378 | $5,536,222 | $7,792,686 | $13,154,414 |

*In April 1970, Carmen issued $1,500,000 in 9 7/8% 10-year debentures.
†Decrease due to stock dividend.
Source: Company records.

# EXHIBIT 6
## Trends in Carmen's shoe sales

| Fiscal year ended December | Leased shoe departments | | | Shoe stores at close of period | Net sales in thousands | | | Total | Sales in thousands | |
|---|---|---|---|---|---|---|---|---|---|---|
| | Opened during period | Closed during period | Number at close of period | | Leased departments | Stores | Miscellaneous* | | Per leased department | Per store |
| 1961 | 12 | 4 | 29 | 1 | $ 2,804 | $ 191 | $313 | $ 3,308 | 97 | 191 |
| 1962 | 17 | 4 | 42 | 2 | 4,006 | 156 | 247 | 4,409 | 95 | 78 |
| 1963 | 21 | 8 | 55 | 1 | 6,575 | 63 | 504 | 7,142 | 120 | 63 |
| 1964 | 10 | 2 | 63 | 10† | 7,641 | 56 | 391 | 8,088 | 121 | 56 |
| 1965 | 9 | 7 | 65 | 11 | 9,052 | 456 | 496 | 10,004 | 139 | 46 |
| 1966 | 10 | 7 | 68 | 22‡ | 10,990 | 1,295 | 12 | 12,297 | 162 | 118 |
| 1967 | 13 | 7 | 74 | 31 | 11,413 | 1,896 | 17 | 13,326 | 154 | 86 |
| 1968 | 13 | 4 | 83 | 33§ | 13,657 | 2,838 | 172 | 16,667 | 165 | 92 |
| 1969 | 18 | 2 | 99 | | 14,930 | 3,458 | 339 | 18,727 | 151 | 105 |

* Includes sales of surplus inventories, sales made to franchisees, Yorkshire, and certain nonshoe products.
† Reflects acquisition of Able Shoe Company.
‡ Reflects acquisition of Orlin Shoes, Inc.
§ Reflects sale of Orlin Shoes, Inc. and acquisition of Factory Cancellations, Inc.
Source: Company records.

the patient's physician. The facilities were designed to supplement general hospital care, not to compete with it. Patients received room, board, nursing care, physical and other forms of therapy, drugs, special diets, and other services as the patient's physician prescribed. Carmed leased the property, buildings, and sometimes the fixtures from nonaffiliated parties such as insurance companies or private owners. In total, eight facilities with over 760 licensed beds and 481 employees were in operation in Texas, six of them in Houston about 400 miles from the Carmed headquarters in Dallas. Occupancy rates in April 1970 were over 80% for all locations except the most recently opened facility (September 1969) which by that time was about one-third filled. For most of the locations, well in excess of 85% of revenues came from government agencies at the state or federal level through Medicare or state programs.

### Toy retailing

Playtime, Inc., operated four toy stores and one children's furniture store in enclosed, temperature-controlled shopping malls in the Minneapolis–St. Paul area and had several new units under construction. Playtime had exclusive toy-store rights in the malls, although other stores could carry toys as part of their merchandise line. The division, with main offices in Minneapolis, had 66 employees and operated its own warehouse and trucks for distributing merchandise to the stores. Toy sales were very seasonal in nature, with the few profitable months carrying the unprofitable ones. Competition came from variety, discount, and department stores. One other company, JELCO, had outlets in several major cities, but no dominant national chain existed in toy retailing in 1970.

### Shoe importing

Yorkshire Shoes, Ltd., imported high-fashion shoes, designed by Rodney Adrian and manufactured in England, for sale to boutiques and shoe stores. It was operated as a "research project" to determine the feasibility of forming a division "to import anything from anywhere." Although revenues were small, the business was complicated by a number of operating characteristics. For instance, to allow for overseas production, shipping, and distribution, product designs had to be completed as much as a year in advance of market introductions. The manufacturers themselves were, by and large, small family companies in Britain. Carmen acted as an importer but did not maintain inventories. For the most part orders were solicited from retail organizations and transmitted to the manufacturer for direct shipment. Carmen arranged for importing and invoiced the customer.

## DR. BORIS CARMEN

Dr. Carmen indicated that his parents had wanted him to enter one of the professions and, with their encouragement, he attended medical school. Reflecting on his decision to become a businessman rather than practice medicine, Dr. Carmen stated that his choice had been a good one: ". . . medicine is too narrow. With a little creativity in business, on the other hand, many avenues may be pursued simultaneously." The recent diversification of the company had been a case in point. Dr. Carmen provided some of the reasoning behind the acquisition of Playtime and Franklin Nursing Homes, the forerunner of Carmed, in these comments:

Closed shopping malls are going to be the wave of the future in retailing. Conventional strip shopping centers are a transient phenomenon. One center is continually subject to the threat of a bigger one that could be built next to it. I am convinced that the next and last step in retailing as we know it will be the malls. After the mall, we will probably have a change in the technology of retailing. People will shop from their homes using computers and visual display devices. I think that will come for my grandchildren, however—not in my lifetime. The regional mall is the opportunity to develop today.

I was also looking for a way to be number one in a business. Partly it was a personal desire, but being number one has a lot of practical advantages as well. For instance, space in regional malls is a seller's market and the promoter would like strong drawing cards. He gravitates toward the industry leaders. Shoes didn't fit on either count; we are about seventeenth in the business, and quite a few shoe stores can be expected in each mall. There aren't any major national chains in the toy field, and no more than one store of this type would be in a mall. When the opportunity to buy Playtime came up, I was interested. . . .

Carmed was founded in a blush of enthusiasm. The market was booming for nursing homes at that time, and I suppose I had a latent desire to participate in the medical field. Robert Norris, one of our directors, had a brother who was a doctor-administrator in Texas and was interested in entering the business. We had a chance to buy Franklin Nursing Homes, a company with four facilities, and out of this we formed Carmed.

While the company was growing and entering new businesses, Dr. Carmen had been attempting to redefine his role in the organization. His efforts reflected both a perceived need to build an organization appropriate for a diversified company and a personal inclination to devote more time to worrying about the future and less to administration.

One of my desires is to have the freedom to be a thinker, to conceptualize the future directions for this company. I would prefer not to become involved in detailed decision making.

As long as the boss is involved, subordinates will compete for his attention and approval; those who get it feel loved, those who don't feel threatened. People have difficulties with the organization and with one another because they conceive their jobs differently. My goal is to create a climate in which each manager knows what he is held responsible for. That implies devising some method of measuring his performance that is as objective as possible. We are moving toward budgets and profit centers which are more impersonal, more professional, and which help to get us away from "buddy-buddy" management.

For the last few years, I have been trying to bring professional management into the organization. At the same time I have been delegating operating decisions and attempting to withdraw from the details of the business. We are on our way to establishing product divisions and a separate headquarters staff. Within the past two weeks Morris Furman has been appointed manager of the shoe operations. Gradually we are forming a corporate management group composed of Paul Platt, Frank O'Connell (the controller), our new real estate man,[4] and myself.

## THE BOARD OF DIRECTORS

Dr. Carmen consulted frequently with the outside members of his board of directors and had relied on their judgment to help guide the company through the period of rapid change. An indication of the activities of the board is provided in Exhibit 7. He commented on this relationship:

I have invited highly skilled men in marketing, finance and distribution to be on my board for a couple of reasons. First, a company of our size can't afford men of their quality on a full-time basis—even if I could get them. Given a choice, I would rather have the best part time than someone mediocre full time. Second, I look to the outside directors for a cold, dispassionate review of our programs and for help in making judgments that, as the guy on the spot, I can sometimes get a bit too involved in. I don't think we should have suppliers on the board, however, and I include banks in that category. I wouldn't like to feel obligated to them when a decision affecting their company comes along.

I am of two minds on the usefulness of insiders on the board. On the one hand, they bring an intimate knowledge of operations to bear on the discussion which hopefully produces better decisions. But on the other hand, they probably won't disagree with the boss. It's been my experience that little can be accomplished with inside board meetings that hinge on their views which couldn't be done in an operating committee of some kind.

Of course there are limitations to outside directors as well, and from my own experience I can appreciate their position. They are increasingly busy men who can't afford to devote a lot of time to the company. What is my life is their sideline. This has been a difficulty for me in the last year; I

---

[4] To begin the following week.

**EXHIBIT 7**

## THE CARMEN COMPANY
### Relative* Involvement of Directors in Past Year

| Director | Age | Percentage of time at company | Term expires March 31 | Involvement† Shoe | Carmed | Toy | York-shire | Corp. and finance planning | Corp. staff admin. | 1970 Special assignments | Time at company versus last year |
|---|---|---|---|---|---|---|---|---|---|---|---|
| Carmen...... | 48 | 100% | 1972 | B | B | C | C | A | B | ... | n.a. |
| Rabinow...... | 49 | 15–20 | 1971 | B | B | B | C | A | C | Legal advice; lease and labor negotiations | Same |
| Norris...... | 38 | 1–2 | 1973 | B | C | C | C | A | B | Computer installation | Less |
| Williams...... | 54 | 1 | 1971 | B | C | B | C | C | C | Evaluation of marketing programs | Less |
| Putnam...... | 42 | 2–3 | 1972 | B | C | C | C | A | A | Evaluation of capital requests; financial control systems; study of long-range potential for leased departments | Less |
| Platt...... | 40 | 100 | 1971 | A | B | C | B | B | A | ... | n.a. |
| Keysor...... | 54 | 100 | 1973 | A | C | C | C | C | C | ... | n.a. |
| Wiess...... | 56 | 100 | 1971 | A | C | C | C | C | C | ... | n.a. |

* Relative to total time spent by the director at Carmen. Therefore columns cannot be compared directly.
† A = considerable
  B = moderate
  C = minimal
n.a. = not available.
Source: Casewriter's notes based on discussions with directors.

haven't been able to get as much of their time as I had in the past or as much as I would have liked. Under these circumstances, outside directors may also be reluctant to disagree with the chief executive. After all, a director agrees to serve because he trusts management, and trust breeds confidence, which tends to end up meaning that they believe us. Their alternative, most likely, is to quit. The other side of the coin, of course, is that they may make a strong recommendation based on other experiences which—because I respect their intelligence—is accepted but turns out not to fit our situation.

Directors were elected for three-year terms, roughly one third of them falling due each year, with the total number limited to 10. Voting was noncumulative, meaning that each share of stock was entitled to one vote for each director.[5] In June 1970 the board was composed of the following people:

> Dr. Boris Carmen,* chairman of the board and chief executive officer
> Mr. Martin Rabinow,* secretary, and a practicing attorney in the city of
> St. Louis
> Robert Norris,* Ph.D., professor of marketing, Graduate School of
> Business Administration, University of Minnesota
> John Williams,* Ph.D., professor and chairman, faculty of marketing,
> University of Missouri
> Philip Putnam,* Ph.D., professor and chairman, faculty of finance,
> University of Missouri
> Mr. Paul Platt,* president and treasurer
> Mr. Allen Keysor, vice president, leased departments
> Mr. Sidney Wiess, vice president, Free-Standing Stores
>    * Member of the executive committee.

An indication of the relationship between the board and the company is provided in the comments below by the four outside directors, covering, in each case, first, the relationships among the director, the board, and operating management; and, second, the views of each on Carmen's growth and diversification.

### Dr. Robert Norris

Dr. Norris was a specialist in physical distribution and marketing. In addition to teaching at the University of Minnesota, he consulted privately with many companies on their distribution problems.

#### The director, the board, and the organization

John Williams, a friend and professional colleague for years, introduced me to Carmen on a consulting problem in distribution in 1966. Carmen had

---

[5] Dr. Carmen owned or controlled 33% of the company's common stock; 11 other officers and directors as a group owned an additional 2%.

an inventory problem. Its system lacked sophistication and the operation relied on Boris' personal talent. The company was too big for this, however, and Boris' interests were extending beyond operations.

I introduced Paul Platt to Boris. I had known Paul from work on distribution economics at Standard Oil while I was completing my doctorate at the University of Minnesota and from my association with UPS,[6] where he worked after that. After Carmen went public, Boris hired Paul to run the operations. There was no specific acquisition strategy at the time, but it was envisioned that Paul would handle more than shoes. That's why we didn't hire an experienced shoe executive. Paul's immediate task was managing the shoe operation.

Everything except the management and merchandising in shoes used to be weak. Now, finance is better, data processing is coming on strong, the warehouse has improved, and Morris Furman has filled the slot in shoes. His promotion was a surprise, but a good move, a good gamble. He was the logical guy, since he has been there through the management transitions in the division. . . .

Our board is a very tight group with no major conflicts. The board wants management to lay out plans and goals and to stick to them. This has drifted in the past, and the directors have expressed their criticisms along these lines: The board took a firm stand against shoe-store expansion as a cure for sinking profits by insisting first on internal strengthening. . . .

### Corporate growth and diversification

When Paul was hired, we wanted to diversify but had no specific plan. We looked at anything within the realm of possibility and pursued several opportunities in detail. All of our acquisitions were organizations in which we banked on a few entrepreneurs in start-up situations. I don't feel this is unusual for a company like Carmen.

I suggested a number of acquisition possibilities, including Carmed. My brother, Dr. William Norris, owned one hospital in Texas and was anxious to pursue the concept of extended-care facilities (ECFs). Carmed has no inventory and provides a service, so it fits our concept. There is a great similarity between running a hospital and running a toy store. The end product is different, but both involve tight controls.

### Dr. Philip Putnam

Dr. Putnam first became involved at Carmen in 1966 when he worked on an in-house management development program on "management by objectives." Dr. Carmen asked him to review some capital expenditure proposals, and they continued their association on other boards of directors. In 1968, Dr. Carmen asked Dr. Putnam to join the Carmen board.

---

[6] United Parcel Service.

### The director, the board, and the organization

Boris is a fascinating and different businessman. Nonstandard situations such as this are a great help to me in teaching. In addition I personally review most major projects as to their financial soundness.

Boris wants outside views from his board. Although the discussion becomes intense at times, our relationships are all cordial. We work well by appreciating each other's strengths and weaknesses and eventually arrive at a consensus out of conflict. The decision to reduce our dependence on leased shoe departments is an example. We were relying on rising volume to pull us through but changed directions and decided to consolidate our operations, eliminating marginal departments and stores. Sid Wiess and Allen Keysor were very cooperative.

### Corporate growth and diversification

We happened into hospitals indirectly and are undecided whether we shall stay. There are no firm plans now, but I feel we should not become too conglomerated. Toy and shoe stores are about the same, but hospitals and nursing homes have other problems. Carmed was an opportunity in which we felt we could use our systems skills to solve its problems. However, shoes will be our principal business for a long time.

Concerning Yorkshire Shoes, Dr. Putnam commented:

Every once in a while you attempt something. The hope was high profit from a small investment with little management input. This hasn't worked in practice yet. Boris is a great guy for trying new things. Yorkshire Shoes will probably never be an important element and receives no board attention.

## Dr. John Williams

Dr. Williams had worked for Dr. Carmen's father as a consultant on store location and merchandising strategy. He and Dr. Carmen had been neighbors since World War II and he had been elected to the board when the company went public in 1962. Dr. Williams was a member of the marketing faculty of the University of Missouri, a well-known author, and a consultant to many companies on marketing and distribution problems.

### The director, the board, and the organization

My interest is in the fast growth of discount and specialty stores. I find this aspect of Carmen exciting. Beyond that, I joined the board because of a long and cordial relationship with the Carmen family and also because I find the association with the other board members personally very rewarding. However, my university responsibilities and other client obligations severely limit the time I have available.

Often the board gives some strong criticism, but Boris is receptive to it. Reducing our dependence on leased shoe departments was an example. We should concentrate on the low-price segment of the free-standing store market. Since we must keep up with fashion trends, the radical changes in the apparel business work against high-price lines.

## Corporate growth and diversification

When Carmed came along, the glamour of the leased department shoe industry was waning. Medical stocks were booming, and we hoped that it would help our P/E ratio.

So far our bread and butter has been a series of good opportunities, not a long-range plan. We must be flexible. If we become too Harvard Business School policy oriented we might find ourselves in a straight-jacket.

## Mr. Martin Rabinow

Mr. Martin Rabinow was a distant relative to Dr. Carmen and had known him all his life as a businessman and family friend. He had been formally involved in the company since 1962 when the board was composed of himself, Dr. Carmen, and Dr. Carmen's wife.

### The director, the board, and the organization

Over the years my relationship with Boris has remained the same but the business has changed. Now there is more at stake in each decision, and better quality demanded. My view of the world and how a business should operate is centered more around profit than professional management. I am conservative and wouldn't risk the business for any venture. My philosophy is, don't get too far afield.

Recently the board decided to hold the sales volume of the shoe division constant. The prior premise had been that if volume went up, so would profits. We are now concentrating more on consolidation. The board at that time also reaffirmed its faith in Playtime and distribution through malls, and a new focus of return on total assets instead of profit as a percentage of sales was adopted.

### Corporate growth and diversification

Carmed came up in a bull market. It looked like a golden opportunity. Medical stocks were riding high, and we were acquisition minded. Boris felt he could create a skilled management team in health care and use equity rather than cash to make acquisitions.

I was cool to the idea. It seemed to me to be a distraction of management time from our real purpose. I view a company as a series of related skills. Carmen's skills seem to me to be in the retail and wholesale distribution of goods. We have no skill in medical affairs. To play that game, we need more chips.

I was never high on acquisitions. They have come in a rather hit-or-miss fashion, and the philosophy seems to be one of knowing nothing about a strange business and its problems and thinking you can run it. Profits, not volume, are our weakness. We have too many shoe clerks with too little training in middle management, and too many low-volume shoe stores spread out all over the place.

### Mr. Paul Platt

Before joining Carmen, Mr. Platt, an MBA from Fordham University, worked first for Standard Oil in research on distribution and marketing economics and then for a consulting firm before joining the United Parcel Service. At UPS he had advanced rapidly, becoming director of business development and corporate planning and then vice president and general manager of the Pacific Region, which had revenues of over $100 million. Mr. Platt explained his association with Carmen and his view of the company in these terms:

I was restless at UPS. I had a large staff, and it seemed the organization would run without me. Robert Norris introduced me to Boris Carmen, and Boris charmed me. It's hard to explain, but why else would I leave a position with the status and benefits I had with UPS in California to come to St. Louis, Missouri?

My role is to direct and manage the operations of the company. I am more involved in movement along a chosen path than in choosing the path. My goal is to build an organization which can grow. I prefer to work with a division head to help him solve problems, to clear organizational hurdles for him, rather than worry about day-to-day administration.

Gradually, the scope of my work is increasing to include longer range concerns, particularly the evaluation of acquisitions and new business opportunities. We can't look at everything. Maybe I'm conservative, but a business has to fit our strengths and weaknesses before I think we should consider it. For instance, we don't know anything about manufacturing and shouldn't consider "going vertical" by making our own shoes. We are basically a distribution and service company.

The chairman asks me to evaluate from an operating viewpoint the ventures he cooks up. By and large, if I don't buy the idea, he will go along with me. Boris is a prolific idea generator, but I have to catch the sparks and work with them. His approach resembles a shotgun, mine a rifle.

### DIVISION MANAGEMENT

The division managers brought to their jobs a variety of backgrounds and experience, as the following table indicates:

| Division | Division manager | Age | Education | Length of time in current position | Previous experience |
|---|---|---|---|---|---|
| Shoe | Morris Furman | 35 | M.B.A. | 2 weeks | Buyer and merchandise manager |
| Toy | Stanley Lynsky | 32 | B.A. | 3 years | Systems engineer, Sperry Rand |
| Carmed | William Norris | 48 | M.D. | 6 months | Medical practitioner and hospital administrator |
| Yorkshire | Rodney Adrian | 44 | B.Sc. | 2 years | Shoe designer |

The divisions, in turn, were each confronted with different problems and opportunities in June 1970. These are developed briefly in the following sections.

## The shoe division

The shoe division had very recently undergone a major organizational change. Although maintaining a strong interest in the warehouse and distribution systems he had designed for the division, Mr. Platt was in the process of disengaging from the day-to-day administration of shoe operations. For Mr. Furman the promotion came unexpectedly:

> My promotion 10 days ago was a real surprise. Six years ago, as a buyer, I aspired to be the merchandise manager and was promoted when the former merchandise manager left. But I never thought I would run the shoe business. My expertise is in merchandising, so I'll need lots of help to learn this job. I'm glad to have some old pros like Allen [Keysor] and Sid [Wiess] with me.

The division had been largely responsible for the earnings decline since 1968. Mr. Keysor discussed some of the factors contributing to the poor performance.

> Our main problems center on expansion and control. Expansion means finding new free-standing store sites. At one time or another most of us have taken a stab at this, but the results haven't been completely satisfactory. Inventories rose last year because orders were placed further in advance than before and additional merchandise was ordered in anticipation of new store openings, some of which never happened. To make matters worse, the decision rules in our computer caused some excessive inventory accumulations in the stores. These mistakes occurred in the face of a softening economy and a violent, unexpected style change which confused consumers, causing them to purchase more slowly.

The leased departments presented an additional series of difficulties. Aside from excess inventory and attendant markdowns, the leased departments had suffered from inventory losses (often running three times higher than in the free-standing stores), from increasing rents, and from high costs for marking and packing the shoes. The result had been deteriorating margins.

Over the long term, Dr. Carmen was concerned about possible consolidations and grinding competition among discounters. Many of the larger chains, including Zayre and Caldor, already owned their own shoe departments, and Dr. Carmen felt a trend in this direction was in the offing. In fact, two discounters, each leasing several departments to Carmen, had merged, thus increasing the company's dependence on a single discounter.

Despite recent setbacks, Mr. Furman maintained that opportunities continued to exist for growth in shoe retailing. He noted his plans for the division:

My most important function is to reestablish a growth pattern for shoes. Our last few leased departments have been bombs, as have our recent free-standing stores. More free-standing stores will be opened, but in larger towns and in clusters of two or more to spread our overhead costs. You have to make lots of noise to sell shoes, and a small town or a one-store operation can't justify the advertising expense needed to generate sales.

Our present low-priced shoe mix does not fit the concept of a mall store. I will move into malls with higher priced lines and more service than our present stores have if we decide to go in this direction.

There has never been a formal long-range plan for the shoe division. The organization has been restructured to meet the needs of different sales plateaus. My promotion is an example. Now we don't have a merchandise manager. I'm filling the slot but will soon have to hire someone to ease my workload, though I don't want to give up my merchandise-policy role. I will probably have to consider hiring a controller as well.

In the first five months of 1970, four unprofitable leased departments had been discontinued and another five were scheduled to close. An abortive attempt to enter the Los Angeles market with leased departments was also discontinued. Mr. Furman hoped to recover the lost volume by opening 10 free-standing stores in the remainder of 1970.[7]

## Toy division

The acquisition of Playtime, Inc., was viewed by many in the company as a natural extension of Carmen's operations. Mr. Platt expressed his views in these terms:

Entering the toy field was a good decision. With increasing leisure time and affluence, the market is going to grow. Toys are not all for kids, either;

---

[7] The cost of opening a free-standing shoe store was estimated by Mr. Furman to be about $40,000 for fixtures and inventory; the lead time averaged about four months.

adult games are popular now as well. Toy stores fit nicely into our existing operations and provide a base for entering related activities, such as children's furniture, records, and ready-to-wear clothing. We can also use our skills in inventory and warehouse management and our distribution facilities. The warehouse doesn't recognize different products; all boxes are the same there.

For Mr. Lynsky, the decision to merge with Carmen was a matter of considerable consequence. At stake, as he saw it, was the future of the company he had started six years before. The background of the business and the reasoning behind the merger reflect some of Mr. Lynsky's expectations for the future. He said:

During college I wrote a report on the birth rate and found rapid growth in areas around Minneapolis. I was looking for my own opportunity and decided that births equaled toys. I noticed that Ma and Pa operations were folding to the discounters and that there were no independents retailing toys. So in 1963 I left Honeywell and opened a store in a strip shopping center. I did well, but there was no real traffic.

Then in 1964 I spotted enclosed malls. I finally convinced one developer that a toy store would benefit his mall.[8] He gave me 2,000 square feet, but put a "kickout clause"[9] in my lease. I did $300,000 sales volume my first year and $400,000 my second, so I was convinced that malls have the traffic.

Dr. Carmen heard of Playtime and asked a developer to approach me. I had not sought such contracts but was willing to talk, since I knew I was undercapitalized. My suppliers were carrying me; my profits were being reinvested; and I knew that two stores would be my limit for awhile without help. I began to look around after that and found that several other parties had their eye on Playtime. The question was whether to be acquired or not and, if so, by whom. Perhaps the question was having a percentage of something or the risk of a lot of nothing.

I had several goals in mind. I wanted to pursue entrances into malls. Being acquired by a bigger company would increase the value of my lease as collateral to a developer. I wanted to be national and needed someone to make this possible. I didn't want working partners, because I wanted to be in charge. Having my brains picked only to be replaced by someone cheaper, or being standardized to fit someone else's idea of how the operation should be run, didn't appeal to me.

I made a table of the pluses and minuses of those interested in me. Most fit, except for the last two points. Some didn't like the mall and wanted free-standing stores. Carmen was looking for anyone with a good business, growth tied to population, and a capital need.

Boris was shooting crap when he bought me. He wanted a concept and good, honest management. I wanted honesty, money, and close proximity to top management. I'll be an important factor in Carmen's growth. My reward is building with someone else's money.

---

[8] Developers want AAA tenants so that the lease can be used to obtain financing.

[9] The developer could evict Playtime at any time if the volume fell below an agreed amount.

The purchase price for Playtime, Inc., was tied in part to the future profitability of the business. Carmen paid 7,500 shares in common stock (valued at $75,000) when the merger was consummated on November 20, 1969, and was to deliver a maximum of 60,000 shares or $1 million in market value, whichever was less, based on Playtime's earnings in the 1970–73 period. Specifically, the additional shares were to be issued in an amount equal to Playtime's profit after taxes for those years provided it exceeded $50,000 in 1970, $100,000 in 1971, $125,000 in 1972, and $150,000 in 1973.[10]

Mr. Lynsky was intent upon expanding the number of stores in his division and enlarging the scope of his product line with a minimum of added administrative expense. Four new outlets in closed malls had already been announced, and Mr. Lynsky hoped to proceed with eight more in the near future. Each store of this type was estimated to require a cash investment of $120,000 in construction, fixtures, and inventory after construction allowances and supplier credit. The timing was critical, as Mr. Lynsky explained:

The most important thing is to be open and ready when the mall's grand opening occurs. From the time I find out about a mall to the grand opening takes about two years. I used to go to a lot of trouble making traffic estimates, but now I use the size and name of the mall's anchor stores[11] as a guide.

He was also seeking volume by expanding his product line and by aggressive merchandising. As he indicated below, locations in shopping malls were an important element in implementing his plans:

I want to serve the children's market from conception through grandparenthood. By that I mean that I hope to eventually supply children's items, such as toys, furniture, and clothes, that will be bought by parents, relatives, or friends for children before and after they are born. My product line will follow the changes in life style. This means higher ticket items, such as scooters and skis, and leisure-time products, such as sporting goods.

Mr. Lynsky indicated that he had considerable autonomy in the management of his division's affairs, including the selection and staffing of new store locations. Reporting to him, in addition to the store managers, were a bookkeeper and a buyer. He summarized his relationship with the corporation in these terms:

My main interactions at the corporate level are usually with Paul Platt about growth. I set my goals for 12 months in advance, plan my attack, and stick to it. The board reviews them but I don't make changes just for their sake. Boris is open, but Paul is cautious. Two members of the board

---

[10] Profit after taxes for Playtime in fiscal years ending August 31 had been: 1967, $2,243; 1968, $1,654; and 1969, $12,781.

[11] Typically the large national chains in the mall.

are very critical and offer their own approaches. I sense these days that expansion projects should have greater than a 20% ROI to vie for funds.

## Carmed

Both the Carmen board of directors[12] and Carmed's operating management had initially favored aggressive growth in extended-care facilities. Mr. Platt felt that, through the application of systems analysis, ECFs could be managed scientifically. He commented:

The control of extended-care facilities is not really different from our other businesses. They are quite predictable and can be programmed precisely. Manpower, meals, and patient services can be based on forecasted bed utilization, and economies of scale can be gained through centralized purchasing. I have been working with the operating people to adopt computer simulation techniques to minimize costs.

Certain weaknesses in the management of the subsidiary had become evident in the spring of 1970, however, highlighted by a series of labor difficulties.

When Carmed acquired Franklin Nursing Homes, the employees were not unionized, although several unions were seeking representation. A union approached the Houston facilities in September 1969, but, according to Mr. Platt, the managers in Houston, who reported to Dr. William Norris in Dallas, felt that the union could not gain enough support to hold a certification election. When the union succeeded in getting the needed support, Houston management felt the union could not win the election. When the union won the election and requested contract negotiations, Mr. Platt and Mr. Rabinow represented the company and eventually settled on a contract in February 1970. Mr. Platt described the subsequent events:

Both our management and the union local had to learn how to handle this new set of relationships. In the process a lot of small grievances were allowed to accumulate. Then in May the union met with the press and threatened a wildcat strike. William Norris felt he could keep the hospitals open and running even if they did strike.

Well, the following Monday morning the wildcat began and the newspapers played it up. Pickets were strung out, and the employees didn't cross the lines. The State of Texas had a man on the scene immediately with authority to remove the state's patients if proper service wasn't available.

I received the news at nine, and by eleven was on a flight to Houston. I had to assess the problem and decide how to deal with it. Old management, and I say old because they have been replaced, felt that the grievances were not proper and needed no more than a verbal answer. After a long

---

[12] Carmed had its own board of directors, consisting of Dr. Carmen, Dr. William Norris, Dr. Robert Norris, Mr. Rabinow, Mr. Platt, and two operating managers.

day and a half we were able to get the problems settled without a disruption of services.

You know, Stanley [Lynsky] and I are the only people here who have experience in labor relations. I still handle labor matters myself. I'm going to make certain the caldron doesn't bubble over again.

In June 1970, Carmed management was considering the initiation of a cluster[13] of hospitals on the West Coast. As in Texas, Carmed would lease the facilities, which would take from one to two years to locate and build. Break even on a cash-flow basis would occur nine months after the facilities opened, on the average, though the time period was dependent on the speed of occupancy. It was felt that the minimum-size facility should be 100 beds and that the cluster should contain from 1,200 to 1,400 beds. Carmed was also exploring the possibility of owning and operating its own drugstores to serve its patients and the public. One such pharmacy had already been established in Houston in November 1969.

## Yorkshire Shoes, Ltd.

Yorkshire Shoes had been in the planning and operational stages for almost two years and was still experiencing problems which Mr. Platt felt required his attention. The project was also the subject of a good-natured difference of viewpoint between Dr. Carmen and Mr. Platt. On one occasion Mr. Platt commented to the casewriter: "Yorkshire Shoes is one of the chairman's creations. He kids me about it because I don't suppose there are any two things in this world Rodney [Adrian] and I would do the same way."

A three-hour meeting was scheduled for a Friday morning early in June 1970 to discuss the status of Yorkshire Shoes. Mr. Adrian and his assistant, Mr. John Carmichael, had spent the previous four days preparing a report on sales and profits. Mr. Platt and Mr. Adrian had then spent four hours together Thursday evening discussing the problems which were to be probed in depth the next day. The meeting itself lasted six hours Friday, was carried over to Saturday, and was concluded on Monday afternoon. Portions of the discussion are reproduced in Exhibit 8.

During a break Mr. Carmichael commented to the casewriter that Mr. Platt was very critical of the operation and spent a lot of time checking its activities. He said that, so far, he and Mr. Adrian had been able to stay one jump ahead by developing sales potential between the time a reporting period closed and the time the report was available for review. As of June 1970 the operation was breaking even and the

---

[13] A concentration of facilities in a geographic area.

**EXHIBIT 8**
**Yorkshire Shoes, Ltd.—review meeting (partial transcript)**

CARMICHAEL° (*report in hand*): Most of the things in this report are facts substantiated by past experience. Our month ended on May 23, 1970. We sold 19,000 pairs for $133,416 against a projected $85,000. These are orders written to be delivered later. . . .

PLATT: What charges remain outstanding against this $90 profit? How do you handle returns?

CARMICHAEL: When people return shoes, accounting takes off the customs charge. Then when they are shipped again, customs is added back on. So we keep our books straight. I never let that money stay out. If the shoes haven't been shipped by the end of the month, I write the customs off against profit. We could, therefore, very easily have $10,000 of merchandise in the warehouse and have paid all of the customs charges.

PLATT: You see, what you are telling me is that $90 of profit—and again I have some questions on the overhead—this $90 could have been increased by $10,000 if you could have controlled that $.30 expense variation which I previously indicated. That's money. Now, in this overhead, I assume you have the salesmen's commission and the 7½% administrative charge from the company.

CARMICHAEL: Yes.

PLATT: (*questioningly*): You do have that? In effect, that $90—an amazingly close number to a break even—if I were a suspicious man, ah . . . . In any event, based on these numbers, $15,000 has been allowed as contribution.

CARMICHAEL: Yes.

PLATT: And direct expenses, yours and Rodney's expenses, are in?

CARMICHAEL: Well, those aren't up to date on this report.

PLATT: What about the interest on loans?

CARMICHAEL: It's included!

PLATT: So you have fully distributed cost here. Then you have an objective of getting this 80% cost of sales figure down to 75%, your target. Do we all understand 75% as the target? Are we all clear on this? Rodney? John?

ALL: Yes.

PLATT: Now, I find it just as dangerous, however, to try and reduce the figure below 75%. If you try to get too much for the shoes, if you try to make too much money on individual sales rather than making money on velocity, you will have fewer sales, which will cause you to raise prices to cover costs, and you will then in turn have fewer sales, until gradually you run this thing underground. I don't think you should run the risk of overpricing in the short run. In all probability, we are talking about market entry and identification of an image. We should go for a profit, a realistic profit, not a high profit. As an example, if you had a 60% there, I would be more alarmed than the 80% because I would be afraid we were missing a tremendous amount of sales.

ADRIAN:† There are two things which will reflect on here somewhat. One, there is a strong movement toward shoes of our quality in the very exciting Corfam materials. They come in at a low rate of 6% import duty.

**EXHIBIT 8** (*continued*)

PLATT: And the Kennedy Round of Tariff Adjustments in January should reduce it another 2%.

ADRIAN: But this Corfam thing with which we are playing carefully should be interesting. . . .

PLATT: Which means, if you hold a relatively fixed price position for next year, you have a 2% reduction to cover your added costs of goods in Europe. . . .

ADRIAN: And we are trying some new suede materials. . . .

PLATT: But I wouldn't try to get your cost of goods much less than what it is now, Rodney. Then you are taking an unrealistic view of what the shoe should sell for.

ADRIAN: So, you say too low is dangerous.

PLATT: There is a very interesting thing on your next report. It shows a rise in the cost of merchandise from 63% to 64%.

ADRIAN: One was 63.4%, the other 63.5%.

PLATT: Then I see that the total cost dropped 2%. I am delighted. The cost of goods goes up, but we still make more money. I don't know how it happens.

ADRIAN: Very easily. The size of orders could do it.

PLATT: What does that mean?

CARMICHAEL: The quantity per order.

PLATT: What does that mean?

ADRIAN: Reduced freight.

PLATT: Reduced freight where?

CARMICHAEL (*to Platt*): No. You see, we have so many little divisions going right now—the slipper division, the boot division, the canvas shoe division. This report should be made out on each division.

PLATT: Spare me!

CARMICHAEL: O.K., spare you, but for my use. . . . But since we do have this, a 1%–2% variance can easily occur.

PLATT: John, back to the question. Why did our cost drop 2%? What do you mean big orders? How does that cause it to drop?

CARMICHAEL: Well, you're talking about the. . . . Actually, if we take an order for 90 pairs we lose money.

PLATT: John. . . . I want you to quit hedging and tell me how you save money on large orders.

CARMICHAEL: I'm not hedging (*laughing*). Well, it's a very minute amount, so small its unbelievable.

PLATT: Two percent is not small on the year to date.

CARMICHAEL: The sales are so small, $250,000, that every time we get one profit-making order, it changes 2%–3%.

PLATT: But how did you get a profit-making order? What was different about this one?

CARMICHAEL: Once in a while we get a lucky one.

PLATT: What? Be more specific.

CARMICHAEL: Rodney, these are the stretch boots; we have the order and can make a very good profit.

**EXHIBIT 8** (*continued*)

PLATT: Why?

CARMICHAEL (*laughing*): Well, it's just the ideal buy and the merchandise is a little cheaper.

PLATT: You didn't buy it cheaper!

CARMICHAEL: Yes.

PLATT: No!! (*Long silence.*) You have indicated a higher merchandise cost.

CARMICHAEL: That's right. One was like 63.4%, the other 63.5%.

PLATT: Assume the cost stayed the same. You can't give me a rounding of two points, can you? You did something right, but you don't know what it was. Well, I want you to find out, and do it again, you hear. . . .

\* \* \* \* \*

PLATT: You mean to tell me that you're going to have $870,000 worth of delivered sales by December with only $254,000 now delivered?

CARMICHAEL: I'm telling you that.

PLATT: Delivered sales?

CARMICHAEL: It works out this way. Rodney asked me that yesterday, and I worked it backwards on paper. Pending sales after this year would just about equal what's been delivered now. Let's. . . .

PLATT: Whoa! If you had $800,000 of delivered sales this year and all your sales in the fall which will be delivered next year—that means your booked sales [delivered plus undelivered] would be greater than $1,300,000.

CARMICHAEL: This is predicted on orders.

PLATT: Then you can't say delivered at the top of the form.

CARMICHAEL: O.K., agreed. You're right.

PLATT: No way you'll get $870,000 delivered this year unless you sell some $100,000 clog orders, because physically it's impossible. Your orders for fall are by and large finished. Right, Clay?

SIEVER:‡ I disagree with you for two reasons. The buying period for fall was very close to the selling season due to economic conditions. Everyone has not bought everything for November and December, either. We hope that the economy will turn up and give people who can deliver shoes a chance.

PLATT: Their track record is that they can't deliver on short notice. Do you really think American buyers with short lead times will buy imports?

SIEVER: If we can deliver, they will buy.

PLATT: John, what do you think?

CARMICHAEL: Yes, sir. I'm convinced. If you look at our track record last fall, you'll see shoes sold last July and August for delivery in November and December.

PLATT: The majority of your selling in September and October of this year will be for spring delivery.

CARMICHAEL: Wrong. Our fall sales for spring delivery will be about 25% of our business.

PLATT: When are you going to sell the spring shoes?

CARMICHAEL: Spring shoes as such—let me interpret the market as I

**EXHIBIT 8** (*continued*)

understand it. You come out at the shoe fair in July. People buy shoes for October, November, December delivery. For Easter selling, with our shoes, it's a very limited market.

SIEVER:    The ready-to-wear field is so mixed up that most buyers have switched to conservative merchandise, skipping fashion completely. This has left footwear buyers in the same way.

PLATT:    I would say that's a correct assessment, Clay. Ready-to-wear is confused. Correspondingly, shoes fall in line behind because we are after-the-fact fashion. We cannot prepare shoes for short hemlines and then find them long. I disagree with John.

CARMICHAEL:    I gave you 20%–25%.

PLATT:    As a matter of fact, John, I would suspect that this Easter will be one of your better Easters. The woman has had no direction for some period of time, and she's been too long with her shoes, and psychologically she buys in the spring.

---

\* Assistant director, Yorkshire Shoes, Ltd.
† Director, Yorkshire Shoes, Ltd.
‡ Prospective sales manager, Yorkshire Shoes, Ltd.

---

company had about $40,000 invested in organizational expenses, with an additional $60,000 in accounts receivable.

## THE STAFF

The staff functions in the company were in a state of transition. Mr. Frank O'Connell, previously the controller of the shoe division, had recently been made corporate controller and given responsibility for short-term cash management. Reporting to him were a data processing department and an accounting analysis section, both of which were still being developed. The remainder of the corporate staff was composed of the new real estate manager and George Carpenter, an MBA who undertook specials studies for Dr. Carmen on corporate development projects and potential acquisitions.

A major part of Mr. O'Connell's time was consumed by efforts to improve the financial reporting system for Carmen's divisions. A description of the reports currently received from the field is shown in Exhibit 9. In Mr. O'Connell's judgment, the weekly shoe division statements provided a comprehensive, timely, and reasonably accurate picture of the performance of individual stores or departments. On the other hand, he felt the information received from the toy division thus far was deplorable, as he maintained below:

They really don't have a decent accountant up there. It's almost impossible to get an accurate picture of inventory or markdowns. It scares me to think that we might be doubling the size of that operation without having a good

**EXHIBIT 9**
**Carmen Division Reports**

| Report | Frequency | Purpose |
|---|---|---|
| **The shoe division** | | |
| Sales analysis . . . . . . . . . | Weekly | To compare actual and budgeted sales by store and district* |
| Overhead analysis. . . . . . . | Weekly | To compare actual overhead expense with budgeted |
| Dollar shortage . . . . . . . . | Weekly | To control money collection from leased departments |
| Accounts receivable . . . . . . | Weekly | To control collection from landlords who pay by check |
| Cash report . . . . . . . . . . | Weekly | To inform top management of planned and actual cash flow |
| Markup, markdown. . . . . . | Monthly | To indicate profitability of shoe lines† by district |
| Retail inventory. . . . . . . . | Monthly | To control the amount of stock at the retail level by store |
| Open to buy. . . . . . . . . . | Monthly | To inform buyers of their order and inventory positions relative to forecast by district and line |
| **Carmed** | | |
| Receipts and disbursements . . | Weekly | To control cash flow and borrowings |
| Census . . . . . . . . . . . . . | Biweekly | To monitor occupancy of hospitals by hospital |
| **Playtime, Inc.** | | |
| Sales analysis . . . . . . . . . | Weekly | To compare actual and budgeted sales by store |
| **Yorkshire Shoes, Ltd.** | | |
| Sales analysis . . . . . . . . . | Weekly | To compare actual and forecast sales in pairs and dollars |

* There were eight districts in the shoe division.
† Women's, men's, children's.
Note: Balance sheets and profit and loss statements were received from each division quarterly except Carmed, which also submitted a profit and loss statement monthly.
Source: Company records.

way of monitoring results. I've been trying to get Stan Lynsky to hire a good accountant, but he's reluctant to take on the overhead.

## THE FUTURE

. Confronted with falling equity markets (Carmen stock had declined from a high of $22 per share in 1969 to $5 in June 1970) and a cost of debt in excess of 10%, Dr. Carmen had become increasingly concerned about the commitment of funds to continued expansion:

The year 1969 was a disaster for the shoe business. The style and economic climates changed violently, but we made some mistakes as well which I took special pains to admit in our last annual report. When the tide comes in, the debris comes with it; but when it ebbs, the clutter is left on the beach. This year we are scrubbing the barnacles off the bottom of the boat and foregoing profits to get our ship in order for a big year in 1971.

Today the dollar is king. I'm trying to recapture dollars by selling off operations that can't justify themselves. I've already disposed of one unprofitable shoe chain. You just can't become committed to dying businesses in a down cycle. I have never seen a business with operating problems that has been able to grow its way out of them. My motto is "beaucoup ROCoup."[14] I want to be ready when the economic climate turns up.

Dr. Carmen continued to be dedicated to long-term growth, however. In addition to providing the opportunity for greater profits, he perceived a number of advantages in managing a larger company.

I would much prefer to run a larger company. It would be a good deal easier, too. I could afford to hire a greater number of competent managers and would have quicker access to the financial markets. To function in a creative way in business is to invite mistakes, and small companies just can't make very many and be successful or survive for that matter. In fact, I would even be willing to consider putting the company into a larger one providing we would be the survivor.

The trying times of 1970 prompted Dr. Carmen to consider again what directions the company should be pursuing. In addition to the matter of growth, he felt a rethinking of the role of his board and the effectiveness of his organization structure was of utmost importance. As the economy recovered, he was anxious to be in a solid position to resume the rapid growth of the mid 1960s.

---

[14] ROC means return on capital.

# Bill Communications, Inc.

TEN YEARS ago Bill was a slowly dying company. Years as a family-run business had left it low on cash, unable to make acquisitions, and with a general climate inconducive to growth. It had only one really first-rate magazine, *Sales Management*. The others were simply not anywhere near being leaders in their markets. Since then we have concentrated on building up property values and on being the best, if not the biggest, in the business magazine industry.

John Hartman, chairman and chief executive officer of Bill Communications, was talking to the casewriter in September 1970 about the changes in the company over the previous dozen years. Revenues had grown from $3,890,000 to $11,335,000 during that period, and the company had moved from a deficit to a profit position, a record Hartman ascribed in part to the philosophy of management he had fostered at Bill. The management group had established difficult goals for the next four to six years and were actively considering the possibility of going public during that time.

For most publishers of business magazines, the recession beginning in 1969 was having an adverse effect on advertising revenues. In fact, a number of magazines had recently been discontinued. Bill was evidently feeling the effects as well; each estimate of 1970 revenues prepared by George Lowden, the senior vice president for finance and planning, indicated a larger decline from the original forecast. Dollar revenues were still projected ahead of the previous year on a slightly lower number of advertising pages, but profits were then thought likely to be down by roughly a third. Hartman was considering how the attention of his line managers might be directed to the need for maintaining short-term profitability. He felt that "the crunch of 1970" provided the first test of his management philosophy.

## COMPANY HISTORY AND ACTIVITIES

The company was founded in 1879 by Colonel Edward Lyman Bill and his cousin, Jefferson Davis Bill, to publish a magazine called *Music Trade Review*. After 10 years of part ownership, J. D. Bill retired from the publishing field, leaving the management of the company to Colonel Bill and subsequently to the Colonel's sons, Raymond and Edward Bill. Before the two brothers died in 1956 and 1957, they agreed that management would remain with those actively engaged in the business. Thus, in 1957, John Hartman, who had been executive vice president and was related to Raymond Bill through marriage, became president of Bill Brothers Publications, Inc., the forerunner of Bill Communications, Inc., a name adopted in 1968 to reflect the widening range of activities pursued by the company.

In addition to publishing nine magazines and special editions, directories, and supplements associated with these magazines, the company had in recent years become active in market research, business services, book publishing, and seminar management. Two magazines had been sold since 1957 and two others started, the most recent in May of 1970. As a result of growth and diversification, the share of total revenues accounted for by *Sales Management* had fallen from 30% to 20% during this period, even though revenues from the magazine had increased by $1 million.

Despite the addition of new activities, Bill remained primarily a publisher of selective business magazines. Moreover, management believed this was a field with substantial growth potential. One officer commented:

Business publications are the best, easiest, and fastest way there is to spread information about specialized jobs and businesses. They keep people up to date on what is going on in their particular lines of work and serve all kinds of jobs and professions. Such publications are the link that connects the businessman with others doing the same work—regardless of where they may be located.

The company's operations and certain other data related to them are described in Exhibit 1; a summary of revenue sources is shown below; pertinent income and balance sheet information is given in Exhibits 2 and 3.

| | 1958 | 1967 | 1968 | 1969 |
|---|---|---|---|---|
| Source of revenue (thousands) | | | | |
| Advertising (gross) . . . . . . . . . . | $3,440 | $7,913 | $ 8,560 | $ 9,700 |
| Subscriptions . . . . . . . . . . . . . | 300 | 561 | 558 | 628 |
| Reprints and special editions . . . . . | ⎰ 90 | 178 | 231 | 267 |
| Books . . . . . . . . . . . . . . . . | ⎱ | 309 | 354 | 310 |
| Other activities* . . . . . . . . . . . | 60 | 263 | 378 | 413 |
| Investments . . . . . . . . . . . . . . | . . . | 18 | 16 | 17 |
| | $3,890 | $9,242 | $10,098 | $11,335 |
| Advertising pages in regular | | | | |
| editions . . . . . . . . . . . . . . . | 6,831 | 7,898 | 8,204 | 8,676 |
| Advertising revenue per page . . . . . . | $ 550 | $1,002 | $ 1,042 | $ 1,120 |

* Includes Plastics Focus Newsletter, Market Statistics, Inc., "Sales Meetings" conferences, "FF" Food Seminars, and Restaurant Business Services.

The principal aim of management since 1957 had been to develop the image of the magazines in terms of editorial content, advertising pages, advertising dollars, and reputation rather than to stress short-term profits. To do so meant reinvestment in the magazines to build circulation, attract advertising and upgrade editorial capabilities. John Hartman said he wanted each property (magazine), acquired or developed internally, to have a minimum potential for one-half million in gross advertising revenues. Thus, one magazine, *Modern Floor Coverings,* had been sold in 1969 because it was perceived to lack this potential. Growth during the Hartman years had been entirely internal, due at least in part to the fact that the company had little excess cash and a privately held stock.

The corporate offices were located in New York, which also served as the headquarters for *Sales Management, Plastics Technology,* and four other magazines, three of them (*Fast Food, Institutional Distribution,* and *Dining*) in another building four blocks from the administrative offices. *Modern Tire Dealer* and *Rubber World* were published in Akron and *Sales Meetings* was published in Philadelphia. Regional sales offices had been opened in Chicago, Los Angeles, and Atlanta as well as in the above cities, though each magazine was not necessarily represented in each office.

## COMPETITION

Bill could be compared generally with McGraw-Hill, Chilton, and Cahners Publishing Company, which had approximately 50, 20, and 25 trade magazines, respectively. Certain financial data on the first two, which were publicly held, are provided in Exhibit 4. Competition, however, was more specific: that is, it took place in each market and varied from the plastics field where there were three high-quality magazines

# EXHIBIT 1

## BILL COMMUNICATIONS, INC.
### Description of Operations

| | Issues/Year | Publisher* | Advertising revenue† (in thousands) | | | Percent increase 1968–69 | Advertising pages‡ | | Percent increase 1968–69 |
|---|---|---|---|---|---|---|---|---|---|
| | | | 1958 | 1968 | 1969 | | 1968 | 1969 | |
| **I. Magazines** | | | | | | | | | |
| *Sales Management:* Edited for sales and marketing executives who are responsible for planning, packaging, advertising, distributing, and selling their company's products and services. In addition to regular issues, there are three annual issues, one of which is the *Sales Management Survey of Buying Power.* | 24 | Randy Brown (46) | $1,170 | $2,190 | $2,290 | 4.5 | 1,562 | 1,512 | (3.2) |
| *Sales Meetings:* Primarily the meeting and exhibit management publication for marketing and association executives who plan and stage conferences, conventions, sales meetings, exhibits, and trade shows. *Sales Meetings* also publishes and sells separately two directories, *Exhibits Schedule* and *Directory of Conventions.* | 8 | Philip Harrison (51) | 330 | 930 | 1,210 | 30.0 | 934 | 1,120 | 19.9 |
| *Incentive Marketing:* Published for executives in a wide variety of industries who buy and use premiums or incentives as a definite part of their sales programs. In addition, there is an annual, *Incentive Marketing Facts.* | 12 | Lawrence Bell (50) | 300 | 1,050 | 1,180 | 12.4 | 1,415 | 1,386 | (2.0) |
| *Plastics Technology:* Reaches all U.S. plastics processing plants (i.e., custom, proprietary, and captive) through their process engineering personnel, including plastics processors at end-user plants. *Plastics Technology* also publishes an annual, *Processing Handbook.* | 12 | . . . | 240 | 770 | 940 | 22.1 | 801 | 868 | 8.4 |
| *Modern Tire Dealer:* Serves as a news, merchandising, and how-to magazine and reaches tire dealers, retreaders, brake-and-front-end shops, and other retailers and wholesalers of tires, batteries, accessories, and undercar services. *Convention Extra* and *Retreadweek,* on-the-scene convention publications, are also published by *Modern Tire Dealer.* | 12 | Bernard Kovach (37) | 210 | 520 | 720 | 38.5 | 761 | 846 | 11.2 |
| *Rubber World:* The interpretive news and technical publication which reaches the scientific, administrative, and commercial executives of the rubber and allied industries in the United States and abroad. The staff of *Rubber World* is also responsible for semiannual reference works on compounding materials and on machinery and equipment for the rubber industry. In addition, *Division Extra,* an on-the-scene convention publication, is published twice a year. | 12 | Robert Miller (49) | 280 | 550 | 610 | 10.9 | 920 | 954 | 3.7 |

*Fast Food:* The magazine of the restaurant business; reaches executives of commercial food-service organizations who are responsible for the food, equipment, supplies, and services required to operate their businesses profitably.

*Institutional Distribution* (first published in 1965): Serves the managers and salesmen of the institutional food wholesalers who annually sell $13 billion worth of products to the away-from-home eating market, i.e., restaurants, schools, hospitals, and other institutions.

*Dining* (first edition in May 1970): Designed exclusively for the leisure-dining or "table cloth" restaurant market.

*Modern Floor Coverings* (sold in 1969).

*Tide* (sold in 1959).

| | Editor (age) | | | | | | | |
|---|---|---|---|---|---|---|---|---|
| 12 | Donald Karas (37) | 560 | 1,910 | 2,160 | 13.2 | 1,256 | 1,436 | 14.3 |
| 12 | Donald Karas (37) | … | 300 | 420 | 40.0 | 447 | 543 | 21.5 |
| 6 | Donald Karas (37) | … | … | … | … | … | … | … |
| | | 160 | 340 | 170 | n.a. | … | … | |
| | … | 190 | … | … | 13.3 | … | … | |
| Total magazines | | $3,440 | $8,560 | $9,700 | (12.5) | 8,096 | 8,664 | 7.0 |

II. *Other activities*

*Book Division:* Publishes a wide variety of books, cassettes, marketing maps, pamphlets, and other printed aids for businessmen. In addition to publishing original material, the Book Division "repackages" in book form editorial material of lasting interest from various Bill publications.

*Market Statistics, Inc.:* Creates the annual *Sales Management Survey of Buying Power* and the *Directory of Key Plants.* This subsidiary also sells specialized data to many of the country's biggest manufacturing and communications corporations as well as to government agencies. Market Statistics serves as an independent research consultant to many of these clients.

*Restaurant Business Services* (including the Test Kitchen): Provides clients in the food, equipment, and restaurant industries with technical and creative guidance and services in all aspects of the clients' marketing programs.

*Seminar Division:* The newest of the service divisions. With several successful seminars as a base, this division is expanding its activities by working with individual Bill publications and outside organizations to develop programs for those areas of greatest information need.

| | | | | |
|---|---|---|---|---|
| Book Division | $ 90 | $ 354 | $ 310 | 19.6 |
| Market Statistics, Inc. | } 60 { 279 | 334‖ | | 19.6 |
| Restaurant Business Services | 25 | 38 | | 52.0 |
| Seminar Division | … | 74 | 41 | (44.7)‖ |
| Total other activities | $ 150 | $ 732 | $ 723 | (1.2) |

* Numbers in parentheses refer to age.

† Before deducting 15% advertising agency commission.

‡ *Magazine Industry Newsletter,* January 28, 1970. Totals differ slightly from those on page 2 of the case.

§ Includes reprints and special editions which are not included in 1968 and 1969 figures.

‖ Includes *Plastics Focus* in 1969.

n.a. = not available.

**EXHIBIT 2**

### BILL COMMUNICATIONS, INC.
Consolidated Statement of Income

| | *Year ended November 30* | | |
|---|---|---|---|
| | *1967* | *1968* | *1969* |
| **Publishing income** | | | |
| *Sales Meetings* | $219,500 | $193,600 | $160,000 |
| *Sales Management* | 213,300 | 190,300 | 177,300 |
| *Incentive Marketing* | 187,100 | 149,100 | 148,100 |
| *Plastics Technology* | (67,100) | (118,600) | (79,300) |
| *Modern Tire Dealer* | 87,000 | 37,200 | 47,900 |
| *Rubber World.* | 35,800 | 36,300 | 77,200 |
| *Fast Food.* | 229,100 | 150,500 | 144,600 |
| *Institutional Distribution* | (17,700) | (64,200) | (86,100) |
| *Modern Floor Coverings.* | 21,400 | 5,300 | (21,400) |
| Total publishing income* | $908,400 | $579,500 | $568,300 |
| **Other divisions** | | | |
| *Restaurant Business Services* | $ (19,200) | $ (13,800) | $ 1,100 |
| *Book Division.* | 20,600 | 32,900 | 3,400 |
| *Market Statistics.* | 5,300 | 32,200 | 23,800 |
| *Seminars* | (1,900) | 16,000 | 1,900 |
| Gross operating income | $913,200 | $646,800 | $598,500 |
| Intercompany profits† | 40,900 | 47,000 | 39,600 |
| Net operating income | $954,100 | $693,800 | $638,100 |
| **Other income** | | | |
| Investments | $ 16,600 | $ 15,600 | $ 18,000 |
| Cash discounts earned | 7,100 | 8,100 | 8,900 |
| Miscellaneous income | (700) | (700) | (4,600) |
| Gross income | $977,100 | $716,800 | $660,400 |
| **Other expenses** | | | |
| Officers' salaries | $ 60,000 | $ 60,000 | $ 60,000 |
| Pensions | 17,800 | 19,100 | 16,700 |
| Interest on long-term notes | 41,300 | 44,100 | 27,500 |
| Abandonment of leasehold improvements | 6,100 | . . . | . . . |
| Income before profit sharing | $851,900 | $593,600 | $556,200 |
| Profit-sharing contribution | 169,000 | 147,000 | 152,000 |
| | $682,900 | $446,600 | $404,200 |
| Management participation | 111,700 | 49,300 | 47,900 |
| | $571,200 | $397,300 | $356,300 |
| Unearned subscription and book income | (30,900) | 27,800 | 6,100 |
| Provision for uncollectable accounts | (4,500) | 14,500 | (9,700) |
| Keyman insurance | (4,100) | (6,900) | (9,300) |
| Income before income taxes | $531,700 | $432,700 | $343,400 |
| City, state, and federal taxes | 278,700 | 191,400 | 165,600 |
| Income before extraordinary items. | $253,000 | $241,300 | $177,800 |
| Gain on sale of MFC–net of income taxes | 129,100 | . . . | . . . |
| Net income | $382,100 | $241,300 | $177,800 |

* Includes all costs and revenues associated with publishing and circulating regular and special editions.
† Paper sales and overabsorbed corporate expenses.
Source: Company records.

**EXHIBIT 3**

BILL COMMUNICATIONS, INC.
Consolidated Balance Sheet

| | *Year ended November 30* | |
|---|---|---|
| | *1968* | *1969* |
| *Assets* | | |
| Current assets | | |
| Cash . . . . . . . . . . . . . . . . . . . . . . . . . . . . . . . | $ 446,500 | $ 488,100 |
| Certificates of deposit . . . . . . . . . . . . . . . . . . . | 190,900 | . . . |
| U.S. Treasury notes—approximate market value . . . . . . | 205,700 | 243,300 |
| Other marketable securities—at cost . . . . . . . . . . . . | 10,400 | 13,100 |
| Accounts receivable—net. . . . . . . . . . . . . . . . . . | 624,100 | 1,380,500 |
| Inventories—at cost. . . . . . . . . . . . . . . . . . . . . | 141,700 | 153,000 |
| Loans and advances to employees . . . . . . . . . . . . . | 25,700 | 25,000 |
| Prepaid expenses and deposits. . . . . . . . . . . . . . . | 153,800 | 156,000 |
| Total current assets . . . . . . . . . . . . . . . . . . | $1,798,800 | $2,459,000 |
| Furniture and equipment—net of accumulated | | |
| depreciation. . . . . . . . . . . . . . . . . . . . . . . . | $ 370,200 | $ 448,600 |
| Other assets | | |
| Cash value of life insurance . . . . . . . . . . . . . . . . | $ 90,000 | $ 114,600 |
| Mortgage receivable—deferred portion . . . . . . . . . . . | 1,200 | . . |
| Stock subscriptions receivable—deferred portion . . . . . . | 20,500 | 24,000 |
| Receivable on sale of publication . . . . . . . . . . . . . . | . . . | 161,000 |
| | $ 111,700 | $ 299,600 |
| Publication titles and goodwill . . . . . . . . . . . . . . . | $ 405,300 | $ 375,300 |
| Total assets . . . . . . . . . . . . . . . . . . . . . . : . . . | $2,686,000 | $3,582,500 |
| *Liabilities and Shareholders' Equity* | | |
| Current liabilities | | |
| Notes payable . . . . . . . . . . . . . . . . . . . . . . . . . | $ 37,900 | $ 38,500 |
| Accounts payable. . . . . . . . . . . . . . . . . . . . . . . | 331,000 | 627,800 |
| Accrued profit-sharing contribution . . . . . . . . . . . . . | 127,000 | 169,000 |
| Accrued expenses. . . . . . . . . . . . . . . . . . . . . . . | 165,600 | 215,500 |
| Accrued taxes . . . . . . . . . . . . . . . . . . . . . . . . . | 196,200 | 256,800 |
| Total current liabilities . . . . . . . . . . . . . . . . . . | $ 857,700 | $1,307,600 |
| Long-term notes payable. . . . . . . . . . . . . . . . . . . | 632,500 | 592,200 |
| Deferred income taxes—sale of publication . . . . . . . . . | . . . | 41,600 |
| Unearned subscription income . . . . . . . . . . . . . . . . | 304,500 | 335,400 |
| Minority interest in preferred stock of subsidiary. . . . . . | 16,400 | 11,500 |
| Total liabilities . . . . . . . . . . . . . . . . . . . . . . . | $1,811,100 | $2,288,300 |
| Shareholders' equity | | |
| Common stock . . . . . . . . . . . . . . . . . . . . . . . . . | $ 180,000 | $ 180,000 |
| Additional paid-in capital . . . . . . . . . . . . . . . . . . | 10,000 | 11,200 |
| Retained earnings . . . . . . . . . . . . . . . . . . . . . . | 739,700 | 1,121,100 |
| Total shareholders' equity . . . . . . . . . . . . . . . . | $ 929,700 | $1,312,300 |
| Less: Cost of common stock in treasury . . . . . . . . | 54,800 | 18,100 |
| | $ 874,900 | $1,294,200 |
| Total liabilities and shareholders' equity . . . . . . . | $2,686,000 | $3,582,500 |

Source: Company records.

**EXHIBIT 4**

McGRAW-HILL AND CHILTON, INC.
Summary Financial Data

|  | 1958 | 1968 | 1969 | Growth 1958–68 | Growth 1968–69 |
|---|---|---|---|---|---|
| **McGraw-Hill** | | | | | |
| Sales . . . . . . . . . . . . . . | $96,241 | $368,109 | $398,292 | 183% | 8% |
| Operating profit . . . . . . . . | 14,230 | 55,443 | 51,192 | 289 | (8) |
| Profit after taxes . . . . . . . | 7,266 | 27,944 | 25,631 | 285 | (8) |
| Assets . . . . . . . . . . . . . | . . . | 306,819 | 333,175 | . . . | 8 |
| Stockholder equity . . . . . . . | . . . | 169,186 | 180,339 | . . . | 7 |
| E.P.S. . . . . . . . . . . . . . | 0.46 | 1.13 | 1.02 | 146 | (10) |
| Operating profit/sales . . . . . | 0.148 | 0.150 | 0.129 | | |
| Profit after tax/sales . . . . . . | 0.075 | 0.076 | 0.064 | | |
| Sales/assets . . . . . . . . . . | . . . | 1.20 | 1.20 | | |
| Profit after tax/equity . . . . . | . . . | 0.165 | 0.142 | | |

P/E ratio: March 2, 1970, 22.6; 1955–70 median, 22.0.

|  | 1958 | 1968 | 1969 | Growth 1958–68 | Growth 1968–69 |
|---|---|---|---|---|---|
| **Chilton, Inc.** | | | | | |
| Sales . . . . . . . . . . . . . . | $13,553 | $ 31,759 | $ 39,619 | 134% | 25% |
| Operating profit . . . . . . . . | n.a. | 1,594 | 1,629 | . . . | 2 |
| Profit after taxes . . . . . . . | 443 | 1,519 | 1,356 | 243 | (11) |
| Assets . . . . . . . . . . . . . | . . . | 26,631 | 27,459 | . . . | 3 |
| Stockholder equity . . . . . . . | . . . | 19,884 | 20,766 | . . . | 4 |
| E.P.S. . . . . . . . . . . . . . | 1.14 | 3.28 | 2.79 | 188 | (15) |
| Operating profit/sales . . . . . | . . . | 0.050 | 0.041 | | |
| Profit after tax/sales . . . . . . | 0.033 | 0.048 | 0.034 | | |
| Sales/assets . . . . . . . . . . | . . . | 1.19 | 1.45 | | |
| Profit after tax/equity . . . . . | . . . | 0.076 | 0.065 | | |

P/E ratio: March 2, 1970, 9.8; 1955–70 median, n.a.

Notes:
1. Sales, income, asset, and equity figures in thousands.
2. McGraw-Hill businesses are approximately 37% magazine publishing, 44% book publishing, and 19% information services.
3. Chilton also had a substantial book publishing business and a large printing operation.

n.a. = not available.
Source: Moody's and Value Line.

to the fast food market where there were about 13. An example of the tactics employed to attract advertisers by *Fast Food,* the most rapidly growing of Bill's publications, is shown in Exhibit 5. In addition, there was competition for advertising dollars from other media.

Complicating the planning process was the fact that Bill's markets were constantly changing and being redefined. For instance, *Modern Tire Dealer* had to adapt to both the concentration of tire production in the hands of a few manufacturers and the increased variety of products handled by the typical tire dealer. Knowledge of the industry and the trends in its environment were prime requisites for success. In addition, markets could become saturated, which meant that the relevant audience was being fully reached, and increases in advertising rates

**EXHIBIT 5**

BILL COMMUNICATIONS, INC.
Trade Advertisement

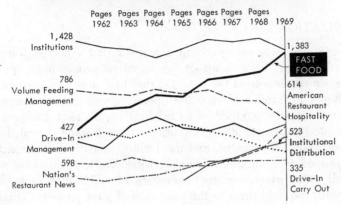

## 8 Big Reasons Why FAST FOOD is the Runaway Leader in the COMMERCIAL FEEDING MARKET

|  | Pages 1962 | Pages 1963 | Pages 1964 | Pages 1965 | Pages 1966 | Pages 1967 | Pages 1968 | 1969 |
|--|--|--|--|--|--|--|--|--|

1,428 Institutions

786 Volume Feeding Management

427 Drive-In Management

598 Nation's Restaurant News

1,383 FAST FOOD

614 American Restaurant Hospitality

523 Institutional Distribution

335 Drive-In Carry Out

### UP 143 ADVERTISING PAGES FOR 1969

**1** THE EXCLUSIVE SPECIALIST—FAST FOOD is the ONLY management-oriented magazine for the high-volume commercial restaurant business.

**2** PACES THE INDUSTRY'S GROWTH—In reach, readership and research, FAST FOOD's growth keeps constantly a step ahead of the dynamic growth of the commercial feeding field.

**3** HOW-TO, PROFIT-MAKING EDITORIAL AUTHORITY—FAST FOOD editorial content gives the professional buyer more profit-making ideas per minute of reading time than any other magazine published—with more useful field-tested information per issue on how to increase sales volume, productivity and effective management.

**4** LARGEST SPECIALIZED CIRCULATION—FAST FOOD delivers the greatest number of purchasing food influentials in commercial feeding—now over 60,000 homogeneous circulation—hand-selected, constantly "requalified," to deliver today's market TODAY!

**5** IN-DEPTH CHAIN PENETRATION—FAST FOOD readership includes more than 20,000 chain executives who influence and control purchasing for some 100,000 restaurant units—an unmatched penetration that is subjected to day-to-day checking.

**6** HIGH VOLUME BUYING POTENTIAL—FAST FOOD readers are the commercial food service men who control the buying for over 135,000 high-volume rapid-turnover units—the cream of the commercial restaurant market.

**7** HIGH READERSHIP ADVERTISING MANAGEMENT STUDIES SCORES—Average reader spends 57 minutes per issue. That's more than 650,000 hours of reading time per year spent with FAST FOOD by this superlative audience for your product or service.

**8** BEST ADVERTISING BUY—FAST FOOD delivers $3,000,000 (estimated) in food purchase potential for each dollar invested. Your specialized message to this highly concentrated buying audience is your most effective buy. It's the reason why FAST FOOD's advertising growth outstrips the entire field.

Source: Standard Rate & Data Service.

simply tended to match increased costs. As Randy Brown[1] said: "Some markets will stabilize, at which point it becomes difficult to register increased profits. Then we try to beat the rap by adding extra communications vehicles like special directories or organizing seminars for that audience." With other magazines, such as *Incentive Marketing*, Bill had sought to define an industry or function. *Incentive Marketing* had been responsible, according to Brown, for expanding the use of incentive programs by many types of organizations.

## ORGANIZATION

The company was organized in a manner that reflected John Hartman's concept of "bottoms-up or participative management, in which decisions do *not* flow from the top." On the "line" side of the organization chart shown in Exhibit 6 were the operating units of the corporation. The magazines were grouped into a publications division. Each magazine was operated independently of the others, though some shared the same publisher, and there was no divisional chief executive. Other activities were grouped into an information division. Once again there was no divisional chief executive; the managers of individual units worked closely with the publishers in the execution of joint projects. There were 13 operating units in all, each accounted for as a profit center.

The "staff" side of Exhibit 6 reflects the other functions, positions and titles in the company. The functions of sales/education, editorial/creative, public relations, executive vice president, and finance/planning were performed by Morgan Browne[2] and George Lowden. These men, with John Hartman, Randy Brown, and Don Karas,[3] comprised the corporate staff. The corporate staff met informally all the time, formally once a month, and made the major nonoperating policy decisions for the company. Reporting to George Lowden were the controller and a production coordinator, and to Morgan Browne individuals responsible for research and development and circulation.

In addition there was the corporate development board, described by George Lowden as "an internal sounding board for top-management people in the corporation. It does not make operating decisions but it does allow the viewpoint of the various people to be presented on such issues as an acquisition." The board was comprised of the four corporate officers (Hartman, Browne, Lowden, and Brown) and six line managers who held various positions in the organization.[4]

---

[1] President of Bill Communications and publisher of *Sales Management*.
[2] Executive vice president.
[3] Publisher of *Fast Food, Institutional Distribution,* and *Dining.*
[4] Donald Karas, Lawrence Bell, Philip Harrison, and Bernie Kovach, all publishers; Robert Smallwood, senior vice president for circulation of *Sales Management;* and Ernie Zielasko, editor of *Modern Tire Dealer.*

**EXHIBIT 6**
**Bill Communications table of organization 1970**

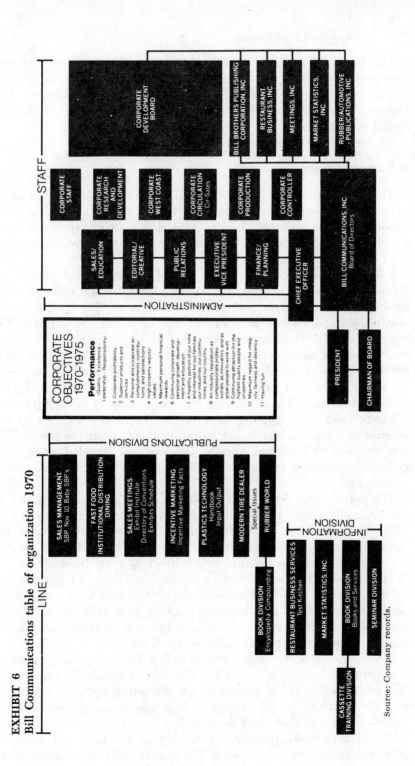

Source: Company records.

The board of directors of Bill Communications included the four corporate officers and one outside director. Approximate ownership of the company as of 1970 was: John Hartman, 42%; Randy Brown, 35%; Morgan Browne, 4%; George Lowden, 4%; the remaining 15% was divided among 40 employees.

## Management team

The four officers had been with Bill Communications for 14 to 25 years. Their offices were spacious, expensively decorated, and in close proximity to one another. They asserted that mutual respect and congenial working relationships had existed among them over the years. Brief descriptions of each follow:

*John Hartman,* 48, chairman and chief executive, had joined Bill Brothers Publications in 1949 as a salesman for *Sales Management.* After serving as sales manager and general manager of that magazine and eventually executive vice president of Bill, he became president of the company in 1957. Hartman was described by his associates as an "active thinker" and a constant writer of memoranda. Many in the company felt that his personal philosophy pervaded the organization and was the source of much of its collective values, style, and objectives. Morgan Browne described him as "having the personality of a high-powered salesman" and as "a guiding force in the corporation but not at the expense of the publishers in the industries their magazines served." He was involved in numerous outside activities and traveled extensively, giving speeches and talking about Bill's progress and his management philosophy.

*Morgan Browne,* 50, executive vice president, had come to Bill as the managing editor of *Tide* magazine which had been acquired in 1956. (It was sold in 1959.) He was the chief editorial officer of the corporation although he indicated that he rarely meddled in the content of the magazines. Randy Brown described Morgan Browne's job as "a staff generalist on everything—a backstop to John—an intermediary between line and staff—and a man aware of the whole business." Browne described his own job as a "collector of ideas" from Hartman and others upon which he took action. He felt his job was "a very good one for which I am paid outrageously well, as we all are."

*George Lowden,* 45, senior vice president for finance and planning, had joined the company in 1946. His tasks included the formulation of financial policy and responsibility for budgeting and planning activities. He described his job in part as "a license to cajole and persuade line managers regarding their decisions."

*Randy Brown,* 46, president of Bill Communications and publisher of *Sales Management,* had joined the firm in 1951 as a salesman for

*Sales Meetings* and was made a vice president in 1960. He had directed *Sales Management* for a number of years and still spent 90% of his time on that magazine. The remainder was consumed by "general administrative duties." Mr. Hartman commented: "We do not feel we are really big enough, yet, to need a chairman and a chief executive officer as well as an operating corporate president. Randy and I decided that he should 'fill' the corporate presidency very simply to 'block it out' for a few years from competitive jockeying."

## Management philosophy

Management at Bill had aspired to define and implement what it felt were the key responsibilities of executives to their corporation and to their associates. Ray Bill in 1957 had defined a manager's responsibilities to be operating profitably, "conscientiously striving to improve everybody serving under him," "helping everybody in the organization, from top to bottom, to live a happy life—a life that gets happier as the years roll on," and "being fair at all times and with all people." He had gone on to enumerate what the company had done in each of these areas. For example, he illustrated the third point, making people happy, by pointing to Bill's pioneering in the industry in the areas of group life insurance, profit sharing, and health and hospital insurance. Bill had also provided attractive and modern working space, offered increased vacation time for longer service, and sponsored "nonshop" social gatherings. In 1970 such practices were widely accepted, but referring back to 1957 Hartman felt that they were then manifestations of the company's character "as a benign, honest, paternalistic corporation— and one only beginning to stir into new ways of doing things."

At this same 1957 meeting, Hartman had also given a speech in which he discussed his feelings about the nature of the business. His talk stressed that the business was different from others; that 12 times a year they had to create and to do "on-the-job-imagineering" and that this had to be done by the operating people, not a special planning or creative group. He felt the trade magazine publishing industry was changing as its markets and customers changed, which led him to state that "at Bill, nothing is sacred . . . we have no sacred cows."

Hartman traced the evolution of his management philosophy at Bill:

I became chief executive officer of Bill Communications over 13 years ago, June of 1957. I was reminded constantly by other chief executives that it was both "professional" and "smart" to "let go" . . . delegate authority and responsibility. I accepted this intellectually, believed it, read all the books on it, and actually thought I was doing it. In fact, I had been only kidding myself. Delegation too often in reality had only meant abdication. Or, on the other extreme, in delegating, but only to the point where things got tight, I was really creating more confusion by then once again dashing in and attempting to be the personal hero rectifying things singlehandedly. I had failed at building a true organization. I had discouraged individual initiative at least as much as I had encouraged it. Most of our potential leaders were working far below their actual capacities. There was no possible successorship developing.

Then an unusual circumstance forced me to spend one third of my time away from the business two successive years [as vice president and then president of the Young Presidents' Organization]. At that time—in 1961—I guess I was vainly concerned enough to feel that my absence might have some very bad effects on my company. In hindsight, it turned out to be the best single thing that ever happened to force real delegation for the company's real growth and manager development. It is more than coincidence, I believe, that ever since those years we have led virtually all of our industry contemporaries with an internal growth rate that has averaged better than 12% per year. On my frequent travels I've been phoned by the office once in six years. I've phoned them maybe six times.

In order to do this, I didn't really "let go." What we did try to do, however, was to completely reverse our traditional approaches of an authoritarian kind of one godlike power at the top . . . and to bring many others into real, meaningful, participative leadership and responsibility. We had to reposition the climate, style, and responsibilities of not just myself . . . but all of our line and staff managers. The challenge was to switch from entrepreneurial to professional management.

Hartman summarized this "repositioning" in a 1968 speech entitled: "How it works: how we do our thing and the care, feeding, climate and results we aim for." It was delivered at the professional hour, a meeting of all Bill associates held regularly for the purpose of communicating ideas both from without and within the organization. The table in Exhibit 7, reproduced from the transcript of that speech, summarizes 10 areas in which Hartman felt Bill Communications was different.

These specific statements illustrated a commitment by Hartman to the "climate" he and his managers sought to create that would permit people to grow, work, and prosper. He described this notion by the equation:

$$B = F(C \times P)$$

which meant that behavior (performance) was a function of the climate (environment) times the personality. Hartman, however, preferred to write it:

$$B = F(C^3 \times P)$$

The corporate officers admitted that, as Morgan Browne put it,

. . . the practice of our philosophy is sporadic and spotty, yet the philosophy pervades. It has served to keep people at Bill. I can't think of a single man we have lost in five years whom we didn't want to lose.

**EXHIBIT 7**
**John Hartman's summary of the "Management Methods We Aspire To"**

| *Traditional Way* | *New Way* |
|---|---|
| 1. Authoritarian planning: "Central Management" makes plans, budgets, forecasts. | Participative planning: Planning and budgeting is decentralized as much as possible. Staff fully participates, but line has last word. |
| 2. Tops-down management: Staff of "corporate" sets goals, controls, checks. | "Bottoms-up" management: Line develops the goals, self-controls, checks. |
| 3. Exaggerated requisitions: Ask for twice as much as you need. | Nonbargaining allocations: Costs mutually arrived at—requests reflect actual needs. |
| 4. Line-staff conflict: All line-staff contact a competitive, win-lose clash. | We win—you win: Line is responsible; its judgment prevails, staff serves and supports. Both aim for common goals. |
| 5. Line fights the system: System imposed by staff to suit its wishes; line tries to beat it. | Line makes the systems: Staff offers innovative, professional support. |
| 6. Minimum supplementary education: either on or off the job. | Maximum education: greatest help possible in meeting new standards, opportunities for seminars, programs. |
| 7. How little can we pay? | What is the MOST a man can make? Pay the most vis-à-vis a man's contemporaries. |
| 8. How far can we go? Line personnel in informal conspiracy to outwit accounting. | Self-controlled expenses: Line profit responsibility and participation creates self-control (or peer-group pressure). |
| 9. Secret financial data: "What you don't know won't hurt you." | Fullest disclosure of any information that affects individual's area of concern or over which he exercises control. |
| 10. Two- or three-party ownership. | Employee equity: 40 employee stockholders, and growing. |

Source: Speech by John Hartman delivered on November 7, 1968.

Moreover, Randy Brown felt that this style of management could be related to Bill's performance:

. . . our philosophy over the years has led to our sales growth while at the same time acting as a depressant to profits. Now that we have dedicated ourselves to more profits, I think we'll be just as successful in doing the one as the other.

As one measure taken to implement the Bill philosophy, management had sent some 60 associates for "grid training" at one time or another. There was also the professional hour, the emphasis on potential stock ownership, and the "Golden Ground Rules among Bill Communications Management" (see Exhibit 8).

**Evaluation and compensation**

John Hartman felt management compensation was higher than the industry average. He wanted to pay now what the job was worth rather

**EXHIBIT 8**

BILL COMMUNICATIONS, INC.
Memorandum to Corporate Development Board

*Subject: Golden ground rules among Bill Communications management*

1. *Always* give your fellow member of top management credit for good intentions. (But allow for the inevitability of occasional poor communications or inadequate execution.) In spite of the best planning . . . best intentions . . . allow for human nature and/or the totally unexpected to foul up our timetable for implementation of new plans on occasion.

2. Whenever we are disagreeing on problem solving . . . Bill Communications top management should make sure it is behind closed doors. (It is not fair to Bill Communications associates *not* on the top-management level to get erroneous impressions, half-baked information, etc.)

3. Once Bill Communications top management "opens that door," regardless of what has developed *behind* the door, we must present a united front. If, after a decision, further information develops which would call for reconsideration, wait until you can again get behind the closed door with your fellow member of top management involved before giving the impression to other associates that the decision will be altered.

4. It will probably be important for us always to remember that it is just plain human nature for the "rank-and-file" to want to do some griping—about even the most minor subject. Further, a certain amount of it is actually healthy. Recognizing this may be helpful at times in avoiding getting tied up in knots and diverting our productive time into nonproductive areas in our attempts to smooth everything over, make everyone 100% happy, 100% of the time.

5. In the home office, the most distant point between any of our top managers' offices is 103 steps—takes about 67 seconds to walk it. With our midwestern top-management associates we have a more complex problem, though hardly insoluble. Let's all remember that before we (*a*) jump to conclusions or (*b*) dictate that searing and soul-satisfying memo . . . we first "put down our ulcers and pick up the phone (or our feet)."

6. Again, to the maximum extent possible, "total truth" . . . candor, honesty, and objectivity . . is the byword among Bill Communications top management. If we remember these so-called ground rules, there should be no healthy change we should not be able to innovate, no honest and realistic goal we should not be able to attain.
Source: John Hartman memorandum.

than use the "carrot" philosophy he perceived to exist in many other organizations.

Editors or publishers were basically evaluated qualitatively. Top management developed a sense of confidence in the man and his knowledge of the market and the competition. They looked at the costs he had incurred, his market share, and his advertising volume. He was paid a salary and a bonus, typically a percentage of his unit's profits.[5] A publisher could choose a higher salary and a lower percentage of profits if he wished. Salespeople, on the other hand, were paid a salary plus a commission for sales in excess of a quota which was set for them. Their performance was evident to them and others, and compensation was tied directly to it, a procedure typical in the industry.

Salary administration was one of George Lowden's functions. He collected information on salaries in the industry and tried to set general compensation guidelines within which each publisher decided the

---

[5] Never above 10% of the magazine's pretax profits.

salaries for the employees of his magazine, subject to Lowden's approval. The publisher's compensation was set by agreement between the individual and Lowden. If a difference of opinion developed, the matter was forwarded to Hartman, although this almost never occurred. Lowden encouraged the publishers to accept a compensation package that included an important performance incentive.

## OPERATIONS

### Distribution

Only two of the magazines had a paid circulation: *Rubber World* and *Sales Management*. The others were "controlled" circulation publications which guaranteed advertisers a certain audience of specific demographic characteristics. Such magazines were mailed to selected recipients and were not sold on newsstands.

### Advertising

While Bill advertising rates were competitive with other trade magazines, they were higher than mass-circulation media on a cost-per-1,000-readers basis. Randy Brown explained that "this disparity is possible because of the quality of our audience. We reach people who *do* read the magazine, and who are in positions where they can act on the things they read and the products they see advertised." Moreover, page rates had been increased for eight consecutive years, and as a result advertising revenues increased by 182% from 1958 to 1969 on a 27% increase in advertising pages. Management was concerned, however, that some peaking out in rates might occur in the future.

The proportion of advertising pages in a magazine was planned by using a rule-of-thumb of 60/40 ad/editorial copy. "In this type of publication," according to Morgan Browne, "advertising can be as important to the reader as editorial copy." On the other hand, the company's emphasis on editorial quality had led to a 57/43 ratio in *Sales Management*, which "cost profit dollars." Aggregate advertising pages were increased substantially by special editions, directories, and, of course, new magazines.

### Editorial

Magazine content was the responsibility of the publisher of each magazine and his editorial staff. These men were expected to be spokesmen for the industries their magazines serviced and as a result they devoted considerable attention to developing relationships in the business and keeping current on trends affecting it. Morgan Browne routinely reviewed each issue and maintained a dialogue with publishers concerning editorial policy and magazine presentation. While at times critical, Browne did not, however, force his views on the line managers.

## Costs

Cost control was considered critical by management, though often neglected in an industry that accorded priority to editorial content and advertising sales. Bill had consistently experienced rising costs for paper, printing, and postage.[6] Sales expense and controllable costs, such as administrative overhead, advertising promotion, travel, and entertainment, had also been rising. In March 1970 Randy Brown emphasized the need to "control, and I don't necessarily mean cut, costs in order to improve profits." In his annual report to management in 1969, George Lowden illustrated the cost trends by the indices and ratios shown in Exhibit 9.

## Investment and growth

Management felt that there was a continuing need at Bill to invest in the growth of publications. Randy Brown described the typical growth process for a magazine as follows:

The first step in beginning a magazine is research to be sure a market exists, that there are people who can benefit from some information either not now available or not available in the form of a business magazine.

Next, we have to deliver the product editorially to make that magazine *mean* something to the reader. We have to be unique or better than the competition, and advertisers will want studies showing that our magazine does have an impact. Controlled circulation doesn't just mean you send it out to a list of addresses. The next step is to sell advertising pages. As we get a higher market share, we can raise our rates. As we become a more attractive marketing vehicle, we can produce more pages or use our reputation to back other related marketing items like a newsletter, or produce cassettes for training in that field, or run seminars.

The typical magazine turns the corner in three to five years: it registers a publishing profit when the ad revenue catches up to the costs of putting together the magazine editorially and producing the physical book.

Once established we need to reinvest in the magazine by upgrading the editorial staff and content. In addition, we occasionally spend money to raise the circulation. For instance, we spent $82,000 more in 1968 than in the

---

[6] All Bill publications were printed on a contract basis by independent printers, but Bill purchased the paper.

**EXHIBIT 9**

BILL COMMUNICATIONS, INC.
Cost and Revenue Analysis

| | Percent of net advertising revenue* | |
|---|---|---|
| | *1968* | *1969* |
| *Cost Ratios* | | |
| Operating costs | | |
| Direct salaries . . . . . . . . . . . . . . . . . | 28.8 | 27.2 |
| Composition, engravings . . . . . . . . . . . | 4.8 | 4.5 |
| Presswork, binding, etc. . . . . . . . . . . . | 13.2 | 12.7 |
| Paper . . . . . . . . . . . . . . . . . . . . . . | 6.3 | 6.4 |
| Bulk postage . . . . . . . . . . . . . . . . . | 4.8 | 4.8 |
| Editorial costs . . . . . . . . . . . . . . . . | 5.8 | 5.4 |
| Sales promotion and advertising . . . . . . | 5.0 | 4.5 |
| Sales travel/expense/conventions . . . . . . | 7.0 | 6.2 |
| General and miscellaneous costs . . . . . . . | 9.4 | 9.4 |
| Administrative budget . . . . . . . . . . . . | 6.0 | 6.2 |
| Circulation costs (net) . . . . . . . . . . . . | 1.6 | 2.1 |
| | 92.7 | 89.4 |
| Publishing income . . . . . . . . . . . . . . | 7.3 | 10.6 |
| | 100.0 | 100.0 |

| *Cost and Revenue Indices* † | *1969* |
|---|---|
| Revenue | |
| Advertising . . . . . . . . . . . . . . . . . . | 116 |
| Subscription . . . . . . . . . . . . . . . . . | 113 |
| Operating costs | |
| Direct salaries . . . . . . . . . . . . . . . . . | 109 |
| Composition, engravings . . . . . . . . . . . | 107 |
| Presswork, binding, etc. . . . . . . . . . . . | 114 |
| Paper . . . . . . . . . . . . . . . . . . . . . . | 118 |
| Bulk postage . . . . . . . . . . . . . . . . . | 117 |
| Editorial costs . . . . . . . . . . . . . . . . | 108 |
| Sales promotion and advertising . . . . . . | 104 |
| Sales travel/expense/conventions . . . . . . | 102 |
| General and miscellaneous costs . . . . . . | 130 |
| Administrative budget . . . . . . . . . . . . | 119 |
| Circulation costs . . . . . . . . . . . . . . . | 121 |

*Excludes *Modern Floor Coverings*.
†1968 = 100.
Source: George Lowden calculations.

previous year to raise the circulation of *Sales Management*. The results were an increase in readership from 39,500 to 41,500. We are now at 43,000. At the same time we were able to raise our ad rates.

George Lowden added:

Investment should perhaps also include the accumulated losses on a new magazine until it's profitable. For instance, losses have been $354,000 on *Institutional Distribution* since 1965 and $1,178,000 on *Plastics Technology* since 1955.

The management of these two magazines mentioned by Lowden are described more fully below.

### Plastics Technology

Plastics Technology had a controlled circulation of 36,000, mostly plastics process engineers. It claimed to have nearly 100% coverage of the plants in the industry and of the particular people who had the power to purchase advertised products. Principal competitors were *Modern Plastics*, published by McGraw-Hill with a paid circulation of roughly 60,000, and *Plastics World*, published by Cahners with a controlled circulation of about 52,000. *Plastics Technology* management said they had 20% of the advertising pages but only 14% of the advertising dollars in this market. While page rates in the magazine were lower than the competition, cost per 1,000 readers was higher than, for example, *Modern Plastics* ($30 to $24). The nature of the competition and differences among them are illustrated more fully in Exhibit 10.

**EXHIBIT 10**

BILL COMMUNICATIONS, INC.
Competitive Characteristics for *Plastics Technology*

I.　*Analysis of editorial content\* (pages 7/68-6/69)*

| | Modern Plastics | SPE Journal | Plastics World | Plastics Technology |
|---|---|---|---|---|
| Markets for plastics . . . . . . . . . . . . . | 307 | 73 | 154 | 10 |
| Design concepts . . . . . . . . . . . . . . . | 52 | 29 | 2 | 2 |
| Processing techniques . . . . . . . . . . . | 218 | 111 | 31 | 124 |
| Engineering articles . . . . . . . . . . . . . | 230 | 83 | 32 | 186 |
| Technical features . . . . . . . . . . . . . | 337 | 140 | 46 | 98 |
| Machinery and equipment news . . . . . . | 96 | 32 | 77 | 88 |
| General news . . . . . . . . . . . . . . . . | 171 | 159 | 151 | 59 |
| All other editorial . . . . . . . . . . . . . . | 315 | 472 | 283 | 153 |
| Total . . . . . . . . . . . . . . . . . . | 1,726 | 1,098 | 776 | 720 |

II.　*Advertising pages—1969†*

| | | | | |
|---|---|---|---|---|
| Pages . . . . . . . . . . . . . . . . . . . . . | 2,424 | 345 | 1,180 | 866 |
| Ad/editorial ratio . . . . . . . . . . . . . . | 1.41 | 0.32 | 1.52 | 1.20 |

III.　*Advertising cost per thousand readers ‡*

| | | | | |
|---|---|---|---|---|
| U.S. circulation . . . . . . . . . . . . . . . | $32.12 | $48.67 | $24.75 | $30.16 |
| All readers . . . . . . . . . . . . . . . . . . | 24.74 | 41.95 | 24.75 | 29.89 |

\*Pages from Market Research Department, *Modern Plastics*.
†*Industrial Marketing*, January 1970; advertising/editorial ratio calculated from I and II above.
‡Based on June 1969 BPA and ABC circulation guarantees and the per-page rates for six insertion, black and white.

*Plastics Technology* was run by two men, both with the title of vice president of *Plastics Technology*. One was responsible for editorial content, the other was in charge of marketing, sales, and advertising. There was no publisher at the time of the case; in mid-1969 the former publisher had become a member of the general administrative staff working with Morgan Browne. Malcolm Riley, editorial vice president, described the magazine in these terms:

I had been plastics editor with another publisher and wanted to start or buy my own magazine. I agreed to take on this one in 1962 only on the condition that money be put into it, for in those days it was a real shoestring operation. One of the first things we did was a market research study to determine the number of plants and people in the industry. Out of this work came our editorial focus on the plastics process manufacturing area. We write for the production engineering departments in the 14,000 fabricating and processing plants around the country.

*Plastics Technology* is a technical magazine. That makes it tough because, to be successful, we are expected to be experts in the industry, which means a lot of time in the field with engineers and attention to gathering news and keeping up to date with the literature. All those things cost money. McGraw-Hill has a worldwide news bureau, for instance, and a number of publications in industries related to plastics and fabrication to share the burden. Here we have an editorial staff of four.

I have thought about starting some new activities; in fact, last year we tried a weekly newsletter but it didn't pay. We could go into market research, special publications, and even special projects for industry clients. As far as new magazines are concerned, ceramics would be a natural as well as metalworking, though the latter is already crowded.

Lee Noe, vice president of marketing, had been with *Plastics Technology* from 1955 until 1958 when he had left .to join the staff of the *Society of Plastics Engineers Journal;* he had returned to Bill in 1963. He described certain other aspects of the magazine's operations and organization:

We have 18 people today—less than we did before. I head up marketing—the other vice president heads up the editorial side. We have equal voices, and both of us operate pretty autonomously of outside control. There is also a managing editor who is in charge of physically getting the copy printed and the magazine produced. As is typical, we have the paper and ink purchased for us through the corporation and contract for outside printing ourselves.

We are responsible for setting our rates, number of pages, and policy for our editorial content. They [the corporate staff] pretty much leave us alone. All I've had to do is show them what I want to do and why it makes sense. Our formal relationship with Bill Communications is that we are owned by them, and they provide space and certain corporate services like circulation and accounting, which we pay for.

We work through George Lowden on budgets and salary administration. I personally negotiate a salary contract each time we have an ad-rate increase. I suppose if George and I can't agree it would go to Mr. Hartman, but

I don't think he likes this kind of issue to come to him. Generally, I have chosen a reasonable salary base and a percentage of sales revenue.

A profit had been forecast for *Plastics Technology* in 1970. However, as the year wore on it became apparent that advertising revenues would not meet expectations while costs continued to rise. Riley commented:

At the moment we are trying to figure out what to clip. Some time ago we let our weakest editor go. We can run on momentum for awhile, but I'm reluctant to cut any further. Looking back on our history, I would have shifted the advertising/editorial page ratio earlier.

### Institutional Distribution

*Institutional Distribution* was one of three magazines in the food-service and restaurant field published under the direction of Don Karas. He described his concept for the business this way:

I came to Bill from the Kellogg Cereal Co. in 1958 at the age of 26. The company had one tired publication in the food business then, called *Fountain and Fast Food,* serving mostly the soda fountain trade. It was run by a couple of old-timers who soon left. I saw my job as fixing an image for the magazine and making it grow. We have since helped shape the fast-food industry and have participated in the boom of the 1960s. It's a pretty amorphous industry, though—there are over 350,000 popularly priced restaurants in the country—and many times we've had to define it for them. I've become a spokesman of sorts and have made a couple of speeches recently on Wall Street to allay the fears about franchising.

By 1965 *Fast Food* was well enough along and had a strong enough staff so that we could support another magazine. *Institutional Distribution* was the second phase of my master plan for the food-service industry (shown below):

| Food Distribution *(Institutional Distribution)* | Popular-Price Restaurants *(Fast Food)* |
|---|---|
| | Top-of-the-Line Restaurants *(Dining)* |
| | Institutions (Schools, Hospitals, etc.) |

The magazine has grown nicely. We had hoped to turn the profit corner this year, though it may have to wait a year now.

Last year I went to John Hartman with five propoals to round out my plan, including two magazines, an annual, and some special projects. The corporation couldn't say no to all of them. I said that *Dining*, aimed at the top-of-the-line restaurant, was the one we really wanted, and they agreed to let us launch it. It's a rough year to start a magazine, and we won't break even as we had hoped, but the first issues have met with excellent response from readers. I'm confident I've got a winner.

Karas had created the position of associate publisher for each of his magazines, though it had only been filled at present for *Institutional Distribution*. Advertising space in *Institutional Distribution* and *Dining* had initially been sold by *Fast Food* salesmen, though by 1970 commission potential was large enough in most areas to support a separate sales force for *Institutional Distribution*. Editorial and production facilities continued to be shared. Karas commented on his organization and his relationship to the corporation:

I like to work—it's my thing—and I've done a lot of the building myself. But I've pushed my organization hard, too. My challenge of the moment is to get good people who are willing to keep up the pace, while at the same time creating an atmosphere that will make working here enjoyable.

Bill has been very satisfying for me so far. A lot of my feeling about it is due to John Hartman. He's a kind, thoughtful person. More than that, he's given me the freedom to make mistakes and learn from them. We have a management philosophy at Bill that I don't think will change, at least not while John is chairman.

## THE CRUNCH OF 1970

Bill management was aware of the need for planning to replace what Hartman referred to as the "old boiling caldron method where the most pressing issues sort of rise to the top." George Lowden coordinated the annual budgeting cycle, a task he described as follows:

First, I prepare a financial forecast for each profit center. The line managers don't have accounting or budget directors, and so the necessary raw data isn't readily available to them. My plan has been the product of their inputs regarding anticipated rates, pages, and circulation.

Each profit-center manager studies the plan, revises it, and then accepts it, which is, in fact, a commitment to the forecast. I then discuss the plans with them and attempt to revise any areas that look unrealistic. Finally, I prepare a consolidated corporate plan and add notes to indicate where I disagree with the individual plans.

In past years, line managers called Lowden when they felt they were off plan. Although there was no formal report of "actual to forecast," comparisons were made to the previous year's results, and Lowden alerted managers when he saw financial problems in their operations. Lowden also prepared updated forecasts of corporate performance for the development board. His reports in 1970 reflected deteriorating market conditions:

ADVERTISING REVENUE
1970 Forecast versus 1969 Actual
(percent changes)

| Forecast date | Pages | Revenue |
|---|---|---|
| March. . . . . . . . . | 8.4 | 14.4 |
| June . . . . . . . . . . | 4.4 | 10.1 |
| August . . . . . . . . | 1.2 | 9.2 |
| September . . . . . . . | (1.1) | 7.4 |

Profits were more difficult to project, though by September it appeared that they would be moderately lower than the previous year.

John Hartman reflected on the implications of the financial situation for the organization:

The crunch is on. It's really the first one we've had in 10 years. We've got to turn our attention to short-term profitability. I've asked George Lowden, who has been working on long-range planning, to step back into operations. He and his controller are going to hold financial review meetings with each of the publishers to see what can be done. Morgan Browne was subsequently added to the review team. I could become a big pooh-bah of some kind but I've deliberately delegated this task. I'm confident that our management philosophy will prevail with our line managers or their successors when we get back on the track.

George Lowden noted three changes that he (Lowden) had already suggested:

One of my worries is cash. With money tight, our advertisers take a little longer to settle their accounts. On the other side, however, we have to be responsive to our printers and suppliers if we are to meet deadlines. As a result, for the time being we have cut off virtually all capital expenditures and new projects that don't yield an immediate profit.

Second, we're thinking about changing the focus in budgeting. Take *Plastics Technology*, for instance. They have been overstaffed for the existing sales revenue. A magazine gets fully established as far as costs go before the revenues really start to build. Even at that, several times they have been near break even but then they reinvested to improve the magazine or to reaim it at a different audience. For next year, we may start with the bottom line, say at break even, and see what has to be done to achieve it.

Third, there is the matter of advertising rates. In the past, we have asked the publisher what he thinks rates ought to be. If we thought they should be higher, we talked about it, but, if the publisher contended for competitive reasons that he ought to hold the line or do something else, we went along with him. Next year we're going to suggest a 6% increase to cover postage, printing, and general cost increases and expect him to add this to any proposed rate increase or, if not, let us know where the savings are going to come from.

Lowden felt that measures such as these would help to "tighten up" the organization and produce more substantial profitability in the future.

## PLANS FOR THE LONG TERM

Despite the difficulties of 1970, John Hartman remained confident that the growth of Bill Communications would continue. Included in his plans for the future was the possibility of going public. The following reasons for taking that step were offered by various members of Bill management:

1. Going public would ease the estate problems of the major stockholders, John Hartman and Randy Brown. It would give them alternatives they would not have otherwise and would provide for their children.
2. Publicly traded stock would enhance the corporate image.
3. Stock could be a vehicle for acquisitions of a tax-free nature.
4. Options on publicly traded stock would provide a stronger incentive for key executives as one part of the compensation package.

John Hartman and Randy Brown concurred that such an offering should not be undertaken until a market value of $10 million could be placed on the company. Hartman felt that a price-earnings ratio of 10 could be expected, necessitating $1 million in after-tax profits, a level of profits he hoped could be obtained in four to six years.

# United Latex Ltd.*

"OUR TASKS are not easy. We have to change attitudes of mind, find and train the right executives, and, most important, completely reorganize our accounting methods to give you measuring sticks," stated Mr. Peter Dudley, deputy managing director of United Latex Ltd. (ULL)[1] in announcing major changes in corporate organization at an executive conference in June of 1968. Mr. Dudley, 44, had joined ULL in late 1966 after holding important technical and executive positions in the chemical industry and was the principal architect of the new structure. He continued:

The ULL organization has grown as a result of the acquisition of a number of companies, many undertaking similar activities. With 9 companies and 11 factories, integration has to come but has lagged. A year or two ago the managing director had, in theory, 36 people reporting to him and received 120 reports each month. Obviously, such a state of affairs was unworkable, particularly because of the interrelation of problems, as business became tougher.

As well as providing a heavy load on top management, the centralized functional organization is defective in the lack of general business training permitted by the system. Even senior executives grow up with just a specialized training in sales or factory matters, without knowledge of each other's problems, and often in a perpetual state of war with each other.

[1] Names, locations, and certain financial information have been disguised.

Our plans provide for a division of company activities into cells of business activity in which those composing the cell will be responsible for the operation, development, and profitability of the company's business allotted to the cell profit centers. The decision to date is to create four operating divisions supported by the usual staff departments. These divisions follow obvious product groupings. The sales turnover of each division is substantial, and the intention is to have divisions operated by a general manager as and when appropriate personnel become available from within and without the organization. For the time being, we may have to improvise and have one executive undertaking more than one job.

For many years we have sold our goods through regional sales offices operated by ULL with certain subsidiaries playing minor sales roles because of traditional goodwill. Today we have created divisions with their own marketing responsibilities which will have to rely on these general offices. Many of the customers of divisions may be important general customers of the company within a region, so knowledge of the customer must be built up for the mutual advantage of the division and the regional sales office. Rivalry must not exist between division and regional sales, and it is hoped that effective teamwork will be forthcoming.

Divisional marketing managers can seek help from our corporate development and market research department, but that department cannot be expected to perform the day-to-day duties of a division; its prime task is to study our long-term problems and interest and pay particular attention to development projects until they are securely placed on a commercial and economic basis.

Ideally, a division—or any other cell of business activity—would operate most efficiently if the prime functions were all at one center, with the factory, the sales office, and the development laboratory under one control. However, we are faced with some large factories which may always have to be subdivided on a divisional basis. What we have to ensure is concentration of like manufacturing activities, and this must be one of the prime tasks of the divisions. But our present location problems and the inevitable consequences of development programs over the next 5 to 10 years render improbable a tidy divisional factory pattern in the sense that the divisions can have control of all our factories.

Our immediate problem is to develop an organizational structure which permits the division to exercise its full responsibility for ensuring that the products required by the division are manufactured at an economic cost and are of adequate quality. Further, the division must be able to exercise its responsibility to improve and develop the line of products allocated to it. These responsibilities can be exercised through a production manager who controls a plant within the jurisdiction of a corporate factory manager. The extent to which the responsibility for operations passes directly from division to production, or from division indirectly to production through factory management, is a matter for determination between divisional heads and factory management. The problem is analogous to that presented by divisional representation and regional sales offices.

So you will note that we have a lot to unravel, but the tasks are not insuperable. To solve them will need the closest cooperation between divisional production control and factory management. Many of you have been brought up just to mind your own business, which is a useful characteristic when interpreted as doing an effective task on your own. Unfortunately, the effect has been to discourage a sense of participation in company, factory, or divisional affairs. This attitude of mind has just got to disappear.

It has been traditional in the rubber industry that the mysteries of rubber processing and compounding are locked in the mind of the works chemist. He has become the technical dictator of control and development activity, and the rest of the organization—unable to understand what he was brewing—tended to keep him divorced from other considerations and perhaps narrowed his outlook. He has been the victim of excessive functionalism.

To be able to exercise our judgment in the techno-commercial field, we have created a corporate development department to stand aloof from day-to-day problems and guide us on how and where to concentrate our future activities. This does not mean that the divisions cannot draw upon the corporate development department. They can, but the case must be justified to corporate development and then corporate development must justify an addition or substitution in their budget.

Divisionalization, with its delegation of authority to perform in a specified area of business activity, cannot work unless those concerned have measuring sticks to control their operations and judge their performance. The essence of the reorganization is to set up profit earning centers. The company as a whole is not accustomed to be judged in monetary terms, but henceforth every senior executive will be responsible for an expense budget, a production cost, or a profit position. To achieve this has required a complete overhaul, rationalization, and modification of our accounting departments and their procedures. Divisional profitability will be judged, therefore, not on profits on sales but upon return on investment based on the fixed and working capital used by the division.

Our accounting team knows the relative importance of time and accuracy in the processing of figures, but they can get nowhere without the data on which to give you figures, and you are the people responsible for supplying the data. If you don't think you are, you had better get moving quickly to find out why you have not recognized this responsibility.

With measuring sticks available to you and to management, you are on the spot, and you will be judged by your performance against a budget you yourselves have compiled. One of our members once suggested we were bottom heavy, and this is generally true by the very fact that we have had a complex organization with considerable duplication of effort. All this is being eliminated.

To succeed we must develop people who have got a little more than other companies have got. Good men are hard to get, and it is true that there are many good men around whom we fail to recognize because we don't put opportunity in their way. Divisionalization will fail if we do not find the right leaders in the first place, and we cannot tolerate the wrong man in the wrong place. This might be management's mistake by placing a man beyond his ability to perform. Recognize your limitations or else you may well be heading for a very unhappy career. Increased responsibility is tough but fun, and we want people who are prepared to have a go at it.

## CORPORATE HISTORY

ULL was a leading manufacturer in the British rubber industry. Its product line included tires, conveyor and power transmission belting, rubber hose, footwear, and a wide variety of industrial rubber products. In recent years ULL had added plastics and synthetic-fiber products to its rubber product line; these materials were replacing rubber in many applications, and their development permitted the company to diversify in associated markets.

During the 1950s and 1960s, ULL had been confronted with increasing competitive pressures resulting from (1) changed and tightened purchasing policies by its major customer, the National Coal Board; (2) the abandonment of price agreements prohibited by the Restrictive Trade Practices Act; and (3) increases in raw material prices and the entry of synthetic substitutes. ULL had entered this period with antiquated and inefficient plants as a result of policies of the then managing director who had limited plant expenditures during the years of high margins and demand. He reasoned that large cash balances were needed to take advantage of all cash discounts and to place the company in a strong bargaining position vis-à-vis its suppliers. (See Exhibit 1 for profit and loss figures from 1959 to 1970 and Exhibit 2 for the balance sheet as of December 31, 1970.)

As these competitive pressures mounted, retirement required a shift in management. The new managing director, Mr. Bradley, had previously been marketing manager. To meet increased competition, he took several steps. Time and motion study projects were introduced in the factories in an effort to increase worker efficiency and reduce costs. Second, increased efforts were made in the export market. Third, a corporate development department was created, which was responsible for handling all major products of the corporation from laboratory and market research to design. And fourth, diversification and expansion projects were undertaken by acquiring manufacturing facilities for the production of plastics and subsequently synthetic fibers. While a large proportion of its sales of these products were to the government, there was an increasing volume of business in the commercial field.

In commenting on the company's internal situation, one executive said:

After Mr. Bradley came in, I think the company tried to change, but it just did not know how. For one thing, we were extremely short of qualified staff as a result of a policy of not replacing retiring executives. Almost all

**EXHIBIT 1**

UNITED LATEX LTD.
Profit and Loss Statements, 1959–70
(thousands of pounds)

| | 1959 | 1960 | 1961 | 1962 | 1963 | 1964 | 1965 | 1966 | 1967 | 1968 | 1969 | 1970 |
|---|---|---|---|---|---|---|---|---|---|---|---|---|
| Sales | | | | | | | | | | | | |
| Belting and hose | 14,719 | 15,694 | 15,899 | 15,193 | 14,617 | 13,934 | 14,306 | 14,881 | 13,224 | 13,198 | 13,727 | 13,994 |
| Tire | 3,120 | 2,334 | 2,689 | 4,189 | 3,157 | 3,558 | 3,528 | 3,177 | 4,764 | 3,702 | 4,164 | 4,212 |
| Industrial products | 4,295 | 4,211 | 5,357 | 5,553 | 5,474 | 6,052 | 6,181 | 6,101 | 6,920 | 7,603 | 8,325 | 8,987 |
| Specialty plastics | .... | .... | .... | .... | 2,132 | 4,404 | 5,407 | 6,263 | 6,315 | 6,690 | 7,257 | 8,113 |
| Total | 22,134 | 22,239 | 23,945 | 24,935 | 25,380 | 27,948 | 29,422 | 30,422 | 31,223 | 31,193 | 33,473 | 35,306 |
| Cost of sales | 19,454 | 19,470 | 20,099 | 21,373 | 22,310 | 24,241 | 25,540 | 26,968 | 28,275 | 28,918 | 31,149 | 32,520 |
| Gross profit | 2,680 | 2,769 | 3,846 | 3,562 | 3,070 | 3,707 | 3,882 | 3,454 | 2,948 | 2,275 | 2,324 | 2,786 |
| Sales, general and administrative | 1,397 | 1,454 | 1,471 | 1,480 | 1,482 | 1,485 | 1,520 | 1,552 | 1,581 | 1,647 | 1,796 | 1,858 |
| Profit before taxes | 1,283 | 1,315 | 2,375 | 2,082 | 1,588 | 2,222 | 2,362 | 1,902 | 1,367 | 628 | 528 | 928 |
| Taxes | 592 | 603 | 1,345 | 1,264 | 886 | 1,193 | 1,117 | 957 | 756 | 215 | 135 | 394 |
| Net profit | 691 | 712 | 1,030 | 818 | 702 | 1,029 | 1,245 | 945 | 611 | 413 | 393 | 534 |

Source: Company records.

**EXHIBIT 2**

UNITED LATEX LTD.
Balance Sheet as of December 31, 1970
(in thousands of pounds)

*Assets*

Current assets
| | | |
|---|---|---|
| Cash | | 306 |
| Investments | | 729 |
| Accounts receivable | | 3,613 |
| Inventories | | 7,096 |
| Total current assets | | 11,744 |
| Fixed assets | | |
| Plant and equipment | 10,112 | |
| Less: Depreciation | 4,363 | 5,749 |
| Total assets | | 17,493 |

*Liabilities and Stockholders' Equity*

Current liabilities
| | | |
|---|---|---|
| Bank overdrafts | | 1,612 |
| Accounts payable | | 2,870 |
| Tax liability | | 512 |
| Other accrued expenses | | 415 |
| Total current liabilities | | 5,409 |
| Stockholders' equity | | |
| Cumulative preference shares | 470 | |
| Common stock | 4,200 | 4,670 |
| Retained earnings | | 7,414 |
| Total liabilities and stockholders' equity | | 17,493 |

Source: Company records.

the executives in the company were advanced in years and were quite overworked.

A second characteristic of the company's management that continued during this time was the centralization of power in the managing director, with little delegation of authority. Thus, it usually took a long time to get any decisions. Furthermore, there was little encouragement for executives to use their own initiative. And finally, I think that one of our most serious problems was that people did not talk about the future. All attention was centered on our day-to-day operating problems.

## SUBSEQUENT ORGANIZATIONAL DEVELOPMENTS

In January 1970 Mr. Dudley assumed the position of managing director and Mr. Bradley became chairman of the board of directors. By March 1971 the organizational changes conceived by Mr. Dudley had been largely implemented, although in a somewhat modified manner. First, the divisions assumed complete marketing responsibility, and the position of regional sales manager was eliminated. Second, the factories were assigned to specific divisions, even though factories producing for more than one division were still operating. And third, a cor-

**EXHIBIT 3**

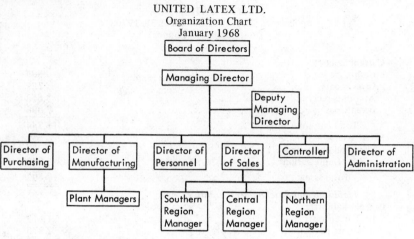

UNITED LATEX LTD.
Organization Chart
January 1968

Source: Company records.

**EXHIBIT 4**

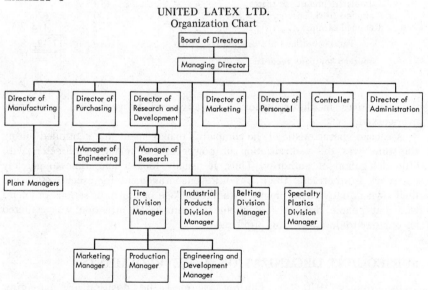

UNITED LATEX LTD.
Organization Chart

Source: Company records.

porate director of technical operations was appointed, and the functions of the corporate development department were assumed by this more comprehensive technical organization.

As Mr. Dudley pressed ahead with his organizational plan, he noted in particular the change in manufacturing:

It became evident that without direct control of production our divisional managers were not going to understand the important production-marketing relationship. Thus, at the beginning of 1971 we assigned each factory to the division receiving the largest amount of its output. Any conflicts which the division managers cannot resolve on an informal basis can be brought to the monthly meeting of the policy committee, which is composed of the division managers and top corporate executives.

**EXHIBIT 5**

UNITED LATEX LTD.
Organization Chart
January 1971

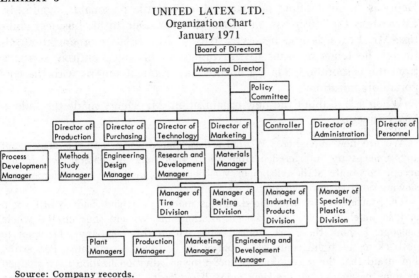

Source: Company records.

(See Exhibits 3, 4, and 5 for organizational charts from January 1968 to January 1971.)

## CORPORATE-DIVISION RELATIONSHIPS

Mr. Dudley, however, stressed that many problems remained to be worked out. He particularly emphasized the issue of corporate-division relationships: "One of my biggest problems is that I don't believe any of our division managers have really resolved this problem." The remainder of this case gives the views on this issue of six ULL executives representing three divisions[2] and two staff departments.

### Mr. Arthur Henry and Mr. Paul Edwards, industrial products division

The industrial products division of ULL produced a broad range of products, including antivibration mountings, industrial belts, rubber

---

[2] The manager of the tire division was on vacation during this period.

and plastic mouldings, extrusions, and rubber hose. The division manager, Mr. Arthur Henry, and the assistant general manager, Mr. Paul Edwards, were interviewed together. Mr. Henry had been in his position since May 1968 and was 39 years old in 1971. Until 1968, he had been the owner manager of a small rubber products company. Mr. Edwards, 35 years old in 1971, had also worked for a small company before joining ULL in 1967.

Speaking of these two men, a corporate executive remarked: "Mr. Henry is an outstanding salesman with a volatile personality, while Mr. Edwards is the 'businessman' of the division. Due to his business abilities, Mr. Edwards is a necessary part of Mr. Henry's organization, although he tends to want to run things on his own, entirely separate from the corporation. Thus, Edwards has frequent run-ins with the corporate organization."

When asked about the new organization, Mr. Henry made the following comments:

We are new men here. We only know our division, and we don't want any unnecessary interference from the corporation. In general, we do not accept corporate staff assistance. We believe it leads to frustration and a slowing down of our operations.

Of course, we are prejudiced in this matter. We have had so little help and so much trouble from the corporation that we are sour on the whole concept. I think there are some people within this company who want to go back to the tight, centralized control we had here at one time. Personally, I'm afraid that the wise efforts to move toward divisionalization have stopped in some cases and we are now going backwards. The staff needs something to do. But Lord, they don't know a thing about industrial belts, or even our new industrial hoses. They try to make us spend more on research as if we were a Du Pont or someone. We think our marketing skill, our ability to move quickly to satisfy customer need, is our greatest asset. But Matthews (the new vice president of technology) wants us to spend as much on research as the specialty plastics division. On the other hand, we can't get any new materials out of specialty plastics because they want to exploit their own developments in some silly esoteric way.

We don't play according to the book in this division. The two of us run the show and pay attention mainly to profits. In some of the other divisions I know that the division manager is not really the boss and that they are run by the division's executive committee.[3]

In response to a question about corporate functions, Mr. Edwards commented in particular on accounting.

---

[3] Each division had an executive committee composed of top divisional managers. However, since Mr. Dudley felt that "a man should not sit in judgment on his own acts," the chairmanship of this committee was given to someone in the division other than the division general manager. In addition, the managing director of the corporation was a member of each committee.

Divisional rather than corporate accounting is absolutely necessary. We get data from the corporate accountants, and we need an interpreter in order to understand what it means. Here we are with a large number of different products and we need to know where the profit is. Yet the corporation insists upon allocating all the corporate overhead against product sales. Sometimes we tell the corporation that we don't believe their accounting data. Then they go to our plants for the information and it is passed back to the division by the corporation. All this is wasted effort and could be handled much more quickly if the divisions did their own accounting. Here's what I mean by some of the worthless information we receive from the corporation.

At this point Mr. Edwards left his office and returned a few minutes later with a 20–30 foot length of computer tabulating paper. After throwing it into the air, collecting it in a large pile on the floor, and placing it in a wastebasket, he continued:

As you can see, there are no words on that paper. There are only numbers because the machine has to work entirely with codes; and it would take me hours to translate the data. Now this is an extreme example, and I don't know why they even sent us that paper, but my point is that when you take the accounting function away from a division, you remove the intimacy with an activity which is essential to business. Unless you have this function within your organization, you are never able to see things realistically.

Mr. Henry continued Mr. Edwards' discussion of corporate functions with a brief comment on research.

Although research and development should primarily be a divisional function, I suppose the corporation can do some long-term development. As for the new function of the vice president of technology, it should not have any line authority. We are willing to accept technical advice if it is offered in the form of a suggestion such as we would get from an outside consultant, but we do not want to take any orders from these people.

## Mr. Charles Whitney, belting division

The belting division possessed a particularly complex manufacturing organization, receiving its production from five plants. Only one of these produced exclusively for the division, and the division was responsible for operating the Sheffield factory, which produced some products for the tire and industrial products divisions.

The manager of the belting division, Mr. Charles Whitney, was a man in his early fifties. He was an engineer by training and had spent most of his career in the rubber industry. He came to ULL in 1958, and before assuming his present position in 1962 was plant manager at the Sheffield factory. Mr. Whitney was described by a corporate executive as follows:

Of all the division general managers, he has the type of background which would lead one to think that he should be the best equipped to run a division. He is a charming person, and although he does not have the dynamic qualities of Mr. Henry, I am sure that he really knows how to implement the divisionalization. On the other hand, he still hesitates to run the division as independently as he should. This is probably because he is a product of the rubber industry, which is an old-fashioned industry. For example, the industry has never paid much attention to developing people in modern management methods, and we face this problem acutely in the belting division.

For example, there is not yet an obvious number-two man in the division; this spot is probably shared by the division's marketing and production managers, neither of whom has yet developed enough drive and knowledge of business management. This is unfortunate, because the future of the division will depend to a large extent on how hard the men under Mr. Whitney set the pace.

The following statements were made by Mr. Whitney as he explained his attitudes toward the relationship he felt should exist between the divisions and the corporate organization.

During my career I have become convinced that it is of the greatest importance for people in any organization to know to whom they are responsible at the top. This is sometimes difficult to ensure in larger companies—as was the case when I first joined United. Thus, I fully supported Mr. Dudley's idea of divisionalization, which would give the divisional managers their individual organizations (rather like little companies) to look after. It seemed to me to be the right and logical thing to do.

### Production

One of our biggest problems arising from divisionalization continues to be the question of how to operate the Sheffield factory. The trouble with our operations there is that the divisions are sometimes inclined to forget that there are other divisions around. We get other divisional people coming down to the plant and talking too much about what they are going to do and how much money they are going to make on their products. The result is that people at the plant sometimes become concerned about the effect of the acts of other divisions on them personally. For example, one divisional manager said that his division was going to do its own production planning. I told Mr. Dudley about this, for I considered this as the kind of case involving a change in policy which should first be discussed at a policy committee meeting. Any change in scheduling practices at the factory level should be made only after an agreement is reached at the policy level.

### Policy committee

I believe the formation of the corporate policy committee was a very wise step because it provides the opportunity for the divisional managers to work together as part of a company team. We discuss each other's projects in the policy committee and we have to defend our projects on economic grounds.[4] Therefore, each divisional manager knows exactly why he does not get something he wants. He also knows that the whole matter was discussed and agreed upon among the divisional managers at this committee.

In the discussion of corporate versus divisional functions, Mr. Whitney made the following remarks:

### Accounting

In the area of finance and accounting, I have no doubt it should be corporate rather than divisional responsibility. Of course, the divisions here never tried to run their own accounting, but I do not think it would be in the interest of the company if they did.

We receive a great deal of accounting information from the corporation, but we have not yet reached the stage where we know the real value of these data. Perhaps we are getting a little too much detail. The main things I want to know as a divisional manager are whether I am meeting my budgets, how much profit I am making, and if I am not making as much as I should, where I am falling down.

### Research and development

The day-to-day technical problems are the responsibility of the divisions, as is divisional long-term development. At the same time, however, we have to get help from the corporation. One thing that supports the need for a corporate technology department is that there are so many technical problems within the divisions that the future seldom receives much attention. Another reason is that the divisions are short of process and design engineers.

I do not mean to say that the divisions are not responsible for performance. For instance, in my division we have just hired our own process engineer. However, as a division we have got so much work to do that we are going to need all the help we can get.

### Mr. George Evans, specialty plastics division

The manager of the specialty plastics division, Mr. George Evans, had assumed this position in late 1970. Before 1968, he had been a plant chemist at one of the United factories and had started his career in one of the company's laboratories as a rubber technologist. From 1968 to 1970, Mr. Evans had held the position of vice president of corporate research and development. In 1971 he was in his middle forties.

---

[4] A division could invest "all its depreciation funds plus about 25% of its net profits before taxes." If additional funds were needed, a formal request was made to the policy committee.

Mr. Evans was described by Mr. Dudley as an excellent scientist with little general experience in business. "He has had no sales experience, and his only line experience was years ago when he was in charge of a small workshop. Nevertheless, I am taking the risk that he has what it takes to become a manager. He has had no opportunity to understand accounting data, but I have hired an accounting assistant for him, who can become the business manager of the division."

In commenting on corporate-division relationships, Mr. Evans made the following remarks:

### Accounting

While I agree that accounting should be primarily a corporate function, I am not completely happy with some of the methods used. For instance, I suspect they are allocating factory overhead costs to products on the basis of their sales revenue. However, this does not give an accurate picture of where the overhead costs were created.

I also have some misgivings about the collection of accounting data for use in our budgetary control system. I see a variance in the red, but since the man who produced the budget is not in my division, he is not close enough to the production problems to really explain why it is in the red. Nor can he always ensure that the figures on which he bases the budget are close enough to reality. I think that the actual collection of data should be a divisional responsibility up to a certain point in order to get better reliability in the data.

### Purchasing

In purchasing, the corporate people are able to get bulk contracts and therefore the divisions should utilize corporate purchasing to take advantage of the reduced prices. Plant supplies and other local purchases must be decentralized, and we have done this in the last six months.

It is also important to have someone in the corporate technical organization to help the corporate purchasing people select the proper materials. This was not so important a few years ago when we were just using natural rubber. But today, when there are three or four hundred types of synthetic materials to choose from, it is very important to have someone with technical competence coordinating these purchases.

### Personnel

As far as personnel and training are concerned, in some locations we are experiencing some slowness in getting information. I also wonder to what extent we should divisionalize our personnel administration. For example, when we have two plants in two different divisions just a mile apart, are we justified in having separate maintenance departments just because the plants are being operated by different divisions? On the other hand, my division has a high number of scientific and technical people, and I find corporate personnel can't recruit the kinds of individuals we need.

### Research and development

In the technical area, I think the corporation should carry out most of the long-term research, although we will also need long-term research associated with the divisions. The development of products is really a joint responsibility of both the divisional and the corporate technical people. We should put products in the corporate laboratory until they reach the stage when they can be placed in the divisions.

### Production

In general, my only complaint about our divisionalization program is that sometimes we get so excited about it that we forget that the plants even exist. One man in the corporate organization made the remark that he thought that in United the tail was wagging the dog, and by tail he meant the production facilities. In my opinion, the factories are the dog and the corporation is the tail.

### Mr. Adams Lowry, corporate controller

Mr. Lowry had joined United in 1953 as an accountant. In 1968 he was made corporate controller. He stated:

I would classify the divisions as being subautonomous. They are reasonably self-contained and have a responsibility for profits. The division managers are free to operate within specified target limits.

I look upon the accountants in the division as people who are under the line authority of the divisional managers. I can say that these people are my accountants, but they are not my men. I see the corporate accounting function as something that can serve as a guide, but improvements should be made by working through the line organizations. In my opinion, the relationship between the accounting people in the divisions and the corporate organization should not be a simple line relationship where a man has no route of appeal except through the line organization. In the area of accounting, a man has a functional responsibility, and he has the right of appeal to the managing director through the corporate accounting function.

You have to realize that this is not a holding company and that the managing director has operating responsibility. If I were going to decide whether to give the accounting function to the divisions, I would consider the economics of this move, and I would look at their accounting methods to see if they were the ones required by the managing director. If all of these points were satisfied, I would be happy to let the divisions handle their own accounting.

When people in the divisions complain about corporate accounting, I ask them what they would do without this central service. It is our function to draw information from the divisions, process it, and then send it back to the line organization, both downward to the divisions and upward to the managing director.

In deciding what information to send to the divisional managers, we use a process of give and take and try to find the best answer. After satisfying the requirements of the corporation, we are perfectly willing to let a man have his own type of information. We send a total of 15 reports to the divisions. Once in a while we will also give them an IBM run with some detailed figures on it, but we never give this information in this much detail unless it is requested.

A few years ago, the divisional managers were given almost no information at all. Mr. Dudley told me that we should give them every piece of information we had until they were overflowing with it. Then, he thought, they would not be able to say that they did not have enough information.

### Introduction of the new system

You should also realize that there are wide differences between the divisions in the extent to which they are able to use information we give them and in the extent to which they accept the central accounting data. The important thing is to get the recipients of the information to the point where they can appreciate what it means. I think the system is working fairly well now, but this is something that takes a very long time.

## Mr. Harold Matthews, director of technology

In November 1970 Mr. Harold Matthews was appointed director of technology for United Latex Ltd. Prior to 1970 Mr. Matthews had worked for a large chemical company. In his new position he had the responsibility for major engineering projects, process and machine experimentation, and the development of new technology relative to plant operations, factory layouts, work methods, and instrumentation in the field of production engineering.

I have joined a company that is still weak in the area of engineering technology. First of all, in the past the company did not employ many graduate engineers. As technical people grew up in the plants, they were trained much like chefs are trained in a London restaurant. Furthermore, the technical side of the rubber business is dominated by the compounders, who are really witch doctors and not engineers. Therefore, one of the first things I want to do is to debunk the theory that the rubber compounder is the key man in the technology of the company when, in fact, he represents only one third of the required technological team. The other two are the process engineer and the machinery engineer.

Though a much younger industry, the plastics industry was until recently just like the rubber industry today, in that it was dominated by one group of specialists—the chemists. The subsequent division of technical responsibility between chemists and engineers, who have much more to contribute to process engineering and machinery engineering, is what has made the plastics industry what it is today—an area of sophisticated processes constantly modified to achieve low cost on high volume.

The fact is, thinking in the corporation is still shaped by experience in the days when proprietary technology and scarce rubber assured it of markets. In those days synthetics were something black that cracked under severe wear. Today the materials industry is a synthetic industry and advanced processes to achieve new low-cost products are key.

Forward thinking about product development also leaves something to be desired. There are not enough people in the company with business judgment. In the past, I think that the top management tended to confuse short-term profitability with technical efficiency. Because the company was profitable, management seemed to assume that it was technically efficient.

One of the things that we must now do is to take a hard look at our present processes to determine their technical efficiency. At every level in the production process this company may need more process control. For instance, when rubber is processed one can expect to get certain variations in the thickness of the rubber, and some of these variations will result in a thickness greater than that required. It will be part of our job to point such things out to divisional management and show them that, if they can further minimize this amount of extra rubber, they will maximize the process efficiency.

I am with Mr. Dudley 100% in his plan to divisionalize the organization of the company. However, I do not think United can go far toward establishing autonomous divisions such as those in large companies. First, the company cannot afford to do this because the divisions are not very large. Second, there are not enough capable people in the divisions to permit them to be completely autonomous.

Another thing that makes divisionalization difficult from a technical point of view is that the company presently operates such an amorphous group of factories. Because the factories are so spread out, there is a serious question of whether the company can afford to put the required high-grade technical people in each unit. Therefore, I expect to take a hard look at factory rationalization.

The relationship between the divisions and the corporation should be one of plural loyalty. The people in the divisions should have their primary loyalty to their division manager. At the same time, however, they should have a loyalty to the functional heads at the corporate level where policy will be set.

In working with the divisions, my job will be primarily an educational one. In the beginning I will try to ensure that the technological structure at the plant level is right. I want to have considerable influence over these divisional technical organizations and who goes into them. For at present there are not enough people in the divisions who are really in a position to judge a person's technological ability. Once I have established satisfactory technical organizations in the divisions, I will delegate control to the divisions, continuing to support them, of course, with professional advice.

I plan to get the cooperation of the division managers by showing them that I shall recruit people with technical competence and that we can help them increase their profits. Some of the division managers have little or no technical knowledge, and these will be the easiest to work with. The hardest will be those who consider themselves to be technologists. Of course, I will also have the opportunity to argue my case with top management and get their support for the implementation of my recommendations.

## The managing director's view

Mr. Dudley summarized his thinking on the status of his organization in the following terms:

As I said some years ago, we were going to try to break the organization up into cells of business activity. We have never shifted from this basic policy, and I am convinced that by so doing we are going in the right direction. I want the responsibility and full authority for operations in the hands of the divisional managers. They are responsible for the profitability and the development of the company's business in those areas allotted to them.

At the same time, however, we have not been able to delegate all functions to the divisions because some are not large enough economically to conduct their own advertising or research and development programs. Therefore, we have centralized certain functions at the corporate level and the divisional managers are expected to look to these corporate functions for help. They, of course, pay for these activities by an allocation of corporate overhead expenses.

The difficulty is that as soon as you make a man a division manager, he fights like hell for everything to be under his control and doesn't like to come to the corporation for help. For example, one of our divisions was headed by an extremely self-sufficient person who had so much a sense of independence that he insisted that his organization perform all its secretarial, accounting, and even research activities. His research activities, however, amounted to over three times his annual net profit.

We finally told him that we would approve the research but that he would have to come to the corporation for support and that the work would be financed out of the central research budget. Even under this arrangement, he wanted to have complete control over everything that was developed as a result of the research, in spite of the fact that some of the products might be more appropriately controlled by other divisions. In time, we had to withdraw the research work from his organization. He just had a tendency to overdo the development function and forget that he had to make a profit in a competitive market. Eventually we were forced to release him.

Mr. Dudley was now particularly concerned about the status of the organization because at the most recent board meeting Mr. Bradley had indicated the need for a review in this area. Mr. Dudley was aware that the chairman talked informally from time to time with members of the executive group but he had no feeling for what bearing, if any at all, these conversations had on Mr. Bradley's desire for an organization review.

# The Peace Corps

THE LATE President Kennedy, in his first State of the Union address, called for the formation of a Peace Corps, "enlisting the services of all those with the desire and capacity to help foreign lands meet their urgent needs for trained personnel. On March 1, 1961, he established the Peace Corps on a temporary basis by executive order. At that time he said:

The vast task of economic development urgently requires skilled people to do the work of the society—to help teach in the schools, construct development projects, demonstrate modern methods of sanitation in the villages, and perform a hundred other tasks calling for training and knowledge. . . . This organization will differ from existing assistance programs in that its members will supplement technical advisers by offering specific skills needed by developing nations if they are to put technical advice to work.

The Peace Corps will not be limited to the young, or to college graduates. All Americans who are qualified will be welcome to join this effort. But undoubtedly the corps will be made up primarily of young people as they complete their formal education. . . . The benefits of the Peace Corps will not be limited to the countries in which it serves. Our own young men and women will be enriched by the experience of living and working in foreign lands. They will have acquired new skills and experience which will aid them in their future careers and add to our own country's supply of trained personnel and teachers. They will return better able to assume the responsibilities of American citizenship and with greater understanding of our global responsibilities.

**EXHIBIT 1**

**Peace Corps volunteers by country at end of fiscal year**

AFRICA

| | 1962 | 1963 | 1964 | 1965 | 1966 | 1967 | 1968 | 1969 | (Now scheduled) 1970 | Est. 1971 |
|---|---|---|---|---|---|---|---|---|---|---|
| Ghana | 51 | 129 | 136 | 110 | 111 | 208 | 242 | 181 | 198 | 190 |
| Nigeria | 109 | 258 | 508 | 634 | 719 | 719 | 248 | 93 | 61 | 10 |
| Sierra Leone | 37 | 120 | 159 | 150 | 233 | 236 | 273 | 258 | 271 | 210 |
| Tanzania } Tanganyika } | 35 | 26 | 125 | 326 | 366 | 290 | 143 | 8 | ... | ... |
| Cameroon | | 39 | 88 | 103 | 118 | 77 | 61 | 50 | 64 | 70 |
| Ethiopia | | 278 | 402 | 565 | 566 | 432 | 389 | 395 | 292 | 100 |
| Gabon | | 41 | 70 | 35 | 49 | 71 | | | | |
| Ivory Coast | | 49 | 51 | 55 | 63 | 71 | 80 | 102 | 102 | 100 |
| Liberia | | 132 | 272 | 335 | 399 | 317 | 299 | 327 | 276 | 250 |
| Niger | | 16 | 12 | 43 | 48 | 129 | 156 | 45 | 44 | 60 |
| Malawi } Nyasaland } | | 42 | 97 | 230 | 231 | 153 | 123 | 140 | 129 | ... |
| Senegal | | 34 | 62 | 51 | 55 | 75 | 119 | 98 | 68 | 80 |
| Somali Rep. | | 35 | | 58 | 80 | 96 | 73 | 51 | ... | ... |
| Togo | | 44 | 59 | 56 | 49 | 109 | 102 | 85 | 84 | 70 |
| Guinea | | | 52 | 95 | 81 | | | 1 | 23 | 20 |
| Kenya | | | | 129 | 197 | 229 | 253 | 277 | 306 | 260 |
| Uganda | | | | 35 | 56 | 118 | 123 | 97 | 88 | 100 |
| Botswana | | | | | | 56 | 50 | 68 | 64 | 60 |
| Chad | | | | | | 30 | 38 | 46 | 55 | 50 |
| Mauritania | | | | | | 11 | ... | ... | ... | ... |
| Gambia | | | | | | | 16 | 14 | 17 | 50 |
| Upper Volta | | | | | | | 44 | 52 | 51 | 50 |
| Lesotho | | | | | | | 66 | 57 | 61 | 55 |
| Dahomey | | | | | | | 26 | 37 | 51 | 55 |
| Swaziland | | | | | | | | 44 | 50 | 50 |
| Congo | | | | | | | | | | 20 |
| Mauritius | | | | | | | | | | 20 |
| Mali | | | | | | | | | | 20 |
| Totals | 232 | 1,243 | 2,093 | 3,010 | 3,421 | 3,427 | 2,924 | 2,526 | 2,355 | 1,950 |

NORTH AFRICA/NEAR EAST/SOUTH ASIA

| | 1962 | 1963 | 1964 | 1965 | 1966 | 1967 | 1968 | 1969 | (Now scheduled) 1970 | Est. 1971 |
|---|---|---|---|---|---|---|---|---|---|---|
| India | 26 | 115 | 153 | 401 | 754 | 1,133 | 750 | 536 | 500 | 595 |
| Pakistan East } | 29 | | | | | | | | | |
| West } | 28 | 172 | 191 | 141 | 35 | | | | | |
| Morocco | | 56 | 102 | 133 | 117 | 83 | 94 | 118 | 124 | 160 |
| Tunisia | | 94 | 48 | 135 | 192 | 252 | 230 | 192 | 135 | 115 |
| Afghanistan | | 35 | 62 | 136 | 181 | 207 | 171 | 164 | 123 | 130 |
| Ceylon | | 36 | | | | | 42 | 30 | 26 | 60 |
| Cyprus | | 23 | | | | | | | | |
| Iran | | 41 | 36 | 149 | 272 | 267 | 167 | 191 | 168 | 170 |
| Nepal | | 65 | 96 | 120 | 150 | 221 | 179 | 185 | 159 | 135 |
| Turkey | | 39 | 114 | 338 | 481 | 225 | 158 | 161 | 60 | 125 |
| Libya | | | | | | 18 | 13 | 161 | | |
| Malta | | | | | | | | | | 10 |
| Totals | 83 | 676 | 802 | 1,553 | 2,182 | 2,406 | 1,804 | 1,738 | 1,295 | 1,500 |

## EXHIBIT 1 (*continued*)

### LATIN AMERICA

| | 1962 | 1963 | 1964 | 1965 | 1966 | 1967 | 1968 | 1969 | (Now scheduled) 1970 | Est. 1971 |
|---|---|---|---|---|---|---|---|---|---|---|
| Brazil | 43 | 168 | 210 | 548 | 639 | 601 | 580 | 456 | 400 | 350 |
| Chile | 63 | 99 | 106 | 294 | 397 | 392 | 254 | 197 | 150 | 100 |
| Colombia | 103 | 229 | 561 | 544 | 506 | 522 | 576 | 467 | 280 | 145 |
| El Salvador | 25 | 21 | 49 | 55 | 51 | 105 | 119 | 87 | 86 | 45 |
| Jamaica | 38 | 32 | 62 | 77 | 70 | 101 | 117 | 112 | 146 | 155 |
| Eastern Caribbean Islands | 15 | 14 | 17 | 5 | 45 | 89 | 124 | 131 | 155 | 175 |
| Venezuela | 23 | 83 | 117 | 265 | 292 | 352 | 262 | 206 | 150 | 175 |
| Bolivia | 35 | 112 | 126 | 220 | 266 | 303 | 219 | 230 | 184 | 145 |
| British Honduras | | 33 | 18 | 49 | 33 | 42 | 45 | 35 | 26 | 35 |
| Costa Rica | | 26 | 65 | 61 | 107 | 154 | 98 | 83 | 88 | 65 |
| Dominican Republic | | 144 | 171 | 85 | 101 | 140 | 161 | 121 | 63 | 45 |
| Ecuador | | 156 | 236 | 309 | 211 | 255 | 247 | 200 | 152 | 150 |
| Guatemala | | 27 | 105 | 83 | 69 | 140 | 151 | 85 | 84 | 75 |
| Honduras | | 27 | 46 | 103 | 107 | 174 | 167 | 152 | 100 | 135 |
| Panama | | 28 | 76 | 133 | 196 | 171 | 174 | 112 | 100 | 105 |
| Peru | | 285 | 293 | 379 | 301 | 349 | 283 | 137 | 185 | 185 |
| Uruguay | | | 18 | 4 | 48 | 65 | 31 | 14 | 21 | 20 |
| Guyana | | | | | | 44 | 51 | 43 | 58 | 50 |
| Paraguay | | | | | | 35 | 56 | 65 | 71 | 80 |
| Nicaragua | | | | | | | | 30 | 51 | 75 |
| Totals | 345 | 1,484 | 2,276 | 3,214 | 3,439 | 4,034 | 3,715 | 2,963 | 2,550 | 2,310 |

### EAST ASIA/PACIFIC

| | 1962 | 1963 | 1964 | 1965 | 1966 | 1967 | 1968 | 1969 | (Now scheduled) 1970 | Est. 1971 |
|---|---|---|---|---|---|---|---|---|---|---|
| Malaysia | | | | 378 | 561 | 583 | 495 | 495 | 417 | 450 |
| Malaya | 67 | 169 | 206 | | | | | | | |
| Sabah/Sarawak | | 91 | 124 | | | | | | | |
| Philippines | 272 | 472 | 286 | 227 | 571 | 601 | 720 | 662 | 309 | 335 |
| Thailand | 45 | 227 | 245 | 242 | 356 | 321 | 228 | 283 | 204 | 180 |
| Indonesia | | 17 | 31 | | | | | | | |
| Korea | | | | | | 92 | 310 | 265 | 179 | 295 |
| Micronesia | | | | | | 448 | 625 | 478 | 200 | 300 |
| Western Samoa | | | | | | | 129 | 115 | 69 | 70 |
| Tonga | | | | | | | 114 | 88 | 68 | 60 |
| Fiji | | | | | | | 51 | 139 | 149 | 160 |
| Totals | 384 | 976 | 892 | 847 | 1,488 | 2,045 | 2,672 | 2,525 | 1,595 | 1,850 |

### SUMMARY

| Year | Number | Year | Number |
|---|---|---|---|
| 1962 | 1,044 | 1967 | 11,912 |
| 1963 | 4,379 | 1968 | 11,115 |
| 1964 | 6,063 | 1969 | 9,752 |
| 1965 | 8,624 | 1970* | 7,795 |
| 1966 | 10,530 | 1971† | 7,850 |

\*projected.
†estimated.

Note: Projections for June 30, 1971, are based on a worldwide position. Regional and country totals, established within the worldwide framework, are based on currently known requirements and projections of June 30, 1970 in-country strength. The actual number of volunteers in each country on June 30, 1971 may vary from these projections as volunteer allocations for each country are made at a later date on the basis of firm host country requests and worldwide comparisons of programs.

Source: Peace Corps 1970 Annual Report to Congress.

The Peace Corps Act, signed into law on September 22, 1961, reflected the multiple objectives for the agency cited by the President. Specifically the act provided that the Peace Corps:

Help the people of [developing nations] in meeting their needs for trained manpower.
Help promote a better understanding of the American people on the part of the peoples served.
[Help promote] a better understanding of other peoples on the part of the American people.

In October 1970 the Peace Corps had almost 9,000 volunteers in the field engaged in roughly 270 projects in 60 countries; a history of Peace Corps involvement by country and project mix is shown in Exhibits 1 and 2. However, after increasing each year through 1967, the number

**EXHIBIT 2**
**Peace Corps volunteer programs**

| | Agri-culture | Community develop-ment | Educa-tion | Health | Other | Total volunteers overseas |
|---|---|---|---|---|---|---|
| I. *Historical summary* | | | | | | |
| 1962. . . . . . . . . . . . . | 14.3% | 1.9% | 64.2% | 10.9% | 8.4% | 1,044 |
| 1963. . . . . . . . . . . . . | 7.6 | 25.6 | 54.6 | 8.2 | 4.0 | 4,379 |
| 1964. . . . . . . . . . . . . | 6.6 | 26.7 | 52.8 | 9.3 | 4.6 | 6,063 |
| 1965. . . . . . . . . . . . . | 7.9 | 26.2 | 51.8 | 9.9 | 4.2 | 8,624 |
| 1966. . . . . . . . . . . . . | 8.2 | 26.5 | 51.4 | 11.2 | 2.7 | 10,530 |
| 1967. . . . . . . . . . . . . | 10.2 | 25.3 | 49.4 | 11.2 | 3.9 | 11,912 |
| 1968. . . . . . . . . . . . . | 10.3 | 25.1 | 48.4 | 11.9 | 4.3 | 11,115 |
| 1969. . . . . . . . . . . . . | 11.2 | 21.7 | 50.2 | 10.5 | 6.4 | 9,752 |
| II. *Scheduled programs—1970* | | | | | | |
| Africa . . . . . . . . . . . . | 20.1% | . . . | 63.8% | 12.1% | 4.0% | 2,355 |
| Latin America . . . . . . . | 32.0 | 30.0% | 20.2 | 9.9 | 7.9 | 2,550 |
| East Asia/Pacific . . . . . . | 10.9 | 5.0 | 70.0 | 9.1 | 5.0 | 1,595 |
| North Africa/Near East/ South Asia . . . . . . . . | 33.7 | . . . | 43.3 | 10.4 | 12.6 | 1,295 |
| Total . . . . . . . . . . | 24.3% | 10.9% | 48.7% | 10.5% | 5.6% | 7,795 |

Source: Peace Corps 1970 Annual Report to Congress.

of volunteers had declined in 1968 and 1969 and a further shrinkage was occurring in 1970. On the other hand, the number of skill classifications had grown to 360, and the proportions of volunteers in these categories had increased, according to Peace Corps officials, from 20% to 60%. Joseph Blatchford, the third director in the agency's history and the first appointed by a Republican President, had launched what was thought by many to be a major departure in the role of the Peace Corps from that envisioned by his predecessors. One commentator summarized the change in these terms.

The typical Kennedy-era volunteer was a clean-cut young American college graduate, long on idealism but short on practical skills. Now the dedicated amateur is gradually being replaced by more mature, highly skilled volunteers, drawn from private enterprise, the farm, and minority groups. In a second major departure, Blatchford is making plans to absorb volunteers from other countries to create a kind of multinational service corps.

Blatchford's critics say the revamping of the Peace Corps is purely political, designed solely to put a Blatchford-Nixon stamp on the old Shriver-Kennedy program. His supporters say he is reacting in the only way possible to the real situation in the developing world. . . .

If Blatchford goes ahead with plans to "professionalize" and "international-ize" the Peace Corps, he may sacrifice some of its idealism along the way. He may also insure the continued existence of the Peace Corps in a world increasingly suspicious of America's claim to altruism in international affairs.[1]

Concurrent with attempts to redirect the efforts of Peace Corps volunteers, Blatchford had engaged a major consulting firm to undertake an organizational study. The consultants recommended the delegation of important operating decisions, notably project selection, to the four regional managers, each of whom supervised about 15 country directors. The consultants also proposed the institution of planning and control mechanisms appropriate in their view for the effective management of a geographically dispersed organization.

The director instituted the suggested changes in responsibilities and authorities almost immediately and proceeded with the implementation of the planning and control system. In October 1970, however, he was reconsidering the role of the regional director. Among his concerns were the needs to adapt the organization to a changing environment and to increase its responsiveness to a set of new Peace Corps objectives. The director's administrative task was complicated by the intensity of staff members' feelings, often conflicting, about the purpose of the Peace Corps.

## THE PEACE CORPS IN GOVERNMENT

The Peace Corps was constituted as a semiautonomous agency in government. The founding legislation provided that "the Secretary of State shall be responsible for the continuous supervision and general direction of the programs authorized by this Act, to the extent that such programs are effectively integrated both at home and abroad and the foreign policy of the United States is best served thereby." The act left wide latitude for interpretation; Dean Rusk, the first Secretary of State having to deal with the agency, helped provide it with an independent posture. He said at one point: "To make the Peace Corps

---

[1] Richard Alfred, Latin American Services, *Newsday*, Garden City, March 7, 1970.

an instrument of foreign policy would be to rob it of its contribution to foreign policy."[2]

On operating matters, Peace Corps programs were submitted to AID[3] for comment and to the State Department for approval, which was virtually always forthcoming. In the field, the Peace Corps was represented by the country director, who was officially subordinate to the ambassador. The ambassador reviewed volunteer programs before final approval was sought in Washington. Typically, however, Peace Corps personnel remained apart from the diplomatic mission, except in times of emergency or during the occasional controversy surrounding the activities of individual volunteers.[4]

In 1965 Sargent Shriver, the first director, secured the removal of the Peace Corps from Civil Service Commission jurisdiction in the hiring of professional staff. Prior to that time, a very limited number of exemptions had been permitted. Concurrently Shriver recommended and obtained passage of an amendment to the Peace Corps Act which limited the time a staff member could stay in the Peace Corps to five years (effective with appointments made after September 1965) "unless the Director of the Peace Corps, under special circumstances, personally approves an extension of not more than one year on an individual basis." The amendment assured a flow of new people and ideas through the organization which Shriver hoped would preserve its vitality. Service as a volunteer did not count in the five years.

Contact with other departments of government concerning Peace Corps operations were infrequent. In fact, in the case of intelligence agencies such as the CIA, President Kennedy had issued a strongly worded order that there was to be no interference (or infiltration) in Peace Corps activities.

## LEADERSHIP

### The Shriver years

Sargent Shriver, then 45, brother-in-law of John Kennedy and former manager of the Merchandise Mart owned by Joseph Kennedy, had been asked by the President on February 1, 1961, to create the task force

---

[2] Robert G. Carey, *The Peace Corps* (New York: Praeger Publishers, 1970), p. 180.

[3] Agency for International Development.

[4] For instance, in 1967, a volunteer led a protest for better streets during President Johnson's visit to one Central American country. When the ambassador reprimanded her, she protested again, provoking the ambassador's expression of displeasure to the director of the Peace Corps. The director in turn contacted the president of that country and was reassured that the volunteer was still welcome.

which developed the Peace Corps program articulated by the President the following month. Subsequently Shriver played a major role in engineering passage of the Peace Corps Act (and a $30 million appropriation) by the second largest margin of any nondefense measure sent to Congress that year. He also made good on his recommendation that the Peace Corps get off to a fast start by assembling a Washington staff of 362 and putting over 600 volunteers, virtually all recruited from the campuses that spring, to work in eight countries in the first six months.[5]

Under Shriver, the Peace Corps experienced rapid, continued growth in appropriations and volunteers. The number of applications received and countries served, on the other hand, leveled off after the first several years. The agency's activities were, in general, favorably received overseas and continued to enjoy the strong support of Congress and Presidents Kennedy and Johnson.

| June 30 | Appropriations (millions) | Volunteers overseas | Countries served | Applications received |
|---------|---------------------------|---------------------|------------------|-----------------------|
| 1962 . . . . . . . | $ 30.0 | 1,044 | 17 | 20,058 |
| 1963 . . . . . . . | 59.0 | 4,379 | 45 | 33,762 |
| 1964 . . . . . . . | 96.0 | 6,063 | 44 | 45,653 |
| 1965 . . . . . . . | 104.1 | 8,624 | 45 | 42,124 |
| 1966 . . . . . . . | 114.1 | 10,530 | 45 | 42,656 |

The organizational response designed and encouraged by Shriver was described by Bill Tebitts,[6] a senior staff member who had served under all three directors as volunteer, country director, and Peace Corps, Washington (PC/W) officer. It was the researcher's impression that his views were widely shared.

In the early years of the Peace Corps there was an overriding desire—to make it bigger faster. The country directors who got attention and promotions were those able to double the size of their programs each year. There was only one unit of measurement. That was great until about '64; after that projects began to get started which were marginal or poorly planned.

Shriver was a great believer in getting good people—lots of them—and letting them fight it out even though sometimes several people might be assigned the same job.[7] However, he gave the organization a spirit which transcended the confusion he sometimes created in it. Responsibilities were

[5] Carey, *The Peace Corps,* p. 22.

[6] Disguised name.

[7] One commentator noted: "Shriver prefers to be the hub of the wheel rather than at the top of the heap." Peter Brastrup, *New York Times Magazine,* December 17, 1961, p. 11.

not very well defined and the wheel was invented more than once, but he knew how to get people to work hard and somehow the job seemed to get done.

In August 1964 Shriver was appointed director of the new Office of Economic Opportunity. For the next year and a half he led both agencies, a dual responsibility that evoked some criticism in Congress. Finally, in March 1966, he relinquished the Peace Corps post to continue with OEO and later as Ambassador to France.

## The Vaughn years

Jack Hood Vaughn, 46, became the second Peace Corps director. He came from the State Department where he had been assistant secretary for Latin America following service as Ambassador to Panama. Earlier, from October 1961 to April 1964, he had been in charge of Latin American activities for the Peace Corps.

In Vaughn's first public address as director, he commented on his vision for the Peace Corps:

. . . the cost of peace is no more than the cost of love itself. And here and now, I suppose, is as good a time as any to break down some embarrassments and inhibitions and give this game a name—for of what have we been speaking, toward what have we been groping, if not toward love? I shall not quarrel if it is your style to mask the word with others, like "understanding," or "giving," or "generosity," or even that half-way mystery, "enlightened self-interest."

But if our task is serving the cause of lasting peace, then we are trying to deliver a coded message without the key—unless we admit that the key is love, and the message is man's belief that he can make himself, and every other man, higher than the animals.[8]

The record in quantitative terms is summarized in the table below. The 1968 annual report to Congress noted that greater stress was being placed on cooperation with host-country officials, incorporation of assignments calling for more highly skilled volunteers, and increased attention

| June 30 | Appropriations (millions) | Volunteers overseas | Countries served | Applications received |
|---------|---------------------------|---------------------|------------------|-----------------------|
| 1966 . . . . . . . | $114.1 | 10,530 | 45 | 42,656 |
| 1967 . . . . . . . | 110.0 | 11,912 | 51 | 36,548 |
| 1968 . . . . . . . | 107.5 | 11,115 | 57 | 31,111 |
| 1969 . . . . . . . | 102.0 | 9,752 | 60 | 24,336 |

[8] Carey, *The Peace Corps,* pp. 39–40.

to matching returned volunteers with domestic programs, particularly in teaching. The report also indicated that "the picture of the average volunteer changes little from year to year. He is 24 and a recent liberal arts college graduate."

Organization transitions under Vaughn were traced by Bill Tebitts in these terms:

When Vaughn came, he said he was going to change the focus of the Peace Corps—to rationalize the administration and emphasize performance. In fact, he didn't for the first year or so, it was run much as before only without the feeling of excitement that Shriver had given it.

When change finally came, the effect was centralization. Program decisions which for all practical purposes were being made by the country and regional directors were vested with PDR.[9] Decisions were made in committee with the PDR people controlling the outcome. My first act as a member of that department, for instance, was to cut off requests for replacements for an English-language education program that had been running for two years in one Latin American country. That was it. The country and regional directors had no recourse.

There had been "country memoranda" outlining the country director's plans for the future, but they were generally not reviewed—certainly not in a way that mirrored the work put into them—and eventually were discontinued. Vaughn got into vast detail and, toward the end, few decisions of consequence were made without him.

When the Nixon Administration took office in January 1969, Vaughn tendered his resignation, as is customary for appointed officials of the outgoing administration, but, according to newspaper reports, he was to be retained.[10] He was then abruptly replaced several weeks later, which, one reporter claimed, Vaughn discovered "by reading the account in a Washington newspaper."[11] At the time of his departure, Vaughn expressed again his continuing belief in the "sharing and loving" nature of the Peace Corps:

If we ever lose track of this vague sharing that has made the Peace Corps what it is—the ambivalent, individualistic, subtle thing of giving and receiving and never knowing who's receiving more—then we're in for a demise that can come pretty fast. This kernel is the magic. It is why voluntarism works. . . . It's the nebulous nature of sharing and loving. We must go about it in our own soft way."[12]

---

[9] Program Development and Review, a department composed of program specialists which reported to the director.

[10] "Nixon Keeping Jack Vaughn as Director of Peace Corps," *Evening Star*, January 8, 1969, p. A-2.

[11] Kay Bartlett, "Is Nine-Year Old Peace Corps Growing or Going?" *Sunday Call-Chronicle*, Allentown, Pa., March 8, 1970, p. A-13.

[12] *The Volunteer*, May 1969.

## The Blatchford years

On March 17, 1969, Joseph Blatchford was nominated as the third director of the Peace Corps and, at 34, was the youngest agency head in the Nixon Administration. In 1959 Blatchford, a lawyer and one-time intercollegiate tennis champion from UCLA, had helped found ACCION, a privately financed volunteer organization devoted primarily to community development work in Latin America. He resigned as president of ACCION in 1968 to run for Congress as a Republican in Los Angeles, losing narrowly in a heavily Democratic district.

On May 5 Blatchford was sworn in by President Nixon, who commented at the subsequent White House news conference: "Despite his very young years, he has the responsibility to come up with new ideas. He has the opportunity to develop new programs . . . [which] will receive the very highest priority within the Administration."

Among the new director's first steps was the creation of nine task forces to reevaluate the objectives of the Peace Corps, or, as one of those involved said at the time, "to set new directions and to squeeze out the water that has built up after eight years. Reorganize it, if necessary, and be ready to present a package of new ideas to the President in the fall."[13] Thomas J. Houser, 39, a Chicago attorney, former campaign manager for Charles Percy in 1964 and 1966, and one of the strategists in President Nixon's 1968 Cook County campaign, was one of the evaluators. In late May he was appointed deputy director of the Peace Corps.

The study teams were quick to point out two characteristics of the Peace Corps world of 1969 that distinguished it from earlier periods. First, host-country expectations were changing. As one senior staff officer noted:

> The early years of the Peace Corps coincided with the first blush of enthusiasm accompanying independence in Africa and Punte del Este[14] in Latin America. Emerging nations were trusting and eager for assistance in community development and primary education that the Peace Corps was able to provide quickly with volunteers right out of college. Times have changed: increased sophistication and better organization on their part, nationalism, the war, and so forth. We found growing opposition, for instance, to the notions of foreign teachers in primary grades and AB generalists [recent liberal arts graduates] as education experts.

Moreover, the image and importance of the Peace Corps and overseas volunteer service among recent or soon-to-be college graduates appeared to be deteriorating for a variety of reasons—distrust of government involvement overseas, Vietnam, primacy of domestic issues, and so forth.

---

[13] *New York Post,* Saturday, May 17, 1969, p. 26.

[14] The Alliance for Progress was an outgrowth of the Inter-American President's Conference in Punte del Este, Uruguay, 1961.

The accelerating drop in applications since 1966 was thought to reflect these changing attitudes.

By late summer 1969, the outlines of the new directions had taken shape. Refined over the next year, they were expressed by Blatchford in October 1970 as follows:

1.  The first of these new directions is to shift more volunteer assignments to the high-priority needs of developing countries. Long-range planning is the first step; country directors have therefore been asked to work out with local leaders a four-year plan to utilize volunteers. We expect this planning to take the Peace Corps more heavily into vocational training, irrigation, small business development, and such hitherto ignored areas as educational television, self-help housing, and urban planning.

In this search we will be making a number of new assumptions.

First, we are willing to seek out and send overseas a single man or woman with a special skill, or to put together a small team of people. Large numbers are not important and can create an unhealthly dependency. What is important is providing people with the particular and often unusual skills found in a modern society, which a developing society cannot afford to educate. . . .

Second, we will work with those private agencies which have standing within the country and work on important needs. In the past the Peace Corps has dealt almost exclusively with central governments.

Third, once a need is identified, we will consult with volunteer-sending agencies in other countries, most of which are in Europe, to put together multinational teams of volunteers. . . .

2.  The second new direction is to recruit the volunteers with the skills which meet these higher priority requests. To attract volunteers from a wide spectrum of American society, the Peace Corps has to broaden its appeal. Many people still think that to serve they must have a college degree or be under 30 years of age. A new message must go out, a new call to all Americans to volunteer. These will, in turn, require new rules and recruiting methods. For example, an experienced engineer, or a machinist, carpenter, or farmer, is more likely to be married than the typical recent college graduate. To enable him to serve abroad, Peace Corps must relax its prohibition against volunteers with families. . . .

3.  The third new direction of the Peace Corps concerns its relationships to the host country. . . . we have taken certain concrete steps to help make the Peace Corps a cooperative venture. Our goal is to fill 50% of the Peace Corps overseas staff positions—including the upper echelons—with local citizens. . . .

4.  Encouraging volunteer service by international and multinational teams is the Peace Corps' fourth new direction. My experience has been that most countries still prefer to receive volunteers on a bilateral basis. However, this is not true in all cases. Sometimes one country cannot supply all of the skills needed in a particular project; sometimes governments—particularly those most sensitive to East-West tensions—prefer to avoid too close an identity with any one other government; and many of today's potential volunteers

prefer to serve under an international flag or in concert with volunteers from other countries. . . .

5. If the first four new directions emphasize a great contribution to the foreign country, the fifth is intended to relate the Peace Corps to the enormous problems in the United States. It is common for Americans to ask today, "Why go overseas when there is so much to be done at home?" . . .

In the future we expect the Peace Corps to play a larger role abroad in population, ecology, and conservation problems, curriculum reform, vocational education, and urban planning. In each of these areas the foreign experience can provide training to meet a need in the United States. We will also undertake programs of "combined service," in which a volunteer would sign up for three years instead of two and serve part of his time in the United States and part of it abroad. . . .

Blatchford was optimistic about the future of the Peace Corps under the new directions and confident that its contribution to developing nations would be significant. He was, however, aware that success was far from assured.

These five new directions are essentially untested, and the test is coming at a time when the political winds are as turbulent for the agency as at any time since 1961. There is bitter disillusionment over the Vietnam war among the Peace Corps' traditional college constituency. For many of these students the Peace Corps is tainted by the war, an arm of the Establishment, merely the most tolerable part of an intolerable government. An organized and vocal minority of returned volunteers call the Peace Corps "the smile on the devil's policy."

Moreover, as the country turns inward, voluntary service at home becomes more attractive than service overseas. In the shifting and often fickle competition among social causes the Peace Corps trails well behind ecology or domestic politics. Then, too, the election of Richard Nixon could alter the traditional allegiances. Some think the President will allow the Peace Corps to die of inattention. In the Congress, the Peace Corps could fall victim to partisan politics. As for the new directions, none of them lack detractors. Some people are opposed to the partnership approach, others to working with international agencies and volunteers from other countries. One critic has already called our recruitment of skilled workers, farmers, and members of minority groups "a disaster," and more charitable commentators are still skeptical that the Peace Corps can recruit in sufficient numbers beyond the campus. To say the least, there is no reason to expect a smooth course for the Peace Corps in the years ahead.

## FINANCING THE PEACE CORPS

The Peace Corps was funded by Congress as a separate agency. The process for the fiscal year beginning June 30 generally was initiated in October of the previous year by a "first look" at the coming year's budget submitted to the President. The figures and supporting data were refined until by late December they were ready for inclusion in the proposed national budget sent to Congress in January. During this period the director received guidance from the executive branch concerning the overall magnitude of spending considered advisable for the Peace Corps. During the spring, the director and his advisers appeared before the Senate Committee on Foreign Relations and the House Committee on Foreign Affairs to present the Peace Corps program for the ensuing year. In due course, following the reports of these committees, Congress authorized a budget which was then referred to the appropriations committees of the House and Senate. The appropriation, which might not be approved by Congress until September or later, constituted the final budget which could then be obligated (roughly meaning spent) in the fiscal year beginning the previous July 1. A history of the 1969–71 budgets is traced in Exhibit 3.

Leon Parker, deputy director of administration and finance, indicated several areas that had been of particular concern to congressional committees.

Congressmen tend to measure the effectiveness of the Peace Corps first in terms of the ratio of administrative to program costs.[15] [See Exhibit 4.] In a way, this penalizes us for our efforts to increase project effectiveness. We typically end up with a very tight administrative budget and a looser program budget.

In the same vein, we are carefully scrutinized for increases in staff levels and average staff salaries, particularly among our senior people. We have a policy of paying for the rank of the man and not for the rank of the job. We will typically compensate a man based on his prior earnings although as a matter of principle we generally insist on a small sacrifice to work for the Peace Corps. The result is that country director salaries, for instance, may vary considerably and not necessarily in relation to the number of volunteers they are responsible for.[16]

Many of our old friends in Congress continue to relate our efforts to the number of volunteers recruited and in the field each year. This feeling persists even though we stress that a greater impact can be made by a smaller number of highly skilled and trained volunteers.

The budget reviewed by Congress did not apportion the funds by project. Parker continued by explaining the role played by financial controls in the management of the Peace Corps.

The budget gets approved so late that it would be very difficult to specify it by project. All you need is one Libya to throw it off.[17] One of the good

---

[15] Includes principally training and overseas costs and the readjustment allowance.

[16] On December 31, 1969, country director salaries ranged from $12,848 in Chad (52) and Somali (42) to $33,495 in Malaysia (313) and Brazil (405). Also the director in the Philippines (410) received $19,704 and in Guinea (19), $32,762. Figures in parentheses indicate the number of volunteers in the country.

[17] Over 300 volunteers were in Libya or in training to go there when the Peace Corps was asked to terminate its activities in September 1969.

**EXHIBIT 3**

Comparison of Peace Corps budgets for fiscal years 1969, 1970 (dollars in millions)

| | Total appropriation | Program funds | Administrative expenses | Est. volunteer & trainee strength by Aug. 31, 1969 | FY 1969 trainee input |
|---|---|---|---|---|---|
| **FY 1969** | | | | | |
| January 1968 President's Budget | $112.8 | $82.5 | $30.3 | 15,200 | 9,200 |
| September 1968 Authorized by the Congress | 112.8 | 82.5 | 30.3 | * | * |
| October 1968 Appropriated by the Congress | 102.0 | 72.5 | 29.5 | * | * |
| December 1968 Adjustment to absorb federal pay raise | ... | – 0.8 | + 0.8 | ... | ... |
| April 1969 Peace Corps financial plan | 102.0 | 71.7 | 30.3 | 12,400 | 7,000 |
| September 1969 Final figures | 100.5 | 70.9 | 29.6 | 10,650 | 6,303 |
| **FY 1970** | | | | *By Aug. 31, 1970* | *FY 1970* |
| January 1969 President's Budget | $109.8 | $78.9 | $30.9 | 13,800 | 8,500 |
| April 1969 Amendment to President's Budget made by Peace Corps | 101.1 | 70.5 | 30.6 | 12,000 | 7,500 |
| October 1969 Authorized by the Congress | 98.5 | 66.4 | 32.1 | * | – |
| November 1969 Appropriated by Congress | 98.5 | 66.4 | 32.1 | * | * |
| April 1970 Peace Corps financial plan | 98.5 | 66.4 | 32.1 | 10,500 | 6,500 |
| September 1970 Final figures | 90.8 | 60.4 | 30.4 | 9,000 | 4,637 |
| **FY 1971** | | | | *By Aug. 31, 1971* | *FY 1971* |
| January 1970 President's Budget | 98.8 | 67.4 | 31.4 | 10,000 | 7,000 |
| September 1970 Authorized by the Congress | 98.8 | 67.4 | 31.4 | * | * |
| October 1970 Appropriated by the Congress | † | † | † | ... | ... |

* Not specified by Congress.

† The Senate Appropriations Committee appropriated $98.8 million; the measure was still before the House Appropriations Committee. The Peace Corps had reduced its request to $94.5 million.

Source: Financial Management Report, September 10, 1969; updated by casewriter.

**EXHIBIT 4**
Summary of Peace Corps obligations by activity—fiscal years (in millions of dollars)

| | 1962 | 1963 | 1964 | 1965 | 1966 | 1967 | 1968 | 1969 | 1970 (est.) | 1971 (est.) |
|---|---|---|---|---|---|---|---|---|---|---|
| Volunteer and project costs | $19.7 | $39.3 | $58.4 | $65.6 | $89.6 | $79.8 | $78.2 | $70.8 | $66.4 | $67.4 |
| | 66.7% | 71.9% | 76.7% | 76.8% | 79.1% | 76.4% | 73.2% | 70.5% | 67.4% | 68.2% |
| Administrative expenses | $9.8 | $15.4 | $17.8 | $19.8 | $23.6 | $24.7 | $28.6 | $29.6 | $32.1 | $31.4 |
| | 33.3% | 28.1% | 23.3% | 23.2% | 20.9% | 23.6% | 26.8% | 29.5% | 32.6% | 31.8% |
| Total | $29.5 | $54.7 | $76.2 | $85.4 | $113.2 | $104.5 | $106.8 | $100.4 | $98.5 | $98.8 |

Permanent full-time personnel employment at end of year

| | 1963 | 1964 | 1965 | 1966 | 1967 | 1968 | 1969 | 1970 (est.) | 1971 (est.) |
|---|---|---|---|---|---|---|---|---|---|
| Overseas posts | | | | | | | | | |
| U.S. Citizens | 165 | 234 | 263 | 308 | 355 | 349 | 322 | 306 | 303 |
| Foreign Nationals | 142 | 122 | 97 | 120 | 144 | 171 | 109 | 100 | 100 |
| Subtotal | 307 | 356 | 360 | 428 | 499 | 520 | 431 | 406 | 403 |
| Washington | 711 | 663 | 668 | 677 | 631 | 691 | 657 | 590 | 590 |
| Total | 1,018 | 1,019 | 1,028 | 1,105 | 1,130 | 1,211 | 1,088 | 996 | 993 |

Source: Peace Corps 1970 Annual Report to Congress.

things about the Peace Corps is its ability to respond quickly; too many controls might inhibit that.

We do have an allotment system, however, which divides the overseas costs among countries, broken down into administrative, program, and in-country training components. Our country directors think about projects, not administration, so they tend to change the former without thinking about the consequences of the latter. There is a feeling in the agency these days that the people at the top are interested in seeing us minimize the cost of running the Peace Corps.

## VOLUNTEER SERVICE

The normal tour of duty for the volunteer was two years, though one-year extensions were not uncommon. While overseas the volunteer received a living allowance averaging roughly $100 a month with considerable variation depending upon the country and the assignment. In theory the allowance was intended to permit the volunteer to live in a manner that was comparable to that of his host-country co-workers which, of course, varied depending on location and occupation. An additional $75 for each month spent overseas was retained in the United States for the volunteer as a "separation allowance."

Volunteer assignments were becoming increasingly varied, though for the most part they fell into four categories:

1. *Education.* Nearly half of all volunteers worked in education. They have helped education ministries develop new curricula and have taught in primary and secondary schools, universities, teacher training institutes, and vocational schools. The Peace Corps has prepared most of these volunteers for their jobs, since fewer than one third had taken education courses previously.[18]

2. *Community development.* In early years, individual volunteers were placed in communities to initiate projects for which they saw a need, such as well digging, construction of community facilities, athletic competitions, credit unions, and so forth. Recently volunteers had been advised to move more slowly and work with local agencies to define and execute recognized high-priority projects. The open-ended nature of these assignments and some confusion over goals (e.g., self-help or a "revolutionary" force) sometimes led to uneven training and frustrating tasks, especially in urban communities.

3. *Public health.* Health programs were aimed at controlling diseases and teaching better hygiene to the people and health-care practices to local public health organizations. Volunteers included specialists, such as nurses, therapists, and x-ray technicians and generalists trained in child care, personal hygiene, family planning, and sanitation.

---

[18] Carey, *The Peace Corps,* p. 115.

**4.** *Agriculture.* Volunteers in agriculture were given widely varying assignments. For instance, they have helped upgrade produce, establish grade standards, improve packaging methods, enlarge markets; others have taught in training centers and helped establish cooperatives and build irrigation systems. Still others have worked with animal husbandry and livestock slaughtering and processing programs. Volunteers, both specialists and generalists trained in cultivation techniques, have been important forces in the successful introduction of "miracle rice" in India.

The volunteer was not an employee of the U.S. government; he traveled on a private citizen's passport and was subject to the laws of the host country. While he did not have the perquisites of government employment overseas, he had more freedom, for instance, to travel and to criticize U.S. policies.

On the job, volunteers were responsible to their host-country supervisors, be they local government agencies, headmasters, or doctors. In this sense, the Peace Corps staff were not project managers but rather constituted a source of personal guidance and administrative support and a high-level contact with host-country government officials.

## OPERATIONS OF THE PEACE CORPS STAFF

The Peace Corps staff numbered about 1,000, of whom about 600 were at Peace Corps, Washington (PC/W) and the remainder in the field. Aside from support functions such as administration and finance, medical care, Congressional liaison, and public affairs, the staff was concerned with three major activities.

### Project development

This activity dealt with identifying, evaluating, and approving projects. Roughly 200 projects were approved each year, of which about 60 were new and the remainder carry-overs, perhaps in modified form, from prior years. The country director was responsible for developing the Peace Corps program in his territory; in turn, he reported to a regional director at PC/W.[19] Since host-country officials had to invite volunteer participation and approve projects, the country director worked closely with government ministries in assessing national priorities and appropriate fields for Peace Corps assistance. If subsequently approved by PC/W, the project was assigned volunteers who then were trained specifically for it. Technical assistance was available to the field from the Office of Program Development Evaluation and Review

---

[19] There were four regions: Africa, Latin America, East Asia/Pacific, and North Africa/Near East/South Asia.

(PDER)[20] which included functional specialists in education, agronomy, public health, urban development, and resource development. In October 1970, PDER had about nine professionals available for such assignments, with the number expected to increase in the future.

Normally PC/W approval came after agreement had been reached in the field, although Michael Agar, special assistant to the director, added: "We sometimes take a calculated risk and approve them ourselves before the host country does. We have found that 8%–15% of the projects undergo major changes or are canceled between approval and initiation." During its history the Peace Corps had been asked to terminate its program in 10 countries. The reasons surrounding these events are summarized in Exhibit 5. In two of these instances, volunteers returned after a lapse of several years.

### Volunteer recruitment, training, and assignment

The Peace Corps had processed over 200,000 applications for volunteer service since 1961, nearly 80% of them from college students. In 1966 the agency ceased to rely on the "campus blitz" by staff members and hired full-time recruiters (largely returned volunteers) who operated from offices in Boston, Atlanta, Chicago, and San Francisco. Applications were first reviewed by "skill desk" officers and then by the regional directors and their staffs who made the final determination about issuing invitations for projects in their regions. Training was performed at one of the three Peace Corps centers or in the host country or a combination of the two. Three volunteer recruiting and training cycles were conducted each year coinciding with the end of college semesters. Correspondingly, there were three project-approval and start-up cycles as well:

| Recruiting | Training | Project start-up | Approximate proportion of volunteers |
|------------|----------|------------------|--------------------------------------|
| Spring     | Summer   | Fall             | 50%                                  |
| Summer     | Fall     | Spring           | 20%                                  |
| Fall-Winter| Spring   | Summer           | 30%                                  |

Three kinds of difficulties in this area had become evident by 1969. First, as requests from the field for specialists of various kinds increased, candidates became less interchangeable and recruiters were forced either to search for specialists to assign to specific projects or to rely on more

---

[20] The successor to the office of Program Development and Review (PDR).

**EXHIBIT 5**
**Countries from which the Peace Corps has withdrawn**

| Country | Withdrawal date | Explanation |
|---|---|---|
| Cyprus | February 1964 | War in Cyprus. |
| Ceylon | June 1964 | A new leftest Prime Minister (Mrs. Bandaranaike) allowed Peace Corps education program to expire. Volunteers in food production and community development returned under Mr. Senanayake's administration in 1967. |
| Indonesia | May 1965 | Peace Corps withdraws volunteers by mutual consent with government because their safety could not be guaranteed. |
| Guinea | November 1966 | Peace Corps volunteers given one week to leave country by President Sekou after a series of incidents. Returned in 1969. |
| Mauritania | June 1967 | Relations with United States broken during Israeli-Arab conflict. Peace Corps given 48 hours to leave. |
| Pakistan | June 1967 | Program closed out because Pakistan "determined that its needs were technicians and specialists of a more sophisticated level than the Peace Corps generally provides." |
| Gabon | January 1968 | Peace Corps given 10 days to withdraw from country. Action subsequently attributed to budgetary deficiencies which made the government's contribution to the program impossible to maintain. |
| Tanzania | October 1969 | Amid a public summons for more "self-reliance" and "Africanization," President Nyerere requested the Peace Corps to phase out its program. |
| Libya | October 1969 | Following a coup d'etat, the Peace Corps contract (mostly to provide English teachers) was terminated. |
| Somalia | December 1969 | Peace Corps activities terminated "probably" for political consideration (the volunteers were to be replaced by Egyptians). |

Source: Hearings before Committee on Foreign Affairs, House of Representatives, April 7, 1970, pp. 48–49.

sophisticated training to provide generalists with the required skills. For instance, the plan for Botswana noted inadequate dams and groundwater facilities among the country's development needs. Peace Corps involvement called for a water technician and a drilling instructor, each with 5 to 10 years' experience, and a civil engineer to act as a water supply adviser.

Concurrently, the timing of the invitation was critical; among college students invitations issued in February for summer training had an acceptance rate of 60%–70%, while for those delayed until May the acceptance rate dropped to 10%–15%. The desirable lead time for noncollege applicants was frequently longer. A substantial proportion of invitations had fallen toward the end of the recruitment period. Third, delays in contracting for training personnel, prompted by uncertainty over projects and manning, narrowed the field of available contractors and presumably led to lower quality instruction.

### Administration

A final group of activities encompassed the support, evaluation, and staffing of ongoing Peace Corps projects and offices. At the country level, this involved overseeing volunteer activities, ensuring that they were given useful assignments, and maintaining contact with government ministries. Larger countries with sizable volunteer populations such as India were divided into several districts, and deputy or associate country directors were assigned the first-line supervisory functions. Depending on the nature of the program, the overseas staffs might include training coordinators and technical specialists for ongoing projects.

At PC/W, supervision of overseas activities was accomplished through periodic field visits by regional directors and evaluators from PDER. More time-consuming was the recruitment of overseas staff, a task that was complicated by the five-year rule and an agency policy of limiting contracts for particular assignments to 30 months. Of a more routine nature were a vast number of administrative requests from the field (e.g., a pair of roller skates for Niger) and other miscellaneous support activities ranging from technical assistance to medical care.

### ORGANIZATION CHANGE—1969

Acting in part on the consultant's recommendations,[21] Blatchford undertook several major organizational changes amounting to a reshaping of the PC/W structure and responsibilities. An organization chart is shown in Exhibit 6. Regional directors were given authority to approve requests for individual projects and were to be held accountable, together with the country directors, for the results. Concurrently, PC/W specialists were grouped together in PDER. While it was not to have

---

[21] The scope of the consultant's study specifically excluded training and overseas activity.

**EXHIBIT 6**
**The Peace Corps organization**

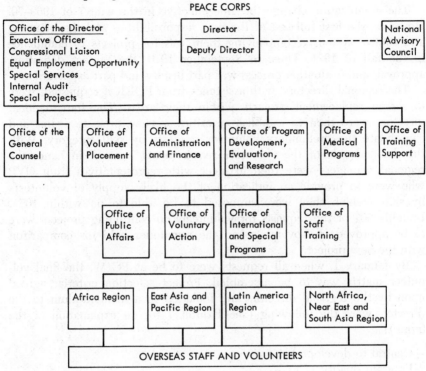

Source: Peace Corps.

decision-making authority over projects, PDER was to assess the impact of resource constraints (e.g., volunteer specialists), provide advice to the director on alternative mixes of projects for achieving Peace Corps goals, suggest professional staff priorities among projects, and provide technical support to country directors on ongoing projects. The evaluation division of PDER was to be responsible for "objectively analyzing and evaluating" projects against host-country needs.

Volunteer recruiting and selection, which had been performed by two departments, were brought together into the Office of Volunteer Placement (OVP) which was charged with the responsibility of providing a sufficient number of qualified volunteers to work on approved Peace Corps projects. However, in-country training which had been increasing in importance continued to be the responsibility of regional training coordinators who reported to the regional directors.

## PROJECT DEFINITION, APPROVAL, AND EVALUATION

The organization changes became effective in the winter of 1969–70. However, the first full test of the new responsibilities and the planning and control system accompanying them was for projects to commence in the fall of 1971. Thus, in September 1970, the project definition, approval, and evaluation process was part history and part expectation.

The regional directors, with assistance from PDER if requested, were to screen replacement projects within their areas. The four regional directors were then to establish priorities, review projects again, and consolidate the preliminary volunteer requests by skill category. With the demand side of the volunteer requirements "matrix" in hand, the regional managers were then to meet with representatives from OVP who were to provide an indication of the likely supply of volunteers by skill (which they were supposed to be able to do within 10%). Roughly 50% of the requests for volunteers on continuing projects were to be approved in November and the remainder held for comparison with the new project.

By January 1, when all requests were to be at PC/W, the final volunteer matrix was to be assembled. Project selection criteria, agreed upon by the regional directors and included in a memorandum to the director, were the following (see Exhibit 7 for an explanation of the terms):

—Central to development
—Program quality
—Multiplier effect

The final matrix was then to be reviewed by PDER and forwarded to the director for final approval. This document provided the basis upon which OVP would recruit volunteers. With an earlier understand-

---

**EXHIBIT 7**
**Criteria for Peace Corps project selection**

*Central to development:* The frame of reference is the specific country and its developmental goals. Need analysis is also taken into account. Clearly, what is central to development in one country may be secondary in another.

*Multiplier:* Multiplier effect exists when:

—Volunteers are training host-country people who will train others. Examples include teacher training, ag extension worker training, and community development leadership training.

—Volunteers are engaged in research and development activity. Examples include ag research, curriculum development, and pilot projects to prove out new techniques in education, ag, etc.

*Quality:* Quality takes into account the traditional factors which make up a good Peace Corps program including clearly defined jobs, integration into host-country structure, good program experience, volunteer satisfaction, etc.*

*Memorandum from regional directors to the director of the Peace Corps, June 12, 1970.

ing of skill needs, OVP would hopefully be in a position to issue invitations to prospective volunteers in February, thus increasing the acceptance rate and improving the opportunities for contacting high-grade training personnel.

The evaluation of Peace Corps programs had not, as yet, been affected by the new planning and approval process. One staff assistant to the director commented on the way it was currently done and on some new steps being implemented:

We get feedback from volunteers,[22] PDER, outside experts, and country nationals. Evaluation is a negative sort of thing. If enough people say it's bad, especially if the volunteer attrition rate is high, then we take it to be a poor project. The dollars expended related to a project budget wouldn't mean much.

On the other hand, we are starting to monitor progress against some of the new directions. For instance, we are requesting data on the number of non-American staff hired and the extent of multinational participation in Peace Corps projects.

Others were more hopeful that measures of effectiveness could be determined. One manager in PDER said:

There's not a damn project overseas that we can't measure objectively on some basis. Take primary-school English teachers, for instance; we could work with the number of students, the hours taught, and the number of instructors and come up with an index. It also ought to be possible to compare effectiveness of various kinds of projects with the cost of training specialists. We might find that nurses are vastly less effective relative to the costs of putting them in the field than agronomists. Just because people say it will never work is no reason to give up trying.

## REGIONAL MANAGEMENT

The regional director had assumed an important position in the revised organization structure. Caleb Roehrig, a 1941 graduate of the Harvard Business School,[23] discussed his job in these terms:

I see this job in four parts. First, I have a responsibility for transmitting the director's goals to the overseas staff. Second, I am responsible for seeing that in-country training is performed satisfactorily—last year we spent about $5 million on 1,700 volunteers. Third, I have to worry about filling and evaluating some 150 staff positions in 20 countries. And fourth, there is the business of program development and review. These last two warrant some elaboration.

---

[22] Mid-service in addition to termination interviews were conducted with volunteers.

[23] Backgrounds of the regional directors and certain other key operating officers are provided in Exhibit 8.

**EXHIBIT 8**
**Selected PC/W staff**

| Name | Age | Education | Position | Date assigned | Previous experience with Peace Corps | Non-Peace Corps experience |
|---|---|---|---|---|---|---|
| William Dyal | 41 | BA MT | Regional director (NANESA) | 1969 | Country director, Colombia, 1967–69 | Director, Baptist Foreign Mission and Christian Life Commission |
| Joseph Kennedy | 43 | BS MA Ph.D. | Regional director (EAP) | 1970 | Country director, Sierra Leone, 1967–70; Deputy director, Africa region, 1965–67 | Research director, American Society of African Culture; Teacher |
| Walter Carrington | 40 | AB LLB | Regional director (Africa) | 1969 | Deputy director, Africa region, 1967–69; Deputy director, PPR, 1967; Country director, Sierra Leone, 1964–67 | Massachusetts Commission against Discrimination |
| Caleb Roehrig | 52 | BA MBA | Regional director (acting) (L.A.) | 1970 | Deputy country director, Tunisia, 1961–64; Deputy director, Latin America region, 1969; Country director, Dominican Republic, 1967–69; Deputy country director, Ecuador, 1965–67 | Department manager, Polaroid |
| James Hawkins | 49 | BS M.Ed. Ph.D. | Director, PDER | 1970 | None | Special Assistant to Secretary, Department of Commerce; Micronesia Administrator, Department of Interior |

| Name | Age | Degree | Peace Corps position | Year | Prior Peace Corps experience | Current position |
|---|---|---|---|---|---|---|
| John Mills | 49 | BA Ph.D. | Director, program development (PDER) | 1970 | None | Development manager, Monsanto |
| Kevin O'Donnell | 46 | BA MBA | Director, admin. and finance | 1970 | Country director, Korea, 1967–69 | General manager, Atlas Alloy Steel Company; Booz Allen and Hamilton |
| William Inglis | 39 | BS | Director, OVP | 1970 | Director, admin. and finance, 1969–70 | Vice president, Irving Trust Co. |
| Leo Gallarano | 29 | BS | Director, assignment division, OVP | 1970 | Country director, Somalia, 1967–70; Volunteer | Ford Motor Company |
| C. Payne Lucas | | BA MA | Director, ORV* | 1970 | Regional director, Africa, 1967–69; Deputy director, Africa, 1967; Country director, Niger, 1965–67; Country representative, Togo, 1962–65 | |

*Office of Returned Volunteers.
Source: Peace Corps.

**Staffing**

Staffing can be a time-consuming task. Our normal contract for an assignment in the Peace Corps is 30 months and we have a turnover rate of over 30% a year.[24] Even with all the turnover, though, I have to depend on my country staffs—the distances are just too great to do otherwise. In particular, I look for country directors who can develop good relationships with volunteers, staff, and host-country officials; who can handle emergencies; who can design programs and get them going; who will learn the language; and who have leadership qualities that will give the country programs a sense of mission. That's a lot to ask, and one of my concerns is figuring out what I can offer in return. One thing, of course, is autonomy; we're the envy of the State Department and AID overseas which helps us recruit top-flight people.

**Program development and review**

Program development is easily as difficult. In Washington, we're a long way from the action and there isn't any balance sheet to help us out. The result is delegation, on the one hand, and subjectivity on the other—the kind of situation that breeds instant opinions and the danger of being charmed into accepting a program on a short trip overseas. I try to judge a program by looking at whether it appears to be as useful for the host country as others we might take on and whether it's the sort of program we can do well. Projects vary so much, however, that it's hard to make judgments on a uniform basis.

Each regional director had a staff of roughly 30 people devoted largely to program coordination, volunteer training coordination, and the "country desks" which handled the liaison with the field. Technical specialists were seldom assigned to the regions. Instead they were more likely to be attached either to the country staffs to assist on large projects or to PDER.

The regional directors were positively disposed to the enlargement of their programming responsibilities. As one observed:

There is a lot more frankness in the regions now that we can decide among ourselves on program priorities. We have our own reviews with the country directors and have fostered competition among them. One concern, though, is the role of PDER. They really haven't "staffed-up" yet and we aren't sure what is going to happen when they do.[25] We hope they will

---

[24] Turnover of regional staff was also considerable. In one region, only six out of 22 positions were filled by the same individual in December 1969 and October 1970. Several people had received new assignments in the region, so the staff retained was somewhat higher than six.

[25] The director of PDER and his principal department heads had come to the Peace Corps from business and other government agencies during 1970. Several positions had not been filled as of October 1970.

help us develop projects and not interfere with the approval process. If they do interfere, then we are back to the conflict-of-interest situation we had before—the same guy who specifies the project approves it.

On the other hand, the revised planning and control system provoked less favorable reactions. Another regional director commented:

The new "professionalism" is difficult for the organization to take. The idea that policy decisions can be made at the top and transmitted down goes against the grain in the Peace Corps. Everyone from the volunteer up wants some participation in policy making. Even the refugees from big business on the staff join the Peace Corps because they have acted on a commitment to their values, and at that point they aren't willingly going to accept somebody else's. The controversy between those who see us providing love and understanding and those who see us exporting development skills continues, and no planning system is going to reconcile them.

## CONCERNS FOR THE FUTURE

Certain of the new directions had been adopted with enthusiasm by the field organizations. For instance, the objective of serving higher priority host-country needs had been reflected in a very large increase in the number and variety of requests for skilled volunteers. In fact, the swing had been so abrupt that OVP was encountering difficulty meeting the demand.[26] Moreover, the effects on volunteer training activities were potentially significant, as one OVP official noted:

In theory, if skilled volunteers are recruited, their training ought to be limited pretty much to overseas orientation and language, the sort of thing that can be done best in the host country and supervised by the country staff. However, there is also the alternative, if we can't find enough experienced people, of taking a relatively unskilled volunteer and trying to make him a specialist, typically in one of our three training centers. Just how much we're realistically capable of doing ourselves is a matter of some debate, though at the moment there aren't any boundaries to the variety of projects we're supposed to be able to provide volunteers to fill.

Other objectives had been less successfully implemented. A case in point was progress against a publicly stated goal of 200 volunteers with families. A program coordinator in one of the regions provided his view of what had happened:

The country directors were aware of Blatchford's commitment in the press last fall, and many had said informally at the time that they would take some volunteers with families. When the country plans and project requests

---

[26] One OVP official estimated that 70% of the 1970 requests from the field specified skills as opposed to 30% the year before. He also indicated that in his view the gross number of volunteers specified in the budget submitted to Congress could be recruited without undue difficulty if skills were not considered.

started to come in, however, we didn't see much follow-through. It appears in this case that the volunteers could be recruited, but we don't have an easy way of getting the field to send us project requests which specify families.

One of the director's chief concerns, then, was getting overseas response on Peace Corps objectives. A senior staff adviser, who had had experience in the field, the regions, and PDER, summarized his views on this issue:

The Peace Corps has come a long way in the last year in systematizing the operation and defining objectives. But some of the tough questions haven't been answered. Fundamentally, there is a split between those who think we have 60 Peace Corps and those who think we have one. There tends to be disagreement over policy on an emotional level that drives out reasoned analysis. In the old days we didn't have much analysis, but at least values were widely shared.

What aren't seen clearly are the implications of the New Directions. What's going to happen if there is a shortfall come May in some skill categories? We have delegated decision making to the regions, but are they really equipped to make judgments on increasingly complex projects? Can Peace Corps/Washington really keep its eye on what's going on in the field without an immense staff? And in that regard, are we trying to produce a specialty project with the old mass-production-type organization?

It was in this context that Blatchford had identified the role of the regional manager as an area for study. The men currently in those positions were nearing the end of their five-year terms with the Peace Corps, a situation presenting the director with an opportune time for introducing change. In one sense, he felt there were only three line positions in the agency—the director, the country director, and the volunteer—and everyone else was essentially there to support the country director in the achievement of agency goals. Yet the organization was governmental, and success depended in part on its ability to respond to constituencies in the United States whose needs and expectations were at times distinct from the problems of host countries. From this viewpoint, substantial control over operating matters ought to remain with senior staff officers in Washington.

# Index

# Index of cases